CIVILIZATIONS OF THE WORLD

CIVILIZATIONS
OF THE WORLD

The Human Adventure
VOLUME TWO: FROM THE MIDDLE 1600s

Richard L. Greaves
Florida State University

Robert Zaller
Drexel University

Philip V. Cannistraro
Drexel University

Rhoads Murphey
University of Michigan

1817

Harper & Row, Publishers, New York
Grand Rapids, Philadelphia, St. Louis, San Francisco,
London, Singapore, Sydney, Tokyo

Sponsoring Editor: Lauren Silverman
Development Editor: Mary Lou Mosher
Project Editor: Susan Goldfarb
Art Direction: Teresa J. Delgado
Text and Cover Design: Delgado Design Inc.
Cover Coordinator: Mary Archondes
Text Maps: Burmar Technical Corp.
Photo Research: Elsa Peterson
Production: Willie Lane

Cover illustration: Wang Da Quang, *Summer in Peking*/E. T. Archive

Part-opening art: Part Four: From preface to *Alzire, ou les Américains,* by
Voltaire, Amsterdam, 1736 (Innervisions/Rare Books and Manuscripts Collection,
New York Public Library, Astor, Lenox, and Tilden Foundations); Part Five:
From contemporary rendering of traditional Japanese Zen Buddhist daily chant
(courtesy of Dai Bosatsu Zendo).

The authors are indebted to Princeton University Press for permission to reprint
the poem "Ithaka" by C. P. Cavafy in the front matter for this book. The poem
appears in *Selected Poems by C. P. Cavafy,* translated by Edmund Keeley and
Philip Sherrard (Princeton, N.J.: Princeton University Press, 1972).

Color atlas in front matter © copyright Hammond Incorporated, Maplewood, N.J.

Title page: Frank Lloyd Wright's Fallingwater; photo by Bill Hedrich, Hedrich-
Blessing.

Civilizations of the World: The Human Adventure (Volume Two: From the
Middle 1600s)

Copyright © 1990 by HarperCollins*Publishers*

Library of Congress Cataloging-in-Publication Data
Civilizations of the world : the human adventure / Richard L. Greaves
. . . [et al.].
    p.   cm.
    Contents: Vol. 1. To the late 1800s—v. 2. From the middle 1600s.
    ISBN 0-06-047358-4 (v. 1).—ISBN 0-06-047357-6 (v. 2)
    1. Civilization—History. I. Greaves, Richard L.
  CB69.C565 1990
  909—dc20   89-24558
                                             CIP

90 91 92 93 9 8 7 6 5 4 3 2

CONTENTS IN BRIEF

Maps and Graphs   xix
Preface   xxi
Supplements   xxv
Acknowledgments   xxvii
About the Authors   xxix
A Note on the Spelling of Asian Names and Words   xxxi
Atlas   *following page xxxii*

21. The Societies of the Early Modern World   501
22. The Age of Absolutism   524
23. Europe's Century of Genius   546

PART FOUR   **TOWARD THE MODERN WORLD   566**

24. Europe and the Americas   568
25. The Enlightenment   593

THE VISUAL EXPERIENCE: Toward Modernity *following page 608*

26. The French Revolution and Napoleon   616

Global Essay: Death and the Human Experience (II)   642

27. Early Modern India and Iran   648
28. Manchu China and Tokugawa Japan   670
29. The Industrial Revolution   692
30. The Age of Ideology   719
31. The Triumph of Nationalism in the West   745
32. Industrial Society and the Liberal Order   768

Global Essay: Writing and Communication (II)   793

33. The Age of Western Domination   799

PART FIVE   **THE TWENTIETH CENTURY   828**

34. Culture, Society, and the Great War   830

Global Essay: The Human Image (II)   855

35. Upheaval in Eurasia and the Middle East 861

36. Fascism and the Crisis of Democracy 886

THE VISUAL EXPERIENCE: The Modern World *following page 896*

37. Totalitarianism and War 908

38. Revival and Revolution in East Asia 936

39. Nationalism and Revolution: India, Pakistan, Iran, and the Middle East 963

40. Decolonization and Development: Africa and Latin America 990

Global Essay: Maps and Their Makers (II) 1016

41. The Age of the Superpowers 1021

Epilogue ▪ Civilization and the Dilemma of Progress 1046

Index I-1

CONTENTS

Maps and Graphs xix
Preface xxi
Supplements xxv
Acknowledgments xxvii
About the Authors xxix
A Note on the Spelling of Asian Names and Words xxxi
Atlas *following page xxxii*

CHAPTER 21 The Societies of the Early Modern World 501
Social Hierarchies 502 ▪ *Caste and the Social Order in India* ▪
Social Hierarchy in East Asia ▪ *Social Hierarchy in Europe* ▪
The European Aristocracy ▪ *Urban Society* ▪ **Marriage and the Family 505** ▪
The Family in Asia ▪ *The Family in Europe* ▪ *Marriage in Asia* ▪
Divorce in Asia and Europe ▪ *Marriage and the Family in Africa* ▪
The Status of Women 508 ▪ *Women in Asia* ▪
Women in the Middle East and Africa ▪ *Women in Europe* ▪
Sexual Customs 511 ▪ **Education, Literacy, and the Printed Word 513** ▪
Learning in Asia ▪ *Learning in the West* ▪ *Education in the Ottoman Empire* ▪
Poverty, Crime, and Social Control 516 ▪ *Causes of European Poverty* ▪
Poor Relief in Europe ▪ *Poor Relief Outside Europe* ▪ *Crime and Poverty* ▪
Controlling Crime

◎ Documents:
Aristocratic Behavior in Japan 502
"Surplus" Daughters 507
Peasant Poverty: France, 1696 517
Capital Punishment and Cruelty 520

CHAPTER 22 The Age of Absolutism 524
France Under Louis XIV 525 ▪ *Provincial Autonomy and Central Control* ▪
Divine Right Monarchy ❧ **JEAN-BAPTISTE COLBERT, MINISTER OF
FINANCE 526** ▪ *Louis XIV and the Bureaucracy* ▪
Versailles: The Sun King Enthroned ▪ **The Wars of Louis XIV 530** ▪

The Dutch War (1672–1678) ▪ *Aggression Without War: Louis Against Germany* ▪ *The War of Five Continents* ▪ *Britain and France: The Contest for Empire* ▪ *Louis XIV and the Climax of Absolutism* ▪
Peter the Great and the Emergence of Russia 533 ▪ *The Tsarist State* ▪ *Peter and the West* ▪ *The Reforms of Peter* ▪ **Austria: The Dynastic State 538** ▪
Prussia: The Garrison State 539 ▪
Eastern European Absolutism in Context 541 ▪
England: The Triumph of Parliamentary Government 541 ▪
The Glorious Revolution and the Revolutionary Settlement **LATE STUART AND HANOVERIAN LONDON 543**

Documents:
On the Nature of Majesty 528
The Disasters of War 532
Law and Justice Under Peter the Great 537
The Right to Alter Government 542

CHAPTER 23 **Europe's Century of Genius 546**
From Ancient Science to the Copernican Revolution 547 ▪
The Legacy of Antiquity ▪ *The Medieval World Picture* ▪ *The Hermetic Challenge* ▪
The New Order of Knowledge 549 ▪ *Galileo and the Copernican Triumph* ▪
Other Scientific Advances ▪ *New Technology* ▪ **Science at the Crossroads 552** ▪
Doubt and Faith: Descartes and Pascal ▪ *Conflicting Roads to Truth* ▪
The Newtonian Synthesis ▪ *The Scientific Method* ▪
Philosophy: The Age of Reason 556 ▪ *Thomas Hobbes and the Natural Man* ▪
John Locke and the State of Nature ▪ *French Skepticism* **THE LENS GRINDER OF AMSTERDAM, BARUCH SPINOZA 559** ▪
Literature: The Triumph of the Vernacular 560 ▪
The Age of the Baroque 562 **ROME: THE REBIRTH OF A CAPITAL 562**

Documents:
On the Infinity of the Universe 550
Pascal on Humankind's Place in the Universe 553
The Scientific Method 556
The Institution of the Commonwealth 558

PART FOUR Toward the Modern World 566

CHAPTER 24 **Europe and the Americas 568**
The Old Colonial System 569 ▪ *Spain and the New World* ▪
Gold and the Expansion of the European Economy 570 ▪
Merchant Capitalism and the Growth of the State 571 ▪
The Economy of the Americas 572 ▪ *The Settlement of North America* ▪
Sugar and Slavery 573 ▪ *The Slave System* ▪ *The Slave Trade* **LIVERPOOL IN THE AGE OF SLAVERY 575** ▪ **The First Age of Global War 577** ▪
The New Balance of Power ▪ *Walpole, Britain's First Prime Minister* ▪
The Triumph of the Elite ▪ *France Under Louis XV* ▪ *Taxation and Finance* ▪

The Wars of Midcentury ▪ *The Seven Years' War* ▪
The Birth of the American Republic 583 ▪
The American Colonies and Britain ▪ *Protest and Rebellion* ▪
The Revolutionary War ▪ *Forming a Nation* ▪
From Confederation to Commonwealth ▪ *American and Canadian Expansion* ▪
**The Abolition of the Slave Trade and the Emancipation of Spanish
America 588** ✤ **SIMÓN BOLÍVAR, THE LIBERATOR 589** ▪
The End of Empire

⊕ **Documents:**
Conscript Labor in Spanish Mexico 570
A Slave's Experience 576
The First Stock Market Crash 581
Bolívar's Message to the Congress of Angostura 589

CHAPTER 25   The Enlightenment 593
The Roots of the Enlightenment 594 ▪ *The God of Reason* ▪
The Idea of Progress ▪ *Locke and Liberty* ▪ **Philosophy in Action 597** ▪ *Voltaire* ▪
The Enlightenment and Society 598 ▪ *Rousseau and the Social Contract* ▪
State and Utopia ▪ *The Philosophes and Their Public* ▪ *Literacy and Censorship* ▪
The Encyclopedia ▪ **The Enlightened Despots 601** ▪ *Catherine the Great* ▪
Frederick the Great ▪ *Joseph II: The Revolutionary Emperor* ▪
Enlightened Despotism in Perspective ▪ **The Counter-Enlightenment 607** ▪
The Revival of Religion ▪ *Skepticism and Idealism* ▪
The Emancipation of the Jews 609 ▪ **The Abolitionist Movement 610** ▪
The Rights of Women 611 ✤ **MARY WOLLSTONECRAFT, FEMINIST
612** ▪ **The Arts: From Rococo to Neoclassical 613** ▪
Vienna and the Golden Age of Western Music 614

⊕ **Documents:**
Rousseau on the Social Contract 599
From Diderot's *Encyclopedia* 602
Frederick the Great on the Enlightened Despot 604
The Romantic Reaction 608
The Revulsion Against Slavery 611

THE VISUAL EXPERIENCE   Toward Modernity *following page 608*

CHAPTER 26   The French Revolution and Napoleon 616
The Crisis of the Old Order in France 617 ▪ *Reform and Reaction* ▪
The Fiscal Crisis ▪ *The Constitutional Crisis* ▪
The Bourgeoisie and the Third Estate ▪ **The Revolution of 1789 619** ▪
From the Estates General to the National Assembly ▪ *The Popular Revolution* ▪
The Abolition of Privilege and the Declaration of the Rights of Man ▪
The New Order, 1789–1791 623 ▪ *The Bourgeoisie in Power* ▪
The Reorganization of Church and State ▪ **The Revolution and Europe 625** ▪
✤ **PARIS AND THE FALL OF THE MONARCHY 625** ▪
The Radical Revolution, 1792–1794 626 ▪ *Reform and Regicide* ▪
Robespierre and the Terror ▪ *The Republic of Virtue* ✤ **MADAME ROLAND:
A WOMAN IN THE REVOLUTION 630** ▪

Conquest and Reaction, 1795–1799 631 ■
The Legacy of the Revolution: Conflicting Interpretations 633 ■
The Napoleonic Era 634 ■ *From Republic to Empire* ■ *France Against Europe* ■
The Grand Empire ■ *The Collapse of the Napoleonic Order* ■
The Bourbon Restoration

⊕ Documents:
France on the Eve of Revolution   618
The Fall of the Bastille: An Eyewitness Account   622
Robespierre on the Principles of Revolutionary Government   629
A Revolutionary's Plea for the Rights of Women   633
Napoleon on Himself   635

〰 GLOBAL ESSAY   DEATH AND THE HUMAN EXPERIENCE (II)   642

CHAPTER 27   Early Modern India and Iran   648
The Mughal Collapse 649 ■ Westerners in India 650 ■
The Early English Presence 651 ■ *Territorial Bases* ■
The Mughal and Post-Mughal Contexts ■
Anglo-French Rivalry and the Conquest of Bengal 655 ■
  ❧ ROBERT CLIVE AND THE BEGINNINGS OF BRITISH INDIA   655 ■
The Establishment of British Rule ■
The Orientalists and the Bengal Renaissance 658   ❧ CALCUTTA,
COLONIAL CAPITAL   660 ■ The Subjugation of India 660 ■
Images of British Rule 663 ■ The Mutiny of 1857 664 ■
Iran in Transition: The Eighteenth Century 665 ■ *Nadir Quli* ■ *Karim Khan*

⊕ Documents:
India in Turmoil   649
Why Calcutta?   652
The British Indicted   659
British Life in India   661
The Charter Act, 1833   662

CHAPTER 28   Manchu China and Tokugawa Japan   670
China Under the Manchus 671 ■
Prosperity and Population Growth 673 ■
The Reigns of Kang Hsi and Ch'ien Lung ■
The Later Ch'ing: Symptoms of Decline ■
New Barbarian Pressures: The Westerners ■ *Stagnation and Vulnerability* ■
The Opium Wars 680 ■
Reunification and the Tokugawa Shogunate in Japan 682 ■
The Era of the Warlords ■ *Tokugawa Rule* ■ *The Expulsion of Foreigners* ■
Culture and Nationalism   ❧ EDO AND THE "FLOATING WORLD"   688 ■
  ❧ HOKUSAI, MASTER ARTIST   688 ■
Foreign Pressures and Domestic Unrest 689

⊕ Documents:
Adam Smith on China   673
Omens of Crisis   679
Hideyoshi Writes to His Wife   683

Tokugawa Ieyasu: Instructions to His Successor   685
Japanese Women: An Outsider's View   686

CHAPTER 29   **The Industrial Revolution   692**
The Background: Population, Energy, and Technology 693 ▪
Commerce and the Formation of Capitalist Society 695 ▪
The Agricultural Revolution 697 ▪ *A New Prosperity?* ▪
Science, Technology, and the State 699 ▪
The Transformation of Britain 700 ▪ *The Organization of Labor* ▪
Industrial Discipline ▪ *Family Life: A Tale of Two Cultures* ▪
Capital, Labor, and the Rights of Man   ❧ ROBERT OWEN, INDUSTRIAL
REFORMER   706 ▪ The Population Explosion 708   ❧ MANCHESTER,
THE FACTORY TOWN   711 ▪
The Spread of the Industrial Revolution 714 ▪ *Exploitation and Resistance* ▪
The German Giant ▪ *Industrial Development After 1850* ▪ *The Harnessing of Science*

◉ Documents:
Malthus on Population   693
Child Labor   703
Luddism   706
Two Views of Manchester   713

CHAPTER 30   **The Age of Ideology   719**
The Legacy of Revolution 720 ▪ The Congress of Vienna 721 ▪
Collective Security ▪ *The Diplomatic Settlement* ▪ Reaction and Revolution 724 ▪
The Overthrow of Ottoman Rule in Greece ▪ *The Troubled 1820s* ▪ *Liberalism* ▪
Romanticism and the Quest for Identity 728 ▪
The Dethronement of Tradition ▪ *The Romantic Hero*   ❧ GOETHE AND THE
ROMANTIC SPIRIT   729 ▪ *The Spread of Romanticism* ▪
Romanticism Beyond the Arts ▪ *Romanticism and the Image of Women* ▪
The Liberal Revival and the Revolutions of 1830 734 ▪
The July Revolution in France ▪ *Revolution East and West* ▪
Britain: Revolution Averted ▪ The Socialist Challenge 737 ▪
The Demand for Reform ▪ *From Reform to Revolution* ▪ *Karl Marx* ▪
The Revolutions of 1848 739 ▪ *The Causes of the Revolutions* ▪
The Collapse of the Old Order ▪ *Counterrevolution in Central Europe* ▪
France: From Revolution to Empire

◉ Documents:
The Mystique of Nationalism   721
Metternich's Plea for the Old Order   725
The Romantic Poet   731
Mazzini's Call to Revolution   735
The June Days   742

CHAPTER 31   **The Triumph of Nationalism in the West   745**
The Politics of National Grandeur: Napoleon III in France 746 ▪
The Second Empire ▪ *The Liberalization of the Empire* ▪
Power Politics and the Unification of Italy 750 ▪ *The Italian Risorgimento* ▪
Cavour the Realist ▪ *The Crisis of Italian Unification* ▪
Iron and Blood: The Making of the German Empire 754 ▪
Nationalism and the German State System ▪ *Bismarck and the Liberals* ▪
The Showdown with Austria ▪

The Franco-Prussian War and the Forging of German Unification ▪
Eastern Europe and the Ottomans 759 ☙ **VIENNA IN THE AGE OF
FRANZ JOSEPH 759** ▪ *Russia Between Reaction and Reform* ▪
Alexander II and the Dilemma of Russian Reform ▪
Turkey: "The Sick Man of Europe" ▪
The Jewish Question and the Birth of Zionism 764 ☙ **THEODOR
HERZL AND THE QUEST FOR A JEWISH HOMELAND 764** ▪
The United States from the Civil War to National Unity 766

◷ **Documents:**
The Napoleonic Myth 747
Cavour Versus Garibaldi 754
Bismarck on Power Politics 757
Tsarist Russia on the Edge of Revolution 761
On Anti-Semitism 765

CHAPTER 32 **Industrial Society and the Liberal Order 768**
Industrial Development and Monopoly Capitalism 769 ▪
The Second Industrial Revolution ▪ *The Rise of Big Business* ▪
The Social Hierarchy 771 ▪ *The Aristocracy: Adjustment and Change* ▪
The Growth of the Middle Classes ▪ *The Decline of the Working Class* ☙ **THE
URBAN LANDSCAPE 773** ▪ **Sexuality, Women, and the Family 774** ▪
Bourgeois Respectability ▪ *Sexual Attitudes* ▪
Liberalism and the Political Order 776 ▪ *Britain in the Victorian Age* ▪
The Third Republic in France ▪ *Germany Under the Reich* ▪
The Liberal State in Italy ▪ *Spain and the Smaller Powers* ▪
The Rise of Feminism 782 ▪ *Social Activism and Women's Rights* ▪
The Suffrage Struggle ☙ **EMMELINE PANKHURST AND THE POLITICS OF
CONFRONTATION 783** ▪ **Science and the Doctrine of Progress 785** ▪
The Darwinian Revolution ▪ *Science and Society* ▪
Culture and Industrial Society 786 ▪ *Painting: New Visions of Reality* ▪
The Literary Response ▪ **Socialism and the Labor Movement 788** ▪
Socialism, Anarchism, and the Paris Commune ▪
Trade Unions and the Labor Movement ▪
Socialist Parties: Between Reform and Revolution ▪ *Women of the Left*

◷ **Documents:**
The Cult of Domesticity 775
The Principle of Utilitarianism 783
The Suffragette Revolt 784
Socialist Women 790

≋ **GLOBAL ESSAY** **WRITING AND COMMUNICATION (II) 793**

CHAPTER 33 **The Age of Western Domination 799**
The New Imperialism 800 ▪ *Conflicting Interpretations* ▪
Economics and Empire ▪ **Africa and the Colonial Powers 802** ▪
Explorers and Missionaries ▪ *The Scramble for Africa* ▪
Britain, France, and the Perils of Empire ▪ *South Africa and the Boer War* ▪
Imperialism and Its Consequences ▪ **The West in Asia 807** ▪
British Imperial India 807 ▪ *Modern Growth* ▪ *Colonial Government* ☙ **NEW
DELHI: INDIAN SUMMER OF THE RAJ 812** ▪
The Rise of Indian Nationalism ▪ **Colonial Regimes in Southeast Asia 814** ▪

The British in Burma and Malaya • *French, Dutch, and American Colonialism* • *Independent Siam* • *Overseas Chinese* • **China Besieged 817** • *Traders and Missionaries* • *The Taiping Rebellion* • *Attempts at Reform* • *Treaty Ports and Mission Schools* • *The Boxer Rebellion* • **Japan Among the Powers 821** • *The Meiji Restoration: Response to the West* • *Economy and Government* • *Japanese Imperialism*   ☙ **ITO HIROBUMI: MEIJI STATESMAN 823** • **Australia and the Pacific Islands 824** • *Australia: Convicts, Wool, and Gold* • *New Zealand: Maori and Missionaries* • *Islands of the Pacific*

◉ **Documents:**
Imperialism and Economics: The Debate 801
Military Revolution in Africa: The Zulu Warrior 802
Women and African Society 806
Opium 818
Through Each Other's Eyes 819

PART FIVE The Twentieth Century   **828**

CHAPTER 34   Culture, Society, and the Great War 830
The Crisis of European Culture 831 • *The Revolt Against Positivism* • *The Dilemmas of Science* • *Realism Abandoned: Literature and Art* • ☙ **BARCELONA AND THE MODERN TEMPER 833** • *Postimpressionists, Cubists, and Futurists* • *Nationalism and Racism* • **The Breakdown of the European Order 836** • *Bismarck and the Concert of Europe* • *The Triple Entente* • *The Arms Race* • *Europe on the Brink* • *Sarajevo: The Failure of Diplomacy* • **The Ordeal of the West 840** • *War of Attrition* • *The Eastern Front and Italian Intervention* • *The War Beyond Europe* • *Agony on the Western Front* • *The Social Consequences of Total War* • *American Intervention and the German Collapse* • **The Reordering of Europe 845** • *The Paris Peace Conference* • *The Treaty of Versailles* • *The Search for Security* • **Society and Culture: The Impact of War 848** • *Social Change and Economic Crisis* • *The New Morality: Women, Work, and Sex* • ☙ **JOSEPHINE BAKER: AN AMERICAN IN PARIS 850** • *Science, Literature, and Art*

◉ **Documents:**
The Futurist Manifesto 835
The Trauma of Trench Warfare 843
The War Guilt Principle 846
Postwar Sexual Mores 850

⚐ **GLOBAL ESSAY**   THE HUMAN IMAGE (II)   855

CHAPTER 35   Upheaval in Eurasia and the Middle East 861
The Russian Revolution 862 • *The Twilight of the Romanovs* • *The March 1917 Revolution* • *Lenin and the Bolshevik Coup* • *Building the Communist State* • *Revolution Under Siege*   ☙ **ALEXANDRA KOLLONTAI AND THE WOMEN'S QUESTION 868** • *Stalin Versus Trotsky: The Struggle for Power* •

The Comintern: Russia Between East and West ▪
China: Rebels, Warlords, and Patriots 872 ▪
Sun Yat-sen and the 1911 Revolution ▪ *The May Fourth Movement* ▪
China and the Marxist Model ▪ *The Nanking Decade* ☙ **SHANGHAI: THE
MODEL TREATY PORT 876** ▪ **India: Toward Freedom 877** ▪
Gandhi and Mass Action ▪ *Hindus and Muslims* ▪
The Nationalist Awakening in the Middle East 881 ▪
The Mandate System and the Palestine Question ▪
The Modernization of Turkey and Iran

◎ **Documents:**
The Bolshevik Strategy 865
What Price Revolution? 867
The Comintern: East Versus West 872
Gandhi's Message to the British 879
The Declaration of Indian Freedom 880

CHAPTER 36   Fascism and the Crisis of Democracy 886
The Nature of Fascism 887 ▪ *General Characteristics* ▪ *The Origins of Fascism* ▪
Italy: The Fascist Triumph 888 ▪ *Benito Mussolini* ▪ *Postwar Crisis in Italy* ▪
The Fascist Movement ▪ *The March on Rome* ▪
Germany: From Weimar to Hitler 892 ▪
Revolution and the Weimar Republic ▪ *Adolf Hitler and the Rise of Nazism* ▪
    ☙ **BERLIN, CAPITAL OF WEIMAR CULTURE 894** ▪
    ☙ **BERTOLT BRECHT AND THE THEATER OF COMMITMENT 896** ▪
The Nazi Seizure of Power ▪ **Fascism as a World Phenomenon 899** ▪
Varieties of European Fascism ▪ *Fascism in Asia* ▪ *Brazil's Estado Novo* ▪
The Great Depression and the Crisis of Capitalism 902 ▪
The Economic Collapse ▪ *Government Response* ▪
Britain, France, and the United States: The Trial of Democracy 904 ▪
Politics and Society ▪ *Toward the Welfare State* ▪
Central and Eastern Europe 905 ▪ *The Successor States* ▪
The Decline of Liberalism

◎ **Documents:**
Theory of the Fascist State 889
Mussolini's Seizure of Power 891
The Nazi State 895
Nazism: The Philosophy of Domination 896
Hitler as Demagogue 899

THE VISUAL EXPERIENCE   The Modern World *following page 896*

CHAPTER 37   Totalitarianism and War 908
Mussolini's Italy 909 ▪ *Economic Policy* ▪ *The Church and Fascism* ▪
Regimentation and Propaganda ☙ **MARGHERITA SARFATTI AND FASCIST
CULTURAL POLICY 910   ☙ ROME, THE FASCIST CAPITAL 911** ▪
The Anti-Fascist Opposition ▪ **Nazi Germany 912** ▪ *The Nazi State* ▪
Economic Policy ▪ *Society and Culture* ▪ *Hitler and the Jews* ▪
Stalin's Russia 915 ▪ *The Five-Year Plans* ▪ *Social Policy* ▪ *The Great Purges* ▪
The Rising Sun: Japanese Expansion in East Asia 918 ▪
Aggression and Appeasement in the West 918 ▪

Europe and Africa: The Axis Advance ▪ *The Spanish Civil War* ▪ *The Czech Crisis* ▪
World War II 922 ▪ *The Nazi Onslaught* ▪ *Allied Resistance and Axis Setbacks* ▪
The United States and Japan: The Road to Pearl Harbor ▪ *The War in China* ▪
⚜ **CHUNGKING: BELEAGUERED WARTIME CAPITAL 926** ▪
India and Southeast Asia ▪ *Japan and the Pacific Theater* ▪
The Price of Victory 928 ▪ *Descent into the Abyss: The Holocaust* ▪
⚜ **ISABELLA KATZ AND THE HOLOCAUST: A LIVING
TESTIMONY 929** ▪ *The Grand Alliance: Victory in Europe* ▪
The Atomic Bomb and the Defeat of Japan ▪ *The United Nations*

◎ **Documents:**
The Nuremberg Racial Laws 914
Guernica 920
Hitler's War Plans 921
Secret Protocol of the Nazi-Soviet Pact 923
The End of Emperor Worship 933

CHAPTER 38 Revival and Revolution in East Asia 936
The Recovery of Japan 937 ▪ *The American Occupation* ▪
Economic and Social Development ▪ *Japan's International Role* ⚜ **TOKYO AND
THE MODERN WORLD 942** ▪ **China in Revolution 942** ▪
Postwar China and the Communist Triumph ▪ *Reconstruction and Consolidation* ▪
The Great Leap Forward ▪ *The Sino-Soviet Split* ▪ *The Cultural Revolution* ▪
China After Mao ▪ **Taiwan and Hong Kong 952** ▪ **Divided Korea 952** ▪
Southeast Asia Since World War II 954 ▪ *The Philippines and Indonesia* ▪
Indochina and the Vietnam War ▪ *Malaysia, Singapore, and Thailand* ▪ *Burma* ▪
Women Leaders in Modern East Asia 958 ▪
Women in East Asian Society 959 ▪
Rewards and Problems of Modernization 960

◎ **Documents:**
MacArthur: An Assessment 939
Attack on the "Revisionists" and "Imperialists" 946
Mao: The Revolutionary Vision 947
Revolution, Chinese Style 949

**CHAPTER 39 Nationalism and Revolution: India, Pakistan, Iran,
and the Middle East 963**
South Asia: Independence and Political Division 964 ▪
The Kashmir Conflict ▪ **India After Independence 968** ▪ *India Under Nehru* ▪
⚜ **INDIRA GANDHI 970** ▪ *The Sikhs* ▪ *India After Indira Gandhi* ▪
Bangladesh and Pakistan 973 ▪ **Sri Lanka 974** ▪
The Turbulent Middle East 975 ▪ *The Establishment of Israel* ▪
The Zionist Movement ▪ *Conflict over Palestine* ⚜ **DAVID BEN-GURION,
ISRAEL'S FOUNDER 978** ▪ *Israeli Society: Challenge and Conflict* ▪
The Arab-Israeli Wars ⚜ **JERUSALEM: A CITY DIVIDED 981** ▪
Arab Nationalism 981 ▪ *Nasser and the Egyptian Revolution* ▪
The Middle East in the Postwar World 983 ▪ *OPEC and the Politics of Oil* ▪
Modernization and Revolution in Iran ▪ *Women and the Islamic Revolution* ▪
The Middle East Today ▪ *Legacy of Violence: The Lebanese Civil War*

◎ **Documents:**
Muslim Solidarity: Jinnah's Call 965
India and the Sense of History 967
India's World Role 970
Israel or Palestine? 977
Militant Islam 986

CHAPTER 40 **Decolonization and Development:
Africa and Latin America** 990
Africa: The Seeds of Revolt 991 ▪
Black Africa: The Challenges of Nationhood 992 ▪
The Achievement of Independence ❦ **JOMO KENYATTA: KENYA'S
FOUNDING FATHER** 995 ▪ **South Africa** 996 ▪ **North Africa** 998 ▪
South America: Reform and Revolution 1000 ▪ *Brazil: The Unstable Giant* ▪
❦ **BRASILIA: THE PLANNED CITY** 1003 ▪
Argentina: Dictatorship and Democracy ▪
Chile and Peru: Socialism and the Military ▪ *Bolivia: Land of Revolutions* ▪
Central America and the Caribbean 1008 ▪ *The Cuban Revolution* ▪
Patterns of Violence ▪ *The Nicaraguan Revolution* ▪
Mexico in the Twentieth Century 1012 ▪
Society and Culture in Latin America 1013 ▪
Women and the Culture of Machismo

◎ **Documents:**
Black Power 995
Apartheid and the Oppression of Women 998
Eva Perón on Peronism 1005
Che Guevara on Guerrilla Warfare 1010
A Sandinista Woman 1011

彩 **GLOBAL ESSAY** **MAPS AND THEIR MAKERS (II)** 1016

CHAPTER 41 **The Age of the Superpowers** 1021
The Cold War 1022 ▪ *Potsdam and the Origins of the Cold War* ▪
From the Truman Doctrine to the Berlin Blockade ▪
The Cold War and American Politics ▪
The Soviet Union and Eastern Europe 1025 ▪
Postwar Reconstruction in the Soviet Union ▪
From National Fronts to People's Democracies ▪ *The Yugoslav Model* ▪
De-Stalinization and the Rise of Khrushchev ▪ *Dissent and Diversity* ▪
Western Europe and North America 1028 ▪ *The Political Revival of Europe* ▪
Women and Social Change in Western Europe and the Communist Bloc ▪
American Society in Transition ❦ **MARTIN LUTHER KING, JR., AND THE
STRUGGLE FOR CIVIL RIGHTS** 1031 ▪
The New Activism and American Women ▪
Canada: Economic Expansion and Social Change ▪
From Brinkmanship to Détente 1035 ▪ *Confrontation and Crisis* ▪
Brezhnev and the Return to Repression ❦ **MOSCOW: RUSSIAN CITY AND
SOVIET CAPITAL** 1038 ▪ *Coexistence and Détente* ▪
The Superpowers Challenged 1040 ▪ *The Growth of European Autonomy* ▪
The Nonaligned World ▪ **The Nuclear Peril** 1043 ▪ *The Quest for Disarmament* ▪
The Gorbachev Era

◉ **Documents:**
The Iron Curtain 1023
Letter from Birmingham Jail 1033
The Cuban Missile Crisis: Two Views 1037
Perestroika: Reform in Gorbachev's Russia 1045

EPILOGUE **Civilization and the Dilemma of Progress** **1047**
History, Time, and Progress 1047 ▪
Global Implications of Progress 1048 ▪
Facing the Future: History as Freedom 1049

Index I-1

MAPS AND GRAPHS

22.1	France Under Louis XIV **525**		32.1	German and British Industrial Production, 1882–1912 **770**
22.2	Europe in 1714 **534**		33.1	Africa on the Eve of World War I **805**
22.3	Russia in the Age of Peter the Great, 1689–1725 **536**		33.2	Growth of the British Empire in India **808**
22.4	The Rise of Brandenburg-Prussia **540**		33.3	Growth of India's Railway Network **809**
24.1	Overseas Trade in the Seventeenth and Eighteenth Centuries **575**		33.4	Major Ports and Commercially Productive Areas in East Asia, 1600–1940 **810**
24.2	The Expansion of Europe, 1715 **578**		33.5	Colonial Empires in Asia **815**
24.3	The British Empire in 1763 **583**		33.6	Colonial Empires in the Pacific, c. 1900 **825**
24.4	The Expansion of the United States **587**		34.1	World War I, 1914–1916 **841**
24.5	Latin American Independence **591**		34.2	Territorial Settlements in Europe, 1919–1926 **847**
25.1	The Partitioning of Poland, 1772–1795 **605**		35.1	Russia in War and Revolution, 1917–1921 **868**
26.1	Paris at the Outbreak of the French Revolution **621**		35.2	China in the 1930s **875**
26.2	The Expansion of Revolutionary France, 1792–1799 **632**		35.3	The Growth of Shanghai **877**
26.3	Europe in 1810 **639**		36.1	Unemployment in Germany, 1929–1934 **898**
27.1	India **654**		37.1	Central Europe, 1939 **922**
28.1	China Proper Under the Ch'ing **672**		37.2	World War II in Europe **924**
28.2	Tokugawa Japan **683**		37.3	The China-Burma-India Theater in World War II **926**
29.1	European Industrialization, c. 1850 **696**		37.4	World War II in Eastern Asia **932**
29.2	Urbanization in Europe **711**		38.1	Modern Japan **937**
29.3	Railways in Great Britain, 1825–1914 **712**		38.2	Modern China **944**
30.1	Europe After the Congress of Vienna (1815) **723**		38.3	Modern Korea **953**
30.2	Ethnic Composition of the Austro-Hungarian Empire **728**		38.4	Southeast Asia **956**
30.3	Parliamentary Representation in Britain Before 1832 **736**		39.1	South Asia Today **964**
30.4	Europe's Revolutions of 1848 **741**		39.2	Major Languages of India **969**
31.1	Europe in 1871 **750**		39.3	Sri Lanka **975**
31.2	The Unification of Italy, 1859–1870 **752**		39.4	The Modern Middle East **984**
31.3	The Unification of Germany, 1866–1871 **755**		40.1	Africa Today **993**
31.4	The Decline of the Ottoman Empire to 1914 **763**		40.2	Modern South America **1001**
			40.3	Mexico and Central America **1008**
			41.1	Europe Since World War II **1041**

PREFACE

Our ability to relate to other cultures and peoples demands some understanding of their history and values; without this understanding there can be no responsible citizenship, no informed judgment, and no effective commitment to seek peace and dignity for all. Americans do not live in isolation from people in Asia, Africa, Europe, and the Middle East. Our ability to understand and respect one another necessitates an awareness of our historical roots.

This text seeks to forge a new path in the way we understand the past. Most textbooks that cover world civilizations were originally European histories to which a few non-Western chapters were added. *Civilizations of the World* was from its beginning a *world* history—a conscious effort to discuss historical events, cultures, societies, and beliefs in a global context, yet built on the Western cultural heritage to which most students have been primarily exposed. At the same time it leads students from their Western orientation to a truly global understanding of the past and the present.

Part Structure and Part Essays

We have divided the text into 41 chapters, enabling the instructor to cover approximately half a chapter in each class hour. We have also grouped the chapters into five parts, each of which is prefaced with a brief essay summarizing the principal themes discussed in that part. Historical divisions, while to a certain extent arbitrary, are essential if students are to organize and analyze what they study.

Biographical Portraits

World histories sometimes fail to give students a sense of personal intimacy with the subject. Migratory movements, famines and plagues, trading patterns, and imperial conquests are all important in history, but the individual also matters. Scholars used to write about the past in terms of its "great men"; that is not our purpose, although great men and women will always be part of any broad historical study. To emphasize the personal element, we have included a biographical portrait in most chapters. The subjects are not necessarily history's most famous personalities, although each made a significant contribution to society. Among them are cultural figures, such as the Greek poet Sappho, the Japanese artist Hokusai, and the German dramatist Bertolt Brecht. Others are religious leaders, such as Gautama Buddha; St. Clare, founder of the Roman Catholic order of Poor Sisters; and the Quaker pamphleteer Margaret Fell. Some were prominent in the political world: the rebel Chinese Emperor Hung-wu; the South American liberator Simón Bolívar; and David Ben Gurion, a founding father of Israel. Others, such as England's Mary Wollstonecraft and the Soviet feminist Alexandra Kollontai, were especially concerned with women's rights. The lives of these people offer special insights into the societies of which they were a part.

Urban Portraits

Civilization begins with the city, and modern society is increasingly urban. We have therefore provided accounts of how cities around the world have developed. We do this not by organizing each historical era around a particular city, for this would distort the past, but rather by making urban portraits an integral part of the historical narrative. Some of the cities—Italy's Pompeii and Mexico's Teotihuacán, for example—are now in ruins, while others—Shanghai, Baghdad, Moscow—are thriving. Jerusalem, Paris, Tokyo (Edo), and Rome are revisited at different periods to give a sense of how they changed over time. Like the biographical portraits, the urban portraits provide instructors with excellent topics for discussion, essay questions, and unusual lecture themes, while students will find them intriguing subjects for term papers.

Women and Minorities

This text is particularly sensitive to women and minorities. The contributions of women to both Western and non-Western societies—whether as rulers, artists and writers, revolutionaries, workers, or wives and mothers—are systematically considered. The biographical portraits featuring women are the most obvious illustrations of the attention given to women, but discussions of their contributions are also interwoven throughout the text's narrative. Consideration is also given to the role of minorities. Four black figures are highlighted in the portraits: the dancer and social activist Josephine Baker, the African monarch Sundiata, Jomo Kenyatta of modern Kenya, and Dr. Martin Luther King, Jr. As one of the founders of Western civilization and a significant force throughout their history, the Jews are covered more fully in this text than in any comparable work. They are followed from their settlement in ancient Palestine to their persecution and exile under the Romans, and from their medieval migrations to their return to Palestine and the founding of modern Israel. By recounting the histories of these groups, we hope to make students aware of their achievements.

Social and Cultural Coverage

Recent scholarship has placed considerable emphasis on social and cultural history. That scholarship is reflected throughout this text, but perhaps most clearly in two chapters that are unique among survey texts. Chapter 7, "The Ancient World Religions," offers a comparative overview of the great religions and philosophies of the ancient world, with a discussion of Islam immediately following in Chapter 8. Chapter 21, "The Societies of the Early Modern World," provides a fascinating overview of such key elements of the world's societies in the sixteenth and seventeenth centuries as marriage, the family, sexual customs, education, poverty, and crime. Moreover, at eight different points throughout the text, we pause to consider four significant sociocultural themes: writing and communication, the human image, mapping, and the human experience of death. Here again are special opportunities for distinctive lectures, discussions, essay topics, and research papers.

Pedagogy

Map Atlas and Full-Color Art Inserts

There are two types of special color inserts in the book. First, included in the front matter, is an eight-page full-color atlas showing the physical characteristics of major areas of the globe. This section is intended as a reference that students can use to improve their knowledge of geography. There are also over 100 maps in the text itself.

In addition to the atlas, in the combined volume there are four full-color inserts titled "The Visual Experience," each insert featuring about 15 illustrations—of painting, sculpture, architecture, and objets d'art—that are related in a meaningful way to the text's presentation of history. In the split volumes, selected color inserts are included. The text illustrations consist of a separate program of close to 400 engravings, photographs, and other images chosen for their historical relevance.

Primary Source Documents

To enhance the usefulness of this text, we have provided not only a generous complement of maps and illustrations but also a comprehensive selection of primary sources. By studying these documents—usually four or five per chapter—students can see the kinds of materials with which historians work. More important, they can interpret the sources and so participate directly in the process of understanding. To emphasize the sense of history as a living discipline, we have provided surveys of conflicting historiographic interpretations of the Renaissance, the French Revolution, imperialism, and fascism.

Reading Lists

The discipline of history goes far beyond merely amassing raw data such as names, places, and dates. Historical study demands analysis, synthesis, and a critical sense of the worth of each source. The discipline of history thus teaches skills important to every citizen. As a guide to students who wish to hone their historical understanding and analytical skills, an up-to-date reading list is provided at the end of each chapter.

The task of writing a world history is both daunting and humbling. This book is the result of not only our own research but also that of many others, all of whom share our belief in the importance of historical study. To the extent that we have succeeded in introducing students to the rich and varied heritage of the past, we owe that success in a very special way to our fellow historians and to the discipline to which we as colleagues have dedicated our careers.

RICHARD L. GREAVES
ROBERT ZALLER
PHILIP V. CANNISTRARO
RHOADS MURPHEY

SUPPLEMENTS

The following supplements are available for use in conjunction with this book:

- The *Instructor's Manual,* by Robert Zaller and Richard L. Greaves, includes lecture themes (especially formatted for the new instructor) and special lecture topics designed to appeal to the more experienced teacher; added topics for class discussion and essays; a list of films; identification items; and map items for study.

- The *Study Guide,* by Robert Zaller and Richard L. Greaves, contains an exceptional number of student study aids. For each chapter there are an overview of the chapter content; map exercises using outline maps; chronologies of key events; identification exercises involving people, places, events, dynasties, and more; definitions; completion exercises; short-answer questions; exercises in understanding the documents in the text; "Points to Ponder"; and topics for term papers.

- *Mapping the Human Adventure: A Guide to Historical Geography,* by Glee Wilson of Kent State University, features 35 sequenced exercises corresponding to the map program in the text. Addressing a renewed interest in remediation in geography, it can be used as a self-contained learning tool or for classroom assignments.

- The *Test Bank of Objective Questions,* by Edward D. Wynot of Florida State University, contains over 2,000 extensively reviewed items for testing factual knowledge, including 50 multiple-choice items for each chapter.

- The *Test Bank of Comparative and Essay Questions,* by Marian Purrier Nelson of the University of Nebraska at Omaha, has over 1,000 items for testing conceptual knowledge, including 20 multiple-choice and 5 essay questions for each chapter.

- *Harper Test,* a highly acclaimed test-generation software package available for IBM computers, allows users to add, edit, delete, and scramble all test items.

- *Grades,* a grade-keeping and class-management system for the IBM-PC and most compatibles, maintains data for up to 200 students.

- *50 Map Transparency Acetates,* for use with overhead projectors, uses maps from the text to reinforce student understanding of historical geography.

World History Media Program

Ask your Harper & Row representative about the following options offered to text adopters as part of Harper & Row's special history media policy:

■ A selection of videos from *The World*. This telecourse was produced by South Carolina Educational Television. The 30-minute programs are based on the *Times Atlas of World History* and include live-action footage, computer-animated maps and graphics, and an emphasis on art and artifacts.

■ *Historical Newsreels*. These authentic newsclips—each just a few minutes in length—offer stimulating lecture openers, a way to convey to students the immediacy and excitement of past events. The clips cover a wide range of historic episodes.

■ Harper & Row Film Rentals. A wide selection of films is available on topics from Western Europe, Africa, and Asia.

■ *World History Media Handbook*. Specially prepared for adopters of *Civilizations of the World,* this brief guide provides descriptions and ordering information for available media resources as well as numerous practical strategies for incorporating media in the classroom.

ACKNOWLEDGMENTS

The authors are grateful to Marianne Russell, Editorial Director at Harper & Row, who not only signed this book but enthusiastically supported it from its inception to its publication. The authors would also like to thank Lauren Silverman, history editor; Mary Lou Mosher, senior development editor; Susan Goldfarb, project editor; and Bruce Emmer, copy editor. This book could not have been completed without the invaluable assistance of Judith Dieker Greaves, editorial assistant to the authors. The authors wish additionally to thank the following persons for their assistance and support: Lili Bita Zaller, Philip Rethis, Kimon Rethis, Robert B. Radin, Julia Southard, Robert S. Browning, and Professors Eric D. Brose, Roger Hackett, Victor Lieberman, William W. Rogers, Donald F. Stevens, Ralph Turner, Thomas Trautmann, and Edward D. Wynot, Jr.

The following scholars read the manuscript in whole or in part and offered many helpful suggestions:

Dorothy Abrahamse
California State University, Long Beach

Winthrop Lindsay Adams
University of Utah

George M. Addy
Brigham Young University

Jay Pascal Anglin
University of Southern Mississippi

Charmarie J. Blaisdell
Northeastern University

William A. Bultmann
Western Washington University

Thomas Callahan, Jr.
Rider College

Miriam Usher Chrisman
University of Massachusetts, Amherst

Jill N. Claster
New York University

Cynthia Schwenk Clemons
Georgia State University

Allen T. Cronenberg
Auburn University

John Dahmus
Stephen F. Austin State University

Elton L. Daniel
University of Hawaii at Manoa

Leslie Derfler
Florida Atlantic University

Joseph M. Dixon
Weber State College

John Patrick Donnelly
Marquette University

Mark U. Edwards, Jr.
Harvard University

Charles A. Endress
Angelo State University

Stephen Englehart
California State Polytechnic University, Pomona

William Wayne Farvis
University of Tennessee

Jonathan Goldstein
West Georgia College

Edwin N. Gorsuch
Georgia State University

Joseph M. Gowaski
Rider College

Tony Grafton
Princeton University

Coburn V. Graves
Kent State University

Janelle Greenberg
University of Pittsburgh

Udo Heyn
California State University,
  Los Angeles

Clive Holmes
Cornell University

Leonard A. Humphreys
University of the Pacific

Donald G. Jones
University of Central Arkansas

William R. Jones
University of New Hampshire

Thomas Kaiser
University of Arkansas at Little Rock

Thomas L. Kennedy
Washington State University

Frank Kidner
San Francisco State University

Winston L. Kinsey
Appalachian State University

Thomas Kuehn
Clemson University

Richard D. Lewis
Saint Cloud State University

David C. Lukowitz
Hamline University

Thomas J. McPartland
Bellevue Community College

Elizabeth Malloy
Salem State College

John A. Mears
Southern Methodist University

V. Dixon Morris
University of Hawaii at Manoa

Marian Purrier Nelson
University of Nebraska at Omaha

William D. Newell
Laramie County Community College

James Odom
East Tennessee State University

William G. Palmer
Marshall University

William D. Phillips, Jr.
San Diego State University

Paul B. Pixton
Brigham Young University

Ronald R. Rader
University of Georgia

Leland Sather
Weber State College

Kerry E. Spiers
University of Louisville

Paul Stewart
Southern Connecticut State University

Richard G. Stone
Western Kentucky University

Alexander Sydorenko
Arkansas State University

Teddy Uldricks
University of North Carolina at Asheville

Raymond Van Dam
University of Michigan, Ann Arbor

John Weakland
Ball State University

David L. White
Appalachian State University

Richard S. Williams
Washington State University

Glee E. Wilson
Kent State University

John E. Wood
James Madison University

Martin Yanuck
Spelman College

About the Authors

RICHARD L. GREAVES Born in Glendale, California, Richard L. Greaves—with Robert Zaller general editor of this text—is a specialist in Reformation and British social and religious history. Greaves earned his Ph.D. degree at the University of London in 1964. After teaching at Michigan State University, he moved in 1972 to Florida State University, where he is now Robert O. Lawton Distinguished Professor of History and Courtesy Professor of Religion. A Fellow of the Royal Historical Society, Greaves has received fellowships from the National Endowment for the Humanities, the American Council of Learned Societies, the Andrew Mellon Foundation, the Huntington Library, and the American Philosophical Society. The eighteen books he has written or edited include *John Bunyan* (1969), *Theology and Revolution in the Scottish Reformation: Studies in the Thought of John Knox* (1980), *Saints and Rebels: Seven Nonconformists in Stuart England* (1985), *Deliver Us from Evil: The Radical Underground in Britain, 1660–1663* (1986), and *Enemies Under His Feet: Radicals and Nonconformists in Britain, 1664–1677* (1990). The Conference on British Studies awarded Greaves the Walter D. Love Memorial Prize for *The Puritan Revolution and Educational Thought: Background for Reform* (1969), and his *Society and Religion in Elizabethan England* (1981) was a finalist for the Robert Livingston Schuyler Prize of the American Historical Association. He has been named president of the American Society of Church History for 1991.

ROBERT ZALLER Robert Zaller was born in New York City and received a Ph.D. degree from Washington University in 1968. An authority on British political history and constitutional thought, he has also written extensively on modern literature, film, and art. He has taught at Queens College, City University of New York; the University of California, Santa Barbara; and the University of Miami. He is Professor of History and former Head of the Department of History and Politics at Drexel University. He has been a Guggenheim fellow and is a member of the advisory board of the Yale Center for Parliamentary History. His book *The Parliament of 1621: A Study in Constitutional Conflict* (1971) received the Phi Alpha Theta prize for the best first book by a member of the society, and he was made a Fellow of Tor House in recognition of his study *The Cliffs of Solitude: A Reading of Robinson Jeffers* (1983). His other books include *Lives of the Poet* (1974) and *Europe in Transition, 1660–1815* (1984). He has edited *A Casebook on Anaïs Nin* (1974), and coedited, with Richard L. Greaves, a *Biographical Dictionary of British Radicals in the Seventeenth Century* (3 vols., 1982–1984). Zaller's most recent publications include studies of Samuel Beckett, Philip Guston, Bernardo Bertolucci, and the English civil war. With Richard L. Greaves he is general editor of this text.

PHILIP V. CANNISTRARO A native of New York City, Philip V. Cannistraro, an authority on modern Italian history and culture, received the Ph.D. degree from

New York University in 1971. Currently Professor of History and Head of the Department of History and Politics at Drexel University, Cannistraro taught at Florida State University and has been a visiting professor at New York University and St. Mary's College, Rome. He has lectured widely in Italy and in the United States and is American editor of the Italian historical quarterly *Storia Contemporanea*. The recipient of two Fulbright-Hays fellowships, Cannistraro is an active member of the Society for Italian Historical Studies and the American Italian Historical Association. His numerous publications include *La Fabbrica del Consenso: Fascismo e Mass Media* (1975), *Poland and the Coming of the Second World War* (with E. Wynot and T. Kovaleff, 1976), *Italian Fascist Activities in the United States* (1976), *Fascismo, Chiesa e Emigrazione* (with G. Rosoli, 1979), *Historical Dictionary of Fascist Italy* (1981), and *Italian Americans: The Search for a Usable Past* (with R. Juliani, 1989). Cannistraro is currently writing biographies of Generoso Pope and Margherita Sarfatti.

RHOADS MURPHEY Born in Philadelphia, Rhoads Murphey, a specialist in Chinese history and in geography, received the Ph.D. degree from Harvard University in 1950. Before joining the faculty of the University of Michigan in 1964, he taught at the University of Washington; he has also been a visiting professor at Taiwan University and Tokyo University. From 1954 to 1956 he was the director of the Conference of Diplomats in Asia. The University of Michigan granted him a Distinguished Service Award in 1974. Currently president of the Association for Asian Studies, Murphey has served as editor of the *Journal of Asian Studies* and *Michigan Papers in Chinese Studies*. The Social Science Research Council, the Ford Foundation, the Guggenheim Foundation, the National Endowment for the Humanities, and the American Council of Learned Societies have awarded him fellowships. A prolific author, Murphey's books include *Shanghai: Key to Modern China* (1953), *An Introduction to Geography* (4th ed., 1978), *A New China Policy* (with others, 1965), *Approaches to Modern Chinese History* (with others, 1967), *The Scope of Geography* (3rd ed., 1982), *The Treaty Ports and China's Modernization* (1970), *China Meets the West: The Treaty Ports* (1975), and *The Fading of the Maoist Vision* (1980). *The Outsiders: Westerners in India and China* (1977) won the Best-Book-of-the-Year award from the University of Michigan Press.

A Note on the Spelling
of Asian Names and Words

Nearly all Asian languages are written with symbols different from our Western alphabet. Chinese, Japanese, and Korean are written with ideographic characters, plus a phonetic syllabary for Japanese and Korean. Most other Asian languages have their own scripts, symbols, diacritical marks, and alphabets, which differ from ours. There can thus be no single "correct spelling" in Western symbols for Asian words or names, including personal names and place names—only established conventions. Unfortunately, conventions in this respect differ widely and in many cases reflect preferences or forms related to different Western languages. The Western spellings used in this book, including its maps, are to some extent a compromise, in an effort to follow the main English-language conventions but also to make pronunciation for English speakers as easy as possible.

Chinese presents the biggest problem, since there are a great many different conventions in use and since well-known place names, such as Peking or Canton, are commonly spelled as they are here in most Western writings, even though this spelling is inconsistent with all of the romanization systems in current use and does not accurately represent the Chinese sounds. Most American newspapers and some journals now use the romanization system called *pinyin,* approved by the Chinese government, which renders these two city names, with greater phonetic accuracy, as Beijing and Kwangzhou but which presents other problems for most Western readers and which they commonly mispronounce.

The usage in this book follows the most commonly used convention for scholarly publication when romanizing Chinese names, the Wade-Giles system, but gives the pinyin equivalents for modern names (if they differ) in parentheses after the first use of a name. Readers will encounter both spellings, plus others, in other books, papers, and journals, and some familiarity with both conventions is thus necessary.

In general, readers should realize and remember that English spellings of names from other languages (such as Munich for München, Vienna for Wien, and Rome for Roma), especially in Asia, can be only approximations and may differ confusingly from one Western source or map to another.

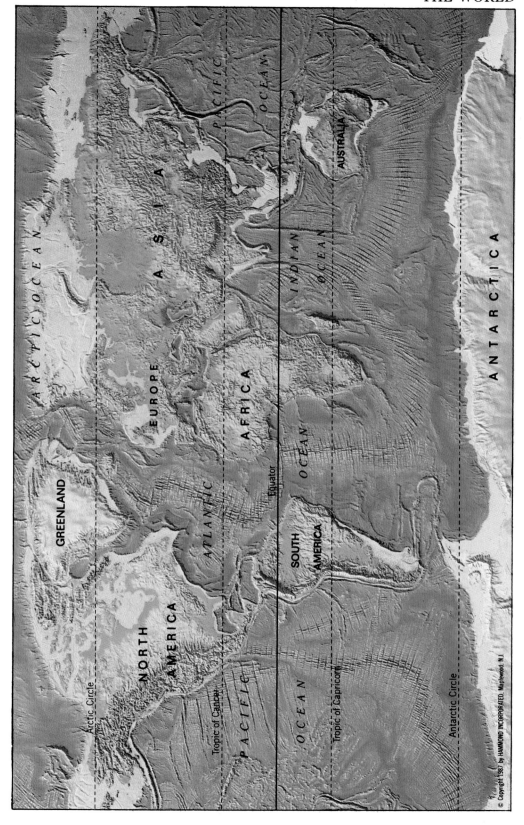

ARCTIC OCEAN

ASIA

EUROPE

AFRICA

PACIFIC

OCEAN

INDIAN

OCEAN

AUSTRALIA

ANTARCTICA

GREENLAND

ATLANTIC

OCEAN

Equator

SOUTH
AMERICA

NORTH
AMERICA

PACIFIC

OCEAN

Arctic Circle

Tropic of Cancer

Tropic of Capricorn

Antarctic Circle

EUROPE

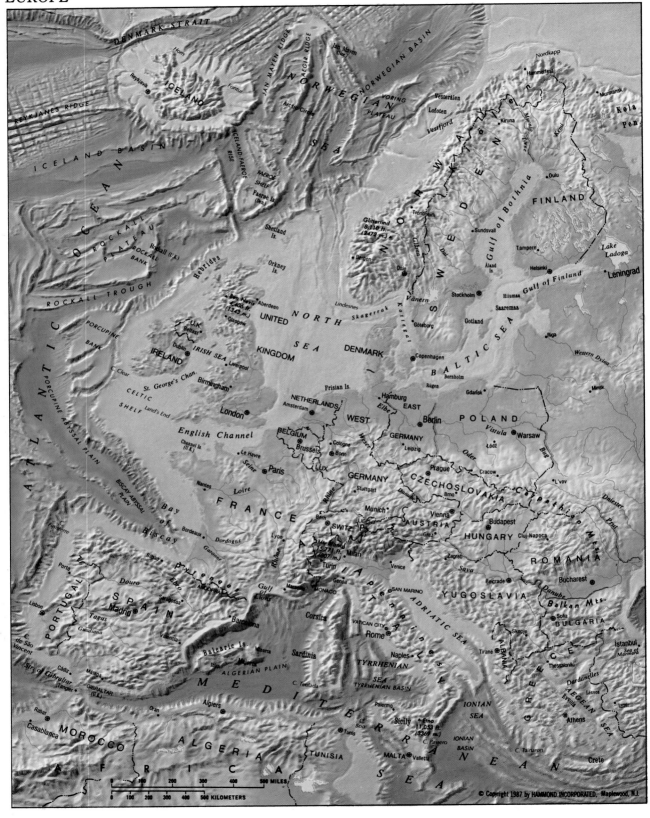

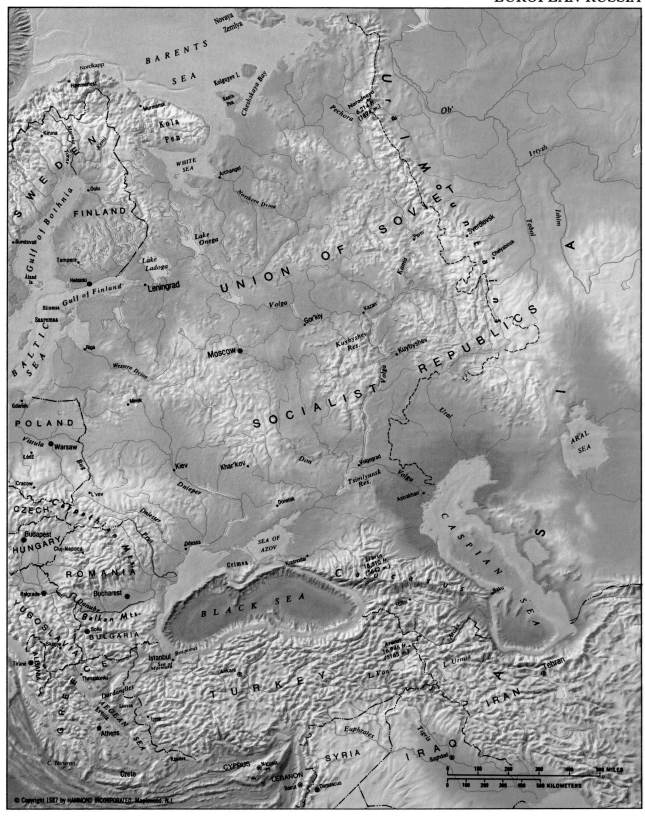

BARENTS

SEA

Novaya
Zemlya

Nordkapp

Kolguyev I.

Hammerfest

Chesha

Murmansk

Kanin
Pen.

Kola
Pen.

WHITE
SEA

Pechora

Norodnaya
21,214 ft.
(1894 m.)

Ob'

Irtysh

Kiruna

Archangel

Ishim

SWEDEN

Northern Dvina

Oulu

FINLAND

Lake
Onega

Perm

Sverdlovsk

Sundsvall

Tampere

Lake
Ladoga

Kama

Chelyabinsk

Tobol

Gulf of Bothnia

Åland
Is.

Helsinki

Leningrad

UNION OF SOVIET

Volga

Gor'kiy

Kazan'

Hiiumaa

Gulf of Finland

Saaremaa

Riga

Kuybyshev
Res.

Kuybyshev

Moscow

BALTIC

SEA

Western Dvina

SOCIALIST REPUBLICS

Gdańsk

Minsk

Ural

ARAL
SEA

POLAND

Vistula

Warsaw

Don

Volga

Łódź

Bug

Kiev

Khar'kov

Volgograd

Cracow

L'vov

Dnieper

Tsimlyansk
Res.

Volga

CZECH.

Dniester

Astrakhan'

CASPIAN SEA

Budapest

HUNGARY

Cluj-Napoca

Prut

Odessa

SEA OF
AZOV

Donetsk

ROMANIA

Crimea

Krasnodar

Elbrus
18,510 ft.
(5642 m.)

Belgrade

Bucharest

Danube

Balkan Mts.

BLACK SEA

Caucasus

Baku

YUGOSLAVIA

Sofia

BULGARIA

Tbilisi

Skopje

Istanbul

Bosporus

Kura

Tirane

Sea of
Marmara

Ankara

L. Urmia

ALBANIA

Thessaloniki

L. Van

Tehran

Dardanelles

IRAN

Lésvos

TURKEY

Ararat
16,946 ft.
(5165 m.)

Évvoia

GREECE

Izmir

AEGEAN

Athens

SEA

Euphrates

Tigris

C. Taínaron

Rhodes

SYRIA

IRAQ

Crete

CYPRUS

Nicosia

Baghdad

LEBANON

Beirut

Damascus

100   200   300   400   500 MILES

100 200 300 400 500 KILOMETERS

AFRICA

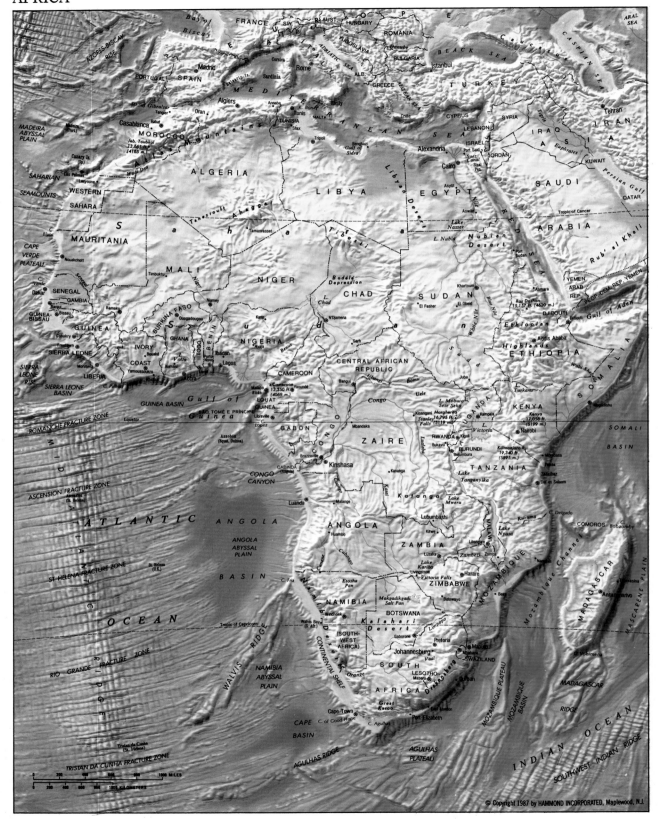

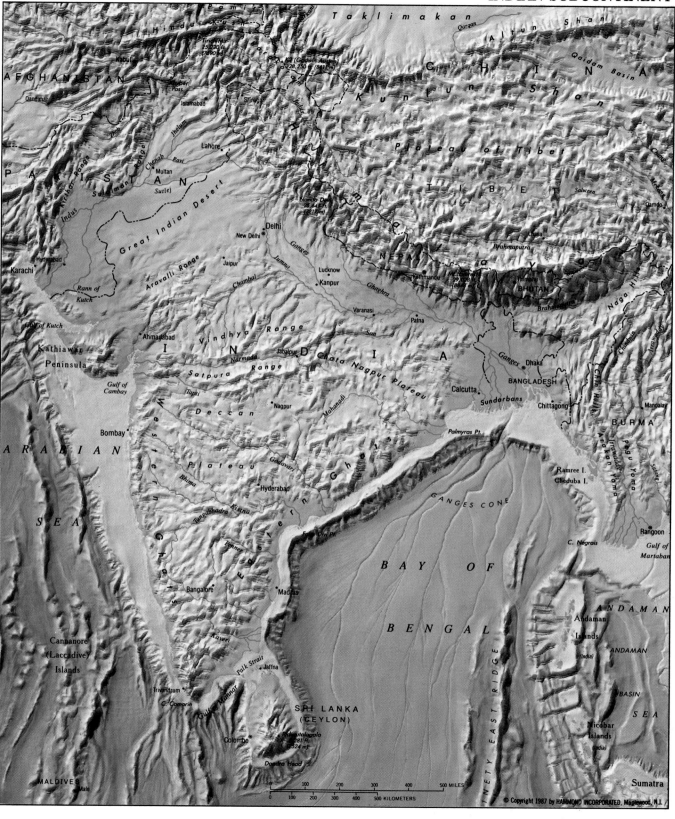

INDIAN SUBCONTINENT

Taklimakan

Qarqan

Altun Shan

Qaidam Basin

AFGHANISTAN

Hindu Kush

Qandahar

Kabul

Khyber Pass

Islamabad

K2 (Godwin Austen)
28,250 ft. (8611 m)

Kunlun Shan

CHINA

Plateau of Tibet

TIBET

PAKISTAN

Kirthar Range

Sulaiman Range

Zhob

Jhelum

Srinagar

Indus

Chenab

Ravi

Lahore

Multan

Sutlej

Nanda Devi
25,645 ft.
(7817 m)

Salween

Chamdo

Mekong

Lhasa

Brahmaputra

NEPAL

Kathmandu

Mt. Everest
29,028 ft.
(8848 m)

Himalaya

BHUTAN

Thimphu

Naga Hills

Hyderabad

Karachi

Rann of
Kutch

Great Indian Desert

Aravalli Range

Delhi

New Delhi

Ganges

Jumna

Jaipur

Chambal

Lucknow

Kanpur

Ghaghra

Varanasi

Son

Patna

Ganges

Dhaka

BANGLADESH

Brahmaputra

Chin Hills

Irrawaddy

Chindwin

Gulf of Kutch

Kathiawar
Peninsula

Gulf of
Cambay

Ahmadabad

INDIA

Vindhya Range

Narmada

Jabalpur

Satpura Range

Tapti

Deccan

Nagpur

Chota Nagpur Plateau

Mahanadi

Calcutta

Sundarbans

Chittagong

Mandalay

BURMA

Pegu Yoma

Arakan Yoma

Bombay

Plateau

Godavari

Western Ghats

Bhima

Hyderabad

Kistna

Tungabhadra

Palmyras Pt.

Ramree I.
Cheduba I.

GANGES CONE

BAY OF
BENGAL

C. Negrais

Rangoon

Gulf of
Martaban

ARABIAN

SEA

Penner

Bangalore

Eastern Ghats

Madras

False Divi Pt.

Sitang

ANDAMAN

Andaman
Islands
(India)

ANDAMAN

Cannanore
(Laccadive)
Islands

Kaveri

Palk Strait

Jaffna

Gulf of Mannar

Trivandrum

C. Comorin

SRI LANKA
(CEYLON)

Pidurutalagala
8,281 ft.
(2524 m)

Colombo

Dondra Head

NINETY EAST RIDGE

BASIN

SEA

Nicobar
Islands
(India)

MALDIVES

Male

Sumatra

100   200   300   400   500 MILES

0

0   100   200   300   400   500 KILOMETERS

© Copyright 1987 by HAMMOND INCORPORATED, Maplewood, N.J.

EAST AND SOUTHEAST ASIA

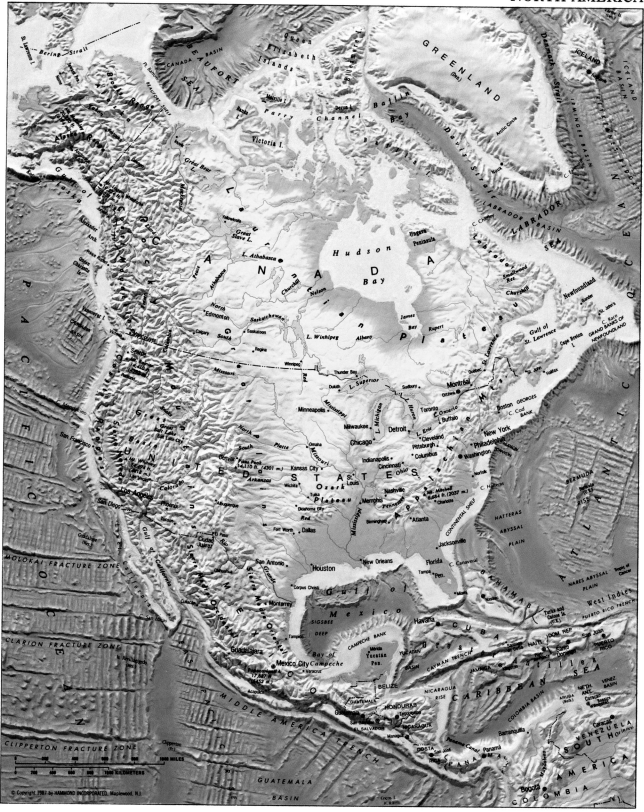

SOUTH AMERICA

Oceans, Seas & Basins: CARIBBEAN SEA, CONTINENTAL SHELF, DEMERARA ABYSSAL PLAIN, PARA ABYSSAL PLAIN, CEARA ABYSSAL PLAIN, AMAZON CANYONS, ATLANTIC OCEAN, ARGENTINE BASIN, PACIFIC OCEAN, PERU BASIN, CHILE BASIN, NAZCA RIDGE, PERU-CHILE TRENCH, CHALLENGER FRACTURE ZONE, MORNINGTON ABYSSAL PLAIN, FALKLAND ESCARPMENT, FALKLAND PLATEAU, FALKLAND RIDGE, NORTH SCOTIA RIDGE, RIO GRANDE PLATEAU, SANTOS PLATEAU, CONTINENTAL SLOPE

Countries: NICARAGUA, COSTA RICA, PANAMA, COLOMBIA, VENEZUELA, GUYANA, SURINAME, FRENCH GUIANA, ECUADOR, PERU, BRAZIL, BOLIVIA, PARAGUAY, CHILE, ARGENTINA, URUGUAY, West Indies, TRINIDAD & TOBAGO

Cities: Barranquilla, Maracaibo, Caracas, Ciudad Guayana, Georgetown, Paramaribo, Cayenne, Belém, São Luis, Fortaleza, Recife, Quito, Guayaquil, Iquitos, Manaus, Teresina, Lima, Cusco, Cochabamba, Salvador, Belo Horizonte, Goiânia, Campo Grande, Brasília, Antofagasta, Asunción, São Paulo, Rio de Janeiro, Curitiba, Córdoba, Santa Fe, Rosario, Santiago, Concepción, Porto Alegre, Buenos Aires, Montevideo, La Plata, Bahía Blanca, Stanley

Physical Features: Orinoco, Amazon, Negro, Japurá, Içá, Juruá, Purus, Madeira, Tapajós, Xingu, Tocantins, Araguaia, Paraná, Paraguay, Pilcomayo, Bermejo, Uruguay, Colorado, Salado, Río de la Plata, Planalto de Mato Grosso, Brazilian Highlands, Gran Chaco, Tropic of Capricorn, Equator, L. Maracaibo, L. Titicaca, L. Poopó, Lagoa dos Patos, Lagoa Mirim, Golfo San Matías, Golfo San Jorge, Pen. Valdés, Bahía Grande, Str. of Magellan, Tierra del Fuego, Cape Horn, Falkland Islands (U.K.), I. de Marajó, Archipiélago de los Chonos, Isla de Chiloé, Juan Fernández Is. (Chile), I. Robinson Crusoe (Chile), Alexandro Selkirk, I. de San Felix (Chile), I. San Ambrosio (Chile), Mt. Roraima, Cerro Aconcagua 22,831 ft. (6959 m.), Chimborazo 20,561 ft. (6267 m.), Huascarán 22,205 ft. (6768 m.), Illampu 21,489 ft. (6550 m.), Vol. Ullailaco 22,057 ft. (6723 m.), Nev. Ojos del Salado 22,573 ft. (6880 m.), Pico de Bandeira 9,482 ft. (2890 m.)

Ithaka

As you set out for Ithaka
hope your road is a long one,
full of adventure, full of discovery.
Laistrygonians, Cyclops,
angry Poseidon—don't be afraid of them:
you'll never find things like that on your way
as long as you keep your thoughts raised high,
as long as a rare excitement
stirs your spirit and your body.

Laistrygonians, Cyclops,
wild Poseidon—you won't encounter them
unless you bring them along inside your soul,
unless your soul sets them up in front of you.

Hope your road is a long one.
May there be many summer mornings when,
with what pleasure, what joy,
you enter harbors you're seeing for the first time;
may you stop at Phoenician trading stations
to buy fine things,
mother of pearl and coral, amber and ebony,
sensual perfume of every kind—
as many sensual perfumes as you can;
and may you visit many Egyptian cities
to learn and go on learning from their scholars.

Keep Ithaka always in your mind.
Arriving there is what you're destined for.
But don't hurry the journey at all.
Better if it lasts for years,
so you're old by the time you reach the island,
wealthy with all you've gained on the way,
not expecting Ithaka to make you rich.

Ithaka gave you the marvelous journey.
Without her you wouldn't have set out.
She has nothing left to give you now.

And if you find her poor, Ithaka won't have fooled you.
Wise as you will have become, so full of experience,
you'll have understood by then what these Ithakas mean.

C. P. Cavafy

CIVILIZATIONS OF THE WORLD

The Societies of the Early Modern World

The richness and variety of the world's societies is abundantly revealed in the period of transition between the medieval and modern worlds that extends from approximately 1400 to 1800. Throughout the Western world in particular, social structures, behavioral patterns, and value systems underwent important changes that helped determine the character of today's societies. The institution of the family also altered, again mostly in the West, whereas in Asia the traditional family remained the bulwark of social hierarchy and stability. The age of women's rights lay in the future, but throughout the world women made significant contributions to their societies, sometimes in terms of political power at the highest levels of government. Women ruled, or were powers behind the throne, in societies as different as western Europe, Africa, and the Ottoman Empire.

The dress and many of the pursuits of the aristocracy—such as hunting, lawn bowling, and formal afternoon promenades—set them apart from the other social classes. This is a detail from *Le Rendez-vous pour Marly* by Moreau le Jeune. [The Metropolitan Museum of Art, Harris Bisbane Dick Fund, 1933]

The early modern period saw dramatic educational expansion in the West and a printing revolution in both the West and Asia. For the most part, neither Africa nor the Ottoman Empire effectively shared in these developments. Although patterns of trade became worldwide in the early modern period, most people lived at or near the subsistence level. To alleviate misery, Asians looked primarily to the family, Europeans to religious, civic, and charitable institutions. In many respects, however, people responded to their social needs in similar ways, as reflected, for example, in the resort of the desperate in virtually all societies to banditry. This was particularly so in areas where governmental power was weak and resentment of urban wealth was strong. Beyond the threads of common human experience, however, differing value systems, rooted in religion and tradition, shaped early modern societies into distinct entities.

Social Hierarchies

Traditional Asian civilizations were hierarchically based, marked not only by the uniquely Indian institution of caste but also by the status groupings associated with kingship, feudal-style relations, occupation, age, gender, and levels of literacy and learning. In general, apart from caste, the importance of the social hierarchy and the emphasis on achieving status through learning remains a distinctive aspect of Indian, Chinese, Korean, and Japanese civilizations to the present day. Perhaps more than any other characteristic, this emphasis on seeking status and advancement through education distinguishes them from most societies elsewhere. For many Asians, an individual's place in the hierarchy is still the most important single determinant of how to behave, and the proper observance of hierarchical rules remains the most basic means of preserving social and political harmony.

Southeast Asia has always been fundamentally different from China, Korea, India, and Japan, partly because of the influences of Buddhism and Islam, both of which stress equality, and partly because of the indigenous nature of Southeast Asian culture. Kingship and the hierarchies related to it, however, were common in Southeast Asia too.

Caste and the Social Order in India

In contrast to the merit system of China and its variants in Vietnam, Korea, and Japan, caste was decreed by birth

◎ Aristocratic Behavior in Japan ◎

The importance of hierarchical order in Japan is revealed in this 1615 decree of a shogun regulating the behavior of the feudal lords, or daimyo, and their retainers, the samurai. *Note the obligation to be aristocrats rather than mere soldiers.*

Literature, arms, archery, and horsemanship are to be the favorite pursuits. Literature first, and arms next to it, was the rule of the ancients. They must both be cultivated concurrently. . . . Drinking parties and gambling amusements must be kept within due bounds. . . . Offenders against the law are not to be harbored in the feudal domains. Law is the very foundation of ceremonial decorum and of social order. To infringe the law in the name of reason is as bad as to outrage reason in the name of the law. . . .

The distinction between lord and vassal, between superior and inferior, must be clearly marked by apparel. Vassals may not . . . wear silk stuffs. . . . Miscellaneous persons are not at their own pleasure to ride in palanquins. . . . Lately even sub-vassals and henchmen of no rank have taken to so riding. This is a flagrant impertinence. . . . The *samurai* throughout the provinces are to practice frugality. Those who are rich like to make a display, while those who are poor are ashamed of not being on a par with others. There is no influence so pernicious as this, and it must be kept strictly in check. . . .

Source: D. Lach, *Asia on the Eve of Europe's Expansion* (Englewood Cliffs, N.J.: Prentice-Hall, 1965), pp. 157–160 passim.

in India. Caste is a sociocultural practice with some religious concepts woven into it. Since it is also practiced by South Asian Muslims, Christians, and Buddhists (in Sri Lanka), it is clearly separable from Hinduism as a nonreligious system evolved later as a means of ordering an otherwise disordered society. The lack of a strong central state was accompanied by chronic disruption. Caste provided a system of social organization, a mutual-benefit society, a trade guild, and a sense of group identity. Ritual pollution and purity became the essence of caste, but its operative units were and are "subcastes," or *jatis*, commonly linked to occupation: potters, weavers, farmers, and so on. Each *jati* was and is endogamous (that is, it restricts marriage to fellow *jati* members), and members are forbidden to eat with or accept food or water from members of other *jatis*. One cannot change one's caste any more than one can change the place where one was born, although caste distinctions seem not to have been observed rigidly until relatively late in Indian history, well after the time of Harsha (seventh century A.D.). However, it has always been possible to escape from caste through religious devotion, again underlining the nonreligious nature of the caste system. The ascetic saddhu, or holy man, was beyond caste and honored by all, regardless of his earthly origins. Such mystics were, and like priests remain, far more numerous in India than elsewhere. South Asians have known for many centuries which *jatis* they were born into, but this is not really part of their religion, any more than genealogy, social class, or occupation are for Christians in the West.

Caste has remained a highly flexible system. Although individuals are born into a given *jati,* by sustained group effort the members of a *jati* can raise its status, often by adopting religious, dietary, and other practices of higher-status groups. This process is called "Sanskritization," from the use of Sanskrit rituals associated with the Brahmins. In addition, the power of group action can be a potent weapon, especially in politics. This is particularly characteristic of Asian societies, where the individual is important primarily as a member of a group, whether family, clan, caste, guild, or regional or linguistic division.

Caste also served the need for some form of hierarchical order in a region of complex divisions. As new religions, cultures, and languages came into India, no single one emerged as permanently dominant. In this bewildering context caste provided a sense of group identity, a means of support and defense, and a cultural vehicle as well, since each caste was necessarily local and shared a common language. Occupational associations for most subcastes meant that they also functioned as the equivalent of guilds and mutual-help societies, serving to arbitrate disputes. Caste was less a matter of religious than of social ordering, and the hierarchy it entailed was perhaps less important than the day-to-day support it gave and the social mobility it made possible for group members.

Social Hierarchy in East Asia

Despite the uniqueness of caste, Indian society conformed in other respects to the dominant Asian social model, of which China is the principal example. Under the empire in China, which lasted from the third century B.C. to 1911, power, responsibility, and status formed a pyramidal structure, with the emperor at the top as a truly absolute monarch. Below him were appointed officials in a series of grades: councillors, provincial governors, and generals, down to the district magistrates in some 2,000 counties, all of whom were selected from the ranks of the scholar-gentry who had passed the third level of the imperial examinations.

But this was not merely a political pyramid, and it did not act alone. The emperor and his officials had as their highest duty the setting of a good example, of "virtuous conduct." They were seen, and saw themselves, as fathers to the people, since the family was the basis of social order in all of Asia to an even greater extent than in most other societies. In theory, if the emperor and his officials behaved properly and responsibly, others in the social hierarchy would do so as well. In practice, social order—in Chinese parlance, the "Great Harmony"—was preserved primarily by the family system; this operated in much the same way in the rest of Asia. Younger people deferred to their elders, wives to husbands, and social "inferiors" to "superiors." This was the Confucian formula for human happiness and social harmony, but it was accepted in India, too, as well as in Korea and Japan as Confucianism spread.

Social Hierarchy in Europe

Europeans likewise attached a great deal of significance to a hierarchical society, which they believed was ordained by both divine and natural law. Civic and religious leaders alike insisted that the duty of each person was to accept his or her place in the social order, an ideal intended to promote social stability and domestic tranquillity. The hierarchical societies of early modern Europe were not, however, structured according to a class system in which groups were defined by similar levels of income and lifestyles, as in the modern West. In the early modern period the common basis of aristocratic power—landed wealth and the control of labor—was modified by the source of one's wealth, the antiquity of one's title, and the number of armed and paid retainers at one's disposal. A noble, though possibly not as rich as an urban businessman, outranked the latter in prestige—so much so that business families often tried to marry their daughters to landed aristocrats as a means of enhancing their social status.

The European system was divided, though less formally than in Asia, into *estates,* or social groups defined by degrees of fixed status. The aristocratic estate was generally expected to possess significant wealth in order to fulfill its social function as leader, exemplar, local ruler, maintainer of order, and reliever of the poor. Whereas in Asia many of these functions resided primarily with the family, in Europe—and among the Aztecs in Mexico—they were largely the province of the aristocracy. It was the duty of the lower orders, both religious and political, to accept the rule of the upper, though in reality there was often resentment and occasionally rebellion. Good behavior demanded deference to superiors, courtesy to equals, and kindness to inferiors. More was expected of, but also tolerated from, the higher orders, where gentility was supposed to entail a combination of birth and virtue.

There are some parallels between social hierarchy in the East and the West, including the importance attached to the idea that status entailed responsibility. Europeans too used the analogy of paternal authority to justify monarchical power, especially in the 1600s, but never to the same degree as in Asia, where the family exercised a greater role in the maintenance of social order. In the West the function of the extended family in this regard declined in the early modern period as the emphasis gradually shifted to the nuclear family on the one hand and the state on the other. Both Europeans and Asians tried to reinforce the social hierarchy by reserving distinctive styles of dress for the upper orders.

In Europe social distinctions were also reflected in numerous other ways, such as the number of a noble's retainers or clients or the number of coaches in his procession. Even funerals were distinctive pageants designed to reflect the social status of the deceased and their families.

The European Aristocracy

Prior to the mid-sixteenth century, the aristocracy generally improved its social position and became more involved in public affairs at the local or state level. Most nobility strove to acquire more land, usually by strategic marriages, or greater status, normally by obtaining more elevated titles of nobility. To meet the demand for status, titles such as duke, marquess, and viscount were created, and new chivalric orders, including the Knights of the Garter in England and the Order of the Golden Fleece in Burgundy, were founded. New nobles were usually recruited from the landed gentry rather than the bourgeoisie, especially in France and England. On the Continent an administrative aristocracy developed in the early modern period. In France and Milan, for example, officials acquired aristocratic privileges and became known as the nobility of the robe, after their gown of office.

Conditions among the gentry varied widely. Whereas the more successful among them could be as wealthy and powerful as some nobles, others, especially on the Continent, sometimes turned to banditry to improve their sagging fortunes. A notorious gang of English robbers followed the lead of two lesser aristocrats, Sir William Bussy and Sir John de Colseby, while in France similar groups tried unsuccessfully in 1560 to end the political dominance of the Guise family, the head of which, the duke of Guise, was the king's chief adviser. Disaffected knights often supported reform movements, including Lutheranism in Germany and Calvinism in France, hoping to better their position.

Beginning in the mid-sixteenth century, the aristocracy entered a period of difficulty. Incomes from landed estates did not keep pace with excessive expenditures on elaborate dress, rich food, fine jewelry, lavish hospitality, and luxurious buildings. Raising funds through the sale of lands only reduced the income from rents. Nor did rents keep pace with the rising cost of living due to inflation, especially since many rents were fixed by custom, and in some areas tenants held long-term leases. The political position of the aristocracy was further undermined by the growing reliance of governments on talent rather than rank, though no Western country came close to establishing a meritocracy such as existed in China.

The prestige of the older aristocracy was harmed when sovereigns in France, Spain, and England sold titles to raise funds and accommodate the demand for status among newly wealthy elites. The upper aristocracy normally suffered more from these problems than the lower; in England much of the lower aristocracy, or gentry, improved its position in this period through careful land management, advantageous marriages, and the purchase of lands from the monasteries dissolved during the Reformation.

Urban Society

The social eminence of urban merchants, or patricians, stemmed from their involvement with long-distance trade, their ownership of city property, and their control of town government. Patricians intermarried to preserve the exclusiveness of their privileges, though some married off their daughters to aristocrats merely to acquire the unique prestige that went with ownership of the land. Townsfolk treated the patricians as a noble class, particularly in republican Venice, where the absence of a monarch or a landed aristocracy elevated their status. In the Netherlands and the German states too the wealthy patricians were virtually a noble class, though their supremacy was disputed by the landed nobility.

In contrast to the patricians, the guildsmen continued, as in the medieval era, to concern themselves primarily with local production and services. In most towns they had considerably less influence than the patricians but were better off than the artisans and unskilled workers, who were poorly organized and had little voice in town government. Only by joining with the guildsmen could the artisans and laborers bring about change. Another urban

An arranged marriage, in this instance between the son of a financially strapped nobleman and the daughter of a wealthy merchant hungry for social prestige, is the subject of one of the scenes from William Hogarth's series of six paintings titled *Marriage à la Mode* (1744–1745). [National Gallery, London]

group, the lawyers, found their services in increased demand as commerce expanded, land transactions became more complex, and landowners sought ways to evade the fiscal payments that were still part of feudal land tenure. Together these middling and upper urban groups began insisting upon a greater share of political power in early modern Europe, particularly in France and England, where their demands contributed to the outbreak of civil war in both countries in the 1640s.

Marriage and the Family

The Family in Asia

The Asian family was a hierarchical structure in which group welfare took precedence over individual preferences. The father was like a little emperor, with absolute power but also with absolute responsibility. Filial obedience was the cardinal Asian virtue; loyalty and obligation to parents and elders was rigid and inflexible, but it produced a tight-knit unit. In family relations age was the major determinant. Three generations commonly lived under one roof, and the grandfather was thus the dominant figure, although his place might be taken after his death by his widow. Younger sons were subject to their older brothers, wives and sisters to their husbands and brothers, and all to the eldest male. Individual initiative other

than by the patriarch was not tolerated; the welfare of the family as he interpreted it came first, and all decisions were accordingly made by the elder members.

A new Asian bride was the servant of the husband's family and was often victimized by a tyrannical mother-in-law. More so than in the West, Asian girls could be married against their wishes and had little or no right of refusal—except suicide. An entire genre of Asian stories was devoted to this theme. In a typical story, an unwilling bride is carried in an enclosed cart or sedan chair to her new husband's family; when the curtains are opened, she is found to have killed herself. Marriage was seen as a business arrangement between families, not as an individual choice or a love match. In later centuries the custom of foot-binding spread through the Chinese population, inflicting dreadful pain on growing girls and emphasizing their role as erotic playthings while reducing them to a hobble that effectively kept them at home. About the same period, the practice of purdah, the veiling and sequestering of women, spread with the Muslim conquerors even through Hindu northern India.

Few Asians questioned the family hierarchy. The family operated as a collective entity; each member was both socially and legally responsible for the behavior of all other members. Collective responsibility, family pride, and the shame of family disgrace are still credited for the relatively low rate of crime in much of Asia. Government from higher levels was far less necessary. Asian societies have been called self-regulating, and to a very large extent that is true. The price of this has been the sacrifice of individual initiative, independence, and self-fulfillment so prized by the modern West and now increasingly attractive in many parts of modern Asia.

Individuals moved through life only as members of families, as did members of larger groups such as castes, clans, or guilds. Yet there was a surprising amount of vertical mobility in Chinese society. Judging from the numerous biographies of successful examination candidates, as many as a third of the gentry group in each generation represented new blood. In Asian countries families and sometimes villages, clans, or guilds squeezed their resources to support promising boys through the lengthy education needed for entry to the scholarly ranks, in effect as their representative and as one who could bring prestige and profit.

The larger society offered few support mechanisms. Without a family or descendants to care for them, the sick, the poor, and the elderly could not survive. In the Hindu and Buddhist countries minimal shelter and food were available to all at temples, as they still are, but in all of Asia the production of offspring, especially sons, was the overriding goal for simple self-preservation. People who did well in life were bound to help not only siblings but also uncles, aunts, cousins, and their families.

The bonds of obligation and collective responsibility reached throughout the extended family, which in Asia included all parental and maternal relatives, or at least those with whom a given nuclear family was in touch. Each Asian society had a complex variety of name designations for each of these graded kin relationships; one did not refer merely to "brother," "sister," "uncle," "aunt," or "grandmother" but to elder or younger brother, first, second, or third paternal aunt, maternal grandfather, and so on. This extended network of relationships put a heavy burden on individuals, but also provided mutual support.

The Family in Europe

Extended family linkages were important in Europe as well at the level of the aristocracy, where patterns of ownership, inheritance, and status were complex. Below this level the conjugal or nuclear family was a more or less self-contained unit. Apart from eastern Europe, most couples married late, in their mid-twenties, by which time they were usually in a position to find living quarters and establish their own households. A widowed parent might subsequently take up residence with a married child, in contrast with the Asian practice of newlyweds moving in with the bridegroom's parents. The prevalence of the nuclear family pattern at the lower social levels was disadvantageous in the sense that mistreated spouses received less kin support, and smaller family units were more vulnerable to economic hardship if a spouse became unemployed.

The large family network common in Asia provided an important support system that commoners in the West often lacked. Conversely, however, the smaller family units in the West presumably made it easier for many couples to make the personal adjustments necessary for a successful marriage without the intervention of relatives and in-laws.

The nature of the Western family underwent a significant change in the sixteenth and seventeenth centuries, particularly among the aristocracy. The late medieval aristocratic family, in return for loyalty and personal attendance by its retainers and servants, provided patronage and hospitality. The aristocratic household was large because it included not only family members and relatives but also a collection of servants and retainers that might number in the hundreds. The importance of preserving the family's status and property led to the practice of the arranged marriage. Often a young person had no choice in the determination of a partner, for matrimony was a collective decision of the family and kin in which the key issues were property and power. Some parents allowed their children a veto over the proposed spouse, and occasionally headstrong young people defied the system by eloping, but only at the risk of losing their inheritance. Young men's acceptance of the arranged marriage was aided by the knowledge that once an heir was born, mistresses could be enjoyed. There was a double standard, however, for wives were denied such freedom and were expected to remain sexually loyal to their husbands.

Daughters were often an economic liability among the propertied classes since a dowry had to be provided for marriage; in return, the groom's father guaranteed the bride an annuity if her husband died before she did. As heirs and potential fathers of future heirs, firstborn sons usually married earlier than other young men. In sixteenth-century England men normally wed at about age 28, but aristocratic heirs typically married at 22 in order to facilitate property settlements and enhance the prospects of providing a male heir in the next generation. Because a younger son had considerably less property and wealth than his elder brother, who benefited from the practice of primogeniture, he faced a decline in social position unless he could find a wealthy bride.

About the middle of the sixteenth century the nature of the family began to change among the upper social orders. On the one hand, more significance was attached to the nuclear core (parents and children), and on the other, affection between spouses apparently became more important as a determinant of family relationships. The decline of kinship dominance is manifested in both decreasing hospitality and the diminishing sense of kin responsibility for individual acts. As states such as France, Spain, and England expanded their control of justice, protection, and the preservation of property, the responsibility for social control shifted from kin to state. Simultaneously, Protestantism increased the significance of the nuclear family by stressing marital affection and by treating the family as a miniature parish, with distinct religious responsibilities in

---

◉ "Surplus" Daughters ◉

In the eyes of both Asians and Europeans, daughters were much less desirable than sons. To avoid the expense of providing dowries, Catholic parents sometimes sought to dispose of "surplus" daughters by coercing them into becoming nuns. Some clergymen strongly protested this practice.

You have no right to dispose of your children by forcing a vocation on them. . . . It would cost money to establish this daughter: reason enough to consecrate her as a nun. . . . But she has no trace of religious calling: the present state of your finances is calling enough for her. . . . And so the victim is led to the temple, hands and feet tied: by which I mean against her will, dumb with fear and awe of a father whom she has always honored. Such murderous fathers are far from imitating Abraham . . . who was ready to sacrifice his son to God: instead they sacrifice their children to their own estate and to their own cupidity.

Source: L. Bourdaloue, *Œuvres complètes,* in *Collection intégrale et universelle des orateurs sacres,* vol. 15 (Paris, 1845), cols. 374 ff.; English translation in *Not in God's Image,* ed. J. O'Faolain and L. Martines (New York: Harper Torchbooks, 1973), p. 270.

---

instruction and worship. These changes brought about a greater and greater divergence from the Asian model and its associated lack of state control.

In contrast to the modern nuclear family, patriarchal authority was reinforced. The Renaissance state supported the domination of the husband-father on the grounds that his authority was analogous to that of a sovereign over his subjects. The decline of kinship could increase the wife's subordination to her husband by leaving her more exposed to exploitation in the nuclear family. Capitalizing on this, the state relied on husbands to keep their wives law-abiding. Yet the development of the nuclear family could also facilitate better relations between spouses by providing them with more time to be alone, away from the prying eyes of relatives, retainers, and servants.

Marriage in Asia

In the societies of early modern Asia marital patterns were similar in many ways to those in Europe, particularly with respect to the arranged marriage, the premium placed on sons, and the use of dowries, although considerably less so in areas such as divorce and remarriage. In Asia, however, the average age at marriage was lower than in the West—approximately 21 for males and 17 for females in China; 16 and 14, respectively, in India; and 20 and 16 in Japan and Southeast Asia.

Except for parts of Southeast Asia and a small region of South India, marriage was and remains patrilocal; that is, the bride, who was almost invariably recruited from another village to avoid inbreeding, left her family and became a member of her husband's family, where she was the lowest-status member until she had borne a son. She might visit her parents occasionally, but she was lost to them as a family member and cost them heavily in dowry. Girls were often loved as much as boys, but on practical grounds they were of far less value, although they were desirable domestic helpers to their mothers. Sons were essential for family continuity and security. Since life was an uncertain business and death rates were high, especially in the early years of life, most families tried to produce more than one son. Girls might be sold in hard times as servants or concubines in rich households.

The childless family was truly bankrupt and might even pay relatively large sums to acquire a son by adoption. A wife who failed to produce a son after a reasonable amount of time was commonly returned to her parents as useless, for the primary purpose of marriage was perpetuation of the male line. It was not understood until quite recently that the sex of a child is determined by the father or that childlessness may result as often from male as from female sterility. In time, however, most women became willing and even enthusiastic members of their husbands' families, passing on these attitudes to their children. Eventually they might become household heads and oldest survivors, thereby sometimes achieving considerable power.

All members of the society regarded marriage as a contract between families for the furthering of their interests. Virtually all marriages were arranged by the families, usually through a go-between. Bride and groom had usually not met before their wedding. Sometimes they might be allowed to express preferences, although these might be overruled in the family interest. Compatibility was rarely considered, and love marriages were extremely rare, although affection might grow in time.

There was a similar willingness to suppress individual wishes among the Incas of South America, where state officials chose mates for young people slow to act on their own. At times the Incas arranged mass marriages. The rulers themselves could marry only their sisters, making the royal family a product of considerable inbreeding.

Divorce in Asia and Europe

Divorce was rare in Asia, difficult but not impossible. Unlike the West, remarriage was even more difficult, and that knowledge probably helped people try harder to make their marriages work. It doubtless helped too that romantic expectations were not as high as in the modern West. People were trained to put individual wants second to family interest. Biographies, memoirs, popular literature, and legal records bear out that most marriages were successful on these terms and that husbands and wives valued and even loved each other and worked together in the family unit to reproduce the dominant social pattern. Divorce was relatively rare in the Islamic world as well.

There was no divorce in the modern sense in the medieval West since the canon law of the Catholic church deemed marriage an unbreakable sacrament. If the existence of an impediment or bar to a marriage could be demonstrated, the marriage could be annulled, but any children resulting from the union were thereby made illegitimate. Annulments were granted in such cases as marriage to relatives or in-laws, impotence, or forced marriage. The only other alternative, separation, did not bastardize the children, but neither did it leave the spouses free to remarry.

The Reformation reduced the grounds for annulment but established divorce in the modern sense only in certain geographic areas, including Geneva. Catholic states retained the medieval canon law, with its absolute prohibition of divorce until modern times, apart from a brief period during the age of the French Revolution and Napoleon. Among Europe's poor, some unhappy spouses ran away; others committed bigamy. From the medieval period into the nineteenth century a dissatisfied husband in England occasionally put a halter around his wife's neck, took her to the local cattle market, and sold her. The practice underscored the notion that a wife was the property of her husband, although common law never recognized this. In rural Greece well into the twentieth century, a bride might

simply be returned to her family if she was discovered or believed to have lost her virginity before marriage.

Marriage and the Family in Africa

Like the Muslims, Aztecs, and Incas, many African tribes practiced polygamy. A man demonstrated his wealth by having several wives, although in reality women, who typically worked beside men, produced so much by their labor that they virtually supported themselves. The perception of wealth was derived from the fact that a man had to pay "bridewealth"—usually livestock—to a woman's father in order to marry her. As in western Europe, men married relatively late, usually about the age of 30, though brides were typically in their late teens. A new wife would be added at fairly regular intervals of a year or two, and because of the importance attached to fertility, the result was normally a large family.

The high birthrate helped to offset the large number of deaths of infants and children and also ensured support for parents in their old age, an ideal no less valued in Asia. Like the early Hebrews, many Africans accepted the practice of leviratic marriage, by which the brother of a deceased man married the widow. In the African family no function was more important for the wife than bearing children, but beyond that she exercised a critical role in providing the food supply and in some instances even conducting local and regional trade.

Throughout the early modern world, the family was the basic unit of social organization. The Western European aristocracy began to distinguish itself in this period by moving away from the extended family, which remained common in Asia and Africa, toward the conjugal or nuclear family, which was probably already the norm among the lower social orders in Europe. Although family structures varied substantially between Muslims and some Africans and Amerindians, with their polygamous marriages, and Asia and Europe, where monogamy prevailed, all societies valued children for a variety of reasons, including, among the lower orders especially, their function as laborers and eventually as providers for elderly parents. Protestant Europe, by establishing the principle of divorce as we now understand it, planted the seeds for the eventual weakening of the family as the fundamental social unit.

The Status of Women

Although many women might have been powers within their families, their role in general was highly subordinate. There is no question that theirs was a male-dominated world and that their chief claim to status was as producers of sons. They were less valued from birth virtually everywhere. Females were subject first to their fathers and brothers, then to their husbands and their husbands' male relatives.

Women in Asia

Unlike their counterparts in the West, Asian widows were not supposed to remarry or even to have male friends. Given the high death rate and the unpredictable fortunes of life, many women—often no more than girls—were thus condemned to celibacy, loneliness, and poverty for most of their lives. "Chaste widows" were praised, and though some managed a little life of their own, most conformed to the expected model and suffered. Some widows committed suicide in China and in the Islamic world; this was carried to its extreme in India, where it often came to be expected among the higher castes. Hindu funeral practice includes the burning of the corpse; a surviving widow was supposed to throw herself on her husband's funeral pyre, a ritual known as *sati* (suttee). Perhaps as many as one-fifth of all childless Indian upper-caste widows actually sacrificed themselves in this way.

As in the West, in hard times female infants might be killed soon after birth so that the rest of the family might survive; Asian female babies could also be sold as servants or potential concubines. The selling of children seems especially heartless, but such a girl might have a better life as a slave-servant or concubine in a wealthy household than starving to death with her own family. Women were rarely given any formal education, and although some acquired it, they were primarily instructed by their mothers and mothers-in-law in how to be good, subservient wives, mothers, and daughters-in-law.

Power within the family brought women rewards that were especially important in this family-centered society. Their key role in ensuring family continuity brought much satisfaction. In most families women, as the chief raisers of children, shaped the future. More directly, they managed most families' finances, as they still do in Asia. Some women achieved public prominence as writers, reigning empresses, and powers behind the throne as imperial consorts or concubines. In India, China, and Southeast Asia, as in England and Scotland, a few women became rulers in their own right, but only in India could one find women who were brilliant generals and cavalry fighters, such as the Rani of Jhansi. Admittedly, these were a tiny handful within Asia and Europe as a whole. In East and West alike, the crucial role of women in what mattered most—the family, its well-being, and its perpetuation—was, within clear status limits, recognized. Among the peasantry, the overwhelming mass of the population, women played a crucial role in helping with the agricultural labor and were usually the major workers in cottage industries, producing handicraft goods for sale or barter. Upper-class women lived a generally idle life and commonly turned their children over to nurses or tutors.

It remained for the twentieth century, spurred by Western influence, to discourage the traditional subjugation of women in Asia and begin the movement toward equality, or at least more equitable treatment. Southeast Asia has traditionally been freer of sex discrimination than India, China, Korea, or Japan, and most of its regional cultures included some matrilocal marriage, female control and inheritance of property, and female dominance within the family. In the rest of Asia the traditional patterns were formed 4,000 years ago and persisted largely unchanged until this century. (See Chapters 38 and 39.)

In this court scene, attributed to Ku Kai-chih (A.D. 344–406), an instructress is writing down directions for her pupils, ladies of the court. In China, as elsewhere, court ladies were expected to be literate and accomplished in several arts. [Trustees of the British Museum]

Women in the Middle East and Africa

In the Islamic societies of the Middle East and North Africa, women were discouraged from participating in activities outside the home by the conviction that females should be secluded as well as veiled. The latter practice was obviously a practical way of enforcing anonymity on them when they did appear in public. Women who engaged in trade or educational pursuits were rare exceptions. As in Asian cultures, the woman's primary task was to marry and raise children, especially boys.

Religion was used, as in the West, to legitimate the subordination of women. This point was succinctly stated by a seventeenth-century Iranian theologian, who asserted that a wife's principal spiritual duty was subservience to her husband: "A wife must obey her husband, never disobey his commands, never leave the house without his permission." As early as the 1200s Islamic society was characterized by a separate social life for men and women, though a small number of women were sometimes able to exert political power in both Ottoman Turkey and Safavid Iran.

In sub-Saharan Africa some tribal societies accorded prominent roles to women. In contrast to the Western world, West African tribes such as the Igbo and Yoruba in Nigeria were organized on a "dual sex" system, in which each sex governed its own affairs at all levels of society. One group of Igbo was ruled by dual monarchs, one female and the other male, each with its own advisory group. The female monarch, or *omu* (literally "mother"), was different from a queen in the Western sense, for she was neither the king's wife nor the reigning daughter of a deceased king who had no male heir. The *omu* represented all women and had special responsibility for the marketplace. Igbo women also had their own organizations at the village level, which functioned as political pressure groups.

Although most African societies were dominated by men, there were important exceptions. Women, for instance, could be chiefs among some of the tribes of West Africa. A number of other West African tribes followed the custom of female descent, by which the throne descended not to the king's son but to the son of his sister. In precolonial African societies, which had no permanent political structure, important matters were routinely decided by a meeting of the heads of households, but because women rarely exercised this responsibility, they were not prominent in making community decisions.

The subordinate role of most African women was underscored by the predominance of patrilineal and patrilocal customs, which traced lineage through the male line and required brides to live in the villages of their husbands. There were exceptions, such as the Senufo of West Africa, whose wives could remain in their native villages and whose divorced women retained custody of the children because the latter belonged to the maternal kin. Generally, however, the traditional African societies treated women as the economic and social dependents of males, as elsewhere.

Women in Europe

In late medieval Europe aristocratic women were regarded largely as bearers of children, sexual companions, and comrades in social functions. Few administered family estates or raised their own children, a task left to nurses and tutors. Nurturing an infant was turned over to a wet nurse, typically a peasant woman hired for the occasion and often blamed for subsequent medical or psychological problems. Wet nursing freed the mother from the inconvenience of nighttime feeding and did not interrupt her social engagements, but the practice largely died out in the 1700s.

Aristocratic women had relatively little to occupy their time apart from such leisurely pursuits as reading, social visits, card playing, and theatergoing, especially since many had stewards to run their households as well as nurses and tutors to care for their children. However, women of the landed gentry often played a major role in the household economy and managed the family estates when their husbands were away. Because of her social status, a gentlewoman or a merchant's wife had little choice of occupation, for manual labor was incompatible with her position, and the professions were closed to women. Some became ladies-in-waiting to aristocratic women, some governesses of children, and a few, such as the English dramatist Aphra Behn (c.1640–1689), authors. Two aristocratic English women—Margaret Cavendish, duchess of Newcastle, and Anne, Viscountess Conway—wrote about the new science, and Katherine Boyle, the sister of the chemist Robert Boyle, took an active part in it. Catholics, of course, had the option of joining a convent or a teaching order.

Near the lower levels of society, the wives of artisans and peasants had to join in their husbands' labor in order to survive, since most Europeans lived at or near subsistence. As in Asia, Africa, and the Americas, peasant women engaged in virtually every aspect of farming from plowing and spreading manure to reaping and threshing, and also handled the household chores and cared for any poultry or dairy animals. In both urban and rural areas many wives supplemented the family income by weaving or other side employments, occasionally even prostitution.

Late medieval craft guilds allowed masters' wives to share in their work, and they often carried on the business when the men died. Although women had been admitted to the guilds, the new forms of business organization were almost exclusively male, and there was mounting hostility to women in the trades because they worked for lower pay. Apart from the cloth industry, women were being pushed out of many trades, such as brewing, at one time largely a female preserve. In England men were even moving into the occupation of midwife. Women could practice folk medicine and compete with barber-surgeons, but they were generally excluded from the profession of physician as well as attorney and minister. Although women found it increasingly difficult to compete for jobs in most trades, they found employment in the cottage industry concerned with cloth manufacturing, but the pay was poor and the hours long. Life was also difficult for single women. Some worked in the coal and iron mines, where they typically received lower wages than their male peers. Most single women earned their living by spinning cloth, a practice that gave rise to the term *spinster* for an unmarried woman.

In certain respects the legal position of European women declined in the late medieval period. Frenchwomen could no longer participate in public affairs, testify before various courts, or even act in place of an absentee or insane husband. Women in Saxony and wives in England were prohibited from undertaking legal actions; an English wife had to be represented by her husband, while a Hamburg statute of 1603 stipulated that "women can neither bring a matter up before the court nor transfer or hand over property without a guardian." Bavarian law prohibited a woman from selling anything without her husband's consent, though beginning in 1616 an exception was made for goods specified for her personal use. In England a husband enjoyed absolute control over his wife's personal property and could profit by leasing her real estate to others. In the seventeenth century, however, marriage contracts guaranteed the wife "pin money" for her personal expenses, and the courts increasingly recognized the existence of her "separate estate," a handy device if her husband was sued for bankruptcy. French courts similarly began to demonstrate greater concern for a wife's rights, including control over her dowry. A French wife whose husband mismanaged her property could win a legal separation, the most she could expect in a society without divorce. By the eighteenth century Russian noblewomen and the wives of artisans and merchants became the heads of their households when their husbands died, although only in urban areas. Legally, then, the decline in women's rights bottomed out in Europe in the 1500s and improved slowly in the seventeenth and eighteenth centuries.

Sexual Customs

Asian women were expected to be modest and chaste. They seldom appeared in public, and any open display of affection with their spouses was taboo. At the same time, the elite Asian cultures, unlike those in the West, are famous for their erotic literature and art and for the development of a courtesan (prostitute) tradition older than any other living civilization. The geisha tradition of Japan

and its original, the "singsong" or "flower boat" women of China, are well known, as is the cult of ritual sex among Indian temple priestesses and the orgies of Tantric Buddhism. Explicit portrayals of sex appear in Indian art, and the classic Indian sex manual, the *Kamasutra*, is world famous. But this behavior was reserved for the privileged few.

In contrast to the Judeo-Christian West, India, Tibet, and parts of Southeast Asia had a religious tradition in which sex was used as ritual, in some ways rather like the ancient cult of Dionysus in classical Greece. Representations of sex in Indian sculpture and painting use gods and goddesses as subjects, not ordinary mortals, and celebrate the divine life force, creation. Tantric Buddhist and some Hindu temple sex rites had the same purpose. Western art, beginning in the Renaissance, was less explicit than Indian art but depicted sensuous nudes in the guise of classical deities. All of this—the pleasures of the elite dallying with their concubines, singsong girls, erotic pictures, and the joys of Islamic rulers in their harems—was beyond the experience of the lower social orders, although at least in the West they might find an outlet for their sexual desires in traditional festivals, such as the May Day celebrations, when promiscuous behavior was reportedly common.

A relationship between sex and religious ritual existed in some African societies, especially in connection with puberty rites. The Kikuyu, who lived in the region of Mount Kenya, not only circumcised boys as part of such rites but also removed the clitoris from girls. This practice is still widespread in eastern Africa today. In both cases the act of cutting symbolized the rite of passage into adulthood. In the case of the Masai, however, puberty initiation for girls involved elongating the labia by massage and teaching the girls movements to enhance their sexual performance.

European attitudes toward sex were generally determined by the teachings of the church, although these were often merely a veneer imposed on centuries of folk custom. For the masses of East and West, sex appears to have been largely oriented toward procreation and usually confined officially to marriage or engagement, although Japanese, Southeast Asian, and Polynesian young people of both sexes were encouraged to experiment with sex before marriage. In the eyes of the medieval Christian church, sexual relations were acceptable only within marriage and were intended primarily for procreation. Little attention was attached to love in a sexual context, and lust was condemned.

During the Reformation, Protestants began to treat love and procreation as related and to regard sexual pleasure in marriage as a legitimate expression of the conjugal relationship. Among the propertied orders, sexual relations before marriage were regarded with disapproval, largely because of the importance of bearing a legitimate heir. Because a woman was regarded as the sexual property of a man, her value diminished if she had been "used" by another man. Despite the church's official disapproval, males of the propertied elite frequently engaged in premarital sex, normally with women from professional or merchant backgrounds whose families had fallen on hard times. The same freedom did not extend to women of their rank. A woman's honor was based on her reputation for chastity, a man's on his word. A wife who committed adultery insulted not only her husband's virility but also his ability to govern her, which resulted in dishonor. In this respect the elites of East and West shared the acceptance of a double standard that enhanced male dominance.

Among the lower orders in Europe, pressure for premarital sex was created by the late ages at which people wed—typically in their upper twenties. Late marriage helped hold down population growth, but figures for illegitimacy indicate relatively little sexual activity apart from engaged and married couples, probably due to religious and socioeconomic pressure. Infanticide may also have contributed to low bastardy levels. The bastardy rate was 3 percent in rural England in the 1590s and 2 percent at Frankfurt in the early 1700s. In contrast, there was considerable sexual activity by engaged couples. Approximately 21 percent of English brides were pregnant at their weddings in the late sixteenth century.

Because the Catholic church considered the sexual act primarily procreative, it regarded most attempts at contraception as mortal sin. By the sixteenth century, however, many Catholics accepted *coitus reservatus*—withdrawal before ejaculation—as a permissible technique for the economically destitute, and people did use a variety of physical contraceptives. The church condemned *coitus interruptus*—ejaculation outside the vagina—as unnatural on biblical grounds.

In Protestant lands religious leaders discouraged birth control methods, believing they were contrary to the biblical command to be fruitful and multiply. Instead, they argued, children should be accepted as blessings from God, a means to maintain the commonwealth and church, and the means for women to recover the honor lost when Eve disobeyed God.

For women with unwanted pregnancies, medical manuals provided information on how to induce an abortion. Interest in the use of birth control methods was undoubtedly strong among women who wanted relief from the repeated cycle of pregnancies that often brought death. In the sixteenth and seventeenth centuries, perhaps one out of every ten pregnancies ended in the mother's death, and 30 to 50 percent of all children died before the age of 5. In France as many as 30 percent were dead before their first birthday.

Because abortion could be so dangerous to the mother, infanticide was a popular alternative, particularly since it could be disguised as accidental "overlaying" or suffocation. The problem was so prevalent that in 1784 Austria made it illegal for parents to take children under 5 into bed

with them. The punishment for infanticide was often harsh; in the German town of Bamberg a convicted person was drowned or buried alive and speared. Infanticide figures for Renaissance Florence indicate that more girls than boys died, presumably reflecting the greater value placed on males, though in eighteenth-century Paris there was no significant discrepancy among victims.

Many parents, already victims of poverty, simply opted to abandon their children in the streets. More foundling hospitals were built to deal with the problem. Milan and Venice had established theirs in the medieval period, and new ones were built in Florence (1445), Paris (1670), London (1739), and St. Petersburg, where two former palaces of the nobility were used to house the children. The availability of the houses seems to have encouraged more parents to abandon their infants. In the 1770s and 1780s the number of children abandoned in Paris reached 4,500 per year, more than double the number at the beginning of the century. By the 1770s more than one out of every five children baptized in Paris had been abandoned. Conditions were so bad in these homes that at times no more than 5 percent of the infants admitted in Paris survived to adulthood.

Catholic and Protestant leaders alike denounced homosexuality. In England the Tudor Parliaments of the sixteenth century made it a capital offense, though the statutes seem not to have been enforced. Magistrates there were more concerned with heterosexual intercourse outside marriage because it could lead to illegitimate children and thus pose a financial burden on the community. Homosexuals were found in the court of Elizabeth I, and especially in that of her successor, James I, himself a homosexual. Homosexuality was common in secondary schools, where boys often shared beds, and in universities. It was probably also common among servants and in tiny rural communities where access to persons of the opposite sex was severely restricted. In London there were homosexual prostitutes as well as "molly houses" where homosexuals gathered for entertainment. Although Islamic religious writings typically disapproved of homosexuality, the practice itself was generally treated with indifference.

By the 1600s organized prostitution was common in European cities such as Paris, Berlin, and Toledo, often with the tacit acceptance of authorities. In Seville brothel keepers and prostitutes were licensed by the city, which even leased houses for this purpose. Church officials tried to close down the brothels, but the city fathers would do no more than require the prostitutes to attend church on Sundays and holy days. In 1676 Cambridge had 13 brothels catering largely to the university community. Many women drawn into a life of prostitution were economically destitute, including unwed mothers and cast-off mistresses, while others opted for it in preference to a 14- to 16-hour day as a seamstress. Some domestics as well were forced out of service and into prostitution when their employers got them pregnant. Other prostitutes were

Brothels such as this one, which catered to the aristocracy, became commonplace in early modern Europe. Note that the nobleman is casually giving alms to a syphilitic beggar. This drawing by Thomas Rowlandson is titled *Charity Covereth a Multitude of Sins.* [Trustees of the British Museum]

wives from poor families. Prostitution was often a criminal offense, for which women were typically pilloried, flogged, imprisoned, and sometimes expelled from a city, though usually to little effect. Nor were punitive measures effective against operators of houses of prostitution.

The late ages at marriage as well as the proximity of family members in small houses tempted some Europeans to commit incest. Apprenticing male children and placing girls in other homes as servants were safety valves, but incest was still sufficiently common to trouble church authorities. Perpetrators caught in the act were usually punished by shaming (public penance), as in the case of other sexual offenses. Usually confined to the lower orders, shaming typically required the offender to appear before the local congregation clad only in a white sheet and to stand in a public place or ride through town in a cart with a sign proclaiming the offense.

Parents of bastards were treated more harshly because their misdeed was a potential burden on the community's funds; such persons were regularly stripped to the waist, whipped, and placed in the stocks. In keeping with the double standard of the age, mothers of bastards were often subjected to punishment while the fathers sometimes escaped, although efforts were made to hold fathers fiscally responsible for their illegitimate children. Whether suffering from the double standard or undergoing frequent pregnancies, sexual experience for the early modern woman was fraught with hazard and anxiety and was potentially life-threatening as well.

The dangers sexual intercourse posed to a woman were real whether she lived in Europe, Asia, Africa, or the Americas. Nevertheless, sex was widely valued as the means for procreation. The way in which sex was viewed varied considerably, depending especially on religious traditions. Whereas Roman Catholicism, for instance, exalted the celibate life, sexual elements were incorporated into religious ritual in parts of Africa, India, Tibet, and Southeast Asia, while Hindu elites embraced concubines and their Muslim counterparts had harems. Although all societies embraced sex as a life force, for procreative purposes, there was considerable disagreement as to whether it should properly serve as a vehicle for pleasure or religious expression.

Education, Literacy, and the Printed Word

Learning in Asia

Respect for learning was universal in Asia. Written texts in particular or even scraps of paper with writing on them were to be treated reverently and preserved. This was partly due to the importance of the philosophical, moral, and religious texts that played so great a part in each Asian cultural tradition but partly also because literacy and learning were the surest and most prestigious paths to worldly success. In the cultures where religion was more centrally important than in China, especially in India and Buddhist Southeast Asia, literacy and learning also led to an honored status as priest or monk; such persons were second only to the ruler in the status hierarchy. The Indian Brahmin combined the role of scholar and priest, while in Buddhist countries the monkhood has remained the most honorable calling of all. Scholars, priests, and monks were exempt from manual labor, whereas in Europe many clergymen farmed to make ends meet, and monastic labor was often a deliberate part of the ascetic regime. In East and West alike, lip service was paid to the worth and importance of peasant labor and agriculture, but the rewards and status went to people who had risen above the necessity of physical work. In Asia even kings and emperors deferred to the learned holy man or the upright scholar.

Freedom from manual labor for the educated was marked by dress, lifestyle, and the deference of others. In Europe and Asia alike, it was the duty of the rest of society to support monks and priests by regular donations and alms and to finance their temples and rituals. Their activities were connected with ordinary life, including weddings, namings of children, funerals, and religious festivals. Officials, drawn from the ranks of the learned, also wore distinctive clothing and enjoyed special privileges, including exemption from corporal punishment. Especially in China, the masses treated them with respect in deference to their awesome authority as the direct representatives of the emperor. The Chinese gentry, from among whom officials were selected, wore the long blue scholar's gown, hem touching the ground and loose floppy sleeves hanging from the arms. Since no physical exertion could be performed in such a garment, it was in effect a badge of their freedom from manual labor. The scholar-gentry also frequently let their fingernails grow to extreme length, sometimes protecting them with special covers, to make the same point.

There were three grades of gentry, reflecting the three levels of the examination system. Only members who had passed the third level could be selected as officials, but those in the two lower grades were also recognized as educated men and followed gentry lifestyles and dress. Many of them served as teachers of the next generation of candidates, running both private and government-financed schools where Chinese boys learned their characters and worked their way through the Confucian classics under stern discipline. Most gentry did not become officials but formed an unofficial local elite, serving as teachers, arbiters of disputes, and managers of local enterprises, deferred to by all below them.

Merchants too needed at least some literacy in all Asian cultures, especially since in most of them merchants also had to deal with the state and the official bureaucracy. In any case, they had to keep records and accounts and communicate over long distances. Some of them also acquired a good deal of classical education, and certainly they read poetry and fiction, both classical and popular, as did the scholars. We have no accurate means of measuring literacy in traditional Asian societies. It may have been as high as a quarter of the population, at least in terms of the most basic ability to read and write. Literacy was much higher in Japan after about 1600, and by 1800 it probably reached 50 percent for males. But even a literacy rate of 25 percent would be remarkable, considering the difficulty of learning Chinese characters, which were also the basis of the Japanese, Korean, and Vietnamese written languages.

The gentry group in China, and comparable elites in other Asian societies, probably never constituted more than about 2 percent of the population. To these must be added merchants and petty traders (who often had at least some degree of literacy), clerks and scribes, and some

village elders. Despite the fact that they did not attend the regular schools, women sometimes acquired literacy from their brothers or fathers or occasionally on their own. The best evidence is probably the respectable number of female Asian authors, including the famous Lady Murasaki, Japanese author of the world's earliest psychological novel, *The Tale of Genji*. Court ladies such as Lady Murasaki had the leisure to learn to read and write. Literacy was expected of them, as were accomplishments in music, painting, and dance. In the Buddhist countries of Southeast Asia the monkhood claimed virtually all young men for at least two years and at any one time may have included, with older monks, 10 or 15 percent of the population, all of whom were literate. In India the Brahmins, as the sole performers of ritual and the keepers of the Great Tradition, had to be literate.

Paper and printing were both invented in China, the former by the first century A.D. under the Han, the latter by T'ang times. Movable type appeared in the Sung dynasty by about A.D. 1100, and shortly thereafter in Korea. These inventions spread rapidly to Japan, more slowly to India, Southeast Asia, the Islamic areas, and the West. The importance of sacred texts and commentaries for Hinduism, Buddhism, and Islam meant that even before printing, large numbers of copies were made by scribes. As in the West, the spread of printing greatly increased the reading public. The most important result was the increased circulation of literature, first in China, then progressively in other parts of Asia. This included copies of the classics; philosophical and religious texts; epic tales, such as the Indian *Mahabharata* and the *Ramayana;* and similar epics and accounts of heroic deeds from the classical traditions of China, Japan, and Korea.

Literature for a mass audience was being printed by T'ang times in China (A.D. 600–900) and soon thereafter in the rest of Asia, including plays, short stories, poetry, and the first novels. Well before the T'ang period in China, in the splendor of Guptan India (A.D. 300–500), the court poet and playwright Kalidasa had created a brilliant series of dramas. With the spread of printing, his plays and poems were made available to a mass audience. Throughout Asia printing also meant that what had long been present as an oral tradition of storytelling and drama took on new life. Much of it has been lost or is available only in much later printed versions, but from T'ang times on there was a vigorous popular literature in the vernacular, less lofty and more down-to-earth than the classics. Stories and plays about universal human foibles—akin to Chaucer's *Canterbury Tales* in the West—were read avidly by a growing number of people, including scholars to whom such works were supposedly prohibited and who hid them under their pillows. In China there were even detective stories. India produced similar tales, and some of the works of Kalidasa are in this genre. Accounts of adventure and intrigue flourished throughout Asia.

Learning in the West

Respect for learning in the West was not as pronounced as in the East, though in the early modern period there was a notable increase in literacy, in the number of schools, and in the continued development of the universities. In keeping with their broad range of intellectual and cultural interests, Renaissance humanists not only founded new schools but also reformed the traditional curriculum by challenging its heavy reliance on Aristotle. The success of Protestant reformers ultimately rested on the ability to educate younger generations in their religious principles, and in turn the Catholics relied heavily on education to thwart Protestant expansion and to provide the foundation for their missionary work.

Both religious groups looked to the universities to provide intellectual leadership. The Protestant stress on Bible reading, especially with the availability of new vernacular translations in the sixteenth century, was a powerful incentive to become literate. The scientific revolution, with its rapid communication of ideas, was also highly dependent on literacy, and the rapid growth of state bureaucracies increased the demand for skilled officials, particularly those with some legal training. In England the early modern period was the golden age of the Inns of Court, where aspiring young men studied the common law.

As in the East, many Western educational developments were closely linked to religion. Catholic orders such as the Jesuits and the Ursulines are famous for their educational work, but other groups were active too. The Oratory of Jesus, a society of secular priests, established colleges and seminaries throughout France, mostly for children of the French nobility, which rejected physical punishment as an educational tool. So did reforming Catholic Jansenists, whose "little schools" normally had no more than 25 boys in classes of six or less. Several Catholic organizations were established in France in the late 1600s to teach the children of the poor. Although Protestants had no teaching orders, they too actively founded schools, including "charity schools" for children of the poor; their curricula concentrated on reading, writing, and religion. One of the greatest Protestant successes was the founding of the University of Halle in eastern Germany in 1694 by Pietists, whose evangelical, devotional faith troubled orthodox Lutherans. By its emphasis on independent thinking, the faculty at Halle helped pioneer the development of modern academic freedom.

The Jewish communities of eastern Europe and Spain were keenly interested in education. At the elementary level, education was mandatory for all boys, and some girls were taught to read, especially after the appearance of printed vernacular literature. Gifted male students were directed into the fields of medicine and religion, the latter being a specialty of rabbinical academies. Because of the importance of rabbinical law in the ghettos, legal studies as well as religion were an important part of the curriculum.

Note the use of corporal punishment as a learning device in this 1592 woodcut of a German classroom. [Bettman Archive]

Progress in the founding of schools and the increase of literacy was pronounced in early modern Europe. Between 1580 and 1650 more than 800 schools were endowed in England and Wales. By the late seventeenth century the number of parishes with schools was near 90 percent in the diocese of Paris and the lowland counties of Scotland, though the figure was only 42 percent in the diocese of Verdun and even less in some areas. French literacy rates were perhaps 20 percent overall in the seventeenth century, but a third of the population was literate by 1789. The reformer John Knox proposed a program of universal education in the 1560s, but the Scottish Parliament refused to fund it. Nevertheless, a century later Scotland had an impressive system of parish schools where even the poor were welcome.

Universal education effectively began when Prussia made attendance at elementary school mandatory in 1717. The founding of new schools was accompanied by substantial increases in literacy. By 1800 the literacy rate for males approached 90 percent in Scotland and 67 percent in France, whereas in 1600 only one in six Frenchmen had been able to read. Among women, whose educational opportunities were more restricted, literacy rates generally rose more slowly. Only 5 percent of the women in the English counties of East Anglia were literate, compared to 35 percent of the men in the period from 1580 to 1640. In Amsterdam, where literacy greatly enhanced employment opportunities, the rates were 57 percent for men and 32 percent for women in 1630. Because the Swedes required literacy for confirmation and marriage, by the 1690s at least one Swedish diocese had achieved a rate approaching 100 percent, though for many this may have represented little more than the ability to sign one's name. As in the East, the growth of literacy helped spur the printing industry, which published inexpensive books, ballads, and newspapers, the latter appearing for the first time in the seventeenth century. The dramatic increase in Western literacy was not matched in Asia; in Japan, which had the best record, 45 percent of the men and only 15 percent of the women were literate as late as the mid-nineteenth century.

Education in the Ottoman Empire

Unlike eastern Asia or the West, the Turks, who opposed the publication of Islamic religious literature, did not allow printed books until 1728, with the exception of a small number of presses in the non-Muslim communities. The first Turkish newspaper did not appear until 1861. Religious influence dominated the Turkish educational system; most schools were attached to mosques, and the ulema typically supplied the teachers. The Jewish and Christian communities had some schools, but generally the Ottomans discouraged education for their subject peoples.

Even among the Muslims, education was essentially the preserve of the well-to-do or the politically important, since the Turks were convinced that too much learning threatened Islam.

Beyond the elementary schools, the more capable Muslim students could pursue the study of Islamic theology, law, and some humanities and science in theological schools known as *medreses*. Here the curriculum lasted as long as 12 years. The sultan also maintained five preparatory and four vocational schools where a full course of study could be as long as 15 years. These palace schools had some Christian teachers, though most of the faculty belonged to the ulema. The curriculum included the study of Turkish, Persian, and Arabic as well as the liberal arts, physical education, calligraphy, and vocational training in such areas as architecture, shipbuilding, and military affairs. There was instruction too in Islam and Turkish etiquette. But the *medreses* and the palace schools were only for the few. The expansion of Islam into North Africa and the Sudan meant that there too education was not encouraged for the masses.

Thus attitudes toward education and learning varied sharply among early modern societies. Until the arrival of Europeans, schools were nonexistent in the Americas and sub-Saharan Africa, while in the Islamic world education was narrowly confined and provided to the few by schools linked to the royal palace or the mosques. The advent of the printing press and the Protestant and Catholic Reformations in Europe spurred the founding of schools, the growth of literacy, and a growing appreciation of learning that has generally continued in the West to the present. Yet nowhere in the early modern world was respect for learning greater than in Asia, both as a means to preserve its philosophical and religious traditions and as a path to achieve worldly success.

Poverty, Crime, and Social Control

It is impossible to measure levels of well-being for most periods in the past. We can calculate living standards only roughly, using such evidence as travelers' accounts, estimates of population and production, trade figures, stories reflecting lifestyles, famine records, and remedial measures. Before the modern period these records are fullest for China, where we have a wealth of official and local documents and an extensive literature. Generally, most Chinese seem to have been materially better off in diet, housing, and clothing than most people elsewhere in the world until perhaps as late as the mid-nineteenth century. But the only real defense against absolute poverty was the family system in Asia, which provided its own mutual-assistance network.

Authorities in France and England in the late 1600s probably exaggerated in estimating that over half of their people lived at or below the subsistence level, but the number was high. In the late 1400s more than two-thirds of the taxpayers in Basel and Augsburg were too poor to survive serious economic adversity. The large number of poor seriously strained the ability of religious and civic authorities to provide assistance. In the plague year of 1580, more than half the population of Genoa was on poor relief. In the last decades of the sixteenth century some 20 percent of the inhabitants of Lyons, France's second largest city, needed assistance.

For the poor the greatest problem was often the uncertainty of the food supply, which was frequently threatened by inflationary pressures as well as natural disasters. Malnutrition and disease were the principal reasons for a life expectancy of only 25 years as late as 1700. The bulk of the world's population still lived in rural areas in the early modern period, often in mud huts with thatched roofs. Living quarters were severely cramped; an entire family often lived in a single room. In towns the poor were victims of polluted water and filthy living conditions.

The diet of the poor was simple and, even in Europe, usually devoid of meat. The more fortunate peasants might occasionally have a little mutton or pork, but the poor usually had to survive on a diet of dark bread, peas, beans, and soup. Many European peasants kept stock simmering in a pot, adding to it whatever foods were available each day. Sometimes cheese, butter, or curds were consumed, but milk was shunned because it was thought to be unhealthy. In general, the lot of the rural poor was marginally better than that of their urban counterparts, since many of the former were able to raise some of their own food. This was not usually true of landless day laborers, who amounted to as much as half the population of some districts in Spain and Switzerland. As the general population increased, it was imperative to find means to relieve the destitute.

Causes of European Poverty

Various factors contributed to the severity of poverty in the early modern period. As the population grew, landlords improved the efficiency of their farms to provide additional food, but industry did not expand rapidly enough to absorb the surplus labor displaced as landowners switched from raising crops to grazing sheep. Inflation itself took a heavy toll as rents and prices rose faster than wages, leaving urban workers particularly vulnerable.

◉ Peasant Poverty: France, 1696 ◉

The famous French military engineer, Sébastien Le Prestre, marquis de Vauban, wrote a moving description of the poor peasants in France in 1696.

All the so-called *bas peuple* [mean people] live on nothing but bread of mixed barley and oats, from which they do not even remove the bran, which means that bread can sometimes be lifted by the straw sticking out of it. They also eat poor fruits, mainly wild, and a few vegetables from their gardens. . . .

The general run of people seldom drink [wine], eat meat not three times a year, and use little salt. . . . So it is no cause for surprise if people who are so ill-nourished have so little energy. Add to this what they suffer from exposure: winter and summer, three fourths of them are dressed in nothing but half-rotting tattered linen, and are shod throughout the year with *sabots* [wooden shoes], and no other covering for the foot. . . .

The poor people are ground down in another manner by the loans of grain and money they take from the wealthy in emergencies, by means of which a high rate of usury is enforced, under the guise of presents which must be made after the debts fall due, so as to avoid imprisonment. After the term has been extended by only three or four months, either another present must be produced when the time is up, or they face the *sergent* [debtors' bailiff] who is sure to strip the house bare.

Source: Vauban, "Description géographique de l'élection de Vezelay," in P. Goubert, *The Ancien Régime: French Society, 1600–1750,* trans. S. Cox (London: Weidenfeld & Nicolson, 1973), pp. 118–119.

Short-term increases in poverty were caused by extreme fluctuations in the cloth industry, which was adversely affected by such things as plague, war, and bad harvests. Whereas rural textile workers might weather a slump by finding temporary farm work, urban laborers were typically reduced to poor relief or begging. When harvests failed, the plight of the poor often became desperate. In England from the late fifteenth to the early seventeenth century, harvests failed on an average of every four years. When the harvests were bad several years in a row, the problem was acute, and food riots were common. Finally, as the size of European armies expanded in the early modern period, the number of demobilized and often unemployable soldiers increased, adding burdens to relief rolls.

Poor Relief in Europe

Various attempts were made to deal with the poor in this period. In the late 1400s local authorities ordered beggars to leave their districts, although exceptions were sometimes made for local beggars who were handicapped, ill, or elderly. In Brabant, France, and Venice, vagabonds provided oarpower for the galleys, while in England a 1495 law ordered that the idle be whipped, placed in the stocks for three days, and then returned to their parishes of origin. Intended to keep the destitute from flooding into the towns, virtually all early measures to deal with the poor relied on some form of coercion but failed to provide organized means to relieve the needy.

The widespread social unrest sparked throughout Europe by the harvest failures of the 1520s brought major changes in social policy. Between 1531 and 1541 some 60 cities reformed their welfare policies, and there were state-imposed reforms in the Netherlands, England, France, Scotland, and Spain. The governments of the first three states prohibited begging and insisted that the able-bodied poor work. Funds for those unable to work were raised through taxes or donations, but there was a clear shift in emphasis from private charity to public welfare. The English Poor Law of 1601, for example, prohibited begging, required the able-bodied poor to work on local projects, centralized poor relief, and provided for the education of paupers' children. Where there was industry to employ the able-bodied at low wages, as in Flanders, France, and England, the new system achieved some success. In Scotland and Spain, however, there was little need for the labor of unskilled paupers, and licensed begging was used in an attempt to keep them under control.

Because employment could not always be found for the able-bodied poor, many European cities established workhouses to discipline the poor as well as to provide job training and moral instruction. Although these institutions could not accommodate all the able-bodied poor, officials hoped to coerce the remainder into finding employment. Some workhouses, such as Bridewell in London and those

In early modern Europe many indigent persons took to the highways in search of employment, but in so doing they risked severe punishment as vagabonds. This 1520 engraving is by Lucas van Leyden. [Staatliche Museen Preussischer Kulturbesitz, Kupferstichkabinett, West Berlin/Jörg P. Anders]

founded by the papacy in Rome, became little more than places of punishment, while others, such as those in the Netherlands, Scandinavia, and Germany, were sources of cheap labor for private employers. French workhouses at first were used to benefit private business, but after 1640 they were employed primarily to control rebellious peasants and workers. The inmates of these institutions rarely benefited from their enforced stays.

Poor Relief Outside Europe

The towns of coastal West Africa similarly developed a system of poor relief in the late sixteenth and seventeenth centuries. As the rural poor fled to the towns in search of better opportunities, the number of the indigent was often as high as 40 percent, and in the port of Shama on the Gold Coast it reached 70 or 80 percent.

There were, however, no professional beggars because of a rather extensive system of poor relief. The wealthy took some of the poor into their personal service, while others received assistance from special funds raised by taxes or court fines. Some of the offerings given to priests made their way to the poor as well. Local authorities were required to provide gainful employment for young men, the physically handicapped, and the elderly, usually in the crafts, food processing, and market vending. Because the rural poor who faced severe economic hardship sometimes opted for banditry rather than migration to the towns, in the early 1600s brigandage reached near-epidemic levels in parts of West Africa. By striking at the trading caravans transporting rural produce to the towns, the brigands effectively symbolized the resentment of peasants at their growing subservience to urban merchants, a development that was also common in much of Europe.

In South America the Incas addressed the problem by systematic regimentation and care of the needy. The state itself owned the land and apportioned it to families based on their size, with a substantial portion of the crops going to storehouses to supply the nobility, the military, state workers, and priests. The government also took much of what the artisans produced. Although the masses were thus deprived of both freedom and initiative, in times of famine or natural disaster the state provided them with food from the public warehouses.

The larger Asian society had pitifully inadequate means beyond the family level to intervene on behalf of the poor. In China the imperial bureaucracy did what its limited local powers allowed, including the remission of taxes, the control of floods, the keeping of order, and the storing of grain for distribution in lean years at uninflated prices, a policy called the "ever-normal granary system." Such efforts flagged or failed when the dynasty was weak or collapsed—perhaps a third of the time—and even in strong periods the state could not cope with a major catastrophe. In India and Southeast Asia, and to a lesser degree in the Buddhist areas of Korea and Japan, temples provided some refuge for the destitute, but this too was inadequate. In general, the family system of mutual support could keep most people from total destitution most of the time, but no means were adequate to deal with the recurrent large-scale disasters to which all premodern societies were subject, such as drought-induced famine, major flooding, or long periods of civil disorder. In the Islamic world, the poor could look to social-service institutions funded primarily by charitable legacies and the obligatory tax, or *zakat,* which was one of the principal duties of a Muslim.

Crime and Poverty

One of the most striking differences between East and West was in the treatment of crime. In general terms, Asian thought made no place for the Judeo-Christian concept of sin. Correction and, if possible, reform through reeducation or renewed piety were stressed more than repayment or punishment, although these were certainly used and frequently harsh. The incidence of crime or social deviance was almost certainly less in Asia than in other areas, thanks to the self-regulating mechanism of the family and the deterrent power of the shame that individual misbehavior might bring on the group. It is sometimes said that whereas Western societies emphasized individual sin and guilt, the East stressed the unacceptability of antisocial behavior and used shame to enforce moral codes. In addition to the social stigma of misbehavior, public shaming was commonly used as an official punishment both in Asia and in Europe. Both Asian and European criminals were publicly exhibited, often paraded through the streets carrying placards indicating their offenses, and sometimes executed.

As the living standards of European workers and peasants deteriorated, criminal activity increased, especially after the mid-1500s. In rural areas there was a clear connection between crime and destitution. Records for the Spanish province of Toledo show that nearly all defendants in larceny cases came from the lower ranks of society. Theft was often the most common crime; in the English county of Sussex in the early 1600s stealing accounted for nearly two-thirds of all indictments. Theft was a capital offense, though the death penalty was rarely applied. Most rural felons were common laborers who did not repeat their criminal activity after once being caught.

Larceny changed somewhat in the early modern period. In medieval times thieves stole mostly subsistence items—food, clothing, and tools—but later they began to prefer luxury goods, increasingly available in the expanding towns. Whereas the poor had hitherto stolen mostly from other poor, they began more and more to rob the rich. A major exception to this pattern of crime occurred during the unsettled times of fourteenth- and fifteenth-century Europe when bands of lawless nobles and gentry engaged in robbery and extortion. Victims who refused to pay often had their crops destroyed and their homes burned. Not even the wealthy were immune, for they provided tempting targets for kidnapping and extortion. Known as "fur-collar criminals" because of their noble garb, the culprits thrived until governments were strong enough to stamp most of them out in the 1500s.

Banditry did not cease with the decline of fur-collar crime, but henceforth nearly all bandits were from the lower ranks and included many men unable to find employment. As major roads were more effectively patrolled by the seventeenth century, most of these bandits were forced into remote areas. Russia, however, experienced considerable turmoil throughout the 1600s because of large roving bands.

In Asia, too, banditry was a common response by people reduced to absolute poverty. It was especially frequent in periods of political disorder and hence virtually endemic in parts of India, while its incidence rose and fell in China with the changing effectiveness of the imperial government and the levels of peasant distress. Bandits operated most successfully on the fringes of state-controlled areas or in frontier zones between provincial jurisdictions, areas that were often mountainous or forested. Bandits exacerbated the poverty of their prey. Although their prime targets were the rich and the trade routes, these were often better protected than the common people and their villages. Some bandit groups turned into rebels, who built on the support of the disaffected majority to overthrow the government and found a new order that could better serve mass welfare. Much popular fiction dealt with the adventures of bandit groups, often depicted as Robin Hood–type figures but in any case regarded as heroes rather than criminals.

In the West a new literary form, the picaresque novel — celebrating the adventures of an urban rogue, or *picaro* — developed in connection with a trend toward more sophisticated urban crimes. In addition to the usual larceny, physical assault, homicide, and arson, early modern towns were increasingly troubled by business fraud and swindlers. By the mid-1600s novels about these rogues were popular in Spain, from whence they spread to Germany and England.

Another facet of urban crime was the growth in the larger European cities of neighborhoods where a genuine underworld existed. In Paris the criminal sector near the Porte St.-Denis was so extensive that officials dared not enter it until it was subdued by an army detachment in 1667. Curtailing crime in the cities was nearly impossible because the poor were packed into grossly overcrowded slums where shanties filled even the narrow alleys.

Controlling Crime

European states responded to the rise in crime by reorganizing the personnel and procedure necessary to control it. In the medieval period criminal control was based on the existence of small populations in compact, mostly isolated areas. As the population expanded and interregional contacts increased, it became imperative to develop more effective government controls beyond the local level. In France this need was met by expanding the powers of the royal *procureur*, who handled the prosecution in criminal proceedings. In England the Tudors, who had no police force, enlarged the role of the justices of the peace, who, as unpaid agents of the crown, had the authority to arrest, indict, and grant bail. They also enforced labor codes and social laws, which governed such things as alehouses and unlawful games. By the late sixteenth century justices of the peace were responsible for enforcement of the poor law.

◉ Capital Punishment and Cruelty ◉

European justice entailed not only the use of torture to extract confessions but also the application of capital punishment for various crimes against property as well as human life. Here is the account of a French observer sensitive to the cruel suffering inflicted on criminals in eighteenth-century Paris; note his opposition to capital punishment as contrary to natural law.

I went home by way of rue Saint-Antoine and the Place de Grève. Three murderers had been broken on the wheel there, the day before. . . . As I crossed the square I caught sight of a poor wretch, pale, half dead, wracked by the pains of the interrogation inflicted on him twenty hours earlier; he was stumbling down from the Hôtel de Ville supported by the executioner and the confessor. These two men, so completely different, inspired an inexpressible emotion in me! I watched the latter embrace a miserable man consumed by fever, filthy as the dungeons he came from, swarming with vermin! And I said to myself, "O Religion, here is your greatest glory! . . ." I saw the other as the wrathful arm of the law. . . . But I wondered: "Have men the right to impose death . . . even on the murderer who has himself treacherously taken life?" I seemed to hear Nature reply with a woeful no! . . . "But robbery?" "No, no!" cried Nature. "The savage rich have never felt they devised enough harsh safeguards; instead of being friends and brothers, as their religion commands, they prefer the gallows. . . ." This was what Nature said to me. . . .

Source: Nicolas-Edmé, Restif de la Bretonne, *Les Nuits de Paris, or The Nocturnal Spectator,* trans. L. Asher and E. Fertig (New York: Random House, 1964), pp. 7–8.

Throughout Europe revised criminal procedures had the effect of depersonalizing the judicial process and treating criminal activity as an offense against society rather than the individual. Punishment became more severe. In contrast to the relatively mild medieval system, where justice was intended to settle disputes between persons, the new criminal proceedings punished the guilty but ignored compensation for the victim. Unlike medieval justice, corporal punishment became more common, though a status distinction was generally made in meting out justice; the rich were often fined, the poor imprisoned or mutilated. The increased severity of punishments was intended to discipline the lower orders and curb the increase in crimes by the poor against the rich. Public punishment thus had a twofold purpose: to deter crime and to demonstrate the authority of the state to regulate the behavior and command the obedience of its citizens.

Chinese punishment for minor offenses. The heavy wooden collar, the *cangue*, was a burden to support and also prevented the criminal from reaching his mouth with his hands, which meant that he would starve if not fed by others. This man's crime is recorded on the inscription, but all that shows here is the official title and seal of the imperial magistrate at Shanghai in 1872. [Photo by John Thomson; Harvard-Yenching Library, Harvard University]

In both Asia and Europe criminals were tried and laws and punishments enforced by civil courts run by the state and presided over by magistrates, rulers or their representatives, community elders, or learned men. In both Asia and sometimes in Europe there was no prior assumption of guilt or innocence; judgment was made and sentences arrived at on the basis of evidence, including the testimony of witnesses. Asians had no lawyers standing between people and the law; plaintiffs and defendants spoke for themselves. In China and most of the rest of Asia, people charged with criminal behavior could be found guilty and punished only if they confessed their guilt. If they refused to do so despite the weight of evidence against them, they were often tortured to extract a confession. Torture was also used in early modern Europe, though confession was not essential for a conviction. Asian law and the system of official justice, like its European counterpart, was designed to awe all who appeared before its majesty. Plaintiffs, defendants, and witnesses knelt before the magistrate or judge and could be whipped if they were not suitably reverential—another expression of a strongly hierarchical, authoritarian society.

In both Asia and Europe punishment for major crimes of violence was almost invariably death, commonly by beheading or strangulation. Death could also be imposed for many minor crimes. For especially dreadful crimes, such as parricide, treason, rebellion, or, in Asia, other forms of filial and political disloyalty, more gruesome punishments were used: dismemberment, the pulling apart of limbs by horses, the Chinese "death of a thousand cuts," or in India impalement or trampling by elephants. In Europe dismemberment by "drawing and quartering" (sundering limbs from the body) was imposed for treason.

Punishments were seen as deterrents to would-be criminals; the heads of the executed were exhibited on poles until they rotted. For lesser offenses Asian criminals were displayed in painfully small cages or mutilated, practices also used in Europe, or forced to wear a heavy wooden collar that prevented them from feeding themselves. In East and West alike prisons were often dreadful places where inmates might starve if they were not fed by relatives. For what we might call misdemeanors, Asian sentences tended to stress reeducation and reform. Criminality, or at least misbehavior, was seen as potentially correctible, especially with family help.

People naturally worried about falling into the machinery of the law and courts, especially in criminal cases. Two important points need to be made. In Asia probably considerably fewer than 10 percent of disputes and minor crimes—perhaps most crimes of all sorts—ever reached the courts since they were settled through family, village, gentry, or other local networks. Second, modern Western scholars conclude that justice was done by that system, perhaps more consistently than in the West. Most magistrates were judicious, diligent with evidence, and concerned to see justice done, not only to avoid the censure that could ruin their careers but also because of the sense of responsibility they bore. But there was, particularly in the West, a double standard of justice, which was much harder on the poor, whose crimes generally stemmed from poverty, than on their social betters. Laws were made and administered by elite groups, whose interests in the preservation of their privileged status and property were at least as great as their devotion to justice.

Surveying the societies of the early modern world, perhaps most striking is the contrast between the relative stability of Asian society and the volatility of Europe. As Europeans made crucial economic, political, and educational advances in the early modern period, Western society altered substantially, beginning in western Europe and spreading to the Americas through colonization. Nevertheless, the strikingly numerous social parallels between the different parts of the world in this period underscore the commonality of much historical development and human experience. Societies were structured hierarchically and embraced the principle that social status entailed special responsibility. In Asia and Europe alike, arranged marriages were common, and precedence was accorded to sons. Capital punishment was commonly imposed for major crimes, and some of the poor in all societies periodically resorted to banditry. Moreover, in their treatment of women, most Asian and Western societies were alike in not granting even a modicum of social equality to women until the twentieth century.

Conflicting religious tenets were responsible for some of the most basic social differences in the early modern world. Religious considerations explain at least in part why Aztecs, Incas, Muslims, and some Africans practiced polygamy, whereas non-Muslim Asians and Europeans were primarily monogamous. Religion was also a key factor in views on sex. Many East Asians and Africans, unlike Christians, for instance, linked sex and religious ritual. Religious changes were responsible for altering the way some Westerners viewed marriage: divorce (other than through annulment) was not possible in Europe until the Protestant Reformation in the sixteenth century; in Asia, divorce did occur, though rarely. The relative importance attached to education, particularly in Asia, stemmed partly from the desire to preserve its religious and philosophical traditions. The same can be said of Judaism and later of Christianity.

Suggestions for Further Reading

Buxbaum, D., ed. *Chinese Family Law and Social Change*. Seattle: University of Washington Press, 1978.

Ch'u, T. *Law and Society in Traditional China*. Paris: Mouton, 1961.

Cohn, B. S. *India: The Social Anthropology of a Civilization*. Englewood Cliffs, N.J.: Prentice-Hall, 1971.

Davidson, B. *The African Genius: An Introduction to Social and Cultural History*. Boston: Little, Brown, 1969.

Dumont, L. *Homo Hierarchicus: An Essay on the Caste System*, trans. M. Sainsbury. Chicago: University of Chicago Press, 1970.

Forster, R., and Forster, E., eds. *European Society in the Eighteenth Century*. New York: Walker, 1969.

Foucault, M. *The History of Sexuality*, trans. R. Hurley. New York: Pantheon, 1977.

Fraser, A. *The Weaker Vessel: Woman's Lot in Seventeenth-Century England*. London: Weidenfeld & Nicolson, 1984.

Freedman, M., ed. *Family and Kinship in Chinese Society*. Stanford, Calif.: Stanford University Press, 1970.

Goubert, P. *The French Peasantry in the Seventeenth Century*, trans. I. Patterson. Cambridge: Cambridge University Press, 1986.

Greaves, R. L. *Society and Religion in Elizabethan England*. Minneapolis: University of Minnesota Press, 1981.

Hanawalt, B. A., ed. *Women and Work in Preindustrial Europe*. Bloomington: Indiana University Press, 1986.

Ho, P. *The Ladder of Success in Imperial China*. New York: Columbia University Press, 1964.

Hunt, D. *Parents and Children in History: The Psychology of Family Life in Early Modern France*. New York: Basic Books, 1970.

Kea, R. A. *Settlements, Trade, and Politics in the Seventeenth-Century Gold Coast*. Baltimore: Johns Hopkins University Press, 1982.

Ladurie, E. L. *The French Peasantry, 1450–1660*. Berkeley: University of California Press, 1986.

Lannoy, R. *The Speaking Tree: Indian Culture and Society*. New York: Oxford University Press, 1971.

Laslett, P. *The World We Have Lost Further Explored*, 3d ed. London: Methuen, 1983.

Le May, R. S. *The Culture of Southeast Asia*. London: Allen & Unwin, 1954.

Lerner, G. *The Creation of Patriarchy*. New York: Oxford University Press, 1986.

Lewis, R. *Everyday Life in Ottoman Turkey*. New York: Putnam, 1971.

Macfarlane, A. *Marriage and Love in England: Modes of Reproduction, 1300–1840*. New York: Basil Blackwell, 1986.

McKnight, B. *The Quality of Mercy: Amnesties and Traditional Chinese Justice*. Honolulu: University Press of Hawaii, 1981.

Mandelbaum, D. G. *Society in India: Continuity and Change.* 2 vols. Berkeley: University of California Press, 1970.

Maynes, M. J. *Schooling in Western Europe: A Social History.* New York: State University of New York Press, 1985.

Norberg, K. *Rich and Poor in Grenoble, 1600–1814.* Berkeley: University of California Press, 1985.

Ozment, S. *When Fathers Ruled: Family Life in Reformation Europe.* Cambridge, Mass.: Harvard University Press, 1983.

Pike, R. *Aristocrats and Traders: Sevillian Society in the Sixteenth Century.* Ithaca, N.Y.: Cornell University Press, 1972.

Pollock, L. A. *Forgotten Children: Parent-Child Relations from 1500 to 1900.* Cambridge: Cambridge University Press, 1984.

Prior, M., ed. *Women in English Society, 1500–1800.* London: Methuen, 1985.

Rawksi, E. S. *Education and Popular Literacy in Ch'ing China.* Ann Arbor: University of Michigan Press, 1979.

Rose, M. B., ed. *Women in the Middle Ages and the Renaissance: Literary and Historical Perspectives.* Syracuse, N.Y.: Syracuse University Press, 1986.

Schalk, E. *From Valor to Pedigree: Ideas of Nobility in France in the Sixteenth and Seventeenth Centuries.* Princeton, N.J.: Princeton University Press, 1986.

Shorter, E. *The Making of the Modern Family.* New York: Basic Books, 1977.

Stone, L. *The Family, Sex and Marriage in England, 1500–1800.* New York: Harper & Row, 1977.

——, and Stone, J. C. F. *An Open Elite? England, 1540–1880.* New York: Oxford University Press, 1984.

Traer, J. F. *Marriage and the Family in Eighteenth-Century France.* Ithaca, N.Y.: Cornell University Press, 1980.

Wakeman, F., ed. *Conflict and Control in Late Imperial China.* Berkeley: University of California Press, 1975.

Wiesner, M. E. *Working Women in Renaissance Germany.* New Brunswick, N.J.: Rutgers University Press, 1986.

Woodbridge, L. *Women and the English Renaissance and the Nature of Womankind, 1540–1620.* Champaign: University of Illinois Press, 1984.

CHAPTER 22

The Age of Absolutism

The sixteenth century had witnessed the emergence of the nation-state in western Europe. The seventeenth and eighteenth centuries saw its consolidation. By the end of the Thirty Years' War, it was clear that the future lay with the powers capable of mobilizing their resources most effectively for both war and peace. From the middle of the seventeenth century to the end of the eighteenth, the major states of Europe embarked on a variety of programs designed to increase centralized political and economic control. On the political level, this process generally took the form of absolutism; on the economic level, that of mercantilism. Each of the major states took a somewhat different path to these ends. What proved workable in the France of Louis XIV required a different approach in England or in the Russia of Peter the Great. But by the mid-eighteenth century, every major power had succeeded in its program of centralization, or had paid the price of failure.

The professionalization of the military coincided with the growth of standing state-supported armies. The elaborate costume of the Prussian grenadiers, the most elite corps of the eighteenth century, set them distinctively apart from the civilian population, impressing the authority of the state on them in peace as well as in war. [Granger Collection]

524

This process was not accomplished without difficulty. Merchants generally welcomed the economic initiatives of the state, and in some cases actively sought them. The landed aristocracy, fearful of losing its privileges and jealous of its traditional authority, often opposed centralization. Workers demanded wage and price controls, a dependable supply of bread, and restrictions on cheap imported labor. Peasants sought relief from the onerous burdens of taxes and traditional obligations. Thus the state's quest for political unity and economic control raised a host of demands from competing constituencies. It sharpened the differences between the estates and led eventually to the demand for political representation. By the eighteenth century some European rulers frankly regarded themselves as arbiters between the competing interest groups in their countries. But the centralizing states were not always able to control the forces they had unleashed. By the late eighteenth century, absolutism had created the conditions that would lead to its demise and its replacement by the modern state.

France Under Louis XIV

Of all the absolute monarchs, none stamped his age as decisively as Louis XIV of France. No other Western European ruler exerted greater or more uncontested control of his country during the 1000-year period between the reign of Charlemagne and the French Revolution of 1789. Yet even Louis faced daunting obstacles and resistance in his efforts to bend the people and institutions of France to his will, and even he was forced to acknowledge the limitations of his power.

Provincial Autonomy and Central Control

The France of Louis XIV was not a unitary state but a patchwork of widely varying provincial customs and pow-

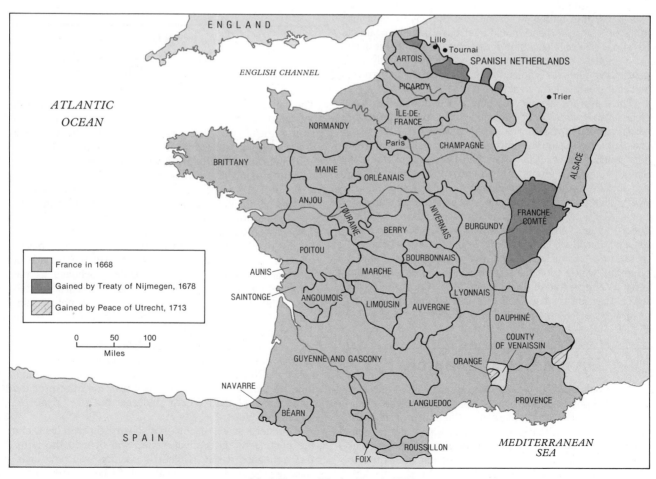

22.1 France Under Louis XIV

ers. In many respects, the crown's relations with the larger and older provinces, called *pays d'état* because they had their own representative assemblies or estates, resembled treaties with quasi-sovereign powers. These provinces set their own tax rates and passed laws independent of and often at odds with those of the central government. As late as 1661 Louis was acknowledged as no more than count of Provence and duke of Brittany in those two provinces. Many of the towns as well enjoyed not only their own councils and magistrates but also levied their own customs duties and raised their own militias. A good number of them were wholly exempt from the basic property tax of the realm, the *taille*. So were whole classes of the population, notably the clergy and, in at least some of the forms in which it was levied, the nobility. On the other hand, the taille was imposed directly and unilaterally on the newer provinces. The hated excise tax on salt, the *gabelle*, was applied so unequally that the price of this vital commodity was as much as 25 times higher in one province than in another.

Armed rebellions often broke out when the central government attempted to impose a new tax. Some of these rebellions went on for years and cost the government far more to suppress than it could ever have hoped to gain in revenue. The only constant in the system was that it bore most heavily everywhere on the poor, particularly the peasantry. Thus it combined both the greatest unfairness and the greatest inefficiency.

The basis for a policy of effective centralization was clear: standardization of laws and taxes, reduction of internal tariffs, promotion of key industries, and the neutralization of seigneurial courts and provincial legislatures. The foundations for this policy had been laid in the previous two reigns. Henry IV had curbed the power of the provincial estates and established government monopolies over mining and the production of gunpowder and salt. Louis XIII's minister, Cardinal Richelieu, had dispatched special agents, the *intendants*, to oversee provincial administration. Both Henry IV and Louis XIII had studiously ignored the national representative assembly, the Estates General, which met only twice during their combined reigns. The revolt of the Fronde (see Chapter 18), in which the nobility had made its last serious attempt to assert power on a national level, had ended in failure.

Divine Right Monarchy

It was Louis XIV, however, who most successfully exploited the powers of personal monarchy to create a centralized state. For Louis, increasing the power of the state was not merely a matter of policy. It was a natural consequence of his authority as a divine right king. Whether Louis actually made the famous statement attributed to him, "I am the state," he clearly lived by the thought. Louis identified himself wholly with the French state. Even

his private life was lived in public, among a throng of courtiers; for him, there was no distinction between the man and the monarch. Fortunately, Louis had the ideal temperament for a king. He was highly conscious of his dignity; it was said that even as a child he seldom laughed. But Louis did not experience the cares of state as a burden. "The calling of a king is great, noble, and delightful," he said. Louis took his pleasures and his responsibilities with the same equanimity. In 54 years of active rule, he never lost his zest for governing.

For Louis, the aim of the state was *gloire*—glory. *Gloire* was both an attribute of persons—the dignity of a nobleman, the majesty of a king—and the collective aspiration of a nation. The glory of France was in its wealth and productivity, its technology and engineering, the splendor of its arts. Even more, in an age that valued military prowess above all else, its glory was measured by its power. France was already the richest and most powerful state in Europe at the accession of Louis XIV. For Louis that was only the measure of its potential for further achievement and greater *gloire*.

❦
JEAN-BAPTISTE COLBERT, MINISTER OF FINANCE

The king assembled around him a small group of ministers recruited not from the nobility but the bourgeoisie. Chief among these was Jean-Baptiste Colbert. The son of a draper, Colbert shared his master's vision of glory. From 1661 until his death in 1683, he was the most important man in the kingdom after Louis himself.

Colbert had entered government service when not yet 20, and his talents and capacity for hard work soon commended him to the secretary of state for war, Michel Le Tellier, who made him his private secretary. By 1649, at the age of only 30, Colbert had become himself a councillor of state, and two years later he entered the service of Cardinal Mazarin, who had succeeded Richelieu as the dominant figure in French politics. Mazarin at first treated the upstart young bourgeois with reserve, if not disdain, but he soon found Colbert's services indispensable, as Le Tellier had. As the cardinal's health began to fail, Colbert took on more and more responsibility. By the late 1650s he was charged with suppressing a major revolt of the nobility in Normandy, Anjou, and Poitou, while at the same time he drafted an ambitious new plan for reform of the king's finances that directly undercut his chief rival, Nicholas Fouquet.

Fouquet learned of Colbert's scheme through his friend the postmaster general of Paris, who opened the letter that contained it. But Colbert's position was now unassailable, and at Mazarin's death in 1661 he had the professional and no doubt personal pleasure of arresting Fou-

Jean-Baptiste Colbert, the consummate bureaucrat, in a portrait by Lefebvre. Colbert's financial and organizational genius made the splendor of Louis' reign possible. [Giraudon/ Art Resource]

quet. The fallen minister, who had grossly enriched himself, narrowly escaped execution. Colbert also used his position to enrich himself and his numerous family, but with a difference: he enriched the king as well.

Colbert's title was controller-general of finances, but his mandate embraced the economy as a whole, including trade and commerce, the merchant marine and the navy, the colonies, and internal security. Colbert found that the crown's deficit was nearly a third of its income and that its revenues were pledged as much as three years in advance. Worse still, barely a third of the taxes levied by the crown found their way into the treasury due to fraud and evasion.

While actually decreasing the taille, Colbert was able to double the overall tax yield within six years by curbing the abuses of tax collectors, tightening exemptions, exploiting the royal demesne more efficiently, and compelling the *pays d'état* to increase their share of taxes. He presided over a council of commerce consisting of prominent merchants, which charted a course for France's commercial and industrial supremacy. Disdainful of agriculture, he pointed to the example of the Dutch, who had gained wealth and world power by commerce despite a land area and population barely a tenth the size of France. He established and subsidized hundreds of new workshops and

factories, either under direct royal control or licensed as monopolies. His agents scoured Europe to recruit the most skilled technicians—dyers, glassblowers, gun founders. At home, meanwhile, he tried to organize all French craftsmen into guilds, subject to minute regulations and supervised by an army of state inspectors.

The purpose of new industry was to provide material for commerce; the purpose of commerce was to amass wealth; and the purpose of wealth was power. Economic activity was thus for Colbert, as for Louis, both a preparation for war and a kind of warfare in itself. By fostering new trades and erecting tariff barriers, France would reduce its dependence on imports and prevent the drain of its bullion. By increasing production, expanding the navy, and creating large overseas trading companies, it would penetrate markets, drive off rivals, and extend French power on a global scale. To all of this, centralized organization and control was the key. "If your Majesty could constrain all your subjects into these four kinds of profession," Colbert wrote the king, "agriculture, trade, war by land or by sea, it would be possible for you to become the master of the world."[1]

Colbert was particularly active on behalf of maritime trade and warfare. Within France, he built canals and modernized ports. He created a flotilla of trading companies for both the West Indies and the East Indies that were designed to extend French power and wealth no less than its fleet. He was the real founder of the French navy, and he searched the prisons and poorhouses of France to man his new ships. In some cases he commuted death sentences to procure sailors, but in many others he arbitrarily lengthened prison terms, compelled judges to sentence convicts to the galleys, and forcibly impressed beggars and vagrants. Such actions showed the darker side of a man obsessed with the goals of power. Assiduous in cultivating his superiors, he seemed a tyrant to many when at last he had no superior but the king. When he died in 1683, his body was buried secretly lest his tomb be desecrated by his enemies. Yet he was France's greatest economic statesman, and perhaps its greatest cultural patron as well.

Louis XIV and the Bureaucracy

Ironically, the chief obstacle to the king's dreams appeared to be his own bureaucracy. According to one contemporary estimate, the number of government offices in France had increased by 50,000 during the first half of the seventeenth century. There were nearly 2,000 officers in the Court of Chancery, and almost 1,000 tax collectors for the taille (at least on paper) in the province of Normandy alone.

The reason for this explosion of bureaucrats lay in the nature of officeholding itself. Each occupant of a venal office bought and owned it. In return for his investment, he acquired a blue-chip property that yielded a handsome income in fees and whose resale value was very likely to appreciate. There was status value too, since even minor offices often entitled the holder or his heir to ennoblement.

The entire system constituted a form of indirect taxation. Purchasers advanced a lump sum to the crown, and recouped their outlay by charging the public for their "services." For the financially pressed monarchy, the lure of ready cash was irresistible. Administratively, however, the system was a nightmare. The number of offices created bore no relation to function or need. The public business was intolerably delayed, and the king's own edicts were lost in the maze of clerkships. Once entrenched, the officeholders resisted any attempt at accountability or reform. In return for short-term financial relief, the crown had traded long-term political paralysis.

In contrast to this bloated bureaucracy, Louis XIV gathered around him a tiny nucleus of advisers. Besides Colbert, the only important ministers were Lionne for foreign affairs and Le Tellier for war. The king made all decisions of state with these three. Another 30 councillors of state and fewer than 100 masters of requests prepared material and executed orders, assisted by scribes, ushers, and other minor functionaries. All in all, the royal executive consisted of fewer than 1,000 persons.

By streamlining his government at the top, Louis was able to act swiftly and in secret and to keep all major threads of policy in his own hands. If there was chaos at the extremities of the state, the king was determined to counteract it by command at the center.

The key to the royal strategy was the revived use of intendants, who were handpicked from among the masters of requests. At first, as under Richelieu, they were sent out on specific assignments to the provinces. Later, however, they took up permanent residence. Their commissions were all-embracing, and their powers superseded those of all other officials, including the provincial governor. Not since Roman times had central authority exerted such continuous and effective control at the local level.

By such means Louis was able to cut through his own bureaucracy and impose his will on France. To be sure, he often met stubborn resistance. Local noblemen, jealous of their independence, made common cause with local officials to frustrate his intentions. Proud Brittany did not submit to the yoke of an intendant until 1689. But in the last analysis, there could be no disputing the command of a divinely anointed king. As God's representative on

---

◉ On the Nature of Majesty ◉

Jacques-Bénigne Bossuet (1627–1704), bishop of Meaux and tutor to the royal family, was the foremost spokesman for the divine right of kings in seventeenth-century France and its last great apologist in Europe. In this characteristically titled work, Politics Derived from the Words of Holy Scripture *(published posthumously in 1709), Bossuet describes the quality of "majesty" in kingship as the reflection and transmission of the power and glory of God on earth.*

By majesty, I do not mean that pomp which surrounds kings, or that show of brilliance which dazzles the vulgar. This is but the reflection of majesty, and not majesty itself.

Majesty is the image of the glory of God in the prince. God is infinite; God is all. The prince, in his capacity as a prince, is not considered an individual man: he is a public person, the whole state is in him, the will of the whole people is contained within his own. As all perfection and all virtue are united in God, so is the entire power of individual persons united in the person of the prince. What greatness is it for a single man to hold such power!

God's power makes itself felt in an instant from one end of the world to the other. Royal power acts simultaneously throughout the realm. It keeps the whole realm in its proper state, just as God does for the whole world. Let God withhold his hand, and the world would collapse again into nothingness; let authority cease in the realm, and everything would be in confusion.

Source: K. M. Baker, ed., *Readings in Western Civilization,* vol. 7 (Chicago: University of Chicago Press, 1987), p. 39.

earth, his will was supreme. Bishop Bossuet (1627–1704), Louis' chief spiritual adviser, went so far as to declare that the king was God himself. It is not recorded that Louis denied it.

Versailles: The Sun King Enthroned

For the king's power to be felt, it had to be visible. Louis had his architects and decorators turn the royal hunting lodge at Versailles, 10 miles from Paris, into the most splendid palace in the Western world. Surrounded by formal gardens and artificial lakes, it stretched in a great semicircle for more than a quarter of a mile. Fountains and statues adorned it on all sides. Inside, a hall of mirrors lit by thousands of candelabras led to the main apartments. Louis himself was portrayed in triumph everywhere, ruling over Europe, Asia, and the Americas in the frescoes that lined the halls of state or garbed as a Roman emperor surrounded by classical gods and goddesses. The king had taken the sun as his personal emblem early in the reign, and every aspect of Versailles, from the smallest decorative details to the long, tree-lined avenues that spread out from the palace like the rays of a great orb, reflected the solar theme. An army of workmen and engineers the size of a city—36,000 were counted on the site at one time—toiled to construct this ultimate monument to *gloire*, digging trenches and canals, erecting pagan temples, stocking the game parks, and trimming the gardens to create a perfect world where nature as well as man obeyed an absolute ruler.

This artificial paradise enclosed one of the most artificial societies ever created. The most distinguished noblemen of France vied for the honor of living in the cramped and squalid conditions of an overcrowded court. Proximity to the king determined one's status. Personal attendance on him was the most coveted honor of all. Great dukes fought for the right to serve as his footmen, adjusting his livery or holding his candlestick. Louis lived in Versailles not as a man but as an idol, displaying himself to the privileged few permitted to worship him in person. In this way, he tamed his nobility. Absorbed in etiquette, obsessed with their own vanity, they neglected the most important aspect of status: power.

As Voltaire remarked, "Louis liked the ladies, and it was reciprocal." The prominence of women in the court life of Versailles reflected the general softening of manners that had come to the French court with its increasing refinement and sophistication of taste. But royal favor, once withdrawn, could be devastating. Louis' first mistress, Louise de la Vallière, had to endure the ignominy of watching him pass through her apartments to visit his new favorite, Madame de Montespan, until she was permitted to retire to a Carmelite nunnery.

The king was finally tamed by a remarkable woman, Madame de Maintenon (1635–1719). Born Françoise d'Aubigné, she was taken to the Caribbean island of Martinique as a child and left penniless at her father's death. She struggled back to France with her mother and, soon

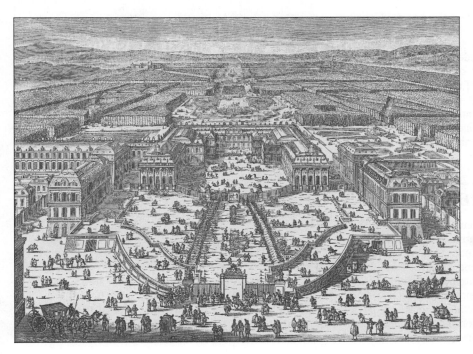

This contemporary engraving of the palace at Versailles gives a good idea of the vast extent of the royal complex and grounds and the throngs of courtiers, suitors, officials, and ladies of fashion that made up its daily traffic. [Bettmann Archive]

orphaned, escaped the fate of a poor relation by marrying the poet Paul Scarron. After Scarron's death, a chance connection brought her the estate of Maintenon and a position at court, where she became governess to Madame de Montespan's bastards and eventually the king's confidante. When Queen Marie-Thérèse died in 1683, Louis secretly married the woman now called Madame de Maintenon, and although the wedding was never acknowledged, she was the dominant presence at Versailles until his death.

Under Maintenon's influence, the court, still brilliant, took on a more pious and sober tone. Remembering the hardships of her own life, Maintenon had begun to educate poor children as early as 1674, and in 1686 she opened a school exclusively for the daughters of impoverished nobility, St. Cyr. For the remainder of her life she visited it nearly every day, directly overseeing the development of its curriculum and the welfare of its pupils. St. Cyr was an immense success, a training college whose graduates spread the spirit of reform into old-fashioned convent schools and a milestone in the history of women's education. Maintenon was buried in the school's chapel, beside her beloved children. St. Cyr itself was closed during the French Revolution, and in 1794 some workmen, engaged in demolishing the chapel, discovered her grave, pulled out her preserved body, dragged and kicked it about the grounds, and threw it into a pit.

The Wars of Louis XIV

If Versailles was the image of *gloire*, war was the practice of it. Louis waited until Colbert had filled the treasury before embarking on his first military adventure, an attack on the Spanish territories of Flanders and the Franche-Comté, which he claimed by right of inheritance through his wife, Marie-Thérèse. This brief contest, the so-called War of Devolution (1667–1668), gained him a dozen towns, including the important commercial centers of Lille and Tournai. It also provoked an alliance between England and the Netherlands, which had only recently completed a war of their own.

The Dutch War (1672–1678)

For Louis, the Dutch were both commercial rivals, whose defeat would open up their lucrative carrying trade to French shipping, and religious heretics, whose Calvinism he was planning to suppress among his own Protestant subjects, the Huguenots. The Dutch had personally offended him at the end of the Flanders campaign with a cartoon that portrayed his sun emblem eclipsed by a wedge of Dutch cheese. More important, the Dutch alone stood between Louis and his long-range goal to dominate

the Low Countries and Germany, and even—as a book published under royal sponsorship in 1667 declared—to revive the empire of Charlemagne in the West.

Louis struck in the spring of 1672. The French occupied three of the seven Dutch provinces, and Amsterdam was saved only by opening the dikes and flooding the province of Holland. The Dutch offered to concede all their strongholds in Flanders and to pay an indemnity of 10 million livres. This would have given Louis victory and left the Dutch frontier defenseless. But Louis demanded a virtual surrender of sovereignty: major territorial concessions within the seven provinces themselves, French commercial and religious penetration, an indemnity of 24 million livres, and most insulting of all, an annual embassy to present a medal in tribute to Louis, like a Roman satellite acknowledging its emperor.

These humiliating demands may have been the worst mistake of Louis' career. The Dutch dug in, determined to resist to the end. The republican Regime of True Liberty that had governed the Netherlands since 1650 was overthrown; its leader, Jan de Witt, was torn to pieces by an angry mob, and the 22-year-old Prince William of Orange was summoned as stadholder and captain general of the army. Louis thus raised up his own worst enemy, for

William of Orange, stadholder of the Netherlands and later, as William III, king of England, was the heart and soul of European opposition to Louis XIV for thirty years. [Scala/Art Resource]

the dour but capable William was to be the heart and soul of European resistance to Bourbon France for the next 30 years. With French troops stalled by the floodwaters, he gained support from Spain and Austria. By 1674 the French had withdrawn from Dutch soil. The Treaty of Nijmegen (1678) not only affirmed Dutch independence but forced the French to lower their own tariffs against Dutch goods. Louis had lost the war.

Aggression Without War: Louis Against Germany

Despite this check, the French state, with its army of 250,000 men, was the strongest not just in Europe but probably in the world. The Dutch were exhausted, the Spanish enfeebled under their last Habsburg king, the ailing and incompetent Charles II, and the Austrians preoccupied by a new Turkish advance along the Danube that brought Ottoman armies under the grand vizier, Kara Mustafa, to the gates of Vienna by 1683 for the first time in a century and a half. Only a relief army commanded by the king of Poland, Jan Sobieski, saved the imperial capital. Louis, meanwhile, continued his war of nerves along the Rhine. He claimed any area on or near his borders that had ever been French by law or custom, a tactic not unlike the one Hitler employed in Germany in the 1930s. Accordingly, French troops occupied large parts of Flanders, Luxembourg, Alsace, and the Saarland after 1680, as well as the free city of Strasbourg. Even Casale Monferrato in northern Italy admitted a French garrison.

Louis insisted that these actions were in accordance with the treaties of Westphalia and Nijmegen. He certified each claim in special courts set up for that purpose, the Chambers of Reunion. In the absence of any international court of arbitration, what better title could be established? But as his courts and armies pushed farther and farther into the heartland of Germany, the princes of the Holy Roman Empire became alarmed. Alarm turned to panic when, in 1685, Louis revoked the Edict of Nantes, which had guaranteed freedom of worship to French Protestants. If the French king's worst diplomatic miscalculation was to have rejected the Dutch peace terms of 1672, the revocation of the Edict of Nantes was his greatest domestic blunder. The thousands of refugees who fled across the border with their tales of persecution were among Louis' most productive subjects, and their skills were soon enriching his enemies. Meanwhile, under Habsburg leadership, the German princes hastily formed a defensive alliance, the League of Augsburg (1686).

The War of Five Continents

When Louis entered the Rhenish Palatinate in September 1688 to support his claims in the region, he began a war that was to outlast all the protagonists but himself. Ranging over five continents and lasting 25 years, it was the first truly global war in history. No war of comparable scale was to be seen again until the twentieth century. For the first time, the quarrels of Europe became the affair of the world.

The 1683 siege of Vienna, here depicted in a composite view, marked the last great Muslim advance in Europe, although the Turks remained a presence on the continent until the early twentieth century. [Austrian National Library, Vienna]

The conflict had two distinct phases. The Nine Years' War (1688–1697) was fought largely along the disputed frontiers of Flanders and Germany, though it reached as far afield as North America, where it was known as King William's War. At first the French had the advantage. But Louis had too many enemies now to win a decisive victory. The Anglo-Dutch alliance was revived in the most dramatic way when William of Orange, responding to a secret invitation from a coalition of English lay and religious leaders, sailed to England in November 1688 and deposed James II. William became king of England (as William III), reigning jointly with his wife Mary (1689–1695), James' elder daughter, while continuing to govern the Netherlands through his able regent, Antonius Heinsius. With such a base, William soon brought Spain, Austria, and Savoy together in a grand anti-French alliance. By the end of the war virtually all of Europe east of the Elbe was fighting France. Louis could not be dislodged from his strong defensive position. But the war took a terrible toll within France itself. Poor harvests, soaring grain prices and military requisitions caused a devastating famine in 1694–1695. Before it had run its course, 2 million French subjects—one-tenth of the population—had died. It was a man-made disaster comparable in its effects on France only to World War I.

The Treaty of Ryswick (1697) compelled Louis not only to restore almost all the territories he had occupied since 1678 but also to withdraw recognition from his hapless guest and pensioner, the former James II, and to acknowledge his archenemy William III as king of England. But a new round of warfare was in the offing, for even higher stakes. For a third of a century, the dynastic politics of Europe had swirled about the fate of the Spanish throne, whose feeble and childless occupant, Charles II, had presided helplessly over the ruin of a once-great power. When Charles died at last in 1700 his government was so impoverished that it could not pay for masses for the repose of his soul. Yet Spain still held much of the southern Netherlands and most of Italy, as well as its great empire in the Americas. In the hands of a competent ruler, it might still regain its former glory; in the hands of a foreign one, it was an incomparable asset.

So thought both Louis XIV and his Habsburg contemporary and antagonist, the Austrian emperor, Leopold I (1658–1705). Since neither was willing to concede control of the whole Spanish patrimony, either by themselves or through dynastic proxies, they had begun to negotiate for Spain's division as early as 1668. As Charles II's death at last became imminent, an effort was made to find a compromise candidate for the throne. This failed, however,

◉ The Disasters of War ◉

In 1695, at the height of the great famine, which had been induced by a combination of bad harvests, wartime requisitions, soaring inflation, and speculation and hoarding, a remarkable open letter circulated among elite circles in France. Addressed to Louis XIV, it was probably the work of an outspoken clergyman, François Fénelon (1651–1715). Its view of the king's pursuit of gloire *is a very different one from that offered by Bossuet.*

Your people, Sire, whom you should love as your children, and who up to this time have been so devoted to you, are dying of hunger. The land is left almost untended, towns and countryside are deserted, trade of all kinds falls off and can no longer support the workers; all commerce is at a standstill. . . . For the sake of getting and keeping vain conquests abroad, you have destroyed half the real strength of your own state. Rather than take money from your poor people, you ought to feed and cherish them. . . . All France is now no more than one great hospital, desolate and unprovided. . . . And it is you, Sire, who have brought these troubles on yourself. . . . Little by little the fire of sedition catches everywhere. The people believe that you have no pity for their sufferings, that you care only for your own power and glory. They say that if the king had a father's heart for his people, he would surely think his glory lay rather in giving them bread and a little respite after such tribulations than in keeping hold of a few frontier posts which are a cause of war.

Source: P. Goubert, *Louis XIV and Twenty Million Frenchmen* (New York: Pantheon, 1970), p. 220.

and when Charles died, he unexpectedly willed his throne and all his dominions to the Bourbon claimant Philip of Anjou, Louis' grandson, who became Philip V of Spain (1700–1746).

Britain and France: The Contest for Empire

The result was the second phase of the great war of France against Europe, the War of the Spanish Succession (1701–1713). Louis moved quickly to consolidate his hold on Spain and its possessions. It was a foregone conclusion that Austria would resist. England and the Netherlands were even more directly menaced. With the occupation of the Spanish Netherlands, the last buffer between French and Dutch territory had been stripped away. The English found their access to the Mediterranean cut off and their empire in the New World threatened.

William III swiftly organized a new Grand Alliance against Louis. It was his last accomplishment. In March 1702 he died following a fall from his horse, to be succeeded in England by James II's younger daughter, Anne (1702–1714), while in the Netherlands Heinsius remained the dominant figure until his death in 1720. The Anglo-Dutch alliance held, though England was now decidedly the senior partner. The English general John Churchill, duke of Marlborough (1650–1722), the greatest soldier of his age, turned back Louis' thrust into Bavaria at Blenheim (1704) and crushed French armies at Ramillies (1706) and Oudenaarde (1708) in Flanders. Meanwhile, the superior Anglo-Dutch fleet kept France at bay in the New World and Africa. By 1709 Louis' position was desperate. Allied armies were poised on the borders of France itself, the treasury was empty, and famine ravaged the land. A bitter parody of the Lord's Prayer circulated at court: "Our father who art at Versailles, whose name is no longer hallowed, whose kingdom is no longer large, give us our daily bread. . . ."

Louis held out, stiffened by demands not only that he surrender all the conquests of his reign but that he help drive his grandson from the Spanish throne as well. At Malplaquet, the bloodiest battle on European soil up to that time, he blunted the allied advance. Thereafter, the Grand Alliance dissolved and the war wound down. The cluster of treaties known as the Peace of Utrecht (1713) left Spain and its overseas dominions to Philip V, though on condition that his throne never be united with that of France. Spain's possessions in the Netherlands and Italy were given to Austria, partly to compensate it for the lost Spanish throne and partly as a buffer against French expansion, though the Dutch received so many concessions in the former area that they actually dominated it. England's prizes reflected its increasing concern with empire. Gibraltar and Minorca gave it control of the Mediterranean, Nova Scotia and Newfoundland entrenched it

on the North American coast, and trading concessions offered a foothold in the lucrative slave trade of Spanish America.

The wars of 1688–1713 were fought to contain the territorial ambitions of the French in Europe. In retrospect, however, they marked the first stage in the great contest of empire between England and France that, resumed in the war cycles of 1740–1763 and 1792–1815, would end only with Wellington's defeat of Napoleon at the Battle of Waterloo. They marked as well the final eclipse of Spain as a great power. The Austrians gained the most territory in Europe itself, but their greatly distended borders were to prove more of a burden than an asset in the long run.

Louis XIV and the Climax of Absolutism

Despite its defeat, France was still the greatest power on the European continent. When Louis XIV died on September 1, 1715, he had reigned longer than anyone else in the history of the world and had dominated his time more completely than anyone since Charlemagne. If he had failed ultimately to impose his will on Europe, it had taken the united strength of his adversaries to contain him. Yet the sum of Louis was more than his parts. He was neither a great soldier nor a genuine innovator. His economic views were firmly rooted in the rigidly protectionist doctrines of mercantilism, and his persecution of the Huguenots drove away many of his most productive subjects. Although he personified divine right kingship, his religion was conventional and often opportunistic. Even his administrative reforms looked backward to the traditions of personal monarchy rather than forward to the modern bureaucratic state. If he showed what could be accomplished by a determined royal absolutism, he showed the limitation of such a system as well. It was left to his arch-rivals, the English, to develop on a large scale what the Dutch polity had already suggested: that a politically stable oligarchy with a moderate representative base could be a far more effective instrument of government than an absolute monarchy dependent on the will and energy of a single man.

Peter the Great and the Emergence of Russia

As forceful as Louis XIV and far more despotic, Peter I (1682–1725), called the Great, consolidated autocracy in Russia and brought his country into the European state system. From its modest beginnings in the fourteenth-century duchy of Muscovy, Russia had become the largest

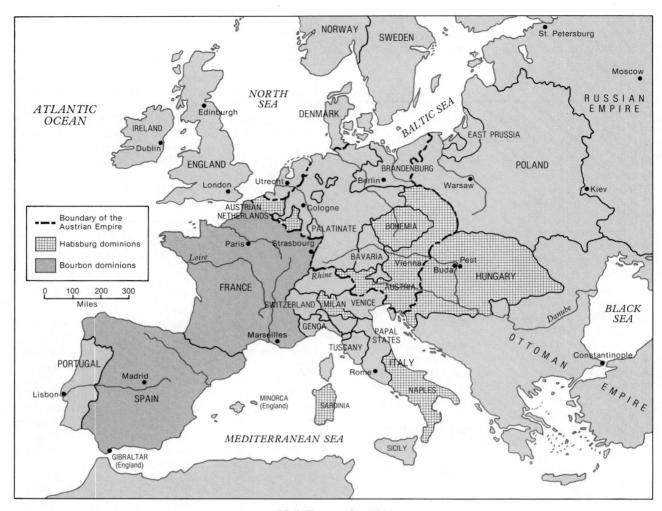

22.2 Europe in 1714

state in the world by Peter's time. Three times the size of Europe, it spanned the Eurasian landmass from the Polish steppe to the Pacific Ocean, embracing some 5.7 million square miles. Much of this expansion had taken place in the seventeenth century, culminating in the first Russian settlement on the Pacific (1647), the reconquest of the ancient Rus' capital of Kiev (1654), and the pacification of the Siberian tribes.

The Tsarist State

This vast land had a population of only 14 million, only one-fortieth the density of France or Italy. Grain yields were comparable only to those of pre-Carolingian agriculture in the West, compelling almost the entire population to farm; only 2 percent lived in towns. The tsarist state and its

nobility had undertaken to control this scarce labor supply since the late fifteenth century, first restricting and at last completely eliminating all freedom of movement. By the seventeenth century the Russian peasantry had been fully enserfed except in some frontier areas, and for all practical purposes enslaved. The great law code, or *Ulozhenie*, of 1649, which served as the basis of Russian society for the next 200 years, formalized its rigid, castelike divisions. Each person's status was fixed by law down to the last detail. Townsmen as well as peasants were bound to their dwellings and occupations. The nobility had become a civil service class since, apart from the clergy, only those who performed state service were permitted to own land. Few societies have ever been more tightly controlled. The concept of personal rights, so important to the development of the West, simply did not exist. Authority could be questioned only by authority. Only the tsar was free, and his freedom—that is, his power—was absolute. What an Austrian ambassador to Russia said in the early sixteenth century was if anything even more true at the end of the seventeenth:

> In the sway the tsar holds over his people, he surpasses all the monarchs of the whole world. . . . He uses his authority as much over ecclesiastics as laymen, and holds unlimited control over the lives and property of all his subjects; not one of his counsellors has sufficient authority to dare to oppose him, or even differ from him, on any subject. They openly confess that the will of the prince is the will of God, and that whatever the prince does he does by the will of God.[2]

Peter and the West

This was the throne that passed to Peter the Great. Like Louis XIV, he experienced a turbulent minority. At the death of his father, Alexis (1645–1676), his half brothers Feodor (1676–1682) and Ivan (1682) succeeded, but both were incompetent, and in 1682 the nobility proclaimed the 9-year-old Peter tsar instead. The country was saved from civil war only by Peter's sister, Sophia, who ruled in his name until 1689. The Peter who came to young manhood then needed no help from anyone. Nearly 7 feet tall and with strength and appetites to match, he was no less ambitious than the ruler of Versailles but far less prudent. All but one of his 36 years of active rule were spent at war. Military expenditures consumed more than 80 percent of his revenue. Even church bells were melted down into cannon. The Russian state was turned into a gigantic battering ram, and it was aimed west.

At the same time, Peter was deeply impressed by the advanced technology and warcraft of the West. He studied tactics and fortifications and built a standing army of 300,000 that, despite Russia's acute manpower shortage, was made up largely of his own subjects, whom he conscripted for life. In 1697–1698 he became the first Russian prince to visit the West, where he and his entourage made a sensation. A bemused William III was his host in Holland and England, where he ignored protocol by touring and even working in foundries and dockyards. The ruler of the world's largest landmass was fascinated by the sea and proudly flourished a certificate declaring him a master shipwright. William invited him to attend a session of England's Parliament. Peter was impressed by the sight of subjects speaking openly to their sovereign, but constitutional monarchy was not one of the Western innovations he brought home with him.

Peter's first military efforts were directed against the Ottoman Turks, from whom he wrested Azov on the Black Sea in 1696. His attention than turned to the Baltic. Here, 1,000 miles from Moscow, he built a new capital, St. Pe-

tersburg, whose royal residence, the Winter Palace, rivaled Versailles in its splendor.

But Peter still lacked a secure northern seaport except at Archangel (Arkhangelsk) on the White Sea, whose harbor was frozen nine months a year. Access to the Baltic was blocked by Sweden, whose territory enclosed it on three sides. The eastern end of the Swedish triangle included the traditionally Russian Karelian peninsula, which Sweden had occupied during the Time of the Troubles. Tsar Alexis, Peter's father, had failed to recapture it. The time now appeared ripe. Sweden's hardy but scattered population of 1.5 million seemed insufficient to defend it against a concerted attack. Its new ruler, Charles XII (1697–1718), was still a boy. With Denmark, Poland, and Brandenburg-Prussia as allies, Peter declared war.

The result was the Great Northern War (1700–1721). After swiftly dispatching Denmark, the warlike Charles, not yet out of his teens, humiliated Peter at Narva (1700), crushing an army five times the size of his own. Muscovy lay defenseless before him. But Charles turned to secure his rear in Poland, giving Peter time to rebuild. By 1704 Peter had retaken Narva. Not content merely with fighting a major war, however, he was simultaneously building his new capital and attempting to join the Don and Volga rivers by a canal, thus giving full access to his port at Azov.

Peter's insatiable demands on the country at last provoked revolt. Invoking the name of the rebel Stenka Razin, the Cossack chieftain Kondraty Bulavin rose in 1707. He burned villages along the whole length of the Don, and cannon were mounted on the Kremlin walls. At the same time, Charles began his long-awaited invasion, striking south into the Ukraine. Peter himself lay ill. Desperately seeking help, he turned to his old ally, England. But the English, fighting their own war with Louis XIV and fearing that Charles might turn against Austria if not otherwise occupied, sent Marlborough the length of Europe personally to persuade the Swedish king to attack Russia.

Victory at Poltava (1709) saved Peter. While Charles was forced to seek refuge in Turkey, Peter overran Karelia and the Baltic provinces of Ingria, Estonia, and Livonia, securing the ports of Revel and Riga. These gains were confirmed by the Treaty of Nystad (1721), which established Russia as the major power in the Baltic. Peter celebrated by assuming the titles of father of his country and emperor and accepted formally the appellation of "the Great." "By our deeds in war," he exulted, "we have emerged from darkness into the light of the world."

The Reforms of Peter

Peter dreamed of yoking the great rivers of Russia together by a system of canals, thereby linking the vast expanses of his realm to his new outlets on the sea. Azov was lost to the Turks in 1711, and with it ten years' labor on the Don-Volga canal. Undaunted, Peter linked the

22.3 *Russia in the Age of Peter the Great, 1689–1725*

Volga to St. Petersburg's river, the Neva, thus uniting the Caspian Sea with the Baltic. Thousands of lives were lost on the project, but within a decade of Peter's death flotillas of flat-bottomed barges were moving the grain and oak timber of central and southern Russia steadily to market.

Peter reorganized his government on the latest Western models. He replaced the old boyar duma (council of nobles) with a nine-member senate, in effect a supreme council of state, and reduced the 40-odd ministries to 12, each headed by a "college" of senior officials reporting to the senate. The countryside was also divided into new provinces and districts. The purpose of the whole, as Peter straightforwardly told the senate, was "to collect money, as much as possible." In this it was successful; tax revenues tripled over the course of the reign.

Foreigners were at first brought in to coordinate the new system and even to staff it. But Peter had always intended that his boyars be bound, as before, to state service. To learn Western ways, he compelled them to adopt Western food and dress and to shave their beards, personally shearing off any he saw in his presence. There were grislier acts of submission as well. When his palace guard, the *Streltsi*, rebelled in his absence, Peter forced the palace nobility to participate in their executions.

In 1722 Peter capped his administrative reforms with the Table of Ranks, which created a new hierarchy of 14

◉ Law and Justice Under Peter the Great ◉

Ivan Pososhkov (1652–1726) was a Russian merchant and entrepreneur who was frequently in trouble with the law and ultimately died in prison. This passage reflects both his own frustration with an often arbitrary and capricious judicial system and the horrific abuses to which it could easily give rise.

There is no man more excellent and judicious than Prince Golitsyn, yet in 1719 I petitioned him for permission to build a distillery and for a license to supply vodka for sale, but he had me put under arrest for no known reason. I remained in custody for a whole week and began to get impatient at being there so long without knowing why. On the eve of the Lady Day fast I asked the corporal of the guard to inform the Prince of my case and Prince Golitsyn said: "Has he been in custody long?" And the corporal said: "A whole week, Sir." And he at once ordered my release. Now I am not entirely without position, I think, and Prince Golitsyn knows me personally; yet I was detained for a whole week for no reason at all. How much worse is the case of a man of no account who will be arrested and forgotten about? In this way a great number of innocent folk languish in prison and die there before their time. . . . I am truly astounded that judges are in the habit of holding men in prison for five or six years or more. If judges and governors were to inspect the new prisoners daily this would no longer happen and there would be no possibility of an innocent man being imprisoned or kept in custody.

Source: I. Pososhkov, *The Book of Poverty and Wealth* (Stanford, Calif.: Stanford University Press, 1987), p. 207 (modified slightly).

military and civil service grades. It permitted commoners as well as nobles to enter state service, ennobling them either upon receiving an officer's commission or attaining the civilian rank of collegiate assessor. In this way Peter broadened the base of the landowning class and gave room to talent from below, though the most privileged positions were still reserved for the old nobility. This system remained essentially intact down to 1917.

The church was also thoroughly restructured. The office of patriarch, assumed by the metropolitan of Moscow in 1589, had in the hands of such men as Philaret (1619–1633) and Nikon (1652–1666) rivaled the power of the tsar, as Peter himself complained. In 1700 he permitted it to lapse, and in 1721 he replaced it with the Holy Synod, a body closely tied to the state. He reduced the number of monasteries and nunneries as well and diverted much of their income into his own coffers, though they were too much a part of the fabric of Russian life to be done away with altogether, as he would probably have wished. For Peter, all idle hands were useless, and praying hands were idle.

Peter the Great, himself clean-shaven after the fashion of the West, decreed that his nobility must shear off the beards that were a traditional mark of their status. Recalcitrant nobles were fined or, as here, subjected to compulsory barbering. [Granger Collection]

There were perhaps 3,000 foreigners in Russia at the beginning of Peter's reign, many of whom lived in the so-called German suburb of Moscow. Peter brought in many more to staff his ministries and run his new technical schools and fledgling industries. Their heathen mores aroused the ire of churchmen and nobles, and native merchants resented their privileges; they even sometimes inspired actual panic in the countryside. At one point a wild rumor circulated that Russian men would be forbidden to marry for seven years so that foreigners imported by Peter (himself viewed by many as the Antichrist) could take their women instead. One of the rallying cries of the Cossack rebellion was a demand for the expulsion of all foreigners.

Despite this, Peter persisted in his attempts to westernize Russia. He reformed the calendar and redesigned the alphabet, ordered translations of the Greek and Roman classics, and hired a German troupe to perform French comedies in the Kremlin Square. In 1703 he introduced the first newspaper into Russia, which he edited himself. He built the first Russian greenhouses and laboratories and in 1724 established the Russian Academy of Sciences, though its first members were all Germans.

Peter died in February 1725, leaving an unsettled succession and an exhausted realm. But he had created the foundations of a modern state and economy and made Russia a permanent part of Europe. The Western powers were not slow to recognize this. Peter's ambassador in Vienna reported after Poltava, "It is commonly said that the tsar will be formidable to all Europe, that he will be a kind of northern Turk." By 1711 Prussia was already proposing an anti-Russian alliance, and the British fleet appeared in the Baltic to challenge Peter's presence.

In many ways, Peter's life was a struggle to tame himself as well as Russia. The young tsar who loved to trick his courtiers by signing decrees with pseudonyms became the statesman who introduced orderly, bureaucratic government to his realm. The man who corresponded on politics with the great philosopher Leibniz had ungovernable fits of rage and beat his ministers. As a foreign visitor observed, "He is a prince at once very good and very bad; his character is exactly that of his country." In his passionate contradictions, Peter mirrored the conflicts of a Russia torn between the isolation of its past and the world presence of its future.

Austria:
The Dynastic State

After the division of the Habsburg crown in 1555 between its Spanish and Austrian branches, the Austrian monarchy consisted of three major units, the hereditary provinces of Austria itself; the so-called crown of St. Wenceslas, comprising Bohemia, Moravia, and Silesia; and the crown of St. Stephen, including Hungary, Transylvania, and Croatia. Bohemia and Hungary had become part of the Habsburg dominions in 1527 after the Battle of Mohács, though much of Hungary was still contested. Indeed, only the continuing threat of the Turks in southeastern Europe could have united so disparate a group of peoples—Germans, Czechs, Magyars, Croats, Slovaks, Slovenes, Italians, Romanians, Ruthenians—under a single head. Turkey may in this sense be said to have engendered the Austrian monarchy; nor was it a coincidence that the final expulsion of Turkey from Europe in the early twentieth century should have been followed shortly after by the collapse and dismemberment of the Habsburg empire. The histories of Turkey and Austria rose and fell together.

Austria in the seventeenth century might be described as a power but not a state. The imperial title was recognized only in the Austrian provinces proper; the Habsburg emperor was separately king of Bohemia and Hungary. The chief unifying factor in this strange entity, whose ruler lacked a single title and whose lands lacked a common name, was the person of the monarch himself. His government was actually a series of ongoing negotiations with the provinces of his realm, whose noble estates possessed extensive powers, including the right to veto imperial taxes and, in Hungary, even to rebel.

After the failure of Ferdinand II's attempt to reassert his power as Holy Roman Emperor in the Thirty Years' War, his successors, Ferdinand III (1637–1657) and Leopold I, concentrated on achieving internal consolidation. The Counter-Reformation in Austria was, in its political dimension, a struggle against the Protestant nobility who were dominant in Bohemia and Hungary. Bohemian Protestantism had been ruthlessly suppressed after 1620, and the native nobility was replaced by Catholic loyalists. A similar policy was applied in Hungary after 1671 following an abortive rebellion. While the zeal to root out heretics tended to diminish in states that had achieved political stability, the Habsburgs continued their efforts to impose religious uniformity and, with it, centralized control. Such persecution fell most heavily on the Jews, who were expelled from all of Lower Austria as a pious act by Leopold I despite the fact that his principal financier, Samuel Oppenheimer, was and remained a Jew.

Religious orthodoxy was linked to what the Habsburgs saw as their special mission: the defense of Christian Europe against the menace of the Ottoman Turks. After a period of quiescence following the Treaty of Sitva-Torok (1606), the Turks crossed the Danube in strength in 1663, ravaging Hungary, Moravia, and Silesia. Repulsed at St. Gotthard by a papal-sponsored and Austrian-led army, they acceded to the Truce of Vasvar (1664). This treaty formally divided Hungary, which, though nominally a Habsburg principality, had long enjoyed semi-independence as a border region between the two great powers. When the Turks renewed the war in 1683 with an army of 200,000 men, the Hungarians, preferring the Ottoman yoke to what they had seen of the Habsburg, joined forces with the invaders. The Turks were also assisted by Louis XIV, who saw the attack as a welcome opportunity to divert Leopold's attention from his own aggression on the Rhine, though he temporarily suspended aid as a gesture to European public opinion when the Turks stormed up to the very gates of Vienna, subjecting it to a two-month siege.

The relief of the Habsburg capital by John III Sobieski of Poland (1673–1696) was hailed throughout Europe as a miraculous deliverance. It was a historic moment, for it marked the last great thrust of Muslim power that had threatened Europe for nearly 1,000 years. In the war that ensued, climaxed by Prince Eugene of Savoy's great victory at Zenta (1697), the Turks were driven permanently from the Danube basin and back upon the Balkans. They might have been expelled completely from Europe had France heeded the appeal of Pope Innocent XI to join the Habsburg alliance. But the bitter rivalry between Bourbon and Habsburg prevented any such union, leaving a significant Turkish presence on the continent for more than two centuries.

The Treaty of Karlowitz (1699) gave the Habsburgs possession of virtually all of Hungary, Transylvania, and Croatia. Hungary's crown of St. Stephen was declared hereditary in the Habsburg family (1687). The Magyar nobility was not purged, as in Bohemia, and it was permitted to retain its provincial assemblies and national diet. But its power was curbed, and non-Magyar nobles were settled in the new lands, as well as German and Slavic peasants. The result was a new Magyar rising under Prince Ferenc Rakoczi, which lasted from 1703 to 1711. The defiant Magyars, with their proud sense of isolation among the surrounding Slavic populations, remained the most refractory of the Habsburg empire's many peoples.

The Habsburgs thus faced three major problems during the long reign of Leopold I and after: in Germany, to contain Louis XIV and to restore the influence if not control of the emperor; in the east, to defend the frontier, first against Turkey and later Russia; and at home, to assert the imperial authority over a fractious and independent nobility. Each of these tasks seemed beyond their strength. French influence appeared well on the way to replacing Austrian in Germany. The timid Leopold had fled Vienna at the approach of the Turks, and only the courage of a foreign prince had saved the empire. The monarchy's plight at home was symbolized by the efforts of Charles VI (1711–1740) to gain support for the Pragmatic Sanction, which tried to establish the principle of a common succession in all Habsburg lands and thus ensure a single rule.

Yet the unwieldy Habsburg state continued to grow. Its victories against the Turks had doubled its effective size during the reign of Leopold I. The Treaty of Rastatt (1714) brought it the Spanish Netherlands and most of Italy. Another brief war with Turkey (1716–1718) pushed its borders into the Balkans. Even Prince Eugene, who conducted this campaign, expressed misgivings about the acquisition of so much territory. A swollen empire now stretched from the Carpathian Mountains to the North Sea. The Habsburgs had multiplied their subject populations but had devised no strategy for integrating them.

Prussia: The Garrison State

A very different course was pursued by Prussia, which emerged from the rubble of post-Westphalian Germany to become a major European power and the ultimate unifier of Germany as a whole. Prussia had its origin in the electoral mark of Brandenburg, a flat, sandy terrain south of the Baltic coast that passed in 1417 to the princely house of Hohenzollern. In 1618 the elector of Brandenburg acquired the duchy of Prussia, then a fief of Poland, giving the dynasty its first access to the sea. At about the same time (1614) he fell heir to Cleves, a small duchy on the Rhine. These three entities were widely separated on the map. Their populations, half German and half Pole, half Lutheran and half Catholic, half serf and half free, had nothing in common but their ruler. During the Thirty Years' War, all three territories were overrun by foreign armies. Brandenburg was occupied between 1627 and 1643, and the population of its capital, Berlin, fell from 14,000 to 6,000. Many towns were destroyed completely.

Under these circumstances 20-year-old Frederick William (1640–1688), later known to history as the Great Elector, succeeded to the Hohenzollern legacy. By 1648 he had built up an army of 8,000, a small force but one sufficient to obtain for him a part of the coastal region of Pomerania and the ecclesiastical principalities of Magdeburg and Halberstadt at the Conference of Westphalia. Frederick William had the means of a prince but the ambition of a great dynast. When Pomerania and East Prussia were menaced by a war between Sweden and Poland in 1655, he ignored the refusal of the Brandenburg estates to vote new taxes and collected them by force. Though he lacked a royal title, he considered himself as much a divine right ruler as Louis XIV, demanding recognition of this from the estates of Prussia and landing 2,000 troops in its capital, Königsberg, to enforce his claim. Frederick William found the key to state-building in the maintenance of a standing army, which he swelled to 30,000. The army was both his excuse for raising taxes and his means of compelling payment. His soldiers collected taxes directly and exercised police powers as well. Thus from the first, the Great Elector broke down the distinction between civilian and military functions.

Frederick William was not uniformly successful. He made no further territorial gains after 1648 despite participating in two major wars and was thwarted in his lifelong goal of connecting Prussia with the rest of his dominions,

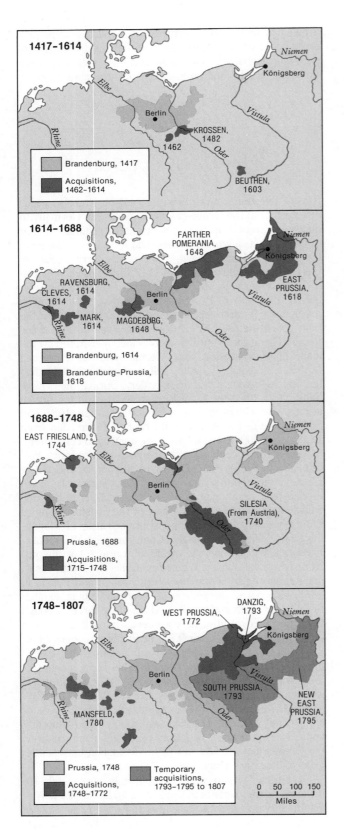

a task not accomplished until 1772. Though he tripled his tax revenues, he remained dependent on foreign subsidies to maintain the army. To conciliate the nobility, he exempted them from his new taxes. These fell mainly on the towns instead, thereby frustrating his goals of commercial and industrial development. Like Peter the Great, however, he required service of the nobility, particularly in the army. Thus while curbing the nobility's privileges on a political level—that is, their power to obstruct him—he confirmed their social preeminence and integrated them into his absolutist state.

The elector Frederick III (1688–1713) was recognized as King Frederick I of Prussia in 1701 in return for his participation in the War of the Spanish Succession against Louis XIV, though Prussia contributed little. The task of state-building was resumed by his eccentric but capable successor, Frederick William I (1713–1740). The Great Elector had seen the army as an instrument of state power; under his grandson and namesake, the army to all intents and purposes became the state. With the establishment of the General Directory in 1723, which combined the functions of the war and finance councils, the entire governing apparatus down to the lowliest tax collector or quartermaster in the provinces revolved about the needs of the army. Frederick William divided the country into recruitment districts and regimental cantons. The army was not segregated in barracks but billeted among the general population, so that civilians, particularly in the towns, were continuously exposed to the impress of military discipline and drill. No sight in Prussia was more common than a parade. In addition to the regular career army, every Prussian male was subject to three months of military service a year. By this means Frederick William was able to maintain a standing army of 80,000 men on a population base of only 1.5 million. Not since ancient Sparta had a society lived so completely by the military ideal.

Under Frederick II (1740–1786), also called "the Great," Prussia reached the full status of a great power. Frederick was the most impressive monarch of the eighteenth century, and at least for the first half of his reign he dominated continental politics almost as completely as Louis XIV had done. Frederick broke with the personal austerity and Calvinist piety of his father. He was a son of the Enlightenment who flirted with atheism and entertained the philosopher Voltaire; a soldier-king whose armies, like Louis XIV's, held off half of Europe. In his social policies, however, he adhered closely to the practice of his father. Each class was assigned its duties from above. The higher ranks in the army and the state bureaucracy were reserved for the nobility. Merchants and townsmen were obliged to accept a subordinate position. They could

22.4 The Rise of Brandenburg–Prussia

neither purchase noble land nor aspire to noble status. Frederick had kind words for the peasantry, which, he declared, deserved the greatest respect because it carried the heaviest burdens. He did little to relieve those burdens however, even in East Prussia, where peasants were enserfed and in many respects little better than enslaved by the local nobility, known as Junkers.

Eastern European Absolutism in Context

Vast Russia, divided Austria, and militarized Prussia took different routes after 1650 toward a common goal: the centralization of authority. All three were landlord states where peasant labor was largely unfree and trade and industry were largely undeveloped. All three lacked suitable outlets to the sea until the eighteenth century, and despite the efforts of Peter the Great to build a Russian navy, none became a true maritime power. Thus the commercial pressures that spurred the development of centralized (though not necessarily absolutist) authority in western Europe were not directly present. But the impressive wealth and power of the Atlantic states—England, France, and the Netherlands—were very much on the minds of Romanov, Habsburg, and Hohenzollern sovereigns. Peter the Great's visit to the West in 1697–1698 determined him to modernize his country. The Great Elector had been educated in the Netherlands and dreamed, though in vain, of emulating its commercial success. The Habsburgs, too, sought to encourage mining and industry and even attempted to establish overseas trading companies as the Dutch and English had done. Mercantilist doctrines that equated the amassing of treasure and the increase of state power took hold in the east just as they had begun to give way to more sophisticated models in the west. In England, particularly, a more flexible political and financial system emerged in the wake of a second rebellion to give it a signal advantage in the new global context of European state competition.

England: The Triumph of Parliamentary Government

The Stuart monarchy had been restored in 1660 under a formula that defined the government as consisting of king, lords, and commons. But it was not clear where the balance of authority lay among these three elements. A newly constituted Convention Parliament, composed chiefly of nobles and other great landowners, compelled the new king, Charles II (1660–1685), to accept its terms. The crown could no longer create special courts outside the jurisdiction of the common law, nor could it collect taxes not authorized by Parliament. The king was obliged to issue a general amnesty for all but those directly responsible for his father's death. In all, 13 persons were executed, an astonishingly small number in view of the scale of the rebellion and the customs of the age. Finally, Charles agreed to exchange his traditional feudal revenues for a permanent grant of customs and excise taxes, thus freeing the magnates from all restrictions on the ownership of their estates and shifting the tax burden from the landed classes toward the towns.

Charles was not even able to reward those who had supported him. Royalists whose estates had been confiscated during the revolution were permitted to sue for their recovery, but those who had sold them, even under duress, received no compensation. This too confirmed the rebel gentry in their gains and accelerated the tendency toward concentration of land ownership. Charles' promise of religious toleration was swept away by his first elected parliament. This "Cavalier" Parliament, as it was nicknamed for its initially reactionary tone, restored the supremacy of the Anglican church and placed severe restrictions on all other forms of worship. Some 1,200 ministers were ejected from their parishes for refusing to accept a new prayer book and to take an oath of conformity, creating a schism within English Protestantism that persists to the present day.

Charles' return was generally popular at first, though a republican underground persisted. But his honeymoon was short-lived. An unsuccessful war with the Dutch resulted in the fall of his chief minister, the earl of Clarendon (1667), and a similar fate befell his successor, the earl of Danby (1678). Charles' most persistent problem was money. The grant of taxes he had received in 1660 was calculated to meet his expenses. It proved insufficient, however, and he remained financially and therefore politically dependent on Parliament. Charles sought to escape this dependence by obtaining a French subsidy in return for supporting Louis XIV's war against the Netherlands (Treaty of Dover, 1670). But Charles also agreed secretly to announce his conversion to Catholicism and, if necessary, to accept French troops to impose it on the country. The rumor of this agreement poisoned the remainder of his reign. Parliament responded in 1673 by passing the Test Act, which barred all religious dissenters from public office. The real object of attack was the king's younger brother and prospective heir, the openly Catholic duke of York. After a wave of anti-Catholic hysteria following allegations in 1678 of a Jesuit plot to assassinate Charles, three successive parliaments attempted to ram through an act excluding the duke of York from the throne. The country seemed again on the verge of civil war. But the opposition party, called the Whigs, was divided in its aims, some members favoring alternative candidates to the throne and some the establishment of a republic. The king was able to rally his own supporters, the Tories, behind the principles of direct hereditary succession and divine right. The leading Whigs were banished or executed, and, on his deathbed, Charles was finally received into the Catholic church.

The Glorious Revolution and the Revolutionary Settlement

The duke of York succeeded peacefully as James II (1685–1688). He promised to preserve the constitution and the supremacy of the Church of England. He was already 51, and without a male heir. The country hoped that his brief Catholic reign would pass without serious incident.

But James soon revealed his true intentions. He placed Catholics in key civil and military positions. This violated the Test Act, but James claimed that he was not bound by former acts of Parliament. He camped Irish troops above London, allowed Jesuits to proselytize freely, and imprisoned seven Anglican bishops for refusing to read a proclamation giving freedom of worship to Catholics and Protestant nonconformists. When James reported the birth of a son in June 1688, thus opening the possibility of a Catholic dynasty, Whigs and Tories swiftly united. They called on William of Orange to free the country.

William's invasion was one of the great gambles of history. Victory meant the possibility of combining England and the Netherlands into a force capable of resisting Louis XIV; defeat meant the loss of his fleet and, most likely, his country. Landing on the coast of Devon in the southwest on November 5, William was hailed as a liberator. Most of James' army deserted him, and James was forced to flee into exile.

William summoned a parliament, which declared him jointly sovereign with his wife, Mary. Over the next dozen years they built a new constitutional order that, much modified by time and circumstance, has remained both the basis of English government itself and the primary model of representative government the world over. The Bill of Rights (1689) declared the supremacy of all law passed by Parliament. Henceforth, no king could levy taxes, maintain an army, or create new organs of government without

◉ The Right to Alter Government ◉

In 1688 England deposed a king for the second time in 40 years. Writing to justify the right of a sovereign people to alter its institutions of government, John Locke (1632–1704) offered what would become a classic defense of revolution.

The reason why men enter into society is the preservation of their property, and the end why they choose and authorize a legislature is that there may be laws made and rules set as guards and fences to the properties of all the members of the society. For since it can never be supposed to be the will of the society that the legislative should have a power to destroy that which everyone designs to secure by entering into society and for which the people submitted themselves to the legislators of their own making: whenever the legislators endeavor to take away and destroy the property of the people or to reduce them to slavery under arbitrary power, they put themselves into a state of war with the people. . . . By this breach of trust they forfeit the power the people had put into their hands for quite contrary ends, and it devolves upon the people, who have a right to resume their original liberty and the establishment of a new legislative (such as they shall think fit), to provide for their own safety and security, which is the end for which they are in society. . . . What I have said here, concerning the legislative in general holds true also concerning the supreme executor, who having a double trust put in him, both to have a part in the legislative, and the supreme execution of the law, acts against both when he goes about to set up his own arbitrary will as the law of the society.

Source: J. Locke, *Two Treatises of Government,* ed. P. Laslett (Cambridge: Cambridge University Press, 1964), pp. 430–431 (spelling and punctuation modernized).

Parliament's consent. No Englishman could be arrested without legal warrant, detained by excessive bail, or subjected to "cruel and unusual punishments"—a phrase incorporated directly into the American Bill of Rights a century later. Though they lacked the phrase for it, the framers of this new order—which came to be known as the Revolutionary Settlement—worked to contain executive authority by a separation of powers. The king might not tamper with elections or interfere with free speech in Parliament, nor might royal officials sit in the House of Commons. Similarly, judges could no longer be removed by the king, only through parliamentary impeachment. Some of these ideas proved unworkable, such as the ban on electioneering and the exclusion of officials from Parliament, and others were modified in practice. But the essential principles of legislative and judicial independence remained.

The new system worked awkwardly at first. With the threat of James removed, Whigs and Tories fell out with each other over the spoils of power. There were genuine differences between them as well, however. Though both derived from the landed gentry, the Whigs tended to embrace the great London merchants who believed in commercial and colonial expansion and eagerly supported parliamentary supremacy. The Tories, by contrast, were reluctant revolutionaries, rural and isolationist, who regarded 1688 as a tragic necessity rather than a brilliant opportunity. William naturally tended to rely on the Whigs, and with their support he chartered the Bank of England (1694). Private banks had been in operation in England since the 1650s, and the Bank of Amsterdam (1609) was the most important commercial institution in Europe. The Bank of England, however, represented a new kind of marriage between private capital and government. It was established for the specific purpose of lending William £1.2 million—nearly a year's ordinary revenue—to help finance the war against Louis XIV. By borrowing rather than taxing, William was able to tap an almost limitless source of funds. Thus was born the idea of a permanent national debt and with it the power of modern government.

By 1713 the public debt stood at £54 million, nearly 100 times more than in 1688. This was the money that defeated Louis XIV. Some feared that without the need to rely on Parliament for taxation, the monarchy would soon become independent of any control. But the Whig magnates who funded William through the bank were the same men who supported him in Parliament. The struggle between crown and Parliament had ended in the discovery of common interests: war, empire, and profit.

The only thing that threatened this new partnership was the fragility of the Stuart line in England, represented by Queen Mary. At William III's death, he was succeeded by Mary's sister Anne (1702–1714), none of whose 16 children had survived. Parliament settled the succession on the electoral house of Hanover in Germany, distantly related to the Stuarts through the daughter of James I. At

the same time, it declared that no Catholic could ever sit on the throne of England, thus barring James II and his son, James Edward. As a further precaution, the Whigs united Scotland with England in 1707, thus creating the modern Great Britain. When Anne died, some Tory leaders, unwilling to relinquish divine right, rashly backed an invasion attempt by James Edward. The Whigs, who staunchly supported the new dynasty, were more firmly entrenched than ever and remained the dominant political force in the country until 1760.

♣ LATE STUART AND HANOVERIAN LONDON

If Paris was the cultural capital of Europe and Amsterdam its financial center, London's time was fast approaching in the late seventeenth century. With a population of about 500,000 to 600,000 by 1700, it was, with Paris and Edo (Tokyo), one of the three largest cities in the world. Whereas only one of every 40 or 50 Frenchmen was a Parisian, however, one of every ten Englishmen lived in London, fully half the urban population of the country.

The magnet of London was trade. People engaged in commerce and manufacturing averaged four times the income of those who farmed. The wealth and produce of the entire country flowed daily into the city: great droves of turkeys who walked the roads from Norfolk and Suffolk, sheep from Lincoln and Leicester, cattle from Wales and the Scottish Highlands, corn from the midland counties, cheese from Cheshire, fish from Kent, coals from Newcastle, stones from Dorset. London "sucks the vitals of trade in this island to itself," wrote Daniel Defoe, the author of the immensely popular *Robinson Crusoe* (1719). Daily, 3,500 boats and barges plied London's river, the Thames; in 1700, 77 percent of England's foreign trade and nearly 60 percent of its shipping passed through the city.

By the late seventeenth century a lively business culture had grown up around a new London institution, the coffeehouse. Over 500 of them flourished in the reign of Queen Anne. Merchants wrote maritime insurance at Lloyd's, and brokers traded stocks and securities at Jonathan's and Garraway's in Exchange Alley (a formal stock exchange was finally licensed by the government in 1697; the first crash followed in 1720). Noblemen and men of fashion, artists and scholars had their favorite houses too. Here men exchanged news and gossip; read the daily newspapers, which, beginning with *The Daily Courant*, had reached a circulation of 67,000 by 1714; and avidly consumed political pamphlets and the popular periodicals, *The Tatler* and *The Spectator*. But the new climate of business so evident after 1688 predominated. As Defoe, himself the editor of an influential journal, *The Review*, put it

simply, "the main affair of life" appeared to be "getting money."

The face of London also changed in this period. The Great Fire of September 1666 burned down 13,000 of the city's old timbered houses. Most were rebuilt with brick and mortar, many in the classical style popularized by Sir Christopher Wren (1632–1723), England's greatest architect. The new West End suburbs of Bloomsbury, Piccadilly, and St. James' were marked by splendid squares and esplanades down which the rich and fashionable paraded or were carried in coaches or sedan chairs. But the vast majority of the population lived quite otherwise, in one-room tenement apartments without water or sanitation on streets so crowded and obstructed by carts, overhangs, basements, and open sewers that movement was next to impossible. The working poor of the city—porters, coal heavers, dockworkers, scavengers, domestics—lived hand to mouth in squalor and filth. An underworld of thieves and cutthroats preyed on this population, their activities all but uncontrolled in a world where life was cheap, riot common, and policing virtually nonexistent. (By contrast, Paris had instituted an effective police force as early as 1667.) The introduction of cheap gin in the second quarter of the eighteenth century sent the death rate soaring, particularly among the destitute. The London magistrate and reformer Henry Fielding observed that gin was "the principal sustenance . . . of more than a hundred thousand people in this metropolis." A man too poor to eat could drink himself into a stupor for a penny. Even after an act of Parliament regulated the consumption of gin, 1,000 people a year starved to death in the richest city of the world.

The state system of Europe in the second half of the seventeenth century and the first half of the eighteenth century was characterized by the tension between monarchies that attempted to extend and centralize their authority, often by appeal to divine right, and landed aristocracies that generally resisted them, seeking to reassert traditional privileges. In most cases the monarchies prevailed to a greater or lesser extent, sometimes by coercion, sometimes by cooptation, and sometimes with the assistance of a new elite of merchants, bankers, and bureaucratic office-holders. In France, the leading power on the Continent throughout the period, this process was clearly visible in the policies of Louis XIV, who placed men of bourgeois origin in the most important offices of state and kept his nobility in opulent idleness at Versailles.

In England, by contrast, the landed and mercantile elites united to create through revolution a uniquely successful partnership between limited monarchy and a broad governing class. In Russia the absence of constitutional tradition enabled Peter the Great to subordinate his nobility and to replace Sweden as the major power in the north, while the retreat of Turkish power left Habsburg Austria, despite its diffuse political structure, dominant in southeastern Europe. The most extraordinary example of state building was in Prussia, where a series of able and determined rulers welded a scattered and unpromising patrimony into a formidable military machine. These new patterns of power produced a Europe more politically complex, competitive, and interdependent than ever before.

Notes

1. G. Treasure, *Seventeenth Century France* (New York: Barnes & Noble, 1966), p. 334.
2. R. K. Massie, *Peter the Great* (New York: Knopf, 1980), p. 177.

Suggestions for Further Reading

Anderson, P. *Lineages of the Absolutist State*. London: N.L.B., 1974.

Baxter, S. B. *William III and the Defense of European Liberty, 1650–1702*. New York: Harcourt, Brace & World, 1966.

Blum, J. *Lord and Peasant in Russia from the Ninth to the Nineteenth Century*. Princeton, N.J.: Princeton University Press, 1961.

Carsten, F. L. *The Origins of Prussia*. Westport, Conn.: Greenwood Press, 1981.

Clark, G. N. *The Later Stuarts, 1660–1714*. 2d ed. Oxford: Clarendon Press, 1958.

——. *War and Society in the Seventeenth Century*. Cambridge: Cambridge University Press, 1958.

Evans, R. J. W. *The Making of the Habsburg Monarchy, 1550–1700*. New York: Oxford University Press, 1979.

Goubert, P. *Louis XIV and Twenty Million Frenchmen*. New York: Pantheon, 1972.

Greaves, R. L. *Deliver Us from Evil: The Radical Underground in Britain, 1660–1663*. New York: Oxford University Press, 1986.

——. *Enemies Under His Feet: Radicals and Nonconformists in Britain, 1664–1677*. Stanford, Calif.: Stanford University Press, 1989.

Hatton, R. M., ed. *Louis XIV and Absolutism*. Columbus: Ohio State University Press, 1977.

Hellie, R. *Slavery in Russia, 1450–1725*. Chicago: University of Chicago Press, 1982.

Kamen, H. *Spain in the Later Seventeenth Century*. London: Longman, 1980.

Kann, R. A. *A History of the Habsburg Empire, 1526–1918*. Berkeley: University of California Press, 1974.

Kenyon, J. P. *Revolution Principles: The Politics of Party, 1689–1720*. Cambridge: Cambridge University Press, 1977.

Laslett, P. *The World We Have Lost*. London: Methuen, 1965.

Massie, R. K. *Peter the Great*. New York: Knopf, 1980.

Plumb, J. H. *The Growth of Political Stability in England, 1675–1725*. London: Macmillan, 1967.

Riasonovsky, N. V. *The Image of Peter the Great in Russian History and Thought*. New York: Oxford University Press, 1985.

Rosenberg, H. *Bureaucracy, Aristocracy, and Autocracy: The Prussian Experience, 1660–1815*. Boston: Harvard University Press, 1958.

Rude, G. *Paris and London in the Eighteenth Century*. New York: Viking Press, 1971.

Rule, J., ed. *Louis XIV and the Craft of Kingship*. Columbus: Ohio State University Press, 1970.

Spielman, J. P. *Leopold I of Austria*. London: Thames & Hudson, 1977.

Sumner, B. H. *Peter the Great and the Emergence of Russia*. New York: Macmillan, 1951.

Wolf, J. B. *Louis XIV*. New York: Norton, 1968.

Europe's Century of Genius

Science is the systematic attempt to understand the world and to adapt it to human uses. As such, it is as old as culture itself. The establishment of the first major civilizations was concurrent with the Neolithic revolution that occurred about 8000 B.C. The advances made in China between the third and thirteenth centuries A.D. may be considered a second scientific revolution. But the development of modern science that began in Europe in the sixteenth and seventeenth centuries and, having spread across the globe, continues today at an accelerating pace has transformed not only our relation to the environment but the environment itself. It thus stands as one of the most momentous changes in human history.

This illustration from Vesalius' *De Fabrica* (1543), the first great textbook of modern anatomy, shows the sheaths of muscle beneath the skin. The body is posed upright against a typical Renaissance landscape, as if to emphasize the relationship between a human's natural elements and those of the world. [Lynn Mooney/College of Physicians and Surgeons]

From Ancient Science to the Copernican Revolution

It is often assumed that the scientific revolution was a sudden breakthrough that cleared away the mists of legend, superstition, error, and ignorance with which the human imagination had cloaked the world and revealed the physical universe in its true light. Nothing could be further from the truth or indeed further from the nature of modern science itself. The scientific revolution was the product of particular historical circumstances and imperatives and the culmination of a rich and varied intellectual tradition. Without the circumstances and the tradition, its achievement would have been impossible.

The Legacy of Antiquity

Classical antiquity had bequeathed a rich scientific heritage to Western civilization. Mathematics, astronomy, biology, and medicine were all highly developed. Much about the physical world was accurately known, and many modern theories had their origin in Greek science. Pythagoras had deduced that the earth was a sphere in the sixth century B.C., and Eratosthenes in the third century B.C. measured its diameter to within 90 percent accuracy. Anaximander, a contemporary of Pythagoras, offered the first theory of the earth's evolution, based on his discovery of fish fossils in mountain areas far removed from the sea. A century later, Leucippus and Democritus put forward the first atomic theory of matter. These theories were not universally accepted however. Aristotle put the great weight of his authority behind the rival theory of Empedocles that matter consisted not of complex structures of atoms but of compounds of the four primary elements of earth, air, fire, and water. Similarly, the third-century B.C. speculation of the astronomer Aristarchus that the sun rather than the earth was the center of the universe was rejected in favor of the geocentric view Aristotle sponsored, and given its classical expression in the work of Ptolemy of Alexandria (second century A.D.).

The Romans made little contribution to scientific theory, although their technological achievements—dams, irrigation, road building, engineering, plumbing, and heating—were unequaled in the West until the Renaissance. The period after the fall of the Roman Empire in the West, with its erosion of civic life and loss of records, interrupted the literate culture and the social and state patronage on which scientific development depended. The heritage of Greek science was continued in Byzantium, however, and even more intensely in the Arab world. Following the Arab conquests of the seventh century, Islam served as a focal point for Greek, Egyptian, Persian, and Indian traditions of thought. The introduction of paper from China provided the means of transforming the largely oral Arab culture into written form. The result was an enormous diffusion of knowledge. Whereas the sixth century Roman historian Cassiodorus had access to only one treatise by Galen (c. 130–200), the greatest physician of the ancient world, by 900 the Arabs had translated some 129 of his works. Arabic science improved on Greek measurements and astronomical calculations and built the world's first observatories in the ninth century. It culminated in the career of Ibn Sina or Avicenna (c. 980–1037), whose breadth of interest and learning in philosophy, medicine, natural history, physics, chemistry, astronomy, mathematics, and music rivaled that of Aristotle. (See Chapter 8.)

The Medieval World Picture

By the twelfth century Arab science had begun to decline, in part because of the breakup of what had been a unified empire into warring principalities. Shortly after, however, a revived and expanding western Europe began to cull its fruits. Arab scientists and their Greek predecessors were both translated into Latin. Aristotle's prestige was so great in the medieval West that he was referred to simply as "the Philosopher," as if no rival could exist, and indeed none challenged him until the sixteenth century.

Reassimilating Greek science into the western tradition meant reconciling it with Christian doctrine. Fortunately, Ptolemy's geocentric model of the universe proved readily compatible with Christian notions about man's central position in the divine order. The cosmos was held to consist of an arrangement of ten concentric spheres rotating around a fixed, motionless earth. The first two of these spheres carried the moon and the sun. The next five were occupied by the known planets, and the eighth, like a giant diadem, carried all the stars. The last two spheres were dark, but their rotation was held to account for apparent changes in the positions of the stars. Beyond the tenth sphere, whose distance from the earth was estimated by Campanus of Novara (c. 1205–1296) at 73 million miles, was the throne of God, surrounded by his angels and the souls of the righteous. The spheres themselves were moved by angels, since according to Aristotle all bodies not activated by a constant external force would come to rest. In keeping with the perfection of the heavens, the celestial bodies were composed of a pure, unchangeable substance, the quintessence. For this reason any alteration among the celestial bodies, such as the appearance of a comet or the great explosion of the Crab nebula in 1054, was looked upon as a divine portent, since they could not naturally alter by themselves. On earth, humans were locked in the prison of time and decay, but when they looked up, what they saw was the picture of eternity.

This view of the heavens was deeply satisfying. It combined a credible explanation of the natural world with a religious view of the cosmos as the theater of human redemption, in which humankind was the center of God's concern just as the earth was the center about which the heavens revolved. Medieval maps showed Jerusalem as the center of the earth and therefore of the universe, completing the perfect symmetry of the cosmos. It was true that certain details refused to fit in. Some physical bodies, such as projectiles, failed to behave as the Aristotelian theory of motion said they should. Some of the planets and fixed stars appeared to be wayward in their orbits. But these problems did not seem enough to shake an edifice built up over the centuries, hallowed by tradition, and deeply entwined with the belief and value systems of Christianity.

But new currents were running beneath this placid surface. The fourteenth and fifteenth centuries saw serious challenges to the authority of the church during the Babylonian captivity and the Great Schism. The French philosopher and bishop Nicholas of Oresme (c. 1323–1382) observed that it was fortunate that faith instructed people that the earth could not rotate on its axis and that there could be no bodies beyond the fixed stars, for it could not be demonstrated either by argument or observation. Oresme's comment illustrated the loss of confidence in the belief of men such as Thomas Aquinas that reason and revelation both disclosed the same truth about the world. A century later, the German Nicholas of Cusa (1401–1464) asserted the rotation of the earth despite official doctrine. With the Reformation, there was no longer a single authority to interpret the Christian faith. By the early seventeenth century the Jesuit Cardinal Robert Bellarmine (1542–1617) felt obliged to concede that in cases where reason and the Bible differed about the natural world, reason must be accepted. For the first time in the history of the church, faith was no longer the final arbiter of knowledge.

The Hermetic Challenge

At the same time, the authority of Aristotle was being questioned as well. The Greek scholars who fled after the fall of Byzantium in 1453 brought with them texts not previously known in the West. Prominent among these were the writings of Hermes Trismegistus ("thrice-great"), believed to be an Egyptian who had received divine revelations about the physical world at the time Moses had been given the Ten Commandments. In fact, Hermes was fictitious, and his texts were the product of third-century A.D. Neoplatonists working in Alexandria. The so-called Hermetic doctrine viewed the material world as an emanation of divine spirit. All objects were related to each other by sympathy or antipathy through the energies of this spirit, which could be released and manipulated by those who knew how to pair the right objects. Humans, the highest compound of matter and spirit, were destined

This mosaic from the cathedral in Siena, Italy, depicts the legendary lawgiver of ancient science, Hermes Trismegistus, with a figure who is probably meant to be Moses, giver of the moral law. The paired sphinxes in the lower-right-hand corner represent Hermes' allegedly Egyptian origins. The mosaic dates from the 1480s, when the Neoplatonic revival that so influenced Copernicus was at its height. [Alinari/Art Resource]

to command the forces of the natural world by learning to read the book of nature and to decipher its hidden codes.

The Hermetic doctrine greatly stimulated interest in chemistry, botany, metallurgy, and astronomy, since the celestial bodies were believed to be the agency by which the divine spirit was transmitted. The sun, as the most important of these, was held to be at the center of the universe, rather than the earth, as in Ptolemaic theory. Hermeticism thus revived the heliocentric theory of Aristarchus, although on a mystical rather than a mathematical or mechanical basis. But mathematics was crucially important for the Hermeticists too. They believed, as Plato and Pythagoras had, that the universe was ultimately constructed in terms of mathematical proportions and harmonies. As the medieval mystic had sought to know the God of love by prayer and meditation, the disciples of Hermes sought to understand the Divine Mind through the mathematical harmonies by which it expressed itself. Mathematics was the highest form of understanding, both of the physical world and of the God who manifested himself in it.

Much of Hermeticism tended to degenerate into the cruder forms of magic, alchemy, and astrology. But the image of man as a natural magician calling forth the hidden powers of the world had great appeal. It suggested that there was still much to be learned about the world beyond the categories of Aristotelian science. Shakespeare's hero Hamlet reflects this new sense of possibility when he tells his loyal but conventional friend, "There are more things in heaven and earth, Horatio, than are dreamt of in your philosophy," and Prospero, the hero of his last play, *The Tempest* (1611), is a portrait of the Renaissance man as a Hermetic magician.

The Neoplatonic revival was only one element that contributed to the crisis of knowledge and belief in the sixteenth century. The Reformation had deeply unsettled people's assurance about the nature of grace and salvation and undermined their faith in those who had interpreted spiritual knowledge. The discovery of the New World shattered their faith in the adequacy of their knowledge of the physical world as well. The scientific revolution was a product of this upheaval and shared in its difficult birth the tensions and contradictions of the age.

The New Order of Knowledge

The most important convert to the Hermetic doctrine was the Polish astronomer and mathematician Nicholas Copernicus (1473–1543). Born in Toruń on the Polish-German frontier, he imbibed Hermeticism in the course of a ten-year sojourn in Renaissance Italy. Copernicus was convinced that the majesty of the cosmos demanded that the sun be at its center rather than the earth. As he explained his conception:

> **In the middle of [the cosmos] sits the Sun enthroned. . . . Could we place this luminary in any better position from which he can illuminate the whole at once? He is rightly called the Lamp, the Mind, the Ruler of the Universe; Hermes Trismegistus names him the visible God. . . . So the sun sits as upon a royal throne ruling his children, the planets which circle around him.[1]**

Copernicus devoted the rest of his life to proving not only that the heliocentric theory of the Hermeticists was preferable to that of Ptolemy on aesthetic and religious grounds but also that it offered a better account where Ptolemy's theory was weakest, in explaining celestial motion. This claim was reflected in the title of his treatise, *On the Revolution of the Heavenly Spheres*, whose publication he authorized only on his deathbed in 1543. Copernicus assumed that only the earth and the five planets actually moved. The sun was motionless at the center of the universe as the fixed stars were at the periphery, their apparent motion being accounted for by the rotation of the earth. This was a great theoretical simplification, although the mathematics necessary to calculate the actual position of the stars relative to a moving earth were hardly less complex than Ptolemy's. Copernicus was also able to dis-

JOHANNIS HEVELII
COMETOGRAPHIA.

This engraving, from Johannes Hevelius' *Cometographia* (1608), shows the excitement generated by Copernican astronomy. In the foreground, three scholars compare their calculations; in front of them is an armillary sphere representing the celestial globe, together with a sextant, while on the roof of the building in the background observers train a telescope and measuring devices on the heavens and the comet coming into view. Comets were of intense interest for both scientific and superstitious reasons, as they were held to portend great events. [Department of Special Collections and University Archives, Stanford University Libraries]

pense with the idea of giant crystalline spheres moved by angels, which Christian doctrine had superimposed on Ptolemy's original theory. Heavenly bodies moved and rotated because it was their nature to do so; put a globe in space, Copernicus argued, and it will spin. Such an idea contradicted the Aristotelian notion that bodies not externally propelled would come to rest, but it did not explain why some bodies—the earth, the moon, and the planets—were in motion, while the sun and the stars were not.

The Copernican theory offered a credible but not compelling alternative to the Ptolemaic system. Its calculations of the celestial orbits were no less complex, and it created as many mathematical and physical problems as it solved. Martin Luther's reaction was typical. "That is how things go nowadays," the great German reformer said. "Anyone who wants to be clever must not be satisfied with what others do. He must produce his own theory as this man does, who wishes to turn the whole of astronomy upside down."[2] No other astronomer accepted Copernicus, and his theory was kept alive only in Hermetic circles. One such convert, the Italian philosopher Giordano Bruno (1548–1600), argued that the sun around which the earth revolved was only one of innumerable suns in an infinite universe, each of which might harbor planets and species like our own. Bruno fell into the hands of the Inquisition and was burned at the stake. Such were the perils of unguided speculation on the basis of Copernicus' theory. Catholics and Protestants alike condemned it. The greatest astronomer of the late sixteenth century, Tycho Brahe (1546–1601), explicitly rejected it.

But the Copernican theory did not die. The appearance of a bright new star in the sky in the 1570s, followed by a brilliant comet, reminded people that there were phenomena not explained by Ptolemy's static system. Tycho Brahe's meticulous celestial observations served a young German astronomer, Johannes Kepler (1571–1630), who had come to Copernicus through his own Hermetic beliefs. Kepler made the crucial discovery that the orbits of the planets were not circular, as both Ptolemy and Copernicus had assumed, but elliptical. This enabled him to simplify

---

◉ On the Infinity of the Universe ◉

The Copernican displacement of the earth from the center of the universe led the Italian philosopher Giordano Bruno to question the very notion of a "center" in space and to contend for the idea of an infinite universe that reflected the infinite power and glory of God.

How is it possible that the universe can be infinite? . . . I say that the universe is entirely infinite because it has neither edge, limit, nor surfaces. But I say that the universe is not all-comprehensive infinity because each of the parts thereof that we can examine is finite and each of the innumerable worlds contained therein is finite. I declare God to be completely infinite because he can be associated with no boundary and his every attribute is one and infinite. And I say that God is all-comprehensive infinity because the whole of him pervades the whole world and every part thereof comprehensively and to infinity. . . . What argument would persuade us that the Agent capable of creating infinite good should have created it finite? And if he has created it finite, why should we believe that the Agent could have created it infinite, since power and action are in him but one?

The influence of Bruno's daring hypothesis can be seen in the work of a contemporary scientist, William Gilbert.

Who has ever made out that the stars which we call fixed are in one and the same sphere, or has established by reasoning that there are any real and, as it were, adamantine spheres? No one has proved this, nor is there a doubt but that just as the planets are at unequal distances from the earth, so are these vast and multitudinous lights separated from the earth by varying and very remote altitudes. . . . How immeasurable then must be the space which stretches to the remotest of fixed stars! How vast and immense the depth of that imaginary sphere! How far removed from the earth must be the most widely separated stars and at a distance transcending all sight, all skill, all thought!

Source: D. W. Singer, *Giordano Bruno: His Life and Thought* (New York: Schuman, 1950), pp. 66–67, 250, 257, 262.

Copernicus' calculations, giving him for the first time a decisive advantage over Ptolemy. Ironically, however, Kepler's discovery was itself rejected by the man whose work finally undermined the Ptolemaic theory, Galileo Galilei.

Galileo and the Copernican Triumph

Galileo (1564–1642) was born in Pisa, Italy. After completing studies in mathematics and natural philosophy, he joined the faculty of the University of Padua, where Copernicus had studied a century before. Galileo was the first important figure to accept Copernicus outside the Hermetic circle. His own inspiration was the ancient Greek mathematician Archimedes (287–212 B.C.), whose works had been republished in 1543. Archimedes, like Pythagoras, had attempted to describe the world in purely mathematical terms. Unlike Pythagoras, however, he attributed no mystical significance to the mathematical proportions he found in nature, and unlike the Neoplatonists, he posited no spiritual basis in matter. For him, and for his latter-day disciple Galileo, the world was best

Galileo's espousal of the Copernican theory and his own celestial discoveries were decisive in gaining acceptance for the new astronomy, while his strict adherence to a mechanistic view of the cosmos purged it of lingering Hermetic elements. [Art Resource]

thought of as a gigantic machine operating by simple principles expressible in geometric ratios.

In such a world there was no room either for Aristotle's mythical quintessence or for the medieval angels who moved the stars. Galileo's own most important work was his discovery of the principle of accelerated motion, in which he brilliantly connected velocity and distance to the variable of time. But he caused a sensation when in 1609 he turned a newly invented instrument, the telescope, on the heavens. Galileo discovered four moons in orbit around the planet Jupiter, and so many hundreds of previously undetected stars that he declared them to be innumerable. This seemed to suggest a startling confirmation of Bruno's belief in an infinite universe. Galileo also demonstrated that the surface of the moon was rough and eroded, thereby demolishing the theory of a perfect and unchanging heaven.

Copernicus had disclosed his findings only with great caution during his lifetime, but Galileo, armed with his new observations, rushed boldly into print. He claimed that the truth of the Copernican theory had now been established, and when confronted with the familiar scriptural story of Joshua making the sun stand still, he retorted that the Bible might be adequate for ignorant laymen but could hardly qualify as a scientific treatise. This was too much for the Catholic church. Despite the burning of Bruno, it had never officially condemned the Copernican theory. It did so now, however (1616), and when Galileo defiantly published a further defense of Copernicus in his *Dialogue Concerning the Two Chief World Systems* (1632), he was arrested by the Inquisition, threatened with torture, and obliged to recant his belief in the heliocentric system. But though Galileo might be silenced, his challenge to received authority could not. What he represented was not the familiar problem of the heretic who challenged Christian doctrine on its own terms but a rival system of truth that bypassed it as irrelevant to the description and understanding of the physical world. For Galileo, observation was the guide, experiment the test, and mathematics the language of physical reality. No other form of understanding was necessary, no other authority acceptable.

Thus Copernicus, who believed that the sun was the lamp of nature and the image of God, was vindicated by the mystic Kepler, who believed that the planets and stars were souls who danced to the music of the spheres, and by the rationalist Galileo, who banished spirit and purpose from the world of matter and left only physical bodies obeying the mechanical laws of motion. What all three held in common was the language of mathematical proof. It was by mathematics that Copernicus turned the Neoplatonic doctrine that the sun was the center of the universe into a plausible description of the actual cosmos, by mathematics that Kepler was able to demonstrate the superiority of that description to its rivals, and by mathematics that Galileo was able to begin constructing the new physics of motion that the Copernican universe required.

Other Scientific Advances

If the common language of mathematics made astronomy and physics the cutting edge of the scientific revolution, chemistry, medicine, anatomy, and biology all advanced as well. As in the case of astronomy, the impetus for development often came from Hermetic and Neoplatonic doctrine. The Swiss-born German physician Theophrastus Bombastus von Hohenheim (1493–1541), called Paracelsus, launched a one-man crusade against the influence of Aristotle and Galen in medicine. Paracelsus was imbued with the spirit of medieval and Renaissance magic. He believed that occult forces were at work everywhere in nature and that demons could even divert the courses of the stars. It would be hard to imagine a mind further removed from the cool, rational skepticism of Galileo. Yet Paracelsus' very belief in the omnipresence of magical forces led him away from the traditional textbooks—he is said to have burned all the medical classics before delivering his introductory lecture at the University of Basel in 1527—and back to nature. In accordance with Hermetic doctrine, he believed that the structure of the human organism was directly analogous to that of the natural world and that specific organs of the body were sympathetically related to specific plants, minerals, chemical substances, and even stars. The disorders of the body came from disturbances in the natural harmony between the body and the world, and their remedies were thus to be sought in identifying and applying substances that could correct the balance. This meant constant search and experimentation. "A man cannot learn the theory of medicine out of his own head," Paracelsus declared, "but only from that which his eyes see and his fingers touch. . . . Theory and practice should together form one, and should remain undivided."[3]

The emphasis on direct observation of nature produced the first great textbook of anatomy, the *De fabrica* (1543) of the Fleming Andreas Vesalius (1514–1564), and the discovery of the circulation of the blood (1628) by the Englishman William Harvey (1578–1657). The results of these discoveries, as in the case of astronomy, proved contrary to the theories that had originally inspired them. Vesalius believed that the structure of the human head, as the temple of reason, was necessarily different from that of animals, and Harvey saw the heart as the source of spiritual as well as physical life. What they showed instead was that the anatomies of humans and animals were similar in structure and function. Harvey became an enthusiastic disciple of comparative anatomy, remarking tartly that had the anatomists paid as much attention to animals as to humans, the mysteries of the body would have been solved long before. Indeed, the last element in the circulation of the blood unsolved by Harvey himself, the transfer of blood from veins to arteries by capillary action, was discovered in 1661 by the Italian Marcello Malpighi (1628–1694), who examined a frog's lungs with the aid of another optical instrument, the microscope.

New Technology

New inventions and techniques were stimulated not merely by the requirements of scientific curiosity but also those of practical activity. The great voyages of trade and discovery that began in the late fifteenth century are a case in point. Until that time, European ships seldom ventured out of sight of land and could proceed by pilotage, or reckoning by coastal landmarks. But when they sailed out into open and uncharted seas, they required navigation, or reckoning by the sun and the stars. For this purpose seamen adapted instruments previously used by astronomers, the quadrant and the astrolabe. The problem of plotting straight-line courses on two-dimensional maps representing a three-dimensional earth was solved by the Fleming Gerhard Kremer, called Mercator, whose map was first published in 1569 and in modified form is still used today. In 1484 King John III of Portugal appointed a commission of mathematicians to work out tables of latitude, and when Gresham College was founded in England in 1597, one of its three scientific chairs was reserved for an astronomer whose duties included the teaching of navigation. Sixteenth century interest in theories of the cosmos thus had a very practical basis. In similar fashion, the development of the cannon took ballistics, the science of calculating the trajectory of missiles, out of the realm of academic theory and on to the battlefield, while the extraction of gold and silver from the Indies stimulated the development of chemical separation processes and mining technology such as subsurface ventilation and hydraulic pumps.

Science at the Crossroads

The new scientific theories were disturbing to established authority, particularly in the universities and the churches. The new ideas were often associated with political subversion and black magic, inflammatory charges in an age marked by civil unrest and witchcraft persecution. Galileo had already been driven from the University of Padua before his arrest by the Inquisition, and Kepler was expelled from the Protestant faculty of the University of Tübingen. Jewish elders were hostile to the Cabala, a system akin to Hermeticism that claimed to decode secret meanings in the Old Testament.

The authorities' concern about the new science and the esoteric doctrines that swirled about it was not unfounded. The confidence of educated laymen in the traditional picture of the world had already been eroded by the late sixteenth century. "The more I think, the more I doubt," the Jesuit Francisco Suárez confessed in 1581, and 30 years later the English poet and divine John Donne summarized the anxieties many people felt about humanity's

◎ Pascal on Humankind's Place ◎ in the Universe

The notion of an unlimited cosmos seemed to reduce humanity to insignificance and to call into question the idea of God's love and purpose for humankind. Such feelings were given unequaled expression by the great seventeenth-century mathematician and philosopher Blaise Pascal.

When I consider the brief span of my life absorbed into the eternity which comes before and after—*as the remembrance of a guest that tarrieth but a day*—the small space I occupy and which I see swallowed up in the infinite immensity of spaces of which I know nothing and which know nothing of me, I take fright and am amazed to see myself here rather than there: there is no reason for me to be here rather than there, now rather than then. Who put me here? By whose command and act were this time and place allotted to me? . . .

The eternal silence of these infinite spaces fills me with dread.

Source: B. Pascal, *Pensées*, trans. A. J. Krailsheimer (Baltimore: Penguin Books, 1966), pp. 48, 95.

---

loss of its privileged place in the cosmos in "An Anatomy of the World" (1611):

> *And new philosophy calls all in doubt;*
> *The element of fire is quite put out,*
> *The sun is lost, and the earth, and no man's*
>   *wit*
> *Can well direct him where to look for it*
> *And freely men confess, that this world's*
>   *spent*
> *When in the planets and the firmament*
> *They seek so many new; then see that this*
> *Is crumbled out again to his atomies*
> *'Tis all in pieces, all coherence gone;*
> *All just supply and all relation.*

Donne's poem is remarkable in demonstrating the speed with which scientific ideas were circulating, since Galileo had announced his discovery of new celestial bodies only a year before. His familiarity with the dispute about "the element of fire" (challenged by Paracelsus and his followers) and with the revival of interest in Democritus' theory of atoms can also be glimpsed in his lines.

Doubt and Faith: Descartes and Pascal

More extreme reactions to the new science can be seen in the Frenchmen René Descartes (1596–1650) and Blaise Pascal (1623–1662). As Descartes himself related his ex-

perience, he was assailed one night by a sudden, paralyzing doubt about the possibility of knowledge. The senses, he felt, deceived us, faith was undermined by doubt, and the authorities were only people like ourselves. How could one be sure of the existence of the world, of God, or even of oneself? Descartes' famous reply—"I think, therefore I am"—was the starting point of his extraordinary attempt to reconstruct all knowledge from the ground up on the basis of simple, self-evident propositions.

Pascal, a brilliant mathematician and a man of great religious sensitivity, felt the vast new spaces of the Copernican universe as a terrible silence in which humans were alone with their frailty and doubt and God had become a remote conjecture. He was one of the first men of his time to realize that the traditional conception of God no longer fit the world revealed by science. But he argued, in his famous "wager" with skeptics, that it was better to affirm the existence of a just and merciful God in whom one might no longer fully believe than to deny him, since there was everything to gain if he did in fact exist and nothing to be lost if he did not.

Conflicting Roads to Truth

Science itself had arrived at a crossroads by the mid-seventeenth century. The scientific enterprise was a Babel of languages from which no common grammar had yet emerged. The Aristotelian tradition was largely in shambles, but nothing had appeared to replace it. An English

The great French skeptic René Descartes in a confident pose by Frans Hals. Descartes' separation of mind from matter marked the beginning of a crisis in Western thought. [Lauros-Giraudon/Art Resource]

participant in an early scientific meeting has left us a catalog of the subjects discussed that suggests both the excitement and confusion of the new science:

> We discoursed of the circulation of the blood, the valves in the veins, the *venae lacteae,* the lymphatick vessels, the Copernican hypothesis, the nature of comets and new stars, the satellites of Jupiter, the oval shape (as it then appeared) of Saturn, the spots in the sun, and its turning on its own axis, the inequalities and selenography of the Moon, the several phases of Venus and Mercury, the improvement of telescopes, and the grinding of glasses for that purpose, the weight of air, the possibility, or impossibility of vacuities [vacuums], and nature's abhorrence thereof, the Torricellian experiment in quick-silver, the descent of heavy bodies, and the degrees of acceleration therein; and divers other things of like nature.[4]

Especially lacking was a common standard of judgment and proof. Although important discoveries had been made by scientists working from both Hermetic and mechanistic assumptions, in the last analysis they were incompatible

as ways of seeing the world. The cosmos could be a living organism or an enormous machine, but not both. A similar division existed regarding scientific method. The English philosopher and jurist Sir Francis Bacon (1561–1626), Lord Chancellor under King James I, argued for the deductive or empirical method, by which knowledge was gained through systematic observation of the world and tested by experiment. The inductive method was championed by Descartes, who, as we have seen, rejected the senses as a basis for knowledge and argued that reality could be known only by reasoning from axiomatic principles. Descartes took a step that was decisive in the intellectual history of the West. He divided reality into two distinct entities, spirit, which was characterized by the power of thought but was without physical properties, and matter, which was substance extended in space and the capacity that that implied, motion. In doing so, he completely separated matter and spirit, rejecting the Hermetic vision of the world as a fusion of the two. He was thereby able to treat the material world in completely mechanical terms, while reserving an independent realm for spirit. Spirit meant in effect intelligence for Descartes, and the greatest intelligence was that of God, who had created the physical universe of matter in motion and designed the laws by which it operated. By studying and understanding those laws, humankind could understand God. Thus Cartesianism, as Descartes' philosophy came to be called, made science into a religious quest, but one that proceeded in terms not of theology but of mechanical engineering and mathematical reasoning.

The immediate importance of Descartes' work was that it gave impetus to the mechanistic conception of the world, where the most fruitful line of scientific advance actually lay, while avoiding the charge of black magic on the one hand and of atheism on the other. Cartesian science itself had serious drawbacks. It was well suited for physics but completely useless for biology, since it could provide no convincing explanation for the phenomenon of life. It relegated observation and experiment to matters of secondary detail at best, thus failing to provide an independent standard of proof for anyone who did not accept the premises of the system. Brilliant strategically as a means of breaking the impasse between Hermeticism and mechanism, it was still inadequate as a general model for science itself.

The Newtonian Synthesis

Sir Isaac Newton finally carried out the task Descartes had set: to provide a clear and comprehensive explanation of the physical universe in mathematical terms, a universe created by the will of God but fully subject to the laws of nature. Newton's work was a synthesis of all the elements of the scientific tradition. His solution to the problem of gravity, which he had made the key to his system, illustrates this. In Aristotelian physics, gravity was the inherent tendency of physical bodies to fall toward the earth as the center of the universe. The Englishman William Gilbert (1540–1603) had advanced the argument by his discovery that the earth itself acted as a magnet, drawing bodies to itself. But this left a serious problem in a Copernican universe where the sun was the center of the cosmos or (as both Descartes and Newton assumed) there was no center at all. Even granting the principle of inertia—that bodies set in motion would continue along the same path—how could it be explained that heavenly bodies did not simply drift randomly through space but described regular orbits about one another? Descartes rejected the idea of gravity as attraction at a distance because it seemed to him too close to the Hermetic idea of a force inherent in matter emanating from a divine source. Newton, however, had no trouble accepting such a notion, provided that it could be given an adequate mathematical basis—that is, provided that it could be shown to describe the actual orbits and positions of heavenly bodies. But classical mathematics, like classical physics, had always assumed the existence of a stable center. There was no mathematics capable of describing the interaction of independently moving bodies. Newton thereupon invented a new mathematics, called calculus, to deal with these relations.

Using the assumption of gravity as a universal constant, Newton was able to reduce the movement of all bodies in heaven or on earth to three basic laws. The elements of the system were as simple as the proofs were painstaking and complex. When Newton published his findings in his *Mathematical Principles of Natural Philosophy* (1687), he completed the work begun by Copernicus a century and a half earlier in replacing the Ptolemaic system. But Newton's model was even further from that of Copernicus than the latter's had been from Ptolemy's. Copernicus had still assumed that the universe had a definite center and a final boundary. Newton's cosmos was infinite and centerless. The speculation for which Bruno had been burned at the beginning of the seventeenth century had become scientific orthodoxy by its end.

The great success of Newton's synthesis was to reconcile not only the conflicting traditions of the new science but its competing methodologies as well. The conceptual simplicity of his system was a triumph of inductive logic, yet it was fully supported by the most up-to-date astronomical observations. This combination brought about ultimate acceptance of his system after the initial skepticism of men like the German mathematician Gottfried Wilhelm von Leibniz (1646–1716), who had independently worked out calculus at the same time as Newton but rejected his notion of gravity. The Newtonian model was not only mathematically convincing as Descartes' was not, but for the next 200 years every empirical observation and experiment confirmed it in detail. After Newton, scientific method was not a matter of theory or observation, but

both. By his death in 1727, his prestige was so great that the poet Alexander Pope could write:

> *Nature and nature's laws lay hid in night;*
> *God said, Let Newton be! and all was light.*

The Scientific Method

Newton himself remarked, "If I have seen further [than others], it is by standing on the shoulders of giants." Indeed, the most impressive aspect of the scientific revolution was less an increase in knowledge about the world than the creation of a new method for understanding it. The ancient world had stressed the primacy of reason as a means of knowledge. The Middle Ages, while accepting reason, had insisted on the primacy of God's word as revealed in the Bible and interpreted by the church. The Reformation had changed that. Faith in God's word might be as strong as ever, but faith in its interpretation by the clergy was not. No longer was a single standard of truth acceptable to all.

The result, in part, was a return to reliance on reason. Descartes was a clear and radical example of this. What he wanted of reason was what he could no longer find in faith: certain and irrefutable truth. But the scientific method, as it had actually developed, offered both something less and something more. It was something less because science could not claim, even with Newton, to have arrived at a final truth about the world (though some of his eighteenth-century admirers would assert as much). It was something more because it amounted to a redefinition of truth itself. Henceforward, truth was not something to be revealed at once and in its entirety, whether by the sacred word or by direct intuition. Rather, truth was to be discovered and refined piecemeal, with each new stage in understanding serving as a step toward the next one. Through individual trial and error, collective truth was to be won.

For this reason, science became more and more a collabortive effort after the mid-seventeenth century. The first scientists had worked alone, like Copernicus and the reclusive Tycho Brahe, who built an observatory on his private island and jealously guarded the results of his work. Gradually, these isolated individuals became linked by chains of correspondence, such as the one set up in Paris in the 1630s by the friar Marin Mersenne (1588–1648), an enthusiast of the new science and friend of Galileo's. From this grew scientific meetings such as the one we glimpsed earlier, and finally formal societies. Among the first of these was the Royal Society of London for Improving Natural Knowledge, founded in 1662, of which Newton was an early member and later president. Four years later Colbert founded the French Academy of Sciences under state patronage, and similar societies were soon established in Berlin, Uppsala, Stockholm, Copen-

◉ The Scientific Method ◉

As received ideas of truth and knowledge were cast into doubt by the scientific revolution, a new method for ascertaining truth slowly evolved, stressing the importance of observation, experiment, and mathematical reasoning. The English philosopher Sir Francis Bacon stressed the importance of controlled experiment.

But by far the greatest impediment and aberration of the human understanding proceeds from the dullness, incompetency, and errors of the senses; since whatever strikes the senses preponderates over everything, however superior, which does not immediately strike them. Hence contemplation mostly ceases with sight, and a very scanty, or perhaps no regard is paid to visible objects. The entire operation, therefore, of spirits enclosed in tangible bodies is concealed, and escapes us. . . . Again, the very nature of common air, and all bodies of less density . . . is almost unknown; for the senses are weak and erring, nor can instruments be of great use in extending their spheres or acuteness. All the better interpretations of nature are worked out by instances, and fit and apt experiments, where the senses only judge of the experiment.

Of equal importance, the Frenchman René Descartes stressed the use of deductive reasoning.

By [deduction] we mean the inference of something as following necessarily from some other propositions which are known with certainty. . . . This distinction had to be made, since very many facts which are not self-evident are known with certainty, provided they are inferred from true and known principles through a continuous and uninterrupted movement of thought in which each individual proposition is clearly intuited. This is similar to the way in which we know that the last link in a long chain is connected to the first: even if we cannot take in at one glance all the intermediate links on which the connection depends, we can have knowledge of the connection provided we survey the links one after the other, and keep in mind that each link from first to last is attached to its neighbor.

Sources: F. Bacon, *Novum organum*, in *Great Books of the Western World*, vol. 30 (Chicago: Encyclopaedia Britannica, 1952), p. 111; *The Philosophical Writings of Descartes*, trans. J. Cottingham, R. Stoothoff, and D. Murdoch, vol. 1 (Cambridge: Cambridge University Press, 1985), p. 15.

hagen, and St. Petersburg. By the last decades of the seventeenth century we can speak of a scientific world, international in scope and cosmopolitan in character, in which knowledge could be systematically communicated, new theories debated, and new talent recognized.

Philosophy: The Age of Reason

In the seventeenth century no strict distinction was made between philosophy—inquiry into the limits of human knowledge as such—and science, the branch of knowledge that addressed itself to the natural world. In that sense, the attack on Aristotle, Ptolemy, and Galen that characterized the scientific revolution was part of a wider movement in European thought that questioned traditional authority in general. But there can be no doubt that the success of science in dethroning medieval cosmology gave impetus and urgency to the development of critical philosophy as a whole.

The two traditions of philosophy that were most influential in the seventeenth and eighteenth centuries were the English and the French. German philosophy, which began its modern career with Leibniz and Samuel Pufendorf (1632–1694), began to dominate European thought only in the late eighteenth and nineteenth centuries. In English and French philosophy, speculation adhered to the norms set down respectively by Bacon and Descartes. The English tended to begin from concrete observation of the world, the French from a priori assumptions about it.

Another broad distinction between English and French philosophy can be drawn in terms of subject matter. The English, preoccupied with the revolutions of 1640 and 1688, concentrated on the problem of people's relation to the civic orders of state and society, whereas the French, inheriting the skepticism of Descartes, focused on humanity's relation to the cosmos.

Thomas Hobbes and the Natural Man

The Englishman Thomas Hobbes (1588–1679), writing in the tumultuous 1640s, produced in *Leviathan* (1651) the most important work of Western political philosophy since Machiavelli's *The Prince*. Hobbes argued that human beings are social by necessity rather than by nature, as Aristotle had thought. He started from the mechanistic assumption that humans, like all other entities, could be described in terms of matter and motion and that their thoughts, feelings, and desires could be explained as responses to external stimuli, differing in degree but not in kind from those of animals. Even reason, the glory of the mind, was only a complex form of calculation, and the will, which attested to human freedom, was defined simply as the last appetite before choice. Hobbes professed to believe in God, the soul, and the workings of Providence, but, like Descartes (whom he knew and admired), he separated the realms of matter and spirit so sharply that his view of society appeared purely secular. That, combined with the fierce anticlericalism that ran through all his political writings, led to his condemnation as an atheist.

In Hobbes' view, human beings strive to maximize pleasure and minimize pain. This brings them into conflict with others who, acting on the same principle, compete for scarce goods. The result, Hobbes declared, was a "war of all against all," a condition in which the life of men was, in his pithy phrase, "solitary, poor, nasty, brutish and short." To avoid this, they gave up their natural freedom and entered society, as rational animals might enter a zoo. Hobbes' zookeeper was the sovereign, who had absolute power to order all social arrangements, allotting each person a share of goods and duties. Only in this way, he believed, could order be guaranteed and the anarchy of the natural human condition avoided. Society was in effect a contract in which freedom was exchanged for security, or at least the hope of security, since the subject, in surrendering all natural rights, had also surrendered the means to enforce the bargain. To critics who complained that this created a license for tyranny, Hobbes replied that it was better to be subject to the arbitrary will of a single individual than to the potential violence of all.

The famous frontispiece of Hobbes' book *Leviathan* shows his absolute sovereign as a giant who incorporates the entire body politic. The Latin quotation at the top, from the Book of Job, reads: "There is not his like upon earth." [Granger Collection]

Hobbes insisted that his theory was not an abstract blueprint but an actual description of power in society. Whether monarchy, aristocracy, or democracy, the core of every government was an absolute, unchallengeable sovereignty that could not be divided or infringed without destroying the state and consequently the social order. He therefore rejected all theories of "mixed" government or separation of powers as a confusion between real and delegated powers.

Hobbes' theory scandalized everyone. Liberals rejected it because it left no place for political dissent. Conservatives liked it no better because, although Hobbes condemned rebellion as the greatest of political evils, he accepted all changes of government in a spirit of pure pragmatism. The only test of a regime was its ability to

◎ The Institution of the Commonwealth ◎

The English philosopher Thomas Hobbes described the origin of the state in the agreement of sovereign individuals to merge their natural rights in a single person acting in the name of all.

It is manifest, that during the time men live without a common power to keep them all in awe, they are in that condition which is called war, and such a war, as is of every man, against every man. For war consisteth not in battle only, or the act of fighting; but in a tract of time, wherein the will to contend by battle is sufficiently known. . . . The only way to erect such a common power, as may be able to defend [individuals] from the invasion of foreigners, and the injuries of one another . . . is to confer all their power and strength upon one man, or upon one assembly of men, that may reduce all their wills, by plurality of voices, unto one will: which is as much as to say, to appoint one man, or assembly of men, to bear their person. . . . This is . . . a real unity of them all, in one and the same person, made by covenant of every man with every man, in such a manner, as if every man should say to every man, *I authorize and give up my right of governing myself, to this man, or to this assembly of men, on this condition, that thou give up thy right to him, and authorize all his actions in like manner*. This done, the multitude so united in one person, is called a commonwealth. . . . This is the generation of that great Leviathan, or rather (to speak more reverently) of that mortal God, to which we owe under the immortal God, our peace and defense.

A very different view of the state as originating in force and fraud was offered by Hobbes' contemporary Gerrard Winstanley (c. 1609–c. 1676).

In the beginning of time, the great creator Reason, made the earth to be a common treasury, to preserve beasts, birds, fishes, and man, the lord that was to govern this creation; for man had domination given to him, over the beasts, birds, and fishes; but not one word was spoken in the beginning, that one branch of mankind should rule over another. . . . But . . . selfish imagination taking possession of the five senses, and so ruling as king in the room of Reason therein, and working with covetousness, did set up one man to teach and rule over another, and thereby the spirit was killed, and man was brought into bondage, and became a greater slave to such of his own kind, than the beasts of the field were to him.

Sources: T. Hobbes, *Leviathan*, ed. A. R. Walter (Cambridge: Cambridge University Press, 1904), pp. 83, 118–119 (modernized); G. H. Sabine, ed., *The Works of Gerrard Winstanley* (Ithaca, N.Y.: Cornell University Press, 1941), pp. 251–252.

provide security. A government that could not do so forfeited all claim to loyalty, while any government that could possessed a sufficient title to be obeyed.

John Locke and the State of Nature

Writing 40 years later, John Locke (1632–1704) took a very different view of human society. Locke started from the premise that human beings in their natural condition—

what had come to be called the state of nature—were not competitive but cooperative. Such persons entered society to gain the benefits of communal organization. Their natural rights were not surrendered but rather enhanced in society. Government on this view was merely an instrument of common social purpose, and the ruler was entrusted with such powers as were necessary to provide for the general welfare but no more. Should he abuse this trust, he might be replaced or deposed without doing violence to the constitution and certainly without dissolving society as Hobbes had thought. This was what had happened to James II in 1688, and English society, far from being destroyed or hurled back into anarchy, had been strengthened and renewed.

Locke's view of politics derived from his assumptions about human psychology, expressed in the *Essay Concerning Human Understanding* (1690). Taking a radically empirical stance, he argued that the mind at birth was a *tabula rasa,* or blank slate, on which experience inscribed itself. It followed from this that careful education could develop the mind in almost any desired direction. Thus, although reason in the state of nature suggested the desirability of human cooperation, people could easily be trained to obey the far more complex rules of society.

French Skepticism

In France a vein of skepticism ran through philosophy from the essayist Michel de Montaigne (1533–1592) to Descartes to Pierre Bayle (1647–1706). Descartes dealt with his own crisis of belief by asserting the power of reason to validate the world, including the existence of God. The idea of an infinite being, he argued, is spontaneously present in the human mind; yet since it would never have occurred of itself to a finite, limited consciousness, it could only have been placed there by God. But Descartes insisted on excluding God from any direct responsibility for the material universe, remarking that his readers could substitute "the mathematical order of nature" for "God" wherever he used the latter term.

For Pascal the absence of God from the material universe was the very source of human despair. Descartes' cool, rational conception of a God who made himself known as an idea but could not be reached as a person had no interest for him. The force of Pascal's argument was that Descartes, by exalting the powers of the mind, had excluded God, reducing him to a meaningless abstraction. It was only by admitting one's frailty and need that it was possible to reach the Christian God who had extended himself to humankind by his own suffering.

Pascal was closely associated with the religious circle at Port-Royal, a Cistercian abbey a few miles southwest of Paris that had embraced the teachings of the Dutch theologian Cornelius Jansen (1585–1638). Jansenism was a reaction against the scholastic tradition maintained by the Jesuits. Stressing individual piety and personal election rather than outward good works and conformity to church doctrine, it was viewed as a "protestant" heresy within Catholicism, although Jansen claimed his inspiration from St. Augustine rather than Calvin. Opposed by Richelieu and Louis XIV no less than by a succession of popes, it maintained itself as a religious and political counterculture well into the eighteenth century.

The skeptical tradition nonetheless continued to gain ground in France. In his *Critical History of the New Testament* (1678), the Oratorian priest Richard Simon sub-

jected the Bible to an exhaustive textual scrutiny, exposing hundreds of errors and discrepancies. Shocked by the audacity of anyone—no less a priest—treating Holy Writ by the standards of ordinary literature, Bishop Bossuet ordered the book burned. Simon protested that his aim was not to cast doubt on the essential truth of the Bible but to purge it of human error. No such redeeming purpose could be attributed to Pierre Bayle, who satirized biblical and pagan figures side by side in his *Historical and Critical Dictionary* (1697). For Bayle, whose book profoundly influenced such eighteenth-century skeptics as Voltaire, reason and religion were mortal enemies fighting "for possession of men's souls."

THE LENS GRINDER OF AMSTERDAM, BARUCH SPINOZA

The philosophical and religious issues of the seventeenth century were perhaps nowhere better epitomized than in the life of Baruch Spinoza. Spinoza was born in Amsterdam in 1632, the son of a prosperous Jewish merchant whose family had emigrated from Portugal at the end of the sixteenth century. The Amsterdam of his youth was the most cosmopolitan city in Europe. The Jewish community mixed freely with the general population, adopting its manners and dress (as the portraits of Rembrandt show), intermarrying, and imbibing liberal social and religious ideas. This freedom created great tension within the Jewish community itself, which conservative members feared would soon lose its identity. The brilliant young Spinoza was a case in point. While the elders of the community supported the House of Orange and the Dutch East and West India companies, Spinoza backed the republican revolution of 1650 and advocated the dissolution of the trading companies and the abolition of their privileges. Above all, he rejected his Jewish heritage, abjuring the synagogue and denying that the Jews were a chosen people. The Amsterdam synagogue responded by excommunicating him in 1656. He was formally cursed, and Jews were forbidden all contact with him. Spinoza renounced the career in commerce he had begun and earned his living by grinding and polishing lenses, a job of deliberately low status but symbolically appropriate for a man determined to see the world by no light but his own.

In his major work, the *Ethics,* Spinoza proposed a radical solution to the central seventeenth-century question of the relation between God and nature. Traditional philosophy had distinguished between substance, the stuff of the universe, and cause, the external agency that acts on it and shapes it. Spinoza rejected this distinction as false. There could be no separation between God as cause and nature as substance. It followed that God *was* the world,

The great Jewish philosopher Baruch Spinoza saw God and nature as indivisible. Contemporaries found his ideas "frightening," but he was a hero to later generations. [Collection Haags Gemeentemuseum, The Hague]

He that knows himself to be upright does not fear the death of a criminal, and shrinks from no punishment; his mind has no remorse for any disgraceful deed: he holds that death in a good cause is no punishment, but an honor, and that death for freedom is glory.[5]

Spinoza was not entirely isolated. He had friends and even disciples in the Netherlands and carried on a wide correspondence. Leibniz, who visited him, professed admiration for the rigor of his thought but finally concluded that the *Ethics* was "a frightening work" and spoke of the "monstrous opinions of this Jew expelled from the Synagogue." When Spinoza died from a longstanding tubercular condition in 1677, he had no defenders, and his work fell into obscurity until Goethe rediscovered it in the eighteenth century and the Romantics made him a hero in the nineteenth. Since then he has found his place among the great Western philosophers and the champions of freedom—honored at last, but still alone.

which was contained in him though he was not confined by it. It is hard to imagine an idea more calculated to give offense. Religious thinkers had speculated that the human soul might be regarded as a spark of divinity within humankind. Spinoza denied the existence of the soul, since there could be no distinction between matter and spirit; but on the other hand he asserted that God was present not only in humans but in the lowest and most degraded phenomena of the world as well. To accept God was to accept everything, and once that was done, false categories such as sin and salvation, which separated man from God, lost all meaning and fell away. Descartes, daring as he was, never left the Catholic church. Spinoza's metaphysics made all religious doctrine irrelevant.

Spinoza's political ideas were equally radical. Like Hobbes, he argued that sovereignty was absolute and indivisible and denounced clerical influence in the state; unlike Hobbes, Spinoza demanded complete freedom of thought. "The rights of the individual," he declared, "extend to the utmost limits of his power," and freedom was the final, indispensable human value:

Literature: The Triumph of the Vernacular

Latin was still the language of educated Europe in the sixteenth and seventeenth centuries, the language of international diplomacy, of scholarship, and of the Catholic church. As late as the early eighteenth century, when the elector of Hanover came to Britain to reign as King George I with no knowledge of the English language, he conversed with his chief minister, Sir Robert Walpole, in Latin. But the sixteenth century saw the beginning of a sustained tradition of vernacular literature, that is, literature in the popular spoken tongue. It began in Italy with the immensely popular chivalric poems of Ludovico Ariosto (1474–1533) and Torquato Tasso (1544–1595); in France with the prose epics of François Rabelais (1494–1553), *Gargantua* and *Pantagruel*; and in Germany with Luther's translation of the Bible, which went through 377 printings in his own lifetime. But the development of vernacular literature was particularly associated with the theater, the most popular of all art forms. The late sixteenth and seventeenth centuries were a golden age of theater in England, France, Spain, and the Netherlands, unrivaled from the time of ancient Greece and unequaled since.

The first of these national theaters was the English, where licensed companies of actors appeared from 1574. Two years later James Burbage built the first public theater in London, a roofless wooden amphitheater similar to the open spaces in inns and bull and bear-baiting arenas. Large enclosed theaters were built in the 1590s, of which the most famous were the Swan (1596) and the Globe (1599), which boasted seating capacities of 3,000. The basic price of admission was a penny for "groundlings" or standees; a seat in the lower galleries cost 2 pence, one in the upper ones 3, and a private box, usually reserved for a nobleman, was 6. The audience thus represented every element of Elizabethan society, and what it saw was the reflection of its own world, from cobblers to kings: Thomas Dekker's *Shoemaker's Holiday* (1599) depicted an upwardly mobile craftsman who becomes Lord Mayor of London; Thomas Middleton's *Chaste Maid in Cheapside* (1613), a goldsmith; Ben Jonson's *Bartholomew Fair* (1614), Puritans and pickpockets. Well might the greatest of these playwrights, William Shakespeare (1564–1616), whose imaginative world was perhaps larger than that of any person who ever lived, boastfully declare:

> *All the world's a stage,*
> *And all the men and women merely players.*
> *They have their exits and entrances,*
> *And one man in his time plays many parts.*[5]

The English stage exhibited not only great variety but also astonishing boldness and freedom. Topical and political satire abounded. Jonson was in trouble early in the reign of James I for attacking the vices and corruption of the court, and Middleton later on for a thinly veiled attack on the king's foreign policy. Shakespeare himself was paid to perform *Richard II*, his play about the fall of the fourteenth-century English tyrant, on the eve of the earl of Essex's rebellion against Queen Elizabeth in 1600. Actors, authors, and producers were often just a step ahead of the censor, until at last the Puritan revolutionaries, so often the butt of the London stage, closed it down in 1642.

Civic theater also flourished in the Netherlands, where it produced a major figure in Joost van den Vondel (1587–1679), a committed republican who protested against the rigidities of Dutch Calvinism. The playwrights of the Spanish school—Lope de Vega (1562–1635), Tirso de Molina (1571–1648), and Pedro Calderón de la Barca (1600–1681)—were immensely prolific; Lope claimed to have written over 1,500 plays, and the titles of nearly 1,000 survive. Performances were held outdoors in the public square, with seats arranged around the stage and rooms rented in private houses to provide the equivalent of boxes for noblemen and ladies. Male and female spectators were strictly segregated, and though the monarchy was often the subject of the Spanish theater, it was considered improper for the king and queen to attend. The French theater of Pierre Corneille (1606–1684) and Jean Racine (1639–1699), in contrast, was court-sponsored and reflected its patronage in its choice of classical themes, its emphasis on honor and the renunciation of the passions, and its formal, chiseled verse line. But the French produced their comic genius too in Jean-Baptiste Poquelin,

called Molière (1622–1673), who mocked the social pretensions of his own bourgeois class, although he stopped carefully short of satirizing his aristocratic audiences.

The seventeenth century saw the entry of women into literature for the first time, particularly in France. Women writers of note, such as Christine de Pisan, Marguerite of Navarre, and the English mystic Juliana of Norwich, had occasionally emerged before, as had even the stirrings of a feminist literature in Elizabethan England, but not until the accession of the Bourbon dynasty in France did women begin to occupy an important place in literature and literary life. Madeleine de Scudéry (1607–1701) created a new genre with her *Grand Cyrus* (1649–1653), a historical romance that portrayed the protagonists of the Fronde in the fictional guise of ancient Persians. Similarly, Marie de Sévigné (1626–1696) established letter writing as a literary art; her volumes of correspondence, ranging in their description from court life at Versailles to peasant rebellion, are the most rounded portrait we possess of life in the age of Louis XIV. No less important to the emerging cultural prominence of women was the literary salon, pioneered by the elegant Catherine de Rambouillet (1588–1665), at whose private gatherings aspiring writers came to establish their reputations. Even so, however, literature was not yet a respectable pursuit for women; Scudéry's *Grand Cyrus*, certainly the most popular and influential French novel of its time, was published under the name of her brother George, a mediocre playwright.

The last of the great epic poets was the Englishman John Milton (1608–1674), a lonely figure despite his service in the revolutionary regimes of the 1650s. Milton's *Paradise Lost* (1667), a poem not surpassed since in any language for its breadth and ambition, looked back to the model of Dante in its account of the fall of Adam and Eve, although its powerful portrayal of the character of Satan anticipates the rebellious Romantic hero of the nineteenth century. A new medium for narrative had begun to emerge, one that would dominate the literature of the West: the novel. The rambling adventure tales of Rabelais had anticipated the form in the sixteenth century, but the first true example is Miguel de Cervantes' *Don Quixote*. Cervantes intended to satirize the chivalric tales still popular in his native Spain, but he accomplished much more. His two wandering heroes, the idealistic nobleman Don Quixote and his worldly but faithful servant, Sancho Panza, are not mere stock figures on which a tale of adventures can be strung but living, individual characters whose success arises from their vivid contrast of temperament. The English drama was accomplishing much the same thing at the same time, but 100 years were to pass before anyone was able to capture the necessary balance of character and plot again in prose. With Daniel Defoe's enormously popular *Robinson Crusoe* (1719), however, a story not for the old world of chivalry but the new one of capital formation and commercial enterprise, the age of the novel had begun.

The Age of the Baroque

The origin of the term *baroque* is obscure, but may come from the Portuguese *barroco,* an irregularly shaped pearl. It has come to define the very distinctive art of the seventeenth century, though originally, like the adjective *Gothic,* it was a term of derision. Certainly, to those whose ideal was the serene beauty of a Raphael or the monumentality of a Michelangelo, the dramatic, swirling lines of baroque architecture and the darkened palette of baroque painting, with its abrupt contrasts of light and shadow and the brooding intensity of its portraits, could not but seem strained, distorted, and profoundly disturbing. Yet the baroque, like every major art style, had complex and subtle affinities to the wider culture of the age. In its restless, probing, and essentially theatrical nature, it reflected a period of conflict, exploration, and doubt, while in its bold redefinition of space, it suggests a response to the vision of Copernicus, Bruno, and Galileo.

The baroque originated as a style in Italy. Its first patrons were the Jesuits, and Gesù, the church of the order in Rome, is commonly accepted as the first full-fledged example of baroque architecture. Certainly the sense of spiritual quest and renewal emphasized by the Jesuits can be seen in such works as the *St. Theresa in Ecstasy* of Gianlorenzo Bernini (1598–1680) or the somber ecclesiastical portraits of Francisco de Zurbarán (1598–1664), but the baroque soon stepped across national and religious frontiers. The spiritual and the sensual, moreover, often blended into one another, as Bernini's *St. Theresa* vividly illustrates, or settled down happily side by side, as in the fleshily exuberant biblical scenes of the Flemish painter Peter Paul Rubens (1577–1640).

Dutch painters carried the new chiaroscuro style of the Italian Michelangelo Merisi, called Caravaggio (1573–1610), back from Rome. Caravaggio's work, with its dramatic interior lighting, often from no visible source, was soon reflected in the work of artists all over Europe, including Diego Velázquez (1599–1660) in Spain and George de la Tour (1593–1652) in France, but it found its apotheosis in the Dutch Mennonite artist Rembrandt van Rijn (1606–1669). Rembrandt was the greatest of a remarkable series of painters who captured the variety and vitality of seventeenth-century Dutch society, leaving an unmatched record of the everyday life of their time. Rembrandt's own work reveals this same curiosity about the unusual and even (by classical standards) the bizarre, as in his *Anatomy Lesson of Dr. Tulp* (1632), in which an anatomist dissects the cadaver of an executed criminal before the Surgeons' Guild of Amsterdam. But his genius was too impatient for the landscape and genre scenes preferred by his contemporaries; as his drawings reveal, he could capture the essence of a landscape more surely in a few quick strokes of brush or pen than most of them in elaborate and painstaking canvases. He spent his own immense gifts of color and composition on individual portaits, including a series of self-portraits that, begun in a vigorous and commercially successful youth, continued up to the year of his death when, unfashionable and destitute, he painted largely for himself alone. In Rembrandt's portraits, something of what Spinoza may have meant by the "soul that lives in all things" is visible, for no other artist has ever revealed so much of our common humanity.

The music of the baroque, like its art and architecture, tended toward the dramatic. Sung texts and spoken words had largely existed apart before Claudio Monteverdi (1567–1643), who fused them into a new theatrical form, the opera. By the 1630s Italian opera had become a lavish spectacle; Cardinal Barberini sponsored one performance at his palace in Rome before an audience of 3,500, with stage designs by Bernini. Much of seventeenth-century music remained dominated by Italian models, particularly in the secular forms of the oratorio, the cantata, and the concerto. In Germany the tradition of church music introduced by the hymns of Martin Luther produced a series of important composers, including Heinrich Schütz (1585–1672). Later baroque music developed in the direction of elaborate ornamentation and contrapuntal complexity, reaching its climax in Johann Sebastian Bach (1685–1750), in whom the Lutheran tradition achieved a universality that, like the art of Rembrandt, reaches across all ages and cultures.

The state gradually superseded the Catholic church in the role of patron of baroque art. Rubens was commissioned to paint a series of allegorical portraits glorifying Marie de' Medici of France and her son, Henry IV, and he was also employed (with his younger colleague Anthony van Dyck) in making equestrian portraits of the ill-fated Charles I of England, who took the extraordinary step of knighting him for his services. It was Louis XIV, however, who saw most clearly the possibilities of bringing art to the service of the state. In Versailles the dramatic, heaven-storming qualities of baroque art (suitably refined by French taste) and the pomp of divine right monarchy came together in an image of absolute secular power. Other rulers rushed to follow his example—Leopold I in Austria, Charles XII in Sweden, Peter the Great in Russia, Frederick the Great in Prussia, Augustus the Strong in Saxony, and a host of lesser princelings, neither great nor strong, who felt that no reign could be complete without a palace to attest to its *gloire.*

❦
ROME:
THE REBIRTH OF A CAPITAL

Rome, for most of the population of Europe still the center of Christendom, recovered slowly from the sack of 1527 and the subsequent Spanish occupation. With the new energies of the Counter-Reformation, however, the city began to revive. Work on St. Peter's, still without a facade or dome, was the first order of priority. Pope Sixtus V, working men around the clock for 22 months, finished Michelangelo's dome in 1590. The architect Carlo Maderna (1556–1629) designed the new facade, and Bernini spent nearly a decade (1657–1666) completing the great colonnaded square in front. Maderna departed radically from Michelangelo's original designs, widening and opening the central nave and replacing Michelangelo's facade with columns whose variable spacing produced a fluid effect. Bernini's undulating columns in the nave and his daringly open square—the first such space in any European city—completed with baroque exuberance and novelty the great edifice that had been begun in the High Renaissance. In no other building is the contrast between the aims and aspirations of the two epochs more strikingly visible.

With St. Peter's in progress, Popes Paul V (1605–1621) and Urban VIII (1623–1644) undertook the reconstruction and beautification of Rome, giving it the squares and fountains—many designed by the ubiquitous Bernini—that still distinguish it today. With these came new churches as well, notably Bernini's San Andrea al Quirinale (1658–1670) and Francesco Borromini's San Carlo alle Quattro Fontane (1638–1641), whose interior represents the first completely undulating wall space since the reign of the Roman emperor Hadrian. In Borromini (1599–1666), the greatest Italian architect of the century, the flowing space of the baroque—like the post-Copernican universe, itself never defined by any single perspective—achieves its most characteristic form.

By the early eighteenth century the rebuilt city had become a major tourist attraction for Protestants and Catholics alike, an obligatory stop on the grand tour by which elegant young ladies and gentlemen put the finishing touches to their education. One such traveler, the French magistrate Charles de Brosses, declared that Rome was "the most beautiful city in the world." St. Peter's was "the finest thing in the universe." Like a jewel, its facets were endlessly fascinating: "You might come to it every day without being bored. . . . It is more amazing the oftener you see it." Most impressive of all, he thought, were the fountains and firework displays that played constantly and

The revival of Rome was marked by completion of the colonnaded square of St. Peter's, the masterpiece of the greatest architect and sculptor of the baroque, Gianlorenzo Bernini. The church of St. Peter's, seat of the Vatican, appears at the left rear. [Granger Collection]

The restless, aspiring spirit of the baroque is well illustrated in this detail of the curving facade of Borromini's church of San Carlo at the Four Fountains in Rome. Massive but supple form and a dramatic use of interior space characterized the architecture of the baroque. [Wim Swann, New York]

gave the city an air of perpetual festivity. This impression was not far from wrong, as Rome celebrated no fewer than 150 holidays a year, not to mention occasional pageants, local processions and fairs, and weekly summer festivals that included water jousts and mock sea battles in the flooded Piazza Navona.

Rome's population grew steadily during this period, from approximately 80,000 in 1563 to 118,356 in the census of 1621 to about 150,000 by 1709. This included some 8,000 priests, monks, nuns, and other religious who staffed the almost 400 churches of Rome and a nearly equal number of monasteries, convents, and seminaries. The papacy dominated the political and economic life of Rome just as the dome and square of St. Peter's did its skyline. It governed the city as the capital of the so-called Papal States, a band of territories that stretched across the middle of Italy, and was far and away its chief employer, dispensing charity and relief as well to the poor. What the papacy did not provide directly it did indirectly, in the services that were needed for the hordes of pilgrims, estimated at 100,000 per year in 1700, that formed the bulk of the tourist trade. The result was that Rome's was almost entirely a service economy, living on papal wealth and foreign income. Life was casual if not indolent; even at the Vatican, washing was hung out to dry from the windows. At the bottom of the social scale, Rome's easygoing ways tailed off into squalor, and its poor, favored at least by the climate, spent as little time as possible in their wretched hovels. The very openness of life acted as a safety valve for discontent; there was always distraction in the street, even for the most extreme misery, and, in a city full of wealthy strangers, always opportunity as well.

One group that stood apart from the ministrations of the church was the Jewish community. Yet it, too, was noted in the papacy's ubiquitous accounts, and when Paul V planned his new fountains for Rome, one was duly provided for the city's synagogue. A more curious and less benevolent example of Rome's uneasy relationship with its Jews was in the ceremony that opened the Roman Carnival, the eight-day pre-Lenten celebration that was the most elaborate and tumultuous holiday of the year. The Jews were taxed the cost of the prize money for the horse races and, assembled as a group, were thanked for their "gift" to the city by a pretended kick in the small of the chief rabbi's back.

The seventeenth century has rightly been called the century of genius. Shakespeare, Milton, Cervantes, Rembrandt—these men shaped the image of humankind in the West and still stand at the frontier of its cultural heritage, their works undimmed by time. Bacon, Hobbes, Descartes, Pascal, and Spinoza shaped the modern quest for knowledge, and the questions they posed, about humankind and the cosmos, about freedom and government, are still alive today. Copernicus, Kepler, Galileo, Newton, and many others of lesser ability created the scientific revolution and with it transformed humankind's capacity to know, to create, and to destroy.

The effects of the changed intellectual climate were visible by the end of the century. The triumph of the mechanistic vision of nature over Aristotelian physics and cosmology and the rival tradition of Hermetic natural magic had a decisive influence on popular superstition as well as educated thought. The beginning of the century had seen the last upsurge in witchcraft persecution, affecting some 100,000 persons between 1580 and 1650. By the end of the century belief in witchcraft itself was largely extinct, and faith in astrology and magic healing had declined sharply. The view of the cosmos as a web of hidden affinities and powers on which such beliefs depended was no longer credible, and so they silently faded away.

The cultural shock that greeted man's dethronement from his position at the center of the universe gradually gave way to a new pride in the power of human knowledge. Until the nineteenth century the scientific revolution had little practical consequence, and few of the technological advances of the

1700s owed themselves to the abstruse physics of Newton. Nonetheless, the new science came to symbolize faith in the improvement of the human condition, a faith that for some in the eighteenth century took on the quality of religious conviction itself. At the same time, the mathematized God of Newton and Descartes was gradually detached from sci- *ence. For them, God had still been the ultimate guarantor of the truth of their universe. A century later, asked why he had omitted God from his system, the French astronomer Pierre Simon de Laplace (1749–1827) would answer coolly, "I have no need of that hypothesis."*

———

Notes

1. T. S. Kuhn, The *Copernican Revolution* (Cambridge, Mass.: Harvard University Press, 1957), p. 128.
2. H. F. Kearney, *Science and Change, 1500–1700* (New York: McGraw-Hill, 1971), p. 101.
3. A. R. Hall, *The Scientific Revolution, 1500–1800* (Boston: Beacon Press, 1956), p. 132.
4. Martha Ornstein, *The Rôle of Scientific Societies in the Seventeenth Century* (Chicago: University of Chicago Press, 1938), p. 95.
5. *The Chief Works of Benedict de Spinoza*, ed. R. H. M. Elwes, 2 vols. (London: G. Bell, 1917, 1919), vol. 2, p. 263.
6. *As You Like It*, act 2, scene 7.

Suggestions for Further Reading

Butterfield, H. *The Origins of Modern Science*. New York: Macmillan, 1957.

Cohen, I. B. *The Birth of a New Physics*. New York: Norton, 1985.

Feuer, L. S. *Spinoza and the Rise of Liberalism*. Boston: Beacon Press, 1966.

Friedrich, C. J. *The Age of the Baroque*. New York: Harper, 1952.

Gillespie, C. C. *The Edge of Objectivity: An Essay in the History of Scientific Ideas*. Princeton, N.J.: Princeton University Press, 1960.

Hall, A. R. *The Scientific Revolution, 1500–1800*. Boston: Beacon Press, 1956.

Kearney, H. F. *Science and Change 1500–1700*. New York: McGraw-Hill, 1971.

Koyre, A. *From the Closed World to the Infinite Universe*. Baltimore: Johns Hopkins University Press, 1957.

Krautheimer, R. *The Rome of Alexander VII, 1655–1667*. Princeton, N.J.: Princeton University Press, 1985.

Kuhn, T. S. *The Structure of Scientific Revolutions*. Chicago: University of Chicago Press, 1970.

MacPherson, C. B. *The Political Theory of Possessive Individualism: Hobbes to Locke*. New York: Oxford University Press, 1964.

Mesnard, J. *Pascal, His Life and Works*. New York: Philosophical Library, 1952.

Nash, J. M. *The Age of Rembrandt and Vermeer: Dutch Painting in the Seventeenth Century*. New York: Holt, Rinehart and Winston, 1972.

Ornstein, M. *The Role of Scientific Societies in the Seventeenth Century*. Chicago: University of Chicago Press, 1928.

Palisca, C. V. *Baroque Music*. Englewood Cliffs, N.J.: Prentice-Hall, 1981.

Popkin, R. *History of Scepticism from Erasmus to Spinoza*. Berkeley: University of California Press, 1979.

Santillana, G. de. *The Crime of Galileo*. London: Heinemann, 1958.

Spear, R. E. *Caravaggio and His Followers*. Cleveland, Ohio: Cleveland Museum of Art, 1971.

Strauss, L. *The Political Philosophy of Hobbes*. Chicago: University of Chicago Press, 1966.

Thomas, K. *Religion and the Decline of Magic*. New York: Scribner, 1971.

Warnke, F. J. *Versions of Baroque: European Literature in the Seventeenth Century*. New Haven, Conn.: Yale University Press, 1972.

Westfall, R. S. *Never at Rest: A Biography of Isaac Newton*. Cambridge: Cambridge University Press, 1980.

Wilson, M. D. *Descartes*. Boston: Routledge & Kegan Paul, 1978.

Yates, F. A. *Giordano Bruno and the Hermetic Tradition*. Chicago: University of Chicago Press, 1964.

PART · FOUR

Toward the Modern World

The modern world that came of age in the eighteenth century was marked by rapid and revolutionary change. In Europe a century of imperial expansion and development abroad and unprecedented social criticism at home was climaxed by the French Revolution, which at a stroke abolished feudal tenures and the hierarchy of orders in the continent's most powerful state. The French Revolution paved the way for economic modernization and political centralization throughout Europe, the latter also assisted by the rising sentiment of nationalism. By the second half of the nineteenth century the two largest territorial blocks in central Europe, Germany and Italy, had been unified politically for the first time since the Middle Ages, while the growing power of Russia, the protracted collapse of the Ottoman Empire, and the increasing demands for national independence among the minorities of the Austrian empire had created an unstable zone of contending powers and client states. These complex power realignments, tied to imperial and commercial rivalry, resulted in a conflict of global magnitude, World War I.

While these changes were taking place, a far wider transformation of the human situation was under way. Beginning in the mid-eighteenth century, the number of humans began to expand at an increasing rate, a phenomenon, uninterrupted and accelerating to the present day, known as the population explosion. At the same time, new sources of mechanized power exploiting steam, coal, and other natural elements were being devised on the island of Britain, which, closely tied to the imperatives of capitalism and state power, produced the most significant development in human technology in 10,000 years, the Industrial Revolution. That process, like the population explosion, has now become a global phenomenon that continues to transform our material culture.

The decisive advantage lent to Europe by its aggressive organization and superior technology was translated into global hegemony in the nineteenth century. The European states claimed large portions of Africa and Asia as colonies, protectorates, or spheres of interest. The British completed a conquest of India begun in the mid-eighteenth century and fanned out from there to dominate much of Southeast Asia and the Middle East, creating the largest empire the world had ever known. China was forced to accept humiliating infringements of its economic and territorial sovereignty. Weakened by a terrible civil war in the mid-nineteenth century that undermined the declining Manchu dynasty, it took the first painful steps toward modernization. Only two major states remained outside the European orbit: the United States of America, founded by rebellion in the late eighteenth century and, by the end of the nineteenth, the dominant force in the Western Hemisphere and the world's greatest industrial power, and Japan, which, startled from feudal isolation by the imperial challenge, rapidly transformed itself into first the equal and ultimately the superior of any European state.

These changes in politics and technology were accompanied by far-reaching transformations of the social order. Slavery was formally abolished in Africa and the Americas, although other forms of labor coercion remained. In Europe and later in the Western Hemisphere the industrial working force began to organize in its own behalf under the banner of a new doctrine, socialism, which consciously opposed itself to the capitalist and imperialist order. The great movement for gender equality known as women's liberation began in the industrial nations and spread rapidly across the globe. In Europe the Jews were emancipated after centuries of enforced isolation, and other minorities began to claim their rights to equality and free expression. By 1900 a majority of the population in the leading industrial nations lived in cities, creating a new and distinctive urban culture, and despite the continuing economic struggle of many, improvements in sanitation and health care had begun dramatically to increase the average life expectation in the developed countries. ∎

Europe and the Americas

By the eighteenth century the economy of western Europe had become worldwide in scope. Large regional economies, integrated by trade patterns and dominated by strong states, had existed since ancient times. China had long been the center of such an economy in East Asia. The Indian Ocean and Red Sea area constituted another large system. In Europe itself, the Mediterranean had provided a natural focus of economic integration under the successive dominion of Egyptians, Phoenicians, Greeks, Romans, Arabs, Venetians, and, most recently, Spaniards.

But Spain had begun to decline in the seventeenth century, and by the early eighteenth the Mediterranean was dominated for the first time by a power not based geographically in the region, Britain. At the same time, the center of European gravity had shifted to the Atlantic states. Britain, France, and the Dutch Netherlands were not merely the dominant economic powers of Europe, but their scattered overseas possessions, a source of persistent though relatively peripheral rivalry in the seventeenth century, became the focus of a much more intense competition in the eighteenth. Those possessions, increasingly consolidated in political terms and increasingly

William Pitt the Elder, Britain's choleric but brilliant statesman and architect of its North American empire. A contemporary described him as "imperious, violent ... implacable [and] ... despotic," yet also as "a man of veracity and a man of honor." [National Portrait Gallery, London]

valuable in economic ones, became themselves the springboard for further expansion and conquest. The slave trade directly linked four continents — Europe, Africa, and North and South America — in a complex and highly coordinated relationship. After 1750 India and to a lesser extent Indonesia were drawn more and more into the web of European-dominated exchange, and by the end of the century the British were knocking at the gates of China. As the importance of the world market grew, Britain and France clashed repeatedly for control of it. After three major cycles of warfare spread across 125 years, the British emerged victorious, though shorn of what had been their largest New World colony, the newly independent United States of America.

The Old Colonial System

The new global economy consolidated by Europe in the eighteenth century had its roots as far back as the crusades, when the potential for profit in overseas trade first became apparent. This economy was based on the establishment of colonies, used both as forward bases for trade, exploration, or further conquest and as passive markets and sources of raw materials. The crusader colonies in Palestine, Cyprus, and Greece were prototypes of the later and much larger Spanish, Portuguese, Dutch, and English colonies in the New World, Africa, and Asia. A second type of colony, developed by the Genoese in the fourteenth century, was based on control by a private trading company operating under a government charter. The English and Dutch East India companies, founded in 1600 and 1602, respectively, administered large territories under such arrangements, as did the Virginia and Massachusetts Bay companies on the Atlantic seaboard of North America. Yet a third type of colony was based on an agreement between individuals for the settlement of a territory; the Mayflower Compact was an example.

The nature of a given colonial enterprise depended on the territory to be settled and the general approach of the colonizing center, or "metropolis." In the New World tiny bands of adventurers such as those commanded by Cortés in Mexico and Pizarro in Peru, exploiting native rivalries, were able to conquer vast areas through mobile tactics, skillful use of Indian auxiliaries, and technological superiority. The urban civilizations of the Aztecs in Mexico and the Incas in Peru were in many respects the equal of Europe's, but their weapons were those of the Stone Age. Elsewhere in the Americas, Europeans confronted only scattered tribes which were quickly exterminated, enslaved, or driven into wilderness areas.

The peoples of Africa were nearly as vulnerable to European penetration as those of the Americas. The Portuguese established their influence along the Congo and Zambesi rivers in the early sixteenth century, but the un-

attractiveness of the climate for Europeans deterred large-scale settlement except at the Cape of Good Hope on the southern tip of the continent, where Dutch colonists arrived in the seventeenth century. For the most part, Europeans were content to barter for slaves, gold dust, and ivory with African middlemen, and apart from establishing coastal bases for commerce they made little attempt to explore the continent.

In Asia, where Europeans possessed no significant technical or military advantage except in ship design, conquest and hence colonization were out of the question. Here the Portuguese and the Dutch competed with Asian and Arab merchants for a share of the lucrative spice trade, often financed by piracy. At the beginning of the eighteenth century, however, the European presence in Asia was still marginal.

Spain and the New World

Spain ruled its colonies in the New World through its Council of the Indies, although its powers were gradually dispersed among other ministries in the eighteenth century. With the immense bureaucratic patience typical of the Spanish Old Regime, it attempted — for the first time in Europe in 1,000 years — to govern a territory and population far exceeding its own, a challenge compounded by the distance of several thousand miles of ocean. From Madrid it sent out an endless stream of edicts covering the minutest details of colonial life; by 1700 more than 400,000 of these were still technically in force, and a digest of the more important ones contained 11,000 laws.

To ensure conformity with its regulations, the council relied on the *residencia*, a review of all senior colonial officials at the end of their service, and the *visita*, irregular inspections that might produce temporary improvements but more often, as one viceroy put it, did little more than raise the dust on the streets. The empire was formally divided into the viceroyalties of New Spain and Peru, the former encompassing Mexico and most of the western two-thirds of the present-day United States. In addition, there were three captaincies general, Santo Domingo, Guatemala, and New Granada, the last of which, centered in what is now Colombia, became a viceroyalty in 1739. The viceroyalties were divided into provinces, but the basic unit of administration, as in Spain itself, centered on the municipality, governed by an official usually called the *corregidor*. The corregidor was the backbone of the colonial system, and the day to day lives of most of the population depended on his performance.

The primary purpose of the empire was the exploitation of its wealth. This required the mobilization of its inhabitants. In the early years of the sixteenth century the Spaniards enslaved the island populations of the Caribbean and worked them literally to extinction in the gold mines; by midcentury the population of Hispaniola had been reduced from several hundred thousand to a few hundred. The inhabitants of Cuba and Puerto Rico suffered a similar fate, while smaller islands, which the Spanish did not bother to settle, were stripped of their populations by raiding parties. Reports of these atrocities, and the complaints of Spanish priests that the native population was dying off before it could be converted to Christianity, prompted the Spanish government to issue an edict regarding its treatment:

> **Because of the excessive liberty the Indians have been permitted, they flee from Christians and do not work. Therefore they are to be compelled to work, so that the kingdom and the Spaniards be enriched, and the Indians Christianized. They are to be paid a daily wage and well treated as free persons, for such they are, and not slaves.[1]**

These instructions had no discernible effect on the extermination of the Caribbean Indians. In Mexico labor was at first directly enslaved. This was modified by the introduction of the *encomienda*, a type of manorial system whereby Spanish settlers were given responsibility for protecting and "civilizing" native communities in return for their labor. As mining developed in Mexico and particularly in Peru, the system proved inadequate to the demands for a mobile labor force that could be transported from site to site and was supplemented by a conscript system, the *repartimiento*, in which Indian community chiefs were required to provide a stipulated amount of labor to the authorities, who distributed the workers to Spanish contractors. Nominal wages were paid, but they were so low that they were often a mere pretext to force Indian workers into debt and peonage. Although conditions varied from region to region with the requirement of a work force (being worst where economic activity was most intense), the *repartimiento* tended to become indistinguishable from forced labor. In its brutally efficient regimentation of labor, it became the prototype of colonial capitalism, and its techniques eventually found their way home to the metropolis with the advent of the Industrial Revolution.

Gold and silver brought Europeans to the Americas in the sixteenth century. The great silver mountain at Potosí, 10,000 feet above sea level, gave rise to a city whose population eventually reached 160,000, rivaling at one point the size of London and exceeding Madrid, Paris, and Rome. Its 36 churches, with their splendid baroque ornamentation, were matched by 36 gambling casinos, no less grandly adorned. Its mines consumed the lives of an estimated 8 million Indian workers before they gave out.

Gold and the Expansion of the European Economy

The importation of massive quantities of precious metals, ferried home by an annual treasure fleet, had a profound

◉ Conscript Labor in Spanish Mexico ◉

A seventeenth-century Spanish commentator, Antónío Vásquez de Espinosa, describes the operation of a textile mill in the city of Puebla.

There are in this city large woolen mills in which they weave quantities of fine cloth, serge, and grogram, from which they make handsome profits. . . . To keep their mills supplied with labor . . . [the operators] maintain individuals who are engaged and hired to ensnare poor innocents. Seeing some Indian who is a stranger to the town, with some trickery or pretext, such as hiring him to carry something, like a porter, and paying him cash, they get him into the mill. Once inside, they drop the deception, and the poor fellow never again gets outside that prison until he dies and they carry him out for burial. In this way they have gathered in and duped many married Indians with families, who have passed into oblivion here for 20 years, or longer, or their whole lives, without their wives and children knowing anything about them. . . . And although the Royal Council of the Indies . . . has tried to remedy this evil with warrants and ordinances . . . and the Viceroy of New Spain appoints mill inspectors to visit [the Indians] and remedy such matters, nevertheless, since most of those who set out on such commissions aim rather at their own enrichment . . . and since the mill owners pay them well, they leave the wretched Indians in the same slavery . . . as if it were not a most serious mortal sin.

Source: A. V. de Espinosa, *Compendium and Description of the West Indies* (Washington, D.C.: Smithsonian Institution, 1942), pp. 133–134.

effect on the European economy. The Mediterranean region, whose weak bullion base had been further eroded by the decline of imports from its previous supplier, the Sudan, suddenly burgeoned. From Seville to Antwerp, the ports of western Europe teemed with new shipping and trade, presaging the great shift of power to the Atlantic economies that occurred within the next two centuries. Transatlantic trade multiplied eightfold between 1510 and 1550 and tripled again between 1550 and 1610. Through trade and smuggling, a considerable quantity of the new bullion found its way to Asia and the Levant, and at one time a direct transpacific trade developed between Acapulco and Manila in the Philippines. Gold and silver from the New World created a network of worldwide commerce on a scale and of a complexity never seen before.

The gradual exhaustion of the mines of Mexico and Peru brought this first, precocious global economy to an end. Asia had no interest in Western goods comparable to the European demand for silks and spices, which therefore had to be paid for almost entirely in bullion. As new supplies tapered off, the Asian trade dwindled. At about the same time, the European economy, so powerfully stimulated by the influx of precious metals, began to contract. European states blamed the prolonged depression that set in between 1619 and 1622 on their shrinking bullion reserves, although this was only one factor in a complex

A woman weighing gold looks thoughtful in this painting by Rembrandt. Gold was vital to commercial and industrial expansion in early modern Europe and the chief spur to exploration and colonization in the Americas. [Marburg/Art Resource]

process of overproduction, diminished population growth, and a long-term pattern of severer climate. The anxiety of states to protect their bullion supplies led to import restrictions, thus hindering trade and deepening the slump. This in turn heightened the tensions surrounding the Thirty Years' War, which itself produced ruin in much of Europe.

Merchant Capitalism and the Growth of the State

Nonetheless, the great sixteenth-century boom had permanent effects. The sharp rise in profits and prices enriched the merchant bourgeoisie, whose new political importance was clearly manifested in Britain, France, and the Netherlands. The value of estates and rents tended to fall, thus putting pressure on the landed nobility. In eastern Europe the demand for foodstuffs and raw materials to stoke the expanding Atlantic economies stimulated the enserfment of scarce peasant labor, an apparently "backward" step that was, like the regimentation of Indian labor in the Americas, in significant part a response to growth in the core economies of the West. The results of this were profound. It immobilized the peasant population, stunting urban growth and confirming the power of the landed nobility at a time when it was under challenge in the West. From the sixteenth century onward, the development of eastern and western Europe increasingly diverged; their present political and economic divisions are a consequence.

The growth of the economy was linked to that of the state. The expansion of the latter was most visible in palace building and the development of a court-based culture, which reached their climax in the Versailles of Louis XIV. These self-conscious displays of power were accompanied by a proliferation of state offices and the gradual transformation of royal attendants serving the king's pleasure into bureaucratic functionaries performing regular and prescribed duties. At the same time, the state took a greater interest in economic development, which provided it with a larger tax base. The fiscal demands of the state stimulated the growth of banking and credit, and these in turn expanded the state's capacities further.

The development of merchant capitalism and of centralized political authority was thus reciprocal. The establishment of centralized authority was essential to peaceful commerce at home and the protection of colonial ventures abroad. Often, as in the development of the silk and glass industries in France or of mining in Austria and Hungary, the state allied itself directly with business interests, and the entire process of exploration and colonization in the sixteenth century may be considered as a partnership between the state and private entrepreneurs in which the state provided venture capital in return for a fixed share of the profits. War itself took on a more overtly commercial tone, as states fought over trade routes, commercial privileges, and control of profitable or potentially profitable territories.

This did not mean that the interests of rulers and merchants were necessarily harmonious. Their partnership was always an uneasy one, and by the eighteenth century some merchants felt that the state had become unduly restrictive and even oppressive, hampering rather than fostering economic development with its rigid controls and regulations. On balance, however, the state and merchant capitalism were mutually supportive during the first stages of global economic growth in the West. If the merchant bourgeoisie had developed to the point where state intervention was perceived as a handicap, it was only because state power had nurtured it to the point of self-generating growth.

The Economy of the Americas

The principal economic activity of Spanish America, even in the headiest days of gold and silver production, was agriculture. Spanish colonial society quickly reproduced the patterns of the home country, with large estates worked by native labor. The government made land grants of immense size as a means of encouraging new settlements, and great cattle herds pushed the frontiers of New Spain beyond Mexico into what is now the southwestern United States. The Spaniards supplemented the native crops of maize, beans, and squash with wheat and a variety of fruits. Sugar was grown from early on in the Caribbean islands and on the Mexican lowlands, and olive and vine culture was successfully established in Peru. Cortés, seeking a profitable crop, introduced the silkworm into Mexico in 1523. The most successful export over the next three centuries of Spanish dominance in America, however, was cochineal, an insect used in red dyes.

In Portuguese Brazil, where no precious metals were discovered until 1690 and the native population was inadequate as a labor force, a plantation society quickly developed based on sugar, tobacco, cocoa, and cotton, employing black slave labor. This pattern was repeated by the British, French, and Dutch in the Caribbean and the southern colonies of North America, where similar climatic and demographic conditions prevailed. Farther up the North American coast and along the rivers of the interior, notably the Mississippi and the St. Lawrence, a settler society developed in the absence of readily exploitable labor or natural resources. The most populous of these settlements were the British colonies along the Atlantic sea-

board, although the most far-flung geographically was the long arc of French trading stations and fortifications that extended from the Gulf of Mexico to Hudson's Bay. The principal Dutch base on the North American mainland was New Amsterdam, at the mouth of the Hudson River. From here the Dutch conducted a lucrative fur trade and an even more profitable smuggling operation until the settlement was conquered by the British in 1664, who renamed it New York.

The Settlement of North America

British settlement in North America proceeded fitfully. After several false starts, a small colony was established at Jamestown on the Potomac River in 1607. By 1733 the number had grown to 13 colonies along the coast and the adjacent river valleys from New England to Georgia. The northernmost of these colonies, particularly Massachusetts, Rhode Island, and Connecticut, were essentially subsistence economies of slight value to the mother country. They served, together with the Quaker colony of Pennsylvania, primarily as a dumping ground for religious and political dissidents, some 20,000 of whom migrated to New England between 1629 and 1642 in the wave of repression that preceded the English revolution. In the Middle Atlantic and southern plantation colonies, indigents and convicts (frequently transported as an alternative to hanging) joined religious exiles as settlers, together, of course, with imported slave labor.

Since Britain's mainland colonies were at first perceived largely as a safety valve for excess population or unwanted social groups, the crown exerted relatively little control over them. The French, in contrast, never thought of allowing their colonies to be peopled by paupers, felons, and dissidents. Great efforts were made to procure suitable migrants, down to the provision of tools, seed, stock, and even free passage to Canada for women willing to marry settlers. The crown first subsidized and controlled the companies formed to plant settlements and then, under Jean-Baptiste Colbert, relieved them of all administrative responsibility, placing each colony under a military governor. Nonetheless, the combined French and British presence in the New World in the seventeenth century was only a fraction of Spain's in size, population, and wealth—and that in spite of the loss in Spanish America, mostly to epidemic disease, of some nine-tenths of its preconquest population of 20 million or more, one of the greatest demographic extinctions in history. It was not, however, the vast expanses of the North American continent that were to make the New World profitable for Britain and France in the late seventeenth and early eighteenth centuries but the small sugar-producing islands of the Caribbean.

Sugar and Slavery

Sugar had been grown in the New World almost from the beginning of European colonization. As early as the 1510s sugar cultivation had been introduced into the Caribbean islands, where it was harvested by black slaves imported from Africa to replace an Amerindian population already decimated by white settlers. The Portuguese were the first to introduce sugar on a relatively large scale in Brazil, where some 60 mills were in operation by 1580. Most of the export trade was carried on by Dutch merchants, one of whose spokesmen, Willem de Usselincx, farsightedly pointed out that plantation crops such as sugar had a far greater long-range profit potential than the Spanish bullion that so dazzled his contemporaries. The Dutch themselves were driven out of Brazil by 1654, but their role in spreading the sugar trade in the West Indies by means of shipping and selling the product, introducing the processes that turned brown sugar into the much more popular white variety, and supplying African slaves, was crucial.

The replacement of the Dutch as middlemen and their defeat as competitors marked the coming of age of the British and French imperial systems. The British moved swiftly to consolidate control of their colonial trade. The Navigation Acts of 1651 and 1660 provided that colonies could trade certain "enumerated" products—sugar, tobacco, cotton, indigo, ginger, and dyewoods—only with the mother country or other British colonies and only on British ships. In return they were to accept manufactured goods from Britain. This closed system of trade exemplified the economic theory of mercantilism, which sought to enhance the wealth of the mother country by acquiring a captive source of supply for its commodity needs and a compulsory outlet for its manufactures. The French were never able to develop a system as fully integrated as that of the British, partly because of the absence of a mainland population sufficient to promote intercolonial trade, but as commodity suppliers alone their major West Indian possessions—Guadeloupe and Martinique, settled in 1635, and Santo Domingo, acquired from Spain in 1697—had an increasing impact on the metropolitan economy.

The phases of sugar harvesting and processing are shown here in a print representing a slave plantation in the West Indies. At right raw cane is being brought in from the fields; it is crushed in a roller mill, mixed with lime and egg white, and left to crystallize. The profitability of sugar, and of the slave trade that supplied the labor it demanded, resulted in one of the greatest forced migrations in history. [Bettmann Archive]

Of all British and French colonial products, sugar was by far the most important. Its cultivation required not only suitable colonies but also a heavy investment in land and labor. Wealthy royalist exiles from the English civil wars provided this in the 1640s and 1650s, driving out poorer white settlers and consolidating their land into large plantations. By 1673 sugar production on tiny Barbados was one-quarter that of Brazil's, and by 1700 the economic value of the West Indian islands exceeded that of all the mainland colonies combined. Jamaica, acquired by Britain in 1655, did not develop into a major supplier until the early eighteenth century, but by 1770 it was producing half of all British sugar and was incontestably the single most valuable colonial territory in the New World. Despite some price fluctuation, the demand for sugar remained extraordinarily high for well over a century, particularly in Britain itself, where per capita consumption was eight times that in France. Overall, the production of sugar in the Americas rose from 20,000 tons per year in 1600 to 200,000 tons on the eve of the American Revolution.

The Slave System

The labor required for sugar cultivation on this scale could have come only from slaves, and as the pace of importation quickened, the free white population of the West Indies fell dramatically; some 30,000 whites left Barbados alone between 1650 and 1680. Seen in this perspective, the "settlement" of the New World in the seventeenth, eighteenth, and much of the nineteenth century was overwhelmingly by African blacks. A million blacks had been imported into the Americas by 1700, and 6 million more arrived in the course of the eighteenth century, a number nearly equaling both the partially recovered remnant of the original Amerindian population and that of white settlers combined. Half of this number was funneled into the West Indies alone, where the permanent British and French population was less than 100,000. Yet despite the 3 million black men, women, and children who entered the Caribbean during this period, the net population increase was only 700,000. The vast majority of slaves perished within ten years of arrival. In part this may be accounted for by disease, the major factor in the destruction of the native population in the sixteenth century. But the primary reason was exploitation. Blacks were systematically worked to death.

At first glance this appears difficult to explain. Slaves were an expensive investment; they accounted for 90 percent of the capital value of Jamaican plantations in the eighteenth century, exclusive of land. Nonetheless, in the calculus of profit, they were expendable. It was cheaper to replace than to maintain them, which meant supporting those too young and too old to work.

The Slave Trade

The mechanism of replacement, the great wheel that turned all of eighteenth-century colonial commerce, was the slave trade. Slaving was a textbook example of what mercantilist economists called the "triangular trade." Ships from Liverpool or Nantes exchanged cheap textiles, gunpowder, or gin for slaves provided by native traders at stations on the West African coast. As new cargo, the slaves were transported to the West Indies. Allowing for a 15 to 20 percent mortality rate en route, the survivors would sell for approximately five times their original purchase price. The ships would then fill up with sugar and return home.

The transatlantic voyage, known euphemistically as the "middle passage," took two months. The slaves were segregated by sex and packed together below decks in chains, helpless amid vermin and rats. In fair weather they were exercised on deck, under the lash; when seas were rough, they were kept below with the portholes shut. The tensions of the voyage provoked insane acts of cruelty. The captain of one ship flogged a 10-month-old child with a cat-o'-nine-tails for refusing to eat, then plunged it into scalding water, tied it to a log, flogged it again to death, and forced its mother to throw it into the sea.

Once ashore, the slaves in Britain's Caribbean colonies possessed neither legal nor moral rights. A planter who flogged a 14-year-old girl to death was actually tried for murder in Jamaica but was acquitted on the ground that "it was impossible [that] a master could destroy his own property." The Spaniards had tried to justify their conquest of the Americas by the necessity to convert the heathen, but eighteenth-century missionaries were forbidden to proselytize among blacks, and one slave caught going to church in Grenada was given 24 lashes.

In assessing the mutual dependency of sugar and the slave trade and its overall economic impact, it would be a mistake to focus too narrowly on the calculations of the plantation owner, crucial though they were. Only by bringing profitable cargo into the New World on a large scale and a regular basis could the European sugar market be developed, since merchant fleets would not risk the journey across the Atlantic with empty hulls, and the sugar islands were hardly major consumers of manufactured products. Thus slaves were vital not only to the production of the tropical economy but also to its marketing process. If black mortality in the New World had not exceeded reproduction, a saturation level would have been reached, and the slave trade would have died. From this perspective, the sugar market could only have been sustained by genocide.

Much attention has been focused on the economic marginality of the slavers themselves. It is true that while the opportunity for great profit existed, the risk of great loss was also present, as on any long-distance voyage. The

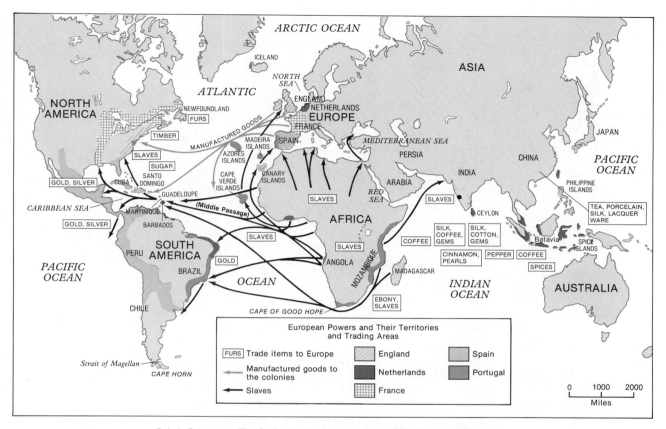

24.1 Overseas Trade in the Seventeenth and Eighteenth Centuries

significance of the triangular trade itself, however, did not lie in the reliability of profit in any single component but in the profit-generating capacity of the whole. The existence of the trade meant a steady demand for shipping; the feeding and clothing of millions of slaves was a major stimulus to textiles and agriculture. The capital spinoff into the European economy was therefore of considerable importance; and it was with the mechanization of the textile industry, financed in part by the slave trade, that the Industrial Revolution began.

LIVERPOOL IN THE AGE OF SLAVERY

Even before industrialization, the influx of slave-generated wealth was very evident. Liverpool, an English coastal town on the Irish Sea with a population of barely 500 in the sixteenth century and only 28 streets in the late seventeenth, became the chief slave port of Europe, carrying at its height almost two-thirds of the British and nearly half of the total European slave trade. The town's rise to success was in part the result of the bankrupting of the London slave merchants in the South Sea Bubble of 1720. Enterprising Liverpudlians soon took over from them, taking advantage of the port's westerly location. The profitable War of the Austrian Succession in the 1740s also enabled trade, in the words of a local merchant, "to spread her golden wings." By 1750 a flotilla of nearly 200 ships directly served the slave trade, and four years later a splendid new exchange opened on Castle Street—as if to emphasize the alliance of commerce and government, it also housed the town hall. No expense was spared, as the town fathers sought to emulate the Greek columns and the imposing cupola of the Royal Exchange in London. A week of boat races, public breakfasts, and balls celebrated its opening. An observatory and an academy of arts came soon after, a regular stagecoach run to London, and in 1768 representation in Parliament, the final mark of new status.

Fourteen banks graced the town by midcentury as well, none with fewer than £200,000 in assets. Most banks were founded by the slave merchants, who also operated their own insurance companies, collected the excise, and

◉ A Slave's Experience ◉

Olaudah Equiano (c. 1745–1797), an Ibo born in eastern Nigeria,
near Benin, was abducted into slavery at the age of 10. He survived a
transatlantic crossing and a series of masters, eventually bought his
own freedom, worked as a barber, a domestic servant, and a sailor,
and in 1789 published, in English, a two-volume memoir of his life as
a slave, from which these excerpts are taken.

The first object which saluted my eyes when I arrived on the coast was the sea, and a slave ship which was then riding at anchor and waiting for its cargo. These filled me with astonishment, which was soon converted into terror when I was carried on board. I was immediately handled and tossed up to see if I were sound by some of the crew, and I was now persuaded that I had gotten into a world of bad spirits and that they were going to kill me. Their complexions too differing so much from ours, their long hair and the language they spoke (which was very different from any I had ever heard) united to confirm me in this belief. . . . When I looked round the ship too and saw a large furnace or copper boiling and a multitude of black people of every description chained together, every one of their countenances expressing dejection and sorrow, I no longer doubted of my fate. . . .

The stench of the hold while we were on the coast was so intolerably loathsome that it was dangerous to remain there for any time, and some of us had been permitted to stay on the deck for the fresh air; but now that the whole ship's cargo were confined together it became absolutely pestilential. The closeness of the place and the heat of the climate, added to the number in the ship, which was so crowded that each had scarcely room to run himself, almost suffocated us. This produced copious perspirations, so that the air soon became unfit for respiration from a variety of loathsome smells, and brought on a sickness among the slaves, of which many died. . . . This wretched situation was again aggravated by the galling of the chains, now become insupportable, and the filth of the tubs, into which the children often fell and were almost suffocated. The shrieks of the women and the groans of the dying rendered the whole a scene of horror almost inconceivable.

Source: P. Edwards, ed., *Equiano's Travels: His Autobiography* (New York: Praeger, 1967), pp. 25, 28–29.

guaranteed the municipal finances. They were, in fact, Liverpool. The city maintained its traditional trade with Ireland, chiefly in cattle, and it produced pottery, glassware, and salt. But these activities were dwarfed by the slave and sugar trade and gradually strangled by it. The banks, the warehouses, and the dockyards formed a commercial trinity that dominated the city's life as it did its skyline. Until 1772 it was also possible to see slaves in their iron collars being sold for domestic use at the city market, but in that year Lord Chief Justice Mansfield ruled in the court of King's Bench that no person could be subjected to slavery in Britain. Liverpool's slave market disappeared, but not its slave trade; it was to be 61 years before the slaves in Britain's colonies were likewise freed.

From Liverpool the prosperity produced by the slave and sugar trade spread visibly across the English landscape in the form of great country houses and the mer-

chant mansions of London and Bath. As early as 1729 the pamphleteer Joshua Gee noted that "all the great increase in our treasure proceeds chiefly from the labor of negroes in the plantations." But conspicuous consumption by the rich was not the principal result of the commerce in human lives. The new wealth was to lay the ground for Britain's rise to world power.

From the sixteenth century on, the European economy had become significantly entwined for the first time with that of a region thousands of miles away that provided it with the means of capital expansion, first through the importation of bullion from Spanish America and later primarily through the trade in sugar and slaves. The importance of this new global economy was great. So, too, was its human cost. It destroyed by direct or indirect means much of the native population of two continents and substantially depleted that of a third.

Liverpool was the chief port of terminus for the sugar and slave trades, and it prospered accordingly. The corner of Tithebarn Street is shown, with the back of the Town Hall at right. Behind the hall, space is being cleared for the erection of a new commercial exchange, in which the man with the wheelbarrow is presumably employed. [Herdman Collection, Liverpool Public Library]

The First Age of Global War

"It is a notorious fact that the history of colonial expansion is also the history of incessant warfare," the historian Walter Dorn observed.[2] The wars of the early modern period, particularly in what has sometimes been called the era of the second Hundred Years' War (1689–1815), were fought for a variety of reasons, including religion, dynastic rivalry, and positional advantage on the European continent. Increasingly, however, the major wars of Europe involved conflict in four overseas areas as well—North America, the West Indies, Africa, and India. By the time of the Seven Years' War (1756–1763) these external theaters had become more important than the European struggle itself.

The wars of Europe were, then, in part the effect of expansion; but they were a cause of it as well. The use of firearms and cannon in European warfare became decisive between 1460 and 1540, and during that time iron production rose by as much as 500 percent and copper by even more. The mechanization of war made it the monopoly of the state. As heavy field pieces replaced horses, armor, and crossbows as the major capital investment in warfare, private noblemen could no longer afford the personal armies that had been the hallmark (and often the bane) of the late medieval period. A modern arsenal containing furnaces, forges, foundries, gunpowder mills, and saltpeter shops might employ, as the French arsenal at St. Étienne in the early seventeenth century did, 700 workers or more. The building of warships, which carried two or three banks of cannon and often exceeded 1,000 tons, was an even more complex activity, requiring specialized skills and materials that might come from halfway around the world. The state alone possessed the resources for such investment, and this in turn spurred its own growth. The increasing scale of warfare, the expanding role of the state, and the widening arc of commerce

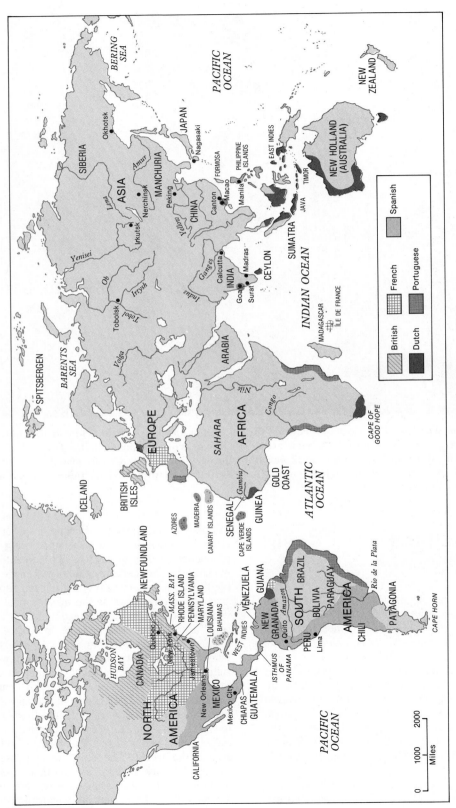

24.2 The Expansion of Europe, 1715

were all part of the dynamic that made Europe's wars, as well as its economic activity, worldwide.

The New Balance of Power

The wars of Louis XIV marked a turning point in the European balance of power. France remained, as it would for the next century and a half, the dominant land power on the Continent. Its main rival, however, was no longer Spain, its great antagonist in the Thirty Years' War, or Austria, the chief barrier to its expansion in Germany, Italy, and the Low Countries, but Britain. Britain owed its new international prominence to its naval supremacy, its commercial wealth, and, perhaps most important, its access to that wealth through the working partnership of the landed elite, the financial community, and the organs of government.

Walpole, Britain's First Prime Minister

The stability of the new system was epitomized by the man who made it function for two decades, Sir Robert Walpole (1676–1745). The son of a prosperous Norfolk squire, Walpole rose steadily through the Whig hierarchy. He sat in Parliament for 40 years, held high office for 30, and for some 20— from 1722 to 1742—was the effective ruler of the country, the first prime minister of Britain in fact if not in name.

Walpole grasped the fact that the Glorious Revolution of 1688 had settled the basic issues of seventeenth-century British politics, creating a limited monarchy firmly subject to the wishes of the landed gentry. What remained, with rising prosperity and a stable dynasty on the throne, was to organize the division of spoils. Walpole's command of the system was based on his control of its three major components, the crown, Parliament, and patronage. The support of the first two Hanoverian kings, George I (1714–1727) and George II (1727–1760), was his anchor. He consulted their wishes, cultivated their prejudices, and flattered their mistresses; through them, he consolidated and controlled all honors, promotions, offices, and contracts, scrupulously rewarding his friends and punishing his enemies. This monopoly of favor enabled him in turn to ensure a comfortable majority in Parliament, for although the principle of ministerial responsibility—that the king's ministry must retain a working majority in the House of Commons—was not firmly established until the nineteenth century, it was already true that no government could survive for long without such support. That this support was based more or less openly on bribery and corruption did not bother Walpole. If corruption was required to ensure stable government and general prosperity, he argued, then corruption was a political virtue, if not a moral one.

The Triumph of the Elite

The real stability of the British system, however, was in the unchallenged dominance of the landed elite, particu-

In this contemporary print, the way to favor under Sir Robert Walpole's rule is graphically illustrated. [Culver Pictures]

larly its uppermost stratum. The government of eighteenth-century Britain, superficial political scrimmaging apart, rested securely with some 400 families, who independently controlled one-quarter of the arable land in the country. This striking concentration of ownership, which had been achieved largely since the Restoration of 1660, was the result of several interrelated factors. Large estates were protected from partition by laws that required that they be passed on to a single heir, who was prohibited from selling off parcels except under strict conditions. The value of land had been enhanced by increased productivity, in part the result of agricultural improvements, in part of laws that encouraged the cultivation of grain for export. This spurred the process known as enclosure, by which common grazing land and individual farm plots were fenced in by wealthy landowners armed with sheriffs' writs or private acts of Parliament. By 1840 fully 6 million acres had been enclosed in this fashion, bringing another quarter of Britain's farmland under elite control. The small independent farmer or yeoman, once the backbone of English agriculture, had become an endangered species by the eighteenth century and virtually extinct by the nineteenth, disappearing into the mass of wage laborers and tenant farmers who worked the great estates of the few.

Such a far-reaching and traumatic centralization of ownership might have been expected to produce unrest and even rebellion, yet Britain's countryside was for most of the eighteenth century among the most peaceful in Europe. This was partly due to the unique nature of its aristocracy. Only about 200 families in England held formal titles of nobility (as opposed to half a million each in France and Spain), and the only distinct advantage such titles conveyed was the right to sit in the House of Lords. It entailed no other significant legal privileges such as marked off Continental elites from the mass of the population, particularly exemption from taxation. Indeed, the difference between Britain and the other European monarchies might be summarized by saying that whereas on the Continent the landed elite tolerated royal control of taxation on the condition that it fall chiefly on others, in Britain it accepted the burden of taxation in return for the right to control it through Parliament.

The absence of a status system based primarily on graded titles of nobility and distinguished by special privileges meant that wealth itself was the basic criterion for membership in the British elite. This encouraged entrepreneurship and investment in mining, industry, canal building, and urban real estate as well as colonization and agriculture, and the ever-expanding wealth of this elite provided the sinews of empire. At the same time, it was a true governing class that controlled and unified the instruments of social order from the pay of the local justice of the peace to the provision of the Royal Navy. Few aristocracies in history had exercised so clear and thorough a dominion over their societies as that of eighteenth-century Britain.

France Under Louis XV

The situation of France was quite different. Louis XIV had devoted much of his energy to reducing the nobility to political impotence. He had worked all his life to create a system of government dependent on the will and capacity of the sovereign, only to leave his throne to a 5-year-old boy, Louis XV. Power devolved upon his elder cousin, Philip, duke of Orléans, as regent. With a nobleman heading the government, the aristocracy reasserted its claims to power, with disastrous results for central authority. By 1723 Louis XV had proclaimed his majority; but in a real sense he never grew up. Though rather bright and served by some able ministers—Cardinal Fleury, the duke of Choiseul, and René de Maupeou—he lacked the discipline and the character to impose his will on the government, and so faint was his impress on the history of his long reign (1715–1774) that the age is better remembered for a shrewd and vivacious royal mistress, Madame de Pompadour, than for its titular ruler. Without forceful leadership, the bureaucracy became slack and unresponsive, the intendants pursued policies at variance with those of the government, and the parlements openly defied the crown, supporting opposition groups such as the Jansenists and successfully resisting all efforts to raise taxes.

Taxation and Finance

A pair of similar incidents early in the reigns of Louis XV and George I demonstrated the growing difference between the pace of development in France and Britain. In 1716, while Orléans was regent, he gave permission to a Scottish speculator, John Law (1671–1729), to found a private bank whose notes could be used as legal tender to pay taxes. Orléans hoped in this way to centralize tax collection and to avoid the rapacity of the tax farmers, who even under Louis XIV had kept a third of all receipts for themselves. At the same time, Law was given a chartered monopoly of all overseas French commerce, the Mississippi Company, whose profits were to secure the bank's notes. Wild reports of gold and diamonds in French Louisiana, some deliberately fabricated, drove the price of Mississippi stock up from 500 to 15,000 livres. By 1720 Law had been appointed controller general of France, with virtual control of the nation's economy. His fall was as dramatic as his rise. The profits of overseas trade lagged behind expectations, and the rumor of a bonanza in Louisiana was soon dispelled. Mississippi stock plummeted, Law's bank collapsed, and by the end of the year he had fled the country, leaving French finances as before in the hands of the tax farmers.

What the French had sought in Law's bank was to emulate the success of the Bank of England in providing regular, low-interest credit to the crown. It failed in part because of opposition by the tax farmers, who preferred to siphon off one-third of French tax revenues rather than settle for the 8 percent per annum paid by the Bank of England, and in part because of the suspicion of the nobility that Law's scheme was simply a device to abolish their tax privileges. In Britain, where the landed elite controlled the taxing power and taxes were collected directly instead of through farmers, there were no vested interests to overcome or privileges to be protected.

What did concern Britons, however, was the size of the public debt, which had risen from £644,000 in 1688 to £54 million in 1713. This represented more than the gross annual product of the economy, and many Englishmen wondered how they could owe more than they were worth. It was at this point that the South Sea Company, a trading company set up to exploit the South American slave trade, put forward an audacious proposal to assume the entire public debt from the Bank of England on the strength of its anticipated profits and to pay it off by establishing a sinking fund equivalent to 2 percent of the value of the debt per year. For a time it appeared that the company might replace the bank as the leading credit institution of the country. Its board of directors included prominent Whig politicians, and George I himself consented to become its honorary head. But as with Law's Mississippi Company, the profits on which its scheme was

to be capitalized proved illusory, and after a similar run-up, the value of its stock collapsed in the spring of 1720. The company went into receivership, and a number of smaller firms set up by using its stock as collateral failed, ruining thousands of investors. Thus the first two great financial panics of modern times occurred almost simultaneously in Paris and London. Their consequences, however, were far different. The Bank of England, having weathered the challenge to its supremacy, emerged stronger than ever, and the expanding British economy absorbed the effects of the panic with relative ease. In France, the failure of Law's bank set back the development of modern credit for 70 years, condemning the crown to an escalating spiral of debt.

The Wars of Midcentury

Europe enjoyed a generation of relative calm after the Peace of Utrecht. But the death of two kings brought war again in 1740. Frederick II succeeded to the throne of Prussia, where his father, Frederick William I, had drilled and perfected an army he had never used. Maria Theresa (1740–1780) became empress of Austria and queen of Hungary, the first female sovereign in the history of the

◎ The First Stock Market Crash ◎

The rage for speculation and the lust for profit, which at its height inflated stock values on the London Exchange to five times the estimated cash reserves of the entire continent of Europe, was well described by a contemporary observer, William Chetwood. Shortly after, the South Sea Bubble collapsed, ruining thousands and threatening the Bank of England itself.

The whims of the stocks in this kingdom [are] of late so far cultivated and improved from a foreign example [Law's Mississippi Company in France], that one might reasonably conclude the numerous inhabitants of this great metropolis had for the most part deserted their stations, business, and occupations; and given up all pretensions to industry, in pursuit of an imaginary profit.

If your occasions are never so urgent for a mercer, a tailor, a shoemaker, etc., they are nowhere to be met with but at the Royal Exchange. If you resort to any public office or place of business, the whole enquiry is, How are the stocks? If you are at a coffee-house, the only conversation turns on the stocks. . . . If you repair to a tavern, the edifying subject (especially to a philosopher) is the South Sea Company; if you wait on a lady of quality, you'll find her hastening to the House of Intelligence in Exchange Alley. . . . Even smocks are deposited to help make up the security for cash; jewels pawned to raise money for the purchase of ruin—and, perhaps, wives and daughters have been mortgaged for the very same purpose.

Source: L. Melville, *The South Sea Bubble* (London: O'Connor, 1921), pp. 78–79.

Habsburg dynasty. Her father, Charles VI (1711–1740), had spent the better part of his reign trying to get the princes of Europe to recognize her right to succeed him through the document known as the Pragmatic Sanction. Their promises were worthless. Charles Albert, the elector of Bavaria, immediately claimed the Austrian throne. Bavaria, in turn, was considered a mere stalking-horse for Austria's arch-rival, France. At the same time, Frederick II sought to take advantage of Austria's disarray by seizing the rich province of Silesia, which Prussia had long coveted. This was the signal for a general conflict, the War of the Austrian Succession (1740–1748).

The war soon turned into another chapter in the great imperial war of the century between Britain and France. Britain entered it on the side of Austria, while France supported Prussia and Bavaria. The Anglo-French conflict once again extended to North America, where fighting ranged from the isthmus of Panama to Cape Breton Island off the coast of French Canada. In Europe the chief battles were fought in Flanders, where the French sought to dislodge Austria. In the end, France's success on land was checked by Britain's supremacy at sea. The Treaty of Aix-la-Chapelle (1748) restored Britain and France to their original positions, as the British surrendered Fort Louisburg, taken by colonial militia, in return for their trading station at Madras on the east coast of India. The only belligerent to come out ahead was Frederick of Prussia, who, having realized his objective in the conquest of Silesia, had dropped out of the war six years before.

The Seven Years' War

The absence of a clear winner ensured an early resumption of the conflict. The Seven Years' War (1756–1763) marked the decisive triumph of the British Empire over that of France on all fronts, in North America, Africa, and India. It also marked the end of the rivalry between Habsburg and Bourbon that had been the polestar of European politics for the previous 2½ centuries. This was the achievement of the brilliant, eccentric Count Wenzel von Kaunitz, who was to direct Austrian foreign policy until his death in 1794. Kaunitz' chief objective was the recovery of Silesia from Prussia. Austria's former allies, Britain and the Netherlands, had forced it to give up Silesia and to fight instead for Flanders, a policy that suited their interests but not Austria's. The solution was simple. In return for French troops and money against Prussia, Austria would cede Flanders, a territory it could neither usefully exploit nor properly defend. Thus the alignment of the previous war was completely reversed. All former friends were now enemies, all former enemies friends.

Kaunitz completed the diplomatic isolation of Prussia by entering into an alliance with Russia, which thus joined the European concert of powers for the first time. For five years Frederick fought a war of survival against apparently hopeless odds, earning the appellation "the

Great." Each year defeat seemed inevitable; each year—at Rossbach, Leuthen, Zorndorf, Leignitz, Torgau—he staved it off with a last-ditch victory. The toll on Prussia, fighting virtually alone against the three largest powers in Europe, was immense. The Prussian army was reduced from 150,000 in its first campaign to 90,000 in its last. Frederick himself despaired of the final outcome. "To tell the truth," he wrote a minister, "I believe all is lost. I will not survive the ruin of my country."

For Britain, too, the war at first went badly. The French began their drive into the Ohio valley in North America two years before the formal outbreak of hostilities in Europe. They built a line of forts to block British expansion in the region and repelled expeditionary forces sent against them under General Edward Braddock and the young colonial colonel, George Washington. While Indian raids harassed the British frontier, the French seized Oswego on Lake Ontario and captured the strategic Mediterranean island of Minorca when Admiral John Byng abandoned its defense. The British hanged Byng, "to encourage the other admirals," as Voltaire remarked dryly, and in June 1757 replaced the inept ministry of the duke of Newcastle with one headed by William Pitt (1708–1778).

Pitt, the son of a great merchant in the Indian trade, was a leader born for crisis. Magnificent in debate, possessed by his vision of Britain's imperial destiny, he had been for 20 years the most dominant personality in the House of Commons. Yet power had eluded him. Harsh and uncompromising, often ill and frequently unstable, he had none of Walpole's managerial skills, and George II despised him. In the crisis of 1757, however, no one else would do. For the next four years he ruled with almost dictatorial powers and brought Britain victory.

Pitt's strategy was to keep Frederick the Great in the field against the French and the Austrians while he applied Britain's naval superiority against France's North American empire and plundered its trade. In effect, while the French refought the Hundred Years' War in Flanders, Britain would fight for everything else. The French fleet was bottled up in Brest and Toulon and was destroyed at Quiberon Bay and at Lagos off the coast of Portugal when it attempted to break out. Relief expeditions to North America were turned back, and the sheer weight of numbers—the 13 colonies now had a combined population of 2.5 million, against only 70,000 permanent French settlers—told at last. The French forts on the Great Lakes and the St. Lawrence River fell, and the Ohio valley was evacuated. Quebec was captured after a daring campaign in 1759, and with the fall of Montreal in 1760, the last French army in North America surrendered. The West Indian island of Guadeloupe was taken too, as well as the African slaving stations of St. Louis and Gorée. French aggression also backfired in India, where the British found themselves after their victory at Plassey in 1757 not only in possession of the rich Carnatic coast but of the entire hinterland of Bengal.

Pitt resigned in 1761 when his cabinet balked at his plans to conquer the whole of the French West Indies. The Peace of Paris (1763) reflected the view of more cautious men that Britain could not hold on to all it had conquered (which now included Havana and Manila, taken from Spain in 1762) and that any attempt to do so would shortly provoke another war. Guadeloupe was restored, its sugar having proved a glut on the British market, and the French were permitted again to trade in India and to fish off Newfoundland, though not to maintain garrisons. Havana and Manila were returned to Spain in exchange for Florida. From his back bench seat, Pitt denounced the treaty as a betrayal of Britain's blood and treasure. Nonetheless, victory over France was complete and decisive. Britain had gained all of Canada, doubling the size of its American territories. France would never, as it seemed, pose a threat to its hegemony in the New World again. The significance of the unexpected British victory in India would prove even greater, as Britain's wealth provided much of the capital for the Industrial Revolution a generation later. If Britain had not achieved all that Pitt desired, it had accomplished more than anyone but Pitt would have thought possible.

With the hope of winning Flanders gone, the French deserted their Austrian allies. Russia too pulled out in 1762. With no hope of accomplishing alone what it had failed to do with two powerful allies, Austria reluctantly made peace with Prussia (1763). Frederick the Great retained Silesia, although it had cost him the near-destruction of his country to do so, and the remainder of his reign was spent largely in rebuilding it. The transfer of this single province from the Habsburg to the Hohenzollern crown was the only territorial result of two great wars in Europe. Those wars were the last to be fought over questions of dynastic succession and among the first to be fought for the high stakes of overseas empire.

The Birth of the American Republic

If the map of Europe had been little altered by the Seven Years' War, that of North America had been substantially redrawn by the British capture of Canada from France and

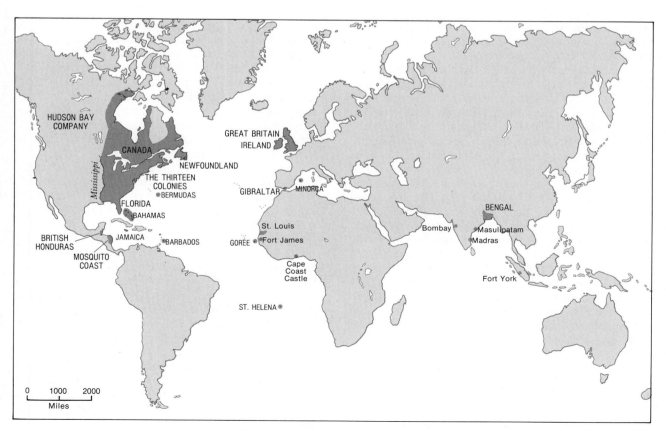

24.3 The British Empire in 1763

Florida from Spain. The British prepared to exploit and extend their new conquests, but they failed to take into account the existing colonies, whose inhabitants, themselves largely of English and Scots-Irish stock, had reached a point of economic and political maturity at which they were no longer prepared to subordinate their interests to those of the mother country, with which they had already begun aggressively to compete. The result was rebellion and the creation of the first independent nation in the New World, the United States of America.

The American Colonies and Britain

By 1763 the 13 colonies of the Atlantic seaboard had become an important market for British manufactures, and if they could not yet compete with the West Indian sugar islands in sheer profitability, their size and the potential for expansion opened up by the conquest of Canada ensured that they would eventually dominate Britain's American empire. Yet within 13 years those colonies would begin the first successful rebellion in the New World, within 13 more they would have established the first indigenous non-European republic in history, and little more than three decades later, with their example and in part with their support, the whole of the Western Hemisphere south of Canada would have thrown off the European yoke brought in with the Spanish conquest.

In might be said with justice that the cause of the 13 colonies' rebellion was Britain's attempt actually to govern them. Until 1763 they had enjoyed an extraordinary degree of independence. Though theoretically subject to the British Parliament, they were exempt from British taxation and had their own assemblies, legal systems, and finances. Instead of serving the home economy as envisioned by mercantile theory, the colonists competed with British ships in the Newfoundland fisheries, built their own vessels in competition with British shipyards, and carried on a lively smuggling trade with the West Indies. The crown had made sporadic attempts between 1685 and 1714 to revoke colonial patents and charters with a view to governing the colonies more directly, but these had foundered on the refusal of Parliament to tamper with what it regarded as property rights. The American colonists saw this as a vindication of their autonomy. They considered themselves not a subject people but Britons with the same rights and entitlements as anyone living in Britain itself.

The crown viewed matters differently. It regarded the colonies as a dominion or possession, united to it like Ireland but distinct from the realm of Britain itself, which after 1707 had consisted of England, Wales, and Scotland. Ireland too had its own lawmaking assembly, the Irish Parliament, but its subservience to the acts of the British Parliament had been spelled out in the Declaratory Act of 1719. But whereas Ireland was a plantation economy in which an Anglo-Scottish minority ruled a subject population of Catholic tenantry, the Middle Atlantic and New England colonies in particular consisted largely of independent freeholders and a mobile class of wage earners. And while Ireland was geographically in Britain's shadow, the American colonies were 3,000 miles away.

America's distance from Britain made it difficult not only to control but also to defend. Even after the defeat of the French, the western frontiers were insecure, as the general rising of Indian tribes under Pontiac in May 1763 made clear. In theory, the colonial militias could have looked to their own defense, but their performance in the war against the French had been reluctant and halfhearted. Moreover, the British government was anxious to prevent uncontrolled settlement beyond the Appalachian Mountains, which was certain to provoke further Indian attacks. Accordingly, it placed the trans-Appalachian west under direct royal control, although several of the colonies had already claimed the Mississippi River as their border. At the same time, it proposed to maintain a permanent army of 10,000 to guard the frontier and levied new taxes, notably on all stamped or licensed paper, to help pay for it.

Protest and Rebellion

The British were quite unprepared for the explosion of protest that greeted these acts. Rioters burned the official stamps and formed resistance groups called the Sons of Liberty, merchants boycotted British wares, the colonial assemblies passed resolutions denouncing taxation without representation in Parliament, and nine colonies sent representatives to a Stamp Act Congress in New York. The British reacted uncertainly. On the one hand, they affirmed parliamentary control of the colonies, arguing that the colonists were "virtually" represented in Parliament in the same way as Britons at home who lived in boroughs that lacked a parliamentary franchise. On the other hand, they repealed the Stamp Act and reduced the much hated customs levy on sugar to a token penny per gallon.

Britain's policy continued to vacillate in the next several years, in part because of a rapid turnover of ministries until 1770, when the new king, George III (1760–1820), finally settled on the conciliatory but ineffective Frederick Lord North to serve as prime minister. The American colonies were importing almost £2 million more in British goods by 1770 than they were shipping back across the Atlantic. If they could not recoup that sum in trade with the West Indies, legally or illegally, their economy, particularly that of the mercantile Northeast, could not survive. Britain's vague but alarming gestures in the direction of new taxes and import duties as well as its sweeping assertions of jurisdiction over colonial trade threatened America's economic viability. Concern for prosperity merged with concern for legal rights. The closing of the western frontier and the policing of the Caribbean menaced two freedoms that Americans valued highly indeed: freedom of movement and freedom of trade.

A clash between British soldiers and a mob in Boston that left five colonists dead sobered both sides momentarily. North withdrew all British taxes except that on tea and announced that no further ones would be levied. When, however, in 1773 he permitted the East India Company to dispose of a tea surplus in America, it was promptly interpreted as a new attempt to raise revenue. The Bostonians dumped the company's tea in their harbor. North responded by closing it and imposing martial law on Massachusetts. At the same time, Parliament passed the Quebec Act, extending the Canadian frontier southward to the Ohio River. Unrelated in British eyes, these actions signaled a new campaign of repression to the colonials. As a sympathetic Englishman, Edmund Burke, observed, "Any of these innumerable regulations, perhaps, would not have alarmed alone; some might be thought reasonable; the multitude struck them with terror."[3]

Events now moved swiftly. An assembly of all the colonies calling itself the Continental Congress met in Philadelphia in September 1774. Although it still acknowledged the authority of the crown, its very meeting was regarded as an act of rebellion in Britain. Sporadic fighting broke out in Massachusetts in the spring of 1775, and in May the Continental Congress voted to raise an army in defense of the colonies. Much of the hardening on the British side came from George III himself. Burke and others opposed the drift to war, but North, who lacked the stomach to fight it, found himself without a politically acceptable way to back down.

The Revolutionary War

On July 4, 1776, the Continental Congress declared the independence of the 13 colonies in a document, drafted largely by Thomas Jefferson of Virginia, whose tone was more of sorrow than anger. The colonials had little choice but resistance or surrender. Strong forces had already landed from Canada, with reinforcements from Britain. Inferior in numbers and training, with British troops in possession of Boston, New York, and Philadelphia, the colonial army fought at first merely to survive. But in October 1777 a British army unit of 7,000 men under General John Burgoyne, intended as part of a pincer movement to cut the northern colonies in two, blundered into a trap in the wilderness near Saratoga, New York, and was forced to surrender.

This defeat changed the character of the war. Until Saratoga, France and Spain had limited themselves to offering aid and financial credits to the rebels. Now they entered the war actively, France in 1778 and Spain a year later. America's war for independence had become an international struggle in which Britain found itself rapidly isolated. Control of not only the Atlantic seaboard but also the West Indies, the Mediterranean, and even India was at stake. Gibraltar withstood a three-year siege (1779–1782) that was, militarily, the largest operation of the war, and a French thrust at Jamaica was repelled by Admiral George Rodney in the great naval Battle of the Saints (1782). But the French fleet, temporarily gaining control of the waters off Virginia, forced the surrender of another large British army at Yorktown in October 1781.

With their empire threatened on all fronts, the British could no longer continue the luckless and draining struggle in America. The independence of the colonies was recognized in the Treaty of Paris (1783); Minorca and East Florida were returned to Spain, and the French recovered some West Indian islands and their former strongholds in Senegal. A shattered Britain was left to redirect its imperial energies toward India and the Far East, where in 1788 it began to colonize Australia. The French could now reflect that the loss of Canada had at least been balanced by the separation of the 13 colonies from Britain. But victory would prove dear. France's habitually insolvent treasury, taxed by the demands of another major war while still burdened with the debts of previous ones, soon tottered into bankruptcy, bringing the French state, and with it the entire Old Regime in Europe, to crisis.

Forming a Nation

Having won their independence, the 13 colonies set about the task of forming themselves into a nation. The Declaration of Independence had boldly asserted that "all men are created equal"—a revolutionary sentiment in a world ruled by monarchy and nobles, although America had never had a hereditary aristocracy—yet the new nation was clearly dominated by a landed and mercantile elite, and one-fifth of its total population (one-third in the plantation states of the south) consisted of black slaves. But the revolution liberalized white American society to a significant degree. Primogeniture and entail, which protected large estates from division, were swept away; Anglican and Congregationalist churches lost their privileged positions, paving the way for the complete separation of church and state that would be one of the most radical features of the American constitution; and the electoral franchise was widened in a number of states. These represented concessions won by workers, farmers, frontiersmen, and religious dissidents in return for support of the rebellion.

Though America was far from having achieved true egalitarianism and though the cloud of slavery, already troubling to many, hung over its future, it was incontestably the most democratic state in the world and the first since the short-lived English Commonwealth of the 1650s to proclaim the sovereignty of the people, or at least those who were free and male. As such, it was a potent inspiration for reformers in Britain and elsewhere in the Old World, a unique experiment that embodied much of the advanced political thought of the century.

From Confederation to Commonwealth

At first the 13 states were individually sovereign entities that associated themselves loosely under the so-called Articles of Confederation. Each state had its own constitution, civil laws, militia, and currency. The Continental Congress continued as a national organ, but it lacked the power to tax or to raise an army and could order nothing without the approval of all 13 states. There were no central courts to resolve disputes between the states, most of which had rival territorial claims, and no agency existed to provide for common trade policy, diplomacy, and defense. As John Adams of Boston remarked, trying to provide for any collective interest was like trying to get 13 clocks to chime at once. In addition, the elites feared that continued popular pressure on weak state governments for political and economic reform would lead to anarchy. In 1786 farmers threatened by foreclosure rebelled in Massachusetts under a former militia captain, Daniel Shays. To men such as the Virginia patrician Edmund Randolph, Shays' rebellion was a perfect example of "the turbulence and follies of democracy."[4]

The result was a convention that met in Philadelphia in the summer of 1787 with the approval of the Continental Congress to amend the Articles of Confederation. The leading members of the convention, including George Washington (1732–1799), the former commander in chief of the revolutionary army, who chaired it, and James Madison (1751–1836), a brilliant young lawyer and fellow Virginian, scrapped the articles completely and, defiantly exceeding their mandate, devised an entirely new constitution. This created a new federal entity, the United States of America, with a bicameral legislature composed of a House of Representatives and a Senate empowered to levy taxes, raise an army, regulate commerce, fix a uniform national currency, and, in a sweeping grant of authority, "make all laws necessary and proper for carrying into execution" these powers. A strong executive was also provided, consisting of a president and vice-president, as well as the foundation of a national court system. In a frankly revolutionary gesture, the convention discarded the requirement that any act at the national level have unanimous consent, declaring that approval by any nine states would ratify the constitution. If there had been a national government worthy of the name, the actions of the convention would have constituted a coup 'd'état against it.

Historians of the American Revolution have been divided ever since the publication of Charles A. Beard's *Economic Interpretation of the Constitution* in 1913 over whether the U. S. constitution was a betrayal of the democratic promise of the new republic by a cabal of rich men anxious to protect their property through a strong government. Unquestionably, the new system reflected suspicion if not hostility toward popular democracy. It was warmly welcomed by the elites and viewed with skepticism by wage earners and small farmers. But the inconveniences of the Articles were real, and some of the more drastic proposals at the convention—such as the abolition of the states altogether and life terms for the president and the members of the Senate—were rejected. Madison, the constitution's most articulate defender, argued that no lesser degree of centralized authority would suffice to govern a state larger than any in Europe except Russia and larger than any republic in history. After turbulent debate, the constitution was ratified (in the event by every state), and the new republic was inaugurated in 1789 with George Washington as its first president.

American and Canadian Expansion

The United States contained 3 million persons at its first census in 1790, including 600,000 Afro-American slaves. Approximately three times as many American Indians were dispersed within its borders and across the remainder of the North American continent. The new nation was expansionist from the start. As early as 1787 plans were laid in the Northwest Ordinance for the development of new states in the territory west of the Alleghenies, and new land was systematically acquired, by purchase (Louisiana, Florida, Alaska), annexation (Texas), settlement and negotiation (Oregon), and conquest (New Mexico, California). By the mid-nineteenth century Americans had fulfilled what they called their "manifest destiny" of becoming a transcontinental power with a larger territorial mass than any other nation save Russia and China.

The chief obstacle to the expansion of the United States was the native Amerindian population. Although less sophisticated than the Mayans, Aztecs, and Incas of pre-Columbian America, the Indians of North America were far from primitive: they farmed as well as hunted, formed complex political and commercial networks, and often lived in towns. The Iroquois Confederation under Pontiac had allied with the French in an effort to resist British expansion during the Seven Years' War, and 50 years later the Shawnee chieftain Tecumseh (1768–1813) allied with the British during the Anglo-American War of 1812 to resist the United States. Tecumseh dreamed of a united Indian nation strong enough to drive whites off the continent altogether, but the withdrawal of the British ended all practicable hopes of resistance. The Indians were largely decimated by war, forced migration, disease, and starvation, and by 1890 only a million were left in the territorial United States.

Visiting the United States in the 1830s, the French observer Alexis de Tocqueville ventured the bold prediction that the United States would have a population of 100 million within 100 years and would be, with Russia, the great power of the twentieth century. America, Tocque-

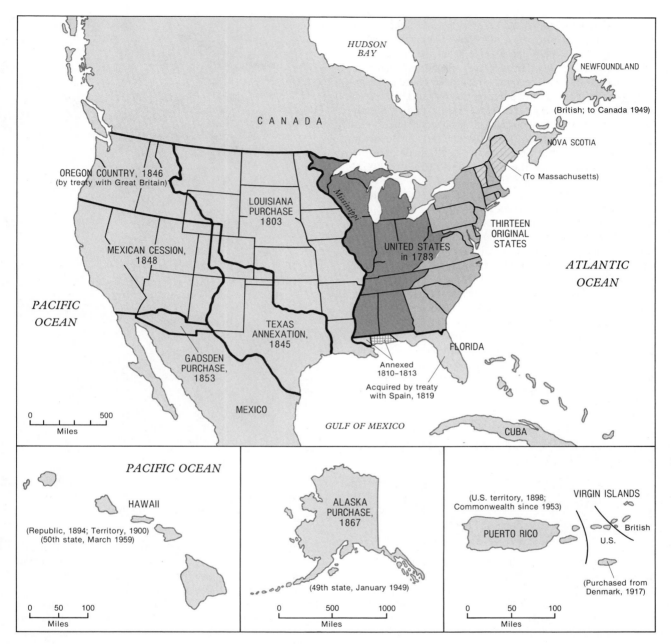

24.4 The Expansion of the United States

ville asserted, represented the triumph of equality and of the democratic revolution that he believed was destined to sweep the globe. By almost every yardstick, the new society appeared to be a success: "While all the nations of Europe have been ravaged by civil strife," he wrote, "the American people alone in the civilized world have remained pacific. Almost the whole of Europe has been convulsed by revolutions; America has not even suffered from riots."[5] But sectional antagonisms between the urban north and the plantation society of the south, particularly over the issue of the westward expansion of slavery, undermined the seeming tranquillity of the Union. By 1861 it collapsed, following the secession of the ten southern states, in a civil war that left more than 600,000 dead.

Many former Loyalists—supporters of the British cause in the American Revolution—had fled to Canada at the conclusion of that war. The British, attempting to deal with a still preponderantly French population, divided Canada into two jurisdictions in 1791. English-speaking Upper Canada, the future province of Ontario, retained English laws and institutions, while French-speaking Lower Canada, now Quebec, kept French law, seigneurial land tenures, and an officially recognized Catholic church. An invasion by the United States during the War of 1812 united the inhabitants of both Canadas briefly, but a steady stream of immigrants from Britain aroused French fears of cultural submergence. Following the Durham Report in 1839, Britain reunited Upper and Lower Canada over the latter's opposition, and the British North America Act of 1867 created the Dominion of Canada, a fully self-governing entity within the British Empire. This voluntary granting of independence, called "devolution," was to be applied later to Australia (1901), New Zealand (1907), the Union of South Africa (1910), India and Pakistan (1947), and the other former colonies in the Caribbean, Africa, and Asia that remain associated in what is today the British Commonwealth of Nations.

Canada expanded rapidly westward after 1867, linking both oceans by rail in 1885. Comparable in size to the United States, its population has never been more than a tenth as large, with most of it clustered in the more temperate coastal regions and the southern plains. Generally stable and prosperous, its chief problems have been intercommunal tensions with the French-speaking minority of Quebec and the economic and cultural dominance of the United States.

The Abolition of the Slave Trade and the Emancipation of Spanish America

The last quarter of the eighteenth century witnessed a revulsion against the Atlantic slave trade. Testimony before the British Parliament in 1788 laid bare the inhuman conditions under which millions of slaves had been transported, and revolutionary France in the 1790s found slavery incompatible with its professions of universal brotherhood. The slaves, for their part, were unwilling to wait for the enlightenment of their masters; a major rebellion broke out in Jamaica in 1760, and in 1791 half a million blacks under Toussaint L'Ouverture drove the French out of Haiti. At the same time, the profitability of the slave trade declined sharply with the collapse of sugar prices in the 1790s. The framers of the American constitution agreed to abolish the slave trade after 1807, and Britain outlawed it as well in that year, soon to be followed by most other European states. Slavery itself, however, remained legal in the British Empire until 1833, in the United States until 1863, and in Brazil and Cuba until 1886 and 1888, respectively. The slave trade continued to flourish

Toussaint L'Ouverture, the leader of the second successful colonial rebellion in the Americas and the first great black revolutionary of modern times. [Mansell Collection]

illegally for most of the nineteenth century, and a British commission reported in 1844 that more slaves were being transported than at any time in the previous century.

What doomed the slave trade—at least in the West Indies, where the advanced economies of Britain and France predominated—was the obsolescence of the old colonial system itself. As the Scottish economist Adam Smith argued persuasively in *The Wealth of Nations* (1776), free trade was far more profitable to a state such as Britain than a rigid protectionism that tied down capital, engendered pointless wars, and leaked away profits in smuggling. With the loss of the 13 colonies by Britain and of Haiti by France, the futility of a closed labor and commercial system became apparent.

The economy of Spanish America had gradually been reorganized in response to pressures from the more advanced imperial powers, but politically it was as tightly ruled from Madrid as before. Despite earlier rebellions in Peru and Colombia and the spread of republican ideas among some of the Creole (American-born) class, however, disaffection was not widespread until disaster struck the mother country itself. That disaster was Napoleon's conquest of Spain in 1808. For the next six years the American colonies refused to recognize the occupation ruler, Joseph Bonaparte, and were left to fend for themselves. When the Bourbon ruler Ferdinand VII was restored in 1814, most of the colonies swore renewed allegiance to him. In the six years of Ferdinand's absence, however, they had come of age politically. Competing parties and improvised organs of government, or *juntas*, had been formed, the latter often based on extensions of the municipal councils traditionally dominated by Creoles. The experience of self-government had changed the chemistry between Spain and its colonies. When Ferdinand, blind to the new situation, attempted to reimpose royal government and commercial monopoly in its old form, there was widespread resentment.

❦
SIMÓN BOLÍVAR, THE LIBERATOR

Disillusionment with Ferdinand was exploited by republican nationalists, who had staged several abortive revolts during the interregnum of 1808–1814, notably in Mexico, Venezuela, and Argentina. Though formally professing loyalty to Spain, the Argentines refused to readmit the old royal officials and declared independence under their leader José de San Martín (1778–1850) in 1816. By 1821 San Martín had occupied Lima and declared Peru liberated. Royalist forces soon retook it, however, and the real work of revolution was left to another Creole leader, Simón Bolívar.

Bolívar was born in Caracas, Venezuela, in 1783, the fourth child of one of the oldest and wealthiest noble families in the city. Orphaned at an early age, Bolívar was fired as a young man by the republican ideals of the American and French revolutions. Like most Creole aristocrats, he completed his studies in Europe and was present in Paris when Napoleon was crowned emperor. He brought a young wife, Maria Teresa del Toro, back with him from Madrid, but she died of yellow fever. Bolívar kept his vow never to marry again, although it did not prevent him from enjoying a number of passionate love affairs.

Bolívar began his revolutionary career in an abortive uprising at Caracas in 1810, in which he played a leading role. After toying with the idea of accepting a commission in the British army in Spain, he raised a new rebel army, declaring war to the death against the Spanish empire. By

◎ Bolívar's Message to ◎ the Congress of Angostura

Simón Bolívar's message to the congress that had gathered in 1819 to consider a proposed constitution for the new state of Venezuela reflects the disillusionment he already felt for the revolution he had led and his foreboding for the future stability of the South American republics.

America, in separating from the Spanish monarchy, found herself in a situation similar to that of the Roman Empire when its enormous framework fell to pieces in the midst of the ancient world. Each Roman division then formed an independent nation in keeping with its location or interests; but this situation differed from America's in that those members proceeded to reestablish their former associations. We, on the contrary, do not even retain the vestiges of our original being. We are not Europeans; we are not Indians; we are but a mixed species of aborigines and Spaniards. Americans by birth and Europeans by law, we find ourselves engaged in a dual conflict: we are disputing with the natives for titles of ownership, and at the same time we are struggling to maintain ourselves in the country that gave us birth against the opposition of the invaders. Thus our position is most extraordinary and complicated. But there is more. As our role has always been strictly passive and our political existence nil, we find that our quest for liberty is now even more difficult of accomplishment; for we, having been placed in a state lower than slavery, had been robbed not only of our freedom but . . . we were deliberately kept in ignorance and cut off from the world in all matters relating to the science of government.

Source: V. Lecuna, comp., and H. A. Bierck, Jr., ed., *Selected Writings of Bolívar*, vol. 1 (Caracas: Banco de Venezuela, 1951), pp. 175–176.

Proud, imperious, and mercurial, Simón Bolívar liberated a continent from three centuries of foreign rule and lived to regret his own work. [Granger Collection]

January 1814 he had returned to Caracas, declaring Venezuela a republic with himself as its head. Rather than choosing a more conventional name as head of state, he adopted the title of "liberator," symbolizing his commitment to the freeing of all of New Granada. Driven out by the Spaniards six months later, he fled to Jamaica but returned to Venezuela in 1817 and, raising an army of native forces and British soldiers of fortune, staged a daring invasion of Colombia. By August 1819 the entire province was in his hands, and three months later he proclaimed a constitution for the United States of Colombia, including Venezuela, where the last pro-Spanish resistance was extinguished in 1821. Ecuador fell in 1822, and Peru was conquered in 1824.

Bolívar hoped to unite this entire area—virtually all of South America apart from Brazil, Argentina, and Chile—into a single great republic. His enemies attacked him for his apparently boundless ambition; "I am tired," he complained to Bernardo O'Higgins, the liberator of Chile, "of hearing men call me tyrant, that I wish to make myself King, Emperor, the Devil." But his brutal methods of conquest, the indiscipline of his armies, and his undoubted dictatorial tendencies ultimately defeated what remained a noble if tarnished dream. By his death in 1830 the provinces of what he called "Gran Colombia" had splintered again into their old imperial configurations. "He who serves a revolution," he wrote in one of his final letters, "ploughs the sea."

The End of Empire

Backward Brazil, a slave society with few cities worthy of the name, had an even more passive revolution. The regent John came to it in exile after Napoleon's conquest of Portugal, and when he attempted to recall his son Pedro home again in 1822, the Brazilians refused to let him go, raising him to the position of emperor and driving Portuguese troops out of the country. In the viceroyalty of New Spain, a rebellion that had broken out in Mexico in 1810 under the leadership of a Creole priest, Father Hidalgo, was brought to completion in 1821 by a renegade royalist, Agustín de Iturbide, who proclaimed himself emperor. The remaining provinces of New Spain—Honduras, Nicaragua, San Salvador, and Costa Rica—all became independent at the same time, rejecting union with Mexico or each other.

Within ten years Spain had been divested of an empire it had ruled with remarkable equanimity for three centuries, retaining only Cuba and Puerto Rico of its former possessions in the New World. Unlike the newly fledged United States of America, Spain's colonies were neither prepared for independence nor particularly desirous of it. External events had weakened Spain's grip on the New World, and when it attempted to reimpose it without suitable consideration for the developments that had taken place in the interim, it was easily shaken off. The Spanish were never able to send large forces to combat the rebels, and the wars of liberation were essentially fought between native loyalists and republicans. The factor that tipped the balance in favor of the latter was the support of the British, who, seeking to break up Spain's commercial monopolies for good and for all, permitted irregular land and naval forces to assist Bolívar and San Martín openly and threw up a virtual blockade against the feeble Spanish navy. Britain, having lost its own most important American colonies in a bitter and protracted war, thus emerged, ironically, as the patron of liberation. But the new societies of Central and South America, where a 20 percent white minority continued to perpetuate oligarchic rule over a majority population of native and mixed (*mestizo*) blood, subsided into a period of political oppression, governmental instability, and economic exploitation from which they began to emerge only in the twentieth century.

24.5 Latin American Independence

The colonies of the New World became a critical element in the advanced European economies of the eighteenth century, and the character of European warfare was gradually reshaped by the struggle for possession of them. By the end of the first quarter of the nineteenth century, most of those colonies had gained their independence, and what remained in European hands—Canada and most of the West Indies—had become relatively insignificant in economic terms.

Nevertheless, the wealth derived from them was a crucial factor in the development of the new global economy and of capitalist enterprise, particularly in Britain. The transportation of millions of blacks across the Atlantic constituted *the largest involuntary migration in human history up to this time, and their settlement throughout North and South America profoundly altered the demographic and social structure of the New World.*

Notes

1. R. Davis, *The Rise of the Atlantic Economies* (Ithaca, N.Y.: Cornell University Press, 1973), p. 43.
2. W. D. Dorn, *Competition for Empire, 1740–1763* (New York: Harper, 1940), p. 13.
3. D. K. Fieldhouse, *The Colonial Empires* (New York: Delacorte Press, 1967), p. 109.
4. W. U. Solberg, ed., *The Federal Convention and the Formation of the Union* (Indianapolis: Bobbs-Merrill, 1958), p. xc.
5. A. de Tocqueville, *Democracy in America* (New York: Anchor Books, 1969), p. xiv.

Suggestions for Further Reading

Brown, P. D. *William Pitt, Earl of Chatham: The Great Commoner*. London: Allen & Unwin, 1978.
Butler, R. *Choiseul*. New York: Oxford University Press, 1981.
Curtin, P. *The Atlantic Slave Trade: A Census*. Madison: University of Wisconsin Press, 1969.
Davis, D. B. *The Problem of Slavery in the Age of Revolution*. Ithaca, N.Y.: Cornell University Press, 1966.
de Vries, J. *The Economy of Europe in an Age of Crisis, 1600–1750*. Cambridge: Cambridge University Press, 1976.
Dickson, P. G. M. *The Financial Revolution in England: A Study in the Development of Public Credit, 1688–1756*. London: Macmillan, 1967.
Dorn, W. D. *Competition for Empire, 1740–1763*. New York: Harper, 1940.
Fieldhouse, D. K. *The Colonial Empires: A Comparative Survey from the Eighteenth Century*. New York: Delacorte Press, 1967.
Fox-Genovese, E., and Genovese, E. D. *Fruits of Merchant Capital: Slavery and Bourgeois Property in the Rise and Expansion of Capitalism*. New York: Oxford University Press, 1983.
Frank, A. G. *World Accumulation, 1492–1789*. New York: Monthly Review Press, 1978.
Heckscher, E. *Mercantilism*. New York: Macmillan, 1955.
Lynch, J. *The Spanish American Revolutions, 1808–1826*. London: Weidenfeld & Nicolson, 1973.
McDonald, F. *We the People: The Economic Origins of the Constitution*. Chicago: University of Chicago Press, 1958.
McKeown, T. *The Modern Rise of Population*. New York: Academic Press, 1976.
Madariaga, S. de. *Bolívar*. New York: Farrar, Straus & Cudahy, 1956.
Mintz, S. W. *Sweetness and Power: The Place of Sugar in Modern History*. New York: Viking, 1985.
Morgan, E. S. *Birth of the Republic, 1763–1789*. Chicago: University of Chicago Press, 1977.
Nef, J. U. *War and Human Progress*. New York: Russell & Russell, 1968.
Parry, J. H. *Trade and Dominion: European Overseas Empires in the Eighteenth Century*. New York: Praeger, 1971.
Plumb, J. H. *Sir Robert Walpole*. 2 vols. Boston: Houghton-Mifflin, 1956, 1960.
Shennan, J. H. *Philippe, Duke of Orléans, Regent of France, 1715–1723*. London: Thames & Hudson, 1979.
Wallerstein, I. *The Modern World System*. 2 vols. New York: Academic Press, 1974, 1980.
Wood, G. S. *The Creation of the American Republic, 1776–1787*. Chapel Hill: University of North Carolina Press, 1969.

The Enlightenment

REFLECTIONS

ON THE PRESENT CONDITION OF THE

FEMALE SEX;

WITH

SUGGESTIONS FOR ITS IMPROVEMENT.

BY

PRISCILLA WAKEFIELD.

LONDON:

Printed for J. JOHNSON, in St. Paul's Church-yard;
and DARTON and HARVEY, in Gracechurch Street.

1798.

The eighteenth century was characterized by a wide-ranging critique of the social and intellectual bases of European culture to which contemporaries gave the name of the Enlightenment. Unlike other movements of renewal and reform in the West since the advent of Christianity, the Enlightenment did not take the form of a religious revival. It grew instead out of the new methods of inquiry bequeathed by the scientific revolution and the questions that its view of the cosmos posed to traditional religion. The thought of the Enlightenment was frankly secular and rationalist, and this, in a society where all art, science, morality, and political authority had acknowledged the primacy of religious truth for 1,500 years, posed a revolutionary challenge to the social order. At the same time, the Enlightenment was a response to economic and political changes at work in European society. Some of the most influential thinkers of the Enlightenment were men of bourgeois origin. Unattached to church or court, they heralded the coming of a new secular society, and their demands for freedom and toleration, their conception of a worldwide human community, and their contempt for inherited privilege echoed the interests of free trade, unfettered enterprise, and an expanding global economy.

The cover of an early treatise on women's rights, dated 1798. [Library Company of Philadelphia]

The Roots of the Enlightenment

The scientific revolution gravely undermined a set of closely interlocked assumptions on which the traditional social order rested. According to the traditional view, all created things had their place on the universal ladder of existence that ultimately led to God. The angels were subordinate to God as humankind was to the angels, beasts to persons, and inanimate matter to living, in a descending scale of natural value. Each order of being had its own internal hierarchy as well. There were superior and subordinate angels, higher and lower animals, and nobler and baser persons. The human order was part of the harmony ordained by God for the universe, and anyone who attempted to disturb it was defying God as well as humankind. The historian Arthur O. Lovejoy has named this complex of ideas the "great chain of being."

In social terms, the great chain of being entailed a general principle of subordination, by which women and children were subject to the authority of men, commoners to noblemen, and all subjects to their rulers. This notion culminated in the idea of the divine right of kings. Monarchs received their authority directly from God as a means of enforcing his will on earth. Since kings had no superior but God, their actions could not be questioned by anyone on earth, and their commands must be treated as if coming directly from God. If a king were a tyrant, he should be regarded as a scourge sent by God to chastise people for their sins. God would hold the tyrant accountable, but subjects could not.

In practice, the absolute power of kings was often subject to challenge. The church of the Counter-Reformation insisted that heretical rulers might be deposed or even killed; in 1570 Pope Pius V absolved Queen Elizabeth I's English subjects of their allegiance to her, and in 1610 Henry IV of France was assassinated by a deranged priest. The English in 1649 had executed their own king, Charles I, after trying him before an extraordinary tribunal, and even Louis XIV had known rebellion in the early years of his reign. Further down the social scale, desperate peasants rebelled frequently against oppressive taxes and other burdens, and such customs as the English practice of ducking scolds who beat or abused their husbands in the local pond or river showed that women did not always passively accept the roles imposed on them.

Although resistance might be offered in particular cases, most women continued to regard their subservience to men, and peasants to their lords, as part of the natural order of things. This pattern of submission, called *deference,* was instilled in the lower orders of society from an early age. Here is the journalist Richard Steele's description of the proper attitude of the tenant farmer, written in 1672:

A just fear and respect he must have for his landlord, or the gentleman his neighbor, because God hath placed them above him and he hath learnt that by the father he ought to honor is meant all his superiors.[1]

These words were written in England. Even there, where the attempt to impose absolute monarchy had been curbed by the revolutions of 1640 and 1688, the social supremacy of the nobility was not merely undiminished but greater than ever. This was generally true of the privileged orders throughout eighteenth-century Europe. Beneath the surface, however, the Old Regime was not only being reshaped by the stresses of imperial competition and the emerging global economy but also being undermined by the intellectual consequences of the scientific revolution.

The most immediate of these consequences was a weakening of faith in the traditional Christian God of salvation, at least among the more educated classes. It was true that nothing in the new science directly contradicted the tenets of Christianity. But it was difficult to reconcile the biblical God who regularly manifested his presence in the world through signs, wonders, and miracles with the expanded Newtonian universe of self-regulating mechanical motion. Such a God seemed not so much incompatible with this universe as irrelevant to it.

The revolution in the Western concept of space was soon matched by a corresponding revolution in the concept of geologic time. Just as the cosmos had been thought to be contained within the ten heavenly spheres of the Ptolemaic universe, so its age, reckoned by the creation of Adam and Eve, was thought to be no more than 6,000 years. A seventeenth-century English theologian, James Ussher, calculating by biblical genealogies, had even announced the precise date of creation to have been October 23, 4004 B.C.

The God of Reason

As scientists began to turn their attention to the natural history of the earth, it was soon apparent that a far longer span was necessary to account for the evolution of its features. The God who had already been exiled to the outer edges of a vast and perhaps boundless universe now seemed to recede as well from the intimate scale of human history to that of a remote, geologic time. Such a God might be conceived of as a creator, but in what sense was he still a father? Yet if the idea of a paternal God had begun to lose its credibility, what would become of the divine right monarchs who ruled in the name of that God? The theories of Newton might have seemed very far removed from the glitter and pomp of Louis XIV's court, but their implications for royal absolutism and noble privilege were serious and ultimately fatal. In pulling the linchpin of a traditional Christian God from the great chain of being, the new mechanical universe had called into question the entire justification for the social order that rested on it.

For some thinkers, such as Pascal, the erosion of faith in a personal God of salvation was profoundly disturbing. But for many others in the late seventeenth and eighteenth centuries, the biblical God died a natural death with the view of nature and the cosmos of which he had been part, to be replaced by one more in keeping with the rational world of the new physics. Thus was born what was called "natural religion," or Deism. Deism rested on a variant of the old scholastic argument from design. The rational universe revealed by science, the Deists contended, could never have organized itself by accident and was thus necessarily the product of a rational, divine mind. Having created an orderly and self-perpetuating universe, this intellectual God had no need to intervene in it, and his apparent absence from it reflected merely his repose in its perfection. What God did in the world, in effect, was to contemplate it. He had no need to force notice of himself on it, since his presence was implicit throughout its design. It followed that the proper way to worship such a God was to study the world itself.

Deism appeared on the surface to reject and even scorn Christianity. For the cultural outsider Spinoza or for a cool, rationalist skeptic such as the third earl of Shaftesbury (1671–1713), this was a matter of indifference if not pride. But many people anxious to embrace Deism wished to save as much as possible of Christianity within it. They found their spokesman in John Locke, who argued in *The Reasonableness of Christianity* (1695) that Christian ethics reflected divine reason. What Christianity could not claim to possess was an exclusive revelation of truth. All religions reflected the "natural religion," which recognized and worshiped the divine intelligence in the world. This was the valid core of each religion, underneath the impurities of dogma and superstition. For this reason, as Locke argued in *An Essay on Toleration* (1689), all religions were worthy of respect, none of priority. Toleration thus emerged as a positive virtue, not merely a truce in a war to the death between rival systems of belief.

The argument that each religion should be sifted for the truth it possessed was akin to the method of science in testing different theories by experiment. Common to both was the assumption that truth was not discovered all at once through external revelation but rather acquired slowly by applying reason to the facts of experience, in the manner of fitting together the pieces of a jigsaw puzzle. The scientific revolution itself was the most triumphant demonstration of this process. Newton's synthesis, "the true system of the world," as an eighteenth-century admirer called it, had been built on the earlier theories of Copernicus, Galileo, and Kepler, each of which had contributed its partial truth to the final discovery of the whole. If the truth about the physical cosmos, obscured even to the greatest minds of antiquity, had been disclosed at last by this method, what mystery could not be made to yield

to it? Reason, perfected by the method of science, seemed poised to unlock the final secrets of heaven and earth.

The Idea of Progress

The upshot of these developments was the idea of progress, a notion that changed an entire civilization's conception of itself. For more than 2,000 years, the West had thought of its world as the shrunken remnant of a glorious past. The Greeks had looked back to a mythical world of gods and heroes, the Romans of the empire to the virtue of the republic, the Middle Ages to the sanctity of the apostles, and the Renaissance back again to Rome. Most important of all was the Judeo-Christian myth of humankind's fall from grace in the Garden of Eden. In the Jewish version of the fall, redemption was still conceived in secular terms as a return to the promised land. But for Christians, human sin could not be eradicated in historical time; indeed history, time itself, was the punishment inflicted on humanity for its sins.

The notion of secular progress, the improvement of the human condition in the world through human effort alone, thus required a radical transformation in Western thinking. The scientific revolution, and the Deist faith in a rational God to which it gave rise, provided the basis of this transformation. The success of the scientific method in explaining the cosmos generated great confidence in its ability to resolve social, political, and even moral problems as well. If humankind could unlock the secrets of the natural world, why should it be unable to master its own human one? At the same time, the God of Deism freed humankind from the Christian preoccupation with sin, and it became possible to think of human nature positively. The human race was not born with an innate propensity to sin, but it could be animated, even in the absence of divine grace, by feelings of benevolence and a disinterested desire for the welfare of others. "I have seen some take on the feelings of others," declared the French poet Saint-Lambert, "espouse the interests of others, and enter into their situation to the point of losing their own feelings, of forgetting their own interests and situation."[2] A Deist, Saint-Lambert believed that contemplating the goodness of God was necessary to the cultivation of moral sentiments. Established churches, however, were actually harmful to them, since they substituted formal duties and barren rituals for natural and spontaneous feeling.

The possibility of progress was the subject of a famous literary debate in late seventeenth-century France, the so-called quarrel of the ancients and the moderns. The ancients upheld the view that modern man could never duplicate the achievements of classical Greece and Rome, while the moderns asserted that the age of Louis XIV was the equal if not the superior of any previous period in history. The most persuasive of the moderns' spokesmen, Bernard de Fontenelle (1657–1757), argued that whereas great works of art required only individual genius, the

The idea of progress spawned a number of amusing fantasies, such as this alleged flight from "Plazentia" to "Coria" in Spain. By the end of the eighteenth century, balloon flights had already been made and observation balloons were being used in battle. [Musée Carnavalet, Paris; Photographie Bulloz]

growth of knowledge was a collaborative effort and thus cumulative over time. Although history suffered periods of reversal as well as advance, the attainments of the past always remained to be built on and surpassed by the present. An enthusiastic popularizer of the new science, Fontenelle believed that his own time represented a new peak of human achievement. In the perspective of centuries to come, he declared, the fifth century before Christ and the seventeenth after would both be seen as points on a line of ascending progress. The time of Christ himself was pointedly absent from this reckoning.

If each period could build on the past, each individual represented a new and untested set of possibilities. The traditional Christian view had assumed that the individual was born in a state of sin and that the primary task of education was to control a natural inclination to evil. In the view suggested by Deism, however, humankind was morally neutral if not instinctively good, and the proper function of education was to maximize society's potential for progress by developing each individual talent to the fullest. Once again, John Locke provided the most popular account of this new psychology. In *Essay Concerning Human Understanding* (1690) he argued that the mind at birth was a blank slate that registered the experience of the senses passively. These sensations were organized by simple categories and processed by reflection. The result was a product called knowledge or understanding. Locke viewed the mind of the child as fluid and malleable. Bombarded by sense impressions and relatively unorganized, it was, he said, "as easily turned this way or that, as water itself." This meant that education was critical in determining human development. Properly guided, the mind could realize its full powers, both for its own benefit and that of society. Deprived of such guidance, or purposely misled, it was prey to superstition, intolerance, and tyranny.

Locke and Liberty

John Locke (1632–1704) was a member of the Whig opposition to Charles II and James II and for a time went into exile under an assumed name. After the Glorious Revolution, he published *Two Treatises of Government* (1690), intended to defend the deposition of James II and to refute the theories of Thomas Hobbes.

Hobbes had argued that people contract with a sovereign whose unchallengeable authority erects a society that protects them from one another. Although Hobbes, like Locke, explained human psychology from a materialistic standpoint, his view of the antagonism between individuals reflected traditional Christian pessimism about the depravity of human nature. For Locke, by contrast, reflecting the new Deism, humans were innately peaceful, rational, and gregarious in the state of nature, enjoying their natural rights to life, liberty, and the fruit of their own labors. They entered society not from fear but from the desire to increase their wealth and happiness by cooperation with their fellows. The social contract thus involved not a surrender of natural rights but the protection and enhancement of them. Society itself was the voluntary association of free, equal, and separate individuals into the free, equal, and united members of a group.

The first task of society was to establish a rule-making authority or government. Locke rejected Hobbes' assertion that sovereignty must reside in a single person or institution. As each individual had been sovereign over himself or herself in the state of nature, so all were now jointly sovereign over the society they had created together. This was the very meaning of their union as a people. It followed that government was first and foremost an instrument of the people's will. If the particular government they had chosen proved tyrannical or otherwise defective, they might amend it or cast it off. Thus the right of rebellion was implicit in the formation of society itself. Far from dissolving the social order, as Hobbes had argued, rebellion was a means of renewing and reaffirming the ends for which it had been instituted. Nothing could dissolve the union of a free people as long as they elected to remain together.

Locke's *Treatises* provided what still remains the classic foundation of the liberal state, with its emphasis on associative community, representative government, and natural rights. His view of society as an act of collective decision making by free and unconstrained individuals reflected both the Deist vision of man as a rational being and the values of an emerging secular society with its emphasis on choice and satisfaction. His influence on the American Revolution, with its claim to a people's right to rebel on behalf of their inalienable rights, was obvious, and the convention of the founders who drafted a constitution for the 13 former colonies might almost have stepped from the pages of the second *Treatise* as an illustration of society in the making.

Locke's views remained open to objection however. His picture of the human mind as a bundle of sensations acted on by "reflection" did not explain how the capacity to reflect could arise. By locating political sovereignty in the people as a whole, he begged the question of how power is actually exercised in society. In asserting that natural rights disclosed themselves intuitively, he assumed that everyone would agree what they were. But the English revolutionary Gerrard Winstanley had already rejected one of Locke's rights, the right of property, as incompatible with true liberty, and the abuse of property was to be denounced by Jean-Jacques Rousseau and others in the eighteenth century as well.

Philosophy in Action

The Enlightenment was a broadly based intellectual movement whose avowed goal was to apply reason to society for the purpose of human betterment. It was led by the *philosophes,* a loose coalition of thinkers and critics who were not philosophers in the traditional sense but social activists for whom knowledge was something to be converted into reform. Many of the leading philosophes were French, but they came from virtually every country in Europe, and their ideas carried everywhere. The philosophes saw themselves not as subjects of a particular country but as citizens of the world, or, in Peter Gay's phrase, as "the party of humanity." They claimed to speak on behalf of all oppressed by tyranny or blighted by ignorance, and their goal was nothing less than a world where reason alone was sovereign.

The philosophes prided themselves on their political and intellectual independence. The bible of their movement, Denis Diderot's *Encyclopedia,* defined the philosophe as one who, "trampling on prejudice, tradition, universal consent, authority, in a word all that enslaves most minds, dares to think for [himself] . . . [and] to admit nothing except on the testimony of his experience and his reason." The philosophes did not seek specific political reform so much as fundamental changes in values and attitudes that would bring reform about. Their motto, coined by the German philosopher Immanuel Kant, was "Dare to know," and their object, Diderot boasted, was to make "a revolution in men's minds."

Voltaire

The most famous and influential of the philosophes was François-Marie Arouet (1694–1778), known to history by his pen name of Voltaire. Born in Paris, Voltaire was, like many of the philosophes, of bourgeois origin; his father was a notary. He began his career as a satiric playwright but ran afoul first of the regent, who imprisoned him for 11 months in the Bastille, and then of a prominent nobleman, the Chevalier de Rohan, who had him caned in the street and imprisoned again when he protested. Forced into exile, Voltaire spent three years in England. This experience was the turning point of his career. Voltaire was deeply impressed by the relative freedom he found in England, and his *Philosophical Letters on the English* (1734) praised that nation's institutions. He was influenced as well by Lockean psychology and Newtonian physics, and his *Elements of the Philosophy of Newton* (1738) is one

Frederick II of Prussia visits Voltaire in his study during the latter's residence at Frederick's court. In this extraordinary image, it is Voltaire, pen in hand, who remains seated while his royal host bends forward in greeting. Only the rearing horse outside conveys the image of bridled majesty and hints at the stormy rupture that was to part the two men later. [Bettmann Archive]

of the clearest and most direct links between the scientific revolution and the thought of the Enlightenment.

Unable to publish freely in France, Voltaire accepted an invitation from an admirer, Frederick the Great of Prussia, at whose court he spent two years (1749–1751). He then retired with his niece and mistress, Madame Denis, to an estate at Ferney, just over the French border in Switzerland, where he spent the last third of his life. There he functioned as a one-man republic, entertaining a steady stream of visitors, firing off as many as 30 letters a day, and carrying on a tireless series of campaigns for justice. The most famous of these was to clear the name of Jean Calas, a French Protestant put to death on the trumped-up charge of having murdered his son to prevent his conversion to Catholicism. As a Deist, Voltaire had no more use for one form of Christianity than another; his interest was in exposing the consequences of bigotry. *"Écrâsez l'infame!"*—crush the infamy!—he cried, and no one did more, by anger or ridicule, to expose intolerance and to undermine the authority of established religion in Europe. The compliment was returned: his last major work, the *Philosophical Dictionary* (1764), was burned in Paris, Ge-

neva, and Rome, and Voltaire observed wryly that the authorities would gladly have burned the author as well.

Satire was Voltaire's special forte, and his wit was turned against his friends as well as his enemies. His novel *Candide* (1759), the most popular and enduring of all his works, was a satire on the faith of his contemporaries in automatic or unlimited progress. There was a dark side to Voltaire; that God was good, he believed, did not protect humankind from evil. What people could do was to minimize the evil they inflicted on one another, and they could do this best by coming to understand their common heritage. In a sense Voltaire is the father of this book; his *Essay on Custom* (1756) was the first survey of the history of world civilization, beginning with that of ancient China. As always, Voltaire's purpose was didactic, to show that no culture had a monopoly on beauty or value, just as no religion had a monopoly on truth. In his last years he was able to return to Paris in triumph. He described himself as bowed down with every infirmity of old age; but nothing, he added, "can deprive me of hope."

The Enlightenment and Society

When the philosophes put their own society under the lens of reason, they found it seriously wanting. Superstition abounded; free thought was stifled; education was in the hands of the established churches. Idleness had been elevated to a way of life by the aristocracy, while the efforts of the most productive class, the bourgeoisie, were for the most part scorned.

At the same time, the idea that the structure of society reflected the hierarchical order of the universe was under attack. "No society can exist without justice," Voltaire had written; yet could a God of reason have created a society where justice was so perverted? Some of the more radical philosophes had already gone beyond Deism, however. For such openly avowed atheists as the Frenchmen Denis Diderot (1713–1784) and Julian La Mettrie (1707–1747) or the Baron d'Holbach (1723–1789), a wealthy German nobleman living in Paris, the idea of God itself was the last superstition. Humankind, they declared, was alone in the universe, the author of its own destiny. Society, its own creation, should respond to its needs. If it did not, the answer to the problem had to be sought in humankind itself, for the only law to which humanity was subject was that of its own nature.

Rousseau and the Social Contract

These questions led the philosophes to investigate the origins of society. The most radical analysis was offered by Jean-Jacques Rousseau (1712–1778). Born in Geneva, Rousseau was, unlike most of the philosophes, poor and ill-educated. He ran away from home at the age of 16 and remained a misfit all his life, betraying friends and even abandoning his own children. Rousseau's personal discontents were reflected in his view of society. "Man is born free," he declared, "yet everywhere we find him in chains." Society had not fulfilled human nature but perverted it. In his *Discourse on the Origin of Inequality* (1755), he found the origin of injustice in the institution of property:

> **The first man who, having enclosed a piece of ground, bethought himself of saying *This is mine*, and found people simple enough to believe him, was the real founder of civil society. From how many crimes, wars and murders, from how many horrors and misfortunes might not someone have saved mankind, by pulling up the stakes and filling in the ditch, and crying out to his fellows, "Beware of listening to this impostor; you are undone if you once forget that the fruits of the earth belong to us all, and the earth itself to nobody."**

Rousseau depicted the state of nature as an idyllic primitive communism, corrupted by the sin of possession. That original transgression created the basic institution of society, property. This in turn led to greed, the source of all oppression. The love of gain made sons wish for the death of their fathers and helped speculators profit from plague, famine, and war. Far from being an absolute natural right, as Locke had thought, property, when perverted by greed, was the evil that usurped and destroyed all other rights.

The solution, Rousseau argued in *The Social Contract* (1762), was to create a society in which private interest was subordinated to the common good. This, he asserted, could be accomplished only if each individual agreed to give up the final determination of his interest to the collective whole. Rousseau saw in this not loss but a gain of freedom. Since each person, while giving up his own rights, received at the same time the surrender of everyone else's, his original rights were actually returned many times over. Yet since everyone had made the same exchange, all persons remained exactly equal to one another. This was the true meaning of the social contract. In Hobbes' version of it, all persons were equal in their subordination to an absolute ruler, but none were free. In Locke's version, all persons were free to pursue their private interests, which led inevitably to inequity, oppression, and the loss of freedom. Only by guaranteeing both freedom and equality, Rousseau believed, could the conditions for a just society be met.

Rousseau called the collective entity in which all individual rights were vested the *general will*. Rousseau took the general will (as opposed to the will of any segment, including a majority) to mean both the permanent interest of the entire community and the course of action that represented its best interest at any given moment.

Ideally, the general will would be enacted by the unanimous consent of the entire community. In practice, however, it could not be expected that all citizens would be able to transcend their private interests, and to wait for unanimity on every question would, Rousseau admitted, reduce the social contract to an empty formula. It would therefore be necessary at some point to oblige dissenters

◉ Rousseau on the Social Contract ◉

Rousseau, agreeing with Hobbes that society had been founded by compulsion but with Locke that it ought to be founded on consent, argued that a properly constituted social order was the instrument for converting natural into civil freedom.

Man is born free, and everywhere he is in chains. One thinks himself master of others, but is himself the greater slave. How did this change take place? I do not know. What can render it legitimate? I believe I can answer this question.

If I were to consider nothing but force and its effects, I should say: "As long as a people is compelled to obey, and does so, it does well; as soon as it can shake off the yoke, and does so, it does even better; for in recovering its liberty on the same grounds on which it was stolen away, it either is right in resuming it, or was wrongly deprived in the first place." But the social order is a sacred right which serves as the basis for all others. And yet this right does not come from nature; thus it is founded on conventions.

Source: J. J. Rousseau, "The Social Contract," in *Rousseau: Political Writings,* trans. and ed. F. Watkins (Edinburgh: Nelson, 1953), pp. 3–4.

to comply with the general will, for their own good as well as the community's. In the last analysis, Rousseau declared, citizens who could not recognize where their real freedom lay must "be forced to be free."

State and Utopia

Rousseau's insistence that freedom and equality were inseparable was echoed in the famous assertion of the American Declaration of Independence that all men were created free and equal. But Rousseau never clearly explained how the general will was to be recognized. The American founders therefore turned instead to the ideas of another philosophe, the Baron de Montesquieu (1689–1755), who argued in *The Spirit of the Laws* (1748) that liberty was best secured by a separation of the powers of government. Montesquieu's influential notion found its way not only into the checks and balances of America's constitution but into the French constitution of 1791, the Prussian Code of 1792, the Spanish constitution of 1812, and the short-lived revolutionary constitutions of 1848.

If Montesquieu had the more practical effect on political reform, Rousseau expressed the more fundamental tension that lay at the heart of Enlightenment thought. If men were created equal in rights and yet unequal in the wealth, power, and interest by which those rights were to be enjoyed, how was society to achieve justice and promote the common welfare? For the Abbé Morelly, author of the *Code of Nature* (1755), the only answer was to abolish all property and commerce and to establish a rigidly egalitarian society in which each individual was allotted a specific quota of production and consumption. The late Enlightenment figure Simon-Henri Linguet, a lawyer disbarred

for his attacks on the property system, predicted a widening gap between rich and poor that would lead to general revolution: never, he wrote, "has Europe been nearer to a complete upheaval."

The majority view, expressed by Bernard de Mandeville (1673–1733) and Adam Smith (1723–1790), remained optimistic. In his *Fable of the Bees* (1714), Mandeville argued that just as bees building a hive contributed to the greater good without being aware of it, so even vices such as vanity, envy, and pride were useful because they promoted commerce and industry and gave employment. Adam Smith, expounding a similar view more systematically in *The Wealth of Nations* (1776), asserted that public wealth (and thereby private benefit) was maximized by allowing each individual to pursue his or her own selfish interest. Just as the Newtonian universe produced balance and harmony by obeying its own laws without the need of special divine intervention, so the market was a self-regulating mechanism that functioned best when left alone. As Alexander Pope expressed it in verse, "God and Nature link'd the gen'ral frame, / and bade Self-love and Social be the same."

The Philosophes and Their Public

The philosophes spoke to and largely for the new commercial classes and their interests. But their ideas were also disseminated in the salons of the liberal aristocracy. At these large and semipublic social gatherings, where wit rather than birth was the criterion for admission, they held forth as the guests of such influential tastemakers as Madame du Deffand and Madame Geoffrin. The salons served

A lively conversation among the philosophes, dominated as usual by Voltaire, whose arm is raised. International celebrities, the philosophes are each identified by number. Diderot, the editor of the *Encyclopedia*, is seated at Voltaire's left. [Mansell Collection]

to domesticate the ideas of the Enlightenment and also to make them more acceptable. These ideas in turn undermined the social dominance that the French court had enjoyed in the days of Louis XIV and thus some of its power as well. The salons gave the leading figures of the Enlightenment both a prestige and entrée into circles of the highest influence they could not have attained without them, a point ruefully acknowledged later by the conservative Joseph de Maistre when he remarked that "an opinion launched in Paris was like a battering ram launched by thirty million men."

Literacy and Censorship

The principal vehicle of Enlightenment thought, however, was the printing press. In the 100 years before the French Revolution, 18 more men and 13 more women in every 100 became literate in France, and comparable increases were recorded in England, Austria, Denmark, and parts of Germany. The philosophes rode the crest of a great wave that created a new kind of public in Europe: the reading public. For the first time, literature had not merely a circulation but a market, and this market created a new profession, that of the independent writer. Newspapers and periodicals flourished, among them the remarkable *Journal des dames* ("Ladies' Journal"), whose feminist tone was ringingly set by its first female editor, Madame de Beaumer: "Be silent, all critics, and know that this is a *woman* addressing you!"

One indication of the burgeoning appetite for serious discussion, particularly in France, was the emergence of provincial literary academies that sponsored essay competitions on such subjects as the nature of the passions, the influence of Christianity, and the condition of philosophy. Rousseau himself first gained recognition through a competition offered by the Dijon Academy, and the future revolutionary Robespierre was secretary of the one at Arras in the 1780s. Lower down on the social scale, but still appealing primarily to a bourgeois audience, were less formally organized reading clubs and social groups such as the Freemasons, a social brotherhood dedicated to celebrating human dignity whose members included figures as diverse as Mozart and Benjamin Franklin.

The governments of the Old Regime tried vainly to stem the spread of new and seditious ideas through the licensing of printers and booksellers, censorship, confiscation, and in the case of notorious figures such as Voltaire, burning books by the common hangman. In Austria under Maria Theresa, even foreign ambassadors had their luggage searched for forbidden books, and Prussia under Frederick William I exiled its foremost philosopher, Christian Wolff. Nor did governments alone exercise censorship; the Catholic church maintained its *Index of Prohibited Books,* and such bodies as law courts and universities could also order the suppression of printed works. Universities, with few exceptions, played little part in the Enlightenment. The Austrian reformer Joseph von Sonnenfels lamented that the universities in his country were a century behind the times, but the same could be said for Paris, Cambridge, and Oxford.

The philosophes used great ingenuity in getting around the various forms of censorship. Some of them used the device of the fictional reporter, as Montesquieu did in his *Persian Letters,* or science fiction, as Voltaire did in his Utopian fantasies *Zadig* and *Micromegas* and the satirist Jonathan Swift (1667–1745) in *Gulliver's Travels.* A large underground book trade also flourished, fed by presses in Switzerland and the Low Countries that supplemented their business in serious social criticism with scandal, gossip, blasphemy, and pornography. One enterprising Spanish editor even established a journal called *El Censor.*

The Encyclopedia

The most important and embattled publishing project of the Enlightenment was the great *Encyclopedia,* conceived and edited by the versatile Diderot. The son of a provincial artisan and himself the author of philosophical and mathematical treatises as well as plays, essays, and novels, Diderot commissioned a veritable Who's Who of the Enlightenment, including Voltaire, Rousseau, and Montesquieu, to contribute thousands of articles on every aspect of human knowledge. The result was the largest publishing venture up to that time in Western history. The first volume, containing controversial articles on atheism and the human soul, appeared in 1751. It was pounced on by the censors, who first suspended and later revoked the publisher's license. The attorney general of France denounced it as a conspiracy against public morals, and the pope declared anyone buying or reading it to be excommunicated. When the coeditor, Jean d'Alembert, dropped out, Diderot continued alone, issuing further volumes despite the ban, filling in the gaps when contributors defaulted, and even setting up the plates himself. By 1765 the 17 volumes of text were complete, and in 1772 the last of 11 volumes of illustrations appeared. In the end, the *Encyclopedia* was a great commercial success, although Diderot himself saw little of its profits. By 1789 an astonishing 20,000 full sets had been sold, and many more circulated in abridgments, extracts, and pirated editions. Modern public opinion—the reaction of an audience too large and too independent to be controlled by any institution of church or state—was born in the eighteenth century. No single book did more to create and mold it than Diderot's *Encyclopedia.*

The Enlightened Despots

One of the most remarkable aspects of the Enlightenment was the adoption and espousal of many of its ideas and

In addition to its often provoc-ative articles, Diderot's *Ency-clopedia* offered hundreds of unique illustrations of the in-dustrial and mechanical arts of the eighteenth century, such as the brass foundry pictured here, whose workers seem dwarfed by the giant machines and implements they ply. The horse pictured at left turns wheels that crush crude zinc. The workmen in figure 6 crank a barrel that mixes the zinc with copper to make the brass alloy. The brass is then stamped in a mold and cut by giant shears. [Granger Col-lection]

◎ From Diderot's *Encyclopedia* ◎

Denis Diderot, whose multivolume Encyclopedia *was the largest, most daring, and most influential single work of the Enlightenment, here de-fends his project against the censors.*

We have already remarked that among those who have set themselves up as censors of the *Encyclopedia* there is hardly a single one who had enough talent to enrich it by even one good article. I do not think I would be exaggerating if I should add that it is a work the greater part of which is about subjects that these people have yet to study. It has been composed with a philosophical spirit, and in this respect most of those who pass adverse judgment on us fall far short of the level of their own century. I call their works in evi-dence. It is for this reason that they will not endure and that we venture to say that our *Encyclopedia* will be more widely read and more highly appreciated in a few years' time than it is today. . . . Some . . . were once praised to the skies because they wrote for the multitude, following the prevailing ideas, and accommodated their standards to those of the average reader, but they have lost their reputations in proportion as the human mind has made progress, and they have finally been forgotten altogether. Others, by contrast, too daring for the times in which their works appeared, have been little read, hardly understood, not appreciated, and have long remained in obscurity, until the day when the age they had outstripped had passed away and another century, to which they really belonged in spirit, overtook them at last and finally gave them the justice their merits deserved.

Source: D. Diderot, *Encyclopedia*, ed. and trans. S. Gendzier (New York: Harper & Row, 1967), p. 95.

principles by some Old Regime rulers themselves, a phe-nomenon known as "enlightened despotism." This was less surprising than it might seem. The Enlightenment was a general movement that penetrated the most entrenched bastions of tradition and privilege; even rulers were not immune to new ideas. Moreover, some monarchs saw the

philosophes as potential allies in their struggles with the nobility, which almost everywhere resisted the centraliz-ing tendencies of royal governments. Thus it was that Voltaire could be the guest and companion of one king at the same time that his works were being burned by order of another.

For their part, the philosophes welcomed enlightened despotism as the most efficient means of realizing their objectives. Although Locke and Rousseau had championed popular sovereignty, neither was a democrat; Rousseau, despite his humble origins, scorned the masses. Most philosophes were ready enough to welcome a despot, provided that he was willing to use his power in the service of reason and reform.

Catherine the Great

Russia, still in many respects on the margins of European society, seemed a particularly unlikely setting for enlightened despotism. In the 37 years following the death of Peter the Great, it had had six rulers, including a boy of 12, an infant, and a half-wit. Some observers believed that the country was headed toward the kind of aristocratic anarchy that had befallen Poland, whose elective king was a mere figurehead. The Russian nobility had largely emancipated itself from the code of state service Peter imposed on it, and the status of the peasantry had deteriorated even further. The criminal code of 1754 listed serfs only under the heading of property; they had lost even the legal status of human beings.

Strong rule returned to Russia in 1762 when Catherine the Great (1762–1796), the German-born wife of Tsar Peter III, organized his assassination and seized the throne for herself. Few rulers have ever matched Catherine's blend of cosmopolitan charm, instinct for publicity, and ruthless opportunism. She described herself, somewhat disconcertingly, as "every inch a gentleman," but certainly there were at least a few that were not; she had 21 attested love affairs during her reign, and doubtless more of briefer duration.

In the early years of her sovereignty, Catherine was oriented almost wholly toward the West. She founded new schools and stimulated the nascent publishing industry. While neighboring states were banning the philosophes, she read Voltaire openly and admiringly, and she subsidized the publication of the *Encyclopedia*. In 1767 she summoned a legislative commission of 560 delegates, of whom half were commoners, including peasants, to revamp the Russian legal code. Catherine herself drafted an elaborate "instruction," including long passages cribbed from her favorite philosophes, expressing her commitment to reform.

The Instruction was a remarkable document in many ways, although some of its more liberal provisions, especially concerning the reduction of serfdom, were cut out of the final draft. The sections on legal procedure were particularly novel. Catherine declared that all persons should be equal before the law. Reflecting her reading of the seminal reform treatise by Cesare Bonesana, marquis de Beccaria, *Of Crimes and Punishments* (1764), she called for the abolition of torture and the reduction of capital punishment. The Instruction was translated into the major languages of Europe; Voltaire received a personal copy. Catherine's fellow enlightened despot, Frederick the Great, was so delighted with it that he made her a member of the Berlin Academy. The most flattering response came from France, where it was banned as subversive.

Despite this fanfare, the legislative commission was a disappointment if not a fiasco. The delegates, most of them inexperienced in public affairs, were bewildered as to what was expected of them, as well they might have been, since Catherine's proposals would have stood much of Russian society on its head. The commission divided bitterly over the issue of serfdom, with the peasants and a few of the liberal nobility opposed stoutly by the landed interest, and produced only minor reforms in provincial administration. It was adjourned at the outbreak of war with Turkey in 1768 and never reconvened.

The Russo-Turkish war of 1768–1774 marked a turning point in Catherine's reign. Her dalliance with reform was now over, and she devoted herself instead to the more familiar business of power politics. In this and a subsequent war with Turkey (1787–1792), Catherine annexed the north shore of the Black Sea, although her goal of conquering Constantinople itself—the oldest and hardiest of all Russian imperial dreams—remained unfulfilled. The false hopes of reform Catherine raised were also largely responsible for the great rebellion of Emilian Pugachev (1773–1774), a Cossack chieftain who declared himself to be the murdered Tsar Peter, set up a court with the "true" Catherine, and promised an end to serfdom, taxation, and conscription, as well as the abolition of the landed aristocracy. For a time much of southern Russia was aflame, and refugees streamed into Moscow; but Pugachev was defeated at last in a series of pitched battles, brought to Moscow in a cage, and, like Stenka Razin a century before, quartered in the Kremlin Square.

Pugachev's Rebellion confirmed the mutual dependence of Catherine and her nobility. As the nobility needed the strength of absolute despotism to protect their privileges, so they alone stood between the empress and peasant anarchy. Their common interest was sealed in the Charter of the Nobility (1785). The charter completely freed the nobility from imperial service, giving it instead sole responsibility for provincial administration. In this way the nobility, in looking after their own interests as landowners, exercised direct political control of the countryside on behalf of the state. Content with their powers, they ceased to meddle in palace affairs, while the imperial government no longer concerned itself with serfdom, human and political rights, and other unpalatable subjects. The few intellectuals who still did, such as the educational reformer Nikolai Novikov (1744–1818) or Alexander Radischev (1749–1802), author of the bitterly critical *Journey from Moscow to St. Petersburg* (1790), soon found themselves in exile or in prison. It was of no avail for Radischev to point out that he had said nothing that Catherine herself had not affirmed in her days of Enlightenment. In the end, she even banned her old friend Voltaire.

Frederick the Great

A far more sophisticated example of enlightened despotism was Frederick the Great of Prussia. Frederick was the most admired monarch of the eighteenth century. He dominated it, by reputation if not by the actual strength of his country, much as Louis XIV had dominated the Europe of his time. Frederick liked to encourage the parallel, although he was certainly Louis' superior both as a soldier and as a man of intellect. Not only did Frederick speak the rhetoric of the Enlightenment, but he was a philosophe of sorts himself. He scorned divine right kingship, declaring that his power rested on his service to the people; a ruler, he said in a famous phrase, was only "the first servant of the state." In effect, Frederick replaced the divine right notion of a mystical relation between the ruler and God with an equally mystical relation between the ruler and his people. He identified the king with what Rousseau was to call the general will, for the monarch alone, he argued, standing above all parties and interests, could legislate for the common good. For that reason too, although the monarch's power derived from the people and was exercised solely on their behalf, they could never recall or revoke it. Their interests being partial, they could never be in a correct position to judge the whole; only the ruler could see the common interest.

Such a ruler, restrained by neither God nor man, might turn tyrant with impunity. But, Frederick argued, having already all the power he could desire and all the wealth he could consume, he was beyond ordinary temptation. Frederick himself seemed the perfect illustration of this. He built a palace at Potsdam in imitation of Versailles but found little time to enjoy it. No breath of scandal ever touched him; he had no private vices and, it almost seemed, no private life. His energies, apart from philosophy, literature, and music, were wholly absorbed in Prussia. He drained its swamps, encouraged its industry, and expanded its agriculture. Within the country, he promoted education, welcomed religious refugees of every stripe, and undertook a codification of the laws. "My chief obligation," he wrote, "is . . . to make [my people] as happy as human beings can be, or as happy as the means at my disposal permit."

The people Frederick wished to serve were not the free and equal citizens of Rousseau's commonwealth, however, but the hierarchically divided subjects of an Old Regime society. Prussians were not free; although Frederick, like Catherine, was opposed to serfdom in theory, he did little to alleviate it. Nor were Prussians equal. Frederick favored the nobility even more than his father had, reserving the officer corps of the army and the upper levels of the civil service exclusively for them. Because the army and the bureaucracy dominated Prussian society

◉ Frederick the Great ◉ on the Enlightened Despot

Frederick here offers the classic justification for the traditional sovereign who, by comprehending all interests, is alone qualified to promote the common interest.

The sovereign is attached by indissoluble ties to the body of the state; hence it follows that he, by repercussion, is sensible to all the ills which afflict his subjects; and the people, in like manner, suffer from the misfortunes which affect their sovereign. There is but one general good, which is that of the state. . . . The sovereign represents the state; he and his people form but one body, which can only be happy as far as united by concord. The prince is to the nation he governs what the head is to the man; it is his duty to see, to think, and act for the whole community, so that he may procure it every advantage of which it is capable. . . . Such are in general the duties imposed upon a prince, from which, in order that he may never depart, he ought often to recollect that he himself is but a man, like the least of his subjects. If he be the first general, the first minister of the realm, it is not so that he should shelter in the shadow of authority, but that he should fulfil the duties of such titles. He is only the first servant of the state, who is obliged to act with probity and prudence; and to remain as totally disinterested as if he were each moment liable to render an account of his administration to his fellow citizens.

Source: Frederick the Great, *An Essay on Forms of Government,* trans. T. Holcroft, in E. Weber, ed., *The Western Tradition,* 3d ed. (Lexington, Mass.: Heath, 1972), pp. 539, 544.

between them, this meant that little initiative and less authority was left for the fledgling merchant class. At Frederick's death, Prussia was the most aristocratically controlled society in Europe. The long-term consequences of this, for Prussia and for Germany, were severe.

If Frederick believed in service to inferiors, he had few behavioral scruples toward his fellow monarchs. Even Louis XIV had attempted to rationalize his aggressions by legal claims, but when Frederick attacked Silesia in 1740, he blandly justified it on the grounds that it was in the nature of states to expand up to the limit of their ability. In 1772 he joined Catherine and Maria Theresa of Austria in carving up a helpless Poland in order to "adjust" the balance of power in eastern Europe in the wake of Catherine's gains against Turkey. Poland lost a third of its territory and half its population in this so-called Partition Treaty. Despite desperate attempts to strengthen itself by constitutional reform, it was wholly swallowed up by the subsequent partitions of 1793 and 1795 and ceased to exist as an independent nation. Enlightened despotism might sometimes aim at making states more rational and efficient; it did not make them more peaceful.

Joseph II:
The Revolutionary Emperor

If Catherine and Frederick were essentially conservative rulers who used the rhetoric of the Enlightenment to main-

tain traditional autocracy, the Austrian emperor Joseph II (1780–1790) was the one sovereign who seriously embraced its principles and unreservedly attempted to put them into effect. The eldest of Maria Theresa's 16 children, Joseph grew up unhappily in the shadow of a court whose dull and devout propriety was far removed from the witty, urbane skepticism of the philosophes. In 1765 he became Holy Roman emperor and coregent of Austria, but his desire for reform was frustrated during his mother's lifetime. When he succeeded her at last, he had a 15-year backlog of frustrated projects and ambitions.

The empire Joseph inherited was a crazy quilt of territories and populations that spread across Europe from Flanders on the North Sea to the borders of Russia and Turkey. Its various peoples—Flemish, Italian, German, Czech, Croatian, Magyar, Polish—had little in common, and their loyalty to the Habsburg throne had been purchased only by conceding a large measure of self-rule, especially in Hungary and Bohemia. Joseph set out to compress this explosive mixture into a single political and social order and to transform some of the most backward regions of Europe into instant models of progress and enlightenment.

In her quiet way, Maria Theresa had done much to put the Austrian empire on the path to modernization. Administration had been centralized in Austria proper and Bohemia, creating a model for the whole empire. Guild monopolies and tariff barriers had been overthrown, establishing the largest free trade zone in Europe. Church

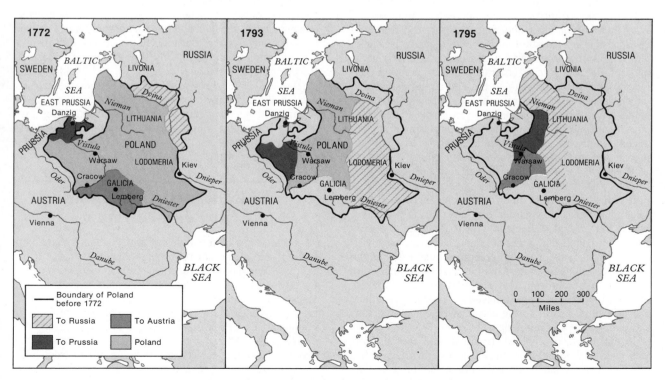

25.1 The Partitioning of Poland, 1772–1795

Joseph II and Catherine the Great, two of the Enlightened Despots and rivals in power politics as well as reform, met in 1787. By this time Catherine had long abandoned her liberal pose, while Joseph's attempt to remodel the Austrian Empire had driven many of its provinces to the verge of revolt. [Historisches Museum der Stadt Wien.]

land had been expropriated, and despite Maria Theresa's own hostility to secularism, the church's grip on education had been broken. For Joseph, however, the work of reform had barely begun with these steps. In ten years of ceaseless activity, he issued 6,000 edicts covering every aspect of life in the empire. What Catherine and Frederick had only talked of doing, Joseph decreed with the stroke of a pen. Serfdom was abolished, censorship lifted, and freedom of religion instituted. Jews were given civil rights and permitted to intermarry with Christians. Marriage itself was declared a civil contract, to the horror of conservatives and the outrage of the church. Apostasy and witchcraft were stricken from the legal code. Capital punishment was limited, and judicial torture was abolished. Equality before the law was not only proclaimed but enforced; Vienna was shocked by the sight of a young nobleman sweeping the streets in a chain gang.

There can be no doubt of the sincerity of Joseph's intentions. Although many of the changes he introduced were similar to those of other centralizing eighteenth-century monarchies, he regarded his power as an instrument for the betterment of humanity. He considered the existence of serfdom an "incredible and inexpressible evil," was outraged by bigotry and intolerance, and regarded the task of reform as an almost holy calling. "The service of God is inseparable from that of the state," he declared, and he wrote to one of his ministers, "Hasten everything that brings me nearer to the accomplishment of my plans for the happiness of my people."

Joseph brushed privilege, tradition, and special interests aside in the spate of his reform, boasting that he had made philosophy alone the legislator of his empire. The result was to unite the nobility, the church, and the pro-

vincial estates against him. Even the peasants, bewildered by the mass of edicts meant for their benefit and often sympathizing with the local priest or noble whom Joseph declared to be their oppressor, failed to support him.

Faced with almost universal opposition, Joseph redoubled his efforts. He reimposed censorship in an effort to dampen criticism, suspended due process, and set an army of spies on the population. The reactionary Count Pergen, his minister of police, became the most powerful man in the government and ultimately the only one he trusted. Rebellion flared in Hungary, the Tirol, and Flanders, and by the end of Joseph's reign, large parts of the empire were held down only by force. He died a broken man at 48, and within a few years the entire edifice of his reforms collapsed. Serfdom was restored, to survive in parts of the empire as late as 1867, and the nobility and clergy resumed their sway.

Enlightened Despotism in Perspective

The creed of enlightened despotism was best summed up in the motto of another reforming monarch, Charles III of Spain (1759–1788): "Everything for the people, nothing by the people." The enlightened despots represented a stage in the transformation of the personal monarchy of the old dynastic states to the impersonal rule of modern bureaucracies. Their very success in consolidating the power of the central state proved to be their undoing. It was true that the nobility and the church had frequently stood in the way of their ambitions. But in the long run absolute monarchy depended on these institutions as much as they did on it. Together, the church, the aristocracy, and the crown had made up the hierarchical order of authority whose ultimate expression was the divine right of kings. In undermining the foundations of that order, the enlightened despots eroded the ground on which they stood. There was no particular reason why their functions could not be exercised by someone else, and in fact similar programs—freeing trade, secularizing education, curbing privilege, modernizing the law, and guaranteeing basic rights—were carried out in Portugal and Denmark by ministers rather than by the feeble monarchs they served. When the French Revolution broke out in 1789, Joseph II condemned it bitterly, even though its authors sought many of the same goals as he. Joseph, who had wanted to do so much for the people, could not accept the fact that they might at last do something for themselves.

The Counter-Enlightenment

Reason was not triumphant everywhere in the eighteenth century, nor were its claims accepted uncritically. In his enormously popular novels, *The New Heloise* (1761) and *Émile* (1762), Rousseau argued that feeling was as important as intellect in the development of moral sentiments. He praised nature not merely as a clever mathematical arrangement but also as a source of beauty and wonder whose effect on human emotions was as crucial as the operation of its laws on reason. *The New Heloise* went through 70 editions by 1789 and became the bible of people who saw in unspoiled nature a haven from the corruptions of society and a model for the pure and simple life. *Émile,* by stressing the importance of developing each child's individual character and ability and the role of the teacher as a sympathetic guide rather than as a taskmaster, inspired a new movement in education, carried forward by the Swiss reformer Johann Heinrich Pestalozzi (1746–1827) and the Germans Johann Basedow (c. 1742–1790) and Friedrich Fröbel (1782–1852), and eventually a new view of childhood altogether. Instead of seeing the child as an immature and refractory adult, these educators emphasized the unique and distinctive character of childhood and the various phases of the child's development.

The middle and upper classes sought relief from the rationalism of the Enlightenment in a cult of sentiment, fed by popular novels such as Samuel Richardson's *Pamela* and *Clarissa* and Pierre de Marivaux's *Marianne.* But the official culture left deeper needs unmet. Established religion, buffeted by attacks on the tenets of its faith no less than on its wealth and privilege, was everywhere on the defensive. The Jesuits were so fiercely assailed that their order was temporarily dissolved in 1773, while theologians such as Samuel Clarke (1675–1729) and Joseph Butler (1692–1752) in England tried to anchor morality in reason and prudence rather than revelation.

The Revival of Religion

Such ideas were cold comfort to Europe's laboring millions, who sought in religion the promise of salvation and the only hope and consolation in their lives. What they could no longer get from their betters they soon began to make for themselves. Grass-roots religion—a phenomenon previously associated with periods of upheaval such as the Reformation or the English revolution—spread out from late seventeenth-century Germany across Protestant Europe and even to the New World. As Pietism in Germany, Methodism in England, and the Great Awakening in America, it had the same general goal: to revitalize religion by encouraging personal piety, good works, and a communal, often highly emotional experience of worship.

The roots of Pietism lay in the German mystical tradition, revived in the early seventeenth century by Jakob Böhme (1575–1624) and popularized by the evangelist Philip Jakob Spener (1635–1705). As with popular religious movements during the midcentury English revolution, Spener's preaching was attacked by the clerical establishment; the University of Wittenberg found 250 alleged errors in his doctrine. Nonetheless, by the end of the century Pietism had become the dominant spiritual movement in Protestant Germany. It found academic support in the newly established University of Halle (1694) and an aristocratic patron in Count Nicholas von Zinzendorf (1700–1760), who sheltered the Moravian Brethren, a radical Pietist sect, on his estate. It was a Moravian Pietist who counseled the spiritually troubled young English clergyman John Wesley (1703–1791), who with his brother, Charles, and a charismatic preacher, George Whitefield, took the evangelical message to the mine pits and the open fields when the churches closed their doors to him. Wesley's conversion experience was typical. On an evening in May 1738, he wrote, "I felt my heart strangely warmed. I felt I did trust in Christ, Christ alone, for salvation, and assurance was given me that . . . saved me from the law of sin and death." Never faltering in this conviction thereafter, Wesley tramped the English countryside for 50 years, delivering by his own estimate some 40,000 sermons. His followers, called Methodists, embraced the lower-middle-class virtues of thrift and toil, but their social horizons were limited, and they tended to be hostile to Catholics and Jews.

Catholicism produced its own reform movements, beginning in the seventeenth century with Quietism in Spain and Jansenism in France, Flanders, and Italy. Because of the greater organizational unity of the Roman church, these movements, unlike the various forms of Pietism, were of elite rather than popular origin, although in some areas they spread more widely among the population; in

The charismatic John Wesley was one of the most important figures in the religious revival that spread widely among those whose spiritual hunger was served neither by the established churches nor by the Deist God of Reason. [National Portrait Gallery, London]

spite (or perhaps because) of papal and royal opposition, two-thirds of Paris was Jansenist in 1730. Like Pietism, the Catholic reform stressed personal faith, emancipation from dogma, and the right of individual conscience.

Skepticism and Idealism

Reason itself was subjected to criticism by the Anglo-Irish philosopher George Berkeley (1685–1753) and the Scotsman David Hume (1711–1776), who cast doubt on the simple model of sensation and reflection proposed by Locke. Both stressed that ideas developed in the mind on the basis of sense impressions did not necessarily correspond to the world as it actually existed. Immanuel Kant (1724–1804), the greatest philosopher of the age, went even further. Kant argued that the mind imposed its own structure on experience, creating a picture with which it then lived. This picture could be tested and refined—for example, by science—but the mind could never go beyond it to know what the world was really like in itself. Kant's *idealism,* as his philosophy came to be called, was devastating to the claims of both science and religion; neither faith nor reason, he suggested, could lead to a knowledge of reality in itself.

Both skeptical philosophy and popular religion stressed the subjective experience of the individual, and both laid the ground for the new Romantic sensibility that began to develop in the eighteenth century. We must not, however, think of the Enlightenment in terms of rationalism and the reaction against it. Rather it must be seen as a great current whose very strength created countercurrents that are

◉ The Romantic Reaction ◉

The rationalism and skepticism of the philosophes produced a powerful reaction in favor of emotion and religious sensibility, expressed in these verses by William Blake (1757–1827).

> Mock on, Mock on Voltaire, Rousseau:
> Mock on, Mock on: 'tis all in vain!
> You throw sand against the wind,
> And the wind blows it back again.
>   And every sand becomes a Gem
> Reflected in the beams divine:
> Blown back they blind the mocking Eye,
> But still in Israel's paths they shine.
>   The Atoms of Democritus
> And Newton's Particles of light
> Are sands upon the Red Sea shore,
> Where Israel's tents do shine so bright.

Source: W. Blake, *The Commonplace Book.*

The personification of divine right monarchy, a mature Louis XIV, king of France, poses in the full pomp and regalia of his office in this portrait by Hyacinthe Rigaud. During Louis' reign, France was the greatest power in continental Europe. [1701, oil on canvas, $9'1\frac{1}{2}'' \times 6'2\frac{5}{8}''$ (278 × 190 cm.); Louvre/Réunion des Musées Nationaux]

THE VISUAL EXPERIENCE
Toward Modernity

The dramatic transformation of the world's civilizations is vividly captured in the art of the early modern period. Political unification, the great voyages of exploration, and the growth of commercial capitalism provided the means for economic and colonial expansion, particularly as Westerners sought new lands, new markets, and the products of non-Western societies. The prosperity of the period was not, however, shared by all; political inequality, grinding taxation, bitter warfare, and slavery cast a long shadow over the lives of millions, driving some into revolution. Nevertheless, these were centuries of human triumph, as witnessed in such consummate achievements as the scientific revolution and the unsurpassed beauty of the prints of Hiroshige and the paintings of Rembrandt and Delacroix.

Sir Isaac Newton's grand synthesis capped the scientific revolution by reducing the explanation of all motion in the material world to three simply stated laws. [National Portrait Gallery, London]

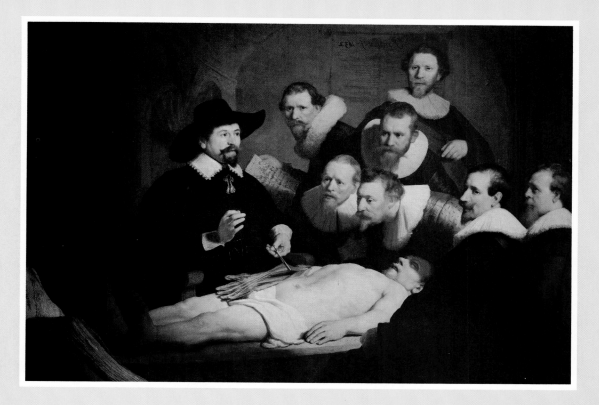

The Anatomy Lesson of Dr. Tulp. The dramatic interior lighting and the contrast between the animated postures and formal attire of the physicians and the stiff, livid corpse mark this early masterpiece by Rembrandt as a typical production of the baroque. Frequent public executions, often for petty crimes, insured a ready supply of cadavers. [1632, oil on canvas, 5′3⅜″ × 7′1¼″ (161 × 217 cm.); Mauritshuis, The Hague; Scala/Art Resource]

The ornate, elegant Hall of Mirrors of the Amalienberg, a summer house on the grounds of Nymphenburg Palace in Munich, is a fine example of the intimate yet airy style of the rococo, which originated in France and spread to Germany in the 1730s. [1734–1739; Michael Holford, London]

John Trumbull's famous portrait of the Founding Fathers. The drum, trumpets, and crossed flags on the wall symbolize resolve for the war of independence yet to be fought in America. This war launched the era of revolution. [Yale University Art Gallery]

Symbolically an attack on the monarchy itself, the fall of the ancient fortress called the Bastille in July 1789 soon led to a general revolt against seigneurial privilege throughout France. [Giraudon/Art Resource]

Jacques-Louis David's remarkable portrait of a woman of Paris' working class shows the anxiety and suffering but also the dignity and determination of those who struggled in the French Revolution, not merely for survival but also for justice. [Musée des Beaux-Arts, Lyon]

Horace Vernet's portrait of Napoleon in battle at Jena catches the intensity and concentration that made him a great field commander, but also the arrogance that presaged his ultimate downfall. [Château de Versailles/Réunion des Musées Nationaux]

Christianity's major rival, Islam, shared its belief in life after death. This illustration from the Khamsa of Nizami, a Persian manuscript of the mid-sixteenth century, shows Muhammad, astride his mare, being guided into heaven by the archangel Gabriel. [Bridgeman/Art Resource]

A Durbar (celebratory festival) in formal procession, in the traditional Indian style, in Calcutta. Note that Indians are the only ones who are walking (or carrying arms), although some Indian notables and guests are riding on the elephants with the top-hatted British. [India Office Library of the British Library]

The East India Company Docks in London by Samuel Scott. This deceptively quiet scene actually teems with activity. Cargo is drawn up and lowered from an upper-story window as an agent makes out his bill of lading; barrels are rolled and caulked; crowded ships maneuver in the harbor. In the foreground, a twist of calico cloth and packets of tea symbolize the goods prized by British consumers, while the cocker spaniel stamps the scene as unmistakably English. [Victoria and Albert Museum, London]

Burgeoning global trade in the eighteenth and nineteenth centuries influenced both East and West. Japanese woodblock prints of the late Tokugawa period, for example, had a marked impact on Western art. One of the best known was *A Sudden Shower at Ohashi* by Hiroshige (1797–1858), a contemporary of Hokusai. [The Metropolitan Museum of Art, purchase, 1918, Joseph Pulitzer Bequest]

The artists of the Romantic era sought not only to understand nature but also to commune with it. This classic image of the Romantic solitary—*The Traveler Above the Sea of Clouds* by Caspar David Friedrich, the leading German painter of his time—shows a climber on a mountaintop, above the material strife and illusion of the world, at peace with himself and nature. [Kunsthalle, Hamburg]

Eugéne Delacroix, *Liberty on the Barricades.* In this famous depiction of the 1830 French revolution, perhaps the most celebrated of all images of revolution, an idealized woman of the people leads a charge of workers whose ranks include a single bourgeois. [1830, oil on canvas, 10′10″ × 8′6″ (300 × 259 cm.); Louvre/Réunion des Musées Nationaux]

inseparably linked to it. In this respect, its most characteristic figure is perhaps Rousseau, who dreamed of an ideal community yet found himself always an outsider and insisted on the submission of the individual to the general will while exalting the rights of personal feeling and a liberated human nature. If the eighteenth century has with justice been called the age of reason, it was also a time that knew, in the words of Pascal, that "the heart has its reasons, that reason knows nothing of."

The Emancipation of the Jews

The decline of traditional Christian faith among the elite, the general questioning of the political and social order, and the concept of a secular brotherhood that animated the Enlightenment at its best led to a gradual reassessment of groups that had long been on the margins of European society. Prominent among these were the Jews. There were perhaps a million Jews in eighteenth-century Europe. The overwhelming majority were the Ashkenazim, who lived mainly in the small towns and villages of eastern Poland and Lithuania and spoke the mixed German-Polish dialect called Yiddish. Confined in ghettos, shunned and subjected to periodic outbreaks of looting and massacre known as pogroms, and for the most part desperately poor, they lived in almost complete isolation from the surrounding Christian community, marked off by their distinctive dress, beards, and speech, striving to live by their ancient biblical and rabbinical precepts, and nourishing the secret, never-extinguished hope of a messiah who would lead them out of exile and back to the Holy Land.

By contrast, the Sephardim, mostly the descendants of Jews expelled from Spain and Portugal in the sixteenth century and settled largely in such urban centers as Amsterdam, Venice, London, Frankfurt, and Bordeaux, were more prosperous and cosmopolitan. But Jews everywhere, still commonly blamed for Jesus' death and disliked for their distinctive practices, were subjected to restrictions and prohibitions of every kind. They were periodically driven from anyplace where their numbers seemed alarming, as in Vienna in 1421 and 1669 and Prague in 1557 and 1744. Elsewhere they were restricted by quota; the city of Ulm permitted exactly one Jewish family to reside there. In central and eastern Europe, Jews were forbidden to engage in agriculture and most ordinary trades and were confined to banking, commerce, moneylending, and peddling. They were subject to special taxes and assessments and often pure blackmail: Maria Theresa forced the Jews of Bohemia to pay 3 million florins to spare the community from expulsion. They were barred everywhere from public office, and a bill to naturalize British-born Jews in 1753 was withdrawn in the face of a violent public outcry.

A few Jewish financiers attained great wealth and on occasion political influence. The so-called court Jews of the seventeenth century were merchants and bankers who played a vital role in raising credit, supplying armies, and serving as financial advisers to rulers in Spain, Germany, and Austria. Samuel Oppenheimer (1630–1703) of Heidelberg organized the defense of Vienna against the Turks in 1683. The river fleet he constructed enabled the Austrian army to besiege Budapest and Belgrade, and when the victors brutally sacked the Jewish communities there, he provided for their relief. During the 1690s, as imperial armies fought both Louis XIV in Germany and the Turks in Hungary, Oppenheimer was given the title of director general of war supply. This so scandalized the Viennese that a mob was permitted to attack and loot his mansion, though not, to be sure, until the war was over.

The Sephardic Jews in the west were spared the more horrific experiences of their eastern brethren, such as the pogrom at Uman near Kiev in 1762, when 20,000 Poles and Jews were massacred by peasants and Cossack tribesmen. But all Jewish communities lived in perpetual fear and anxiety. When in 1665 a charismatic Jew of Syrian origin, Sabbatai Zevi (1626–1676), proclaimed himself the messiah, a wave of millennial fervor swept over European Jewry. It gripped not only the poor and downtrodden Ashkenazim of eastern Europe but the wealthiest Jewish families of Amsterdam and Hamburg as well. Tens of thousands of Jews sold their belongings and prepared to march east. Their hopes were tragically disappointed. The Turkish sultan, alarmed at the commotion Zevi's activities had aroused in his dominions, forced him to convert publicly to Islam on pain of death, and his movement collapsed.

Traditional anti-Semitism was at first reinforced by the Enlightenment. Christian anxiety at the weakening of faith was easily deflected toward the Jews; the Hebraic scholar Johann Andreas Eisenmenger (1654–1704) published a 2,000-page anti-Semitic tract in 1699, *Judaism Discovered,* a source frequently mined by later authors. Many of the philosophes were unsympathetic toward the Jews as well, taking up Spinoza's attack on their adherence to the Mosaic law as an enslavement to a dead past. But others, such as Locke and Montesquieu, promoted their cause as victims of the church. In *The Persian Letters,* Montesquieu's fictional correspondent upbraided the conduct of Christian Europeans: "You Christians complain that the Emperor of China roasts all Christians in his dominions on a slow fire. You behave much worse toward the Jews, because they do not believe as you do." The German playwright and critic Gotthold Ephraim Lessing (1729–1781) made a Jew the hero of his drama *Nathan the Wise* (1779). Joseph II saw toleration in more practical terms: "It is our purpose," he wrote, "to make the Jews more useful and serviceable to the state." Though even this most enlightened of despots did not grant Jews full equality, he removed most of the customary disabilities against them, encouraged them to enter agriculture and the crafts, and permitted them to enroll at academies and universities. The poll tax levied against Jews was remitted in France in 1784 and in Prussia in 1787, and the marquis de Pombal, the reforming minister of Joseph I of Portugal, promulgated the first laws against anti-Semitism.

Jewish emancipation was a special case of the more general extension of religious toleration in eighteenth-century Europe. After a long crusade, French Protestants regained in 1787 the civil rights and freedom of worship they had lost by the revocation of the Edict of Nantes in 1685, while in England the first legal Roman Catholic chapel since the mid-sixteenth century opened in Westminster in 1792. The Prussian Law Code of 1794 summed up the fruits of a century of agitation by declaring that "every inhabitant of the state must be granted complete freedom of conscience and religion."

But toleration was a two-edged sword for the Jews. Some embraced it fully, such as the philosopher Moses Mendelssohn (1729–1786), a colleague of Kant's and reputedly the model for *Nathan the Wise*. Mendelssohn founded the Haskalah movement, which attempted to reconcile Enlightenment thought with Jewish tradition. Conservatives, however, viewed such overtures with horror. They feared that what centuries of persecution had failed to do, toleration would at last achieve instead: the destruction of the Jewish community and its assimilation into the dominant Christian culture. The fear of losing Jewish identity also stimulated the growth of Hasidism, a popular religious movement akin to Pietism that emphasized the *aliyah,* or return to Israel. But neither tradition nor nostalgia nor the revival of Judaism's most ancient dream could prevent the incursion of the new secularism into even the most closed quarter of European society. After centuries, the Jews were being forced out of their isolation into a future of uncertain promise.

The assimilation Mendelssohn favored was the main goal of the Reform movement of the early nineteenth century. The first Jewish Reform temple was founded in 1810 in Brunswick, in northern Germany; the service was conducted in German as well as Hebrew, and an organ was used, a musical instrument hitherto associated with Christian churches.

The aim of the Reform movement was to demonstrate that the Jews had lost any sense of nationalism and had become a purely religious sect. Within the movement itself there was considerable debate about the authority of the Hebrew Bible and the Talmud, together with the value of retaining the use of the Hebrew language in religious worship. This challenge to tradition provoked strong reactions, with those who upheld the traditional point of view becoming known as Orthodox. In its present form, Orthodox Judaism combines a strict observance of traditional beliefs and observances with an awareness of their applicability to modern living.

An attempt at compromise inspired the development of the Conservative movement, which began in the United States at the end of the nineteenth century. Both Reform and Conservative Jews worship in synagogues in which the sexes are not segregated and in which prayers in the vernacular are used. Conservative Jews follow the Orthodox tradition of accepting the entire rabbinic tradition of the Talmud, although they interpret it more flexibly; they also promote Jewish aspirations to be recognized as a nation.

An offshoot of the practical aims of Conservatism was the development of the Reconstructionist movement, whose members interpret Jewish traditional practices as folkways acquired over the centuries and religion as only one aspect of the Jews' existence as a people. The Reconstructionist God, far from being the supreme creator and legislator of the Old Testament, is perceived as a cosmic process. Like other splinter movements, Reconstructionism has generally failed to establish itself on a widespread basis, and most practicing Jews today are either Orthodox or Reform, except in the United States, where Conservatism has a large number of followers.

The Abolitionist Movement

The contradiction between the ideals of freedom and equality expressed by the Enlightenment and the reality of eighteenth-century practice was most glaringly evident in the case of slavery. This contradiction was explained away by the assumption of black inferiority. Blacks, it was held, were less developed than whites both biologically and intellectually; thus they felt physical and mental hardships far less keenly. Perpetual children, they were incapable of taking independent responsibility for their lives and hence of genuine liberty. Their management by whites was actually a kindness; one slave ship was piously named the *Social Contract.*

The myth of the happy slave ran aground on the fact of black rebellion. The critic Samuel Johnson shocked a literary gathering at Oxford by offering a toast to the next slave revolt in the colonies. The pamphleteer Thomas Paine asked Americans in 1775 how they could rebel against the British while still keeping slaves themselves. But it was not until nearly the end of the century that a movement to abolish slavery and the slave trade gathered force. Significantly, it was led not by the philosophes but by dissenting English Protestant groups such as Quakers and Baptists as well as a group of Anglicans seeking to revitalize their church, the Clapham sect. The sect's leaders, William Wilberforce (1759–1833) and Thomas Clarkson (1760–1846), lobbied Parliament and campaigned vigorously in the press and in the pulpit, demonstrating again the growing importance of popular opinion. Clarkson, the first reformer to make abolitionism a professional career, interrogated seamen on the Liverpool docks and tracked down witnesses who could testify to the evils of the slave trade. Not to be outdone, the republican leaders of France's National Convention declared slavery abolished

◎ The Revulsion Against Slavery ◎

The opposition to slavery, muted at best in the writings of the philosophes, gained ground in the late eighteenth century and culminated in the abolition of the slave trade in the early nineteenth. The new revulsion was well expressed in this letter of 1778 describing a slave auction in Kingston, Jamaica.

Early this morning a Negro went through all the streets ringing a little bell. He had a slip of paper in his hand and called out something for sale. I asked what he was calling out, and someone answered: "People."

I got dressed and went to the market. There a whole mass of black people was standing about, old and young, men and women, all stark naked, just as God had made them. Each had a card hung around his neck with a number written on it.

Dear God, I thought, here people sell human beings just as we sell geese and pigs.

By nine o'clock, everything was sold, and everyone made his preparations to carry off his newly acquired goods. The little black girl kissed her little brother once again and cried; the old Negroes embraced one another and howled their goodbyes. As they were going, there suddenly started up a dull roaring among them. At first I thought it was just more howling. Then I realized they were singing a song in their Guinea language which would go something as follows:

Far from my homeland
I must languish and die,
Without comfort, amidst struggle and shame.
O the white men, so clever and handsome!
Yet I have done these pitiless white men no harm.
You, there, in heaven, help me, a poor black man!

Source: A. L. von Scholzer, "A New Year's Letter from Jamaica," trans. R. Gay, in P. Gay, ed., *The Enlightenment: A Comprehensive Anthology* (New York: Simon & Schuster, 1973), pp. 688–689.

Am I Not a Man and a Brother? This medallion, struck by Josiah Wedgwood and adopted as the seal of the Slave Emancipation Society, may be regarded as a prototype of the modern political issue button. It was a powerful propaganda weapon in the abolitionist campaign of the late eighteenth century. [Culver Pictures]

outright and all former slaves citizens in 1794, although this edict was never put into effect, and Napoleon later reestablished slavery in the colonies. British abolitionism proved a longer-lasting cause. It gave religious dissenters their first major social cause in 100 years and a chance to show that Christianity too could take its place in the vanguard of progress. If the actual achievement of abolition owed more to the decline of slavery's profitability than anything else, the abolitionist role in forging the political consensus necessary to act was a crucial one.

The Rights of Women

John Adams, replying in 1776 to a suggestion from his wife, Abigail, that the American revolutionaries "remember the ladies" in their new charter of rights, observed with uneasy humor that her letter "was the first intimation that another tribe more numerous and powerful than all the rest were grown discontented." The debate on the rights and status of women already had a long history when Abigail Adams spoke up to her husband. As early as 1589, a woman suitably named (or calling herself) Jane Anger had written a spirited defense of women. During the English revolution some women had preached from the pulpits of Independent congregations, and the colonist Anne Hutchinson (1591–1643) was expelled from Massachusetts Bay for demanding religious freedom; she and five of her children were later murdered by Indians. By the end of the seventeenth century a number of women, including Aphra Behn, Susan Centlivre, Mary de la Riviere Manley, and Eliza Haywood had begun to earn independent livings as writers. Catherine Macaulay (1731–1791) wrote an eight-volume *History of England* as well as pamphlets denouncing the British monarchy and defending the French Revolution, and the educational reformer and abolitionist Hannah More (1745–1833) earned more than £30,000 by her writings. These, however, were exceptions to the norm. Although Daniel Defoe had urged wives to participate actively in their husbands' businesses and a remarkable article in *The Gentleman's Magazine* in 1739 by an anonymous woman writer deplored the fact that the economic helplessness of women forced them to marry against their will, respectable tradesmen preferred to keep their spouses at home, and working women were severely stigmatized.

As we have noted, some women played important roles as hostesses of salons during the Enlightenment, and writers such as Locke, Montesquieu, and Voltaire occasionally commented on the legal disabilities of women. Significant changes were also taking place in the most important institution that touched on women, the family. The emphasis on romantic love and companionship first advanced by writers such as the poet John Milton had become general by the late eighteenth century, and with it, women's expectations in marriage had begun to rise. At the same time, the attack on divine right hierarchy shook traditional notions of male dominance in the family. The entry for "Women" in the *Encyclopedia* pointed out that marriage was a legal contract with mutual rights and responsibilities. The extension of the idea of a contract to marriage and the family had profound social implications. Its consequences are still unfolding today.

But the status of eighteenth-century women, even of the most privileged classes, is better summarized in the careers of two Englishwomen, Lady Mary Wortley Montagu (1689–1762) and Mary Wollstonecraft (1759–1797). Montagu, a woman of great energy and independence, associated on terms of equality with such leading literary figures as Alexander Pope and edited a journal supporting Sir Robert Walpole. Her husband was British ambassador to Constantinople, and in her "Turkish letters," which circulated only in manuscript, she contrasted the freedom of Turkish women to carry on adulterous affairs under their veils with the restraints on women of her own class and nation. Montagu's intention, like Montesquieu's in *The Persian Letters*, was of course satiric, but she had a serious purpose underneath. Before her marriage she had written to her fiancé that wealthy young women were sold by their fathers into marriage "like slaves, and I cannot tell you what price my master will put upon me." Montagu's father had in fact attempted to force her to marry a man she could not love. She had educated herself against his wishes, and when she eventually separated from her chosen husband, she was forced to live the remainder of her life in Italy. Her own experience of oppression gave her sympathy for that of others, and she praised the Roman critic Longinus for having chosen as examples of the best writing of antiquity the work of "a Jew . . . and a woman."

MARY WOLLSTONECRAFT, FEMINIST

Mary Wollstonecraft was the daughter of a tradesman who squandered an inheritance and abused his wife. From an early age she showed signs of rebellion against the conventions of dress and behavior expected of respectable girls. She was also precociously aware of the ill treatment of servants, widows, and the poor generally. Leaving home, first as a lady's companion and then as a schoolmistress, she struck up a passionate friendship with a girl two years her senior, Fanny Blood. It was the first of her many attempts to find the affection and understanding that had been so painfully absent in her family.

At this time too, Wollstonecraft began to find the first adult role models with whom she could identify herself. Respectable society had been shocked by the elopement of Lady Eleanor Butler and Sarah Ponsonby, who set up house together in a remote Welsh valley where they received selected visitors in an exquisitely arranged house and garden. For Wollstonecraft and for many other young Englishwomen, they represented an ideal of companionship and personal freedom.

Escape to Wales was impracticable, but in the London suburb of Newington, Wollstonecraft met the Unitarian minister and political radical Richard Price, whose circle included women writers such as Ann Jebb and Anna Barbauld. Like Lady Montagu, Wollstonecraft soon found her professional outlet in writing. Her first essay, *Thoughts on the Education of Daughters*, was largely conventional in tone, but it contained a bitter complaint against the lack of occupations open to women that clearly echoed her own situation. This was followed by an autobiographical novel that she called simply *Mary*. In it the author advocates both social reform and sexual liberation, and in an uncompleted second novel, *Maria, or the Wrongs of Women*,

John Opie's portrait of the great English feminist Mary Wollstonecraft shows a powerful, mature woman in her mid-thirties whose introspective expression is tinged with sadness and disillusion. Mary may have been pregnant with her second child when this portrait was painted. [National Portrait Gallery, London]

that women have been as brutalized as black slaves and degraded almost beneath the status of reasonable beings:

> The *divine right* of husbands, like the divine right of kings, may, it is to be hoped, in this enlightened age, be contested without danger . . . . I love man as my fellow, but his sceptre, real or usurped, extends not to me, unless the reason of an individual demands my homage; and even then the submission is to reason, and not to man.

It was time, she asserted, not to make place for "a small number of distinguished women" in society but to demand liberation for all.

Wollstonecraft won support in radical circles, but Horace Walpole's denunciation of her as "a hyena in petticoats" was typical of conservative reaction. Her personal life also shocked respectable opinion. She bore a daughter out of wedlock in 1794 and lived openly with the anarchist William Godwin (1756–1836), who opposed marriage on philosophical grounds but agreed to a wedding upon learning of her second pregnancy. Wollstonecraft died ten days after the birth of another daughter, Mary. These scandals, revived by the publication of Godwin's memoirs, led nineteenth-century feminists such as Harriet Martineau to shun her as an unsafe example for the women's movement. It was not until 1889, when Susan B. Anthony and Elizabeth Cady Stanton published the first volume of their *History of Woman Suffrage,* that Mary Wollstonecraft's name was redeemed, and given first place among the pioneers to whom the book was dedicated.

Wollstonecraft makes the latter point even more strongly: "When novelists and moralists praise as a virtue a woman's coldness of constitution and want of passion, I am disgusted."

Like many other British radicals, Wollstonecraft placed great hopes in the French Revolution. Her eye, however, was as much on what could be done in Britain as on what was happening in France. In *A Vindication of the Rights of Man,* written in answer to Edmund Burke's attack on the revolution, she called for the breakup of large estates as a means of relieving urban poverty and denounced Burke's notion of liberty as a cloak for the defense of property interests. She traveled alone to Paris in December 1792 to observe the revolution at first hand and returned to publish a defense of it. "The will of the people," she declared, "is always the voice of reason."

Wollstonecraft's most famous and most important work, however, was *A Vindication of the Rights of Woman,* published in 1792 and now regarded as the true beginning of the modern women's movement. The *Vindication* is a work of passionate indignation; Wollstonecraft declares

The Arts: From Rococo to Neoclassical

The dramatic style of the baroque gave way in the eighteenth century to the smaller-scaled and more refined rococo. With its often elaborate ornamentation, rococo was most effective in intimate, interior forms, and it is for the elegance of its aristocratic drawing rooms, furniture, and porcelain that the period is best remembered. The hold that French culture had taken on Europe during the reign of Louis XIV continued up to the French Revolution. French painting at last displaced Italian and Spanish in the work of Antoine Watteau (1684–1721), Pierre Chardin (1699–1779), François Boucher (1703–1770), and Jean-Honoré Fragonard (1732–1806) and in the vogue enjoyed by the earlier landscape painter Claude Lorrain (1600–1682). Watteau, Boucher, and Fragonard have left us a pictorial record of what Baron Talleyrand meant when he said that no one who had not lived before 1789 had tasted the true sweetness of life. Their aristocratic lords and ladies disport themselves against a pastoral background from which all hint of those on whose labor they existed has been removed. French, too, was the language of the Enlightenment. By the end of the seventeenth century, it had already begun to replace Latin as the language of diplomacy and learning, and it was a disgrace to be unable to speak it in society. Its influence was particularly strong in countries such as Poland, Russia, Sweden, and the German states, whose national literatures were just beginning to develop.

The chief rival to French culture was that of Britain. The brilliant satirist of London life, William Hogarth (1697–1764), showed a world in all its strength and brutality that the French court painters had so carefully eliminated, although Britain's aristocracy too had its chroniclers in Thomas Gainsborough (1727–1788) and Sir Joshua Reynolds (1723–1792). Defoe's *Robinson Crusoe* was translated into French, German, and Swedish, and the novels of Samuel Richardson (1689–1762), Henry Fielding (1707–1754), Laurence Sterne (1713–1768), and Tobias Smollett (1721–1771) had great success. Italy was still regarded as the ultimate finishing school for the cultured European, and a fresh revival of interest in antiquity led to the first excavations of Herculaneum and Pompeii and the beginnings of modern archaeology. European taste was growing more sophisticated and for the first time conscious of artistic history as a sequence of styles and traditions, each with its own value. This led to the emergence of a new kind of literary authority, the critic, whose task was to give perspective to cultural experience and to shape public taste. The critics Lessing, Johann Joachim Winckelmann (1717–1768), and Johann Gottfried von Herder (1744–1803) did much to shape an emerging national consciousness in Germany, while Samuel Johnson (1709–1784), whose life, faithfully chronicled by his admirer James Boswell, is one of history's best-known biographies, reigned for more than two decades as the literary dictator of London. Johnson, stung by the rejection of an early aristocratic patron, exemplified the new bourgeois man of letters who made his own way and owed his position to his own wit and force.

The heroic period of European exploration was largely over, to be replaced by an age of travel. One of the fruits of this was the great enthusiasm for China and its civilization displayed by Leibniz, Voltaire, Diderot, Christian Wolff, and others, a compliment, to be sure, that the Chinese did not return. On an artistic level this expressed itself in a craze for all things Chinese, particularly fine silks and porcelain, that went by the name of *chinoiserie*. Wallpaper and watercolor paints were also introduced from China, and the influence of Chinese painting was particularly evident in the work of Watteau. The European conception of China, based on reports by earlier Jesuit missionaries, was hardly an accurate one; Confucius, who was translated and widely admired, was read as a kind of philosophe. Nonetheless, the fascination with China marked a stage in Europe's expanding consciousness of the outside world; a global culture, as well as a global economy, was taking its first uncertain steps.

Vienna and the Golden Age of Western Music

Of all the forms of art, the only one that produced names to rank with the greatest figures of the seventeenth century was music. The baroque forms that had culminated in Bach and George Friedrich Handel (1685–1759), who adapted the Italian forms of the opera and the oratorio to northern tastes with great success, gave way to a more linear, less ornamental style in the works of Jean-Philippe Rameau (1683–1764) in France and Christoph Willibald von Gluck (1714–1787) in Germany. Bach's eldest son, Carl Philipp Emanuel (1714–1788), in his lifetime far better known than his father, was a crucial link in the development of what came to be called the classical style. This style, which came to fruition in the latter half of the century, was based on the elaboration of an old seventeenth-century form, the sonata. As applied in the orchestral forms of the symphony and the concerto, it produced a music that combined wit, elegance, and formal symmetry in a manner that reflected the balance of intellectual thrust and emotional restraint characteristic of much of eighteenth-century culture. Yet it was capable, too, in the hands of its greatest masters, of achieving extraordinary poignancy and depth.

The leading exponents of the new style were the Austrians Franz Joseph Haydn (1732–1809) and Wolfgang Amadeus Mozart (1756–1791), the latter an astounding prodigy who composed musically mature works from the age of 9 and works of profound originality from his teens. Haydn, slower to develop but immensely prolific in every form of the period, was employed by the greatest noble family of Hungary, the Esterhazys, who maintained a private orchestra for his use. Haydn remained with the Esterhazys all his life, although in later life he traveled widely and accepted commissions from all over Europe. Mozart's patronage was much less secure, and he depended for his living on a fickle public, for whom he turned out music with astonishing speed.

For both men, the Viennese public was the ultimate test of success. The growth of the bourgeoisie in the later reign of Maria Theresa and that of Joseph II had stimulated the development not only of music halls and theaters but also of a very lively salon culture. What verbal display and wit were to the salons of Paris, music was to those of Vienna. There were thousands of amateur musicians and singers in the city, and a British traveler remarked on provincial schools full of young children learning to read, play, and write music. The young Ludwig van Beethoven (1770–1827) came to Vienna at the age of 16, returned to stay permanently at 21, and dominated Viennese musical life for 30 years. His death, and that of Franz Schubert (1797–1828), the only native Viennese among these composers, marked the end of the golden age of Vienna's music. For Beethoven, who burst the bounds of classical tradition to forge the new Romantic style and who commanded an audience throughout Europe, Vienna was merely a stage; but Schubert, who lived his short life in the shadow of his great elder contemporary, was nurtured by the salon culture and the small circle of friends and admirers for whom he wrote his songs, sonatas, and chamber works.

ꟷꟷꟷ

The Enlightenment had a profound and lasting effect on Western culture. It called into question the basic institutions of European society, subjecting them to the test of reason and condemning whatever fell short by its measure. On the surface, it seemed the work of a small, self-appointed band of critics, the philosophes, who for the most part lacked status and position and were frequently hounded, censored, and even imprisoned. Yet the philosophes themselves represented only the cutting edge of the great transformation of Western thought that had begun with the Reformation, the commercial expansion of Europe, and above all the scientific revolution. If they succeeded despite such apparent odds, it was largely because their conservative opponents had capitulated to their values and ambitions or found it imprudent to resist. This was most evident in the phenomenon of enlightened despotism. If the seventeenth century had marked the triumph of a new order of the universe, the eighteenth produced a new vision of humanity to complement it. To many, this vision was troubling. But even those who continued to seek comfort in a traditional Christianity were forced to redefine it in terms of achieving secular progress on earth.

Notes

1. R. Zaller, *Europe in Transition, 1660–1815* (New York: Harper & Row, 1984), p. 12.
2. L. G. Crocker, *An Age of Crisis: Man and World in Eighteenth-Century French Thought* (Baltimore: Johns Hopkins University Press, 1959), p. 328.

Suggestions for Further Reading

Beales, D. *Joseph II*, vol. 1. Cambridge: Cambridge University Press, 1987.

Bernard, P. P. *Joseph II*. New York: Twayne, 1968.

Besterman, T. *Voltaire*. New York: Harcourt, Brace & World, 1969.

Cassirer, E. *The Philosophy of the Enlightenment*. Boston: Beacon Press, 1951.

Comini, A. *The Changing Image of Beethoven*. New York: Rizzoli, 1987.

Crocker, L. G. *An Age of Crisis: Man and World in Eighteenth-Century French Thought*. Baltimore: Johns Hopkins University Press, 1959.

Darnton, R. *The Business of Enlightenment: A Publishing History of the Encyclopedia, 1775–1800*. Cambridge, Mass.: Belknap Press, 1979.

———. *The Literary Underground of the Old Regime*. Cambridge, Mass.: Harvard University Press, 1982.

Ferguson, M., ed. *First Feminists: British Women Writers, 1578–1799*. Bloomington: Indiana University Press, 1984.

Gay, P. *The Enlightenment: An Interpretation*. 2 vols. New York: Knopf, 1966, 1969.

Gelbart, N. R. *Feminine and Opposition Journalism in Old Regime France: le Journal des dames*. Berkeley: University of California Press, 1987.

Gough, J. W. *The Social Contract*, 2d ed. Oxford: Clarendon Press, 1957.

Hazard, P. *The European Mind, 1680–1715*. New Haven, Conn.: Yale University Press, 1935.

Israel, J. I. *European Jewry in the Age of Mercantilism, 1550–1750*. New York: Oxford University Press, 1985.

Jacob, M. *The Radical Enlightenment: Pantheists, Freemasons and Republicans*. Boston: Allen & Unwin, 1980.

Jones, R. E. *The Emancipation of the Russian Nobility, 1762–1785*. Princeton, N.J.: Princeton University Press, 1973.

Krieger, L. *An Essay on the Theory of Enlightened Despotism*. Chicago: University of Chicago Press, 1975.

Lough, J. *The Encyclopedia*. New York: McKay, 1971.

Madariaga, I. de. *Russia in the Age of Catherine the Great*. London: Weidenfeld & Nicolson, 1981.

Manuel, F. *The Eighteenth Century Confronts the Gods*. Cambridge, Mass.: Harvard University Press, 1959.

Rendall, J. *The Origins of Modern Feminism: Women in Britain, France and the United States, 1780–1860*. New York: Macmillan, 1984.

Ritter, G. *Frederick the Great: A Historical Profile*. Berkeley: University of California Press, 1968.

Rogers, K. *Feminism in Eighteenth-Century England*. Urbana: University of Illinois Press, 1982.

Shklar, J. *Men and Citizens: A Study of Rousseau's Social Theory*. London: Cambridge University Press, 1969.

Spencer, S. I., ed. *French Women and the Age of the Enlightenment*. Bloomington: Indiana University Press, 1985.

Tomalin, C. *The Life and Death of Mary Wollstonecraft*. New York: New American Library, 1974.

Wade, I. O. *The Intellectual Origins of the French Enlightenment*. Princeton, N.J.: Princeton University Press, 1957.

Wilson, A. *Diderot*. 2 vols. New York: Oxford University Press, 1957, 1972.

The French Revolution and Napoleon

Great transformations had taken place in Western society between the beginning of the sixteenth century and the end of the eighteenth. The Reformation had shattered the unity of Christendom, and the Enlightenment had challenged the roots of Christian belief itself. The European economy had acquired a global dimension through the conquest and exploitation of the New World and the expansion of its markets in Asia and Africa. The scientific revolution had reordered Western people's views of the cosmos and themselves. Yet the political order of Europe had remained relatively static. The nations of Europe were still governed by kings and princes. The nobility was still predominant, its privileges seemingly more entrenched than ever.

The French Revolution challenged all that. Within a matter of weeks in the summer of 1789, a social and political edifice that had stood for 1,000 years was torn down, and for a generation all of Europe was caught up in the convulsive changes that ensued. From the very beginning, the revolution was recognized as the most important event of the age. In its turmoil and agony the shape of the modern world first became visible. Two centuries later, historians are still debating its nature and its impact.

An engraving of the pamphleteer and power broker Abbé Sieyes, who was a major force in the atmosphere of intrigue that surrounded the Directory in its last days. [Granger Collection]

The Crisis of the Old Order in France

The revolution began as an uprising not by the poorest segment of French society but by its richest and most privileged one. It was inevitable that the nobility would react against the autocratic rule of Louis XIV and seek to reassert their power. The long reign of the indolent Louis XV (1715–1774) provided them with an opportunity to do so. Thus while in most other places the privileges of the nobility were being reshaped and in many cases curtailed by enlightened despots, in France they remained unchecked. The intendants whom Louis XIV had sent to break the nobles' control of the provinces had been neutralized. The nobility's monopoly on the best and most lucrative offices in the church, the army, and the government was growing more and more restrictive; by the 1780s, for example, it required four generations of noble blood to qualify for an army commission. The parlements, the chief courts of the realm, had regained much of their old power to challenge and obstruct royal edicts, claiming broad powers of judicial review. By the 1760s they had grown bold enough to imprison provincial governors and military commanders who attempted to execute royal orders that they held to be illegal.

Of all their privileges, the one the nobility defended the most stubbornly was their exemption from most forms of taxation. Attempts to levy even token amounts in 1726 and 1749 met with furious resistance and had to be dropped. For the nobleman, taxation was the ultimate insult: like public flogging, it was something properly inflicted only on commoners. The bourgeoisie or upper merchant and professional class—a steadily expanding group in the eighteenth century—also sought to avoid taxation as a mark of status and in large part succeeded. The result was that while the privileged classes grew richer, the state became poorer, obliged as it was to rely on the poorest and most depressed sectors of the economy for support.

Reform and Reaction

Stung by the open defiance of his authority, Louis XV at last attempted to act. Guided by a reforming minister, René Charles de Maupeou (1714–1792), he took the daring step of abolishing the parlements outright and exiled their former judges to remote parts of the country. In their place he created new courts whose members would no longer have life tenure in office but could be removed at pleasure. At the same time, he undertook reforms to reduce the public debt to manageable proportions and to put the state's finances in order.

These measures were greeted by a storm of protest. Louis and Maupeou were attacked as despots bent on overthrowing the constitution. The king, however, remained firm. After nearly 60 years, he had finally decided to govern. It was too late. His death in 1774 brought his 20-year-old grandson, Louis XVI (1774–1792), to the throne. Louis was an affable, pious young man, fond of hunting and gardening and eager to please. He was soon persuaded to abandon his father's reforms and to restore the old parlements.

The Fiscal Crisis

The new king was ably served by his chief ministers, the philosopher Turgot (1774–1776) and the banker Necker (1776–1781). Both sought to relieve the chronic indebtedness of the crown by easing trade restrictions, abolishing guild monopolies, and raising new taxes. The need for reform was clear and had now become urgent. The 26 provinces of France represented a hopeless tangle of conflicting laws and jurisdictions. Taxes levied in one were prohibited in another. Commerce was impeded everywhere by customs and tolls; even a uniform system of weights and measures was lacking. But Turgot and Necker found themselves stymied. The revived parlements rejected their proposals out of hand, and factional intrigue undermined their position at court. Each in turn was forced from office, having accomplished nothing of substance.

The crown's plight was worsened by its participation in the American War for Independence, which added considerably to the debt burden. By 1786 interest payment on the existing debt amounted to half the royal budget, and the treasury was borrowing to meet that. At last it could obtain no further credit at any price. The king's comptroller, Charles de Calonne, informed his master that the state was bankrupt.

A new tax was the only possible solution. To circumvent the inevitable opposition of the parlements and to appeal directly to the more liberal nobility, Calonne proposed that Louis call a handpicked Assembly of Notables. This body convened in February 1787, but, suspicious of Calonne's motives and unwilling to bypass the parlements, it refused to support his program. Louis dismissed Calonne and dissolved the assembly.

The Constitutional Crisis

The financial crisis now became a constitutional one. The parlements now insisted that new taxes could be granted only by the representative assembly of the whole realm, the Estates General. This ancient feudal body had not met since 1614, but the judges made it into a symbol of popular liberty. Adopting the language of the Enlightenment, they insisted that law was the expression of reason, the general will, and the rights of man. It could no longer be accepted as the will of a single individual.

The crown found itself isolated, the natural focus of all discontent. The nobility feared it as the usurper of its privileges. The peasantry, ground under by taxes, resented it as the expropriator of its labor. The bourgeoisie saw it as a barrier to wealth and status. Its problems were blamed not on genuine need but on the extravagance of the court. Whereas the pomp of Versailles under Louis XIV had reflected the glory of France, it now symbolized the decadence of personal monarchy.

Louis finally attempted to suppress the parlements as his father had done and set up new courts in their place. But the tide of reform could no longer be stopped by a show of force. Rioting and near-rebellion broke out in the provinces, and committees of correspondence were formed on the model of the American Revolution. The clergy threatened to reduce their annual "gift" to the treasury, and the king's own courtiers opposed him. Louis backed down. In July 1788 he recalled the parlements, whose judges returned as heroes, and agreed to summon the Estates General. The revolt of the nobility had triumphed.

Progressive opinion now looked for a system of constitutional government to emerge, with the Estates General evolving into a more or less modern representative body like the British Parliament or the American Congress. But the progressives were in for a shock. The judges of the parlements may have spoken the language of Rousseau and Thomas Jefferson, but they had no intention of sharing the powers they had pried from the crown. The Parlement of Paris ruled at once that the new Estates General must have the same form as the old, with three separate chambers representing the clergy, the nobility, and the commoners of the realm. Because each chamber voted as a separate unit, the two privileged orders could always outvote the Third Estate of the commons, which in fact was made up of merchants, financiers, petty officials, and members of the professions, the group loosely referred to as the bourgeoisie. Except in theory, none of these groups represented the actual majority of peasants and workers who made up four-fifths of the population.

The Bourgeoisie and the Third Estate

The situation now boiled down to a three-cornered struggle among the king, the nobility, and the bourgeoisie. The resentment of this last group was of long standing. The bourgeoisie regarded themselves as the most productive element in society. They chafed at economic restrictions which they saw as largely designed to protect the interests of the nobility and, though some of them had acquired fortunes as great as any nobleman's, they were bitter at their exclusion from the highest echelons of status and power. As the political debate widened, they also came to

◎ France on the Eve of Revolution ◎

The English traveler Arthur Young gives a vivid impression of the ferment in pre-revolutionary France in his account of a dinner party in 1787.

Dined today with a party, whose conversation was entirely political. . . . One opinion pervaded the whole company, that they are on the eve of some great revolution in the government: that everything points to it: the confusion in the finances great; with a deficit impossible to provide for without the states-general of the kingdom, yet no ideas formed of what would be the consequence of their meeting: no minister existing, or to be looked to in or out of power, with such decisive talents as to promise any other remedy than palliative ones: a prince on the throne, with excellent dispositions, but without the resources of a mind that could govern in such a moment without ministers: a court buried in pleasure and dissipation . . . a great ferment amongst all ranks of men, who are eager for some change, without knowing what to look to, or to hope for: and a strong leaven of liberty, increasing every hour since the American revolution; altogether form a combination of circumstances that promise ere long to ferment into motion, if some master hand, of very superior talents, and inflexible courage, be not found at the helm to guide events, instead of being driven by them.

Source: A. Young, *Travels in France During the Years 1787, 1788, and 1789,* ed. C. Maxwell (Cambridge: Cambridge University Press, 1950), pp. 84–85.

see themselves as speaking, through the Third Estate, for the nation as a whole. Their position was eloquently summarized in a pamphlet circulated early in 1789 by a liberal clergyman, the Abbé Sieyès (1748–1836), which asked:

> *What is the Third Estate? Everything.*
> *What has it been thus far in the political*
> *   order? Nothing.*
> *What does it demand? To be something.*[1]

The Third Estate's discontent was the king's opportunity. If he could exploit it properly, he could outflank the opposition to tax reform and break the back of the nobles' revolt. Urged on by Necker, who had been restored to power, Louis decreed that the Estates General be popularly elected: nobles by nobles, clergy by clergy, and the Third Estate by all other males over 25 whose names appeared on the tax rolls. With a stroke of the pen, the king had enfranchised millions of Frenchmen for the first time.

In deference to this greatly expanded electorate, Louis agreed to "double the Third," that is, to permit twice as many representatives to be chosen for the Third Estate as for the other two orders. But this did not affect the voting balance of the three estates. Each order would still vote as a separate unit. In terms of actual power, therefore, the Third Estate's position remained that of a minority.

Louis' position was bound to leave the Third Estate unsatisfied. But the concessions he had made also aroused fierce opposition from the nobility, the Parlement of Paris, and even the royal family. The king was caught between a bourgeoisie he dared not trust and a nobility he dared not abandon.

In the meantime, an election fever swept over France. In 40,000 electoral districts all over the country, lists of grievances were compiled to be sent along with the delegates; the lists revealed widespread dissatisfaction with the social system. The same demands were repeated insistently: popular representation, legislative control of taxation, and a limitation of the monarchy. Also bitterly attacked were church tithes; traditional payments by peasants to the local lord, which ranged from a tenth to a third of the value of their crop; and hunting rights that enabled the nobility to trample across fields and vineyards in pursuit of game. The lists of the Third Estate were virtually unanimous in demanding full civil equality for all Frenchmen.

In these grievances and demands lay the seeds of a social revolution. The nobility had wanted to protect its privileges, the bourgeoisie to share them. What arose from the countryside was a cry of protest at the exploitation that the peasantry had suffered at the hands of both. Throughout the eighteenth century noble and bourgeois landholding increased, as the peasants were squeezed onto smaller and smaller plots and sometimes entirely off them. In the region of Toulouse in the south, for example, where a capitalist, market-oriented agriculture had developed, wage-earning laborers made up a majority of the rural population 50 years before the revolution. Many of those peasants who still owned land could not produce enough on it to feed themselves and their families, and they too depended on wage labor for survival. This meant that more Frenchmen were vulnerable to a subsistence crisis—crop failure compounded by price rises and hoarding—than ever before.

As it happened, the worst political crisis in the nation's history coincided with the worst subsistence crisis of the eighteenth century. Following a period of expansion in midcentury, France had entered a long cycle of depression after 1770. This was aggravated by a series of bad harvests, culminating in that of 1788. Starving peasants fled to the towns, swelling the urban unemployment rate to as high as 50 percent. Even people who had work found up to 80 percent of their earnings consumed by the price of bread. By the spring of 1789 there were violent uprisings against grain prices and shortages, and wandering bands roved the countryside, attacking the castles of the nobility.

The Revolution of 1789

France had known periods of disorder before, but the circumstances that now converged on it—a constitutional crisis that was a thinly veiled struggle for power among contending political and economic groups, a monarchy enfeebled not only by an incompetent ruler but also by attacks on its fundamental legitimacy, a widespread sense of social injustice and an assumption that radical change was inevitable—all combined to bring about the collapse of the government, the destruction of the manorial order, and the replacement of a society based on the division of estates and orders into one predicated, at least in theory, on the legal and political equality of all citizens. This was the revolution of 1789.

From the Estates General to the National Assembly

The 1,165 delegates to the Estates General were the focus of all hopes when they came together at Versailles on May 5, 1789. The First Estate of the clergy consisted of 291 delegates, of whom 46 were bishops; the majority were hardworking and underpaid parish priests, close to the peasantry they served and sympathetic to reform. The 270 nobles of the Second Estate also included a vociferous reform group. Among its number was the marquis de Lafayette (1757–1834), already celebrated as a hero of the American Revolution. Of the 578 commoners who com-

Louis XVI presides from his raised throne at the opening of the Estates General on May 5, 1789. Louis' failure to provide a credible reform program or to resolve the issue of whether the estates would vote by number or by order ended the last royal hope to control events. [Photographie Bulloz]

prised the Third Estate,* well over half were lawyers, most of whom also held government jobs, and another quarter were merchants, businessmen, and rentiers, persons who lived off the profits of feudal dues. Despite the wide franchise, not a single worker or peasant had been elected. This was partly because the final selection of delegates took place at only 200 district assemblies, where the influence of local notables predominated, and partly because of the traditional deference of the electorate to its social superiors. The result was that the full Third Estate was represented only by its narrowest elite, although an elite angry and embittered at its rebuff by the nobility.

Had the crown been able to assert itself at this point, a compromise might still have been found. But Louis and Necker had no program to present, no solution to offer. The king spoke of caution, his minister of deficits. Leaderless, the Estates General fell to wrangling over the question of voting by orders, with the Third Estate insisting that the three orders merge into a single body. As this not only would have given the Third Estate a numeric voting majority but would also have abolished the principle

of separate orders on which the privileges of the clergy and the nobility rested, it was stoutly resisted. On June 17, after weeks of deadlock, the Third Estate took the decisive step toward revolution: it declared itself an independent body, the National Assembly, with the right to legislate alone in the public interest. Three days later the members of the Third Estate found themselves locked out of their chamber. They gathered in a nearby indoor tennis court, where in great passion and excitement they vowed not to disband until they had given France a constitution.

Louis now acted. He told the Estates General that he would give it a permanent place in the state, with wide though unspecified rights over the administration and the budget. In this he seemed to accept the principle of a limited monarchy that had been demanded on all sides. But he also declared the self-created National Assembly (whose numbers had now been swollen by dissident clergy and nobility) null and void and ordered the Estates to return to their separate chambers. The nobles were elated. The king had come down for the principle of blood privilege on which his own throne ultimately rested. But the Third Estate remained defiant. Facing mutinous soldiers and an angry populace, Louis backed down. On June 27 the first two Estates united with the Third. The National Assembly was now a fact.

---

*The remaining 26 delegates were unclassified.

The Popular Revolution

The revolution now moved into the streets. The workers and tradesmen of Paris, fearing both rural mobs and military repression, broke into the civic arsenals and armed themselves. On July 14 they stormed the ancient fortress of the Bastille and seized its weapons after a pitched battle in which 98 of the attackers were killed. This event, still celebrated annually in France, was of enormous symbolic significance. It gave the revolution its baptism of blood and resulted in the final collapse of the king's authority. Riots broke out and arsenals were pillaged in Bordeaux, Lyons, and other large cities. In some eastern towns, such as Sedan, Nancy, and Troyes, there were violent clashes, but elsewhere, as in Strasbourg and Rennes, the army defected en masse. In many places the intendants and municipal officials simply fled, leaving the local population to organize citizen militias and revolutionary committees, or *communes,* on the model already established in Paris.

Disorder broke out simultaneously in the countryside, often triggered by a wave of rumor and hysteria, the so-called Great Fear, which centered around reports of advancing royalist or bandit armies. From town to town the cry went up, "The brigands are coming!" Since there were enough bandits in the best of times, these fears were not without foundation. They soon became a pretext for looting, and by late July a full-scale agrarian insurrection was in progress. Peasants broke into the manor houses of the nobility, systematically destroying the legal records of debts and feudal dues. What went up in flames was more than paper. In the high summer of 1789 the Old Regime itself was dying in a thousand bonfires throughout France.

The Abolition of Privilege and the Declaration of the Rights of Man

The bourgeois members of the National Assembly were far from pleased with this wholesale destruction of property rights. But they quickly moved to ratify what they were powerless to prevent. On the night of August 4 two liberal noblemen, coached by leaders of the Third Estate, moved to abolish all compulsory labor service, such as road maintenance, and to offer redemption for all other dues and obligations. What can only be described as a

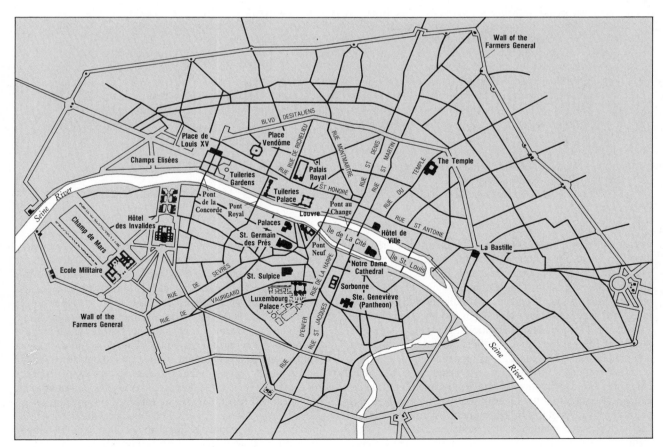

26.1 Paris at the Outbreak of the French Revolution

◎ The Fall of the Bastille: ◎
An Eyewitness Account

*Jean-Baptiste Humbert, a Parisian watchmaker who claimed to have
been the first to scale the walls of the Bastille on July 14, 1789, provides a vivid account of the excitement and confusion of that day.*

I followed the crowd, to get to the cellar where the arms were kept. On the staircase
leading to the cellar, seeing a man armed with two muskets, I took one from him, and
went up again; but the crowd at the top of the stair was so great that all those who were
climbing up were pushed down again, and fell right into the cellar. . . . In spite of this
horrible tumble, the crowd persisted in going down the stairs, and as nobody could get
up again, there was such a crush in the cellar that people were shrieking and gasping for
breath. . . . Afterwards I went to the cannon that stood just above the drawbridge of the
Bastille, in order to push it off its guncarriage and render it unusable. But as I stood for
this purpose with my shoulder under the mouth of the cannon, someone in the vicinity
fired at me, and the bullet pierced my coat and waistcoat and wounded me in the neck; I
fell down senseless; the Swiss soldier whose life I had spared dragged me on to the staircase, still clutching my gun, so he told me. . . . On my way home I remembered some
friends who lived in the rue de la Ferronnerie; I had left them that morning, and they had
seemed anxious about the dangers which they foresaw my zeal might lead me into. I
went to their house, and four armed bourgeois escorted me to the rue du Hurepoix. I was
greeted with praise wherever I went; but when we reached the Quai des Augustins, we
were followed by a crowd of people who mistook me for a malefactor, and twice attempted to put me to death. As I could not explain things to everyone, I was about to be
seized, when I was recognized by a bookseller on the Quai, who rescued me from the
hands of the crowd and took me into his own home. . . . I rested until about midnight,
when I was woken by repeated cries of *to arms! to arms!* Then I could not resist my
longing to be of some further use. I got up, armed myself, and went to the guardroom,
where I found M. Poirier, the Commanding Officer [of the National Guard], under whose
orders I remained until the following morning.

Source: J. Godechot, *The Taking of the Bastille, July 14th, 1789*, trans. J. Stewart (New York: Scribner,
1970), pp. 281–286 passim.

psychological stampede ensued. Member after member
arose to volunteer renunciation of his own privileges and
those of cities, corporations, and provincial estates.
Hoarse and exhausted, the delegates adjourned at 2 A.M.
with the declaration, "Feudalism is abolished." By morning
many had repented their enthusiasm and tried to reinstate
various qualifications and exemptions. It was too late. The
people of France took them at their most generous word
and simply ceased to pay all former dues.

The assembly's next step was to issue a constitutional
blueprint, the Declaration of the Rights of Man and the
Citizen (August 26). Its 17 brief articles summarized the
political principles of the Enlightenment. All men, it stated,
"are born and remain free and equal in rights." Those
rights were defined as "liberty, property, security, and

resistance to oppression," which it was the duty of every
state to preserve. Sovereign power was declared to be
vested in the nation as a whole, and law was to be the
expression of the general will. Freedom of speech and
religion were guaranteed, and liberty—the right "to do
anything that does not harm another person"—could be
abridged only by due process of law, before which all men
were to be regarded as equal. The declaration was to
remain the basic document of the revolution, however far
subsequent regimes departed from its principles in practice. At one stroke it eliminated the archaic, cumbersome
divisions of French society. It replaced the system of orders by one based on formal civil equality and cleared the
ground for the modern political and economic development
of France. It also made devastating propaganda. Trans-

Classical and biblical symbols entwine in this engraved representation of the Declaration of the Rights of Man. The preamble and the seventeen articles of the document are depicted as the tablets of a new Mosaic law, while two female deities appear against a sky whose parting clouds reveal the light. The figure on the left holds the broken chains of privilege, while the winged figure on the right holds the staff of popular sovereignty. A luminous eye representing the God of Reason completes the trinity. [Historical Pictures Service, Chicago]

lated into every major European language, it shook the established order and galvanized demands for reform across the Continent.

The king alone remained passive and aloof in the face of these developments. This led to the last of the revolutionary tremors of 1789. On October 5 a contingent of Parisian housewives, having previously invaded the mayor's office to protest food shortages and the continuing high price of bread, marched to Versailles and demanded that Louis return to the capital. They were soon backed up by the arrival of the newly formed National Guard under Lafayette, 20,000 strong. Virtually defenseless, the royal family was forced to accompany this motley procession back to Paris, where they took up residence in the Palace of the Tuileries. The National Assembly followed a few days later, and Louis gave his unhappy consent to the August 4 decrees and the Declaration of the Rights of Man.

The New Order, 1789–1791

The poet Chateaubriand was later to remark that the nobility had begun the revolution and the people had finished it. But despite the slogan that now epitomized the goals of the Revolution—"Liberty, fraternity, equality"—there was no single "people" of France, only groups with divided and often bitterly contending interests. On one extreme were the 20,000 people, mostly aristocrats, who had left the country and rejected the revolution. On the other were those, especially the *sans-culottes** or working class of the towns, who had gained theoretically but not materially from it and continued to demand both relief from high prices and scarcity and representation of their interests. In between were the great mass of the peasants, who wished chiefly to consolidate the fruits of their rebellion in July, the destruction of the manorial regime and the freeing of their title to the lands they farmed.

The Bourgeoisie in Power

Actual power was in the hands of none of these groups, however, but rather those of the bourgeoisie, the unexpected beneficiaries of the collapse of royal authority and the abolition of the order of the nobility. The bourgeoisie dominated the National Assembly or, as it called itself from October 1789, the Constituent Assembly. The assembly had two crucial tasks: to write a new constitution for France and to govern the nation while doing so. Having achieved power and control of the king by mass action, it wanted no further interruption of its business by the sans-culottes. Its first acts from its new base in Paris were to declare martial law and censorship of the press, and on October 21 a young laborer, Michel Adrien, was hanged for sedition. The honeymoon of the Third Estate was over.

---

*Literally, "without breeches." For practical reasons, workingmen wore long pants instead of the silk or muslin stockings and breeches of the nobility and the bourgeoisie.

The assembly's desire to insulate the new government against undue popular influence was reflected in the constitution of 1791. Contrary to Article 6 of the Declaration of the Rights of Man, the constitution distinguished between "active" and "passive" citizens. Both groups enjoyed full civil rights, but only the actives, those meeting a minimum property qualification, had the right to vote for some 50,000 electors, who in turn chose the 500 representatives of the Legislative Assembly. About two-thirds of the adult male population qualified for active citizenship and fewer than half of it for nomination as electors. This was still a far wider franchise than in England, and the property qualification for voting was lower than in some states in America. But since the electors were obliged to spend several days choosing representatives at their own expense and often at a considerable distance from home, the process ensured that they would necessarily be men of means and leisure—in short, men of the bourgeoisie.

The Reorganization of Church and State

The most pressing issue before the Constituent Assembly was the unresolved crisis of the public debt. The simplest recourse was to repudiate it as a legacy of the discredited Old Regime. As a substantial portion of the debt was owed to members of the bourgeoisie, however, there was no question of doing that. Instead, the assembly decided to pay the debt off by selling the lands of the church, which it declared to be confiscated in the name of the nation. A special currency called *assignats* was issued to facilitate the purchase of these lands. In this way some 10 percent of the real estate of France was redistributed to deserving—that is, chiefly bourgeois—revolutionaries.

This massive transaction destroyed the financial independence of the church and made it a ward of the state. Clergymen became salaried officials, chosen from a qualified slate by popular election like other state functionaries. Archbishoprics were abolished, and the number of bishops was reduced from 135 to 83. Monasteries and nunneries were dissolved, and the taking of religious vows was prohibited. The pope was to be informed as a matter of courtesy when a bishop was installed, but his authority was in no other way recognized.

These changes were embodied in the Civil Constitution of the Clergy (1790). They were less drastic than they seemed, for the Gallican church might have been expected to respond favorably, since clergymen's salaries were to be nearly doubled under the new dispensation. The problem was ratification. The church wanted to adopt the Civil Constitution on its own authority, thereby affirming its continued identity as a corporate body. To the assembly, this would have been tantamount to recognizing the existence of a First Estate again, when all estates and orders had been abolished. It therefore promulgated the new constitution alone and backed it up with an oath of allegiance that all clergy were required to swear.

The assembly perhaps could not have acted otherwise, since Pope Pius VI, whose antagonism to the revolution was fanned by émigré agents in Rome, was preparing to denounce the Civil Constitution. The result, however, was to divide the French church. Half the lower clergy refused to take the new oath, and all but seven of the bishops as well. The "refractory" or "nonjuring" clergy, as they were called, emigrated or went underground, where, protected by loyal parishioners, they formed a natural focus of resistance to the revolution. Far from becoming an obedient servant of the state, the church would henceforth be its bitterest enemy.

Equally far-reaching was the assembly's reorganization of administration and government. All former courts and jurisdictions were abolished. A uniform code of administration was instituted for the 44,000 rural and urban districts of the country. The 26 old provinces, many of them rich with history (and memories of previous rebellions), were replaced by 83 "departments," all newly named and democratically equal in size. An independent judiciary was established, with elected judges and juries for criminal trials. Yet, although the administration was thus radically standardized, it was actually less centrally controlled than under the Old Regime. Local and regional officials were to be elected from below rather than appointed from above, and they were left essentially on their own in the work of government. In this respect, the Constituent Assembly's reforms did not go nearly far enough. Anxious to avoid the charge of despotism leveled at the Old Regime, it left the implementation of its decrees in the hands of officials over whom it had little effective control. Had the revolution been securely established, such a system might have been workable. As matters stood, with an embittered nobility, a divided church, a suspicious peasantry, and an unsatisfied proletariat, it was an open invitation to resistance. Counterrevolutionary disturbances broke out in the region of the Midi around Toulouse, Nîmes, and Montauban in the spring of 1790, precursors of full-scale rebellion to come.

The status of the king posed a difficult question. It was inexpedient to depose Louis, as republican members of the assembly wished. He was the only remaining link between the old France and the new and the only valid symbol of authority for millions of French citizens. At the same time, despite his grudging approval of the Declaration of the Rights of Man and the Civil Constitution of the Clergy, his hostility to the revolution was plain. His powers were therefore restricted to a three-year suspensive veto over the Legislative Assembly.

But Louis refused to play the role assigned him. On June 20, 1791, he attempted to flee the country with the royal family. Captured by peasants at the border town of Varennes, they were forced to return to Paris in a humiliating procession. The assembly accepted the fiction that the king had been "kidnapped." It was clear to all, however, that even before its formal adoption, the new constitution had been repudiated by the man intended to serve as its head of state.

In the long run, the work of the Constituent Assembly was of great importance. It dissolved and replaced the institutions of the Old Regime and laid the foundations of the modern French state. But it failed to solve almost all the immediate problems before it. It passed out of existence on September 30, 1791, leaving behind a sharply polarized nation, mounting political and economic chaos, and a constitution that, satisfying no one, survived it by barely ten months.

The Revolution and Europe

At first many people outside France greeted the revolution with enthusiasm and even rapture. "How much the greatest event that has happened in the world, and how much the best!" exulted the British politician Charles James Fox. The poet William Wordsworth later recalled the sense of liberation and almost limitless hope inspired by the French revolution:

> *Bliss it was in that dawn to be alive*
> *But to be young was very heaven!*

Elsewhere, too, the reformers rejoiced. In Germany the elderly philosopher Kant and the young nationalist Johann Fichte both sang the revolution's praises, and the bourgeoisie of Hamburg turned out to celebrate the first anniversary of the fall of the Bastille. Societies and clubs in support of the revolution were founded in Switzerland, Savoy, the Netherlands, and Britain, and many of them engaged in revolutionary activities themselves. An uprising in the Austrian Netherlands drove the imperial army out of Brussels in December 1789, while in the Rhineland peasants refused to pay seigneurial dues to their lords. Not content to admire from afar, many activists gathered in Paris to participate directly in the revolution, including the American pamphleteer Tom Paine and the Prussian Anarchasis Cloots, who styled himself the "representative of the human race."

Not all reaction was favorable, however. The British statesman and orator Edmund Burke (1729–1797), who had supported the American Revolution, wrote a highly effective rebuttal in his *Reflections on the Revolution in France* (1790), which remains to this day a classic statement of the conservative view of history. Burke argued forcefully against the assumption that all men possessed identical natural rights. Not men, he contended, but nations were the basic units of history. Each nation was a unique cultural entity shaped by its distinctive historic ex-

perience. Reforms that respected the time-tested institutions of the nation were right and proper. But for a single generation to destroy those institutions and to attempt to substitute some abstract formula of justice for the collective wisdom of all its predecessors was an act of folly and arrogance, a "fond election of evil" that could bring only ruin.

The émigrés who fled France brought their own tales of horror, and the monarchies of Europe were soon alert to the danger the revolution posed. Bavaria, Sardinia, Spain, and Portugal took steps to suppress all expressions of revolutionary solidarity within their own borders, and Spain posted troops along its frontier to keep out the "French plague." Not until August 1791 were the two largest Continental powers able to agree on a joint statement of policy toward France. The Declaration of Pillnitz, issued by Frederick William IV (1786–1797) of Prussia and Leopold II (1790–1792) of Austria, stated as its goal the restoration of the French monarchy, by force if necessary. A declaration without an act of war, it served only to strengthen the republicans in France, who argued that the revolution would never be complete or secure as long as Louis remained king.

♣ PARIS AND THE FALL OF THE MONARCHY

Paris was the nerve center of the revolution, the seat of national government and the home of the volatile sans-culottes, who comprised half its population of 600,000. The city had enjoyed its own revolution in July 1789 when it overthrew its royal administration and improvised, almost on the spot, a new governing authority, the Commune, based on representation from the electoral districts set up to choose delegates to the Estates General. These districts, subsequently reorganized into 48 "sections," remained the heart of the city's political activity. Although the Constituent Assembly attempted to restrict the franchise to the communal assembly, which was the city's official governing body, to so-called active citizens, the section assemblies themselves, open in practice to all comers, were at their best schools of democracy in which, in the words of a contemporary petition, "there reigns that equality, that fraternity of the golden age that our benevolent laws are seeking to restore."

Political activism in the city spilled over into numerous popular clubs and societies, of which the most famous, the Jacobins,* had more than 400 provincial affiliates by 1791 and debated before audiences of up to 2,000. By 1793 half a million people were enrolled in such clubs. Some of them

---

*So named from their original meeting place in the former convent of the Jacobin order.

functioned as interest groups or embryonic political parties; the Jacobins themselves had originated as a caucus of liberal members of the National Assembly. To such groups were added the *fédérés,* or "federations," spontaneous unions of the municipal councils and militias of the provinces that converged on Paris on the first anniversary of the fall of the Bastille to affirm their loyalty to the revolution. When not gathered in the large crowds and assemblies so characteristic of the revolution, Parisians themselves avidly consumed the scores of newspapers, pamphlets, and petitions that poured forth daily from the press.

One of the first newspapers, *l'Ami du peuple* ("The Friend of the People"), was founded by Count Mirabeau (1742–1791), who, boycotted by his fellow noblemen, had won election as a member of the Third Estate and emerged as a leader of the National Assembly. Other journalists such as Camille Desmoulins and Jean-Paul Marat (1743–1793) won wide public followings and often exercised considerable political influence. Thus was born the modern power of the press, whose nickname, the "Fourth Estate," still attests to its revolutionary origins.

The Parisian sans-culottes were the most radical element in the revolution, in part because of the idealism with which they embraced their first experience of politics and self-government, in part because their concrete interests clashed with those of the bourgeoisie who dominated the Constituent Assembly. The assembly, as we have seen, had sought to deny sans-culottes the vote; by the Le Chapelier law (1791) it had outlawed all workers' unions, and, in a direct confrontation, 15 sans-culottes had been killed in an antimonarchical demonstration on the civic parade ground, the Champs de Mars, in July 1791.

By the summer of 1792 the revolution had reached a new flashpoint. Swept on by a combination of ideological fervor and traditional anti-Habsburg sentiment, the new Legislative Assembly had declared war on Austria in April. It was a disastrous decision. The army was bereft of commanders, two-thirds of its officers (all former nobles) having deserted or quit. The country was in the grip of renewed inflation, in part the result of the government's failure to remove assignats from circulation as church lands were sold off. As their value depreciated, peasants refused to accept them as payment for their crops, creating food shortages and riots. When the war proved a fiasco, the public mood turned grim. Amid a general breakdown of order, there were rumors of counterrevolutionary plots. The Jacobin republicans blamed the failure of their crusade on Louis. How, they demanded, could a war against all kings be led by a king?

By the end of July, 47 of the 48 Paris sections had declared against the monarchy. The city was in an uproar as military recruits from the provinces mingled with the sans-culottes. Agitation was particularly severe in the district of St.-Antoine, whose working-class inhabitants had led the assault on the Bastille. The Jacobin leadership, alarmed by the prospect of a new popular insurrection,

now backtracked and offered Louis support. But a more radical faction, led by Maximilien Robespierre, threw its lot in with the crowd. On August 10 Louis and his entourage were driven from the Tuileries by an armed mob, with heavy loss of life. It was an event as crucial as the fall of the Bastille. A new revolutionary council, composed largely of sans-culottes and lesser bourgeoisie, seized control of Paris. The constitution was suspended, the Legislative Assembly was dispersed, and a new National Convention was summoned to create a republic.

The Radical Revolution, 1792–1794

The National Convention, elected by all French males, met on September 20 in an atmosphere of near anarchy. Earlier in the month hysterical mobs had rampaged through the prisons of Paris in search of "counterrevolutionaries," killing between 1,100 and 1,400 inmates, including 37 women. A Prussian army had penetrated deep into northern France and was stopped at Valmy, only 200 miles from Paris, on the very day of the convention's first meeting. The convention had deliberately taken its name in reference to the American constitutional convention, which had written the modern world's first democratic constitution. But Paris in the early autumn of 1792 bore little resemblance to Philadelphia in the summer of 1787.

Reform and Regicide

Nevertheless, the convention set to work undaunted. It not only abolished the monarchy but the calendar, declaring September 22 the first day of Year I of the republic. Later it scrapped the entire Christian calendar of months and days, commissioning a poet, Philippe Fabre d'Églantine, to rename them. Fabre decided to call his months by their seasonal characteristics; thus July 27 was to be the ninth of Thermidor, the month of heat; November 10 became the eighteenth of Brumaire, the month of fog; and so on. The year was to consist of 12 equal months of 30 days each, with five leap days at the end to be celebrated as revolutionary holidays. Each month consisted of three weeks or "decades" of ten days each, which meant, among other things, a nine-day workweek. Saints' days, used for festivity and rest, were eliminated as well. This calendar remained in effect until 1804, although it was never adopted beyond official circles.

The convention's faith in the future was soon repaid. French armies, fired by patriotic ardor and reorganized under officers promoted from the ranks, drove the Austro-Prussian invaders out and swept across the border, occupying Frankfurt and Brussels. In two months they conquered more territory than Louis XIV had in 50 years.

The convention decreed feudal dues and services abolished in all areas occupied by French forces and offered "liberation" to any people wishing it. On February 1, 1793, war was declared on Britain, Spain, and the Dutch Netherlands.

The king remained to be dealt with. Alive, he was a magnet for counterrevolution, and his incriminating correspondence with the Austrians had been discovered. Placed on trial for treason, he was condemned to death by a single vote in the convention, 361 to 360. On January 21, 1793, Louis went to the guillotine. Ten months later, his Austrian queen, Marie Antoinette, followed him.

The revolution now entered its climactic phase. It was a time of great passions and great excesses. The men who

The condemned queen, Marie Antoinette, dressed in a prisoner's smock and ironically crowned with a liberty cap, was sketched by Jacques-Louis David on her way to execution. [Photographie Bulloz]

A satirical print entitled "Exercise of the Rights of Man and of the French Citizen" depicts the violence that erupted at the fall of the monarchy in September 1792. Murder by every means is attempted: shooting, hanging, stabbing, clubbing. The victims in the foreground include a gentlewoman, a bishop, and a child; in the background, a nobleman's house and a church are burning. [Photographie Bulloz]

ruled France often worked around the clock, facing political, military, and economic crises all at once. At the same time, they were conscious of living at a historic moment and making decisions that would stamp generations to come. Out of what they did, and what they failed to do, came much of the shape of the modern West.

The center of this activity was the National Convention. Only 286 of its 750 members had served in the previous two assemblies of the revolution, although socially they had the same predominant makeup of lawyers, merchants, businessmen, and officials. Despite the fact that the convention had been created by the insurrection of the sansculottes, it contained only two workers, a munitions maker and a wool comber. The peasants, who comprised 80 percent of the population, had no representative at all.

Politically, the convention was divided between what had emerged as the two warring factions of the Jacobin club, with the great mass of delegates in the middle. The Girondins, so called because many of their leaders came from the southwest department of the Gironde, had been the war party of the Legislative Assembly, but in the eyes of their opponents their revolutionary purity had been compromised by their attempt to deal with the king the previous summer. The more radical faction was the Montagnards (the "mountain men"), so called because they sat in the upper tiers of the convention, whose base of support was among the sans-culottes of Paris. Their leaders were Robespierre, the journalist Marat, and the worldly politician Georges Danton. The two parties were separated by no great issues or principles. Both accepted the republic, both had shed the king's blood, and both believed in the mission of the revolution to liberate Europe. But the Montagnards proved more adept at riding the tiger of mass politics that the second revolution of August 1792 had unleashed. On June 2, after a spring of military reverses, renewed inflation, and a major royalist uprising in the western region of the Vendée, Robespierre led a purge of Girondist leaders by the sans-culottes.

The Montagnards were now in power, though largely at the sufferance of their working-class allies, who came daily to the convention to harangue them. The sans-culottes demanded, and for the first time got, price controls on bread, flour, and other commodities, as well as a general increase in wages. The speech of the radical street leader and ex-priest Jacques Roux on June 25 was typical:

> **Liberty is nothing but a figment of the imagination when one class can deprive another of food with impunity. Liberty becomes meaningless when the rich exercise the power of life and death over their fellow creatures by means of monopolies. . . . Have you outlawed speculation? No. Have you decreed the death penalty for hoarding? No. Have you defined the limits to the freedom of trade? No. . . . Deputies of the Mountain, why have you not climbed from the third to the ninth floor of the houses of the revolutionary city? You would have been moved by the tears and sighs of an immense population without food and clothing . . . because the laws have been cruel to the poor, because they have been made only by the rich and for the rich . . . [but] the salvation of the people . . . is the supreme law.[2]**

The deputies of the convention were shocked by this oration, because Jacques Roux was telling them that their revolution had accomplished nothing of substance and that liberty without bread was a fraud. Roux was removed bodily from the convention and later committed suicide in prison. But his challenge would remain to haunt the politics of liberal democracy.

Robespierre and the Terror

Maximilien Robespierre now emerged as the most conspicuous figure of the revolution. Robespierre was born in 1758 in the coastal town of Arras, the son of a lawyer and a brewer's daughter. Abandoned by his father at the age of 8, he was raised by aunts and educated in the school of

Maximilien Robespierre, the leading figure in the National Convention and the principal architect of the Terror. [Mansell Collection]

the Oratorian order. Robespierre was nicknamed "the Roman" by his classmates, for both his gravity of manner and his command of Latin. He grew up a reserved and serious young man, followed his father's profession, and became a judge in the local episcopal court. Fond of pets, he kept pigeons but had no close friends. He remained unmarried, and his sister Charlotte kept house for him. Elected to the Estates General in 1789, he caught the eye of Mirabeau, who remarked cynically, "He will go far; he believes everything he says." Above all, Robespierre believed in himself: "You have no idea," he said, "of the power of truth or the energy of innocence when sustained by an imperturbable courage."

Robespierre's ability to formulate and even personify the ideals of the revolution brought him to prominence. He lived for the revolution and had no life apart from it. By the end of 1792 he was the dominant figure in the Jacobin club; by the following summer he stood at the forefront of events. The convention had just finished drafting the new Constitution of the Year I. It provided for the most democratic system of government since that of ancient Athens, with a broader definition of natural rights, a ballot based on universal manhood suffrage, and a popular referendum. As Robespierre himself declared, it contained "the essential basis of public happiness." But with foreign armies still pressing against French borders and armed resistance to the government flaring across three-quarters of the country, there was no question of putting it into effect. The convention, like the Constituent Assembly before it, had attempted to govern the country by a system

---

◉ Robespierre on the Principles ◉ of Revolutionary Government

In this, one of his many speeches to the National Convention, Robespierre attempts to define the nature of the revolutionary government.

The defenders of the Republic must adopt Caesar's maxim, for they believe that *nothing has been done as long as anything remains to be done.* . . .

The object of constitutional government is to preserve the Republic; the object of a revolutionary government is to establish it.

Revolution is the war waged by liberty against its enemies; a constitution is that which crowns the edifice of freedom once victory has been won and the nation is at peace.

The revolutionary government has to summon extraordinary activity to its aid precisely because it is at war. It is subjected to less binding and less uniform regulations, because the circumstances in which it finds itself are tempestuous and shifting. . . .

Under a constitutional government little more is required than to protect the individual against the abuses by the state, whereas revolutionary government is obliged to defend the state against the factions that assail it from every quarter.

To good citizens revolutionary government owes the full protection of the state; to the enemies of the people it owes only death.

Source: G. Rudé, ed., *Robespierre* (Englewood Cliffs, N.J.: Prentice-Hall, 1967), pp. 58–59.

---

of councils and committees. To one of these, a body with rather vague supervisory functions called the Committee of Public Safety, Robespierre was elected on July 27. Galvanized by his presence, it soon became the focal point of the revolution.

Steps were now rapidly taken to put down the revolts in the Vendée and elsewhere. Draconian punishment was meted out to rebels, as at Lyons, where nearly 2,000 people were executed in the wake of a Girondist uprising. So-called representatives on mission, armed with almost unlimited authority, struck terror into the provinces. At the same time, a *levée en masse,* or general conscription of all able-bodied men, was decreed. Of all the acts of the convention, this was perhaps the most significant. War was no longer to be the sport of kings and nobles but the sacred cause of the nation, a mass mobilization of all human and material resources. Young men who could not fight were to make weapons, munitions, clothing, and banners; women were to serve as nurses; elderly men were to make patriotic speeches.

Out of this fevered atmosphere was born the Terror, a systematic attempt to root out and destroy all enemies of the revolution. To catch these enemies, special tribunals were set up and new categories of counterrevolutionary offense established so broad as to include almost everything. A certain Monsieur Blondel was arrested, for example, for "thoughtlessness and indifference," a Citizen Lachapelle because he "did not lose much sleep over the

revolution." These denunciations were made not by secret police but by zealous sans-culottes who were genuinely puzzled that anyone could lack enthusiasm for the revolution. Who but an enemy of the republic would not lose sleep over it?

Robespierre defended the Terror in a famous speech: "If the basis of popular government in time of peace is virtue, the basis of popular government in time of revolution is both virtue and terror: virtue without which terror is murderous, terror without which virtue is powerless." Terror was merely inflexible justice applied to the enemies of the people, and so "an emanation of virtue." As Robespierre's young colleague Saint-Just put it more succinctly, "Between the people and its enemies there is only the sword." In the ten months between September 1793 and July 1794 perhaps 300,000 people were arrested and 40,000 executed. Of these, only 15 percent were ex-aristocrats or priests and another 15 percent bourgeois, mostly members of the Girondist resistance in the south. The overwhelming majority were ordinary workers and peasants caught up in the whirlwind of revolutionary self-purification.

The Terror had another aim: to centralize all authority in the revolutionary government and to eliminate all opposition and dissent. By the law of 14 Frimaire (December 4, 1793), all subordinate authorities were placed under the direct control of the Committee of Public Safety, to which they were ordered to report every ten days. All local officials became "national agents," subject to immediate removal by Paris. Committees of surveillance—that is, teams of spies—were placed over government functionaries at every level. The law of 14 Frimaire became the real constitution of France.

The Republic of Virtue

The revolution produced not only a new political apparatus but a new political culture as well, the "Republic of Virtue." Styles of dress, which had indicated differences of social position under the Old Regime, now proclaimed differences of political position as well. The color of one's clothes or the length of one's trousers might touch off a quarrel or even a riot. Even common objects such as plateware, calendars, or playing cards became ways of displaying commitment, and the popular symbols of the revolution—the red, white, and blue ribbons or "cockades" worn on the hat, the liberty trees planted in the tens of thousands all over France—became enduring badges of republican affiliation that long outlived the revolution itself. The government soon began to channel spontaneous activities such as dances and celebrations into organized festivals. These centered at first around mass loyalty oaths but soon became replacements for the old religious festivals on which the regime now frowned. Thus the veneration of the Virgin Mary was deflected into that of the goddess of Liberty, popularly called Marianne, and the worship of the Christian God became that of a Deist supreme being or, even more abstractly, Reason itself. As patriotic outlets, as propaganda forums, and as a means of surveillance, the festivals were no less important than the guillotine in maintaining political discipline.

By the spring of 1794 order had been restored and the armies of the *levée en masse*, 850,000 strong, poured victoriously again into the Low Countries. Yet the Terror, like a mindless machine, ground on. Danton and Desmoulins went to the guillotine for suggesting that too much blood had been shed, the ultra-left Enragés and their leader, Hébert, for complaining that there had been too little. The Enragés were to get their wish. The law of 22 Prairial (June 10) declared spreading rumors and defaming patriots to be capital crimes and limited the Revolutionary Tribunal to two verdicts: acquittal or death. In the next six weeks more people were guillotined in Paris than in the entire preceding year. Even the members of the all-powerful Committee of Public Safety walked in fear of one another, especially of Robespierre. A group of them conspired to denounce him before the convention on 9 Thermidor (July 27). Robespierre attempted to defend himself but was shouted down and arrested. The next day he and Saint-Just were executed.

His enemies called Robespierre a tyrant who sought supreme power for himself. When he participated in the Festival of the Supreme Being, an attempt to set up a Deist god of reason as a revolutionary religion, many were convinced that he aimed to be not merely the dictator of the revolution but its high priest. Yet he never held any title but delegate to the convention, and his estate at his death came to barely 100 livres. A disciple of Rousseau, he believed that he embodied the general will. Among the corrupt and disillusioned, and even at last the horrified, he retained absolute faith in the justness of the revolution. As its tragedy unfolded, he foresaw his own martyrdom. "The founders of the Republic," he wrote, "can only find peace in the tomb."

❧ MADAME ROLAND: A WOMAN IN THE REVOLUTION

Few women not of royal blood came closer to the center of political power in the eighteenth century than Marie-Jeanne Phlipon (1754–1793), better known by her married name, Madame Roland. The daughter of a Parisian engraver, Manon—as family and friends called her—exhibited her gifts early and was taught to read before the age of 4. Profoundly influenced by Rousseau, she found a

Madame Roland, a woman of the revolution.
[**Photographie Bulloz**]

kindred feminine spirit as well in the writings of Madame de Sévigné. The American Revolution fired her enthusiasm as a war against kings, and she followed its progress eagerly. At about the same time, she composed an essay deploring the gulf between the rich and the poor in France, the absence of representative government, and the monarchy's use of force to stifle dissent, which, in a prophetic phrase, she denounced as a "reign of terror." In revolution alone did the 20-year-old Manon see any hope for her country's future.

In 1780 Manon married Jean-Marie Roland de la Platière, the inspector of manufactures for the province of Picardy, 20 years her senior. With characteristic frankness, the young bride described her wedding night as "surprising and disagreeable," but a daughter, Eudora, soon resulted from the union. Madame Roland threw herself into her husband's career, collaborating on his technical studies and polishing his awkward literary style. When Roland was transferred to Lyons, she was appalled at the condition of the local peasantry, tending so assiduously to the sick among them that Roland feared for her own health.

From the moment the revolution began in 1789 Madame Roland lived for little else. She chafed at her provincial isolation, wrote to warn her friends in Paris of the reactionary tendencies of the smaller cities, and urged from the beginning the abolition of the monarchy. The Rolands returned to Paris in 1791, where Manon, with her vivacity, ambition, and charm, created a salon that attracted such figures as Robespierre and Tom Paine. Roland became minister of the interior and a member of the war party led by his patron, Jacques Brissot. In June 1792 he delivered a letter to the king, actually written by Manon, demanding that he revoke his veto of the legislation against nonjuring priests. Louis responded by dismissing Roland, and the entire Girondist ministry soon fell. This triggered an attack on the royal palace and, following a summer of heated intrigue in which Madame Roland took an active part, the fall of the monarchy, the September massacres, and the summoning of the National Convention.

When it was moved in the convention that Roland be invited to resume his ministry, Georges Danton, a political opponent, suggested that the invitation be extended to Madame Roland as well. The convention, knowing her influence, burst into laughter. But Roland's star was already on the wane, while Manon, appalled by the September massacres and now deeply distrustful of Robespierre, began to waver for the first time in her belief in the revolution. She so triumphantly acquitted herself of charges of conspiring with royalist émigrés that she received a standing ovation from the convention, but six months later she was arrested in the coup of May 31, 1793. Imprisoned for five months, she hastily composed her memoirs, knowing that she would be permitted no other defense. Condemned and executed on the same day, November 8, she showed great courage and composure on the scaffold, and uttered before the guillotine fell what have come down as the most famous words of the French Revolution: "O Liberty, what crimes are committed in thy name!" Roland, who had gone into hiding, committed suicide at the news of her execution.

Madame Roland was a heroic figure to nineteenth-century historians, with their tendency to idealize women of passion and character. Her powers were not always matched by her judgment, but her integrity was unquestioned, and her career was astonishing and unprecedented. Not until the emergence of organized feminist politics in the late nineteenth century would any woman put a comparable stamp on the events of her time.

Conquest and Reaction, 1795–1799

The fall of Robespierre was followed by a sharp swing to the right, known as the Thermidorian reaction. Men were tired of terror and virtue alike. Political opportunists, money men, and speculators abounded. Aristocratic styles and even sentiments returned to fashion among the *jeunesse dorée,* or "gilded youth," of the bourgeoisie. Ex-Robespierrists in the provinces were purged by a semiofficial White Terror that rapidly degenerated into a brutal settling of scores with radicals in general. The democratic Constitution of the Year I was shelved for good, and with surviving Girondists readmitted to the convention, a new constitution was devised in 1795 that reinstated the old system of electors, with a property qualification so high that only 20,000 men in France met the test. The electors chose all department officials and a new Legislative Assembly, which in turn chose a five-member executive, the Directory, from which the new regime was to take its name. As a precaution against future reprisal, the convention decreed that two-thirds of the new assembly must be made up of its own members.

These events spelled final defeat for the sans-culottes. The convention removed economic controls, prices skyrocketed, and the bread ration was cut to 2 ounces a day. Concluding not unreasonably that they were being deliberately starved into submission, the sans-culottes stormed the convention in May 1795, crying, "Bread or death!" It was less a demand than a simple statement. But loyal units of the National Guard dispersed them, and, leaderless, they were henceforth spent as a political force.

Despite this, however, the Directory was inherently unstable. It had neither the ideological attraction of Jacobinism nor the traditional appeal of monarchy. It was particularly vulnerable to attacks from royalists, who denounced its bourgeois leadership as a would-be aristocracy without the courage to choose its king. A royalist uprising in October was put down only by the presence of mind of a decommissioned young brigadier of artillery named Napoleon Bonaparte who happened to be in Paris at the time, but the threat remained. When elections in April 1797 produced startling gains for the right, the results were annulled, and the Directory declared that anyone advocating either the monarchy or the democratic constitution of 1793 would be shot on sight. With this, it shed its last pretense to legitimacy. What remained was simply a cabal in search of a strongman.

Despite its difficulties at home, the revolution went militarily from success to success abroad. Its conquering armies annexed the Austrian Netherlands, the left bank of the Rhine, and the Mediterranean principalities of Nice and Savoy to France outright and turned the proud Dutch republic into a satellite state after exacting an indemnity of 100 million livres. A daring foray by Napoleon in 1796 produced a string of new satellite republics in Italy, all grandiloquently named: the Cisalpine (Milan), the Ligurian (Genoa), the Roman (the Papal States), and the Parthenopean (Naples). The Swiss cantons were also herded into

a so-called Helvetic Republic. Austria was compelled to recognize these conquests, as well as the annexation of its province in the Netherlands, by the Treaty of Campo Formio (October 1797). As a sop, the Austrians received Venice, thus extinguishing the independence of Europe's oldest republic.

Propped up by this success, the Directory drifted on for two more years. But the outbreak of war again in 1799 made a strong government imperative. A group led by the Abbé Sieyès put forward Napoleon Bonaparte, whose rapid rise to military prominence seemed to make him an ideal front man for a reorganized and strengthened executive. A coup in November 1799 ousted the Directory and dispersed the Legislative Assembly. It was the eighth major change of power in the revolution. Napoleon rapidly dispensed with his civilian allies and assumed complete power. For the next 15 years he governed France alone as first consul, consul for life, and finally emperor of the French. The revolution was over.

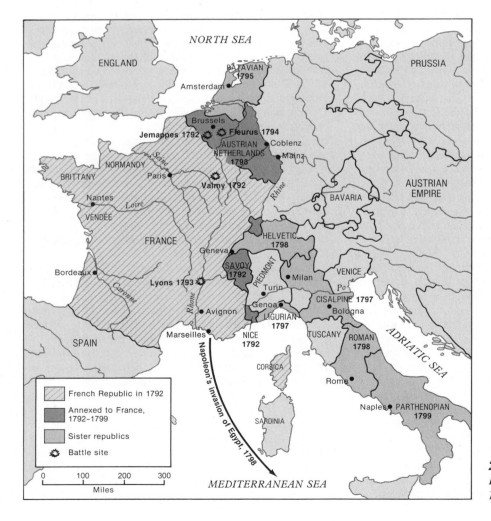

26.2 The Expansion of Revolutionary France, 1792–1799

The Legacy of the Revolution: Conflicting Interpretations

The men and women who experienced the French revolution can be broadly classified into three groups. Some wished it had never occurred and wanted only to turn the clock back before 1789; some were satisfied with their gains at a given point and wished it to go no further; and some felt that it had not yet accomplished its task. The first group was composed chiefly of the nobility and the nonjuring clergy, the second of the peasants and the bourgeoisie, and the third of the sans-culottes and their allies among the liberal nobility and bourgeoisie. From these differing attitudes emerged the right, center, and left of nineteenth-century European politics.

Historians too, depending on their own political sympathies, have seen in the revolution either a great calamity, a necessary adjustment to changing circumstances, or a vision of social justice as yet unrealized. The first view was best represented in the nineteenth century by Hippolyte Taine (1828–1893), who feared a new revolution in his own time and wished to warn his fellow countrymen of the evils he felt it would unleash, and in more modern form by J. L. Talmon, who saw in the revolution a false dream of secular salvation that could lead only to tyranny. The second view is identified with Alexis de Tocqueville (1805–1859), who argued in his highly influential *The Old Regime and the French Revolution* (1856) that the revolution was not so much a break with the Old Regime as a development of the tendencies toward centralization and bureaucracy already inherent in it. From this perspective, the constructive work of the revolution was essentially complete by 1791, and the radical or Jacobin phase was an aberration caused by the instability of the constitutional monarchy that the Constituent Assembly had attempted to set up.

The third view, associated with the work of Jules Michelet (1798–1874) and, later, Albert Mathiez and Albert Soboul, argues to the contrary that the Jacobin republic was the climax of the revolution, which by exposing the hollowness of a formal political equality unaccompanied by a redistribution of the wealth on which actual political power depends set the agenda for modern mass politics and the demand for social justice. This view was first put forward during the revolution itself by the left-wing ideologue and conspirator Gracchus Babeuf (1760–1797), who predicted in his *Manifesto of the Equals* (1796) that "the French Revolution is but the forerunner of another, far more grand, far more solemn, which will be the last."

The group least satisfied by the revolution was women, particularly those of the urban working class. Although women bore the brunt of the revolution's hardships at all times and at least at one point, in the march on Versailles in October 1789, played a critical role in events, their interests were not addressed by any of the dominant factions of the revolution. Very few were in the position of Madame Roland, whose salon was a center of revolution-

◉ A Revolutionary's Plea ◉ for the Rights of Women

In On the Admission of Women to the Rights of Citizenship, *the marquis de Condorcet, one of the few French noblemen to give his unqualified support to the revolution, chided the authorities for failing to provide for the rights of women as well as those of men.*

Is there a stronger proof of the power of habit, even among enlightened men, than to hear the principle of equality invoked in favor of 300 or 400 men deprived of their rights by an absurd prejudice [against counting all votes in the Estates General equally] and forgotten in the case of some 12 million women? . . .

    Women are superior to men in the gentle and domestic virtues. Like men, they know how to love liberty, although they do not share all its advantages; and in republics they have often been known to sacrifice themselves for it. They have demonstrated the virtues of citizens whenever chance or civil troubles have brought them upon a scene from which the pride and the tyranny of men have excluded them in all nations.

Source: Marquis de Condorcet, *Selected Writings*, ed. K. M. Baker (Indianapolis: Bobbs-Merrill, 1976), pp. 97, 99.

ary intrigue; most spent their days on ration lines, often to receive spoiled or unpalatable goods, or nothing at all. Women and children were the first to succumb to starvation or malnutrition, as local records clearly show, and one can only imagine the desperation of the mothers of Masannay who in May 1794 demanded the elimination of all people over 60 so that the young might be fed enough to survive. When the women of Paris tried to organize their own clubs, they were shut down by the procurator of the Commune, who observed that sans-culottes had a right to expect their wives to keep house while they attended political meetings.

The legacy of the revolution remains a matter of debate among historians as they continue to discuss the precise composition of the groups we call "bourgeois," "aristocratic," and "sans-culotte," to study the complex interactions and alliances among these groups, and the relationship between Paris and the countryside and between France and Europe. There are still many questions to be answered about the actual redistribution of land, wealth, and power in the revolution; about the functioning of revolutionary institutions, especially outside Paris, and the effect of those institutions on conquered territories abroad. Some conclusions, however, seem unlikely to be seriously modified.

The revolution destroyed the localism of Old Regime France, welding it into a single political and economic unit and opening it to the forces of market capitalism while giving impetus to similar developments elsewhere. It produced the first citizen army of modern times and showed for the first time what an entire society mobilized for war and driven by ideology could achieve. It introduced modern mass politics and made the sovereignty of the people, already proclaimed in America, the fundamental legitimating principle of Western governments. It also introduced in the name of the people the suspension of all legal rights and forms and the elimination of all dissent by genocide, a practice that began with the Jacobins but was equally characteristic of the Directory and has since become an increasingly casual weapon of modern regimes. In that respect the revolution may be said to have opened up the Pandora's box of modern politics in which, as the Russian novelist Feodor Dostoevsky remarked, "everything is permitted." But it also, like Pandora, gave the great mass of the human race what it had never had before except from religion: hope.

The Napoleonic Era

It was not immediately clear that Napoleon's coup d'état would be very different from the previous changes of government of the past ten years, let alone that it would usher in a new era both for France and for Europe. As Napoleon slowly but firmly drew the reins of power into his own hands, however, and as his campaigns of conquest brought more and more of the continent under French sway, it became apparent that France had a master, and Europe a ruler, such as neither had known before.

From Republic to Empire

The Abbé Sieyès had brought Napoleon to power under the slogan, "Confidence from below, authority from above." Napoleon took the slogan and dropped his ally. Born in 1769 into a family of impoverished minor nobility on the island of Corsica, he was barely 30 when he became master of France. Italian by descent (Napoleon dropped the *u* in the family name Buonaparte when he invaded Italy in 1796), he was French only by virtue of Corsica's annexation to France in 1768, and his first adventure was fighting for his island's independence in 1789. Soon swept up in the revolution on the mainland, he gained notice by taking the royalist port of Toulon in 1793, and after the stroke of luck that put him in Paris during the revolt of October 1795, he became a central figure in the political upheavals of the Directory. His brilliant campaign in Italy made him the man of the hour, and despite the failure of a campaign against the British in Egypt in 1798, his reputation was undimmed.

Napoleon promulgated a new constitution, which created an enfeebled legislature whose three chambers could respectively debate, enact, and veto laws but do nothing together and centralized executive authority in the hands of three "consuls." Napoleon took the title of first consul, with full authority to appoint all officials and magistrates, conduct diplomacy, declare and wage war, and protect the public safety. Napoleon had vowed to keep the republic, but all that remained of it was a facade. The powers he gave himself made him an uncrowned king. In a masterful stroke of public relations, he submitted the constitution to a popular referendum, although he had already proclaimed it in effect. The result was predictably lopsided, with 3,011,007 votes counted for and 1,562 against. Napoleon could now claim his "mandate" from the people. In 1802 he extended the term of his consulship from ten years to life, and in 1804, after making peace with the church, he assumed the title of emperor. Both acts were ratified by popular referendum, but for his coronation Napoleon summoned Pope Pius VII to Paris, and in a gesture deliberately reminiscent of Charlemagne's at his coronation as Holy Roman emperor 1,000 years before, he took the crown from the pontiff's hands and placed it on his own head. Shortly afterward he created an aristocracy, mostly from the upper bourgeoisie. The revolution against kings, priests, and nobles had come full circle.

Napoleon ruled through propaganda, press censorship, a highly efficient secret police, and, on occasion, acts of political terrorism such as the kidnapping and execution of the young Bourbon duke of Enghien in 1804. Yet his popularity was genuine, and he enjoyed the broad support of all classes almost to the end. Only diehard royalists and

---

◎ **Napoleon on Himself** ◎

Napoleon's boundless ego and lack of ethical principles are clearly re-
flected in his many statements, a sample of which follow.

My policy is to govern men the way the great majority wants to be governed. This, I
believe, is the only way in which it is possible to acknowledge the sovereignty of the
people. By making myself Catholic I brought the war in the Vendée to an end. By becoming a Muslim I established myself in Egypt. By acting ultramontane I won the minds
of the Italians. If I governed a nation of Jews, I should restore the temple of Solomon.
Thus I shall talk freedom in the free part of Santo Domingo; I shall confirm slavery in the
Île de France and even in the slave part of Santo Domingo—with the reservation that I
shall soften and limit slavery wherever I maintain it and shall restore order and discipline
wherever I maintain freedom.

   You must know that I am not in the least afraid of committing an act of cowardice if it
were useful to me. Look here, at bottom there is nothing either noble or base in this
world. My character possesses all those qualities that are capable of strengthening my
power and of deceiving those who imagine that they know me. Frankly, I am a coward,
indeed I am—essentially a coward. I give you my word of honor that I would not experience the least repugnance toward committing what the world calls a dishonorable action.

   Don't talk to me of goodness, of abstract justice, of natural law. Necessity is the highest law; public welfare is the highest justice. Unto each day the evil thereof; to each
circumstance its own law; each man according to his own nature.

Source: J. C. Herold, ed. and trans., *The Mind of Napoleon* (New York: Columbia University Press, 1955),
pp. 79, 160.

---

republicans refused to accept him. Simply stated, Napoleon gave the rich what they wanted, the poor what they
would accept, and, through an unprecedented career of
conquest, a measure of glory to everyone such as Louis
XIV had only dreamed of.

   Napoleon centralized political control as thoroughly as
the Jacobins had ever done in the days of the Terror. All
officials from the lowest level were responsible to the national state and ultimately the emperor himself through a
clear chain of command. The judiciary, declared independent in 1791, was brought back under executive control. The economy was similarly taken in hand. Napoleon
applied price controls as he saw fit, promoted new industry, and built an extensive network of roads and canals.
The Bank of France was chartered in 1800 to free the
government from reliance on private credit. Thus the
French began to catch up with the fiscal system developed
by the English more than a century before.

   Napoleon capped his reforms with the Civil Code of
1804, known, with later additions and modifications, as the
Napoleonic Code. The code was the culmination of efforts
to produce a digest of French legal and administrative principles dating back to the sixteenth century, and it became
the most influential code of secular law outside the Anglo-
Saxon tradition since Roman times. The main principles of

the early revolution—civil and legal equality, religious toleration, and the abolition of feudal obligations and legally
privileged orders—were confirmed. Beneath the veneer
of formal equality, however, the code envisioned a hierarchical society based on subordination to wealth and gender. The emphasis, as in the Old Regime, was on the flow
of authority downward from the state to the patriarchal
family. Women were enjoined to obey their husbands and
prevented from acquiring property without written consent and from administering joint property. Children might
be imprisoned for up to six months on the mere word of
their father and had to gain his consent to marry up to the
age of 30. A similar hierarchy was established in the workplace; for example, the word of an employer automatically
prevailed over that of a worker in court. The code was
extremely detailed in its guarantees of property rights and
its provisions for contracts and debts, but as for labor,
denied as before the right of association, it was merely
"free"—free to survive or perish as market conditions
might dictate.

   Napoleon's other major settlement was with the
church. By the Concordat of 1801, the Vatican recognized
the confiscation of its lands and tithes as permanent,
thereby accepting the role of the clergy as salaried employees of the state. It even consented to a catechism in

which disobedience to Napoleon was declared to be grounds for eternal damnation, something no divine right monarch had ever succeeded in making a part of religious instruction. Napoleon himself had no religious convictions whatever. "I was a Muslim in Egypt," he remarked in a famous moment of candor; "I shall be a Catholic here for the good of the people . . . and had I to govern a nation of Jews I would rebuild Solomon's temple." In return for his concessions, the pope was recognized as head of the church, and Catholicism was declared to be the religion "of the majority of Frenchmen." By this careful formulation, Napoleon stopped short of making Catholicism the official state church, thus preserving the principle of religious toleration; yet it served that function in effect. With the Concordat, the empire, and the code, his structure of authority was complete.

France Against Europe

Napoleon inherited command of the war France had been fighting since 1792, which by 1815 ranged over the entire globe and brought such consequences as the conquest of India, the liberation of South America, and the doubling of the size of the United States. Despite its complexity, however, it had, like the wars of Louis XIV a century before, a single dominant element: the containment of France.

The French had gone to war in 1792 to extend the revolution abroad and to maintain its momentum at home. By 1795 this initial enthusiasm was largely spent, and the French pursued the war for more traditional imperial and commercial goals. They were opposed by a shifting coalition whose only stable member was Great Britain. The Continental powers were slow at first to react to the French threat. Informed military opinion, far from considering France a menace, dismissed the revolutionary army as a leaderless mob. It was a measure of their preoccupation with more important matters, such as the partition of Poland, that Austria and Prussia did not even think this defenseless France worth attacking and confined themselves at first to diplomatic gestures such as the Declaration of Pillnitz.

The success of French forces took Europe wholly by surprise. No one had ever seen an army like this, which broke all the rules of military practice yet kept on winning. New recruits picked up their training on the march, discipline was negligible, and supplies were always short. Promotions were made on the basis of merit rather than birth: Napoleon's marshals included former coopers, millers, masons, and stable boys. Their average age was about 30; most of Prussia's generals were over 60.

But Europe could not long tolerate a French frontier that ran from the North Sea to the Ionian. Backed by British money and Russian troops, a second coalition drove the French back on a broad front in 1799. If the original revolutionary impetus of the French army was exhausted, however, it was now replaced by an equally pow-

erful force: Napoleon's own dream of world empire. Napoleon smashed the Austrians at Hohenlinden and Marengo, forcing them to sue for peace (Treaty of Lunéville, 1801) on even worse terms than at Campo Formio, and with the fall of the 18-year ministry of William Pitt the Younger, the son of the hero of the Seven Years' War, the British made a reluctant peace at Amiens in 1802.

Full-scale war resumed in 1805 with Britain, again under Pitt, subsidizing Russian troops to the tune of £1,250,000 per each 100,000 recruits. But at Ulm on October 15 an Austrian army, completely outgeneraled, surrendered without firing a shot, and six weeks later, on the first anniversary of his coronation (December 2), Napoleon won the greatest of all his battles over a combined Austro-Russian force at Austerlitz. Prussia, neutral since 1795, blundered into war alone in 1806, only to have its reputedly invincible army destroyed in two simultaneous battles 12 miles apart at Jena and Auerstadt. The French now pursued Russia along the Baltic shore into East Prussia, where after bloody battles at Eylau (February 1807) and Friedland (June), Tsar Alexander I (1796–1825) too offered peace. Napoleon was unsuccessful only at sea, where his plan for invading Britain was dashed by the fleet under Lord Horatio Nelson at Cape Trafalgar off the coast of Spain. Nelson sank or captured 18 French ships without the loss of a vessel but was himself slain in the battle.

The Grand Empire

European politics had long been predicated on maintaining a balance of power between its major states. This principle was formally incorporated into the Peace of Utrecht (1713), and it appeared so self-evident to eighteenth-century commentators that one even likened it to gravity as a law of nature. The French Revolution had challenged it with the idea that all states might be compelled to respect natural rights, if necessary by force. Napoleon openly rejected the balance of power. "Europe," he declared, "cannot be at rest except under a single head who will have kings for his officers." Clearly he saw himself as that head.

After the defeat of the Third Coalition in 1805, Napoleon began to construct his Grand Empire. The debris of petty German principalities was swept away, to be replaced by the Confederation of the Rhine, a satellite entity whose 38 members acknowledged Napoleon as their protector and agreed to furnish troops for his army. The 1,000-year-old Holy Roman Empire, once the symbol of German nationality and latterly of Austrian domination, was summarily abolished in 1806. Only Prussia retained its nominal independence, but shorn of half its territory and with its army reduced to a mere 42,000 men. Prussian Poland was reconstituted as the Grand Duchy of Warsaw, another satellite. Napoleon created a kingdom of Italy for his stepson Eugène, later annexing some of it to France and imprisoning Pius VII when he objected to the occupation of the Papal States. Similarly, a kingdom of Holland was created for Napoleon's brother Louis but absorbed outright four years later. Using his siblings essentially as prefects, Napoleon made his brother Jérome king of the German satellite of Westphalia in 1807 and his brother Joseph king of Spain in 1808, deposing the reigning Bourbon dynasty.

By the time this structure of satellite kingdoms was complete, however, Napoleon considered it obsolete. National entities, even ruled as the private preserve of the emperor's own family, were still too insubordinate, too conscious of their separate historical identities. As the Constituent Assembly had abolished the old provinces of France, so Napoleon decided to abolish the nations of Europe, replacing them with a single imperial administration. But events overtook him, and this last design was never carried out.

The Napoleonic Code was used as the basis of administration in the Grand Empire, from whence its influence spread throughout Europe and beyond, reaching places as far distant as Bolivia, Egypt, and Japan. By abolishing serfdom, dissolving the Old Regime system of orders, and introducing public education, it opened careers in commerce, industry, and government to men of talent. If the code represented the revolution at its least liberal, it was still often startlingly new and progressive elsewhere in Europe, and its importance as a solvent of feudal structures and as a model of modern society can scarcely be exaggerated.

Despite the order and prosperity Napoleonic government introduced, it provoked reactions ranging from passive resistance to outright rebellion everywhere. The chief common grievance was the Continental System, an attempt by Napoleon to close the ports of the empire to British commerce. This exposed such ports to reprisals by the British, who wholly dominated the seas, as well as to a counterblockade that had a crippling effect on European commerce. The deeper reason for resentment, however, was the suppression of national culture in the subject territories, the dominance of French officials and the presence of French troops and police, and the exploitation of the wealth and resources of a continent for the benefit of a single nation and ultimately a single family. In the Dutch Netherlands, where French aggression had been resisted for centuries, the occupation was particularly severe. The use of Dutch was discouraged, and all books were rigidly censored. Unhappy Westphalia rebelled no fewer than seven times against Napoleonic rule, while Rome bitterly resented the humiliation of the papacy. But by far the most serious resistance came from Spain. Spaniards of all classes rose up spontaneously against the French occupation and waged a fierce guerrilla war for six years whose atrocities were recorded for all time by the painter Francisco Goya. Spain was the stanchless wound in Napoleon's side. He thought that 20,000 men could hold the country; ten times that many failed. A British army under Arthur Wellesley, later duke of Wellington, linked up with the Spaniards through Portugal in what came to be known as the Peninsular War. By early 1814 southern France itself was under attack. The war ended with the British in Toulouse.

A more lasting effect of the Napoleonic occupation was the stimulation of national feeling, particularly in Italy and

"And They Are Like Wild Beasts." Spanish women, virtually unarmed, give battle to Napoleon's troops in this print from Goya's series of etchings *Disasters of War.* No other artist has ever captured so directly the naked ferocity of war. [Metropolitan Museum of Art, Rogers Fund, 1922]

Germany. Passed from hand to hand since the sixteenth century, Italy had been parceled out in bits and pieces to in-laws and even cabinet ministers by Napoleon. But despite heavy taxes and a general distaste for the French presence, Italian commerce and industry benefited from the abolition of tariff barriers, the building of new roads, and the introduction of uniform weights and measures. It is significant that many of the future leaders of the movement for Italian unification were descended from families that became rich under Napoleon. These new industrialists and financiers were not prepared to return to the inefficiencies of the traditional economy after 1815, and they chafed under its reimposition.

National consciousness had been promoted in eighteenth-century Germany by the philosopher Johann Gottfried von Herder, who argued that each people had a separate and unique historical destiny shaped by its *Volksgeist,* or inner spirit. But most German intellectuals of the Enlightenment prided themselves on a lofty cosmopolitanism instead. Their ideal was the tiny, idyllic dukedom of Weimar, whose ruler, Karl August (1775–1828), had gathered around him a brilliant court crowned by the great poet Goethe. They despised Prussian militarism in particular, and many initially welcomed the Napoleonic invasion; on the eve of the Battle of Jena the philosopher Hegel, himself a Prussian, wrote, "As I [did] formerly, now everybody wishes success to the French army."

The collapse and dismemberment of the Prussian state changed all that. Defeat brought Prussia what victory never had: a sense of nationhood. As French troops paraded through the streets of Berlin, the philosopher and publicist Johann Gottlieb Fichte (1762–1814) delivered a series of "addresses to the German nation" in which he argued that the German Volksgeist was intrinsically superior and must protect itself from contamination by outside cultures. Fichte denounced the petty sectionalism of German politics and called for a national movement to drive out the French oppressor. The dramatist Friedrich von Schiller also preached national liberation in his patriotic odes and plays, and freedom from oppression was the thinly veiled message of Beethoven's opera *Fidelio.* In Prussia itself, meanwhile, the crown ministers Baron Stein and Prince Hardenburg initiated significant land reforms, including the abolition of serfdom, liberalization of land tenures, and the reform of the bureaucracy.

For the moment, however, liberation seemed far away. From the Atlantic to the Polish steppe, from the Baltic to the Mediterranean, Napoleon ruled or dominated the whole of Europe. A swollen France itself stretched from the north German port of Lübeck to south of Rome. When Austria, which like Prussia had been reduced to dependent status, rebelled in 1809 and called on the former states of the Holy Roman Empire to assist it, not a single one responded. The Habsburg army was quickly crushed at Wagram, and it was now Vienna's turn to entertain a triumphal parade of French troops.

Yet Napoleon's empire was inherently unstable. As the flush of idealism and reform it had borrowed from the revolution wore away, the cynical and exploitive nature of its administration was increasingly apparent. It preached human equality but demanded permanent subjection. It violated the entire history and tradition of the European state system. It was not even in the interest of France, whose distended borders now resembled a jaw open on the whole continent. As early as 1808 Napoleon's foreign minister, Talleyrand, had made secret overtures to Tsar Alexander. Even at the height of the empire, Talleyrand did not believe it would last.

Napoleon himself was aware of the weakness of his position. He became obsessed with founding a dynasty. When his first wife, Joséphine de Beauharnais, failed to provide him with an heir, he divorced her in favor of Princess Marie-Louise of Austria. In 1811 she bore him a son, whom Napoleon grandly called the king of Rome. But nothing could obscure the fact that Napoleon, who had so often humiliated Austria, felt compelled to buy legitimacy by mixing his blood with that of the Habsburgs.

The Collapse of the Napoleonic Order

Of the major states of Europe, only Britain and Russia remained outside the Grand Empire. Britain continued its struggle with Napoleon alone, resulting in a war with the United States over its naval blockade of the Continent in 1812. Russia, by contrast, was formally a French ally. By the Treaty of Tilsit (1807), which the tsar and the emperor had negotiated in person on a barge in the middle of the Niemen River, Alexander agreed to join the Continental System if his efforts to mediate between Britain and France failed, and he also accepted French intercession in his conflict with the Turkish sultan. Superficially, this seemed to be an agreement between equals to assist each other in disputes with their neighbors; in reality, it obliged the tsar to recognize the Napoleonic order while giving Napoleon an entrée into a traditional Russian sphere of interest.

An uneasy truce prevailed for the next five years, as both sides probed for each other's weaknesses. Alexander attempted to gain control of the Grand Duchy of Warsaw, which under Napoleonic rule was a dagger pointed at Russia itself. Napoleon in turn sought influence in Constantinople, which he regarded as the "center of world empire," an empire presumably to be controlled by himself.

When Russia reopened trade with Britain and erected tariffs against French goods, Napoleon resolved on war. In June 1812 he crossed the Niemen into Russia with over 600,000 men, the largest army ever assembled for a single campaign. Napoleon envisaged a quick victory. His troops carried only four days' rations and the supply convoys

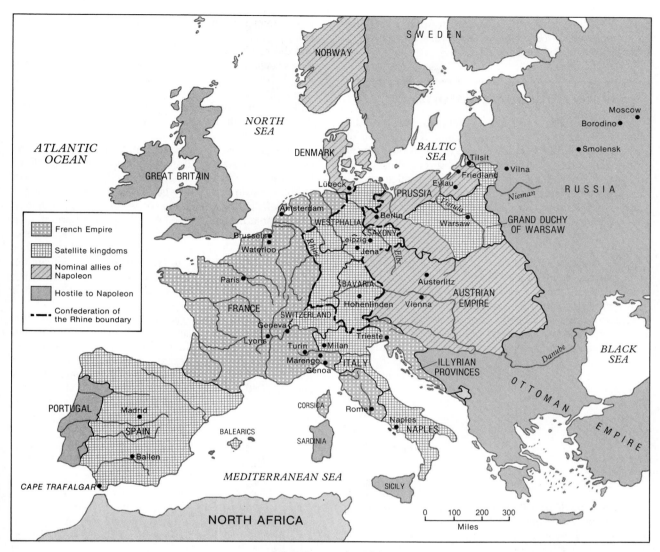

26.3 Europe in 1810

three weeks' more. But the Russians gave ground instead of fighting, leaving behind only scorched earth. They surrendered Moscow after an indecisive but bloody battle at Borodino, and Napoleon entered it unopposed on September 14. What had been a city of 300,000 was all but deserted. Fires had already begun, and within a week three-quarters of it had burned down. Without food or shelter, Napoleon could not winter in the devastated city. On October 19 he began a retreat. Mired in snow and mud, dogged by Russian sappers, his army laid a 1,000-mile track of corpses along its way. More than half a million men died, deserted, or disappeared.

Abandoning his army to its fate, Napoleon raced back to Paris. He raised a new army of 250,000 to face a re-

vived coalition of Russia, Prussia, Austria, and Sweden, with Britain as usual footing the bill. After several indecisive victories, he was defeated outside Leipzig in the great three-day Battle of the Nations (October 1813) and thrown back upon France. The Austrian foreign minister, Count Klemens von Metternich, alarmed at Prussia's new nationalism and eager to have the Russians out of Europe, offered to guarantee the French borders of 1792, including the former Austrian Netherlands and the left bank of the Rhine. Napoleon refused. For the emperor of the French, the only stakes were all or nothing. Allied armies now poured into France from Belgium, the middle Rhine, and Switzerland, with Wellington attacking from the south. Napoleon's defensive campaign was the most brilliant of his career, but the result was foregone. On April 4, 1814, he abdicated as emperor in favor of his 3-year-old son, a day after his Senate had deposed him.

The Bourbon Restoration

The victorious allies, aided by Talleyrand, restored the Bourbon dynasty in the person of Louis XVIII, count of Provence,* who signed the Treaty of Paris on May 30 that ended France's 22-year war with Europe. Wishing to support the new monarch, the allies demanded no indemnities or reparations. France was simply required to return to its prewar boundaries. Even Napoleon was treated leniently. He was exiled to the island of Elba off the west coast of Italy but permitted to retain the title of emperor and granted a pension of 2 million francs a year.

Louis XVIII was in theory an absolute king, but he confirmed the revolutionary land settlement and the Napoleonic Code and issued a Constitutional Charter that provided for a bicameral assembly chosen by a restricted suffrage of large landowners. But thousands of vengeful émigrés returned with him who would be satisfied by nothing less than a complete restoration of the Old Regime.

---

*The son of Louis XVI, who died in prison at the age of 10 without ever reigning, was recognized as Louis XVII.

The activities of these Ultraroyalists, or Ultras, as they were popularly called, together with economic depression and the inevitable letdown from the excitement of Napoleon's reign, cost the Bourbon regime whatever credibility it had. Napoleon, sensing his opportunity, returned with a small flotilla and with 1,000 veterans marched unopposed on Paris. The Bourbons fled to Belgium, and the emperor declared himself restored "by the unanimous wish of a great nation."

The allies, who had gathered in Vienna to discuss the settlement of postwar Europe, promptly declared Napoleon a public outlaw. Napoleon himself, courting support at home, made conciliatory gestures both to the right and to the left. But only a trial by battle could reestablish him. Raising an army, he crossed into Belgium, where on June 18, 1815, he met a combined force under the duke of Wellington and the Prussian general Gerhard von Blücher at Waterloo on the road to Brussels and was defeated in daylong combat. Returning to Paris, he was met with a stony demand for abdication. His second reign had lasted exactly 100 days.

Napoleon was now exiled to St. Helena, a bleak, tiny island in the south Atlantic, 4,000 miles from Europe, where in 1821 he died of stomach cancer. His legend lived on in France, where a veritable cult grew up around him that was climaxed by the return and reentombment of his body in 1840.

ᛀᛃᛀ   ᛀᛃᛀ   ᛀᛃᛀ

Napoleon himself said that the man of genius is a meteor who illuminates his time but does not transform it. Talleyrand, who knew him as well as anyone, thought that he had squandered an opportunity to create a lasting political equilibrium in Europe. Yet Napoleon did leave a permanent legacy. His code became the basis of modern French society. His conquests stimulated both anti-French nationalism and aspirations for a liberal society on the French model. His suppression of the Holy Roman Empire was the first step toward the unification of Germany. If the ideas he spread were those of the revolution rather than his own, they might never have traveled as far as they did without him. Napoleon failed to make Europe a province of France, but he did much to make the French Revolution European.

Notes

1. J. H. Stewart, *A Documentary Survey of the French Revolution* (New York: Macmillan, 1951), p. 42 (modified slightly).
2. R. Zaller, *Europe in Transition, 1660–1815* (New York: Harper & Row, 1984), p. 130.

Suggestions for Further Reading

Bergeron, L. *France Under Napoleon.* Princeton, N.J.: Princeton University Press, 1981.

Blanning, T. C. W. *The Origins of the French Revolutionary Wars.* London: Longman, 1986.

Cobb, R. C. *The People's War.* New Haven, Conn.: Yale University Press, 1987.

Cobban, A. *The Social Interpretation of the French Revolution.* Cambridge: Cambridge University Press, 1964.

Doyle, W. *Origins of the French Revolution.* Oxford: Oxford University Press, 1980.

Furet, F. *Interpreting the French Revolution.* New York: Cambridge University Press, 1981.

Geyl, P. *Napoleon: For and Against.* New Haven: Yale University Press, 1967.

Godechot, J., Hyslop, B., and Dowd, D. *The Napoleonic Era in Europe.* New York: Holt, Rinehart, and Winston, 1971.

Hampson, N. *A Social History of the French Revolution.* Toronto: University of Toronto Press, 1963.

Hunt, L. *Politics, Culture and Class in the French Revolution*. Berkeley: University of California Press, 1984.

Jones, P. M. *The Peasantry in the French Revolution*. Cambridge: Cambridge University Press, 1988.

Jordan, D. *The Revolutionary Career of Maximilian Robespierre*. New York: Free Press, 1985.

Kennedy, M. *The Jacobin Clubs in the French Revolution*. 2 vols. Princeton, N.J.: Princeton University Press, 1981, 1988.

Lefebvre, G. *The French Revolution*. 2 vols. New York: Columbia University Press, 1962, 1964.

————. *The Great Fear of 1789: Rural Panic in Revolutionary France*. New York: Pantheon, 1973.

————. *Napoleon from Tilsit to Waterloo, 1807–1815*. New York: Columbia University Press, 1969.

May, G. *Madame Roland and the Age of Revolution*. New York: Columbia University Press, 1970.

Palmer, R. R. *The Age of the Democratic Revolutions*. 2 vols. Princeton, N.J.: Princeton University Press, 1959, 1964.

————. *Twelve Who Ruled: The Year of the Terror in the French Revolution*. Princeton, N.J.: Princeton University Press, 1970.

Rose, R. B. *The Making of the Sans-Culottes: Democratic Ideas and Institutions in Paris, 1789–92*. Manchester: Manchester University Press, 1983.

Rudé, G. *The Crowd in the French Revolution*. Oxford: Oxford University Press, 1959.

Schama, S. *Citizens: A Chronicle of the French Revolution*. New York: Knopf, 1989.

Soboul, A. *The Sans-Culottes and the French Revolution*. Princeton, N.J.: Princeton University Press, 1980.

Thompson, J. M. *Napoleon Bonaparte: His Rise and Fall*. New York: Oxford University Press, 1969.

Death and the Human Experience (II)

Throughout history, every society has grappled with the fact of death and speculated about what may lie beyond the grave. Thus death is a common human bond, linking the most primitive societies with the most advanced. While all of the major world religions have offered explanations of death and hypotheses about subsequent existence, each has, in practice, been forced to accommodate its tenets to folk customs and popular mores. In so doing, religion has borne witness to the universal human effort to find a satisfying way to cope with death and dying. Reformers, in their quest to purify religion, have periodically attempted to purge funeral rituals of these culture-bound practices, thereby forcing their followers to rethink the question of death. Missionaries made similar efforts, attempting to replace folk customs with their own conceptions of death and the afterlife. Thus history is in part the story of conflicting attitudes about the common human experience of mortality.

The fundamental need to render death less fearful led orthodox Muslims to embellish the tenets of the Koran. Gradually Muslims came to believe that as a believer neared death, white-faced angels descended and sat before him. When he died, the Angel of Death gently extracted his soul from the corpse and gave it to other angels (see the third color insert). They in turn carried the soul, wrapped in a perfumed shroud, to the seventh heaven, where the beliefs and deeds of the deceased were recorded. The soul then rejoined the body in the grave for an interrogation on those beliefs and deeds by two blue-eyed, black-faced angels named Munkar and Nakir. To prepare the dead person for this Trial of the Grave, mourners sometimes whispered advice—the Instruction of the Deceased—to the corpse at the funeral. After the Trial of the Grave, the soul was comforted by Munkar and Nakir and allowed to enjoy a virtually limitless garden before its resurrection from the grave.

For an unbeliever the routine was superficially similar, though the angels attending him were black-faced and his soul could only be dragged from his body with enormous difficulty. The soul was borne only to the gate of the lowest heaven, bound in haircloth that reeked like rotting flesh. Following the questioning by Munkar and Nakir, this soul would be sentenced to a period of torment in a grave filled with heat and smoke. The point of adding these details was to help the living deal with the demise of others as well as to prepare for their own deaths. Such details made the account more memorable as well as more familiar in experiential terms.

A comparable phenomenon occurred in Japan as traditional folk belief was blended with Buddhism. According to folk religion, death occurred when the soul left the body; hence as a person lay dying, his or her friends beseeched the soul not to depart. Following death, a bowl of cooked rice for sustenance and a sword or other sharp object for protection were placed beside the corpse. As happens occasionally in the West, family members sat with the corpse the night before the funeral. The service itself was conducted by Buddhist priests, one of whom gave the deceased a new name for use in the afterlife seven days after his or her death. Formal mourning lasted 49 days, on the last of which a commemorative service was held. As in Roman Catholicism, requiem masses were observed for the deceased at specified intervals. The last of these, held 33 or 49 years after the person's death, marked the point at which the spirit lost its individuality and merged with the ancestral diety (*kami*), following which reincarnation in a newborn child could occur. The family of the deceased could take comfort that through its ritual observances the soul of the dead could enhance its status until it united with the ancestral *kami*. Thus not only was death familiarized, but the bereaved could find comfort in their efforts to aid the soul in the afterlife, much as Roman Catholics pray for the speedy passage of souls through purgatory.

While many sought to familiarize death by blending spiritual tenets with folklore, reformers periodically tried to purge religion of these customs. In Europe, for example, the Protestant reformers of the sixteenth century denounced requiem masses, prayers for the dead, monthly and yearly "minds" (commemorative services for the dead), purgatory, and extreme unction on the grounds that they were superstitious and without foundation in the Bible. In India the bhakti movement, a religious renewal in the fifteenth and sixteenth centuries, similarly deemphasized ritual in favor of devotion to the Godhead. The poet-reformer Kabir (died 1518), for instance, criticized traditional Hindu death rituals, holy places, and the doctrine of reincarnation. Taking a less extreme position, devotional cults in northern India retained simplified funeral rites but insisted that they were meaningful only if infused with love for God.

Colonial expansion brought Europeans into contact with many new perceptions of death and, to them, exotic burial customs. But there were also some striking resemblances. African folklore, for instance, included numerous myths to explain the origin of death, some of which were similar to Judeo-Christian concepts. As in the ancient Hebrew belief in a fall from a pristine state, some Africans suggested that death was the consequence of a fall from morality or disobedience to specific commandments. A number of African myths

The Indonesian island of Sumba provides another illustration of the conflict between Christian and native burial customs. Like the Chinese, the Sumbanese believed that the dead engaged in social relations with the living; in fact, the dead enjoyed greater power because they could enforce supernatural sanctions in dealings with their descendants. Missionaries discouraged such beliefs, especially when Sumbanese diviners began reporting that deceased converts to Christianity were demanding reburial according to traditional customs, including interment of their corpses in megalithic tombs. The diviners buttressed their claims by blaming illness and hardship among descendants on their failure to bury their ancestors in the traditional manner. Numerous converts finally left the church in order to reinter their forebears in their ancestral villages.

Sometimes the customs associated with death

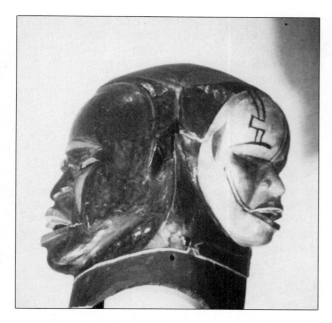

This mask from the Ikoi tribe in Nigeria illustrates death (the dark male face to the left, with eyes closed) and life (the lighter female face to the right). This was a way of expressing belief in life after death. [Werner Forman Archive]

are essentially variations of the "forbidden fruit" theme of Genesis, but others attribute the origins of death to such things as family discord, disease, sexual intercourse, or a natural longing to die.

The spread of Western imperialism starkly juxtaposed Christian beliefs and funeral rites with those of other religions. In northern India the imposition of British rule beginning in 1763 actually sparked a revival of Hindu funerary practices, including pilgrimages to holy places associated with death rituals. But the British in turn tried to prohibit "unnatural" funerary customs. Among them was suicide at holy places, which could be undertaken for a variety of reasons, including a desire to be reincarnated in a higher state or, for Muslims, entry into paradise. British authorities also tried to limit the practice of *sati*, insisting that a widow could not be forced to cast herself into the flames of her husband's pyre. British Baptist missionaries in Bengal attempted to stop the Hindus from leaving the terminally ill beside a river without food or shelter. From a Hindu perspective, to allow such a person to die in a home would mean lengthy and expensive purification rites. Though in some respects colonial rule brought modifications in burial customs, Indians who resented imperialism clung resolutely to traditional rites, at least in part to defy their colonial overlords.

An eighteenth-century illustration of the Hindu practice of *sati*. [Granger Collection]

shocked Westerners. In the seventeenth century French Jesuits were scandalized by the practices of the Huron Indians of southeastern Canada. According to the Hurons, at death the soul is separated from the body and enters an afterlife akin to the world of the living. It was therefore important to participate in a ritual known as the Feast of Courage to enable one's soul to be powerful in the afterlife. In this feast the Hurons drank the blood and ate the flesh of an enemy warrior who had died valiantly after being cruelly tortured; by this act, they believed, they incorporated his courage within themselves.

The Hurons also observed the Feast of the Dead, which was held every 10 or 12 years with the intent of binding the people together. At heart, the ritual entailed a second burial. Family members began by retrieving the bodies of deceased relatives that had been stored on scaffolds in a cemetery, after which the women cleaned any remaining skin and flesh from the bones. The bones were then wrapped in furs and taken back to the village houses, where the families dined in their presence. Only then were the bones taken to a circular burial pit, over which they were suspended on poles for as long as a week while the

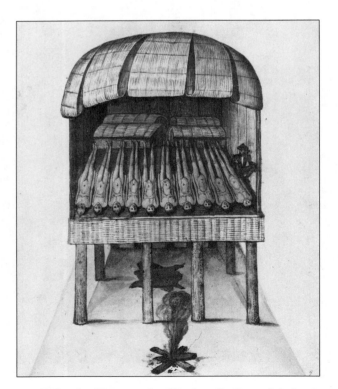

Like the Hurons, the Natchez Indians dried their corpses on frames. [Watercolor by John White; British Museum]

people played games, gambled, danced, and feasted. After an elaborate ritual, the bones were buried in the pit along with various gifts. When the Hurons were defeated by the Iroquois, they began to lose faith in the Feast of Courage, and when, in the nineteenth century, they were forced to move to reservations in Oklahoma, they left behind their dead and thus their sense of identity as a people.

The use of death to heighten the sense of community is present in other cultures. This is true, for example, of the Christian community's commemoration of the death and resurrection of Christ, a ceremony sometimes linked to passion plays and realistic reenactments of the crucifixion. Among Shi'ite Muslims, the annual performance of rites to commemorate the death of Muhammad's grandson, Husein, underscores the historical continuity of the Shi'a movement and deepens its sense of community.

In the Iraqi cities of Nejev and Karbala, pilgrims honoring Husein annually crowd the streets. Their buildings are draped in black, and the cafés, bars, and theaters are closed, as religious processions command attention. As in Christian lands, there are dramatic reenactments of the last days and death of the religious leader. The public ceremonies climax with a procession reputedly bearing Husein's head, followed by flagellants, bare to the waist, thrashing themselves with chains. Other ritual sufferers bear swords, periodically striking themselves on the forehead or scalp until blood gushes forth. Some worshipers have died, among them actors who, for the sake of realism, had depicted Husein's decapitation by burying their own heads or bodies in the scorching sand. Others engage in knifing rituals, the object of which is to stab oneself in the stomach without bleeding, thereby demonstrating a higher spirituality.

The ultimate self-punishment is, of course, suicide, as sometimes occurred among Hindus in India or by believers in other countries who burned themselves to death to dramatize their message. The public suicide of Buddhist monks in Vietnam helped bring about the fall of the American-sponsored Diem government in 1963. Closely related to these practices is the deliberate courting of martyrdom. In Islam this has been a means of immediate entry to paradise and has been fairly common among such diverse groups as modern terrorists and Iranian soldiers willing to sacrifice themselves in the Iran-Iraq war. From time to time Christianity too has experienced this phenomenon, particularly during the period of the church's persecution in the late Roman Empire and again during the crusading movement that commenced in the 1090s. Thus many have courted death at the hands of others to advance their cause or obtain spiritual rewards.

Martyrdom of a different sort has been practiced among the Jews, who, though in no sense seeking death, have confronted a death inflicted by others with a commandment known as the *Kiddush Hashem,* the sanctification of God's name. During the Holocaust there were numerous instances of Jews going to their death singing religious songs, radiating spiritual ecstasy, or performing ritual dances. As one rabbi wrote in 1939, "Every Jew [is prepared to] be killed for *Kiddush Hashem,* happy in the privilege of sanctifying, by his own means, the Name of Heaven."[1]

For many modern Westerners, death has become something to shun or even deny. The roots of this attitude can be found in a number of complex changes that occurred in the early modern era. During the Reformation, Catholics, Lutherans, and Puritans called for simple funerals and greater attention to the spiritual truths involved in death and resurrection; physical death was deemphasized. At the same time, artists and writers began consciously linking death and love, sometimes in an openly sensual way, making death at once a thing of beauty and a sudden rupture between this world and an alluring afterlife. In the seventeenth century Baroque playwrights staged love scenes in tombs, and Bernini's statue of St. Theresa's mystical union with God simultaneously depicted physical death and a spiritual ecstasy suggestive of sexual fulfillment. Death and resurrection, death and ecstasy— the tendency of the new sensibility was to play down the cruder physical aspects of dying by associating death with life and especially pleasure.

During the Enlightenment this trend culminated in attempts to suppress the awareness of death. Mourning, said the Abbé Coyer, a French priest, only encourages a cruel image of death, when in fact dying is "agreeable." Some chose to speak not of death but of a journey, a voyage, a refuge, a harbor, or sleep. Efforts were made to halt burials in churches and churchyards within the cities, partly for health reasons, thus symbolically expelling the dead from the community of the living. Corpses were to be interred in public cemeteries, enabling families to visit specific grave sites as distinct from vaguer burials under church floors or in charnel houses. The grave plot became in effect a piece of family property, keeping the deceased "at home." In rare instances this was carried to the point that bodies were preserved for viewing in huge containers of alcohol or as mummies in the home. More often, loved ones contented themselves by keeping an embalmed heart at hand; it was the wish of one Frenchman that his be kept in his mother's sewing basket.

Attitudes shifted again in the late eighteenth and nineteenth centuries, primarily due to the rise of the modern nuclear family with its heightened sense of personal affection. Concern now focused more on the family survivors than on the deceased. Even wills changed, becoming merely a record of the disposition of property, as in our time; the more personal elements, such as expressions of religious faith or decisions about burial, were discussed with family members, who thus became more intimately involved in the process of dying.

A change also occurred with respect to the manifestation of grief. From the late medieval period to the eighteenth century, mourning was socially controlled: excessive grief was frowned upon, but some manifestation of sorrow was expected even if it was not genuine. In the nineteenth century the restraints were dropped, sometimes leading to hysterical mourning. Unleashed feeling was but one manifestation of the emotion so fundamental to Romanticism. Another was the exaltation of death as a thing of eerie beauty, a means to attain reunion with loved ones, a path to eternal peace. The English author Emily Brontë wrote:

> Oh, not for them should we despair,
> The grave is drear, but they are not there;
> Their dust is mingled with the sod,
> Their happy souls are gone to God![2]

The age of Romanticism also produced the cult of the hero, and this too was reflected in funerary practices, including the Pantheon in Paris and the monuments to George Washington, Thomas Jefferson, and Abraham Lincoln in Washington, D.C., to Victor Emmanuel II in Rome, and to Lord Nelson in London.

The Romantic vision of death as at once emotional, beautiful, and perhaps heroic could not survive World War I. Death in the trenches was indescribably ugly, as reflected in soldiers' memoirs:

> Each body was covered, inches deep, with a black fur of flies which blew up into your face, into your mouth, eyes, and nostrils, as you approached. The bodies crawled with maggots. . . . We worked with sandbags in our hands, stopping every now and then to puke.[3]

It was again time to rethink death. Dying became ugly, death itself a taboo. Efforts were made to protect the dying person from a knowledge of her or his condition, and the place of death was transferred from the home to the hospital or sanitarium. As belief in life after death declined, there was a growing tendency to downplay the reality of death itself. Mourning was sharply curtailed as too upsetting, a sign perhaps of mental instability; tears were banished to the privacy of solitude. The practice of cremation, which had revived amid considerable controversy in the late nineteenth century, became popular. As the founders of the Cremation Society of England candidly asserted, this method of disposing of corpses did not offend the living and rendered the remains "innocuous." Especially in America, people began to "depart" rather than die; their corpses became "remains" taken to "funeral homes" or "parlors," from thence to be placed in "memorial parks" for their "eternal rest."

But the effort to hide from death is simply one more manifestation of the diverse human experience in coping with an inescapable fact of nature.

The Funeral of Attala by Girodet illustrates the Romantic tendency to make death both sensual and a thing of beauty. [Art Resource]

The tendency to romanticize death made no sense in the trenches of World War I. Shown here is a German corpse from the battle of the Somme. [Imperial War Museum, London]

Notes

1. F. E. Reynolds and E. H. Waugh, eds., *Religious Encounters with Death: Insights from the History and Anthropology of Religions* (University Park: Pennsylvania State University Press, 1977), p. 174.
2. P. Ariès, *The Hour of Our Death,* trans. H. Weaver (New York: Knopf, 1981), p. 438.
3. S. Cloete, *A Victorian Son: An Autobiography, 1897–1922* (Collins: London, 1972), p. 237.

Suggestions for Further Reading

Abrahamsson, H. *The Origin of Death: Studies in African Mythology.* New York: Arno Press, 1977.

Ariès, P. *The Hour of Our Death,* trans. H. Weaver. New York: Knopf, 1981.

———. *Images of Man and Death,* trans. J. Lloyd. Cambridge, Mass.: Harvard University Press, 1985.

———. *Western Attitudes Toward Death: From the Middle Ages to the Present,* trans. P. M. Ranum. Baltimore: Johns Hopkins University Press, 1974.

Gillon, E. V. *Victorian Cemetery Art.* New York: Dover, 1972.

Gorer, G. *Death, Grief and Mourning in Contemporary Britain.* Garden City, N.Y.: Doubleday, 1965.

Greaves, R. L. *Society and Religion in Elizabethan England.* Minneapolis: University of Minnesota Press, 1981.

Harrah, B. K., and Harrah, D. F. *Funeral Service: A Bibliography of Literature on Its Past, Present and Future, the Various Means of Disposition and Memorialization.* Metuchen, N.J.: Scarecrow Press, 1976.

Kipp, R. S., and Rodgers, S., eds. *Indonesian Religions in Transition.* Tucson: University of Arizona Press, 1987.

McManners, J. *Death and the Enlightenment.* Oxford: Oxford University Press, 1981.

Miller, A. J., and Aèri, M. J. *Death: A Bibliographical Guide.* Metuchen, N.J.: Scarecrow Press, 1977.

Mitford, J. *The American Way of Death.* New York: Simon & Schuster, 1963.

Morley, J. *Death, Heaven and the Victorians.* Pittsburgh: University of Pittsburgh Press, 1971.

Reynolds, F. E., and Waugh, E. H. *Religious Encounters with Death: Insights from the History and Anthropology of Religions.* University Park: Pennsylvania State University Press, 1977.

Stannard, D. E. *The Puritan Way of Death.* Oxford: Oxford University Press, 1977.

———, ed. *Death in America.* Philadelphia: University of Pennsylvania Press, 1975.

Watson, J. L., and Rawski, E. S., eds. *Death Ritual in Late Imperial and Modern China.* Berkeley: University of California Press, 1987.

Whaley, J., ed. *Mirrors of Mortality: Studies in the Social History of Death.* London: Europa, 1981.

Wolf, A. P., ed. *Religion and Ritual in Chinese Society.* Stanford, Calif.: Stanford University Press, 1974.

Early Modern India and Iran

The collapse of Mughal power in India after 1707 was not followed by the rise of a new Indian order. The subcontinent's legacy of cultural diversity and intergroup rivalry worked against unity, and there was no single effective successor to the Mughals. In this confused setting, the English East India Company began to extend the position it had slowly built up as a trading agent on both coasts, first to protect its merchants, trade partners, and goods against banditry and civil war, then to take on the actual function of government. By 1800 or so the Company was the most powerful single force in the country, and it had become the real sovereign over most of India. In the course of the next half century, a series of military campaigns, more peaceful takeovers, and treaties with local Indian rulers left the Company as the direct administrator of about half the subcontinent and indirectly the dominant power in the rest. The development depended to a large degree on Indian collaboration, but in 1857 dissidents

Colonel James Todd, an East India Company official, on tour "upcountry" c. 1800, by an Indian artist. Many Company officials took on the trappings of traditional Indian potentates and performed many of their functions, such as hearing cases and settling disputes. [E. T. Archive]

joined forces in supporting a mutiny by some of the Indian troops in the Company's army. This was put down after much bloodshed, and the British asserted dominance over the whole of India.

Iran in the eighteenth century had to withstand powerful Ottoman efforts to conquer the country, which the orthodox Sunni Ottomans considered a stronghold of heretical Shi'ite Islam. After early Ottoman successes, Nadir Shah came to the Iranian throne in 1736 and regained the lost territories but presided over a bloody period of internal repression. His successor, Karim Khan, restored peace until his death in 1779, when Iran was again torn by internal rivalries.

The Mughal Collapse

India had been left in chaos at the death of Aurangzeb in 1707. His military campaigns in the south and his continued persecution of Hindus and Sikhs had brought most of the country to rebellion. His successors on the throne at Delhi were far weaker men. Aurangzeb's three sons fought each other in the usual battles of the Mughal succession. After 2½ years of civil war, the victor was then virtually besieged by a Sikh uprising that swept the Punjab and by guerrilla warfare to the west and south. His death in 1712 brought on another struggle for the throne among his sons. They were outmaneuvered by a cousin, who captured and killed the Sikh leader only to be poisoned by his own courtiers in 1719.

The authority of the once great Mughals was by now irretrievably lost, and it no longer mattered to most people what feckless creature sat on the Peacock Throne, dreamed away his days in the imperial harem, or smoked opium. But even Aurangzeb could never have reestablished control over Rajasthan, Maharashtra, Gujarat, Punjab, or Bengal, let alone the Deccan or the south. Only a remnant of the former empire remained around Delhi and Agra. Most of the rest of India was also torn by factional fighting, civil war, and local banditry, with widespread raiding by Maratha cavalry all over the Deccan and into the north.

Aurangzeb's immediate successors had officially recognized the Maratha Confederacy (so called, although it never really achieved unity) and its extensive conquests in Mysore and on the southeast coast. The Marathas were made nominally tributary allies of the Mughals but controlled their own territories and revenues. They were in effect given thus both the means and the license to extend their raids or conquests into still more of central, southern, and eastern India, whose revenues could further augment their power. They continued to nibble away at the

◉ India in Turmoil ◉

The Muslim Indian historian Khafi Khan, writing in the 1720s, gives a vivid picture of the chaos following the death of Aurangzeb in 1707.

It is clear to the wise and experienced that . . . thoughtfulness in managing the affairs of state and protecting the peasantry . . . have all departed. Revenue collectors have become a scourge for the peasantry. . . . Many townships which used to yield full revenue have, owing to the oppression of officials, been so far ruined and devastated that they have become forests infested by tigers and lions, and the villages are so utterly ruined and desolate that there is no sign of habitation on the routes.

This is matched by English descriptions of late seventeenth-century Bengal, which had broken away from Mughal control.

Bengal is at present in a very bad condition by means of the great exactions on the people. . . . There are no ways of extortion omitted . . . [which] makes merchants' business very troublesome. . . . The king's governor has little more than the name, and for the most part sits still while others oppress the people and monopolize most commodities, even as low as grass for beasts . . . nor do they want ways to oppress people of all sorts who trade, whether natives or strangers.

Sources: I. Habib, *The Agrarian System of Mughal India* (New York: Asia Publishing House, 1963), p. 186; H. Yule, ed., *Diary of William Hedges*, vol. 2 (London: Barlow, 1887), pp. 237, 239.

remaining shreds of Mughal authority in the north and Hindustan, ultimately raiding Agra and Delhi itself as well as deep into Bengal as far as Calcutta, though English defenses kept them out of the city.

For a time it looked as if the Marathas might inherit the former Mughal position, but they proved incurably divided into contending factions, and no leader emerged who might have welded them into a coalition. The Maratha cavalry operated more and more as bandits and plunderers, rarely attempting to set up any administration in the areas they swept for loot and then left in chaos. In the south, Hyderabad became a large and wealthy kingdom independent of both the Mughals and the Marathas, while in the central Ganges valley the independent kingdom of Oudh with its capital at Lucknow also emerged from the breakup of the once great empire. In many parts of India cultivated areas were abandoned by peasants unable to defend their crops or their homes against raiders and bandits. Trade dwindled, famine increased, and India slipped further into impoverishment and anarchy.

The last shreds of Mughal power were swept away when a Persian army sacked and looted Delhi in 1739, massacred its inhabitants, and took back with them the famous Peacock Throne. Iran's powerful ruler, Nadir Shah, upon seizing the Persian throne in 1736, asked for Mughal help to crush Afghanistan, formerly a part of the Mughal Empire. But the Mughals were by now hard pressed to defend even Delhi against Maratha raiders. In 1738 Nadir Shah, acting alone, conquered Afghanistan and went on to Lahore and Delhi, leaving them in smoldering ruins. The dynasty continued in name, and successive Mughal emperors sat in state in Delhi's Red Fort until 1858, when the last of them was banished by the British.

After 1739 few people in India or elsewhere took the Mughals seriously. This was the harvest of Aurangzeb's cruel reign, which had condemned most of India to chronic civil war, local disorder, and impoverishment. Unfortunately, Rajputs, Marathas, Sikhs, Gujaratis, Bengalis, and other regional groups who had fought against the Mughals saw each other as rivals and indeed as enemies rather than as joint Indian inheritors of power. Their languages, though related like those of Europe, were different, and they differed culturally as well. Their divisions now made it possible for the English and French to make a place for themselves and to increase their commercial and political power.

Westerners in India

The story of the Portuguese arrival in India and their establishment of a major base at Goa on the west coast has been briefly told in Chapter 17. For about a century after Vasco da Gama's voyage to Calicut in 1498, the Portuguese dominated Western trade with India, as well as with Southeast Asia, China, and Japan. In India they competed with Indian and Arab traders and increasingly after the end of the sixteenth century with Dutch and English merchants and their ships. But no Westerners even thought about contending for political power in India for another 250 years, until the latter half of the eighteenth century. Although the Portuguese arrived well before the establishment of the Mughal Empire in 1526, they were a tiny handful with no effective means of confronting any of the Indian states of the south, let alone the soon-triumphant Mughals.

Westerners fought among themselves for control of the sea routes, but their objectives in India were purely commercial, except for the early Portuguese interest in converting the few Indians they encountered to Catholicism. In their competition for trade, the Europeans offered local rulers guns and naval help for use against their neighbors, together with a share of their profits, in exchange for commercial privileges or the use of a port. Small numbers of Europeans might involve themselves on opposite sides of such inter-Indian conflicts, seeking further influence or advantage. Once the Mughals became the dominant force in India, such power brokering largely subsided, and European merchants became humble petitioners before the Peacock Throne, whose influence was so much greater than their own.

The Portuguese were first in India and hence obtained the largest number of concessions, including a base at Goa. Concessions elsewhere included the rights to warehouses, residences and commercial rights of way at small ports on both east and west coasts, as well as at sites inland in Bengal, source of the finest cotton textiles for export and the richest and biggest market. By the early seventeenth century, however, the Portuguese were rapidly losing ground to Dutch and English traders. Their ships were outclassed in size, speed, maneuverability, firepower, and numbers, and their poor and tiny home base could no longer sustain the effort of maintaining an overextended commercial empire. The Portuguese also suffered from political miscalculations. Vijayanagar, for example (see Chapter 10), actively sought Portuguese help in its efforts to fight off its ultimate conquest by a coalition of Muslim sultanates in the northern Deccan. The Portuguese had earlier provided Vijayanagar with imported horses and cannon and had benefited commercially from their association with this dominant state of the south, but the ruler's urgent request for more aid in his greatest hour of need was shortsightedly refused. After the defeat of Vijayanagar in 1565, Portuguese trade and the Portuguese position in India rapidly declined.

The Dutch and later the English were able to move into the Indian market by making their own agreements with local rulers or with the Mughals and to begin to establish their own trade bases. The interest of the Dutch in Asia was from the beginning centered on the spice trade and its sources in the Indonesian archipelago, but they established several bases in small ports along the east coast of

India, retaining many of them until late in the eighteenth century. There they competed vigorously against the Portuguese and later the English. The Dutch involvement in Ceylon, however, was far more extensive. The Portuguese had fortified a base at Colombo some years after arriving there in 1502 and controlled large parts of the lowland west coast of the island, including the profitable trade in cinnamon bark from the Colombo area. Their efforts to extend their control inland were repelled by the Sinhalese* kingdom of Kandy in the central highlands, which had become the chief power in Ceylon after the collapse of the classical and medieval state based at Anuradhapura and Polonaruwa (see Chapter 10). But the Portuguese did succeed in converting many of the west coast Sinhalese to Catholicism, at first often by force, and Portuguese surnames remain widespread there, as in parts of Southeast Asia.

The Dutch drove out the Portuguese between 1640 and 1658 and established their own more extensive position in Ceylon, including bases on the east as well as the west coast. Although they too failed in several attempts to conquer the mountain-girt Kandyan kingdom, they made Ceylon an even more profitable commercial enterprise, setting up a plantation system for coconuts and later for coffee, imported from their territories in Java. Like the Portuguese, they often intermarried with the Sinhalese, producing a Eurasian group still known as "Burghers." By the 1630s Dutch ships dominated the Indian Ocean and its approaches and were even able to blockade Goa. Ceylon was an obvious prize, both for its trade profits and for its strategic role along the route eastward from India, in sight of the southern tip of the subcontinent and only three or four days' sail from Goa. The Dutch were to remain in control of the trade of Ceylon from their several coastal bases until the Napoleonic wars, when the British took over the island and in 1815 finally conquered the Kandyan kingdom.

The Early English Presence

England, like other European trading nations, learned about Portuguese profits in India and began to seek a northeast passage to India by sea around Russia and Siberia in 1553. The expedition was found two years later frozen into the Arctic ice, all aboard dead. A later effort to run the Portuguese blockade in 1583 in the ship *Tiger* ended in Portuguese capture of the vessel, but one of the English merchants aboard, Ralph Fitch, escaped and went on to India, where he visited Akbar's capitals of Agra and

Fatehpur Sikkri as well as Goa, returning to London in 1591 with firsthand accounts of India's wealth. Portugal was dynastically united with Spain in 1580, but this tended to weaken rather than strengthen the Portuguese effort in Asia, and with the defeat of the Spanish Armada in 1588 the way eastward was more open to England.

The English East India Company was founded in 1600. Its first two ventures were aimed at the spice trade in Southeast Asia, but the third went to India, reaching Surat, the major port of Gujarat, in 1608. Gujarat had been absorbed into the Mughal Empire in 1573, and Captain William Hawkins, who commanded the fleet of three English ships, carried presents and a letter from King James I to the Mughal emperor, Jahangir, requesting a trade treaty. Hawkins claimed that the Portuguese, especially the Jesuits who were already ensconced at the Mughal court, conspired against him, but in any case he was kept waiting for over two years and was finally obliged to return home empty-handed. A second English envoy reached Agra in 1612 but was sent away even more summarily after the Jesuits there urged the emperor not to deal with him.

However, later in 1612 a single English ship defeated and dispersed four Portuguese galleons and a number of frigates off Surat, in view of those on shore, a feat that was repeated in 1615. Indians now saw that the English were more valuable clients than the Portuguese and better able to defend Indian shipping and coasts from pirates and from rival Europeans, whose tactics were often indistinguishable from those of pirates. The Indian market had little or no interest in trade with England and was not impressed by the samples of goods it was offered from what was, after all, a much less advanced economy.

The lack of goods attractive to the Eastern market was indeed to hamper European and American trade in India until the British conquest and trade with China and the rest of Asia until well into the nineteenth century. The Mughals, however, had no navy and had to depend on foreigners for protection against piracy; of these, it now seemed clear, the English were the least troublesome and the most effective. In 1616 King James sent another ambassador, Sir Thomas Roe, who finally won permission from Jahangir for the East India Company to build a warehouse in Surat. Seven years later the Dutch massacred ten English merchants who had been sharing the spice trade of eastern Indonesia, signaling the end of the Netherlands' willingness to allow any European competition in what thus became their private preserve. The English were obliged to abandon their effort to penetrate Dutch territory and to concentrate on India.

Territorial Bases

From Surat, English ships completed the elimination of Portuguese power at sea, and English merchants became the main traders in the port. They then sought bases on

---

*The Sinhalese are the dominant inhabitants of Ceylon (Sri Lanka), having invaded and settled the island, probably from northern India, in the seventh century B.C.

the east coast and in Bengal, where they could buy the finest-quality cottons more directly as well as the indigo and saltpeter produced in the lower Ganges valley. After their early attempts had been driven off by the Dutch, English negotiations with a local ruler to the south led to their purchase of land in 1639 around a small harbor that later became the city of Madras. Here they immediately built Fort St. George. Madras became their chief base in eastern India, from which they had access to south Indian cottons and other goods. From Madras they made repeated efforts to trade directly in Bengal and finally established a warehouse up river near the provincial capital. They found, however, that such proximity to the Mughal and Bengali authorities exposed them to arbitrary taxation and even sometimes expropriation, and on at least one occasion the Company's agent was publicly whipped and expelled. Accordingly, they sought a more secure position. They had traded periodically at a small market half a day's sail up the Hooghly River, one of the lesser mouths of the Ganges, and in 1690 decided to make a settlement there where they felt their ships could protect or rescue

them if needed. There they were also more distant from Indian authority. Soon thereafter they received permission to build a fort. The new settlement, called Fort William (after the English monarch William III), was shortly to be known as Calcutta.

At Surat the English remained among many merchant groups and were dependent on the fickle pleasure of Mughal and Gujarati powers. But Bombay, originally a chain of small islands enclosed in a large bay, was ceded to the English crown by Portugal in 1661 as part of the marriage contract of the Portuguese princess Catherine of Braganza and Charles II. The Portuguese had built no settlement there and used it only occasionally, since it was vulnerable to piracy, cut off from landward access to markets by the rampaging Marathas, and had a harbor too big for the small ships of the time. But the quite different drawbacks of Surat and the attractions of a more nearly independent and protected base, as at Madras and Calcutta, led the Company to move its western India headquarters to Bombay in 1687.

With the founding of Calcutta in 1690, the English now

◎ Why Calcutta? ◎

Before the founding of Calcutta, the English had tried to use several other harbors on the seaward edge of the Ganges delta. Here is a 1689 description of the problems at Ballasore, one of those harbors, and of the plan to make a base instead at Calcutta.

Our ships in Ballasore road do generally ride in a hard and dangerous roadstead and many of our men come to sickness and death by the constant labor of rowing so far in such a rough sea, which we would willingly prevent all that in us lies, and therefore if the Moors [Mughals] will allow us to fortify ourselves at Chutanutee [the village that became Calcutta] where our ships may go up and ride within the command of our guns it would be much better for us, though it should cost us a bribe of thirty or forty thousand rupees to the great men to be paid when we are possessed of the Mughal's Phirmaund [charter of trading privileges] for that and for the twelve articles made with Mr. Charnock [the Company's chief agent in Bengal], but the confirmation of these articles we insist on in right and will not purchase them.

But Calcutta had other problems. Here is a description in 1703.

[Mr. Charnock chose the site] for the sake of a large shady tree, though he could not have chosen a more unhealthful place on all the river, for three miles to the northeast is a salt water lake that overflows in September and October and then prodigious numbers of fish resort thither, but in November and December when the floods are dissipated those fishes are left dry and with their putrefaction affect the air with thick stinking vapors which the northwest winds bring with them to Fort William [where] they cause a yearly mortality.

Sources: C. R. Wilson, *Old Fort William in Bengal* (London: Murray, 1906), p. 5; J. N. Das Gupta, ed., *India in the Seventeenth Century* (New Delhi: Associated Publishing House, 1976), p. 232.

had three small territorial footholds, well placed to tap the trade of India in each of its major segments, west, south, and east. But like all other foreigners in India, they remained petitioners, dependent on the favors of the Mughal state or of local rulers and liable to be driven out, expropriated, or denied trading privileges. No one as yet anticipated the imminent collapse of Mughal power.

Even after the death of Aurangzeb, there was little recognition of the changed situation. The East India Company sent an embassy to the by then virtually powerless Mughal emperor in 1714; the embassy's leader prostrated himself before the throne as "the smallest particle of sand" giving "the reverence due from a slave," asking for additional trade privileges. Significantly, however, the agent also sought the right to collect revenues in the immediate areas around Madras and Calcutta, where the Company was by now the de facto government. The embassy was largely ignored and would probably never have been even acknowledged if the emperor had not fallen ill and asked for treatment from the embassy's English doctor. His success led to the embassy's reception, and in 1717 all its requests were granted.

The Mughal and Post-Mughal Contexts

The Mughals, like many premodern states, were used to such arrangements with various groups or individuals to whom they in effect farmed out the collection of taxes and the administration of local areas that the taxes supported. In their view, the English were little different from scores of others who had long been granted such rights, equivalent to the Mughal *jagir* or *zamindari* (see Chapter 19), and Delhi attached little importance to the 1717 concession. Indeed, it seems important now only because we know what followed and can recognize it as the first step toward English territorial sovereignty in India.

After the death of Aurangzeb, the Mughals as well as local and provincial authorities had ceased to maintain order. In this context, the English East India Company was at least able to keep up a semblance of government in its fortified bases, and, with the help of small private armies, in the areas immediately around the bases as well. The embassy to Delhi in 1714 had to fight off large armed robber bands even on the imperial road from Agra. Most of the rest of India was in even worse condition. The Company could survive and prosper only if it could create security for trade goods in storage and in transit and could offer its Indian partners similar security. Areas of production could generate trade commodities also only if they could be kept orderly. The main consequence of the fading of Mughal power was thus not that the English rose politically in India, but that they were driven increasingly to provide their own defense, policing, revenue collection, and local government. They did this well enough to survive and to attract Indian merchants to deal with them and even become residents of the English bases, where their profits and property could also be secure.

Within a few years Madras, Calcutta, and Bombay were overwhelmingly Indian in population, home to many laborers and servants as well as numerous merchants, artisans, bankers, and agents, all having selected the still tiny English-dominated world of the fortified ports over any Indian alternative. Apart from the Mughals, who counted for little in any case, local states and rulers were often also willing to have the Company manage trade, collect taxes, and keep order. Civil order and healthy conditions for trade, which the English offered, were more than enough to ensure the cooperation of most Indians.

The Company prospered, and Indian cottons became so popular in England that Parliament in 1701, concerned to protect English textiles, prohibited their import. When that ban was ignored, a parliamentary ruling in 1720 prohibited their use or wear, but reexport to the Continent continued and even domestic consumption could not be prevented. Indian cottons were clearly superior to Western products, and the finest of them have never been surpassed. A widely repeated story told how the emperor Aurangzeb had reproved his daughter for appearing naked at court, to which she is said to have replied that she was wearing seven thicknesses of Dacca muslin.

Bombay Green in 1767, with the buildings, servants, and troops of the East India Company. Note the Western-style architecture of the buildings, including the church in the center. [Granger Collection]

The Company was not alone in its prosperity. From the first factory at Surat to Indian independence in 1947, Indians found employment in the expanding economy of what became the colonial ports and later their inland equivalents, as well as in the colonial bureaucracy. English and Scots who prospered were greatly outnumbered by Indians, but most of the biggest gainers were British. Most Indians remained poor, and most of those who prospered did so as junior partners, especially after 1830, despite British economic and social discrimination against them.

For most peasants the gradual spread of Company rule meant at least protection against banditry or Maratha raids and a growing new market within India and abroad for their commercial crops. Commercialization of agriculture proved ruinous to some but profitable to many. In any case, the Company could never have succeeded without extensive Indian collaboration, particularly the connections with domestic trade networks and production provided by Indian merchants, agents, and bankers. All were dependent on the Company's ability to maintain order.

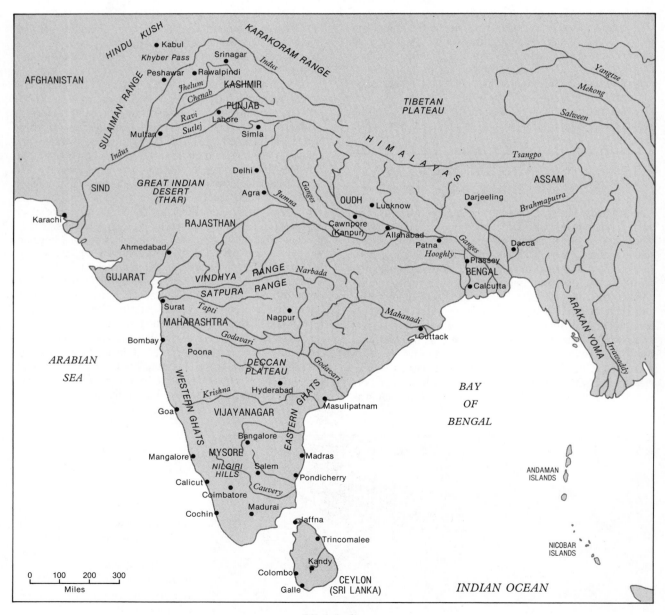

27.1 India

Anglo-French Rivalry and the Conquest of Bengal

The French had also been active contenders for the trade of India since the founding of the French East India Company in 1664 and had established a warehouse of their own at Surat, an east coast base at Pondicherry, south of Madras, and another warehouse just up river from Calcutta. The French bases, in India as in all their overseas ventures, were government-sponsored and controlled. They had the advantage of superb leadership under Joseph Dupleix (1697–1764), who favored an expansionist policy. He was supported by able military and naval commanders. Their forces captured Madras in 1746 and went on to defeat the local Indian ruler of the southeast, becoming the dominant power in the whole of south India. Unfortunately for them, they got little support from home, and the Treaty of Aix-la-Chapelle in 1748 restored Madras to the English. Two years later the English trader Robert Clive defeated both the French and their southern Indian allies with a small force.

When the Seven Years' War (1756–1763) erupted in Europe, fighting spread to India as well as North America, and the British and French provided troops and ships to supplement the Indian forces who did most of the actual fighting. Now deprived of the leadership of Dupleix, who had been called home for allegedly spending too much of the French company's resources in "unprofitable adventures," the French lost out in this struggle. A major lesson of the conflict was that very small numbers of European troops, operating with somewhat larger numbers of Indian soldiers trained in Western methods, could repeatedly defeat enormously larger Indian armies. Those on the European sides were disciplined to fire regular volleys on command and to plan and coordinate their actions. Their guns and cannon were better, but organization and leadership made them more effective, as did morale enhanced by regular pay and uniforms.

Western military power was, however, tested most severely by a Bengali challenge to the growing English position in and around Calcutta. As their local authority increased, the English became less deferential to the still technically sovereign rulers of Bengal, now independent of the Mughals. No longer humble petitioners who had regularly kissed the feet of the *nawab* (king) of Bengal, their independent behavior and their addition to the fortifications of Fort William offended the new nawab, Siraj-ud-Dawlah, who came to the throne in 1756. In a last flash of imperial fire, his army and war elephants overwhelmed Calcutta and its small corps of defenders in June 1756. Some escaped in boats and fled to Madras, but about 60 were left behind, to be thrown into the fort's tiny, airless dungeon. Next morning two-thirds of them were dead of suffocation. The incident of the so-called Black Hole of Calcutta became infamous. It seemed the end of the English position in Bengal, but appearances were deceiving. Within four months an expedition sailed from Madras under the same Robert Clive who had earlier ousted the French from the south. In January 1757 he retook Calcutta and then drove the French from their remaining bases in Bengal. With support from Indian groups, he defeated the huge army of the nawab at the battle of Plassey in June, some 75 miles northwest of Calcutta.

Although no one seemed fully to realize it at the time, the English were now masters of Bengal. They had no effective rivals, nor were there viable alternatives to British rule. Their military victory was, however, due in large part to Indian collaboration, including, perhaps most important, bankers who had lent money to both sides and who calculated that an English victory was more desirable on practical grounds. The English paid their debts, as the nawab did not, and as a merchant group the English East India Company furthered trade rather than preying on it. The leading Indian banker in fact paid very large sums to troops on the nawab's side to persuade them not to fight; the reserves, which were to have swept the field at Plassey when the battle hung in the balance, never came. But the traditional Indian armies of the day were usually composed of different groups who were often rivals and were rarely effectively led. Contingents often deserted, failed to appear, or decided to throw their lot in with another side.

❁
ROBERT CLIVE AND THE BEGINNINGS OF BRITISH INDIA

Robert Clive (1725–1774) had shipped out to Madras as an East India Company clerk but he soon developed a reputation as an adventurer. He found his clerk's job so boring that he tried unsuccessfully to blow his brains out with a pistol that misfired. Adventure soon came when the French captured Fort St. George in 1746 and he was taken prisoner. He escaped and took a commission in the Company's small army. His first military expedition, against a powerful southern kingdom allied with the French, was won by brilliant strategy even though his opponents outnumbered his forces 20 to 1. Clive was acclaimed as a hero and repeated his success by driving out the French and their Indian allies in the major Deccan kingdom of Hyderabad. Still only 27 years old, he was praised as a deliverer and granted two years' home leave. Sent out again with the rank of colonel in 1756, he reached Madras just as Calcutta was being overwhelmed by the armies of the nawab of Bengal.

Already known to Indians by a nickname roughly translatable as "He Who Is Daring in War," Clive sailed north with a small force. He recaptured Calcutta, defeated the greatly superior army that tried to stop him just north of

Robert Clive accepting tribute from Mir Jaffar, the puppet whom he had placed on the throne of Bengal after the battle of Plassey, as depicted in an oil painting by Francis Hayman, c. 1760. [National Portrait Gallery, London]

the city, and four months later met the main Bengali contingent at Plassey. By this time he had just over 1,000 British troops and about 2,000 Indians under his command. The Bengali army totaled 18,000 cavalry and 50,000 foot soldiers, with more than 50 field guns managed by French artillerymen. Again Clive's tactical genius won the day, confusing, outmaneuvering, and finally routing the enemy. He then marched to the Bengali capital, where he installed his own Indian client and ally as ruler.

Clive and his English and Indian colleagues helped themselves to the provincial treasury, and the Company too was richly repaid in reparations and new revenues now under its control. After consolidating his conquests with further victories against Indian and French forces, Clive devoted his enormous energy to strengthening the Company's army, refortifying Calcutta, and administering the new domains. Four years of incessant activity broke his health, and he spent five years in England. He was sent back to India in 1765 to try to check the plundering excessses of his successors and to reorganize what now amounted to the Company's government of Bengal.

Two years later he was back in England to face charges in Parliament that he had defrauded the Company and enriched himself by extortion. The accusations were brought by many of the same people whom he had tried to restrain from similar behavior and who were jealous of his successes. Although in the end he was cleared, he brooded over his grievances, and still suffering from poor health, he shot himself in 1774 at the age of 49. The same mer-

curial temperament that had made him try suicide as a young man and then carried him to the heights of success proved his undoing. Yet more than any one person, he began the process that was to end in British rule in India. He was far more than a brilliant field commander and was concerned about the implications of British policy in India. His immediate successors were more interested in personal enrichment.

The Establishment of British Rule

With Bengal now in their hands, many of the English turned to plunder as well as trade, extorting silver and jewels from the rich and also demanding what amounted to protection money. After a few years this brought severe criticism from home, parliamentary inquiries, and finally, in 1784, the India Act, which created a board of control for India in London. Meanwhile, beyond Bengal, the rest of India remained in turmoil. Afghan armies repeatedly laid waste the northwest and looted Delhi again in 1757, slaughtering most of the inhabitants. A huge Maratha army gathered to repel yet another Afghan invasion in 1760 was crushed in a great battle near Delhi early in 1761. The Afghans then withdrew, but they had in effect removed the only Indian power able to contest the English. Three years later outnumbered Company forces soundly defeated a final Indian coalition organized by leading Bengalis, ending the last serious challenge to their power in the north.

From this point on the policy of both the Company and its London supervisors was to acquire no more territory but to achieve their ends through alliances with Indian princes, offering them military protection in exchange for trading rights. In Bengal as in the smaller areas around Madras and Bombay, they continued to collect taxes and run the administration as nominal agents of the local or regional Indian rulers. Administration was expensive and distracted from the Company's main business, trade. The collection of rural taxes was farmed out to Bengali agents, or *zamindars*. The zamindars, with British encouragement, seized land from defaulting taxpayers, thus allying themselves with the new company administration. Calcutta was made the capital of all of British India; after 1785 the Company, under parliamentary supervision from London, concentrated on promoting trade but also administered justice and defense. Indian agents were necessarily employed in the lower echelons of government; all higher administrative and military posts were reserved for the British.

The official policy of discouraging further direct conquest yielded in the 1790s to the strategic pressures of the Napoleonic wars. The French still had small footholds in South India and a history, like that of the English, of alliances with various Indian rulers. Successive heads of state in Mysore had had some dealings with the French and had also periodically threatened Madras. In 1799 Mysore was overwhelmed by Company troops. Half of it, including the commercially important coastal strip, was annexed outright, thus linking the Madras area to the west coast. Most of the rest of it was given to a loyal Indian ally, the neighboring state of Hyderabad, which was to remain nominally independent until 1947. The peninsular south was now firmly under Company control, but the Marathas remained a formidable power, and their home base in Maharashtra blocked Bombay's access to inland markets. Taking advantage of internal Maratha division, the Company signed a treaty with one side in 1802 promising military support in exchange for territorial rights. When the Maratha puppet the British had installed tried later to revive his power, the Company defeated his forces and took over all Maratha domains in 1818, soon joining them to Bombay Presidency, the major British territory in western India.

The central Ganges valley west of Bengal, through which India's major trade route ran, was too important to be left uncontrolled. In 1801 the ruler of the state of Oudh was forced to accept British protection, although he remained nominally sovereign. The same arrangement was made with the Mughal emperor for his domains in the Delhi-Agra area. Southern Gujarat, including the commercially important port of Surat, was also brought under Company control. Only Rajasthan, the Indus valley and Sind, Kashmir, and Punjab remained outside the British sphere. Much of what the British controlled was, however, nominally ruled by allied Indian princes.

The British, troubled by the French threat and reminded of French naval successes in the Bay of Bengal 50 years earlier, moved on Dutch-held Ceylon after Napoleon's occupation of Holland. Their first concern was to take over the fine natural harbor of Trincomalee on the east coast of Ceylon, where they could base their naval vessels. There were no harbors safe to enter or leave during the northeast monsoon or winter anywhere on the Indian east coast, nor were any of them large enough for the fleet, which had to be withdrawn to winter haven in distant Bombay. Trincomalee filled this urgent need, and the British occupied it in 1795, subsequently taking over all of the other Dutch holdings in Ceylon.

As the French threat faded, British attention shifted to the far more productive southwestern lowlands of Ceylon, and the colonial capital was fixed at Colombo. From there roads were built crisscrossing the island and, after the final conquest of the Kandyan kingdom in 1815, into the central

Cultural blending in colonial India: an Indian ruler in Rajasthan in British uniform, by an Indian artist. [Victoria and Albert Museum, London]

highlands, followed by railways after 1858. Coffee plantations spread rapidly with this improved access to export markets, as did coconut production, and by midcentury Ceylon had the plantation economy it retained until after independence. Tea was introduced after a disastrous coffee blight in the 1870s, and rubber was added at the end of the century. Tamil laborers were brought in from overpopulated South India to build roads and railways and to provide labor for the new plantations. Ceylon was designated a crown colony separate from British India and was administered as such despite its long and close Indian connections.

The conquest of India by a relative handful of British settlers, merchants, and troops, at first almost a private venture, could not have happened without native support or without the factional divisions that fatally weakened Indian resistance. Most people accepted Company control either because they benefited from it as merchants, bankers, collaborators, agents, or employees or because they saw it as preferable to control by the Mughals, the Marathas, or any of the local rulers, whose record was not attractive. Most contemporary Indian states were oppressive, taxing merchants and peasants unmercifully and often arbitrarily, while at the same time failing to keep order, suppress banditry, maintain roads and basic services, or administer justice acceptably. Revenues went disproportionately to support court extravagances and armies, which spent their energy more in interregional conflict than in genuine defense. This was partly the legacy of the Delhi sultanate and particularly of the Mughals. It became clear to most Indians that, in fact, only the British were both willing and able to protect them from banditry, ensure the security of life and property, and foster conditions under which trade and agriculture could again prosper. That was enough to win their support or at least ensure their acquiescence. At any rate, nearly a century was to pass between the last Bengali resistance in the mid-1760s and the first major uprising against British rule in 1857.

The Indians accommodated themselves to the British as they had to foreign conquerors in the past. Mindful of the early English rapacity in Bengal, the Company generally tried as much as possible to avoid displacing or offending Indians or disrupting local customs except for slavery and *sati* (widow burning). This maturation of policy was illustrated in a letter from the directors to the company offices in Bombay in 1784:

> By the exercise of a mild and good government people from other parts may be induced to come and reside under our protection. Let there be entire justice exercised to all persons without distinction, and open trade allowed to all.[1]

Such a plan reflected the original exclusive aim of trade profits, more bluntly stated almost a century earlier: "Merchants desire no enemies, and would create none."[2]

The Orientalists and the Bengal Renaissance

As British administration was extended, more and more company employees were not merchants or clerks but officials and magistrates. British and Indian merchants had obvious common interests, and many even appreciated each other's culture. Some Company traders and officials, such as Sir William Jones (1746–1794), found themselves fascinated by the rich variety of the Indian tradition. Jones, a judge in late eighteenth-century Bengal, had the usual classical education in England and then had to learn Persian (still used for Mughal law), Sanskrit (the classical language of India and of Hindu texts, which were often cited in law cases), and the modern languages of North India spoken by those who appeared in court: Bengali, Hindi, and so on. He began to realize after his arrival in 1783 the close connections among them and between them and Greek, Latin, and the languages of modern Europe, including English. In 1786 he published a paper that convincingly made the case for an Indo-European language family, thereby earning himself the nickname "Oriental" Jones. Other Englishmen studied and translated the Indian classics and the great traditions of Indian religion and art and carried out archaeological work of great importance, including the later rediscovery of Harappa, Mohenjo Daro, and the Mauryan empire.

British scholars of Indian culture and history founded the Asiatic Society of Bengal in Calcutta in 1784, whose *Journal* published Jones' paper and many others on a wide variety of Indian topics. Most of the members and contributors were Company employees or officials who pursued their research on the side, but some found their Indian studies so engrossing that they retired to devote all their time to what was now known as Indology. Many took Indian wives, though few brought them home in retirement.

These British Orientalists, as they were called, were matched by Indian scholars who learned perfect English, studied Latin and Greek, wrote in the English literary and academic tradition, and also produced what is labeled both the Hindu Renaissance and the Bengal Renaissance, begun primarily by the work of the Bengali Ram Mohun Roy (1772–1833). Roy and others who followed him—some Company employees, others private scholars—sought their own cultural identity as well as Western learning and helped to restore the pride of educated Indians in their rich religious, philosophical, and literary heritage.

Roy founded a society in Calcutta to pursue these efforts, which made a deep impact on successive generations of Bengalis and Indians everywhere. Members of the society and like-minded Indians studied India's classical texts and led a revival of interest in the power and virtue of the Indian cultural tradition. H. L. Derozio

◉ The British Indicted ◉

In 1772 one of the early Orientalists, Alexander Dow, criticized the English.

Posterity will perhaps find fault with the British for not investigating the learning and religious opinions which prevail in those countries in Asia into which either they or their commerce or their arms have penetrated. The Brahmins of the East possessed in ancient times some reputation for knowledge, but we have never had the curiosity to examine whether there was any truth in the reports of antiquity upon that head. . . . Literary inquiries are by no means a capital object to many of our adventurers in Asia.

But William Jones was soon to join Dow and others. This is what he wrote in 1783.

It gave me inexpressible pleasure to find myself . . . almost encircled by the vast regions of Asia, which has ever been esteemed the nurse of science, the inventress of delightful and useful arts, and scene of glorious actions, fertile in the production of human genius, . . . abounding in natural wonders, and infinitely diversified in the forms of religion and government, in the laws, manners, customs, and languages as well as in the features and complexions of men. . . . [Later he wrote:] It was my desire to discharge my public duties with unremitted attention, and to recreate myself at leisure with the literature of this interesting country. . . . I am no Hindu, but I hold the doctrine of the Hindus concerning a future state to be incomparably more rational, more pious, and more likely to deter men from vice than the horrid opinions inculcated by Christians on punishments without end.

Sources: A. Dow, *History of Hindoostan* (1772), p. 107; P. Mudford, *Birds of a Different Plumage* (London: Collins, 1974), pp. 88–90 passim.

(1809–1831), of mixed Indian and British parentage, became in his short life a brilliant teacher and poet, inspiring young Bengalis to pursue, as he had done, learning in both the Indian and the Western or British traditions. He thus served to promote a true meeting of East and West, as his British counterparts among the Orientalists also attempted to do.

One prominent member of the society was Dwarkanath Tagore (1794–1846), an outstanding Western-style entrepreneur, banker, merchant, and industrialist who became,

An East India Company official studying an Indian language with a *munshi* (a native language teacher), c. 1813. Especially after 1800, the Company began to require all of its officials to learn at least one Indian language fluently, an obvious necessity for those who dispensed justice and managed administration as well as traded. [British Library]

like Roy and many others, an Anglicized Indian. These Western and Eastern synthesizers of the two cultures worked together, especially in Calcutta, to promote the similar education of young upper-class Indians, founding schools and libraries and publishing jointly a number of journals and books. Their efforts foreshadowed the full-scale emergence of the Westernized Indian middle class of intellectuals and business people later in the nineteenth century, including Tagore's grandson Rabindranath Tagore (1861–1941), India's greatest modern literary figure, who devoted most of his life to bridging East and West. The Hindu Renaissance was also concerned to reform what in the perspective of the nineteenth century had come to seem the less desirable aspects of Hinduism, such as suttee and child marriage, and in time to make Hinduism an appropriate vehicle for modern Indian nationalism.

❀ CALCUTTA, COLONIAL CAPITAL

By 1810 Calcutta's population had reached a million, and it was already being labeled "the second city of the British Empire," a title it retained until Indian independence in 1947. It was also known as "the city of palaces," adorned not only with government buildings and the governor's residence but also with the mansions of rich British and Indian merchants, which made an imposing facade along the river. Behind the facade was the reality of mass squalor. Rudyard Kipling was later to call Calcutta "the City of Dreadful Night" for its hot, humid climate and the vast slums and shanty settlements that sat back from the river. From the beginning, it was overwhelmingly Indian in population. British residents found its tropical environment a trial, the more so because fashion required them to wear the woolen outfits expected of a gentleman at home, to overeat, and to consume large quantities of wine and whiskey. Anyone who aspired to a position in society had to keep a carriage, dress in fashion, and entertain lavishly. Westerners also had no immunity to regional diseases, and the death rate among them was high until well into the twentieth century. Malaria, dysentery, typhoid, and cholera were the major killers; it was in Calcutta in 1899 that Sir Ronald Ross first proved the theory that malaria was carried by mosquitoes and began preventive measures. Home leave was not common until after the opening of the Suez Canal in 1869, but the colonial administration, which remained in Calcutta until 1912, retired to the cool foothills of the Himalayas for the hottest summer months.

Calcutta was picked in 1690 for the site of the Company's trading base in Bengal, in part because the Hooghly River, one of the many mouths of the Ganges, widened a little there and formed a deep pool where the ships of the time could anchor. There was a small trading fair there already where Indian merchants periodically brought their goods, but Calcutta probably took its name from the nearby shrine to the goddess Kali at Kalighat. It prospered from the start and became the predominant trading center first for Bengal and then for all of eastern India. It enjoyed an advantageous position in the Ganges delta with easy access to inland routes and coastal shipping. After 1850 a network of railways was built with Calcutta as the major hub, and textile and metalworking factories rose beside the Hooghly, joined toward the end of the century by a wide range of other industrial enterprises. The biggest industry was the weaving of jute, a coarse fiber from a plant grown along delta streams and made into gunnysacks and twine, of which Calcutta had a near world monopoly. The city became the largest industrial center in India, as well as its biggest city. Kipling wrote a short poem about it in 1905 that caught it well:

> *Me the sea captain loved, the river built,*
> *Wealth sought and kings adventured life to*
> *   hold.*
> *Hail England! I am Asia, power on silt;*
> *Death in my hands, but gold!*[3]*

Calcutta was the major base for the English plunder of Bengal after 1760, and many fortunes made in those chaotic years were reflected in the splendid houses along the river. This was the extravagant culture of the people called "nabobs" (a corruption of the Indian title *nawab*, "ruler"), who had "shaken the pagoda tree" in India and displayed their new wealth ostentatiously. As Calcutta grew and industrialized, it became mainly a city of dingy warehouses, factories, and slums. It was also, however, the scene of the Bengal Renaissance, a remarkable flowering of the blend between Western and Indian cultures. The present-day city remains India's most lively literary, intellectual, and cultural center. Western visitors find its grimy slums depressing, like those of any Third World city, but it is still, as for all of its short history, an immensely vigorous and creative place.

The Subjugation of India

Until well into the nineteenth century much of British rule in India was conducted through the formal sovereignty of the so-called Princely States and their Indian rulers and was to a large extent collaborative. Even in recently conquered Maharashtra, as elsewhere, the British attracted support by their suppression of banditry and furthering of production and trade. Most elite Indians who had any dealings with the British were content with their new rulers, and many were enthusiastic. Peasants who had been accustomed to the harsh exactions of Indian states had come

---

*Jute was often referred to in India as "gold on silt."

◎ British Life in India ◎

The English who succeeded in trade or in the higher administration of the East India Company lived luxuriously and affected an extravagant style. Here are some sample accounts, the first describing the governor's entourage in Madras about 1710.

The governor seldom goes abroad with less than three or four score peons armed; besides the English guards to attend him he has two union flags carried before him. . . . He is a man of great parts, respected as a prince by the rajahs of the country, and is in every way as great.

The secretary to a high Company official in Calcutta in the mid-1770s voiced complaints.

The cursed examples of parade and extravagance they [the Indian servants] are holding up forever to us. "Master must have this. Master must do that." A councillor never appears in the street with a train of less than twenty fellows, nor walks from one room to another in his house unless preceded by four silver staves. . . . What improvement India may make in my affairs I know not, but it has already ruined my temper.

Another account of Calcutta in the 1770s describes the life of the colonialists.

Most gentlemen and ladies in Bengal live both splendidly and pleasantly, the forenoon being dedicated to business, and after [midday] dinner to rest. . . . On the river sometimes there is the diversion of fishing or fowling or both, and before night they make friendly visits to one another, when pride or contention do not spoil society, which too often they do among the ladies, as discord and faction do among the men.

Things were much the same at Bombay in 1812, according to a visiting English lady, who might have been describing pretentious expatriate society anywhere and at any time, including the present.

With regard to the Europeans in Bombay, the manners of the inhabitants of a foreign colony are in general so well represented by those of a country town at home that it is hopeless to attempt making a description of them very interesting. The ladies are underbred and over-dressed, ignorant, and vulgar. The civil servants are young men taken up with their own imaginary importance.

Sources: C. Lockyer, *An Account of the Trade of India* (London: Crouch, 1711), p. 24; B. Francis and E. Kean, eds., *Letters of Philip Francis,* vol. 1 (London: Murray, 1901), p. 219; J. T. Wheeler, *Early Records of British India* (Calcutta: Newman, 1879), p. 53; J. Forbes, *Oriental Memoirs,* vol. 1 (London: White, Cochrane, 1813), p. 42.

to distrust all government. Most, indeed, were only dimly aware at first that a new group of foreigners now dominated politics, especially since local administration was left largely in Indian hands. Indirectly, however, peasant welfare was increasingly affected by the spread of zamindar landlordism encouraged by the British and by the spread of commercial crops and market forces. Freedom from banditry and from arbitrary or excessive taxation were important gains, but there was a significant rise in tenancy and a decline in net economic well-being for many who lost their land or were exploited by new commercialization, such as the notorious indigo plantation system, which ruined many thousands of Indian peasants.

Just as the British worked largely through native rulers, so, at first, they left the structure of Indian society intact. Except for their suppression of *sati*, banditry, and slavery,

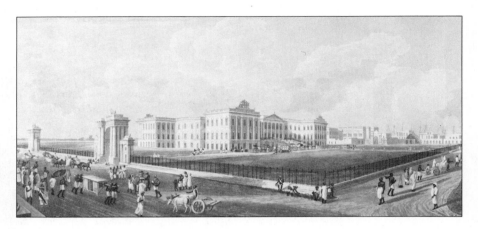

Government House, Calcutta, in 1826: all very Western in style, although the sedan chair (left foreground) was a traditional Asian institution too. [British Library]

the British did not tamper with Indian customs. Even Christian missionaries, whom the Company had excluded as "disruptive" until 1813, were limited for some time to running schools, which attracted many young Indians as a means of rising in the new colonial society and gaining employment in the colonial system. Rooted in commerce, the Indian middle class made money in the expanding trade promoted by the British order, and they too founded or joined as partners in new Western-style banks, corporations, agency houses, and joint-stock companies. In 1833 Parliament abolished the Company's previous monopoly of all trade in and with India in response to the demand for entry into this vast and lucrative market, and India was opened to all kinds of private enterprise.

As the nineteenth century wore on, however, and industrialization and technological progress brought Britain unprecedented wealth and power, British attitudes began to change. The growing conviction that Britain was the appropriate leader of the world in all things replaced the earlier interest in Indian culture with a new ethnocentric arrogance. The domination of the Indian economy and its subjection to British interests at home had similarly deleterious effects. Machine-made cloth from the mills of Lancashire ended the Indian cotton exports that had for so long been the chief basis of trade. Mass-produced British cloth invaded the Indian market, throwing millions of Indian hand spinners of cotton out of work, although raw cotton continued to be shipped to supply British looms.

◉ The Charter Act, 1833 ◉

The rise of humanitarianism and liberalism in Britain led to a new Charter Act for India in 1833 when the Company's monopoly was removed. This was often cited later by Indian nationalists as showing the hypocrisy of British rule, but it stated a principle that many colonial administrators made an effort to follow.

No native [of India], nor any natural-born subject of His Majesty resident therein, shall by reason of his religion, place of birth, descent, color, or any of the above, be disabled from holding any place, office, or employment under the Company. . . . On a large view of the state of Indian legislation, and of the improvements possible in it, it is recognized as an indisputable principle that the interests of the native subjects are to be consulted in preference to those of Europeans whenever the two come in competition, and that therefore the laws ought to be adapted to the feelings and habits of the natives rather than to those of Europeans.

Source: S. Wolpert, *A New History of India* (New York: Oxford University Press, 1982), p. 213.

At the same time, British policymakers for India decided that it was the chief duty of government to "civilize" and "improve" Indians, that is, to bring them into conformity with British cultural norms. Such policymakers included a series of governors general, beginning with William Bentinck in 1828, who were followers of the new British school of utilitarian liberalism. It was decreed in 1835 that English and Western learning should be the main objects of education, in order, in the words of the Liberal spokesman Thomas Babington Macaulay, "to form a class who may be interpreters between us and the millions whom we govern, a class of persons Indian in blood and color, but English in taste, in opinions, in morals, and in intellect."[4] The views of the Orientalists and their admiration of Indian civilization were set aside; Indians were now to be educated along British lines. A new law code was devised for all of British India, which incorporated many aspects of Indian tradition but created an essentially British system of law and jurisprudence. Although from 1809 all British recruits to the East India Company and later to the Indian civil service were required to learn at least one Indian language and something of the country's history and culture, fewer and fewer bothered to learn Sanskrit or to study the Indian classics.

After midcentury, British control of India was extended and facilitated by improvements in transportation and communication. The first rail lines were begun in 1850, reaching inland from Calcutta and Bombay. By 1855 all of India's major cities had been linked by telegraph and by postal service down to the village level. Railways and telegraph service were soon to be of vital importance to the British in suppressing the mutiny of 1857, but their primary use was to haul raw materials and agricultural goods to the rapidly expanding urban markets. Many had doubted that caste-conscious Hindus would crowd together on trains, but rail travel was popular from the start and indeed typified the flexibility of caste in a changing environment.

At the same time, British ambition faced potential competition. The British watched with growing concern as Russia successively took over the independent kingdoms of central Asia. Soon only Afghanistan stood between the two empires. To block Russian influence there, the British ill-advisedly sent an expedition to Kabul in 1839, assuming control of the lower Indus valley (the province of Sind) along the way. Afghan guerrilla resistance finally forced the British to retreat in 1841 through the wild mountain and gorge country along the route to India, a natural setting for a devastating ambush. Only one British survivor of the nearly 20,000-man Army of the Indus reached safety. Fierce Afghan tribal warriors had humbled yet another proud empire, but Sind was brutally reconquered in 1843 as "strategic territory."

The Sikhs of Punjab had refused passage to the ill-fated expedition to Afghanistan, and now Punjab challenged the British as the only part of India not under their direct or indirect control. Factional conflicts over the political suc-

cession there gave the British a chance to intervene in 1845–1846. The Sikhs were defeated and Punjab and Kashmir were formally annexed, although the British had to mount a second campaign and did not finally prevail until 1849. Having won the war, the British, appreciating the military skills of the Sikhs, offered them a prominent place in their army. This was the beginning of a long partnership that paid an early dividend in Sikh support for the British in the mutiny of 1857.

Images of British Rule

Until the nineteenth century the British had been far from seeing themselves as conquerors, nor had they planned to govern India. By 1800, however, they had achieved dominance, and by 1818 their empire had been largely established. Having acquired an Indian empire, the British then had to decide how to rule it. Part of the debate centered on what sort of educational and legal system would best serve British interests as well as those of the new dominions. The Orientalists, who had learned to admire and study Indian civilization, argued that young Indians should be educated in their own culture and its great tradition, which they regarded as the moral equivalent of Christianity. This included the study of Sanskrit, the Indian counterpart of Latin or Greek, and of the classical Indian texts.

Orientalists saw the study of the Hindu cultural and religious legacy as valuable for its own sake, but also as a guide to proper social behavior. One of the British members of the Asiatic Society of Bengal wrote:

> **Hinduism little needs the ameliorating hand of Christianity to render its votaries a sufficiently correct and moral people for all the useful purposes of a civilized society. . . . In the vast region of Hindu mythology I discover piety in the garb of allegory, I see morality at every turn blended with every tale. . . . It appears the most complete and ample system of moral allegory that the world has ever produced.[5]**

The contrary view, which ultimately became the dominant one, argued that Britain had "a moral duty to perform" in "civilizing" India according to the modern British model. This meant that English would replace Sanskrit and that Western subjects would replace the traditional Indian curriculum for those Indians being trained for careers in business and government.

Governor-General William Bentinck chose the young Thomas Babington Macaulay, later famous as a historian, to preside over the education committee, which was attempting to resolve the debate between the two sides and to plan British India's education system in 1834. Macaulay asserted that "a single shelf of a good European library is worth the whole native literature of India," and Governor Bentinck in the end declared that "the great object of the British government ought to be the promotion of European literature and science among the natives of India." The education system that resulted from such official designs was strongly English in character and content, although most upper-class Indians continued to study their own culture and linguistic tradition as well. Macaulay also drafted virtually single-handedly a new penal code for British India that produced legal uniformity for the first time throughout India. Many punishments under the new code were less severe than those under the English law of the time. Indian judges, trained in both Indian and Western-style law, were made part of the system, and by the end of the colonial period they constituted the great majority of the bench.

English-style education and law had a lasting impact on India. Both have been retained with relatively little change in modern India, adapted by Indians to their own uses. Most educated Indians became as familiar with English literature and history as educated Englishmen. Many members of the Indian upper classes went on to British universities, where they competed successfully with English students and often outdistanced them. The Hindu Renaissance, which was partly a reaction to English influence, helped to balance it, and as a result most Indians also learned about their own cultural tradition.

Indians had never been effectively unified politically or culturally in the past. British education accomplished this for the elite, and national integration was greatly facilitated by modern means of transport. Before the nineteenth century the strength of Indian regionalism resulted in part from the great difficulty of communication among its parts, given India's size and topography and the absence of navigable rivers in most of the country. The rail and road systems built after 1850 tied India together and brought most educated or commercial Indians into contact with each other; and English gave them a single common language for the first time.

Early British officials frankly acknowledged Indian hostility to their presence and argued for fair administration on the grounds of expediency. Charles Metcalfe, the British resident at Delhi, wrote in 1835:

> Our dominion in India is by conquest; it is naturally disgusting to the inhabitants and can only be maintained by military force. It is our positive duty to render them justice, to respect and protect their rights, and to study their happiness. By the performance of this duty, we may allay and keep dormant their innate dissatisfaction.[6]

Some farsighted Britons recognized that these processes must bring about a demand for national independence. Charles Trevelyan, a secretary in the political department of the government in Calcutta, wrote in 1838:

> The existing connection between two such distant countries as England and India cannot in the nature of things be permanent; no effect of policy can prevent the natives from ultimately regaining their independence. But there are two ways of arriving at this point. . . . One must end in the complete alienation of mind and separation of interests between ourselves and the natives; the other in a permanent alliance, founded on mutual benefit and goodwill.[7]

For much of the final century of British rule, particularly after 1857, the first way seemed all too likely an outcome.

The Mutiny of 1857

The arrangement that left Indian princes in formal control of much of India, although under British supervision, was in many ways unsatisfactory to the new imperialist policy. Using the pretext that disputes over succession were disruptive of political order (as they often were), the Company assumed direct sovereignty over several central Indian states in the 1850s, and in 1856, despite earlier treaty promises, annexed the rich kingdom of Oudh in the central Ganges. Mounting British arrogance had already provoked discontent among Indian troops, and the new territorial seizures had created potentially powerful enemies among deposed elites, who made common cause with the disgruntled soldiery. The hereditary aristocracy saw not only that they had been displaced as rulers by the British but also that their place in Indian society was being taken by the upstart collaborators of a rising commercial and Westernized Indian middle class. Many of the troops were incensed at being required to accept service overseas, which was forbidden to caste Hindus.

Conditions were ripe for an explosion, and a pretext soon arrived. Early in 1857 an improved rifle was introduced. It was rumored that the cartridges were coated in pork lard and other animal fat and had to be bitten off before loading, something deeply offensive to vegetarian Hindus and to Muslims. That had indeed been so originally, but although the process was quickly changed, the rumor persisted. The outcry of protest was met not by concession or explanation but by rigid insistence on following orders. Those who refused were dishonorably discharged, many of them men from Oudh.

Several regiments mutinied and killed their British officers. The mutineers captured Delhi and "restored" the last surviving Mughal emperor, now an old man, who had never been formally removed by the Company. Mutineers on the rampage slaughtered the British population of Delhi and of outlying districts there and in Oudh, massacred those who had surrendered from their encampment in the city of Cawnpore (Kanpur), and besieged the somewhat

A drawing by C. F. Atkinson, "Repulse of a Sortie," depicting an incident in the Mutiny of 1857. [British Library]

larger group of men, women, and children, including loyal Indians, who had fortified themselves in the grounds of the British Residency in Lucknow, the capital of Oudh.

During the summer of 1857 the British lost control of major portions of the Ganges heartland in northern India and, temporarily, parts of the Punjab and central India. Panic was widespread within the European communities. But most army units remained loyal, and most Indians took no part in the struggle or stood by the British. Once the British recovered from their initial shock, the outcome of the uprising was not in doubt. By July 1858 the British governor general, Lord Canning, had proclaimed victory, although resistance continued in small pockets in northern and central India until later in the year.

The British repaid the atrocities they had suffered in kind. Captured rebel soldiers were strapped to cannon and blown away, and entire villages were put to the torch. Fear and hatred created a permanent gulf between rulers and ruled. The British were henceforth frankly an occupying power, despite their continued reliance on native elites. Intermarriage and fraternization greatly decreased, and the colonial regime became more like a walled community that held itself stiffly apart from what some of its members called the "nigger natives." The feeble Bahadur Shah, last of the Mughal emperors, was exiled to Burma,

where he died in 1858, and a British captain named Hodson, taking his cue from the early Mughal dynasts themselves, murdered Bahadur Shah's sons in cold blood. Although most Indians remained collaborators, and some of them enthusiastically, and many British continued to pursue more tolerant and more positive attitudes and policies, the dream of an equal Anglo-Indian partnership was largely over.

Iran in Transition: The Eighteenth Century

For the Iranians the eighteenth century was a period of transition. The corrupt vestiges of the Safavid dynasty were swept away, and, after a period of violent internal struggle, a new dynasty emerged and undertook an expansionist foreign policy, mostly at the expense of the Ottomans. The stage was set for these developments by Ottoman aggression. The Shi'ite militancy of the Safavids had increasingly antagonized Sunni Muslims, especially the Ottomans, whose sultans regarded themselves as the protectors of the Sunnis. The Ottomans, moreover, were eager to reverse their fortunes after disastrous territorial losses to European states in the late seventeenth and early eighteenth centuries, and Iran seemed an obvious place to expand in the 1720s. With their Sunni allies in Afghanistan, the Ottomans went to war against the Iranian Shi'ites. The Iranians repulsed the Afghans and Ottomans and checked a Russian assault under Peter the Great as well. Much of Iran's success was due to an ex–robber baron turned general, Nadir Quli (1688–1747), known to history as "the Napoleon of Iran."

Nadir Quli

When the Safavid shah, Tahmasp II, accepted a humiliating peace with the Ottomans in 1732, Nadir ousted him from the throne and governed as regent for Tahmasp's infant son. Four years later the ambitious Nadir had himself crowned as Nadir Shah Afshar. The same year he concluded a series of military campaigns to recover Iranian provinces from the Ottomans, and, exploiting Russo-Turkish rivalry, he persuaded the Russians to cede Iranian territory in their possession. Unsatisfied with these striking gains, he launched an expansionist war against India, defeating the Mughal emperor, Mohammed Shah, in 1739. Nadir's troops plundered Delhi and Lahore, slaughtering some 20,000 people and seizing even the Peacock Throne. Because India was too large for him to hold, Nadir left all but the provinces on the west bank of the Indus in the hands of a subdued Mohammed Shah and returned to Iran with an enormous booty in 1740. Ties with the defeated Mughals were cemented by the marriage of Nadir's second son to the granddaughter of Aurangzeb.

Like the great Indian ruler Akbar, Nadir Shah was interested in finding the common truth he believed was at the heart of competing religions, though he made no attempt, as Akbar did, to found an ecumenical faith. He did, however, order the Bible and the Koran translated into Persian. In the hope of easing tensions between Sunni and Shi'ite Muslims, he ordered a halt to the persecution of Sunnis in Iran, while demanding that the Shi'ites be given special accommodations at Mecca. His scheme to reunify Islam was based on having his Shi'ite people embrace the newly created Ja'fariyah sect, which he insisted should be officially recognized as a Sunni group. But the Ottoman Sunnis branded the new sect unacceptable and authorized their adherents to kill Iranians. In Iran itself any hope of bridging the Sunni-Shi'ite gulf was doomed by the hostility of the Shi'ite religious leaders, who bitterly resented Nadir's attempts to reduce their power.

The influence of such religious leaders was but one of several effective checks on any shah's pretension to absolute power. In theory the shah continued to govern by divine right, though in reality no post-Safavid shah ever regained the spiritual aura that had once been accorded the early Safavids. By the eighteenth century the shah was no more than a political despot, akin to the Ottoman sultan. The shah's influence was checked as well by regional loyalties and poor communications, both of which encouraged the decentralization of power. Thus the authority of any shah ultimately depended on his personal abilities as well as his relationship with Muslim leaders.

Nadir's military talents had enabled him to extend the Iranian frontiers beyond those of the Safavid era, but like Napoleon, this reckless military adventurer had no sense of when to stop. Instead of turning his attention to economic growth and administrative reform, he squandered human and material resources on ruinous military campaigns. He met his match in the Caucasus against the Lezgian tribe, whom he failed to conquer and whose success against Nadir encouraged subject peoples in Iran to revolt. Although the rebels were savagely repressed, Nadir himself became increasingly vindictive, unstable, and vicious, executing many of his own advisers and military officers. In 1747 he was assassinated, a victim of the atmosphere of terror he had created.

For a decade Iran was plunged into strife as rival claimants fought for the throne, sometimes deposing and blinding each other. As in the Safavid era, fratricide and the execution of one's opponents was commonplace. Nadir's nephew and successor, having learned of his new position by an invitation accompanied with Nadir's severed head, ordered the execution of Nadir's children and the disemboweling of those of his widows and concubines believed to be pregnant. He in turn was eventually murdered by supporters of Nadir's grandson, a luckless fellow who was deposed and restored to the throne twice and blinded in the process.

Karim Khan

Order was finally restored in 1757 by the more temperate Karim Khan, who governed not as shah but as *vakil*, or deputy, a title once used for the chief officer of state. He was, he insisted, the shah's steward, a position reminiscent of the Ottoman vizier. This was only in part a charade, for Karim Khan was genuinely interested in social justice. He earned his reputation as the "advocate of the peasants" by terminating Nadir Shah's disastrous policy of inducting large numbers of peasants into the army, thereby forcing those who remained in the fields not only to compensate for the lost labor but to pay higher taxes to support the growing military. Although the state granaries that Karim Khan constructed in every province were primarily to feed his army, he used the stockpiled grain to relieve the poor when famine struck.

Karim Khan's era was one of peace and relative prosperity, notable in part for his beautification of the capital, Shiraz, with new buildings and gardens and for his construction of a palace and new fortifications at Tehran. The key figures in this building program included artists and craftsmen that Nadir Shah had brought from India. Under both Nadir and Karim Khan the artisans of the royal workshops produced sumptuous tapestries, carpets, miniatures, liveries, and artistic calligraphy. But unlike Europe or India, Iran in the eighteenth century could not boast great literary achievements.

Under Karim Khan religious minorities enjoyed substantial toleration, not least because of their economic productivity. As in the Safavid period, representatives of Roman Catholic orders such as the Benedictines and the Jesuits were free to live, worship, and trade as they wished, so long as they did not offend the Shi'ites. Native, or Armenian, Christians were also tolerated and in fact had to be restrained from harassing Latin Christians. Iranian Jews periodically suffered persecution in the eighteenth century, though Karim Khan allowed them to have their own quarter in the capital in return for paying a special tax. After his death, however, the Jews were again persecuted.

Although Nadir's military adventurism and the ensuing period of civil chaos had had an adverse impact on the Iranian economy, conditions improved during the rule of Karim Khan. Trade with Russia periodically thrived, as the Iranians shipped raw silk, madder (for red dye), cotton and silk cloth, rice, and dried fish in return for such goods as iron, steel, mirrors, hides, and sugar. But the Russo-Iranian trade again declined when Russia's hostile relations with the Ottomans threatened the overland routes in the 1760s. Iran's other major trading partners were the Ottomans, the Indians, and, increasingly, the Europeans. In the eighteenth century approximately a third of Iran's foreign commerce was with the Ottomans, who traded such items as cashmere shawls, cotton, silk, and tobacco for Syrian textiles, European manufactures, jewels, and dyestuffs.

There was an equivalent trade with India, whose peoples were active in all spheres of Iranian commerce, serving even as bankers, brokers, shipping agents, and sailors. In turn the Iranians and Turks played an important role as middlemen in trade between India and Europe. Some of this trade was conducted through the Persian Gulf; most was in the hands of Asian merchants, though a quarter of it was with Europeans, such as the British Levant and East India companies. Trade relations between the Iranians and the Europeans were often strained, yet throughout the century each was irresistibly drawn to the other— the Iranians by the technological superiority of the West-

Karim Khan, as depicted by a contemporary artist. [British Library]

erners, the Westerners by the lure of trade profits and imperial gains.

Karim Khan sought to tame the bloody nature of Iranian politics, in part by treating one potential enemy, Agha Muhammad Qajar, more like a guest in his home than the traditional hostage he actually was. When, however, Karim Khan lay dying in 1779, Agha Muhammad escaped to launch his own bid for power. After a renewed period of fratricidal fighting, he crowned himself shah in 1794, inaugurating the long Qajar dynasty, which governed Iran until 1924.

Both India and Iran had enjoyed periods of political vigor under strong rulers, accompanied by cultural brilliance and economic revival. The Mughal dynasty in India, especially under Akbar's long reign, was one of the most splendid periods in Indian and world history, and India in those years was one of the greatest and richest of empires. In Iran,

Nadir Shah drove the Ottomans out of the Iranian territories they had occupied and even sacked and looted Delhi, but his ruthlessness and repression led to his own assassination and to civil war. His ultimate successor, Karim Khan, restored peace, but on his death, fighting resumed, and Iran never recovered its former glory. Similar bloody struggles over the succession to the Mughal throne in India deeply marred the century after Akbar, whose successors also plundered and neglected the empire while building their gorgeous palaces. Aurangzeb exhausted the country in his fruitless efforts to conquer the south and to persecute Hindus, leaving India at his death in 1707 torn by civil war and economic devastation.

In this critically deteriorating situation, the English East India Company, which had established small trading positions on both west and east coasts in the seventeenth century, began after 1700 to fortify and develop its bases at Bombay, Madras, and Calcutta, becoming the de facto rulers of small areas around each base. As India sank ever deeper into chaos, the Company's small army of mixed Indian and British forces began to acquire control over more territory, primarily to protect trade routes and the storage of trade goods.

Clive's victory at Plassey in Bengal in 1757, in retaliation for the Bengali capture of Calcutta the previous year, opened a new phase in which the Company began to take over larger areas in both the north and the south. By 1800 the foundations of a British Indian empire had been laid, in part as the result of the British defeat of French ambitions and the rivalries of the Napoleonic wars. Imperial aims were accompanied by considerable blending of British and Indian cultures and interests, especially on the part of the Orientalists, as they were called, and of the Indian response in the Bengal Renaissance. But as British power and confidence rose, fed by growing industrialization, wealth, and technological progress at home, British arrogance in India increased, culminating in the mutiny of 1857, exactly a century after Plassey. The mutiny was not yet a national war of independence, but it did express long-standing grievances and foreshadowed the later rise of an Indian nationalist movement that would demand the country's freedom. The nation's political, economic, legal, and cultural institutions would evolve substantially within the patterns worked out during the colonial period.

Notes

1. From Company records, in S. N. Edwardes, *By-ways of Bombay* (Bombay: Tara Porevala, 1912), pp. 170–171.

2. From Company records, reproduced in C. R. Wilson, ed., *Old Fort William*, vol. 1 (London: Murray, 1906), p. 33.

3. R. Kipling, "Song of the Cities," in *The Five Nations and the Seven Seas* (New York: Doubleday, 1915), p. 183.

4. From T. B. Macaulay's "Minute on Education," in S. Wolpert, *A New History of India* (New York: Oxford University Press, 1982), p. 215.

5. G. Moorhouse, *India Britannica* (New York: Harper & Row, 1983), p. 89.

6. Ibid., p. 84.

7. Ibid., p. 97.

Suggestions for Further Reading

India

Bearce, G. D. *British Attitudes Towards India, 1784–1858*. Oxford: Oxford University Press, 1961.

Bhattacharya, S. *The East India Company and the Economy of Bengal, 1704–1740*. London: Luzac, 1954.

Broehl, W. G. *Crisis of the Raj: 1857 Through British Eyes*. Hanover, N.H.: University Press of New England, 1986.

Chaudhuri, K. N. *The Trading World of Asia and the English East India Company, 1600–1760*. Cambridge: Cambridge University Press, 1978.

Das Gupta, A. *Malabar in Asian Trade, 1740–1800*. Cambridge: Cambridge University Press, 1967.

Farrell, J. G. *The Siege at Krishnapur*. London: Weidenfeld & Nicolson, 1973. (A lively novel of India in 1857.)

Fawcett, C., ed., *The English Factories in India*. Oxford: Clarendon Press, 1952.

Furber, H. *Bombay Presidency in the Mid-Eighteenth Century*. New York: Asia Publishing House, 1965.

Hibbert, C. *The Great Mutiny: India 1857*. New York: Viking, 1978.

Kincaid, D. *British Social Life in India, 1608–1937*. London: Routledge & Kegan Paul, 1973.

Kling, B. *The Blue Mutiny: The Indigo Disturbances in Bengal*. Philadelphia: University of Pennsylvania Press, 1966.

———. *Partner in Empire: Dwarkanath Tagore and the Age of Enterprise in Eastern India*. Berkeley: University of California Press, 1976.

———, and Pearson, M. N., eds. *The Age of Partnership*. Honolulu: University Press of Hawaii, 1979.

Kopf, D. *British Orientalism and the Bengal Renaissance, 1773–1835*. Berkeley: University of California Press, 1969.

Laird, M. A. *Missionaries and Education in Bengal, 1793–1837*. Oxford: Clarendon Press, 1972.

Marshall, P. J. *East Indian Fortunes: The British in Bengal in the Eighteenth Century*. Oxford: Clarendon Press, 1976.

———, ed. *Problems of Empire: Britain and India, 1757–1813*. New York: Barnes & Noble Books, 1968.

Mudford, P. *Birds of a Different Plumage: A Study of British and Indian Relations from Akbar to Curzon*. London: Collins, 1974.

Mukherjee, S. N. *Sir William Jones: A Study in Eighteenth Century British Attitudes to India*. Cambridge: Cambridge University Press, 1968.

Murphey, R. *The Outsiders: The Western Experience in India and China*. Ann Arbor: University of Michigan Press, 1977.

Raychaudhuri, T. *Jan Company in Coromandel, 1605–1690*. The Hague: Nijhoff, 1962.

Sinha, D. P. *The Educational Policy of the East India Company in Bengal to 1854*. Calcutta: Punthi Pustaic, 1964.

Sinha, N. K. *The Economic History of Bengal*. Calcutta: K. L. Mukhopadhyay, 1956.

Spear, P. *Master of Bengal: Clive and His India*. London: Thames & Hudson, 1975.

———. *The Nabobs: A Study of the Social Life of the English in Eighteenth Century India*. London: Oxford University Press, 1963.

———. *Twilight of the Mughals*. Cambridge: Cambridge University Press, 1951.

Stokes, E. *The English Utilitarians and India*. Oxford: Clarendon Press, 1959.

Tripathi, A. *Trade and Finance in the Bengal Presidency, 1793–1833*. Bombay: Orient Longmans, 1956.

Watson, F. *A Concise History of India*. London: Thames & Hudson, 1979.

Iran

Armajani, Y. *Iran*. Englewood Cliffs, N.J.: Prentice-Hall, 1972.

Perry, J. R. *Karim Khan Zand: A History of Iran, 1747–1779*. Chicago: University of Chicago Press, 1979.

Ramazani, R. K. *The Foreign Policy of Iran: A Developing Nation in World Affairs*. Charlottesville: University of Virginia Press, 1966.

CHAPTER 28

Manchu China and Tokugawa Japan

On the eve of the modern world, China and Japan both emerged, in their separate ways, from periods of decay, rebellion, and civil war to found vigorous new orders. In China this occurred with the beginning of the Ch'ing (Qing) or Manchu dynasty, which took power in 1644 and ruled the empire until 1911. Under Manchu rule, China became once again the greatest power in the world as well as its richest and most sophisticated society. Despite their nomadic origins in northern Manchuria and their role as alien conquerors, the Manchus quickly adopted Chinese culture. This began even before 1644 as they built their power base in southern Manchuria, which had long been part of the Chinese system. They called their new dynasty Ch'ing, meaning "pure," in an effort to give legitimacy to their rule; in fact they governed China completely in the Chinese mode and with widespread Chinese cooperation.

Under Ch'ing government, China prospered. The commercialization and urbanization begun under the Sung and the Ming dynasties developed still further, while agricul-

Official court painting of the emperor Kang Hsi (1661–1722) by an unknown artist. Note the imperial dragon robes. [Metropolitan Museum of Art, New York]

ture became far more productive, with total output at least doubling. But population growth, in itself a result of prosperity, began to exceed production, and in the nineteenth century the Ch'ing regime also slowly lost its effectiveness. Peasant poverty bred rebellion, while China was at the same time unable to resist foreign pressures for trade concessions. In the early 1840s the Chinese were humiliatingly defeated by the British in the so-called Opium War. With the 1850s China entered a steep decline that left it largely at the mercy of Western incursions.

In Japan centuries of conflict among rival clans degenerated into open civil war in the sixteenth century. In 1600 a strong new centralized government, the Tokugawa shogunate, emerged to unify the country for the first time. Under Tokugawa control, Japan enjoyed more than two centuries of order, prosperity, and economic growth. But the regime rested on a revived system of feudal ties, and as the economy matured and a new merchant class became more prominent, pressure for change increased. Foreign demands for trade concessions, as in China, finally broke down Japan's self-imposed isolation in 1853. This Western pressure revealed Japan's weakness while feeding domestic discontent with the Tokugawa rulers. The shogunate was ended in 1868 by what is called the Meiji Restoration; although it ostensibly did restore the emperor, it is more accurately seen as a nonviolent revolution that brought to power a new group of radical reformers who set Japan on a course of rapid modernization, while China continued to flounder.

China Under the Manchus

Manchu rule, established in 1644, was only slowly consolidated. Scattered groups of Ming loyalists and others, including former Manchu allies who had been granted fiefs in the south, fought the new conquerors until the 1680s. Once resistance had been crushed, however, the new dynasty made a genuine effort to win not just Chinese support but actual partnership, a far more successful approach than that of the Mongol dynasty four centuries earlier. With Chinese collaboration, the Ch'ing gave the country order and tranquillity under which it prospered as never before.

Like the Mongols, the Manchus, who totaled only a little over a million people, or some 2 percent of the empire, could not hope to rule without the cooperation of the Chinese, who filled about 90 percent of all official posts throughout the dynasty. Manchu aristocrats dominated the top military positions, but the body of the army, militia, and police were predominantly Chinese, as were many generals. Provincial administration was headed by two-man teams of Chinese and Manchu governors working in tandem—and, of course, checking on each other. The gen-

try, who provided unofficial leadership and authority at all local levels, remained almost entirely Chinese. The gentry continued to supply nearly all of the officials through the imperial examination system, which the Manchus retained and expanded. At the capital in Peking (Beijing), the Grand Secretariat, the various ministries, and the imperial censorate were staffed equally by Chinese and by Manchus. The Manchu spoken language continued to be used, but all Manchus were by now equally at home in Chinese.

The Manchus succeeded also because they had become, even before 1644, as thoroughly Sinified as their "subjects"—indeed, they had long been an outlying part of the Chinese empire themselves. They came from an area of Manchuria where pastoral nomadism merged with Chinese-style intensive agriculture in the Liao valley and where Chinese cultural dominance dated back at least to the Han dynasty. To protect their homeland and their identity, they discouraged further Chinese emigration to Manchuria until around 1870, and kept northern Manchuria as an imperial hunting preserve.

In their administration of China itself, however, they maintained continuity with the now long established imperial structure and its institutions. The emperor appointed all officials down to the level of the county magistrates and presided over a mobile body of civil and military servants who owed direct loyalty to the throne. These officials were rotated as a rule every three years to emphasize their imperial rather than local or regional roles. The emperor was accessible to all his officials, who could send confidential memoranda (known as "memorials") for the emperor alone and to which he could reply in confidence to the sender only. The emperor personally had to approve all policy matters, to sign all death sentences, and to hear appeals.

The Chinese imperial structure was top-heavy, but on the whole it worked at least as well as the administration of other large empires and better than most. Each official had an extensive unofficial staff to help with the otherwise unmanageable burden of administrative routine and paperwork. But even so, it was a thinly spread system and grew progressively more so as a relatively static number of about 30,000 imperially appointed officials served a growing population. Most of China, still over 90 percent rural, continued to govern itself through the Confucian system of the "self-regulating society." But there was a huge amount of imperial administrative business too. Communication was essential among the widely scattered provinces and districts of this enormous empire, considerably larger than the modern United States and far more populous, and between each of them and the capital, where most important decisions had to be made or approved. The Ch'ing established some 2,000 postal stations along the main and feeder routes of the imperial road system, much of which was paved. The network extended into Manchuria, Mongolia, Sinkiang, and Tibet. Less urgent communications and shipments traveled by water wher-

28.1 China Proper Under the Ch'ing

ever possible, but for emergency messages or documents mounted couriers using relays of fast horses could cover 250 miles a day or more. This still meant nearly a week of travel from Canton to Peking, but it was almost certainly faster than anything in the West and was rivaled, at least before the end of the eighteenth century, only by the courier system of the Roman Empire at its height.

We know more about Ch'ing China than about any previous imperial period, partly because its recency means that far more of the documentation is still available. But we also have a great many foreign accounts, especially after the late eighteenth century. The Europeans were fascinated by China, and they can give us a perspective, and a comparative dimension, lacking for earlier periods. Their accounts help to establish a picture of Manchu China as the largest, richest, best governed, and most sophisticated country in the world of its time. European thinkers of the Enlightenment, including Leibniz and later Voltaire

◉ Adam Smith on China ◉

The founder of classical Western economics and advocate of the free market, Adam Smith, commented on China in his Wealth of Nations, *published in 1776, which was based on the accounts of Europeans who had been there.*

The great extent of the empire of China, the vast multitude of its inhabitants, the variety of climate and consequently of productions in its various provinces, and the easy communication by means of water carriage between the greater part of them, render the home market of that country of so great extent as to be alone sufficient to support very great manufactures, and to admit of very considerable subdivisions of labor. The home market of China is perhaps in extent not much inferior to the market of all the different countries of Europe put together.

Source: A. Smith, *The Wealth of Nations*, vol. 2 (New York: Dutton, 1954), p. 217.

and Quesnay, were much influenced by what they knew of Ch'ing China. They were struck in particular by its emphasis on ethical precepts as opposed to the commands of revealed religion and on selection for office through competitive examination. China, they thought, avoided the evils they ascribed in Europe to a hereditary officeholding nobility. To them China seemed close to the Platonic ideal never achieved in the West, a state ruled by philosopher-kings.

The Ch'ing compiled a vast new law code, dealing mainly with criminal offenses; most civil disputes continued to be handled locally through family, clan, and gentry networks. It too impressed European philosophers and legal scholars for its grounding in Confucian ethics. Admiration of China led also to a European vogue for Chinese art, architecture, gardens, porcelains, and even furniture and wallpaper (another Chinese innovation), all of which became the height of fashion for the upper classes, especially in France and England. The foreign perspective on China began to change in the nineteenth century as China declined and the West entered its steep modern rise. But traces of the original admiration long remained, for those less blinded by Victorian imperialist arrogance.

Prosperity and Population Growth

The first 150 years of Ch'ing rule were an especially brilliant period, marked by the long reigns of two able and dedicated emperors, Kang Hsi (Kang Xi, 1661–1722) and Ch'ien Lung (Qian Long, 1735–1796). As a direct consequence of the order and prosperity they established, pop-

ulation began an increase that continued until about 1850, probably nearly tripling over two centuries. Until late in the eighteenth century production and the growth of commerce more than kept pace. Even by the 1840s and 1850s, when per capita incomes had probably been declining for two generations or more, British observers agreed that most Chinese were materially better off than most Europeans. Robert Fortune, a well-informed traveler and resident in China, writing in 1853, succinctly summarized the prevailing view by saying that "in no country in the world is there less real misery and want than in China."[1] Fortune wrote from the perspective of industrializing England, with its repressed proletariat, but his judgment about China was probably accurate and is corroborated by other Western observers.

The massive growth of population and production is a good measure of the success of Ch'ing rule and the confident spirit of the times. Government officials diligently promoted improvements in agriculture, new irrigation and flood prevention works, roads, and canals. More new land was brought under cultivation to feed the rising population, and more new irrigation projects were constructed than in the whole of previous Chinese history. The Ch'ing period also saw the Chinese agricultural conquest of the cultivable areas of the south and southwest, at the expense of the remaining minority non-Han inhabitants (see Chapters 3 and 11). Much of the new tilled land was in the hilly south, where terracing was often pushed to extremes, driving the indigenous population into still more mountainous areas, especially in the southwestern provinces of Szechuan (Sichuan), Yunnan, and Kweichou (Guizhou). Large new acreage was also brought under the plow in the semiarid margins of northern China. Yields everywhere rose with new irrigation, increased fertilization, better seeds, and more intensive cultivation.

Merchants were also allowed a broader scope under the Ch'ing even than under the Ming. Trade with Southeast Asia grew still further, and permanent settlements of Chinese merchants grew with it. Domestic commerce and urbanization reached new levels and remained far more important than overseas connections. Merchant guilds proliferated in all of the growing Chinese cities and often acquired great social and even political influence. Rich merchants with official connections built up huge fortunes and patronized literature, theater, and the arts. Fleets of junks (Chinese-style boats) plied the coast and the great inland waterways, and urban markets teemed with people and goods. General prosperity helped to ensure domestic peace. Silver continued to flow in to pay for China's exports to the West, now including tea and silk, leaving a large favorable trade balance. Cloth and handicraft production boomed with the sophisticated division of labor and an increasing market.

Along with silver, other New World goods entered the China market through Manila. These included new and highly productive crops from the Americas, including sweet and white potatoes, maize, peanuts, and tobacco. All had been unknown in Asia before, and in many cases they supplemented the staple agricultural system of rice, wheat, and the other more drought-tolerant cereals, such as millet and sorghum, grown in the drier parts of the north. Potatoes could be raised in sandy soils unsuited to cereals, white potatoes in the colder areas, sweet potatoes in the south. Both produced more food energy per unit of land than any cereal crop. Corn yielded well on slopes too steep for irrigated rice. Peanuts and tobacco filled other gaps and added substantially to total food resources or to the list of cash crops, such as cotton.

Early-ripening rice introduced from Southeast Asia in the Sung and Ming periods was further developed under the Ch'ing, and the period from sowing to harvest was progressively reduced. In the long growing season of the south, this meant that more areas could produce two crops of rice a year and some could manage three. The practice of transplanting rice seedlings in spaced rows set in irrigated paddies became universal in the Ch'ing period. This greatly increased yields and shortened the time to harvest.

Food and nonfood crops were now treated with the kind of care a gardener uses for individual plants, fertilized by hand, weeded at frequent intervals, with irrigation levels precisely adjusted to the height and needs of each crop as the season advanced. The use of human manure now also became universal, and the amounts increased as the population rose, providing both the source and the need for more intensive fertilization. Rice yields were more than doubled by a combination of all these methods, and the total output also rose as the result of double and triple cropping and the addition of newly cleared land. Improvements in rice cultivation, China's major crop since Han times, as well as new irrigation and other techniques, were probably the chief source of food increases. Rising population provided both the incentive and the means for im-

proved crop yields under the management of local magistrates and gentry. The irrigation of rice was finely engineered, permitting the alteration of water levels and the draining of the paddies in the last few weeks before harvest. These improvements required immense amounts of labor and organization, but they paid handsomely in increased yields.

These changes, improvements, and additions to the system help to explain how an already large population could double or triple in two centuries and still maintain or even enhance its food and income levels. Agriculture remained the heart of the economy and the major source of state revenue, but its surpluses created a growing margin for both subsistence and commercial exchange. The population figures the Ch'ing compiled, like those of earlier

As population increased and demand for food rose, agriculture was pushed up onto steeper and steeper slopes, as in this photograph from the southwestern province of Yunnan. Terracing required immense labor but could create only tiny strips of level land, and water for irrigation was a major problem. Terracing was necessary because by the late Ch'ing period all gentler slopes had been occupied, while the population continued to rise. This is an extreme example, but such terraces were not uncommon. [Rhoads Murphey]

dynasties, were not designed as total head counts and were based on local reports by village headmen enumerating households and adult males fit for military service. Land ownership and output were also recorded for tax purposes, and for a time, as in previous centuries, there was also a head tax. Since everyone knew that population figures were used for calculating taxes and for conscript labor, there was an understandable tendency for local headmen and households to understate the true numbers.

Early in the dynasty it was announced that the head tax would never be raised, and it was later merged with the land tax and a levy on crops. At the same time, the Ch'ing made it plain that reports of population increase were welcome evidence of the prosperity of their reign. Reports showing little or no gain would reflect on the effectiveness of the local magistrate. For these and other reasons having to do with the imprecision, inconsistency, and incompleteness of the count (which often but not always excluded women, servants, infants, migrants, and non-Han people), Ch'ing population figures must be used cautiously, but the long-term trend is clear. From roughly 150 million in the late seventeenth century, the population had reached 400 or possibly 450 million by 1850. The official figures, almost certainly an undercount at first and possibly an overcount after 1750 or so, show 142 million in 1741 and 432 million in 1851. The rising population was indeed strong evidence of the success of Ch'ing rule, but in time it became a burden that the system could no longer carry successfully, leading to increasing poverty, disorder, and bureaucratic breakdown.

The Reigns of Kang Hsi and Ch'ien Lung

The emperor Kang Hsi, completely Chinese in culture and even an accomplished poet in that language, encouraged literature, art, printing, scholarship, and artisan production. He revived and enlarged the Imperial Potteries, which with other centers turned out great quantities of beautiful porcelain for the palace and court, the rich merchant elite, and the export trade. A patron of learning, Kang Hsi studied Latin, mathematics, and Western science with Jesuit tutors at his court and corresponded with European monarchs. Toward the end of his reign he lost patience with the sectarian quarreling of the Catholic missionaries and was incensed that a foreign potentate, the pope, should presume to tell the few Chinese Christian converts what they should and should not believe. He remained interested in a wide variety of things, however, and is described by his Jesuit tutors as insatiably curious.

Kang Hsi was a conscientious and able administrator of boundless energy who tried to ensure honesty in government and a harmonious partnership among Chinese and Manchu officials. He went on six major state tours around the empire and showed a great interest in local affairs. He commissioned an ambitious new encyclopedia of all learning, updated and greatly expanded from Yung-lo's compilation under the Ming dynasty. Running to 5,000 volumes, it was probably the largest such work ever written anywhere. The huge dictionary of the Chinese language that Kang Hsi also commissioned, which still bears his name, remains the most exhaustive and authoritative guide to classical Chinese up to his own time. He also supervised the compilation of a voluminous administrative geography of the empire. He encouraged the further spread of private academies for the sons of the gentry and state-supported schools for worthy but poorer boys, to spread classical learning and to open the way to office for those who mastered it. Older scholars and retired officials were sent around the empire at government expense to lecture to the populace on morality and virtue.

Kang Hsi was equally effective in military affairs. He supervised the reconquest of Taiwan, restored Chinese control over Mongolia and eastern Sinkiang, and in 1720 mounted an expedition to put down civil war in Tibet, where he established firm Chinese authority. His armies had earlier chased the Russians out of the Amur region of northern Manchuria. He then negotiated the Treaty of Nerchinsk in 1689 with the tsar's representatives, confirming Chinese sovereignty in the Amur valley and southward. This was both China's first significant engagement and its first treaty with a Western power. The Ch'ing clearly emerged as victors, successfully defending China's traditionally threatened landward frontiers. The Russian negotiators were kept on the frontier and not received in Peking; Nerchinsk was a minor border post, and relatively minor Chinese officials were sent to deal with them, assisted by Jesuit interpreters.

Far less attention was paid to the Westerners already attempting to trade at Canton and to extend their efforts farther northward along the coast. These traders, mostly Portuguese, Dutch, and English, were regarded as a minor nuisance in the same category as bandits or pirates. They were certainly not perceived as representatives of civilized states with whom China should have any dealings. The difference in response to the Russians reflected the perennial Chinese concern about their continental borders, the source of so much trouble in the past, as compared with the maritime frontier, which had never presented any major security problem. Their defenses, their front doors, and their military priorities faced westward toward the great Eurasian landmass whence the Mongols and other invaders had come.

Ch'ien Lung, Kang Hsi's grandson, succeeded him in 1735. He might have reigned officially until his death, but filial piety prompted him to retire in 1796 after 60 years so as not to stay on the throne longer than his grandfather. However, he remained the real power until his death three years later at the age of 89. Less austere and more extroverted than Kang Hsi, Ch'ien Lung, with his grand manner, has often been compared to King Louis XIV of France. Until his last years Ch'ien Lung was a diligent and

Ch'ing glory: the Altar of Heaven, just outside the Forbidden City in Peking, originally a Ming structure but rebuilt by the Ch'ing. Here the emperor conducted annual rites to intercede with Heaven for good harvests. The temple roofs are covered with magnificent colored and glazed tiles. [Bildarchiv Foto Marburg]

humane ruler who continued his grandfather's administrative and patronage model in all respects; comparison with Louis XIV does him less than justice. He commissioned the collection and reprinting of an immense library of classical works in over 36,000 volumes. But his support for learning was marred by the destruction of more than 2,300 books that he thought were seditious or unorthodox.

Ch'ien Lung was, of all Chinese emperors, probably the greatest patron of art. He built up in the imperial palace a stupendous collection of paintings and other works of art from all past periods as well as his own. Most of it is still intact. Ch'ien Lung also spent huge sums on refurbishing, embellishing, and adding to the imperial buildings inherited from the Ming.

Militarily, too, he was an aggressive and able leader. Despite Kang Hsi's expeditions, the Mongols had remained troublesome. Ch'ien Lung completely and permanently destroyed their power in a series of campaigns in the 1750s, after which he reincorporated the whole of Sinkiang into the empire. A revolt in Tibet shortly afterward led to a Ch'ing occupation that fixed Chinese control there even more tightly. Punitive expeditions were launched against Nepal, northern Burma, and northern Vietnam to compel tributary acknowledgment of Chinese overlordship.

Until the 1780s Ch'ien Lung, like the men who preceded him on the Dragon Throne, dealt personally with an immense mass of official documents and wrote his own comments on them. One of the Grand Council secretaries remarked in wonder at his diligence: "Ten or more of my comrades would take turns every five or six days on early morning duty, and even so would feel fatigued. How did the Emperor do it day after day?"[2] But as Ch'ien Lung grew older, he became more enamored of luxury and sur-

rounded himself with yes-men. In old age he left matters of state increasingly in the hands of his favorites. His chief favorite, the unscrupulous courtier Ho-shen (He shen), entered the palace in 1775 as a handsome young bodyguard of 25 and, becoming Grand Councillor within a year, built up a clique of corrupt henchmen and plundered the empire. At his fall after Ch'ien Lung's death, the private wealth Ho-shen had extorted was said to be worth the equivalent of a $1.5 billion, an almost inconceivable sum for that time and probably a world record for corrupt officials. He concentrated all power in his own hands, holding in time as many as 20 different positions simultaneously. He betrothed his son to the emperor's daughter and clearly intended to take over the dynasty.

Ho-shen's rise was symptomatic not only of Ch'ien Lung's growing senility but also of the deterioration of the administrative system as a whole. The army, too, was neglected. A major rebellion by the White Lotus sect (see Chapter 20) erupted in 1796. The rebels were finally put down only after Ho-shen's fall by the new emperor, Chia Ch'ing (Jia Qing). In 1799 he quickly moved against Ho-shen, stripping him of his power and wealth.

Ho-shen's career illustrates the importance of personal connections in imperial China (and to some degree in China now), despite the merit system of examinations. Corruption, connections, and nepotism (favoring one's relatives) were aspects of China, and of Asia generally, that Westerners criticized as more widespread than in their own political and economic systems. Westerners were at least embarrassed by it at home; Asians supported it as proper. Family loyalties and the ties of friendship were valued as the highest goods. Anyone with wealth or power who did not use it to help relatives and friends was considered morally deficient. The family was the basic cement of society and with its support system of mutual aid was regarded as a microcosm of the empire as a whole, in which the emperor was seen as the nurturing father of his people as well as his officials. The connections of friendship were also part of the Confucian-sanctified "five relationships" (see Chapter 7) and took precedence over other considerations. In addition, political office was relatively poorly paid, and it was expected that officials would use their position to provide for their families and friends by diverting funds or receiving "presents." People of rank were expected to live well, in keeping with the dignity of their position. Even now one hears repeated the traditional saying, "Become an official and get rich." Ho-shen was only the most extreme example of a normal practice that was grossly abused.

The Later Ch'ing: Symptoms of Decline

By the 1750s the Ch'ing dynasty was already well into its second century. The eighteenth century saw the pinnacle of its glory, prosperity, and harmony, but even before the death of Ch'ien Lung, decline had begun. Prosperity remained widespread, accompanied by a major output of art and literature. This included new popular novels such as *The Dream of the Red Chamber* (also known as *Story of the Stone*), which prophetically dealt with the decline and degeneracy of a once great family and is still widely read.

Part of the government's problem was the failure of its officialdom to keep pace with the growth in population. Despite the rapid increase in overall numbers, there was only a small increment in the number of official posts, perhaps 25 percent versus a 200 to 300 percent boost in the population as a whole. This had an obviously negative effect on both governmental effectiveness and morale. A prestigious career in the bureaucracy, once a reasonable ambition for able scholars, became harder and harder to obtain. At the same time, the imperial examinations became still more rigidified exercises in old-fashioned orthodoxy and the memorization of traditional texts. These were to be commented on in the infamous eight-legged essays (see Chapter 20), allowing no scope for imagination or initiative. "Men of talent," as the best of the scholar-gentry had been called since the Han period, were often weeded out by this process. The examination failure rate climbed rapidly, and only students who lacked or suppressed all creativity could hope to pass.

Disappointed examination candidates and others who passed but were not called to office became a larger and larger group of alienated intellectuals. Paradoxically, the problem was only made worse by the earlier Ch'ing efforts to expand education and to open it to larger sections of the population. Learning had always been the key to advancement. Now, however, it was far from necessarily so. The system had hardened just when flexibility was most needed. Instead of preserving the Great Harmony, it bred discontent. One result was new corruption. Degrees, once attainable only by examination, and occasionally even offices, began to be sold. Failed candidates and disappointed office seekers provided the leadership for dissident and ultimately rebellious groups, whose numbers increased rapidly after 1785.

The lack of firm leadership and virtuous example, under Ho-shen and again after the death of the emperor Chia Ch'ing in 1820, aggravated the burdens of overworked officials. A magistrate of the Sung dynasty 500 years earlier had been responsible for an average of about 80,000 people in his county. By the end of the eighteenth century the average county, still administered by a single magistrate and his staff, numbered about 250,000; many were larger, and the average rose to about 300,000 in the nineteenth century. Local gentry, landlords, merchant guilds, and sometimes dissident or even criminal groups began to fill the vacuum. This led to a revival of anti-Manchu sentiment, for the Ch'ing was, after all, an alien dynasty of conquest.

The most basic and intractable problem the dynasty faced was a product of its own earlier success. By the last quarter of the eighteenth century population growth had probably outrun increases in production. Per capita incomes stabilized and then began slowly to fall. The poorest areas suffered first, and local banditry started to rise. By the end of the century open rebellions were breaking out. The secret society of the White Lotus, revived from a long quiescence, reemerged in a major uprising in 1796. Its reappearance tended to suggest to many Chinese that once again the ruling dynasty was perhaps losing the Mandate of Heaven. The secret and semi-Buddhist rituals of the White Lotus and its promise to overthrow the Ch'ing attracted many followers, including distressed peasants. Until 1804 the rebels defied the imperial army from mountain strongholds in the upper Yangtze valley along the borders of three provinces. The enormous expense of suppressing the White Lotus bled the treasury and fed corruption in the military. The unnecessarily long campaign also revealed the decline in the effectiveness of the army, which ultimately prevailed only with the help of some 300,000 local militiamen.

New Barbarian Pressures: The Westerners

Despite these mounting problems, China was still able to awe Westerners, who now appeared in unprecedented numbers and who tried to deal with the Dragon Throne as an equal and to obtain trading privileges. Like all foreigners, they had from the beginning been fitted into the tributary system, the traditional Chinese way of dealing with outsiders. At Canton, the only port where Westerners were permitted to trade, they could stay only for the trading season of about six months and were forbidden to bring in firearms and women, to enter the city proper, or to trade elsewhere on the China coast. They were obliged to deal only with the official monopoly that controlled all foreign trade, a restraint that they found galling in view of the huge potential market that China represented. Westerners were seen as potential troublemakers and perverters of Chinese morality. They should, it was felt, be kept on the fringes of the empire and walled off from normal contact with its people.

Various attempts by the British and the Dutch to trade elsewhere or with other merchants were rebuffed. In 1755 the English trader James Flint had sailed into several ports north of Canton, including Shanghai and Tientsin (Tianjin), in an effort to establish trade there. He was jailed and then deported, but the emperor ordered execution for the Chinese who had served as his interpreter and scribe. By the 1790s the restrictions at Canton seemed intolerable, especially to the British, then in their own view the greatest mercantile and naval power in the world and tired of being treated like minor savages.

In 1793 Britain's King George III sent an embassy to Ch'ien Lung led by a British nobleman, Viscount Macartney, to request wider trading rights and to establish relations with China as an equal power. He brought with him samples of British manufactures as presents to convince the Chinese of the benefits of trade with the West; these articles were not yet refined enough to impress the Chinese, though they included samples of the contemporary pottery of Josiah Wedgwood—hardly likely to appeal to the inventors of porcelain. The Chinese could still make most of the things Macartney brought better and cheaper and saw no need for British goods. The mission was a comedy of errors on both sides, since both were still profoundly ignorant of each other and lacked any standard of comparison. The Chinese interpreted the visit and the presents as a standard tribute mission, although from an especially distant and hence backward group of people, too far from China to have picked up any civilization. Chinese politeness obliged them to accept the presents, but with the kind of tolerance a kindly parent might display for the work of children.

The Chinese expected Macartney to perform the *k'e t'ou* (kowtow), or ritual submission, as all tribute missions did, before the Son of Heaven. Macartney, a typical Georgian aristocrat in his satin knee breeches who also suffered from gout, refused. He offered instead to bend one knee slightly, as he would to his own sovereign. Macartney further offended his hosts by pompously saying that he was "sure the Chinese would see that superiority which Englishmen, wherever they go, cannot conceal." One can almost hear him saying it! As a result, he never had a real audience with Ch'ien Lung, although he was kept waiting in Peking for over a month. Instead Ch'ien Lung sent him a letter for George III that was a masterpiece of crushing condescension:

> I have already noted your respectful spirit of submission. . . . I do not forget the lonely remoteness of your island, cut off from the world by intervening wastes of sea. . . . [But] our Celestial Empire possesses all things in abundance. We have no need for barbarian products.[3]

One can imagine the reaction of George III and Macartney.

In 1793 it was still possible for China to get away with such haughty behavior, and it was true that China was happily self-sufficient. A Dutch embassy of 1795 that also asked for better trade conditions was similarly rejected, even though the Dutch, perhaps less concerned with power or dignity than with profits, vigorously performed the kowtow several times as they lined up at court with other representatives from other countries sending tributary missions. A later British embassy under Lord Amherst in 1816 had a similarly humiliating experience. Amherst had the bad luck to turn up just when the British in India were fighting the Gurkhas of Nepal, a Chinese tributary since 1792, and was ordered out of the country by the emperor without an audience.

Nevertheless, the accounts of China given by members of the Macartney and Amherst parties as they traveled south from Peking to Canton, nursing their rage at the way they had been treated, were still strongly positive. They found China prosperous, orderly, and agriculturally productive, with an immense commerce and numerous large cities. Here are a few samples from the diary kept by a member of the Amherst mission in 1816:

> Tranquility seemed to prevail, nothing but contentment and good humor. . . . It is remarkable that in so populous a country there should be so little begging. . . . Contentment and the enjoyment of the necessities of life [suggest that] the government cannot be a very bad one. . . . The lower orders of Chinese seem to me more neat and clean than any Europeans of the same class. . . . Even torn, soiled, or threadbare clothing is uncommon. . . . All the military stations are neatly whitewashed and painted and kept in perfect repair, and instead of mud cabins the houses of peasants are built in a neat manner with brick. The temples are also handsome and numerous.[4]

Stagnation and Vulnerability

China may have declined from its eighteenth-century peak, but it was far from collapse. Although the emperors after Ch'ien Lung fell short of his level of brilliance, they were conscientious and honest. The corruption that had marred Ch'ien Lung's last years was greatly reduced, his scheming favorites were disposed of, and a renewed atmosphere of responsibility and service was established. The official salt monopoly, which had become semiparalyzed by corruption, was totally reformed in the 1830s. This was one indication that the imperial bureaucracy still had resilience and the power to correct weaknesses.

◉ Omens of Crisis ◉

For all his pompousness and the failure of his mission, Viscount Macartney was an astute observer. Though he was impressed by China's productivity and its well-ordered society, he accurately saw political trouble ahead.

The empire of China is an old first-rate man of war, which a succession of vigilant officers has continued to keep afloat for these 150 years past, and have overawed their neighbors merely by her bulk and appearance. [Here, of course, he spoke also from his own humiliating experience.] But whenever an insufficient man happens to have command on deck, adieu to the discipline and safety of the ship. She may perhaps not sink outright; she may drift for a time as a wreck, and then be dashed to pieces on the shore; but she can never be rebuilt on the old bottom.

But the economy continued to flourish well into the nineteenth century. Here is part of the account of a French traveling priest, the Abbé Huc, written in 1850.

European productions will never have a very extensive market in China. . . . China is a country so vast, so rich, so varied that its internal trade alone would suffice abundantly to occupy that part of the nation which can be devoted to mercantile operations. . . . Foreign commerce cannot offer them any article of primary necessity which they do not already produce themselves, nor even of any real utility, and they would see it stopped altogether . . . with a certain feeling of satisfaction.

Sources: J. L. Cranmer-Byng, ed., *An Embassy to China* (London: Longman, 1962), pp. 212–213; E. R. Huc, *The Chinese Empire* (London: Longman, 1855), p. 365.

At its best Ch'ing art remained magnificent, although much of later Ch'ing painting, decoration, and ceramics lacked originality and toward the end became overly ornate. Like much of the scholarship and philosophy of the time, it was technically accomplished but without the exuberance or imagination of earlier periods. Urban culture continued to thrive as merchant wealth was more widely diffused and city dwellers could read the new vernacular literature, enjoy the art of the time, and attend popular plays. China remained a sophisticated society as well as a prosperous one, still generally confident, even complacent. Imperial slights to barbarian upstarts like the British were in keeping with what most Chinese thought.

Yet the state really had no adequate long-run means to respond to the relentless pressures of increasing population. Decline was slow at first. China was immense, and its society and economy, largely independent of state management except for the official monopolies, took time to decay. Signs of trouble here and there did not mean that the whole system was rotten—not yet. Nor did governmental or military inefficiency or corruption among some officials mean that the whole administration was in trouble.

Most of the Chinese world was only indirectly affected by the political sphere and continued to flourish after political decay was far advanced. Government was a thin layer on top of traditional controls.

Both foreign and Chinese critics were often misled by signs of administrative weakness into concluding that the whole country was falling apart. But the basic problem of growing rural poverty, especially after 1850, remained, as population continued to rise faster than production. Traditional agricultural technology had reached its limit of productivity, and all usable land had been pressed into cultivation. Only new technology could break this jam. Chinese agriculture, only a century before the most advanced in the world, was now rapidly falling behind the West's but showed no readiness to adapt. There was little interest in the now superior technology of Europe, and especially not in the disruption that would inevitably have accompanied its spread. China continued to protect itself against any ideas or innovations of foreign origin that might disrupt traditional ways. A different sort of response might have come from a new and vigorous dynasty, but the Ch'ing was now old, rigid, and fearful of change. Always sensitive about their alien origins, they feared to depart in any way from their self-appointed role as the guardians of the ancient Chinese way in all things.

The growing wealth of commercial elites did not fuel other kinds of growth or change, as it did in Europe. Individual or family wealth came not so much from increasing production as from acquiring a greater share of what already existed, through official connections or through managing the state monopolies. Merchants and their guilds never became an independent group of entrepreneurs or sought to change the system to their advantage, as their European counterparts did. In the Chinese view, they prospered by working within the existing system and had few incentives to alter it. For long-term investment, land was the preferred option since it was secure and offered social prestige as well. Capital earned in trade went into land, moneylending at usurious rates, or luxurious living but rarely into manufacturing or new technology.

Leisure and gracious living in gentry style were more valued in China than in the modern West, and there was less interest in further accumulation for its own sake. The gentry and the scholar-officials dominated Ch'ing China as they had since at least the Han dynasty, leaving little separate scope for merchants, who were still looked down on as parasites and who depended on their gentry or official connections to succeed. They neither could nor wished to challenge the Confucian bureaucracy but were content to use it for their own ends. All of this discouraged or prevented the rise of private capitalism and the kinds of new enterprise and investment that were basic to the commercial and industrial revolutions in the modern West.

Until the eighteenth century China had been in most respects the world's most technically advanced society. Iron-chain suspension bridges, canal locks, mechanical threshers, water-powered mills, looms, clocks, and the basic technology of the motor—crankshaft, connecting rods, and piston rods for converting rotary to longitudinal motion and back—all originated in China and were still spreading under the Ch'ing. But Chinese accomplishments, like those of earlier periods, were primarily a catalog of cumulative empirical discoveries rather than the result of systematic or sustained scientific inquiry. Confucianism offered little scope for abstract theorizing or empirical investigation. Learning concentrated on the Confucian classics and on records of the past as the proper guide for the present and the future.

The tradition of the learned man as a gentleman also created a deep division between those who "labored with their minds," as Mencius put it, and those who worked with their hands. Chinese craftsmen were highly skilled and ingenious but rarely engaged in theory or experiments, and most were not even literate. Scholars regarded all manual work, even experimental work, as beneath them, whereas the joining of theory, design, experiment, and practice from the time of Leonardo da Vinci produced the achievements of modern science and technology in the West. No such fusion occurred in China, which rested on its already high level of development.

It seems easier to understand why China did not become capitalistic or move on from its early achievements in science and technology than to understand why Europe did. The abrupt break with its own past that the transformation of the modern West involved and the explosion of modern science are harder to explain. China remained sufficiently successful not to seek or require such fundamental change. To a poorer and less developed Europe, change was more compelling, as the means to "progress." By the nineteenth century, however, China had fallen critically behind the insurgent West and was ruled by a dynasty old in office and suffering from complacency and loss of efficiency. The weakened government faced a population bigger than ever before and now sliding into economic distress, as well as a threat posed by militant Westerners. Neither was adequately dealt with.

Corruption is endemic in all systems; its seriousness is only a matter of degree. As the nineteenth century wore on, corruption in China became a growing cancer sapping the vigor of the whole country. Confucian morality began to yield to an attitude of "devil take the hindmost." People and families with connections had their lands and fortunes removed from the tax rolls, as in the last century of all previous dynasties. This put a heavier burden on the decreasing number who had to provide the state's revenue, mainly peasants. The strain on their already marginal position led many of them into banditry and rebellion. In all of these respects, late Ch'ing China was especially unprepared to meet the challenge of an aggressive, industrializing West. It was hard also to readjust Chinese perspectives, which had always seen the landward frontiers as the major area of threat. China was slow to recognize that external danger now came from the sea and along the coast.

The Opium Wars

China's resources, and those of the economy as a whole, were also depleted by a reversal of the earlier flow of silver that accounted for its favorable export balance. Exports of tea, silks, porcelain, and other wares continued, but imports of opium rose dramatically after 1810, mostly from India, where the British East India Company encouraged its cultivation as a cash crop for exchange on the Chinese market. By the 1820s opium imports exceeded China's total exports in value, and a heavy drain of silver flowed out, disrupting the economy.

Opium had been imported from Persia and was later grown in China for many centuries. It was widely used medically, but it began to be smoked as a recreational drug on a large scale in the late eighteenth century. Chinese addicts and their merchants and middlemen created the booming market for imported opium, which was thought to be superior to the domestic variety. No foreign pressure was necessary to encourage its use.

Although the imperial government declared opium smoking and traffic a capital offense, the profits of the trade were high, and the ban was ineffective. Westerners, including American as well as European traders, delivered opium to Chinese smugglers on the coast, who distributed it throughout the country through a vast network of dealers. Most of the fortunes won by early American traders to China rested on opium. Its growing use in China was a symptom both of the growing despair of the disadvantaged and of the degeneracy of a once proud and vigorous system, including many of its now self-indulgent upper classes.

Meanwhile, opium provided the occasion for the first Anglo-Chinese war of 1839–1842, popularly called the Op-

ium War. Nearly 50 years had passed since Ch'ien Lung's rebuff of Macartney and his trade requests. Opium was the immediate issue that sparked the outbreak of hostilities, but much larger matters were involved. British patience was wearing thin; the British wanted freer access to the huge Chinese market as well as diplomatic recognition, as equals, by its government. They saw China as out of step with a modern world where free trade and regular diplomatic relations were the common ground of all "civilized" nations. China's resistance to such demands was taken as proof of its backwardness, and as India had been brought under the blessings of Western civilization, now, they thought, it was China's turn. China's arrogance toward the West was now matched by the West's toward China.

In 1838 the Chinese sent an imperial commissioner, Lin Tse-hsu (Lin Zexu), to Canton to stop the traffic in opium. Lin ordered stocks of the drug burned as contra-

The Opium War: the British steam-powered paddle wheeler *Nemesis* destroying a Chinese fleet in a battle on January 7, 1841, near Canton. The *Nemesis* was one of the first iron-hulled steam vessels; it was designed with a shallow draft so that it could attack inland shipping. Its guns had far greater range and accuracy than those of Chinese ships or shore batteries, and its name as well as its devastatingly easy success made it a symbol of Western naval and military ascendancy. [Bettmann Archive/BBC Hulton]

band. The British regarded their lawful property as having been destroyed and used the incident as a pretext to declare war. A small mobile force sent mainly from India soon destroyed the antiquated Chinese navy, shore batteries, and coastal forces. With the arrival of reinforcements it attacked Canton, occupied Shanghai and other ports northward on the coast, and sailed up the Yangtze River to Nanking (Nanjing) to force the Chinese government to grant what the British wanted. Because of distances, supply problems, and the stubbornness of the Chinese government, the war dragged on fitfully for more than three years. Each encounter ended in a Chinese rout that demonstrated the overwhelming superiority of Western military technology. The Chinese finally capitulated in the Treaty of Nanking (1842). Signed on board a British naval vessel, the agreement was the first in a long series that the Chinese came to call "the unequal treaties." Western imperialism had come to China.

Reunification and the Tokugawa Shogunate in Japan

Late medieval Japan under the Ashikaga shogunate had been marked by the rise of regional feudal lords and their armies, as summarized in Chapter 11. Ashikaga rule from Kyoto became increasingly ineffective in the sixteenth century. Although the shogunate had never been in control of more than central Japan, even areas beyond the immediate vicinity of Kyoto became more and more independent under their own *daimyo* (feudal lords), each with an army of *samurai* based in impressive fortified castles. Fighting between such armies became chronic, and with the final collapse of the Ashikaga shogunate in 1573, Japan dissolved into civil war.

Japan was still a small, poor, relatively backward country on the edge of the major Asian stage, divided among warring clans. The settled area of the country was only a fraction of the whole, and its total population was about 15 million, the size of a single Chinese province. The refined court and urban culture of Kyoto was luxurious, and technologically Ashikaga Japan had made much progress, even surpassing China in such fields as steelmaking and the production of fine swords.

Trade with the rest of East Asia was extensive, and Japanese shipping by the fifteenth century dominated the East China Sea. Japan's relatively small size and population and its weak central government worked to its advantage in this respect, making it easier to develop a national commercial system and a strong and semi-independent merchant class, unlike China or India. Foreign trade was proportionately more important than in China or India, more nearly on the scale of European countries. Most rural areas, by contrast, were isolated and lagged culturally and economically behind the urban centers. The political chaos of the late sixteenth century tore Japan apart once more, but it was to emerge from its troubles to find a new national unity.

The rising power of the daimyo destroyed the Ashikaga. The continued growth of their feudal domains, each more and more like a state in miniature, needed only common leadership to turn Japan into a national political unit. That was essentially the nature of the Tokugawa regime. The Tokugawa founders started out as daimyo like any of

Daimyo castle, Nagoya. This is a typical example of the fortresses built during the last troubled decades of the Ashikaga dynasty and in the early Tokugawa period by local lords who then were conquered by or swore allegiance to the Tokugawa shogunate. The massive wall was surrounded by a moat. Such castles could usually be taken only by a long siege leading to the surrender of the starving defenders. [Wim Swann]

the others. Over about a generation a series of three exceptionally able leaders progressively conquered all their daimyo rivals and superimposed their dominance on an essentially unchanged feudal order. The subject daimyo were given substantial authority in their areas in return for formal submission to the Tokugawa shogun and periodic attendance at his court. Tokugawa central authority was far stronger and extended over a much larger area than any government in previous Japanese history. Despite its feudal trappings, it was in many respects in a class with the emerging national states of contemporary Europe. Samurai served not only as military officers but also as administrators. The flourishing merchant group provided revenue to add to land or agricultural taxes and also transported troops and supplies.

The Era of the Warlords

The process of unification began even before the formal end of the Ashikaga shogunate when Oda Nobunaga (1534–1582), a powerful daimyo who ruled the area around Nagoya, seized Kyoto in 1568 and became supreme in central Japan. He later captured the great temple-castle of Osaka, until then the independent seat of the militant Shin Buddhist sect. Nobunaga was murdered by a vassal in 1582, but his place was assumed by his chief general, Toyotomi Hideyoshi (1536–1598), born a peasant, who rose to the top through his ability and driving ambition. Hideyoshi soon eliminated the remaining faction of Nobunaga's family, subdued its vassals, and rebuilt the castle at Osaka as the base of his military government. In a campaign westward, he crushed the Satsuma clan on the

28.2 Tokugawa Japan

◉ Hideyoshi Writes to His Wife ◉

Hideyoshi wrote to his wife while he was besieging a daimyo castle in the spring of 1590.

Now we have got the enemy like birds in a cage, and there is no danger, so please set your mind at rest. I long for the Young Lord [his son], but I feel that for the sake of the future, and because I want to have the country at peace, I must give up my longing. So please set your mind at rest. I am looking after my health. . . . There is nothing to worry about. . . . Since as I have thus declared it will be a long siege, I wish to send for Yodo [his concubine]. I wish you to tell her and make arrangements for her journey, and tell her that next to you she is the one who pleases me best. . . . I was very glad to get your messages. We have got up to within two or three hundred yards and put a double ditch around the castle and shall not let a single man escape. All the men of the eight eastern provinces are shut up inside. . . . Though I am getting old, I must think of the future and do what is best for the country. So now I mean to do glorious deeds and I am ready for a long siege, with provisions and gold and silver in plenty, so as to return in triumph and leave a great name behind me. I desire you to understand this and to tell it to everybody.

Source: G. B. Sansom, *Japan: A Short Cultural History,* rev. ed. (New York: Appleton-Century-Crofts, 1962), p. 410.

island of Kyushu. In 1590 all of eastern and northern Honshu submitted to him after he had defeated the chief daimyo in the Edo (Tokyo) area. Hideyoshi scorned the title of shogun (the emperor's military adviser) and ruled instead as a dictator, although warlord is probably a more appropriate title.

With a large and unified army of professional fighters, Hideyoshi now looked abroad for more worlds to conquer. China was an obvious target, but to reach it he needed passage through Korea. When this was refused, he invaded Korea in 1592 and made rapid progress until a joint Korean and Chinese army forced him back almost to the coast.

Hideyoshi's death in 1598 ended this wasteful and destructive adventure, and his troops welcomed the chance to return home. His place was soon taken by one of his leading vassals, Tokugawa Ieyasu (1542–1616). Ieyasu had already built a castle-headquarters at Edo, where he had served as Hideyoshi's deputy. In 1600 he won a great victory in the battle of Sekigahara, near Nagoya, over a coalition of rivals. This established his power as Hideyoshi's successor, and he solidified it by capturing Osaka Castle in 1615.

Tokugawa Rule

Ieyasu wanted to build a strong, centrally controlled political system. He and his able Tokugawa successors largely achieved this, creating stability and peace for the next 250 years. They did so by enforcing a set of rigid controls on society as well as on political behavior and by repressing change. Tokugawa feudalism was even more hidebound than that of earlier eras, and the shoguns also tried to control dangerous thought with the help of a fearsomely efficient secret police. They themselves administered the central core of the country, from the Edo area to Kyoto, Osaka, and the peninsula south of Osaka, placing members of their own clan in the key centers of Mito, Nagoya, and Wakayama. This was, then as now, the economic heart of Japan, containing most of its best farmland and most of the commercial towns and cities. Other loyal allies and early supporters of Ieyasu were given fiefs in the rest of this central area. Beyond it, to the north and to the west, the Tokugawa bound other daimyo to them by feudal ties, helping to ensure their loyalty by requiring them to leave members of their own families, including wives and sons, in Edo as hostages. Daimyo were required to keep a permanent residence in Edo and to alternate their time between attendance at court and service in their distant fiefs, but armies were not permitted to leave their fiefs. The expenses of this required travel, with their retinues, and of maintaining two residences, which were often luxurious, put the daimyo increasingly in debt to merchants, whose unofficial power thus slowly rose.

A close eye was kept on the construction or repair of daimyo castles to keep them from becoming potential bases for rival military power, as they had been in earlier centuries. The shogunate created a new group of officials who acted as censors, on the Chinese pattern, and the secret police watched for any threats to Tokugawa rule. At Edo a new castle was built as the shogun's headquarters, a vast fortress inside massive walls and moats arranged in a series of concentric rings about 2 miles across. The innermost ring, with its moat and walls, remains as the imperial palace in the center of downtown Tokyo to-

The procession of a daimyo and his retainers along their journey from his local domains to take up the required period of residence at Edo. [Bildarchiv Foto Marburg]

◉ Tokugawa Ieyasu: ◉ Instructions to His Successor

Tokugawa Ieyasu was a careful planner, a good judge of men, and one who understood the virtue of patient waiting until the time was right for action. Here is one of the instructions he left to his successors.

The strong manly ones in life are those who understand the meaning of the word patience. Patience means restraining one's inclinations. There are seven emotions: joy, anger, anxiety, love, grief, fear, and hate, and if a man does not give way to these he can be called patient. I am not as strong as I might be, but I have long known and practiced patience. And if my descendants wish to be as I am, they must study patience.

Source: A. L. Sadler, *The Maker of Modern Japan* (London: Allen & Unwin, 1937), pp. 389–390.

---

day. The emperor was left in place with his court at Kyoto, and the ancient fiction of imperial divinity and supremacy was preserved. Technically, the shogun was only the emperor's military chief of staff; in reality, he was the acknowledged ruler of the country.

By the time Ieyasu died in 1616, having prudently transferred power to his son so as to avoid a dispute over the succession, the new feudal order was firmly established. It is called feudal because it preserved many feudal forms, but the new central authority of the Tokugawa makes the label only partly appropriate. A new post of prime minister was created, assisted by a council of state, in part to ensure that the system would not weaken or collapse under a less effective shogun. In time a relatively complex central administration grew up, with posts filled first largely by able members of the Tokugawa clan or from the families of loyal daimyo and later from the expanding group of gentry in the central area.

Merchant groups and other commoners had begun to acquire new power and even some independence as Ashikaga rule deteriorated. Large-scale trade centered in the Osaka area. The neighboring commercial center of Sakai, now part of greater Osaka, was actually a self-governing city run by merchants with their own army, like a Renaissance city-state in Italy. The Tokugawa suppressed the rising political power of the middle and lower classes as a threat to their authority. Merchants were restricted and supervised in their activities and were made subservient to the new aristocratic order. Sakai's walls were demolished, its armies were dissolved, and its government was absorbed into the Tokugawa system.

The same order was brought into the countryside. Peasants were made to surrender their swords and other weapons to the government, and the hereditary warrior class of samurai was left in complete charge of military affairs. Swords became the badge of the samurai and came to symbolize their dual role as "gentlemen warriors" and as administrators. Firearms, which the Japanese knew of both from the Chinese and from the Portuguese and Dutch, were also seen as potentially disruptive. They too were successfully outlawed, and Japan remained free of them for the more than two centuries when foreigners were also excluded. Swords became even more an exclusive hallmark of the aristocracy, not easily challenged by unarmed peasants. In isolation from the world, Japan prolonged a medieval technology and the social system that went with it.

Peasants and artisans were essential producers, but merchants, despite their obvious accomplishments, literacy, cultivation, and wealth, were regarded as parasites and put into the lowest social order of all. This reflected classic Confucian values, revived by the Tokugawa, which admirably suited their feudal and hierarchical system. Merchants were forbidden to wear the fine clothes or materials of the upper classes, to ride in sedan chairs, or to omit the groveling and subservient bowing also required of peasants and artisans to samurai or other aristocrats whom they encountered. Those who did not bow low enough might have their heads chopped off by samurai guards.

The Expulsion of Foreigners

The Portuguese had reached Japan by 1543, and for nearly a century they and later the Spanish and the Dutch carried on an extensive export and import trade. Catholic missionaries came too and made numerous converts. Japan was more curious about Westerners than China was, having long understood the value of learning from others. But the Tokugawa grew irritated by the factional bickering among the different missionary orders and the allegiance converts had to give to a distant and alien pope. The foreigners and their intrigues were disturbing to the smooth order the Tokugawa had worked so hard to establish. In the years after Ieyasu's death in 1616, all missionaries were killed or expelled and converts executed or forced to recant. The persecution culminated in the suppression of a rebellion by impoverished Christian peasants in the area of Nagasaki, which had been the chief trade port for Westerners, in 1638. The survivors were slaughtered and thousands were crucified, but a few escaped and kept Christianity alive on an underground basis until the reappearance of Western missionaries in the 1860s.

All Western merchants were expelled by 1638, and Portuguese envoys who came in 1640 to ask for a reopening of trade relations were executed. Japanese were forbidden to go abroad, and no ships capable of overseas trade were built. In order not to lose complete touch with what was happening in the rest of the world, one Dutch ship a year was permitted to come for trade, on the island of Deshima in Nagasaki harbor, remote from the main centers of Japanese population.

Culture and Nationalism

With such an array of controls over people's lives, the Tokugawa did indeed ensure peace and stability. For about two centuries they also largely succeeded in retarding most change, especially in social or political matters. Economically, however, Japan continued to develop, and now, under the long Tokugawa peace, more rapidly than ever before. Production and internal trade grew, and with it, despite their low status in Tokugawa society, an expanding

---

◉ Japanese Women: An Outsider's View ◉

From the early accounts of the Dutch at Deshima, some American authors in 1841 compiled this account of the state of women in Japan.

The position of women in Japan is apparently unlike that of the sex in all other parts of the East, and approaches more nearly their European condition. The Japanese women are subjected to no jealous seclusion, hold a fair station in society, and share in all the innocent recreations of their fathers and husbands. The minds of the women are cultivated with as much care as those of men; and amongst the most admired Japanese historians, moralists, and poets are found several female names. The Japanese ladies are described as being generally lively and agreeable companions, and the ease and elegance of their manners have been highly extolled. But, though permitted thus to enjoy and adorn society, they are, on the other hand, during their whole lives, kept in a state of tutelage: that is, of complete dependence on their husbands, sons, or other relatives. They have no legal rights, and their evidence is not admitted in a court of justice. Not only may the husband introduce as many unwedded helpmates as he pleases into the mansion over which his wife presides but he also has the power of divorce, which may be considered unlimited, since he is restrained only by considerations of expediency. The Japanese husband, however, is obliged to support his repudiated wife according to his own station, unless he can allege grounds for the divorce satisfactory to the proper tribunal; among which, the misfortune of being without children takes from the unhappy wife all claim to maintenance. Under no circumstances whatever can a wife demand to be separated from her husband. At home, the wife is the mistress of the family; but in other respects she is treated rather as a toy for her husband's amusement, than as the rational, confidential partner of his life. She is expected to please him by her accomplishments, and to cheer him with her lively conversation, but never suffered to share his more serious thoughts, or to relieve by participation his anxieties and cares. She is, indeed, kept in profound ignorance of his business affairs; and so much as a question from her in relation to them would be resented as an act of unpardonable presumption.

Source: P. F. Siebold, *Manners and Customs of the Japanese in the Nineteenth Century* (London: Murray, 1852), pp. 122–124.

merchant class. A truly national market developed for many basic commodities, aided by the use of a system of paper credit. None of this fit well with the formally feudal arrangement of the social and political systems, and in the long run it had the same disruptive effects on Japanese feudalism as the revival of trade, towns, and merchants had in late medieval Europe. As rich merchants began to lend money to needy or extravagant noblemen and then to marry their daughters, they could no longer be treated as beneath the notice of daimyo and samurai. The cultural life of Tokugawa Japan was largely urban, and merchants came to dominate it as a new bourgeoisie.

The amusement quarters in the cities, especially Edo, were patronized mainly by merchants and by occasional samurai who sought relaxation from the stiff conventions of aristocratic society. This was the great age of the geisha, women carefully trained to cater to a male clientele as entertainers who specialized in singing, dancing, lively

Tokugawa splendor: a view of the main audience hall at Nijo Castle, Kyoto. The superb screen paintings, beautifully set off by the plain *tatami* (rush mat) floor, are a fine example of early Tokugawa decorative art for the elite. [Anne Kirkup]

conversation for male patrons, and sometimes sex. Artists and novelists loved to depict geisha scenes, which became a distinct genre of refined eroticism.

The arts, too, produced relief from a highly conventionalized society. These included popular puppet plays and, from the seventeenth century, a new dramatic form, *Kabuki*, which is still popular in Japan. Kabuki catered to less refined tastes than the classical *Noh* theater and emphasized realism, comedy, and melodrama. Classical poetry, based on Chinese models, was reduced to three-line miniatures, the *haiku*, which at their best were superb snapshots of a moment of thought or feeling. Painting became more flamboyant, colorful, and grand, but still in keeping with the remarkable Japanese sense of good taste. Magnificent decorated screens and wall panels were produced for the palaces of the shogun and of noblemen, who wore gorgeous silk brocades and furnished their tables with beautiful lacquer ware and porcelain. In time, much of this splendor could also be found in the houses of rich merchants, but popular art became more important, and commoners' houses were more often decorated with woodblock prints. This is probably still the Japanese art best known abroad; it reached the climax of its development in the work of Hokusai and Hiroshige in the last decades of the Tokugawa regime early in the nineteenth century.

A good deal of information about the outside world continued to filter in by way of the Dutch at Nagasaki, including Western advances in medicine, shipbuilding, and metalworking. A few Japanese scholars began to study Western science; they compared Dutch texts on anatomy with traditional Chinese medical texts, for example, and through their own dissection of the corpses of executed criminals, demonstrated as early as 1771 that the Dutch version was accurate, whereas the Chinese was not. The Chinese rejected dissection, taboo in light of Confucian respect for the body. The Japanese also acquired a new national consciousness, thanks to the Tokugawa unification. They were able to adopt ideas and techniques from foreign sources, as they had long done from China, without in any way diluting their own cultural and national identity. Japan's separateness as an island nation further reinforced its sense of uniqueness.

Together with a renewed interest in things foreign, the late Tokugawa period saw a nationalist-inspired revival of Shinto, the ancient Japanese worship of natural forces. Shinto legends and naive myths about the divine origin of the emperor, and through him of the Japanese people, appealed more to the new nationalist attitudes, although Shinto never replaced Buddhism or the Confucianism of the upper classes and intellectuals as the dominant religion. These and other developments were slowly transforming Japan, despite its unchanging surface, toward modernity, including a commercial economy and society that would soon be ready to burst the artificial restraints imposed on them.

❀
EDO AND THE "FLOATING WORLD"

By 1770 it is probable that the population of Edo and its immediate environs had reached a million, rivaled only by Peking and larger than any city in Europe. This urban concentration (the population of Japan by then was about 30 million) resulted from a combination of administrative centralization under the shogunate and the rapid commercialization of the economy. Edo and Osaka were the major centers of a national trade system and the headquarters of large merchant groups. The requirement that all daimyo had to maintain households in Edo, where they left their wives and family members as hostages, further swelled the population, as did their regular formal visits with their large retinues. Daimyo family estates, the large court of the shogun, and rich merchant families employed very large numbers of servants and artisans who provided them with luxurious furnishings and works of art.

Edo was also a major port; much of Japan's coastal trade passed through it, in addition to the trade that came by land. Much of the site had originally been swampy or prone to flooding, and large new tracts were drained and reclaimed as the city grew. Areas were set aside for daimyo and merchant residence and for shops, open-air markets, temples, and amusement quarters around the landward sides of the huge new castle built by Ieyasu. Thousands of soldiers based in Edo added to the numbers, as did the even more numerous laborers whose work supported the huge population.

Merchants dominated the bourgeois culture of Edo. Rich commoners wore forbidden silk under their plain outer clothing. The arts and amusements centered around what was called the Floating World, a pleasure quarter of theaters, restaurants, baths, and geisha houses. The main pleasure quarter was at the northern edge of the city, outside the official limits. Lesser aristocrats and their retainers, and even artisans, frequented this quarter, mingling with merchant patrons on a temporary basis of equality.

Rapid growth and crowding made for many problems, not the least of which was fire. Except for the shogun's castle and a few daimyo mansions, Edo was built almost entirely of wood, like all Japanese cities of the time, and fires often could not be controlled. The city burned down almost completely several times, but on each occasion it was rebuilt, larger and grander.

This was a new urban age of great cultural vigor, reminiscent in some ways of Sung dynasty Hangchow but increasingly dominated by bourgeois tastes. Culture was not necessarily vulgarized; merchants in fact often insisted on high aesthetic standards.

❀
HOKUSAI, MASTER ARTIST

Probably the best known of Japanese woodblock printmakers under the Tokugawa was the man called Hokusai (1760–1849), whose astonishingly fertile career spanned eight decades. He was born in Edo of unknown parentage and was adopted at age 3 by a craftsman named Nakijima, who made mirrors for the shogunate. The boy seems to have shown a talent for drawing by the time he was 5, and by the age of 13 he had been apprenticed to an engraver of woodblocks. Hokusai was a devout Buddhist and chose the name by which he is known, which means "north studio," to honor a Buddhist saint who was thought to be an incarnation of the North Star. His early work centered on book illustration, and he also made many portraits of contemporary actors. His prints are very Japanese in style but had become enormously popular in the West even before the end of Japan's seclusion policy.

Hokusai emerged at a period when Japan's arts had again begun to penetrate an international market. Japanese craftsmen had begun to copy the Chinese blue-and-white porcelain ware, so popular with Westerners that it became, together with silk and tea, an important Japanese export. It did not occur to the Japanese that Westerners would find their art desirable, although the woodblock prints in which their artists specialized were turned out in large numbers, sold very cheaply, and could easily be duplicated from the original block. But the freshness, color, and simple lines of Hokusai's work, like that of many of his contemporaries, appealed strongly to a Europe already impressed and influenced by Chinese art. The European craze for chinoiserie in the late eighteenth and early nineteenth centuries was joined by an enthusiasm for "japonoiserie." Many Japanese prints in fact arrived in Europe as wastepaper, used for wrapping porcelain and other export goods, but they soon became prized and collected. Return trade to Japan brought, among other things, the color and materials for Prussian blue, which Hokusai and others soon used to brighten and enliven their work.

Perhaps the best known of Hokusai's prints in the West is his *Thirty-six Views of Mount Fuji*. His style and that of his contemporaries had a great influence on Western artists, especially in late-nineteenth-century France. Most of the impressionists acknowledged their debt to Hokusai, and many of them painted pictures in an avowedly Japanese style during the craze for things Japanese after 1870, including Vincent van Gogh's careful copy of a print by Hokusai's great contemporary Hiroshige (1797–1858). Thus while Meiji Japan was busily adopting Western ways as fast as it could, Western artists were returning the compliment.

Hokusai: "The Breaking Wave," from *Thirty-six Views of Mount Fuji*: perhaps the woodblock print best known outside Japan. Note Mount Fuji in the background. [Metropolitan Museum of Art, Henry L. Phillips Collection]

Foreign Pressures and Domestic Unrest

The political system controlled so tightly from Edo ran relatively smoothly through the first half of the nineteenth century, and there were few outward expressions of dissent. In time the pressures building up behind the orderly facade of Tokugawa life would probably have forced basic change. As it happened, an outside force provided the impetus that destroyed the shogun's power and compelled Japan to face the world fully. It is not surprising that, having been so long suppressed, the change that resulted was on a truly revolutionary scale.

Among the outsiders, Americans were most eager to open Japanese ports to foreign trade. First American whalers, then clipper ships plying the China trade, then steamships in need of coal supplies sought permission to obtain provisions in Japan. The Tokugawa response was sharply negative. American and European sailors shipwrecked on Japanese shores were often handled roughly. American, British, and Russian expeditions after 1800 were repelled by the Edo government, and their requests were rejected. Finally, the American government took matters in its own hands. In 1853 it sent a small but powerful naval force under Commodore Matthew Perry with a letter to the shogun demanding trade relations and better treatment of foreign castaways.

Perry's squadron anchored in Tokyo Bay, in full view of Edo. The government was duly impressed by the size and the guns of the Americans' steam-powered "black ships," against which they realized Japan was defenseless. The Japanese tried to stall, and conservative forces, which dominated the Tokugawa, urged that the foreigners be refused and ejected. When Perry renewed the show of force the next year, the government capitulated. It signed a treaty, opening two ports and allowing a limited amount of regulated trade. Similar treaties ensued with European powers, and in 1858 a set of more detailed commercial treaties followed.

Foreigners could now reside in five ports as well as Osaka and Edo and could trade with whom they liked. The political backlash was severe. Many Japanese still felt strongly that the foreigners must be expelled before they further sullied the sacred soil of Japan. The official who had signed the trade agreements was assassinated by conservative elements in 1860. Other extreme nationalists murdered an Englishman near Yokohama, a former fishing village that had become the main foreign settlement. There were, of course, reprisals, and the Tokugawa government was caught in a dilemma. It was neither able to resist foreign pressures nor to control its own subjects, who increasingly felt that the government had failed them and revealed its impotence. The outer daimyo domains in western Japan had always been restless under Tokugawa domination and now saw their chance to challenge it. They and others began to intrigue at the court in Kyoto and finally confronted Edo's forces militarily.

When the emperor died in 1867, the shogun, bowing to the general pressure, formally handed over power to the new boy emperor, Meiji, and his advisers, among whom samurai from rebellious western Japan had a prominent place. A little over a year later they persuaded the outer daimyo to offer their domains to the emperor, and feudal lords in the rest of Japan followed suit. The emperor moved to the more modern Edo, which thenceforward was known as Tokyo ("eastern capital"). This largely nonviolent revolution of 1868 is known as the Meiji Restoration, for technically the emperors of Japan had never surrendered their sovereign powers. But it was a revolution nonetheless, and it brought to power new forces bent on rapid and radical change. The daimyo were compensated for their surrendered lands, and some remained as governors and other officials of the new government. Feudalism in Japan was over; the way was clear for the wholesale remaking of the nation as a modern industrial power.

王 王 王

The growth of cities, trade, and merchants and the rise of a strong centralized government helped make it possible for Japan to modernize itself rapidly along Western lines while Manchu China floundered. Tokugawa rule had been profoundly conservative, even hidebound in its feudal forms, but its often harsh political controls had created the stability that made economic development possible. Antiquated though the feudal forms seemed, late Tokugawa Japan, like late medieval Europe, was a society on the eve of economic revolution.

In China late Ch'ing rule was also conservative, but its central administrative controls weakened after 1800, and

Western penetration accelerated its collapse. The economy remained dominated by peasant agriculture, and urban life was never more than a small part of a basically agrarian system. China was too big to be affected by new trends except very slowly. The inherent conservatism of both the peasants and their rulers worked against change. But none of this was clear as of 1860 or even 1870. Most foreign observers still looked to China as the dominant force in the East Asian economy. Within the next century, however, Japan, with a population still less than a tenth of China's, was to outstrip its neighbor in productivity, wealth, and power.

Notes

1. R. Fortune, *Three Years' Wanderings in the Northern Provinces of China* (London: Murray, 1853), p. 196.
2. J. K. Fairbank, E. O. Reischauer, and A. Craig, *East Asia: Tradition and Transformation* (Boston: Houghton Mifflin, 1978), p. 228.
3. J. L. Cranmer-Byng, ed., *An Embassy to China* (London: Longman, 1962), pp. 212–213.
4. G. Stanton, *Notes of Proceedings During the British Embassy to Peking in 1816* (London: Murray, n.d.), pp. 153–225 passim.

Suggestions for Further Reading

China

Fairbank, J. K., ed. *The Cambridge History of China*, vol. 10: *Late Ch'ing*. Cambridge: Cambridge University Press, 1978.

Fay, P. W. *The Opium War*. Cambridge: Cambridge University Press, 1975.

Greenberg, M. *British Trade and the Opening of China, 1800–1842*. Cambridge: Cambridge University Press, 1951.

Ho, P. T. *Studies on the Population of China, 1368–1953*. Cambridge, Mass.: Harvard University Press, 1959.

Kahn, H. L. *Monarchy in the Emperor's Eyes: Image and Reality in the Ch'ien Lung Reign*. Cambridge, Mass.: Harvard University Press, 1971.

Lach, D. *Asia in the Making of Europe*. 2 vols. Chicago: University of Chicago Press, 1965, 1978.

Metzger, T. *The Internal Organization of Ch'ing Bureaucracy*. Cambridge, Mass.: Harvard University Press, 1973.

Miyazaki, I. *China's Examination Hell: The Civil Service Examinations in Imperial China*, trans. C. Schirokauer. New York: Weatherhill, 1976.

Perkins, D. *Agricultural Development in China, 1368–1968*. Chicago: University of Chicago Press, 1969.

Rawski, E. *Education and Popular Literature in Ch'ing China*. Ann Arbor: University of Michigan Press, 1978.

Rozman, G. *Urban Networks in Ch'ing China and Tokugawa Japan*. Princeton, N.J.: Princeton University Press, 1973.

Spence, J. *Ch'ing Sheng-tsu, Emperor of China*. New York: Knopf, 1974.

Van der Sprenkel, S. *Legal Institutions in Manchu China*. London: University of London Press, 1962.

Wakeman, F. *The Great Enterprise: The Manchu Reconstruction of Imperial Order in Seventeenth-Century China*. Berkeley: University of California Press, 1986.

Wong, R. B., Will, P. E., and Lee, J. *State Granaries and the Food Supply of China, 1650–1850*. Ann Arbor: University of Michigan Press, 1987.

Japan

Barr, P. *The Coming of the Barbarians*. London: Macmillan, 1967.

Bix, H. P. *Peasant Protest in Japan, 1590–1884*. New Haven, Conn.: Yale University Press, 1986.

Bolitho, H. *Treasures Among Men: The Feudal Daimyo in Tokugawa Japan*. New Haven, Conn.: Yale University Press, 1974.

Dore, R. P. *Education in Tokugawa Japan*. Berkeley: University of California Press, 1965.

Dunn, C. J. *Everyday Life in Traditional Japan*. London: Batsford, 1969.

Elison, G., and Smith, B. *Warlords, Artists, and Commoners: Japan in the Sixteenth Century*. Honolulu: University Press of Hawaii, 1981.

Michener, J. A. *The Floating World*. Honolulu: University Press of Hawaii, 1983.

Reischauer, E. O. *Japan: The Story of a Nation*. New York: Knopf, 1970.

Storry, R. *A History of Modern Japan*, rev. ed. New York: Penguin Books, 1982.

Totman, C. *Politics in the Tokugawa Bakufu, 1600–1843*. Cambridge, Mass.: Harvard University Press, 1967.

———. *Tokugawa Ieyasu: Shogun*. San Francisco: Heian, 1983.

The Industrial Revolution

From the beginning of history to the nineteenth century, all physical labor was accomplished by human hands, either directly or with tools held or rigged by human hands or with animals guided by human hands. Power was supplied by muscle reinforced by levers, pulleys, and weights and supplemented by running water, moving air, or fire. Since then, work has been performed increasingly, and in the more developed regions of the world predominantly, by machines powered by steam, electricity, combustible gases, and the exploding atom. The use of new power sources to drive increasingly complex machines is still developing, as may be seen in such contemporary devices as computers and lasers. The enormous consequent increase in productive capacity and technical mastery of the resources of the globe has transformed work, society, and the face of the planet itself more than any single development since the introduction of agriculture. This process is still known by the name given to it by the nineteenth-century British historian Arnold Toynbee: the Industrial Revolution.

An early steam-powered engine, based on English design and built in 1727, pumps water from a Swedish mine. Impressive in scale, it could pump 100 gallons a minute out of flooded shafts. [Trustees of the Science Museum, London]

The Background: Population, Energy, and Technology

The Industrial Revolution began in western Europe, specifically in Great Britain. Europe had achieved an aggregate growth of population, commerce, and energy between the fifteenth and the eighteenth centuries. Such growth, at an even faster relative rate, had been experienced between the eleventh and thirteenth centuries, only to be succeeded by the demographic catastrophe of the fourteenth. Some observers, such as the Englishman Thomas Robert Malthus (1766–1834), feared at the end of the eighteenth century that Europe was on the brink of such a catastrophe again. In his *Essay on Population* (1798), Malthus noted with alarm the surge in Europe's population, apparent since the middle of the century. Asserting that population tended to increase geometrically while production grew only arithmetically, he calculated that Europeans would soon outstrip their resources. The result would be scarcity, famine, and war.

Had the Industrial Revolution not transformed Europe's productive capacity, Malthus' dire prophecy might have come true. By the end of the eighteenth century, its once

◎ Malthus on Population ◎

The English clergyman and economist Thomas Malthus, writing at the beginning of the population explosion, concluded that the permanent pressure of population would frustrate all efforts to achieve a more perfected society, and that only sexual abstinence could prevent widespread misery.

In plants and irrational animals, the view of the subject is simple. They are all impelled by a powerful instinct to the increase of their species; and this instinct is interrupted by no doubts about providing for their offspring. Wherever therefore there is liberty, the power of increase is exerted; and the superabundant effects are repressed afterwards by want of room and nourishment.

The effects of this check on man are more complicated. Impelled to the increase of his species by an equally powerful instinct, reason interrupts his career, and asks him whether he may not bring beings into the world for whom he cannot provide the means of support. If he attend to this natural suggestion, the restriction too frequently produces vice. If he hear it not, the human race will be constantly endeavoring to increase beyond the means of subsistence. But as, by that law of our nature which makes food necessary to the life of man, population can never actually increase beyond the lowest nourishment capable of supporting it, a strong check on population, from the difficulty of acquiring food, must be constantly in operation. This difficulty must fall somewhere, and must necessarily be severely felt in some or other of the various forms of misery, or the fear of misery, by a large portion of mankind.

That population has this constant tendency to increase beyond the means of subsistence, and that it is kept to its necessary level by these causes, will sufficiently appear from a review of the different states of society in which man has existed. But, before we proceed to this review, the subject will, perhaps, be seen in a clearer light if we endeavor to ascertain what would be the natural increase of population if left to exert itself with perfect freedom; and what might be expected to be the rate of increase in the productions of the earth under the most favorable circumstances of human industry.

It will be allowed that no country has hitherto been known where the manners were so pure and simple, and the means of subsistence so abundant, that no check whatever has existed to early marriages from the difficulty of providing for a family, and that no waste of the human species has been occasioned by vicious customs, by towns, by unhealthy occupations, or too severe labor. Consequently in no state that we have yet known has the power of population been left to exert itself with perfect freedom.

Source: T. Malthus, *An Essay on Population* (London: Dutton, 1914), pp. 6–7.

abundant forests had been seriously depleted by industrial demand and agricultural clearance. The average Parisian, for example, was consuming 2 tons of fuel per year by 1789, almost all of it wood, and French forests had already shrunk to their present-day size. At that rate, the exhaustion of France's major energy source and chief industrial material seemed inevitable.

The solution was the replacement of wood by coal. Coal had become an important fuel source in the sixteenth century in Liège, where it was mined in the surrounding basin, and even more so in Newcastle on the Tyne basin in England, where after 1600 it was used extensively in the production of salt, glass, bricks, and tiles, in metal and sugar refining, and in baking and brewing. But its more general use was restricted by the difficulty and danger of mining it, the lack of overland transportation to distribute it, and the foul-smelling sulfur released in burning it.

One of the chief hazards of coal mining was subsurface water. At the beginning of the eighteenth century, Thomas Savery, a London inventor, and Thomas Newcomen, a Dartmouth blacksmith, developed a steam-powered pump that Savery called "the Miners' Friend." The efficiency of this pump was increased fourfold by the introduction in the 1770s by the Scotsman James Watt (1736-1819) of a condenser that kept the steam from being dissipated into the atmosphere, and demand for it jumped. Dissatisfied with what was still essentially a simple pump, Watt continued to experiment until by 1782 he had converted it into a double-action rotary engine capable of turning heavy machinery. By 1800, 500 such engines were in use in Great Britain.

Just as industrial progress was limited by the use of wood as its primary source of energy, so too was it limited by its dependence on wood and stone as its chief construction materials. Running a poor third to these, though indispensable for such everyday products as nails, needles, wire, spurs, buckles, and rings, as well as heavier implements such as stoves and weapons, was iron. Smelting iron, which involved separating it from its ore, was a complex, labor-intensive process (the Italian city of Brescia, a major iron center, was said to employ 60,000 people to manufacture iron in the late fifteenth century), requiring heavy machinery and great amounts of fuel. The product itself, like coal, was difficult to transport, and most iron for domestic use was produced in small quantities on the village level.

Smelting was accomplished by the use of charcoal, which required that all large ironworks be located near forest areas. The search for an alternative fuel as the forests dwindled led to coke, a waste product obtained from coal essentially as charcoal is from wood. Its high sulfur content resulted in an unacceptably brittle product, however, until the Quaker ironmaster Abraham Darby was able to produce a coke-smelted iron suitable for heavy utensils and military ordnance in 1709. The demand for munitions during the Seven Years' War led to a consid-

erable expansion of coke-fed blast furnaces in Great Britain. But it was not until 1784, when Henry Cort introduced the puddling process for converting crudely cast pig iron into the lighter and more tensile wrought iron necessary for most domestic products, that the iron industry was freed from its dependence on wood.

The result of these technical innovations was that by the 1780s Europe stood on the verge of a great breakthrough in its industrial capacity. The use of steam facilitated the extraction of coal; the use of coal made possible the increased production of iron; and iron (with other metals) was first to supplement and then to replace wood and stone as the prime industrial material. At the same time, transportation was improved by new highways called turnpikes that could bear far heavier loads and by canals that turned Britain's waterways into an integrated transport system. The symbol of the new age was the great iron bridge that Abraham Darby III built across the Severn River in Shropshire in 1779; 50 years later, the first phase of the Industrial Revolution was to culminate in the locomotive, which, made of iron and powered by steam and coal, was to provide industry with an incomparably cheap and efficient method of transportation.

These neatly interlocking developments suggest that the Industrial Revolution was a more or less straightforward consequence of certain technical improvements in mining and metallurgy, prompted by a threatened scarcity of traditional resources. But such an explanation by itself would be misleading. Other societies, including previous European ones, had faced scarcity without finding a key to increased productivity. Other societies had achieved technical levels comparable to those of eighteenth-century Europe without an industrial breakthrough. The Chinese had used coal for domestic heating for several thousand years and for metalworking from about 500 B.C. Their smelting processes were far more sophisticated, and they were able to produce wrought iron and steel of far higher quality. The swords forged with this steel, proceeding westward along the trade routes, had enabled Persian cavalrymen to rout Roman legions in the third century A.D. Western metalworking, despite considerable advances between the eleventh and eighteenth centuries, was still in fact inferior to that of China and India; and when in 1591 the Portuguese captured a cargo of Indian steel, no blacksmith in Lisbon or Spain was able to forge it. Yet at the same time the fine silks and cottons of China and India, so much in demand in eighteenth-century Europe, were woven on looms whose crudeness astonished Western visitors. Clearly, the relation between craft and technology was complex; nor do we fully understand the social processes that inhibited technology in China after the thirteenth century at just the moment it had begun to advance in what had only recently been one of the most backward sectors of the globe, western Europe.

The technical breakthrough of eighteenth-century Europe should therefore be seen not as the beginning but as

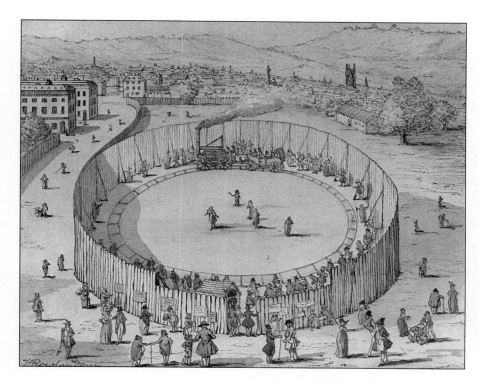

The first railway track was laid inside this circular enclosure near what is now the site of the great Euston train station in London to demonstrate Richard Trevithick's steam locomotive in 1808. The first commercially practical engine was built in the 1820s, and by the 1840s rail networks had begun to span Europe and the United States. The enormous capital outlays forced business, industry, and the state into partnership on an unprecedented scale. The drawing is by Thomas Rowlandson. [Trustees of the Science Museum, London]

the end product of a complex process of social change. That process had at least three distinguishable components: commercial, agricultural, and scientific.

Commerce and the Formation of Capitalist Society

Before the term *Industrial Revolution* had been coined, the nineteenth century social critics Karl Marx (1818–1883) and Friedrich Engels (1820–1895) had identified the banking and commercial classes of Europe—the bourgeoisie—as critical in the development of the new industrial society. "The bourgeoisie," they wrote,

> has subjected the country to the rule of the towns. It has created enormous cities, . . . agglomerated population, centralized means of production, and has concentrated property in a few hands. . . . [It] has created more massive and more colossal productive forces than have all preceding generations together.[1]

Marx and Engels saw the bourgeoisie as a group unique to modern Western society, differing from merchant elites in all previous societies in its ability to grasp, organize,

and exploit the basic elements of production: capital, land, and labor. Exaggerated though this view may be, it is certainly true that the development of business and commerce had become critical to the prosperity and expansion of Europe.

Commerce becomes a specialized economic function when consumers no longer obtain their goods directly from producers. In commercial economies, producers and consumers typically consummate their exchange through a person appropriately called a *middleman,* or merchant. In the simplest case, the commercial exchange involves a seller (the producer) and a buyer (the consumer) linked by a person who both buys (from the producer) and sells (to the consumer). By extending the links in this chain— by adding more intermediaries—goods can be shipped around the world, joining producers and consumers who share no common language or currency or even knowledge of one another's concrete existence. In such a case, the producer produces for a wholly abstract market, the size and nature of which is defined by the number of men in the middle.

What expands this number, and hence the economy itself, is capital. Capital can be defined in stocks of goods or resources, in warehousing and shipping facilities, in command or control of a labor supply. But its simplest form is money, since money is freely interchangeable into all the other elements. The term *capital* in this sense was first used in the West in the twelfth and thirteenth centuries. A *capitalist,* as the term emerged by about the mid-

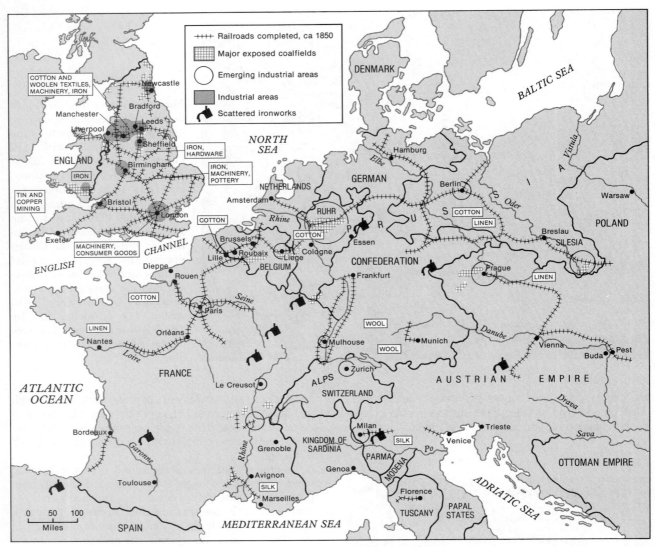

29.1 European Industrialization, c. 1850

seventeenth century, was someone who possessed a large stock of money, whether or not he chose to invest it. Although the term *capitalism* can be found as early as 1753, it emerged as a description for an economic system characterized by control of the means of production (capital in its modern sense) by a distinct group of private individuals (capitalists) only in the early twentieth century. Marx himself never used the term.

Capitalist society—the distinctive form of the modern West—may then be understood as one in which economic relations are integrated by those who possess, as personal or corporate property, the means of production, through which they command both the labor force and the range of consumer choice. In this sense, capitalism as a fully developed system cannot be said to have existed before

the transformation of European society by the Industrial Revolution in the nineteenth century. Yet if the Industrial Revolution made capitalism possible as a distinctive economic system, the capitalist element in the preindustrial economy—the activity of the bourgeois or merchant class—was the most dynamic element in that economy, the activity that enabled it to grow.

Preindustrial capitalism was, in short, commercial capitalism, a capitalism not of producers but of distributors. The two states of eighteenth-century Europe where this capitalism was most advanced were Great Britain and the Netherlands. Dutch prosperity, the envy of Europe in the previous century, was chiefly the result of commercial activity. The Dutch had been merchants and seafarers since the Middle Ages. The Bank of Amsterdam was the greatest commercial institution on the Continent. Through joint-stock companies—limited-liability partnerships of merchants and investors—it financed a worldwide traffic; at its height, Dutch shipping carried half of the world's trade, exclusive of China. Though Dutch industry and agriculture were also advanced, it was the trading of other people's goods that gave the Netherlands the highest standard of living in the seventeenth-century West and enabled it to enjoy great power status with a population barely an eighth the size of France's, and a land area—largely barren of resources—no more than a twentieth that of France.

The culture of early modern capitalism was nowhere better displayed than in the Netherlands. The Dutch republic was dominated by its town life; as early as 1500, more than half the population of its largest province, Holland, was urban. Dutch towns, with their meandering waterways, humpbacked bridges, and the mellow red brick of their pavements and houses, were connected by a web of canals plied constantly by barges, ferries, and flyboats. Their harbors were crammed with the treasures of the Americas and the Indies—sugar, silks, spices, cocoa, tobacco; its shipyards launched 2,000 new seagoing vessels each year. Cloth manufacture and finishing remained the staple industry, as it had been since the Middle Ages, but there were hundreds of other industries and specialized trades such as diamond cutting, lens grinding, and bookmaking (Amsterdam alone had between 40 and 50 presses). Business was serviced by a host of bankers, factors, jobbers, and commodity and discount brokers.

The great commercial families, the so-called regent class, ruled with all the aplomb of the traditional European aristocracies. As their city grew, the merchant oligarchs of Amsterdam conceived the bold plan of virtually quadrupling its area by constructing three new concentric canals linked by a system of cross canals and streets. They carried out this extraordinary project in the midst of their war of independence against Spain, and with their own profits on it built sumptuous houses for themselves along the new canals. But population pressure on the towns was continuous. A shantytown arose beyond the northern boundary of Haarlem, where, it was reported in 1643, there was "much disorder and mischief not only by night, when the gates of this city are closed, but at all times."[2] The modern problems of overcrowding, poverty, and violence were already in evidence.

The Dutch had had a miniature Industrial Revolution of their own in the sixteenth and seventeenth centuries. The introduction of a movable cap to the windmill, traditionally an important power source in the Netherlands, meant that the central drive shaft no longer had to be turned, only the sails. Windmills and their sails could henceforth be much larger, making them both more powerful and responsive to lighter airs. In the 1590s Cornelis Cornelisz attached a crank to the drive shaft that transformed the rotary motion of the sails into a reciprocating motion driving a series of vertical saw blades. This enabled the Dutch to hew the giant Baltic timbers they used in shipbuilding

with far greater precision and efficiency. By adapting the crank to other kinds of implements—hammers, rams, paddles—they were able to convert the windmill to a host of industrial uses: hulling, oilseed crushing, fulling, boring, and paper and dye preparation, among many others. Even more significant was the development of the water-pumping mill, which enabled the Dutch to drain lakes and marshes and thus to add significantly to their land-poor country. Such large-scale reclamation projects were financed by groups of wealthy merchants, particularly Amsterdammers; thus once again commercial capital, industrial innovation, and economic development went in tandem.

The British were slower to develop as a commercial power, but during the eighteenth century their growing naval and imperial supremacy, their control of the lucrative slave trade, and the systematic creation of capital and credit through the expansion of the national debt enabled them to outstrip the Dutch. In 1688, before the creation of the Bank of England, the public debt was £688,000; by 1713, after the wars against Louis XIV, it had grown to £54 million; in 1815, after the defeat of Napoleon, it stood at £861 million. At first much of this expansion was financed by the Dutch themselves, who as late as 1776 held 43 percent of the British debt, but this share rapidly declined thereafter. By 1815 it was held almost entirely by the British upper classes themselves: noblemen, gentry, and well-to-do merchants. This oligarchy not only determined the expenditure of the debt through their control of the government but also reaped a direct return through the payment of interest on it, estimated in 1815 at nearly a tenth of the government's revenue. In effect, the British state itself had been converted into a giant corporation paying dividends to its wealthy shareholders. This great capital, the spoil of commercial profit, war, and empire, was a fuel that stoked the engines of the Industrial Revolution no less than coal and steam.

The Agricultural Revolution

The backbone of European society was the traditional peasant village, typically structured around open fields divided into narrow, unfenced strips. These strips were worked by individual peasants, but since they comprised a single large field, the strips were all plowed, sown, and harvested as one. These rhythms enforced the communal cooperation and solidarity that characterized peasant society. The peasants' life was the life of their villages: traditional, conservative, immemorial as the soil and the seasons, and highly resistant to change. But that life was soon not only to change but within a few generations actually to disappear.

The two necessities of the peasant's life were to feed his family and to pay his dues and taxes—to his lord, the church, and the state. These two necessities constituted the task of subsistence—survival—since peasants who could not meet their obligations to the lord would lose the use of the land. Subsistence was difficult in the best of times, and only the wealthiest of peasants could think of producing for the market. The majority dared not experiment with new crops or techniques that promised greater productivity. Their existence held no margin for error.

But changes in both demography and the structure of land ownership undermined these traditional patterns. The general surge in population in the sixteenth century had put great pressure on the food supply, driving up land and food prices. This made life harder for the average peasant, whose increased cost for seed was not compensated by higher food prices, since he did not produce for the market and indeed was often a purchaser of food himself. But it opened great opportunities for those able to speculate in land and sell grain. In England this class of substantial landowners, the gentry, had already been enriched by the purchase of church lands at the time of the Reformation. In the seventeenth and eighteenth centuries they set out to maximize their profits, partly through land acquisition and enclosure and partly through the importation of new techniques developed by the Dutch and the Flemish.

Simply defined, enclosure was the process of appropriating a portion of the village commons, usually by the manorial lord or chief local landowner, by erecting a fence or a hedge. Enclosure removed pastureland and sometimes plowland from the community. The result was hardship and sometimes devastation. Resistance was often violent. A major rebellion in 1549 following a period of heavy enclosure climaxed in an attempt to set up a communistic peasant community in Norfolk under the leadership of Robert Kett.

Most enclosure before the seventeenth century was for the purpose of pasturing sheep, which the gentry raised for market. Thereafter it was increasingly justified as a means of raising agricultural productivity to feed a growing population through the introduction of crops and fertilizers on land that peasants lacked either the means or the desire to "improve." But when the increase in population temporarily leveled off, as it did in the late seventeenth century, the lure of profit did not. Agrarian capitalism—the replacement of small-scale farming for subsistence by large-scale farming for the market—had begun to transform the traditional village; it would end by destroying it.

The improvement of enclosed land involved a variety of new techniques. As in the Low Countries, marshland was extensively drained and filled in. Marl and clay were mixed in sandy soils to make them more productive. Jethro Tull (1674–1741) introduced the planting of seeds in straight, even rows in place of the wasteful old method of sowing them at random (broadcast), while Lord Charles Townshend—"Turnip" Townshend, as he came to be nicknamed—demonstrated that yields could be signifi-

cantly improved by rotating crops and planting with turnips and clover fields that had previously lain fallow. Both plants replenished the soil and provided winter fodder to sustain animals that would otherwise have been slaughtered for lack of feed. Not only did this substantially increase the size of herds, but thanks to the tireless experiments of the Leicestershire breeder Robert Bakewell, they became larger and heavier as well: between 1710 and Bakewell's death in 1795 the average weight of sheep had trebled and cattle doubled. By the mid-eighteenth century, a veritable craze for agricultural improvement had swept the country. More than 1,000 books, pamphlets, and journals on agricultural subjects had been published by the end of the century, 250 of them alone by Arthur Young, at whose urging the governmental Board of Agriculture was established (1793). King George III himself contributed to Young's journal under the pen name "Farmer George."

Spurred by personal competition and the quest for profits, improving landlords hastened to acquire and enclose more and more land. The unquestioned control of Parliament by the gentry facilitated a policy of legalized confiscations. Between 1760 and 1815 some 3,600 acts of Parliament enclosed 6 million acres of land, or roughly a quarter of the arable land in England. By 1840 the communally farmed open field had ceased to exist.

What emerged in its place was a system of great estates worked by tenant farmers and hired laborers—no longer a peasantry but an agricultural work force. This system, with its vastly greater productivity and efficiency, enabled Britain to feed a population that had begun to grow at an unprecedented rate. In 1700 the population of England was about 5.5 million; by 1801 it had increased to 9 million and by 1851 to 18 million. This growing population provided both the work force and the primary market for the products of the Industrial Revolution, while at the same time the profits of the new agricultural economy, together with those of commerce and empire, constituted yet another major source of capital.

A New Prosperity?

Analysts have vigorously debated whether Britain's new wealth resulted in a higher general standard of living. Certainly the disparity between the immense wealth of the propertied few and the mass of the population had never been greater. Even more significant was the sense of dispossession many English men and women felt from their own country. The small independent proprietor or yeoman sank with the more ordinary village peasant to the status of a mere laborer, no longer owning the land he worked or entitled, even in part, to its fruits. The poet Oliver Goldsmith caught the popular sense of alienation and bitterness in "The Deserted Village," which went through five editions in the year of its publication, 1770:

Ill fares the land, to hastening ills a prey
Where wealth accumulates and men decay.
Princes and lords may flourish, or may fade
A breath can make them, as a breath has
*   made*
But a bold peasantry, their country's pride
When once destroyed, can never be supplied.

Even Arthur Young, the foremost propagandist of the new agriculture, came at last to deplore its human cost. "I had rather," he wrote at the end of the eighteenth century, "that all the commons were sunk in the sea than that the poor should in future be treated as they have generally been hitherto."

Apart from Britain, the Low Countries, and Denmark (where Dutch methods were also introduced), the agricultural revolution was slow to spread. Enthusiasm for agricultural improvement ran high in France, particularly among the group of reformers called the Physiocrats, led by François Quesnay (1694–1774); Louis XV wore a potato flower in his lapel in an attempt to popularize the plant. But the French aristocracy was not eager to disturb the system of seigneurial dues that constituted its chief profit from the peasantry, and the peasant insurrection of July 1789 (see Chapter 26) that led to the abolition of the manorial regime left France a nation of small proprietors and delayed the introduction of large-scale capitalist agriculture for a century. Elsewhere, despite some interest in the new methods, change was retarded by the ingrained conservatism of lords and peasants, especially in eastern Europe where serfdom was still widespread. The agricultural revolution was bound up with the existence of commercial capitalism and the habits of a developed market economy; where these were lacking, little headway was made.

The agricultural revolution was a revolution in soil management and animal husbandry rather than mechanization. The scythe gradually replaced the sickle in the eighteenth century, but it was not until the nineteenth that threshers and reapers were introduced, and their use spread slowly. The abundance of cheap labor—and the necessity to absorb a rapidly growing population—made the introduction of laborsaving machinery in agriculture not only less necessary but also politically dangerous. No similar inhibitions were at work in industry, where machines created more work than they destroyed. But if the agricultural revolution was not in this sense a part of the Industrial Revolution, at least until the introduction of combine harvesters in the 1880s, it was an indispensable precondition of it.

Science, Technology, and the State

The last major element in the Industrial Revolution was the development of machine technology itself. As will now be clear, the new technology was not a cause but rather an effect of conditions that favored and to some degree compelled an attempt to expand productive capacity—the extension of a market economy and the pressure of a growing population.

Technology itself must be viewed not as the mere sum of new methods and inventions but as the outcome of a complex social process in which need precedes opportunity and opportunity precedes design. Time and again in history, seeming technological breakthroughs had failed to yield significant results for lack of sustained economic demand; even in Britain itself, the Newcomen steam pump and Darby's coal-smelting process had little impact for half a century until the need for new energy sources spurred further development.

Nonetheless, cooperative interest in new industrial processes and techniques was growing. The Royal Society (1662), which served as a general clearinghouse for scientific ideas, provided the model for bodies such as the national Society of Arts, which sought improved methods of production. Informal groups of scientists and manufacturers in England and Scotland coordinated efforts to find solutions for specific industrial problems and sponsored prize competitions. Each such solution set a potential agenda for the next.

A case in point was the mechanization of the textile industry. Textiles were the most important element of the European economy after agricultural products. In the early eighteenth century they accounted for three-fourths of all English exports. Traditionally, England had specialized in woolens, but the leading edge of the industry was in cotton, stimulated by the popularity of fine calicoes from India and by the supply of raw cotton provided by slave labor in the colonial plantations. Raw materials were thus available, and a market was waiting, but productive capacity lagged. The first breakthrough occurred in 1733 when a Lancashire clockmaker, John Kay, invented the flying shuttle. This device enabled weavers to drive the shuttle across their looms by pulling strings attached to hammers. At one stroke it doubled the capacity of the loom. Yet the weavers could produce their cloth no faster than spinners could provide them with thread. The Royal Society offered a prize for a spinning machine, but not until James Hargreaves startled his wife at work on her wheel one day in 1764 was a solution found. Jenny Hargreaves' wheel overturned, but it continued to revolve on its side even though the spindle remained upright. Hargreaves envisioned a set of spindles driven by a single wheel, and thus the "spinning jenny" was born. A former barber, Richard Arkwright, attached the jenny to the water frame, a system of rollers that drew the thread taut before it was spun. The supply of thread now exceeded loom capacity until the clergyman Edmund Cartwright invented a power loom that could be operated by water or steam. Arkwright made a fortune and was rewarded with a knighthood in 1786, the first ever given to an industrialist, while Cartwright was voted £10,000 by a grateful House of Commons.

The official recognition given these men of humble status indicated the importance the state attached to commercially viable inventions. Yet the British government was far less directly involved in promoting industrial development than mercantilist France, with its state-sponsored factories, or the Prussia of Frederick the Great. The British concentrated instead on seeking raw materials, opening markets, and securing naval supremacy. From the age of the Navigation Acts (1651–1660), designed to ensure control of the colonial trade, the government pursued a consistent policy of commercial advantage. Britain's wars were fought not for *gloire* but for trading posts and privileges; what it sought above all from the wars against Louis XIV was penetration of the rich market of Spanish America, and when, 70 years later, it obtained logging rights along 300 leagues of wooded Mexican coastline, a British diplomat noted sagely, "If we manage this area wisely, there ought to be enough wood for eternity." If free enterprise and laissez-faire, the gospel so compellingly preached by Adam Smith in *The Wealth of Nations,* were to prove the formula for industrial expansion at home, it was within the framework of unfettered access to world markets and vital resources opened up by a century and a quarter of conscious government policy.

The Transformation of Britain

Between about 1780 and 1830 Great Britain was transformed more profoundly than any nation in recorded history. This transformation affected the size of the population and the distribution and living conditions of the vast majority. It altered the nature and in some respects the very notion of family life, work, and leisure. It profoundly affected the bonds of social organization and even the physical face of the land itself. From Britain the effects of this transformation rippled outward, first to the rest of Europe and then, through the mechanism of imperialism, to the furthest corners of the globe.

During this same period, the eyes of all Europe were fixed not on Britain but on the revolutionary upheavals in France—the great revolution of 1789, the meteoric career of Napoleon, the Bourbon restoration, and finally, in 1830, yet another round of revolution (discussed in Chapter 30) that overthrew the ruling dynasty once more and shook European politics as far away as St. Petersburg. Yet economically and even socially, France in 1830 was still in many respects the France of 1780, a nation of peasant proprietors tilling the soil much as their ancestors had done for hundreds of years.

The events in France were significant, certainly, and indeed they were broadly related to the great transformation in Britain. But if we can in the last analysis see the same fundamental change at work in both countries—the triumph of the capitalist mode of production and its integration with the powers of the state—the method of this change was very different in each. In France, owing to the survival of the seigneurial regime until 1789 and the relative underdevelopment of commercial capitalism, the drama was played out as a contest for control of the state, while in Britain, where the interests of the commercial classes and the state had been completely harmonized, a social transformation of unprecedented magnitude was achieved with relatively little political disturbance, and virtually none at all at the level of national authority. Britain saw only two monarchs between 1780 and 1830, George III and George IV, and even more remarkably, the office of prime minister was occupied for 35 of those 50 years by only two men as well, the brilliant William Pitt the Younger and the colorless Lord Liverpool.

The magnitude of economic change in Britain can best be suggested by statistics. In 1700 Britain produced 2.5 million tons of coal; in 1815 it mined 16 million. Pig iron production rose from 17,000 tons in 1740 to 125,000 in 1796 and then doubled again to 256,000 tons in 1806. Much of this production went to service the booming cotton industry, where output rose from 21 million yards of cloth in 1796 to 347 million by 1830. During this period cotton cloth rose from ninth to first place in the value of British manufactures, accounting for almost half of all exports. Even after 1830 textiles in general and cotton in particular constituted the essential product of the Industrial Revolution.

The Organization of Labor

The enormous increase in production attested by these figures entailed not only new energy sources and new machines but also new methods of commercial and industrial organization. Thus arose the two distinctive institutions of the Industrial Revolution: the bank and the factory. The function of banks was to concentrate capital; of factories, to concentrate labor. There were still only 12 banks in Great Britain outside London in 1750; by 1793 there were nearly 400, and by 1815 about 900. The intimate connection between banking and industrialization was demonstrated by the fact that some of the leading inventor-industrialists of the period—Richard Arkwright and James Watt among them—formed banks of their own as their business expanded.

The modern factory was the result of the machine. Previously, production had been carried on by four more or less distinct means of organization: the small workshop; the "cottage" or "domestic" system of home labor; the urban "manufactory" (to use Marx's term), which concentrated large numbers of workers under the same roof; and the preindustrial factory, or "arsenal," which assembled workers on an open-air site such as a mine, dockyard, or foundry.

Of these four, the first two were by far the most important. The small workshop, consisting typically of a master craftsman, two or three journeymen, and a like number of apprentices, had been characteristic of the medieval city. The workshops were organized on the basis of craft or trade into guild associations, which set general conditions of work and wages and standards of production. The guild system was in decay in the eighteenth century and in Britain had been legally abolished, although the workshop itself, with its distinction among master, journeyman, and apprentice, still remained. The result was that journeymen increasingly tended to organize in defense of their working conditions and wages, a phenomenon noted with deep disapproval by the German Imperial Diet in 1731.

The cottage or domestic system was particularly widespread in the clothing trade, although it was common as well in metalworking and other pursuits. Under this arrangement the clothier provided the yarn and the looms to spinners and weavers who worked at home and whose product the clothier then collected and marketed, thus combining the function of capitalist and merchant in one. On his travels in the English countryside in the 1720s Daniel Defoe noted that the population of whole villages was engaged in cloth production, "so that no hands being unemployed, all can gain their bread." Cloth-producing centers on the Continent were similarly organized. At its

most developed, the domestic system converted rural hamlets into integrated productive units in which the workers were separated only by walls.

The urban manufactory was typical of more specialized textile production such as hat, lace, and tapestry making; the Gobelins tapestry works established by Colbert was perhaps the most famous example. The manufactory concentrated as many as 500 workers under a single roof, thus making possible a greater division of labor and a closer supervision of the productive process—both typical of the nineteenth-century factory. The manufactory differed from a factory in the modern sense, as the etymology of its name implies, in that machinery was still directly hand-operated and hand-powered; human muscle still supplied the energy.

The eighteenth century reserved the term *factory* itself for industrial or mining operations in which human energy was supplemented by wind, running water, or fire. Iron foundries, arsenals, and shipyards were typical examples, while large-scale water-powered mining was well established in central Europe by the sixteenth century. Yet even though the concentration of labor and the increasing sophistication with which it was organized laid the basis for an industrial breakthrough, it could not of itself bring it about. Far greater concentrations could be found in China, for example, where in Songjiang south of Shanghai

Coal-mining operations such as the one depicted here in the county of Northumberland, belching their black smoke for miles around, transformed much of the British landscape in the early nineteenth century. [Trustees of the Science Museum, London]

over 200,000 workers were employed in the cloth trade. What made the difference was the development of iron machinery powered by coal and steam and the expanding market economy prepared by commercial capitalism. China had neither. Its immense productive base was turned inward on primarily domestic consumption, and its unexcelled craftsmanship had been developed at the expense of its technology.

The factory system of the Industrial Revolution was essentially an adaptation of the urban manufactory to the new machines. These machines doomed the domestic system. The engines that powered them required buildings of unprecedented size and complexity of design. Andrew Ure described one such factory at Stockport:

> **The building consists of a main body, and two lateral wings, the former being three hundred feet long, and fifty feet wide, the latter projecting fifty-eight feet in front of the body. There are seven stories, including the attics. The moving power consists of two eighty-horse steam-engines, working rectangularly together, which are mounted with their great gearing-wheels on the ground floor . . . and are separated by a strong wall from the rest of the building. This wall is perforated for the passage of the main horizontal shaft, which, by means of great bevel wheels, turns the main upright shaft, supported at its lower end in an immense pier of masonry, of which the largest stone weighs nearly five tons.[3]**

Ure described the steam engines as the "two-fold heart" of the factory, whose alternating pulsations caused "an uniformity of impulsive power to pervade every arm of the factory." As this language suggests, the factory was conceived as a giant organism whose lifeblood was the surging force of its engines and whose vital activity—production—depended on the coordination of all its parts. This was why the factory was, much more than a gigantic enclosure for heavy machinery, an integrated system of production. Ure himself defined the nature of this system: "The term *Factory System* . . . designates the combined operation of many work-people, adult and young, in tending with assiduous skill a series of productive machines continuously impelled by a central power."[4]

Industrial Discipline

Ure's words reflected a profound transformation in attitudes toward work itself. The work patterns of an agrarian society had been dictated by the rhythms of nature. People satisfied with subsistence quit when they had achieved it. But production for the market was open-ended, and long before the advent of the modern factory, entrepreneurs such as the Scotsman John Law had deplored the fact that many agricultural laborers were "idle one half their time." From this equation of leisure time with idleness it was only a short step to regarding the typical worker as lazy and unwilling to work—especially for his employer's

profit—except when goaded by necessity. Daniel Defoe was irked when "strolling fellows" refused his offer of day labor, replying that they could earn more money by begging. This did not suggest to prospective employers the desirability of offering better wages; rather, most agreed with Samuel Johnson that "raising the wages of day laborers is wrong for it does not make them live better, but only makes them idler."

In fact, few workers could afford "idleness" in the market-oriented British economy of the eighteenth century, where most of the rural population could make ends meet only by entering the cottage system. But the productivity of workers in their own homes could be imperfectly supervised at best; only in factories could a genuine work discipline be enforced. Long before such discipline came to Britain, Colbert had applied it to his state factories in France. Overseers pounced on every defect; at the third mistake, a worker would be put in irons for two hours next to a sample of the faulty work. No swearing or idleness was permitted; only hymns might be sung, in a low voice that would not disturb the other workers.

The mechanized factory carried this process to its logical conclusion. Instead of assigning one class of worker, the overseer, the task of imposing discipline on the rest of the work force, such discipline was now imposed by the rhythm of the machine itself. No longer did the laborer work a machine; rather, the machine worked the laborer. The penalties for slackness were savage. "Idlers"—often women and children, who comprised the majority of the work force in the textile mills—were flogged, tortured, and hung with weights, had vises screwed to their ears, or were tied three or four at a time "on a crossbeam above the machinery, hanging by our hands," as a witness told an investigating commission in 1835. Sixteen-hour workdays were not uncommon, and many workers toppled from weariness into their machinery: the grisly image of a worker falling into a vat of lard and becoming a part of the product in Upton Sinclair's novel *The Jungle* (1906) had its counterpart in fact. Some commentators compared the treatment of factory workers unfavorably to that of West Indian slaves, and conditions were even worse in the mines.

Family Life: A Tale of Two Cultures

The early Industrial Revolution had a devastating effect on traditional patterns of child rearing and family life among the rural poor. Child labor among the poor had been common in preindustrial Europe, but parents maintained direct supervision of their children in the field or, in the cottage system, at the wheel or loom. Once families were brought under the discipline of the factory, however, it was no longer the father but the overseer who determined the nature, duration, and rhythm of work. Adult males were indeed a minority in the typical textile mill. Employers preferred women and children, the younger the better; Andrew Ure confessed that it was "near impossible to convert persons past the age of puberty . . . into useful factory hands." At the factory of Samuel Greg, seven workers in ten were under the age of 18, one in six under the age of 10. Children entered the factory at the age of 5 or 6, as they enter school today; in some mills children as young as 3 were employed, and in one recorded case a child of 2. Ure depicted these children as "lively elves" whose work "seemed to resemble a sport." Unfortunately, the elves seemed not to live very long; the child mortality rate among Britain's working poor in the mid-nineteenth century was two to three times that of the suburban middle class, and the average life expectancy of the poor in the working-class district of Bethnal Green in London was two years lower than that estimated for Cro-Magnon man. Children who emerged from what the poet William Blake (1757–1827) called the "dark Satanic mills" of early industrialism were so puny and stunted that they seemed to many observers to belong to a separate race.

The relative underemployment of adult males in the factories left many fathers to serve as "house-husbands" while their wives and children worked. Many young women went into domestic service in middle- and upper-class households; by the middle of the nineteenth century, female servants made up the second largest occupational category in Britain, after farmworkers. Such women were often sexually exploited by their employers; others went into prostitution in the new factory towns. Under these circumstances the male-dominated family unit that had been characteristic of early modern Europe at all social levels was gravely undermined among the new working class. Many of what we regard as typical family problems of the modern poor—single-parent, female-headed households, high rates of illegitimacy and child delinquency, participation in the underground economies of prostitution and theft—were already in evidence in early industrial Britain. The Poor Law of 1834 was the culmination of this process. The assumption behind it was that unemployment and destitution were the result not of low wage rates and violent fluctuations in the industrial economy but of personal idle-

◉ Child Labor ◉

This testimony was given by Joseph Hebergam, age 17, before a select committee of Parliament in 1832.

Q.: You had fourteen and a half hours of actual labor at 7 years of age?
A.: Yes
Q.: What means were taken to keep you at your work so long?
A.: There were three overlookers; there was a head overlooker, and then there was one man kept to grease the machines, and then there was one kept on purpose to strap.
Q.: Was the main business of one of the overlookers that of strapping the children up to this excessive labor?
A.: Yes, the same as strapping an old restive horse that has fallen down and will not get up.

                    *   *   *

Q.: How far did you live from the mill?
A.: A good mile.
Q.: Was it very painful for you to move?
A.: Yes, in the morning I could scarcely walk, and my brother and sister used out of kindness to take me under each arm, and run with me to the mill, and my legs dragged on the ground. . . .
Q.: Were you sometimes too late?
A.: Yes; and if we were five minutes too late, the overlooker would take a strap, and beat us till we were black and blue.

Source: "Report of the Select Committee on the Factories Bill," in Industrial Revolution: Children's Employment, vol. 2 (Shannon: Irish University Press, *British Parliamentary Papers,* 1968–1972), 2: 157–159.

ness and unwillingness to work. Paupers were herded into workhouses where husbands were separated from wives, as if in jail, and parents from children. Those who died there were denied church burial. For the first time, poverty itself was made a crime.

In contrast to the working-class family, the bourgeois household was becoming more closely knit. It was also more child-centered than ever before. Children had been viewed traditionally as miniature adults. They were neither the object of family life nor the prime focus of its concern. In peasant families children were put to work as soon as they were able; in aristocratic ones they were boarded out at the age of 7 or 8. But in the wake of such reformers as Rousseau and Pestalozzi childhood was not only defined negatively as the absence of such adult traits as size, strength, and rationality but also seen as distinct phase of life with its own experiential value. Rousseau and Pestalozzi were succeeded by a torrent of popular manuals on child rearing with titles such as *The Parents' Handbook.* "The child," declared the poet Wordsworth, "is father to the man," and the bourgeois household was gradually redefined as a kind of factory whose product the child was, an attitude still reflected in our language today when we speak of children as "products" of either good or broken homes.

While thus internalizing the values of industry within the home itself, the bourgeois household was also viewed as a refuge from the competitive pressures of society, "a tent pitch'd in a world not right," in the picturesque phrase of Coventry Patmore. The influential Victorian poet and critic John Ruskin called it "the place of peace; the shelter, not only from all injury, but from all terror, doubt, and division." This idealized vision of "home, sweet home" implied a domestic division of labor between a male breadwinner and a woman whose function as wife and mother was to maintain a secure and idyllic refuge. This reinforced the patriarchal dominance of the bourgeois household just when it was being shattered in the working-class one.

The bourgeois wife and mother was expected to subordinate herself totally to her husband and to have no thought or interest beyond his welfare and comfort. Such subordination began in the bedroom. The Victorian woman was taught not merely to put her husband's pleasure before her own but to experience no pleasure at all. As one physician wrote, "A modest woman seldom desires any sexual gratification for herself. She submits to her husband, but only to please him; and, but for the desire of maternity, would far rather be relieved of his attentions."

In every respect then, the working-class and bourgeois family experience was as different as possible. In the bourgeois home the husband was the master and sole provider; in the working-class one it was often the wife who found employment while the husband maintained whatever home life was possible. The bourgeois family exalted the child as the "product" for which it existed, while the children of the working class were expendable units in the dredging

of coal or the making of textiles. The result, wrote the novelist and later statesman Benjamin Disraeli, was that Britain had become

> **two nations between whom there is no intercourse and no sympathy; who are ignorant of each other's habits, thoughts and feelings, as if they were dwellers in different zones, or inhabitants of different planets, who are formed by a different breeding, are fed by a different food, are ordered by different manners, and are not governed by the same laws.**[5]

Capital, Labor, and the Rights of Man

Disraeli's two nations might also be given another name: capital and labor. Writing in the 1830s, the French novelist Honoré de Balzac (1799–1850) remarked that the three orders of Old Regime society "have been replaced by what we nowadays call classes. We have lettered [professional] classes, industrial classes, upper classes, middle classes, etc." Balzac's *etc.* would include the growing army of industrial laborers, which Marx would call the proletariat and others, more simply, the working class.

The very different thing about the new social division between classes instead of orders was that it no longer assumed a harmony but rather a conflict of interests between the various groupings, particularly between the two broad categories known as capital and labor. The traditional medieval distinction among those who work, those who fight, and those who pray—the peasantry, the aristocracy, and the clergy—was based on the ideas that each order had a distinctive function that was essential to the good of the whole and the glory of God and that if the role of the fighters and prayers included command over the bodies and souls of the workers, it was on behalf of a common welfare that embraced all. Martin Luther, whose revolution shattered the unity of the priesthood, reinforced the idea of subordination when he preached that each man had a vocation prescribed by God in which it was his duty to labor and to remain content. But the Enlightenment brought with it a fundamental change of attitude. The Declaration of the Rights of Man asserted the political equality of all men, even as the economic inequality between them continued to widen. Adam Smith declared that the public interest was not something that could be determined in advance and hence worked toward as a common goal but the result of each person pursuing his or her private interest in an arena of competitive equality.

Taking this a step further, Smith's successors, notably David Ricardo (1772–1823), argued that capital and labor were governed by natural laws as fixed and immutable as the laws of physics. Those laws enshrined the clash of interests at the heart of society. Competition, not cooperation, was the law of social life.

WOMAN DRAGING COAL   OLD WOMEN AT WORK   CHILDREN PICKING UP

These horrific images of work in a British coal mine of the 1840s, recorded by a French visitor, speak for themselves. Women and children were preferred for work in the coal galleries because of their smaller stature and greater docility. Notice that the woman in the left frame is chained to her cart so that she can drag it forward on all fours. The height of the galleries was approximately that of the holds on slaving vessels. [Mansell Collection]

For anyone unable to compete, there could be only a struggle to survive. Long before the new proletarians began to perceive their employers as class antagonists, however, the spokesmen of the new industrial order had portrayed them as enemies of progress. In effect, the working class was defined negatively as having no interests and hence no social existence. Its only desire, according to writers such as William Temple, was to be as idle as possible. "Great wages and certainty of employment render the inhabitants of cities insolent and debauched," Temple declared. He concluded that "the only way to make [the poor] temperate and industrious is to lay them under a necessity of laboring all the time they can spare from meals and sleep, in order to procure the common necessities of life." Ironically, both Adam Smith and David Ricardo regarded labor as the source of all economic value, an idea that was to be crucial to the thought of Karl Marx. But Smith and Ricardo failed to relate the abstract value of labor to the actual toil of the laborer. In effect, labor was seen as something to be extracted from the recalcitrant body of the worker as coal was hacked out of the side of a hill.

At first workers' resistance to the new industrial order was directed chiefly at the introduction of new machinery or the importation of foreign labor or products. As early as 1675 the silk weavers of East London smashed 35 mechanical looms imported from Holland. In 1719 the weavers rose again to protest the importation of cheap calico fabrics from India and secured an act of Parliament against them. The use of Irish immigrant labor occasioned the riots of 1736, which included a bomb blast in the houses of Parliament. Anti-Irish feeling also sparked the great Gordon riots of 1780, when London burned for six days.

The most sustained violence occurred between 1811 and 1817, a period marked not only by an intensive mechanization of textile production that threw tens of thousands of traditional weavers out of work but also by the general depression that set in with the end of the Napoleonic wars. A destitute rioter in East Anglia summed up the plight of many in 1816: "Here I am between Earth and Sky, so help

me God. I would rather lose my life than go home as I am." The rioters were called Luddites after a legendary figure, Ned Ludd, who may have destroyed stocking frames in Yorkshire in the 1780s. *Luddism* has gone into the dictionary as a synonym for mindless opposition to change. In fact, the Luddites were chiefly artisans and skilled workers who put forward a platform of political grievances and demands, including the right to organize. More generally, machine breaking was often used as a bargaining tool in industrial disputes, and workers were surprisingly sophisticated in targeting machines that threatened their livelihood.

Industrialists opposed worker organization for obvious reasons of self-interest, but also on the grounds that it interfered with the working of the "objective" laws of economics to the detriment of productive efficiency and hence general prosperity. The doctrine that the free interplay of private market interests produced maximum public benefit in the form of wealth and happiness was known generally as economic liberalism or, in a phrase borrowed from the French, *laissez-faire* (roughly, "leave it alone").

The philosopher Jeremy Bentham (1748–1832) argued that it was actually possible to calculate social benefits on an arithmetic scale and thereby determine objectively what constituted the public good, which Bentham defined as "the greatest happiness of the greatest number." Bentham agreed with Smith and Ricardo that this happiness could be achieved only by noninterference in economic activity, especially by the state. "Every law is an evil because every law is a violation of liberty," he wrote, "so that the government can only choose between evils."

But if nonintervention was enjoined on the state, it applied equally to organizations, such as guilds or unions, that attempted to raise wages artificially or to reduce working hours. The chief economic role allotted the state in the laissez-faire dispensation was to prevent such organizations from arising to do mischief, and the only good laws the state could enact in the economic sphere were those suppressing them. The government did indeed act, spurred in the 1790s by fear of political clubs organized on

◉ Luddism ◉

This declaration by framework knitters, a formerly prosperous class of artisan workers who possessed a royal charter regulating their production of hosiery, illustrates the grievances of skilled craftsmen, which included complaints about the inferior quality of machine-made goods as well as fears of depressed wages and unemployment. "Ned Ludd" was a symbolic signature, referring to an already mythic figure, and "Sherwood Forest" was meant to evoke not only the legend of Robin Hood but also the freedom and independence traditionally associated with England's woodsmen.

Whereas by the charter granted by our late sovereign Lord Charles II, by the Grace of God King of Great Britain, France, and Ireland, the framework knitters are empowered to break and destroy all frames and engines that fabricate articles in a fraudulent and deceitful manner and to destroy all framework knitters' goods whatsoever that are so made. . . . And we do hereby declare that we will break and destroy all manner of frames whatsoever that make the following spurious articles and all frames whatsoever that do not pay the regular prices heretofore agreed to by the masters and workmen—All print net frames making single press and frames not working by the rack and rent and not paying the price regulated in 1810: warp frames working single yarn or too coarse hole—not working by the rack, not paying the rent and prices regulated in 1809. . . . All frames of whatsoever description the workmen of whom are not paid in the current coin of the realm will invariably be destroyed. . . .

Given under my hand the first day of January 1812. God protect the Trade.

Ned Ludd's Office
Sherwood Forest

Source: A. Aspinall and E. A. Smith, eds., *English Historical Documents*, vol. 11: *1783–1832* (Oxford: Oxford University Press, 1959), p. 531.

the Jacobin model by the London shoemaker Thomas Hardy and by tracts such as Tom Paine's *The Rights of Man*, which demanded popular rights, including reform of the House of Commons and abolition of the monarchy and the House of Lords. In 1799 and 1800 it passed the Combination Acts, which forbade workers to organize for any purpose whatever. However, it did nothing about industrial lobbies such as the General Chamber of Manufacturers, organized by Matthew Boulton and Josiah Wedgwood. Nor did most advocates of laissez-faire seem to regard the thousands of enclosure acts passed by Parliament on behalf of private interests as state intervention.

As the catastrophic effects of industrialization on the working class became apparent, however, widespread demand arose for government regulation of at least the conditions of child and female labor. "A feeling very generally exists," the conservative Thomas Carlyle remarked, "that the condition and disposition of the Working Classes is a rather ominous matter at present; that something ought to be said, something ought to be done, in regard to it."

That "something," largely the work of reformers such as Francis Place (1771–1854) and the earl of Shaftesbury (1801–1885), was a series of Factory Acts, of which the most significant included the Factory Act of 1833 and the Mines and Collieries Act of 1842, which prohibited the employment of children under the age of 9 in textile mills and children under 10 and women underground in mines, and the Factory Act of 1847, which established a ten-hour day for women and children. Slowly, the pulverizing conditions of industrial labor were relaxed, and its devastating impact on the working-class family was mitigated.

❧
ROBERT OWEN,
INDUSTRIAL REFORMER

The most sustained opposition to laissez-faire economics came from Robert Owen (1771–1858), industrialist, philanthropist, and founder of British socialism. "Under this system," he declared,

> there can be no true civilization; for by it all are trained civilly to oppose one another by their created opposition of interests. It is a low, vulgar, ignorant and inferior mode of conducting the affairs of society; and no permanent, general and substantial improvement can arise until it shall be superseded by a superior mode of forming character and creating wealth.[6]

The strength of Owen's attack was that it rejected the claim of laissez-faire economics to scientific status. Far from being, as its disciples argued, an objective conformity to the immutable laws of economics, it was only one possible means among many for ordering society, in fact a "low" and "inferior" one that created not wealth and harmony but misery and conflict. It was possible to do much, much better; and, being possible, it was morally obligatory.

Owen was born in a small Welsh town, the son of a saddler and ironmonger and a local farmer's daughter. At the age of 15 he migrated to Manchester. Here he shared rooms at one point with Robert Fulton, the inventor of the steamboat, whom he lent £100 out of his first savings. Shy and diffident, Owen was nonetheless manager of a cotton mill employing 500 people by the age of 19. In 1794 he became a partner in the Chorlton Twist Company, one of Manchester's principal textile firms, and five years later he persuaded his fellow partners to purchase the New Lanark spinning mills near Glasgow from the industrialist David Dale, whose daughter Caroline he married.

Thus far Owen's career resembled that of many of the other self-made industrialists of the era. But he was already a member of the Manchester Board of Health and keenly interested in reform. New Lanark, with its 2,000 employees, one-fourth of them children, was well run by the standards of the day, and David Dale was considered an enlightened employer. But Owen had plans that went far beyond Dale's kindly paternalism. He was horrified by child labor and refused to employ anyone under the age of 10. He rebuilt the workers' houses, cleaned and paved their streets, provided cheap coal for heating, and opened a company store that sold goods at cost.

As Owen's views grew more radical (and his profit margins lower), his business partners became restive. In 1813 he bought them out and formed a new company whose partners, including Jeremy Bentham, agreed to limit themselves to a 5 percent return. This enabled him to carry out the educational theories he had gradually developed, which he first spelled out in *A New View of Society* (1813). Owen argued that people were wholly the products of their environment and education; this alone, he said, made the difference between judges and the persons they sentenced to be hanged or deported. He built a large educational complex at New Lanark, characteristically named the Institute for the Formation of Character, the heart of which

was the first nursery school in Great Britain. Owen's theories anticipated much of progressive education. His school was run on the principle of play; no child was forced to do anything against his or her wishes, and no punishment was ever imposed. New Lanark became a mecca for reformers of every stripe and a major tourist attraction as well: between 1816 and 1826 nearly 20,000 visitors streamed through its gates.

Owen himself had meanwhile turned his interests to reform on a national level. His agitation was largely responsible for the passage of the early (though ineffective) Factory Act of 1819. By now he had become convinced of the radical injustice of contemporary society. Always a religious skeptic, he openly denounced the clergy from 1817, thus parting company with mainstream reformers such as William Wilberforce, who sought to mitigate the evils of the Industrial Revolution by an appeal to Christian ethics. Owen shocked a meeting of his fellow magnates by declaring that it would be better for the cotton industry to perish altogether than to be carried on under conditions that destroyed the health of its workers.

Between 1817 and 1820 Owen put forward a sweeping plan to reorganize society on the basis of small, cooperative communities. Each community would contain 500 to 2,000 members and would be both agriculturally and industrially self-sufficient. The major buildings, suitably spaced and landscaped, would be contained in a large rectangle, giving everyone access to light and air. Production for profit was prohibited; goods were to be distributed on the basis of labor performed, an anticipation of Marx's formula, "From each according to his abilities, to each according to his needs." Each community was to be completely self-governing. Owen suggested that such communities might be set up by private philanthropists, by parishes or counties seeking relief from the burden of their poor, or by associations of tradesmen, workers, and farmers who wished to escape "the evils of the present system." He envisioned such communities as establishing regional and national federations and, ultimately, a worldwide one. It was, he fervently believed, the social, economic, and political form of the future.

Owen traveled widely over the next several years in Ireland and on the Continent to promote his plan, and in 1825, convinced that the New World was a more fertile ground for his ideas than the Old, he set up the model community of New Harmony on a 20,000-acre site in Indiana. Despite initial enthusiasm, it collapsed after three years, having cost Owen himself the bulk of his fortune.

Owen returned to England in 1829 to find that in his absence he had become a hero to the nascent British labor movement, which, coming into the open after the repeal of the Combination Acts in 1824, had adopted his call for worker self-governance. Owen once more threw himself into reform agitation. He now saw that the potential for organizing a great federation of the producing classes actually existed in the trade union movement, and in October 1833 he launched what was to become the Grand National

Stedman Whitwell's conception of one of Robert Owen's utopian communities is a cross between a medieval fortress and a planned city, with its fanciful architecture and rigidly straight thoroughfares. The idyllic pastoral scene in which it is so incongruously set emphasizes its rejection of commerce and the corrupt world beyond. Such communities were designed as self-sufficient living systems for 500 to 2,000 persons. [Granger Collection]

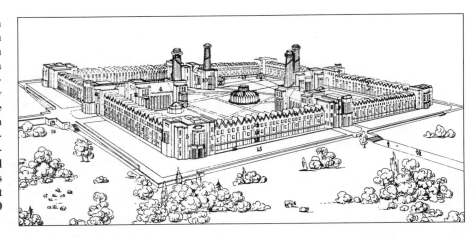

Consolidated Trades Union, the first nationwide confederation of labor in history. For a few heady months Owen was the acknowledged leader of the worker movement, and as local unions and associations rushed to join, the Grand Union claimed no fewer than 500,000 members by the spring of 1834. Thoroughly alarmed, employers initiated lockouts of workers who joined the Union, and the government cracked down as well, hastily deporting seven Dorset workers who went down in labor history as the Tolpuddle martyrs. What doomed the Grand Union, however, was the very speed at which it had grown, outstripping both its organizational resources and its agreed-on goals. Owen himself was disillusioned as the Union, far from evolving peacefully toward communal living, appeared bent on a bloody confrontation with capital. By late 1834 it had ceased to exist in all but name, and embittered labor militants turned their backs on socialism in Britain for the next 50 years.

Owen continued to travel and speak widely on behalf of his ideal communities (seven more were founded in Britain between 1825 and 1847). An exchange founded by the flannel weavers of Rochdale in 1844 became the basis of the modern cooperative movement, which still flourishes in the midwestern United States. Owen himself continued to see America as the best hope for the realization of his principles. All four of his sons became U.S. citizens; the eldest, Robert Dale Owen, served in Congress and had a distinguished career as an advocate of educational reform and women's rights. Active to the end, Owen addressed public meetings into his eighty-eighth year. Carried home to die in his native town, he spent the last day of his life planning the reform of education in the parish. The liberation of women was an abiding concern as well, and it is appropriate that the best summation of Owen's character and influence should have come from a pioneer feminist, Harriet Martineau. He was, she said,

always a gentle bore in regard to his dogmas and expectations; always palpably right in his descriptions of hu-

man misery; always thinking he had proved a thing when he had only asserted it in the force of his conviction; and always really meaning something more rational than he had actually expressed.[7]

The Population Explosion

An observer visiting our planet about 250 years ago and returning today would probably be struck by two things: first, by how many more human beings were inhabiting it, and second, by how densely concentrated they were in specific areas. The first of these phenomena goes popularly by the name of the population explosion; the second is called urbanization. Both of them are related to the Industrial Revolution, though they are by no means simply its result.

The human population of the earth was probably well under 10 million at the time of the neolithic revolution—the cultivation of plants and the domestication of animals—about 10,000 years ago. Agriculture made historical civilization possible, and civilization, from a very early point, was marked everywhere it developed by city-dwelling. Thus a continuous rise in population and a propensity to urbanization have been characteristic of civilization from the beginning. What has been unprecedented is the steady rise and concentration of population since about the mid-eighteenth century. In 1750 the world population was under 800 million. It reached 1 billion by about 1830, 2 billion in 1930, 3 billion in 1960, 4 billion in 1975, and 5 billion in 1986. At the same time, the number of persons engaged in agriculture has been steadily diminishing. In most places, at least 80 percent of the population was engaged in agriculture in 1750; in most industrialized nations today, the percentage is less than 5 percent.

These numbers suggest some obvious conclusions. The population explosion began before the advent of the Industrial Revolution, and it was well under way as a worldwide phenomenon long before the effects of industrialization reached beyond Europe. However, its continued rate of increase has unquestionably been sustained by the Industrial Revolution, including the continuous transformation in the productive capacity of agriculture known today as the "green revolution." Despite the fears of Malthus and of many neo-Malthusian commentators today, the food supply has kept pace with population growth; indeed, most of the industrially developed nations suffer at present from excess productive capacity, which has led them to warehouse enormous quantities of food and to subsidize farmers to keep large portions of their acreage fallow—a development that would no doubt have seemed like a world turned upside down to "Turnip" Townshend. It remains true that world nutritional levels are declining as a whole and that patches of famine have even broken out in places like the Sahel region of Africa, but it is quite clear that this is the result of unequal economic development and wealth and not of inadequate productive capacity as a whole.

Although there is much debate about the causes of the population explosion, it has everywhere been associated not with an increase in fertility but with a decrease in mortality. The difference may be summarized by a single statistical comparison. In 1700 only 475 of every 1,000 persons born live would reach the age of 20; by the midtwentieth century 960 would do so. The sharp decline in the death rate was essentially the result of a reduction in mortality from infectious diseases and (after the introduction of modern contraceptive devices) infanticide. At the same time, increases in agricultural capacity enabled more developed nations to sustain population growth. The population of England and Wales increased from 5.5 million to 18 million between 1700 and 1850, yet, thanks to the agricultural revolution, food production kept pace. Emigration and the settling of new lands also relieved population pressure; some 60 million Europeans left the continent between 1846 and 1924, mostly for the Western Hemisphere, the Siberian hinterland of Russia, and Australasia. Not all of this resulted in net population gain. White settlers in Australia completely exterminated the native population of the large island of Tasmania, and four-fifths of

the Maori population of New Zealand and three-fourths of the Indian population of the United States had been destroyed by the 1870s.

The first great surge in population was to a large extent a European phenomenon. In the absence of reliable data (only Sweden kept mortality statistics before 1800), we can only speculate that a cyclic remission in the incidence of microbic diseases combined with the increase in agricultural productivity in northern Europe generated sufficient thrust to trigger growth. Given the enormously high level of mortality, even a marginal increase in the survival rate could have had a significant impact on population.

Not until after 1850 was control of infectious diseases made possible by the introduction of hygiene and sanitation, particularly in the purification of water supplies and the disposal of waste. These two measures did (and continue to do) more to reduce mortality rates than any others, including the development of vaccines and so-called wonder drugs (the sulfa family in 1935 and antibiotics, most notably penicillin, in the 1940s). The concern for sanitation was at first provoked by the appallingly high mortality rates among workers in early industrial towns, but it was extended systematically only after the scientific connection between dirt and disease had been established by the research of Pasteur in France, Lister in Scotland, and Koch in Germany in the 1860s and 1870s. The results were dramatic. Typhoid deaths fell by more than 85 percent in England over a 35-year period, malaria by nearly as much in Italy over 20 years. It was not the ability to cure infectious disease but the simple reduction of exposure to it that accounted for this progress.

The population of Europe (including Russia) roughly quadrupled between 1650 and 1900, from about 100 to some 430 million, exclusive of emigration. From less than a fifth of the world's population in the mid-seventeenth century, Caucasians had become a third of it by the dawn of the twentieth. This was the high-water mark of European demographic advance. The introduction of Western standards of sanitation to other areas of the globe—essential to preserve the health of European colonizers in the heyday of imperialism—ignited a similar population explosion in Asia and Africa. By the 1980s non-Western peo-

POPULATION GROWTH, 1750–2000 (IN MILLIONS)

	1750	1800	1850	1900	1950	2000 (projected)
Asia (excluding Russia)	498	630	801	925	1,381	3,458
China	200	323	430	436	560	1,200
India and Pakistan	190	195	233	285	434	1,269
Africa	106	107	111	133	222	768
Europe (including Russia)	167	208	284	430	572	880
North America	2	7	26	82	166	354
South and Central America	16	24	38	74	162	638
Australasia and Pacific Islands	2	2	2	6	13	32
World	**791**	**978**	**1,262**	**1,650**	**2,515**	**6,296**

ples again accounted for approximately four-fifths of the world's population.

Perhaps the most significant and far-reaching effect of the Industrial Revolution was the urbanization of Western society. The city had occupied a distinctive place in the West since the Middle Ages. With its walls and towers, it stood off boldly from the surrounding countryside. No less important were the charters and privileges, often won by long struggle, that gave it a unique degree of self-government and political importance. The late medieval city-states of Italy and the free imperial cities of Germany were the finest flowering of this proudly independent civic culture, and neither the Renaissance nor the Reformation would have been conceivable without them. But the new state-centered global economies that had begun to develop by the late sixteenth century were inimical to them, and their decay was shortly evident. Machiavelli had written with admiration of the vigor and independence of the German cities of his time; 200 years later Frederick the Great could reply that a word from the emperor sufficed to control them.

The great eighteenth-century cities of London, Paris, and Amsterdam, with their worldwide commercial and financial connections, were prototypes of a new kind of city, the global metropolis. But such cities were still exceptional. With nearly a million inhabitants by 1800, London was ten times larger than the next British city and 100 times or more the size of the majority of Britain's towns, which still served as they had for hundreds of years primarily as markets for the local countryside. Although urbanization had reached 50 percent or more in some highly commercialized regions of the Low Countries, in Britain less than a third, and in France less than a quarter of the population lived in towns.

The Industrial Revolution changed all that. Factory towns like Huddersfield sprang up overnight near the coalfields and iron mines of Britain's industrial heartland. The pulse of manufacture turned regional marketing centers like Northampton into points on a nationwide distribution grid and old coastal towns like Bristol into international seaports. These in turn were now linked by a new mode of transportation ideally designed for hauling large quantities of goods, the steam locomotive. The British census of 1851 distinguished between manufacturing, mining, and hardware towns, regional centers and seaports, and spas and coastal resorts. Like everything else, the city was now a specialized category, a part of the universal division of labor.

And it was to the city that the rapidly growing British population now came. To London above all: from under a million inhabitants in 1800 it swelled to 2.5 million by mid-century and 4.5 million by the early 1900s. Half again as many people lived in its suburbs. No city of its size had ever been seen before in the world. No other British city approached it, but many others achieved rates of growth that were proportionally no less impressive; Sheffield, for example, grew from 111,000 to 285,000 over a 40-year period, Nottingham from 52,000 to 187,000. By 1851 half the population lived in urban areas, and that number would grow to three-quarters by 1900. The percentage of farm laborers declined correspondingly. In 1851 only two of every nine working Britons were engaged in agriculture; 30 years later that number was 2 of every 16; and on the eve of World War I fewer than two out of 25 members of the work force remained on the farm. As the British commentator Robert Vaughan wrote as early as 1843, "If any nation is to be lost or saved by the character of its great cities, our own is that nation."[8]

A river of humanity streams up this impossibly congested street in Gustave Doré's depiction of nineteenth-century London. The vividly gesturing porters and drivers suggest the vigor and tumult of a great commercial metropolis, and the Dickensian fat boy asleep on the pile of cargo in the center adds a touch of humor, but the picture recedes darkly into a sea of anonymous human faces and forms— an ominous comment on the mass society Doré already saw taking shape in his time. [Mansell Collection]

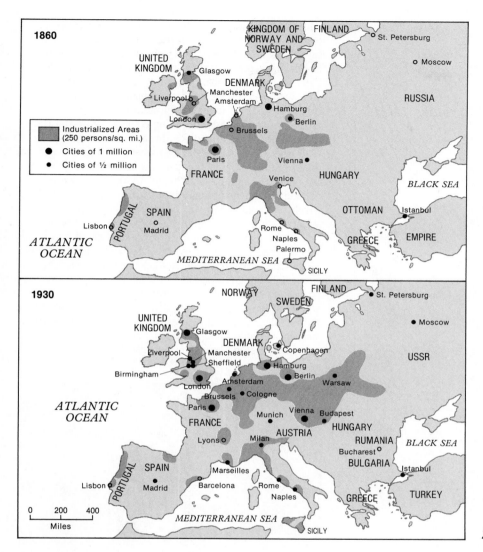

29.2 Urbanization in Europe

MANCHESTER, THE FACTORY TOWN

If any city might have served as a test case for Vaughan's assertion, it was industrial Manchester. Situated in Lancashire west of the Pennine mountains and connected to the port of Liverpool by the river Mersey, Manchester had long been a modestly prosperous regional marketing center whose population on the eve of the Industrial Revolution was about 17,000. The cotton industry transformed it in the 1770s and 1780s, and the grim, grime-blackened factories with their surrounding slums, which seemed to mushroom overnight, made it the prototype of the new industrial city. By the 1780s its population had grown to 40,000, by 1801 to 70,000, and by 1831 to 142,000: an eightfold increase in 80 years. Visitors commented on the new appearance of what had once been described as the "fairest" town in the region, and as late as 1784 it had seemed attractive to a French tourist. By 1814, however, a Prussian visitor noted the pall that hung over the town. "The cloud of coal vapor may be observed from afar. The houses are blackened by it. The river . . . is so filled with waste dye-stuffs that it resembles a dyer's vat." Another visitor proclaimed it "abominably filthy" and obnoxious to the senses: "the Steam Engine is pestiferous, the Dyehouses noisesome and offensive, and the water of the river as black as ink or the Stygian lake." The Frenchman Alexis de Tocqueville summed up contemporary opinion in 1835 when he wrote of Manchester, "Civilization works its miracles, and civilized man is turned back almost into a savage."

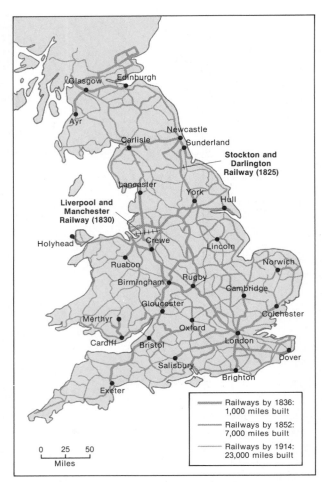

29.3 Railways in Great Britain, 1825–1914

Nowhere else was the confrontation between the classes more starkly posed. A local clergyman noted:

> There is no town in the world where the distance between the rich and the poor is so great. . . . There is far less *personal* communication between the master cotton spinner and his workmen . . . than there is between the Duke of Wellington and the humblest laborer on his estate.

When Friedrich Engels, the colleague of Karl Marx and himself a Manchester industrialist, tried to engage a "middle class gentleman" in conversation about the condition of the city's slums, he received the brusque reply, "And yet there is a great deal of money made here. Good morning, sir."[9] It was no doubt the existence of such attitudes that made an American visitor "thank Heaven that I am not a poor man with a family in England."

Such despair, as the reformer Francis Place noted, had turned large sections of the Manchester working class into potential revolutionaries. In 1817 a band of destitute weavers set out for London to protest their wages, only to be turned back by force. Two years later, in August 1819, troops fired point-blank into a mass rally at St. Peter's Field in the city, killing 11 persons and wounding some 400, including 113 women and children. It was the first battle of modern labor history, and the "Peterloo Massacre," as it was called in mocking comparison to the Battle of Waterloo, symbolized the threat of class war.

In the 1830s and 1840s Manchester often seemed on the verge of anarchy. Popular unrest exploded again with the economic slumps of 1829 and 1836. These were compounded by devastating outbreaks of typhoid and cholera, which were added to the normal toll of respiratory and intestinal diseases taken by air and water pollution and by the appalling lack of sanitation: it was estimated that there was one indoor toilet for every 212 inhabitants of the city. Moreover, despite its phenomenal growth, Manchester was still being governed as if it were a village. There was no regular police force, no provision for social services, and no attempt to regulate growth. Not until 1853, when the population, now in excess of 300,000, had begun to sprawl over into suburbs as chaotic as the center itself, was Manchester formally incorporated as a city.

Raw industrial waste was dumped directly into Manchester's river, the Irwell, whose still and blackened waters are captured in James Mudd's 1854 photograph. [The Manchester Public Libraries]

◉ Two Views of Manchester ◉

Two highly contrasting views of Manchester were provided by John Aikin and, some 40 years later, by James Kay.

The prodigious extension of the several branches of the Manchester manufactures has likewise greatly increased the business of several trades and manufactures connected with or dependent upon them. The making of paper at mills in the vicinity has been brought to great perfection, and now includes all kinds, from the strongest parcelling paper to the finest writing sorts, and that on which banker's bills are printed. To the ironmongers' shops, which are greatly increased of late, are generally annexed smithies, where many articles are made, even to nails. A considerable iron foundry is established in Salford, in which are cast most of the articles wanted in Manchester and its neighborhood. . . . The tin-plate workers have found additional employment in furnishing many articles for spinning machines; as have also the braziers in casting wheels for the motion-work of the rollers used in them; and the clockmakers in cutting them. . . . To this sketch of the progress of the trade of Manchester, it will be proper to subjoin some information respecting the condition and manners of its tradesmen, the gradual advances to opulence and luxury. . . . Within the last twenty or thirty years the vast increase of foreign trade has caused many of the Manchester manufactures to travel abroad. . . . And the town has now in every respect assumed the style and manners of one of the commercial capitals of Europe.

The township of Manchester chiefly consists of dense masses of houses, inhabited by the population engaged in the great manufactories of the cotton trade. Some of the central divisions are occupied by warehouses and shops, and a few streets by the dwellings of some of the more wealthy inhabitants; but the opulent merchants chiefly reside in the country. . . . Manchester, properly so called, is chiefly inhabited by shopkeepers and the laboring classes. . . . The rapid growth of the cotton manufacture has attracted hither operatives from every part of the kingdom, and Ireland has poured forth the most destitute of her hordes to supply the constantly increasing demand for labor. . . . The population . . . is crowded into one dense mass, in cottages separated by narrow, unpaved, and almost pestilential streets, in an atmosphere loaded with the smoke and exhalations of a large manufacturing city. . . . The houses . . . are too generally built back to back, having therefore only one outlet, no yard, no privy, and no receptacle for refuse. Consequently the narrow streets, in which mud and water stagnate, become the common receptacle of offal and ordure.

[These] districts . . . are inhabited by a turbulent population, which, rendered reckless by dissipation and want, . . . has frequently committed daring assaults on the liberty of the more peaceful portions of the working classes, and the most frightful devastations on the property of their masters. Machines have been broken, and factories gutted and burned at mid-day. . . . The police form . . . so weak a screen against the power of the mob, that popular violence is now, in almost every instance, controlled by the presence of a military force.

Sources: J. Aikin, *A Description of . . . Manchester* (London: John Stockdale, 1795), pp. 176–184 passim; J. Kay, *The Moral and Physical Condition of the Working Classes Employed in the Cotton Manufacture in Manchester,* 2d ed. (London: Cass, 1970), pp. 20–43 passim.

As the historian Asa Briggs explained:

All roads led to Manchester in the 1840s. It was the shock city of the age, and it was just as difficult to be **neutral about it as it was to be neutral about Chicago in the 1890s or Los Angeles in the 1930s.[10]**

Reformers focused on it and novelists such as Mrs. Gaskell in *Mary Barton* and Charles Dickens in *Hard*

Times depicted it, as Mrs. Gaskell said, to "give utterance to the agony" of the poor. Manchester's mill owners, protesting the unflattering portraits of themselves in such social novels, complained that their services to the nation in creating new wealth and new opportunity were unfairly disparaged. But whichever side one took in the great class debate, all agreed that Manchester was the crucible of an unprecedented phenomenon, as prodigal of energy and power as it was of misery and despair: the industrial city.

Ironically, Manchester itself had already passed the peak of its industrial importance. Its factories were obsolescent in comparison to newer models elsewhere, and its prosperity rested increasingly on its importance as a trading center. The Manchester Exchange, first opened to the public in 1809 and greatly expanded in 1838, was the largest brokerage facility in Europe. With economic maturity came at least the beginnings of civic responsibility. A local sanitary code, one of the first in the country, was drafted in 1845. The next year Manchester got its first public parks and a bequest to found what became the greatest of the early civic universities. In 1857 it held an exposition that drew more than 1.3 million visitors and led to the founding of an orchestra. By late Victorian times the city that had been described as "the entrance to hell" by the commander sent to quell its disturbances in 1839 had become respectable and almost staid.

The Spread of the Industrial Revolution

The rest of Europe was not economically idle while Britain was undergoing its great revolution. Population and production, both agricultural and industrial, was rising on the Continent between 1780 and 1830, and cities were growing as well. Arthur Young was impressed with the progressive nature of farming in parts of France on his travels in the 1780s, while German farmers introduced a variety of new crops into their country, including potatoes, beets, hops, and tobacco. Nor were industrial improvements confined to Britain. In France new methods of iron and steel production were developed, and Joseph-Marie Jacquard invented a silk loom. In Germany the world's first sugar-beet refinery began operation. Moreover, interest in the new developments in Britain was intense. British factories drew thousands of foreign visitors, and details about British inventions and techniques spread rapidly. In other respects, too, much of the infrastructure of the Industrial Revolution was in place on the Continent. Swiss and Dutch banking were highly developed, and the eighteenth century saw major improvements in roads, bridges, and harbors and extensive canal-building projects in northern France and Prussia. An observer looking for the likeliest

place for the Industrial Revolution to begin would probably have suggested the Netherlands in 1700 or France in 1750.

Exploitation and Resistance

Nonetheless, it was in Britain that the spark caught fire. In France a largely parasitic aristocracy drained off capital investment, a top-heavy governmental bureaucracy often crushed the initiative it was trying to promote, and the absence of a central banking system hampered the flow of credit. Germany suffered from its division into hundreds of tiny principalities and the chaos of internal customs barriers and road and river tolls that this engendered. The Dutch republic, the great commercial success of the seventeenth century, had exhausted itself in struggles with Louis XIV. In eastern Europe, including Prussia, Austria, and Russia, the persistence of serfdom hamstrung the movement of labor so critical to industrial development.

Thus it was not until about 1830 that industrialization per se—the use of power-driven machinery and the organization of labor and production in factories—came to the Continent. It appeared first along a belt that included the Low Countries, northeastern France and western Germany, and northern Italy, where the concentration of a skilled and urbanized work force, plentiful deposits of coal and iron, good road and river communications, and access to seaports were most favorable. Its spread, however, was notably uneven. It advanced most rapidly in Belgium, which profited not only from its commercial connections with the Netherlands but also from its rich deposits of coal, which the Dutch lacked.

France, despite its partial development, remained primarily a nation of small farmers throughout the nineteenth century; in 1881 its population was still two-thirds rural. A key variable was social attitude. French capital, long sheltered behind government subsidies and high tariffs, was far more timid and less entrepreneurial than its British counterpart; the Parisian banker Seillière was all too typical when, returning from a visit to an ironworks in 1836, he was reported "scared out of his wits by the investment going on." Large-scale financing was still a novelty in France, and much of it was introduced by foreign firms, such as the great international banking house of Rothschild. French industry, which specialized in luxury items—silks, carpets, tapestries, porcelain, fashion clothing, vintage wines, and brandies—was craft-oriented and not easily adaptable to mass production. A British visitor at a French industrial exhibit in 1802 remarked that there was not a single item of ordinary consumption on display.

In fact, it was British entrepreneurs who introduced the first power machines into France. William Wilkinson set up the first coke furnace in the country at Le Creusot in 1785; not until 1819 was another built. John Holker, who settled in France in the mid-eighteenth century, was almost single-handedly responsible for setting up a modernized textile industry in Rouen, and as late as 1840 it was observed that the majority of foremen in its plants were from Lancashire. The pace of British investment stepped up considerably in the 1820s. Aaron Manby and Daniel Manton set up a large ironworks plant at Charenton in 1827 that became an industrywide model, and the same partners introduced the first gas lighting in Paris two years later.

As in Britain, industrial expansion in France was at first largely confined to textile manufacture; cotton production doubled between 1830 and 1846. A railway building boom in the 1840s brought increased demand for iron and steel as well. At the same time, high tariffs and other barriers to trade began to give way before the increasingly direct control of the levers of government exercised by the commercial bourgeoisie and, especially, banking interests. The ascendancy of such interests was even more open after the revolution of 1848. In the two decades that followed, the French economy entered the industrial era, although many small-scale enterprises continued to flourish. The value of industrial production doubled, foreign trade trebled, internal commerce quadrupled, and railway mileage and total industrial horsepower quintupled.

As in Britain, industrialization was accompanied by ruthless exploitation of the work force, including women and children. Conditions in France had never been idyllic; in 1776 the bookbinders of Paris had struck to *win* a 14-hour day. But the regime of the factory intensified the worst abuses of the preindustrial workshop. An observer in the department of Nord described working conditions in 1826:

The greed of the manufacturers knows no limits; they sacrifice their workers to enrich themselves. They are not content with reducing these poor creatures to slavery by making them work in unhealthy workshops from which fresh air is excluded, from 5 A.M. to 8 P.M. (and sometimes 10 P.M.) in the summer, and from 6 A.M. to 9 P.M. in the winter; they force them to work a part of Sunday as well. From bed to work and from work to bed—that sums up the life of their victims. . . . They never have a moment for their private affairs; they always breathe a polluted atmosphere; for them the sun never shines.[11]

France, too, had its outbreaks of machine breaking, as at Viennes in 1819, and the industrial riots in Lyons in 1831 and 1834 paralleled those in Manchester. In Charles Fourier (1772–1837) it had its own utopian reformer as well. Fourier, a mathematician who had been head of the statistical office in Lyons during Napoleon's Hundred Days in 1815, proposed a network of small, self-contained communities called phalansteries similar to Owen's experiments at New Lanark and New Harmony; like Owen's, attempts to found such communities were short-lived. More modest goals of reform lagged behind the British example. Despite official concern about the high rate of physical rejection among French army conscripts, the only

industrial legislation passed in the first half of the nineteenth century was the Factory Law of 1841, which prohibited the employment of children under the age of 8 in factories.

The German Giant

The Napoleonic wars had been a watershed in German economic development. They had caused serious dislocation, but German industry, sheltering behind the Continental System, had benefited by a respite from competition with British products. They had also radically simplified Germany's political geography, reducing its hundreds of principalities to 39 states, of which an enlarged Prussia, now in control of the coalfields of the Ruhr and the Saar, the main river systems of the north, and the prosperous cities of the Rhineland and Westphalia, was the most important. The most important single item on the economic agenda was the removal of internal tolls and tariff barriers. Under Prussian leadership, a great free trade zone, the Zollverein, or Customs Union, had been established by 1834, embracing some 34 million people. This formed the basis for a sustained industrial expansion whose rate of growth was unsurpassed on the Continent.

Textiles and metallurgy flourished, and new mining techniques opened up the great coal deposits of the Ruhr. Railways were introduced in 1835, eight years after the French had built their first line; by 1850 there were twice as many miles of track in Germany as in France. Private and public capital were symbiotic in Germany to an extent unparalleled except in tiny Belgium, which was for all practical purposes an extension of Germany's western frontier. By the 1820s and 1830s the great industrial pioneers—Krupp, Stinnes, Mannesmann—had already made their mark. Major capital construction, such as railways, was financed by joint-stock ventures underwritten in part by government funds, and by the late 1840s the first state railways were built. By virtually every measure—population, production, urbanization—Germany was the most economically powerful nation on the Continent by 1850, and within a generation it would be challenging the lead of Britain itself.

Industrial Development After 1850

The wealth and productivity of the West increased exponentially after 1850. In part this increase was stimulated by the same factor that had fueled the economic boom of the sixteenth century: the discovery of gold in the New World. The discovery of gold in 1848 at Sutter's Mill in California (and sizable deposits later in Australia) added as much gold to the world's stocks in the next 20 years as in the preceding 350. As the new supply leveled off, the European economy contracted in the 1870s and 1880s,

Flags fly proudly over the Crystal Palace, built to house the world's first international industrial exhibition in London in 1851, while a festive bourgeois crowd takes its ease outside the monument. The palace itself, constructed of cast iron and glass, was a triumph of the new technology. [Bettmann Archive/BBC Hulton]

only to surge forward again with fresh supplies from South Africa and the Klondike. A second source of capital, particularly for Britain and, to a lesser extent, France, was the profits of trade and empire. The traffic of European commerce had constituted 75 percent of the world's trade by 1800. The volume of that trade now skyrocketed, increasing at least 1,200 percent between the 1840s and 1914.

Much of this trade was with the United States, which, already a major economic force by 1860, had become the world's leading industrial power by 1900. The industrialization of the United States marked the triumph of Alexander Hamilton's vision of an America founded on commercial and industrial prosperity over Thomas Jefferson's dream of a pastoral democracy based on independent yeomen. Numerous factors created an ideal climate for expansion: vast deposits of iron, coal, and petroleum, which, with a plenitude of gold and silver, provided an unsurpassed source of both raw materials and specie; a domestic labor and consumer market continually fed by immigration; and a political system firmly controlled by northern banking and industrial interests after the Civil War. By

1890 American iron and steel production had surpassed that of Britain; by 1900 the United States was making more steel than Britain and Germany combined; by 1910 its rail network was carrying a billion tons of freight per year. Huge trusts and monopolies dominated the economy, exploiting the cheap labor drawn primarily from southern and eastern Europe. When the United States Steel Corporation was organized in 1901, it was capitalized at $1.4 billion—a sum greater than the total wealth of the country a century before.

The Harnessing of Science

At the same time, new technological developments greatly extended the scope of the Industrial Revolution. A new age of steel resulted from the refining processes introduced by Sir Henry Bessemer in the 1850s, Werner von Siemen in the 1860s, and the cousins Percy Gilchrist and Sidney Thomas in the 1870s, which permitted both much higher temperatures in blast furnaces and the use of lower grades of ore. In the last three decades of the nineteenth century world steel production increased fiftyfold, as steel, both lighter and more tensile than iron, began to replace it everywhere in rail, ship, and building construction.

For the first time as well, applied science and engineering began to feed directly and systematically into technological development, creating new products, processes, and sources of energy. The age of the amateur inventor, the inspired tinkerer working alone, was rapidly drawing to a close; the American Thomas Alva Edison (1847–1931) was the last and greatest of the type. Large firms began to employ their own scientists and engineers, working directly on product development and production improvement. At the same time, the lag time between basic scientific discovery and its technological application was sharply diminished. As crucial to the nineteenth century as steam had been to the eighteenth was electricity, which as a natural phenomenon had attracted the interest of a host of scientists from Benjamin Franklin to Alessandro Volta. Following the conversion of mechanical motion into electric current by Michael Faraday in 1831, the American Samuel F. B. Morse produced the first practical telegraph in the 1840s. The telegraph was the beginning of a communications revolution that paralleled that of the steam locomotive in transportation. The telephone followed in 1879, and in 1896 the Italian Guglielmo Marconi adapted radio waves, discovered by Heinrich Hertz a decade before, to a new mass communications device.

The development of electromagnets, the electrolytic process, and the modern dynamo paved the way for the use of electricity in public places such as railways, docks, theaters, and markets, as well as in some factories. The incandescent light bulb, invented independently by Edison in America and Sir Joseph Swan in Britain, brought electrical illumination into the home and the office in the 1880s. In the same decade the steam turbine began to replace the old reciprocal-action engine. It was soon adapted to coal and then to the fuel source that would power the twentieth century, petroleum. The combustion engine followed in 1886, the airplane in 1903. By the early 1900s, European and American cities were lit electrically by huge generating systems, and their streets were crowded with trams and, increasingly, automobiles. At the same time, organic chemistry (the chemistry of carbon compounds), developed especially in Germany, produced a whole range of synthetic dyes, textiles, paints, and other products. No longer were humans confined to working, blending, crushing, and refining the given raw materials of nature; by manipulating the basic organic components of these materials, new, artificial products could be created.

By every measure—energy produced, goods and services distributed, miles of railway track and telegraph, telephone, and cable line laid—industrialization and the new, unprecedented standards of living it made possible increased by quantum leaps in Europe and the United States during the nineteenth century. But industrial development remained unevenly distributed geographically, and industrial wealth was even more unequally shared socially. Moreover, the disparity between worker and owner in Europe and the United States was greater still between colonizer and colonized as capital penetration and imperial expansion brought the mines, factories, technical processes, and industrial discipline of the West to the far corners of the globe. As this process intensified during the last decades of the century, social and political dislocation, and in some cases devastation, occurred on a scale that dwarfed the changes that had taken place in Britain and on the Continent. Only a few places outside Europe achieved industrialization on their own before 1900. Chief among them was North America, and particularly the United States, where, with a population nearly equal to that of France or Germany by 1850 and a role as the principal supplier of raw cotton to the European market, integration with the new industrial economy was a foregone conclusion. Beyond the North Atlantic trade circuit, however, only Argentina in the Western Hemisphere and Japan in the Far East had developed a significant industrial base on their own. As the twentieth century dawned, European economic and political hegemony in the world was at its zenith.

The Industrial Revolution and the population explosion that accompanied it both began, independently, in the middle of the eighteenth century, and both continue unabated the processes of change and upheaval that have transformed the globe. Population pressure spurred agricultural and industrial development, at first in Britain and then elsewhere, and success in sustaining an ever-expanding population generated the market and product demand that fed technological growth. When in 1851 Britain celebrated its role as the "workshop of the world" with a great international in- *dustrial exhibition at the Crystal Palace in London, the most important technological advance in humanity's recorded history was already an accomplished fact. The windmill and the waterwheel had given way to the steam engine, the domestic workshop to the factory, the horse and cart to the locomotive and the telegraph. Metals had replaced wood in the construction of harbors, bridges, buildings, and machinery, as coal had replaced it as the source of power. Petroleum in turn was soon to supplement and then largely replace coal, as petroleum itself, having succeeded animal and vegetable oils for lighting, was soon to be replaced by electricity. At the same time, the nature of work and of the social organization that revolved around it was no less radically transformed. The artisan who saw a job through from start to finish was replaced by the skilled factory worker who was confined to a single part of a process and integrated into a complex market structure that dictated the wages, conditions, and availability of employment. The family circle, the*

primary preindustrial work unit the world over, began to give way to an impersonal industrial discipline that reshaped and often shattered traditional relationships and modes of living at the most basic level. Inexorably, these changes radiated outward from their European origins to embrace the entire world and to create not merely a new global economy but a new global culture as well.

Notes

1.   K. Marx and F. Engels, *The Communist Manifesto* (New York: New York Labor News Co.), pp. 13-14. First published in 1848.

2.   A. M. Lambert, *The Making of the Dutch Landscape* (New York: Seminar Press, 1971), p. 195.

3.   A. Ure, *Philosophy of Manufactures* (New York: Kelley, 1967), p. 109. Originally printed in 1861.

4.   Ibid., p. 13.

5.   B. Disraeli, *Sybil, or, the Two Nations*. In *The Works of Benjamin Disraeli,* (New York: M. W. Dunne, 1904–1905), Book II, Chap. 5.

6.   R. Owen, *Life of R. Owen, by Himself* (London: Bell & Sons, 1920), pp. 122–123.

7.   M. Cole, *Robert Owen of New Lanark* (New York: Oxford University Press, 1953), p. 152. First published in 1857.

8.   A. Briggs, *Victorian Cities* (London: Odhams Books, 1965), p. 55.

9.   Ibid., p. 102.

10.   Ibid., pp. 92–93.

11.   W. O. Henderson, *The Industrial Revolution in Europe, 1815–1914* (Chicago: Quadrangle Books, 1961), p. 107.

Suggestions for Further Reading

Ashton, T. S. *The Industrial Revolution 1760–1830*. London: Oxford University Press, 1961.

Braudel, F. *Civilization and Capitalism*. 3 vols. London: Collins, 1979–1985.

Briggs, A. *Victorian Cities*. London: Odhams Books, 1965.

Chambers, J. D., and Mingay, G. E. *The Agricultural Revolution, 1750–1850*. New York: Schocken Books, 1966.

Clapham, J. H. *The Economic Development of France and Germany, 1815–1914*. Cambridge: Cambridge University Press, 1928.

Cipolla, C. M., ed. *The Industrial Revolution, 1700–1914*. London: Penguin Books, 1973.

Cole, M. *Robert Owen of New Lanark*. New York: Oxford University Press, 1953.

Crafts, N. F. R. *British Economic Growth During the Industrial Revolution*. New York: Oxford University Press, 1986.

Dennis, R. *English Industrial Cities of the Nineteenth Century*. Cambridge: Cambridge University Press, 1984.

Harrison, J. F. C. *The Early Victorians, 1832–1851*. New York: Praeger, 1971.

Henderson, W. O. *The Industrial Revolution in Europe*. Chicago: Quadrangle Books, 1961.

Hobsbawm, E. J. *Industry and Empire*. London: Penguin Books, 1970.

Landes, D. *The Unbound Prometheus: Technological Change and Industrial Development in Western Europe from the Seventeenth Century to the Present*. London: Cambridge University Press, 1969.

Mathias, P. *The First Industrial Nation: An Economic History of Britain, 1700–1914*. New York: Scribner, 1969.

McKeown, T. *The Modern Rise of Population*. New York: Academic Press, 1976.

Perkin, H. *The Origin of Modern English Society, 1780–1860*. London: Routledge & Kegan Paul, 1969.

Thompson, E. P. *The Making of the English Working Class*. Harmondsworth, England: Penguin Books, 1964.

Weber, A. F. *The Growth of Cities in the Nineteenth Century*. Ithaca, N.Y.: Cornell University Press, 1969.

Wilson, C., and Parker, G. *An Introduction to the Sources of European Economic History, 1500–1800*. London: Weidenfeld & Nicolson, 1977.

Zaretsky, E. *Capitalism, the Family, and Personal Life*. London: Pluto Press, 1976.

CHAPTER · 30

The Age of Ideology

In the wake of the French Revolution and the Napoleonic conquests, Europe experienced some of its most turbulent and troubled decades. The statesmen of the victorious allies, meeting at Vienna, sought to restore the Old Regime and to find an antidote to revolution. Their attempts foundered on the continuing demands for representative government, free competition, and social justice, often expressed through a fervent desire for national independence or unity. This was in turn linked to the wider cultural movement of Romanticism, which, in its emphasis on the free expressive powers of the individual, questioned traditional values and undermined traditional authority. By 1830 the fragile détente between the old noble elites and the increasingly powerful bourgeoisie had broken down, and a new wave of revolutionary disturbance swept Europe. This was only the precursor of the far more widespread and violent revolutions of 1848, in which the industrial proletariat, fired by the doctrines of socialism, played for the first time a leading role. These revolutions ended largely in apparent failure, but they confirmed the ascendancy of the bourgeoisie as the only barrier to the demand for a new social order.

Detail from Honoré Daumier's *Les Divorceuses*. At an impassioned meeting of women, one of many such during the Revolution of 1848, a feminist spokeswoman, probably Jeanne Derain, demands reform of the divorce laws. Daumier's portrayal typified the derisive reaction of the press to the new and disturbing phenomenon of feminist activism. [Musée Carnavalet/Photographie Bulloz]

The Legacy of Revolution

The American Revolution, in declaring all men born "free and equal," and the French Revolution, in asserting liberty, equality, and fraternity to be the goals of a just society, had propounded new political values to the Western world. Freedom or liberty, as the Old Regime understood these terms, meant not general rights applicable to all but franchises or exemptions enjoyed by particular individuals or corporate groups: the right of a town or locality to charge bridge, river, or road tolls, for example, or the exemption of the clergy from the jurisdiction of secular courts. The foundation of Old Regime society was not equality but hierarchy and subordination; its members were not citizens but subjects.

Even more foreign to the old order was the new revolutionary ideal of fraternity, the voluntary solidarity of all citizens with one another and their patriotic identification with the nation and, beyond borders, with all humanity. In America these principles had inspired the first nation ever created on the basis of citizen equality, though it still excluded women and blacks. The founding of the United States had in turn been a powerful inspiration to the French revolutionaries of 1789. But whereas the United States, an ocean away, had been able to export its revolution only by precept and example, the armies of the French republic, crossing the Alps and the Rhine, had brought theirs by force to much of Europe.

The champions of the old order, led by Britain—whose own revolutions of 1640 and 1688 had been the antecedents of both the French and American ones—had fought and finally defeated the armies of France. Long before Waterloo, however, the ideals of freedom and equality had been tempered both in revolutionary France and democratic America. In the United States the election of senators by state legislatures and of the president and vice-president by an electoral college represented a barrier to direct citizen control of the legislative and executive branches of government. In France a similar retreat was visible as early as 1791 in the distinction between active and passive citizens, and by the time of Napoleon, passive acquiescence in a dictatorial regime was the only function left to citizenship.

Despite this, the ideals of representative government and an egalitarian society remained alive. No longer could the rulers of Europe rely on obedience to authority based on the unquestioned subordination of subject populations to their natural masters, and political agitation everywhere now took the form of demands for basic rights and representation. Of no less importance were the values of freedom and equality to dissolve the traditional barriers to state centralization. The reduction of many particular and individual freedoms was a tedious and sometimes impossible task; the removal of a single set of generalized freedoms required only the suspension of constitutional guarantees by an emergency decree, as first Robespierre and then Napoleon had shown. Liberties extended to all and tyranny exerted over all lay uncomfortably close together as the legacy of the democratic revolutions of the late eighteenth century.

The demand for liberty and equality was often linked to another pervasive political sentiment of the early nineteenth century, nationalism. In its simplest terms, nationalism was a sense of cultural and political identity among a given people. Cultural identity was manifested in shared traditions and the possession of a common language; political identity was expressed in the association with or residency in a particular region or territory. The ultimate expression of a people's identity was the possession of a state.

Nationalism first expressed itself in Germany. The philosopher-critic Johann Gottfried von Herder (1744–1803) argued in the 1770s and 1780s that each people had its own organic development and must pursue its own individual destiny. This contention, like many other early manifestations of Romanticism, went counter to the Enlightenment ideal of a universal reason that would bring an identical justice to all. Herder urged his compatriots to look to their own cultural heritage for meaning and direction, rather than to an imported French model that could only be valid for the French, not the Germans.

Herder's work stimulated a cultural nationalism that was displayed in patriotic literature; research into German philology, folklore, and legend (including the famous collections of the brothers Jacob and Wilhelm Grimm); and attempts to define the German "soul." The Napoleonic conquests galvanized political nationalism in Germany as well. Johann Gottlieb Fichte (1762–1814) called on the people of Prussia to regenerate the lost honor of their fatherland, while his fellow Prussian, the philosopher Georg Wilhelm Friedrich Hegel (1770–1831), claimed that the historical dichotomy between the individual and the community was overcome in the unity of the modern nation-state. The highest manifestation of this unity was not, as Fichte expressed it, in the securing of particular benefits such as life, liberty, and personal well-being, as in the Anglo-American tradition, but in a noble patriotism and love of country.

This almost mystical sense of the union, or perhaps submersion of the individual in the nation, suggests that nationalism was not an essentially liberal cause, even though liberals often expressed their aspirations through it and used it as a vehicle of rebellion against the established order. In Russia nationalism would be invoked in the 1840s both by liberal Westernizers who wished to see Russia become modern and competitive by adopting western European values and institutions and by conservative Slavophiles who believed that Russia could fulfill its mes-

◉ The Mystique of Nationalism ◉

The nationalist fervor that Napoleon stimulated and that ultimately overthrew him was powerfully fed by the antirationalist elements that also produced the Romantic movement. In this passage, the French philosopher Joseph de Maistre (1753–1821), a conservative opponent of the Enlightenment and of the French Revolution, expresses his sense of the "national soul" inherent in all peoples.

Human reason left to its own resources is completely incapable not only of creating *but also of conserving any religious or political association*, because it can only give rise to disputes and because, to conduct himself well, man needs beliefs, not problems. . . . Religion and political dogmas, mingled and merged together, should together form a *general* or *national mind* sufficiently strong to repress the aberrations of the individual reason which is, of its nature, the mortal enemy of any association whatever because it gives birth only to divergent opinions. . . .

What is patriotism? It is this national mind of which I am speaking; it is individual *abnegation*. Faith and patriotism are the two great wonder-workers of the world. Both are divine. All their actions are miracles. Do not talk to them of scrutiny, choice, discussion, for they will say that you blaspheme. They know only two words, *submission* and *belief*; with these two levers, they raise the world. Their very errors are sublime. These two infants of heaven prove their origin to all by creating and conserving; and if they unite, join their forces, and together take possession of a nation, they exalt it, make it divine and increase its power a hundred-fold.

Source: J Lively, ed., *The Works of Joseph de Maistre* (New York: Macmillan, 1965), pp. 108–109 (modified slightly).

sianic destiny in the world only by remaining true to its traditions. In short, nationalism appealed across the spectrum from economic rationalists, who saw the nation-state as an efficient market mechanism, to religious enthusiasts, who saw it as a communal salvation; from Friedrich List, who dreamed of a tariff-free greater Germany, to Adam Mickiewicz, a Polish poet who identified the history of his nation with the passion of Christ and its longed-for independence as the resurrection.

The result of these conflicting ideologies—civil freedom against local and traditional rights, a society conceived as a body of equal citizens or as a patriotic community versus one conceived as a set of hierarchical orders—was a new and uncertain age in which, for the first time, the very basis of the social order was in dispute. In the aftermath of Napoleon's defeat, the victorious allied powers set about to restore the world they had known before 1789 as far as they could. Their attempts to do so, against not only the countervailing forces unleashed by the French and American revolutions but the as yet unreckoned ones of the Industrial Revolution, determined the course of Euro-

pean politics to the middle of the nineteenth century and beyond.

The Congress of Vienna

The major European powers met in Vienna in September 1814 to try to untangle 20 years of war and revolution. It was the first such general congress of the powers since the one that had settled the Thirty Years' War at Westphalia in 1648. Every state on the Continent sent representatives, including defunct members of the old Holy Roman Empire seeking reinstatement. But only five parties really counted—Austria, Britain, Prussia, Russia, and France, represented, respectively, by Prince Metternich, Viscount Castlereagh, Baron Hardenberg, Tsar Alexander I (the only sovereign taking direct part in the proceedings), and the ubiquitous Baron Talleyrand, who after deserting Napoleon had brokered the return of the Bourbon dynasty to France.

The Congress of Vienna, which redrew the map of Europe in the wake of the Napoleonic era. Metternich stands in the left foreground; Castlereagh is seated in the center with his legs crossed; Talleyrand is seated to the right with his right arm on the table. [Photographie Bulloz]

Collective Security

What the allies wanted at Vienna, broadly speaking, was to restore the old order of kingship and aristocracy, to prevent the domination of Europe by any single state, and to contain the virus of revolution wherever it might spread. To accomplish this, they created a structure of collective security that was essentially a classical balance-of-power system tinctured by the agreement to suppress all forms of radical activity. This meant that collective security would be brought to bear not only against states that threatened the stability of the system by external action but also against those whose internal stability was threatened by domestic discontent.

The framework for this sytem was already in place in the wartime coalition that had defeated Napoleon; formalized as the Quadruple Alliance in 1815 and extended, after a suitable period of probation, to include France in 1818, it formed the basis of the so-called Concert of Europe, which kept the peace of the Continent, or at any rate took the credit for doing so, down to 1914. The novelty of the system was the recognition that war, because it had the potential to unleash revolution, had become too dangerous a luxury for Europe to afford. Alexander I, for whom it represented not merely a political instrument but a spiritual compact, managed to bully his fellow sovereigns (with the exception of the pope, the Turkish sultan, and the regent of Britain) into signing a "holy alliance" against war and for Christian concord. On a more mundane level, Prince Metternich conceived it as a sanction to intervene in the affairs of any state threatened by revolution. The British were suspicious of the uses to which such an unlimited warrant might be put, however. Reverting to a lone hand after years of marshaling coalitions on the Continent, they refused to commit themselves to any joint command. Prussia, too, was skeptical of any rapprochement between its two powerful eastern neighbors, Austria and Russia.

The Diplomatic Settlement

The strains among the allies at Vienna came into the open over the Polish-Saxon question, which nearly torpedoed the congress. Napoleon had taken away almost all the territory gained by Austria and Prussia in the partitioning of Poland to create a satellite entity, the Grand Duchy of Warsaw. Its collapse with the defeat of his empire again left a power vacuum in eastern Europe. Alexander I insisted on restoring the original prepartition Poland, with himself as king. To win Prussia's support, he offered to cede it Saxony, which had become vulnerable as the last German state to desert Napoleon. Metternich, appalled, sought out Castlereagh and Talleyrand, who agreed to resist the Russian plan, if necessary by force.

The Polish-Saxon question was finally settled by compromise. Alexander received a reduced "congress" Poland that was roughly equivalent to Napoleon's Grand Duchy, and Prussia was compensated with two-fifths of Saxony. But the whole episode pointed up the inherent contradiction of the congress system, which presupposed lasting cooperation between historical rivals whose interests were fundamentally opposed.

The Congress of Vienna did, however, decide a wide range of issues, which set the diplomatic framework of the nineteenth century. Uppermost in the minds of the allies was the creation of buffer zones, primarily against France but more subtly against Russia as well, whose steady westward encroachment had become a major concern over the preceding 100 years. A new Belgo-Dutch kingdom of the Netherlands was erected as a barrier on France's northern frontier, and Prussia was given a solid bloc of territory along the Rhine to perform a similar function. With the acquisition of the Rhineland—which, with the Saxon strip, made it the largest territorial gainer at the congress—Prussia now overarched all of northern Germany, facing France to the west and Russia to the east. Austria was reinstalled in northern Italy and expanded

***30.1** Europe After the Congress of Vienna (1815)*

along the Dalmatian coast, where, from a southern vantage, it could serve as a check against Russian designs on Turkey and French ones on Italy. The British, following the policy they had adopted at the Peace of Utrecht a century before, sought no territory on the Continent but added several key islands and stations in the West Indies and the Far East to their unrivaled sea empire. They now controlled the Mediterranean through Gibraltar, Malta, and the Ionian islands, the South Atlantic through the West Indies and the Cape of Good Hope, and the Indian Ocean and the South China Sea through Ceylon, Mauritius, and Singapore. Bestriding the major ocean arteries of the world, they were uniquely situated to exploit the productive expansion of the Industrial Revolution and to enjoy a century of extraordinary world dominion.

The thorniest single issue facing the powers was the settlement of Germany. Beset by the rival demands of nationalists who dreamed of a unified German state and the claimants of liquidated states who wanted a return to the benevolent chaos of the Holy Roman Empire, they chose to preserve the states carved from the empire by Napoleon, loosely linked in a federation whose main function was to keep the smaller states from gravitating toward France. It was a pragmatic solution that left Prussia in a position of greatly augmented influence and postponed for 50 years the final confrontation between Prussia and Austria for control of Germany.

France itself was treated leniently in an attempt to shore up the restored Bourbon monarchy, whose representative, Talleyrand, was treated nearly as a partner in the peacemaking. The dramatic return of Napoleon from Elba and the ensuing Hundred Days compelled the allies to harsher sanctions. The Congress took away some snippets of French territory, imposed an indemnity of 700 million francs, and posted an army of occupation in France for three years. Nevertheless, France's treatment was exceedingly lenient. Events bore out the wisdom of the allies' moderation; the age of French aggression and French preponderance in Europe was over.

By their lights, the diplomats at Vienna accomplished a good deal. They cleared away the debris of a generation of war and converted a wartime coalition into a permanent instrument for maintaining order. The instrument was flawed, and the values it sought to defend—monarchy, aristocracy, and hereditary privilege—were already in eclipse, but the goal of regulating interstate conflict was a first step toward the recognition of the historical obsolescence of war.

What the men at Vienna were unwilling to recognize was the change of their own time. Formed under the Old Regime, their conception of society was still patriarchal; in the words of the Holy Alliance, the sovereigns of Europe were "as fathers of families towards their subjects and armies." In redrawing the map of the Continent, they acted in the high-handed manner of old, parceling out peoples and territories solely according to the abstract scales

of power. It would never have occurred to them to ask the Belgians whether they wanted to be under the Dutch, the Venetians under the Austrians, or the Poles under Russia. They rightly calculated that nationalism, the new sentiment that a land belonged to its people and not to its ruler, was incompatible with the preservation of the existing order; they wrongly concluded that they could contain it with treaties, armies, and spies.

Reaction and Revolution

The notion of collective security against revolution—what came to be known as the Congress System—was the brainchild of Prince Klemens von Metternich (1773–1859), who as foreign minister of Austria from 1809 to 1848 put his stamp on the diplomacy of the age. Metternich envisioned the system operating through periodic meetings of the great powers that by monitoring developments in each state could scotch any activity that threatened either internal or external stability. As the Troppau Protocol of 1820 put it,

> **States which have undergone a change of government due to revolution, the results of which threaten other states, *ipso facto* cease to be members of the European alliance. . . . If owing to such alterations immediate danger threatens other states, the powers bind themselves, by peaceful means, or if need be by arms to bring back the guilty state into the bosom of the Great Alliance.**

The opportunity soon arose to test the system. The restored regimes in Spain and the Kingdom of the Two Sicilies were violently unpopular. The Spanish had waged a heroic resistance against Napoleon on behalf of the Bourbon regime to which, after a century, they had transferred their loyalty. When King Ferdinand VII returned to Madrid in 1814 after a six-year exile, he was welcomed rapturously. But enthusiasm for the symbol of Spanish monarchy was not the same as a desire to turn back the clock. The Enlightenment had penetrated Spain, particularly during the reign of Charles III (1759–1788), and the Napoleonic administration, however despised on nationalist grounds, had left its mark in the form of greater tolerance and bureaucratic efficiency. An elected national body, the Cortes, meeting in the free city of Cadiz in 1812, had adopted a liberal constitution on the basis of which Ferdinand had been recalled. But the king swiftly dissolved the Cortes, nullified its acts, scrapped its constitution, and threw its chief leaders and supporters into jail. Restoring the Inquisition and the lands of the church and the aristocracy in full, he proclaimed a return to divine right absolutism. It was a formula for revolution. The economy languished; Seville and Cadiz were full of merchants ruined by the long

◉ Metternich's Plea for the Old Order ◉

Count Metternich, the preeminent figure in European politics between 1815 and 1848, here forcefully expresses his conservative credo.

Drag through the mud the name of God and the powers instituted by his divine decrees, and the revolution will be prepared! Speak of a social contract, and the revolution is accomplished! The revolution was already completed in the palace of kings, in the drawing-rooms and boudoirs of certain cities, while among the great mass of the people it was still only in a state of preparation. . . .

The first and greatest concern for the immense majority of every nation is the stability of the laws, and their uninterrupted action—never their change. Therefore let the governments govern, let them maintain the groundwork of their institutions, both ancient and modern; for if it is at all times dangerous to touch them, it certainly would not now, in the general confusion, be wise to do so.

Source: K. von Metternich, *Memoirs*, trans. Mrs. A. Napier, vol. 3 (London: Richard Bentley & Son, 1881), pp. 461, 474.

---

wars and the revolts of the American colonies, against which the regime seemed helpless to respond. Discontent spread to the military, and secret societies sprang up in defiance of the censorship. Rebellion broke out in early 1820, and Ferdinand, made a virtual prisoner, was compelled to summon the Cortes and to reinstate the constitution of 1812.

Portugal, Spain's Iberian neighbor, was soon touched by an uprising as well when rebels demanded the return of King John VI, who was still in exile in Brazil, but also a constitutional government. At the same time, a series of revolts and disturbances broke out on the Italian peninsula aimed against both Spanish and Austrian rule. They began in Naples, where King Ferdinand I, like his nephew Ferdinand VII in Spain, had abrogated reforms and alienated both the army and the bourgeoisie. Sardinia next attempted to depose its reactionary monarch, Victor Emmanuel I, and there were threats of rebellion in the Papal States as well.

The Overthrow of Ottoman Rule in Greece

A more complex—and far more broadly based—rebellion broke out in Greece in 1821, which soon became a revolution against 3½ centuries of Ottoman rule. Within the space of a year, insurrection had sparked across the entire Mediterranean coast from Cape Finisterre to the eastern Aegean.

Metternich called for action but met a divided response. The British dissented from the Troppau Protocol, and the French, unwilling to serve as the agent of Austrian interests in Italy, sat idle. Metternich was more successful with Prussia and Russia, with whose assent an Austrian army descended on Italy and speedily crushed the rebellions in Naples and Sardinia. France was more amenable to action in Spain, where it was anxious to restore its influence, and when the revolutionary government in Madrid rejected an ultimatum to modify its reforms in 1823, it sent troops across the Pyrenees to restore the king it had deposed 15 years before. Despite promises of clemency, Ferdinand VII carried out a bloody purge and plunged Spain back into a civil and clerical autocracy that left a bitter legacy.

The case of Greece was more complicated. The Ottoman Empire had revived in the seventeenth century to make a last great assault on Europe, only to be driven back from the walls of Vienna and deep into the Danube basin (see Chapter 19). Battered by the southward expansion of Russia in the eighteenth century, it now faced revolt among the subject peoples within its own borders. The Serbians had risen in 1804 in the beginnings of a struggle for nationhood that was to have profound consequences for all of Europe. Their rebellion aroused little interest, but when the Greeks of the southern Peloponnesus raised the flag of independence in 1821, the Continent took sudden notice. The so-called Phanariot Greeks of Constantinople had become effectively the governors of Turkey's Balkan provinces, where their suppression of native culture had been bitterly resented and had indeed contributed to the Serbian rebellion. Greek merchants dominated the trade of the eastern Mediterranean, sometimes flying a Russian flag. At the same time, the Greeks were engaged in a great revival of their own culture, largely dormant since the conquest of Crete in 1669. The Society of Friends, a secret organization supported by Alexander I (whose horror of rebellions stopped short at those that advanced Russian interests), engineered an uprising after a number of false starts.

Under heavy pressure from his alliance partners, Alexander withdrew his support from the rebels, and the powers waited for the Greek insurrection to burn itself out. But they failed to take into account both the resolve of the Greeks and a new force that the very idea of collective security had helped create—public opinion. A new classical revival had begun in the mid-eighteenth century, spurred chiefly by German scholars and archaeologists, that merged with the nascent Romantic movement to produce a fascination with things Greek. The British government paid £35,000 to acquire the friezes of the Parthenon known as the Elgin marbles, and the French installed the Venus de Milo in the Louvre. "We are all Greeks," the poet Shelley enthused, and his great Romantic contemporary, Lord Byron, putting the fervor of many thousands of "philhellenes" (lovers of Greece) into practice, fought and died beside the Greek rebels. Committees to support the Greek cause sprang up spontaneously all over western Europe and the United States, furnishing desperately needed funds and supplies. In the face of this, the calculated indifference of the powers could not be kept up. Britain, France, and Russia attempted to impose an armistice on Turkey in 1827 and, that failing, sent out a squadron that first blockaded and then destroyed the Turkish fleet at Navarino in the Peloponnesus. King George IV of Britain apologized to the sultan for this attack on "an ancient ally," but Russia reverted to its open support of the Greeks and soon declared war. The Turks, galvanized by new nationalist and religious energies of their own, put up surprising resistance but were compelled to recognize Greek independence by the London Protocol of 1830. Two German princes refused the crown of the new kingdom before it was finally accepted by Otto, the son of King Ludwig of Bavaria, in 1832.

The Troubled 1820s

The revolt of the Greeks was the political cause célèbre of the 1820s. It gave heart to nationalist movements everywhere, although it showed too that such movements could not hope to succeed merely on the basis of elite elements such as the bureaucracy and the officer corps but required mass support. It left the Congress System in ruins as well. The spectacle of an allied fleet playing midwife to a revolutionary state demonstrated that Metternich's dream of a perpetual status quo could not withstand a united demand for change and that in a crisis each power would consult its own interest first and its treaty obligations second. What emerged was a looser, more informal understanding, the Concert of Europe, by which the great powers would attempt to resolve their major differences and attempt to avoid general war.

While only Russia among the major powers underwent an actual rebellion within its borders between 1815 and 1830—the Decembrist revolt of 1825—all experienced significant unrest. We have touched on the Luddite attacks and urban agitation in Britain. In retrospect, it was remarkable that unrest was contained as well as it was in Britain, given the unprecedented social transformation of the Industrial Revolution, whose maximum impact was being felt in these years. It seemed serious enough, however, to the Tory government of Lord Liverpool. In the wake of the Peterloo Massacre, the government passed a series of repressive measures through Parliament, the Six Acts, which suppressed public meetings, curbed the press, and speeded up procedures for prosecuting offenders against the public order. Waterloo's hero, the duke of Wellington, expressed the hope that Britain's example of firmness would be followed by others so that the world might escape "the universal revolution which seems to menace us all." Three months later, in February 1820, a plot to assassinate the entire cabinet and seize control

The poet Byron in Greek dress. His struggle on behalf of Greek independence symbolized the Romantic quest for freedom and the recovery of the heroic ideal. [National Portrait Gallery, London]

of the government was "discovered," although the conspirators' arms had actually been supplied by the government. It was not until the late 1820s that a less hysterical atmosphere began to prevail.

In France, Louis XVIII (1814–1824) sought a middle ground between the reactionary Ultraroyalist party, which wanted to turn the clock back literally to 1789, and the ex-Bonapartists and republicans, whom Louis knew he would have to conciliate to stabilize his regime. He offered a charter that in essence preserved the structure of the Napoleonic code and set up a bicameral assembly that could veto royal legislation. The Hundred Days brought a violent Ultra reaction in which hundreds of suspected Jacobin and Bonapartist sympathizers were massacred. No sooner had Louis regained a measure of control than the assassination in 1820 of the duke of Berry, the heir to the throne, set off a new wave of reaction. As Louis' reign ebbed, power passed to his intransigent brother, the count of Artois, who succeeded him as Charles X (1824–1830). A new spate of legislation enacted the program of the Ultras. The Law of Indemnity (1825) compensated nobles who had lost their estates during the revolution by devaluing government bonds held by the bourgeoisie, and the Law of Sacrilege, passed in the same year, imposed the death penalty for the theft of sacred objects and other vaguely defined offenses against the church. When members of the Jesuit order, still officially banned in France, appeared openly in Catholic schools, liberals concluded that they were now directing the government.

Despite its greatly strengthened geopolitical situation, Prussia was content to allow Metternich to play ideological policeman to the rest of Germany, a role he assumed with relish. By the Carlsbad Decrees of 1819, Metternich suppressed the student societies that had taken up the aspirations for national unity thwarted at the Congress of Vienna. These societies were in turn the successors of the quasi-military gymnastic clubs founded by Friedrich Ludwig Jahn (1778–1852) during the Napoleonic wars, whose members, wearing gray-shirted uniforms and imbued with a hatred of "foreign" (including Jewish) influence, strikingly foreshadowed elements of Nazi ideology and practice. Student groups that gathered at Wartburg Castle near Eisenach to commemorate the tricentennial of Luther's Ninety-five Theses in 1817 toasted unity and freedom but also burned conservative and antinationalist books after a torchlight procession, a rather dubious way to protest censorship.

In Austria itself Metternich's chief concern was to suppress nationalist stirrings among the many minority groups that comprised the Habsburg empire. The very name *Austria* had been adopted no less recently than 1804 to describe the patrimonial lands of the emperor, and whereas the yearning for national identity might encourage a sense of unity in such regions as Germany and Italy and strengthen it in states such as Britain, France, or Spain already established on the basis of a common language and

heritage, it could only foster division and separatism in such an amalgam of peoples and tongues as the Habsburg state represented. By skillfully playing rival minorities off against one another, Metternich delayed his day of reckoning for more than 30 years; by failing to provide a genuine accommodation for nationalist aspirations within the framework of the empire, he ensured that that day would come.

Russia was still by far the most autocratic of all European states. Like Catherine the Great, the eccentric Alexander I (1801–1825) began his reign with a flourish of reform. Men of all classes were legally entitled to hold land for the first time, and masters were encouraged to free their serfs. New schools were founded, including six universities, and new ideas entered the country, particularly through the medium of the Freemasons and other secret fraternities, much in vogue at the time. Leo Tolstoy has left a vivid picture of liberal ferment among the early nineteenth century urban aristocracy in his novel *War and Peace* (1869). The reforming Count Speransky even drafted plans for a system of representative bodies culminating in a national assembly, though without real legislative power. But the Napoleonic invasions blew away these fair hopes like petals before a storm, and a chastened Alexander, regarding his country's disaster as a providential judgment, lapsed into a reactionary mysticism that made him Metternich's most zealous if not always most reliable ally in the war against reform.

Frustrated liberal aspirations among the officer corps in conjunction with a succession crisis in December 1825 provoked Russia's first attempt at revolution. Alexander's heir, the Grand Duke Constantine, had secretly resigned his claim to the throne in favor of his brother Nicholas, but when the tsar died suddenly, each brother proclaimed the other. In the resulting chaos, some of the disaffected officers raised the standard of "Constantine and constitution," which some of the soldiers apparently thought referred to the tsar and his wife.

Whatever the comic overtones of the Decembrist uprising, it was ruthlessly suppressed. Hundreds were imprisoned or exiled, and five officers were executed; these officers' courageous bearing made them symbols of resistance under the dreary and despotic reign of Nicholas I (1825–1855). The latent genius of the Russian people flowered in an extraordinary literary generation that included the poets Alexander Pushkin (1799–1837) and Mikhail Lermontov (1814–1841) and the novelists Nikolai Gogol (1809–1852) and Ivan Turgenev (1818–1883). Gogol in particular caught the spirit of Nicholas' Russia in his comic novel *Dead Souls* and his play *The Inspector General*, while the young Feodor Dostoevsky (1821–1881), later one of the century's greatest novelists, began his career by facing a mock firing squad in Siberia for allegedly "socialist" activities. Others, like the journalist Alexander Herzen (1812–1870), sought haven abroad, thus initiating the long tradition of the Russian exile.

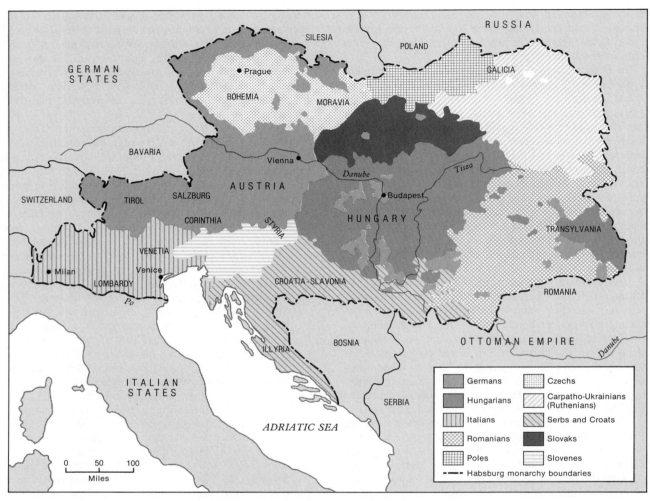

30.2 Ethnic Composition of the Austro-Hungarian Empire

Liberalism

The term most frequently used to describe the varied forms of opposition to the Restoration regimes was *liberalism*, a word that has and continues to bear many different and sometimes contradictory meanings. The origins of liberalism go back to the British philosopher and political theorist John Locke (see Chapter 25), who argued for the supremacy of society over the state or, in practical terms, the control of the Stuart monarchy by the propertied classes. Adam Smith drew out the implications of Locke's argument for the freedom of commerce from state interference, or what the modern neoliberal philosopher Robert Nozick has called "capitalist acts between consenting adults." Having picked up much of the freight of the Enlightenment as well, liberalism by the early nineteenth century had come to stand broadly for free trade in a laissez-faire marketplace, the limitation of state authority by written constitutions, secular education, and national self-determination. In a general sense, nineteenth-century liberalism may be said to have represented the interests of capitalist enterprise and the aspirations of the commercial bourgeoisie. This was how Karl Marx took it; for him liberalism was simply the ideology of the bourgeoisie. But it was merged as well with a profound change in cultural sensibility, Romanticism, to form a complex and potent mixture whose appeal extended far beyond narrow economic interests.

Romanticism and the Quest for Identity

Romanticism may be viewed in many ways. The term *Romantic* is often contrasted to the term *classical* to express a mood or movement of art, thought, and cultural sensibility in which feeling and imagination shape form instead of the other way around and in which the expression of individual personality is valued above conformity to established norms of taste and style. As such, it is a tendency that may be observed in many cultures and periods, particularly in the arts.

The Dethronement of Tradition

Historically, the Romantic movement that began in the West in the mid-eighteenth century and continues as its dominant cultural style to the present day represented a final emancipation from the authority of ancient Greece and Rome. That legacy lay heavily over the medieval period in terms of its religion (Christianity, the faith of the late Roman Empire), its law (largely based on the Code of Justinian, itself an adaptation of the Roman civil code), and its thought (influenced first by Aristotle and later by Plato and his followers). So deeply was the culture of the West permeated by the influence of antiquity that even the reaction against scholastic thought and institutions that we call the Renaissance took the form of a renewal of the classical tradition. A similar movement on a smaller scale took place with the classical revival that began in the mid-eighteenth century. This time, however, the reinterpretation of the Greco-Roman tradition took place in the context of a far wider shift in the perspective of Western culture.

Many things contributed to this development. The Renaissance emphasis on the value of the individual and the Reformation idea of personal responsibility for one's own salvation (and one's ethical conduct in the world) laid the first basis for this shift. The scientific revolution, with its revolt against the cosmogony of the ancient and medieval worlds and the traditional Christianity that rested on it, was a second important step. By the end of the seventeenth century, in the debate between the Ancients and the Moderns (see Chapter 23), it was being confidently asserted for the first time that the modern world was equal if not superior to the ancient one, and by the mid-eighteenth, the doctrine of progress, with its assumption of the inferiority of the past and the indefinite improvement if not ultimate perfectibility of the species, had become widely prevalent. The French Revolution was the political expression of this hope, and it persisted in the utopian schemes of Owen, Fourier, and others.

The result of all this was a new view of human possibility. At the same time, however, the embarkation on an uncertain and uncharted future provoked deep anxiety. The past was no longer the model for the present but merely a record of progress to date; culture was not to be inherited but to be created. For the first time the West took on the burden of originality, of the new and avant-garde, that has characterized its culture ever since. Each generation, each decade, was to be reckoned in terms of its difference from its predecessors. The demand for progress and the measure of progress (whether in art, science, politics, or fashion) by originality speeded up the experience of time no less than the factory whistle, the locomotive, or the newspaper.

The Romantic Hero

The dethronement of tradition and the quest for the new put extraordinary emphasis on the role of the individual. A single person, properly placed, could change the destiny of a nation; a single idea could create a new product or industry or a new artistic form: thus the philosophes exalted the enlightened despot; thus the solitary inventor, like Edison, became a hero; and thus too the lonely artist in his garret or lost amid the wilds of nature became the very symbol of the creative process. Yet these images betrayed pathos too. The great political figure, like Napoleon, might suffer ignominy and exile; the inventor might fail; the starving artist might die in obscurity. Emancipated from tradition, society was now dependent on genius; and genius, wayward and unpredictable, was to be found only in the individual.

What emerged was a confidence in the collective destiny of Western culture—whether in the form of nation building, utopian experiment, missionary zeal, or imperial expansion—that rested paradoxically on the talent and initiative of the isolated individual. The cultural expression of this paradox was Romanticism. The Romantic hero was typically a sensitive, misunderstood young man (much less often a woman) in revolt against his surroundings or a man of destiny boldly seeking knowledge and power no matter what the cost. In the former type, Romanticism portrayed the sense of anxiety and vulnerability that beset the individual in a time of change; in the latter, the vaunting self-confidence of a society that had laid claim to the secrets of nature and would soon take the dominion of the earth.

❦ GOETHE AND THE ROMANTIC SPIRIT

Both kinds of heroes were represented in the work of the great German poet and dramatist Johann Wolfgang von Goethe (1749–1832), whose career spanned the last decades of the Enlightenment and the first ones of Romanticism. Goethe was the son of a town councillor of Frankfurt. He studied and briefly practiced law before turning to a literary career, which by 1775 was prominent enough to secure him an invitation from the young duke of Weimar, Karl August, who had chosen him to be the star of what he hoped to make the most brilliant court in Europe.

This depiction of the great Goethe with his wife and children is much more than a fancy-dress family portrait. By situating himself in a pastoral setting typical of eighteenth-century aristocratic portraits, Goethe symbolizes the emergent power of his own bourgeois class and its appropriation of the political and material source of aristocratic power, the land. At the same time, the towering ruin symbolizes Romantic aspiration and hence Goethe's personal claim to status as an artist. This oil painting is by J. K. Seekatz. [Freies Deutsches Hochstift—Frankfurt am Main]

Arriving with little thought except to gain a temporary sinecure that would free him for writing, Goethe was to remain at Weimar, with the exception of a critical two-year sojourn in Italy in 1786–1788, for the rest of his life.

Goethe was not merely the founding figure of modern German literature but also an artist and natural scientist of distinction. Like Rousseau, he was a keen student of botany, and he put forward an elaborate theory of color in opposition to Newton's. Science in his day had not yet become professionalized, and amateurs continued to dominate it, such as the minister Joseph Priestley, who discovered oxygen, and William Herschel, the organist-astronomer who found Uranus and Neptune, the first

planets discovered since antiquity. Goethe's scientific pursuits, however, were closely tied to his conception of nature as a unity composed of innumerable individual elements. "Every living thing," he wrote,

is not a single unit but a plurality: even if it seems to be an individual, it nevertheless remains an association of living, independent entities, which are similar in idea and plan, but which in appearance may be like and similar or unlike and dissimilar.

From this sprang Goethe's profoundly Romantic idea of the cosmos itself as the ultimate living organism, a notion that nationalist thinkers would find easy to apply to the relationship between the individual citizen and the nation.

But it was as an author that Goethe exerted his greatest influence. His early novel, *The Sorrows of Young Werther* (1774), brilliantly captured the mood of the so-called *Sturm und Drang* (storm and stress) years of the early Romantic movement in Germany and portrayed its quintessential hero in the student Werther, who commits suicide out of frustrated love. *Werther* was a best-seller all over Europe and sparked a rash of real suicides; its fame was so great that the Chinese painted the young hero and his love, Lotte, on porcelain for the export trade. But Werther's sorrows were as much metaphysical as amorous, and as such he embodied the Romantic sense of the individual at odds with a world he never made.

Goethe himself was very much the rebellious young man he wrote about in his early years, tempestuous in his love affairs and radical in his politics. It was only much later, as the venerable Sage of Weimar, that he acquired the image of Olympian wisdom and detachment that has been historically associated with his name. Yet a single work that preoccupied him for six decades gave continuity to his entire career as well as matchless definition to the Romantic movement itself, his dramatic poem *Faust*. The Faust legend originated in a sixteenth-century German physician, astrologer, and magician, probably named Sabellicus but who called himself Faustus, who was reputed to have made a pact with the Devil. Contemporary writers used his story as a cautionary tale, though the English dramatist Christopher Marlowe, himself a reputed atheist, made him a semiheroic figure in his *Tragical History of Dr. Faustus* (1592). But Goethe rescued Faust the bogeyman from the carnivals and shows of his day and made him the very symbol of the Romantic quest for forbidden knowledge and experience. Equally important, Goethe's literary Devil, Mephistopheles, is not merely an evil tempter but a tormented being who is a larger symbol of Faust himself. Goethe's difficulty in finishing the poem stemmed from his rejection of the legend of Faust's ultimate damnation; like his fellow Romantics, he believed that the quest for knowledge was the essence of man's being and that good and evil could not be disentangled from it. In the end his Faust finds salvation rather than punishment, though not before coming to understand the limitations of all knowledge and the abiding mystery of existence.

In his later years Goethe was the cultural arbiter of Europe, whose favor and blessing was sought by the great and near-great; Napoleon, who met him at Erfurt in 1808, confessed to having read *Werther* seven times. No other poet since Shakespeare had so profound an influence on his fellow artists; the Romantic composers Beethoven, Schubert, Berlioz, Liszt, Mendelssohn, Schumann, and Wagner were only some of the musicians who found inspiration in his work, particularly *Faust*. Goethe himself had a wide and sympathetic interest in younger artists, and he was particularly taken by the English poet Lord Byron (1788–1824), whose death he memorialized in the second part of *Faust*. But his main influence was on his fellow German poets and dramatists.

The Spread of Romanticism

The generation that came to maturity with Goethe in the 1770s and 1780s included the playwrights Gotthold Ephraim Lessing (1729–1781) and Friedrich von Schiller (1759–1805). In these authors particularly the link between Romantic individualism and Romantic nationalism can be seen clearly. In his *Laocoön*, Lessing called for the creation of a national, heroic literature and the rejection of classical models, which were likened (as in the ancient statue from which he drew his title) to a giant serpent strangling human creativity. Schiller, who was particularly close to Goethe, answered that call in plays such as *William Tell* and *The Maid of Orleans* that described charismatically led movements of national liberation.

Goethe remained the mentor and example for the most important German writers of the next two generations, including the poets Friedrich von Novalis (1772–1801), Friedrich Hölderlin (1770–1843), and Heinrich Heine (1797–1856) and the playwright Heinrich von Kleist (1777–1811). The last decade of the eighteenth century also saw the advent of Romanticism in Britain, with the poetry of William Wordsworth (1770–1850) and Samuel Taylor Coleridge (1772–1834) and the immensely popular novels of Sir Walter Scott (1771–1832). Coleridge's still widely-read *Rime of the Ancient Mariner* (1798) combined Christian symbolism with Romantic quest and atonement; Wordsworth's epic verse autobiography, *The Prelude* (1807), offered the artist himself as hero, a theme that was to preoccupy both the nineteenth and twentieth centuries. These poets' successors, the tragically short-lived John Keats (1795–1821), Percy Bysshe Shelley

◉ The Romantic Poet ◉

In the preface to his Lyrical Ballads *(1798), William Wordsworth describes the poet as a kind of universal lawgiver, what his younger contemporary Percy Shelley would later call "the unacknowledged legislator of the human race." This proclamation of the sovereign genius of the solitary poet was crucial to the development of Romantic individualism and to the notion of the artist as a uniquely privileged figure in society.*

What is meant by the word Poet? What is a Poet? To whom does he address himself? And what language is to be expected from him? He is a man speaking to men: a man, it is true, with more lively sensibility, more enthusiasm and tenderness, who has a greater knowledge of human nature, and a more comprehensive soul. . . . He is the rock of defense of human nature; an upholder and preserver, carrying everywhere with him relationship and love. In spite of difference of soil and climate, of language and manners, of laws and customs, in spite of things silently gone out of mind and things violently destroyed, the Poet binds together by passion and knowledge the vast empire of human society, as it is spread over the whole earth, and over all time. The objects of the Poet's thoughts are everywhere; though the eyes and senses of men are, it is true, his favorite guides, yet he will follow wheresoever he can find an atmosphere of sensation in which to move his wings. Poetry is first and last of all knowledge—it is as immortal as the heart of man.

Source: The Complete Poetical Works of William Wordsworth (Philadelphia: Porter & Coates, 1851), pp. 664, 666.

(1792–1822), and Byron, brought English Romantic poetry to its finest flowering.

It is arguable that France produced the first truly Romantic figure in Jean-Jacques Rousseau, whose call for a return to nature as a refuge from the evils of a corrupt civilization and whose candid autobiography, the *Confessions*, were the earliest models of Romantic quest literature. However, the neoclassicism that dominated the arts through most of the eighteenth century retained its hold longer in France than elsewhere. The French Revolution harked back to Rome and Greece for its symbols of republican virtue and patriotism, and Napoleon, giving these a skillful imperial twist, adapted them for his own purposes. Not until after 1815, when defeat had turned France's mood inward, did it produce its first Romantic generation. The crucial transitional figures were the novelist Benjamin Constant (1767–1830), the poet and historian François-Auguste-René de Chateaubriand (1768–1848), and Madame de Staël (1766–1817), whose immensely influential book *On Germany* (1813) popularized German Romantic philosophy in France. Chateaubriand in particular was the herald of a Catholic revival in France that rejected the Deism of the Enlightenment and the revolution and signaled a renewal of interest in medieval piety, soon reflected in a neo-Gothic movement in architecture. Madame de Staël caught this new mood as well: "I do not know exactly what we must believe," she declared, "but I believe that we must believe! The eighteenth century did nothing but deny. The human spirit lives by its beliefs." This new, if rather vague, religiosity blended well with Romantic self-absorption, but it clashed with liberalism. The result was that the Romantics tended to sort out either on the extreme right (Chateaubriand in France, Novalis in Germany) or on the extreme left (Shelley in England), with very few in the political middle.

The post-1815 generation in France included the novelist Stendhal (Marie-Henri Beyle, 1783–1842), whose great novel *The Red and the Black* gave the French their own Werther in the character of Julien Sorel; the painter Eugène Delacroix (1798–1863), whose depiction of a Turkish atrocity during the war of Greek independence, *The Massacre at Chios*, profoundly influenced European opinion; and the composer Hector Berlioz (1803–1869), whose *Symphonie fantastique* (1830), with its lavish orchestral coloration and rather fevered literary program, was the prototypical Romantic symphony.

Romantic music reached its unquestioned apogee in Germany and Austria, where in the period between 1770 and 1830 four of the greatest geniuses in musical history appeared: Franz Joseph Haydn (1732–1809), Wolfgang Amadeus Mozart (1756–1791), Ludwig van Beethoven (1770–1827), and Franz Schubert (1797–1828). Haydn and Mozart were the supreme masters of the classical style that reigned for most of the latter half of the eighteenth century, with its emphasis on clarity of structure and texture, but their work exhibited elements of the nascent

Ludwig van Beethoven bridged not only the classic and Romantic periods in music but also, as the first musician to support himself primarily by the sale of his own work, the era of aristocratic patronage and that of the artist-entrepreneur. [Mansell Collection]

Romantic sensibility as well. Beethoven bridged the classic and Romantic eras, particularly in the nine symphonies that remain to this day the most admired synthesis of personal expression and formal control in music. Beethoven was a critical transitional figure in another respect as well. Whereas Haydn had worn the livery of his aristocratic employers, the Esterhazys, for most of his life, and Mozart too had been at the mercy of his patrons, Beethoven was the first composer to make an independent living by the sale of his music. The artist, too, no longer sheltered (and subordinated) by clerical or noble patrons, had entered the marketplace.

Romanticism Beyond the Arts

Romanticism touched not only the arts but philosophy, history, religious thought, and the natural sciences as well. Even as the Enlightenment proclaimed the sovereignty of reason, the German philosopher Immanuel Kant fatally undercut its claims by arguing that the human mind was no mere passive sorter and recorder of experience, as Locke and other empiricists had believed, but a complex mechanism that gave form and shape to phenomena according to its own internal laws. Accordingly, the world could not be experienced as it was "in itself" but only as filtered through the processes of intellect and emotion and therefore subjectively. There could be no objective and impersonal description of the world, even in science, because no one—except perhaps God—could overcome the limitations of individual perception. Like the blind, we touched a world that was truly real but could never be seen as it really was.

Kant's philosophy went by the name of idealism, after his distinction between the "ideas" we form of reality through the interaction of world and mind and the world as it exists independently of our perception of it. The implications of Kantian idealism were powerfully but controversially explored by the Prussian philospher Georg Wilhelm Friedrich Hegel (1770–1831). Hegel argued that all of human history was a great unconscious drama that tended toward the realization of human freedom, which he called the spirit of reason. The agents of this drama were great individuals such as Caesar or Napoleon, through whose personal passions and ambitions this spirit acted; thus Caesar had created the first world empire, and Napoleon had stimulated the sense of national self-identity that Hegel saw as the final phase of the development of freedom.

Hegel's emphasis on the role of great men in history dovetailed neatly with Romantic individualism, while his identification of nationalism with the progress of freedom had immense appeal to liberals in Germany and elsewhere. He also gave great impetus to the development of nationally oriented histories, such as those written by Jules Michelet in France and Leopold von Ranke in Germany, as well as such cognate disciplines as ethnology (the study of humankind by racial and cultural divisions) and philology (the study of particular languages). No other thinker of the period made so strenuous and systematic an effort to reconcile the two opposite poles of Romantic thought, the attempt to define oneself in opposition to society, whether as explorer, entrepreneur, or artist, and the desire for patriotic identity within the national group.

Romanticism and the Image of Women

The beginnings of modern feminism coincided with those of Romanticism and may be seen as part of the same process of social transformation. Prior to this time the few women who by sheer force of personality had been able to distinguish themselves were regarded as oddities or freaks; Samuel Johnson's cruel jest that a woman preaching was like a dog walking on its hind legs summarized the dominant male attitude toward female intellectual activity in general, even during the Enlightenment. But with the nineteenth century women began to appear for the first time on a plane of equality with men in a major cultural movement. If Mary Wollstonecraft still had to struggle for recognition because of her sex in the 1790s, Madame de Staël was much more readily accepted only 20 years later, and in the succeeding decades women came to occupy an increasingly prominent place in the arts, particularly literature. We have noted the immense popularity of the British novelist Elizabeth Gaskell in the 1840s and 1850s (see Chapter 29). An analogous position was occupied by the American author and abolitionist Harriet Beecher Stowe, best known for her novel *Uncle Tom's Cabin* (1852), and the French novelist Aurore Dupin (1804–1876), who, taking the pen name of George Sand, became as famous for her daring private life—which included a highly publicized liaison with the great Polish composer-pianist Frédéric Chopin—as for her voluminous literary output. At least four Englishwomen stand in the front rank of nineteenth-century literature: Jane Austen (1775–1817), whose social novels reveal a psychological penetration equaled among her contemporaries only by

Classical philosophy culminated in the work of Georg Wilhelm Friedrich Hegel, whose conception of history as a struggle between dialectically opposed forces embodied Romantic notions of quest and struggle and profoundly influenced Karl Marx. [Mansell Collection]

Goethe; the Brontë sisters, Charlotte and Emily; and Mary Anne Evans (1819–1880), known by the pen name of George Eliot, whose novel, *Middlemarch*, is rivaled only by the major works of Charles Dickens. At the same time the reclusive New Englander Emily Dickinson (1830–1886) was writing some of the finest lyric poetry since Sappho.

Nevertheless, the disabilities faced by women attempting to compete in what was still a man's world were obvious. Elizabeth Gaskell was never known by her own forename but simply as "Mrs. Gaskell"; Dupin and Evans both adopted masculine pen names in an effort to gain more serious attention for their work; and Emily Dickinson's poems were never published in her own lifetime. If, moreover, a place in literature and to a lesser extent in the other arts was reluctantly conceded to women, it served only to confirm age-old prejudices against them in the fields of philosophy, politics, and the professions. The German nationalist philosopher Johann Gottlieb Fichte (1762–1814) argued that women lacked the "speculative aptitude" for either philosophical inquiry or public office. Hegel made what was to be the fundamental nineteenth-century bourgeois distinction between a public world of work and struggle, in which only men were fit to compete, and the private sphere of "piety and domesticity," for which women were intended by nature. The Frenchman Auguste Comte (1798–1857) doubted that women could be entrusted even with running a household except under male supervision. If women excelled in literature, it only confirmed the prevailing stereotype of them as creatures in whom the imagination prevailed at the expense of the intellect.

The rejection of marriage by women like Mary Wollstonecraft and George Sand and their demand for free sexual companionship reinforced the widespread male belief that women should be confined as tightly within the bounds of "piety and domesticity" as possible. Yet the image of woman had come to stand allegorically for revolution itself. In 1792 the new French republic decreed that it was to be represented officially by a seal that bore the likeness of a woman dressed in ancient style holding a pike. This popular figure of "Marianne," which blended the image of Roman virtue and Joan of Arc with secular allusions to the cult of the Virgin Mary, reached its apotheosis in Delacroix's famous painting of the revolution of 1830, *Liberty on the Barricades*. The painting shows a semiallegorical female figure leading a charge over the bodies of fallen sans-culottes, a top-hatted bourgeois at her side. Her bared breast recalls the classical image of the Amazon warrior, but the realistic touches—the stained petticoats, the hair under the arms—proclaim her as well to be a woman of the people. At the same time, her nudity carries an implicit message of sexual aggressiveness that is only partly offset by her averted, impassive gaze. Far more powerfully than the seal of Marianne, Delacroix's figure conveys the conflicting impulses behind the early

Romantic image of woman: the idealized warrior-goddess and the available woman of the street, the symbol of liberation who remains chained in her petticoats, who leads a battle that will be fought by the sans-culottes but won by the bourgeoisie.

The Liberal Revival and the Revolutions of 1830

By the late 1820s dissatisfaction with the reactionary Bourbon dynasty in France and the slow pace of reform in Britain had reached the flashpoint of revolution. A neutral observer, asked to predict where it would actually occur, would probably have chosen Britain. The British political system, unreformed since 1689, had refused even a token accommodation to the new social reality created by the Industrial Revolution. The great new cities, half-anarchic, had virtually no representation in Parliament and no access to central government. Yet Britain alone, of all the major states of Europe, was to avoid revolution in 1830 and the years to come. Not London but Paris was to provide the impetus for the next wave of insurrection.

The July Revolution in France

The new revolutionary crisis began in March 1830 when the French Chamber of Deputies, led by the bankers Jacques Lafitte and Jean-Paul Casimir-Perier, voted no confidence in the government of Charles X and its policies of censorship, suffrage restriction, and clerical control of education. Charles dissolved the assembly, but new elections, even though limited to an electorate of 100,000, produced a decisive opposition majority. The king wavered, but spurred on by his chief minister Polignac, the archbishop of Paris, and Metternich, he responded on July 26 by dissolving the just-elected Chamber before it could meet, imposing new press censorship, reducing the electorate to a hard core of 25,000 aristocrats, and announcing fresh elections on this basis.

The target of these edicts was the regime's bourgeois opposition, but the reaction came from the working-class sections of Paris. The very next day barricades appeared spontaneously in the streets, and the army, called out to clear them, refused to do so. Faced with anarchy, Charles abdicated two days later in favor of his grandson and fled into exile. France was left without a government.

The sudden vacuum of power revealed the clear-cut divisions of the French political spectrum. The bourgeois opposition—bankers, industrialists, and merchants—wanted not the overthrow of the Bourbon monarchy but greater favor within it for themselves. The Parisian workers, students, and radical intellectuals who had taken to the barricades and made the revolution wanted a republic, headed by the venerable marquis de Lafayette as president. A compromise was hastily brokered behind the scenes. The duke of Orléans, a collateral relative of the Bourbons but a republican soldier in the army of 1792, was put forward as a constitutional monarch by a coalition consisting of Talleyrand, the liberal journalist Adolphe Thiers, and Lafitte, the duke's personal banker. When Lafayette publicly endorsed him, the republican opposition melted away. Louis-Philippe, as the new king was called, promised to abide by the charter of 1814, flew the tricolor flag of the 1789 revolution rather than the Bourbon lily, and was the first monarch to wear the contemporary equivalent of a business suit in public. With his paunch and umbrella, he was indistinguishable from the bourgeois interests that had brought him to power and whose interests he faithfully served.

Revolution East and West

The three-day revolution in France was the signal for major uprisings across the border in Belgium and, for far different reasons, in Poland. The union of Belgium and the Netherlands, arranged at Vienna, had much to recommend it in theory, as the two nations formed a natural economic and geographic unit. The Catholic Belgians, however, long accustomed to relative autonomy under the rule of Spain and Austria, chafed under the domination of a Protestant Dutch king, William I. Heartened by the French example, they rose up in August 1830 and, after fruitless efforts at conciliation, proclaimed independence under a liberal monarchy of their own. When Dutch troops failed to quell them, a hastily arranged big power conference in London recognized the new government to forestall French intervention.

The Polish rebellion was triggered by the news that Tsar Nicholas I, who was also king of Poland, was planning to send Russian troops through that country on its way to help suppress the Belgians. Russian rule was desperately unpopular, however, and almost any pretext might have served. The Polish Diet declared Nicholas deposed, but the tsar's army speedily crushed the revolt. Poland was absorbed directly into the Russian empire and ruled under a state of military emergency that lasted technically from 1833 until the First World War. Thousands of Poles were executed, imprisoned, or banished to Siberia, and many more fled to the West, among them Chopin.

◉ Mazzini's Call to Revolution ◉

Despite the failure of the revolutions of 1830, young nationalists took heart at the year that had rocked the kings of Europe on their thrones. Giuseppe Mazzini, the leader of Young Italy, an organization dedicated to the liberation and unification of Italy, here declares both the faith and the method of his revolutionary band. The emphasis on education and guerrilla tactics sounds a particularly modern note.

Young Italy is *Republican*. . . . Republican—because theoretically every nation is destined, by the law of God and humanity, to form a free and equal community of brothers; and the republican is the only form of government that insures this future. . . .

The means by which Young Italy proposes to reach its aims are—education and insurrection, to be adopted simultaneously, and made to harmonize with each other.

Education must ever be directed to teach by example, word, and pen the necessity of insurrection. Insurrection, whenever it can be realized, must be so conducted as to render it a means of national education. . . .

Insurrection—by means of guerrilla bands—is the true method of warfare for all nations desirous of emancipating themselves from a foreign yoke. This method of warfare supplies the want—inevitable at the commencement of the insurrection—of a regular army; it calls the greatest number of elements into the field, and yet may be sustained by the smallest number. It forms the military education of the people, and consecrates every foot of the native soil by the memory of some warlike deed.

Source: N. Gangulee, ed., *Giuseppe Mazzini: Selected Writings* (London: Lindsay Drummond, 1945), pp. 129–134 passim.

Lesser disturbances also shook Germany, Italy, Switzerland, Spain, and Portugal, though for the most part without significant result. Yet liberals could, with the tragic exception of Poland, count 1830 as a year of victory. The bourgeoisie had reclaimed political primacy in France and, no longer dependent on a dictator such as Napoleon to retain it, had cut a king to their own measure. The powers had been forced to acquiesce in an independent Belgium, nominally a monarchy, whose constitution acknowledged its origin in the sovereignty of the people and provided what was to be for many years the widest electoral franchise in Europe. The autocratic William I was forced to embrace reform in the Netherlands, and liberal gains were made in Switzerland. Above all, 1830 marked the year when history seemed to move again in Europe. The liberal triumph was far from complete, but its outlines at last seemed visible.

Britain: Revolution Averted

Britain accomplished revolutionary change without revolution. The settlement of 1689 had confirmed the supremacy of Parliament over the king. But neither the size of the electorate—less than 4 percent of the population—nor the distribution of seats had changed in nearly a century and a half, and both were now profoundly unrepresentative of the urban, industrialized society that Britain had become. The long and almost unbroken Conservative domination of British politics from 1760 to 1830 had hardened the nation's rulers in their belief that, as the duke of Wellington put it, the British constitution was already more perfect than any human intelligence could contrive to improve.

In fact, reform had already begun during the ascendancy of George Canning, Castlereagh's successor as foreign minister in Lord Liverpool's government. Tariff duties and colonial trade restrictions, some in effect since the seventeenth century, were relaxed, and the Test Act, which had barred Catholics and Dissenters from public life since 1673, was at last repealed (1829). A gesture was even made toward the lower orders; unions were recognized, and the number of offenses punishable by death was cut by 100—which nevertheless left another 100 on the books. But the one issue that had become symbolic of the liberal cause as a whole—parliamentary reform—remained unaddressed.

The reformers' moment came in 1830, when Wellington's government fell and a Whig ministry under Lord Grey came to power. Despite bitter Tory opposition, Grey at last steered a parliamentary reform bill through both houses in 1832, although the Lords acquiesced only when faced with the king's threat to create enough Whig peers to override them. It was just in time; riots had broken out all over the country, a tax strike was being organized, and

radicals urged a run on the Bank of England as a means of bringing the properties classes to their knees.

The Reform Bill was as important for the revolution it averted as for the rather modest alterations it produced. It changed the image but not the reality of power in Britain. Some 143 seats in the House of Commons, about a quarter of the total, were redistributed. Slightly fewer than half of these went to new industrial towns, such as Manchester, which had previously lacked representation of any kind. Some, but by no means all, of the "rotten boroughs"—decayed constituencies that continued to return members to Parliament with a largely phantom electorate—were eliminated. The franchise was extended from slightly under 500,000 to just over 800,000 voters, still little more than 5 percent of the population. The net effect was a token recognition of the industrial bourgeoisie

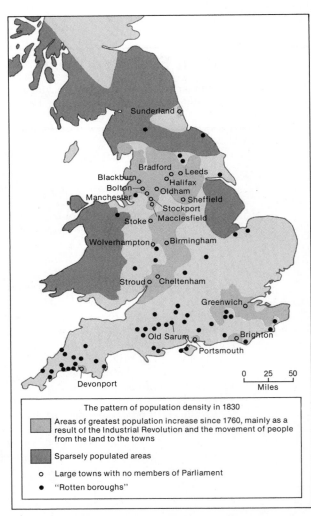

30.3 Parliamentary Representation in Britain Before 1832

that kept the balance of electoral power safely in the hands of the gentry and nobility. But while on some issues the interests of the two groups were genuinely divided, it would be a mistake to see them as fundamentally opposed. The new magnates of industrial capitalism, like their eighteenth-century predecessors in commerce and finance, had little need of parliamentary representation to make their weight felt. The propertied classes in town and country had adjusted their mutual relations in a manner that more adequately represented the influence of the former. Both agreed that the reins of government would continue to rest with them to the exclusion of the vast majority. The Reform Bill of 1832, like the regime of Louis-Philippe in France, reflected that broad consensus.

The Socialist Challenge

It would be accurate to say that the working classes had fought the revolutions of 1830 and the bourgeoisie won them. The sans-culottes on the barricades in Paris, the workers who defied the Dutch king in Brussels and Antwerp, and the British laborers who seized Bristol and threatened other towns in their demand for parliamentary representation had all taken an initiative that their betters were quick to convert to their own advantage. Nothing could symbolize the irony of mass politics in the early industrial age more than the spectacle of elderly aristocrats like Lafayette and Lord Grey stage-managing the transference, or at any rate the sharing of power between the traditional nobility and the industrial bourgeoisie at the behest of the workers.

The Demand for Reform

The experience of the 1830s and 1840s taught at least the more advanced elements of the working class that their interests could not be encompassed by those of the bourgeoisie. The mass movement that Robert Owen led briefly from 1833 to 1834 (see Chapter 29) was prompted in part by disillusion with the Reform Bill, and by the end of the 1830s the first sustained workers' movement had emerged in Britain, the Chartists. It began in 1836 when a small shopkeeper, William Lovett, founded the London Workingmen's Association. The association's relatively modest initial demands were presented in the tradition of social deference to one's superiors. Its tone, however, soon grew more radical. In 1838, with the assistance of the veteran reformer Francis Place, it drew up the first People's Charter. This document rejected the piecemeal reform of Parliament, which was all conventional politics could offer. It demanded a secret ballot, equal electoral districts, annually elected Parliaments on the basis of universal manhood suffrage, the removal of property qualifications for office, and payment for all members of Parliament. The effect of this would have been fully to democratize the political system (at least for men) and to enable workers themselves to stand for and occupy seats in Parliament. Here was a genuine break with the politics of deference, with its assumption that the interest of the working class could be represented satisfactorily by its social betters.

In February 1839 a self-styled workers' convention met in London to press for the People's Charter, now attached to a petition that had gained a million signatures. The delegates called themselves "Members of the Convention," both in evident allusion to the French National Convention of 1792 and to Parliament itself. When the House of Commons rejected the charter, a general strike was proposed. Lacking organization and experienced leadership, it petered out in sporadic agitation from which many existing unions held aloof. Unlike Owen's Grand Union however, the Chartist movement did not collapse with its first defeat but remained a powerful force throughout the 1840s.

A similar rethinking of worker interests was going forward in France, where, having consolidated its position, the government of Louis-Philippe set its face against even token reform. In 1839 the journalist Louis Blanc (1811–1882) argued in a widely read book, *The Organization of Labor*, that the state should socialize all major economic services, including banking, transportation, and insurance, and establish "social workshops," or cooperative factories operated by and for workers. Blanc's reformism derived from the Saint-Simonians, followers of the influential Count de Saint-Simon (1760–1825), who had advocated control of public services and enterprises by a technocratic elite of scientists and engineers. What both Saint-Simon and Blanc ignored, however, like more "utopian" socialists such as Owen and Fourier, was the problem of actual political power. The state, whether controlled by aristocrats, by bourgeoisie, or, as in much of western Europe, by an uneasy combination of both, was highly unlikely to cede authority to either workers or engineers.

From Reform to Revolution

Such was the conclusion drawn by revolutionaries such as Louis-Auguste Blanqui (1805–1881) and Pierre Proudhon (1809–1865), who in turn derived from the martyred Gracchus Babeuf (see Chapter 26) and his Italian disciple, Filippo Maria Buonarotti (1760–1837). Proudhon, unwilling to compromise with any scheme of state ownership, declared roundly that all property was a theft of the value created by labor. He envisioned the abolition of the state in favor of a system of decentralized cooperative enterprises that would produce and exchange goods noncompetitively on the basis of social need. For Blanqui, such an arrangement, however desirable in principle, begged the fundamental question of power: how was such a peaceful system to be established against the resistance of the properted classes and the state machinery they controlled? Blanqui's answer was armed revolution aimed at establishing a "dictatorship of the proletariat," a phrase he coined. Like his mentor Buonarotti, Europe's first professional revolutionary, Blanqui spent most of his life in jail or on the run; Tocqueville, observing him in 1848 at a rare moment of liberty, said that he had the appearance of a man who had passed his life in the sewers. But with Buonarotti and Blanqui, a new kind of person had appeared on the European scene, convinced of the inevitable struggle between the classes and dedicated to revolution at any cost.

All the thinkers and political activists just considered subscribed to a common critique of the capitalist system. They accepted Adam Smith's definition of labor as the source of all productive value and believed (as Smith did not) that the wealth produced by this labor should be owned socially or collectively: hence the name *socialism* applied to their ideas and demands. The socialists' beliefs were clear-cut: private ownership was the appropriation by force of an excess share of the common social wealth (in the pithy formulation associated with Proudhon, "property is theft"), and unregulated capitalism was the equivalent of unrelieved exploitation. But they disagreed about the remedy. Owen, Fourier, and Proudhon put their faith in small, collectively owned enterprises linked voluntarily into cooperative associations; Saint-Simon and Blanc believed that only state power could break up existing concentrations of private capital and ownership; and Blanqui added that only revolution from below could give the proletariat access to that power. What they all lacked was a theory of social action or, more simply, a credible plan for overthrowing the existing order.

Karl Marx

Karl Marx supplied the theoretical basis for socialism. Until Marx, the socialists had produced no thinker who could conceptually challenge the defense of capitalism put forward by Adam Smith and David Ricardo. For both Smith and Ricardo, private enterprise—economic competition for individual profit—maximized the production of wealth and hence the aggregate social good. Ricardo in particular was sensitive to the high social cost of capitalism: the exploitation of child and female labor, the tendency of worker income to remain at subsistence level, and the "business cycle"—the abrupt spasms of boom and bust to which the industrial system had already shown itself to be vulnerable. These costs were regrettable but, Ricardo felt, for the most part unavoidable. This was particularly true for income stagnation, which Ricardo formulated as the "iron law of wages." In times of industrial expansion when the demand for labor exceeded the supply, Ricardo argued, wages would tend to rise above subsistence level; but the result of relative prosperity was a higher birthrate,

which produced excess labor capacity, depressed wages, and caused starvation and misery. For this reason, worker demands for higher wages were self-defeating. Marx was the first socialist thinker to challenge this and similar "laws" of economics on their own ground and in his major work, *Capital*, to advance a comprehensive countertheory to demonstrate that capitalism was not merely unstable but inherently self-destructive as well.

Marx was born in Trier in the rapidly industrializing Rhineland. He was descended on both sides from a long line of rabbis, but his father, like many other Jews of the time, had submitted to Christian baptism to gain entry into the legal profession. Marx studied philosophy at Bonn and Berlin, drank and dueled, and wrote bad poetry, a comic novel, a tragic play, and a doctoral dissertation on the

The founder of modern communism, Karl Marx, in a photograph taken in the mid-1870s. [Globe Photos]

difference between the atomic theories of Democritus and Epicurus. He also became part of a circle of young radicals who were attempting to extend Hegelian philosophy in a leftward direction. As a correspondent for the *Rheinische Zeitung*, he exposed the wretched poverty of the wine-growers of the Trier region in an article that helped lead to the suppression of the newspaper. Quitting Germany in disgust, he settled in Paris, where he produced a series of extraordinary and prophetic essays on worker alienation and shed his last attachments to Hegelian idealism. With his friend and lifelong collaborator, Friedrich Engels, he hailed the coming of a new socialist order in *The Communist Manifesto*, but the failed revolutions of 1848 led him into exile instead.

Marx took refuge in London with his large and needy family, living under the watchful eye of the local police and the spies of a dozen nations and on the bounty of Engels, who owned a factory in Manchester. Marx was not embarrassed to live on the profits of capital and himself speculated on the stock market. The task of philosophy, he said, was not to understand the world but to change it, and the man who meant to make that philosophy was not worried about being judged by the rules of the world that would be left behind.

Dismissing his predecessors and rivals, Marx declared his work to be the only "scientific" socialism. It was founded on a grand theory that, arguing humanity's intellectual and social development from its material struggle to wrest the necessities of life from nature, proceeded to describe the stages of history in terms of a social struggle for control of the technical means of production—land, labor, and machinery. Marx described ancient society as founded on slavery, the medieval West on feudalism, and capitalism on wage labor, which he saw as a modern form of slavery. Since, like other socialists, Marx regarded labor as the only source of productive value (capital itself, whether in the form of money, machinery, or tilled lands, was only labor in objectified or symbolic form), all profit extracted from labor by means of the wage system was "surplus" or appropriated value.

Marx praised the bourgeoisie for having greatly expanded the material base of civilization by industrialization and urbanization, even as it simultaneously debased its human content by forcing the great mass of the population to live in conditions of unparalleled exploitation and misery. The contradiction between the prosperity of the few and the poverty of the many would, however, ultimately be too evident to ignore. At the same time, the inherent tendency of capitalist competition to contract and profit margins to shrink would lead to ever shorter and severer contractions of the business cycle and the growth of monopoly, until the conditions for socialist revolution were ripe.

But revolution could be neither prepared nor accomplished without active class struggle. Marx collaborated (and ultimately quarreled with) all the leading social activists of his day, including the Frenchman Proudhon, the Russian anarchist Mikhail Bakunin (1814–1876), and the German trade unionist Ferdinand Lassalle (1825–1864). Yet he continually stressed the cooperative nature of the proletarian struggle across all borders, rejecting nationalism as a bourgeois phenomenon that reflected the divisive, competitive nature of capitalism itself. In 1864 he was instrumental in founding the International Workingman's Association, later known as the First International, to promote the proletarian cause throughout Europe and America. At his death in 1883, he was clearly the foremost figure of European socialism, as both a thinker and an activist.

Marx never managed to put his mature ideas into finished, comprehensive form. Half his manuscripts lay unpublished at his death, many to remain unknown for decades; even his masterpiece, *Capital*, the first part of which was published in 1867, was only a torso. In part this reflected his own refusal to settle into any mold, even his own; as he once wittily remarked, "I am not a Marxist." Yet, though always controversial and frequently misinterpreted, his thought has been more decisive than anyone else's in the shaping of the modern world, and in the universality of his influence he may be regarded as the first nonreligious thinker of world significance. Certainly he takes his place as one of the most important figures in the Western tradition. Before Marx no theory of societal development had advanced much beyond Plato and Aristotle 2,000 years before. There was no theory of historical change that dealt adequately with the concrete problems of subsistence, organization, or technological innovation. There was no theory of the Enlightenment that portrayed humanity as anything more than orphans of reason or suggested the possibility of a truly just society. As with all revolutionary thinkers, time continues to winnow away what was local and circumstantial in his thought from what remains of continuing significance and value. The Russian émigré Annenkov described Marx as unkempt, domineering, and very nearly offensive in manner; but, he added, "he looked like a man with the right and power to demand respect, no matter how he appeared before you and no matter what he did," a man with "the firm conviction of his mission to dominate men's minds and prescribe them their laws." More than a century later, the world still responds to that force.

The Revolutions of 1848

When late in the year 1847 the young Marx warned of the imminence of revolution in *The Communist Manifesto*, he may have been the only person in Europe to expect it. Yet within the first four months of 1848 the Continent was rocked by almost 50 separate revolutions in France, Prussia, Austria, and almost all the lesser German and Italian states. Surveying the wreckage of monarchies, Tsar Nicholas I wrote to Queen Victoria that Russia and Britain seemed to be the last two states standing in Europe. The exaggeration in that statement was slight.

The Causes of the Revolutions

Some general causes of the revolutions can be discerned, although they differed with the circumstances of each state or region. The Industrial Revolution, which had begun in earnest on the Continent after 1830, had shaken social and demographic patterns and profoundly altered political ones. Unfulfilled nationalist aspirations were a primary impetus in Germany, Italy, and eastern Europe. These tensions and grievances were also exacerbated, as before 1789 and 1830, by hard times. Harvests were poor in the three years preceding 1848; the Prussian peasantry, lacking bread, survived on potatoes, while in Ireland, the failure in 1845 of the potato crop—the last resort of the poor—led to mass starvation and emigration, which between them reduced the population of the country from 8.5 million to 6.5 million in five years. Urban workers were also squeezed by the rising price of food, and the agricultural crisis soon produced industrial depression as well. The integration of agricultural and industrial markets through capitalist development meant that any disturbance in one sector of the system had immediate repercussions in the rest of it, while the new concentration of population in towns and cities provided natural foci of discontent.

The single most pervasive element in the revolutions of 1848, however, was a general questioning of the existing political order. The monarchs of the Old Regime had based their authority on appeals to divine right and a traditional social order, but divinity no longer shielded a ruler who could be forced off his throne by a three-day riot as Charles X had been in 1830 or set up like Louis-Philippe by a backstairs cabal consisting of a diplomat, a journalist, and a banker. Nor could such a ruler appeal to traditional values or deference in a society where the most basic relations of property, production, and authority were being transformed and a new financial, commercial, and industrial elite was busily accumulating power. Still less could rulers legitimate themselves where, as in most of Italy, they served not a native but a foreign interest.

The new bourgeois or quasi-bourgeois regimes established by the events of 1830–1832, though based explicitly or implicitly on popular sovereignty and constitutional guarantees, had proved singularly unwilling to embrace the vast majority of the people in the political process. In no European nation with a representative system did the electorate exceed 5 percent of the population. The Chartists pursued their demand for universal manhood suffrage in Britain with petitioning campaigns of 3 million signatures in 1842 and five million in 1848, only to meet with con-tinuing rejection in Parliament, while in France, with only 300,000 electors in a population of 30 million, the government of François Guizot set itself resolutely against even a token extension of the franchise. After two revolutions and 60 years, the French Assembly was a less representative body than the Estates General of Louis XVI had been.

The Collapse of the Old Order

The revolutions began with a stirring in Italy, where on January 12 the people of Sicily rose against Ferdinand II. By the end of the month Milan and Venice had proclaimed their ancient independence as republics and called on King Charles Albert of Piedmont and Pope Pius IX to help unify the entire peninsula. The French were not far behind. Liberal reformers, blocked from public demonstrations, had adopted the British tactic of holding banquets that were in effect mass political rallies on behalf of a modest extension of the franchise. When the authorities sought to ban one such banquet in Paris in late February, the events of 1830 swiftly repeated themselves. Riots broke out, barricades went up, and the National Guard, called out to quell the disturbances, joined in instead. Louis-Philippe dismissed the unpopular Guizot in a bid to regain middle-class support. But the Parisian workers were not to be duped a second time. Breaking into the Chamber of Deputies, they forced the proclamation of a republic, and Louis-Philippe fled into exile in London.

The news from Paris galvanized dissidents in Germany and Austria. In Berlin the irresolute Frederick William IV (1840–1861) found himself a virtual prisoner of nationalists who demanded that Prussia take the lead in unifying Germany under a liberal constitution. Student rebels and workers joined in Vienna to extract a promise of reform from the emperor, Ferdinand I, and the aged Metternich fled the city in disguise to join Louis-Philippe in exile. More serious were nationalist uprisings by the Bohemians in Prague and the Hungarians in Budapest. The latter, under the leadership of the fiery journalist and orator Louis Kossuth (1802–1894), demanded virtual independence from Austria, with a separate army, government, and system of finance. In addition, the Hungarian Diet, composed exclusively of noblemen and long one of the most reactionary assemblies in Europe, voted for constitutional government, the abolition of serfdom, and the imposition of taxes on the nobility. By the end of March the Austrian empire was prostrate, while in Germany a group of liberals, meeting spontaneously in Heidelberg, called for the election of an all-German parliament on the basis of universal manhood suffrage and under the supervision of an electoral body, the *Vorparliament*, summoned directly by them. So great was the enthusiasm for unity throughout the country, and so paralyzed were the existing governments, that the election was duly carried out, and on May 18 the 830

30.4 Europe's Revolutions of 1848

delegates of the new parliament convened in Frankfurt to make Germany a nation.

The single most evident fact about this whirlwind of revolutions was the weakness and prostration of the established governments. As Charles X had fallen at what seemed the merest touch in 1830, not only had his successor been toppled, but what seemed the most rock-solid thrones in Europe, Prussia and Austria, had shaken in their foundations before relative handfuls of protesters who made up their demands as they went along. Nothing could have more conclusively demonstrated the ideological bankruptcy of these regimes and their helplessness in the face of even the most disorganized challenge. At the same time, however, the revolutionaries, united for the moment in the flush of success, were soon as divided from one another as they had been from the kings who served as the common target of their discontent.

Counterrevolution in Central Europe

Among the first of the revolutions to unravel occurred within the Austrian empire. In Italy, Charles Albert had no sooner assumed leadership of the anti-Habsburg coa-

lition when it began to collapse; a counterrevolution restored Ferdinand II in Sicily, while the Venetians made it clear that they had no intention of abandoning their republic to merge with the House of Savoy. In July, Austria badly defeated Charles Albert's forces at the battle of Custozza, and a last attempt to resuscitate the cause ended in disaster at Novara in March 1849. The Italian conflagration was not quite over; in November 1848 Pius IX fled Rome after the assassination of his chief minister, and a republic was proclaimed in February headed by Giuseppe Mazzini (1805–1872), whose impassioned vision of a united, democratic Italy had made him a hero to a generation of young nationalists. Mazzini's government immediately announced the confiscation of church lands and their redistribution to the peasantry, as well as a program of public housing for the urban poor. Although it controlled only the city of Rome and its immediate environs, the republic declared itself the nucleus of a united Italy. But it fell to a French army in July despite stubborn resistance, and with the fall of Venice a month later, the collapse of the revolutionary cause was complete.

In Hungary the Magyar majority under Kossuth rapidly alienated the various minorities under its control by proclaiming what amounted to racial hegemony: it abolished local assemblies in non-Magyar provinces and prescribed that Hungarian be the exclusive language of all higher education as well as of the Diet. This stimulated Slavic nationalism, which culminated in a pan-Slav congress that convened in Prague in June, only to be suppressed by troops under General Alfred Windischgratz still loyal to the Habsburgs. This victory emboldened the court party to attempt the liberation of Vienna. In October, Windischgratz occupied the city after a bombardment and executed or exiled its radical leaders on the spot. Two months later the feebleminded Ferdinand I was induced to step down in favor of his 18-year-old nephew, Franz Joseph I (1848–1916), who, unhampered by his predecessor's promises to the liberals, completed the process of restoration the following summer by crushing the Hungarian revolt with the aid of 140,000 Russian troops.

In Germany, meanwhile, the Frankfurt Assembly set to its task of providing the country with a national government and a constitution. The fundamental anomaly of its position, however, was soon apparent. Almost all the delegates were university-educated members of the upper bourgeoisie: lawyers, doctors, scholars, ministers, bankers, merchants, and manufacturers. Their vision was of a world made safe for bourgeois opportunity: free trade, untrammeled growth, an end to the political monopoly of the aristocracy, and a liberal regime presiding benignly over a swelling gross national product. But the masses, whose rebellion had cleared the ground for them, wanted none of these things. They were peasants clamoring for land, artisans demanding protection for their trades, and workers who wanted higher wages and industrial regulation. Free enterprise only meant new chains to them, and free speech was less important than bread they could afford to eat.

While the Frankfurt delegates attempted to thrash out their own manifold differences—whether the new Germany should be a federation or a unitary state, a monarchy, an empire, or a republic, and above all whether it should seek to incorporate German-speaking areas of Austria, Denmark, and Poland within its borders—the existing governments of the German Confederation, supposedly waiting for final extinction but still in control of their armies, slowly recovered their authority. By the time the Assembly had drafted its constitution, which included provisions for freedom of speech, assembly, and the press, religious toleration, and public education, both Prussia and Austria had become strong enough to reject it out of hand. When Frederick William IV, no doubt with memories of being forced to ride through the streets of Berlin with a revolutionary tricolor in his hat the previous spring, was approached in April 1849 to become "emperor of the Germans," he replied loftily that he would not pick up a crown from the gutter. At that the Frankfurt Assembly began to collapse. The more moderate delegations, unwilling to contemplate a republic, went home, and the radical remnant was dispersed by force in June. The revolution in Germany was over.

◉ The June Days ◉

The French liberal Alexis de Tocqueville describes the June Days of 1848.

I come at last to the insurrection of June, the most extensive and the most singular that has occurred in our history, and perhaps in any other: the most extensive, because, during four days, more than a hundred thousand men were engaged in it; the most singular, because the insurgents fought without a war-cry, without leaders, without flags, and yet with a marvellous harmony and an amount of military experience that astonished the oldest officers.

What distinguished it also, among all the events of this kind which have succeeded one another in France for sixty years, is that it did not aim at changing the form of government, but at altering the order of society. It was not, strictly speaking, a political struggle, in the sense which until then we had given to the word, but a combat of class against class. . . .

It must also be observed that this formidable insurrection was not the enterprise of a certain number of conspirators, but the revolt of one whole section of the population against another. Women took part in it as well as men. While the latter fought, the former prepared and carried ammunition; and when at last the time had come to surrender, the women were the last to yield.

Source: A. T. De Mattos, trans., *The Recollections of Alexis de Tocqueville* (New York: Columbia University Press, 1949), pp. 150–151.

France: From Revolution to Empire

In France the course of events was quite different. Here alone (apart from Mazzini's short-lived Roman republic), the monarch of an independent state had actually been deposed and a new provisional government established. A hasty compromise among revolutionary factions, it consisted of seven moderate and three radical (socialist) republicans. Among the latter was Louis Blanc, who urged immediate relief for the unemployed through a Ministry of Progress that would establish his workshop system. Behind Blanc was the specter of Blanqui, white-haired and black-clad, "the most complete revolutionary of his time,"[1] who showed his power by mounting a demonstration of 100,000 workers in Paris in March 1848. When Blanc failed to win them the concessions they demanded, one of the marchers denounced him as a traitor. The revolution had already been split.

Most of the wealthier bourgeoisie and nobility had already fled Paris, and the United States was the only foreign power to recognize the French republic. The moderates in the government placed their hopes in speedy elections, which they expected to produce a conservative majority that would isolate the radicals. A Constituent Assembly, elected by universal manhood suffrage in April, convened on May 4 and immediately replaced the provisional government with a five-man executive of its own that contained no socialists. On June 22, following an abortive coup led by Blanqui, the government announced the dissolution of the workshop program, which had been set up as a sop to Blanc but had provided only ill-paid road work for the 200,000 unemployed of Paris. The reaction was immediate. The workers took up arms, the government proclaimed martial law, and the class war heralded only six months before by Marx in *The Communist Manifesto* became bloody reality in the streets of Paris. Ten thousand people were killed or wounded in a three-day struggle without quarter (June 24–26) until troops under General Louis Cavaignac regained control of the city. Capping victory with vengeance, the Assembly decreed that the 15,000 prisoners taken be deported. An army of 50,000 occupied the French capital until October.

The so-called June Days sent a shudder of terror throughout bourgeois Europe; one woman likened the strife in Paris to the siege of Rome by the barbarians. The feeling was reciprocated, and not by French workers alone. "Every proletarian," wrote the editor of *Red Revolution* in London, "who does not see and feel that he belongs to an enslaved and degraded class is a *fool*." The ideological breach between the classes was complete, and that division remains the formal posture of western European politics to this day.

Looking back on the revolutions of 1848, Karl Marx observed wryly that history repeats itself: the first time as tragedy, the second as farce. There was more than a touch of farce about many of them, but there was much tragedy too, and in the June Days of Paris, an ominous portent of the future. But perhaps the dominant emotion was frustration. For a glorious moment, liberals had dreamed of constitutions, nationalists of unification, and radicals of a classless society in which the workers of every land could embrace as comrades. These dreams were not as yet to be.

The European elite of the mid-nineteenth century—an amalgam of the upper bourgeoisie and the traditional landed aristocracy—was still powerful enough to maintain itself, while its opponents were too diffuse in their aims, too divided among themselves, and too little rooted in the political and social realities of the mass of the population they claimed to represent. Yet the demands they made—political equality, national consolidation, and social justice—reflected deeply felt ideological contradictions within European society. Inherited privilege, the basis of political dominance in Europe for centuries, was no longer self-justifying, while acquired privilege—the accumulation of wealth and capital by the bourgeoisie—was equally suspect as a mandate to rule. If the revolutionaries of 1848 had failed to topple the existing order, they had exposed the essential hollowness and vulnerability of any authority not based on popular consent.

Notes

1. P. Robertson, *Revolutions of 1848* (New York: Harper & Row, 1960), p. 61.

Suggestions for Further Reading

Abrams, M. H. *The Mirror and the Lamp: Romantic Theory and the Critical Tradition.* New York: Oxford University Press, 1953.

Artz, F. B. *Reaction and Revolution 1814–1832.* New York: Harper & Row, 1963.

Chevalier, L. *Laboring Classes and Dangerous Classes in Paris During the First Half of the Nineteenth Century.* New York: Fertig, 1973.

Clark, K. *The Romantic Rebellion.* New York: Harper & Row, 1973.

Dakin, D. *The Greek Struggle for Independence.* Berkeley: University of California Press, 1973.

De Ruggiero, G. *The History of European Liberalism,* trans. R. G. Collingswood. Boston: Beacon Press, 1959.

Droz, J. *Europe Between Revolutions, 1815–1848.* New York: Harper & Row, 1967.

Friedenthal, R. *Goethe. His Life and Times.* Cleveland: World Publishing Co., 1965.

Hammond, J. L., and Hammond, B. *The Age of Chartism.* Hamden, Conn.: Archon Books, 1962.

Hobsbawm, E. J. *The Age of Revolution: Europe, 1789 to 1848.* New York: New American Library, 1962.

Kohn, H. *The Idea of Nationalism.* New York: Collier Books, 1967.

Krieger, L. *The German Idea of Freedom.* Boston: Beacon Press, 1957.

Lichtheim, G. *A Short History of Socialism.* New York: Praeger, 1970.

McLellan, D. *Karl Marx: His Life and Thought.* New York: Harper & Row, 1973.

Manuel, F. E. *The Prophets of Paris.* Cambridge, Mass: Harvard University Press, 1962.

Nicolson, H. *The Congress of Vienna.* London: Constable, 1946.

Pinkney, D. H. *The French Revolution of 1830.* Princeton, N.J.: Princeton University Press, 1972.

Pointon, M. "Liberty on the Barricades: Women, Politics and Sexuality in Delacroix," in S. Reynolds, ed., *Women, State and Revolution.* Brighton: Wheatsheaf, 1986.

Robertson, P. *Revolutions of 1848.* New York: Harper & Row, 1960.

Stearns, P. N. *1848: The Revolutionary Tide in Europe.* New York: Norton, 1974.

Taylor, A. J. P. *The Habsburg Monarchy, 1809–1918.* New York: Harper & Row, 1965.

The Triumph of Nationalism in the West

The failure of the 1848 upheavals represented at once a crushing blow to the ideals of romantic revolution and the last desperate stand of the conservative order established by the Congress of Vienna. In the decades that followed, the forces of order gave way to those of change as a powerful, rapidly spreading nationalism triumphed in Europe.

As the dominant theme of European history over the next half century, nationalism had a powerful appeal to a broad cross section of society, from workers to industrialists and from merchants to aristocrats. Many factors explain the success of nationalism in the post-1848 period. Unlike the abortive nationalist movements of the 1820s and 1830s, it now combined the Romantic celebration of the past and its tortured search for self-identity with a new realism based on the understanding and use of power. Moreover, artists, writers, and musicians explored nationalistic themes in their work, while both higher literacy rates and more skillful propaganda made ever-larger numbers of the middle and lower classes sensitive to nationalist

Princess Victoria of Hohenzollern, the wife of Emperor Frederick William IV of Germany, was at the center of liberal opposition to Bismarck's domestic policies. [Mansell Collection]

symbolism. Most important, in regions where nationalistic aspirations were frustrated by foreign domination, a new generation of practical, tough-minded leaders came into power. Raised during the turbulent days of the Napoleonic empire, these men admired the methods of modern warfare and diplomacy, appreciated the benefits of efficient government, and understood the principles of liberal economics and industrial development. Cavour in Italy and Bismarck in Germany were the two most outstanding examples of this marriage between nationalism and power politics. In an age increasingly under the influence of science and technology, Bismarck and Cavour successfully translated the ideals of an earlier generation into the concrete action of the new.

Although all-pervasive, nationalism reflected local conditions. In Italy and Germany it assumed the form of nation building. Where centralized states already existed, as in Britain, nationalism merged with liberalism to forge a new ruling elite dedicated to industrial and commercial expansion through overseas empire or, as in the case of France, to economic development under a restored empire. In the Austrian, Russian, and Ottoman empires, despotic but ineffectual monarchies struggled to control ethnically diverse populations clamoring for independence or self-determination, while the young republic of the United States struggled to restore unity after a destructive civil war. Finally, the international Zionist movement added a new element to nationalism as it sought to give expression to the centuries-old quest for a Jewish homeland.

The emergence of nationalism in the second half of the nineteenth century is a development of immense importance. As a worldwide phenomenon, its long-range repercussions would be felt in the national antagonisms that twice in the twentieth century erupted into global war, in the twisted ideas that fed the ideologies of fascism between the wars, and in the national rivalries over which the United States and the Soviet Union have fought a dangerous ideological war. Ironically, nationalism also inspired the revolt of former colonies against Western rule, which was itself partly a consequence of nationalism.

The Politics of National Grandeur: Napoleon III in France

Nowhere after 1848 was the beguiling appeal of nationalism stronger than in France. In December 1848, partly as a result of the gruesome violence of the June insurrection, French males overwhelmingly chose as the president of their new Second Republic Louis-Napoleon Bonaparte, the enigmatic nephew of Napoleon I. Much to everyone's amazement, General Louis-Eugène Cavaignac, the conservative republican hero who had crushed the June riots,

received only 1.5 million votes, the socialist Alexandre Ledru-Rollin and the poet Alphonse de Lamartine even less, whereas the virtually unknown Louis-Napoleon won the trust of more than 5.5 million Frenchmen.

Louis-Napoleon (1808–1873) had almost no political experience, but the magic of his name was irresistible. For years he had lived abroad, a dreamy youth caught up in the euphoria of revolutionary romanticism. Implicated in the 1831 revolt in the Papal States and in two ludicrous plots to overthrow Louis-Philippe, he spent time in exile and then in prison until his escape to England in 1846. French and English reactionaries funded his return to Paris in the midst of the 1848 revolution, whereupon he campaigned for the presidency by invoking the theme of national unity.

Louis-Napoleon's platform, designed to appeal to a strife-torn society, argued that the country needed an authoritarian leader. Like many modern politicians, however, Louis-Napoleon was duplicitous. While appealing to Catholics and other proponents of authority, he also cultivated the support of the working classes.

He proposed to eliminate a corrupt Parliament and political parties to open the way to a direct relationship between the citizens and himself through plebiscites based on universal male suffrage. Unlike the role of the aristocratic Old Regime or the upper-middle-class government of Louis-Philippe, the proper role—indeed, the duty—of government was, in Louis-Napoleon's mind, to wipe out poverty and provide prosperity for all citizens.

These views, first expressed in two pamphlets he wrote while in prison, *On Napoleonic Ideas* and *The Extinction of Poverty*, formed the core of Louis-Napoleon's political thought. But his popularity was derived in large measure from the memory of national greatness attached to Napoleon I. Despite a stocky build and an exaggerated mustache and goatee, Louis-Napoleon had a charismatic appeal that transcended class and social status. He also realized that public opinion could be a powerful instrument of authority. He knew almost by instinct what later, twentieth-century dictators would discover, that an authoritarian state based on nationalist pride and popular consensus and promising both social tranquillity and economic prosperity had a strong appeal in times of stress.

The Second Republic lasted three years. Although its constitution provided for a strong president, the chief executive could serve for only one term. Louis-Napoleon therefore played to the conservatives who dominated the National Assembly by enacting measures in favor of the Catholic church, reducing the suffrage, and restricting freedom of education and the press. When the legislature refused to amend the constitution to permit him a second term, Louis-Napoleon seized power. On December 2, 1851, he illegally dissolved the Assembly and proclaimed a temporary dictatorship in the name of the people. With the support of the army, he arrested his opponents and crushed an uprising of the workers. In a plebiscite held that same month, 92 percent of the voters gave him the power to draft a new constitution that made him president for ten years. A second plebiscite a year later confirmed by an even greater margin the hold of the Napoleonic legend on the national psyche: Louis-Napoleon was proclaimed Napoleon III, emperor of the French.*

The Second Empire

The structure of imperial government, inspired by the constitution of Napoleon I, was designed to give the impression of a regime responsive to the popular will. An appointed senate was balanced by an assembly chosen every six years by carefully manipulated elections based on universal male suffrage. Parliament could, however, only dis-

*Napoleon II, son of Napoleon I, died in 1832 without having served as emperor.

cuss items submitted by the emperor and had to debate behind closed doors. Napoleon personally controlled the army and the budget and conducted foreign affairs, advised by a handpicked Council of State.

Napoleon's domestic policies, resting on vigorous government intervention in the economy, produced unparalleled prosperity. The emperor deliberately strengthened the middle class by encouraging investment and the modernization of industry. The state-owned railroad increased its mileage fivefold during the first decade of imperial rule, thus stimulating industrial development and commerce. A law passed in 1865 introduced the concept of limited liability to protect corporate stockholders from excessive risk. Investment capital was raised through the *Crédit Mobilier*, a banking institution that sold shares to the public. A free trade agreement with Britain in 1860 resulted in an increase in French exports and eventually a favorable balance of trade. In an effort to advance commerce with the East, French capital financed—and a French engineer, Ferdinand de Lesseps, constructed—the Suez Canal in the decade between 1859 and 1869. These measures bound

◎ The Napoleonic Myth ◎

In 1839, while living in exile in Great Britain, Louis-Napoleon wrote a pamphlet titled On Napoleonic Ideas. *Praising the reign of his uncle as having been founded on the will of the people, Louis-Napoleon contributed to the popularization of the Napoleonic myth on which he was to base his own rise to power.*

The Emperor Napoleon has contributed more than any other person to hasten the reign of liberty, by preserving the moral influence of the revolution, and diminishing the fears which it inspired. . . .

The government of Napoleon, better than any other, could have sustained liberty, for the simple reason that liberty would have strengthened his throne, though it overthrows such thrones as have not a solid foundation.

Liberty would have fortified his power, because Napoleon had established in France all that ought to precede liberty; because his power reposed upon the whole mass of the nation; because his interests were the same as those of the people; because, finally, the most perfect confidence reigned between the ruler and the governed. . . .

There is no longer any necessity to reconstruct the system of the emperor; it will reconstruct itself. Sovereigns and nations will concur in re-establishing it; because each one will see in it a guaranty of order, of peace, and of prosperity. . . .

In conclusion, let us repeat it, the Napoleonic idea is not one of war, but a social, industrial, commercial idea, and one which concerns all mankind. If to some it appears always surrounded by the thunder of combats, that is because it was in fact for too long a time veiled by the smoke of cannon and the dust of battles. But now the clouds are dispersed, and we can see, beyond the glory of arms, a civil glory greater and more enduring.

Source: L. N. Bonaparte, *Napoleonic Ideas,* trans. J. Dorr (New York: Appleton, 1859).

Napoleon III and the Empress Eugenie with their son. Napoleon III dreamed of imperial grandeur, but this photograph shows the Bonapartes as a proper bourgeois family. [Culver Pictures]

a massive rebuilding program. Narrow but picturesque medieval streets and unattractive neighborhoods were demolished to make way for 85 miles of broad boulevards and tree-shaded pavements. Along with large squares and stately new buildings, Haussmann also built sewers to provide drainage. Although costly and controversial, these projects not only created jobs but also gave the emperor better security because the wider avenues made it difficult to erect barricades against government troops, as the Parisians had done so often in the past. This experiment in urban renewal transformed Paris into a well-ordered and elegant city. It also created a vast stage on which Napoleon and his consort, the empress Eugénie, performed lavish public ceremonies befitting the renewed splendor of France.

Born Eugénia de Montijo (1826–1920), Eugénie was the beautiful, ambitious daughter of a Spanish father and a Franco-American mother. When she met the French president in 1850, she judged him a man of greatness and offered to finance his *coup d'état* the next year. They were married in January 1853, after Napoleon became emperor, in a sumptuous ceremony in Notre Dame Cathedral. Together they presided with great elegance over the Second Empire. Just as Napoleon dreamed of the reemergence of his nation as a great power, so Paris was to become once again the arbiter of Europe in matters of taste and culture. After the drab years of Louis-Philippe's bourgeois monarchy, the new imperial court gave at least the appearance of grandeur.

Despite the considerable domestic achievements of the Second Empire, the economic conditions of the working class were depressed and Napoleon III did nothing to improve the condition of French women. Although his uncle's civil code had declared the equality of all French citizens, women were not included in the definition of citizenship, with the result that the power of men over them was actually strengthened. For example, after marriage, women could not control their own property, engage in a business or profession, or administer children's financial affairs without the consent of their husbands. Divorce laws favored men, and adultery had significantly more serious consequences for wives than for husbands. The law codes thus reinforced women's legal inequality and subordination.

Uniting with the utopian socialists in the 1830s and with the republican socialists in 1848 and 1849, the French feminist movement had been one of the most vigorous and advanced in Europe, pushing hard for women's rights and social reform in general. But the censorship and restrictive domestic policies of the Second Empire repressed the feminists along with other opponents of Napoleon III's rule. Feminist views were therefore restricted largely to the liberal salons of Paris and the underground press, where women writers—notably Juliette Lamber and Jenny Héricourt—fought against conservative patriarchy and the equally antifeminist views of former socialist and republi-

the middle class to the government, for industrial production had doubled and the vitality of the economy seemed to confirm the wisdom of the French people in putting another Bonaparte on the throne.

Working-class support for Napoleon III was almost as strong as middle-class enthusiasm, for wages kept pace with inflation and the emperor sponsored government health programs, low-cost housing, and numerous public works projects. Despite the fears of many businessmen, in the 1860s he even permitted the formation of trade unions and legalized the right to strike.

The vigorous economic life of the Second Empire was accompanied by a deliberate effort to drape the public image of France in a grand, if at times gaudy, style. The results were most stunning in the imperial capital, where Napoleon appointed Baron Georges Haussmann to direct

Renovation of a Paris neighborhood, as ordered by Baron Haussmann. [Granger Collection]

can allies such as Pierre-Joseph Proudhon and the historian Jules Michelet. Lamber and Héricourt argued for women's rights in education, the professions, and government and exposed the contradictions implicit in the prevalent attitudes toward marriage, divorce, and the double sexual standard. They and women like them kept social debate alive until the repressive phase of the empire came to an end in the 1860s.

The Liberalization of the Empire

Napoleon III protested that he was a man of peace, but foreign entanglements often threatened to disrupt the stability of the Second Empire. Almost unavoidably, the invocation of the Napoleonic legend raised the specter of war, although Napoleon III had neither the military genius nor the diplomatic astuteness of his uncle. French participation in the Crimean War had been popular, and colonial forays in Africa and Indochina had limited success. But his intervention in Italian affairs backfired when it resulted in the loss of papal territory. More damaging was the disastrous attempt in the 1860s to impose French control over Mexico; even worse was Napoleon's failure to obtain territorial gains from the unification of Germany. The cumulative effect of these mistakes gave rise to domestic criticism, and Napoleon's sensitivity to public opinion led him to make reforms intended to soothe the discontent.

This process of liberalizing the empire, against which Eugénie counseled her husband, began by granting the Assembly increased powers and permitting his political enemies—especially liberals, republicans, and legitimist monarchists—to criticize the government openly. He next lifted the restrictions on parliamentary debate and freedom of the press, a move that encouraged the opposition. The

lifting of censorship also led to the emergence of a reinvigorated feminist movement. Women such as Maria Deraismes debated the issue of inequality before large audiences, published feminist newspapers, and established the Association for the Rights of Women. Although Deraismes and her friends were few in number and it would be many decades before their movement scored significant victories, they contributed much to the quality of French political life in the last years of the Second Empire. By 1869, when national elections were held, it became clear that the emperor had lost control of the political situation—almost half of the voters supported opposition candidates and elected 30 republicans to the assembly. Early in 1870 Napoleon institutionalized these changes in a new constitution that for all practical purposes created a parliamentary government with the emperor serving as head of state. In May the last of Napoleon's plebiscites showed 7.5 million citizens in favor of the new regime but only 1.5 million against.

Whether these sweeping changes reflected Napoleon III's desire to bring France closer to democracy is uncertain, but his days as emperor were numbered. In the summer, drained and in ill health, he went to war against Prussia, and before it was over the Second Empire had collapsed in defeat and the French people had once again turned to a republic.

Material progress made the first decade of Louis-Napoleon's reign among the best years economically in the history of modern France, at least for the bourgeoisie, yet the price of prosperity was the suppression of political freedom. The second half of his rule saw the gradual restoration of liberty accompanied by imperialism and war. Once admired as one of the great rulers of the mid-nineteenth century, he died a broken man, scorned by European opinion and repudiated by the French people. He was the victim of the very Napoleonic legend that he represented.

Power Politics and the Unification of Italy

If nationalist pride had made and then destroyed an emperor in France, its impact was even more dramatic in central and southern Europe. There, by 1871, two new nation-states, Italy and Germany, appeared. Italy, in Metternich's famous phrase, had been merely a "geographical expression." The Italian peninsula comprised a dozen or so independent states; Germany was, at the same time, little more than a name used to describe the region between France and Austria that consisted of some 38 separate kingdoms, principalities, and duchies. Both had had

glorious pasts, Italy as the center of the ancient Roman empire and the land of the Renaissance humanists, Germany as the core of the medieval Holy Roman Empire and the site of Luther's Protestant Reformation. But circumstances and history combined to keep each divided and subject to foreign intervention and manipulation.

Nationalism in Italy and Germany was aroused by the French invasions and the wars of Napoleon I. Bonaparte had reduced and rearranged the states in each region and thereby suggested the possibilities of national unification to Italians and Germans, but their nationalism was in part a reaction against foreign occupation. After Waterloo, the Congress of Vienna restored almost all the original rulers of these states to their thrones and replaced French occupation with Austrian influence. In the 1820s and 1830s

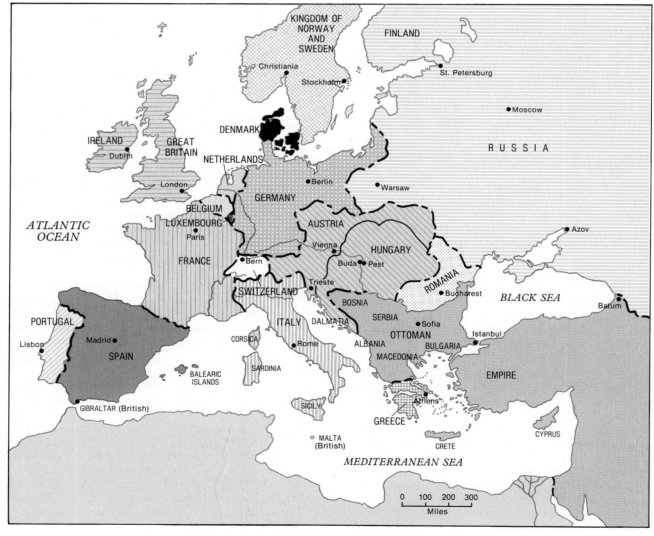

31.1 Europe in 1871

revolutionary Romanticism failed to bring down the status quo so anxiously guarded by Metternich, although national feeling continued to mature during the next decade. As we have seen, the 1848 revolutions gave rise to the first serious attempts to achieve unification in Italy and Germany, but again Austrian military intervention crushed nationalist hopes.

Out of the defeats of 1849 came one positive result: Piedmont-Sardinia emerged as the only viable Italian state to champion national independence, while Prussian leadership became the focus of the unification effort in Germany. In the 1850s Cavour as prime minister of Piedmont and in the 1860s Bismarck as chancellor of Prussia gave their national movements strong leadership that easily matched Napoleon III in cunning and ambition and, by substituting the principles of power politics for Romantic idealism, achieved unification at last.

Nation building in Italy and Germany demonstrated that midcentury nationalism had secured the consensus of large portions of the middle classes and eventually the nobility. By 1871, when the process was complete, the entrance of Italy and Germany into the European state system profoundly altered the balance of power on the Continent.

The Italian Risorgimento

Strong local traditions and competition characterized the politics of the Italian peninsula since the appearance of city-states in the Middle Ages. Despite some changes wrought at Vienna in 1815, the congress restored the overall structure of the Italian state system. In the south the Kingdom of the Two Sicilies (including Naples and Sicily) was ruled by a branch of the Bourbon dynasty related through marriage to the Austrian Habsburgs. In central Italy the Papal States remained the temporal possession of the Catholic church and were ruled from Rome by the popes. The north-central region consisted of a patchwork of small states dominated from Florence by the Grand Duchy of Tuscany, where dynastic and political arrangements also gave the Habsburgs considerable influence. In northeastern Italy the Vienna settlement gave the Habsburgs direct control over the provinces of Lombardy and Venetia, which were ruled from Milan by an Austrian viceroy. Finally, in the strategically important northwest corner lay the Kingdom of Sardinia, consisting of the Piedmont and Savoy regions and the island of Sardinia, ruled by the House of Savoy. This ambitious dynasty had pursued a long-standing policy of expansion in Italy, and in the first half of the century Charles Albert had made two dramatic but unsuccessful bids to oust Austria from the peninsula.

Italian nationalists debated a variety of programs that shared the common goal of an Italian "resurgence," or *Risorgimento*, as the movement for independence and unity was known. Giuseppe Mazzini (1805–1872), one of the great European theorists of nationalism, preached a revolution aimed at creating a united Italian republic based on popular sovereignty and universal suffrage. Mazzini's idealistic propaganda, which educated a generation of Italians to the cause of freedom, posed a radical democratic alternative to the more conservative programs of his contemporaries. The Neo-Guelph* movement, founded by the Piedmontese priest Vincenzo Gioberti, advocated a federation of Italian states led by the papacy and protected by the king of Sardinia. The election of Pope Pius IX in 1846 gave brief impetus to Gioberti's plan, but ultimately his effort to reconcile Italian unification with the temporal interests of the church proved unrealistic. The third alternative, known as the moderate program, was the work of a group of liberal Piedmontese noblemen. Opposed to the revolutionary tactics and democratic principles of Mazzini, the moderates championed a unification imposed from above by Piedmontese armies and a constitutional monarchy under the House of Savoy. The Risorgimento was the climax of Italian nationalism, but from another perspective it was also an ideological civil war fought between radicals and moderates deeply divided over the form and purposes of the unified state that all desired.

---

*In the Middle Ages the Guelphs were supporters of the papacy against the ambitions of the Holy Roman Emperor.

Cavour the Realist

Charles Albert's valiant war against Austria in 1848 and 1849 had given credibility to the moderate program. De-

Count Cavour, whose shrewd policies ultimately unified Italy, is depicted here in a photograph taken at the Congress of Paris in 1856. [Mansell Collection]

spite his abdication in 1849, the hapless monarch had left his kingdom a constitution that became the symbol of Italian liberal hopes and that his son, Victor Emmanuel II (1849–1878), refused to rescind despite Austrian pressure. In 1850 the young king appointed to the cabinet Count Camillo Benso di Cavour (1810–1861), a brilliant statesman into whose hands the leadership of the Risorgimento passed.

Although born into the nobility, Cavour was also the epitome of the nineteenth-century businessman. Portly, nearsighted, and a dull orator who spoke French better than Italian, Cavour was nonetheless crafty and steel-willed. Above all, he was a master of power politics, unwilling to allow principle to interfere with objectives and capable of outwitting Europe's shrewdest diplomats. With a successful background in agriculture, industry, and bank-

ing, he developed an abiding belief in economic liberalism. First as minister of agriculture and commerce in 1850 and then as prime minister from 1852, he modernized Piedmont's economy and forged an alliance of moderate forces within parliament that was responsible for progressive legislation. He understood fully that Piedmont lacked the strength to rid Italy of the Austrians alone, and his policy hinged on securing the support of powerful foreign allies. Nevertheless, Cavour's view of unification was more limited than Mazzini's, for his goal was originally the creation of a large Piedmontese kingdom covering northern Italy but excluding the Papal States and the Bourbon south.

Cavour's first step in the realization of his plan was a masterstroke of political cynicism. Although Piedmont had no apparent interest in the Near East, in 1854 he intervened in the Crimean War on the side of Britain and

31.2 The Unification of Italy, 1859–1870

France, thus securing a place for himself at the Paris peace talks that followed. Cavour not only succeeded in raising the "Italian question" at the conference but also won the admiration of Napoleon III. The French emperor, who in his youth had developed a strong affection for Italy, believed that his sponsorship of the Italian cause would further his own prestige. In July 1858 he and Cavour negotiated the secret Treaty of Plombières. The agreement pledged French military support for a war against Austria, the goal of which would be Piedmont's annexation of Lombardy and Venetia. Victory was to result in the creation of a kingdom of upper Italy and an Italian federation under the presidency of the pope. For its help, France would receive from Piedmont the provinces of Savoy and Nice. Cavour and Napoleon further agreed to manufacture a suitable pretext for war with Austria, and they promised not to make a separate peace until their goals had been reached.

In the tension-filled months that followed, efforts to settle the Italian problem peacefully threatened to wreck Cavour's plans. In April 1859, however, the Austrians played into his hands by issuing an ultimatum demanding that Piedmont demobilize its armies. The French declared war and, taking advantage of Austrian delays, quickly moved into Italy to join their Piedmontese allies. Lombardy was liberated, but as the allies prepared to press into Venetia the unpredictable Louis-Napoleon suddenly announced the conclusion of an armistice at Villafranca with the Austrian emperor, Franz Joseph. It clearly violated Napoleon's agreement with Cavour, for the Austrians were forced only to surrender Lombardy. Nevertheless, Victor Emmanuel accepted the terms, and the outraged Cavour resigned in protest.

Yet all was not lost. During the fighting in Lombardy, moderate nationalists and liberal businessmen secretly worked in cooperation with Cavour to stage a series of revolts that unseated the rulers of the central Italian duchies. Then, in the wake of the armistice of Villafranca, they engineered popular demonstrations in favor of union with Piedmont. Returning to office in January, Cavour suppressed his anger and struck a bargain with Napoleon that permitted the Piedmontese annexation of these territories. Borrowing one of Napoleon's favorite political tactics, Cavour engineered plebiscites to confirm popular enthusiasm for his territorial aggrandisement. Thus by 1860 Piedmont had been considerably enlarged by the addition of Lombardy and the duchies of central Italy. The first step in the unification of Italy was over.

The Crisis of Italian Unification

Until the plebiscites in central Italy, the astute Cavour had managed to shape the course of events, but now the initiative was seized by Giuseppe Garibaldi (1807–1882). A hero in the age of power politics, a determined Romantic in the face of Cavour's cynicism, Garibaldi was nevertheless the greatest guerrilla fighter of the century. Although he believed in Mazzini's republican doctrines, he was above all a patriot determined to see Italy free and united. With a death sentence on his head for having taken part in a Mazzinian plot, Garibaldi fled to South America in 1834 and fought against authoritarian government in the jungles of Uruguay. He returned to Italy in 1848 to fight along with Charles Albert and then went to Rome to lead the dramatic defense of Mazzini's republic against the French troops sent there by Louis-Napoleon to restore the pope. By 1859, when Garibaldi again commanded a volunteer army against Austria, he was a popular figure with a rapidly growing following.

Garibaldi's vision of unification encompassed the entire Italian peninsula. In 1860 he decided to complete the process begun by Cavour with a daring military expedition against the Kingdom of the Two Sicilies. Cavour not only mistrusted Garibaldi's republican sentiments but also feared that Napoleon III would intervene if Garibaldi attempted to seize Rome. He therefore played a double game, secretly encouraging Garibaldi's 1,000-man army of "Red Shirts" while simultaneously preparing to stop the guerrilla leader with force should he threaten Rome. Landing in Sicily in May, Garibaldi outmaneuvered the Bourbon armies, recruited additional volunteers among the disaffected peasants, and captured the island. By September he had crossed to the mainland and taken the Neapolitan capital, declaring a provisional dictatorship over the entire Italian south. In the meantime, a worried Cavour had persuaded Napoleon III to agree to the passage of Piedmontese troops through the Papal States in order to protect the pope. Instead, Victor Emmanuel seized all the papal lands except for the area around Rome. In October, as the Risorgimento reached its climax, Victor Emmanuel and Garibaldi met just south of Naples, thus bringing the moderate and the radical forces face to face. Determined to make Italy a nation rather than plunge it into civil war, Garibaldi relinquished his conquests to the king. In March 1861 the Piedmontese sovereign was proclaimed Victor Emmanuel II, king of Italy. Two months later Cavour died.

The euphoria of the Risorgimento quickly faded as the Italians encountered the problems of nationhood. Indeed, the kingdom was still incomplete—Venetia was not incorporated until the Austro-Prussian War of 1866, and Rome itself was not seized until the Franco-Prussian War in 1870. When it did occur, the annexation of Rome produced deep hostility between the Catholic church and the new state that plagued Italian affairs for the next half century. Regional differences and local loyalties remained strong, and the gap between the developing industrial interests of the north and the depressed agricultural economy of the south widened. A host of vital public policy issues that included illiteracy, disease, and extreme poverty, placed

⊚ Cavour Versus Garibaldi ⊚

*Throughout 1860, while Garibaldi's volunteer army seized the island
of Sicily and then the mainland portion of the Kingdom of Naples,
Count Cavour, the Piedmontese premier, tried to prevent Garibaldi
from seizing control of the Italian unification movement. In this letter
Cavour describes his political calculations and his efforts to stop
Garibaldi.*

If Garibaldi proceeds to the mainland of southern Italy and captures Naples just as he has
already taken Sicily and Palermo, he will become absolute master of the situation. King
Victor Emmanuel would lose almost all his prestige in the eyes of Italians. . . .

We would be forced to go along with his plans and help him fight Austria. I am therefore convinced that the king must not receive the crown of Italy from Garibaldi's
hands. . . .

I have no illusions about the grave and dangerous decision I am advocating, but I
believe it is essential if we are to save the monarchic principle. Better a king of Piedmont
should perish in war against Austria than be swamped by the revolution. The dynasty
might recover from a defeat in battle, but if dragged through the revolutionary gutter its
fate would be . . . sealed.

Although I have made up my mind how to act if Garibaldi reaches Naples, it is nevertheless my first duty to the king and Italy to do everything possible to prevent his success
there. My only hope of foiling him is if I can overthrow the Bourbon regime before Garibaldi crosses to the mainland—or at least before he has had time to reach Naples. If the
regime falls, I would then take over the government of Naples in the name of order and
humanity, and so snatch out of Garibaldi's hands the supreme direction of the Italian
movement.

Source: C. B. di Cavour, letter to Costantino Nigra, August 1, 1860, in D. Mack Smith, ed., *Garibaldi*
(Englewood Cliffs, N.J.: Prentice-Hall, 1969), pp. 44–45.

enormous pressure on a national debt already burdened
by the costs of the wars of unification. Added to these
difficulties was an often corrupt parliamentary regime that
remained unresponsive to the needs of the largely unenfranchised poorer classes and a ruling elite bent on making
Italy a great power. The challenge for Cavour's successors, then, would be to resolve these problems of national
development and move Italy toward political democracy.

Iron and Blood: The Making of the German Empire

In Germany, as in Italy, the Congress of Vienna mandated
a restoration designed to prevent national unification as
well as to guarantee Austrian preponderance in German
affairs. The creation of the German Confederation, with a
diet, or parliament, at Frankfurt representing 38 sovereign
states, recognized the irreversibility of Bonaparte's destruction of the Holy Roman Empire and his simplification
of the German state system. The new German Confederation included small states with only a few hundred
square miles of territory, such as the Thuringian principalities, and much larger units such as the Kingdom of
Bavaria, which comprised more than 10,000 square miles.
Religious differences reinforced political divisions, for
while northern Germany was Protestant, the predominantly Catholic South tended to regard Austria as a bulwark against Protestant Prussia. In these circumstances,
Austria dominated the divided German states.

Nationalism and the German State System

The Kingdom of Prussia, with considerably enlarged territories and a formidable army, was the second most powerful state in the German Confederation. Its autocratic and

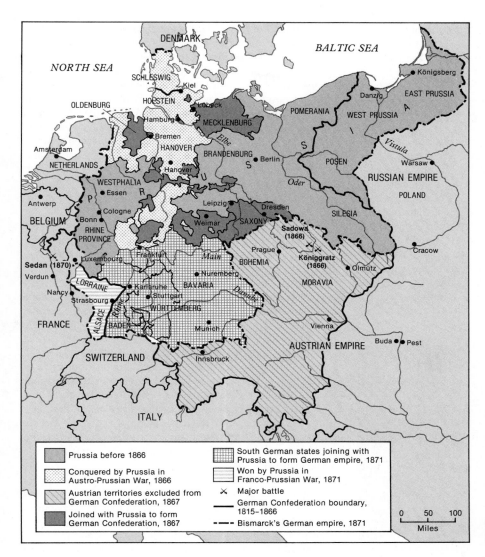

*31.3 The Unification
of Germany, 1866–1871*

unstable monarch, Frederick William IV (1840–1861), aspired to expand the Hohenzollern position in Germany. Just as Piedmont vied with Austria for mastery in Italy, so Prussian-Austrian rivalry was the heart of the German power struggle after 1815. The stronghold of German nationalism, however, was not the Prussian monarchy, whose motivation was largely one of dynastic power, but the rapidly growing liberal middle class. The Prussian-sponsored *Zollverein* (customs union) that developed after 1818 not only stimulated trade throughout Germany and underscored the economic advantages of unification but also anticipated the so-called *kleindeutsch* (small German) solution that sought to exclude Austria from German affairs.

By 1848 these middle-class elements hoped that Prussia would provide the leadership to unify Germany and give

it a constitutional monarchy. Twice during the revolutions of 1848, however, these expectations were dashed by the military-aristocratic forces that ruled Prussia. In the fall Frederick William, encouraged by the army and reactionary elements in his court, withdrew his promise to allow an elected constituent assembly to draft a liberal constitution. In March 1849, when the Frankfurt assembly elected him emperor of Germany, he rejected the "crown from the gutter," later issuing a more conservative constitution of his own. This royal document provided for a two-chamber parliament, an appointed upper house and a lower house elected by an unequal and indirect system of universal male suffrage. Although the constitution was ambiguous about the role of the lower house (*Landtag*) in formulating budget laws, it was clear that the king retained extensive authority. Yet Frederick William's efforts to unify Germany failed. In 1850, when he attempted to solicit an imperial crown from his fellow German monarchs, Austria and Russia coerced him to abandon the plan in a humiliating confrontation at Olmütz.

Bismarck and the Liberals

Despite its commerical and industrial primacy, Prussia's repressive domestic policies, together with Frederick William's timidity in foreign affairs, cast doubt on its ability to bring about German unification. These tendencies were reinforced when William, the monarch's brother, became regent in 1858 and then king in 1861. William I (1861–1888) precipitated a constitutional crisis in Prussia that changed the course of German history.

In February 1860 William presented a bill to the Prussian Landtag that proposed to double the size of the regular army and increase compulsory military service from two to three years. Most controversial, perhaps, was the fact that the king, himself a professional soldier, wished

Bismarck, who forged the modern German state, is shown in 1871, the year the new empire was proclaimed. [Culver Pictures]

to reduce the role and independence of the civilian militia, whose lack of discipline he regarded with contempt. The liberal middle classes—who, because of the elitist nature of the suffrage law, dominated the Landtag—saw these measures as a constitutional challenge, for they wished both to assert the power of parliament over the king and to reduce the influence of the military in Prussian society. As a result, the military bill was eventually withdrawn. When a later version of the same bill was voted down in 1862, William dissolved the Landtag, but the new elections only increased the liberal majority. Torn between abdicating and forcing a showdown with the liberals, the king appointed Count Otto von Bismarck (1815–1898) as his new minister-president.

Bismarck ranks as one of the dominant figures in modern German history. Although a member of the conservative *Junker* class of aristocratic landowners, he was neither provincial in his outlook nor ideologically wedded to the past. He cut an imposing figure, stubborn, fiercely combative, and oblivious to the constraints of tradition and constitutional theory. Bismarck was also a master political strategist. His early career had given him wide experience in diplomacy, first as a Prussian delegate to the Frankfurt Diet and then as ambassador in St. Petersburg and in Paris. While he disdained the parliamentary demands of the liberals, he recognized that they had embraced nationalism and that Prussia needed their industrial skills and wealth. Bismarck's view of unification was at first limited—the imposition of Prussian mastery over largely Protestant northern Germany, a goal he eventually came to believe would require the expulsion of Austria from the German state system.

For Bismarck, the German question and the conflict with the Landtag were linked, for a strong army was needed to deal with Austria. When he found that compromise with the liberals over military reform was impossible, he reorganized the army with funds earmarked for other purposes. The liberals denounced Bismarck's high-handed tactics, and the issue was further complicated by public criticism from Frederick, the heir to the throne, who had been influenced by his liberal-thinking wife, Victoria (1840–1901), the oldest daughter of Britain's Queen Victoria and Prince Albert. Victoria envisioned a unified Germany ruled not by the military but by the best traditions of German culture. Her role in the constitutional crisis resulted in her exclusion from public life for many years.

Not only was Bismarck oblivious to the protests of the liberal opposition, but he lectured them on *Realpolitik*. In blunt speeches before the Landtag, he declared that only a policy of "iron and blood" would yield results, that power rather than principle determined the outcome of conflict, and that results justified means. A vigorous program in foreign affairs, he believed, would win over many liberals and critics of his violation of constitutional procedure. Moreover, since the defeats of 1848, the German intellectuals had either emigrated or abandoned politics. Bis-

◉ Bismarck on Power Politics ◉

On September 30, 1862, Bismarck made the following remarks before the Prussian Landtag in order to secure approval of the military reorganization bill proposed by King William I. His words were the quintessential statement on the nature of power politics.

While it is clear that we cannot avoid complications in Germany, we do not seek them. Germany does not look to Prussia's liberalism but to her power. Because the southern states of Germany—Bavaria, Württemberg, and Baden—would like to indulge in liberalism, Prussia's role will not be assigned to them! Prussia must gather her forces and hold them in reserve for the right moment, which we have already missed several times. Since the Treaty of Vienna, our borders have not been designed to ensure a healthy body politic. Not by speeches and majorities will the great questions of the day be decided—that was the mistake of 1848 and 1849—but by iron and blood.

Source: H. Kohl, ed., *Die politischen Reden des Fürsten Bismarck* (Stuttgart: Cotta, 1892–1905). Translated by P. Cannistraro.

marck thus set the terms on which German unification would be achieved, for just as Cavour's actions intensified the ideological struggle between Italian moderates and radicals, so Bismarck polarized the German unification movement between liberals and the advocates of power politics.

The Showdown with Austria

Bismarck's determination to extend Prussian authority over northern Germany made a military confrontation with Austria all but inevitable. The showdown evolved between 1863 and 1866 and resulted from a situation involving Schleswig and Holstein, two northern duchies controlled by the king of Denmark although not an actual part of his kingdom. Holstein, inhabited almost entirely by Germans, was part of the Confederation, whereas Schleswig's mixed population of Danes and Germans fought bitterly over the issue of membership. When Denmark moved to annex Schleswig in 1863, Bismarck persuaded the Austrians to join Prussia in what proved to be a short and successful war to reclaim the two provinces. The Peace of Vienna that ended the war against Denmark provided that Austria and Prussia would administer the provinces jointly. Discussion as to their future resulted in a deadlock when the Austrians insisted that the provinces become a single state ruled by a German prince, while Bismarck demanded extensive commercial rights that would have made them virtual Prussian provinces. A temporary agreement was established in 1865 according to which Holstein would be run by Austria and Schleswig by Prussia. This awkward arrangement led to continued quarrels between the two al-

lies and eventually gave Bismarck the excuse to provoke a war with Austria.

Like Cavour, Bismarck understood that *Realpolitik* required careful diplomatic preparation among the other European powers. Prussia needed assurance that other nations would not come to Austria's assistance. Because he had offered to help Russia put down a Polish uprising in 1863, Bismarck was fairly certain that Tsar Alexander II would not interfere, but Napoleon III was the unknown element. In the fall of 1865 Bismarck and Napoleon held a secret meeting reminiscent of the Plombières encounter between Napoleon and Cavour. Bismarck secured Napoleon's promise of neutrality in the event of an Austro-Prussian war with vague promises of territorial compensation for France along the Rhine. The following year he negotiated an alliance with Italy that promised Italian military assistance in return for the Austrian-held province of Venetia. After years of preparation, the war came suddenly. On June 1, 1866, the Prussians sent troops into Holstein in protest over what Bismarck claimed was an Austrian violation of their agreement. In response, the Austrians persuaded the German Confederation to vote military action against Prussia. Bismarck's answer was to declare the Confederation dissolved and order Prussia's armies into action.

The Austro-Prussian War was important for several reasons. Bismarck tried to make the point that the "national development of Germany" was at stake, although in truth Prussian aggression was the real issue. After seven weeks of fighting, Austria was defeated at the Königgratz in Bohemia. The Prussian victory was due to the ability to deploy troops rapidly by railroad, to the use of a new breech-loading gun, and to the brilliant strategist Count

Helmuth von Moltke. The king's controversial military re-organization bill had proved itself. Although the war was fought against the other states of the German Confederation as well as Austria, the latter had been poorly prepared and had to fight on both the German and the Italian fronts. By imposing deliberately moderate peace terms on Austria in the Treaty of Prague (August 1866), Bismarck demonstrated once again his mastery of *Realpolitik*. No reparations were extracted from Austria, and a separate agreement forced it only to cede Venetia to the Italians. Bismarck's real goal was achieved by the dissolution of the Confederation and Austria's withdrawal from German affairs. The Austrians also had to recognize Prussia's annexation of Schleswig-Holstein and a number of German states in the north. While the southern Catholic states remained independent, they had to pay indemnities and sign military alliances forcing them to fight on Prussia's side in any future war.

After the war, Bismarck presided over the creation of the North German Confederation. Dominated by Prussia, it included all German states north of the river Main. A constitution made the king of Prussia its president and Bismarck its chancellor. Local affairs remained in the hands of each state, but foreign policy and military authority were controlled by the central government. The parliament of the North German Confederation consisted of the *Bundesrat*, or upper house, representing each of the states, and a *Reichstag*, or lower house, elected by universal male suffrage. This system, which later provided the model for the constitution of united Germany, reflected the wide powers of the Prussian king and limited such parliamentary principles as ministerial responsibility. But the liberalized franchise created the sense that wide strata of the people, not just the middle class, now had a stake in Germany's future.

The Franco-Prussian War
and the Forging of
German Unification

It is difficult to say just how long Bismarck intended the North German Confederation to remain in place. As a Prussian rather than a German nationalist, his vision of unification may well have remained limited despite the events of 1866. But just as Garibaldi had forced Cavour to broaden his view of Italian unification in 1860, so now the diplomatic blunders of Napoleon III pushed Bismarck to complete the process he had begun.

Austria's defeat at the hands of Prussia shocked Napoleon, who had underestimated Prussian power. The suddenness of the Austrian collapse prevented him from intervening, and Prussia's victory had been so complete that Bismarck did not grant the territorial rewards that he had vaguely promised Napoleon. Napoleon's failure to ex-tract concessions from Bismarck, compounded by fiasco in Mexico, stimulated the emperor's opponents at home, who argued that the war represented a severe blow to French prestige. Napoleon became convinced that the consolidation of German strength on France's borders had to be stopped. For his part, Bismarck came to realize that a war with France would inflame German nationalism and push the southern states, where business circles already favored unification, into a united Germany.

Friction between the two countries mounted steadily, with both Napoleon and Bismarck contributing to the tension. The pretext for war arose from a dispute over whether a German prince related to William I would become king of Spain. The immediate cause for the outbreak of the Franco-Prussian War was the so-called Ems dispatch. When William I agreed to withdraw his support of the Hohenzollern candidate, Napoleon demanded that the Prussian king apologize and promise not to raise the Hohenzollern candidacy again. Meeting with the French ambassador at Ems in July 1870, the Prussian ruler refused to give such a promise and telegraphed the details of the talk to Berlin. Bismarck had the dispatch published in the press after changing the wording to create the impression that William had insulted the French. Newspapers in Paris and Berlin sensationalized the telegram and enraged public opinion. On July 19 the French declared war.

As in the case of the struggle with Austria four years earlier, the swiftness of the Franco-Prussian War and the superiority of Prussia's military forces stunned Europe. Thanks to Bismarck's lenient treatment of Austria in 1866, it remained neutral, as did the other great powers; moreover, the military treaties he had forced on the southern German states brought them into the war on the side of Prussia, so that the war became, at least in name, a "national" one. On September 1 the Prussian armies captured Napoleon III along with more than 100,000 French soldiers at Sedan. The news of Napoleon's surrender was followed a few days later in Paris by the proclamation of a republic. The republican forces continued to fight for five additional months despite the siege of the capital and the outbreak of an uprising in March known as the Paris Commune. While Paris held out against starvation and the violence sparked by the Commune, Bismarck consolidated Germany. On January 18, 1871, in the Hall of Mirrors in the palace of Versailles, William I was proclaimed German emperor, and all of Germany was at last unified under a political system virtually identical to the one that had governed the North German Confederation.

At the end of the month the French republic capitulated, and in February a National Assembly was elected and the liberal monarchist Adolphe Thiers chosen as chief executive. Thiers, who made peace with the Germans, had little room to negotiate, for Bismarck was in no mood to be generous. The peace of Frankfurt, signed on May 10, was harsh—France had to pay an indemnity of 5 billion francs and accept German occupation until it was paid.

Most distressing to the French, however, was the loss of Alsace and most of Lorraine to Germany. These provinces, which contained iron deposits and a prosperous textile industry, were inhabited by German-speaking people who preferred the French to the Prussians, and their annexation remained for the next half century a source of bitterness between Germany and France.

The Franco-Prussian War had profound repercussions. Along with the unification of Germany came the victory of Bismarck's political strategy, which had wedded German nationalism to the conservative-aristocratic forces that ruled Prussia and cowed the liberals into abandoning their opposition in the face of unification. The completion of Italian territorial unity was an unexpected by-product of the Franco-Prussian War, for when Napoleon III brought home the troops stationed in Rome to protect the pope, King Victor Emmanuel III seized the city and made it the capital of Italy. Most immediately the war led to the collapse of Napoleon's Second Empire. Perhaps its most far-reaching result was the shift in the balance of power. By 1871 Italy was demanding recognition as a great power, and the collapse of Austria and France demonstrated that Germany had emerged as the most powerful European state. The Treaty of Frankfurt confirmed the end of the Concert of Europe created by the Vienna peace settlement in 1815, for not only had Austria and France been defeated by the new German colossus, but Britain and Russia had remained aloof from the wars. Napoleon III, Cavour, and Bismarck, each in his own way an embodiment of the nationalist doctrines that dominated the age, had wrought profound changes in the structure of the European state system.

Eastern Europe and the Ottomans

Austria's role in Italian and German affairs after 1815 was symptomatic of its status as a multiethnic empire in an age of rising nationalism. This last dynastic state, ruled by the Habsburgs since the Middle Ages, survived the waves of Romantic nationalism of the 1820s and 1830s, as well as the upheavals of 1848, but its existence was seriously challenged in midcentury as its many nationalities clamored for independence. Twelve million Germans controlled political power and enjoyed special status in a state that reached 50 million by 1914 and included 24 million Slavs to the south, 10 million Magyars and 4 million Romanians to the east, as well as Czechs, Slovaks, Poles, Croats, Serbs, Italians, and a variety of other ethnic groups. The Habsburgs made a number of attempts to bring the forces of nationalism under control, but neither reforms, the granting of limited provincial autonomy in 1859, nor the new constitution of 1861 was effective.

The Austro-Prussian War of 1866 demonstrated just how divided and weak the Austrian Empire was, and defeat provoked still one more effort at reform. After difficult negotiations, the emperor Franz Joseph reached a compromise (*Ausgleich*) with Hungarian leaders. The new constitution created the Dual Monarchy, in which Franz Joseph was both king of Hungary and emperor of Austria. Foreign affairs, finance, and military matters were conducted by common ministers, but otherwise the two parts of the monarchy were autonomous, each with its own constitution, official language, and parliament.

The *Ausgleich* did not, of course, eliminate the serious problems facing the empire but merely enabled the Hungarians to share with the Germans in its rule. The other nationality groups continued to demand their freedom. Some industry and a middle class thrived in Bohemia and the area surrounding Vienna, and serfdom had been abolished in 1848. However, in both halves of the Dual Monarchy most inhabitants were landless, backward peasants burdened by conservative landowners and heavy taxes. Despite the ancient lineage of the Habsburgs and the importance of its strategic position in Europe, the Dual Monarchy remained an anachronism in a Europe rapidly dividing along national lines.

VIENNA IN THE AGE OF FRANZ JOSEPH

As the capital of Austria, Vienna was a microcosm of the empire, reflecting its strengths and weaknesses, its brilliance and its contradictions. Since 1278, when the Habsburgs selected the town on the banks of the Danube for their capital, the city was a center of bureaucracy and aristocratic splendor. Vienna grew rapidly in the modern period, and by the opening of the nineteenth century it contained more than a quarter of a million people. Yet although the Habsburg capital was the government center for a vast multiethnic empire, it remained an essentially German city in language and culture.

Because its economy was built around the court and the government, Vienna had little industry or industrial proletariat until the mid-nineteenth century. It collected and spent tax revenues, and its economic life centered on banking, crafts, and the production of luxury goods, including silk and porcelain. Similarly, the social structure of the city included a wealthy aristocracy, a variety of civil servants, artisans and shopkeepers, a small but prosperous business class, and workers. With the coming of the Industrial Revolution to Vienna in the 1830s and 1840s, tens of thousands of peasants streamed into the city, and by the eve of the revolutions of 1848 its population had increased to 400,000.

As long as Austria remained a great European power, Vienna was a center of European diplomacy, a role it played never more splendidly than as host of the great peace settlement following the Napoleonic wars. In the generation before the revolutions of 1848, the city of Metternich became the capital of the European conservative order, crowded with diplomats, reactionary politicians, and police agents bent on uncovering revolutionaries. Metternich's office, and therefore the nerve center of the bureaucracy, was housed in the Ballhaus chancery, built in the early eighteenth century, but the true grandeur of the Habsburg empire was displayed in the rich array of luxurious royal palaces. The emperor Franz Joseph, who died in 1916 after 68 years on the throne, was installed in the vast Hofburg Palace and moved in the summer months to the ornate Schönbrunn Palace. The important aristocratic families of the realm built lavish residences, of which the most remarkable was the Belvedere, the summer palace of Prince Eugène of Savoy. While the bulk of the population lived in middle-class housing and ugly tenements, much of the European nobility that visited Vienna saw only the splendors of the ruling class. In the 1860s Vienna's beauty was enhanced still further by the demolition of the city's medieval wall and the building of the Ringstrasse, a majestic tree-lined boulevard encircling the city that rivaled Haussmann's work in Paris.

Vienna's importance to Western culture was unequaled in the sphere of music. The city nurtured the greatest concentration of musical brilliance in modern times, for the patronage of the Habsburgs and the nobility attracted the musical giants of Europe—Mozart and Haydn, Beethoven, Schubert and Schumann, Johann and Richard Strauss, Brahms and Mahler. Although the second half of the nineteenth century was a period of crisis and decline for the Habsburg empire, its capital thrived as a refined city basking in sentimentality. The light operatic themes of Franz Lehar's *Merry Widow* (1905), together with the late Romantic lushness of the music of Anton Bruckner and Gustav Mahler, had wide popular appeal. The aging emperor Franz Joseph, who stood stiffly in uniform braced by his sword while the imperial court danced to the waltzes of Johann Strauss, was the symbol of a fragile and once great empire.

In this time of unabashed nostalgia, Vienna also gave birth to avant-garde movements that challenged the values of the past. Richard Strauss' *Der Rosenkavalier* (1911) represented the swan song of Romantic opera in the classical style—a young composer, Arnold Schönberg, had already broken from the Western tradition of tonality, and two young followers, Alban Berg and Anton Webern, were pushing the revolution in music even further by abandoning the standard conception of keys. Painters and writers were experimenting with new forms of expression that would later lead to the movement in the arts known as the Vienna Secession. But it was perhaps in the study of a Viennese physician named Sigmund Freud that the most profound transformation was taking place. Freud's investigations suggested that deep-rooted instincts struggled for release and dominance within the human psyche, and the popularization of his work shattered nineteenth-century rationalism.

Vienna also saw the emergence of political movements that challenged the roots of European liberalism, among them the Christian Socialist party of Karl Lüger and the Social Democratic party led by Victor Adler. But whereas the Social Democrats appealed to the city's growing industrial working class, Christian Socialist membership came largely from the petty bourgeoisie. Lüger and his followers identified closely with a growing anti-Semitic sentiment in the city. Lüger was mayor of the city when, in 1907, a teenage German first came to Vienna to study painting. In Vienna the young man discovered anti-Semitism and came to loathe the mixing of nationalities that he saw in the capital. His name was Adolf Hitler.

Russia Between Reaction and Reform

The dilemmas facing a multiethnic empire such as Austria were perhaps more serious still in Russia, where the problems of national minorities were compounded by the vast size of its territory and the complexity of its population. Stretching thousands of miles across two continents, the peoples of the Russian empire included a wide diversity of Europeans and Asians, and for centuries Russia struggled unsuccessfully to define its national identity between the pulls of two civilizations.

Despite its complexity, the social structure of Russia's population was rigidly divided between a small and highly privileged nobility and a huge, impoverished peasant population. Perhaps 95 percent of Russian subjects fell into the peasant category, the great majority of them serfs with no civil rights or property who owed heavy dues and services to the landowning masters. The wealthy nobility owned almost all the land and were exempt from taxes and military service. Because Russia's economy was predominantly agricultural throughout most of the nineteenth century, a small middle class existed only in the larger cities.

In an age when autocracy was disappearing in Europe, the Russian tsar remained an absolute monarch. His will was law, and only the poverty, backwardness, and ineffective bureaucracy of imperial Russia limited his authority. Because no legitimate forms of protest existed, conspiracy and local insurrection were frequent. When faced with such threats, the Romanov dynasty swung between extremes of enlightened reform and brutal repression.

Tsar Alexander I (1801–1825), who recognized that the political and social structure of the empire needed to be modernized, had experimented with constitutionalism and

◉ Tsarist Russia on the Edge of Revolution ◉

In 1881 Tsar Alexander II was assassinated by an anarchist group known as "The Will of the People." In March of that same year the terrorist organization addressed an open letter to the new tsar, Alexander III, of which the following is an excerpt.

A dispassionate glance at the grievous decade through which we have just passed will enable us to forecast accurately the future progress of the revolutionary movement, provided the policy of the government does not change. The movement will continue to grow and extend; deeds of a terroristic nature will increase in frequency and intensity. Meanwhile the number of the discontented in the country will grow larger and larger; confidence in the government, on the part of the people, will decline; and the idea of revolution—of its possibility and inevitability—will establish itself in Russia more and more firmly. A terrible explosion, a bloody chaos, a revolutionary earthquake throughout Russia, will complete the destruction of the order of things. Do not mistake this for a mere phrase. We understand better than any one else can how lamentable is the waste of so much talent and energy—the loss, in bloody skirmishes and in the work of destruction, of so much strength which, under other conditions, might have been expended in creative labor and in the development of the intelligence, the welfare, and the civil life of the Russian people. . . .

These are the reasons why the Russian government exerts no moral influence and has no support among the people. These are the reasons why Russia brings forth so many revolutionists. These are the reasons why even such a deed as killing a Tsar excites in the minds of a majority of the people only gladness and sympathy. Yes your Majesty! Do not be deceived by the reports of flatterers and sycophants; Tsaricide is popular in Russia.

Source: J. H. Robinson and C. Beard, eds., *Readings in Modern European History,* vol. 2 (Boston: Ginn, 1909), pp. 364–366.

---

federalism before reverting to autocracy. His brother, Nicholas I (1825–1855), was so obsessed by the fear of revolution that he appointed secret police to hunt down subversives. Nicholas proclaimed the principles of "autocracy, Orthodoxy, and nationalism," by which he meant obedience to the Romanov dynasty, adherence to the Russian Orthodox church, and the advancement of Russian national interests. Censorship and restrictions on intellectual life were combined with the exile of political prisoners to Siberia.

The tsar also ordered a program of Russification of ethnic minorities and supported the Slavophiles, who believed that Russia should live according to its traditional Slavic values in an agrarian society based on Orthodoxy, mysticism, and despotism. Opposed to this position were the Westerners, who argued that Russia should modernize by adopting the European model of industrial society built on rationalism. This debate split the *intelligentsia,* Russian intellectuals who wanted to achieve political goals.

Alexander II and the Dilemma of Russian Reform

The great issues confronting Russian society in the mid-nineteenth century came to a head after Russia's defeat in the Crimean War. The crisis began when Russia and Turkey went to war in 1853 over the Balkan territories of Moldavia and Wallachia. The next year Britain and France, concerned over Russian attempts to control the Christian holy places in Jerusalem and Palestine and to expand into the eastern Mediterranean, came to the aid of the Turks by invading Russia's Crimean peninsula in the Black Sea. Eventually Piedmont and Austria also sided against Russia, thus involving most of the European powers in a military conflict for the first time since the Congress of Vienna. The Crimean War ended in 1856 with Russia's defeat on the battlefield and diplomatic losses at the Paris peace conference.

Nicholas I died during the war. Like many other Russians, his more liberal son, Alexander II (1855–1881), realized that the Crimean disaster was due in part to the country's military and industrial backwardness, and he at last gave in to demands for reform. In 1861 he issued an imperial edict that emancipated more than 22 million serfs and gave them communal title to a portion of the land on which they worked. A system of local government was begun at the level of the village commune (*mir*), which held the land in common. District councils administered the courts and collected taxes, while indirectly elected provincial councils (*zemstvos*) acted as forums for open discussion of political and social issues and provided elementary education. But the emancipated serfs were forced to compensate their former lords and their land parcels were generally too small for profitable cultivation. The emancipation edict was thus a step forward in relative terms only, for most of the former serfs quickly fell into debt and wound up as agricultural laborers on the estates of their former masters. Moreover, Alexander began to doubt the wisdom of some of his measures after an assassination attempt in 1866, and in the mid-1870s he reimposed censorship on the press and the universities and curtailed freedom of debate in the *zemstvos*.

The new wave of repression sparked widespread discontent. Socialists such as Alexander Herzen (1812–1870) inspired many of the radical intelligentsia to live in the small villages in an attempt to raise peasant political consciousness. But as these so-called *Narodniki* (from the Russian word *narod*, "people") became disillusioned by the obstacles they faced, many began to proclaim themselves "nihilists," who believed in nothing. In the face of Alexander's return to repression, some of the nihilists came under the influence of the anarchist Mikhail Bakunin (1814–1876), who preached the destruction of the government through "propaganda of the deed," by which he meant individual acts of violence. In 1881 Alexander II was assassinated by such a terrorist act.

Russia descended into deep reaction during the reigns of Alexander III (1881–1894) and his son, Nicholas II (1894–1917). The only positive developments were the economic reforms carried out in the 1890s by Count Sergei Witte (1849–1915), a tough finance minister bent on modernizing the Russian economy along Western lines. Under Witte's leadership, government initiative rather than private capital stimulated industrialization. Until reactionary agrarian interests forced his dismissal in 1903, Witte succeeded in attracting Western investments by putting Russia on the gold standard, launching the trans-Siberian railroad, and stimulating industry. The French, eager for an alliance with Russia, poured capital into the empire. According to one estimate, industrial production doubled in a decade. Yet Witte's programs did not begin to come to grips with the monumental social and political problems the country faced.

Turkey: "The Sick Man of Europe"

By the start of the nineteenth century, the Ottoman Empire still ruled an estimated 40 million people, but corruption and administrative chaos were rife and, as in the Austrian Empire it bordered, the nationalist aspirations of its subject populations were already threatening to tear it apart. Revolts by Serbs and Greeks were followed later in the century by Bulgarian and Romanian uprisings, while some of the sultan's ambitious regional commanders, such as Muhammad Ali, governor of Egypt, pursued independent policies. The Western view of the Ottoman Empire was summed up by Tsar Nicholas I, who during a state visit to England in 1844 referred to it as a "dying man."

While nationalist movements challenged the unity of the Ottoman Empire, the great powers posed a more serious threat to its existence. By 1830 the Russians had occupied the Danubian principalities of Moldavia and Wallachia, the French had seized Algiers, and with the help of foreign intervention the Greeks had won their independence. As the internal decay of the Turkish system accelerated and the territorial ambitions of the European states grew, the so-called eastern question emerged. Although on one level it involved the interaction between the Ottoman Empire and the great powers, the eastern question may more clearly be understood as the conflict among the great powers over the future of the sultan's domains. One major complication arose from the growing competition between Austria and Russia for predominance in the Balkans; another was due to the centuries-old Russian ambition to gain control over the Turkish Straits in order to have free access from the Black Sea into the Mediterranean. The fate of the Ottoman possessions in the Middle East interested both Britain and France, for the British regarded the area as the gateway to India and the French were concerned over the protection of Christian holy places. Similarly, in North Africa the French were intent on expanding their foothold in Algiers into Morocco and Tunisia at the same time that the British consolidated their interest in Egypt following the completion of the Suez Canal.

The web of competing interests that comprised the eastern question made the Ottoman Empire a sensitive issue in European diplomacy. The Crimean War and the Paris peace conference of 1856 confirmed the neutrality of the Black Sea, ended the Russian occupation of Moldavia and Wallachia—the provinces were merged into the Kingdom of Romania a few years later—and left the protection of the Christian populations of the Middle East to the sultan. But if the peace conference basically preserved the Ottoman Empire, succeeding events speeded its disintegration. In 1875 revolts against Turkish rule in Bosnia led to a declaration of war against Constantinople by the semiautonomous states of Serbia and Montenegro, which

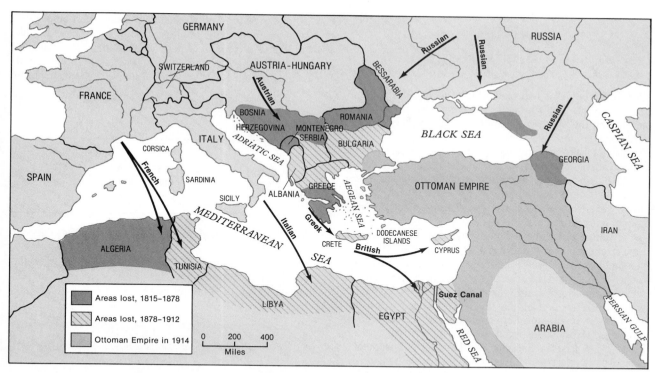

***31.4** The Decline of the Ottoman Empire to 1914*

were eventually assisted by Russia. When the resulting Treaty of San Stefano (1878) threatened to shift the balance of power in the Balkans in favor of Russia, Austria and Britain became alarmed. That summer, therefore, the Russians were forced to the conference table at the Congress of Berlin. Despite Bismarck's claim that he would act as an "honest broker" at the conference, Russian gains from the Treaty of San Stefano were severely reduced. Serbia, Montenegro, and a new state, Bulgaria, were recognized as fully independent from Turkish rule, while the provinces of Bosnia and Herzegovina were placed under Austrian administration. The Ottoman Empire lost half of its European territory. During the next 30 years European powers would strip Turkey of its remaining possessions in North Africa.

The dismemberment of the Ottoman Empire aroused discontent among the sultan's younger, Western-educated subjects and in the army, where opposition to the inefficient rule of the sultans was growing. In 1856 a far-reaching reform edict, the Hatt-i Humayun, established a progressive political structure for the empire, but a new sultan, Abdul Hamid II (1876–1909)—known for his brutal tyranny as "Abdul the Damned"—crushed the hopes of the reformers. After issuing a new constitution, Abdul Hamid reimposed tyranny. In the Ottoman Empire, as in Russia, the weight of centuries of repression seemed to move toward revolution.

Abdul Hamid II, a cruel despot, ruled the Ottoman Empire until the Young Turks deposed him in 1909. [Bettmann Archive]

The Jewish Question and the Birth of Zionism

The Enlightenment had significantly advanced the theoretical equality and the actual emancipation of the Jews, and during the nineteenth century the remaining legal restrictions on them were eliminated in virtually every major country of Europe, although quasi-official sanctions such as educational and professional quotas remained. Despite the fact that religious and social prejudices against them were still deeply rooted in Europe, most Jewish populations were being assimilated into Europe's social, economic, and cultural life.

In an age of self-conscious nationalism, however, the Jewish question grew increasingly complicated. The development of "scientific" theories of race in the late nineteenth century and the resulting merger of nationalism and racism stimulated anti-Semitic discussion. In countries where Catholic and Christian influence blended with political conservatism, anti-Semitism emerged as a political movement with widespread appeal. In Germany, Adolf Stöcker's Christian Socialist Workingman's Union, the Conservative party, and even an Anti-Semitic League advocated an end to Jewish influence in national life, and in 1882 an international anti-Semitic congress was held in Dresden. In France, Edouard Drumont's book *La France juive* (1886) inflamed popular attitudes, and the shocking Dreyfus affair revealed the depth of anti-Semitic sentiment. In the Dual Monarchy, the Christian Socialist party elected Karl Lüger mayor of Vienna on a distinctly anti-Semitic platform.

It was in Russia, where the partitions of Poland in the late eighteenth century had made millions of Jews subjects of the tsar, that systematic repression became state policy. Anti-Semitic measures coincided with the reactionary policies of Alexander I and Nicholas I, and in the wake of the assassination of Alexander II in 1881, violent anti-Semitic campaigns, or pogroms (*pogrom* is Russian for "devastation"), were unleashed, often with official connivance, as Jews were killed and beaten and their homes and shops burned and looted. The infamous May Laws of 1882 provided the basis for the expulsion of Jews from villages and rural centers outside Poland, and even fiercer pogroms broke out in 1902 and 1903. In the period from 1881 to 1910, millions of Russian Jews fled, most of them to the United States.

As a reaction to these persecutions and a defense against the assimilation and secularization of Jewish life, the end of the century saw the development of an organized movement of Jewish nationalism called Zionism. Advocates of Zionism argued that Jews would never find justice and equality until they returned to their biblical homeland and formed their own national state. Rabbi Zevi-Hirsch Kalischer and a number of other Jewish thinkers had already proposed the establishment of a homeland in Palestine, and in 1869 an agricultural colony named Mikveh Yisrael ("Hope of Israel") was founded there. In 1882 Leo Pinsker, a Russian Jewish physician, published an influential pamphlet, *Autoemancipation,* advocating a similar program.

❀ THEODOR HERZL AND THE QUEST FOR A JEWISH HOMELAND

The founder of modern political Zionism was Theodor Herzl (1860–1904). Against overwhelming odds, and at times almost singlehandedly, Herzl set in motion the movement that years after his death resulted in the establishment of the state of Israel.

The founder of the modern Zionist movement, Theodore Herzl, was driven by the revival of anti-Semitism in the late nineteenth century as well as by the centuries-old aspirations of Jews for a homeland in Palestine. [Granger Collection]

◉ On Anti-Semitism ◉

The reemergence of anti-Semitism assumed new and more virulent forms in the late nineteenth century and led Jewish leaders such as Theodor Herzl and his friend Max Nordau to found the Zionist movement. Here are two moving statements by them on the nature of anti-Semitism.

Stunned by the hailstorm of anti-Semitic accusations, the Jews forget who they are and often imagine that they are the physical and spiritual horrors which their deadly enemies represent them to be. The Jew is often heard to murmur that he must learn from the enemy and try to remedy the faults ascribed to him. He forgets, however, that the anti-Semitic accusations are meaningless, because they are not a criticism of facts which exist, but are the effects of a psychological law according to which children, wild men, and malevolent fools make the persons and things they hate responsible for their sufferings.

I believe that I understand Anti-Semitism, which is really a highly complex movement. I consider it from a Jewish standpoint, yet without fear or hatred. I believe that I can see what elements there are in it of vulgar sport, of common trade jealousy, of inherited prejudice, of religious intolerance, and also of pretended self-defense. I think the Jewish question is no more a social than a religious one, notwithstanding that it sometimes takes these and other forms. It is a national question which can only be solved by making it a political world-question to be discussed and controlled by the civilized nations of the world in council.

   We are a people—One people.

Sources: M. Nordau, speech to the First Zionist Congress, 1897, in A. Hertzberg, ed., *The Zionist Idea* (Garden City, N.Y.: Doubleday, 1959), p. 241; T. Herzl, *The Jewish State: An Attempt at a Modern Solution of the Jewish Question* (New York: Maccabaean Publishing Co., 1904), pp. 4–5.

Herzl was born in Budapest in a merchant family of assimilated Jews. After taking a law degree from the University of Vienna, he turned to writing, immersing himself in the world of sentimental, bourgeois culture that characterized the Austrian capital in the 1880s. Although he wrote successful plays, journalism was Herzl's real talent, and he made an international reputation as foreign correspondent for the prestigious *Neue Freie Presse*. A handsome man with a Romantic, narcissistic personality, he moved in literary and aristocratic circles. But in 1891 his Viennese paper sent Herzl to Paris, where his life took a sudden and dramatic turn. In Paris, Herzl discovered his identity as a Jew. France was then in the throes of the Dreyfus scandal, and Herzl witnessed the anti-Semitic frenzy firsthand. Thereafter, Jewish issues began to preoccupy him. The result was his famous pamphlet, drafted in a few intense months in late 1895 and published the following year as *Der Judenstaat* (*The Jewish State*).

   Written in a powerful, crisp style, *The Jewish State* was a radical analysis of the Jewish question. Herzl argued that although many Jews had attempted to assimilate into Euro-

pean society, anti-Semitism had made this impossible. "I consider the Jewish question," he wrote, "neither a social nor a religious one, even though it sometimes takes these and other forms. It is a national question." His solution, therefore, was that Jews all over the world should organize to obtain a land of their own. In his mind, Palestine was the natural site for a Jewish state. But unlike earlier leaders, he insisted that Palestine should be secured not through unofficial immigration and infiltration but rather through an international charter.

   Herzl threw himself into the task. Sacrificing his marriage, his wealth, and eventually his health, he spent the rest of his life in a tireless campaign to convince his fellow Jews and to secure the support of world opinion. His efforts resulted in the establishment of the World Zionist Organization. In 1897 he presided over the First Zionist Congress, in Basel, Switzerland, which proclaimed that "Zionism seeks to establish for the Jewish people a publicly recognized, legally secured home in Palestine" and to strengthen "Jewish self-awareness and national consciousness." By 1901 there were local Zionist organizations throughout the world, including 1,034 in Russia and 135 in the United States, and branches as far afield as New Zealand, Chile, and India. Herzl gained the help of influential Jewish leaders and met with heads of state, including Kaiser William II and the Turkish sultan, in efforts to realize the Basel program. In 1903 the British government offered part of its East African possessions as the basis for a Jewish state. Through the work of Herzl's successor, Chaim Weizmann (1874–1952), and the support of the British statesman Arthur Balfour, the British government became increasingly sympathetic to the Zionist cause, but not until World War I did it support a Jewish homeland in Palestine.

Herzl's program provoked great controversy, even within the ranks of the Zionist movement. Some biographers have portrayed him as a man with a messianic complex—he demanded blind obedience from his followers, and everywhere he traveled, especially in eastern Europe and Russia, throngs of poor Jews greeted him with adulation. His argument that assimilation had failed suggested to many that he despaired of liberalism, yet his vision of the new Jewish state was so grounded in tolerance and progressive ideals that it often provoked resentment from cultural Zionists who saw nothing specifically Jewish about it. Similarly, he failed both to understand the importance of socialism within the Zionist ranks and to anticipate the clash between Jews and Arabs that would result from the occupation of Palestine. Yet his methods yielded results, and he galvanized millions of Jews the world over. His despondency over the failure of assimilation, together with his warnings about the dangers of anti-Semitism, gave an urgency to his search for a solution to the Jewish question. Some of his critics charged that he was obsessed by the Zionist program, but his forebodings about the fate of Europe's Jews would prove tragically prophetic.

The United States from Civil War to National Unity

The struggle for national identity in the nineteenth century was by no means limited to Europe, and similar developments were occurring as far away as China and Japan. Perhaps the closest parallels were to be found in the newly formed United States, for the American government had been set up by people who considered themselves European in culture and values and who were inspired by the same Enlightenment principles that nourished the French Revolution.

Even after the American union had adopted its constitution in 1787, the United States continued to wrestle with ideological issues concerning the nature of its democracy.

Indeed, the struggle between the Federalists, who represented the conservative northern landowners and the commercial classes, and the southern landowner Democratic-Republicans, who championed the small yeoman farmers of the young republic, was not unlike the European conflict between liberalism and conservatism. The passage of the Bill of Rights in 1791 and the subsequent election of Thomas Jefferson (1801–1809) as president signaled the rejection of a powerful central government dominated by privilege and wealth, a tendency later confirmed in the democratic principles of Andrew Jackson (1829–1837).

The advance of democratic attitudes in the United States went hand and hand with its territorial expansion. In less than half a century huge tracts of land, each larger than most European countries, were added to the United States. The Louisiana Purchase in 1803, the settlement of the old northwestern territories, and the conquest of Texas and California in the Mexican-American War, all fulfilled what Americans came to call their "manifest destiny," an attitude first expressed by the Russians in their expansion across Siberia. As more settlers pushed westward into the frontier territories, the pioneer values of hard work, individual worth, and self-reliance were deemed more valuable than birth and status. The seemingly unlimited American continent, with its fertile farmland and natural resources, gave Americans self-assurance and unbridled optimism.

Yet the American experience was not without serious problems. Sectional disputes, particularly between the agricultural south and the industrializing north, threatened to disrupt the republic. By the 1850s the institution of slavery, on which the southern economy depended, had become a deeply divisive issue. The test of nationhood came in the bitter civil war between 1861 and 1865, waged by Abraham Lincoln (1861–1865) to preserve national unity just when Cavour had forged an Italian state and Bismarck was striving to create a united Germany. The defeat of the secessionist Confederacy not only ended slavery in the United States long after it had been abolished in most other places in the Western world but also preserved the American union.

In the decades following the civil war, the United States entered a period of unrestrained economic development and industrialization. By the end of the century almost 200,000 miles of railroads crisscrossed the continent, and American mills produced a third of the world's steel. The population of the nation, swelled by almost 30 million immigrants from Europe and Asia between 1860 and 1914, settled hundreds of millions of acres of land in the west and swarmed into the burgeoning cities. On the eve of World War I almost half of the nation's 100 million people lived in urban centers. The rapid transformation of the American continent from a frontier society to an industrial giant, and the resulting leap in America's status to global power, was to have profound consequences for the world.

In the second half of the nineteenth century European history was largely shaped by triumphant nationalism, which underwent a profound transformation. In midcentury a proponent of nationalism such as Giuseppe Mazzini saw no contradictions between his demands for Italian national liberation and the aspirations of other nationalities. Indeed, Mazzini had cast his nationalist ideas in broad international terms, envisioning an interdependent Europe in which free, equal, self-governing peoples cooperated in a spirit of harmony. Mazzini, who died in 1872, lived to see nationalism triumphant in Italy and Germany, yet by the end of the century he would hardly have recognized the concept as the same idealistic doctrine he had once preached.

Nation building had been a complex interaction in which patriotism and middle-class liberalism had first joined forces against conservatism. Ironically, however, success subverted nationalist movements, for as military, industrial, and conservative aristocratic elites embraced nationalism, many liberals subsumed or abandoned their political values to the more immediate goal of unification. Once national unity was achieved under the leadership of men such as Bismarck and Cavour, the Mazzinian vision of a new European civilization nurtured by a spirit of freedom and equality gave way to an aggressive chauvinism that perceived history as the struggle between nations for power and dominance. Bitter national rivalries resulting from the wars of unification gave concrete form to the larger political and intellectual changes taking place in Europe. The nationalists of the postunification period absorbed and twisted the theories spawned by the Darwinian revolution in science, substituting the doctrine of supremacy for belief in equality, rejecting cooperation in favor of competition, and preaching imperialist expansion instead of self-determination. By the end of the century nationalism, which once had promised a new age of peace and security for Europe, pointed to an unstable and dangerous future.

Suggestions for Further Reading

Binkley, R. C. *Realism and Nationalism, 1852–1871.* New York: Harper, 1935.

Crankshaw, E. *Bismarck.* New York: Macmillan, 1981.

Emmons, T. *The Russian Landed Gentry and the Peasant Emancipation of 1861.* Cambridge: Cambridge University Press, 1968.

Florinsky, M. T. *Russia: A History and an Interpretation.* New York: Macmillan, 1953.

Griffith, G. O. *Mazzini: Prophet of Modern Europe.* London: Hodder & Stoughton, 1932.

Hamerow, T. S. *The Social Foundation of German Unification, 1858–1871.* 2 vols. Princeton, N.J.: Princeton University Press, 1969.

Hertzberg, A., ed. *The Zionist Idea.* Garden City, N.Y.: Doubleday, 1956.

Kohn, H. *The Idea of Nationalism.* New York: Macmillan, 1944.

Mack Smith, D. *Cavour.* London: Weidenfeld & Nicolson, 1985.

———. *Garibaldi.* London: Hutchinson, 1957.

Mosse, W. E. *Alexander II and the Modernization of Russia.* London: English Universities Press, 1958.

Pflanze, O. *Bismarck and the Development of Germany.* Princeton, N.J.: Princeton University Press, 1963.

Schorske, C. E. *Fin-de-Siècle Vienna.* New York: Knopf, 1979.

Seton-Watson, H. *The Decline of Imperial Russia, 1855–1914.* New York: Praeger, 1952.

Shaw, S. J., and Shaw, E. K. *History of the Ottoman Empire and Modern Turkey.* 2 vols. Cambridge: Cambridge University Press, 1977.

Stavrianos, L. S. *The Balkans, 1815–1914.* New York: Holt, Rinehart, & Winston, 1963.

Taylor, A. J. P. *Bismarck: The Man and the Statesman.* New York: Knopf, 1955.

———. *The Habsburg Monarchy, 1809–1918.* New York: Harper & Row, 1965.

———. *The Struggle for Mastery in Europe, 1848–1918.* Oxford: Clarendon Press, 1960.

Thompson, J. M. *Louis Napoleon and the Second Empire.* New York: Norton, 1967.

Williams, R. L. *Gaslight and Shadow: The World of Napoleon III.* New York: Macmillan, 1957.

Woolf, S. *A History of Italy, 1700–1860.* London: Methuen, 1979.

Wright, G. *France in Modern Times.* Chicago: Rand McNally, 1960.

CHAPTER · 32

Industrial Society and the Liberal Order

In the years from 1871 to 1900 Europe achieved a higher level of material well-being than any previous civilization. Its population was healthier, more nutritiously fed, better educated, and longer-lived, and it enjoyed more physical comforts than any other people in history. Europeans of this generation made remarkable progress in understanding and controlling the physical world. By the end of the century they moved themselves and the products of their industrial culture efficiently not only by steam but by the internal combustion engine; they turned machines with steam turbines and electrical energy, communicated rapidly around the globe with the telegraph, underwater cable, and telephone, and illuminated the darkness with the light bulb.

These astonishing advancements in science and technology, together with unprecedented prosperity, determined how the post-1871 generation thought about itself. Most Europeans looked at the world with a faith in the limitless capacity of reason to solve problems. "Progress," inexorable and continuous, was their religion. Believing

The British naturalist Charles Darwin revolutionized science with his theory of evolution. [National Portrait Gallery]

that they were moving steadily toward an ideal future, Europeans were self-assured about the achievements and superiority of their civilization.

The materialist culture of the era reflected the fact that the middle class had become an influential elite in European life. Liberal doctrines shaped the governments of most Western nations, while entrepreneurs and industrialists extolled unregulated, growth-driven capitalism. As the middle class achieved status and political power, bourgeois notions of order and respectability defined public attitudes toward family, sexuality, the roles of men and women, and social behavior. Middle-class values also set standards of style and comfort as well as artistic taste.

Still, the age was by no means as well ordered as many contemporaries believed. Industrial capitalism spawned unanticipated problems. Beneath the surface of middle-class prosperity lay widespread poverty and dehumanizing drudgery in the workplace, loudly denounced by social critics. Some demanded social and political reforms and a wider suffrage. As the right to vote spread, radical opponents of liberalism, inspired by the Marxist critique of capitalism, joined industrial workers in forming labor unions and socialist parties in an effort to wrench power from the bourgeoisie.

The social implications of the industrial system were enormous. By the end of the century factories had drawn millions of farmers from the countryside and had transformed a once rural and agricultural Europe into a predominantly urban civilization with pressing problems of public welfare. Higher factory wages had also attracted women to the workplace in large numbers, altering the pattern of family life, modifying sexual behavior, and challenging traditional models of male-female relationships.

Industrial Development and Monopoly Capitalism

In the last third of the nineteenth century, Europe's economy was transformed in three important ways: the Industrial Revolution spread more widely to other European nations, new sources of energy and products were developed, and business elites evolved new forms of control over industry and capital. These trends brought the earlier industrialization process to a climax and shaped Western economic life for generations.

The Second Industrial Revolution

The first phase of industrialization led by Great Britain had been marked by the application of steam power in the manufacturing of two important commodities—iron and textiles. Subsequent changes in science and technology led to a "second industrial revolution." Although steam remained the major source of industrial energy until 1914, electric power and internal combustion engines fueled by petroleum products increasingly replaced steam-driven machinery. The new energy sources led to the development of more sophisticated machines that greatly expanded efficiency and output and lowered production costs.

During the second industrial revolution, steel replaced iron as the basic metal and the chemical industry grew rapidly. Both developments resulted from the application of scientific discoveries to industry. Through the process developed by Henry Bessemer (1830–1898) at midcentury, steel could now be manufactured in large quantities. The greater strength and flexibility of steel had a profound impact on construction, manufacturing, and transportation. As railroad networks spread across the European and American continents, the production of locomotive engines, cars, and tracks became a major impetus to industry and capital investment and opened significant new markets. In Europe the rail network doubled between 1890 and 1914. In addition, methods for the mass production of chemical substances revolutionized industry by allowing for the creation of such new products as fertilizers, dyes, explosives, plastics, synthetic fabrics, and medicines such as aspirin.

Germany, France, Italy, Russia, the United States, and Japan became industrial nations. Coal and steel provided useful indices of the growth of production during the second industrial revolution. Between 1870 and 1913 world output of coal had risen from 230 million to more than 1.5 billion metric tons, while steel production rose from 550,000 to more than 80 million tons. By 1914 the "inner zone" of Britain, Germany, and France produced 80 percent of Europe's coal, steel, and machinery and 70 percent of its manufactured products. Germany soon emerged as Europe's industrial giant and rapidly outdistanced Britain. By 1900 German steel production had outpaced Britain's, and on the eve of World War I it was more than double that of Britain and second only to the United States, which manufactured almost twice as much as Germany. Germany also led the field in the cast-iron and chemical industries. In the four decades after 1870 Britain's annual growth rate was 2.2 percent, compared to 2.9 percent for Germany and 4.3 percent for the United States.

The sharp increase in productivity that characterized the post-1870 period was made possible not only by new energy sources and the spread of industrialism but also by more efficient machines that reoriented production techniques toward standardized parts and specialized tasks. Pioneered by the American automobile manufacturer Henry Ford (1863–1947), the division of labor on assembly lines made cheaper, mass-produced consumer goods available on a wide scale. Although these trends contributed

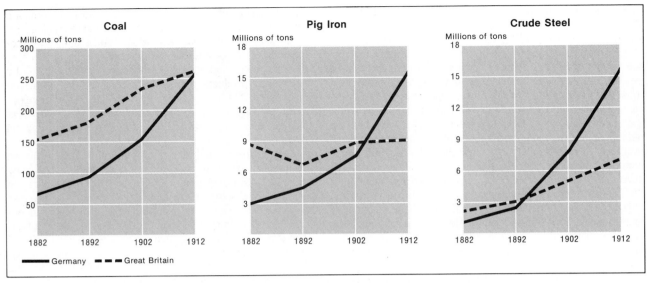

32.1 German and British Industrial Production, 1882–1912

to the material improvement of daily life, they also resulted in overproduction, the further dehumanization of the work process, and a decline in the quality of many products.

The Rise of Big Business

The second industrial revolution bore out Karl Marx's prediction of a trend toward the concentration of wealth in fewer hands. The large numbers of small factories and businesses characteristic of early industrialization gave way to fewer, larger concerns. Business legislation encouraged the trend by extending the concept of "limited liability," which insured the personal assets of investors against business losses. The pattern was not, however, due simply to competition such as took place in retail sales, where department stores forced many independent shopkeepers out of business by buying in large quantities and selling at lower prices. As the cost of such large-scale operations as steel foundries and chemical refineries increased, entrepreneurs required enormous capital, which smaller producers could not afford. Partly for this reason, but largely because competition drove down the margin of profit, investors created monopolies.

Entrepreneurs often operated through a process known as "horizontal integration," whereby they achieved control over a sector of industry or business such as steel, coal, or oil. Such huge combinations—called amalgamations in

The giant Krupp manufacturing complex at Essen, Germany (1912), reflected both the new era of early-twentieth-century industrialization and the industrial power of Germany. [Brown Brothers]

Britain, cartels in Germany, and trusts in the United States—dominated industry by the end of the century because they absorbed or drove out competitors and could limit production, fix prices, divide markets, and control labor. By means of "vertical integration," steel manufacturers could buy up coal and iron mines, chemical plants, blast furnaces, and rail companies to ensure manufacturer control over the entire industrial process.

Unregulated, monopoly capitalism had long-range implications. Investment banking grew in importance, especially with the adoption of the international gold standard for all major currencies. John Pierpont Morgan (1837–1913), the famous American banker, financed governments as well as railroads and steel companies through his firms in New York and London. Industrial monopolies were the work of "captains of industry" such as Andrew Carnegie (1835–1919), who controlled the United States Steel Corporation, and John D. Rockefeller (1839–1937), owner of the Standard Oil trust, or Alfred Krupp (1812–1887) and August Thyssen (1842–1926) in Germany. Such men were ruthless in their pursuit of profit and accumulated vast fortunes that enabled them to wield unprecedented economic and political power. The social ramifications of the second industrial revolution were far-reaching, especially as the emergence of the private-sector bureaucracy enlarged the white-collar class.

The Social Hierarchy

The political and economic changes that transformed Europe in the nineteenth century profoundly affected society. Despite unprecedented material progress, social and economic differences remained sharp, and the quality of life varied greatly between classes.

The Aristocracy: Adjustment and Change

The aristocracy had been the dominant elite before 1789. Most nobles, whose wealth and status had been determined by land ownership, failed to make the transition to modern capitalist agriculture or industrialization. Although land continued to be important, the real wealth of the aristocracy declined along with their income and access to liquid capital. In countries that remained predominantly agricultural, competition from cheaper overseas grain further reduced farm income. Yet in Britain the aristocracy remained stable well into the nineteenth century. The declining influence of the aristocracy appeared sharper than it actually was because of the rapid rise of the middle class. Liberal constitutions gave the bourgeoisie political power, but aristocrats dominated the upper chambers in parliaments. While the spread of civil service examinations and higher education opened administrative positions to the middle classes, there was little competition with the aristocracy for such positions. Ancient lineage and access to royal courts sustained the status of nobles, who remained the point of reference in matters of social prestige and style.

After 1870 the line separating the aristocracy and the upper middle class began to blur, as it had in the sixteenth and seventeenth centuries, as industrial wealth and noble titles sometimes came together through mutually advantageous marriages. Businessmen with surplus capital often bought sumptuous estates as symbols of their rising status. Increasingly, the upper levels of the industrial class copied the living standards of the aristocracy.

The Growth of the Middle Classes

While the aristocracy underwent adjustment in the late nineteenth century, the middle classes enjoyed expansion, though not uniformly. Grouping economic interests and social strata so diverse that they were often mutually antagonistic, the middle classes included wealthy industrialists and bankers as well as shopowners and white-collar workers. In industrialized countries the middle classes represented perhaps one-fifth of the inhabitants, although the powerful industrial and banking families formed a very small percentage of the general population. This elite reaped great benefits from expanded industrial production, earning a third of all national income. Consisting of no more than several hundred families in any given country, this group tended to merge with the old aristocracy, aping their manners and elitist attitudes.

Most middle-class Europeans were members of less wealthy and powerful subgroups: the middle middle class of small entrepreneurs, professional experts, and managers or the lower middle class of shopkeepers and white-collar workers. The ranks of the middle range swelled after 1870 with scientists, engineers, lawyers, and accountants—whose occupations grew more professional—as well as with corporate managers and bureaucrats.

The number of shopkeepers and small business owners grew along with teachers, nurses, and other salaried, nonpropertied members of the lower middle class. The most dramatic increase, however, was among the white-collar employees—clerks, salespeople, secretaries, and low-ranking bureaucrats, most of whom came from the ranks of the working class. White-collar wages were sometimes less than those of skilled workers, but the status of carrying a briefcase, wearing a tie, or having uncallused hands was often seen as compensation for low salaries. The lower middle class expanded rapidly between 1870 and 1900, doubling in Britain to 20 percent of the population.

Although middle- and lower-middle-class groups did not control great wealth, they tended to lead comfortable lives that reflected the values and aspirations of the upper-class bourgeoisie. Yet the status of most of the middle class was precarious in comparison to other groups. Easy social mobility encouraged the lower ranks to strive for greater status and income, but tensions were equally strong. Economic pressure from large industries and corporations threatened small businessmen and shopkeepers, while people living on fixed incomes from savings and pensions feared that business cycles and recessions could suddenly wipe them out. For white-collar employees, who made every effort to distance themselves from the workers, the greatest fear was that economic adversity would force them back to their working-class origins.

The Decline of the Working Class

Most people—four-fifths of them—lived by physical labor. Industrialization made Europe a predominantly urban civilization, so by the end of the nineteenth century agricultural workers were a distinct minority in most western and central European countries. The agricultural crisis that began in 1873 as a result of huge imports of wheat from the United States reduced the price of European grains. Landowners cut wages and pushed peasants, many of whom already lived close to subsistence, into more ex-

This photograph of an upper-middle-class English family at tea reveals the Victorian ideal of social and domestic propriety. [Culver Pictures]

treme poverty. The decline in agricultural earnings, compounded by natural disasters in the 1870s and 1880s, also struck peasant owners, whose land decreased in value.

Behind the exuberant prosperity of Victorian London lay the poverty of much of Britain's working class. This photograph shows an alley in a working-class section of the city. [Snark/ Art Resource]

The rural standard of living improved after 1890 with changes in crops and cultivation methods, as well as the introduction of protective tariffs, but agricultural wages remained less than half the average of factory rates.

In industrialized countries the urban working class represented the largest single social stratum and was even more diverse in composition than the middle classes. Among skilled workers, industrialization brought stressful changes as artisans gave way to factory workers who required less skill. Yet there was also a growing need for new kinds of skilled jobs, including metalworkers, machine tool makers, and locomotive engineers. Skilled workers, whose wages were at least twice as high as those of unskilled laborers, saw themselves as an elite with middle-class pretensions. Semiskilled and unskilled workers vastly outnumbered the artisans and the skilled elite. The semiskilled, such as masons, carpenters, plumbers, and some factory workers, earned less money, while the unskilled workers, among whom the largest number were domestic servants, were the lowest paid.

Between the years 1873 and 1896 the West experienced a series of economic crises known collectively as the Long Depression. Primarily an agricultural phenomenon sparked by competition from North American farms, the Long Depression nevertheless affected industry and trade. Rising costs, increased competition, and shrinking markets reduced profits and triggered stock and bank panics. Periods of high unemployment resulted. In Britain, for example, unemployment among unionized workers rose from 1 percent in 1872 to 11 percent in 1879, from 2 percent in 1882 to 10 percent in 1886, and again from 2 percent in 1890 to 7.5 percent in 1893. Such sharp cycles of unemployment not only caused severe hardships among working-class families but also fanned enthusiasm for militant labor unions. Yet even though fluctuations in wages accompanied the crises, during the three decades after 1870 real wages rose by about 37 percent, increasing by a third in France and Germany and by more than half in Britain.

Urban working-class diets improved and became more varied as food prices declined and purchasing power increased, and health conditions in the cities improved with the development of sewage systems, clean water supplies, and the scientific control of disease. Industrial productivity reduced the cost of clothing, so workers were better dressed. The expansion of urban construction made less cramped housing available, and the development of inexpensive railway, subway, and tram services gave workers access to better housing in the suburbs, although they still had to devote large portions of their budgets to rent.

Despite advances in the standard of life for urban workers, production outpaced wages. Although working-class purchasing power expanded and living standards improved for all social groups, the gap between workers and the middle classes widened.

❦
THE URBAN LANDSCAPE

The urbanization of European society—the movement of people from country to city, the growth in the number of urban centers, and the dense concentration of huge populations in them—continued well beyond 1900. Between 1871 and 1911 England's urban population rose from 62 to 78 percent of the whole and France's from 33 to 44 percent. In Germany, which was rapidly industrializing, the increase was spectacular—from 36 to 60 percent. Moreover, 90 percent of Germany's population growth in the same period was in cities. The culture of western Europe had become predominantly urban.

Improved transportation, particularly the railroad, spurred urban growth, and most important cities became hubs of rail lines or port facilities, and frequently both. In large cities the basic infrastructure—drainage systems, water supply, police and fire protection—had already been established by midcentury, and these services were expanded.

Baron Haussmann's redevelopment of Paris during the Second Empire provided the model for a similar project in Vienna, whose Ringstrasse was inspired by Haussmann's grand boulevards. London and Berlin permitted the reconstruction of inner-city zones in the 1870s, when town planning revived. By the end of the nineteenth century

POPULATION OF THE MAJOR CITIES OF CONTINENTAL EUROPE AROUND 1910

City	Population	City	Population
Paris	2,888,000	Turin	428,000
Berlin	2,071,000	Rotterdam	418,000
Vienna	2,031,000	Frankfurt	415,000
St. Petersburg	1,908,000	Lodz	394,000
Moscow	1,481,000	Düsseldorf	359,000
Hamburg	931,000	Lisbon	356,000
Budapest	880,000	Stockholm	347,000
Warsaw	781,000	Palermo	342,000
Naples	723,000	Nuremberg	333,000
Milan	599,000	Riga	318,000
Madrid	598,000	Charlottenberg	306,000
Munich	596,000	Antwerp	302,000
Leipzig	590,000	Hanover	302,000
Barcelona	587,000	Bucharest	295,000
Amsterdam	568,000	Essen	295,000
Copenhagen	559,000	Chemnitz	288,000
Marseilles	551,000	Stuttgart	286,000
Dresden	548,000	Magdeburg	280,000
Rome	539,000	Genoa	272,000
Lyons	524,000	The Hague	270,000
Cologne	517,000	Bordeaux	262,000
Breslau (Wroclaw)	512,000	Oslo	247,000
Odessa	479,000	Bremen	247,000
Kiev	469,000		

advances in engineering, building materials, and construction techniques began to change the face of cities. Reinforced concrete and steel permitted multistory office and apartment buildings, and both the American skyscraper and the metal tower designed by French engineer Gustav Eiffel in the 1890s became symbols of the new, aggressive city. Sewers, sidewalks, and electric lights made urban centers more pleasant places to live and work.

France led the way with other distinctive features of the modern city. Using wrought iron and steel, Parisian developers built large, glass-covered galleries in which independent shops and cafés were situated, and by the 1880s Moscow had followed the example. The first major department store was the Bon Marché in Paris. By buying in quantity, department stores could sell a wide range of mass-made goods inexpensively, thus making the products of industrial civilization available to workers and the lower middle class.

Working-class housing, which in the early industrial revolution had consisted of squalid, crammed tenements, improved considerably in this period as a result of health and welfare legislation. The French pioneered middle-class apartment complexes, New York exploited that concept, and British cities added the notion of garden apartments. As urban transportation systems grew, more people escaped urban living for tranquil suburbs, and the city became the metropolis.

Everywhere cities adopted from each other, equipping themselves with London-style parks and suburbs, Paris-style boulevards and cafés, and New York–style office blocks and gridded street plans. All of them acquired grand public buildings and cultural centers such as opera houses, concert halls, museums, and public libraries, and all were afflicted with pollution, noise, and overcrowding. By the end of the century the urban landscape had assumed its modern appearance.

Sexuality, Women, and the Family

The Industrial Revolution and the consequent movement of populations from the country to the cities had significant repercussions on the relationship between men and women, as well as on the family. Urban life tended to erode moral codes and traditional forms of courtship and marriage that were more easily enforced in small villages. At the same time, the employment opportunities and higher wage scales that drew workers to the factories often enabled young men and women to escape family supervision. In the period before 1850 the result had been a dramatic increase in premarital sex (among partners who intended to marry), illegitimate births, and common-law

marriages, but this pattern diminished by the last third of the century.

The spread of birth control information contributed to the decline of the birthrate. The French took the lead in contraception, and such traditional methods as the sponge, sheepskin condoms, and the vinegar douche were widely used among the upper classes. In Britain laws prohibited the publication or distribution of contraceptive information until Annie Besant, a socialist, and Charles Bradlaugh, a radical, won a celebrated court case in 1878. Between 1880 and 1900 they distributed more than a million copies of birth control pamphlets that advocated the use of the sponge, syringing with zinc or alum solutions, cervical caps, and rubber condoms. Although Besant aimed her information at the poor, it was the middle class that first made widespread use of these methods, and only by the end of the century did they spread among urban workers. Moreover, middle-class men could more easily afford recourse to brothels, where they found women who were often driven to prostitution by unemployment and poverty.

Industrialization brought mixed results. During the nineteenth century roughly two-thirds of all single women and more than a quarter of married women worked. Life was especially difficult for working women, for most also had to function as mothers and wives. Married generally in their early and mid-twenties after experiencing the relative independence derived from their jobs, working women subordinated themselves to their husbands. The men ate better food, dressed better, went out without their families in the evenings, and often abused their children and wives. Yet despite the grueling physical and psychological pressures, working mothers managed to keep the basic family structure intact.

The principal female employment categories—domestic service, textile work, and garment making—remained fairly constant into the early twentieth century, but the female work force consisted increasingly of single women; by 1911 only 9.6 percent of married women were employed. The notion that women should "retire" when they married was a product of urban industrial culture. In the cities domestic service employed more women than any other activity in the nineteenth century. Because it promoted such virtues as hard work, cleanliness, and obedience, domestic service was regarded as ideal training for future wives of the working class.

Bourgeois Respectability

The expanding demand for domestic servants reflected both the growing prosperity of the middle class and the new ideal of womanhood that it cultivated. The separation between the male sphere of work and business and the female sphere of home and family reached its most fully developed form among the middle class. Bourgeois respectability required that the home be comfortable, well

◉ The Cult of Domesticity ◉

The development of the cult of domesticity, which limited women largely to home maintenance and child rearing, contributed greatly to the social construction of gender roles. In this nineteenth-century handbook for housewives, Mrs. Isabella Beeton explains the principles of household management.

Of all those acquirements, which more particularly belong to the feminine character, there are none which take a higher rank, in our estimation, than such as enter into a knowledge of household duties. . . .

Early rising is one of the most essential qualities which enter into good household management, as it is not only the parent of health, but of innumerable other advantages. Indeed, when a mistress is an early riser, it is almost certain that her house will be orderly and well-managed. . . .

Cleanliness is indispensable to health, and must be studied both in regard to the person and the house, and all that it contains. Cold or tepid baths should be employed every morning, unless, on account of illness or other circumstances, they should be deemed objectionable. . . .

Frugality and economy are home virtues, without which no household can prosper. . . . The necessity of practising economy should be evident to every one. . . .

The treatment of servants is of the highest possible moment, as well to the mistress as to the domestics themselves. On the head of the house the latter will naturally fix their attention; and if they perceive that the mistress' conduct is regulated by high and correct principles, they will not fail to respect her.

After this general superintendence of her servants, the mistress, if the mother of a young family, may devote herself to the instruction of some of its younger members, or to the examination of the state of their wardrobe, leaving the latter portion of the morning for reading, or for some amusing recreation.

Source: I. Beeton, *Book of Household Management* (London: Beeton, 1861), pp. 2–9 passim.

furnished, and characterized by an atmosphere of warmth and safety from the outside world. Middle-class sensibilities idealized women as gentle and virtuous creatures devoted to bearing and raising children and looking after their husbands. The Victorians evolved a "cult of domesticity" for women that stressed duty, submissiveness, and devotion. A close and emotionally intimate family life was extolled as the social bedrock of the age.

The middle-class family concentrated legal power in the hands of the husband and father. Until midcentury contracts were often used in upper-class families to safeguard the property rights of daughters about to be married, for a husband ordinarily gained control of a wife's property. Most states in America passed married women's property acts, as did Britain in 1882, but these were designed largely to enable fathers who had no sons to pass inheritances to their daughters. Widows almost always had to defer to the relatives of their deceased husbands regarding such matters as their children's education and upbringing.

Similarly, divorce was still generally obtainable only by women who could prove that their husbands were impotent or unfit fathers; in most countries husbands could gain a divorce on the grounds of adultery, but women could not. Educational patterns perpetuated the inferior status of women. While middle-class boys usually went to school to receive classical education or professional training in law, medicine, or accounting, girls stayed home to learn painting, needlework, and religion.

Sexual Attitudes

The ideology of bourgeois respectability had a powerful impact on attitudes toward sexuality, though not on its practice. Sexual pleasure was regarded as a male preserve. The assumption that women were not supposed to enjoy sex was a powerful form of male dominance. Public attitudes toward sexuality encouraged a double standard according to which men might, with proper discretion, visit brothels and maintain mistresses to fulfill their "natural" needs. Victorian moral strictures were also imposed on children, whose clothing and physical activities were regulated to repress masturbation and sensations that might lead to sexual arousal. Menstruation—known as "the curse"—was little discussed, and pubescence was regarded as a profoundly disturbing and disagreeable experience.

Diaries and letters, the proliferation of sex manuals and pornography, and the literature of the period demonstrate that despite the strictures fostered by middle-class sexual codes, men and women continued to enjoy sex. The sensational trial and imprisonment in 1895 of the writer Oscar Wilde (1854–1900) because of his love affair with Lord Alfred Douglas made Victorians uncomfortably aware of other sexual orientations. Wilde's account of this experience, *The Ballad of Reading Gaol* (1898), had to be published anonymously, and his "open letter" to Douglas, *De profundis* (1905), did not appear until after his death. The tension created by the dissonance between moral theory and behavior produced a pyschological anxiety that pervaded the late Victorian age.

Liberalism and the Political Order

The middle class had been a driving force behind the political upheavals that stretched from the American Revolution in 1776 to the revolutions of 1848. They had reacted strongly against the excesses of the French Revolution, but their demands for a share in political power, expressed through the doctrine of liberalism, had made them the foe of absolutism and aristocracy. After 1815 the bourgeoisie stood in sharp opposition to the conservative political principles of the Restoration. In France they brought the "bourgeois king" Louis-Philippe to power in 1830, while in England, where the 1832 Reform Bill had enfranchised the industrialists, the propertied classes enjoyed significant political influence. In 1848 and 1849 they came close to establishing constitutional regimes in central and eastern Europe.

The political triumph of the middle classes came after 1850, when they joined forces with elements of the aristocracy in supporting unification movements in Germany and Italy and Napoleon III in France. Thereafter, as the middle classes gained power, they reversed their historical role—whereas once they had acted as a powerful force for change, now they emerged as the champions of order. Liberalism, the doctrine that expressed middle-class aspirations, changed as well.

Over the course of the nineteenth century liberalism had proved to be a flexible doctrine capable of encompassing a wide range of objectives, from the Enlightenment belief in individual rights to romanticism, and from nationalism to Bismarck's *Realpolitik*. After 1870 the industrial and financial bourgeoisie began to appropriate political liberalism as their special preserve, making it the philosophy of the capitalist establishment.

Though liberalism underwent a transformation after 1870, it continued to stand for the basic premise that government should be based on a written constitution—except in Britain, where an unwritten agreement prevailed—with the middle classes and aristocracy represented in parliamentary institutions elected by limited male suffrage. Liberal parliamentary systems reflected a number of trends: a widening suffrage that eventually encompassed most of the working classes, the appearance of modern political parties representing a range of class and special interests, free elementary education, compulsory military service, the secularization of national culture, and the growing role of the state in social legislation and public policy. Individual countries produced variations in this pattern, but as the century drew to a close, liberalism had permeated the political culture of western Europe almost everywhere. By 1900 all but one of the great European states were part of the "liberal" order; Russia alone stood outside the system.

Britain in the Victorian Age

No nation more completely represented the liberal order than Britain, and no European monarch symbolized that ideal more completely than Queen Victoria (1837–1901). She inherited the throne from her uncle, William IV, at the age of 18. In 1840 she married a German cousin, Prince Albert of Saxe-Coburg-Gotha, who had a formative influence on her character. She learned to express her wishes and opinions forcibly to her ministers and had a strong though discreet influence on politics. After Albert's death in 1861, Victoria lapsed into seclusion as the "widow of Windsor." Her 64-year reign as queen (she was also crowned empress of India in 1876), together with the fact that she was the grandmother of both Kaiser William II of Germany and Tsar Nicholas II of Russia, made Victoria the venerable matriarch of Europe's royalty. But as the symbol of Britain's political stability and industrial power, she was no glittering incarnation of imperial splendor—when she reappeared in public in the 1880s, it was as a matronly icon of bourgeois virtue, dressed in black and wide in girth.

Midway through Victoria's reign, British politics underwent a crucial transformation that resulted in the emergence of new leaders at the head of modernized political parties. Under William Gladstone (1809–1898), the old

Queen Victoria and her husband, Prince Albert, were the ideal royal couple, in love with each other and serious about their duties. [Victoria and Albert Museum, London]

pealing to the middle classes. After a successful record of leadership in the House of Commons, he overcame the suspicion of his colleagues, who regarded him as opportunistic, and eventually won the support of Queen Victoria, who preferred the Conservatives to the Liberals.

Gladstone and Disraeli made possible the passage of the Reform Act of 1867. After Gladstone had tried without success to secure passage of a similar bill in 1866, Disraeli—who saw an opportunity for the Conservatives to reap the political credit—maneuvered the measure through the House of Commons. By giving the vote to all middle-class males and the highest-paid urban workers, the second Reform Act doubled the size of the electorate by adding almost a million voters to the rolls.

From 1868 to 1914 the Liberal and Conservative parties alternated in power. First Disraeli and Gladstone, and then their successors, outdid each other in sponsoring political and social legislation. Competitive civil service examinations were introduced in 1870, the secret ballot a year later. After 1884, when Gladstone passed another reform bill that increased the electorate by the addition of 2 million agricultural laborers, Britain continued to evolve toward parliamentary democracy, at least for men.

Before the end of the century the great mass of British workers and farm laborers benefited from a range of reforms— largely modeled on similar legislation introduced in Germany by Bismarck—that included free elementary education; minimum-wage laws; accident, health, and unemployment insurance programs; old-age pensions; and a graduated income tax. Marxist socialism, which was gaining a foothold in less democratic Continental states, had little appeal in Britain. By the eve of World War I, England's upper bourgeoisie believed that their country offered compelling testimony of the wisdom of the alliance between political liberalism and industrial capitalism. Still, as late as 1892 a report found that almost a third of the inhabitants of London—Britain's largest city and the hub of the British empire—lived in poverty.

Whig-radical coalition evolved into the Liberal party. An eloquent orator, Gladstone, the pious son of a merchant, was trained as a classical scholar before entering politics. As chancellor of the exchequer, he had pushed for a policy of free trade as well as reforms that included a postal savings and insurance system widely used by workers and a reduction in taxes. In 1864, when only one adult male out of six had the right to vote, Gladstone pressed for an extension of the franchise, which had not changed since 1832.

At this time Benjamin Disraeli (1804–1881) was molding the aristocratic, agrarian-based Tories into the new Conservative party. More flamboyant than Gladstone, the brilliant Disraeli was the descendant of Spanish Jews and the author of political novels. He was convinced that the Conservatives needed to broaden their support by ap-

The Third Republic in France

For 70 years after 1870 France was governed by a republic born out of military defeat and civil war. The French surrender following the battle of Sedan had resulted in the overthrow of Napoleon III and the proclamation of a republic (see Chapter 31). The National Assembly chose the liberal royalist Adolphe Thiers (1797–1877) as president. Thiers negotiated the humiliating peace terms with Bismarck that ended the Franco-Prussian War.

In March 1871 the National Assembly moved the government to Versailles, the traditional seat of the French monarchy. There the liberal-monarchist majority further aroused the fury of the Parisians by canceling the debt

After toppling this column bearing a statue of Napoleon I in Paris, the communard rebels erected the red flag of revolution in its place. [Musée Carnavalet/Photographie Bulloz]

moratorium and the pay of the civilian National Guard, measures that had kept tens of thousands from starvation during the Prussian siege of the capital. Thiers then tried to confiscate the 200 cannon that had been cast by public subscription during the siege. Angry mobs dragged the cannon to safety and drove off government troops.

Civil war erupted. Extremists in Paris took control of the rebellion and established a "Commune," modeled on the revolutionary government of 1792. When the regular army broke through the city's defenses in May, the Communards executed hostages, including the archbishop of Paris, while the Assembly's soldiers summarily shot everyone found with weapons. By the time government troops had secured the city, as many as 20,000 Communards had been executed and twice that number were deported to penal islands. The repression of the Commune had been bloodier than any civil clash in modern French history. It left a permanent legacy of class bitterness that polarized French politics and intensified social division.

The Third Republic proved both politically unstable and unpopular. Although the monarchists had a majority in the

National Assembly, they could not agree on a suitable candidate for king and continued the republic in effect by default. The constitution of 1875 created a democratic government in which the prime minister and his cabinet were fully responsible to Parliament, whose lower house, the Chamber of Deputies, was elected by universal male suffrage.

Unlike the British, the French failed to develop modern political parties until the end of the century. Poorly organized political groups were held together only by immediate concerns. Royalist sentiment, which remained strong, was the focus of opposition to the Third Republic, but the monarchists remained divided on whether to support the Bourbon, Orléanist, or Bonapartist claimant to the throne. Republican supporters were equally divided. Radical republicans, led by Georges Clemenceau (1841–1929), were anticlerical and anti-German. Moderate republicans were more willing to compromise on major issues. Together, the moderate royalists and the republicans represented the liberal tradition in French politics. The left, which took more than a decade to recover from the disaster of the Commune, was also split into factions. In Parliament, majorities were difficult to form and still more difficult to maintain. More than 50 coalition cabinets governed France during the first 40 years of the republic.

The republic was no friend of social revolution. Reform legislation was slow in coming, and it was 1910 before earlier work and health laws were complemented by accident and social insurance programs. Still, moderates established the supremacy of Parliament and a system of secular state education that slowly engendered republican values in the post-1870 generation.

The strange career of General Georges Boulanger (1837–1891) mirrored the discontent that beset the Third Republic. Originally a radical republican and protégé of Clemenceau, Boulanger became war minister in 1886. He was a popular figure who made a habit of riding a magnificent black horse through the streets of Paris. Chafing under the humiliation of defeat in the Franco-Prussian War, royalists and patriotic admirers saw him as a symbol of French glory. Boulanger lost his cabinet position in 1887 and was sent to the provinces, where he drummed up support for a new constitution and a more authoritarian regime. With the help of right-wing politicians, he planned a coup d'état in 1889 but lost his nerve at the last minute and fled to Brussels.

More serious in its repercussions was the dramatic Dreyfus affair. In 1894 Captain Alfred Dreyfus (1859–1935), a Jewish officer attached to the French General Staff, was court-martialed for treason on charges that he had supplied military secrets to the Germans. A military court ignored evidence that another officer had been the guilty party. This aroused the radical republicans, who believed the military had falsely condemned Dreyfus while protecting the real traitor. While Dreyfus languished in prison on Devil's Island, the notorious penal colony, Clemenceau and the novelist Émile Zola (1840–1902) took up his cause and accused the General Staff of harboring clerical, royalist, and anti-Semitic prejudices. In 1899 the army found Dreyfus guilty "with extenuating circumstances" and pardoned him, but his supporters continued to demand a full acquittal, which came only in 1906.

The episode widened the wedge that already separated radicals, socialists, and intellectuals from army leaders, monarchists, and the Catholic church. The crisis unleashed a wave of anti-Semitism that fueled right-wing forces. The Dreyfus case, like the Boulanger affair, revealed that the enemies of the government were strong. Yet the legacy of the French Revolution was equally powerful, and the Third Republic survived for another half century.

Germany Under the Reich

Liberalism in Germany was weaker than in Britain or France because it had been tied so closely to the triumph of Bismarck's unification program. Bismarck had been appointed minister of Prussia to overcome a deadlock between the king and the liberals in the Landtag, which he did by circumventing its control of the budget. In September 1866, however, after his stunning victory over the Austrians, the liberals and others sanctioned his violation of the Prussian constitution.

While Bismarck cowed the liberals, he also forged a powerful alliance between bourgeois industrialists and aristocratic landowners that enabled him to impose political unity on the German states. Prussia ran the federal structure of the German empire through its monarchy, bureaucracy, and army, and, with 236 of 397 seats in the lower house of parliament, the Reichstag, dominated the national assembly. Outwardly, the German parliament conformed to the liberal formula: the Reichstag was elected by universal male suffrage. The Reichstag approved laws and budgets, but it had no real authority over foreign affairs or the imperial ministers. The upper house, the Bundesrat, represented the 26 federated units of the empire and could initiate laws and block measures proposed by the Reichstag. The powers of the emperor were extensive, for he was commander in chief of the army and, in his role as king of Prussia, remained an absolute monarch. Moreover, the kaiser appointed the imperial chancellor, who was responsible to him alone.

Bismarck presided over the empire as chancellor for 19 years. Distainful of his critics, the "iron chancellor" rammed his programs through parliament with the support of the conservative landowners and the upper middle class. The interests of the industrialists and bankers were represented by the National Liberals, while the great landowners backed the Conservatives. The Progressives, who spoke for the more radical liberals who had initially opposed Bismarck; the Center party, which spoke for the Catholics; and the Social Democrats, representing the socialist party, were Bismarck's chief sources of opposition.

Bismarck's ruthless methods and high-handed policies were designed to forge a single nation out of the patchwork of states that made up the new empire. He tried to extinguish local loyalties and crush opposition to the central state.

The first target of this policy was the Catholic church, against which he unleashed the so-called *Kulturkampf*, or "battle for civilization"—a campaign to make loyalty to Germany supreme over devotion to the Catholic church. Although the *Kulturkampf* was an extreme example of a growing trend toward secularization all over Europe, Bismarck saw it essentially as a political issue. Germany was predominantly Protestant, but Catholics comprised a third of the population and were strong in Alsace-Lorraine. Bismarck clashed with the church when he sponsored laws that abolished religious orders, imposed state supervision over Catholic education, made civil marriage compulsory, and required government approval of ecclesiastical appointments. When he removed bishops and hundreds of

The headstrong Kaiser William II dismissed Bismarck in 1890 and assumed personal direction of German affairs. [Mansell Collection]

other political disaster, Bismarck switched his tactics in the 1880s by sponsoring social welfare programs designed to wean the workers away from the socialists while keeping the antisocialist laws intact. Bismarck's social security laws, the most advanced in Europe, provided workers with accident and health insurance and retirement benefits. After 1890 workers were given additional rights, including labor arbitration and better working conditions. These measures failed to reduce working-class support for the socialists, but they did demonstrate that organized political pressure could win substantial material benefits for workers without revolution. As a result, the Social Democratic party grew enormously in electoral strength and by 1912 was the largest party in the Reichstag. At the same time, however, it lost much of its revolutionary impetus.

Bismarck virtually ruled the German empire until 1890, when Kaiser William II (1888–1918) forced him to retire. As erratic as Bismarck was strong-willed, William had come to the throne when he was 29. Strict training had made him deeply attached to military discipline and the spirit of manly virtue that infused the aristocratic Prussian officer corps. Determined to rule Germany himself and unwilling to be dominated by Bismarck as his predecessors had been, William proclaimed, "There is only one master in the Reich, and that is I." Heaping honors on Bismarck, the kaiser retired the man who had created the German empire.

In assuming command of the Second Reich—German nationalists considered the medieval Holy Roman Empire to have been the first—William II now ruled the most powerful state in Europe. Its population was large and growing rapidly, and its modern industrial plant was outpacing other nations in the production of coal, steel, chemicals, and electrical energy. Spectacular economic growth combined with a system of higher education that stressed technical training and produced the most literate and scientifically advanced population in Europe. The German army was the most efficient military force in the world. Stridently nationalistic, the kaiser launched Germany on a new and dangerous course in world affairs.

The Liberal State in Italy

Britain and Germany offered examples of the liberal order at its extremes, one strong and stable, the other weak and shallowly rooted. Italian liberalism evolved between the two extremes. As in the case of Germany, Italian unification owed a great deal to the efforts of one man, Count Cavour. Unlike Bismarck, however, Cavour had been an admirer of British political traditions and was a moderate liberal by conviction.

Much as Prussia had done in Germany, Piedmont had essentially imposed its traditions and institutions on the Italian states along with unification. The king was com-

priests, Bismarck succeeded only in making political martyrs of them and found that German Catholics rallied to their church. In the next elections, the Catholic-oriented Center party nearly doubled its representation in the Reichstag. Always the realist, Bismarck eventually reached an accommodation with Pope Leo XIII (1878–1903).

Bismarck also dealt with what he considered the other major national problem, the threat of socialism. The formation of the Social Democratic party in 1875 led him to fear that the socialists would capture the loyalties of workers for the cause of revolution and internationalism. He persuaded the Reichstag to pass legislation restricting socialist activities. Denied an open forum, the socialists organized support underground and elected their candidates to the Reichstag in ever larger numbers. Faced with an-

mander in chief of the armed forces and had the authority to declare war and make treaties. He also appointed the prime minister, who was declared to be "responsible," although whether to the king or to parliament remained unstated. The Chamber of Deputies, or lower house of the Italian parliament, was elected on the basis of limited manhood suffrage, with only 2 percent of the population able to vote. The Chamber controlled budget appropriations and could initiate legislation. The Senate, or upper house, could veto measures passed in the Chamber, and its members, appointed by the king for life, tended to be conservatives, nobles, and public officials.

As in France, organized political parties did not emerge in Italy until after the turn of the century.* Instead, parliamentary deputies considered themselves members of either the right or the left. These were largely meaningless labels that had been used during the unification struggle to describe, respectively, the supporters of Cavour's program of constitutional monarchy and Mazzini's republican followers. After 1870 the terms denoted degrees of liberalism, although the differences in outlook were often more a matter of emphasis than substance. In the first years of the kingdom, when the Right was in power, the government pursued a fiscally conservative program of high taxation and low expenditure for social reform. When the Left came into power in 1876, it repealed some of the more onerous taxes, widened the suffrage, and instituted compulsory elementary education. Significant social and economic progress came slowly. The lack of clearly defined political parties and programs contributed to the practice of *trasformismo*, whereby prime ministers formed coalitions that changed constantly, depending on the specific issue and the patronage to be distributed.

The euphoria that had accompanied unification quickly faded as Italians faced the problems of nationhood. The annexation of Rome in 1870 produced deep hostility between the Catholic church and the new state that was to plague Italian politics for the next half century. Through the Law of Guarantees, parliament recognized papal sovereignty over Vatican City and offered financial compensation to the church. But Pius IX, who declared himself a "prisoner of the Vatican," would not compromise. He refused to recognize the kingdom and prohibited Italian Catholics from taking part in political life. The stalemate, known as the "Roman question," weakened the legitimacy of the new state in the eyes of Italy's overwhelmingly Catholic population.

Regional differences and local loyalties remained strong in Italy after unification. The gap between the industrial interests of the north and the depressed agricultural economy of the south widened after 1870, and illiteracy, disease, and poverty put pressure on a national debt already burdened by the costs of the wars of unification. Despite the reforms of the left after 1876, the ruling liberal elite remained unresponsive to the needs of the unenfranchised poor for many years. Unemployed migrant workers turned increasingly to brigandage in the south, while peasant anarchism was widespread in Sicily and central Italy. In the industrial centers of Milan and Turin, workers turned to socialism.

The last two decades of the century were a period of crisis that tested liberalism. From 1887 to 1891 and again from 1893 to 1896 leadership was in the hands of Francesco Crispi (1819–1901). Like Bismarck, Crispi was determined to stem the rise of socialism by suspending constitutional rights and smashing the Socialist party with massive arrests and police harassment. He was also anxious to make Italy a great power through military alliances and colonial conquest, but scandals and military defeat in Africa brought him down. Vigorous action against socialists and anarchists by Crispi's successors climaxed in the bloody suppression of labor demonstrations in 1898. The liberal state in Italy demonstrated its deep hostility to working-class movements.

The accession of Victor Emmanuel III (1900–1946) to the throne in 1900 brought Giovanni Giolitti (1842–1928) to the forefront of national politics. Giolitti served off and on as prime minister for most of the years before World War I. A shrewd politician, he toned down the level of confrontation with labor, coopted moderate socialists into the parliamentary system, and ended strikes through negotiation. Giolitti sought a reconciliation with the church, presided over the development of industry, and sponsored significant factory and social legislation. Finally, in 1911 Giolitti introduced near-universal manhood suffrage. The liberal state had begun its first tentative steps toward democratic reform when the First World War interrupted its progress.

Spain and the Smaller Powers

Instability and unrest, due largely to intrigues surrounding the succession to the throne, marked Spanish political life in the mid-nineteenth century. After a revolution unseated Queen Isabella II (1833–1868), a number of governments—first under the Cortes, then under a king imported from Italy, and finally as a republic—failed to find support and encouraged the church and the army to interfere in politics. Only when Alfonso XII (1874–1885) became king under a liberal constitution did a measure of stability return.

Thereafter, Spain struggled with the problems of social and economic modernization. Small areas of industry existed within an agrarian nation dominated by conservative landed interests. Anarchist and regionalist movements were strong, especially in the Basque region and Catalonia, while industrial growth in Barcelona prompted the rise of socialism. In 1890 universal male suffrage was in-

---

*The Italian Socialist party, founded in 1892, was the exception.

stituted, but the constant struggle between the Liberal and Conservative parties made social reform difficult.

Events in Spain's colonies added to the nation's problems. When a combination of repressive policies and ineffective administration led to the outbreak of guerrilla resistance in Cuba in 1898, the United States seized the opportunity to wage war with Spain over its possessions. The Spanish-American War resulted in the loss of Cuba and the cession of the Philippines, Puerto Rico, and Guam to the United States. By the end of the century intellectuals known as the Generation of 1898 were engaged in reassessing Spain's culture and turned increasingly to mystical nationalism in their search for national purpose.

Belgium, the Netherlands, Denmark, Sweden, and Norway followed a more stable pattern. All were constitutional monarchies that by 1914 had introduced universal manhood suffrage. Belgium was the most industrialized region on the Continent, but the other states underwent rapid economic development that enlarged the middle class.

By 1900 Britain, France, Italy, and Germany represented the range of liberal experience in the European political order. Almost without exception, other nations were variants on the liberal theme. The pace of social and political change differed, depending on the strength of liberalism and the ability of elites to maintain their authority against the emerging political challenge of the working class. As widening suffrage laws involved larger numbers in political life and as governments assumed a greater responsibility for social welfare, the state also claimed more loyalty from its citizens.

The Rise of Feminism

In 1879 the Norwegian dramatist Henrik Ibsen (1828–1906) published a play, titled *A Doll's House*, which exposed the frustration of a wife who felt trapped in what appeared to be a "perfect" marriage. The play ends with Nora, the wife, walking out of her husband's house and slamming the door. Nora became a symbol of female independence for women who sought to escape patriarchy and the middle-class family.

Modern feminism has its roots in the social transformations caused by industrialization as well as in the rebellion against the constraints imposed on women by the ideology of bourgeois respectability. The gulf separating lower-class from middle-class women widened, and not simply because of differences in income and status. Prosperity increased the leisure of middle-class females, who were relieved of household tasks by servants and labor-saving devices. Yet many bourgeois women resented their removal from the workplace, their inferior education, and their confinement in the home.

Social Activism and Women's Rights

To escape their constricted lives, bourgeois women sought outlets in such activities as philanthropy, church work, and temperance drives. British and American women were zealous proponents of abolitionism, although they were forced to take second place to males in abolitionist groups. In the second half of the nineteenth century they did volunteer duty in workhouses, hospitals, and urban tenements, thereby opening up new professions for women in nursing and teaching. After Jane Addams (1860–1935) had established Hull House, Chicago's famous social welfare center, and Beatrice Potter Webb (1858–1943) had disguised herself as an unemployed worker in order to investigate poverty in London's slums, social work also gave women employment opportunities.

Women could not help but be struck by the bitter irony of their efforts to combat racial and industrial slavery while they themselves remained oppressed, and many turned from social activism to feminist militancy in an effort to secure political equality. The beginnings of the modern women's liberation movement can be traced to the world antislavery convention that met in London in 1840, where Elizabeth Cady Stanton (1815–1902) and other women delegates were forced to sit in a curtained galley, separate from the men. In July 1848 Stanton organized a women's rights convention in Seneca Falls, New York, which issued an 18-point Declaration of Sentiments demanding the vote, property and divorce rights, and equal employment opportunities.

In Europe feminists found support in the British reformer John Stuart Mill (1806–1873). Mill was a disciple of the philosopher Jeremy Bentham, who had argued that the best government was one that gave its citizens access to the greatest pleasure and the least pain. In 1859 Mill published *On Liberty*, which posited that society should permit every individual the fullest degree of liberty consistent with the freedom of others. Government, argued Mill, may restrict freedom only to protect society. Conversely, Mill's democratic sentiments led him to urge government action to eliminate poverty, the exploitation of child labor and economic injustice, and the repression of women.

During the debate over the Reform Act of 1867, Mill, a member of the House of Commons, introduced an amendment to give women the vote. Though defeated 194 to 73, the minority vote was surprisingly large. With contributions from his wife, Harriet Taylor (1807–1859), Mill incorporated the women's rights issue into his theory of liberty in a ground-breaking essay, *The Subjection of Women* (1869). The principle of utility, said Mill, demanded that society eliminate inequality and prejudice, which had prevented women from bringing their talents to bear on public issues. Mill had been arrested in his youth

◎ The Principle of Utilitarianism ◎

The philosophical basis of nineteenth-century Liberalism owed much to the work of John Stuart Mill, whose "utilitarian" theories were based on the principle of the greatest good for the greatest number of people. Here Mill explains what he meant by "good."

The creed which accepts as the foundation of morals, Utility, or the Greatest Happiness Principle, holds that actions are right in proportion as they tend to promote happiness, wrong as they tend to produce the reverse of happiness. By happiness is intended pleasure, and the absence of pain; by unhappiness, pain, and the privation of pleasure. To give a clear view of the moral standard set up by the theory, much more requires to be said; in particular, what things it includes in the ideas of pain and pleasure; and to what extent this is left an open question. But these supplementary explanations do not affect the theory of life on which this theory of morality is grounded—namely, that pleasure, and freedom from pain, are the only things desirable as ends; and that all desirable things (which are as numerous in the utilitarian as in any other scheme) are desirable either for the pleasure inherent in themselves, or as means to the promotion of pleasure and the prevention of pain.

Source: J. S. Mill, *Utilitarianism,* 15th ed. (London: Longman, 1907), pp. 9–10.

for advocating birth control methods and was convinced that women were the victims of sexual domination. His essay pointed out that men had convinced women of their own inferiority. Later the social scientist Lester Ward (1841–1913) extended Mill's arguments by asserting in *Dynamic Sociology* (1883) a theory of the natural superiority of women.

The Suffrage Struggle

The women's movement spread throughout Europe in the nineteenth century. Often divided over tactics and goals, feminist leaders nevertheless constituted a kind of women's international as they fought against male privilege, government and church policy, and tradition. In 1868 British women founded the National Society for Women's Suffrage. The following year Susan B. Anthony (1820–1906) and Elizabeth Stanton established the National Woman Suffrage Association, which merged with other groups in 1890 to form the National American Woman Suffrage Association. By the 1870s unmarried propertied women received the municipal franchise in Britain, Sweden, and Finland, and American women gained the suffrage in a few states.

On the European continent, especially where the Catholic church was strong, the women's movement generally incorporated the suffrage into broader campaigns.

In France two generations of feminist activism had been repressed after the 1848 revolutions, but the women's rights struggle revived during the Third Republic under the leadership of Hubertine Auclert, who demanded the vote on the principle of "perfect equality of the sexes before the law and before customs and morality."[1] Anna Maria Mozzoni translated Mill's essay on women into Italian and published a women's journal, while Luise Otto-Peters, who had fought for women's rights during the 1848 revolutions, cofounded the General Association of German Women in 1865. Efforts to forge unity among suffrage forces climaxed in 1902 in the International Alliance of Women, which held congresses in Berlin, Copenhagen, Amsterdam, London, Stockholm, and Budapest.

♔
EMMELINE PANKHURST AND THE POLITICS OF CONFRONTATION

The suffrage movement captured public attention in Britain after the turn of the century under the fiery leadership of Emmeline Pankhurst (1858–1928). She was a woman of immense determination and eloquence. The daughter of a Manchester textile printer, Pankhurst was educated in Paris and was influenced by French feminists. In 1879 she married Richard Pankhurst, an advocate of women's suffrage with whom she promoted the Women's Property Act.

After working with suffrage groups in Manchester, Pankhurst became convinced that women had to use confrontational, and at times violent, tactics to publicize their cause and win the right to vote. In 1886 she participated in a strike of female workers in a London match factory, an experience that taught her the advantages of direct action. Three years later she helped establish, in affiliation with the Liberal party, the Women's Franchise League. Because it met with resistance from the Liberals, she subsequently switched her political allegiance to the Independent Labour party. When the death of her husband in 1898 left her alone to raise a son and three daughters, she took a civil service job but was fired because of her suffrage work.

Inspired by her daughter Christabel, also an ardent feminist, in 1903 Pankhurst created the Women's Social and Political Union (WSPU), a London-based suffrage organization without party affiliation. The WSPU opposed candidates for elected office who did not support the women's vote. Together with her daughters Sylvia and Christabel, Pankhurst led an army of women—called "suffragettes" to distinguish them from the "suffragists" of the moderate National Union of Women's Suffrage Societies—in public meetings, marches to Buckingham Palace, and demonstrations before Parliament.

In 1911, after the government's continued refusal to adopt a prosuffrage platform, Pankhurst took control of the WSPU and, with Christabel, directed a window-smashing campaign along fashionable shopping streets, for which Emmeline received a nine-month prison term. Nevertheless, the WSPU's tactics grew more violent. One woman chained herself to the railings at 10 Downing Street, the residence of the prime minister, while shouting "Votes for women!" Some resorted to bombings and arson; one woman smashed the Rokeby Venus, a painting in the Na-

◈ The Suffragette Revolt ◈

The radical suffragettes of the pre–World War I period declared a feminist war against middle-class society in their efforts to win the vote for women. In this speech, made in London in 1912 after having been released from prison, the British suffragette Emmeline Pankhurst delivered her challenge in no uncertain terms.

Ladies and gentlemen, the only recklessness the militant suffragists have shown about human life has been about their own lives and not about the lives of others, and I say here and now that it never has been and never will be the policy of the Women's Social and Political Union recklessly to endanger human life. We leave that to the enemy. We leave that to the men in their warfare. It is not the method of women. . . . There is something that governments care far more for than human life, and that is the security of property, and so it is through property that we shall strike the enemy. From henceforward the women who agree with me will say, "We disregard your laws, gentlemen, we set the liberty and the dignity and the welfare of women above all such considerations, and we shall continue this war as we have done in the past; and what sacrifice of property, or what injury to property accrues will not be our fault. It will be the fault of that government who admits the justice of our demands, but refuses to concede them. . . ."

Be militant each in your own way. Those of you who can express your militancy by going to the House of Commons and refusing to leave without satisfaction, as we did in the early days—do so. . . . Those of you who can express your militancy by joining us in our anti-government by-election policy—do so. Those of you who can break windows—break them. Those of you who can still further attack the secret idol of property, so as to make the government realize that property is as greatly endangered by women's suffrage as it was by the Chartists of old—do so.

And my last word is to the government: I incite this meeting to rebellion! . . . Take me, if you dare, but if you dare I tell you this, . . . you will not keep me in prison.

Source: E. Pankhurst, *My Own Story* (New York: Hearst's International Library, 1914), pp. 264–266.

Emmeline Pankhurst, whose radical strategies emboldened British suffragists, was repeatedly arrested. [Culver Pictures]

tional Museum, and another tried to strike the Tory Winston Churchill with a horse whip. Following an attempt to bomb the house of Lloyd George, Pankhurst was sentenced to three years' penal servitude. During repeated jail terms, she and her daughters went on hunger strikes to dramatize their cause and had to be force-fed. In 1913 Emily Davison was killed after flinging herself in front of King George V's horse at the Epsom Derby. As the American suffrage leader Carrie Catt observed, the Pankhursts were "in a state of insurrection" against the British government.[2]

The efforts of Emmeline Pankhurst and other courageous women contributed to the development of feminist consciousness as well as to the vote issue, but the women's movement achieved only limited success before World War I. Pankhurst threw herself into war work after 1914 despite her fading health. Her lifelong struggle for women's suffrage bore fruit in 1918 with the passage of the Representation of the People Act.

Science and the Doctrine of Progress

The worship of science and the belief in progress that marked European attitudes in this period weakened the eighteenth-century emphasis on the efficacy of human will.

In broad terms, the Enlightenment had taught that people could shape their own destinies and mold society to their needs. Nineteenth-century developments, by contrast, reinforced the view that the scientific method could merely reveal the laws governing the physical and social environment. The process of discovery offered the promise of unending material improvement, but the laws of science could not be changed or suspended. Hence the optimism of the eighteenth century was replaced by a vision of perfectability that portrayed humans as part of a larger process of change.

The Darwinian Revolution

Scientific discoveries and technological advances had made possible Europe's Industrial Revolution and the improvement in its standard of living. The growth of literacy encouraged the popularity of science and the spread of its methods to other disciplines. The French philosopher Auguste Comte (1798–1857) was the first major figure to apply scientific principles to the study of society. In his *System of Positive Philosophy*, worked out in the 1830s, Comte argued that laws of social behavior paralleled the physical laws governing the universe and that both were discoverable through the study of specific data. Observation of individual phenomena, he believed, would demonstrate the similarities between them, which would in turn reveal natural laws. Comte described human thought as having moved from an early "theological" stage in which it was believed that the world operated by divine action to a "metaphysical" phase that sought to understand nature through abstract principles. Comte saw the thought of his own day as the final, "positive" stage, when observable data rather than metaphysical forces explained human behavior and the physical world.

Although Comte rejected theories of evolution, his work dovetailed with that of a number of natural scientists. Jean-Baptiste Lamarck (1744–1829) had tried to show that plants and animals—including humans—had evolved by adjusting to the environment. Sir Charles Lyell (1797–1875), in his *Principles of Geology* (1830–1833), explained the formation of the earth as the result of a slow process of geologic evolution rather than a sudden cataclysm or act of creation. Lamarck and Lyell relied on the painstaking accumulation of evidence in the development of their theories.

These theories formed the intellectual climate in which the British naturalist Charles Darwin (1809–1882) formulated his theses about evolution. His famous book *On the Origin of Species by Means of Natural Selection* (1859) was not the first work to posit a theory of evolution, but it explained in unprecedented detail how the evolutionary process worked. Darwin's principle of natural selection involved a number of points. Because every species produced more individual life forms than could survive, a struggle for existence took place within and between species. Variations, he asserted, gave some organisms advantages in the competition, so that only the fittest survived. But changing environmental conditions demanded alterations in the definition of fitness. In *The Descent of Man* (1871), Darwin argued that, like other forms of life, humans also evolved—from an ancestral type common to anthropoid apes—by the same principle of natural selection.

Darwin's theory was startling because it challenged both the deistic notion that the universe had been designed by God as well as the biblical account of creation. By claiming that the survival and development of organisms was a mechanistic process, Darwin rejected the notion of divine purpose in nature. His vision of a constantly changing world in which humans were simply another form of animal life seemed to support the spirit of materialism.

Science and Society

Darwin had been influenced by social theorists, including Thomas Malthus, whose *Essay on the Principle of Population* (1798) had predicted that population growth would outstrip food supplies. Social scientists, in turn, used Darwin to support their arguments, but in doing so they took evolution far beyond Darwin's intent. The British political philosopher Walter Bagehot (1826–1877) applied natural selection to politics, asserting the superiority of nations

that conquered others. His fellow countryman Herbert Spencer (1820–1903) made the classic case for what, ironically, came to be called Social Darwinism—Darwin himself never endorsed this doctrine. In his *Synthetic Philosophy,* Spencer contended that the economic competition of individuals advanced social progress by eliminating the weak. His arguments reflected an extreme form of laissez-faire liberalism that opposed state assistance to the poor and similar social legislation. By the end of the nineteenth century the Darwinian concept of the survival of the fittest had even been used to justify imperial conquest and racism.

Culture and Industrial Society

European artists and writers were profoundly affected by the new culture of science and industry. The contradictions of industrial civilization gave rise to two opposing trends in the arts during the second half of the nineteenth century. The idealistic fervor of Romantic painting was replaced by an "academic" style descended from the official canons of seventeenth- and eighteenth-century painting that deemphasized the individual's quest for meaning through an encounter with nature. Academic portraits conveyed the values of the middle class, while bucolic landscapes presented orderly treatments of nature.

Other artists responded to industrial society with a powerful "realism" that rejected an idealized version of industrial civilization. The call for a new artistic conscience was sounded by critics such as John Ruskin (1819–1900), who, like many of the realists, was influenced by socialist critiques of industrial capitalism and sought to make painting and literature responsive to the problems of the age.

Painting: New Visions of Reality

Scientific developments affected culture profoundly. Some artists saw the development of the camera in the early decades of the century—the first photograph dates from around 1826—as a threat to painting, especially if they defined art as the reproduction of observable experience. But artists such as the Frenchmen Édouard Manet (1832–1883) and Edgar Degas (1834–1917) and the American Thomas Eakins (1844–1916) used photography to study form and motion. Moreover, the realist painters found inspiration in daily life and approached their subject matter with sensitivity.

The British artist J. M. W. Turner (1775–1851) had taken an important step in this direction with his controversial *Rail, Steam and Speed, The Great Western Railway*

(1845). Although Turner claimed that the scene represented a literal depiction of a train in a snowstorm, the public rejected his energy-charged treatment of a locomotive as subject matter unsuited to true art. The French painters Gustave Courbet (1819–1877) and Honoré Daumier (1808–1879) were the major proponents of realism. Courbet believed that the search for truth required the artist to reveal the ugly as well as the beautiful. Influenced by socialism, Courbet made the working class the focus of his work because modern life relied on its labor. He was a realist not in the sense that he rendered the details of every object but in that he portrayed the harsh reality of workers and peasants without idealizing his subjects. *The Stonebreakers* (1849) depicts two workers whose hidden faces speak to the anonymity of grueling labor. Daumier, who had been a cartoonist for a radical newspaper, executed watercolors and drawings of common people that deliberately avoided a romanticized vision of poverty.

In the last third of the nineteenth century some artists moved beyond realism under the impact of scientific theories. From recent discoveries in optics, artists learned that air and light are waves of color joined by the human eye into patterns. Their use of short, broken brushstrokes and specific hues captured the way in which changing sunlight affected objects. In doing so, these artists rejected a frozen rendering of reality in favor of a view that was at once scientific and subjective.

The painting by the Frenchman Claude Monet (1840–1926) titled *Impression: Sunrise* (1873) inspired a hostile critic to dub the new style "Impressionism." Monet's fellow Impressionists, including Camille Pissarro (1830–1903), Auguste Renoir (1841–1919), Henri de Toulouse-Lautrec (1864–1901), and Edgar Degas, were similarly committed to these concerns. The Impressionists depicted subject matter that varied from Monet's early railroad station, *Gare Saint-Lazare, Paris,* to the chorus girls of Lautrec's posters and Manet's *Bar at the Folies-Bergères*. While their vision still concerned how the world appeared to the human eye, it was sharply different from that of realists such as Courbet and Daumier.

The Literary Response

If poetry was the major literary mode of the Romantic era, the novel best suited the industrial age. By midcentury an older generation of writers such as Honoré de Balzac (1799–1850) and Victor Hugo (1802–1885) was already making a transition from romanticism to realism to express injustice. Whereas Hugo's *Les Misérables* (1862) combined political radicalism with emotionally evocative social criticism, Balzac and Gustave Flaubert (1821–1880) shaped a consciously unromantic form. Balzac launched the realist movement with a series of novels collectively entitled *The Human Comedy*, while Flaubert's *Madame Bovary* (1857), which was prosecuted for its candid treatment of adultery,

revealed the sordid underside of bourgeois life. One of the most powerful works in this genre was Émile Zola's *Germinal* (1885), a portrayal of socialist hopes among French miners. Flaubert and Zola led the way from realism to naturalism by applying the principles of scientific observation to the human condition. Influenced by Darwin, the naturalists demonstrated the effect of social environment on personality.

The works of two Russian writers, Ivan Turgenev (1818–1883) and Leo Tolstoy (1828–1910), and of the Norwegian dramatist Henrik Ibsen revealed the universal character of realism. Flaubert had a pronounced influence on Turgenev. Turgenev's first important work, *A Sportsman's Sketches* (1852), was a strenuous protest against serfdom. His novel *Fathers and Sons* (1862) introduced the term *nihilism* to express his protagonist's rejection of all forms of authority. In the tragic story of *Anna Karenina* (1877), Tolstoy depicted a character similar to Flaubert's Madame Bovary, but his masterpiece was *War and Peace* (1869). Set against the background of the Napoleonic wars, this monumental novel reflected his sense of Russian nationalism as well as the detailed analysis of characters and events many realists employed.

Ibsen's plays explore the conflict between individual freedom and the bourgeois, materialist culture of the late nineteenth century. While Flaubert and Tolstoy examine the theme of adultery, *A Doll's House* (1879) portrayed a wife who suddenly realizes that she has been living for years with a distant husband who considers her simply a precious possession. Like Mill, Ibsen believed in the obligation of society to further individual freedom, but he was disillusioned by political theories. In *An Enemy of the People* (1882), Ibsen lashed out at the cupidity of the majority who, because their income is endangered, refuse to accept a physician's discovery that the mineral waters of their town are polluted.

The greatest popular success of the realist genre was achieved by the British writer Charles Dickens (1812–1870). His novels were widely read through serialization in newspapers and magazines. His grotesque characters and often improbable plots took Dickens beyond the realm of conventional realism. Yet his novels vividly portrayed the social problems of his times, and his most compelling plots were set in the cities, where social classes played out the contradictions of industrialism. The protagonist of *Oliver Twist* (1838) is an orphan brought up in a workhouse for pauper children, where he is mistreated by a cruel master. Dickens reveals how poverty leads to injustice, crime, and tragedy. In *Hard Times* (1854), Dickens deals with the human consequences of aggressive economic individualism in an industrial city called Coketown, where a selfish businessman obsessed with sales and money destroys the lives of his children.

From industrial Britain to agrarian Russia, nineteenth-century novels and plays came to grips with the harsh realities of industrial capitalism and bourgeois society, adding a powerful voice to the protests of the working class.

Socialism and the Labor Movement

Working-class militancy in Europe struggled against the misery and alienation of industrial capitalism. The sansculottes of the French Revolution and the Luddites of eighteenth-century Britain, like the utopian idealism of Robert Owen and Saint-Simon or the British Chartists and the revolutionaries of 1848, had been expressions of worker rebellion against exploitation. As liberalism triumphed after 1850, some of the harsher aspects of industrialism were blunted by reforms. Nevertheless, laborers devised strategies aimed at improving working conditions, and some advocated the elimination of capitalism itself.

In the second half of the nineteenth century the working-class movement focused around three traditions: trade unionism, anarchism, and the scientific socialism derived from the principles of Karl Marx and Friedrich Engels. Unionism accepted industrial capitalism as a permanent feature of modern life but sought to mitigate its impact by improving wages, benefits, and working conditions. Unionists gradually won a legal basis for organizing and the right to strike. Anarchism and Marxist socialism, by contrast, rejected the permanency of capitalism and saw private property as a source of repression and inequality that could not be reformed. Although Marx himself in later life advocated a political path to socialism, many of his followers continued to believe in violent revolution. Anarchists and Marxists were divided in their attitudes toward the state. Anarchists, rejecting all forms of authority, sought to destroy government, while Marxists wanted to seize control of the state and install the proletariat in power, leaving the destruction of the state for a later stage. These divisions weakened the working-class movement.

Socialism, Anarchism, and the Paris Commune

Initially, socialists, anarchists, and other radicals collaborated in the creation of the International Workingmen's Association, founded in London in 1864. The First International, as it was generally known, tried to coordinate labor activities throughout Europe and provide a vehicle for socialist debate. Marx, who gave its inaugural address and was its dominant figure, clashed with Mikhail Bakunin (1814–1876), the exiled Russian anarchist, and eventually drove nonsocialists from the International.

Marx's triumph came a year before the the Paris Commune, a pivotal event in international socialism. Marx contributed to the legend surrounding the Commune with a pamphlet titled *The Civil War in France*, in which he ar-

gued that it represented the first clear-cut case of proletarian violence. A few international socialists and anarchists had been involved in the Commune uprising, along with large numbers of radicals and ordinary citizens who had no clear program, but the Commune was by no means a Marxist revolution. Yet socialists everywhere came to regard it as a symbol both of the class struggle and of the bourgeois determination to crush worker agitation. Throughout Europe liberal governments reacted to the Commune by imposing restrictions on the working-class movement.

The First International dissolved in 1876 in the wake of the Commune and the socialist-anarchist split. For two decades thereafter, militant action remained largely in the hands of the anarchists, who increasingly adopted terrorist tactics, which they termed "propaganda of the deed." Anarchists tried twice in the 1870s to assassinate Kaiser William I and succeeded in killing a number of statesmen and heads of state, including Tsar Alexander II of Russia (1881), the French president François Sadi-Carnot (1894), the Spanish prime minister Antonio Cánovas del Castillo (1897), the empress Elizabeth of Austria-Hungary (1898), King Umberto I of Italy (1900), and the American president William McKinley (1901). Despite these acts of terrorism, many anarchist leaders repudiated violence. Prince Peter Kropotkin (1842–1921), a Russian noble exiled in London, argued for peaceful cooperation among workers, and the Italian anarchist Errico Malatesta (1853–1932) stressed the humanitarian nature of anarchism and saw himself as an antiauthoritarian socialist.

Trade Unions and the Labor Movement

Although Marx had predicted the growth and concentration of capitalist wealth, the condition of the working class itself did not worsen. Indeed, the general prosperity that began in the 1850s improved the standard of living of most workers, moderating the attitudes of labor and slowing the growth of unions. By the latter part of the century, however, craft unions, representing skilled trades, were again organizing. In the 1870s the Liberal ministry of Gladstone recognized such unions and legalized the strike. The London dockworkers' strike of 1889 provided the impetus for the organization of unskilled laborers and gave rise to industrial unions representing both skilled and unskilled workers throughout an entire industry. By the end of the century Britain's 2 million union members represented the largest and most successful union experience in Europe.

Beyond Britain, modern unions developed largely during the two decades of economic depression that stretched into the 1890s, largely under the banner of socialism. Napoleon III had permitted unions in 1864 in France, but they were suppressed after the Commune, and only in 1884 did the Third Republic grant them legal status. In Germany, Bismarck's antisocialist campaign retarded their formation until the Imperial Industrial Code of 1891 permitted the right to strike. By 1900 organized labor counted some 850,000 members in Germany and 250,000 in France, while in Italy and Austria-Hungary unions were slower to develop.

In the 1890s unionism on the Continent took a more radical turn under the influence of syndicalist leaders. The Frenchman Georges Sorel (1847–1922) was the major proponent of syndicalism (from the French word *syndicat*, "trade union"). He argued that unions rather than political parties were the logical institutions through which working-class leaders could take power from the middle class and reorganize society. In 1895 syndicalists formed the General Confederation of Labor, a union umbrella organization that undertook strike action and rivaled the socialists for leadership of the labor movement. Syndicalism spread to Italy, where leaders attempted an unsuccessful general strike in 1904. After the 1905 Russian revolution, Rosa Luxemburg (1870–1919), a Polish Jew active in politics, published a pamphlet titled *The Mass Strike, the Party, and the Trade Unions* (1906) in which she defined the strike as a political weapon. In *Reflections on Violence* (1908), Sorel proclaimed the general strike as the only means of achieving socialism. The general strike, he argued, would provoke violent state repression, which would incite the workers to revolt.

Socialist Parties: Between Reform and Revolution

Socialist parties grew rapidly in the years after the Paris Commune. Despite Bismarck's efforts to crush it, German socialism flowered. In 1869 two Marxists, August Bebel (1840–1913) and Wilhelm Liebknecht (1826–1900), founded the Social Democratic Labor party, which elected several deputies to parliament. In 1875 the Social Democrats joined forces with the more moderate followers of Ferdinand Lassalle (1825–1864) to issue the so-called Gotha program, combining Marxian theory with pragmatic Lassallian reforms. Although Marx denounced the mixture of revolutionary doctrine and reformist objectives, the resulting German Social Democratic party (SPD) became the strongest socialist party in Europe.

The German example inspired socialists elsewhere. In Belgium socialists founded a party in 1879. A non-Marxist Italian Worker party developed in 1882, although the socialists did not develop an organization of their own until ten years later. Meanwhile, Russian exiles in Switzerland formed the Russian Social Democrats in 1883. In both Italy and Russia police repression against socialists and anarchists was particularly severe and forced many radicals to spend years in exile. In France doctrinal disputes led to the creation of separate parties that did not unite until 1905.

Women were active in organizing labor unions and in strike activity. Here is a women's labor parade in New York City, 1913. [UPI/Bettmann Newsphotos]

◉ Socialist Women ◉

The Russian-born Angelica Balabanoff (1869–1965) was one of the most important figures in the prewar socialist movement. After leaving her wealthy family, she studied and worked in the movement throughout Europe, serving on the executive committee of the Second International for many years. Here she describes her early collaboration with Maria Giudice, an Italian socialist, while both were in St. Gall, Switzerland, in 1904.

One day . . . I received word that a young Italian teacher, an ardent propagandist for Socialism, was coming to St. Gall. She had only recently fled from Italy to escape imprisonment for an article she had written. I wrote the comrades at St. Gall that Maria was to have the use of my room. When I returned I found . . . Maria was experiencing her first pregnancy. She eventually became the mother of seven children and the object of considerable gossip. . . . Several years later, in Italy, the editor of a clerical journal made slurring remarks about Maria's morals. Meeting him in the marketplace one day, Maria, in a loud voice that all round her could hear, inquired of a vegetable woman if this was the man who had gossiped about her. The startled woman . . . nodded her head affirmatively. Maria then stepped in the path of the astonished editor and, before the crowd which had already assembled, gave him a resounding slap in the face. There was little more talk of Maria and her children after that. . . .

At the time Maria lived with me in St. Gall, the Italian Socialists had no special propaganda paper for women. We conceived the notion that one should be started. . . . Both Maria and I were hostile to any form of "feminism." To us the fight for the emancipation of women was only a single aspect of the struggle for the emancipation of humanity. It was because we wanted women, particularly workingwomen, to understand this, to learn that they had to fight not *against* men but *with* them against the common enemy, capitalist society, that we felt the need of this paper. Moving to Lugano, Maria and I founded *Su, Compagne!* (*Arise, Comrades!*). It was an almost instant success. . . .

Source: A. Balabanoff, *My Life as a Rebel* (New York: Harper, 1938), pp. 34–35.

British socialism followed the same moderate path as its unions. In 1884 a group of middle-class intellectuals founded the Fabian Society.* Led by the Irish playwright George Bernard Shaw (1856–1950), Sydney Webb (1859–1947), Beatrice Webb, and the novelist H. G. Wells (1866–1946), the Fabians rejected violent revolution. In 1900 socialists formed the Labour party.

As socialist parties gathered strength throughout Europe, their leaders attempted to reawaken international solidarity with the creation in 1889 of the Second International. It served largely to organize congresses, coordinate May Day celebrations, and provide a forum for con-

sultation. National parties continued to provide the impetus for the socialist movement.

In the two decades before World War I the international working-class movement was dominated by the opposing models offered by German and French socialists. In 1899 Éduard Bernstein (1850–1932) published a theoretical work titled *Evolutionary Socialism*. Bernstein, who had been influenced by the British Fabians, was both a revisionist and a reformist. His revisionism derived from his conviction that Marxist doctrine had to evolve as social, political, and economic conditions changed. In the context of a parliamentary system and an expanding industrial economy such as prevailed in Germany, Bernstein challenged Marx's beliefs in the coming crisis of capitalism, the increasing polarization of classes, and the certainty of working-class revolution. This position led him to abandon revolutionary tactics in favor of achieving concrete gains

---

*Named after the ancient Roman general Quintus Fabius Maximus, who avoided pitched battles with the Carthaginians in favor of harassing operations.

for workers through parliamentary reform and collaboration with non-Marxist parties. In effect, Bernstein's arguments reflected German socialist policy since the 1870s, although his reformism was bitterly denounced by orthodox Marxists. Indeed, the reformist-revolutionary controversy split socialist parties everywhere.

Bernstein's counterpart in France was Jean Jaurès (1859–1914), a fiery speaker and humanist scholar who urged socialist collaboration with middle-class governments to secure reforms. Under pressure from the International, which condemned revisionist "opportunism" and urged French socialists to unite into one party, Jaurès reverted to orthodoxy.

Women of the Left

The development of socialist political parties gave added impetus to the women's movement. Although women experienced resentment even within socialist parties and did not often rise to top positions in labor organizations, they found more acceptance from male comrades than in other parties. Socialists eschewed civil marriage as a bourgeois institution and practiced free love in radical circles. Most socialist parties eventually advocated universal suffrage, divorce laws, and birth control.

Despite German laws that prohibited women from engaging in political activity, the SPD took the lead in organizing women. After the party accepted their right to work, a law forced the creation of separate groups for women. In 1878 Bebel issued his *Women in the Past, Present, and Future*, the first sustained study of the women's question from a socialist perspective. Six years later Engels published *The Origins of the Family, Private Property, and the State*. The core of their arguments remained the idea that the suppression of women evolved as the concept of private property developed.

The party's major theoretician of Marxist feminism was Clara Zetkin (1857–1933), who pioneered female militancy within the SPD as well as in the Second International and edited the magazine *Equality*. Zetkin's theories of female emancipation started out from Marx and Engels' position concerning the nature of the middle-class family. She argued that housework and child rearing represented exploitation in the form of unpaid labor. Bourgeois morality had made women little more than property controlled by men. Hence women's liberation was impossible in isolation but had to take place as part of the broader socialist struggle against capitalism. Because Zetkin believed that female labor was a precondition for the liberation of women from sexual slavery, she urged them to participate in the work force as well as in socialist politics.

The Gotha Program of 1875 had advocated universal suffrage but refused to support more radical feminist views. Zetkin and other women eventually forced the SPD to adopt a broader feminist position. In 1894 SPD deputies in the Reichstag first proposed a bill for women's suffrage, although it was defeated.

Together with Rosa Luxemburg, Zetkin opposed Bernstein's revisionist principles. Their denunciations of reform socialism separated them from other women in the SPD as well as from nonsocialists because they argued the incompatibility of the socialist women's movement and bourgeois feminism. Nonsocialist feminists, they argued, sanctioned capitalism, a system of exploitation that repressed men and women alike. While Zetkin made the feminist cause the center of her professional life, Luxemburg subsumed women's issues into the larger question of revolution. The hostility of the revisionist leadership drove Zetkin and Luxemburg further to the left, and on the eve of World War I they were among the extremists who formed the German Communist party.

The rise of feminism and socialism after 1870, like the work of realist painters and novelists, revealed the deep contradictions that beset the liberal order in Europe. The political order moved toward democracy, while advances in education, health, and communications contributed to the modernization of a society in which workers and peasants were more fully integrated into national life. Yet industrial capitalism, which had produced remarkable prosperity, also engendered economic and cultural oppression in the organization of work, gender and family relations, and the

accumulation of unprecedented wealth by a new business-financial elite. Nor was the prosperity of the period evenly distributed. Workers' wages rose except during the Long Depression, but poverty was still widespread. Illiteracy, infant mortality, and illness remained higher among the workers than in the middle classes.

Constitutional monarchies and parliamentary regimes based on universal male suffrage had replaced absolute monarchy almost everywhere in Europe by the opening of the twentieth century. Nevertheless, in some Western states lib-

*eral governments proved no less vigorous than the old au-
tocrats in preserving a stable social order and protecting the
interests of industrial capitalism and patriarchy. While Europe remained generally at peace for almost a half century,*
*the international order spawned by liberalism also produced
militarism and new forms of nationalism, racism, and
imperialism.*

Notes

1. C. G. Moses, *French Feminism in the Nineteenth Century*
(Albany: State University of New York Press, 1984), p. 213.
2. E. F. Hurwitz, "The International Sisterhood," in R. Bridenthal
and C. Koonz, eds., *Becoming Visible: Women in European History*
(Boston: Houghton Mifflin, 1977), p. 337.

Suggestions for Further Reading

Bridenthal, R., and Koonz, C., eds. *Becoming Visible: Women in
European History*. Boston: Houghton Mifflin, 1977.

Burrow, J. W. *Evolution and Society: A Study in Victorian Social
Theory*. Cambridge: Cambridge University Press, 1966.

Clark, M. *Modern Italy, 1871–1982*. London: Longman, 1984.

Girouard, M. *Cities and People: A Social and Architectural History*.
New Haven, Conn.: Yale University Press, 1985.

Harrison, F. *The Dark Angel: Aspects of Victorian Sexuality*. New
York: Sheldon Press, 1977.

Hayes, C. J. H. *The Generation of Materialism, 1871–1900*. New
York: Harper, 1941.

Joll, J. *The Second International, 1889–1914*. New York: Harper &
Row, 1966.

Landes, D. *The Unbound Prometheus: Technological Change and
Industrial Development in Western Europe from 1750 to the Present*.
Cambridge: Cambridge University Press, 1969.

Milward, A. S., and Saul, S. B. *The Development of the Economies
of Continental Europe, 1850–1914*. Cambridge, Mass.: Harvard
University Press, 1977.

Mosse, G. L. *The Culture of Western Europe*. Chicago: Rand
McNally, 1961.

Pugh, M. *The Making of British Politics, 1867–1939*. Oxford: Basil
Blackwell, 1982.

Rewald, J. *The History of Impressionism*. New York: Museum of
Modern Art, 1961.

———. *Post-Impressionism*. New York: Museum of Modern Art,
1978.

Sheehan, J. J. *German Liberalism in the Nineteenth Century*. Chicago:
University of Chicago Press, 1978.

Stearns, P. N. *European Society in Upheaval: Social History Since
1800*. New York: Macmillan, 1967.

Thoennessen, W. *The Emancipation of Women: The Rise and Decline
of the Women's Movement in German Social Democracy,
1863–1933*. London: Pluto Press, 1973.

Thompson, D. *Democracy in France Since 1870*. New York: Oxford
University Press, 1969.

Vicinus, M., ed. *Suffer and Be Still: Women in the Victorian Age*.
Bloomington: Indiana University Press, 1972.

Writing and Communication (II)

Throughout the ancient and medieval world, literacy was relatively uncommon, but in time improved printing techniques encouraged its spread. In the Arab world and in Europe the production of books was limited by two factors: each copy of a text had to be written by hand, and the material used for manuscripts was generally either parchment, made from split sheepskins, or vellum (calfskin), both of which were expensive. These limitations were first overcome in China, where paper had been manufactured since the first century A.D. Around the eighth century the Chinese invented a system of printing using blocks of wood. The idea of binding several sheets of paper together followed shortly; the first printed book, consisting of six pages, was published in 868.

The notion of movable type originally had little appeal to the Chinese, whose script is made up of thousands of different characters. But in the eleventh century the Chinese developed movable type in wood, a technique later adopted by the Koreans, who were the first to use it on a large scale. Both the Chinese and the Koreans soon made metal type, which obviously lasted longer and made mass printing possible.

By the eighth century the Arabs had borrowed the Chinese method of manufacturing paper, but they had little interest in block printing, perhaps because the art of writing had become an important skill in itself. Toward the end of the twelfth century the Arabs introduced papermaking into Spain, from where the technique spread slowly into northern Europe; by the beginning of the fifteenth century it had reached Germany and Switzerland. There is no evidence, however, that the Europeans knew anything about Chinese printing methods, since almost their only contacts with Chinese culture were through Arab traders.

The invention in Europe of movable type occurred much later than in China and Korea, in the mid-fifteenth century. The material used for the type was metal, since medieval craftsmen were skilled at engraving medals and coins. The first printed book, the so-called Gutenberg Bible, was published in 1455 at Mainz.

In China the production of books had generally been limited to works for the educated classes. The first major printing project was an edition of the Confucian classics in the tenth century, followed by the Buddhist scriptures, and during the Sung period books on art, literature, science, and philosophy appeared in large numbers. Literacy remained primarily an elite preserve, given the difficulty of the written language, but popular fiction began to grow, and literacy rose among the urban merchants, themselves an expanding group.

The effects of printing in Europe may have been more widespread or immediate than in Asia, especially as universities and other schools enlarged their enrollments to educate the children of merchants and craftsmen. The demand for texts could now be met. Furthermore, the process was self-reinforcing: the more books there were, the more people learned to read. Thus the impact of printing was not merely to facilitate the circulation of ideas among educated people but also to make available on a popular level a vast range of material to which access had formerly been difficult, such as almanacs, herbals, and prophecies.

It soon became apparent that the new technology could be employed in conducting political, religious, and scholarly debate, and controversial positions were circulated quickly. Among the first masters of the medium was the Protestant Martin Luther, who published a series of printed tracts on church reform in 1520, and a German translation of the Bible (New Testament in 1522, Old Testament in 1534) that became a cornerstone of the Reformation. The Reformation introduced printed pamphlets, hymns, religious texts, and sacred pictures to much of northern Europe, calling not only for religious changes but social ones as well. Subsequently, debate in the Western world has been conducted in large measure in print, now supplemented by radio and television. Print has not been replaced for scholarly, scientific, or religious debate, and access to the media on social issues (except for talk shows) is generally limited to those who have established their positions in print. Only political debate has partly replaced print as the medium of prime communication, and even here it remains indispensable.

Between the Reformation and the French Revolution mass literacy began to develop in Europe and spread among European colonizers elsewhere in the world. The first battleground for printed texts had been a sacred one, but pamphlets could now be distributed and books published to advocate or even galvanize social and political change, and the spread of popular literature had an enormous impact on the English, American, and French revolutions. Not only did pamphleteers advance specific causes or claim individual wrongs; they also served to make accessible at a popular level ideas that had hitherto been limited to intellectuals.

The pamphleteers of the French wars of religion at the end of the sixteenth century and the English Revolution in the mid-seventeenth argued fundamental religious and political ideas, and their works, often cheaply printed, attracted wide circulation. The London bookseller George Thomason collected nearly

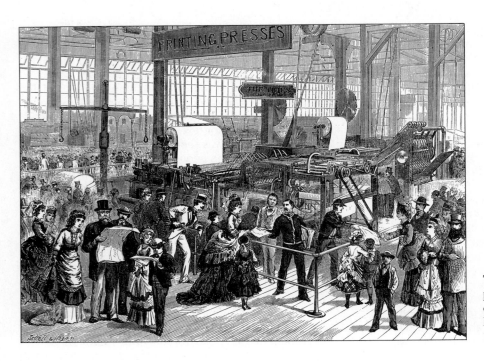

This web press, which was capable of printing on both sides of the paper, was featured at a Philadelphia exhibition in the 1870s. [Granger Collection]

30,000 books, pamphlets, broadsides, and newssheets published in England between 1640 and 1661, an astonishing output in a country of only 5 million people. The appetite for news persisted, and the seventeenth century saw the first newspapers established in Augsburg, Strasbourg, London, and Paris. The role of print expanded in the eighteenth century, making it possible for growing numbers of Westerners in particular to keep abreast of public events and political issues. "Every Englishman, nowadays," said Samuel Johnson, "expects to be promptly and accurately informed upon the condition of public affairs." But not until the advent of the "penny press" in the next century were newspapers fully accessible to the masses. Such exposure required not only literacy and the availability of an extra penny to spend for a paper but also a desire to use the money to acquire the news rather than other goods.

The Enlightenment would have been unthinkable without the printing press, which enabled the philosophes to appeal over the heads of established authority for fundamental reform. Often, however, the most radical thought became available on a popular level only in times of crisis. Tom Paine crystallized revolutionary attitudes in America with a pamphlet appropriately titled *Common Sense,* and the ideas of Jean-Jacques Rousseau became crucial to the thinking of French revolutionaries when they were expressed in popular form by Sieyès in his pamphlet *What Is the Third Estate?* published in January 1789. In China,

with its far greater population, there was from the eleventh century a major increase not only in popular fiction but also in printed manuals and pamphlets, although, unlike their European counterparts, they were rarely critical of the established order.

At the same time, the growth of knowledge and its relatively easy transmission were fundamental to the sudden surge of scientific development in the West. In the eyes of thinkers such as Francis Bacon and René Descartes, it was pointless to continue to depend on ancient writers and their books: new research was needed, and fresh ideas had to be circulated. In medicine and astronomy, chemistry and physics, the basis of modern scientific practice was laid in books published as early as the sixteenth and seventeenth centuries.

Popular literacy was also responsible for something less awesome in scope but equally valuable: instruction and pleasure. From the beginning, many of the most popular books were horoscopes and prophecies, cookbooks, collections of tales, and reports of extraordinary events. New literary forms such as the novel, the short story, and science fiction were created to meet popular demand for fiction and to express new social values and aspirations. All of these forms, including manuals, novels, and even detective stories, appeared in print in China several centuries earlier than in the West, although total literacy in China probably lagged behind after A.D. 1600. In the nineteenth century, the great age of the novel in the West, New

York's dockside was often crowded with readers eagerly awaiting the arrival of the latest installment of a Charles Dickens book from England.

If the invention of writing and the discovery of printing represent two giant steps in the development of world civilization, the mass communication systems of the twentieth century represent a third. The virtually instantaneous global communication that is possible today was foreshadowed in a series of nineteenth-century inventions that did much to change the role of the written word. A government postal system was introduced in Britain in 1840, which was much facilitated by the rapid growth of the railway system. Four years earlier, in 1836, the stamp tax on newspapers had been reduced, and by the middle of the century press circulation was three times its former level. The American Samuel Morse invented the telegraph, first used in 1844, and it soon became a valuable means of communication for Julius Reuter's news agency, the first international news service. The Prussian chancellor Otto von Bismarck effectively combined the telegraph and the press in 1870 when he edited a captured French telegram, the Ems dispatch, for publication, knowing that it would probably provoke the French to declare the war he sought; he was right, and the way was prepared for the completion of German unification.

The laying of the first permanent transatlantic cable in 1866 and Alexander Graham Bell's invention of the telephone a decade later made direct, instantaneous communication between Europe and North America possible. During World War II British prime minister Winston Churchill and American president Franklin Roosevelt conferred frequently by telephone, using the undersea cable. In the aftermath of the 1961 Cuban missile crisis, Soviet and American leaders approved the creation of a direct communications link, or "hot line," between the Kremlin and the White House to facilitate rapid discussion in the event of future crises.

Another revolutionary development in communications involved the technology of the camera and film. Graphic materials, of course, had been reproduced on printing presses for centuries, but beginning in the 1830s it was possible to transmit, through the new process of photography, the immediate pictorial image of an event. Photographs were vehicles of emotion as well as information, reaching the illiterate as well as the educated. The photographs of Mathew Brady (c. 1823-1896) enabled Americans to grasp the horrors that were occurring on the Civil War battlefields; his work laid the foundation for modern newsphoto services. Cameras could do more than record battles; they could shape them, particularly after aerial photography became practicable. Although the first aerial shots (from balloons) dated from 1858, the develop-

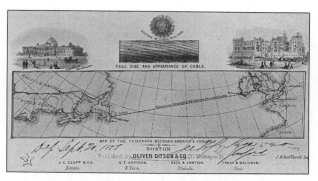

This detail from a sheet music cover commemorated the laying of a transoceanic telegraph cable in 1858. The cable failed after operating only one month. [Granger Collection]

ment of the airplane half a century later permitted extensive use of aerial photographs for military purposes, a vital advantage in World War I. Aerial photography has also played an important role in mapping and surveying natural resources, thus facilitating communication about our physical environment.

The initial impact of these changes was limited to Europe and North America, but they were spread elsewhere in part by the Western colonial powers. In India the British founded universities in Calcutta, Bombay, and Madras, and public opinion expressed itself through newspapers. In China the foreign-run Maritime Customs Service began an efficient Western-style postal and telegraph system after 1860, while missionaries published huge numbers of tracts and founded Western-style schools, colleges, and universities. The Dutch colonial administration of Indonesia, the British in Burma and Malaya, and the Americans in the Philippines did much the same. Japan was first widely exposed to Western influence in 1853 and soon began to employ Western technology.

In Africa the principal beneficiaries of technological progress were the colonial powers themselves. Many parts of Africa had a rich tradition of song and story that went back centuries, but little of it became known beyond the immediate oral range until the twentieth century. In general the African communicative tradition was a spoken one; some of the works of Somali and Swahili poets of the eighteenth and nineteenth centuries were written down, but virtually everything else that is known of earlier times was collected by modern anthropologists. With the arrival of European colonizers and missionaries, a limited number of Africans learned the languages and writing systems of their conquerors, but only the liberation struggles of the twentieth century produced any level of general

Alexander Graham Bell demonstrates the telephone by calling Boston from Salem, Massachusetts, on March 15, 1877. [Granger Collection]

literacy. Many African writers were thus faced with the dilemma of deciding whether to produce works in an alien language for the outside world or use their own tribal language. The same problem still confronts writers in other areas whose native languages and cultures—Basque, Gaelic, and Welsh for example—struggle to survive in the face of more widely spoken rivals.

The appearance of new inventions—radio, movies, the phonograph—combined with earlier changes to enhance the ability to communicate. In the case of sound transmission, war was again crucial in accelerating the technological development that had begun in the mid-nineteenth century. The transmission of sound using light waves rather than wires was discovered by the Italian Guglielmo Marconi in 1895, and within 20 years transmission was possible across both the Atlantic and the Pacific. After World War I, the radio came into common use, bringing with it revolutionary possibilities for political leaders to communicate directly with the masses of their people. Among the early masters of this medium were Franklin Roosevelt, who used the radio for his "fireside chats," and Josef Goebbels, Hitler's propaganda minister. The integration of sight and sound in the cinema was achieved in 1927, when Al Jolson spoke and sang in the first "talkie," *The Jazz Singer*, and by 1930 silent pictures were antiquated. The stage was set for the filming of not only movies for entertainment but also the massive spectacles staged by Hitler at Nuremberg and the patriotic newsreels shown in movie theaters that bolstered morale during the Second World War.

The phonograph also had roots in the mid-nineteenth century, though only in the 1890s did serious manufacturing commence. Improved electrical reproduction came in the 1920s and fine-grooved records in the following decade. Culturally, it was now possible for people in one part of the world to hear and appreciate music from other continents. Perhaps there is no better example of this than the present Japanese fondness for Beethoven's Ninth (Choral) Symphony, performances of which are widespread in Japan each year. Moreover, Japanese and Korean conductors and soloists are now some of the best performers of Western music.

Perhaps the most revolutionary development in communications has been television. Although development of electronically transmitted images was under way as early as 1924, only after World War II was intercity network television launched, using coaxial cables. Microwave radio transmission began the same year, 1946, and in 1951 microwave relay made possible the first coast-to-coast television broadcast. The historical ramifications were enormous. In addition to the educational and cultural possibilities television afforded, the medium's ability to provide viewers with virtually immediate coverage of major events created new pressures as well as opportunities for political leaders. Mounting American anger over military involvement in Vietnam in the 1960s resulted at least in part from what people saw on their television screens. The widespread outpouring of sympathy and aid for famine-stricken areas in North Africa in the 1970s and

Roving photographers such as this one provided valuable documentation for social historians. This photograph was taken at a summer resort in France. [Culver Pictures]

early 1980s was triggered by television pictures of the victims.

Improved communications are changing modern society. Radio and especially television have substantially altered industrial societies by creating mass markets, which have in turn altered labor-management relations and created a greater homogeneity of manufactured goods. Mass communications also facilitate the creation of a consensus for action, while simultaneously providing minorities—in the absence of censorship—with the means to alter majority thinking and behavioral patterns, as Martin Luther King, Jr., demonstrated in the civil rights movement of the 1960s. Through modern technology, ideas and tastes can be increasingly homogenized, yet it is also possible to use the same means to facilitate the rapid acceptance of new styles and ideas. Television and the movies have even intensified urbanization by popularizing the lure of the cities, which are increasingly attractive not only because of their employment possibilities but also for their culture and lifestyle.

The pace of the communications revolution still varies considerably from region to region. For every 1,000 people in the United States, for example, there were 408 televisions and 1,417 radios in 1968, compared to 208 and 255, respectively, in Japan and 3 and 74 in South Korea. Indonesia and India lagged

even further behind, with only 14 and 13 radios per 1,000 people, respectively; Nigeria had only one television set for every 1,000 persons in 1968. Such countries are only now experiencing the full brunt of the print revolution. In the period between 1948 and 1968 the number of daily newspapers declined slightly in the Western industrial countries of the United States, Great Britain, France, Italy, and the Netherlands, while they doubled in India, nearly tripled in Pakistan, and jumped nearly sevenfold in Turkey. There are, of course, exceptions to these patterns, often because of political factors such as the rise or fall of authoritarian regimes. The main problem facing developing countries seeking to implement new communications technology is the extraordinary capital outlay required, a problem that will perpetuate the communications gap in the forseeable future.[1]

Nevertheless, the introduction of communication satellites in the 1970s made possible an operational communications network that is worldwide. Even in areas without electricity, a transistor radio can enable people to hear the news, political messages, and cultural events. But instantaneous communications can complicate international relations. In the nineteenth century reports of hostile action on another continent could take a week or more to reach a concerned government, but at least that provided time for a consid-

In the early 1920s the radio became very popular. Primitive sets required the use of headphones. [Culver Pictures]

ered response. With the advent of the telegraph, and now communication satellites, the pressure for rapid decisions at the expense of deliberate analysis is increased, thereby intensifying the risks of war.

The ability of computers to store and retrieve information is a recent technological advance with major implications for communications. Computers can be programmed with artificial languages to facilitate high-speed transmission of information. Used responsibly, computers are valuable for uses ranging from complex mathematical calculations to scientific experiments.

But computers can also be programmed to act in the absence of human reflection, as in the case of the massive computer-generated trading that triggered enormous losses on the New York Stock Exchange in 1987 and the computer-geared nuclear arsenals of the superpowers. Ironically, revolutionary advances in communications technology, often generated by wartime research, have simultaneously presented the world with possibilities both deadly and visionary.

Notes

1. Statistics in this paragraph from W. P. Davison, ''The Media Kaleidoscope: General Trends in the Channels,'' in *Propaganda and Communication in World History*, ed. H. D. Lasswell, D. Lerner, and H. Speier, vol. 3 (Honolulu: University Press of Hawaii, 1980), pp. 191–248.

Suggestions for Further Reading

Abel, E., et al. *Many Voices, One World: Communications and Society*. Paris: UNESCO, 1984.

Craig, J. *Thirty Centuries of Graphic Design: An Illustrated History*. New York: Watson-Guptill, 1987.

Frawley, W. *Text and Epistemology*. Norwood, N.J.: Ablex, 1987.

Lasswell, H. D., Lerner, D., and Speier, H., eds. *Propaganda and Communication in World History*, vols. 2 and 3. Honolulu: University Press of Hawaii, 1980.

Logan, R. K. *The Alphabet Effect: The Impact of the Phonetic Alphabet on the Development of Western Civilization*. New York: Morrow, 1986.

Lowenthal, L. *Literature and Mass Culture: Communication in Society*, vol. 1. New Brunswick, N.J.: Transaction Books, 1984.

Schiller, H. I. *Information and the Crisis Economy*. Norwood, N.J.: Ablex, 1984.

Siegel, L., and Markoff, J. *The High Cost of High Tech: The Dark Side of the Chip*. New York: Harper & Row, 1985.

Whalley, J. I. *Writing Implements and Accessories: From the Roman Stylus to the Typewriter*. Detroit: Gale Research, 1975.

The Age of Western Domination

Contemporary world history began during the last three decades of the nineteenth century, when a handful of European countries imposed their domination over huge portions of the globe. Britain, France, Germany, and to a lesser extent Italy and Belgium completed control of a large proportion of the earth's land surface and population. Russia continued to push its borders eastward into Asia, while the United States and Japan extended their presence into the Pacific region. One result of this sudden grab for colonial possessions was the establishment of complex forms of interdependency among world civilizations that still shape our lives. This first major phase in the creation of a "global village" as a product of imperialism is the background of the contemporary age.

The battle of Omdurman (1898), in which General Kitchener's army decisively defeated a Muslim force in the Sudan. [The Mansell Collection, detail from a painting]

799

The New Imperialism

The process by which this transformation took place is known as the new imperialism, to distinguish it from the previous phase of European colonial expansion that took place between the sixteenth and eighteenth centuries. This newer form of imperialism was characterized not only by its rapid and intense pace but by other unique features as well.

The earlier overseas empires lay chiefly in the Americas and included extensive European-run areas in India and Southeast Asia as well as footholds on the East Asian and African coasts. After 1870 the Western powers moved deep into the interiors of Asia and Africa. Although the older empires traded with local populations, they were generally regarded as sources of direct revenue for the home country—tribute from native rulers, taxation from the local populations, and the expropriation of gold and silver.

Because the new imperialism was the work of advanced industrial-capitalist nations rather than of mercantile economies, it involved the commitment of significant financial investment as well as the deliberate exploitation of the material and human resources of the colonial areas. The economic function of the new imperialism, whether real or perceived, led in turn to the establishment of direct political control over the colonies, administered through elaborate bureaucracies. By the opening of the twentieth century, therefore, a new and direct relationship of unequal exchange had been established among the civilizations of the world, marked by a vast difference between the industrial and technological power of the West and the relative weakness of less technologically developed cultures.

Conflicting Interpretations

Scholars debate the causes and consequences of the new imperialism. One basic fact appears to be generally accepted: by 1870 conditions in Europe were ripe for overseas expansion. The breakdown of the Concert of Europe and the creation of nation-states in Germany and Italy heightened aggressive national rivalry. Moreover, power status was increasingly equated with the possession of overseas colonies, so empire became a matter of national honor. The Long Depression of 1873–1896 convinced some business and government leaders that overseas colonies would solve the problems caused by shrinking European markets and increasingly higher wages. Though policymakers often used economic arguments to explain the necessity for expansion, imperialism had support among all classes, including workers. Even trade union leaders and some socialists were enthusiastic about colonial expansion.

Economics and Empire

Economic rivalry between older industrial states such as Britain and France and newly industrializing states such as Germany and the United States added to the competition for colonies, especially as tariff barriers restricted European markets after 1880. Unprecedented prosperity and military-industrial power produced by the second industrial revolution and advances in science, technology, and industrial organization gave Europeans confidence in the superiority of their civilization. The climax of European development in the last decades of the century thus brought together a growing concern over national pride and security, the desire for continued economic expansion, and an appetite for cultural dominance.

The connection between economics and imperialism is hardly in doubt, although its exact nature is debated. The economic slump that began in the 1870s had increased unemployment, pushed prices for manufactured goods down, and diminished exports, making industrial nations compete fiercely over markets for their manufactured goods at a time when the abandonment of free trade limited the European market. This competition prompted some observers to argue for sheltered colonial markets limited to trade with the home country. An additional stimulus to imperialism arose from the demand for raw materials unavailable in Europe, especially copper, rubber, tin, cotton, jute, and petroleum, as well as foodstuffs such as coconut, coffee, and tea, on which Europeans had come to rely. Not only raw materials were necessary to the new industrial products, but their value was enhanced because cheap colonial labor made mining, extraction, and agriculture especially profitable.

The debate over economic factors centers on accumulated surplus capital. This argument, which later became the major interpretation of Marxist writers, was first proposed in 1902 by the British economic liberal John A. Hobson (1858–1940) in *Imperialism: A Study*. Hobson believed that capitalism suffered from underconsumption—that is, wealth in capitalist societies was poorly distributed as a result of overaccumulation by the rich. The business and financial interests that controlled such surplus capital soon discovered that it could be more profitably invested overseas, where cheap labor and raw materials made a greater return possible. Hobson saw imperialism as the effort of capitalists to find investment outlets for their surplus wealth. He argued that surplus capital could be eliminated if workers were paid higher wages and the rich taxed more heavily; because these measures would result in greater purchasing power for the working class, the need for new markets—hence imperialism—would disappear.

In 1916 V. I. Lenin (1870–1924), the future Communist leader of the Russian Revolution, wrote the classic Marxist analysis of the subject, *Imperialism: The Highest Stage of Capitalism*. The scramble for colonies, Lenin noted, coincided with the change in Europe's economy from a phase of free competition to one of intense monopoly through combines, trusts, and the control of finance capital. Imperialism emerges from this "highest" stage of capitalism when business and financial interests in each country seek to extend their monopolies overseas in the search for greater profits. Imperialism was therefore an inevitable response to the "internal contradictions" of monopolistic capitalism. For Lenin, imperialism would result in the breakdown of the capitalist system.

Hobson and Lenin were partly correct. Between 1860 and 1900 the value of British capital invested abroad grew from $7 billion to $20 billion. By the eve of World War I, a fifth of the foreign investments of France and Germany was in colonial regions, while about half of Britain's overseas investments were in the colonial world. In many instances, however, foreign rulers needed and requested Western capital, and financial investment hardly explained the imperialist expansion of less developed nations such as Italy and Russia, which had little surplus capital. Nor does colonialism explain the equally large British investments in non-colonial areas, such as Latin America and the United States. Finally, although some colonial possessions were profitable, the military and bureaucratic costs of occupation sometimes exceeded the financial return.

However important the economic motives behind imperialism, it caught the imagination of the European mind and responded to a popular thirst for the exotic. Scientists, missionaries, hunters, and adventurers poured into Africa and Asia in the late nineteenth century. Yet even the humanitarian instincts of the missionaries, intent on bringing Christianity and modern medicine to "heathens," involved a conviction about the superiority of their own civilization. When the British writer Rudyard Kipling spoke of the "white man's burden," he reflected the view of many Europeans that the civilizing mission was a sacred duty of more advanced races—a view supported in more ruthless fashion by those who believed in Social Darwinism.

◎ Imperialism and Economics: The Debate ◎

Among analysts of the economic causes of the new imperialism, two major authors stand out: Hobson and Lenin.

By far the most important economic factor in imperialism is the influence relating to investments. The growing cosmopolitanization of capital is the greatest economic change of this generation. Every advanced industrial nation is tending to place a larger share of its capital outside the limits of its own political area, in foreign countries, or in colonies, and to draw a growing income from this source.

Imperialism is capitalism in that stage of development in which the dominance of monopolies and finance capital has established itself; in which the export of capital has acquired pronounced importance; in which the division of the world among the international trusts has begun; in which division of all territories of the globe among the great capitalist powers has been completed.

More recent students of imperialism, however, have questioned these earlier views.

In the second half of the twentieth century, it can be seen that imperialism owed its popular appeal not to the sinister influence of the capitalists, but to its inherent attractions for the masses . . . and the adoption of a creed based on such irrational concepts as racial superiority and the prestige of the nation. . . . Imperialism cannot be explained in simple terms of economic theory and the nature of financial capital.

Sources: J. A. Hobson, *Imperialism: A Study* (New York: Pott, 1902), p. 30; V. I. Lenin, *Imperialism: The Highest Stage of Capitalism* (New York: International Publishers, 1939), p. 89; D. K. Fieldhouse, "Imperialism: A Historiographical Revision," *Economic History Review*, 2d ser., 14 (1961): 209.

Africa and the Colonial Powers

The most intense phase of the new imperialism unfolded in Africa, a continent four times the size of Europe. For centuries Westerners had viewed sub-Saharan Africa as the "Dark Continent," a vast, unexplored expanse where inhospitable climate, diseases, and geography conspired to keep them out. Muslim traders criss-crossed much of West Africa and the Sahara, but as late as the mid-nineteenth century only the coastal settlements and a few interior regions were represented on European maps. Despite Western ignorance, however, Africa had undergone major transformation in the centuries before the new im-

perialism. Iron metallurgy, agricultural techniques, and the introduction of new crops had spread across the continent, and a large increase in population had caused migrations into central and southern Africa. Diversity of geography and ethnocultural patterns determined development. Sophisticated cultures and effective states marked some regions, especially in the savannah zone of West Africa, where the kingdoms of Ghana, Mali, and Songhai had once flourished, and in Zimbabwe and the Swahili city-states of Southeast Africa. In the rain forests and southern regions, inhabited mainly by San, Pygmies, and Khoikhoi, political organization revolved around village communities that relied on primitive food-gathering techniques.

Changes in military techniques and weaponry also affected conditions in Africa. The earliest of these innovations were the tactics developed by the Zulu, a warlike

◉ Military Revolution in Africa: ◉ The Zulu Warrior

In the 1820s African warfare underwent a major transformation that altered the balance of power among the Bantu-speaking peoples of the southeast. Shaka, the ruler of the Zulu, introduced highly disciplined infantry regiments that were protected by shields and used short, stabbing spears instead of the traditional throwing type. Here is an account of these warriors by Robert Moffat, a British missionary who visited the Zulu a number of years after Shaka's death.

Some thousands of the Matabele [Zulu], composing several regiments, are distinguished by the colour of their shields, as well as the kind and profusion of feathers which generally adorn their heads, having also a long feather of the blue crane rising from their brows, all which has an imposing effect at their onset. Their arms consist of a shield, short spear, and club. The club, often made of the horn of a rhinoceros or hard wood, they throw with unerring precision, so as even to strike dead the smaller antelope. The spear is not intended for throwing, but for close combat, and such being their mode of warfare, the tribes accustomed to throw their light javelins to a distance, are overtaken by these organized soldiers and mowed down. They must conquer or die, and if one return without his shield or spear, at the frown of his sovereign he is instantly despatched by another. They look best in their war dress, which is only worn on great occasions, and without which they are like the Kafir tribes in a state of nudity. They rarely use a war axe, which distinguishes the Bechuana warrior, and which he only uses when brought into embarrassed circumstances, when his spears are expended, or when butchering the vanquished enemy. Their shields, made of the thickest part of the ox hide, are very different in size and shape. That of the Matabele is sufficiently long to cover the body, while the other is light, and easily manoeuvred so as to throw off the missles of the enemy. That of the Basuto is smaller still, and seems only capable of defending the left hand, which grasps the spears, and a rod bearing a plume of black ostrich feathers.

Source: R. Moffat, *Missionary Labours and Scenes in Southern Africa* (New York: Carter & Brothers, 1855), p. 351.

Bantu-speaking people in the southeast. Under their ambitious leader, Shaka (1817–1828), the Zulu steadily conquered new territory. Shaka armed infantry troops with spears designed for fighting at close range. The subsequent introduction of firearms by the British and the Muslims had even more serious consequences. The breech-loading rifle and the Gatling gun, for example, enabled the British to subdue the Zulu in a series of bloody wars in the 1870s. In the hands of Westerners and Africans, modern weapons unsettled the political life of numerous African states, which were either consolidated under new native rulers or subjugated by foreigners. Thus Sayyid Said, a Muslim contemporary of Shaka, became sultan of Zanzibar in 1806 and for 50 years controlled a vast commercial domain in East Africa. Similarly, the rifle enabled the Boer settlers in South Africa to push into the interior in the face of British and Bantu resistance.

Explorers and Missionaries

Western interest in Africa intensified in the early nineteenth century as a result of the debate over the abolition of the slave trade. Curiosity about the interior of the Dark Continent combined with humanitarian concerns to bring a host of explorers and missionaries to Africa. Exploration focused on two unsolved geographic mysteries: the source of the Niger River in West Africa and the source of the Nile in East Africa. As early as 1795 Mungo Park, a Scottish doctor, led an expedition up the Niger, but not until 1830 was the river fully traced. Successive British adventurers made their way from the coast of East Africa in search of the sources of the Nile, including Sir Samuel White Baker and his wife, Lady Florence Baker. In 1864 the Bakers at last arrived in the vicinity of Lake Albert, which they discovered and named. The most famous African explorer of the period was David Livingstone, whose humanitarianism and courage caught the imagination of Europe. His expeditions in the 1850s sparked public interest. From 1857 to 1863 Livingstone explored the Zambesi River region and in 1866 set out on his last journey, intending to settle the question of the source of the Nile. When no word reached the outside world for five years, an American newspaper sent Henry M. Stanley, a well-known correspondent, to find the lost missionary. The two men met in 1871, but Livingstone, sick and exhausted, refused to return to Britain. When Stanley returned to the Congo in 1878 on behalf of King Leopold of Belgium, he paved the way for a new phase in the history of Western imperialism.

The Scramble for Africa

Portugal had held Angola and Mozambique since the age of exploration, but before 1870 European powers had seized only a few footholds along the coast. France had occupied Algeria and portions of the Senegal, and Britain already controlled the Cape of Good Hope, Gambia, and Sierra Leone and had imposed its commercial influence on the Niger River region and Zanzibar. Following the mid-century explorations, the pace of expansion became intense as Western powers scrambled for territory.

The race for colonies was sparked by King Leopold, who planned to exploit the Congo through the privately financed International Congo Association. Establishing a pattern that would be used by other entrepreneurs, hundreds of tribal chieftains were tricked into signing treaties granting the association some 900,000 square miles of land. Karl Peters, founder of the German Colonization Society, followed suit in East Africa, and the Germans seized Southwest Africa; the French army officer Pierre de Brazza secured control over vast tracts north of the Congo.

In 1885 Bismarck called a conference in Berlin to establish international guidelines for the acquisition of African territory. The conference recognized the Congo Free State as a neutral region. Although the Congo was to be governed by the Belgian King, all nations were to have free access to trade and navigation, and the slave trade was to be suppressed. The diplomats agreed that henceforth a power with coastal possessions had a right to the adjacent hinterland only if it effectively occupied the territory. Future disputes were to be settled by arbitration.

The Congo under Leopold's rule suffered unimaginable exploitation. Private firms used forced labor to squeeze maximum profit out of the rich rubber and ivory resources. Atrocities committed by the labor overseers, together with the toll of disease and climate, claimed more than 10 million lives during the next 20 years. Conditions did not improve until Leopold turned his private ownership of the Free State over to the Belgian government in 1908, when it became the Belgian Congo.

Following the Berlin conference, nine-tenths of the African continent was rapidly divided among the European powers. Italy and Germany joined the scramble. When France blocked Italy's ambitions in Tunisia, Italy instead occupied Eritrea and Somaliland, desolate areas along the Red Sea. In 1896 the Italians attempted to conquer the Christian state of Abyssinia (Ethiopia), but the emperor Menelik's forces, four times the size of the Italian army, defeated the invaders at Adowa. By the end of the century Abyssinia and the American-sponsored nation of Liberia on the west coast remained the only nominally independent states on the continent. Although Bismarck was personally opposed to African colonization, he yielded to domestic pressure. Germany proclaimed a protectorate over Southwest Africa and German East Africa (Tanganyika) and eventually added Togoland and the Cameroons to its empire. When Kaiser William II dismissed Bismarck in 1890, German colonial activities intensified.

Britain, France, and the Perils of Empire

The largest empires in Africa were acquired by France and Britain, whose conflicting ambitions at times brought the two powers to the brink of war. The de Brazza expedition had enabled France to claim a huge portion of Equatorial Africa, and by 1896 France had occupied Madagascar as well. The focus of French efforts, however, was in the Sahara. From Algeria, Senegal, and the Ivory Coast the French pushed south, east, and north across the great desert, establishing military outposts while fighting nomads. In 1881 they occupied Tunisia, and by the end of that decade they had gone beyond Lake Chad to the borders of the Sudan. Eventually the French hoped to reach the Nile and perhaps the Red Sea, a plan that brought them into conflict with British aspirations.

By the time the Berlin conference convened, Britain held the Cape Colony in southern Africa and had imposed its control over Egypt. In 1875 Ismail, Egypt's ruler, was unable to repay huge loans from French and British bankers. When, as a result, he was forced to sell his stock in the Suez Canal Company, representing 44 percent of all shares, British prime minister Benjamin Disraeli bought them, giving Britain a vital stake in the strategic waterway. The next year Ismail suspended interest payments on Egypt's foreign debts, and France and Britain assumed joint control of its finances. Foreign intervention sparked nationalist reaction among Egyptian intellectuals and army officers, and in 1882 riots in Alexandria led to a British bombardment of the city and the establishment of a protectorate over the country. For the next 25 years Egypt was ruled by a British governor.

The British next moved to secure the Sudan, an Egyptian dependency to the south. In 1885 a British garrison at Khartoum under General Charles ("Chinese") Gordon was massacred by the armies of the Mahdi, the leader of fierce Muslim tribesmen. Not until 1898 did the British send an expeditionary force, commanded by General Horatio Kitchener, to retake the Sudan. This time the nationalist fervor of the Muslims was no match for the new British machine guns—more than 10,000 tribesmen were wiped out at Omdurman. A few months earlier a French expedition under Captain Jean-Baptiste Marchand had arrived at Fashoda, where it planted the French flag. On September 18, only a few weeks after Omdurman, Kitchener, with a superior force, met Marchand there. An open clash was avoided only when the French government backed down.

British and French imperial plans ran directly counter to each other, for while France sought to create an east-west empire that stretched from the Atlantic to the Red Sea, Britain dreamed of a north-south domain that reached from Egypt to Cape Town. Along with Egypt and the Sudan, they already controlled Uganda and British East Af-

rica (Kenya), and a determined British push north from the Cape might connect the parts.

South Africa and the Boer War

The British Cape-to-Cairo scheme was the brainchild of Cecil Rhodes (1853–1902), who had become fabulously wealthy in diamond and gold mining. A fierce nationalist and social Darwinist, in 1890 Rhodes became prime minister of the Cape Colony and began to formulate a scheme to bring more of Africa under British rule.

The other European powers represented less of an obstacle to Rhodes than did internal conditions in South Africa. The Cape had been settled in the seventeenth century by Dutch immigrants, staunchly independent Calvinist farmers and cattlemen. When Britain annexed the colony after the Napoleonic Wars, these Afrikaners—the British called them Boers, from the Dutch word for farmer—migrated north in the Great Trek, eventually establishing the Orange Free State and the Transvaal Republic. As they carved out new settlements, the Boers encountered opposition from the Bantu and Zulu populations as well as from the British, and more than 30 years of continuous fighting ensued. Just when a compromise appeared possible, the discovery of gold and diamonds

Paul Kruger, prominent Boer politician and President of the Transvaal. [Bettmann Archive]

intensified the conflict between the British and the Boers. In the 1880s and 1890s hundreds of thousands of Englishmen poured into the mining towns of the Transvaal, Bechuanaland, and the area later known as Rhodesia, overwhelming the Boers and making open conflict all but inevitable.

The principal Boer spokesman was Paul Kruger (1825–1904). As president of the Transvaal, Kruger pressured

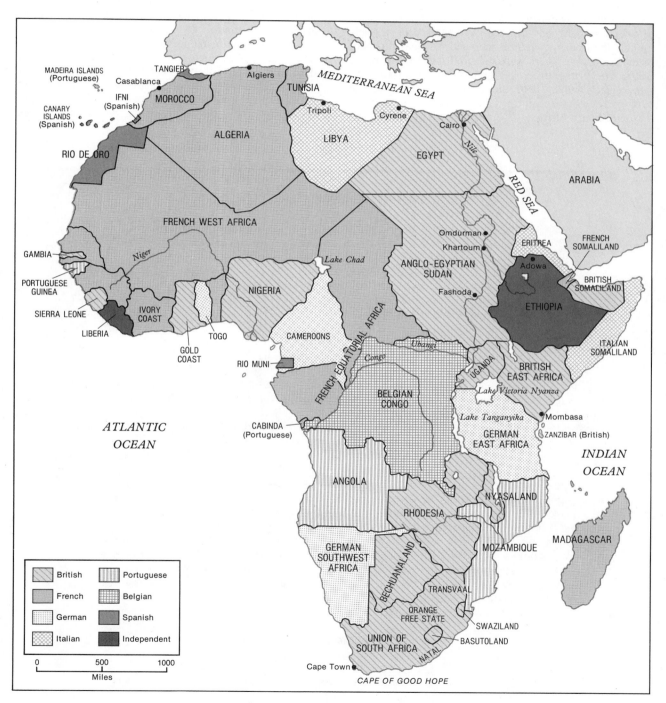

33.1 *Africa on the Eve of World War I*

the *Uitlanders* ("foreigners") by levying discriminatory taxes on them, curbing the use of English, and curtailing the exercise of political rights. In 1895 Rhodes and his agents attempted to overthrow Kruger when a small British force invaded the Transvaal under the command of Dr. Leander Jameson. The Jameson raid failed, but public opinion in Europe condemned the British, and Kaiser William II telegraphed Kruger that the Germans had been ready to help the Boers. In 1899 Britain and the Boer republics went to war; the Boers were defeated and surrendered in 1902. The British eventually granted self-government to the region, and in 1910 the Cape Colony, Natal, the Orange Free State, and the Transvaal were joined as the Union of South Africa.

Imperialism and Its Consequences

Imperialism affected both the European conquerors and their colonial subjects. Economic and industrial development in the West responded to the influx of raw materials and the opportunities for overseas investment, and it is probable that the resulting lower prices had a positive effect on the real wages of some European workers. On the diplomatic level, however, competition for colonies increased tensions among the great powers. The impact on Africa was incalculable as the full weight of Western technology descended on the continent, which for centuries

◉ Women and African Society ◉

Travelers in precolonial Africa encountered long-established social customs that appeared alien to them and that their own cultural arrogance or ethnocentrism made them perceive as primitive. Even David Livingstone, who had a deeper respect for African traditions than most Westerners of his day, sometimes misunderstood the import of what he found. This anecdote, which Livingstone's Victorian mind found humorous, revealed the strength of women's roles in one African community.

The person whom Nyakoba appointed to be our guide, having informed us of the decision, came and bargained that his services should be rewarded with a hoe. I showed him the article; he was delighted with it, and went off to show it to his wife. He soon afterward returned, and said that, though he was perfectly willing to go, his wife would not let him. I said, "Then bring back the hoe"; but he replied, "I want it." "Well, go with us, and you shall have it." "But my wife won't let me." I remarked to my men, "Did you ever hear such a fool?" They answered, "Oh, that is the custom of these parts; the wives are the masters." . . . When a young man takes a liking for a girl of another village, and the parents have no objection to the match, he is obliged to come and live at their village. He has to perform certain services for the mother-in-law, such as keeping her well supplied with firewood; and when he comes into her presence he is obliged to sit with his knees in a bent position, as putting out his feet toward the old lady would give her great offense. If he becomes tired of living in this state of vassalage, and wishes to return to his own family, he is obliged to leave all his children behind—they belong to the wife. This is only a more stringent enforcement of the law from which emanates the practice which prevails so very extensively in Africa, known to Europeans as "buying wives." Such virtually it is, but it does not appear quite in that light to the actors. So many head of cattle or goats are given to the parents of the girl "to give her up," as it is termed, i.e., to forego all claim on her offspring, and allow an entire transference of her and her seed into another family. If nothing is given, the family from which she has come can claim the children as part of itself: the payment is made to sever this bond.

Source: D. Livingstone, *Missionary Travels and Researches in South Africa* (New York: Harper, 1858), pp. 667–668.

had been relatively undisturbed by outside influences. In less than a generation Africans found their social and political structures shattered, their agrarian economy transformed, and their values undermined. Europeans exploited the natural and mineral resources of Africa, extracting huge quantities of gold, diamonds, ivory, rubber, and copper. White settlers seized fertile agricultural land formerly occupied by tribal communities, especially in southern and eastern Africa. The construction of roads, railroads, and telegraph lines stimulated internal trade across long distances and, together with the introduction of a wage-earning structure, transformed the barter economy into a monetary system. Yet enormous manpower was needed to reshape the African economy and build an infrastructure, and the labor supply, poorly paid, was often conscripted by force and treated brutally.

The "modernization" of the continent took a terrible toll on the cultural and political pattern of African life. Broken family and kinship patterns often resulted as workers were required to move over wide distances and tribal communities were stripped of their land. Moreover, imperialism resulted in artificially drawn political boundaries that divided many tribes and merged hostile groups. Even Western humanitarian programs had a mixed impact on local populations. The missionary efforts improved sanitation and agricultural methods and provided Africans with Western education. But these benefits also subverted African identity and undermined traditional values and social mores, for young Africans exposed to Western education or converted to Christianity often rejected family and tribal authority.

The speed and relative ease of European conquest obscures the fact that Africans resisted imperialism. The nomads of the Sahara, the Muslims of the Sudan, and the Zulus of southern Africa fought vigorously against Europeans. After the conquest, resistance took more subtle forms. A new class of Westernized Africans, many trained in European universities and then appointed to posts in the colonial administrations, eventually emerged. Ironically, these Africans, having absorbed Western political attitudes and values, returned home to provide leadership for their people and sometimes spearheaded the drive for independence.

could more readily resist or choose from among Western ideas and institutions. For example, a major Christian missionary effort was made, but it produced few converts, although as in Africa it was an important means of introducing Western medicine and education. Much of traditional Asian culture remained vigorous, especially the family system. At the same time, many Asian institutions were remade under Western influence or were augmented by new ones introduced by Westerners.

The arrogance as well as the success of Western imperialism was galling to most Asians, especially given their own pride in their ancient traditions of greatness. Western colonialism, and the unequal treaties forced on Siam (Thailand), China, and Japan, stimulated a renewal of the national Asian traditions and an effort to make them relevant to a world dominated by the West and its standards. Thus India saw the Hindu Renaissance and related movements (often under British pressure) to eliminate or restrict institutions now seen as unacceptable, such as *sati* and child marriage. In China similar movements arose against footbinding, chaste widowhood, and concubinage, in Japan against premarital promiscuity, class-based restrictions on clothing, and more or less open pornography (known as "spring pictures").

Asians found this forced reexamination of much of their cultural heritage under the eyes of an alien conqueror deeply disturbing. Now more than ever they needed to hold their heads up, convinced that to be Indian or Chinese or Japanese or Southeast Asian was something to be proud of. Many convinced themselves that while the West might have a temporary material advantage, the East was still superior spiritually and in the arts of civilization.

Industrialization was in time pursued vigorously, first in India, then in Japan, and finally in China, although it lagged in Southeast Asia. At least as important as technological change were institutions such as banking and joint-stock companies and the particularly Western idea of nationalism. The great Asian empires and states of the past had been cultural and bureaucratic structures different from the nation-states of modern Europe, whose national coherence and drive Asians rightly saw as a source of strength that they lacked but that they must have if they were again to be masters in their own house.

The West in Asia

Many of the same trends were set in motion by the pressures for Westernization in Asia. This was most true in the countries incorporated in Western colonial systems — India, Ceylon, Burma, Malaya, Indochina, Indonesia, and the Philippines — but similar trends were evident in China and even in Japan. Traditional Asian cultures and states were, however, more highly developed than in Africa and

British Imperial India

A divided and weakened India had progressively fallen under the domination of the English East India Company (as described in Chapter 27), and by 1857 most of it was being administered, directly or indirectly, as a single unit. Most Indians exposed to the new British model of Western-style progress admired it, but in the long run being united for the first time yet treated as second-class citizens in their

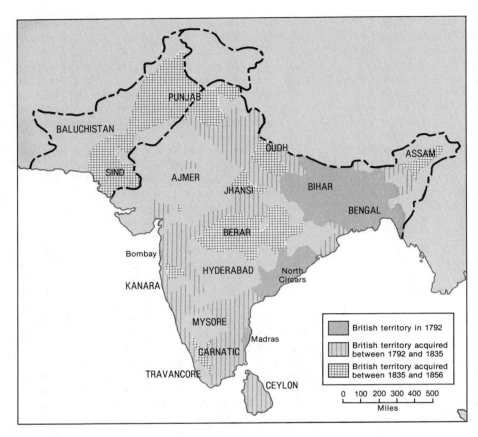

33.2 Growth of the British Empire in India

own country led to the emergence of Indian nationalism. The insurrection of 1857 was not yet a war of independence, but it marked the beginning of Indian response to a foreign control increasingly tinged with arrogance. In the wake of the insurrection, the English East Company was dissolved and the so-called Dual System abolished.

The mutiny marked a watershed between the earlier stages of company rule, which saw considerable racial and cultural mixing, and the rise of full-blown imperialism. The British crown assumed direct imperial authority under the Government of India Act (1858), although the facade of Indian principalities was maintained until independence. To complete the transformation, Queen Victoria adopted the title Empress of India in 1877. She took a special interest in her new dominions, which her prime minister, Benjamin Disraeli, called "the brightest jewel in the crown," and is said to have prayed nightly for her Indian subjects. Although she never went there, many Indians revered her as their own empress, part of the long Indian imperial tradition even under alien rulers, and her picture was widely displayed in people's homes.

The British were careful not to displace any more of the native rulers or to take over more territory, a policy kept until Indian independence in 1947. British residents were placed in each of the hundreds of small and a few large Indian-ruled states, but intervention or threats were rarely needed to keep the roughly half of India still formally in native hands in line with British policy. The army remained largely Indian, but the proportion of British officers and troops was increased, and elite regiments of Sikhs, Rajputs, and Gurkhas (from Nepal) were formed. Indians joined the colonial civil service as well and held responsible positions in all fields under overall British supervision.

Modern Growth

The opening of the Suez Canal in 1869, the shift to steam navigation, and the rapid spread of railways brought India much closer to Europe, greatly accelerating the commercialization of the economy. By the end of the century India had by far the largest rail network (25,000 miles) in all of Asia, on a par with many European countries but on a far bigger scale. This too had obvious commercial consequences, but there were social ones as well. British women could now join their husbands more easily in India and raise their families there, thus creating another wedge of separation between the races and cultures. Colonial social life centered in the buildings and grounds of the British

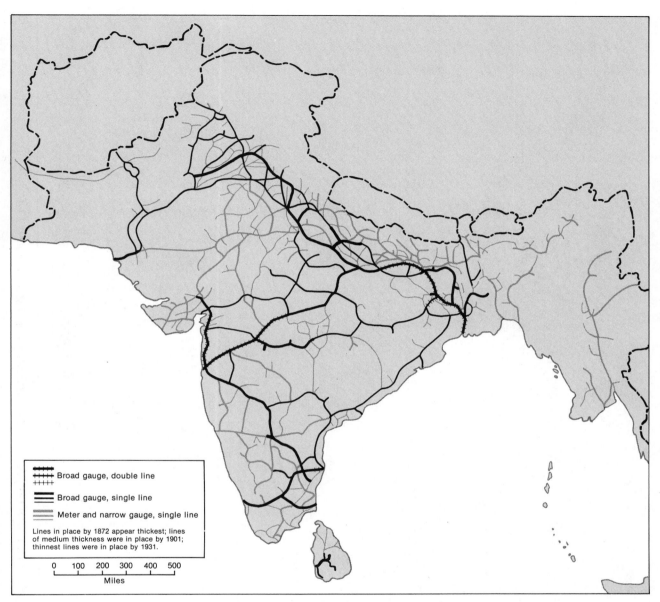

Broad gauge, double line

Broad gauge, single line

Meter and narrow gauge, single line

Lines in place by 1872 appear thickest; lines of medium thickness were in place by 1901; thinnest lines were in place by 1931.

0 100 200 300 400 500
Miles

33.3 Growth of India's Railway Network

Club in each city or town, from which Indians were excluded. This social barrier not only delimited the Indians' inferior status but also kept many of the British in a kind of prison of their own making, cut off both from the subjects they ruled and from fresh ideas and attitudes from home. Thus developed what came to be called the colonial mentality, which preserved a mid-Victorian code of conduct and mores well into the twentieth century.

Indians were the first Asians to experience the impact of Western capitalism and industrialization in their country on a large scale. Many of them were quick to respond as entrepreneurs to the new economic opportunities in com-

merce and machine manufacturing. As in Britain, industrialization began first with machine-made textiles in Bombay and Calcutta, then in a widening range of other manufacturing. Railways stimulated the growing commercialization of agriculture, especially in industrial crops such as jute (fibers), cotton, indigo, and new plantation production of tea, grown mainly in the hills of Assam, which captured most of the world market. New irrigation projects, especially in the semiarid Punjab and the Indus valley, opened productive farming areas to feed India's booming cities, and increased output elsewhere. By 1900 India had the world's largest irrigation system.

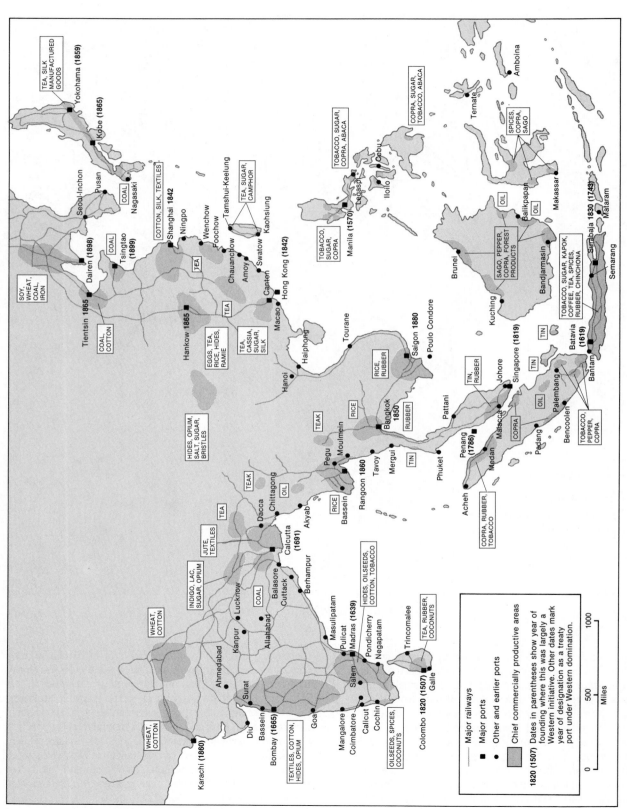

33.4 Major Ports and Commercially Productive Areas in East Asia, 1600–1940

Calcutta remained the country's largest city, closely followed by Bombay and then by Madras. Bombay, with its magnificent harbor and its closeness to cotton-growing areas in Gujarat and Maharashtra, became the premier port and the chief center of Indian-owned textile manufacturing. Large new industrial cities also grew inland as the railway linked most of the country in a single market: Ahmedabad in Gujarat, Lucknow, Kanpur, and Allahabad in the central Ganges, Salem and Coimbatore in the south, and many more. Karachi became the port for cotton and wheat from the Indus valley. British industrial and commercial investors, managers, and traders made money and sold goods in this vast new market, but Indians were increasingly prominent as well in the growing modern sector. Indians also entered and in time dominated the new Western-style professions such as law, medicine, engineering, and education. By 1900 India had the world's fourth largest textile industry and by 1920 the biggest steel plant in the British Empire, both, like many other industries, owned and managed largely by Indians.

Colonial Government

The British saw themselves as the bringers of order and "civilization" to their empire, a role that many of them likened to that of the Romans 2,000 years earlier in Europe. Britain was the greatest power in the world from the mid-eighteenth century to the early twentieth. It was also the nursery of industrialization and modern representative government. These things bred a sense of pride and greatness. Britons were fond of describing theirs as an empire on which the sun never set, since it stretched almost around the globe. Indians, they felt, should be grateful to be included, and indeed many were.

British-style education, conducted in English, continued to shape most Indian intellectuals and literate people to a large degree in the British image. The law of British India, based on English common law, was practiced and administered overwhelmingly by Indians themselves. Nonetheless, the British retained firm control of all senior positions. The prestigious Indian civil service (ICS), staffed until the twentieth century almost entirely by Britons trained in Indian affairs, long remained an exclusive supervisory group under the viceroy, the effective head of state in India appointed by London. The ICS was referred to proudly as the "steel framework" whose roughly 900 members ensured the smooth operation of the colonial government.

Despite colonial achievements in agriculture, public health, education, and transportation, however, most Indians remained poor, illiterate, and powerless. Occasional regional famines continued, as in China. Tenancy and landlessness grew with the increasing commercialization of agriculture, and industrial growth was far too slow to absorb or produce adequately for the rising population.

Between 1800 and 1947 the total population of India probably at least doubled, in itself a sign of order and greater economic opportunity, as in eighteenth-century China. The official census begun in 1871 showed a more or less continuous growth of population together with a falling death rate. But this surge in population was barely matched by overall economic growth, which was in any case unbalanced. There was thus little new margin for improved living standards, and while some commercial, professional, and landed groups prospered, much of the peasantry sank deeper into poverty. India remained poor in part because it was poor to begin with after the extravagances, exploitation, and collapse of the Mughals. Industrialization and commercialization directly impoverished some groups and benefited others, as happened in the West too. The hand spinners of cotton, India's single largest manufacturing work force, were devastated by factory production and British imports, although hand weavers benefited from the cheaper machine-spun yarn. The widening market also gave new employment to many farmers, craftsmen, factory or railway workers, and laborers. The pattern in textiles was repeated in other industries and markets and occurred in China as well.

The colonial government was chronically pinched for funds; London insisted that all expenses had to be covered from Indian revenues. The army took much of these, in part for the conquest of Burma, and there was little to spare. Planning was thus difficult, and problems were addressed piecemeal or not at all. Reformers accused the government of playing the role of night watchman while most Indians remained in poverty. Even so, the colonial administration required indirect support, costs that were necessarily borne by ordinary British taxpayers. Thus the imperial system was supported by the middle and lower classes of both countries for the benefit of British and Indian elites.

It would have been impossible for the relative handful of British in India to control the subcontinent and its 350 million people by the 1930s without the support or the active help of most Indians. The British officer contingent in the Indian army reached 40,000 only in the special circumstances of World Wars I and II. The total number of Britons of all levels and in all branches of the civil service, including district officers, judges, and police, was never more than 12,000. In short, colonial India was run mainly by Indians, who until relatively late willingly supported the British raj or government. By 1910, for example, the police force comprised about 5,000 Britons and over 600,000 Indians. The rest of the civil service employed about 600,000 Indians with only some 5,000 Britons, and the army consisted of about 150,000 native troops and approximately 25,000 British officers.

In contrast, the higher echelons of government remained a British preserve. As if to show their aloofness from the country, they governed in the blazing hot months of summer from hill stations in the Himalayan foothills,

Social life in the hill stations: a fete at Simla, in a glade nostalgically named "Annandale," painted by A. E. Scott c. 1845. [India Office Library of the British Library]

first at Darjeeling in northernmost Assam and later from Simla, north of Delhi. From both they enjoyed spectacular views of the snow-covered mountains, cool, bracing air, Western-style lodges and cottages that reminded them of home, and a round of parties, picnics, and receptions.

As more colonial officers served longer, young British women came or were sent out to India to find a husband, an annual migration at the beginning of the cool weather in autumn irreverently referred to as the "arrival of the fishing fleet." Those who remained unspoken for by the time the hot weather resumed in mid-March often went back to England as "returned empties." As the British community grew, many families by the twentieth century had lived in India for several generations and thought of it as home. They called themselves Anglo-Indians, and they lived in separate residential areas built for them some distance from the Indian town where they worked. These were known as "civil lines" or "cantonments," since many of them had begun as quarters for troops or garrisons. Each of their households was waited on by large numbers of Indian servants, whose labor was extremely cheap.

Another group was also known as Anglo-Indians. These were the products of intermarriage, which had been common in the eighteenth and early nineteenth centuries and still occasionally took place in later years. These Anglo-Indians were rejected by both the Indian and British communities, but they usually tried to pass as English and spoke wistfully of "home," meaning an England that most of them had never seen. Many of them became Christians in an effort to raise their status, as did many untouchables. Missionary efforts made few converts otherwise, although mission schools remained an important means to Western education for many non-Christians as well as for the few Christians.

NEW DELHI: INDIAN SUMMER OF THE RAJ

Calcutta had long seemed inappropriate as the capital of a British India that had expanded to cover the subcontinent, thousands of miles from Bengal. Although now a thoroughly Indian city, it had been founded by the British themselves and had no indigenous roots or history. Its marginal coastal site further emphasized the foreignness of British rule. For several years after 1900 alternative capital sites were considered, and Delhi, the former Mughal capital, was chosen. At the head of the Ganges valley, Delhi controlled routes from both east and south to the heart of India. Successive invaders had to capture Delhi first, mounting their campaigns and ruling their empires from there. The British raj moved too in 1911 to rule from where so many others had before.

It was decided to build a new planned city as an imperial statement, adjacent to the old city and with open space around it but still well within sight of Shah Jahan's Red Fort (see Chapter 19). The remains of other imperial Delhis of the past also showed on the skyline. An artificial hill was built as the setting for the monumental residence and gardens of the viceroy, flanked on each side by two large and stately government buildings known as the Secretariat. From this low rise, broad boulevards and wide vistas led to other buildings and monuments to empire, including the parliament house, by the 1920s filled with mainly Indian members.

Like Paris and Washington, New Delhi was planned before the age of mass transit and the automobile. It was essentially built in a star-shaped pattern with broad tree-lined streets intersecting at angles and punctuated by circles of green area around which traffic had to move. The plan included a large separate commercial and shopping district, with buildings in neoclassical and Anglo-Indian styles, grouped around an immense circle, still called Connaught Circus. Related enterprises lined the streets leading into it at various angles. Pleasant shaded avenues with British names occupied most of the rest of the new planned city, most of them filled with gracious residences and beautiful gardens for civil servants, Indian princes (most of whom maintained extensive establishments in New Delhi), and other members of the upper classes. Lesser officials, workers, and servants commuted the mile or so from Old Delhi, mainly by bicycle, or were housed in the unplanned developments that soon grew around the edges of New Delhi.

The ambitious building plans of 1911 and 1912 were delayed by World War I, but by 1930 the new imperial capital was complete. The architects of New Delhi were of course British, but they made a generally successful effort to combine Western and Indian monumental and imperial traditions, consciously using the same red sandstone of which the Red Fort had been built and creating buildings that fit their Indian setting far better than the earlier Victorian extravagances in Calcutta and Bombay. Old Delhi remains a traditional Indian city, centered around the Red Fort. A confusing maze of tiny streets and alleys surrounds the bazaar near Shah Jahan's great mosque, the Jama Masjid. The large unbuilt area in front of the Red Fort remains a vast open-air market and a frequent scene of political rallies. New Delhi became almost automatically the capital of independent India, with no sense of inappropriateness for the world's largest parliamentary democracy, still based on British colonial foundations. Since 1947 Delhi has boomed and become a major industrial center. But Old and New Delhi represent different strands in India's varied past and now also show the two faces of contemporary India, traditional and modern.

An example of colonial architecture: Victoria Station, Bombay, with a statue of Queen Victoria on the top of its dome. [Rhoads Murphey]

The Rise of Indian Nationalism

British-educated Indians, despite their prosperity, were increasingly resentful of the racial discrimination to which they were subject. Many began to demand a larger role in their country's government. Gradually a movement for independence developed. Liberal Englishmen agreed, contending that alien rule was contrary to the British tradition of representative government and political freedom. Gestures toward increasing the participation of Indians in the administration and civil service and elections for some officials and advisers came too slowly to satisfy either Indian or British critics.

The Indian National Congress, which was to become the core of the independence movement, was actually founded by an Englishman in 1885. Indian political leaders made nationalist appeals, among them highly effective and articulate figures such as M. G. Ranade (1842–1901), B. G. Tilak (1856–1920), G. K. Gokhale (1866–1915), and Motilal Nehru (1861–1931), the father of Jawaharlal Nehru (1889–1964), independent India's first prime minister. Their language, culture, and education were as much English as Indian, and they could speak eloquently in terms of British tradition itself against the colonial rule of their country.

Meanwhile, fear of the still expanding Russian empire in central Asia prompted yet another disastrous invasion of Afghanistan in 1878 to install a British puppet on the throne of Kabul. The Afghans murdered the British resident and his entire staff and military escort within a year, and guerrilla fighters stalemated a second invasion until it was withdrawn in 1880 and the Afghans again were "permitted" to choose their own ruler. Opinion in Britain was outraged by both the brutality and the cost of this futile military adventure, and the Disraeli government fell as a result.

The colonial government in India spearheaded other costly ventures as well. In addition to the conquest of Burma, it launched an armed reconnaissance against Tibet in 1903 and 1904 to forestall illusory Russian influence there. The mission showed the flag and obtained an agreement about the frontier. While imperial posturing preoccupied the colonial government and drained the country's resources, poverty in India remained largely unaddressed. Indian nationalists blamed the severe economic distress in many areas on colonial rule. Boycotts of British imports were begun, cutting their value by 25 percent between 1904 and 1908. The government's response was often repressive, and many political leaders were jailed. There

were still many British in government with more liberal ideas, and many more outside government, who strove to reduce racial discrimination and urged Indian self-government as Britain's ultimate goal. In 1883, for example, it was agreed that Indian judges could preside over cases involving Europeans. But imperialist attitudes and bureaucratic inertia retarded the giving of Indians a larger and more appropriate role in their own government.

Over a million Indian troops and noncombatants served the British effort in World War I in Europe and the Middle East. Many hoped that this would speed progress toward self-government. When change lagged after the war, civil disobedience movements spread, now led by Mahatma Gandhi (1869–1948), among others, only to be met by more government repression. In 1919 Indian troops under British command, called in to put down rioting in Amritsar near Lahore, fired on a peaceful and unarmed crowd celebrating a festival, leaving 400 dead. The massacre was a watershed in Anglo-Indian relations. It turned most Indians away from the idea of reform and toward the goal of full independence, creating almost overnight a greatly expanded nationalist movement.

In 1907 the British Parliament had declared that independence was Britain's objective in India, a point the British government reaffirmed in 1917 and 1921, but the colonial administration remained slow to move. Although the electoral system was greatly broadened in the 1920s and 1930s and Indian legislatures and officials were given far more power and responsibility, it was too little, too late. Time had run out for British rule in India.

The Amritsar Massacre of April 1919 was followed by further repression in the wake of renewed protests and demonstrations. Here British police officers in Amritsar watch while their Indian assistants search a demonstrator. [Bettmann Archive/BBC Hulton]

Colonial Regimes in Southeast Asia

The Dutch came to control the largest amount of territory and population in Southeast Asia, incorporating the whole of what is now Indonesia in their colonial empire, from which they largely excluded other Western trade or investment competition. Large numbers of Chinese were already there, however, and their numbers increased to some 3 million as they expanded their control of smaller-scale domestic trade and retailing. The British, along with other Westerners, had been trading in Burma since the seventeenth century, but as their Indian empire, and their imperial ambition, grew, they progressively annexed Burma to their colonial holdings. Malaya was thinly settled and unimportant in trade until the tin and rubber boom of the late nineteenth century, but the British hoped to use bases there in an effort to tap the trade with Southeast Asia and with China, a role ultimately performed by Singapore. By the end of the nineteenth century all of Malaya was under British colonial administration, but primarily on an indirect basis through local Malay sultans. French and

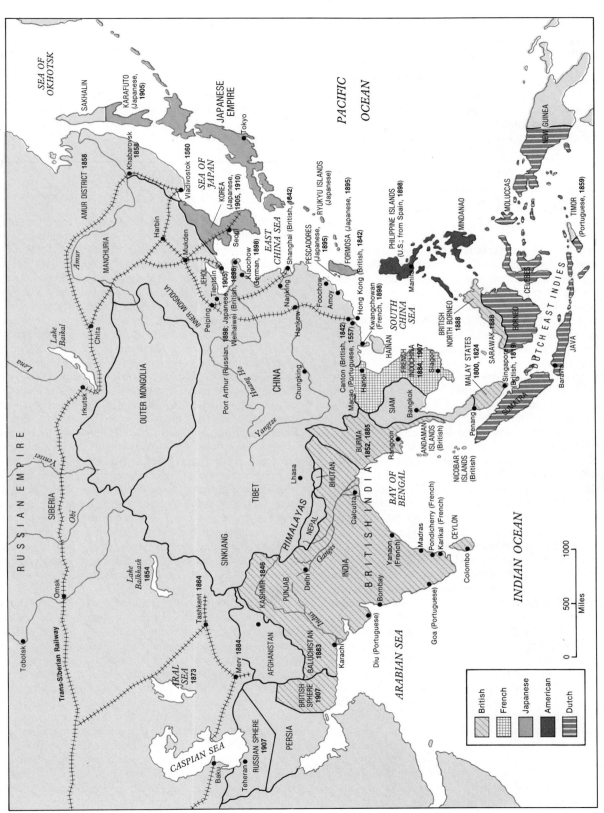

33.5 Colonial Empires in Asia

American colonialists arrived late on the scene. France acquired the Indochinese states of Vietnam, Cambodia, and Laos through conquest by 1885, and the Americans inherited control of the Philippines as a consequence of their defeat of Spain, the former colonial master of the area, in 1898. Each of these Western colonial regimes followed policies with many similarities and some differences. Siam (now Thailand) remained independent as a buffer between rival colonial empires but had to accept the same set of "unequal treaties" as was imposed on China and Japan.

The British in Burma and Malaya

Britain's activity in Southeast Asia had been incidental to its concerns in India and its efforts to break into the China market. It was at first confined to founding bases on the fringes of Dutch power in Malaya. In 1786 a settlement was made at Penang on the northwestern Malay coast, where the British hoped to attract Chinese traders. This was only moderately successful, and they established what soon became their major Southeast Asian trade base at Singapore in 1819.

From the start, Singapore was a commercial center for all of Southeast Asia. Malaya itself remained thinly populated and largely undeveloped until the end of the nineteenth century. Burma was India's immediate geographic neighbor to the east. Its antiquated monarchy periodically made difficulties for British merchants and ignored or insulted British representatives. A brief war from 1824 to 1826 added the important coastal provinces of Burma to the East India Company's territories. Two more minor wars in 1852 and 1885–1886, largely provoked by the British, annexed the rest of the country. Burma was then administered as a province of British India until it was granted separate colonial status in 1937.

Burma and Malaya were rapidly commercialized after 1880 under British rule. Railways were built and steam navigation developed. The Irrawaddy delta in lower Burma, including much newly cultivated land, became a major exporter of rice. Upper Burma produced timber, especially teak, for export, and the central valley yielded oil from wells drilled by the British. All this moved out for export through the port of Rangoon, which served as the colonial capital. In Malaya were found rich deposits of tin, a metal in great demand in the industrializing West, and toward the end of the century Malaya also became the world's major producer of plantation rubber. Labor for tin mining and rubber tapping had to be imported, since the local Malays, subsistence farmers, were not interested in such work. The gap was filled mainly from overcrowded South China, and Chinese settlers soon comprised nearly half the population of Malaya. In time many of these Chinese immigrants, who also entered the booming commercial economy of Singapore, became wealthy. The Malays increasingly resented Chinese domination of the commercial economy. Indians also entered, as both laborers and merchants, and with the Chinese and the British controlled the commercial production and foreign trade of both Burma and Malaya. The colonial government of Malaya ruled as much as possible through local sultans and tried to preserve traditional Malay culture, but both countries were economically transformed.

French, Dutch, and American Colonialism

Largely eliminated from India by the end of the eighteenth century, the French sought their own colonial sphere in Asia. They used the persecution of French Catholic missionaries in Vietnam as a pretext for conquering the southern provinces in 1862, including the port of Saigon. Later they annexed Cambodia and Laos, and in 1885 took over northern Vietnam after defeating Chinese forces sent to protect their tributary state. Under French control, southern Vietnam became a major exporter of rice and rubber grown in the delta of the Mekong River. They were exported through the chief port of Saigon, which was made the colonial capital. Cambodia and Laos remained little developed commercially. Northern Vietnam was already too densely populated to produce surpluses for export, but there was some small industrial growth around the city of Hanoi and in the northern port of Haiphong. The colonial administration tried to impose French culture on these territories, collectively called Indochina.

French rule was oppressive and often ruthless in suppressing all gestures toward political expression. The army was augmented by special security forces and had much of the apparatus of a police state, which executed, jailed, or drove into exile most Vietnamese leaders. These included the young Ho Chi Minh (1890–1969), later the head of the Vietnamese Communist party, who went to Europe in 1911 and later from Paris to Moscow and Canton.

The Dutch left most of Indonesia to native rulers until late in the nineteenth century, content with controlling trade from Batavia (now Djakarta), their colonial capital. Batavia was situated on the tropical island of Java, which produced a variety of plantation crops the Dutch promoted after 1830, including sugar, coffee, tea, and tobacco. By the early 1900s rubber was an important commodity, and Indonesia was second only to Malaya in its production. Oil was also found and exploited. The discovery of more oil and tin and the cultivation of prime land for rubber and tobacco prompted the Dutch to increase their control, first of the neighboring island of Sumatra, and then of Borneo, Celebes, the Moluccas, Bali, and the hundreds of smaller islands in the archipelago south of the Philippines. New railways and ports were built to expedite trade.

Dutch rule was fiercely contested on some of the islands, especially Sumatra, and it never penetrated effectively into the mountain and jungle interior of Borneo. The northern coast of Borneo was controlled by the British. Dutch rule became increasingly oppressive. Indonesians were excluded from participation in government and the exercise of political rights and were denied access to more than elementary education. Java was systematically exploited by forcing its peasants to grow export crops for Dutch profit. Production and population grew very rapidly, but living standards and the quality of life declined.

In 1898 the United States went to war with Spain over Cuba and acquired the Philippines as its first overseas colony. The 43 years of American control had a greater effect on the culture and economy of the islands than 450 years of Spanish rule. The Americans built roads and hospitals and established an education system up to the university level. Literacy and public health rose to levels second only to Japan in Asia. But America's economic impact was exploitive. In partnership with rich Filipinos, it concentrated on growing commercial crops for export, especially sugar, and often neglected the basic needs of the people as a whole. Manila, the colonial capital, became a rapidly growing commercial center and the chief base of the Filipino middle class and educated elite. The Americans declared as their goal the creation of a democratic society in their own image. To a degree this was achieved, but Philippine politics remained under the control of a landed elite supported by others who profited from the American connection and paid little attention to the dominantly peasant population, who remained exploited. The country had been subjugated only by a brutal war against Filipino nationalist resistance from 1899 to 1902 in which the Americans pursued policies that foreshadowed their later misadventures in Vietnam. Most peasants, still largely illiterate, could hardly take advantage of free public education and free expression. The United States granted independence to the Philippines in 1946 on terms that ensured its continuing influence and left huge American military bases there.

Independent Siam

While the rest of Southeast Asia was being taken over by imperialist powers, the Thais kept their independence. This was in part the result of geography. Siam lay between the British in Burma and Malaya and the French in Indochina. Neither was willing to let the other dominate the country. British preponderance in Thai foreign trade and investment was balanced by French annexation of territory claimed or occupied by Siam in western Cambodia and Laos. British Malaya detached Siam's southern provinces. Nonetheless, the Thais benefited from a series of able kings who adroitly played the French off against the British and urged the advantages to both of leaving at least part

of their country as a buffer state. They had to grant special trade, residence, and legal privileges to the colonial powers, a system like that imposed on China, but there was no foreign effort to take over the government. Nevertheless the Thai economy developed along the same lines as colonial Southeast Asia, with a big new export trade in rice from the delta area, followed later by rubber and tropical hardwoods. Bangkok, the capital, grew rapidly as the chief port for foreign trade and spreading commercialization.

Overseas Chinese

Western development had important demographic consequences for Southeast Asia. Immigrant Chinese began to flood into all the commercially developed parts of the region in growing numbers after 1870, as plantation and mining labor and as traders. They soon largely monopolized the retail trade in all the cities of Southeast Asia, although they shared it with immigrant Indians in Burma and Malaya. In Bangkok they constituted over half the population and, as in Burma and Vietnam, controlled most of the large export trade in rice. Southeast Asians resented them, especially since they also served as moneylenders and owned most of the shops, but they were often welcomed by the colonialists as useful labor and commercial agents. In Siam, unlike the rest of Southeast Asia, most Chinese were quickly assimilated into Thai society through intermarriage and acculturation. Elsewhere they tended to remain confined to their own quarters and suffered discrimination from the local people. Altogether, Chinese settlers in Southeast Asia totaled about 15 million by the outbreak of World War II.

China Besieged

The Treaty of Nanking, which ended the Anglo-Chinese Opium War of 1839–1842, granted Britain most of its demands for trading rights and concessions. The port of Hong Kong was ceded outright, and five mainland ports, including Shanghai and Canton, were opened to British trade and residence. Other Western powers, including the United States, negotiated similar treaties the following year. These included the right of extraterritoriality, whereby foreign nationals in China were made immune from Chinese jurisdiction and were dealt with according to their own laws. The war had finally cracked China's proud isolation.

Foreign trade immediately began a rapid increase that continued until the world depression of the 1930s. Tea and silk remained the dominant exports and opium the main import, although it was overtaken after 1870 by cotton yarn, textiles, kerosene, and a variety of other foreign

◉ Opium ◉

The imperial commissioner sent to Canton in 1839 to stop the opium trade wrote a letter in the same year to the young Queen Victoria that read in part as follows.

Magnificently our great emperor soothes and pacifies China and the foreign countries. . . . But there appear among the crowd of barbarians both good and bad persons, unevenly. . . . There are barbarian ships that come here for trade to make a great profit. But by what right do they in return use the poisonous drug [opium] to injure the Chinese people? . . . Of all that China exports to foreign countries, there is not a single thing which is not beneficial. . . . On the other hand, articles coming from outside China can only be used as toys; they are not needed by China. Nevertheless, our Celestial Court lets tea, silk, and other goods be shipped without limit. This is for no other reason than to share the benefit with the people of the whole world.

Source: S. Y. Teng and J. K. Fairbank, *China's Response to the West* (Cambridge, Mass.: Harvard University Press, 1954), pp. 24–26.

manufactured goods. The treaties further impinged on China's sovereignty by limiting the import tariffs it might impose to 5 percent. This had the effect of giving Western goods virtually unrestricted access to the vast Chinese market. Although China continued to provide most of its own needs, the treaties reduced the country to semi-colonial status.

Peking's reluctance to abide by the terms of the treaties led to a second war from 1858 to 1860. British and French troops captured Tientsin (Tianjin) and Peking and burned the imperial summer palace. They saw this as retaliation for Chinese "treachery"—the breaking of successive agreements to observe earlier treaties and to receive the British ambassador in Peking, as well as firing on British forces and imprisoning their representatives.

Traders and Missionaries

The Treaty of Tientsin, which ended this second war, opened still more ports to residence and trade and allowed foreigners, including missionaries, free movement and enterprise anywhere in the country. Missionaries often served as a forward wave for imperialism, building churches and preaching the Gospel in the interior and then demanding protection from their home governments against Chinese protests or riots. Trouble missionaries or foreign traders encountered might be answered by sending a warship to the nearest coastal or river port to threaten or shell inhabitants, a practice known as "gunboat diplomacy." When antiforeign mobs assulted missionaries

or their converts, Western governments often used this as a pretext for extracting still more concessions.

Most Chinese were not receptive to the Christian message, especially in the evangelical form of most missionary preaching, and they resented foreigners with special privileges and protection encroaching on their country. Nor did they understand the missionary practice of buying or adopting orphans for charitable and religious purposes and so assumed the worst motives for these practices. Stories circulated that they ate babies or gouged out their eyes for medicine. In 1870 a mob destroyed a French Catholic mission in Tientsin and killed 10 nuns and 11 other foreigners; gunboats and heavy reparations followed.

Unlike the British, the French had no important trade with China and often used protection of their missionaries as a means of increasing their influence. In 1883 they went to war with China over Vietnam when Chinese troops crossed the border to eject them. The French destroyed part of the new Western-style Chinese navy and the dockyards at Foochow on the South China coast, which they had earlier helped to build. China was humbled again.

The Taiping Rebellion

Meanwhile, the greatest of all uprisings against the Ch'ing government erupted in 1850, the Taiping Rebellion. Westerners tend to overemphasize their own role in China as the major influence on events after 1840. China was huge, Westerners were few, and their activities were limited to the treaty ports and outlying mission stations. China con-

---

◉ Through Each Other's Eyes ◉

After the Opium War, foreign arrogance increased. Here is a sample from 1858.

It is impossible that our merchants and missionaries can course up and down the inland waters of this great region and traffic in their cities and preach in their villages without wearing away at the crust of the Chinaman's stoical and skeptical conceit. The whole present system in China is a hollow thing, with a hard brittle surface. . . . Some day a happy blow will shiver it [and] it will all go together.

But the Chinese returned the compliment.

It is monstrous in barbarians to attempt to improve the inhabitants of the Celestial Empire when they are so miserably deficient themselves. Thus, introducing a poisonous drug for their own benefit and to the injury of others, they are deficient in benevolence. Sending their fleets and armies to rob other nations, they can make no pretense to rectitude. . . . How can they expect to renovate others? They allow the rich and noble to enter office without passing through any literary examinations, and do not open the road to advancement to the poorest and meanest in the land. From this it appears that foreigners are inferior to the Chinese and therefore must be unfit to instruct them.

Sources: G. W. Cooke, *China: Being the Times Special Correspondence from China in the Years 1857–58* (London: Routledge, 1858), p. v; "A Chinese Tract of the Mid-Nineteenth Century," in E. P. Boardman, *Christian Influence on the Ideology of the Taiping Rebellion* (Madison: University of Wisconsin Press, 1952), p. 129.

---

tinued to respond primarily to its own long-standing internal problems, chief among which was a burgeoning population. Having outstripped production, it was falling into poverty and distress in many areas. The Taiping leader, Hung Hsiu-Ch'uan (Hong Xiuquan), was a frustrated scholar who had failed the rigid imperial examinations several times and then espoused an idiosyncratic version of Christianity adapted from missionary teaching. Hung became the leader of a largely peasant group from the impoverished mountain region of southern China, which resented its exclusion from the treaty ports and sought the overthrow of the Manchus. The rebels picked up massive support as they moved north and captured Nanking (Nanjing) in 1853. A northward thrust from there was turned back later that year near Tientsin, but rebel forces won at least a foothold in 16 of China's 18 provinces and dominated the rich Yangtze valley.

The efforts of the Taiping rebels to govern were relatively feeble. Large-scale fighting against the imperial forces continued without significant breaks until its final suppression in 1864. The cost in destruction and loss of life was horrendous. As many as 40 million people died, and much of the productive lower Yangtze region was laid waste. During the same period the Ch'ing also faced three other mass uprisings, in the north, the southwest, and the northwest. The latter two were primarily Muslim rebellions against Ch'ing rule, which lingered until 1873. As one Ch'ing official said, these revolts were like a disease of China's vital organs. In contrast, the activities of the Western powers were a marginal affliction only of the extremities.

Attempts at Reform

One foreign power, however, was still advancing by land: the Russians. Sensing China's weakness, they penetrated the Amur valley in northern Manchuria, from which they had been excluded in 1689. In the treaties following the war of 1858–1860 they detached the maritime provinces of eastern Manchuria and added them to their empire; among their acquisitions was the port of Vladivostok. Muslim rebellion in the northwest after 1862 served as a pretext for Russian intervention in northern Sinkiang (Xinjiang). The Ch'ing government decided that this threat must be met head on, marched an army 2,500 miles from its base in eastern China, and to general surprise defeated both the rebels and the Russians by 1878.

Survival of the Ch'ing regime against the appalling challenges it faced showed that it was still capable of successful action. After 1860 it undertook a policy of "self-strengthening," which included the establishment of new Western-style arsenals, gun foundries, and shipyards. These and other efforts to modernize were handicapped by government red tape, but they achieved some progress. Several outstanding senior officials who realized the need for change rose to power. For a decade or two the Ch'ing seemed to have a new lease on life and to show surprising vigor.

It was not to last. The reformers never won full support from the still archconservative throne or from most of the people. Both remained essentially antiforeign and opposed to adopting Western tactics even to fight Westerners. In 1862 a weak boy-emperor came to the throne, dominated by his scheming mother, Tz'u Hsi (Cixi, 1835–1908), a former imperial concubine who had plotted her way to the top. When the emperor died in 1875 at the age of 19, she put her 4-year-old nephew in his place, retaining all real power for herself as the empress dowager until her death in 1908. Tzu Hsi was clever and politically masterful but narrow-minded and deeply conservative. She had no understanding of what was required to cope with the foreign threat to Chinese sovereignty.

China's first tentative efforts at change were thus for the most part aborted. The Confucian reactionaries, who with few exceptions again dominated the government, grudgingly acknowledged the potency of Western arms but insisted that there could be no abandoning or even altering the traditional Chinese view of the world to deal with them.

The empress dowager Tzu Hsi (Cixi). She was a powerful and unscrupulous ruler, but in keeping with the degeneracy of the late Ch'ing period favored the over-ornate style in which she decorated many rooms in the imperial palace in Peking, as shown here. [Freer Gallery of Art, Smithsonian Institution]

Treaty Ports and Mission Schools

Meanwhile the treaty ports, which numbered over 100 by 1910, grew rapidly, attracting Chinese as merchants, partners, and laborers. Manufacturing also began to grow in the treaty ports, especially after 1895 when the Japanese imposed a new treaty that permitted foreign-owned factories to operate in the ports; these produced mainly textiles and other consumer goods. This was the real beginning of modern industrialization in China.

Chinese entrepreneurs and industrialists, many of whom had been blocked or discouraged by the conservative government, welcomed the more enterprising world of the treaty ports. As elsewhere in Asia, imperialist arrogance was growing, and the Chinese found themselves excluded from foreign clubs and parks and treated as second-class citizens in their own cities. Many of them were torn between their ancient cultural pride and their sense of humiliation by Westerners on the one hand and their reluctant admiration for the West's power and success on the other. As with their Indian counterparts in colonial Calcutta and Bombay, these conflicts produced the first stirrings of modern nationalism.

The most widespread Western influence on Chinese society came through the efforts of missionaries. The total number of Chinese Christians remained discouragingly small, and many, perhaps most, of them were so-called "rice Christians," who attended church for handouts. Most Chinese looked down on Christian converts as traitors or simply as the dregs of society. Many of the missions came to realize that education and medical help were more attractive than Christian doctrine and might pave a smoother path toward the goal of conversion. Mission-run schools spread rapidly, as did their hospitals. The schools drew many students, in time most of the young Chinese who wanted to study English and Western learning or science. Although most graduates did not become converts, they adopted Western ways of thinking in many respects. Most twentieth-century Chinese nationalists were influenced by mission schools, and nearly all of China's universities were founded by missionaries.

Government schools that included Western curricula were also established, and in 1905 the traditional examination system was abolished. Missionaries and others translated a wide range of Western works, which were read avidly by the new generation of Chinese intellectuals. Many of them began to call for the overthrow of the Ch'ing regime. Ironically, they used the treaty ports, notably Shanghai, as their base, where they were protected from Ch'ing repression by living under foreign law.

The Boxer Rebellion

Missionaries in rural areas continued to provoke antiforeign riots as their activities spread. In the late 1890s the empress dowager adroitly turned a group of impoverished bandits and rebels in eastern North China against the missionaries instead of against the dynasty, and by extension against all foreigners. By early 1900 this group, which called itself the "fists of righteous harmony" but was known more simply to Westerners as the Boxers, went on a rampage, burning mission establishments and killing missionaries and Chinese converts. Converts were resented for their use of foreign intervention in their disputes with other Chinese. By June 1900, with covert imperial support, the Boxers besieged the foreign legations in Peking, which barely held out until relieved by a multinational expedition in mid-August. Having earlier declared war officially against all the foreign powers, the court fled to Sian (Xian). After brutal reprisals, the Western powers (now including a large Japanese contingent) withdrew, and a peace was patched up a year later. A staggering indemnity was forced on China, on top of one already extracted by Japan in 1895. The empress dowager and her reactionary councillors, who had seen the Boxers as the final solution to the "barbarian problem," were left nominally in power.

The Ch'ing dynasty was moribund, but no workable alternative was yet at hand. China had still to learn the lessons of national unity and shared political purpose, which had been unnecessary in the past when the empire controlled "all under heaven" and China had no rivals. The government finally fell in 1911, more of its own weight and incompetence than because of the small, disorganized group of revolutionaries whose uprising joined the defection of disgruntled troops. The fall of the Ch'ing dynasty was hardly a revolution, but it ended the imperial rule by which China had been governed for more than 2,000 years and opened the way for fundamental change.

Japan Among the Powers

As indicated in Chapter 28, the antiquated Tokugawa shogunate was toppled in 1868 and 1869 by a new group of reformers. Their goal was the rapid modernization and Westernization of Japan in order to save their country from colonialism and to remove the unequal treaties that had been forced on it. That effort was spectacularly successful. By 1895 new Western-style technology and industry had progressed far and had given Japan new power. With power came new ambition. In a conflict over dominance in Korea, Japan's new navy and army easily defeated China's poorly coordinated forces in 1894–1895 and detached both Korea and Taiwan from Chinese control, adding them to what was now the Japanese colonial empire. In 1904–1905 Japan's new strength enabled it to win early victories against a more formidable opponent, Russia, and then to conclude a treaty that replaced Russian dominance in Manchuria with Japanese. Confidence was high, as Japan was clearly established as a major power in East Asia, and by the early years of the twentieth century Japan was able to get rid of the unequal treaties and to deal with Western powers as an equal. But imperial ambition and military adventuring led the nation into what the Japanese call the "dark valley," beginning with their efforts to take control of much of eastern China in 1915, their formal takeover of Manchuria as part of their empire in 1931, and the morass of their full-scale invasion of China from 1937, a road that led to Pearl Harbor and Hiroshima. Nevertheless, the Meiji period, from 1868 to 1912 (the death of the Meiji emperor), was one of great and constructive progress that laid the foundation of modern Japanese society and economy.

The Meiji Restoration: Response to the West

In contrast to China, the Meiji Restoration in Japan ushered in a period of rapid change and wholesale Westernization. Meiji was the reign title of the young emperor, who moved to Tokyo ("eastern capital") in 1869 as the restored head of state, although his role remained symbolic only. He and his successors served as a rallying point for new nationalist sentiment, and most Japanese took inspiration from the fact that their country was once again under imperial rule.

The goal of the new government was to strengthen and modernize Japan and thereby to free it from the unequal treaties (see Chapter 28). Like China, Japan had suffered loss of control over its tariffs and had been forced to concede extraterritoriality and other special privileges to the Western powers. In contrast to the Chinese, however, Japan's leaders realized that regaining their independence depended on mastering Western technology. They also saw that military technology could not be separated from overall industrialization or from the institutional structures that had produced and accompanied it in the West.

Whereas pride rendered these truths unacceptable to the Chinese, Japan showed little hesitation after 1869 in transforming or abolishing traditional institutions. Many Japanese urged wholesale Westernization, arguing, "If we use it, that will make it Japanese." Some radical enthusiasts in the early years of Meiji actually tried to destroy traditional temples in their zeal to sweep away the old and make way for the new Japan. Japanese national pride did not rest so much in the culture as in the people's sense of themselves. Although change proved largely bloodless and was accompanied by relatively minor political reorganization, Meiji Japan produced in many ways a real revolution.

Economy and Government

The first priority was rapid industrialization, especially in heavy industries and armaments. Foreign advisers were hired to expedite this growth—from Britain for a modern navy, from Germany for a modern army and armaments industry, and so on. Railways were quickly built to link the major cities, and new ports and facilities were created. The machinery of government and law was wholly remade, modeled on a judicious combination of Western systems. What emerged was a modified constitutional monarchy with a parliament and a largely Western-derived legal system. Such change was important also to demonstrate that Japan was a "civilized" country where foreigners did not need extraterritoriality to protect them.

All Western institutions, and even such details of Western culture as dress and diet, were seen as sources of strength. Samurai discarded their swords and picturesque garb, put on Western business suits, learned to waltz, and dominated the new bureaucracy. Some samurai found careers as officers in the new army, and others went into business or manufacturing. The ranks of the army were filled with peasant conscripts; war was no longer a gentlemen's preserve.

The Japanese were rapidly mobilized toward the new goals. They were accustomed to direction, from daimyo, samurai, or other hierarchical superiors, and most came to share the national objectives with genuine enthusiasm. Japan's almost ready-made nationalism, the fruit of an island country with a long history of separateness, was a strong asset. Its people were also racially and culturally homogeneous (as the Chinese and Indians were not), and the country was small and more easily integrated as a unit. In landmass and population, approximately 50 million by 1910, it was about the size of one of China's larger provinces, and some 90 percent of its people were concentrated in the corridor between Tokyo and Osaka. What was decided in Tokyo was quickly carried out everywhere as national policy. Farm output tripled between 1870 and 1940 with the use of new Western technology as well as hard work. In many ways it was the latter that accounted for Meiji Japan's astounding success.

Japanese Imperialism

By the 1890s Japan had a modern navy and army and a fast-growing industrial base. Japanese steamships had won a major place in East Asian trade, and Japanese merchants had acquired a rising share of the China market. In 1894 Britain agreed to relinquish the unequal clauses of the old treaty with Japan by 1899, and other nations soon followed suit.

Having followed the Western lead in modern development, Japan now joined the other imperialist powers in colonial conquests. Korea was the handiest target, and in brief campaigns in 1894 and 1895 the new Japanese fleet and army demolished Chinese forces sent to protect China's tributary dependency. The peace treaty made Japan dominant in a still nominally independent Korea; the Chinese also ceded to them the island of Taiwan (Formosa), a huge indemnity, and the right to operate factories in the China treaty ports.

At the same time, the Russians were extending their influence, railways, and concession areas in Manchuria, whose southern tip they leased from China. The Japanese saw this as a threat to their position in Korea, but in any case they had their own plans for Manchuria. They struck there in 1904 without declaring war, winning a rapid series of land and naval battles against Russia by a combination of dash and willingness to take heavy casualties. The Russians were far from their home base and inadequately prepared; in time, their much greater resources would have prevailed, but the Japanese persuaded the American president, Theodore Roosevelt, to arrange a peace at Portsmouth, New Hampshire, in 1905. The Russians were concerned by then with the first stirrings of revolution at home, and the war was expensive and unpopular in Russia. Japan inherited Russia's position in Manchuria and tightened its grip on Korea, which in 1910 became an outright colony in a growing Japanese empire.

Japan's first steps toward empire profited from the tacit support of the Western powers, who saw it as a counterweight against Russia's geographic advantage in the Far East. Japan had been encouraged to attack Russia by the Anglo-Japanese treaty of alliance and friendship signed in 1902, which was welcomed in Japan as a mark of international equality. Theodore Roosevelt saw the Japanese as promising allies, "bully fighters," as he called them. The Russo-Japanese War of 1904–1905 inaugurated a period of new pride, confidence, and continued economic progress.

Japan joined the Allies in World War I, ostensibly as an equal partner, although it took no part in the fighting in Europe apart from sending a few destroyers to join the British Mediterranean fleet. The opportunity was instead used to take over the German concession areas in China, centered in the province of Shantung in eastern North China. In 1915 Japan presented China with a list of 21 demands that would have made it in effect a Japanese colony. By such bullying tactics, Japan quickly lost the admiration and goodwill built up by its progress since 1869. The Twenty-one Demands also infuriated Chinese patriots and more than any other event spurred the rise of broad-based Chinese nationalism. The Demands were rejected, although Japan hung onto the German concessions in Shantung. Meanwhile, the Japanese continued to develop Taiwan, Korea, and Manchuria.

Taiwan offered rice, sugar, and tropical crops to feed Japan's booming population. Korea had rich resources of coal, iron ore, and timber, which Japan appropriated. The Japanese drained the country of every useful commodity, including food crops, to support their growth, leaving the Koreans as an impoverished and exploited labor force. Koreans were forced to adopt Japanese names, and most were denied even elementary education; the public use of their own language was forbidden. Manchuria, still formally part of China but in effect a Japanese sphere, was a storehouse of coal, ores, timber, productive agricultural land, and potential hydroelectric power. Japan exploited all these resources while building an infrastructure of railways, mines, irrigation systems, dams, port facilities, and a colonial administration. In Korea too, railways, mines, factories, and roads were built and basic economic growth begun, although for Japanese benefit. In Taiwan the infrastructure for economic redevelopment was also laid, primarily in agriculture, leading to new prosperity.

In Manchuria the Japanese built the largest single industrial complex in Asia, including closely integrated mines and factories in the Mukden (Shenyang) area, a dense rail network, and a highly productive commercialized agriculture that generated large surpluses of wheat and soybeans for export to Japan and to world markets through the port of Dairen. Large power dams were built on Manchuria's rivers. The population increased by nearly a million a year from 1900 to the outbreak of the Pacific war in 1941, consisting almost entirely of Chinese who migrated from a disordered and impoverished North China in search of new economic opportunity. Japan's huge investment in Manchuria laid the basis for China's industrialization after Japan's defeat in 1945. But Japan's record as a colonial power, despite the constructive achievements, was marred, as in Korea, by an exploitive approach as well as a disregard for local interests or aspirations.

ITO HIROBUMI: MEIJI STATESMAN

The leading statesman of Meiji Japan, Ito Hirobumi, was born in one of the outer daimyo domains of southwestern Japan in 1841. As a youth, he wanted passionately to save his country from the foreign threat, and at the age of 21 tried to burn the newly established British embassy in Tokyo. But when he visited Britain the next year, he realized that it was impossible to drive the Westerners out by such tactics, and he returned to work for Japan's modernization. After the Meiji Restoration, he went with government missions to Europe and America to learn how to make his country strong and in 1881 became Japan's first prime minister under the new Western-style government. A later visit to Prussia convinced him that a constitutional monarchy was best suited to Japan. Ito was the chief architect of the new constitution proclaimed by the emperor in 1889, which contained many elements of the German imperial constitution. He understood, however, that constitutional government, and the cooperation of the new parliament, could not be made to work without political organization and popular support. In 1898 he left office to form a political party for that purpose, which was dominant in Japan until 1941.

After the Russo-Japanese War in 1905, Ito became the first Japanese resident-general in Korea. The Koreans deeply resented Japanese control, but Ito saw a civilian-based policy as preferable to the complete military occupation urged by powerful voices at home and hoped, against the odds, that he could win the Koreans' goodwill and cooperation in developing their country. In 1909 he was assassinated by a Korean patriot while on a visit to northern Manchuria—an abrupt end to the career of a man who might have played a vital moderating role in subsequent Japanese policies. Ito was an enthusiastic modernizer, especially after his visits to the West, but he also understood the need for compromise in politics and for adapting Western ways to Japanese traditions, circumstances, and values. In some ways he remained at least as traditional as he was modern. His objective was the preservation and development of his country, and Westernization was only a means to that end. He believed deeply in the restoration of the emperor's personal rule and aimed to accomplish his goals by working through the throne. But he also understood the rising yearning for a less authoritarian form of government, the need for political parties, a constitution, and a parliament. These aspirations he served well, never letting personal ambition or power cloud his judgment or his dedication to the public welfare.

Australia and the Pacific Islands

Western expansion came late to the Australian continent and most of the Pacific islands. Australia, however, had been inhabited by aborigines for some 50,000 years, and more recently peoples from Southeast Asia had migrated to Australia and the myriad islands of the Pacific. The culture of these peoples varied from that of the aborigines, who lived until Western colonization very much as their paleolithic ancestors had, to the Maori of New Zealand, skilled seamen whose delicate, filigreed woodcarving was the equal of craftsmen in any part of the world. Western explorers called this region Oceania. In addition to Australia and New Zealand, Oceania included Melanesia, extending from New Guinea to Fiji; Micronesia, to the north, embracing the islands from the Marianas to the Gilberts; and Polynesia, the easternmost islands, encompassing Samoa and Hawaii.

Australia: Convicts, Wool, and Gold

Although Spanish explorers and traders had plied the Pacific throughout much of the sixteenth century, the Dutch were the first Westerners to reach Australia, which they called New Holland, in the early 1600s. The English displayed some interest late in the same century, but not until 1770 did a British expedition under James Cook discover land suitable for settlement and claim Australia for Britain. Because the great island continent was not astride the trade routes, it had hitherto been ignored, but the British soon found a use for the latest acquisition to their empire. Having lost the war with the American colonists and having failed to establish penal settlements in West Africa, they could dump unwanted convicts in Australia.

The first British colony was founded at Sydney on the southeast coast in 1788 by Captain Arthur Phillip, who became the first governor. Because the colony was so distant from Britain and so difficult to supply, it was slow to attract free settlers. Many of the earliest free colonists were soldiers who decided to stay in Australia after serving in the British garrison, notwithstanding the fact that the land was described by one officer as "very barren and forbidding." By the mid-nineteenth century it had become the home of some 160,000 transplanted convicts, many of whom were assigned to work a specified number of years for the free colonizers. New South Wales, as the region around Sydney was called, was difficult to farm, especially because of insufficient water, but in the early 1800s the woolen industry developed rapidly, aided by the British government's termination of import duties on colonial wool. Between 1821, when wool was first shipped to Brit-

ain, and 1845, wool export increased from 175,000 to 24 million pounds.

By that point exploration was moving rapidly forward, and there were key settlements at Melbourne in the south, Perth in the southwest, and Brisbane to the north. Interest in Australia increased substantially when gold was discovered in New South Wales and its southern neighbor, Victoria, in 1851, two years after the great rush had begun in California. In the ensuing decade the population of New South Wales jumped from 200,000 to 350,000, while Victoria's rose from 77,000 to 540,000. As the population of the continent as a whole passed 1 million, more attention had to be given to food production, especially when the supply of gold dwindled. As in the American west, bitter conflicts arose between ranchers and farmers, with the latter additionally plagued by water shortages and inadequate transportation facilities. The crisis was gradually resolved only as roads, railways, and irrigation systems were built and as farmers learned to dry-farm and apply chemical fertilizers.

During the late nineteenth century interest grew in uniting the six Australian colonies, each of which had been given its own legislature by an 1850 British statute. Federation would not only eliminate internal economic barriers but also enhance Australia's ability to withstand potential aggression from one or more of the imperial powers. The resulting commonwealth of Australia, founded in 1901, was a constitutional federation, with the central government, as in the United States, possessing only limited authority.

New Zealand: Maori and Missionaries

The Australian aborigines had been spread too thinly and were too pacific to have posed a serious threat to colonizers. In New Zealand, however, the native Maori were not only relatively more populous, considering New Zealand's smaller size (one-thirtieth the size of Australia), but much better organized and temperamentally more militant. Although Captain Cook had claimed New Zealand for Britain in 1769, interest in settling the island was slow in developing. Missionary efforts to the Maori, begun in 1814, made striking progress by midcentury. Simultaneously, however, some of the Maori began acquiring European guns, which they turned against rival tribes in an orgy of violence. The island also became a battleground in a different kind of war—one fought ideologically and politically between missionaries, who wanted the land preserved for Christianized Maori, and imperial colonizers, who envisaged a country dominated by white settlers.

Matters came to a head in 1840, thanks largely to the colonizing schemes of Edward Gibbon Wakefield and his New Zealand Land Company. The island, he truthfully told a parliamentary committee, was "the most beautiful coun-

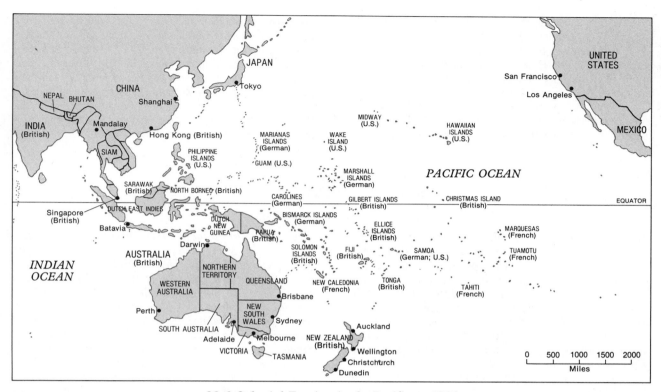

33.6 Colonial Empires in the Pacific, c. 1900

try" with a fine climate and productive soil. The British decision to annex New Zealand may have been stimulated as well by a French show of interest in the island nation. The British government formally annexed New Zealand in 1840; the newly appointed governor negotiated a treaty with the Maori, obtaining their recognition of British sovereignty and promising them secure land tenure. But many of the Maori were soon disillusioned as whites from Australia and Britain poured into the island, and fighting was frequent until 1872, when the Maori finally accepted defeat. By that point the population of the island was approximately 250,000, of whom less than 40,000 by one estimate were Maori. They were victims not only of the fighting but, like the Australian aborigines and the Amerindians, of the new diseases transmitted by Europeans. Peace provided fresh opportunities for growth, and in the next 30 years the population more than tripled, modern transportation and communications systems were developed, and a democratic political constitution evolved that in 1893 extended suffrage to women.

Islands of the Pacific

Although Spanish and Dutch explorers had discovered some of the islands of Melanesia, Micronesia, and Polynesia, it was not until the late eighteenth century that Europeans began to show serious interest in them. At first their motives were largely economic: whalers and sealers from America, Britain, and France used some of the islands as bases, while merchants traded tools, cloth, and guns for the sandalwood that found a ready market in China. As in New Zealand, much of the early interest in the islands was also religious. Spanish missionaries sought converts in the Marianas, while British Protestants in 1797 launched their campaign in Tahiti, and American Protestants began working in Hawaii in 1820. Where the missionaries went, the political interests of their home governments were usually quick to follow. In Tahiti, however, the English Protestants who virtually ran the island were ousted by the French navy in 1843, after which Catholic missionaries taught the natives their version of Christianity.

As imperial rivalry intensified among the great powers in the late nineteenth century, the Pacific islands were increasingly coveted. The interest in converting the native populations continued but was clearly subordinate to economic considerations and imperial advantage. Britain, France, the United States, and Germany competed for the spoils, toppling native states, such as the kingdom of Fiji, in the process. The most notorious example of this occurred in 1893, when American planters, aided by a contingent of 150 marines, overthrew Hawaii's Queen Liliuokalani (1891–1893). Despite the fact that the United

States had recognized Hawaii's independence in 1842, the American government waited only until 1900 to annex it, as it had annexed the Philippines and Guam two years earlier. "We need Hawaii just as much and a good deal more than we did California," insisted President William McKinley; "it is manifest destiny."

Thus in 1900 every island in Polynesia, Micronesia, and Melanesia was a colonial possession of Britain, France, Germany, or the United States. Once-mighty Spain, after losing the Philippines and Guam, had sold its remaining Pacific islands—the Carolines, Marianas, and Marshalls—to Germany the previous year. The Germans, however, would lose those islands to Japan in 1914, the same year they lost northeastern New Guinea to Australia and their part of Samoa to New Zealand. Less than three decades later, conflicting Japanese and American ambitions in the Pacific resulted in the attack on Pearl Harbor that propelled the United States into World War II.

ॲ ॲ ॲ

The age of domination saw European powers take control of most of Africa, India, Ceylon, Burma, Malaya, Indochina, Indonesia, and the Philippines, while they and the Americans exercised a strong influence and enjoyed special concessions in Thailand, China, and Japan. The Japanese, taking a lesson from their Western teachers, created their own colonial empire in Korea, Taiwan, and Manchuria.

Imperialism radically challenged the traditional values and structures of the societies it conquered or dominated. The result was dislocation, suffering, and cultural trauma. Much of value was weakened or destroyed. But the West also brought advances in technology, productivity, and medicine that raised the standard of living and increased life expectancy. For better or worse, the colonial impulse united most of the globe in a broad, overarching web of economic and political interdependency for the first time in history.

Some of the West's values would be adopted, some contested, some rejected. Many of them would be accepted only after being assimilated to the older cultural patterns that reasserted themselves as the yoke of Western dominance was shaken off. The four great civilizations of Asia each responded differently to the Western challenge. British dominion in India stimulated the development of a nationalist movement that created a modern state on the subcontinent. Similar developments came later in Southeast Asia and were retarded by repressive French and Dutch colonial policies. China, too large to be conquered, would find its own path to modernity after a century of confusion and anarchy. Japan made the most rapid and apparently the easiest transition from a traditional society to a modern, industrial one and in mere decades achieved the status of a world power.

Suggestions for Further Reading

Imperialism and Africa

Curtin, P. D. *Africa and the West: Intellectual Responses to European Culture*. Madison: University of Wisconsin Press, 1972.

Fieldhouse, D. K. *Economics and Empire, 1830–1914*. Ithaca, N.Y.: Cornell University Press, 1973.

Hallett, R. *Africa Since 1875*. Ann Arbor: University of Michigan Press, 1974.

Langer, W. L. *The Diplomacy of Imperialism, 1890–1902*, 2d ed. New York: Knopf, 1965.

Oliver, R. and Atmore, A. *Africa Since 1800*, 3d ed. Cambridge: Cambridge University Press, 1981.

Perham, M., and Simmons, J., eds. *African Discovery: An Anthology of Exploration*. London: Faber & Faber, 1961.

India

Embree, A. T. *1857 in India: Mutiny or War of Independence?* Boston: Heath, 1963.

Forster, E. M. *A Passage to India*. New York: Harcourt, Brace, 1924. (Fiction)

Mason, P. *The Men Who Ruled India*, rev. ed. New York: Norton, 1985.

Seal, A. *The Emergence of Indian Nationalism*. Cambridge: Cambridge University Press, 1968.

Southeast Asia

Bastin, J., and Benda, H. J. *A History of Modern Southeast Asia*. Englewood Cliffs, N.J.: Prentice-Hall, 1968.

Hall, D. G. E. *A History of Southeast Asia*, 4th ed. New York: St. Martin's Press, 1984.

Harrison, B. *Southeast Asia: A Short History*. London: Macmillan, 1968.

Orwell, G. *Burmese Days*. New York: Harcourt, Brace, 1934.

Steinberg, D. J., ed. *In Search of Southeast Asia*. Honolulu: University Press of Hawaii, 1987.

China

Fairbank, J. K. *The Missionary Enterprise in China and America*. Cambridge, Mass.: Harvard University Press, 1974.

Gasster, M. *China's Struggle to Modernize*. New York: Knopf, 1972.

Hsu, I. *The Rise of Modern China*. New York: Oxford University Press, 1975.

Murphey, R. *Shanghai: Key to Modern China*. Cambridge, Mass.: Harvard University Press, 1953.

Pruitt, I. *Daughter of Han*. New Haven, Conn.: Yale University Press, 1945.

Schrecker, J. *Imperialism and Chinese Nationalism.* Cambridge, Mass.: Harvard University Press, 1971.

Japan

Beasley, W. G. *The Meiji Restoration.* Stanford, Calif.: Stanford University Press, 1972.

Borton, H. *Japan's Modern Century.* New York: Ronald Press, 1955.

Myers, R. *The Japanese Empire.* Stanford, Calif.: Stanford University Press, 1984.

Storry, R. *A History of Modern Japan,* rev. ed. New York: Penguin Books, 1982.

PART · FIVE

The Twentieth Century

In 1910 King Edward VII of Great Britain died. At his funeral a stately procession of Europe's reigning monarchs—including George V, Edward's successor; Tsar Nicholas II of Russia; Kaiser William II of Germany; Crown Prince Karl of Austria-Hungary; and King Albert of Belgium—paraded on horseback, their helmets and swords glittering in the sun. Looking back on it from the perspective of the present, we are tempted to see great symbolism in the event—the mourning, as it were, for a world that was dying. Within four years the monarchs who had posed so congenially with each other, many of whom were related by marriage or blood, were at war with each other. When that struggle—the "Great War"—was over, some of them had lost their thrones, and those who remained would reign over states with sharply diminished power and prestige.

The world changed rapidly after the Great War of 1914–1918. Revolutionary upheavals in Russia and new ideologies in Italy and Germany proclaimed the entrance of the masses onto the stage of history and the demise of the old liberal order. These Western transformations were accompanied by equally momentous events in India, China, and the Middle East, where anticolonial movements sought both liberation from Western domination and national regeneration. Within twenty years economic crisis and a second world war had completed the decline of Europe as the center of world power. The influence of the traditional European powers was quickly replaced by the emergence of the Soviet Union and the United States as "superpower" states whose military-industrial strength has dominated world affairs ever since.

By 1945 the twentieth century had assumed the broad contours that we now find familiar. A fundamental shift had occurred in the relationship between the West and the rest of the world as Asia, Africa, and Latin America completed the transition from colonialism. If the first half of the century began with a few European states controlling huge colonial empires across the globe, the second half draws to a close with a world community consisting of more than 150 independent nations. Indeed, those newer states today play an increasingly more prominent role in shaping a common destiny through a joint international posture of nonalignment, seeking thereby to mitigate the effects of superpower hegemony.

If, then, there is a sequel to the funeral of Edward VII that vividly symbolizes this dramatic change, it is perhaps to be found in the gathering of nonaligned states that met in New Delhi, India, in 1983, where Cuba's Fidel Castro, dressed in guerrilla fatigues, passed the gavel of the meeting to India's Indira Gandhi, resplendent in the silk sari of her country.

While the twentieth century saw the end of European political supremacy, it also witnessed the extension of Western technology, institutions, and ideas to these very same newly independent nations. The adoption of Western models of development was both a deliberate weapon in the struggle against colonialism and a legacy of their former subordinate status. But as traditional societies experience the disruptive stresses of modernization, developing nations are searching for alternatives more appropriate to their own cultures.

As we move toward the twenty-first century, a host of vital issues—social and political justice, peace, human rights and equality, and economic well-being—loom ever larger as the joint responsibility of an increasingly interdependent global community. ■

Culture, Society, and the Great War

Until a second global conflict erupted in the 1930s, modern memory recalled only the "Great War" of 1914–1918. World War I was called "great" because its toll on human life, its monetary cost and physical destruction, and the human trauma it caused made all others pale in comparison. It started because rulers and government officials blundered in the summer of 1914, but a half century of diplomatic and cultural history lay behind the immediate events. Many artists and writers had rejected traditional moral and social values, and some glorified violence as a catharsis that would strengthen what they believed was a civilization in decay. Such views anticipated the political breakdown of Europe by creating a climate in which war seemed acceptable, even desirable.

Although the fighting stopped in November 1918, its impact was felt for decades. Four empires disappeared as a result of the conflict—Hohenzollern Germany, Habsburg Austria-Hungary, Ottoman Turkey, and Romanov Russia. This last was replaced by the world's first state to describe itself as socialist with the goal of transforming itself into a communist society. The shock of the war experience, no less than the conditions of peace imposed on the vanquished, helped shape the twentieth century.

Women served at or near the front lines in a number of capacities during World War I. Here a British ambulance driver is shown in France. [Bettmann Archive]

The Great War was not the first worldwide war, for earlier struggles had also been waged on several continents and oceans. In this war military engagements took place in Africa, Asia, and the Middle East, but the fighting was concentrated in Europe. Although imperialism formed part of the background to the war, its causes were almost entirely in the West. Nevertheless, the Great War had worldwide repercussions. In its aftermath, Europe's overseas empires disintegrated as its global supremacy collapsed.

The Crisis of European Culture

In the three decades preceding World War I, European culture underwent a revolution that transformed thought: antirationalists challenged the optimism inherited from the Enlightenment and the materialism of the nineteenth century, while the literary and artistic avant-garde experimented with new ways of experiencing time and space. Philosophers increasingly favored instinct over reason to explain human behavior, while students of the mind proclaimed that beneath the fragile veneer of civilization lurked dark forces. Scientists, who had previously explained the physical world through the observation of recordable data, confronted a universe in which measurement itself was relative to the observer. Literary narrative, which once expressed motives and character, spoke increasingly in the language of ambiguity. The crisis also overturned aesthetic values as artists questioned conventional expressions of reality. Most disturbing, new strains of antidemocratic and racist thought were introduced into politics.

The Revolt Against Positivism

The intellectual rejection of materialism and reason is known as the antipositivist revolt. Its most outspoken proponent was the German Friedrich Nietzsche (1844–1900). A philosopher repelled by the hypocrisy and pettiness of his time, Nietzsche assaulted traditional morality. His scathing criticism of bourgeois values extended to the roots of Western culture, from Greco-Roman rationalism to the Judeo-Christian belief in compassion, sin, and humility—concepts he said were more suitable to slaves and weaklings than the free and the strong.

To realize freedom and human potential, Nietzsche urged the abandonment of these traditions in favor of instincts and emotions. He called on heroic leaders to guide the masses: "All gods are dead," he proclaimed, "so we now want the superman to live." While he condemned democratic liberalism and equality, he also repudiated nationalism, militarism, and anti-Semitism, although apologists for Nazism later seized on his writings as justification for their doctrines of national and racial superiority. These justifications were part of the philosophical underpinning for European anti-Semitism. Misunderstood during his lifetime, Nietzsche's ideas had a profound influence on European culture. Literary and artistic rebels drew inspiration from his attack on the establishment, and in the 1920s political demagogues were influenced by his concept of the superman.

Nietzsche's stress on the irrational was echoed by the French philosopher Henri Bergson (1859–1941). Distinguishing between the rational intellect and intuitive understanding, Bergson believed the former a useful tool for analyzing knowledge but not for understanding reality. Only intuition could grasp the "life force," which informed all experience and expressed itself in a continuum, or "duration," that instinct alone could describe. Bergson's chief influence lay in underscoring nonrational experience. Although he did not reject science, he undermined the scientists' claim to a monopoly on knowledge.

Sigmund Freud (1856–1939), a Viennese physician, confirmed Bergson's arguments about the limits of reason. Freud's treatment of psychiatric disorders, based on clinical data, convinced him that behavior is the result of powerful and primitive desires such as aggression and sex. These drives usually remain in an irrational unconscious, which he called the *id*. Freud believed that the id struggles constantly against the *ego*, which rationalizes and channels these desires according to the constraints of reality and the socially implanted values of the *superego*.

The superego functions as a kind of conscience, but instead of reflecting absolute moral values or rational truths, it is the product of social conditioning. Because the mind tends to repress the id, the conflict generally remains unconscious. Nevertheless, the resulting tensions can cause crippling experiences of guilt and fear or even mental breakdown. Freud's theories, particularly those concerning infantile and childhood sexuality, shocked bourgeois notions of human nature. Moreover, by positing the notion that some people live emotionally in a frozen past, Freud and other psychoanalysts altered human perception of time as a forward-moving concept.

Like Nietzsche, Freud emphasized the irrational basis of human behavior and social values. For Freud, civilization is built on the repression of powerful individual urges, particularly sexual ones. Socialization, and hence "progress," rests not on reason but on the frustration of instincts that, held continually in check, threaten to overwhelm it. Nietzsche had questioned whether civilization was worth its cost in terms of human fulfillment. Freud assumed that repression and self-denial are the necessary price of society. World War I seemed to bear out his pessimism about human nature and the stability of civilization, and his influence on postwar thought was enormous.

Freud's leadership within the movement he founded for the study and treatment of the human psyche—psychoanalysis—was challenged by his former disciple, Carl Jung (1875–1961), who elaborated his own theory of a collective unconscious. In recent decades Freud's theories have been sharply challenged. Nonetheless, he has remained one of the most influential thinkers of the century, and his indirect impact on sexual attitudes, artistic expression, and the concept of mental illness has been incalculable. Perhaps no one has done more to change the modern conception of human nature.

The Dilemmas of Science

Ironically, advances in the realm of physical science seemed to reinforce antirationalist arguments. Since the days of Newton, science had sustained the idea that the physical world operated according to immutable laws and predictable mechanical processes. The modern scientific age, which began with investigations into the nature of matter following the discovery of X-rays in 1895 by Wilhelm Röntgen (1845–1923), shattered these illusions. Experiments by Marie Curie (1867–1934) and her husband, Pierre (1859–1906), showed that the atomic weight of elements such as radium changed as they emitted energy in the form of "subatomic" particles. These findings suggested a relationship between matter and energy. By the end of the 1920s a radical revision of the basic assumptions of classical physics had totally recast scientific understanding of the universe.

Early in the twentieth century the German physicist Max Planck (1858–1947) conducted studies of radiation that revealed that contrary to earlier theories, light energy moves not in steady waves but in discontinuous yet calculable spurts, which he called *quanta*. Working independently, Albert Einstein (1879–1955) also began to revolutionize physics. His "Special Theory of Relativity," published in 1905, rejected the notion that space and time were absolutes, suggesting instead that both were relative to the position of the observer. Einstein showed that light moves through space in particles known as photons and calculated that the energy contained in a photon was equal to its mass multiplied by the square of the speed of light—a concept expressed in his famous formula, $E = mc^2$. Hence not only do mass and time vary with velocity, but energy and mass are interchangeable. In 1915 Einstein's "General Theory of Relativity," which explained gravitation, further shook standard views of the physical world: it described the universe as curved, so that when light waves are deflected as they pass through a gravitational field, they eventually return to their point of origin. Einstein's universe was a four-dimensional one in which length, breadth, and height also had to be conceived in terms of time.

Albert Einstein, whose theories of relativity revolutionized our concepts of the universe, is shown here in his middle years. He received the Nobel Prize for physics in 1921. [Granger Collection]

In the years between the evolution of Einstein's theories of relativity, Ernest Rutherford (1871–1937) forced contemporaries to abandon still another basic assumption about matter. Rutherford theorized that the atom, which since ancient times had been regarded as a solid, indivisible mass, was actually an arrangement much like a solar system, consisting of a central particle (the nucleus) with a positive electrical charge, surrounded by orbits of negatively charged electrons. He demonstrated that by bombarding substances with subatomic particles, the structure of atoms could be changed.

In the popular mind these theories and findings led to a doubly disturbing conclusion about the physical universe: that it was not unchangeable but shifting and uncertain, and that perhaps knowledge of it lay beyond human comprehension. While almost all countries, in an effort to coordinate wireless communications and transportation schedules, were adopting World Standard Time at the beginning of the twentieth century, scientists such as Einstein were shattering the concept of a uniform public time into the infinite variations of private times relative to each individual.

Realism Abandoned: Literature and Art

The revolt against positivism was reflected in literature and painting. Writers and artists not only expressed the social criticism that rejected the values of materialist culture but also probed beyond the conscious mind. Alienation impelled literary figures to take refuge in obscure symbolism, decadence, or aestheticism, while artists provided visual evidence of the breakdown of traditional forms.

The rebellion in literature had begun at midcentury with the publication of *Flowers of Evil* (1857) by the French poet Charles Baudelaire (1821–1867). Like the British poet Algernon Swinburne (1837–1909) and others, Baudelaire was hostile to bourgeois values and deliberately shocked conventional morality. The 1880s saw the birth of the Decadents and Symbolism, two literary movements derived in part from these earlier sources. The Decadents were sophisticated aesthetes such as Oscar Wilde (1854–1900), J. K. Huysmans (1848–1907), and Gabriele D'Annunzio (1863–1938), who extolled the idea of art for art's sake and cultivated exoticism and artificiality.

The Symbolists, represented by Stéphane Mallarmé (1842–1898) and Paul Verlaine (1844–1896), sought to express the inexpressible in experimental verse that relied on symbols to convey images that logic alone could not fathom. They rejected conventional perception in favor of a subjective, inner world. Often proclaiming the values of aestheticism and decadence, the Symbolists portrayed emotions derived from immediate experience, much as Bergson had urged.

In the 1870s Impressionism assaulted both realism and academic art by depicting the disintegrative effects of light. By the 1880s Impressionism was under attack by Postimpressionists, who, like the Symbolists, were moving away from the outer world of visible reality to an inner realm of the individual artist. In his later years, Claude Monet (1840–1926), the leading Impressionist, painted huge canvases depicting waterlilies. These shimmering pools of color, almost devoid of form, represented a transition between the perceived reality of Impressionism and the emotion of Postimpressionism.

One of the most powerful Postimpressionists was Vincent van Gogh (1853–1890), whose works conveyed an imaginative vision of the world. Like Paul Gauguin (1848–1903), who left the materialistic society of France to settle in Tahiti, van Gogh was interested in using the formal, abstract elements of art—line, color, and form—to express an intensely personal view of truth. Paul Cézanne (1839–1906), however, wanted to free art of subjectivity and emotionalism. Following classical principles, he used color to stress the underlying weight and volume of objects. His landscapes define objects only in the most general sense by using contour, color, and mass to convey abstract equivalents for conventional objects.

BARCELONA AND THE MODERN TEMPER

No city better reflected the cultural ferment of turn-of-the-century Europe than Barcelona. Located on Spain's northeastern plain at the edge of the Mediterranean Sea, Barcelona was the center of Catalan regionalism. In many ways the capital of Catalonia province represented the outstanding example of a modern European city, an innovative, rapidly modernizing enclave in a traditional, agrarian nation. By the late nineteenth century Barcelona had become a city marked by bold cultural experimentation.

Founded at the end of the first century B.C. as a Roman administrative center, the town had grown up in the Middle Ages around a military fortress. Its location on the sea made it a natural focus of trade and shipbuilding. The Industrial Revolution reached Spain through Barcelona, where an enterprising middle class emerged in the late eighteenth century. By the 1850s chemical and machinery manufacturers had joined bankers, shipping magnates, and textile producers in forming a powerful liberal oligarchy. Although its members pressed for urban development and economic modernization, they also fought the labor and socialist movements with support from the government.

At midcentury greater Barcelona had a population of several hundred thousand that exhibited the class characteristics of an advanced capitalist society. Demographic growth forced the adoption in 1859 of a new town plan, similar to the plans followed in Paris and elsewhere, that consisted of a square grid pattern of streets and parks cut across by broad diagonal avenues. Less than a generation later, when more than 500,000 people lived there, Barcelona hosted the Universal Exhibition of 1888. The project, which incorporated a huge complex of exhibition halls, hotels, apartment buildings, factories, and urban services into the city plan, gave a strong thrust to construction and the arts.

Despite their reactionary politics, the economic elites that sponsored the Universal Exhibition encouraged an atmosphere of cultural innovation that made Barcelona synonymous with the most avant-garde trends in Europe. Brilliant local architects, working in the so-called *modernista* style, designed new buildings in a wide range of exciting idioms. This eclectic movement found inspiration in Moorish, Romanesque, and Gothic patterns, in the strong craft tradition of Catalonia, and in the international Art Nouveau style of the period.

The most creative architect of the period, Antonio Gaudí (1852–1926), developed a unique style that reconciled form with function and expressed his militant Catholic beliefs. Gaudí's creations, such as the Guell Palace, incorporated organic forms that resembled sculptural modeling. While his designs were derived from both Gothic and Art Nouveau styles, they represented an original architectural vocabulary that was a reaction against what he saw as the falsity of *fin-de-siècle* design. Many of his ambitious creations remained unrealized or only partially complete; a society exists even to this day that seeks to finish his most famous project, the Church of the Holy Family.

While Gaudí and other architects gave the city a bold new face, Barcelona also became a haven for the avant-garde, which included some of Europe's major artists and writers. Four important Spanish-born artists lived and exhibited in Barcelona in the early years of the twentieth century: Pablo Picasso (1881–1973), usually associated with Paris, executed his first mature works in Barcelona, along with Joan Miró (1893–1983), pioneer abstract painter and a native of the city, Julio Gonzalez (1876–1942), a craftsman turned sculptor, and Salvador Dalí (1904–1989), the famed Surrealist painter. The economic boom that Barcelona experienced during World War I

drew many foreign artists from war-torn countries to neutral Spain. The French Dadaist and Surrealist painter Francis Picabia (1879–1953) came into contact with Dalí, and worked in Barcelona, and was later joined by the Belgian Surrealist René Magritte (1898–1967). In the 1930s the American photographer and painter Man Ray (1890–1976), the Italian sculptor Alberto Giacometti (1901–1966), and the German painter Max Ernst (1891–1976) all exhibited there.

While these and other creative talents pushed art and design toward modernism, the Spanish writer Eugenio d'Ors (1882–1954) founded a more conservative cultural movement known as *Noucentisme* ("Twentieth Century"), which stressed a revival of Mediterranean classicism in the arts. Nevertheless, as Spain headed toward dictatorship and conflict in the 1920s, Barcelona remained a bastion of cultural discourse. The International Exhibition of 1929 was the last symbol of Barcelona's cultural primacy. The brilliant architect Mies van der Rohe designed the exhibit's German pavilion in the Bauhaus style, which had come to stand for internationalism and modernity. Ironically, his "Barcelona chair," a pivotal example of modern furniture design, was intended as the official seat for King Alfonso XIII.

Postimpressionists, Cubists, and Futurists

Postimpressionists such as Cézanne brought painting to the edge of modernism. At the Paris Salon of 1905, the works of a number of Postimpressionist artists—Matisse, Rouault, and others—were hung together because of certain common characteristics. Their distortions, flat patterns, and preoccupation with line and form rather than objective reality, combined with violent, bold colors and stark contrasts, earned these men the title of *fauves* ("wild beasts"). Closely related to Fauvism were two German Expressionist groups, the Bridge and the Blue Rider, formed between 1905 and 1911, whose proponents emphasized bold colors and psychological portraiture.

The most significant step away from the traditional portrayal of reality came with Cubism, launched in Paris by the Spaniard Pablo Picasso and the Frenchman Georges Braque (1882–1963) in 1907. Influenced by Cézanne, Picasso and Braque developed a concept of form and context that enabled them to render the whole structure of an object as well as its position in space. Abandoning the bright colors and striking contrasts of the *fauves*, they focused on the subtleties of intersecting lines and angles and the reduction of objects to abstract forms. The Cubists not only set in motion the revolution in abstract painting, but by fracturing objects into separate elements and fixing them in time-space relationships, they transformed traditional views of reality.

The highly original talent of the Barcelona architect Antonio Gaudí is seen here in a photograph of the Casa Milá, an apartment house completed in 1910. [Giraudon/Art Resource]

The only major prewar art movement to develop independently of Paris was Futurism, founded by Filippo T. Marinetti (1876–1944) and a group of young Italian writers and artists in 1909. In contrast to most of the avant-garde of the period, the Futurists rejected humanist culture in the name of the machine and industrial civilization. Exalting the speed and energy of modern life, painters such as Umberto Boccioni (1882–1916) and Carlo Carrà (1881–1966) moved toward the elimination of traditional forms. Futurists advocated the destruction of libraries and museums and, influenced by the ideas of Nietzsche, Sorel, and Bergson, preached violence as an act of liberation.

◎ The Futurist Manifesto ◎

The Futurists were symptomatic of the crisis of prewar European culture. Not only did they rebel against reason, tradition, and conventional standards of beauty, but they also demanded a new civilization based on the aesthetic of the machine. Here is the first Futurist manifesto, drafted by Filippo T. Marinetti and originally published in Paris on February 20, 1909.

We want to praise the love of danger, the attitude of energy and fearlessness.

Courage, audacity, and revolt will be essential elements of our poetry.

Until now literature has exalted pensive immobility, ecstasy, and sleep. We want to exalt aggressive action, a feverish insomnia, the racer's stride, the mortal leap, the punch, and the slap.

We assert that the beauty of the world has been enriched by a new beauty: the beauty of speed. A racing car . . . is more beautiful than the *Victory of Samothrace*.

We want to praise the man at the wheel, who hurls his spiritual lance across the earth, along the circle of its orbit.

The poet must give himself with ardor, splendor, and generosity, to swell the enthusiastic fervor of the primordial elements.

There is no beauty except in struggle. No work without an aggressive character can be a masterpiece. Poetry must be conceived as a violent attack on unknown forces, to reduce and prostrate them before man.

We stand on the last promontory of the centuries! . . . Why must we look back, when what we want is to break down the mysterious doors of the impossible? Time and space died yesterday. We already live in the absolute, because we have already created eternal, omnipresent speed.

We want to glorify war—the world's only hygiene—militarism, patriotism, the destructive gesture of liberators, beautiful ideas worth dying for, and scorn for woman.

We want to destroy museums, libraries, academies of every kind, and want to fight moralism, feminism, every opportunistic or utilitarian cowardice.

We will sing of great crowds excited by work, by pleasure, and by riot; we will sing of the multicolored, polyphonic tides of revolution in modern capitals; we will sing of the vibrant nocturnal fervor of arsenals and shipyards blazing with violent electric moons; of hungry railway stations that devour fire-breathing serpents; factories hung on clouds by the twisted lines of their smoke; bridges that stride the rivers like giant gymnasts, gleaming in the sun with a glitter of knives; adventurous steamers that cut the horizon; deep-chested locomotives whose wheels gallop along the tracks like the hooves of huge steel horses bridled by tubing; and the sleek flight of planes whose propellers flutter in the wind like banners and seem to cheer like an enthusiastic crowd.

Source: L. De Maria, ed., *Per conoscere Marinetti e il futurismo* (Milan: Mondadori, 1973), pp. 5–7. Trans. P. Cannistraro.

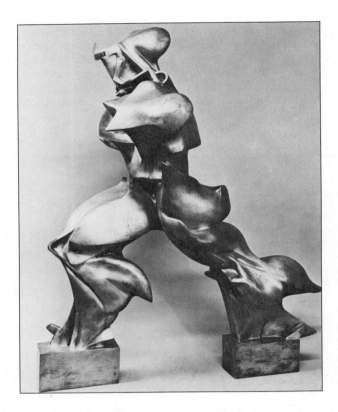

Umberto Boccioni's sculpture *Unique Forms of Continuity in Space* (1913) typifies the Futurist concern for motion and action. It is bronze and measures $43\frac{7}{8} \times 34\frac{7}{8} \times 15\frac{3}{4}$ wide. [Museum of Modern Art, New York; acquired through the Lillie P. Bliss Bequest.]

Futurism found other disciples in art and literature, notably in the English painter Wyndham Lewis (1882–1957) and the Russian poet Vladimir Mayakovsky (1893–1930).

Nationalism and Racism

The Futurists may have been the most extreme example of the crisis of European culture, but such disturbing concepts also affected public affairs. Some political theorists and social critics rejected the positivist doctrines on which both liberalism and socialism were based. Georges Sorel founded his syndicalist theories on the belief that the working masses could be stimulated to violent action by the idea of the general strike. Sorel's ideas were reinforced by the psychologist Gustav Le Bon (1841–1931), whose book *The Crowd* (1895) argued that mobs responded to pathological suggestion, and by others who maintained that instinct determined social conduct.

The characterization of mass behavior as essentially irrational led the Italian sociologist Vilfredo Pareto (1848–

1923) to assert the need for government by an elite rather than by the people. The French monarchist Charles Maurras (1868–1952) founded a reactionary political organization known as *Action française* on the theory that "the mob always follows determined minorities." Such thinking would influence important political leaders of both the right and the left, from Benito Mussolini to V. I. Lenin.

A further manifestation of these trends was the rise of racism and a new form of nationalism. Whereas nationalists of the 1830s and 1840s fought oppression on behalf of subjected peoples, a chauvinistic nationalism now pitted races and nation-states against one another. Influenced by Social Darwinism, the virulent nationalism of the late nineteenth century preached aggression and dominance. In the 1870s the pan-Slav movement proclaimed Russia's historic mission to unite all Slavic peoples into a great federation for an inevitable struggle against the West, while the Pan-German League, founded in 1893, demanded territorial expansion and a German-dominated central Europe.

The exaggerated nationalism of the period was linked to racist doctrines, which owed much to the Frenchman Arthur de Gobineau (1816–1882), author of "An Essay on the Inequality of the Races." Gobineau argued that the white races—especially the "Aryans" descended from Germanic tribes—had created civilization but had degenerated as a result of intermingling with "inferior" races. His theories impressed the German musical genius Richard Wagner (1813–1883), who condemned "Jewish" influence in music and whose cycle of four powerful operas in *The Ring of the Nibelungen* (1848–1876) glorified Germanic mythology. Wagner's son-in-law, the British expatriate Houston Stewart Chamberlain (1855–1927), espoused the creation of a superior race through genetic breeding. Chamberlain's *Foundations of the Nineteenth Century* (1899) blamed Europe's racial "degeneration" on the Jews.

Although anti-Semitism had existed for centuries, it reappeared in the vicious Russian pogroms of the late nineteenth century and as the basis for political movements spawned by racial doctrines. In Germany political parties inspired by Adolf Stöcker (1835–1909) elected deputies to the Reichstag on anti-Semitic platforms, while the mayor of Vienna, Karl Lüger (1844–1910), used anti-Semitism to generate popular support for his Christian Socialist party. In France, Charles Maurras led a campaign against the Jews during the Dreyfus affair. Nazi anti-Semitism was rooted in the racist atmosphere of the 1890s.

The Breakdown of the European Order

Few topics in modern history are more controversial than the causes of World War I. During and after the conflict, governments on both sides issued volumes of documents to justify their positions. In the wake of the Allied victory, a defeated Germany was forced to accept the blame. Since then, historians have taken a more balanced view of the war's origins, separating the long-range developments in which all European nations had participated from the immediate circumstances that led to its outbreak. The controversy erupted again in the 1960s when a German scholar, Fritz Fischer, maintained that his country had deliberately planned a far-reaching program of conquest before 1914. The response to Fischer's thesis has been heated, and today most historians would argue that his explanation focused too narrowly on Germany and underemphasized the broader European causes of the war.

For decades historical antagonisms, colonial rivalries, economic competition, and expansionist aspirations, all fueled by chauvinistic nationalism, had propelled Europe into an arms race and hostile alliances. Diplomatic confrontations increased tensions among the powers, so that most nations came to believe that only military alliances provided safety. When the final crisis came in the summer of 1914, the diplomatic order collapsed through a combination of fear and miscalculation. Science and technology, the twin sources of power and pride that had enabled the West to dominate the globe, made what most statesmen hoped would be an easy war a long and agonizing ordeal from which Europe never fully recovered.

Bismarck and the Concert of Europe

For more than half a century after the defeat of Napoleon in 1815 Europe's international system had been based on the notion that the great powers would act "in concert" to keep the peace established by the Congress of Vienna. The system worked remarkably well until the creation of the German empire in 1871 drastically altered international politics. Bismarck's triumph, won on the ruins of the second French empire, gave birth to a powerful state whose unsurpassed military strength was quickly equaled by its industrial and economic power.

The rapid emergence of Germany upset the European balance of power. Upon achieving unification, Bismarck denied having any further territorial ambitions. For the next 20 years his foreign policy goals remained the preservation of the concert of Europe and the protection of Germany. Bismarck saw two potentially troublesome situations. On the western frontier the French were obsessed with achieving revenge against Germany after their humiliating defeat in the Franco-Prussian War. For the Iron Chancellor the worst scenario was a military pact between France and Russia that would sandwich Germany between them in a two-front war. To avoid such a "nightmare," as he described it, Bismarck sought to keep France isolated from diplomatic alliances with other powers.

The east presented a more complicated security problem. The rise of nationalism threatened to destabilize east-central Europe and the Balkans by pulling apart both Austria-Hungary, which had been severely weakened by Prussia's lightning victory in 1866, and the deteriorating Ottoman Empire. The Balkans became the focus of this regional instability, for there Austria-Hungary and Russia competed for territory and influence at the expense of the Turks. Conflict between Vienna and St. Petersburg over the Balkans could drag Germany into a major war in the east and allow France to invade from the west. Bismarck responded by creating secret and often mutually contradictory diplomatic and military pacts. His strategy placed Berlin at the center of a complicated web of alliances that exploited competing national interests and fears.

Bismarck took his first step in 1873, when he concluded a mutual consultation treaty, the League of the Three Emperors, with Russia and Austria-Hungary. The league faced a serious crisis in 1877 and 1878. Russia, motivated by a desire for expansion, joined Serbia, Montenegro, and Bulgaria in a war against Turkey. The Treaty of San Stefano freed the Balkan states from Turkish control and gave the tsar a foothold in the region. Assuming the self-professed role of an "honest broker," Bismarck tried to engineer peace at the congress of Berlin and redress the balance of power. Austria secured the right to administer the provinces of Bosnia and Herzegovina, which technically remained Ottoman possessions, and the size of Bulgaria was reduced. Nevertheless, the Berlin congress aroused Slavic hostility against Germany and Austria-Hungary, for the Russians were angered by what they considered Bismarck's perfidy, while Serbia and Montenegro were bitter over Austria's occupation of Bosnia and Herzegovina. Romania and Greece were disappointed at not having gotten territories from the Turks. The Balkans had become a powder keg.

Bismarck moved immediately to protect Germany from reprisal. In 1879 he concluded the Dual Alliance with Austria-Hungary, a defensive military pact. The Russians, sensing their isolation, responded in 1881 by agreeing to a mutual-security pact with Germany. Not only did this ease Russia's fears of encirclement, but it also gave Germany a measure of security by reducing the possibility of a joint attack by France and Russia. Bismarck had successfully played off Austria and Russia.

Two additional treaties closed the circle of Bismarck's diplomatic policy. In 1882 the Triple Alliance drew Italy into a defensive agreement with Germany and Austria. Finally, in 1887 Bismarck secretly negotiated the Reinsurance Treaty with Russia, guaranteeing neutrality by one power if the other were attacked. Thus Russia did not have to worry about Germany in the event of a war with Austria, while Germany no longer feared what Russia would do in case of a war with France. Bismarck could now be confident that German interests were protected—at least as long as he managed German affairs.

The Triple Entente

When Kaiser William II forced Bismarck into retirement in 1890, German foreign policy changed drastically. The new emperor rejected the necessity of an alliance with Russia and friendship with Britain, two vital premises of Bismarck's diplomacy. Convinced that Austria was Germany's natural ally, William refused Russian requests to renew the Reinsurance Treaty. The inevitable happened: in 1894 France and Russia signed a defensive military agreement that created the "nightmare alliance" Bismarck had dreaded.

Britain had remained aloof from Continental alliances, adhering instead to its traditional "balance of power" policy. But the kaiser, who resented Britain's preeminent world position, was determined to raise German prestige by winning colonial territories and brandishing German power. Britain, whose industrial growth had fallen behind Germany's, grew alarmed at the kaiser's hostility. Abandoning Bismarck's opposition to imperial conquest, William attempted to block the consolidation of British interests in Africa and in 1896 enraged London by expressing pro-Boer sentiments. Between 1898 and 1900 British security interests were again put at risk when Germany began constructing a powerful fleet that challenged Britain's goal of maintaining a two-to-one margin over Germany's naval forces.

German aggressiveness forced Britain to end its diplomatic isolation. An Anglo-Japanese agreement in 1902 was followed two years later by the Entente Cordiale ("friendly understanding") with France, which settled colonial disputes between the two nations. France agreed to a British sphere of influence in Egypt in return for French predominance in Morocco. Outraged by this, Kaiser William visited Tangier to support Moroccan independence. The Algeciras conference of 1906 affirmed the Entente agreements, rebuffing Germany.

In 1906, in the wake of the Moroccan crisis, the British launched the first of a series of battleships known as dreadnaughts, with greater range, speed, and firepower than any previous type of military vessel. The next year the Germans followed suit, unleashing a costly naval race between the two powers. Tensions increased as German plans to construct a Berlin-to-Baghdad railroad made Britain, France, and Russia uneasy over their interests in the Middle East. Encouraged by the French, Russia and Britain negotiated a treaty in 1907 that settled colonial rivalries in Tibet, Afghanistan, and Iran and, like the Entente Cordiale, made possible closer cooperation in Europe.

In the 20 years after Bismarck's retirement, Europe's great powers had aligned themselves into two blocs. Germany, Austria, and Italy were bound by the terms of the Triple Alliance, while Britain, France, and Russia were tied less formally by treaties that together formed a Triple Entente. Separating these military and diplomatic blocs was a pattern of growing hostility. Disputes between members of the rival blocs heightened tensions and made the alliance systems more rigid, for the fear of being left without the protection of friends led nations to support their partners, regardless of the merits of the issue. The most dangerous consequence of this development was that in times of crisis the alliances limited the options available to each power.

The Arms Race

Even before the division of Europe into opposing blocs, firms such as Krupp in Germany, Schneider in France, and Armstrong-Whitworth in Britain reaped enormous profits from the sale of weapons and exercised great influence on the defense policies of their governments. International rivalries over colonies and markets stimulated armaments industries and were used to justify huge military expenditures. French per capita arms spending more than doubled between 1870 and 1914, while Germany's increased more than sixfold. By the eve of World War I both countries were spending almost 5 percent of their national income on weapons.

Improvements in weapons advanced rapidly, yet the nature of technological development made permanent advantage impossible. Reinforced concrete and steel alloys improved defensive systems. Nevertheless, the enormous firepower of heavy artillery—especially long-range howitzers—and more powerful explosives made impregnable fortresses a thing of the past. The British dreadnaughts, designed to revolutionize sea warfare, were mounted with ten 12-inch guns, each capable of hurling an 850-pound shell 10 miles. But the thick armor plating and turbine engines of the dreadnaughts were vulnerable to enemy guns as well as to torpedoes from newly developed submarines and destroyers. Military planners were convinced that the outcome of warfare on land and sea would be determined by artillery.

Despite the technology, infantry soldiers were the basis of war strategy. By 1874 all of the great powers except Britain had introduced compulsory military service. France and Germany doubled their standing armies between 1870 and 1914, each keeping almost half a million men under arms in peacetime. The function of the infantry was modified in the 1880s with the introduction of the magazine rifle and the machine gun, which gave great advantage to defensive positions and guaranteed huge casualties to attacking armies. Despite these changes, European tactics were still based on the Prussian campaigns of 1866 and 1870, with their emphasis on speed, mobility, and surprise. Military plans, based on elaborate transportation networks and exact timetables, contributed to the possibility of war, for generals insisted on rapid mobilization during international crises.

Such was the case with the Schlieffen Plan, worked out

in 1905 by the German general staff. Based on the likelihood of a two-front war against France and Russia, the strategy assumed that the Russians would take longer to mobilize than the French. Hence, Schlieffen proposed that while Germany remained on the defensive against Russia, two armies—a powerful one sweeping through Luxembourg and Belgium and a weaker force moving from the south to lure the French away from the real attack—would swing rapidly around a central "hinge" and crush the French in a giant pincer. Having defeated France, the Germans could then concentrate their military strength against Russia.

With mass conscription came the introduction of the general staff, also based on the German model, and the growing prestige of a professional officer caste. Although strongest in Germany, the link between the landed nobility and the military command was present in every country. Their aristocratic lineage gave high-ranking officers special access to and influence over their sovereigns, even in representative governments, while their conservative outlook in domestic politics weakened the position of liberal civilians in government circles.

Government propaganda, the sensationalism of the press, and the nationalism imbued in citizens by universal elementary education conditioned the public to conscription and the high cost of armaments. Compulsory military training in turn convinced the public to accept the possibility of war.

Europe on the Brink

Relations between the Triple Alliance and the Entente deteriorated as one international crisis succeeded another. The Austro-Russian struggle for hegemony stirred nationalist fervor in the Balkans, where Serbian nationalists sought to create a united Slavic state and looked to Russia—the Slavic "big brother"—for support. Austria-Hungary, which regarded Slavic nationalism as a threat to its multinational empire, opposed Serbia. These forces came to a head in 1908 when Austria attempted to prevent Serbian expansion to the Adriatic Sea by annexing Bosnia and Herzegovina. The angry Serbs, who had hoped to incorporate Bosnia into their greater Slavic state, could do little without Russia, which felt too weak to respond in the face of British and Austrian pressure.

European aggression speeded the disintegration of the Ottoman Empire. In 1911 the kaiser dispatched the *Panther* gunboat to the Moroccan port of Agadir under the guise of protecting German nationals, but his real purpose was to challenge French and British domination in Africa. The crisis dissipated when the French agreed to cede part of the Congo to Germany, but it had the effect of alarming British opinion and solidifying the Anglo-French Entente. Later that year Italy went to war against the Ottoman Empire and wrested Libya from the Turks.

Encouraged by these events, the Balkan states attacked Turkey in 1912. The Balkan League, consisting of Serbia, Bulgaria, Greece, and Montenegro, easily defeated the Turks. Bulgaria emerged with the lion's share of the spoils. Austria intervened again to prevent the Serbs from gaining access to the Adriatic Sea, and when Russia protested, an international conference resolved the dispute by creating the state of Albania and compensating Serbia with inland territory. No one was satisfied. A month later, in June 1913, a second Balkan war erupted in which Serbia, Romania, Greece, and Turkey stripped Bulgaria of many of its territorial gains.

The Serbs, who had now doubled the size of their country, reoccupied parts of Albania, but their Russian protectors again failed to back them when an Austrian ultimatum forced their withdrawal. In fact, both Vienna and St. Petersburg remained deeply anxious. Throughout 1912 and 1913, the Austrians were bitterly critical of Germany, to whose lack of support they attributed Serbia's expansion. The Russians simultaneously blamed Britain for having prevented Serbia from gaining access to the sea. On both sides an uneasy feeling prevailed that neither the Triple Alliance nor the Entente could survive further internal tensions.

Sarajevo: The Failure of Diplomacy

On June 28, 1914, three students assassinated Archduke Franz Ferdinand (1863–1914), nephew of the emperor of Austria-Hungary and heir to the throne, while he attended military maneuvers in Bosnia. The three terrorists—members of Young Bosnia, a Slavic nationalist group—had been trained by Serbian army officers in a secret organization called Unity or Death (also known as the Black Hand). The Austrians did not know that Serbian cabinet members had been aware of the plot for some weeks, although they had not approved of it. Nevertheless, the Austrians expressed outrage and accused Serbian officials of complicity in the assassination. Some officials pushed for quick military action, hoping to crush Serbia permanently. The danger lay in the probability that conflict with Serbia would spark Russian intervention. Austria thus sought the support of Germany before acting.

In response, Kaiser William gave Austria-Hungary a "blank check" on July 5—that is, clear assurance of military support, along with advice to strike while world opinion was still hostile to Serbia. His chancellor, Theobald von Bethmann-Hollweg, acknowledged the risk of a general European war but believed that decisive Austrian action supported by Germany would deter Russia. Britain, he assumed, would not intervene. On July 23 Austria presented Serbia with a stiff ultimatum, including a demand that Austria be permitted to hunt for Franz Ferdinand's assassins on Serbian territory. Although Belgrade's reply

One of the conspirators responsible for the assassination of Archduke Franz Ferdinand is shown here being taken into police custody. [Granger Collection]

was conciliatory, the Serbians refused to accept this provision, which would have undermined their independence. On July 28 Austria declared war on Serbia.

When a reluctant Tsar Nicholas II ordered partial Russian mobilization on July 30, General Helmuth von Moltke, the kaiser's chief of staff, appealed for an immediate German mobilization in order to put the Schlieffen Plan into operation. Bethmann-Hollweg belatedly tried to persuade the Austrians to negotiate, to no avail. The Austrians announced mobilization against Russia on July 31, and Nicholas responded in kind. The Germans immediately demanded that the tsar pull back, but before he could reply, Germany declared war on Russia on August 1.

The elaborate diplomatic calculations continued to go awry. On August 2 the German ambassador in Brussels delivered an ultimatum demanding free passage through Belgian territory, presaging a preemptive strike against France. The British foreign secretary, Sir Edward Grey (1862–1933), intimated to Berlin that a violation of the international treaty guaranteeing Belgian neutrality would be regarded as a serious matter, but Bethmann-Hollweg ridiculed the idea that Britain would fight over "a scrap of paper." Two days later Germany declared war on Belgium and France and set the Schlieffen Plan in motion. On August 4 Britain declared war on Germany. "The lamps are going out all over Europe," Grey is supposed to have said, and "we shall not see them lit again in our life-time."[1]

The Ordeal of the West

Most countries greeted the coming of war with relief and even enthusiasm, and almost no one thought it would last for very long. Within a few weeks, however, these expectations proved illusory. Europe found itself locked in a prolonged ordeal that brought unprecedented death and destruction.

War of Attrition

The rapid war of movement and assault anticipated by military planners turned into a bloody stalemate almost at once. The German armies crossed into Belgium on August 4, but unexpected resistance and last-minute changes in strategy threw off their timetable. By September they advanced to within 25 miles of Paris, but the French halted them at the Marne River and forced retreat. With the Schlieffen Plan in shambles, the Anglo-French allies and Germany then tried to outflank each other; the line of battle soon reached from the Swiss border to the sea.

Once the Germans failed to strike a death blow against France, their dream of a rapid victory vanished. Instead, the equally matched combatants now faced each other in a war in which defense proved stronger than attack. On either side of the front, the combatants dug hundreds of miles of trenches, protected by barbed wire, land mines, and machine guns, in which millions of infantry soldiers lived and died. After preparatory artillery barrages, soldiers were ordered to charge the enemy trenches and cross the "no man's land" that separated them, only to be cut down by deadly machine gun fire and artillery. The first four months of fighting alone resulted in 1,640,000 casualties, yet after the first battle of the Marne the front line hardly moved. Generals clung stubbornly to the same tactics for 3½ years, squandering the lives of their men. The conflict had become a war of attrition in which the

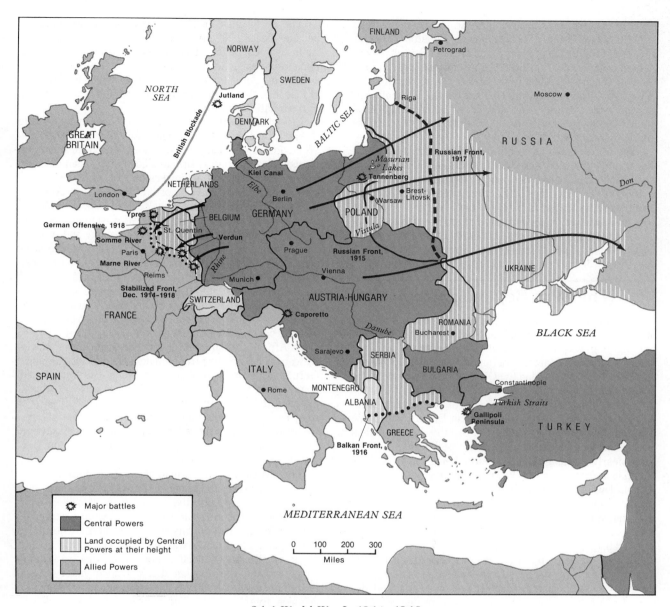

34.1 World War I, 1914–1918

infliction of casualties rather than the capture of terrain became the measure of success.

The Eastern Front and Italian Intervention

Conditions were far different on the eastern front, where men and supplies had to move over vast distances. In August the Russians won unexpected victories by moving two separate armies deep into East Prussia. The Germans panicked and withdrew four divisions from Belgium, while the kaiser put the retired general Paul von Hindenburg (1847–1934) in charge of operations and made the major general Erich Ludendorff (1865–1937) his chief of staff. By dealing separately with each of the Russian armies Hindenburg and Ludendorff won major victories at Tannenberg and the Masurian Lakes, and by mid-September the Russians had lost 250,000 men.

Russia fared better against the Austrians, overrunning Galicia and driving into Hungary. The Austrians suffered further setbacks in the Balkans, where the Serbs twice repelled their armies. But Russian fortunes declined with the entrance of Turkey into the war on the side of the

Central Powers, for the closing of the Dardanelles straits cut Russia off from critical supplies. Winston Churchill (1874–1965), Britain's First Lord of the Admiralty, conceived a daring plan to force the straits open, but a joint Anglo-French fleet failed to break through in March 1915. This effort was followed by landings on the Gallipoli peninsula, which were commanded by Mustapha Kemal (1881–1938), the future dictator of Turkey. By January the British had withdrawn.

The war widened further in 1915. The Germans struck, advancing some 200 miles against Russia, inflicting more than 2 million casualties and capturing or destroying almost a third of its industries. Allied reverses on the eastern front were mitigated in part by Italy's entrance into the war in May in return for promises of territory on the Italo-Austrian border and on the Dalmatian coast. In September, Bulgaria joined Germany and Austria.

The War Beyond Europe

Although military activity beyond Europe was of little importance to the outcome of the war, in the Middle East the fighting was to have a direct bearing on postwar events. Arab nationalists meeting in Paris in 1913 had insisted on autonomy within the Ottoman Empire, but during World War I the British deliberately encouraged the Arabs to revolt, thus foiling Turkish efforts to mobilize them against the Allies. When the Ottoman Empire joined the Central Powers in November 1914, the British Indian army sent an expeditionary force to the Persian Gulf and Iraq, nearly reaching Baghdad before being driven back by Turkish forces. Another Indian force guarded the Suez Canal. During the Gallipoli and Dardenelles campaigns, British diplomats pledged to support an Arab revolt and gained the cooperation of Abdul-Aziz ibn-Saud (1880–1953), the sultan who ruled the Nejd region of south-central Arabia.

British promises to the Arabs were designed to help the war effort, not to bring independence to the region. In 1916 Hussein ibn-Ali (1856–1931), a proclaimed descendant of the prophet Muhammad and protector of the holy city of Mecca, instigated a revolt against the Turks, frustrating efforts to launch a holy war against the Allies. With British approval he declared himself king of the Arabs, claiming control over a vast area stretching from the Hejaz along the Red Sea to the Persian Gulf. That same year the British and French concluded the Sykes-Picot Agreement, which divided much of the region into spheres of influence; France would get Syria and Lebanon while Britain obtained Iraq and Palestine. Throughout 1917 and 1918, T. E. Lawrence (1888–1935), a British archaeologist and soldier—later known as Lawrence of Arabia—assisted Prince Faisal (1885–1933), Hussein's son, who commanded the Arab forces that seized Damascus and Jerusalem.

The dual nature of British policy in the Middle East became clear in November 1917 when Foreign Secretary Arthur James Balfour formally supported Zionist aspirations for a Jewish homeland in Palestine. The Balfour Declaration did not specifically promise Jewish control over all of Palestine, but it contradicted other statements on behalf of Arab nationalist interests.

Elsewhere in the world the war posed a long-range threat rather than an immediate military danger for the West, for Britain and the Dominions feared Japanese expansionism. Allied with Britain since 1902, Japan declared war against the Central Powers in 1914 and swept over the German Pacific islands north of the equator. Australia occupied New Guinea and New Zealand took German Samoa in order to forestall Japanese expansion in the South Pacific. China declared war against Germany and Austria-Hungary only in 1917, but a 200,000-man Chinese labor batallion served with the Allies in Europe. Yet the Japanese seized the German holdings in China's Shantung province and presented China with the infamous Twenty-one Demands (see Chapters 33 and 35). Unlike China or India, Japan took no part in the war in the West beyond sending several destroyers.

In Africa, British colonial armies, made up of Indian, African, and Afrikaner troops, had little difficulty in taking German Togoland and Southwest Africa. But the German commander in East Africa, Paul von Lettow-Vorbeck, matched the daring exploits of T. E. Lawrence in organizing native resistance and conducting guerrilla warfare. He stopped an assault led by the South African general Jan Smuts and invaded Kenya, successfully defending German East Africa until the end of the war.

The British feared German attempts to foment rebellion in Afghanistan and Japanese propaganda in India, but, with minor exceptions, the Indian army remained loyal. More than a million Indian troops and support personnel fought with the British army in France and elsewhere, and India was notified that it was automatically at war as part of the empire. Most Indian nationalists, including Gandhi, supported the war, hoping that a British victory would hasten India's freedom. Yet the contributions made by the colonies, together with Allied promises of "liberation" both in the Middle East and in the German possessions, raised questions about the future.

Agony on the Western Front

In 1916 and 1917 the killing on the western front intensified. In February 1916 the Germans massed their forces for an assault against Verdun, hoping the French would make a costly defense. They were not disappointed. On the first day of the battle the Germans fired about 1 million artillery shells, and when the siege was over months later, 700,000 French and German soldiers were dead. Verdun held, but the bloodletting left deep scars on France. Oblivi-

◎ The Trauma of Trench Warfare ◎

As millions of young men poured into the trenches during World War I, the unimagined horrors of modern warfare crushed both the values and the optimism of a generation of Europeans. Here two British soldiers describe their experiences during the battle of the Somme in the summer of 1916.

There was a terrific smell. It was so awful it nearly poisoned you. A smell of rotten flesh. The old German front line was covered with bodies—they were seven and eight deep and they had all gone black. The smell! These people had been laying since the first of July. Wicked it was! Colonel Pinney got hold of some stretchers and our job was to put the bodies on them and, with a man at each end, we *threw* them into that crater. There must have been over a thousand bodies there. I don't know how many we buried. I'll never forget that sight. Bodies all over the place. I'll never forget it. I was only eighteen, but I thought, "There's something wrong here!"

As far as you could see there were all these bodies lying there—literally thousands of them. . . . Some without legs, some were legs without bodies, arms without bodies. A terrible sight. . . . It didn't seem possible. It didn't get inside me or scare me, but it just made me wonder that these could have been men. It made me wonder what it was all about. And far away in the distance we could see nothing but a line of bursting shells. It was continuous. You wouldn't have thought that anybody could have existed in it, it was so terrific. And yet we knew we were going up into it, with not an earthly chance.

Source: L. Macdonald, *Somme* (London: Michael Joseph, 1983), pp. 113–114.

ous to the lessons of Verdun, the British embarked on an offensive at the Somme River in June. Despite a massive preliminary bombardment, 60,000 British soldiers were cut down the first day. The British introduced primitive tanks into the battle with minimal effect, and by November this offensive too was over with little result but slaughter—600,000 British and French and 500,000 German soldiers had been killed or wounded.

In the spring of 1917 the Allies suffered a major blow in the east. On March 12 St. Petersburg erupted in revolution, and three days later Tsar Nicholas abdicated. While awaiting what they now regarded as an inevitable Russian defeat, the Germans retired behind the Hindenburg Line, a fortified defensive position in the west. The French vainly attacked it in April, suffering 250,000 casualties. From July to November the British fought the Germans at Ypres in the fields of Flanders, despite the new horrors of poison gas. The British suffered another 300,000 casualties.

Europeans could hardly grasp the fearful toll that the fighting had taken—more than 2.5 million dead and wounded alone in the four major western engagements of 1916 and 1917. The enthusiasm of 1914 turned to shock and a sense that civilization had reached the point of collapse. "The higher civilization rises," observed a German general, "the viler man becomes."[2] Churchill, writing

about the war a few years later, was equally bleak: "When all was over, Torture and Cannibalism were the only two expedients that the civilized, scientific, Christian States had been able to deny themselves: and these were of doubtful utility."[3]

The Social Consequences of Total War

The futility of the war brought opposition and sometimes revolt. During the spring 1917 offensive in Champagne, some French units had refused to leave the trenches, and the Russian army was rife with mutiny long before the revolution. The shock of the war also spread defeatism among civilians. In Turin, Italian socialists staged an abortive uprising, and in July the German Reichstag passed a peace resolution.

The collapse of morale on both sides raised serious concerns about the home front, for in a war of such gigantic proportions, industrial production was as important as front-line fighting. Attrition created huge shortages not only of manpower but also of food, clothing, and munitions. To cope with the economic and political strains, leaders formed cabinets of national unity, representing in some cases even socialist parties. Governments instituted rationing, placed controls on prices and wages, restricted union activity, and set up planning boards to coordinate production of war matériel.

The trend toward the greater militarization of society that had begun in the late nineteenth century accelerated sharply. The military assumed more authority in civilian affairs, and governments imposed censorship on the press and suspended constitutional procedures. Official propaganda called for a "total" war effort that demanded the regimentation of civilian life. Soldiers and civilians were regarded as one in the struggle. To dehumanize the enemy, Allied propaganda spread stories of "Huns" committing barbaric atrocities in Belgium and northeastern France. As civilian morale fell in the face of mounting casualties at the front, propaganda increased the stakes in victory so as to justify the enormous sacrifices. Both sides claimed to be fighting not just for national defense but in the name of civilization and democracy.

The ceaseless demands of war resulted in full employment, an unprecedented situation that provided wages for women and the poor. Hundreds of thousands of women left the home for the factories, and by the end of the war they comprised more than a third of all industrial workers in most countries. Women also filled white-collar jobs ordinarily occupied by men. Their independence grew with their importance to the war effort, and they broke social customs that had previously restrained them in behavior and dress. Women also contributed to the war effort by serving as nurses, orderlies, and ambulance drivers. The huge number of casualties created a serious shortage of medical facilities and overwhelmed trained personnel, so that thousands of volunteers staffed field hospitals along with professional nurses. The primitive conditions under which they worked exposed these women not only to infection and disease but also to the dangers of artillery bombardment and the threat of capture, for nursing and Red Cross units were often immediately behind the front.

The most famous nurse of the war was Edith Cavell (1865–1915), a Briton in charge of a Red Cross station in Belgium. She remained at her post to care for the wounded while Germans overran the area. When they learned that she was also helping captured British and French soldiers to escape, they shot her for espionage. Although her nonnursing activities had removed her from the protection of international law, Allied propaganda made her death a symbol of enemy "barbarism."

Class distinctions tended to break down under the impact of the common struggle for survival. Aristocratic ladies volunteered for nursing duties along with working women, and union leaders worked side by side with industrialists on government boards. Moreover, although the enlisted ranks of the armies were filled overwhelmingly with workers and peasants, young aristocrats and educated middle-class men made up the lower officer corps. The dynamics of trench warfare, in which the junior officers led the charges over the top, meant that the upper classes actually spilled a larger proportion of their blood on the battlefields.

Total war targeted civilians as part of an overall military strategy that sought to break morale. German zeppelins dropped bombs over British cities, and Austrian artillery shelled Venice. More effective, however, were efforts to starve entire populations into submission through naval blockades. Britain and France continued to receive food and supplies from the United States and the British Empire, while Russia and the Central Powers, virtually cut off from overseas trade, felt the shortages acutely. Germany instituted rationing as early as 1915. During the bitter winter of 1916–1917, the German people suffered from hunger and cold, subsisting on turnips and synthetic products.

The British violated international agreements by interfering with neutral shipping to Germany. The Germans responded with a major innovation in naval warfare, the U-boat or submarine. To be effective, submarines had to fire on ships by surprise from below the surface, without being able to ascertain whether they were enemy or neutral vessels or whether they were carrying war contraband. Submarine warfare antagonized American opinion, especially after the sinking of a commercial liner, the *Lusitania*, in May 1915 with the loss of over 1,000 lives, 128 of them American. That summer U-boat commanders were given restricted orders.

American Intervention and the German Collapse

The submarine was a devastating weapon, sinking 750,000 tons of shipping in 1915 alone. After the stalemate of Verdun and the Somme, the Germans believed it might be decisive as well, despite the risk of bringing the United States into the war. Unrestricted submarine warfare was unleashed on February 1, 1917, and President Woodrow Wilson broke diplomatic relations with Germany two days later. Allied and neutral shipping losses more than doubled in 1917. The U-boats, together with German diplomatic intrigue, Allied propaganda, and the influence of American munitions manufacturers and other trading and banking interests, influenced Congress to declare war against Germany on April 6.

American supplies began to tip the balance in favor of the Allies, but before the end of 1917 they suffered two serious setbacks. In October the battle of Caporetto nearly knocked Italy out of the war. In March 1918 the new Bolshevik government in Russia signed the Treaty of Brest-Litovsk with Germany, taking Russia out of the war. The events of 1917 were partially offset when Wilson seized the political initiative by announcing American commitment to war aims he hoped would bring "peace without victory." His Fourteen Points, issued in January 1918, included a proposal to end secret diplomacy, freedom of the seas, unimpeded international trade, disarmament, self-determination for the peoples of eastern Europe, the adjustment of imperial claims based on the interests of colonial peoples as well as those of the powers, and the creation of an international peacekeeping organization, the League of Nations.

The last year of the war saw a desperate effort by the Germans to win a military victory. In March, Ludendorff regrouped German troops from the former Russian front and made a massive assault against France, driving once again to the Marne River but failing to break through the Allied lines. On July 18 the Allies, reinforced by some 300,000 American soldiers, began their counteroffensive. By the end of September the German armies, having lost another million men, were in retreat, and civilian morale was on the point of collapse. Convinced that victory was impossible, Ludendorff advised the kaiser to sue for peace.

Germany's request for an armistice on the basis of the Fourteen Points met with a stiff response from Wilson, who demanded that the Germans first make political reforms. In the meantime, Bulgaria, Turkey, and Austria-Hungary collapsed. On November 3 the German fleet at the port of Kiel mutinied, setting off revolutions in Munich and Berlin. Six days later socialists proclaimed a republic in the capital, and the kaiser abdicated. The armistice, signed on November 11, officially ended the fighting.

The Reordering of Europe

At the close of the Great War people knew that Europe would never be the same. Thirty-four nations had been engaged in the struggle. Vast tracts of once productive land lay in ruins, and the populations of cities such as Berlin and Vienna were at the edge of starvation. More than 10 million fighting men and at least 1 million civilians had been killed and 20 million wounded. The war had also bled Europe's financial resources of $3.3 billion, turning a continent that had once exported huge amounts of capital into a debtor to the United States. Disillusioned by the experience of total war, Europeans were hopeful that the peace would bring a better world.

The Paris Peace Conference

In January 1919 representatives from 27 victorious nations assembled in Paris to draw up peace treaties with five vanquished states—Germany, Austria, Hungary, Bulgaria, and Turkey. Two reasons accounted for the air of expectancy that surrounded the conference. First, Wilson's presence suggested that the treaties would be equitable, since both sides had accepted his Fourteen Points as the basis for peace. Second, each nation brought a delegation of technical experts who promised to arrange the

The leaders of the principal Allied powers gather at the Paris peace conference (1919): (left to right) David Lloyd George, Vittorio E. Orlando, Georges Clemenceau, and Woodrow Wilson. [Brown Brothers]

settlements according to objective, "scientific" principles instead of old-fashioned power politics.

Like the Congress of Vienna 100 years earlier, the Paris peace conference was an impressive gathering of national leaders. Britain was represented by its prime minister, the Welsh Liberal David Lloyd George (1863–1945); France by the Republican premier, Georges Clemenceau (1841–1929); and Italy by its prime minister, Vittorio E. Orlando (1860–1952). Most of the major decisions were the result of negotiations among the "Big Three," Wilson, Lloyd George, and Clemenceau.

Operating in the shadow of the Bolshevik revolution in Russia and the fear that its example would spread, the Big Three excluded Lenin's government from the deliberations. Moreover, public opinion among the victors demanded harsh peace terms for the defeated enemy. Unlike the Congress of Vienna, where France was accorded full diplomatic representation, Germany was permitted to have only observers at the conference and to await terms dictated by the Allied Powers.

The Treaty of Versailles

The most pressing problem was what to do with Germany. Three issues were paramount: French insistence on future security against Germany, the disposition of German colonies, and the reparations the Germans would pay. Because France had twice been invaded within 50 years, Clemenceau demanded the creation of a separate buffer state in the Rhineland between his country and Germany. Wilson objected that such a plan would violate the principle of self-determination, and his debate with Clemenceau became so acrimonious that the American president threatened to leave the conference. In the end, Clemenceau compromised: the Rhineland would be demilitarized and occupied by Allied troops for 15 years, during which time the coal-rich Saar region was to be administered by the League of Nations for the economic benefit of France and Britain, and the United States promised to conclude a defensive military alliance with France.

France, Britain, and Japan all coveted German colonies. The "mandate principle" offered a solution under which these powers were each given control over some of the territories under League supervision, with the object of preparing them for independence. The principle did not apply, however, to China's Shantung peninsula, which came under full Japanese authority. Reparations were another contentious issue. Britain and France insisted that Germany be responsible for all damage done to civilians, including pensions and family support. As a result, the Allies drafted Article 231, which held German aggression responsible for the war. The exact amount was fixed two years later at the staggering sum of $33 billion.

John Maynard Keynes (1883–1946), an economist attached to the British delegation, believed the peace treaty put Germany in an untenable position that spelled future disaster. In *The Economic Consequences of the Peace* (1919) he argued that the enormous reparations anticipated were impossible in view of the other economic provisions of the treaty. Large amounts of German coal were allocated to France, many of Germany's ships were given to Britain, and billions of dollars of its foreign assets were confiscated. Territorial losses stripped Germany of half its iron mines and a fifth of its iron and steel industries. The treaty forced Germany to return Alsace and Lorraine to France; on its eastern borders, Germany ceded parts of East Prussia and Upper Silesia to a revived state of Poland, lost the city of Danzig to League control, and gave up territory to newly independent Czechoslovakia. *Anschluss*, or union, was forbidden between Germany and Austria.

Determined that Germany would be in no position to wage another aggressive war, the Allies reduced its army

◉ The War Guilt Principle ◉

The harsh treaty the Allies imposed on Germany at the Paris peace conference contained a unique principle that forced Germany to accept responsibility for having caused World War I. Article 231 of the Treaty of Versailles is known as the "war guilt clause."

The Allied and Associated Governments affirm and Germany accepts the responsibility of Germany and her allies for causing all the loss and damage to which the Allied and Associated Governments and their nationals have been subjected as a consequence of the war imposed upon them by the aggression of Germany and her allies.

Source: U.S. Congress, Senate, *Treaty of Peace with Germany*, 66th Cong., 1st sess., S. Doc. 49 (1919).

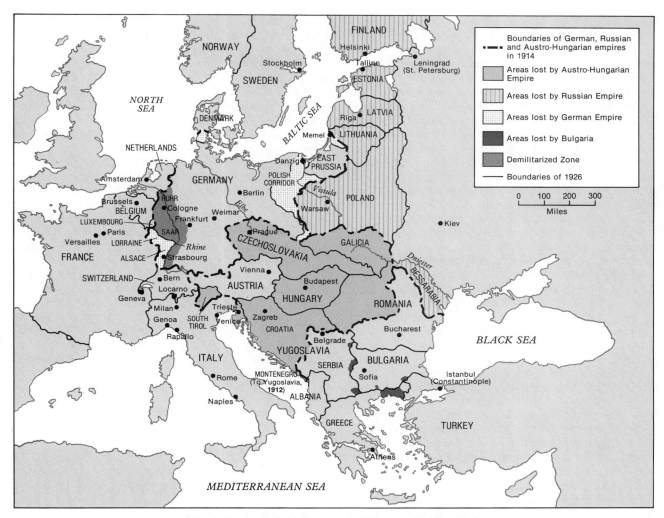

34.2 Territorial Settlements in Europe, 1919–1926

to a 100,000-man volunteer force and limited its navy to a handful of small ships. They also prohibited all offensive weapons, including submarines, airplanes and zeppelins, heavy artillery, tanks, and poison gas. Finally, the treaty provided for the trial of the former kaiser as a war criminal, but the Netherlands, to which he had fled, refused to extradite him. The threat of renewed war forced representatives of the new German government to sign the treaty on June 28, 1919.

The peace terms with Germany's allies were hardly less severe. Austria was reduced to a third of its former size, while Hungary was left with a fourth of its former territory. Bulgaria, too, lost land, and all three states had to reduce their armies. Turkey remained only with Asia Minor and a small strip of territory around Constantinople, and the Turkish straits were demilitarized and opened to international shipping.

The Search for Security

Wilson had insisted that permanent peace rested on the creation of an international body known as the League of Nations. The Covenant, or constitution, of the League was incorporated into each of the peace treaties. It provided for a system of "collective security" by which the League would encourage disarmament and prevent war by arbitrating disputes and applying economic sanctions. The Covenant also established a system of mandates by which the European powers assumed the right to rule a number of non-Western areas that they argued were incapable of self-government. Granting self-determination to some European states, such as Poland and Yugoslavia, while denying the same right to the colonized peoples of Asia, Africa, and the Pacific reflected racist assumptions. Because it had no armed force to coerce violators, the

League lacked the power to enforce its principles. Moreover, when Congress refused to ratify the Treaty of Versailles, the United States itself failed to join the organization; neither Germany nor the Soviet Union was to become a member for years.

France and Germany sought alternatives to the League of Nations to ensure their security. American withdrawal from European diplomatic affairs denied France the defensive treaty that Britain and the United States had promised. Consequently, France created a "little entente" by aligning itself with Czechoslovakia, Romania, and Yugoslavia, hoping thereby to encircle Germany on its eastern borders. Isolated from the community of nations, Germany made common cause with Soviet Russia, another outcast nation. In 1922 they signed the Treaty of Rapallo, opening diplomatic relations and pledging economic cooperation as well as secret military contacts.

France remained uneasy over German intentions, and when the Germans failed to meet their reparations quota in 1923, French and Belgian troops occupied the Ruhr Basin on the eastern bank of the Rhine. Passive resistance among Ruhr factory workers and miners and British and American protests eventually forced a withdrawal, but the fear and hatred between the nations remained deeply rooted.

In 1925 German Foreign Minister Gustav Stresemann (1878–1929) proposed that Germany, France, Britain, Italy, and Belgium guarantee the western European status quo. The result was the Locarno Pact, which relieved some of the international political tension. In 1926 Germany finally joined the League of Nations. In 1927 the French foreign minister, Aristide Briand (1862–1932), and the American secretary of state, Frank Kellogg (1856–1937), sponsored a treaty renouncing war as an instrument of national policy. The Kellogg-Briand Pact of 1928, eventually signed by 65 states, "outlawed" war.

Society and Culture: The Impact of War

A decade after World War I, José Ortega y Gasset (1883–1955), a Spanish philosopher, wrote, "Today, by the very fact that everything seems possible to us, we have a feeling that the worst of all is possible: retrogression, barbarism, decadence."[4] Ortega's irony revealed how deeply disturbed his generation had been by the war. Yet his pessimism makes little sense unless we remember that even as Europeans rebuilt their cities and mourned their dead, they were haunted by the memory of their former confidence in the superiority of their civilization. This explains why the West experienced a profound crisis of belief after 1919 despite the victory of the democracies and the return of peace.

Ultimately, Ortega's foreboding proved justified. Although European intellectual and cultural life in the postwar period was creative and varied, it was marked by a mood of anxiety. The sense of futility was particularly acute among the veterans who returned to a civilian society beset with political and economic problems and intent on getting back to "normalcy." To these dashed hopes was added the horror of modern warfare. The German author Erich Maria Remarque (1898–1970) captured the shock experienced by soldiers in two best-selling novels, *All Quiet on the Western Front* (1929) and *The Road Back* (1931). The mood of despair seemed to confirm the prewar intuitions of Nietzsche and Freud that civilized society was irrational and that humans were unable to control their "primitive" instincts. This atmosphere of skepticism stimulated a transformation of Western culture. A decade after the war's end, the "modern" temper of twentieth-century life had been established.

Distrust of established beliefs, uncertainty about the meaning of life, and anxiety about the future produced what the author Gertrude Stein (1874–1946) termed a "lost generation." The triumph of communism in Russia and the rise of fascism in the 1920s suggested a willingness to abandon democracy. Frustrated material expectations added to the disorientation, for the economic boom after 1919 proved to be only a prelude to the Great Depression.

Social Change and Economic Crisis

The impact of the war was felt differently in each country and class. Everywhere the status and power of the old nobility were seriously weakened, especially in the new states of eastern Europe. The aristocracy had been systematically eliminated in Russia after the Bolshevik revolution, and a large number of young British nobles had been killed in the war. Peasants had been conscripted into military service more heavily than any other class, so the toll in death and disablement among them was also high. After the war many peasants refused to go back to their villages and often formed the rank and file of militant veterans' groups in the cities. When they did go back to the countryside, they frequently led protest movements.

Postwar society in western Europe was predominantly urban. In France, the most agrarian of the industrialized nations, the percentage of the working population engaged in agriculture fell from one-half before 1914 to one-third by 1931. Nevertheless, the number of industrial workers remained fairly stable over the following decades as advances in technology and assembly-line processes made labor more productive. During the first years of the war severe labor shortages had produced higher wages and a modicum of prosperity for the working classes, but government controls and inflation eventually forced wages to lag behind prices, resulting in significant discontent. The support and cooperation socialist parties and unions gave to the war effort had conditioned many labor leaders to moderate policies. Some working-class leaders, however, reverted to more radical doctrines after the war, and many looked to the Russian Revolution for inspiration. As real wages rose between 1924 and 1929, particularly for the unskilled, worker discontent was once again mitigated, a trend reinforced by new social welfare measures in many countries.

The war affected the middle classes most severely. Greater educational opportunities and the growth of the service sector increased the number of white-collar workers, many of whom came from working-class families. The economic slump of the 1920s, however, slowed middle-class mobility. The pressure was particularly acute on the lower middle class, whose opportunities for advancement into managerial positions in the private sector shrank as the economy slowed. Inflation also limited the earning power of this group and threatened its status. The most extreme distress occurred in Germany, where by 1925 inflation had eaten up more than 50 percent of the capital held by the lower middle class. Retirees, widows, and others living on fixed incomes were hit especially hard, as were property owners whose incomes were frozen by rent regulations. Lower-middle-class earnings fell markedly in the 1920s, and millions of workers were forced back into the factories, where salaries equaled or exceeded those of white-collar employees. Hence the lower middle class felt squeezed between two groups: the wealthy capitalists, whose income was still increasing, and the workers from whose ranks many of them had risen. Lower-middle-class resentment of big business and labor often found political expression in radical right-wing groups.

The New Morality: Women, Work, and Sex

The middle class, which had experienced prewar optimism most fully, now found its values under assault. Wartime conditions disrupted social arrangements and family structures: husbands at the front, women in the factories, strangers crowding into the cities, and the uncertainty of survival had loosened the restrictions of bourgeois society and contributed to the breakdown of traditional morality. Psychological and social stress encouraged a new style of life that celebrated "liberation" from conventional behavior. In the 1920s Europeans were caught up in the spirit of the "jazz age," a name reflecting the popular perception that American life was more modern and less tradition-bound.

Public manifestations of the new morality appeared everywhere. Women's skirts were shorter and dresses more revealing, slinky adaptations of the "flapper" style

made famous in Prohibition America. Young people drank and smoked in public, bars and nightclubs proliferated, and dancing took on more expressive—and suggestive—forms. Motion pictures, perhaps the most popular mass entertainment of the period, created the cult of the "vamp," and the private lives of film stars were spread across the front pages of the popular press. The use of chaperons and arranged marriages declined sharply, while illegitimacy and divorce rates rose. Such changes produced a more open attitude toward sexual matters.

Social developments reflected the new morality. Greater tolerance toward sexual minorities evolved. Events once thought sensational, such as Oscar Wilde's trial in the 1890s, seemed quaint to Europeans of the 1920s who openly professed their differing sexual orientation. Paris and Berlin, the two centers of postwar avant-garde culture, were havens for artists, writers, and musicians that included homosexuals as well as American blacks. Gertrude Stein and Alice B. Toklas, the most famous lesbian couple of the period, presided over a brilliant artistic and literary scene in Paris. Sexual minorities still faced formidable obstacles to equality and acceptance, but the more tolerant attitudes of the 1920s brought the issue into the open.

The emancipation of women was another result of the social transformation. An earlier generation of feminist agitation had made important advances in raising the consciousness of women and calling public attention to their demands for equality. Yet despite the work of the middle-class suffragists and the socialist women's movement, Finland and Norway were the only Western nations in which women had won the right to vote before 1914.

Wartime labor shortages created a situation in which women made significant progress toward equality in the workplace. As women crowded into the munitions industries and the service sector, governments made propaganda appeals to them, thus raising expectations for change. Some nations granted women the right to vote: in 1918 the British Parliament extended suffrage to women over 30, and the next year both the United States and the new German republic gave the vote equally to men and women. Austria, Poland, and Czechoslovakia joined Belgium, the Netherlands, Sweden, and Denmark in following suit.

While these were crucial gains, the suffrage was not made universal in Spain, France, Switzerland, and Italy until after World War II. Moreover, in many countries marriage and property laws favoring husbands also remained largely intact. After 1919 more women gained access to educational opportunities and a wider range of jobs, although many were forced out of their wartime work by returning soldiers, and in practice some professions remained closed to women. Nor was progress in regard to the status of women and sexual minorities permanent, for serious setbacks occurred in the interwar years when right-wing regimes repressed both with renewed vigor.

⊚ Postwar Sexual Mores ⊚

In the decade after World War I, many aspects of nineteenth-century codes of social behavior were abandoned in the West as religious belief, defined gender roles, and public morality were consciously rejected by the "lost generation." Here Walter Lippmann (1889–1974), an American social critic, sees changes in the status of women and advances in birth control as the principal reasons for the freer sexual conduct that marked the 1920s.

Until quite recently the main conventions of sex were enforced first by the parents and then by the husband through their control over the life of the woman. The main conventions were: first, that she must not encourage or display any amorous inclinations except where there was practical certainty that the young man's intentions were serious; second, that when she was married to the young man she submitted to his embraces only because the Lord somehow failed to contrive a less vile method of perpetuating the species. All the minor conventions were subsidiary to these; the whole system was organized on the premise that procreation was the woman's only sanction for sexual intercourse. . . . The virtuous man, by popular standards, was one who before his marriage did not have sexual relations with a virtuous woman. . . . These conventions were not perfectly administered. But they were sufficiently well administered to remain the accepted conventions, honored even in the breach. It was possible, because of the way people lived, to administer them.

The woman lived a sheltered life. That is another way of saying that she lived under the constant inspection of her family. . . . She met young men under the zealous chaperonage of practically the whole community. No doubt, couples slipped away occasionally and more went on than was known or acknowledged. But even then there was a very powerful deterrent against an illicit relationship. This deterrent was the fear of pregnancy. That in the end made it almost certain that if a secret affair were consummated it could not be kept secret and that terrible penalties would be exacted. In the modern world effective chaperonage has become impracticable and the fear of pregnancy has been virtually eliminated by the very general knowledge of contraceptive methods.

The whole revolution in the field of sexual morals turns upon the fact that external control of the chastity of women is becoming impossible. . . .

For when conception could be prevented, there was an end to the theory that woman submits to the embrace of the male only for purposes of procreation. She had to be persuaded to cooperate, and no possible reason could be advanced except that the pleasure was reciprocal.

Source: W. Lippmann, *A Preface to Morals* (New York: Macmillan, 1929), pp. 286–291 passim.

❀
JOSEPHINE BAKER: AN AMERICAN IN PARIS

One of the most celebrated figures in Europe between the wars was the black American entertainer Josephine Baker. Born in St. Louis in 1906 to a black mother and a father reputedly of Spanish descent, Baker left school at the age of 8 to help support her family. While living in East St. Louis, she witnessed the race riots that broke out there in 1917, and the sight of white bands burning and killing with impunity left an indelible mark on her.

Baker's talent soon surfaced. She starred in basement musicals as a child and ran away with a vaudeville troupe at the age of 13. Four years later she appeared at Radio City Music Hall in New York in a musical featuring black performers titled, stereotypically, *Shuffle Along*. In 1925

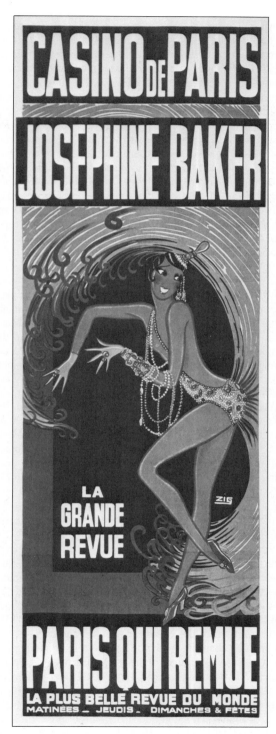

The blues singer and dancer Josephine Baker was a great celebrity in Paris during the years between the wars. [Granger Collection]

she went to Paris with a show called *La revue nègre,* which sought to capitalize on the topical vogue for jazz and for "exotic" black entertainers. The show failed and the company was stranded, but Baker caught on with the Folies Bergère, a club famous for its lavish sets and its scantily dressed performers. She created a sensation in her debut, in which she appeared clad only in a tutu made of rhinestone-studded bananas and three bracelets.

Baker's multiple talents as a singer and dancer, wed to a style of inimitable comic abandon, soon made her an international celebrity. Billed only as Josephine, the former slum child earned and spent enormous sums of money; mimicking her own exotic image, she strolled down the streets of Paris with a pet leopard. After a hugely successful world tour, she appeared in films opposite such French stars as Jean Gabin and ventured into light opera as well.

In 1937 Baker married a wealthy industrialist, Jean Lion, converted to Judaism, and became a French citizen. At the outbreak of World War II she joined the Red Cross and was later recruited into the French Resistance, gathering intelligence and also entertaining Free French forces. At the end of the war she was awarded France's highest decorations, the Croix de Guerre and the Légion d'Honneur, as well as the rosette of the Resistance. Baker's wide travel and her experience of poverty and discrimination led her in 1947 to found what she called a World Village at Les Milandes, her estate in southwestern France. Here, she and her second husband, Jo Bouillon, adopted a "rainbow family" of 12 children of all races and religions. She became a center of controversy in 1951 after she protested the refusal to serve her at the Stork Club in New York, but the National Association for the Advancement of Colored People (NAACP) named her its Woman of the Year. Baker began a crusade against segregation in her native country and succeeded in integrating theaters and nightclubs from Las Vegas to Miami. In 1963 she stood with Dr. Martin Luther King, Jr., at the climax of his march on Washington, D.C., and delivered an impassioned speech in front of the Lincoln Memorial.

Bankrupted finally by her debts at Les Milandes, Baker was provided a villa for herself and her children by Princess Grace of Monaco. In 1973 she triumphed at Carnegie Hall in another comeback tour, and despite failing health she repeated her success in Paris in a performance commemorating her fiftieth anniversary in France on April 10, 1975. Two days later, she died of a stroke.

On or off the stage, in or out of controversy, Josephine Baker was for half a century a uniquely vivid symbol of glamor, vitality, compassion, and commitment to the struggle for human equality. At the end of her life a film biography was planned, but, as she told reporters in a 1973 interview, "I would like to meet the woman who has the courage even to play my life story in a film. . . . I do not believe the woman exists who could have had the courage to have *lived* it as I have done." Certainly, few women of the twentieth century have combined careers and interests so daringly, served the human cause so passionately, and triumphed so indomitably.

Science, Literature, and Art

The postwar crisis of belief was especially acute among artists and writers, whose search for meaning led to creative ferment and experimentation. Proclaiming a "crisis of the mind," the French poet and critic Paul Valéry (1871–1945) articulated the state of anxiety and pessimism. His gloomy prognosis of the future was echoed by the German scholar Oswald Spengler (1880–1936). Spengler's immensely popular book *The Decline of the West* (1918) compared the development of Europe with the historical pattern of other civilizations. He argued that the West had entered a period of decay that could be reversed only by an authoritarian "Caesar" capable of imposing peace and order on a chaotic world. In a similar vein, Ortega y Gasset's *The Revolt of the Masses* (1930) warned that democratic society would result in the decline of education and culture.

Science offered no antidote to these laments. Building on the advances in physics at the turn of the century, the Danish physicist Niels Bohr (1885–1962) had formulated a theory of the atom in 1913 that attempted to reconcile Max Planck's quantum theory with Ernest Rutherford's view of atomic structure. By the mid-1920s, however, more complex ideas challenged Bohr's conclusions. The abstract language of differential equations took the place of concepts such as orbits, while Bohr and others revised their earlier hypotheses. In 1927 the German physicist Werner Heisenberg (born 1901) announced his "uncertainty principle": the behavior of atomic particles did not conform to the laws of cause and effect. The futility of attempting to find a comprehensive explanation of physical phenomena to replace the old Newtonian model became increasingly apparent.

Postwar developments in philosophy both reflected and reinforced the findings of science. Ludwig Wittgenstein (1889–1951), the most forceful advocate of the movement called logical empiricism, maintained that traditional ethical and metaphysical systems were meaningless because philosophy was nothing more than statements of fact clarified by logic. Logical positivists asserted that unless such concepts as "freedom" and "God" could be reduced to the precise language of mathematics and symbolic logic, they were meaningless. Similarly, existentialism, derived from the Danish philosopher Søren Kirkegaard (1813–1855) and later associated with the French philosophers Jean-Paul Sartre (1905–1980) and Albert Camus (1913–1960), presented an image of human helplessness and despair in the face of an existence devoid of meaning and a supreme being. Although the existentialists argued that humans exist without a predetermined purpose, they still asserted the necessity of responsible moral action.

In the world of literature, a no less startling revolution took place. Language and structure gave way to experiments that reflected new theories of the human personality as well as a conscious desire to break away from traditional forms. Authors extended the path opened by Marcel Proust (1871–1922), the French author of *Remembrance of Things Past*, with a new "stream of consciousness" of subjective experience. The year 1922 saw the publication of two influential works in this genre, *Ulysses* by the Irishman James Joyce (1882–1941) and *Jacob's Room* by the Englishwoman Virginia Woolf (1882–1941), followed in 1929 by *The Sound and the Fury* by the American William Faulkner (1897–1962). Each of these works probed the random thoughts and emotions of everyday consciousness and the obscure sources of human motivation that Freud had suggested.

D. H. Lawrence (1885–1930), whose controversial *Lady Chatterley's Lover* (1928) was censored for its explicit description of sexual desire, exemplified the postwar liberation from bourgeois mores. The German Thomas Mann (1875–1955), in *The Magic Mountain* (1924), evoked the collapse of meaning. Franz Kafka (1883–1924), a German Jew who lived in Prague, wrote frightening tales of nightmares that haunt the imagination, most notably *The Trial* (1925) and *The Castle* (1929).

While much of the literature of the period between the world wars was so innovative as to confuse and repel readers, the poetry of the Irishman William Butler Yeats (1865–1939) had a more direct appeal, for he combined traditional lyricism with a stoic view of the world. In a similar manner, the German Rainer Maria Rilke (1875–1926) attempted to evoke harmony with nature.

The Italian dramatist Luigi Pirandello (1867–1936) and the poet T. S. Eliot gave the most representative expression to the concerns of the period. In Pirandello's *Six Characters in Search of an Author* (1918), two sets of players, a family and a group of actors, appear on stage at the same time, with the family members asking actors to portray their roles. Both family and actors present versions of the truth peculiar to their own viewpoints. Much as in Einstein's theories, Pirandello's play offered relative truths from which the observer—or the audience—could choose. The absurdity of a world without fixed guideposts was a pervasive theme of interwar European culture. Eliot, in *The Waste Land* (1922), captured most poignantly the sense of desolation that so many creative thinkers of the postwar world felt. Eliot portrayed the spiritual emptiness of modern London and brought the mood of Symbolism into English poetry. He eventually resolved his personal crisis by joining the Anglican church.

The plastic arts, like literature, caught the spirit of the period. As early as 1915 the horrors of the war had begun to produce the deliberately nonsensical anti-art movement known as Dada (from the French meaning "hobbyhorse").

Other artists embraced a "return to order" that restored representational forms to painting so as to express human alienation and isolation. Surrealism drew from a variety of sources, including the new realism, prewar Cubism, Dadaism, and Freudian psychology. Surrealists such as Salvador Dalí and Giorgio de Chirico (1888–1978) created visions of a dream world and hallucinatory landscapes according to the irrational dictates of the subconscious. Other artists, such as Wassily Kandinsky (1866–1944) and Paul Klee (1879–1940), moved from their earlier Expressionist concerns toward greater abstraction, a trend that Piet Mondrian (1872–1944) brought to its extreme in rigidly nonobjective paintings.

Klee and Kandinsky taught at the Bauhaus, the most famous school of architecture and design in modern times. Founded in Weimar by the architect Walter Gropius (1883–1969), the Bauhaus sought to reconcile art with science and technology. It advanced an architectural style emphasizing functionalism, the use of glass and prefabricated concrete, and a rejection of ornamentation. The Bauhaus "international style," also championed by the French architect Le Corbusier (1887–1965) and the American Frank Lloyd Wright (1869–1959), testified to the triumph of the modern temper.

The generation that grew to maturity between 1890 and 1919 experienced the stress and excitement of living through the end of one historical era and the birth of another. The second half of the nineteenth century had been generally a period of material growth, optimism, and self-confidence. Science and technology had made life in the West more comfortable and had enabled the Western powers to impose their rule over much of the globe.

Many of the same factors that caused European expansion contributed, however, to a mounting crisis among the Western states. To a litany of old grievances were added new rivalries and competition for increasingly limited resources. While political leaders and capitalist entrepreneurs in one nation worked to outmaneuver their counterparts elsewhere, military officers and ideologues planned strategies of defense and domination. Once the crisis erupted, the West discovered that it had become much better at waging war than it had imagined. But unlike the wars of imperial conquest, the great European powers were more or less evenly matched, and the war consequently became an exercise in self-destruction.

The strain of total war had produced major change. Socialists shared power in wartime governments, and monarchies were overthrown in three states. In some countries the bloodletting decimated the ruling classes, while in others revolution eradicated or severely wounded traditional elites. Prewar social arrangements were further altered as a result of the massive conscription of peasants, the mobilization of women into the work force, and the disruption of family life.

The postwar age was a new world. Not only had the European map changed with the shifting of frontiers, but new states appeared on the ruins of old empires. Positive thinkers saw liberal democracy installed in central and eastern Europe for the first time; the more pessimistic questioned the chances for its survival. New forms of political extremism arose everywhere and, in Russia and Italy, soon came to power and threatened to spread. Nor did Europe's world supremacy survive much beyond the war. As the forces of nationalism took hold in the colonies, Western control of the subject peoples of Asia, Africa, and the Middle East weakened.

Science, literature, and art undermined the optimism of an earlier age, expressed the despair of a generation that had experienced shattering trauma, and forged new directions. Some intellectuals turned back to religion as a source of hope and comfort. Even Carl Jung rejected the teachings of Freud, his intellectual mentor, by advocating the therapeutic value of religious faith. In 1934, with the world in the throes of the Depression, the British historian Arnold Toynbee published the first of a series of volumes, entitled A Study of History, *which likened the development of civilizations to the biological process of life, with cycles of birth, growth, and decline. Unlike Spengler, however, Toynbee entertained the prospect that Western civilization might revive itself. In the search for meaning, others turned instead to political movements of protest and violence.*

Notes

1.   Viscount Grey of Fallodon, *Twenty-five Years, 1892–1916,* vol. 2 (New York: Stokes, 1925), p. 20.
2.   K. Robbins, *The First World War* (New York: Oxford University Press, 1984), p. 88.
3.   W. S. Churchill, *The World Crisis* (New York: Scribner, 1923), p. 3.
4.   J. Ortega y Gasset, *The Revolt of the Masses* (New York: Norton, 1957), p. 45.

Suggestions for Further Reading

Calder, N. *Einstein's Universe*. New York: Penguin Books, 1980.

Cantor, N. F., and Wertman, M. S., eds. *The History of Popular Culture Since 1815*. New York: Macmillan, 1968.

Ellenberger, H. F. *The Discovery of the Unconscious*. New York: Basic Books, 1970.

Fussell, P. *The Great War and Modern Memory*. New York: Oxford University Press, 1975.

Hughes, H. S. *Consciousness and Society: The Reorientation of European Social Thought, 1890–1930*. New York: Knopf, 1958.

Hughes, R. *The Shock of the New: Art and the Century of Change*. New York: Knopf, 1981.

Joll, J. *The Origins of the First World War*. London: Longman, 1984.

Kern, S. *The Culture of Time and Space, 1880–1918*. Cambridge, Mass.: Harvard University Press, 1983.

Lafore, L. *The Long Fuse: An Interpretation of the Origins of World War I*. Philadelphia: Lippincott, 1965.

Martin, M. W. *Futurist Art and Theory, 1909–1915*. Oxford: Clarendon Press, 1978.

Masur, G. *Prophets of Yesterday: Studies in European Culture, 1890–1914*. New York: Macmillan, 1961.

Mayer, A. J. *The Politics and Diplomacy of Peacemaking*. New York: Knopf, 1968.

Mosse, G. *The Culture of Western Europe*. Chicago: Rand McNally, 1969.

Pulzer, P. G. *The Rise of Political Anti-Semitism in Germany and Austria*. New York: Wiley, 1964.

Rewald, J. *The History of Impressionism*. New York: New York Graphic Society, 1980.

Robbins, K. *The First World War*. New York: Oxford University Press, 1984.

Sontag, R. V. *A Broken World*. New York: Harper & Row, 1971.

Stearns, P. N. *European Society in Upheaval: Social History Since 1800*. New York: Macmillan, 1967.

Williams, J. *The Other Battleground: The Home Fronts, Britain, France, and Germany, 1914–1918*. Chicago: Regnery, 1972.

Wohl, R. *The Generation of 1914*. Cambridge, Mass.: Harvard University Press, 1979.

The Human Image (II)

Since the primitive carvers of the Old Stone Age some 25,000 years ago, the human figure has been a central theme of artistic representation. Each civilization has accorded it a different emphasis, and artists of every culture have interpreted it from the aesthetic and religious points of view of their times and societies. Throughout much of the ancient period and during the first millennium A.D., the human figure served a number of important purposes, principally as the embodiment of religious themes, as a means of representing notions of beauty, or as a general commentary on the human condition.

While these functions continued to be served by the human image, important changes began to occur in the modern age. The sixteenth century saw a more secularized portrayal of the human figure in cultures as diverse as Europe and India, together with greater stylistic naturalism. At the same time, an exceptionally active artistic patronage began to emerge throughout much of the world. From the court of Ming China to the Mughal Empire in India and the Medici of Florence, rulers turned to painters and sculptors to produce memorials to the greatness of their regimes. Artists had, of course, always served political purposes, but in some cases rulers now developed a new respect for their creative powers. Figures such as Michelangelo achieved the stature of a culture hero in the late European Renaissance, a phenomenon enshrined in Giorgio Vasari's *Lives of the Painters*. Moreover, while patronage elsewhere in the world remained largely in the hands of rulers, in the West private parties began to commission artists to paint their portraits, so in European art the human figure increasingly represented the wider elite.

Mughal culture in India revealed the diversity of Muslim artistic response to figurative art. The court of Akbar and his successors was the center for the production of portrait miniatures, exquisitely delicate works that meticulously recorded their subjects in a narrative style. Unlike Persian miniatures of earlier times, with their fairy-tale decorations, these paintings display an almost unnerving detachment, as in the portrait of a courtier dying of opium addiction. They testify as much to the virtuosity of the artist as to the representation of an individual.

The emperors of Ming China treated artists with less respect than the court of Akbar: Chinese artists worked in palace workshops under tight supervision, a custom that drove many of the more progressive among them to flee the capital for the cities of the south. Free from the demands of the emperors, many painters of the period seem to have deliberately avoided the depiction

Dying Courtier, c. 1618. [Bodleian Library, Oxford]

of human beings, thus reinforcing the Chinese preference for landscapes.

During the Ch'ing dynasty (1644–1912) sculptors reverted to smaller-scale works in porcelain, exceeding the technical skill of earlier Chinese ceramists. A small white porcelain statute of Kuan-yin (the Chinese goddess of compassion) from the seventeenth century reveals the softness of form and the deeply humanized rendering of a goddess achieved in this medium. Large quantities of such ceramics were exported to Europe in the eighteenth century, and to this day the term *china* is used to describe fine ceramic wares, especially porcelain.

In contrast to the detached aestheticism of the Mughal image and the refined delicacy of later Chinese porcelains, artists of the early Edo period in Japan depicted the human figure as a means of preserving historic events. Chinese travelers observed that like their own painters, their Japanese neighbors tended to use scroll paintings to narrate events, often without philosophical meaning. A pair of painted Japanese screens from 1610 depict Westerners playing music. These are among the interesting works that show Portuguese and Dutch influences on Japanese painting as well as Japanese curiosity at the appearance of the "southern barbarians," as the Jesuit missionaries were known. The figures show little interest in the individuals represented but rather depict their customs, together with their costumes, so drab to Japanese eyes.

Toward the end of the seventeenth century the principal artistic medium in Japan shifted from scroll paint-

White porcelain statue of Kuan-yin, the Chinese goddess of compassion. [Barlow Gallery, University of Sussex, England]

Ivory portrait mask, Benin, West Africa. [Trustees of the British Museum]

ing to the woodblock print, which increasingly reflected the lives and tastes of an emerging commercial society. The woodblock allowed for the inexpensive reproduction and wide distribution of popular images and themes, such as the Kabuki actors so admired by the middle class.

When the Portuguese arrived at Benin, West Africa, in the fifteenth century, they found a rich and sophisticated kingdom, whose sculptural tradition may well have been related to that of the earlier civilization of the neighboring city of Ife. Climatic conditions in sub-Saharan Africa have not favored the survival of early wooden carvings, but sculptures made of ivory and metal reveal skillful renderings of the human form both realistically and in more abstract styles. A fifteenth-century zinc brass head is a delicate and idealized portrait of a king. Like the Japanese, Benin artists recorded the appearance of the newcomers, though in a much more symbolic and stylized form. An ivory portrait mask made for a ruler is topped by a crown composed of a band of long-haired, bearded Portuguese. The carver of this piece is more interested in

hairstyles than in dress but shows the same curiosity at strange customs and appearance. The ruler's portrait expresses elegance and power out of all proportion to its size.

No such record survives of the arrival of Westerners in the Americas. The art of the last Aztecs retains a strong element of decoration, as in the statues of deities carved to embellish temples. Yet the last period of Aztec art provides at least one outstanding example of an artist's use of the human figure to depict a primal event: the carving of a woman (perhaps a goddess) giving birth. The realism of the straining and the cold, damp look of the skin, produced by a careful working of the stone, are powerfully contrasted with the stylized miniature adult emerging from the womb.

From the sixteenth to the late nineteenth century European art was molded by the principles of the Italian Renaissance style, which flourished in the fifteenth and early sixteenth centuries. In their efforts to combine the splendors of classical antiquity with Christian values, Renaissance artists turned to the human figure as an image of the highest form of beauty. The face and body reemerged in a way that has been as important for the subsequent development of Western art as its appearance in ancient Greek art in the fifth century B.C. The Renaissance stress on mental and physical prowess and on the ability to control and change environment resulted in the triumph of the human figure as the chief focus of artistic representation in the Western world. Its treatment of the body may best be understood by examining two categories of painting and sculpture: the nude and portraiture.

After centuries of neglect, the female nude was reemphasized in European art in the late fifteenth century. Several of Sandro Botticelli's paintings, including his *Primavera,* were inspired by Hellenistic statuary, especially depictions of Venus, yet they also reflect the early Renaissance philosophical interest in ideal beauty. The classical Venus figure offered the artist an opportunity to depict the female nude, something that could not be done with the Virgin Mary, hitherto the most popular female subject in European art. Titian, the brilliant Venetian painter, displayed the female nude in the reclining form that would remain popular for centuries. His *Venus of Urbino,* vividly and sensuously colored, reflects the Renaissance artist's interest in rendering the human figure in a wholly natural condition, in contrast to the late medieval renditions of naked bodies, often shown at the Last Judgment or in hell. Donatello's famous statue of a virtually nude David is a particularly fine example of the combination of Christian and pagan elements in the Renaissance. The subject is a figure from the Old Testament, but the classical stance and the provocative nudity are Greek.

In portraiture Renaissance painters combined an interest in personality and the external world. Leonardo da Vinci's *The Last Supper* is both the re-creation of a famous biblical episode and a masterpiece of psychological study in which the viewer is implicitly invited to interpret the emotional responses of Christ's disciples through expressions and physical gestures when they learn one of them is a traitor. No less psychological were the late works of Donatello and Michelangelo, both of whom rejected external beauty in their quest to understand the depths of the penitent soul. A half century later, when the art of the late Renaissance had begun to give way to the sophisticated Mannerist style, the Florentine artist Bronzino brilliantly depicted the individualized Renaissance man in his *Portrait of a Young Man.* Here is an elegant, affected youth whose aloof demeanor, handsome face, and elegant hands reveal the haughty arrogance of an educated gentleman of high social position. While Mannerists such as Bronzino emphasized the neck and hands to convey a sense of grace, others, such as El Greco, distorted their figures to highlight the spiritual values of the Counter-Reformation.

Bronzino, *Portrait of a Young Man.* [Metropolitan Museum of Art, Bequest of Mrs. H. O. Havemeyer, 1929. The H. O. Havemeyer Collection.]

The baroque art of the seventeenth century in Europe was characterized by the expression of strong emotions, often religious, and a virtuoso technique. These characteristics can be seen in the works of the Italian sculptor Bernini. In his *St. Theresa in Ecstasy,* the body of the enraptured saint, her robes, and the cloud on which she rests combine to create the illusion of mystical drama. Unlike Michelangelo, Bernini uses the facial expression of his subject, suffused with a passion at once mystical and sensual, to enhance the dramatic effect. Rubens, the Flemish baroque master, concentrated on the human figure as the epitome of the animal body straining against the physical forces around it, whether in the form of soft, luminous female flesh or muscular, tanned male bodies. Unlike the bodies of El Greco or the late works of Donatello and Michelangelo, those of Rubens vividly represent the zest for physical life that was a dominant element of the baroque spirit.

A more traditional use of the human figure as political icon appears in Hyacinthe Rigaud's portrait of Louis XIV (see color insert 3), painted at a time when the grandeur of the baroque style was beginning to yield to the more graceful, intimate rococo. Much rococo art was more concerned with shallow aristocratic pastimes than the use of the human form to explore deeper values. However, a strong interest in portraiture, firmly rooted in the Renaissance, continued throughout the period, especially in Britain.

By the late eighteenth century a similar kind of style had developed in Japan, which depicted day-to-day human activities with a directness that marks a distinctly independent school. Much of earlier Japanese art was strongly influenced by Chinese traditions, but no Chinese artist would have produced prints of the kind known as *ukiyo-e* ("pictures of the floating world") or even recognized them as works of art. One print depicts the scene in a bathhouse, with both naked and dressed figures casually going about their business. In strong contrast to the imposing image of Louis XIV, these figures are given an intentional anonymity, expressing as they do the universality of human experience. This and other prints of the kind made a great impression in Europe when they were first seen there in the nineteenth century. Their influence was strongly felt by the Impressionists.

The later years of the Mughal court saw an increasing informality in the treatment of the human figure,

although eighteenth-century Indian art never approached the candor of the *ukiyo-e* prints. The paintings often deal with romantic themes, as in the depiction of a prince embracing his favorite mistress. Lacking the precision of earlier Mughal art, the work remains within the same framework of stylistic refinement, and a common human experience becomes transformed into an episode of elegance and grace: it hardly seems to matter that the faces of the women in the scene are virtually indistinguishable.

Most of the works discussed so far either commemorated an individual or used the human figure to symbolize universal human experience or values. These traditions continued during most of the nineteenth century. The austere Neoclassicism of Jacques-Louis David, as reflected in *The Death of Marat*, glorified the French Revolution. But by the end of the century Euro-

Detail from bathhouse scene, c. 1800, Japan. [Museum of Fine Arts, Boston; William Sturgis Bigelow Collection.]

Muhammad Yusuf al-Husaini, love scene, c. 1630. [Pierpont Morgan Library, New York]

pean artists had begun to employ human images to express anxiety about the state of their world. There are few more disturbing images of tension and neurosis than *The Scream,* by the Norwegian Edvard Munch, in which the distortions of the human body in the painting are reflected in the cosmic upheaval of land and sky.

The years preceding World War I produced traumatic changes throughout the world, in politics and society as well as in cultural life. Munch's attempt to unify figure and landscape to express a transcendent emotion characterized much of the art of the late nineteenth and early twentieth centuries in Europe. In many respects Munch's projection of human emotion onto landscape recalls fourteenth-century Christian art in Italy, but now devoid of religious context.

Years before Munch, the Frenchman Paul Cézanne had begun the effort among modern Western artists to reduce visual experience to simple, abstract forms. This movement was in turn influenced by European contact with the art of Asia, Africa, and Oceania. Western artists found universal messages in the highly stylized art forms of these regions, an impact that may be clearly seen in the paintings of Picasso and Gauguin and the sculptures of Constantin Brancusi. The brutally stylized representations of prostitutes in Picasso's *Les Demoiselles d'Avignon* caused a great scandal and presaged his even more radical experiments in abstraction a few years later, in which recognizable images disappeared altogether.

The so-called Expressionist style of Munch, which was taken up by German and Austrian artists shortly before World War I; the flat, abstracted style perfected by Picasso and his colleague Georges Braque and known as Cubism; and the wholly abstract canvases and watercolors of the Russian Wassily Kandinsky all foreshadowed a crisis in the representation of the human image in Western art. The cultural shock of World War I and the impact of Freudian psychology brought further distortions of the image in the form of Surrealism, a movement that dominated European art between the world wars. Seeking to penetrate psychological states, Surrealist art was, like Expressionism, an attempt to probe beyond the image into inner realms of feeling, and much of it was overtly erotic. But, although it was often accused of being obscure, Surrealism was also capable of powerful political statement, as in Salvador Dalí's *Soft Construction with Cooked Beans—Premonition of Civil War.*

At the same time, Soviet Russia and Nazi Germany were demanding a new official art that would represent their propaganda objectives—the depiction of happy and contented workers in the first case, racially pure Aryans in the second. Hitler banned all abstract or Expressionist art in the Third Reich, and in 1937 he organized a notorious exhibit of "degenerate" art,

Edvard Munch, *The Scream*, 1893. [Nasjonal-galleriet, Oslo]

which showed the work that had been purged from German museums. The exhibition backfired, as audiences streamed in not to mock but to admire some of the finest German painting of the century.

Some artists of the period, such as the British sculptor Henry Moore (1898—1986), continued to represent the human figure in simplified, monumental forms of great power (see color insert 4), and Picasso, the most protean and prolific painter of the human image in history, returned to it after World War I. The image was banished again when Abstract Expressionism became the dominant international style after World War II, only to return with the Pop Art of the 1960s. Pop Art, whose images were derived largely from advertising and comic strips, sought to satirize consumerism and both cinematic and political cults of personality, as in the portraits of Marilyn Monroe and Mao Tsetung (see color insert 4) by the American Andy Warhol (1928–1987). Pop Art was soon assimilated into a new style of "magic realism," which aimed for photographic illusion, while the former Abstract Expressionist Philip Guston (1913–1980) returned to the image with an effect at once comic and chilling, as in the disembodied head that rolls up an inclined plane in

Philip Guston, *Untitled*, 1980. [David McKee Inc./photo by Bevan Davies]

Untitled. More recently, the German Anselm Kiefer (born 1945) has turned to the long-disfavored genre of historical portraiture in his remarkable representations of German cultural history.

It is hardly surprising that the history of art has been marked by a continual recourse to the human figure as a source of expression and communication. The range of treatment reflects the diversity of human experience. Works have served religious, political, and aesthetic purposes, have documented events, and sometimes have tried to control them, as in fascist and Soviet art. Differences between cultures seem stylistic rather than reflective of profound divergences: the statue of an Egyptian pharaoh and the portraits of a European, Indian, Chinese, or African sovereign reflect a similar political aim, the exaltation and commemoration of the ruler. If anything seems unexpected, it is that at the end of the twentieth century, a period of unprecedented upheaval both in life and in the arts, naturalistic depictions of human beings continue to fascinate us. Such works suggest that the need to ''see ourselves as others see us'' remains constant.

Suggestions for Further Reading

Clark, K. *The Nude: A Study in Ideal Form.* Princeton, N.J.: Princeton University Press, 1956.

De Dilva, A., and Von Simson, O. *Man Through His Art,* vol. 6: *The Human Face.* New York: Graphic Society, 1968.

Garland, M. *The Changing Face of Beauty.* New York: Barrows, 1957.

Lee, S. *A History of Far Eastern Art.* New York: Abrams, 1974.

Man: Glory, Jest, and Riddle—A Survey of the Human Form Through the Ages. San Francisco: M. H. de Young Memorial Museum, California Palace of the Legion of Honor, and San Francisco Museum of Art, 1965.

Mayor, A. H. *Artists and Anatomy.* New York: Artist's Limited Edition, 1984.

Mode, H. *The Woman in Indian Art.* New York: McGraw-Hill, 1970.

Neumeyer, A. *The Search for Meaning in Modern Art,* trans. R. Angress. Englewood Cliffs, N.J.: Prentice-Hall, 1964.

Relouge, I. E., ed. *Masterpieces of Figure Painting.* New York: Viking, 1959.

Rowland, B. *The Art and Architecture of India.* Baltimore: Penguin Books, 1967.

Segal, M. *Painted Ladies: Models of the Great Artists.* New York: Stein & Day, 1972.

Selz, P. *New Images of Man.* New York: Museum of Modern Art, 1959.

Smart, A. *The Renaissance and Mannerism in Italy.* New York: Harcourt Brace Jovanovich, 1971.

Walker, J, *Portraits: 5,000 Years.* New York: Abrams, 1983.

Wentinck, C. *The Human Figure in Art from Prehistoric Times to the Present Day,* trans. E. Cooper. Wynnewood, Pa.: Livingston Publishing, 1970.

Willett, F. *African Art: An Introduction.* New York: Praeger, 1971.

Upheaval in Eurasia and the Middle East

The twentieth century has been characterized by rapid change, particularly in the transformation of the world's biggest countries, China, Russia, and India, and the similar transformation of the Middle East. Together the four regions hold half the world's population. In China and Russia this change has appropriately been called revolutionary, entailing not only the overthrow of old governments by violence and civil war but also a radical restructuring of social, economic, and political systems in a short period of concentrated effort. The upheavals in each country were engineered and directed by native Communist parties, which made use of mass support by workers and peasants,

Leon Trotsky ariving in Paris in 1929, an exile from the Bolshevik USSR he helped to create a decade earlier. ["L'Illustration"/Sygma]

groups that previously had been excluded from power. Each revolution also created a new set of ideological values.

Like the French and American revolutions, those in Russia and China inspired others and served as models for change elsewhere in the world. The Chinese Revolution did not prevail until 1949, but its early stages from 1919 to 1934 were strongly influenced and for a time directly guided by Russian communists. When these early revolutionary efforts failed, China left the Soviet path. The ultimate success of the Chinese Revolution in 1949, and its later development, was far more an indigenous phenomenon than a response to the Russian experience.

Although strong differences marked the struggles for independence in India and the Middle East, neither can properly be viewed as a revolution. The Arabs fought Ottoman control with arms during World War I but then came under British and French authority. Indian protests against the British emphasized a nonviolent strategy. In both regions political power was eventually handed over peacefully to nationalist leaders. In the Middle East the League of Nations mandate system and the influx of Jewish settlers into Palestine, negligible until the rise of Nazism but significant thereafter, stimulated resistance from the native Arab population. Yet in the interwar years Arab nationalism failed to become a genuine mass movement as it did in India. There, the independence effort, as in China and Russia, involved peasants and workers under the direction of political organizers. While the nationalist regimes in Turkey and Iran attempted to modernize their countries after World War I, little effort went into radical restructuring of Indian society or its values.

Nevertheless, the changes that took place in India and the Middle East were in some ways revolutionary, for the awakening of nationalism and the end of the colonial system were to have long-range repercussions. India is the outstanding case of a drive for change that used traditional vehicles and symbols to attract support and to accelerate transformation, a pattern that repeated itself in the form of Muslim fundamentalism among Arab states after World War II.

In all these regions powerful leaders played a key role in planning and directing change, among them Lenin and his successor Stalin in the USSR, Mao Tse-tung (Mao Zedong) in China, Gandhi and his successor Nehru in India, and Faisal, ibn-Saud, Mustapha Kemal, Chaim Weizmann, and Reza Shah Pahlavi in the Middle East. Each of these leaders could claim to have made an enormous impact, not only on his own country but on states far beyond its borders as well. The twentieth century has been called the century of revolution primarily because of the massive upheavals in Russia, China, India, and the Middle East. The ripples that each revolution sent around the world helped to spawn fundamental changes in Asia, Africa, and Latin America. The century of revolution began with dramatic events in Russia in 1917.

The Russian Revolution

In March 1917* the first of two revolutions erupted in war-weary Russia, shattering 300 years of history in the space of a few days: the Romanov dynasty, the last absolute monarchy in Europe, was toppled from the throne it had occupied since 1613. Though laden with drama, the events of March were only a prelude to an even farther-reaching transformation. As if one revolution was insufficient to shift the weight of Russian history, with its virtually unbroken pattern of political and social repression and economic hardship, a second revolution erupted in November. The communist state that arose out of the November revolution became a major force in shaping the twentieth century.

The Twilight of the Romanovs

That the people of Russia were deeply discontented should have come as no surprise to Tsar Nicholas II (1894–1917), for the 1905 uprising had been a clear symptom of crisis. Although Nicholas had given in to demands for the creation of a Duma, the protection of individual liberties, and a broad franchise, within two years imperial decrees undid most of these reforms. Convinced that his power was divinely ordained, Nicholas was determined to restore his absolute authority. After 1911, following the assassination of Peter Stolypin, a reformist minister who had tried to repress terrorists and reactionaries, he further alienated the educated and professional classes by surrounding himself with conservative advisers. By 1914 some ministers even saw a European war as a positive catalyst for national unity.

Nicholas was an indecisive and not very intelligent leader. After the outbreak of war, he took direct command of the Russian armies—the only European head of state to do so—despite his lack of military training. At first his gesture had a positive symbolic value for the millions of peasants who rallied to the call for arms, but as the imperial armies suffered defeat after defeat, even the least sophisticated Russians began to hold the tsar personally responsible. However, most military officers had been poorly trained in modern strategy. Soldiers sent to the German front were among the worst-fed and equipped in Europe. Tens of thousands lacked even a rifle and were told to take one from a fallen comrade or a dead enemy; thus their greatly superior numbers failed to compensate for the country's lack of preparedness. Every setback in

---

*Russia still used the ancient Julian calendar, which had been abandoned in the West centuries earlier. By this time it was 13 days behind the modern Gregorian calendar. Throughout this chapter Gregorian dates will be used.

Tsar Nicholas II and his five children a few years before the revolution that overthrew the Romanov dynasty. [Bettmann Archive]

the field brought greater disenchantment among the troops. In addition to the incompetency of the generals and the enormous logistical problems stemming from Russia's vastness, Russian society was not sufficiently modernized to organize effectively for or sustain a major war effort. The Romanov dynasty collapsed in part because of the retarded development of the country's industries and infrastructure.

While Russia's war effort deteriorated, Nicholas left the government in the hands of his wife, Tsarina Alexandra (1872–1918), a religious zealot and absolutist. Her harsh, uncompromising attitudes were in part shaped by Grigori Rasputin, an eccentric Russian Orthodox monk whose great influence derived from his ability to convince Alexandra he could relieve her son's hemophilia. Rasputin's power over the tsarina and his manipulation of official policy outraged officials and members of the imperial court who hoped that political reforms would defuse popular discontent. Between September 1915 and November 1916 the Duma was suspended, while severe shortages of food and fuel provoked massive resentment in the cities. In December, hoping to free the royal family from his influence, liberal aristocrats murdered Rasputin. By then,

however, the domestic situation had deteriorated so severely that revolution was imminent. Within the reconvened Duma even conservatives and constitutional monarchists opposed the royal family.

The March 1917 Revolution

On March 8, 1917, disorder erupted in Petrograd.* Food riots led by women spread to the workers, and both a factory lockout and a socialist-inspired Woman's Day celebration filled the streets with protesters. The crisis came when the tsar, still at the front, ordered the revolt suppressed. On March 11 troops fired into a crowd, but the government's inexperienced reinforcements then mingled with the demonstrators. As cries of "Down with the tsar!" rang out, officials found their orders unenforceable. The next day the Duma proclaimed a provisional government under Prince Georgi Lvov and called on Nicholas to step down. With the generals unable to assure him of the army's loyalty—indeed, military leaders supported his stepping down—the last of the Romanov tsars abdicated.

After centuries of absolutism and repression, Russia experienced a sudden liberalization. The provisional government planned the election of a constituent assembly on the basis of universal male suffrage and introduced civil liberties. It also implemented the eight-hour workday, ended the persecution of the Jews, and released thousands of political prisoners, although it maintained that only a legally constituted government could resolve the land problem. The new regime enjoyed the support of Western-educated Russians as well as the business and professional classes, while the Duma was dominated by liberals who favored a constitutional monarchy. Even the Entente Powers generally preferred the provisional government to the rule of the tsar, hoping that it would reinvigorate the Russian war effort.

From its inception, however, the provisional government was challenged by the more radical Soviet ("council") of Workers' and Soldiers' Deputies, formed in March. Modeled after the organization that had led the 1905 general strike, the Petrograd soviet was in the hands of workers' representatives who had served on the tsar's War Industries Committee. Its executive committee quickly became a barometer of public sentiment. While hundreds of similar groups soon sprang up in army units, industrial centers, and the countryside, the Petrograd soviet maintained its preeminence because of its location in the capital, where power had traditionally been concentrated.

In contrast to the Duma, led by liberal elements, membership of the soviets consisted largely of socialists of var-

---

*The tsar had changed the name of the city from St. Petersburg to the Russian form, Petrograd, to emphasize the patriotic nature of the war.

ious types. The Social Revolutionaries looked to the Russian peasants and their traditional village councils for instituting fundamental change and favored the use of violence. The Mensheviks and the Bolsheviks, factions within the Social Democratic party, were both Marxist in ideology, though sharp differences divided them. The reform-minded Menshevik ("minority") faction sought to build a large party organization along the lines of the Western social democratic movements. They hoped to achieve their goals through peaceful evolution but did not expect to establish socialism in Russia until industrial development was more advanced.

The Bolshevik ("majority") group accepted Marxist goals but followed the teachings of Vladimir Ilyich Lenin (1870–1924), their exiled leader. Lenin rejected Marx's idea that socialist revolution was premature in an underdeveloped country like Russia, where the industrial proletariat was small. He also opposed the evolutionary strategy of the Mensheviks, arguing that peaceful methods were impossible in the tsarist autocracy and that only violent revolution would achieve socialism. Lenin argued for a "vanguard" of professional revolutionaries that would control a disciplined party, educate the workers and peasants, and prepare to seize the initiative.

The soviets, composed of these competing factions and without a clearly articulated ideology, supported the spontaneous actions of the urban crowds and landless peasants. By so doing, they competed with the provisional government for the people's loyalty. As this struggle progressed, the provisional government found itself at a growing disadvantage. The Bolsheviks, the only major group of the left not represented in the government, remained free of responsibility for unpopular policies.

The weaknesses of the provisional government proved to be fatal. The new leaders made no attempt to address the demands of the urban proletariat or to satisfy the land hunger of the peasants. Of more immediate significance, however, was its war policy. Despite the desperate unpopularity of the conflict, the Duma felt duty-bound to honor the alliance with the Entente against Germany. When the government renewed its pledge to support the war effort in May, popular opposition forced many ranking members to resign.

Lenin and the Bolshevik Coup

The Bolsheviks skillfully exploited the shortsightedness of the provisional government as Lenin began to dominate events. A short, stocky man, mostly bald, with a mustache and a goatee, he did not look charismatic. But John Reed, a young left-wing American writer, understood that although Lenin was a "colorless" man, he had a gift for "explaining profound ideas in simple terms" that any unschooled Russian peasant could understand. He led, said

Reed, "purely by virtue of his intellect."[1] Born Vladimir Ilyich Ulyanov, Lenin had been a radical since age 17, when the government had executed his older brother for plotting to assassinate Alexander III. During his twenties he became a Marxist, and his revolutionary activities brought him nearly five years of imprisonment and exile in Siberia. In 1900 he found refuge in western Europe, where he led the Bolshevik break from the Mensheviks.

When the March revolution erupted, Lenin, still in exile in Switzerland, persuaded the German government to grant him passage to Russia. The Germans, hoping that the Bolsheviks would disrupt the Russian war effort, transported him in a sealed train across their lines to the border, and Lenin arrived in Petrograd on April 20. His famous April Theses declared total opposition to the provisional government and instructed his followers to work for a second revolution in Russia, one that would eventually spread to the more industrialized countries of Europe. A communist victory, he said, would contribute to Russia's industrial base and help sustain Marxist socialism permanently.

Early in July soldiers and sailors led a massive uprising in Petrograd. The provisional government put down the revolt and blamed the Bolsheviks. Lenin, disguised as a locomotive fireman, fled to Finland, while a number of his followers—among them Lev Kamenev and Leon Trotsky—were arrested. When the provisional government launched a final military offensive against the Germans in July, soldiers deserted en masse, while in the countryside millions of peasants seized large estates. In an effort to broaden its support, the provisional government replaced Prince Lvov with Alexander Kerensky (1881–1970), a moderate Social Revolutionary. Kerensky's refusal to negotiate a withdrawal from the war served only to discredit him and his Menshevik allies. The final blunder came in September, when Lavr Kornilov, a reactionary military officer, attempted to crush the soviets. Kerensky appeared to welcome the general's action, but he came to believe that Kornilov intended to turn against him as well; he therefore armed the Red Guards, volunteer units from the Petrograd soviet. Prosoviet railway workers refused to transport Kornilov's equipment, and many of his troops fraternized with the Red Guards.

While Kerensky had prevented a military coup, his power now depended to a great extent on the soviets, which bitterly opposed his determination to continue the war. In the meantime, Bolshevik strength grew rapidly. Lenin's program of "peace, land, and bread" presented a compelling alternative to the provisional government's promises, and his slogan of "all power to the soviets" was a shrewd appeal for popular support. In late October, as the Bolsheviks gained a majority in the Petrograd soviet as well as in Moscow, Lenin secretly returned to Russia.

With Trotsky, now freed from imprisonment, Lenin planned the seizure of power. Trotsky (1879–1940), born Lev Bronstein, was a brilliant intellectual and strategist

◉ **The Bolshevik Strategy** ◉

Lenin's revolutionary theories formed the basis for Bolshevik action during the Russian upheaval of 1917. Here Lenin describes the need for a "professional" revolutionary vanguard.

I assert: (1) that no revolutionary movement can endure without a stable organization of leaders maintaining continuity; (2) that the broader the popular mass drawn spontaneously into the struggle, which forms the basis of the movement and participates in it, the more urgent the need for such an organization, and the more solid this organization must be (for it is much easier for all sorts of demagogues to sidetrack the more backward sections of the masses); (3) that such an organization must consist chiefly of people professionally engaged in revolutionary activity; (4) that in an autocratic state, the more we confine the membership of such an organization to people who are professionally engaged in revolutionary activity and who have been professionally trained in the art of combatting the political police, the more difficult will it be to unearth the organization; and (5) the greater will be the number of people from the working class and from the other social classes who will be able to join the movement and perform active work in it.

Source: V. I. Lenin, "What Is to Be Done?" in D. N. Jacobs, ed., *From Marx to Mao and Marchais* (New York: Longman, 1979), p. 45.

who had spent some of his own political exile in the United States. He was the real architect of the Bolshevik coup. He secured control of military power by persuading the Petrograd soviet, which he headed, to appoint him commander of a military revolutionary committee to protect the city. After winning over the soldiers in the Petrograd garrison, his forces captured the telephone exchange, railroad and electric stations, bridges, and government buildings on the night of November 6. Sailors from the Kronstadt naval base brought the cruiser *Aurora* up the Neva River to within firing range of the Winter Palace, seat of

the provisional government. The Bolshevik majority in the Congress of Soviets, meeting the next morning in Petrograd, proclaimed that power was now in the hands of the soviets and announced that Lenin was the head of the new government. On November 8 Kerensky fled the city. With almost no bloodshed, the Bolsheviks had won control of Russia. Holding that power, however, would prove a formidable task.

Building the Communist State

The seizure of Petrograd and the overthrow of the Kerensky government by no means guaranteed the Bolsheviks a lasting victory. Lenin still had to extend his control to the rest of the country. Setting up an enduring Bolshevik regime would require three more years of bitter struggle amid civil war, political opposition from anti-Bolshevik groups, and invasion by the troops of 14 foreign countries.

Lenin's immediate strategy was to achieve popular support and a measure of stability by ending war, hunger, and peasant unrest. The Social Revolutionaries had the largest following among Russia's landless rural population, but Lenin stole their thunder by declaring the nationalization of all land and its distribution to the peasants. Although in theory the soviets were to keep the large estates intact as collective farms, in practice the peasants, who were already seizing land on their own initiative, were permitted

Lenin and Trotsky planned the Bolshevik revolution and won the Russian civil war. They are shown here in a doctored photo. [Bettmann Archive]

to keep what they had taken. As revolutionary as these actions were, they failed to solve the hunger crisis. Small property holders jealously withheld their crops from urban consumers. Hoarding increased as a result of the civil war and poor harvests; for years starvation plagued millions.

The promise of peace proved costly to keep. The Germans now sensed victory in the east. German peace terms, however, were so harsh that some Bolshevik leaders, including Trotsky and Nicolai Bukharin, wanted to continue the war as a revolutionary struggle. Lenin's insistence on ending the hostilities ultimately prevailed, and on March 15, 1918, his representatives signed the Treaty of Brest-Litovsk. It ceded to Germany all its wartime conquests as well as eastern Poland, the Ukraine, and the formerly Russian areas of Finland, Estonia, Latvia, and Lithuania. Not until the Nazi-Soviet Pact of 1939 would Russia recover its 1914 frontiers, but the treaty provided Lenin with the much needed opportunity to solidify his authority. Lenin quieted opposition to it within the Communist party—the new official name the Bolsheviks adopted in March 1918—by arguing that the spread of "world revolution" into western Europe would eventually render Russia's losses meaningless.

Despite the euphoria that had greeted the reforms and promises of the provisional government following the March revolution, political liberalism had shallow soil in which to grow. Initially the revolutionaries took democracy far beyond conventional practice, with popular choice entering virtually every area of life. In the soviets a kind of direct democracy prevailed, while in army units soldiers elected officers and in the factories workers organized management councils. Yet there was no tradition of self-government above the village level in Russia. The revolution left a vacuum that inexperienced local councils of semiliterate peasants could hardly fill. Into this void Lenin moved his disciplined organization after the November revolution. Yet his own forces were small and lacked administrative experience.

Lenin's victory destroyed the possibility of democratic government. The Bolsheviks had never pretended to value democracy, and Lenin's program demanded peace and economic well-being, not freedom in the traditional Western sense. He knew, too, that after the distribution of land, universal suffrage would produce a majority representing small landowners. In fact, when the elections for a constituent assembly previously scheduled by the provisional government were held in late November, the Social Revolutionaries won nearly twice as many delegates as the Bolsheviks. When the assembly met in January 1918, Lenin swiftly demonstrated his intention to create a Marxist-style "dictatorship of the proletariat," disbanding the assembly after only one day of deliberation. For several months Lenin governed in a coalition with left-wing Social Revolutionaries, but when the latter withdrew their support in June, Russia came under the one-party rule that still governs it today.

During 1918 and 1919, the Bolsheviks began to implement their political and economic policies. Grass-roots government yielded to centralized state administration by the Communist party, soldiers' councils were replaced by appointed officers, and factory committees gave way to trade unions controlled by party officials. In the countryside previously independent peasants now had to deliver their "surplus" produce to hungry urban populations. Advances toward self-determination for ethnic minorities and border peoples were eventually replaced by Russian-dominated centralization thinly disguised as a federal state. Lenin believed this system of "war communism" to be necessary under the dual pressure of civil war and foreign invasion. The pressing need for industrial production was not being met by the factory committees, which often lacked necessary technical skills and sometimes resisted state efforts to coordinate labor. Moreover, Lenin saw industrial cartelization as the basis of a socialist economy. Each branch of industry was therefore nationalized and centralized into state trusts. By 1920 about 90 of these trusts existed, all subordinated to the Supreme Council of National Economy, which attempted to direct industrial production throughout the country.

Revolution Under Siege

Early Bolshevik policies and Leninist authoritarianism were shaped in large part by the return of war and strife to Russian soil. The infant Communist regime had to fight for its survival against an array of domestic and foreign enemies: counterrevolutionary legions made up of conservatives, moderates, and even some Social Revolutionaries, known collectively as the White Army; border nationalities seeking independence from Russia; more than 100,000 troops from 14 foreign nations, including the United States, Britain, France, and Japan; and peasants waging a so-called green revolution against the Reds who requisitioned their crops. Between 1918 and November 1920 the Red Army defended Russia's borders in a desperate effort to save the Communist regime.

A combination of military and ideological motives led to the Allied invasion of Russia. The Entente Powers had supported Kerensky's government in order to bolster the war on the eastern front. Lenin's demands for a separate peace aroused Allied suspicion that he was a German agent, but they failed to convince the Bolsheviks to reject the German peace terms. With their troops no longer tied down on the Russian front, the Germans broke through Allied lines in the west and marched to a position less than 40 miles from Paris. The German advance was repulsed, but the Allies, fearful that the Bolshevik revolution might spread to their own war-weary population, determined on a preemptive strike.

In June 1918 the Allies decided on military intervention.

The French and British sent nearly 24,000 soldiers to Murmansk and Archangel. On July 16 the Bolsheviks, worried that the Allies might try to liberate the tsar, executed the entire royal family. In Siberia 40,000 Czech prisoners of war, formerly Austro-Hungarian conscripts, revolted against their Russian guards and commandeered the trans-Siberian railroad in an attempt to reach their homeland, where they hoped to fight for Czech independence. To assist the Czech legion, President Wilson approved a landing at Vladivostok, where 72,000 Japanese and 8,000 American troops eventually arrived. During the winter of 1918–1919 two British divisions seized the rail lines that connected the Black and Caspian seas along the oil-rich Russo-Turkish border. French units, joined by Greek forces, also landed at Odessa on the Ukraine's Black Sea coast.

Allied soldiers remained in Russia after the armistice was signed in November, giving support to the White Army. Against difficult odds, the Bolsheviks possessed a number of advantages. Party discipline and Lenin's leadership kept their forces together while the White Army factions, united only in their opposition to the Communists, were rent with political division. The Bolsheviks also controlled the Russian heartland and could wage war along interior lines, whereas their enemies were scattered along the periphery. Moreover, the Red Army generally had the support of the peasants, who knew the Bolsheviks would never restore the power of the large landowners. Finally, in ethnically Russian areas Bolshevik propagandists shrewdly combined revolutionary rhetoric with a patriotic appeal in the face of foreign invasion.

Bolshevik military operations were commanded by Leon Trotsky, whose abilities as a speaker and Marxist theoretician were matched by brilliant organizational talent. Trotsky raised, equipped, trained, and directed the Red Army, rushing from one front to another in a special train outfitted as a mobile headquarters. He kept troop morale high by means of political propagandists, called commissars, who were attached to Red Army units. His forces repulsed assaults from Siberia, the Ukraine, and the newly independent state of Poland. Late in 1920 Allied ships evacuated more than 100,000 soldiers from Odessa. By the end of the struggle the Bolsheviks had recovered much of the old imperial lands on the western front, except for the Baltic states and the territory lost to Romania and the new states of Czechoslovakia and Poland. With the civil war won, they also regained control over Azerbaijan, Russian Armenia, and Georgia, which separatist forces had threatened to make independent. These and other nominally autonomous states were eventually incorporated into the Union of Soviet Socialist Republics (USSR), established in December 1922. After two years of desperate fighting against invasion, civil war, and famine, the Communist regime was secure but exhausted.

◉ What Price Revolution? ◉

The great loss of human life during the Russian Revolution and the civil war, criticized by the enemies of bolshevism, was defended by Leon Trotsky as a necessary price for great historical change.

But the misfortunes which have overwhelmed living people? The fire and bloodshed of civil war? Do the consequences of a revolution justify the sacrifices it involves? The question is teleological and therefore fruitless. It would be as well to ask in the face of the difficulties and griefs of personal existence: Is it worth while to be born? Melancholy reflections have not so far, however, prevented people from bearing or being born. Even in the present epoch of intolerable misfortune only a small percentage of the population of our planet resorts to suicide. But the people are seeking the way out of their unbearable difficulties in revolution.

Is it not remarkable that those who talk most indignantly about the victims of social revolutions are usually the very ones who, if not directly responsible for the victims of the world war, prepared and glorified them, or at least accepted them? It is our turn to ask: did the war justify itself? What has it given us? What has it taught?

Source: L. Trotsky, *The Russian Revolution* (Garden City, N.Y.: Anchor/Doubleday, 1959), p. 483. (Originally published in 1930.)

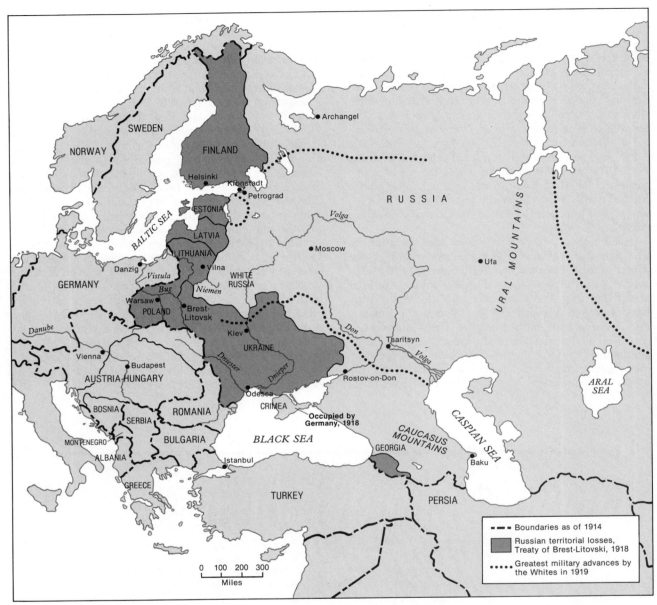

35.1 Russia in War and Revolution, 1917–1921

- – – Boundaries as of 1914
- ■ Russian territorial losses, Treaty of Brest-Litovski, 1918
- ⋯⋯ Greatest military advances by the Whites in 1919

ALEXANDRA KOLLONTAI AND THE WOMEN'S QUESTION

In Russia, as elsewhere in Europe, women had long played an important role in radical movements. Daring women such as Vera Zasulich, who assassinated a cruel provincial governor in 1878, and Olga Liubatovich, who was exiled in Siberia and conspired in St. Petersburg, were but two of the many Russian women active in the revolutionary underground. Others, such as Angelica Balabanoff and Anna Kulischiov, achieved prominence as exiled socialist militants, Balabanoff as secretary to the Second International and Kulischiov as a leader of the Italian socialist women's movement. The career of Alexandra Kollontai (1872–1952) illustrates both the role of women in the anti-tsarist movement and the tense relationship between women's liberation and the Bolshevik revolution.

Born into a wealthy landowning family as Alexandra Domontovich, she married a young engineer but after

An early Bolshevik and ardent feminist, Alexandra Kollontai took part in the first stages of Lenin's government. [Novosti from Sovfoto]

trayed unless it destroyed bourgeois moral standards and the authoritarian family. These ideas and her efforts to establish a state-supported system of maternity and infant care drew sharp criticism from her male comrades, who accused her of wanting to "nationalize" Russian women. Her position was undermined when she joined the anti-Leninist faction and pushed to democratize the Communist party through direct worker participation in policymaking. In March 1918 she resigned from the government and later joined the Workers' Opposition movement. Following the civil war, during which she worked as a propagandist with the Red Army in the Ukraine, Kollontai bitterly criticized the new marriage laws established by the Soviet (Bolshevik) regime, which she felt maintained inequality, and demanded full rights for women. Her controversial ideas on women's liberation and sexual freedom were explained in *The New Morality and the Working Class* (1920), the publication of which alienated her still further from the Communist leadership. Although Kollontai's advocacy of sexual relationships based on affection and equality rather than on socially imposed codes offended her more conservative comrades, many others—especially young urban middle-class Russians and intellectuals—agreed.

When Joseph Stalin became general secretary of the Communist party in 1922, the Workers' Opposition movement was purged and Kollontai's lover, Alexander Shylapnikov, was killed. Kollontai herself was virtually banished for the next two decades: from 1924 until her retirement in 1945 she served as Russian ambassador to Norway, Mexico, and Sweden and as a representative to the League of Nations. In her last lonely years Kollontai suffered from the knowledge that the revolution she had helped to make had fallen short of her hopes.

three years left her husband, who viewed her sympathies for the working class as willful defiance of his authority. After studying in Zurich, she returned to St. Petersburg and joined the Menshevik wing of the Social Democratic party. At the time of the 1905 revolution Kollontai recognized "how little our Party concerned itself with the fate of women of the working class and how meager was its interest in women's liberation." She also came to believe that liberation for women "could take place only as the result of the victory of a new social order and a different economic system."[2] Forced into exile because of her radical activities, she lived in western Europe and the United States from 1908 to 1917. In 1915 she broke with the Mensheviks over the war issue and began to correspond with Lenin, returning to Russia at the outbreak of revolution in March 1917.

As a member of the Bolshevik Central Committee, Kollontai supported Lenin's call for an armed uprising. After the November coup she was appointed commissar for social welfare in Lenin's cabinet. Within the party and the government she argued that the revolution would be be-

Stalin Versus Trotsky: The Struggle for Power

Even without the military struggles of the 1918–1920 period, chaotic economic and social conditions would have threatened the Bolshevik regime. Millions of Russians had died as a result of war, epidemics, and famine. Cities and villages lay in ruin, and the transportation system barely functioned. A lack of managers, technicians, and raw materials had brought factories to a virtual standstill, and industrial production had fallen to about 20 percent of its prewar level. Hoarding and drought continued to cause severe food shortages. In the face of these problems, popular support for the Bolsheviks eroded. A wave of peasant uprisings and factory strikes preceded a military revolt, in March 1921, when sailors at the Kronstadt naval base, once a pro-Bolshevik bastion, seized the Winter Palace and proclaimed a "third revolution" against Lenin's regime. The Red Army crushed the movement with much bloodshed, and Lenin knew he had to act swiftly to restore control.

In March 1921 Lenin announced the New Economic Policy (NEP), a retreat from Marxist orthodoxy. The NEP permitted a degree of private enterprise in small industries and the retail trade, ended food requisitioning, and allowed peasants to sell their produce on the open market after paying a small tax. The state, however, continued to own and operate major industries, banking, and transportation and to control wholesale and foreign trade. The NEP slowly achieved success, and by 1928 agricultural and industrial production had returned to prewar levels. The policy, much debated among Communist leaders, resulted in the revival of the rural middle class of kulaks ("large peasants") that ran counter to the Marxist goal of a classless society.

As long as Lenin lived, he and the Old Bolsheviks—the group that had made the revolution in 1917—retained control of the Communist party, but he was concerned over the increasing number of bureaucratic careerists entering its ranks. The Soviet constitution of 1923 created the All-Union Congress of Soviets, a representative body in which the highest power theoretically resided. The Congress—its name was changed to the Supreme Soviet in 1936—elected a Council of People's Commissars (changed to the Council of Ministers in 1946), the Executive Committee, and the small Presidium, which acted for the Congress between sessions. In reality, however, the Communist party ran the country through its Central Committee, composed of just under 50 members, which met several times each year. The Central Committee in turn elected a ten-member Politburo, which convened weekly and chose a Secretariat of from one to three members to perform executive duties.

In 1922 two strokes removed Lenin from day-to-day leadership. Trotsky appeared to be the logical choice to succeed Lenin, but party members began to unite against him. A temporary *troika*, or three-member leadership, emerged late in 1922 to carry on Lenin's work, consisting of Grigori Zinoviev, party leader in Petrograd (later named Leningrad); Lev Kamenev, the Communist boss of Moscow; and Joseph Stalin, general secretary of the party and the least known of the three.

Tough, clever, and power-hungry, Stalin (1879–1953) was the only Old Bolshevik of lower-class origin. Born Joseph Djugashvili in the province of Georgia, he was the son of a shoemaker and the grandson of serfs. After being expelled from a theological seminary, he joined the Bolshevik movement at the turn of the century and took the underground name of Stalin, meaning "man of steel." He performed some of the party's most reprehensible tasks, including the robbing of treasury transports to acquire operating funds. Hardened in the tsar's prisons and Siberian exile, Stalin possessed none of the broader culture of his colleagues, most of whom had lived in western Europe during the worst years of tsarist repression. As general secretary he dispensed patronage to build a personal following and came to that office at a time when a new generation of bureaucrats was developing within the party.

Lenin recognized Stalin's power at the very time that the other Old Bolsheviks were growing suspicious of Trotsky. After his second stroke in December 1922, Lenin began to consider the problem of succession. With the help of his wife and closest political assistant, Nadhezhda Krupskaya (1869–1939), he dictated a "testament" in which he reviewed the credentials of possible successors, chiefly Trotsky and Stalin. Although he seemed to favor Stalin, he expressed doubts as to whether Stalin knew how to use his power wisely. Less than two weeks later Lenin added a "codicil," or supplement, to these notes denouncing Stalin as "too rude" and advising the party to appoint someone "more tolerant, more loyal, more polite and more considerate to comrades, less capricious, etc."[3]

While Lenin had always held reservations about Stalin, his opinion hardened when he learned that Stalin had tried to intimidate Krupskaya. Following Lenin's death early in 1924, the testament and the codicil were read before the party's Central Committee. That summer Krupskaya attempted to have the documents presented before the entire party congress, but Stalin managed to have only minor commissions hear them. Krupskaya survived Stalin's brutal purges and remained on the Central Committee for the rest of her life, but her husband's denunciations of the man who became the dictator of Soviet Russia went unpublished until after Stalin's death.

In 1924 Stalin, who was never known for his mastery of Marxist theory, put forward the novel concept of "socialism in one country." He argued that the Soviet Union could create the industrial economy necessary to sustain socialism without exporting revolution to the rest of Europe. Against this position Trotsky offered the doctrine of "permanent revolution," an unceasing struggle aimed at the elimination of capitalism everywhere. Stalin believed that the extension of communist revolution to all capitalist societies required resources that Russia did not have and meant continual armed strife with the West. Stalin eventually won the struggle with Trotsky because he secured control over the party apparatus and won the support of other party leaders. Even leftists such as Zinoviev and Kamenev, whose views corresponded more closely to the permanent revolution theory, feared Trotsky's ambitions, and in 1925 they helped the supposedly safer Stalin to strip him of his position as war commissar. In 1929 Trotsky fled into exile, where, after years of opposition to Stalin's regime that won an often sympathetic hearing from Western socialists, he was murdered by a Soviet agent in 1940.

Stalin's skill at maneuvering was consummate. Having used the support of the party's left to weaken Trotsky, he then joined forces with Nicolai Bukharin, leader of the right. Together they removed Stalin's opponents, one by one, from the Central Committee while Stalin increasingly controlled the smaller Politburo. He then turned against his former allies. After the failure of a communist uprising in Bulgaria in 1925, he secured the dismissal of Zinoviev as head of the Communist International and then destroyed Kamenev's authority by having the Moscow party apparatus placed in the hands of the Politburo. In 1928, having crushed the party's left wing, Stalin broke with the right. He did this by favoring the collectivization of agriculture and forced industrialization, positions long associated with the left. When Bukharin opposed these policies, Stalin drove him from office. With Trotsky in exile and the old-guard Bolsheviks outmaneuvered, Stalin emerged as the unchallenged master of the Soviet state.

The Comintern: Russia Between East and West

Stalin's formula for one-country Socialism rejected not only Trotsky's insistence on the need for continuing revolution but Lenin's legacy as well. In March 1919 Lenin had invited the world's socialist leaders to Moscow to create a new global organization known as the Communist International, or Comintern. The purpose of this so-called Third International was to convert the Russian Revolution into a world struggle. The instability of the immediate postwar period, marked by the fall of the monarchies in Austria-Hungary and Germany, riots in China, India, and Japan, the seizure of factories by Italian workers, and the establishment of a Communist regime in Hungary under Béla Kun, gave Comintern leaders hope, for they saw in such events proof that capitalism and imperialism were about to collapse everywhere. Their optimism was, however, premature, for except in the Soviet puppet state of Mongolia, communism failed to seize permanent power beyond Russia. The Comintern sent agents to every corner of the world to organize and strengthen indigenous communist movements, but in the long run Stalin's policies and the organization's internal limitations hampered its effectiveness.

The Comintern had a divisive impact on the European left. Demanding disciplined followers among the socialists in other countries, Lenin established 21 conditions for foreign parties seeking membership in the Comintern. These included purging themselves of reformists, restructuring their organizations along Bolshevik lines, supporting all communist governments, preparing for the seizure of power in their own countries, and fighting social democrats as well as capitalists. Lenin believed the moment for world revolution had arrived, but many Western socialist leaders were reluctant to gamble their previous gains on the chance of revolution. Social democrats preferred to achieve socialism without resorting to dictatorship. The result was that socialist parties outside the USSR split into two camps between 1920 and 1921, with most rejecting Lenin's demands in favor of achieving socialism through parliamentary reform. Lenin accused them of wasting a historic opportunity.

Despite these divisions, the Comintern caused panic in Western countries. In the United States a "Red scare" in 1919 led to a government witch-hunt for radicals of every kind. In Europe many frightened members of the middle class abandoned liberalism in favor of fascism and other anti-Communist movements.

The hysteria the Comintern aroused in the West was ironic in view of the fact that revolutionary communism was so unsuccessful elsewhere in the world. The early socialists were essentially Eurocentric in outlook, a characteristic derived in part from Marx's belief that revolution was likely only in advanced capitalist societies. "The founders of Marxism," noted one scholar, "judged non-European civilizations through the prism of European civilization. The road to progress for the backward peoples they saw as the road of Europeanization, not only from the socio-economic standpoint but also culturally."[4]

Comintern leaders gave little attention to the needs and aspirations of non-Western communists. At the third congress of the Comintern in 1921, the Indian Marxist M. N. Roy attacked the meeting for allowing him only five minutes to report on revolutionary activities in the subcontinent. The next year the Indonesian communist Tan Malaka condemned the Comintern for opposing the pan-Islamic movement, which he said had isolated his party from the Muslim peasants of his country. At the 1924 congress Mexican representatives warned Soviet leaders that they were ignoring potential allies in Latin America, while Sen Katayama of the Japanese Communist party assailed Zinoviev for hardly mentioning the Eastern question. Ho Chi Minh (1890–1969), the Vietnamese activist, complained bitterly that Westerners were ignoring revolutionaries in colonial areas and misunderstood the liberation movements.

When the Comintern did support revolutionary activities in the Third World, its approach reflected Soviet concerns. In 1924 the Comintern sent the able but inexperienced Michael Borodin to China to establish a Communist military college at Whampoa, near Canton. The principal of the college was young Chiang Kai-shek (1887–1975), recently returned from a visit to Russia. Despite Chiang's involvement in the Chinese Nationalist party (Kuomintang) and his close ties to bankers, the Comintern ordered the Chinese Communists to integrate themselves into the Kuomintang. On April 12, 1927, Chiang's troops, aided by gangs hired by Shanghai businessmen, launched a surprise attack against Borodin, the Communists, and the trade unions, murdering thousands and imprisoning many more. Nevertheless, for a time the Comintern attempted to mend the ill-fated alliance with the Kuomintang.

Of all the factors that undermined the Comintern, none was more important than Stalin's rise to power. His one-country socialism was essentially a defensive strategy designed to protect the Soviet state. His concern lest revolutionary activities elsewhere endanger the USSR resulted in his using the Comintern only to keep foreign Communist leaders in line. Under Stalin the Communist International became an anachronism, and in a gesture to antifascist unity during the Second World War, he disbanded it in 1943.

◉ The Comintern: East Versus West ◉

At the Congress of the Peoples of the East, called by the Communist International in 1920, the representatives of non-Western countries complained bitterly that their concerns were being ignored by Russian leaders. One of the most vocal critics was M. N. Roy, an Indian Communist, who argued that the official report on colonial questions maintained that the fate of the revolutionary movement in Europe depended entirely on the course of the revolution in the East.

Without the victory of the revolution in the Eastern countries, the Communist movement in the West would come to nothing. . . . This being so, it is essential that we divert our energies into developing and elevating the revolutionary movement in the East and accept as our fundamental thesis that the fate of world Communism depends on the victory of Communism in the East.

Here is Lenin's response to Roy's arguments.

Comrade Roy goes too far when he asserts that the fate of the West depends exclusively on the degree of development and the strength of the revolutionary movement in the Eastern countries. In spite of the fact that the proletariat in India numbers five million and there are 37 million landless peasants, the Indian Communists have not yet succeeded in creating a Communist Party in their country. This fact alone shows that Comrade Roy's views are to a large extent unfounded.

Source: F. Claudin, *The Communist Movement: From Comintern to Cominform*, vol. 1, trans. B. Pearce (New York: Monthly Review Press, 1975), pp. 247–248.

The inability of the Comintern to establish Communist regimes beyond the Soviet Union should not obscure the profound impact of the Russian Revolution. The Bolshevik seizure of power shook the West to its foundations and altered international relations. Stalin was shortsighted only in failing to recognize the Russian Revolution as the first of a series of momentous upheavals that would transform the world.

China: Rebels, Warlords, and Patriots

In contrast to the Russian Revolution, the upheaval in China began almost tentatively, then sputtered and apparently died, and finally broke out in full force only after nearly 40 years of false starts and setbacks. In China too there were perhaps revolutionary implications in the Taiping Rebellion of 1850–1864. All revolutions have their antecedents, but China's was particularly slow in the making. China had first to develop a national political consciousness and a political organization that could pursue revolutionary change, both of which were lacking in its historical experience. The Chinese were accustomed to the overthrow of dynasties grown old and ineffective and their replacement by a new group, which would then administer the traditional system more successfully. The system itself, however, enshrined by the Mandate of Heaven, appeared to be beyond challenge.

But by the twentieth century the traditional model had lost its ability to deal with the now overwhelming problems of mass poverty, technological backwardness, and political weakness. These problems were vividly symbolized by China's helplessness in the face of the imperial powers of the West. It was to take another century to create a new set of solutions and a political structure to pursue them. Meanwhile, China's material welfare and ancient pride continued to suffer.

The Ch'ing dynasty collapsed in 1911, with the gentlest of shoves from a small and poorly organized group of revolutionaries (see Chapter 33). It was widely seen as a failure and was equally resented as an alien dynasty of conquest. Most of the revolutionary support rested on one or both of these grounds rather than on the still only half-formed plans for change. The end of Manchu rule is considered a revolution because the government was overthrown in an armed uprising by people who called themselves revolutionaries and had some new and radical ideas. But they were too few and too politically inexperienced to establish an effective government of their own, and to make matters worse, they were split into factions. The most important revolutionary organization was the Kuomintang (Guomindang), founded around the turn of the century and led by Sun Yat-sen (1866–1925), an idealist with great personal charisma but little sense of practical politics.

Sun Yat-sen and the 1911 Revolution

Sun was born to a peasant family near Canton (Gwangzhou), traditionally a hotbed of separatism and political ferment. At the age of 13, like many Cantonese, he emigrated, joining his older brother in Honolulu, where he went to a church boarding school and became a Christian. At 16 he returned to study in Hong Kong and finished a medical degree there in 1892 at a British mission hospital. After practicing only briefly in Macao, he founded a secret society to overthrow the Manchus, drawing support from overseas Chinese. In 1895 he was forced to flee to Japan, from where he made repeated trips to build Chinese contacts in the United States, Britain, and Hawaii. Other radical leaders and groups in China were also active, and several abortive attempts were made to seize power until an uprising at Wuhan in 1911 was joined by some troops among its garrison. Its successful defiance brought the fall of the imperial government. Sun returned from abroad and became the first president of the newly proclaimed republic. The last Ch'ing emperor, a 6-year-old boy, abdicated early in 1912, marking the end of an imperial tradition more than 2,000 years old.

China was still hopelessly divided, and even Sun saw that he could not provide unity and strong central government. He agreed to step down in 1912 as president in favor of Yuan Shih-kai (Yuan Shikai, 1859–1916), a leading Ch'ing military man who had thrown his lot in with the republicans. Sun had earlier put together a set of guidelines for a new government called the Three Principles of the People. These were nationalism, democracy, and the people's livelihood, none of which was clearly defined. Nationalism in the modern sense was still a new idea to most Chinese, but they could at least make common cause against the foreign Manchu dynasty in the name of Chinese self-determination. Sun's notion of democracy was heavily indebted to Western models. It implied but did not spell out social and political equality, a notable departure in itself from the hierarchical forms of Confucianism. Democracy was to be assured by a constitution largely on an American pattern, while "livelihood"—a partial redistribution of wealth on behalf of the poorer peasantry—was to be achieved through tax reforms.

China was far from having the requisite basis for democracy, however. There were no true political parties as yet, only a variety of elite or intellectual groups, divided among themselves. When the new Kuomintang won national elections in 1913, Yuan Shih-kai, who had busily concentrated real power in his own hands, arranged the assassination of its leading organizer, Sung Chiao-jen (Song Jiaoren), who had pressed for constitutional government. Sun again fled to Japan, while Yuan tightened his grip as military dictator by force, bribery, and intimidation. In 1915 he had himself declared president for life and took to riding around in an armored car for fear of attack by frustrated revolutionaries. Meanwhile, he dared not confront Western and Japanese imperialism in China because he was dependent on foreigners who looked to him as a strongman who could ensure order. The revolution had been betrayed.

Several southern and western provinces, where disgruntled military men and revolutionaries were active, broke away from Yuan's control. In 1916 he died suddenly after failing to have himself declared emperor. Political and ideological change had gone much too far to permit any return to such traditional forms, although there was still neither a consensus on what should succeed them nor a semblance of national unity. During the next 12 years China dissolved into virtual anarchy, divided among a number of regionally based warlords and other local military leaders. The Kuomintang and the early revolutionaries had a political ideology of sorts but no army; the warlords had armies but little or no program or party organization. Their troops marched around the countryside like a scourge on the peasants, while a bewildering variety of short-lived regimes or political cliques succeeded each other in Peking as the nominal government of China.

In 1917 Sun returned to Canton, formed a rival government, and began building a more effective political organization. He complained that trying to get the Chinese people to work together was like trying to make a rope out of sand. But although he tried to arouse mass support, he appealed mainly to intellectuals and the few Chinese who were as yet politically conscious. What began to spark Chinese nationalism more effectively were new Japanese encroachments on the nation's sovereignty and spontaneous popular protests against them.

The May Fourth Movement

Japan's Twenty-one Demands on China, issued in 1915, provoked immediate protests from patriotic Chinese, especially after Yuan Shih-kai accepted most of them. China joined the Allied side in World War I in 1917, sent labor battalions to the Western front, and hoped thus to get a hearing at the Paris peace conference. But Japan had secretly obtained Allied agreement to keep what it had taken in China's Shantung province, and it soon appeared that the lofty talk about self-determination did not apply to Asia.

When news broke that the warlord government in Peking had also signed secret agreements with Japan, mass demonstrations erupted on May 4, 1919. Chinese nationalism boiled over in what came to be called the May Fourth movement. A new and increasingly radical generation of students in government and mission schools and universities emerged, imbued with Western ideas and dedicated to building a new China. Student protesters beat up a pro-Japanese official and burned a cabinet minister's house. They went on to organize a union and to seek support among the large group of Westernized businessmen, industrialists, and shopkeepers in the treaty ports. Strikes and boycotts of Japanese goods attracted widespread support. The cabinet resigned, and China refused to sign the Versailles Treaty.

The May Fourth movement stimulated renewed intellectual ferment as well, especially in Peking and Shanghai, where hundreds of new political and literary periodicals attacked traditional culture, deplored China's weakness, and advocated a variety of more or less radical solutions. The model of the Confucian scholar steeped in the classics gave way to that of "progressive" thinkers who wrote in the vernacular and tried to appeal not only to fellow scholars or intellectuals but to the people as a whole. Parental and family controls, arranged marriages, and the subjugation of women and the young became targets of attack. Women, especially students, played a prominent part in the May Fourth movement; they and their male colleagues urged full-scale female emancipation and an end to the rigidity of the traditional system as a whole. Lu Hsun (Lu Xun, 1881–1936), the greatest modern Chinese writer, voiced bitter indictments of the old society, whose supposed ideals of "benevolence" and "virtue," he alleged, were hypocritical masks for oppression and exploitation. Foreign imperialism was deeply resented, but such critics as Lu Hsun saw it as the result of China's weakness rather than as the cause. The May Fourth movement sought to build a new China in which modern Western ideas of democracy, equality, science, and nationalism would have a prominent place. The example of Meiji Japan was much admired, despite Japanese aggression against China. Like the Meiji leaders, China's new voices called for a clean slate and a national renewal that would incorporate Western ideas.

China and the Marxist Model

Among the Western concepts with particular appeal was Marxism, especially after the success of the Russian Revolution in 1917. Russia too had been a relatively undeveloped country that had embraced the Marxist-Leninist doctrine of centralized organization and collective effort. The Soviet formula seemed to fit China's circumstances, and

Marx himself had suggested the relevance of his ideas to China many years earlier. In 1921 a small group of intellectuals, including Mao Tse-tung (Mao Zedong, 1893–1976), then a young student, founded the Chinese Communist party. Representatives from the Comintern helped the new party to set up its organization. Soviet experience in political mobilization was also attractive to the Kuomintang, which, like the Communist party, remained largely without any mass base. Sun Yat-sen, still head of the Kuomintang, agreed to an alliance with the Communist party under Comintern direction. Sun's military assistant, Chiang Kai-shek, was sent to Moscow to study Soviet methods. Party dictatorship was seen as necessary in the early stages of national unification, but Sun's Three Principles of the People and some form of representative government were reasserted as the ultimate goal. Sun may have been moving in the direction of socialism during his last years, but he died suddenly in 1925, and party control passed to Chiang Kai-shek. Chiang, despite his Soviet experience, was a far more conservative, even reactionary, figure. With his military background, Chiang saw China's first priority as the achievement of national unity, through force if necessary. He began promisingly by mounting a military and political campaign with Communist help. Moving north from the Kuomintang base in Canton with his Communist allies to defeat the warlords, he established a new national capital at Nanking (Nanjing) in 1927.

The Nanking Decade

Chiang never completely eliminated warlord power in several of the outlying provinces, and although he dominated the Kuomintang, he led it far from its radical origins and progressively lost support. He tried to wipe out his Communist allies in a military coup in Shanghai in 1927 and then in a series of campaigns from 1930 to 1934. Some of the Communists, including Mao, were not in Shanghai in 1927 but in rival areas trying, without success, to organize peasant rebellion. Their small remaining forces retreated to a mountain stronghold in the southeast. Chiang's forces finally drove them out in 1934, forcing them into a retreat known as the Long March. An increasingly ragged column of Communists dodged ahead of Chiang's troops in a zigzag route across western China. The precariously few survivors finally reached a new base area in the remote and mountainous northwest in 1935, centered on Yenan (Yanan). Relatively safe from Chiang's army, they pursued land reform policies and slowly extended their support base in this border area, from which they were to emerge after the Second World War in 1945 to lead a victorious revolution.

The decade of the Nanking government between 1927 and 1937 was, despite its repressive aspects, a period of at least modest recovery and growth. Chiang permitted no genuine democracy, with the excuse that order and

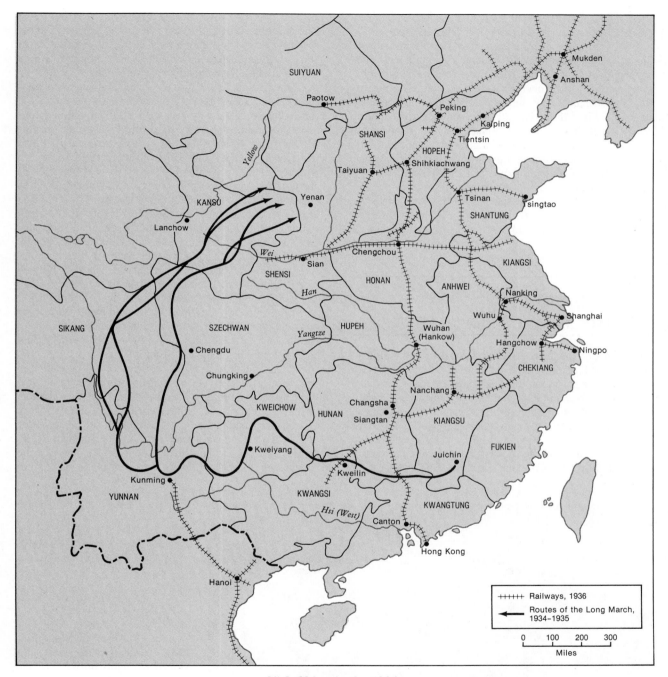

35.2 China in the 1930s

unity must come first. But at least the forms of constitutional government existed, and the economy underwent considerable modernization. Western-trained Chinese developed a central banking system, and a national rail network began to take shape. Industrial growth was still confined almost entirely to the treaty ports but increasingly under Chinese management.

These developments, however, were on a small scale compared to the needs of the country and had little or no impact on most of its predominantly peasant population. Poverty grew in the countryside. The Kuomintang's political base had become largely a coalition of businessmen from the treaty ports and rural landlords, which sought to suppress agrarian reform and prevent the rise of a politicized peasantry. The Communists, meanwhile, clung to their small base in the northwest, biding their time.

The situation was transformed by Japan's invasion of China. The Japanese, having reduced Manchuria to an economic colony, invaded it in 1931 and annexed it outright. They watched with concern as Chiang made progress toward national unification and began to build China's military strength. When the militarists who controlled Japan after 1930 saw their hopes for dominance in China and East Asia threatened, they launched a general assault on China in 1937, attacking first at Peking and then at Shanghai; later in the year they moved on to sack Nanking. With its capital in flames, the Kuomintang retreated up the Yangtze, largely to sit out the rest of the war, while the Communists in the north perfected a guerrilla strategy against the invaders and captured the leadership of Chinese nationalism.

❦
SHANGHAI:
THE MODEL TREATY PORT

While the Communists retreated to remote Yenan behind its mountain barriers and began to work out their program for a new China under the leadership of Mao, Shanghai remained a bastion of foreign privilege and Chinese collaborators. But it also harbored the growing group of Chinese dissidents, radicals, and revolutionaries who lived there under the protection of foreign law. Chinese police could not pursue suspects in the foreign settlements, which were ruled by a foreign-dominated municipal council with its own police. The Chinese Communist party had been founded there in 1921 for that reason, by a small group of revolutionaries and writers, part of the much larger number of political refugees living in the city, many of whom were periodically hounded or captured and executed by the Kuomintang secret police. Chiang Kai-shek's military coup in 1927 killed many of them and drove some of the survivors out, but many remained underground and continued to produce literary and political magazines with titles like *New China, New Youth,* and *New Dawn,* which were avidly read by intellectuals in the rest of China.

After Shanghai passed Peking as China's biggest city about 1910, it became the country's chief center of literature, publishing, and cultural and political ferment. The May Fourth movement spread immediately from Peking to Shanghai; student organizers persuaded many Shanghai merchants to boycott Japanese, and later British, goods. Shanghai joined Peking as a major base for the New Culture movement, sometimes called the Chinese Renaissance, and its efforts to remake Chinese society. Lu Hsun and many other New Culture writers lived in Shanghai.

At the same time, Shanghai remained by far the largest port and commercial center in China, through which over half its foreign trade passed. It also housed over half the country's modern industry. Chinese entrepreneurs, both traditional and Westernized, competed and collaborated with foreigners in trade, banking, and manufacturing, and many of them adopted a Western style of living. The foreign settlements at Shanghai were replicas of the modern Western city and looked physically much like Manchester or Chicago. The muddy foreshores of the Huangpu River, a Yangtze tributary that ran along one edge of the city and constituted the harbor, were covered in the nineteenth

Cosmopolitanism in Shanghai, 1933: from left to right, the American journalist Agnes Smedley, the playwright George Bernard Shaw, Mme. Sun Yat-sen, Ts'ai Yuan-p'ei (a leading intellectual), and Lu Hsun. Shaw was on a visit to China and is here being welcomed by the founders of the China League for Civil Rights. [East-foto/Sovfoto]

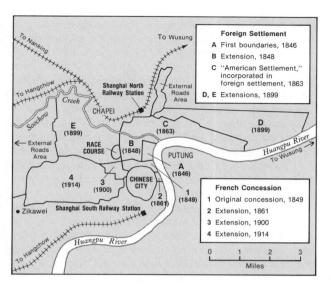

35.3 The Growth of Shanghai

century by an embankment known as the Bund. It became Shanghai's main thoroughfare, lined with imposing Western banks and hotels. Nanking Road, the main shopping street, ran at right angles to it, away from the river, and extensive residential areas featured houses in the Western style. The foreign population peaked at about 60,000 in the 1930s, in a city which by then totaled about 4 million, many of whom lived outside the foreign concession areas in sprawling slums or in the walled Chinese city next to the concessions. But the commercial and industrial heart of Shanghai was largely run by foreigners (the Japanese had edged out the British as the majority interest by the 1930s), and they built it in the Western image. They spoke of it as a beacon of "progress" in a vast Chinese sea of "backwardness."

Shanghai was described as "in China but not of it." The city brought silk, tea, and other agricultural goods from the Chinese hinterland for export in return for metals, machinery, and manufactured goods. Overall, however, Shanghai's economic example made relatively little impact, except in the other treaty ports. Elsewhere, it was largely rejected as alien and unsuited to China. The Communists labeled Chinese collaborators in Shanghai and the other treaty ports "running dogs" of the imperialists and were contemptuous of their departure from Chinese ways in favor of Westernization.

Shanghai and the other treaty ports cut a deep wound of humiliation in the Chinese psyche, but they also offered an example of the kind of industrial and organizational strength without which China could not hope to chart its own destiny. Shanghai played a major role in stimulating the rise of modern Chinese nationalism and with it a determination to rid the country of its foreign oppressors. The foreign way was rejected, but its technological and

industrial achievements were to be adapted to serve Chinese needs. The residents of Shanghai were, of course, the most affected by its example, and it was primarily there that China's modern revolution began. In the end, all foreign privileges were swept away by the revolution, but Shanghai remains China's biggest city and its most advanced industrial and technological center. Shanghai's modernity thus survived the expulsion of the foreigners and shaped basic aspects of the new China.

India: Toward Freedom

In India the pressures for change were narrowly concentrated on winning freedom from colonial rule. Like China, India suffered from mass poverty, technological backwardness, and foreign domination. Indian nationalists tended to blame colonial oppression for their problems and to see the solution as getting rid of their British overlords. But as in China, a new national consciousness had first to be developed and a national political organization built. India had functioned throughout most of its past not as a national political unit but rather, like China, as a cultural tradition. It took time to get Indians or Chinese to work together for a common political goal. The Indian independence movement did respond to the need for attacking poverty and injustice and for pursuing modern development, but the immediate objective was political freedom. While its final achievement was in some ways a revolutionary change, most Indians saw no need to reject either their own tradition or aspects of the British colonial experience that could help the new nation adapt to the modern world.

India's progress toward freedom is in large part the story of the careers of two men, Mohandas K. Gandhi (1869–1948), often called the Mahatma, or "Great Soul," and Jawaharlal Nehru (1889–1964). Gandhi gave the independence movement what it had not yet had, mass appeal and a mass following. Nehru, in close cooperation with Gandhi, gave practical leadership but acknowledged the charismatic power of Gandhi's example. In the years after World War I the Congress party was transformed under Gandhi's direction from a small group of intellectuals into a truly national party representing a wide range of regional interest groups and mobilizing millions of Indians. Gandhi proved adept at using aspects of the Indian tradition as vehicles of protest against British imperialism and as rallying points for nationalist sentiment and organization.

Gandhi and Mass Action

The son of a minor official in commercial Gujarat, Gandhi followed the path of many upwardly mobile Indians in a rapidly changing society. At 19 he went to London to study law and there became thoroughly Westernized. Soon after his return to India, he took a job with an Indian law firm in South Africa, where he spent the next 20 years defending Indian merchants and other immigrants against racist oppression and developing tactics of nonviolent protest and noncooperation.

Back home in 1913, he supported Indian participation in the First World War on the Allied side, hoping, as many Indians did, that loyalty to Britain in its hour of need would be rewarded by self-government. The British secretary of state for India announced in 1917 that the government's policy was "the gradual development of self-governing institutions" and an increase of Indians in responsible positions, but with the end of the war it became clear that such change would be painfully slow. Meanwhile, peasant economic suffering and distress among exploited industrial workers were growing. Gandhi traveled through India dressed as a poor peasant, reaching out to the masses and gaining a reputation for personal sanctity. But he also organized and led successful strikes and protest movements, using nonviolent methods with great effect. These and other signs of ferment appeared to members of the government as "seditious conspiracy." Repression followed, culminating in the Amritsar Massacre of 1919 when Indian troops under British command fired on an unarmed and peaceful crowd, leaving 400 dead.

From then on, few Indians saw accommodation to colonialism as acceptable. The Congress party began to press for independence, and Gandhi's weapon of nonvi-olent protest and noncooperation attracted more and more followers. Gandhi based his tactics on the ancient Hindu idea of *ahimsa*, or reverence for life, and drew on the redemptive power of love to convert even brutal opponents by its "soul force," or *satyagraha*. Traditional Indian values stressed the avoidance of conflict and the importance of self-control, seeking resolution through compromise and consensus. Nonviolent action was also a practical means for unarmed and powerless people to confront an oppressive state. As the American civil rights leader Martin Luther King, Jr., was later to demonstrate, it worked, both to build a dedicated following and to make its protest against injustice effective.

Gandhi organized boycotts of British imports, an action that caught the popular imagination, as it had in China, and helped build a larger following. He urged Indians to wear only their own cottons and wherever possible to spin and weave for themelves. The spinning wheel became a powerful nationalist symbol, linked also to 5,000 years of the country's history. Some of the Congress party's intellectual elite were scornful of Gandhi's methods, the style of a traditional saddhu, or holy man, he adopted, his embrace of the poor, and his personal asceticism. But as both an astute politician and a saintly figure he attracted more support and got more results than the party's politicians had ever done. Gandhi gave the Indian people a sense of their own national identity and inspired them to action through traditional methods and symbols. He succeeded where others had failed in attracting Muslims, Sikhs, Christians, and agnostics to his cause, thus creating India's first truly

Gandhi the ascetic, spinning cotton yarn. He made it a point to spin 200 yards of yarn every day as a symbolic act, no matter how busy he was. ["L'Illustration"/Sygma]

national movement. He urged his fellow Indians to "get rid of our helplessness" and stand together. As Nehru said of him, "He has given us back our courage, and our pride."

Strikes, boycotts, and demonstrations spread in the early 1920s, but with millions of people now involved, Gandhi could not always guarantee nonviolence. Thousands were jailed, violence occurred on both sides, and in 1922 Gandhi was sentenced to prison for six years. He was released for medical reasons after two but did not resume political agitation until 1929, distressed that his nonviolent campaign had gone astray.

Hindus and Muslims

Meanwhile, the government, affected by Gandhi's popular movement, began to implement many of the reforms previously demanded by the Congress party. It greatly in-creased the number of Indian officers in the civil service and the army and moved toward the abolition of the tax on cotton. By 1937 all of the British Indian provinces had become self-governing, with legislatures elected by Indian voters. Nehru became mayor of his home city of Allahabad. During this time, rioting between Muslims and Hindus broke out in many areas, a symptom of the general atmosphere of turmoil but also of the efforts of special groups to ensure a better place for themselves in the independent India that was now clearly coming. Hindus and Muslims had worked together for many years in the Congress party. Now Muslims were warned that they had to safeguard their interests against the Hindu majority and that their own party, the Muslim League, led by Mohammed Ali Jinnah (1876–1948), was their only sure protector.

Jinnah pressed for a separate Muslim electorate to vote for candidates for the new posts being opened to Indian

---

◉ Gandhi's Message to the British ◉

Gandhi knew England and British culture well, in part from his time there as a student, and he had many British friends. In his Hind Swaraj *(Independent India), he addressed them.*

I admit you are my rulers. . . . I have no objection to your remaining in my country, but . . . you will have to remain as servants of the people. . . . We do not need any European cloth. We shall manage with articles produced and manufactured at home. . . . This is not said to you in arrogance. You have great military resources. . . . If we wanted to fight with you on your own ground, we should be unable to do so but [we must] cease to play the part of the ruled. . . . If you act contrary to our will, we will not help you; and without our help, we know that you cannot move one step forward. . . . You English who have come to India are not good specimens of the English nation, nor can we, almost half-anglicized Indians, be considered good specimens of the real Indian nation. If the English nation were to know all you have done, it would oppose many of your actions. . . . If you will search into your own scriptures, you will find that our demands are just. Only on condition of our demands being fully satisfied may you remain in India; and if you remain under those conditions, we shall learn several things from you and you will learn many from us. So doing we shall benefit each other and the world. But that will happen only when the root of our relationship is sunk in a religious soil.

Gandhi's ideas and personal qualities are well brought out in that passage. Nehru said the following of him in 1935.

I have never met any man more utterly honest, more transparently sincere, less given to egotism, self-conscious pride, opportunism, and ambition. . . . It has been the greatest privilege of our lives to work with him and under him for a great cause. To us he has represented the spirit and honor of India.

Sources: W. T. de Bary, ed., *Sources of Indian Tradition*, vol. 2 (New York: Columbia University Press, 1964), pp. 265–266. J. Nehru, "Mahatma Gandhi," *L'Europe* (February 1936), p. 21.

officeholders and Indian voters. Meanwhile, Nehru increased his organizational control of the Congress party, although he maintained his loyalty to Gandhi as India's spiritual and symbolic leader. Nehru insisted that the Congress party was the party of all Indians, including Muslims, and that the independence movement would be weakened by factionalism. He was proved tragically right.

The worldwide depression that began in 1929 bore heavily on India and greatly increased its economic distress. When Gandhi resumed political action in 1930, he chose as his targets the tax the government imposed on salt and the official ban on private saltmaking from the sea, arguing that the tax and the monopoly especially hurt the poor. He led a protest march on foot across India to the coast, where he purposely courted arrest by picking up a lump of natural salt and urging Indians to do likewise, as many thousands did. Gandhi, Nehru, and many others were jailed, and there was a wave of strikes. Gandhi had again stirred the conscience of the nation. After eight months in prison, he was released to meet with the viceroy in New Delhi. Gandhi agreed to discontinue civil disobedience; in return, the government sanctioned a movement to promote the use of Indian-made goods and invited Gandhi to a London conference on India later in 1931, together with Jinnah as a representative of the Muslims.

The conference ended in stalemate, and Gandhi was taken back to jail a week after his return. Boycotts, strikes, and violent demonstrations erupted again without Gandhi to restrain them. Meanwhile, economic distress deepened as world markets for India's exports shrank, and a new, more conservative viceroy was appointed. In England, however, popular and parliamentary opinion was turning more and more toward self-government for India. In 1935 a new constitution for India was announced, followed by nationwide elections in 1937 in which nearly 40 million Indians voted. Congress candidates swept the election, and the Muslim League did not even win most of the seats reserved for Muslims. The new constitution granted "safeguard" powers to the colonial government, but Congress ministries took over the provinces. Jinnah was outraged, and until his death devoted his energies to building first an effective party for Muslims and finally a separate state. Nehru pointed out in reply that the Congress party was a national, not a special interest, party, and that over 100,000 Muslims belonged to it.

By the outbreak of war in 1939, India was well along the road to self-government, but the war brought the pro-imperial Winston Churchill to power in Britain and postponed all talk of independence until fascism could be defeated in Europe and Asia. Indians were informed that they were automatically at war with Germany, and later with Italy and Japan. Neither the Congress party's representatives nor other Indian leaders were consulted. Nationalists once again felt betrayed. The Congress party's provincial ministries resigned in protest, leaving the political field to Jinnah and his Muslim League. A belated British offer, reduced at Churchill's insistence from independence to dominion status once the war was over, was rejected. Gandhi called it "a postdated check on a failing bank." He began a series of nonviolent campaigns, culminating in the "Quit India" movement of 1942, a slogan that was scrawled on walls all over the country and shouted at Britons. Nehru spent most of the war in jail, and Gandhi was confined periodically. Jinnah exploited their absence to

◉ The Declaration of Indian Freedom ◉

Nehru, as president of the Congress party, declared January 26, 1930, a special day for the assertion of India's right to independence and issued this pledge, which was recited throughout India by millions of nationalists. Note the close similarity, quite conscious on Nehru's part, with the American Declaration of Independence.

We believe that it is the inalienable right of the Indian people, as of any other people, to have freedom and to enjoy the fruits of their toil and have the necessities of life, so that they may have full opportunities of growth. We believe also that if any government deprives a people of these rights and oppresses them, the people have a further right to alter it or abolish it. The British government in India has not only deprived the Indian people of their freedom, but has based itself on the exploitation of the masses, and has ruined India economically, politically, culturally, and spiritually.

Source: S. Wolpert, *A New History of India* (New York: Oxford University Press, 1982), pp. 314–315.

press for a separate state for Muslims, to be called Pakistan. Independence would come too late to avoid the bloody tragedy of partition.

The British had begun in India as a small group of merchants competing with Arabs, Portuguese, Dutch, French, and Indians for a share of the trade and a few ports. Trading and maintaining the security of routes and warehouses led imperceptibly to more and more political influence and control in an India that lapsed into chaos after 1707. In time the lure of imperial glory captured the British imagination, but there was a kernel of truth in the observation some made that the Indian empire was acquired in "a fit of absentmindedness." After 1784 Parliament began to supervise the governance of India, and by 1858 virtually the whole of the subcontinent had been brought under direct or indirect British control.

As early as the 1830s, most Britons agreed that India would one day be independent, and long-term British policy should prepare for this. Indians were quick to learn Western ideas and techniques wherever they saw them as useful, including business and industrial methods and British-style education, law, and parliamentary government. India is still governed today by institutions derived from Britain. The assimilation of British ways also greatly enhanced and accelerated the growth of the independence movement, which Indians saw as itself within the British tradition of political freedom.

If independence had come in 1907, when Parliament first declared it to be Britain's objective, or in the 1920s, when the policy was reaffirmed, it would have been possible to look back on the British era in India in relatively positive terms, though marred in the late eighteenth century by plunder and by the arrogance which led to the 1857 mutiny and its bitter aftermath. But however one assesses the balance or weighs it with other aspects of British rule, especially the failure to combat the fundamental modern Indian problem of poverty, Britain's clearest political error was its delay in giving India independence. The bloody consequences that followed might have been avoided had independence come earlier and had the Second World War and Winston Churchill not intervened. Nevertheless, there is little bitterness over the colonial legacy in India, in contrast to much of the rest of Asia, which underwent a harsher rule under the Japanese, French, or Dutch. Many originally British institutions are now firmly a part of South Asian civilization. India has much in common today with other former British colonies, including the United States and Canada, as joint inheritors of many aspects of a common culture.

The Nationalist Awakening in the Middle East

The same nationalist forces that challenged European imperialism in India and China had an equally pronounced impact on the Middle East. Despite ethnic disunity and traditional theological differences within Islam, Arab consciousness had been stimulated by the common experience of Turkish and European exploitation. By the eve of World War I, independence movements, often used as an entering wedge for Western interests, had already dismembered large portions of the weakened Ottoman Empire. The Greeks and most of the Slavic peoples of the Balkans had either freed themselves from Turkish rule or had fallen under Austro-Hungarian control. In North Africa, France had taken Algeria and established protectorates in Morocco and Tunisia, Britain had imposed a sphere of influence over Egypt and the Sudan, and Italy had occupied Libya and Somalia. Besides Turkey proper, only Iraq, Syria, Palestine, and Arabia still remained within the Ottoman sphere.

The Mandate System and the Palestine Question

British success in arousing Arab hostility against the Turks during the war, together with the success of the British adventurer T. E. Lawrence in coordinating Arab resistance, had helped to free most of the Middle East from Ottoman control by 1918. When the war was over, Faisal of Iraq and Lawrence lobbied the Paris peace conference for Arab rights, while Chaim Weizmann, who had succeeded Theodor Herzl as the leader of the Zionist movement, continued to push for the creation of a Jewish state. Neither party succeeded. After Faisal's appeals were rejected, an Arab congress declared him ruler of Syria, Palestine, and Lebanon.

While Faisal and Lawrence were in Paris, Abdul-Aziz ibn-Saud took to the deserts with his troops, extending his control over central Arabia. In 1925 he finally forced Hussein to abdicate as ruler of the Hejaz, which he united with his own Nejd sultanate. The British quickly recognized these conquests, and in 1932 ibn-Saud formally changed the name of his realm to the Kingdom of Saudi Arabia. Vast oil deposits were soon discovered, and ibn-Saud's hereditary absolute monarchy eventually grew wealthy through the concessions granted to Western oil companies.

Although the Saudi dynasty was successful in Arabia, Arab nationalism continued to be frustrated elsewhere. Faisal's rule over Syria was short-lived, for in 1920 the Allies tacitly recognized the terms of the Sykes-Picot Agreement by approving the League of Nations mandate system, and Turkish control formally gave way to Western domination. The French ejected Faisal from Syria, engendering bitter resistance from the Arab population, and created Lebanon as a separate mandate. In 1926 Lebanon was made a republic, with borders similar to those of the now independent state. The roads, buildings, and irrigation systems constructed under French occupation did not make up for the suppression of civil liberties and the divisive efforts to gain the allegiance of the Christian Arabs of Lebanon. The Lebanon mandate had a rich religious diversity, for in ancient times it had been a place of refuge for religious sects of all kinds. The Maronite Christians, a Roman Catholic group that followed Eastern Orthodox rites, had roots that went back to the seventh century; it comprised about 40 percent of the population, while Muslims of various sects made up the bulk of the remaining inhabitants. When the French eventually evacuated the area after World War II, they left behind a legacy of deep hostility.

The British were more successful in their mandate areas. Following an Iraqi rebellion in 1920, which they put down with much bloodshed, they made the popular Faisal king of Iraq, although they continued to run his financial and military affairs for another decade and supervised the creation of a constitutional monarchy. In 1922 Britain granted nominal independence to Egypt but refused to withdraw its troops from the country, and it followed a similar path in Iraq, where independence was recognized in 1930 in exchange for a military alliance that maintained British influence there. Nor did the discovery of rich oil fields in Iraq benefit the population of the region, for foreign companies secured lucrative concessions, further enflaming Arab resentment against the West.

The Palestine problem remained another source of anti-Western hostility as well as a cause of regional unrest. Britain's contradictory policies in the Middle East satisfied neither Arab nor Jewish demands, and throughout the interwar period British governments continued to shift between the two. Arab riots erupted in Palestine immediately after the creation of the British mandate over the area, prompting London to issue assurances that the Balfour Declaration would not be implemented in a way that would damage Arab interests. Yet British statesmen agreed with the Zionist position that the anguished history of the Jews made the creation of an independent Jewish homeland in Palestine a moral necessity. The Jewish community there—the Yishuv—had had a nearly uninterrupted residence since biblical times. It increased as a result of Zionist efforts in the late nineteenth century. By 1919 Jews in the mandate numbered around 60,000, or less than 10 percent of the population. In the early 1920s Britain permitted many Jews to join the Yishuv; by 1939 it had grown to 450,000, almost a third of the total.

Serious violence against Jews, provoked in part by aggressive settlement and the exclusion of Palestinians from newly established factories, broke out in 1929. When Nazi racial policies in Germany and anti-Semitism elsewhere caused another large wave of illegal Jewish immigration in the 1930s, the violence escalated to a virtual state of civil war. The British responded with proposals to create two separate states in the area, but both sides rejected the plan. The bitter struggle between Arab and Jew would reemerge after World War II with far-reaching results.

Despite overwhelming obstacles, Jewish immigrants achieved remarkable success. Although most came from European cities, they adjusted quickly to the rural conditions in Palestine, buying up Arab farmland as well as turning formerly arid terrain into fertile farms and citrus orchards through irrigation, much as the Arabs themselves were doing. The socialist beliefs of many of the early settlers encouraged collective agricultural labor through a farm unit known as the *kibbutz*, where men and women worked on an equal basis and shared nurseries, dining facilities, and schools as well as the defense of the community. Another form of enterprise was the *moshav*, a mixture of capitalist and socialist economic features. By 1939 the Jews had created, on socialist principles, an economic infrastructure that encompassed transportation networks, irrigation schemes, and other forms of industrial and agricultural productivity unique in the Middle East at that time. They also built new and prosperous cities, such as Tel Aviv, where a rich intellectual life thrived, based on the Hebrew language. This intellectual revival was facilitated by a Hebrew-language publishing industry and theater. Other institutions that elaborated biblical and medieval Jewish cultural themes in a twentieth-century context included art and music academies, a philharmonic orchestra, and the Hebrew University of Jerusalem and its Jewish National Library. By the late 1930s Jewish claims to Palestine, both biblical and historical, were reinforced by their achievements in constructing the foundations of a modern society.

The Modernization of Turkey and Iran

In the second half of the nineteenth century internal problems had made it difficult for the Ottoman Empire to deal effectively with external challenges. The reactionary excesses of the Sultan Abdul Hamid (1876–1909) stimulated opposition among Western-educated reformers and army officers (see Chapter 31). These groups formed the Young Turk movement, which in 1908 forced Abdul Hamid to restore the constitution and the parliament. When the sultan attempted a counterrevolution, the Young Turks unseated him. They soon imposed rigid centralization based on Turkish supremacy on a state that included substantial Arab, Armenian, and Slavic minorities. Wooed by German agents, who trained their army, the Young Turks brought Turkey into the First World War on Germany's side.

Military defeat precipitated the final demise of the Ottoman Empire. While the subject Arabs were breaking away from Istanbul, the Allies imposed a harsh peace treaty on Turkey that provided for the partition of its empire. In these circumstances, patriotic Turks turned to Mustapha Kemal (1881–1938), who had defended Gallipoli against the British in 1915. The Western-educated Kemal, charismatic and strong-willed, became the focus of a nationalist movement that revolutionized Turkish life. Setting up a new capital at Ankara, in central Anatolia—a site chosen as deliberately remote from European influence—he won popular acclaim by defying the Allies, abolishing the privileges that foreigners once had in Turkey, and repelling the Greek armies that attempted to wrest further territory from the Turks. While recognizing the inevitability of Arab independence, he was unwilling to surrender Asia Minor, eastern Thrace, or the Dardanelles. In 1923, after creating a republic and defeating a Greek thrust against Asia Minor, he forced a revised peace treaty on the Allies that permitted Turkey to keep Asia Minor and a small strip of territory around Istanbul on the European side of the Turkish Straits.

Kemal—who was given the name Atatürk, or "Father of the Turks"—embarked on a program of massive change designed to bring Turkey into the modern era. Although technically president of the republic, he governed as a dictator under a one-party system with a national assembly elected by indirect vote of a limited electorate, made universal only in 1934. His ability to introduce far-reaching change stemmed in part from an appeal to Turkish nationalism. As the Japanese had done so successfully in their own drive for Westernization, Kemal now played on the fear and resentment that Western imperialism had provoked while simultaneously stressing Turkey's historic role as the dominant force in a region of lesser states. With ruthless determination, he abolished ancient customs and swept away cultural patterns he felt impeded Turkish modernization. Outwardly, the most visible signs of Kemal's revolution were the changes in dress that he decreed. Government officials were required to substitute Western business suits and hats for robes and fezzes. Western-style family names were introduced, and place names were altered to symbolize the break from an archaic past. But other changes had a more profound impact. Kemal, who professed no religious beliefs, struck deeply at Islamic tradition by separating church from state and secularizing the nation's educational and legal systems. A simpler, more phonetic alphabet replaced the intricate Arabic script as the written language, and the government launched a far-reaching educational campaign among millions of previously illiterate Turkish citizens.

Kemal's vigorous social reforms inspired a similar modernization experiment in Iran. In a move much like the revolt of the Young Turks, nationalistic Iranian reformers forced the despotic and backward shah to grant a constitution in 1906. The reform momentum was shattered the next year when the British and the Russians divided Iran into spheres of influence and assumed substantive control of the country. When the British tried to impose their authority over the entire country after the war, Reza Khan Pahlavi (1877–1944), a colonel in the Persian Cossack Brigade, took power and assumed the title of shah in 1925.

Reza Shah Pahlavi greatly admired Kemal Atatürk and imitated his modernization program, though with less success. The shah's secularization efforts met with fierce opposition from the powerful Islamic religious leaders, who resented all Western influence and were as strong as the small group of European-trained reformers. Like Kemal, Reza Shah Pahlavi changed place names and Westernized dress. He built an efficient army and encouraged trade and industry, but he was personally corrupt, and his government proved tyrannical.

In Turkey, Kemal's reforms radically altered the status of women. Polygamy, still practiced by a minority, was abolished in 1926, and marriage laws were modeled after Western examples. Wealthy women began to attend universities and abandoned their veiled costumes in favor of modern European dress. In 1934 women were enfranchised and made eligible for election to the National Assembly. Reza Shah Pahlavi introduced similar policies in Iran, although there Islamic influence kept a stronger hold on women. These and other changes marked a sharp departure from tradition, whose tribal and Islamic practices had kept women in bondage to men, secluded from public life, and confined by strict codes of behavior. The older customs continued to prevail in the Kingdom of Saudi Arabia and elsewhere. Nevertheless, the new social norms fostered by Kemal Atatürk and Reza Shah Pahlavi, to-

Mustapha Kemal Atatürk, the architect of modern Turkey and its first president. [Culver Pictures]

gether with the emergence of a cohesive Jewish community in Palestine where women labored on an equal basis with men, broke the centuries-old pattern of female subservience in the Middle East.

ஷ்ஷ்   ஷ்ஷ்   ஷ்ஷ்

Early in the twentieth century the largest and oldest societies in the world broke sharply with the patterns of the past. In Russia, China, India, and the Middle East, half of the world's people rejected the political systems that had governed them and strove to remake their societies.

In Russia, a corrupt, ineffective, and repressive regime was toppled by an alliance of workers and intellectuals under the charismatic leadership of Lenin. In November 1917 his Bolsheviks swept away the provisional government that had replaced the Romanov dynasty and began a radical experiment in economic and social mobilization. They instituted a program of forced modernization that would enable the Soviet Union, as Russia was now called, to catch up with western Europe and improve the economic condition of its people. On Lenin's death in 1924, leadership passed to the more ruthless, power-conscious Stalin. Lenin's dream of a workers' democracy quickly faded, but Russia's industrial and military power grew rapidly, and the Soviet example of successful revolution and modernization exerted worldwide influence.

In China the revolutionary Kuomintang party succeeded the antiquated Ch'ing dynasty, which collapsed in 1911, but the revolutionaries were too few and too divided to form an effective government. The revolution was betrayed by a military strong man, Yuan Shih-kai, and upon his death in 1916 China disintegrated into a civil war among rival warlords. Under the leadership of Chiang Kai-shek, the Kuomintang managed to form a national government in 1927 but failed to unite the country or to eliminate the rival Chinese Communist party. The Japanese invasion of 1937 mortally weakened the Kuomintang, and civil war after 1945 soon brought the Communists to power with their radical solutions to China's urgent problems of poverty and weakness.

In India the long struggle for independence from British rule made real progress only after 1919, when Mahatma Gandhi greatly widened the movement's support by appealing to mass sentiment. Gandhi restored Indians' pride in their own tradition and identity. With the help of Jawaharlal Nehru, he forged a political instrument, the Congress party, into a successful vehicle for freeing India from colonialism and addressing its inherited problems of economic backwardness and inequality.

In the Middle East both Turkish and European colonial domination was also rejected, and new regimes were created in each country. In 1919 the League of Nations replaced the centuries-long rule of the Ottoman Empire in the Middle East with British and French mandates, designed to provide a transition to independence. The seeds of Arab nationalism grew slowly in the interwar period, for rulers such as Faisal in Iraq and ibn-Saud in Saudi Arabia remained heavily dependent on the European powers, while leaders such as Kemal Atatürk in Turkey and Reza Shah Pahlavi in Iran attempted to modernize their countries according to Western models. The colonization of Palestine by Jewish settlers under British patronage further exacerbated Arab nationalism. Only in the post–World War II era did true independence develop, when several factors combined to bring the new Arab states together against the lingering dominance of the West: the enormous financial strength achieved through the regional coordination of oil resources, a new-found cultural identity inspired by a return to Islamic fundamentalism, and common opposition to the Jewish state of Israel.

Each of these regions linked approaches based on its individual historical experience to the goal of creating new national strength and development. Each swept away unacceptable political systems and built in their place new governments designed to be more effective in responding to urgent national needs. Taken together, the revolutionary changes in these four major regions did indeed shake the world, by fundamentally transforming the half of it that they governed and by inspiring millions in the other half to do the same.

Notes

1.   J. Reed, *Ten Days That Shook the World* (New York: Random House, 1960), pp. 170–171.

2.   A. Kollontai, *The Autobiography of a Sexually Emancipated Communist Woman*, trans. S. Attanasio (New York: Herder & Herder, 1971), p. 13.

3.   D. N. Jacobs, ed., *From Marx to Mao and Marchais: Documents on the Development of Communist Variations* (New York: Longman, 1979), pp. 104–105.

4.   F. Claudin, *The Communist Movement: From Comintern to Cominform*, vol. 1, trans. B. Pearce (New York: Monthly Review Press, 1975), pp. 72–73.

Suggestions for Further Reading

Balfour, Baron J. P. *Atatürk: The Rebirth of a Nation*. London: Weidenfeld & Nicolson, 1964.

Bondurant, J. *The Conquest of Violence: The Gandhian Philosophy of Conflict*. Berkeley: University of California Press, 1969.

Carr, E. H. *The Russian Revolution: From Lenin to Stalin*. New York: Free Press, 1979.

Chamberlin, W. H. *The Russian Revolution, 1917–1921*. New York: Macmillan, 1952.

Chen, J. T. *The May Fourth Movement in Shanghai*. Leiden, Netherlands: Brill, 1971.

Daniels, R. V. *Red October: The Bolshevik Revolution of 1917*. New York: Scribner, 1967.

Deutscher, I. *The Prophet Armed: Trotsky, 1879–1921*. New York: Viking, 1965.

Eastman, L. E. *China Under Nationalist Rule, 1927–1937*. Stanford, Calif.: Stanford University Press, 1974.

Edwardes, M. *The Last Years of British India*. London: Cassell, 1963.

Fischer, L. *The Life of Lenin*. New York: Harper & Row, 1965.

Gasster, M. *Chinese Intellectuals and the Revolution of 1911*. Seattle: University of Washington Press, 1969.

Irving, R. G. *Indian Summer: Luytens, Baker, and Imperial New Delhi*. New Haven, Conn.: Yale University Press, 1982.

Iyer, R. *The Moral and Political Thought of Mahatma Gandhi*. New York: Oxford University Press, 1986.

Low, D. A., ed. *Congress and the Raj: Facets of the Indian Struggle, 1917–47*. Columbia: University of Missouri Press, 1977.

Majumdar, R. C. *History of the Freedom Movement in India*. Calcutta: K. L. Mukhopadhyay, 1962.

Pandey, B. N. *Nehru*. London: Macmillan, 1976.

Reed, J. *Ten Days That Shook the World*. New York: Random House, 1960.

Sachar, H. M. *The Emergence of the Middle East, 1914–1924*. New York: Knopf, 1969.

Sheridan, J. E. *China in Disintegration: The Republican Era*. Glencoe, Ill.: Free Press, 1975.

Trotsky, L. *The Russian Revolution*. Garden City, N.Y.: Anchor/Doubleday, 1959.

Ulam, A. B. *The Bolsheviks*. New York: Macmillan, 1965.

———. *Lenin and the Bolsheviks*. London: Collins, 1969.

Upton, J. M. *The History of Modern Iran*. Cambridge, Mass.: Harvard University Press, 1960.

Von Laue, T. H. *Why Lenin? Why Stalin?*. London: Weidenfeld & Nicolson, 1966.

Wilbur, C. M. *Sun Yat-sen: Frustrated Patriot*. New York: Columbia University Press, 1976.

Wolfe, B. D. *Three Who Made a Revolution*, rev. ed. New York: Dial Press, 1964.

Wright, M. C. *China in Revolution: The First Phase, 1900–1903*. New Haven, Conn.: Yale University Press, 1968.

Young, E. P. *The Presidency of Yuan Shih-kai*. Ann Arbor: University of Michigan Press, 1977.

Fascism and the Crisis of Democracy

The year 1919 opened with general optimism about the prospects for democracy on the Continent. Widespread confidence prevailed that the leaders of the victorious Allied powers who assembled at Paris in January would not only arrange a lasting peace but would also fulfill President Wilson's dream of making the world "safe for democracy." Indeed, the collapse of the imperial autocracies in Russia, Germany, and Austria-Hungary was followed by the creation of parliamentary governments throughout central and eastern Europe. Within two decades, however, liberal ideals and democratic governments were in crisis as fascist movements developed in almost every country and authoritarian regimes emerged in many. By 1933 fascists had seized power only in Italy and Germany, but their appeal was so pervasive that one historian has characterized the entire interwar period as the "epoch of fascism."*

---

*The spelling *Fascism* refers to Italian Fascism, *fascism* to the generic variety.

Adolf Hitler salutes upon emerging from a meeting with his diplomatic corps. [FPG]

Fascism, in contrast to communism, proclaimed itself a spiritual rather than a materialist philosophy, but its appeal nevertheless increased dramatically during periods of economic hardship. The financial crisis that began in 1929 plunged the world into an economic collapse of unprecedented dimensions, causing extreme social distress and challenging capitalism itself. The political consequences of the Great Depression were equally disastrous. The political systems of Britain, France, and the United States, where democracy was deeply rooted, were threatened, though without succumbing to fascism. In the newer states of central and eastern Europe, however, where democracy had been largely the product of the 1919 settlements, liberal governments often fell victim to dictatorship and spawned native fascist movements. Together, fascism and the Great Depression posed a deadly challenge to democracy.

The Nature of Fascism

Many Europeans, dissatisfied with liberal governments but unwilling to adopt communism, regarded fascism as an alternative, a "third way" capable of solving the problems of industrial society. Fascists claimed their system would overcome class struggle and transform society. Over the next two decades, however, fascism inflicted suffering and destruction on millions and collapsed only after the most devastating war in history.

Scholars continue to debate the nature of fascism. Some regard it as a universal phenomenon that transcended national borders and possessed a core of similar characteristics in all countries. Yet most experts concede that despite some similarities, Italian Fascism and German Nazism had deep ideological differences and that each system in turn differed from fascist movements elsewhere. It may be possible to understand fascism only in the context of a particular nation during a specific time. Although the term *fascist* continues to be applied to noncommunist authoritarian regimes, some doubt that we can speak of fascism outside the European setting and beyond the chronological period 1919–1945.

Nor is it easy to classify fascism according to traditional political categories. Was it a movement of the Right or of the Left? Was it a revolutionary, a conservative, or a reactionary force? Some experts suggest that these questions may be resolved in part by recognizing the distinction between fascism as a movement before it came to power and fascism as a regime after it seized control of a government. This approach is based on the fact that once in office, fascist leaders often compromised with traditional power elites in order to consolidate their authority, and these compromises changed the original aims of their movements.

General Characteristics

However difficult it is to define fascism precisely, it is possible to identify characteristics found in virtually all such movements. The fascists rejected the concept of liberty inherited from the French Revolution and nineteenth-century liberalism. They argued that democracy corrupts the human spirit with greed, sacrifices national interests for the sake of party and class concerns, and replaces heroism and honor with alienation and a loss of community. Fascists claimed they would eliminate the materialism and class conflict implicit in Marxism, which divided the national community. The fascist claim that forces of will could create a new age of heroism had its roots in the Romantic rejection of Enlightenment rationalism. In its place they proclaimed the superiority of instinct, feeling, and blood, and they glorified violence and action. The fascists promised to restore idealism, youthful activism, and the spirit of sacrifice and to integrate every class and citizen into the all-embracing "totalitarian" state. As distinct from traditional authoritarian governments, totalitarian regimes attempt to shape minds and attitudes, indoctrinating people and turning them into loyal supporters. To achieve its goals, the totalitarian state employs terror and propaganda.

Dictators such as Benito Mussolini and Adolf Hitler played crucial roles in fascist regimes. These were sustained in large part by the cult of the charismatic leader, whose authority was unquestioned and to whom all loyalty and obedience were directed. Propaganda and public rituals instilled in the population a fanatical faith in the infallible leader, who, with an elite party, ruled in the name of a single national will. Future leaders would be trained through the party, which acted as a link between the people and the state.

The mass base of fascism came chiefly from the lower middle class. White-collar workers, civil servants, artisans, and shopkeepers resented the wealthy, powerful capitalists just as they feared the working classes. This lower-middle-class group, from which the early movements filled their ranks, hoped that fascism would solve the postwar economic crisis and restore traditional values—respect for authority, family, and nation. It shared the fascists' alienation from the existing social and political order, whose elites monopolized power and restricted advancement. Support for fascism was not limited to the lower middle class, however. Fascist programs were tailored to attract diverse interests so that segments of the aristocracy, big business, urban labor, and the peasantry found them appealing.

While fascism incorporated some aspects of socialist thought, its major appeal was to nationalism or racism. Such appeals cut across class lines and economic interests, and fascist propaganda played successfully on the popular desire for national greatness and ethnic dominance. Mussolini's dream of re-creating a Roman empire and Hitler's prophecy of a "thousand-year Reich" reflected the fascist thirst for expansion, and the foreign policies of both dictators were aggressive. For some fascist movements—particularly the German National Socialists—racism was the core of their ideologies, but for others—such as the Italian Fascists—racism represented a later addition. Nevertheless, many fascists emphasized the biological or spiritual distinctiveness of their national "races" and exalted the unity of "blood and soil" in their national histories. Ethnic minorities are usually suppressed in authoritarian regimes, but fascism systematically eliminated entire populations as the extreme logic of its racism unfolded: hundreds of thousands of North African natives were slaughtered by Italian Fascist armies, and millions of Jews were murdered by the Nazis in central Europe.

The Origins of Fascism

In the broadest terms, fascism was the product of crisis—economic, political, social, and cultural. Some historians regard fascism as a reaction against ruling elites, while others consider it as a strategy adopted by those elites to forestall revolution from below. Although a few scholars insist that its origins must be traced back hundreds of years, many agree that we must look for its sources in the nineteenth century. In Italy and Germany the manner and circumstances in which national unification was achieved may have had an important bearing on the origins of fascism. Unification was the work of political and economic elites who excluded the masses from the process of nation building and used the instruments of power politics—war and diplomacy—to achieve their purposes. These elites shaped the new national states according to their own interests to secure power. Large segments of the populations of these countries were therefore unintegrated into national life and looked to fascism as a response to the elitist nature of national unification.

The Marxist interpretation argues that fascism is the product of the class struggle that takes place in all capitalist societies. As the counterrevolutionary form adopted by the capitalist classes to suppress the workers in an effort to prevent the proletarian revolution, fascism, according to the Marxist interpretation, is the last, desperate attempt by the industrial and financial interests to save dying capitalism. While there are many variations of this interpretation, most Marxists now consider fascism an independent force distinct from capitalism itself. In this view, capitalists supported and used fascism as a weapon in their struggle against the working classes. The "Red scare" that spread throughout Europe following the Russian Revolution provided the atmosphere in which fascism rose to power, and the anticommunist thrust of fascism was the capitalist response to that revolutionary threat.

Other scholars defend national unification as the triumph of nineteenth-century liberalism. They argue that the origins of fascism are to be found in the moral and cultural crisis that Europe experienced at the turn of the century. The late nineteenth-century "revolt against positivism" undermined many of the ideals inherited from the Enlightenment and the French Revolution and challenged the underlying Judeo-Christian ethical principles on which Western civilization was based. The decline of these values affected political behavior and produced social disintegration, and World War I was seen as an irrational triumph over reason. Accordingly, fascism emerged out of the dislocation of the postwar period as an extreme revolt against positivist values.

Marxist and non-Marxist scholars agree that fascism was an immediate result of World War I. In the postwar crisis, a number of elements—the presence of numerous unemployed and alienated veterans, thwarted lower-middle-class aspirations, capitalist fears of revolution, the outrage of nations defeated in the war or in the peace settlements—were skillfully manipulated by fascism.

Italy: The Fascist Triumph

The life of Benito Mussolini and the history of Italian Fascism were inextricably linked. Italian Fascism and its regime bore the indelible stamp of his personality and ideas, but he never dominated his movement as Hitler did Nazism.

Benito Mussolini

The founder of Fascism was born in 1883 in a small village in northeastern Italy. Mussolini's father, a blacksmith, was a socialist from whom he inherited a radical, anticlerical bias. He displayed a violent personality but a keen intelligence. His mother, a devout schoolteacher, sent him to a Catholic seminary, from which he was expelled for having stabbed another pupil. By 1901 Mussolini was teaching elementary school and active in local socialist politics. The next year he fled to Switzerland to avoid the draft, remaining there until 1904. As a center for revolutionary exiles from many countries, Switzerland afforded Mussolini the opportunity to develop his socialist ideas. He read widely and worked as a propagandist for the Italian Socialist Party (PSI). After his return to Italy, he distinguished himself as a revolutionary socialist, a public speaker, and a journalist. During the Italo-Turkish War (1911–1912) he appeared as a staunch pacifist and antiimperialist, serving a prison term for inciting antiwar riots. In 1912 he helped the revolutionary socialist faction seize control of the PSI and was made editor of *Avanti!,* the official Socialist party daily.

By the outbreak of World War I, Mussolini had become

a prominent socialist leader. During the "interventionist crisis" (1914–1915), in which Italy remained neutral while arranging to enter the war on the Allied side, he rejected some of his socialist principles, particularly his antiwar stance. Concluding that the war could act as a catalyst for revolution, he advocated Italian intervention and as a result was expelled from the PSI in 1915. That year, with money from industrialists and foreign sources, he founded his own newspaper, *Il Popolo d'Italia*, which became the official Fascist organ.

Following a brief stint as a soldier, during which he was wounded and made a sergeant, Mussolini returned to political agitation. He had meanwhile absorbed nationalist ideas from Cesare Battisti (1875–1916) and abandoned his belief in the class struggle. By the end of the war Mussolini was a revolutionary without an ideology, a leader in search of a movement.

Postwar Crisis in Italy

Peace produced a crisis in Italy. To bolster wartime morale the government had promised land for peasants, jobs for workers, and political and social equality. These promises created heady expectations among Italians of all classes, but postwar realities brought swift disillusionment. Italy's national debt had risen dramatically, the value of its currency had fallen sharply, and foreign trade had been seriously curtailed for more than three years. The spiraling cost of living hit the working and middle classes hard. Demobilized soldiers demanded jobs, many of which had been filled by women during the war, and the difficulties of converting the economy to peacetime production resulted in more than 2 million unemployed by the end of 1919.

◉ Theory of the Fascist State ◉

Fascist political theory rejected nineteenth-century liberalism, which held that government's function was to guarantee the rights and freedoms of individuals. Instead, Fascists argued that service to an all-powerful state was the highest moral goal. In these passages, written in collaboration with the philosopher Giovanni Gentile, Mussolini explained the essence of what he called the totalitarian state.

Against individualism, the Fascist conception is for the State; and it is for the individual in so far as he coincides with the State, which is the conscience and universal will of man in his historical existence. It is opposed to classical Liberalism, which arose from the neccessity of reacting against absolutism, and which brought its historical purpose to an end when the State was transformed into the conscience and will of the people. Liberalism denied the State in the interests of the particular individual; Fascism reaffirms the State as the true reality of the individual. And if Liberty is to be the attribute of the real man, and not of that abstract puppet envisaged by individualistic Liberalism, Fascism is for liberty. And for the only liberty which can be a real thing, the liberty of the State, and of the individual within the state, and nothing human or spiritual exists, much less has value, outside the State. In this sense Fascism is totalitarian. . . .

The Fascist State, the highest and most powerful form of personality, is a force, but a spiritual force, which takes over all the forms of the moral and intellectual life of man. It cannot therefore confine itself simply to the functions of order and supervision as Liberalism desired. It is not simply a mechanism which limits the sphere of the supposed liberties of the individual. It is the form, the inner standard and the discipline of the whole person; it saturates the will as well as the intelligence. . . .

Fascism, in short, is not only the giver of laws and the founder of institutions, but the educator and promoter of spiritual life. It wants to remake, not the forms of human life, but its content, man, character, faith. And to this end it requires discipline and authority that can enter into the spirits of men and there govern unopposed. . . .

Source: B. Mussolini, "The Doctrine of Fascism" (1932), in M. Oakeshott, ed., *The Social and Political Doctrines of Contemporary Europe* (Cambridge: Cambridge University Press, 1939), pp. 166, 168.

Economic hardships were compounded by a crisis of national prestige. The Treaty of London (1915) that brought Italy into the war had committed the Allies to extensive territorial concessions for Italy, including the Trentino and southern Tirol, the port of Trieste, the Istrian peninsula, the Dalmatian coast, and the Dodecanese islands, which the Italians had occupied since 1912. But at the Paris peace conference Woodrow Wilson and Lloyd George not only gave Dalmatia to the new Yugoslav state but also refused to compensate Italy with the port city of Fiume, which Prime Minister Orlando demanded. The Italians felt betrayed, and a patriotic frenzy swept the country. Nationalists blamed Orlando's liberal government for what they termed the "mutilated victory," and Fiume became the symbol of Italy's frustrated hopes.

In September 1919 the nationalist writer and adventurer Gabriele D'Annunzio (1863–1938) invaded Fiume with a group of veterans and set up an independent state. Although the Italian government drove him out after a year, the Fiume adventure set a dangerous precedent for military coups and demonstrated the extent of nationalist sentiment. While he ruled Fiume, D'Annunzio adopted symbols and techniques that Mussolini later copied, including the Roman salute, fiery rhetoric, mass torch-lit rallies, and the title of *Duce* ("leader").

The frustration most Italians felt was directed against the liberal regime. In the postwar elections of November 1919, held on the basis of universal male suffrage, the liberals, who had enjoyed a large majority of seats in the Chamber of Deputies since the unification of Italy, suddenly found themselves reduced to the third-ranking party in Parliament, behind the Socialists and the Italian Popular Party, which combined progressive Catholic principles with demands for social and economic reform. The Socialists and Catholics together held enough seats to control the Chamber of Deputies, but each failed to form a coalition with the other, and King Victor Emmanuel III (1900–1946) continued to select his prime ministers from the ranks of the discredited liberals.

Against this background, industrial and agrarian unrest reached major proportions, with more than 1,600 strikes in 1919 alone. In the impoverished south, landless peasants led by veterans and socialists seized uncultivated land, and in September 1920 a major factory sit-in in the northern industrial centers threatened to develop into a revolution. This "occupation of the factories" helped push the industrialists into the arms of the Fascists.

Mussolini (left) leading the Fascist march on Rome in the fall of 1922. [Brown Brothers]

The Fascist Movement

In this tumultuous context Mussolini founded the Fascist movement. At a meeting of about 100 followers in Milan in March 1919, he established the first *Fascio di Combattimento* ("combat group"), a mixture of nationalist intellectuals, former socialists and syndicalists, and war veterans. The name of the movement was derived from the Latin word *fasces*, a bundle of rods tied around the shaft of an ax, which had been used by the ancient Romans to symbolize unity and authority. As Fascist groups spread throughout northern and central Italy, membership grew from less than 1,000 in the summer of 1919 to 20,000 by late 1920 and to more than 250,000 by 1922. The rank and file were veterans who sought to forge a sense of community based on the "spirit of the trenches"—comradeship, loyalty, bravery, and action. These alienated young men formed Mussolini's paramilitary squads, whose members came to be known as *Squadristi*. Their parades and rallies, black-shirted uniforms, and nihilistic slogans vividly symbolized Italy's postwar crisis.

The *Squadristi* unleashed a reign of terror across the nation under the command of local Fascist chieftains. They launched "punitive expeditions" against socialist and trade union offices, urban strikers, and peasant protesters. By 1921, in the aftermath of the factory occupations, the antisocialist campaign was bringing Fascism financial backing from industrialists and landowners, while the liberal government took no steps to halt Fascist violence. Fascist

◎ Mussolini's Seizure of Power ◎

In late 1924 Mussolini was accused by the opposition of having ordered a secret Fascist police to assassinate socialist deputy Giacomo Matteotti. After weeks of hesitation, during which pressure from both his enemies as well as from radical Fascist leaders mounted, he assumed full authority and declared a dictatorship in a speech on January 3, 1925.

It is I who in this chamber make accusations against myself. . . . If I had founded a secret police, I would have done so through the kind of violence that is an integral part of history. I have always said . . . that violence, to be effective, must be surgical, intelligent, and high-minded. . . .

I declare here, before the entire Chamber and before the Italian people, that I and I alone assume political, moral, and historical responsibility for everything that has happened.

If this surprising statement is sufficient to indict me, then bring forth the scaffolds! If Fascism has been only castor oil and clubs instead of the superb passion of Italy's best youth, the fault is mine. If Fascism has been a gang of criminals, then I am their leader.

If all the violence in this country has been the result of a special historical, moral, and political climate, I am responsible for that climate because I created it. . . .

When two elements are in inevitable conflict, the solution is force. History has never known another solution.

I tell you now that the problem will be solved. Fascism, the government, the party, are all in working order.

You are all under an illusion. You believed that Fascism was finished because I compromised it, but this is not at all the case. Italy wants peace, tranquility, and calm labor. We will give it these things, with love if possible, but with force if necessary.

Rest assured that within the next twenty-four hours the situation will be clarified in every way.

Source: E. Susmel and D. Susmel, eds., *Opera omnia di Benito Mussolini*, vol. 21 (Florence: La Fenice, 1953), pp. 235–241. Trans. P. V. Cannistraro.

assaults were extended to city halls and provincial officials and were followed by open threats to take over the state.

The March on Rome

While the Blackshirts' violent tactics weakened the Socialist party and created the impression that Fascism possessed a strength beyond its actual numbers, Mussolini maintained the profile of a respectable politician. In 1921 he signed a peace pact with the Socialists, which he promptly violated. That same year the Fascist movement, which had been converted into the National Fascist party (PNF), won 35 seats in Parliament. Mussolini now had the prestige of being a deputy. The Liberal premier, Giovanni Giolitti, sought to lure him into a coalition of moderate and conservative parties with offers of a ministerial post, hoping thereby to co-opt the Fascists into the established

order. Like most other liberals, the premier failed to understand that Fascism was not a conventional political force.

In 1922 Mussolini marched on Rome to frighten the government into conceding power to Fascism. Between October 26 and 28, tens of thousands of Blackshirts moved toward the capital while Mussolini waited in his headquarters in Milan. King Victor Emmanuel III, uncertain of the army's loyalty and fearful of civil war, refused to sign a decree of martial law. On October 29 he asked Mussolini to become prime minister. Mussolini arrived in Rome the following day, dressed in top hat and tails, and took the oath of office. Only then did the Blackshirts enter Rome, but now to cheer Mussolini before the royal palace. The liberal state had collapsed in the face of a bluff.

Mussolini took office by legal means, but with only 35 Fascist deputies in a chamber of more than 500, he moved cautiously to consolidate his strength. Over the next year and a half he was granted extensive authority, muzzled the press, and passed a new election law designed to assure Fascists a majority in Parliament. According to this measure, the party that received the largest popular vote, with a minimum of 25 percent, would have two-thirds of the seats in the Chamber of Deputies. In 1924 the Fascists swept the elections by rigging the polls and intimidating opponents with violence, thus securing control of Parliament. Mussolini grew more confident, especially after the army agreed to support the regime in return for the creation of a Fascist militia that would absorb the Blackshirts.

In the summer of 1924 the courageous Socialist leader Giacomo Matteotti (1885–1924), who had exposed the illegality of the Fascist electoral victory, was murdered by Fascist thugs. Popular reaction against Mussolini was so strong that he feared dismissal by the king. Opposition deputies withdrew in protest from the Chamber, and Blackshirt leaders pressured Mussolini to complete the seizure of power. On January 3, 1925, in a forceful speech before Parliament, he assumed total responsibility and proclaimed the Fascist dictatorship. This speech was followed by a "second wave" of violence against the opposition. Over the next four years Mussolini created the institutions of the first fascist regime in history.

Germany: From Weimar to Hitler

Nazism, the German variety of fascism, developed shortly after Mussolini's Fascist group was founded, but it took more than a decade longer to come to power. Outwardly, the two movements appeared to be almost identical—radical parties with ideologies inspired by elements of socialism, syndicalism, and nationalism; the cult of the charismatic leader; a rank-and-file membership consisting largely of the lower middle class and veterans disaffected by the postwar crisis; a paramilitary organization with uniforms, slogans, and a philosophy of violence; resentment toward capitalists and hatred for the communists; and a revolutionary determination to destroy parliamentary government.

Despite these similarities, the Nazi regime was generally acknowledged to have been more thoroughly totalitarian than Mussolini's system. The more overtly racial component in Nazi ideology represented a major difference between the two movements and in part explains the greater brutality of the Third Reich. In its early stages, Mussolini's cabinet included several Jewish ministers, a situation inconceivable in Nazi Germany. During the 1920s Hitler had regarded Mussolini as a mentor, the elder statesman of international fascism; after the Nazi takeover in Germany, however, Hitler emerged as the senior partner in what became known as the Rome-Berlin Axis. This

change was less a result of the personalities of the two men than a reflection of the disparity between the industrial and military capacities of Italy and Germany.

Revolution and the Weimar Republic

The military collapse of 1918 had a profound impact on Germany's political and social fabric. Revolutionary unrest erupted throughout the nation, and worker and soldiers' councils similar to those in Russia were formed. On November 8 Kurt Eisner, a communist leader in Munich, set up a separate Republic of Bavaria that was put down only after his assassination and a civil war between rightists and leftists. When Kaiser William II abdicated on November 9 and his chancellor resigned, the government was placed provisionally in the hands of Friedrich Ebert and Philip Scheidemann, both moderate Social Democrats. That same afternoon Scheidemann proclaimed a republic with Ebert as its first chancellor. Extremists on both the left and the right, however, attempted to seize power. To maintain order, Ebert offered the German high command guarantees of protection if the army remained loyal. Revolutionary Marxists, known as Spartacists (after the Thracian gladiator Spartacus, who led a slave uprising against Rome in 73 B.C.), revolted in 1919 under the leadership of Rosa Luxemburg and Karl Liebknecht. During "Spartacist Week" (January 6–15) they battled the government in the streets of Berlin. Luxemburg and Liebknecht were killed by soldiers sent to arrest them. The government also turned for support to private military groups known as the Free Corps, headed by embittered former officers and armed veterans. The Free Corps, from which would come many of the early adherents to the Nazi movement, would eventually turn against the government itself.

After the Spartacist revolt, an array of moderate political parties—the largest of which were the Social Democrats, the Catholic Center party, and the Democrats—met in the National Assembly at Weimar to draft a new constitution. This document (adopted in July 1919), which created the German Republic, reflected progressive social ideas and democratic principles. It provided for universal suffrage, a cabinet system of government with an elected president and an appointed chancellor, and a bill of rights that guaranteed extensive civil liberties, education, and employment.

Although the so-called Weimar Republic was on paper one of the most liberal governments in central Europe, it was burdened from the start with serious problems. In March 1920, militarists led by Wolfgang Kapp attempted a *Putsch*, or coup, by marching on Berlin. Kapp's putsch was suppressed only by a socialist-led general strike. In the first election under the new constitution, held three months later, the three-party centrist coalition that had dominated the National Assembly fell from 76 to 47 percent of the popular vote, while the parties on the extreme right and left almost doubled their support. Moderate forces never again regained a majority, and the 13 years of the Weimar government produced 20 different cabinets. The German people looked on the republic with suspicion, especially since the collapse of the kaiser's authority had been forced on the country by the Allies. Right-wing reactionaries and leftist extremists regarded the regime as an enemy and plotted against it. Although the army had agreed to protect the government, its high command was uncomfortable with the democratic system and blamed the republic for the humiliating Treaty of Versailles.

Germans found it difficult to understand how their country, once an industrial giant with the best army in the world, could have lost the war. This blow to their national pride was compounded by the fact that the Allies had forced them to accept total responsibility for the war. Right-wing extremists, monarchists, and army officers manufactured the legend that Germany had been "stabbed in the back" by traitors, whom they identified as Marxists and Jews. Reactionaries pointed to the helpless new republic, shorn of its army, as a symptom of decadence. Extremist hatred of the republic led to the assassination of two progressive ministers—Matthias Erzberger, killed in August 1921, and Walther Rathenau, murdered a year later.

The economic problems that beset postwar Germany fueled the feeling that the Weimar Republic was too weak to rule. The government responded to the severe unemployment that struck the country by printing huge quantities of paper currency in order to finance assistance programs and prevent massive starvation. The result was spiraling inflation that devastated much of the middle class,

a condition exacerbated by the French occupation of the Ruhr valley in 1923. The German mark, worth about 12 U.S. cents at the end of the war, was now virtually worthless—German shoppers paid for a loaf of bread or a newspaper with sacks of currency. The almost daily rise in the cost of living left salaries far behind, and people on fixed incomes—pensioners, widows, wounded veterans—were virtually wiped out. By 1925 inflation had destroyed 50 percent of the capital of the lower middle class, more than half a million of whom were forced into factory work. A personal notice in a German newspaper revealed the depth of despair: "30 years old, married, 3 children. Nothing earned for 3 years. Future? Poorhouse, madhouse, or the gas jet."[1] The devastating economic collapse further undermined public confidence in the republic.

Adolf Hitler and the Rise of Nazism

The Nazi movement grew and came to power in the postwar crisis. Adolf Hitler, its founder, was born in 1889 in Braunau, Austria, near the Bavarian border. His father, a minor customs official, was unsympathetic to his son's aesthetic leanings, and the young Hitler was always much closer to his mother. Frustrated by his desire to be an artist, he did poorly in his studies and never graduated from high school. In Vienna, where Hitler lived between 1908 and 1913, he evolved his theories of history, politics, and racism. He lived a harsh, bohemian existence, working odd jobs and earning money by painting watercolors and postcards. Although he developed some skill as an architectural draftsman, his ambitions were frustrated when he was refused admission to the Vienna School of Architecture.

Hitler read voraciously, but his intellectual development was unstructured, and he absorbed a muddle of ideas and attitudes that ultimately formed the basis of Nazi ideology. Racism, in particular anti-Semitism, had the most powerful impact on him. Vienna's population reflected the mixed ethnic composition of the Austro-Hungarian Empire, and in the late nineteenth century two men, Karl Lüger and Georg von Schönerer, channeled Austria's anti-Semitic traditions into political movements. Lüger was the dominant figure in the Christian Socialist party, a Catholic organization supported by reactionary conservatives who elected him mayor of Vienna on an anti-Semitic platform. Schönerer, leader of the lower-middle-class Liberal party and a member of the Austrian Parliament, organized student clubs in Vienna on the basis of anti-Semitism and generated widespread worker support for a campaign against the alleged influence of Jewish bankers in the imperial government. Moreover, he believed that the "superior" German race should rule over the "inferior" Slavs of central and eastern Europe—Czechs, Serbs, Poles, and others.

As unemployment and inflation mounted in postwar Berlin, scenes of poverty became painfully familiar. Here Berliners sell tin cans for scrap during the severe inflation of 1923. [Granger Collection]

Under the influence of these sources, Hitler became obsessed with the idea of race. He came to see Judaism and Marxism as twin forms of degeneracy and to identify the Jews as the principal source of moral and cultural decline and corruption in Europe. From Schönerer's pan-German ideology he concluded that Germany and Austria must be united into a "greater Germany," while Lüger's political success suggested that the key to a radical movement was the ability to generate and channel the enthusiasm of the masses.

When World War I broke out, Hitler volunteered in a Bavarian infantry regiment, for he considered himself a German. He fought at the front, was promoted to corporal, and was twice awarded the Iron Cross. The end of the war found him recuperating in a hospital from the effects of poison gas.

At the end of World War I, Hitler worked in Munich as a political informant for the army. In this capacity he joined a small group known as the German Worker's party, one of many such organizations that sought to stimulate German patriotism and infuse the working class with the spirit of nationalism. Hitler spent the next five years developing his political talents and leadership within the party. Like Mussolini, he had a natural oratorical ability and spoke frequently in public squares, in beer halls, and in the streets, expounding the views he had evolved in Vienna. He was unimpressive in appearance, yet he projected a personal magnetism that gripped a nation. To a far greater degree than Mussolini, Hitler had an uncanny ability to sway the masses and evoke worship. These qualities enabled the Nazi *Führer* ("leader") to convert his small group into a mass party.

In 1920 the German Workers' party was renamed the National Socialist German Workers' party (NSDAP), shortened in popular usage to "Nazi." It acquired its own newspaper, and its 25-point program called for a Greater Germany incorporating all German-speaking peoples, annulment of the Treaty of Versailles, denial of citizenship to Jews, and socioeconomic reforms to benefit the workers and the middle class. Although Hitler himself regarded the socialist provisions as propaganda, some Nazi leaders—such as Gregor and Otto Strasser—took them seriously.

The party also developed a paramilitary wing of storm troopers called the *Sturmabteilung* (SA), with its brown shirts and outstretched arm salute, "Heil Hitler!" greeting, and swastika symbol. Rallies, marches, songs, and banners provided the techniques that Hitler's propaganda machine later developed on a massive scale. The SA membership, like that of Mussolini's Blackshirt squads, consisted of disaffected veterans and Free Corps volunteers, rootless young men, and thugs and criminals. Ernst Röhm, the SA leader, believed that violence and terror would bring about the Nazi revolution.

In 1923 Hitler determined to seize power by force. Inspired by Mussolini's march on Rome, he planned a putsch in Munich with the connivance of local officials and the backing of a popular World War I general, Erich Ludendorff. On the evening of November 8 the Brownshirts surrounded a beer hall in which a political meeting was scheduled. Hitler rushed into the room, jumped onto a table, and fired a pistol in the air, shouting, "The National Socialist revolution has begun!" The putsch ended in fiasco the next day as the police scattered the participants and arrested Hitler. The abortive revolt brought Hitler a five-year prison term, of which he served less than nine months. In jail he wrote his famous testament *Mein Kampf* ("My Struggle"), outlining his racial theories, domestic policies, and plans for world conquest. He also concluded that violence alone would not assure the Nazi conquest of Germany and that the party must combine the legal methods of the election process with the violence advocated by Röhm and the SA.

After the failure of the Munich uprising, Röhm attempted to wrest control of the party from Hitler. Röhm wanted his SA, which he believed would be the instrument for the conquest of the state, to dominate the party. But in Hitler, who wanted to subordinate the SA to the party, Röhm met his match in duplicity. Using murder, blackmail, and slander to reassert his position, Hitler defeated Röhm, who went into exile in Bolivia in 1925. Hitler had become the undisputed leader of the movement.

The inner core of the Nazi leadership, attached to Hitler by bonds of loyalty and fear, began to take shape. The hierarchy included the gluttonous Hermann Göring, future air marshal; the tireless party organizer Rudolf Hess; the brilliant propagandist Joseph Goebbels; the rabid ideologue Alfred Rosenberg; and the chilling technocrat of police terror, Heinrich Himmler. The party also developed its organizational apparatus, creating youth groups and the infamous *Schutzstaffel* (SS), an elite defense corps later used in the mass exterminations of World War II. In 1929 Himmler took control of the SS and turned it into one of the principal instruments of Hitler's power. The black uniforms and death's-head insignia of the SS became synonymous with the Nazi terror state.

❧ BERLIN, CAPITAL OF WEIMAR CULTURE

In contrast to the political and economic turmoil that beset the Weimar Republic, German cultural life between 1919 and 1933 was marked by a feverish brilliance. In theater, cinema, art, architecture, and literature, Germany exploded with a creative energy that was at once modern, experimental, and tormented. Berlin emerged as the center of Weimar's cultural ferment.

Little in Berlin's past suggested that it would be the center of a revolutionary culture. Founded in the thir-

◉ The Nazi State ◉

Although Hitler, like Mussolini, wanted an all-embracing totalitarian government, the Nazi state was to fulfill a special diabolical function—to form and propagate a "master race" that would dominate the world. Hitler explained his view in the pages of Mein Kampf, *which he dictated while in prison in 1925.*

The folkish [*völkisch*] philosophy finds the importance of mankind in its basic racial elements. In the state it sees in principle only a means to an end and construes its end as the preservation of the racial existence of man. Thus, it by no means believes in an equality of the races, but along with their difference it recognizes their higher or lesser values and feels itself obligated, through this knowledge, to promote the victory of the better and stronger, and demand the subordination of the inferior and weaker in accordance with the eternal will that dominates this universe. Thus, in principle, it serves the basic aristocratic idea of Nature and believes in the validity of this law down to the last individual. It sees not only the different value of the races, but also the different value of individuals. From the mass it extracts the importance of the individual personality, and thus, in contrast to disorganizing Marxism, it has an organizing effect. It believes in the necessity of an idealization of humanity, in which alone it sees the premise for the existence of humanity. But it cannot grant the right to existence even to an ethical idea if this idea represents a danger for the racial life of the bearers of a higher ethics. . . .

And so the folkish philosophy of life corresponds to the inner-most will of Nature, since it restores that free play of forces which must lead to a continuous mutual higher breeding, until at last the best of humanity, having achieved possession of this earth, will have a free path for activity in domains which lie partly above it and partly outside it.

We all sense that in that distant future humanity must be faced by problems which only a highest race, become master people and supported by the means and possibilities of an entire globe, will be equipped to overcome.

Source: A. Hitler, *Mein Kampf*, trans. R. Manheim (Boston: Houghton Mifflin, 1943), pp. 383–384.

teenth century along the east-west trade routes, the Hohenzollerns made it the capital of their Prussian domains in 1411. Berlin's importance grew as the ambitious dynasty extended its power, but culturally it remained a dull garrison town. Frederick the Great and his successors improved the appearance and cultural climate of the city by building an opera house, the Tiergarten Park, and Unter den Linden, a magnificent mile-long boulevard planted with lime trees and ending at the neoclassical Brandenburg Gate. Friedrich-Wilhelm University, opened in 1810, boasted the largest student body in Germany and attracted famous scholars that included J. G. Fichte, Georg Hegel, and the Grimm brothers. When Berlin became the capital of the Second Reich in 1871, it was already a city of some 825,000 inhabitants. The huge government bureaucracy and the teeming economic life of the German empire pushed its population to 2 million by the eve of World War I and made it the greatest industrial-commercial city on the Continent.

In 1919 Social Democrats Friedrich Ebert and Philip Scheidemann vied with Spartacists such as Rosa Luxemburg and Karl Liebknecht to seize the revolutionary initiative in Berlin. Although the Weimar Republic represented the triumph of the more moderate Social Democrats, postwar Berlin retained a hectic atmosphere. War, defeat, and revolution had combined to transform the grim solemnity that had once marked the capital into an irreverent spirit that made the city a mecca for young, talented Germans in search of a faster-paced, modern life. By the early 1920s restaurants, bathhouses, dance halls, and nightclubs—including the dozens of gay and lesbian bars described by British writer Christopher Isherwood in his *Berlin Stories*—gave the city a rowdy allure that rivaled even the attractions of Paris. American jazz became the rage, and the iconoclastic atmosphere also gave rise to a peculiar Berlin institution, cabarets in which political and social satire took the form of musical comedy. The air of unreality became starker in the aftermath of the terrible inflation

◎ Nazism: The Philosophy of Domination ◎

The Nazis viewed life—and therefore history—as a Darwinian struggle for existence in which the fittest triumphed over the weak. Hitler's call for German rearmament was therefore only the first step in a plan for world domination. Hitler preached his brutal message in a speech in Munich on March 15, 1929.

If men wish to live, then they are forced to kill others. The entire struggle for survival is a conquest of the means of existence which in turn results in the elimination of others from these same sources of subsistence. As long as there are peoples on this earth, there will be nations against nations. . . .

There is in reality no distinction between peace and war. Life, no matter in what form, is a process which always leads to the same result. Self-preservation will always be the goal of every individual. Struggle is ever-present and will remain. This signifies a consistent willingness on the part of man to sacrifice to the utmost. Weapons, methods, instruments, formations, these may change, but in the end the struggle for survival remains. . . .

One is either the hammer or the anvil. We confess that it is our purpose to prepare the German people again for the role of the hammer. For ten years we have preached, and our deepest concern is: How can we again achieve power? We admit freely and openly that, if our Movement is victorious, we will be concerned day and night with the question of how to produce the armed forces which are forbidden us by the peace treaty. We solemnly confess that we consider everyone a scoundrel who does not try day and night to figure out a way to violate this treaty, for we have never recognized this treaty. . . .

We confess further that we will dash anyone to pieces who should dare to hinder us in this undertaking. . . . Our rights will never be represented by others. Our rights will be protected only when the German Reich is again supported by the point of the German dagger.

Source: G. W. Prange, ed., *Hitler's Words* (Washington, D.C.: American Council on Public Affairs, 1944), pp. 10–11.

---

that struck in 1923 and put a quarter of a million Berliners out of work.

No artist better symbolized Berlin's cultural life than George Grosz (1893–1959). Drafted into the army in 1914, Grosz's hatred of authority had led to his court-martial for insubordination. In Berlin he was a founder of the German Dada movement and was active among the Expressionists. In 1919 he joined the Spartacists and designed illustrations for a communist publisher. Inspired by the bitter irony he saw in the cabarets, Grosz produced political drawings—in series such as *Ecce Homo* and *Café*—that satirized fat industrialists and war profiteers, Junkers, militarists, and corrupt politicians. Grosz gradually rejected Expressionism and joined other artists in the search for a "new objectivity." He continued to assault bourgeois standards of morality and relentlessly indicted the reactionary forces that dominated German society and politics. Grosz detested the Nazis and in 1923 executed a

startlingly prescient drawing of a monocled officer with a swastika, the first of many anti-Nazi works depicting storm troopers and other symbols of the political reaction stalking Germany.

❀
BERTOLT BRECHT
AND THE THEATER
OF COMMITMENT

Grosz's counterpart in theater was Bertolt Brecht (1898–1956), whose plays and poems explored the agony of human isolation and the dilemma of moral and political commitment. A pacifist repelled by the horrors of World War I, Brecht's first critical success came in 1922 with a play titled *Spartacus* (later renamed *Drums in the Night*),

In his stunning painting *Rain, Steam, and Speed: The Great Western Railway,* the English artist J. M. W. Turner used swirling colors to evoke a Romantic vision of a train churning across a bridge. A closer look reveals a rabbit racing ahead of the engine, a scene that symbolizes technology's threat to the environment. [1844, oil on canvas, 3′ × 4′ (91 × 122 cm.); National Gallery, London]

THE VISUAL EXPERIENCE
The Modern World

Artists have been simultaneously fascinated and repelled by the industrialization and technological achievements of the modern world. On the one hand, these developments have made possible improved transportation and communication, better medical care and diet, and physical comforts undreamed of by past societies. On the other hand, they have created the setting for totalitarian dictatorships and unparalleled human destruction even as they have failed to eradicate hunger and homelessness. Not suprisingly, artists have responded to these enigmas by exploring anew the age-old questions of human nature and our relationship to the world in which we live. No single work more fittingly evokes the common human experience than Henry Moore's *Family Group.*

The iron horse in Japan. Early Meiji woodblock artists were fascinated by the new railways, as most Japanese were intrigued with the artifacts of the modern West that flooded into their country. [Asian Art Museum of San Francisco]

William Prinseps' watercolor of the Calcutta waterfront in the early nineteenth century graphically illustrates the link between the old and the new. The small sampan-like boats in the foreground were used as barges to ferry goods to and from the oceangoing ships in the background, which usually had to anchor in deeper water in the Hooghly River. Note the completely European late-eighteenth-century architecture of the buildings. [Spinks & Sons Ltd., London]

Despite its dangerous potential, nationalism could be a constructive force. The meeting of Victor Emmanuel II and Garibaldi at Teano in 1861 was a major step in the process of Italian unification. [Scala/Art Resource]

The works of Gustave Courbet epitomized a new realism that reflected social commentary as well as an aesthetic departure from academic realism. Courbet focused not on the aristocracy and the bourgeoisie but on the proletariat, as in this painting, *The Stone Breakers,* which shows two men building a road. [1849, c. 63″ × c. 102″ (160 × 259 cm.); Oskar Reinhart Collection, Winterthur, Switzerland]

Cezanne's search for meaning led him to impose order on nature. He attempted, he once said, to "treat nature in terms of the cylinder, and the sphere, and the cone," an approach reflected in this painting of Mont Sainte-Victoire.
[1905, oil on canvas; Giraudon/Art Resource]

Like Courbet, Pablo Picasso often painted humble people, but in increasingly abstract forms. In this work, the angular figures, three of whom wear African masks, were prostitutes on Avignon Street in Barcelona. Cezanne's interest in geometric forms was carried much farther by Picasso. [1907, oil on canvas, 8′ × 7′8″ (243.9 × 233.7 cm.). Collection, The Museum of Modern Art, New York. Acquired through the Lillie P. Bliss Bequest.]

This allegorical painting by American artist Peter Blume, titled *The Eternal City* (1934–1937), was intended as a bitter satire on Mussolini's claim that Rome would be the new capital of a glorious Fascist empire. Mussolini's head is the jack-in-the-box. [Oil on composition board, 34′ × 47⅞″ (86.4 × 121.6 cm.). Collection, The Museum of Modern Art, New York: Mrs. Simon Guggenheim Fund.]

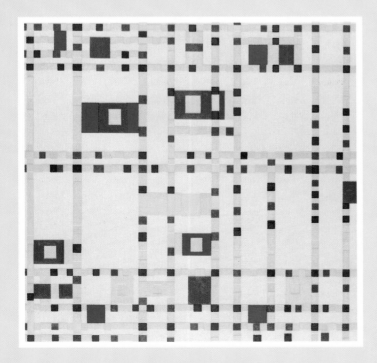

The Dutch painter Piet Mondrian was fascinated by the growth of modern urban centers such as New York City. "The new style," he predicted, "will spring from the metropolis"; its characteristics were broad planes of primary colors dissected by rigid horizontal and vertical lines. This, he claimed, was "pure reality." Shown here is his *Broadway Boogie-Woogie.* [Oil on canvas, 50 × 50″ (127 × 127 cm.). Collection, The Museum of Modern Art, New York.]

No modern artist more effectively merged the classical Western sculptural tradition of Donatello and Michelangelo with the styles of Africa and Latin America, Oceana and the Etruscans, than Henry Moore. His absorption with the human form—as in this sculpture, *Family Group*—stems from his belief in its dignity. [Bronze, $59\frac{1}{4}$ × $46\frac{1}{2}$ × $29\frac{1}{4}''$ (150.5 × 118 × 75.9 cm.). Collection, The Museum of Modern Art, New York; A. Conger Goodyear Fund.]

If Mondrian embraced the great metropolises, the American artist Andy Warhol not only made peace with their blatant commercialism but capitalized on it, in part with his portraits of cinematic and political celebrities. Here he portrays the Chinese revolutionary Mao Tse-tung, a hero of the radical left in the 1960s. [1973; Bruce C. Jones/Leo Castelli Gallery]

One of the leaders of the reaction against abstractionism was Jasper Johns, who, beginning in the 1950s, made distinctive studies of such commonplace objects as beer cans, toothbrushes, and the American flag. His *Target with Four Faces* was completed in 1955. [Collection, The Museum of Modern Art, New York; gift of Mr. and Mrs. Robert C. Scull]

The Mexican painter Diego Rivera, having studied both classical Italian frescoes and Picasso's cubist paintings, developed his own lyrical style in murals featuring the proletariat. Among his best work is this fresco titled *Agrarian Leader Zapata*, which depicts a rebel in the Mexican revolution who seized haciendas and distributed the land to the poor. [7'9¾" × 6'2" (238.1 × 188 cm.). Collection, The Museum of Modern Art, New York; Abby Aldrich Rockefeller Fund.]

In both the Soviet Union and the People's Republic of China, efforts were made to encourage "socialist realism" in art. This slightly idealized but traditional-style Chinese painting depicts a new oil refinery complex. [Shio-yun Ken and Anna Merton, London]

A detail from one of George Grosz's satiric drawings contrasts sober working men with partying "fat cats." [Bildarchiv Preussischer Kulturbesitz]

about a veteran who chose a comfortable life instead of joining the Spartacist uprising.

In 1924 Brecht moved to Berlin, where theatrical producers quickly recognized his genius. Before long he was writing for Max Reinhardt's experimental Deutsches Theater and collaborating with the composer Kurt Weill. In his plays as in his personal life, he struggled to detach himself from the irrationality of violence, sex, and aggression and strove to understand how modern society transformed individuals into groups. In *Man Is Man* (1927), he recognized the powerful forces at work in Germany as he described how a worker had been changed into a bloodthirsty soldier.

After 1929, Brecht's work revealed a growing commitment to Marxism, which he believed to be the only solution to the nihilism of his age. But he saw Marxism as a scientific method of analysis, not as a faith. *The Three Penny Opera* (1928) expressed his cynical distaste for bourgeois materialism by taunting his audiences for their gluttonous appetites and lack of ethical values. Under the growing influence of the German Communist party, Brecht shifted to an austere didactic style. His rigorously controlled language and aesthetic precision urged self-discipline and self-denial in the interests of mankind—he was, he said, interested in the ideas his characters represented rather than in the characters themselves. These influences led him to the development of the Epic Theater, in which plays were conceived on a grand scale and the audience kept at a distance through the use of signs, posters, and light.

In 1932 his full-length play *St. Joan of the Stockyards*—based in part on Upton Sinclair's novel *The Jungle*—depicted the Great Depression as the story of greedy speculation in the Chicago stock market. Despite his Marxism,

Brecht never made himself a blind servant of party discipline. *The Measures Adopted* (1930) brought criticism from German Communist officials because he depicted the murder of a young comrade by party militants. He refused to dramatize revolutionary events, believing that "to requisition the theatre for the purposes of the class struggle is to endanger the true revolutionizing of the theatre."[2]

Darker forces began to encircle Brecht in the early 1930s. The air of creative genius that had given Berlin's cultural life its brilliance seemed unreal in the midst of the Great Depression, which by 1932 had raised unemployment in the city to 636,000. The ironic contrast between Berlin's cabaret culture and Germany's political realities grew sharper as Hitler's storm troopers spread violence and bloodshed. Brecht left Berlin in 1933, living for several years in Denmark and traveling in Europe before emigrating to the United States. He earned a precarious living working on film scripts in Hollywood and on plays in New York. Even after the war, trouble followed him. In 1947 the House Committee on Un-American Activities called him to testify in its investigation of communism in Hollywood.

The day after his testimony, Brecht returned to Europe. He supported the communist German Democratic Republic and worked during his last years for the revived Berliner Ensemble; he was an honored but controversial figure who kept his independence to the end.

The Nazi Seizure of Power

At first the Nazi party's electoral prospects were not promising. When the economy began to recover in 1924, the Weimar Republic's political instability seemed to abate. The next year the country elected a new president, the revered Field Marshal Paul von Hindenburg (1847–1934), who provided middle class Germans with a sense of security. Although Nazi membership increased in 1925 from 27,000 to 178,000 in 1929, the number of Nazi deputies in the Reichstag fell from 32 to 12. By the end of the decade the future of National Socialism was by no means clear. It required the economic shock of the Great Depression to create the mass base Hitler needed to seize power.

No other country suffered greater hardship as a result of the Great Depression than Germany—by 1932 production had fallen by 39 percent and unemployment hit 6 million. The economic collapse encouraged the rapid rise of extremist movements. Although other factors enhanced the appeal of Nazism to many Germans, the severe hardship and pervasive fear generated by the financial crisis produced the ideal environment for Nazi success. The depression polarized German politics. In parliamentary elections held between 1929 and 1932, Nazi representation rose to 230 seats, while the Communist delegation increased from 54 to 89. Moderate elements stepped aside as these two sworn enemies battled physically in the

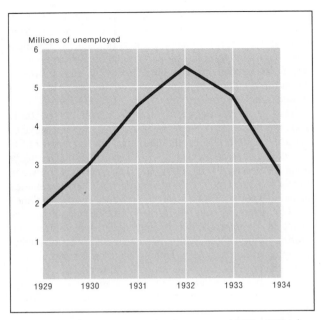

Millions of unemployed

36.1 Unemployment in Germany, 1929–1934

196 seats in the November 1932 elections as the Communists raised their total to 100, encouraging some to believe that the radical left would assume control of a government that was helpless in the midst of economic, political, and social chaos.

Hitler's followers urged him to seize control of the government forcibly in a coup d'état, while conservative antidemocratic forces—aristocratic landowners, army officers, industrialists, wealthy merchants, and financiers—were both terrified at the prospect of a Communist victory and attracted to Hitler's nationalist slogans. Hoping to manipulate him to stem mass discontent and advance their own interests, some began supplying funds to the Nazis.

On January 30, 1933, Hindenburg, fearful of civil war and pressured by his advisers, appointed Hitler chancellor of the German Republic. The new Nazi-dominated cabinet included some members of the Nationalist party. Hitler promptly dissolved the Reichstag and called for new elections, but the parliament building was destroyed in a fire of unknown origin. The Nazis blamed the Communists and conducted the balloting in an atmosphere of anti-Communist hysteria and intimidation. Although the Nazis won only 44 percent of the vote, their Nationalist partners added another 8 percent to give the coalition a legislative majority. Declaring a national emergency, Hitler expelled the Communist deputies from the Reichstag, which then voted him dictatorial powers for four years. After using this authority to outlaw all other political parties, he completed the transition from democracy to dictatorship when he combined the office of president with that of chancellor following the death of Hindenburg in August 1934. Hitler destroyed the short-lived Weimar Republic and became

streets and meeting halls and verbally in speeches, posters, and handbills. When the 85-year-old Hindenburg decided to run for a second term as president in 1932, Hitler and Communist leader Ernst Thälmann opposed him. Hindenburg and Hitler faced each other in a runoff, but although the now senile field marshal won, Hitler had received more than 13 million votes. The Nazis slipped to

A group of young Nazis confiscating books to be taken to the Operplatz in Berlin for burning in May of 1933. [UPI/Bettmann Newsphotos]

◉ Hitler as Demagogue ◉

Hitler was unequaled as a public speaker. His ability to hold huge numbers of people in his spell, to arouse their passions and whip them into a frenzy of adulation, made him a master of political demagogy. Although he was a skillful actor on the political platform, his charisma also derived from his conviction of his own destiny. Konrad Heiden, who witnessed many of Hitler's public speeches, provides a vivid description of his ability to sway audiences.

Hitler's special trait is his concentration on greatness. This is the source of his power. When suddenly this man, who has been awkwardly standing around, now and then muttering a remark that by no means dominates the conversation, is seized with determination and begins to speak, filling the room with his voice, suppressing interruptions or contradictions by his domineering manner, spreading cold shivers among those present by the savagery of his declarations, lifting every subject of conversation into the light of history, and interpreting it so that even trifles have their origin in greatness; then the listener is filled with awe and feels that a new phenomenon has entered the room. This thundering demon was not there before; this is not the same timid man with the contracted shoulders. He is capable of this transformation in a personal interview and facing an audience of half a million. The magic power of this image of greatness emanating from human nullity greatly appealed to the German people after the World War, when this people, oppressed by their own nullity, longed for greatness; but a far deeper and more decisive explanation of Hitler's effect is the soul state of modern man, who, in his pettiness, loneliness, and lack of faith, longs for community, conviction, and greatness. Here he sees greatness emerging from a creature who as a man is smaller than you or I— that is what made Hitler an experience for millions.

Source: K. Heiden, *Der Führer: Hitler's Rise to Power* (Boston: Houghton Mifflin, 1944), pp. 377–378.

the unchallenged ruler of a Germany that was anxious to restore its economy and regain its place in international affairs.

Fascism as a World Phenomenon

In the years after 1919 it appeared to many Europeans that the world was rapidly being divided into two antagonistic systems—communism and fascism. In every European country a struggle unfolded between left and right, between "revolution" and "reaction," that ultimately polarized around these extreme ideologies. Because of their long-range consequences, Italian Fascism and German Nazism were the most serious instances of the triumph of the right in this struggle. But no European nation escaped the trauma of ideological divisiveness or the specter of fascist radicalism. Societies as advanced as Britain's and as underdeveloped as Romania's experienced their own peculiar brands of fascism: in each state segments of the

population looked to extreme solutions for seemingly unmanageable problems.

Varieties of European Fascism

In the strongholds of liberal democracy, France and Britain, fascism was not a genuine threat to the established order, for right-wing movements failed to establish a mass base. But France produced fascistlike political groups that challenged the country's democratic tradition: radical "leagues" proliferated in the 1920s and 1930s, some of which modeled themselves after Mussolini's or Hitler's example—the *Jeunesses patriotes* ("Patriotic Youth"), for instance, and the infamous CSAR, or *Cagoulards* ("Hooded Men"). During the depression the *Parti populaire français* ("French Popular Party") had perhaps as many as a half million members, but it was unable to unify the right. France also produced more traditional conservative movements that capitalized on nationalism and adopted antidemocratic, anti-Semitic principles. Such groups included

Charles Maurras' *Action française* ("French Action") and Colonel de la Rocque's veterans' movement, the *Croix de feu* ("Cross of Fire").

In Britain as well, where Mussolini was a popular figure in the 1920s, fascist organizations were established. In the early 1930s the wealthy aristocrat Sir Oswald Mosley founded the British Union of Fascists. An admirer of Mussolini, Mosley modeled his union, a band of armed thugs, on the Blackshirts. Like Hitler, to whom he gravitated after 1933, Mosley dreamed of a "Greater Britain" in which all citizens were integrated into a regimented society to revive national glory. Mosley's advocacy of political violence resulted in the outlawing of the movement, and during World War II he was imprisoned.

In Spain, where the struggle between right and left was largely the result of a government unable to solve national problems, a military dictatorship under Miguel Primo de Rivera (1870–1930) emerged after 1923. His son, José António Primo de Rivera, created a fascist movement called the *Falange*. In the mid-1930s Spain became the bloody battleground in the conflict between communism and fascism. The Spanish civil war was marked by the military intervention of Hitler and Mussolini on the fascist side as well as that of the Soviet Union on the side of the republican government, and ended with the installation of the dictatorship of General Francisco Franco.

Other varieties of fascism developed in Belgium, Romania, and Austria. In Belgium, a nation bitterly divided between Dutch- and French-speaking ethnic groups, the Rexist movement of Léon Degrelle aimed at national unification in a spiritual and racial sense. A different form of fascism developed in Romania, an agrarian society with a strong Orthodox tradition rooted in peasant society. There Corneliu Codreanu's Iron Guard movement appealed to the traditional associations of soil and religion. In Austria two armed organizations, the urban Social Democratic *Schutzbund* ("Alliance for Defense") and the rural Christian Socialist *Heimwehr* ("Home Guard"), vied with each other and with the Austrian Nazi party. Led by Prince von Starhemberg, the reactionary *Heimwehr* opposed democracy as bitterly as it did Hitler's attempts to Nazify the country. Under the Austrian chancellor, Engelbert Dollfuss, the *Heimwehr* was given representation in the government, which forged a "Fatherland Front" to block the union (*Anschluss*) of Austria and Germany. These movements, together with the Nazis, gained ground with the assassination of Dollfuss in 1934.

Fascism in Asia

Whether or not European fascism had counterparts elsewhere in the world is problematic. In the 1930s there appeared to be at least superficial evidence to justify Mussolini's prediction that fascism would be the dominant political philosophy of the twentieth century, for admirers of fascism were to be found the world over. Demagogues who modeled themselves after Mussolini and Hitler were so popular in the United States that Anne Morrow Lindbergh, wife of the famous aviator Charles Lindbergh, spoke of fascism as "the wave of the future." In India and the Arab countries of the Middle East some nationalist leaders gravitated to fascism in the hope that it would lead to independence from colonial rule. Fascist influence may even have inspired a group of radical army officers in China to establish the so-called Blue Shirts (more properly, the "Cotton Cloth People"), although their militaristic, authoritarian program was little more than a variant of the nation-building doctrine of the Kuomintang regime of Chiang Kai-shek, itself often called fascist.

The most compelling evidence may have been in Japan, where as early as 1934 Marxist writers identified the authoritarian, militaristic, expansionist tendencies of the country as a form of fascism. The code of the samurai and emperor worship also suggest that the roots of a native fascism were to be found in Japanese history. Young army officers and small ultranationalist groups pressed for radical changes in politics and the economy, and the leading nationalist ideologue of the period, Kita Ikki (1883–1937), seemed to be a Japanese counterpart of Mussolini. Kita was a former Marxist socialist who called for nationalization of some industries, state regulation of the economy, authoritarian government under the emperor, and the creation of a greater East Asian empire. Yet unlike Italian Fascism or German Nazism, none of the Japanese groups became a significant party or movement capable of seizing power, and Japan's constitution and political system remained largely unchanged. When Kita Ikki and some of his followers staged a revolt in Tokyo in 1936, they were rounded up and executed. The continuity of Japan's political and cultural traditions proved stronger and more entrenched than the new fascistlike ferment. Moreover, the military aggression of the 1930s was not due to an indigenous Japanese fascism but was rather the result of a broad nationalist consensus in favor of expansion among Japan's traditional political and military leaders.

Brazil's Estado Novo

In Latin America fascistlike military dictatorships were widespread in the years between the wars. The rule of Getulio Vargas (1883–1954) in Brazil offers the best example of a regime strongly influenced by European fascism but shaped largely by local conditions.

The Brazilian republic, founded by the military in 1889 when the emperor Dom Pedro II was overthrown, had proved itself unable to deal with problems of national development. The federal government, in effect a federation of autonomous states, was weakened by regionalism and the power of local bosses. Because the agrarian economy rested largely on coffee production, the conservative plan-

Although technically not a fascist government, Brazilian dictator Getulio Vargas' Estado Novo bore close similarities to the Italian Fascist state. [UPI/Bettmann Newsphotos]

tation owners dominated Brazil's society and its politics. Poverty and illiteracy afflicted the rural population, while the government repressed the labor movement. Only the small Brazilian middle class, represented chiefly by intellectuals and a group of young military officers known as the *tenentes*, wanted industrialization and agrarian reform.

The Great Depression, which ruined the coffee market and made it impossible for the government to repay its staggering foreign debts, brought down the republic. In October 1930 a military coup suspended the legislature and put Vargas in power as provisional president. He was to rule Brazil, with one interval, for almost 20 years.

Vargas came from a wealthy ranching family in the state of Rio Grande do Sul and had run unsuccessfully for president. Vargas had few interests in life other than acquiring and exercising power. A shrewd leader, his enemies denounced him as an unprincipled dictator while his followers revered him as the "father of the poor."

Vargas strengthened the central government by virtually destroying state autonomy. He tried to create worker consensus through labor legislation and government-controlled unions while simultaneously encouraging the development of a strong middle class. Vargas stimulated the economy by diversifying agriculture, limiting coffee production, and extending tax incentives and government loans to business. Like Mussolini, Vargas expanded his personal power by balancing the conflicting economic and political interests that dominated the country. The left-

wing *tenentes* pushed for basic reforms, while the conservatives, resenting his centralization efforts and alarmed by his economic reforms, made an unsuccessful attempt to seize power. On the surface, his reforms seemed to point the way toward greater democracy and social justice—the electorate was expanded and given the secret ballot, women received the vote, social security laws and educational reforms were enacted, and labor unions were formed. In 1934 Vargas pushed through a new constitution that reduced state autonomy and established government authority over the economy. The new Chamber of Deputies reflected Mussolini's corporatist doctrine by providing for the election of representatives not only by population and area but also by class and profession. The Chamber appointed Vargas president for a four-year term.

Vargas thereupon shifted to the right. He gradually stripped the *tenentes* of their influence and suppressed the National Liberation Alliance, a popular-front coalition dominated by the communists. At the same time, he encouraged the growth of *Integralismo*, a fascist movement secretly financed by Mussolini. The Integralists, who adopted green-shirted uniforms and a paramilitary organization, railed against democracy, communism, and Jews while preaching rabid nationalism and "Christian virtues."

Vargas could not succeed himself as president, but as the 1937 elections approached, he dropped all pretense of constitutional rule. Claiming that the army had uncovered a communist plot, he canceled the elections and assumed dictatorial power in November. From 1937 to 1945 Vargas ruled Brazil under the *Estado Novo* ("new state"), a totalitarian government that strongly resembled European fascist regimes. The Estado Novo abolished political parties, imposed rigid censorship, established a special police force to combat "enemies of the state," and filled the prisons with political dissidents. Vargas offered Salgado, the Integralist leader, a cabinet post.

Although Vargas did not attempt the kind of mass mobilization that Mussolini and Hitler had undertaken, he denounced democracy as "decadent" and courted the workers with populist rhetoric. Vargas permitted no alternate sources of power to exist—in 1938 he banned all paramilitary groups, and when the Integralists tried to seize power, he crushed them.

The economic policies of the Estado Novo revealed an affinity to Mussolini's fascist programs. Vargas banned both strikes and lockouts and joined labor laws into a single code that stripped workers of the right to organize independently of the government. The regime set wages and hours, but although industrial workers benefited from some legislation, Vargas appeased the landowners by excluding agricultural workers from the new laws. He succeeded in industrializing Brazil through a policy of economic planning and government investment in development ventures that combined public and private ownership. State technocrats expanded and rationalized Brazilian business, while Vargas preached an economic nationalism designed to free Brazil from dependency on foreign capital. In the end Vargas succeeded too well—he had forced Brazil through a period of rapid social change and economic modernization, and his efforts eventually antagonized the traditional elites as well as his supporters.

During World War II, Vargas attempted to liberalize his regime, but in 1945 the army deposed him in a bloodless coup. Vargas, who kept his popularity among Brazilians, was elected president in 1950. Four years later, when the army tried to force him out of office again, he committed suicide.

The Estado Novo in Brazil, as well as other fascistlike regimes, demonstrates that fascism can be regarded not only as a political movement in individual countries but also as a model for resolving social and economic problems. The spread of the Industrial Revolution and its alteration of traditional society created immense tensions. In such cases fascism was seen as either a means for speeding up the pace of modernization or a method whereby old power elites could retain their authority and status. On still another level, fascism provided an example of how expanded government authority could alter the nature of society. Fascism offered new and brutally direct methods for social organization and control.

While fascism may have been a response to these problems, the question remains why it was so appealing and why it succeeded in some cases in destroying its liberal enemy. In Italy and Germany the answer seems clear. Liberalism was in crisis at the end of World War I in Italy and poorly rooted in Germany, and traditional leaders were incapable of understanding both the new social forces unleashed by the war and the fascist response. On a more general level, the success of fascism was due to the fear and despair among people whose lives and values were threatened by economic collapse and loss of social status. This sense of desperation that led ordinary people to join fascist movements is aptly expressed in the title of the 1932 novel by the German author Hans Fallada, *Little Man, What Now?*

The Great Depression and the Crisis of Capitalism

By the eve of World War I the capitalist system had grown complex and global in scope. In theory, a free international market set the prices of most basic commodities, although imperialism had long since made the law of supply and demand obsolete in many sectors of the world economy. Moreover, some regions enjoyed special status as the sole producers of specific items sold to the rest of the world. Traditionally, industry and commerce were financed through a system of credit resting on the assumption that lenders or investors could collect the money owed them and that borrowers could earn enough income to repay

their loans while continuing to purchase agricultural or industrial products. It was a resilient system, having weathered numerous financial crises—what today might be termed recessions—prior to 1914. But the crisis that erupted in 1929 and lasted in some respects until the outbreak of World War II was more than simply an adjustment in the world economy. Along with major changes in economic theory and practice, it brought untold suffering to millions and raised serious doubts about the viability of capitalism and the liberal political systems on which it rested.

The Economic Collapse

After an initial postwar slump, the 1920s exhibited a surge of economic vitality that brought prosperity to more people than ever before. Much of this growth derived from international trade, construction, and the development of new industries such as the automobile, radio, and motion pictures. While many people believed that the prosperity would last forever, the economic expansion had been financed largely by personal, corporate, and international credit—a shaky foundation whose flaws were exposed in the October 1929 stock market crash. Securities purchases relied heavily on margin trading, whereby investors bought stocks and bonds by putting up only a fraction of the purchase price; the remainder was borrowed from brokers, who in turn obtained credit from banks. Such unregulated practices led to widespread speculation in stocks, whose market value was often many times higher than their actual worth. With installment credit readily available, consumers were encouraged to buy houses, automobiles, and other major items without having the cash to pay for them. Here, too, retailers and wholesalers borrowed funds from banks to pay their suppliers. Manufacturers, in turn, easily obtained credit for plant expansion, and small nations received foreign loans far beyond their ability to repay. If one link in this credit chain suddenly demanded immediate repayment, the others would be forced to produce large amounts of cash to meet their debt obligations.

The availability of easy credit concealed other serious flaws in the post–World War I economy. The new prosperity was not evenly distributed, for profits far surpassed wages for nearly all working people, and farm prices continued to lag far behind those charged for manufactured goods and basic services. Consequently, despite the abundance of credit, mass purchasing power based on solid financial ground never really existed. Furthermore, the economic optimism of the day resulted in high levels of production and huge inventories, with the possibility that unsold goods could force cutbacks and eventual job layoffs. On the international level, the appearance of new states in central and eastern Europe introduced further volatility into the world economy. Since the economies of these states were immature and their finances precarious, their

Anxious crowds gather outside the New York Stock Exchange in October 1929, following the crash. [UPI/Bettmann Newsphotos]

vulnerability to credit difficulties weakened the global economy in times of trouble.

Strictly speaking, the Great Depression began with the financial collapse touched off by the sudden deflation of the New York Stock Exchange in October 1929. In reality, the world agrarian sector had already been experiencing severe hardship as the prices of basic agricultural goods followed an unchecked downward spiral. The stock market crash produced a sudden rush by creditors to call in loans at all levels, and the consequent failure of a major European lender (Austria's *Creditanstalt*) in 1931 gave the crisis an international dimension. The panic soon passed to industry, and even large corporations were forced to halt production as the markets for their goods dried up. By 1933 world production had declined 38 percent and world trade had dropped to one-third its pre-1929 level. When farmers who had escaped previous difficulties were hit by the lack of credit and customers, the collapse of the modern capitalist economy appeared complete.

The resulting Great Depression caused mass suffering, desperation, and fear to an extent hitherto unknown in the modern West. Unemployment reached epidemic proportions—Great Britain reported 3 million unemployed in 1933, Germany 6 million, and the United States 13 million. Worldwide, some 30 million people were without jobs when the depression reached its depth in 1932. People living on fixed incomes or running marginal businesses saw their savings disappear, often literally overnight. Skilled and productive employees were reduced to supporting families on what meager welfare was available. As the depression dragged on, demoralization turned to frustration and resentment. Families disintegrated, suicides rose dramatically, and the very fabric of society seemed torn apart.

Government Response

Nations dealt with the crisis in various ways. The reactions of Britain, France, Germany, Italy, the United States, and the Soviet Union are considered elsewhere in this and the following chapters, but some general observations will prove useful here.

At first governments pursued deflationary policies that made the problem worse but then switched to pump-priming strategies, including deficit spending, in order to stimulate economic revival. All states, whether democratic or totalitarian, undertook measures to generate work for their citizens and limit the economic hardship as much as possible: public works programs, spending cuts, currency controls, and tariffs were among the most widespread efforts. Governments assumed a greater degree of control over economic and social life than ever before as they attempted to come to grips with the immediate consequences of the economic collapse and its long-range implications.

The Great Depression affected the future in ways that were not immediately apparent but had a lasting impact. What had once been an integrated world economy disintegrated into highly competitive national economic systems. Economic competition bred distrust between countries and fostered a spirit of nationalism that shattered postwar dreams of international cooperation. Extremist political movements that promised quick solutions to the crisis spread rapidly. While representative government survived in long-established Western democracies, even France, Britain, and the United States experienced profound trauma that altered their political and social traditions.

Britain, France, and the United States: The Trial of Democracy

The Great Depression challenged liberal democratic systems, yet the problems facing each of the three major democracies were unique. Common to Britain, France, and the United States, however, were an extension of state welfare measures, stronger government control over the economy, and the basic survival of democratic institutions.

Politics and Society

After 1919 Britain had to cope with a serious economic slump brought about by the end of the war and the reorientation of the global economy. In the 1920s British governments, led in succession by the Liberals, Conservatives, and finally by the Labour party, grappled with two closely related issues: chronic unemployment—18.5 percent between 1930 and 1935—and a growing deficit produced in part by social welfare programs. Despite serious labor unrest, most notably a 1926 coal miners' work stoppage that grew into a full-fledged general strike, in periods of severe crisis the Labourites and the Conservatives tended toward ideological convergence. Moreover, the currency policies of successive governments sheltered the British population, particularly its middle class, from the devastating inflationary cycles that ruined other countries.

The postwar period in the United States saw the economic boom of the so-called Roaring Twenties, especially in the construction and automobile industries, and America became obsessed with material success. Under Republican presidents Warren G. Harding (1921–1923) and Calvin Coolidge (1923–1929), the country pursued a "return to normalcy" that aimed at a nostalgic re-creation of the atmosphere of the prewar era. Although Americans were suspicious of foreign political entanglements, government policies spread U.S. economic influence into Latin America and the Pacific. The labor movement found organized action increasingly difficult in the face of government hostility, and the rapid economic growth that produced nearly full employment and better wages undercut the appeal of unions. Only farmers seemed excluded from the prosperity. Facing declining prices and rising costs well before the depression, farmers received little support from the government, and hard times had begun to grip rural America in the early 1920s.

The difficulties experienced by the farmer were often obscured by the glare of Jazz Age life in the big cities. Despite the Eighteenth Amendment to the U.S. constitution, which introduced Prohibition, popular culture was indulgent and iconoclastic. Flashy automobiles, speakeasies, gangster heroes such as Al Capone, and "flappers"—women who wore flimsy dresses and led uninhibited lives—became symbols of America's frenzied modernism, while the election of Republican president Herbert Hoover (1929–1933) epitomized the belief in uninterrupted prosperity.

Aside from the contrasting tone of life in Britain and the United States, both represented relatively stable political states with two-party systems. In France, by contrast, chronic instability had long appeared to be the rule. This was due in part to the tremendous financial investment needed to rebuild the economy after the wartime destruction the country had suffered. Successive cabinets advanced—and then under fierce opposition retreated from—plans for tax increases and other measures designed to finance reconstruction. The result was a large deficit and a serious inflationary spiral. In addition, the electoral system, based on proportional representation, stimulated political factionalism with a multiparty system that necessitated coalition government.

One of the few islands of stability in the period came with the "government of national union" formed in 1926 by Raymond Poincaré (1860–1934). A careful and temperate man, Poincaré governed for three years, during which time he restored a measure of equilibrium to the country. He stabilized the franc, halted the deficit spending programs of previous administrations, and introduced social legislation that rejuvenated the economy and eased social tensions. As living standards improved by the end of the decade, France reestablished its reputation for cultural leadership. Although Paris again became a thriving center of avant-garde artists and writers, its fame in the 1920s rested largely on its large colony of brilliant expatriates, which included the writers James Joyce, Ernest Hemingway, and Gertrude Stein.

Toward the Welfare State

The Great Depression shattered the complacency that had permeated life in the three major democracies. Britain, with the apparatus of the modern welfare state well in place by 1930, endured the economic crisis with the least shock to its political system. British Labour prime minister Ramsey MacDonald (1929–1935) converted his cabinet into a national coalition government in 1931 to eliminate partisan policy disputes. He reduced unemployment compensation in 1931 and sought to stimulate economic recovery by raising taxes, reducing the budget, lowering interest rates, and changing currency and tariff policies. The Conservative governments that followed under Stanley Baldwin (1935–1937) and Neville Chamberlain (1937–1940) continued this approach. Britain weathered the crisis and experienced an economic revival in the late 1930s, based largely on the continued low prices of raw materials from abroad. However, conditions in northern England, Scotland, and Wales remained far more depressed than in the south, encouraging a flight of capital and population from what had once been Britain's industrial heartland that has continued ever since.

Although unemployment in France was not as severe as in other countries, the depression had a critical impact on the country's political system. The government failed to deal effectively with the economic collapse, so as prosperity disappeared after 1932, political tensions resurfaced. The radical right in particular posed such a serious threat that the socialists, communists, and other leftist elements formed a coalition government under socialist Léon Blum (1936–1937), the so-called Popular Front. Social reforms aimed chiefly at the working and lower classes appeared to reduce social stress, but concerted resistance from the financial and business communities halted the recovery program. By the end of the decade France was economically worse off, more bitterly divided, and more politically unstable than any other leading European power.

The United States underwent the greatest transformation as a result of the depression. Firmly committed to the principles of a free enterprise market economy, the Hoover administration did little to halt the financial collapse of the stock market. By 1932 unemployment had reached 25 percent. Yet the mounting despair of the American people, who increasingly demanded action, did not turn against the fundamental principles of the economic and political system. Hence, when Democrat Franklin D. Roosevelt (1933–1945) was elected president by a large majority, he assumed he had received a mandate for fundamental change that would reform capitalism in order to save it.

Roosevelt rejected both socialism and fascism in favor of forceful intervention by the federal government in economic life. Along with regulating the economy and stimulating business recovery through deficit spending, Roosevelt's New Deal introduced several basic social welfare programs. The result was a resurgence of industrial, commercial, and agricultural activity that, while never attaining predepression levels, stimulated significant recovery and partially cushioned the impact of the economic crisis. By 1938, when deficit spending was reduced, a recession had set in, and it required the massive production needs of World War II to pull the nation completely out of its economic slump. Some critics accused Roosevelt of introducing socialism or fascism. Yet except for persistent unemployment, the economic turnabout his policies induced was so successful that most Americans were willing to accept them.

The United States, Britain, and France thus retained both the form and essence of their democratic systems in the face of severe trials. Although fascistlike demagogues developed followings in all three countries, their citizens did not succumb to dictatorship.

President Franklin D. Roosevelt inaugurated major changes in America's economic and social life. [UPI/Bettmann Newsphotos]

Central and Eastern Europe

The strength of liberal institutions in the United States and western Europe was not duplicated in most of eastern Europe. New states had arisen after 1919 out of the remnants of the shattered German, Austro-Hungarian, Russian, and Ottoman empires. These "successor states" were Poland, Czechoslovakia, Yugoslavia, Hungary, Austria, Turkey, and the Baltic republics of Estonia, Latvia, and Lithuania. In these nations democracy proved less resistant to the political and economic stress of the postwar period.

The Successor States

Together with the already independent countries of Bulgaria, Greece, Romania, and Albania, the successor states formed a bastion of small nations in the strategic heartland of Europe. They were governed either by constitutional monarchies with representative institutions or by republican systems modeled after Western democracies. The new democracies were considered important in London and Paris as barriers against the spread of communism and the revival of German power. Most of these states eventually abandoned democracy for authoritarian dictatorship. Although a genuinely fascist regime never ruled in any of these nations prior to World War II, the reactionary right came to dominate the political and economic systems throughout the region. The special circumstances of the successor states demanded unique approaches to governing and to socioeconomic organization that the liberal system often could not manage.

In retrospect, it is surprising that there was such confidence in eastern Europe as a proving ground for democracy. Without exception, these nations faced problems that would have staggered wealthier, well-established states. A variety of factors retarded economic development. Before 1918 the region had functioned, directly or indirectly, as colonial territory for larger powers, which had supplied it with investments and manufactured goods in return for agricultural products and raw materials. When the war ended, the area faced the sudden loss of secure markets and the inexpensive resources necessary for industrial modernization. To these problems were added a lack of native investment capital, outmoded commercial and agricultural structures, and inadequate communication and transportation systems. Indeed, except for portions of Czechoslovakia, Poland, and Austria, the economies of eastern Europe resembled those of colonial areas in Asia, Africa, or the Middle East.

Social weaknesses contributed to the economic difficulties in eastern Europe. These societies had been dominated by landowning or entrepreneurial nobility and a religious hierarchy that ruled peasants who lived as virtual serfs, despite the formal abolition of serfdom in the nineteenth century. Again with the exception of Austria, Poland, and Czechoslovakia, there was no substantial middle class of merchants, financiers, or managers to provide the expertise and resources needed for modern industrial and commercial development. A small but influential intelligentsia provided the real leadership on a local level. Much of the middle class that did exist was German or Jewish. Finally, these nations were beset with problems common to underdeveloped societies. Illiteracy, high birth and death rates, primitive health conditions, and poor nutrition combined to retard modernization and undermine the democratic systems.

In addition to the clash of interests between landowners and peasants or between the emergent urban dwellers and the much larger rural population, these states were characterized by enormous ethnoreligious diversity. For historical reasons, nearly all of them had a heterogeneous population composed of groups whose ethnic and religious affiliations were different from those of the ruling majority. In some cases, notably Poland, Czechoslovakia, Yugoslavia, Hungary, and Romania, these minorities formed a substantial proportion of the inhabitants. Except for Greece and Turkey, which solved this problem by exchanging minority groups, governments faced ongoing challenges from the minorities. The minorities' reluctance to accept the supremacy of national states, coupled with the failure of most governments to treat their minorities fairly, was a major barrier to the formation of integrated societies.

The Decline of Liberalism

Liberal democracy in eastern Europe also suffered from political liabilities. The lack of experience in representative government meant that the normal give-and-take and compromise of parliamentary systems were absent from local and national politics, with the result that policymaking was often paralyzed. Many states had a multiplicity of political parties, which made legislative activity difficult. Perhaps the most serious political liability was the intense nationalism that pervaded the region and colored the perceptions of leaders and common people alike. Some areas, such as Poland, Hungary, and Bohemia, had long-established nationalist traditions, but national animosities were deepened by the wartime experience. Those on the losing side— Austria, Hungary, Turkey, Bulgaria—were determined to regenerate patriotic pride and regain lost territory; the victors who were already independent—Romania, Greece, Albania—viewed nationalism as a device to keep the hard-won spoils of war. In the states formed from territory of the defeated empires—Poland, Czechoslovakia, Estonia, Latvia, Lithuania—an uncompromising nationalism was seen as the basis for protecting their newly won sovereignty. Nationalism in eastern Europe produced aggressive international behavior that impeded cooperation among the countries and rendered impossible the formation of regional organizations that might have resolved economic problems.

It is hardly surprising that parliamentary democracies often failed to cope with these difficulties and gave way to authoritarian dictatorships. The first nation to adopt a dictatorial government was Hungary, which turned to Admiral Miklós Horthy after a short-lived communist regime under Béla Kun in 1919. Authoritarian leaders soon came to power elsewhere: Marshal Józef Pilsudski in Poland (1926), Antanas Smetona in Lithuania (1926), King Zog in Albania (1928), and King Alexander in Yugoslavia (1929). The Great Depression intensified the problems these nations faced and accelerated the trend toward dictatorship. King Carol began to assume dictatorial power in Romania in 1931, and within three years Engelbert Dollfuss in Austria, Konstantin Päts in Estonia, and Karlis Ulmanis in Latvia had followed suit. In 1935 and 1936 King Boris of

Bulgaria and General John Metaxas of Greece completed the transformation to authoritarianism in the region. Only Czechoslovakia, under the leadership of Tomáš Masaryk and Edvard Beneš, managed to retain its democratic government, despite authoritarian tendencies and serious internal problems.

Whether they were royal, civilian, or military dictatorships, these regimes shared certain characteristics. All retained the facade of democratic institutions, but all developed secret police systems, curtailed civil liberties, suppressed political opposition, and relied on centralized bureaucracies to enforce dictatorial decisions. Fascist movements appeared throughout the region, although none came to power before World War II. Instead, the dictators claimed that their regimes represented protection against exploitation, revolutionary unrest, or the persecution of minorities and posed as the embodiment of the national will. The appeals to nationalism and stability in an area beset with competition, mistrust, and insecurity ultimately proved too strong for the democratic experiment in eastern Europe.

As an ideology, fascism drew on the elitist, antidemocratic radicalism and nationalist-racist doctrines that emerged out of Europe's cultural ferment at the turn of the century— although fascist ideologues often claimed descent from prominent intellectuals, such as Nietzsche and Wagner, who had no direct connection with their movements. At the same time, modern concepts of political communication and social mobilization provided skillful leaders with the techniques for developing a power base and a new style of authoritarian leadership. The impact of World War I and the subsequent economic crisis helped to discredit democratic systems and enable these leaders to channel popular discontent into mass movements.

By the mid-1930s the world appeared to be engaged in a series of ideological struggles: for some, the battle was between democracy and fascism, while others saw it as one between capitalism and communism. Fascist victories in Italy and Germany made the prospects for democracy seem dark. The Western democracies came through the economic crisis with their political institutions changed but fundamentally intact. Yet little of the democratic experiment in eastern Europe survived the decade. More dangerous still, in Italy, Germany, and the Soviet Union the totalitarian restructuring of political, social, and economic life offered compelling alternatives to the liberal order. Finally, the spread of totalitarianism had important foreign implications. Both in Europe and in Asia militarism and the thirst for expansion began to undermine peace. With Mussolini and Hitler in power, one of the compelling forces behind the rise of fascism—nationalist frustration over the 1919 settlements—drove the dictators relentlessly toward the destruction of the postwar international order.

Notes

1. P. N. Stearns, *European Society in Upheaval* (New York: Macmillan, 1967), p. 339.
2. K. Völker, *Brecht: A Biography*, trans. J. Nowell (New York: Seabury Press, 1978), p. 116.

Suggestions for Further Reading

Arendt, H. *The Origins of Totalitarianism*, 2nd ed. Cleveland, Ohio: World Publishing, 1958.

Bullock, A. *Hitler: A Study in Tyranny*. New York: Harper & Row, 1964.

Cassels, A. *Fascism*. New York: Crowell, 1975.

De Felice, R. *Interpretations of Fascism*. Cambridge, Mass.: Harvard University Press, 1977.

Dulles, J. W. F. *Vargas of Brazil: A Political Biography*. Austin: University of Texas Press, 1967.

Gay, P. *Weimar Culture*. New York: Harper & Row, 1968.

Greene, N. *From Versailles to Vichy*. New York: Crowell, 1970.

Kindleberger, C. P. *The World in Depression, 1929–1939*. Berkeley: University of California Press, 1973.

Laqueur, W., ed. *Fascism: A Reader's Guide*. Berkeley: University of California Press, 1976.

Larsen, S. U., et al., eds. *Who Were the Fascists?* Oslo: Universitetsførlaget, 1982.

Lyttelton, A. *The Seizure of Power: Fascism in Italy, 1919–1929*. London: Weidenfeld & Nicolson, 1973.

Mack Smith, D. *Mussolini*. London: Weidenfeld & Nicolson, 1981.

Maruyama, M. *Thought and Behaviour in Modern Japanese Politics*. London: Oxford University Press, 1963.

Morris, I., ed. *Japan, 1931–1945: Militarism, Fascism, Japanism?* Boston: Heath, 1963.

Payne, S. G. *Fascism: Comparison and Definition*. Madison: University of Wisconsin Press, 1980.

Seton-Watson, H. *Eastern Europe Between the Wars, 1918–1941*. Cambridge: Cambridge University Press, 1962.

Shannon, D. A. *Between the Wars: America, 1919–1941*, 2d ed. Boston: Houghton Mifflin, 1979.

Taylor, A. J. P. *English History, 1914–1945*. New York: Oxford University Press, 1965.

Toland, J. *Adolf Hitler*. Garden City, N.Y.: Doubleday, 1976.

Totalitarianism and War

Some historians see the 20 years separating the two world wars as little more than a pause in an ongoing conflict. Yet two unique developments made the interwar period different from the years leading up to 1914—the rise of fascism and the emergence of a new form of political organization, the totalitarian state. Experiences as different as Nazi Germany and Soviet Russia demonstrate no causal link between fascism and totalitarianism. Totalitarianism as a form of government imposes complete control over its citizens in order to implement an ideology that seeks to transform society according to supposedly immutable historical laws. Both fascism and communism are totalitarian.

Totalitarian governments are single-party dictatorships in which constitutional rights are severely restricted or eliminated. All political organizations but the official party are outlawed, and in totalitarian states the bureaucracy and the party are closely intertwined. Such regimes are characterized by state terrorism, coercion, police surveillance, government monopoly of the communications media, and strong state economic control. Educational sys-

D day: American soldiers head for the beaches of Normandy as Allied troops assault Fortress Europe. [Brown Brothers]

tems indoctrinate citizens from an early age, while social and leisure organizations are designed to mobilize the masses.

Totalitarian rulers are ideological dictators. Men such as Lenin and Mussolini, Stalin and Hitler were driven by a determination to put their doctrines into practice. While they often compromised for expediency, ideological goals took precedence over traditional moral values. These dictators relied on modern technology—loudspeakers, radio, motion pictures—to achieve social control as well as to reinforce their leadership. In the hands of Mussolini and Hitler the totalitarian state became the instrument for the mobilization of huge industrial, economic, and military resources to unleash wars intended to reshape human life.

Mussolini's Italy

In the two years following the March on Rome in 1922, Benito Mussolini laid the foundations of his totalitarian state. He abolished all political organizations except the Fascist party, censored the press, set up a political police force, instituted loyalty oaths for civil servants, created a military court to prosecute anti-Fascists, and secured power to rule by decree. Once Fascists were installed in key government posts, he set out to forge a broad popular consensus.

On the surface Italy was still a parliamentary state with a monarch. The 1861 constitution remained in force, and Mussolini supposedly held office as prime minister at the pleasure of the king. Imposed above this system was the Fascist Grand Council, which in theory combined party and state functions. The council, appointed by Mussolini, selected candidates for election to the Chamber of Deputies and approved policy decisions. In 1939 this Chamber was replaced by the Chamber of Fasci and Corporations, which represented trades and professions rather than parties. Traditional institutions therefore coexisted with new Fascist bodies, and the totalitarian state never fully superseded them.

Economic Policy

The Fascists established strong state control over the economy while preserving capitalism. Mussolini compromised with the industrialists by agreeing to abolish the non-Fascist unions, prohibit strikes, and recognize the rights of industrial associations. In return, the industrialists supported his regime and dealt only with Fascist unions. Having abolished the economic rights of workers, Mussolini established the "corporate state" in the late 1920s by combining unions and employer associations into "corporations" for each major economic sector and indus-

try. The corporate system was touted as an original form of economic organization, in which state-supervised cooperation between capital and labor would replace class conflict. In reality, private business continued largely unhindered, and the corporate structure had little impact on economic life, except to control workers.

Mussolini failed to solve Italy's economic problems or temper the long-range effects of the Great Depression. Efforts to impose autarchy, or economic self-sufficiency, made matters worse. Marshlands were drained and cultivated, and farmers were coerced into growing more wheat and less of other crops. Nevertheless, overall agricultural production declined. Higher tariffs to stimulate industry increased consumer prices and shortages. Despite welfare programs and subsidies to large families, the standard of living of industrial and farm workers declined throughout the 1930s.

The Church and Fascism

Mussolini was more successful in relations with the Catholic church. Though an atheist, he understood the importance of Catholicism in Italian life and saw the church as a bulwark against communism. He thus ended the hostility that had existed between church and state since 1870, when the Kingdom of Italy seized Rome from the papacy. The Lateran Pacts of 1929 recognized the independence of Vatican City, which became a separate state within the city of Rome; anticlerical laws were repealed; Catholic youth groups were to be free from interference; the Vatican was to have its own newspaper and radio station; religious instruction in state schools became compulsory; and the government paid the Vatican an indemnity. The Lateran Pacts represented a triumph for Mussolini, for they secured the church's cooperation and gave the regime a respectable image. Most important, Mussolini won the support of many devout Italians. Pope Pius XI (1922–1939) proclaimed him "the man sent to us by Providence."

Regimentation and Propaganda

The regimentation of life under Fascism affected both thought and behavior. Mussolini created a secret police agency (called OVRA), spied on anti-Fascists, and introduced a new penal code. Nevertheless, a variety of circumstances—Mussolini's penchant for compromise, a long tradition of Italian resistance to bureaucratic authority, and the more limited ideological goals of Fascism—combined to make his system of terror less severe than that in Nazi Germany or the Soviet Union.

Control of the media and cultural life was placed under the Ministry of Popular Culture. Young people were trained in the party's youth organization, which included separate groups for males and females aged 6 through 17. They provided military training, sports, and political indoctrination and by the mid-1930s had over 3 million members. Leisure activities for workers and peasants were controlled through the party's *Dopolavoro* ("afterwork") organization. By 1940 the party, once an elite vanguard, had been opened to practically all Italians, many of whom viewed membership as a career necessity.

Although Mussolini's early movement had included several female Blackshirts, Fascism held a rigidly chauvinist attitude toward females, who were viewed exclusively as housewives and "mothers of the race." The Duce's highly publicized mistresses enhanced his reputation as a virile lover, and Fascists in general regarded women as objects to be "conquered" by men. The regime fostered conservative social values that reinforced traditional mores. The party trained young females to be wives and mothers, while state agencies provided maternity assistance, hygiene instruction, and child care information. Mussolini had supported giving the vote to women, but once in power he buried political equality. During the Fascist period the percentage of women making up the working population dropped as the depression affected both agriculture and industry.

The party glorified the leader. Mussolini was virtually deified as the farsighted "man of destiny." His skills as an orator, combined with his studied poses and facial expressions, captivated huge throngs. Slogans glorified the Duce and the achievements of Fascism: "Mussolini is always right," "A minute on the battlefield is worth a lifetime of peace," "Believe! Obey! Fight!"

In the mid-1930s the party introduced programs designed to alter Italian customs. Males were to be molded into the Fascist "new man"—obedient, virile, ruthless, efficient, and selfless. The military salute supplanted the handshake, black shirts were to be worn instead of business suits, and bourgeois pastimes such as golf and tennis were replaced with team sports. Many Italians privately scoffed at such measures, which were observed only superficially. The Fascists idealized imperial Rome as their inspiration, and Mussolini promised to create a new empire in which his people would recapture the Roman traditions of sacrifice and discipline. Mussolini was to be Italy's new Caesar.

Margherita Sarfatti, Italian art critic and the author of a popular biography of Mussolini, was the Fascist dictator's lover and cultural mentor for twenty years. [Photograph by Ghitta Carell, 1931, in possession of P. V. Cannistraro]

<h2 style="text-align:center">❦
MARGHERITA SARFATTI AND
FASCIST CULTURAL POLICY</h2>

The first Italian biography of Mussolini, published in 1926 with the Latin title *Dux*, was the work of Margherita G. Sarfatti (1880–1961). It is ironic that the antifeminist Fascist regime owed a considerable debt to a woman, for the best-selling biography promoted the legend of Mussolini as the new Caesar. Born Margherita Grassini, Sarfatti was the daughter of a prominent Venetian Jewish family. Intelligent and sophisticated—she was fluent in five languages—Sarfatti began her career as a socialist art critic. After marrying Cesare Sarfatti, an attorney, she moved to Milan, the center of modern Italian cultural life and socialism. There she was attracted to the Futurist movement, which she encouraged, and became a lifelong advocate of Italy's avant-garde painters and writers.

In 1909 Sarfatti began writing for *Avanti!*, the socialist daily of which Mussolini became editor. The two were immediately attracted to each other and began a passionate romance that lasted for many years. Sarfatti introduced Mussolini to her artistic and literary friends, including the Futurists, and gave the crude revolutionary a veneer of respectability and social grace. Together they agitated for intervention in World War I. The death of Sarfatti's 17-year-old son at the front in 1918—he was the youngest Italian to win the gold medal for bravery—made her personally committed to Mussolini's goal of vindicating Italy's wartime sacrifices. When Mussolini founded the Fascist movement in 1919, Sarfatti became art columnist for his official paper, *Il Popolo d'Italia*. During the March on Rome, she was his constant companion and adviser.

With Mussolini in power, Sarfatti emerged as the most influential woman in Italy, although she held no formal government post. She wrote books on modern art, edited Mussolini's official monthly, and drafted his articles for the foreign press. An international array of prominent writers paid court at her salon in Rome, and she patronized intellectuals and painters, for whom she secured commissions and arranged exhibits. Because of her influence in the art world, she came to be known disparagingly as the "dictator of culture." After World War I many artists had begun to turn away from the abstractionism that had marked prewar artistic modernism. Sarfatti supported this "return to order," advancing painters who remained committed to a modern style while appreciating older Italian traditions, especially perspective, portraiture, and classical landscape.

Sarfatti believed that this transformation could form the basis for an artistic revival that suited the Fascist emphasis on nationalist values. While she championed the cult of Rome, she also promoted modern art, architecture, and literature. In 1922 she organized the artists whose work combined modernism and classical motifs into a movement called the Twentieth Century and persuaded Mussolini to inaugurate its first group exhibit. Until the early 1930s the movement came close to representing Fascism's official artistic style, and thus Mussolini's regime encouraged the kind of avant-garde culture that Hitler condemned as "decadent." In promoting the Twentieth Century, Sarfatti struggled against anti-intellectual Fascists who viewed modernism as a product of a corrupt civilization and wanted a "social realist" art that was little more than posterlike propaganda.

By mid-1930s Sarfatti's star began to wane. Not only had her physical relationship with Mussolini ended, but the Duce had come to believe in his own charismatic abilities. When Mussolini imitated Nazi racial policy by adopting anti-Semitic measures in 1938, Sarfatti (who had converted to Catholicism on the eve of the Lateran Accords) fled to Latin America. She returned to Italy in 1947, after Mussolini had been killed and Fascism destroyed. She spent the rest of her life writing art criticism, never making any public comment about the man she had once loved or the regime she had helped to build.

❦
ROME, THE FASCIST CAPITAL

Sarfatti inspired Mussolini to redesign Rome as the capital of the Fascist state. With its ancient grandeur and rich archaeological remains, Rome was ideally suited for Mussolini's imperial dreams. Its history spanned 2,000 years. A city with a complex physical appearance, its ancient ruins and monuments stood against medieval buildings, Renaissance palaces, and Baroque churches. Fountains and squares provided relief from the winding, dark streets and bustling shopping districts.

Besides its role as a cultural center, Rome was a seat of government. After the collapse of the ancient empire, the city became the site of the papacy and the Catholic church, dominated by the Vatican and St. Peter's Basilica. When Rome became the capital of Italy in 1870, it began to assume its modern appearance. The influx of white-collar workers to staff the bureaucracy increased the size of the urban community significantly. Rome's population of 200,000 in 1870 doubled by the turn of the century, and by 1936 had reached almost 1.2 million. During the reign of King Umberto I (1878–1900) the city underwent a construction boom to accommodate its growing population, and elaborately ornate "Umbertine" architecture took its place alongside older styles.

Like emperors and popes before him, Mussolini determined to redo Rome in order to accent its imperial past, thus making the city the capital of the new Fascist empire. He ordered archaeological excavations and the renovation of ancient sites. He demolished entire residential districts of the inner city to build a grand concourse, the Via dell'Impero ("Imperial Way"), running from the Colosseum along the Forum to the Piazza Venezia, where his office was located. On the walls of the Basilica of Maxentius he placed massive marble maps of the ancient Roman conquests, followed by one showing the Fascist domain. The Piazza Venezia, dominated by the huge monument to Victor Emmanuel II, was the core of Fascist Rome. From the balcony of the Palazzo Venezia, Mussolini harangued enormous crowds. Mussolini also gave the city a modern appearance by constructing monuments and buildings in a modernized classical style characteristic of the regime's taste in architecture. In the 1930s a new complex for the University of Rome was built, as was the Italic Forum, a stadium surrounded by statues of nude athletes intended to symbolize Fascism's emphasis on physical strength. After the Lateran Pacts of 1929, Mussolini again destroyed residential districts to build a wide boulevard from the Tiber River to St. Peter's.

By the end of the decade plans had been laid for a new minicity in the suburbs between Rome and the ancient port of Ostia. Here modern public buildings were designed in the Fascist style for a world's fair in 1942, but the coming of World War II ended the project.

The Anti-Fascist Opposition

In spite of the enthusiasm Mussolini engendered, many Italians opposed Fascism. Mussolini's enemies came from all political parties and walks of life. By 1926 most of the well-known anti-Fascists who escaped Blackshirt brutality had been forced into exile, where they established groups with such names as Justice and Liberty. In the early 1930s an underground Communist network had been set up in

Italy and, together with Justice and Liberty, kept the hope of freedom alive while refuting Fascist propaganda. Mussolini's irresponsible foreign adventures gave anti-Fascism an added impetus, and his anti-Semitic laws alienated many Italians, who regarded the small Jewish population of 50,000 as loyal and productive. The degree to which Italians were repulsed by Mussolini's anti-Semitic policies reflected their humanist traditions.

Nazi Germany

A decade after Mussolini's seizure of power, Adolf Hitler became chancellor of Germany. With greater self-assurance and with clear policies already formulated, Hitler embarked on a total reshaping of German life, thereby establishing the second—and even more brutal—fascist totalitarian state in Europe.

The Nazi State

Hitler created new political and administrative systems. The former states of the German Republic, such as Prussia and Bavaria, were abolished, and a highly centralized government replaced the federal structure established in 1871. Hitler christened his new regime the Third Reich and proclaimed that it would last 1,000 years. He was the *Führer,* the supreme commander who embodied the sovereignty of his nation. Nazi party members replaced high-ranking officials in the central and local bureaucracies. The party itself was reorganized so that local leaders occupied positions equivalent to their bureaucratic counterparts in government. Although the Reichstag remained intact, it served only to provide Hitler with a forum for public declarations and the legitimation of Nazi programs.

The new German legal system also conformed to Nazi philosophy. Law was defined as the will of the German people acting in the interests of the state and its Führer. "People's courts" replaced the regular judicial system to dispense Nazi justice arbitrarily. To enforce compliance, Hitler established a secret political police—the dreaded *Gestapo*—and, six months after the Nazi seizure of power, concentration camps—the first one was at Dachau, outside Munich—to hold political prisoners. Under the command of SS leader Heinrich Himmler (1900–1945), ten or more such centers were built in Germany. Prisoners were used as slave labor, while others were beaten, tortured, or starved to death. Medical personnel performed fiendish experiments on living inmates. The Nazi state deliberately abandoned all traditional moral values.

Hitler was more cautious in dealing with the armed forces. The officer corps, drawn largely from the elite of Prussian society, had been a powerful and independent force in German life. The generals regarded Hitler and his followers as rabble-rousers who could be cast aside once they had generated a renewed sense of patriotism and crushed the communist threat. Hitler brought the generals under his control by compromising his own movement and agreeing to preserve the army's independence.

In 1930 Hitler had persuaded Ernst Röhm, the exiled leader of the SA, to return to Germany and resume command of the Brownshirts. After Hitler became chancellor, Röhm pressed him to eliminate the regular army and turn the SA into a revolutionary people's force. But Hitler needed the army both to consolidate his power and to realize his larger plans for world power. In April 1934 he cut a deal with the officer corps: they would support his policies in exchange for the elimination of the SA. The result was a violent end to a major chapter in the history of National Socialism and a dramatic demonstration of Hitler's ruthlessness. On June 30—the "Night of the Long Knives"—Hitler unleashed a bloody purge of the SA in which Röhm and scores of associates were murdered.

Economic Policy

To pull Germany out of the depression and make it economically self-sufficient, Hitler launched extensive public works programs that changed the appearance of Germany through reforestation, swamp drainage, and the construction of superhighways and housing. Farmers received subsidies and protection against debt foreclosure. To avoid dependence on imported raw materials, German scientists developed artificial rubber, plastics, synthetic textiles, and other substitute products.

While unemployment virtually disappeared and living standards began to rise, both employers and workers lost much of their economic freedom. Strength through Joy, an organization similar to Mussolini's *Dopolavoro*, offered low-income citizens entertainment, vacations, and travel. Industry and commerce remained privately owned but were placed under strict government control. In 1936 Hitler proclaimed the first of two four-year plans that regimented economic life, including wages, profits, and production decisions. Business and professional associations became arms of the Nazi economic system, and independent labor unions were replaced with the National Labor Front, in which membership was compulsory. Strikes were prohibited, and all labor relations were regulated by the state. Hitler's economic policies and rearmament program did pull Germany out of the worst aspects of the depression, restoring relatively full employment. Yet workers paid a heavy price—the destruction of their liberty and a devastating war.

Society and Culture

State coordination also affected social and cultural affairs. Conscious of the need for future soldiers and workers,

Hitler promoted the enlargement of German families through a rising birthrate and improved health care. Some 20 percent of Nazi party members were women in the early 1920s, but once in power Nazi ideologists, like the Fascists in Italy, limited the role of women in national life. In *Mein Kampf,* Hitler had written that for women "the chief emphasis must be laid on physical training, and only subsequently on the promotion of spiritual and finally intellectual values. The goal of female education must invariably be the future mother."[1] Official propaganda projected women as symbols of Germanic female virtue in contrast to the warrior image of men.

Nazi women were generally enthusiastic about restoring traditional social values, and Hitler established a large corps of female officials to organize women in local communities. After 1937, when he began to prepare for war, women were encouraged to work in industry, agriculture, and the service sector.

For males, Hitler removed many of the social barriers that had previously limited economic or political opportunities. Most middle-class citizens perceived the Nazi regime as a promoter and guardian of this social transformation.

Organized religion posed a challenge to the new order and hence came under growing pressure to accept government control. Catholic and Protestant clergy alike were prohibited from criticizing official policies and found it difficult to maintain ties with churches outside Germany. The state discouraged children from attending religious schools while supporting the revival of anti-Christian movements that worshiped ancient Teutonic gods.

The cultural sphere drew special attention both as a means to promote the cult of the *Führer* and to construct the Nazi world view. Under the vigilance of the minister of propaganda, Joseph Goebbels (1897–1945), every facet of intellectual and artistic life was harnessed to generate enthusiasm for Nazi doctrine and its leader. Publishing houses came under the control of the government, which eliminated all literature not conforming to officially endorsed ideas; "offensive" books were publicly burned. The government assigned themes to writers, artists, architects, and musicians. As in Fascist Italy, sports were seen as physical demonstration of Nazi virtues. Radio and film, whose potential for shaping mass opinion was immense, were perhaps Goebbels' most powerful propaganda weapons. Leni Riefenstahl, a talented film director, won international acclaim for the seductive power of her visual imagery in such films as *Triumph of the Will* (1935).

Hitler took a keen interest in art and architecture. Viewing modern styles as alien to the "Germanic spirit," he dismissed modern-minded artists and museum curators and in 1935 regimented artists under Nazi party orders. In his inaugural address at the opening of the House of German Art in Munich in 1937, Hitler denounced Impressionism, Futurism, and Cubism as Jewish-inspired "cultural bolshevism." He demanded an art that reflected German values. To illustrate the "depravity" of modernism, the government set up a permanent Exhibition of Degenerate Art. Nazi painting and sculpture reflected a Romantic hero worship inspired by the themes of Nordic mythology made famous by Wagner's operas. This official art lacked originality or creative expression, let alone aesthetic

Seamstresses sew Nazi flags in 1933. [Landesbildstelle Berlin]

value. Instead, it glorified the *Führer* as a Germanic warrior, extolled the concept of "blood and soil," idealized the image of mothers and children, and depicted muscle-bound nudes as the embodiment of German strength. The Nazis also attacked modern architecture, closing down the Bauhaus and driving its architects out of Germany. Hitler and his architectural consultant Albert Speer planned to erect in Berlin monumental buildings designed in a pseudo-Greek classicism.

Underpinning all these efforts was the educational system. Schools and universities underwent a thorough reconstruction of their curricula and faculties to ensure that all students received indoctrination and only carefully screened information. The Nazi party formed a comprehensive youth movement—the *Hitlerjugend*, or Hitler Youth—that reinforced intellectual, psychological, and political conformity.

Hitler and the Jews

The ultimate horror of the Nazi regime began to reveal itself soon after Hitler came to power. More than any other authoritarian or totalitarian movement, National Socialism was based on racial and ethnic hatred. Nazi ideologues considered the Germans a superior race who deserved to be masters over such "undesirables" as Slavs, gypsies, and Latins. But Hitler, whose anti-Semitism had been formed during his Vienna days, reserved his special animosity for the Jews, whose persecution and ultimate annihilation became his obsession.

◉ The Nuremberg Racial Laws ◉

Hitler incorporated the principles of Nazi anti-Semitism into a series of laws introduced between September and November 1935. The so-called Nuremberg Laws captured the essence of Nazi racism. The following selections are from these infamous measures.

I. The Reich Citizenship Law of September 15, 1935:

A citizen of the Reich may be only that subject who is of German or kindred blood, and who, through his behavior, shows that he is both desirous and personally fit to serve loyally the German people and the Reich.

II. The Law for the Protection of German Blood and Honor, September 15, 1935:

Any marriages between Jews and citizens of German or kindred blood are herewith forbidden. Marriages entered into despite this law are invalid. . . .

Extramarital relations between Jews and citizens of German or kindred blood are herewith forbidden.

Jews are forbidden to employ as servants in their households female subjects of German or kindred blood who are under the age of 45 years.

Jews are prohibited from displaying the Reich and national flag and from showing the national colors.

III. Supplementary decree of November 14, 1935:

A Jew cannot be a citizen of the Reich. He cannot exercise the right to vote; he cannot occupy public office. . . .

A Jew is an individual who is descended from at least three grandparents who were, racially, full Jews. . . .

A Jew is also an individual who is descended from two full-Jewish grandparents if:

(a) he was a member of the Jewish religious community . . . ;

(b) when the law was issued he was married to a person who was a Jew . . . ;

(c) he is the issue from a marriage with a Jew . . . ;

(d) he is the issue of an extra-marital relationship with a Jew. . . .

Source: Reichgesetzblatt (1935), No. 100 (September 15, 1935), 1: 1142–1147.

Hitler swiftly launched a campaign of official persecution against the Jews. In April 1933 the government barred Jews from the civil service, while racial laws forbade them to study or teach in the universities or to practice medicine, law, and other professions. In 1935 the notorious Nuremberg Laws deprived Jews of all civil rights, including the freedom to marry non-Jews. A campaign of terror against German Jews followed. "Jewish" became the characteristic term of official disapproval for everything considered negative in Nazi eyes—democracy, communism, liberalism, or individual rights.

As the anti-Semitic drive intensified, thousands of Jews fled Germany. The assassination of a German diplomat in Paris by a young Polish Jew in 1938 was the pretext for the infamous *Kristallnacht* ("Night of Broken Glass"), a coordinated wave of violence that destroyed Jewish homes, businesses, and synagogues and took many lives; later the Jews were heavily assessed to pay for the damage. The Western democracies, unwilling to assume the burden of caring for millions of refugees, refused to accept mass Jewish immigration. Although some international protests were lodged against these outrages, most Germans either approved or accepted them.

The Jews still in Germany now found it virtually impossible to leave, having become an imprisoned humanity for whom the worst of the horrors still lay ahead. Nazi anti-Semitism drew on a long tradition of persecution, prejudice, and superstition, but the Nazis went far beyond that tradition in their effort to impose the domination of the German "master race" on the "inferior" peoples of Europe. During World War II the fate of Germany's Jews would be tied to that of Jews throughout the Continent as Hitler drove anti-Semitism to its ultimate conclusion: the planned extermination of European Jewry.

Stalin's Russia

Unlike Hitler or Mussolini, Stalin inherited an established, if not completely shaped, revolutionary system. He had several goals, the first of which was the consolidation of his hold over the country and its Communist party. He also wished to make Russia economically independent of the hostile capitalist powers, particularly by modernizing industry. In part he was motivated by ideological considerations. Committed to socialism as they perceived it, Stalin and his supporters were uneasy about the NEP policies introduced by Lenin, which had created a kind of market socialism based on nationalized industry, mixed private retail trade and state distribution, and capitalistic agriculture strongly influenced by state prices and quotas. Eliminating the vestiges of capitalism and introducing a new model of development became a priority, now that the economy had recovered from its wartime prostration and Stalin's political power was secure.

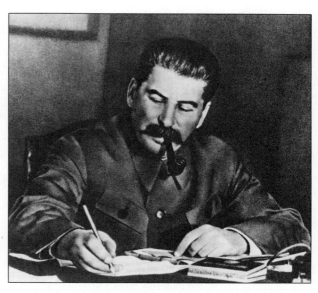

Stalin as the genial leader; a photo of a painted portrait. [Mansell Collection]

The Five-Year Plans

Stalin's device to attain these objectives was the five-year plan. This strategy sought to replace private property and economic activity with a system of production quotas formulated and administered by a central authority under the party's direction. The plan established production goals for every citizen. Heavy industry and transportation received most of the resources at the expense of consumer-oriented manufacturing and agriculture. The quotas were unrealistic—projected increases of 250 percent for heavy industry, 300 percent for steel production, and 150 percent for agriculture. Workers and managers who met or exceeded their targets received bonuses; stiff penalties awaited those who fell short. A new government agency, GOSPLAN, became the vehicle for translating party directives into performance. In sum, the plans attempted to impose centralized state control on resources and manpower that capitalism regulated through such market forces as supply and demand or changes in wages, prices, and interest rates.

The initial plan (1928–1932) had mixed success. Frequent breakdowns in planning and implementation caused waste, surpluses, or shortages, and quotas rarely were met. Moreover, the emphasis on quantity resulted in shoddy products. Nonetheless, due in part to the substantial importation of machinery, skilled workers, and technicians from the advanced industrial countries, production doubled in five years.

Agriculture was another story. Stalin was determined to gain control over the countryside and punish the land-owning peasants who had resisted state authority. Moreover, he wanted to collect grain efficiently and pay for his industrialization programs by controlling grain prices. The method adopted was to consolidate the thousands of small family farms into a few hundred large agricultural enterprises that could use the latest mechanization and management techniques. Each huge farm would focus on a specific crop, which could be grown more efficiently. This would result in agricultural surpluses for sale abroad to finance industrialization.

In 1929 Soviet peasants were ordered to surrender their land and farm animals to the state and to become members of cooperative farms known as collectives. Under state control, each collective would receive quotas, much like factory workers or coal miners. Except for their houses and personal belongings, members were to turn over their property to the collective and to share the work and whatever profit or loss the farm recorded. Much of the peasantry—especially the well-to-do kulaks—rebelled against this system, burning crops and seed reserves or slaughtering livestock rather than surrendering them to the collectives. Across rural Russia detachments of police and, occasionally, Red Army troops attacked villages that resisted collectivization. The most capable farmers were either killed or dispatched to labor camps. The scheme was disastrous for Soviet agriculture. Livestock declined by over one-half, and the output of grain barely increased between 1928 and 1938, when it finally reached the prewar level. A famine swept the country in 1932 and 1933, the direct result of forced collectivization. Together Stalin's agrarian policy and the famine killed between 5 and 8 million persons in the Ukraine alone.

In addition to its social and economic impact, collectivization had important political implications. The systematic and brutal intrusion into the countryside saw a significant extension of the Communist party's power, for until then its direct control over the vast majority of Soviet citizens

had been limited. Stalin's radical measures represented a vital step toward totalitarian control.

Declaring the five-year plan a success, Stalin announced a second in 1932 and a third six years later. In the later versions, steps were taken to improve quality and eliminate shortcomings in production and distribution. The results in industry were impressive. During the first two plans, the output of iron and steel expanded fourfold, that of coal 3½ times; by 1938 the Soviet Union had become the world's largest producer of tractors and locomotives. Many of the new plants featured the latest equipment from America or western Europe. Agriculture, however, continued to present major problems. Grain production crept upward very slowly, and the country faced constant shortages of meat, fruits, vegetables, and dairy products. By the end of 1932 some 60 percent of all surviving peasant families had joined collective farms; by 1938 the proportion reached 93 percent. The government could count on a reasonably steady supply of basic goods for the cities. Collectivization provided Stalin with at least a political triumph.

Industrial expansion coincided with urbanization, as modern cities rose up in previously isolated areas of Siberia and central Asia. To populate them and meet the demand for labor, millions migrated from rural regions to the new manufacturing centers. Workers lost most of their independence as their unions became instruments of the state and their employment was decided by the central authorities.

Life in Stalin's Russia was harsh. Adequate housing was scarce, and wages failed to keep pace with prices—in 1937 a nonagricultural worker could buy about 60 percent of what he could have purchased in 1928. To material hardships was added the psychological strain of political indoctrination. Everyone was required to attend lectures by party activists, who extolled the virtues of Soviet socialism while warning of capitalist plots. Artists, writers, film producers, playwrights, musicians, and other communicators took seriously Stalin's command that they become "engi-

In the Soviet Union women were mobilized into virtually all sectors of the labor force. Here a female tractor driver leads a procession to the fields. [Sovfoto]

neers of human minds" and competed as composers of Communist propaganda.

By the mid-1930s another major propaganda theme was added: virtual deification of Stalin. Unlike other dictators, Stalin shunned public appearances at mass rallies and similar functions. Yet his presence, in the form of portraits, statues, and books, was inescapable. Indeed, he became the focal point of a cult of personality comparable to that in Nazi Germany and Fascist Italy.

Social Policy

Stalin's regime offered positive incentives to labor. Unemployment virtually disappeared, and the basis was laid for free state medical services, old-age pensions, subsidized housing, and day-care facilities for children. Perhaps the most meaningful benefit to many was the extension of free education to all, a policy begun in the 1920s. The government declared war on illiteracy, bringing basic schooling to even the most isolated portions of the Soviet Union. Advanced education was provided free to students demonstrating superior aptitude and ability, and a reward system of high salaries, bonuses, and privileges awaited successful graduates. Indeed, a managerial and technocratic class soon emerged that, together with the political and artistic elites, formed a new aristocracy in this supposedly classless society. The welfare system, combined with fear of the consequences of any criticism, effectively muted discontent among the masses.

The status of women underwent significant change during the Stalinist period. The hopes of early Bolshevik feminists such as Alexandra Kollontai that the revolution would achieve equality for women were never fully realized. In 1918 the *Zhenotdel,* or Party Women's Bureau, was established to educate and recruit women for the Communist party. The Zhenotdel also acted as an advocate for women's interests in the workplace and sponsored women candidates for local elections. Even though it had no powers of enforcement, the Zhenotdel had an uneasy relationship with party officials, and Stalin abolished it in the 1920s.

In that decade, however, Russian women were given legal access to abortion and divorce, and although Stalin minimized the rhetoric of sexual equality, industrial policy and economic necessity resulted in wider opportunities for women. The collectivization of agriculture brought women into the fields in greater numbers, while subsistence salaries for male workers pushed millions of wives and daughters into factory jobs, public works projects, and heavy construction. The most significant change, however, came in educational opportunities, which were now open to women, especially in science, technology, and medicine. Despite the advances in education and employment, the Soviet mobilization of women increased their physical and psychological burdens, for most women were expected to care for children and do housework while working or going to school. Nevertheless, unlike the fascist regimes in Italy and Germany, which relegated women to the roles of wives and mothers, Soviet totalitarianism at least proclaimed the goal of female equality and made important strides in breaking the pattern of traditional roles for women.

The Great Purges

Stalin's development programs had employed totalitarian mechanisms of state control that made wide use of police terror against the peasants. But as uneasiness over his brutal methods mounted, the internal security forces—known as the NKVD—were soon turned against the Communist elite. Between 1936 and 1938 Stalin unleashed an immense reign of terror that engulfed eminent party members, high-ranking administrators, and military leaders. Eventually it expanded to include ordinary citizens, many of whom fell victim to sudden arrest and summary execution or exile to a remote labor camp without apparent reason. The reasons behind these "great purges" remain obscure. There is evidence of at least one serious plot against Stalin; paranoia may have so consumed him that he struck out blindly against presumed enemies.

The terror began with the assassination in December 1934 of Sergei Kirov, a close associate of Stalin's and, according to some, his chosen successor. Claiming that Kirov's murder was part of a vast conspiracy led by supporters of the exiled Trotsky, Stalin, who had in reality arranged for the murder himself, ordered mass arrests. In 1936 there began a series of public trials that captured world attention. Sixteen "Old Bolsheviks"—activists who had joined the party prior to 1917—were charged with conspiring to topple Stalin and restore Trotsky to power. Led by Grigori Zinoviev and Lev Kamenev, all confessed and were executed. Similar trials claimed other Old Bolsheviks, including the theoretician Nikolai Bukharin; all offered identical confessions followed by summary execution. Next the purge reached the army. A secret court-martial in 1937 found Marshal Mikhail Tukhachevsky and other officers guilty of conspiring with the Germans and the Japanese as well as with Trotsky, and all were executed. In addition, thousands of prominent party members, union officials, business executives, and intellectuals lost their liberty or their lives. Stalin culminated the purges by executing the leaders of the very police force that had implemented his program of terror. When the purges were over, millions had fallen victim to his obsession.

The great purges served to remove upper and middle-level officials in the party, state, military, and economic institutions, and Stalin replaced them with younger functionaries who would dutifully obey him. Yet they also had the effect of halting the revolutionary changes that had been going on in the Soviet Union since the early 1920s.

Thenceforth the regime would follow the path set by Stalin's totalitarian dictatorship.

The Rising Sun: Japanese Expansion in East Asia

The Japanese had come to view the large but internally weak Chinese territory as their sphere of interest and had taken advantage of World War I and the Russian civil war to extend their influence on the mainland. In addition to providing an opportunity to seize territory, the war in Europe had also quickened the pace of Japanese industrial growth and enabled Tokyo to capture many regional markets from the Western powers. In the postwar period Japan became the main source of textiles and other consumer products for the rest of Asia.

But this thriving economy rested on a precarious base. Lacking essential raw materials, Japan's chief asset was its highly motivated, well-disciplined work force. Indeed, Japanese leaders were able to mobilize workers even more effectively than Europe's totalitarian dictators, producing a modern industrial machine along with a series of related commercial and financial institutions, largely controlled by a few great family trusts known as the *zaibatsu*. Political and economic leaders realized that their nation would continue to prosper only if it had a guaranteed flow of raw materials from abroad, together with secure foreign markets for its finished products. A disruption of this balance would halt the growth of Japanese power and expose its vulnerability to forces beyond its control.

The Japanese political system vigorously pursued the interests of the nation's economic elite. On paper Japan possessed a government strikingly similar to that of many European powers—a written constitution adopted in 1889, universal male suffrage since 1925, and modern parliamentary and judicial systems. But this institutional structure was largely misleading. The Diet (parliament) had sharply limited powers, and ministers governed in the name of the supreme and holy emperor, to whom they were completely responsible. A spirit of militarism pervaded Japanese life and gave the professional officer corps a political influence comparable to that enjoyed by the German military caste prior to World War I. In the 1930s Japan was the only modern nation that required its war and naval ministers to be generals and admirals on active-duty status. Many of its younger officers, influenced by the national revival that had begun in the mid-nineteenth century, were drawn from a segment of the small landowning nobility that followed the warrior code of the old samurai. The powerful combination of nationalism, militarism, and authoritarianism that dominated Japanese politics deter-

mined that in time of crisis, ultimate authority passed to the military leaders.

After World War I, Chinese tariff barriers and the Great Depression threatened Japan's access to raw materials and markets. Younger army officers proposed the conquest of nearby territory from which materials could be obtained and to which manufactured goods—as well as surplus population—could be sent. Military spokesmen added a messianic tone to these arguments by insisting that the prosperity and progress of all Asia depended on the Japanese, who would liberate Asia from Western exploitation. Japan's imperial program thus assumed the guise of a broader campaign in defense of Asian interests.

Manchuria was the first target of Japanese expansionism. Russia, whose territory bordered Manchuria on the north and east, had dominated the area until its defeat in the 1905 war. Thereafter, although it remained nominally part of China, Manchuria became a Japanese sphere. In September 1931 Japanese colonels took advantage of a minor incident involving the South Manchuria Railway at Mukden to invade Manchuria. The civilian government reluctantly approved the army's initiative, and by early 1932 the Japanese conquest of Manchuria was complete.

When the Chinese responded with a boycott against Japanese goods, Tokyo landed 70,000 troops at Shanghai, then withdrew them under pressure from the Western powers. Japan nonetheless renamed its conquered Manchurian territory Manchukuo ("Country of the Manchus") and proclaimed it an independent state under Henry Pu Yi, the last Manchu emperor, who remained a Japanese puppet. Condemned by the League of Nations, the Japanese withdrew their membership, presenting the League with the first real test of its ability to stop aggression. The League failed to meet the challenge, imposing neither economic nor military sanctions. Japan's ambitions were emboldened by the signing of the Anti-Comintern Pact with Germany in 1936, which bound both partners to withhold aid from Russia should either party go to war with the Soviets.

Aggression and Appeasement in the West

Japan's success in defying the League of Nations encouraged Hitler's and Mussolini's quest for territorial expansion. Mussolini's emphasis on the virtues of war, combined with his dream of creating a new Roman Empire, impelled him toward conquest. Hitler was even more outspoken about his plans for a "Greater German Reich" in Europe, the corollary of a racial policy that aimed at bringing the "inferior" peoples of the Continent under the domination of the "master" Germanic race.

Europe and Africa: The Axis Advance

Hitler laid the groundwork for expansion while rebuilding German military strength. In October 1933 Germany withdrew from the League of Nations and the following July instigated a coup in Austria aimed at bringing about the union (*Anschluss*) of Austria and Germany. The conspirators murdered Austrian chancellor Engelbert Dollfuss but were halted by Mussolini, who intervened to protect Austrian independence, which he considered vital to Italy's security.

In January 1935 Hitler won a huge majority in the Versailles-mandated plebiscite that returned the Saar region to Germany. In March he openly defied the postwar settlement, declaring that Germany had formed an air force and had reinstituted the military draft. Despite protests, Britain tacitly endorsed Hitler's actions in June 1935 by signing a naval agreement with Germany.

In the summer of 1934 Mussolini had begun preparations for the conquest of Ethiopia, one of the two remaining independent nations in Black Africa (the other was Liberia). Arousing enthusiasm with a propaganda campaign at home, the Duce launched his invasion in October 1935. The League of Nations promptly imposed economic sanctions, but it omitted oil from the list of products that member nations could not sell to Italy. This important exception, together with the abstention of the United States, Japan, and Germany from the boycott, virtually assured Italy of victory. In May 1936, when Mussolini proclaimed the incorporation of Ethiopia with Italian Somaliland and Eritrea into a new empire called Italian East Africa, the collective security system created at Versailles crumbled.

Hitler took full advantage of these developments. In March 1936, while the conquest of Ethiopia was under way, he ordered German troops into the Rhineland, which the Versailles treaty had established as a demilitarized zone. At the same time, he repudiated the 1925 Locarno treaties that guaranteed Germany's frontiers with Belgium and France and recognized the demilitarized status of the Rhineland. Although the French mobilized their troops, Britain refused to act. Hitler and Mussolini had shown that the democracies were unwilling to preserve the postwar settlement. In October 1936 the Führer and the Duce agreed to coordinate their foreign policies in what Mussolini called the Rome-Berlin Axis.

The Spanish Civil War

The Axis partnership demonstrated its military capacity during the Spanish civil war. When Spain became a democratic republic after the collapse of the Bourbon monarchy in 1931, the new government launched a campaign of social and economic reform. Conservative elements, especially the military, the Catholic church, and the aristocracy, opposed the reforms and gained control of the government in 1933. In response, leftist and democratic groups formed the Popular Front, which regained power in the 1936 elec-

Franco's victory in the Spanish civil war forced thousands of civilians to seek refuge across the border in France. [UPI/ Bettmann Newsphotos]

◉ Guernica ◉

*The aerial bombardment of the town of Guernica during the Spanish
civil war became a symbol of the horror of modern warfare and inspired Pablo Picasso to paint his wrenching painting by that name.
Here a British correspondent described the event.*

Guernica, the most ancient town of the Basques and the center of their cultural tradition,
was completely destroyed yesterday afternoon by insurgent air raiders. The bombardment
of this open town far behind the lines occupied precisely three hours and a quarter, during which a powerful fleet of airplanes . . . did not cease unloading on the town bombs
weighing from 1,000 lb. downwards and, it is calculated, more than 3,000 two-pounder
aluminum incendiary projectiles. The fighters, meanwhile, plunged low from above the
centre of the town to machine-gun those of the civilian population who had taken refuge
in the fields. . . .

At 2 A.M. today when I visited the town the whole of it was a horrible sight, flaming
from end to end. The reflection of the flames could be seen in the clouds of smoke
above the mountains from 10 miles away. Throughout the night houses were falling until
the streets became long heaps of red impenetrable debris. . . .

In the form of its execution and the scale of the destruction it wrought, no less than in
the selection of its objective, the raid on Guernica is unparalleled in military history.
Guernica was not a military objective. . . .

The rhythm of this bombing of an open town was, therefore, a logical one: first, hand
grenades and heavy bombs to stampede the population, then machine-gunning to drive
them below, next heavy and incendiary bombs to wreck the houses and burn them on
top of their victims.

Source: The Times (London), April 28, 1937.

**In 1937, after the German bombing of the village of Guernica during the Spanish civil war,
Pablo Picasso produced this painting by that name to express the agony. [A&R MAS]**

tions. Unwilling to accept this, army officers under the leadership of General Francisco Franco (1892–1975) revolted in July. Franco was soon joined by extreme nationalists and Spanish fascists, known as the Falange, and the nation was plunged into civil war.

The Spanish civil war was a major barometer of the willingness of democratic and totalitarian forces to act. Hitler and Mussolini poured tanks, planes, and military personnel into Spain on behalf of the Nationalists. Stalin countered by shipping equipment and military advisers to the republican Loyalists. Fearful of escalation, the British and French adopted a policy of nonintervention. Thousands of liberals, socialists, communists, and anarchists from Europe and America who viewed Spain as an ideological battleground fought as volunteers in international brigades against the Franco forces. The agony of the Spanish people was exemplified by the German bombing of the town of Guernica on April 26, 1937. By the beginning of 1939, the Nationalists had won, and Franco became dictator of Spain.

The Czech Crisis

Emboldened by the timidity of the Western powers, Hitler annexed Austria, occupying it with German troops in March 1938. He then turned to Czechoslovakia. The 3 million ethnic Germans who lived in the Sudeten border region had never been reconciled to Czech rule. In the aftermath of the Austrian *Anschluss*, the Czech Nazi leader, Konrad Henlein (1898–1945), demanded autonomy for the Sudetenland, a move that Hitler promptly endorsed. The democratic Czech government, headed by President Edvard Beneš (1884–1948), appealed to France and the Soviet Union, with which it had defensive alliances, and mobilized its own forces. Hitler responded by threatening an invasion. War appeared imminent.

The French, unprepared to fight, yielded the diplomatic initiative to Britain's prime minister, Neville Chamberlain (1869–1940). Determined to avoid war, Chamberlain held a series of meetings with Hitler. A final conference, held in Munich with Mussolini and French premier Edouard Daladier (1884–1970) on September 29 and 30, settled the fate of Czechoslovakia. Chamberlain and Daladier accepted the demand for German annexation of the Sudetenland and forced the Czechs to acquiesce. Chamberlain then returned to London to proclaim "peace in our time." Six months later Hitler violated the agreement, moving German troops into Prague and dismembering what was left of Czechoslovakia. It, like Austria, had ceased to exist as a sovereign state.

The Munich settlement represented the culmination of the Western policy of appeasement. The strategy of appeasement had been calculated to eliminate the dangers of war by satisfying the demands of aggressor states through peaceful negotiation. At the time the policy did not seem as shortsighted as it does in retrospect. Many agreed with Hitler and Mussolini that some aspects of the

◉ Hitler's War Plans ◉

On November 5, 1937, Hitler held a secret meeting with his military leaders in which he sketched his plans for aggression and war. Hitler's comments were recorded by his aid, Colonel Hossbach.

The aim of German policy is to make secure and to preserve the racial community and to enlarge it. . . .

Germany's future was therefore wholly conditional upon the solving of the need for space. . . .

Germany's problem could only be solved by means of force. . . .

If the *Führer* was still living, it was his unalterable resolve to solve Germany's problem of space at the latest by 1943–45.

Our first objective, in the event of our being embroiled in war, must be to overthrow Czechoslovakia and Austria simultaneously. . . . Our agreements with Poland only·retained their force as long as Germany's strength remained unshaken. . . .

Actually, the *Führer* believed that almost certainly Britain, and probably France as well, had already tacitly written off the Czechs. . . .

Military intervention by Russia must be countered by the swiftness of our operations. . . .

Source: Documents on German Foreign Policy, 1918–1945, Series D, I (Washington, D.C.: U.S. Government Printing Office, 1949), Document No. 19.

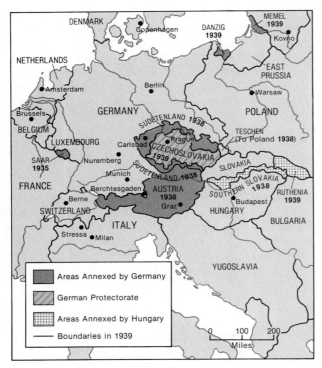

37.1 Central Europe, 1939

postwar peace settlements had been unfair, while others saw the instability of the new states in eastern Europe as proof of the failure of Wilsonian self-determination. Appeasement was the policy of people who had survived the horrors of World War I and were determined to avoid another at almost any cost.

Appeasement was all the more compelling because some European statesmen, still haunted by the specter of the Russian Revolution, believed that the upheavals of war would unleash communism in the West. The Great Depression had seriously weakened the economic and social order of capitalism and had shaken Western faith in democratic political systems. The lack of military preparedness in Britain and France reflected these post-1919 developments, whereas for some Western leaders the armed strength of the aggressors made appeasement seem necessary. The policy, however, only whetted the territorial appetites of Mussolini and Hitler.

World War II

At the end of March 1939—when it was already clear that Poland would be Hitler's next victim—Chamberlain publicly assured Warsaw that Britain and France would defend Polish independence. By then, the dictators had no reason to believe the Western powers meant what they said. On April 3 Hitler secretly ordered the invasion of Poland in September, and five days later Mussolini invaded Albania. In May, after Britain and France extended guarantees to Greece and Romania, Hitler and Mussolini signed the Pact of Steel, a formal military alliance.

In preparation for his assault against Poland, Hitler sought to guard against two possible contingencies: the intervention of Russia and, in the event that the Western powers did fight, a two-front war between Russia in the east and an Anglo-French campaign in the west. The Soviet Union had been negotiating with both sides since early spring, but mutual mistrust in Moscow, London, and Paris ultimately prevented an agreement. From Stalin's perspective, while an alliance with Britain and France might mean a war against Germany with no prospect of gain, Hitler offered him tangible benefits—neutrality in the event of war between Germany and the West and a division of eastern European territory. For Stalin the choice was clear. On August 23 Germany and Russia announced a nonaggression treaty, which contained a secret protocol that divided Poland into German and Russian spheres, gave Lithuania to Germany, and ceded Finland, Latvia, and Estonia to the Soviet Union, thereby almost restoring Russia's 1914 frontiers. The Nazi-Soviet Pact was a consummate act of *Realpolitik* concluded by two bitter ideological enemies. It shattered the loyalty of many Communists and supporters of the Soviets around the world. On September 1 German planes and armored columns attacked Poland. Two days later Britain and France declared war on Germany. World War II had begun in Europe.

The Nazi Onslaught

Poland fell in less than four weeks, in what the Germans called *Blitzkrieg* ("lightning war"), which coordinated air and ground forces in a sudden furious attack. Before the collapse of Warsaw, Stalin rushed troops into eastern Poland to secure the territory promised him in the Nazi-Soviet Pact. Poland, too, was obliterated.

Unable to launch an offensive before the onset of winter, Hitler held back from an all-out assault on the West. Between the end of September 1939 and April 1940, this "phony war" was interrupted only by German-British naval engagements. In the meantime, the Soviet Union moved troops into Estonia, Latvia, and Lithuania and on November 30 invaded Finland, conquering it by March 1940 after unexpected resistance. In April, Hitler suddenly struck at Norway and Denmark. The latter fell in less than a day, Norway by the end of the month. Then, on May 10, the full weight of the German war machine was flung against Belgium and the Netherlands. The same day, Chamberlain resigned and was replaced as prime minister by Winston Churchill (1874–1965).

◉ Secret Protocol of the Nazi-Soviet Pact ◉

*The nonaggression pact Hitler and Stalin signed on August 22, 1939,
contained a secret clause that divided Poland and Lithuania between
the two powers in the event of a war.*

The territory of the Lithuanian state falls to the sphere of influence of the U.S.S.R., while, on the other hand, the province of Lublin and parts of the province of Warsaw fall to the sphere of influence of Germany. . . . As soon as the Government of the U.S.S.R. shall take special measures on Lithuanian territory to protect its interests, the present German-Lithuanian border, for the purpose of a natural and simple boundary delineation, shall be rectified in such a way that the Lithuanian territory situated to the southwest of the line marked on the attached map shall fall to Germany.

Source: R. J. Sontag and J. S. Beddie, eds., *Nazi-Soviet Relations, 1939–1941: Documents from the Archives of the German Foreign Office* (Washington, D.C.: U.S. Government Printing Office, 1948), p. 107.

Although the combined British, French, Belgian, and Dutch forces matched Germany's 134 divisions, the Allies were deficient in planes and antiaircraft power, and overwhelmed by German *Blitzkrieg* tactics. By the end of May the Germans had pushed the Allied armies to the English Channel, where more than 330,000 French and British troops were evacuated from Dunkirk to England. Bypassing the Maginot line, a system of static fortifications that ran north from Switzerland, the Germans pushed rapidly through Belgium into France, outflanking French forces. On June 10 Mussolini, who had kept Italy neutral but now feared that the war might be over before he could act, declared war. French premier Paul Reynaud turned over the government to 84-year-old Marshal Henri Pétain (1856–1951), the hero of Verdun. Determined to salvage what he could, Petain sued for terms. The armistice, signed on June 22, 1940, granted the Germans occupation of more than three-quarters of France, leaving the southern portion of the country to Petain, who established a puppet regime in the city of Vichy. A small resistance group led by General Charles de Gaulle (1890–1970) escaped to London and formed the Free French organization. In less than two months, France, the mainstay of democracy in continental Europe, had fallen.

Allied Resistance and Axis Setbacks

With France defeated, Hitler was certain that Britain would finally seek an accommodation. To hasten this, he unleashed his air force against Britain in July to wreck civilian morale by terror bombing. Churchill, Britain's new

leader, was a veteran of its imperialist wars, having been First Lord of the Admiralty during World War I, and a stirring orator. A convinced anticommunist, he had once expressed admiration for Mussolini but since 1936 had strongly opposed appeasement. Now he personified the British will to resist. Outnumbered by more than two to one, the Royal Air Force (RAF) fought in the skies over London and other cities, inflicting unexpected casualties

**Prime Minister Churchill inspects the damage
from a German air raid. [Brown Brothers]**

on the German *Luftwaffe*. In London, St. Paul's Cathedral remained almost alone in the midst of devastated streets as a symbol of survival, while Churchill rallied the nation in eloquent speeches. Unable to launch an amphibious invasion against a superior navy and facing mounting air losses, Hitler broke off what came to be called the Battle of Britain.

Stymied in Britain, the Axis turned to eastern Europe and North Africa. The Italians assaulted the British stronghold in Egypt in September and were repulsed into Libya, but Hitler salvaged the operation and pushed to within 100 miles of the Suez Canal. The pattern was repeated in October, when Mussolini invaded Greece. Valiant Greek resistance, British aid, and poor Italian equipment required Hitler to intervene again. Together with Hungarian and Bulgarian troops, the Germans overran Yugoslavia and defeated Greece.

As early as July 1940, Hitler ordered preparations for an invasion of Russia. Despite the Nazi-Soviet Pact, Hitler remained obsessed by the desire to destroy Bolshevism and to gain control of the grain-rich fields of the Ukraine. Once Russia was defeated, he believed, Britain would be forced to capitulate. The Russian invasion began on July 22, 1941. "Operation Barbarossa" moved the mightiest army in history—some 175 German divisions—against a vast, unfortified front. The Germans took the Soviets by surprise and, shattering their weak defenses, killed or captured 2 million soldiers in the first months of the campaign. By late October, Russia appeared about to collapse. But instead of allowing his generals to make a concentrated push against Moscow, Hitler insisted on dispersing his forces along the front. An early winter brought the German offensive to a halt, just as it had Napoleon's Grand Army in 1812. When Stalin's troops counterattacked, first

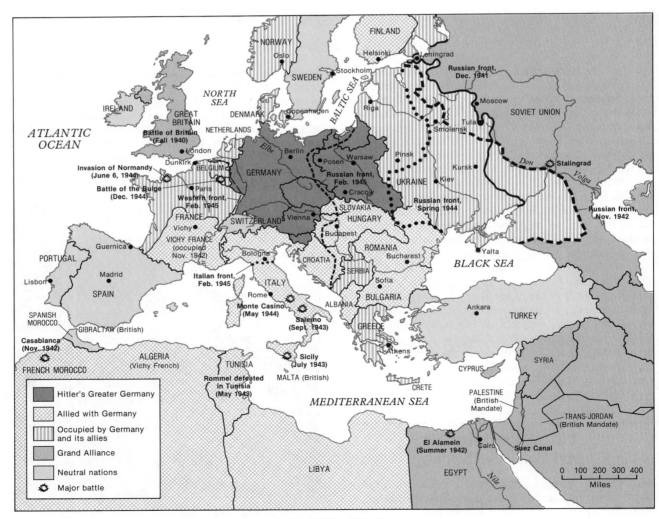

37.2 World War II in Europe

in November and again in December, the Nazi war machine suffered its first setbacks. With Britain holding out in the west and Russia having survived in the east, Hitler now faced the prospect of a two-front war.

The United States and Japan: The Road to Pearl Harbor

Among the great powers of the world, only the United States remained at peace. Disillusionment over the outcome of World War I had nurtured isolationist sentiment among many Americans, and when President Franklin Roosevelt came into office, he moved cautiously to make the nation aware of the precarious state of world affairs. Roosevelt wanted the United States to exert its influence against fascist and Japanese expansionism. But as the threat of war mounted, isolationists in Congress passed neutrality laws that prohibited the export of arms. Nevertheless, the Japanese drive into northern China in the summer of 1937 moved the American government into an openly anti-Japanese position. That October, Roosevelt, in a public statement known as the Quarantine Speech, declared that war was a contagion that had to be contained.

The outbreak of war in Europe found the American public sympathetic to Britain and France but unwilling to become directly involved. Roosevelt, determined to supply France and Britain with weapons, secured a revision of the neutrality laws that enabled the Allies to buy arms on a cash-and-carry basis. As the Nazis stormed across western Europe, he obtained a $1 billion defense appropriation. Public opinion began to rally behind the president during the Battle of Britain, and in September 1940 Congress implemented the first peacetime draft in American history. Two months later, as British resources neared exhaustion, Roosevelt devised the lend-lease program, which extended unlimited goods, instead of credit, to Britain. In the wake of the Nazi invasion of Russia, munitions were also sent to the Soviet Union under the same plan. America had become, in Roosevelt's words, "the arsenal of democracy."

In August, Roosevelt and Churchill met on a cruiser off the Newfoundland coast to sign a statement of principles tantamount to war aims. This Atlantic Charter not only called for national self-determination, disarmament, and "freedom from fear and want" but also looked forward to "the final destruction of the Nazi tyranny" and unconditional German surrender.

Asian events finally brought America into the war. United States policy toward Japan had already hardened over China. Now, with the Western powers fighting in Europe, Japanese expansionists saw their opportunity. In September 1940 Japan signed a defensive Tripartite Pact with Germany and Italy, extending the Axis alliance to Asia. America responded by banning the sale of essential raw materials, including iron, steel, and aviation fuel, to Japan. Negotiations initiated with the United States in the spring of 1941 by Prince Konoye, the Japanese premier, resulted in deadlock. Hitler's invasion of Russia freed Japan to move without fear of Soviet interference, and in July it occupied Indochina. Roosevelt immediately froze Japanese assets and joined with Britain in imposing economic sanctions. The failure of negotiations, together with the stiff American response to Japan's conquest of Indochina, played into the hands of the extremists in Tokyo. In October, General Tojo Hideki (1885–1948), a militarist, became premier. On the morning of December 7— without a declaration of war and while Japanese envoys were meeting with American officials in Washington—two waves of Japanese planes attacked the United States naval base at Pearl Harbor, striking a devastating blow at American power in the Pacific. The next day the United States declared war on the Axis.

The War in China

The Second World War was far more a global conflict than the first, and the major theater outside Europe was Asia. More territory and people in Asia were involved in the fighting than in any other part of the world. Asia experienced the first and so far the only use of nuclear weapons, by the Americans against the Japanese, and China suffered the greatest number of war casualties of any nation.

For China the war had actually begun in 1931 with the Japanese invasion of Manchuria and escalated to an all-out battle for survival when the Japanese attacked Peking and Shanghai in 1937 and fought their way to the Kuomintang capital of Nanking. Japanese troops, with the full knowledge of their commanders, went on an orgy of killing when Nanking fell, vowing to punish the Chinese for holding up the imperial army by their resistance in Shanghai and on the route to Nanking. Chiang Kai-shek had committed most of his best soldiers and modern weapons to slowing the Japanese drive for Nanking, but it was innocent civilians—probably as many as 300,000 dead—who suffered in the so-called Rape of Nanking once the Japanese entered the city. Survivors described horrifying sights of raped women impaled on stakes and children sliced in two.

Chiang's government and the remnants of his army retreated westward to Chungking (Chongqing). The Kuomintang war effort was largely spent, its best troops and equipment gone. New conscription drives in the western provinces brought the army to some 5 million men, but they were poorly clothed and fed, often virtually starved, and tyrannized by their officers; they had few or no weapons and very poor morale. The Japanese invasion was stalled by the mountains of western China, by overextended supply lines, and by the effective guerrilla resistance of the Communists in the north, who pinned down 1 million enemy troops but were never themselves eliminated. Japanese planes bombed the cities left under

Chinese control almost at will after 1937 but had little military effect except to kill many thousands of civilians.

A few small battles took place, largely ineffective retreating actions by demoralized and poorly led Chinese forces easily brushed aside by Japanese columns probing westward. Near the Burma border in the far southwest, periodic artillery duels across the gorge of the Salween River broke out, but no real battles. In the north a different kind of war hurt the Japanese far more. Chinese Communist guerrillas controlled most of the countryside at night, especially west of the coastal plain, bombing bridges, roads, and railways and ambushing Japanese patrols but avoiding pitched battles, given the vast Japanese superiority in equipment. They confined the invaders to the cities and towns, and as the war progressed, they won control of much of the rural north while they too depended on mountains and distance to limit enemy occupation to urban areas in the east. When Japan surrendered in August 1945, its armies still held most of the eastern half of China, from which the Chinese never had the strength to drive them.

But although there were only skirmishes rather than major battles after 1937, more than 20 million Chinese died at Japanese hands from 1937 to 1945, most of them civilians. The occupying army was at least as ruthless as the Nazis in Europe, exterminating whole villages as part of a policy of terror and slaughtering noncombatants indiscrim-

inately. Their officially sanctioned slogan was "Kill all, burn all, loot all!" In the occupied territories the Japanese forced Chinese to bow or even kneel to their officers and beat or shot them if they were not sufficiently deferential. The record of the Japanese was equally bad elsewhere in Asia, but in China they began much earlier and made no real effort to win local support. Like Nazi terror, Japanese brutality stemmed also from a conviction of their own cultural and even racial superiority and from their contempt for those they conquered. It was a grim period in the history of East Asia. At the end of the war, the Kuomintang had been fatally weakened, and the Communists had grown from a tiny and hunted band to a major military presence in the north. Their effectiveness against the Japanese had won them a broad base of popular support even among many in the Kuomintang-controlled areas, and by mid-1945 they were the real government of much of the north.

❀ CHUNGKING: BELEAGUERED WARTIME CAPITAL

Just before the fall of Hankow (one of the three cities now part of Wuhan) on the central Yangtze in October 1938, China's capital moved farther upriver to Chungking, where

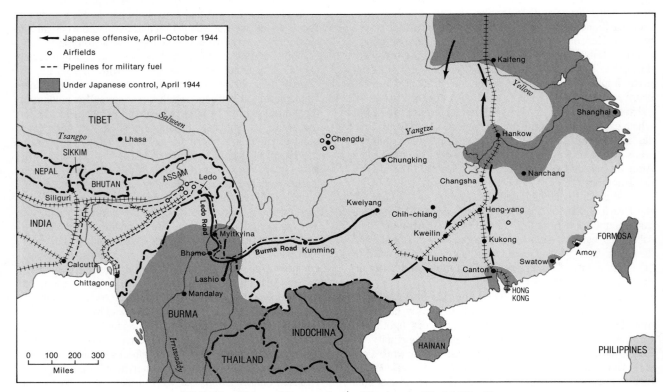

37.3 The China–Burma–India Theater in World War II

it remained for the rest of the war. Chungking sprawled over steep hills at the junction of the Chialing (Jialing) River and the Yangtze near the center of the generally hilly Red Basin of Szechuan (Sichuan), which was in turn surrounded on all sides by mountains. The steep and narrow gorges of the Yangtze about halfway between Hankow and Chungking along the provincial border were easily blocked by a boom. These natural defenses kept Chungking secure from the Japanese army, but it had few defenses against air attack, and Japanese bombing caused great destruction and loss of life. By 1941, before Pearl Harbor, an unofficial American group, the Flying Tigers, paid by the Chinese but with their own fighter planes, had greatly reduced the bombing raids. Chinese morale was high for the first two or three Chungking years, and the wartime capital was a symbol of patriotic resistance. Whole arsenals and factories had been disassembled and carried on the backs of workers to Chungking and elsewhere in Szechuan to escape the Japanese; university faculties and students made the same journey, carrying what they could of their libraries and laboratories. America's entry into the war against Japan in late 1941 gave morale another boost.

But disillusionment spread as the Kuomintang army largely sat the war out while the increasingly corrupt government of Chiang Kai-shek and his cronies stockpiled arms for use against the Communists. Chungking was also notorious for its gray, cloudy weather, its drizzle, its suffocatingly hot summers and cold, damp winters, and its painful overcrowding. More than a million people from all parts of China, including officials and army personnel, were added to the originally smaller population, with too few additions to housing, water supply, and other basics. Fires set by Japanese bombs often burned out of control, and air raid shelters were grossly inadequate. Chungking's main link with the outside world was the extension of the Burma Road through mountainous southwest China and, after the Japanese took Burma, the American airlift from India over the "hump" of the Himalayas. The main airport was a sandbank in the Yangtze hemmed in by steep hills on both sides, flooded every spring and summer by rising river levels, and obscured most of the time by heavy low clouds. The summer airport was on the edge of a cliff above the river, which was equally dangerous. There were no railways anywhere in Szechuan. People understandably felt isolated. Prices for everything skyrocketed through a combination of wartime shortages, government ineptitude, and a swollen population. The Szechuanese blamed it on "downriver people," who in turn were contemptuous of "ignorant provincials."

Tight "thought control" and the secret police suppressed all free political expression, and people with "dangerous thoughts" or caught with "improper" books in their dwellings were jailed or executed. Those with money and connections lived luxuriously in guarded villas with American-made limousines, but most people in Chungking lived in poverty, mud, and squalor. By 1940 inflation began to rise at about 10 percent per month, accelerating wildly after 1943. Currency might lose half or more of its value between morning and afternoon. The government printed more notes of larger denominations, while its finance minister, H. H. Kung, brother-in-law of Chiang Kai-shek, obtained gold from the United States for his own accounts in overseas banks, as did other Kuomintang officials. Salaries and wages fell hopelessly behind inflation, and malnutrition, tuberculosis, and other diseases of poverty were widespread. Furniture, clothing, books, and heirlooms were sold in a vain attempt to stay afloat. Nearly all officials succumbed to bribery and other forms of corruption, whatever their original principles, if only to save their families. By the end of the war the Chinese were universally demoralized and had lost faith in the Kuomintang. The Chungking years saw the death of Kuomintang hopes to remain the government of a China now sick of its ineffectiveness, corruption, and reaction.

India and Southeast Asia

India was only marginally involved in the war, although 2 million Indian troops fought under British command in several theaters, and India itself became a major military base and supply center for the Allied war effort in Asia. A few Japanese bombs fell on Calcutta but the big invasion push through northwestern Burma was stopped by British and Indian troops at Imphal, just inside the Indian border, in the spring of 1944, followed by the accelerating collapse of the Japanese position in Burma as British and Indian forces advanced. Ceylon (Sri Lanka) served as a major Allied base and became the headquarters of the Allied Southeast Asia Command under Lord Louis Mountbatten (1900–1979), who directed the reconquest of Burma and Malaya.

A frustrated Bengali and Indian nationalist, Subhas Chandra Bose (1897–1945), who had been passed over for leadership in the Congress party, saw his chance for power in alliance with the Japanese. Bose had visited Mussolini and Hitler in Europe. He escaped from British arrest in 1941, made his way to Berlin, and in 1943 went by German submarine around Africa to Singapore, where the Japanese gave him command of 60,000 Indian prisoners of war. He called them the Indian National Army for the "liberation" of their homeland, but they were used as cannon fodder in the advance wave for the bloody and fruitless assault on Imphal. Bose escaped and was later killed in an air crash, but he remained a national hero to some Indians.

Japan and the Pacific Theater

The chief military action in Asia took place in the Pacific. Following the attack on Pearl Harbor, the Japanese conquered Malaya, Burma, Indonesia, and the Philippines in rapid succession. This was assisted by Japanese use of French bases in Indochina, granted by the Vichy government in mid-1940 and vital to the assault on Southeast Asia.

The speed of the Japanese advance paralleled that of the Nazis in Europe. Japanese dive bombers destroyed the major ships of the British Asian fleet off Singapore as they had sunk most of the American fleet at Pearl Harbor. The Americans now lacked the naval capacity to defend or supply the Philippines, where much of their air force had been destroyed on the ground a few hours after the Pearl Harbor raid. The Japanese had developed a light, fast, maneuverable fighter plane, the Zero, which gave them air supremacy. The Dutch East Indies (Indonesia) were weakly defended, and no help was available for the greatly outnumbered Dutch. Thailand remained neutral, but at the price of granting Japanese use of bases there. By early 1942 Japan had occupied all the smaller islands in the western Pacific and installed garrisons even in the western Aleutians off Alaska.

Japan's thrust southward had long been planned as part of the "Greater East Asia Co-prosperity Sphere." Japan claimed that it would liberate Asia from Western colonialism, but the real aim was to combine its technological, industrial, and organizational skills with the manpower and resources of the rest of East Asia, thereby creating a single economic unit dominated by Tokyo. Poor in natural resources, especially oil, Japan sought access to the oil, rubber, tin, and rice of Southeast Asia and the iron ore and coal of the Philippines and China. But Japan ignored the rising force of nationalism, first in China and then in its Southeast Asian conquests. Almost from the beginning, Japanese racist arrogance and brutality made a mockery of "co-prosperity" and earned the Japanese bitter hatred everywhere. Western prisoners, including the defeated American forces in the Philippines, were treated with special cruelty. Japan was now master of Asia, and its warrior tradition had only contempt for soldiers who surrendered even when their position was hopeless.

The Price of Victory

The brutality of Japanese rule in Asia occurred on a massive scale, but it lacked the carefully organized, systematic scope of Nazi atrocities in Europe. As the year 1942 opened, Hitler controlled, directly or indirectly, a huge empire that stretched from the English Channel to the gates of Moscow and from Norway to North Africa. His goal, after victory, was to create out of this area a "New Order" with Germany as its center and around which Europe and the world would revolve. Hitler never developed detailed plans for his empire. Yet the war provided ample evidence of what the New Order would have entailed.

Descent into the Abyss: The Holocaust

Hitler's plans derived from his notions of race, which he believed held the key to world history. Nazi racial ideologues divided Europe's population into three broad categories: the master "Aryan" race of German-speaking or related peoples, below which stood the Latins, and at the bottom the Slavs, Jews, and gypsies. Hitler dealt with the conquered territories according to this scale of values. The inferior populations of the eastern regions would provide Germany with *Lebensraum* ("living space") and a huge supply of cheap or slave labor. Immediately after the conquest of Poland, pockets of German colonists were established there, while more than 1 million Poles were brought to Germany as forced workers. Later even greater numbers of Russian prisoners suffered the same fate.

Nazi policy in eastern Europe was a vital part of Hitler's geopolitical scheme, but the Jews were at the core of his obsession about race. He spoke repeatedly of making Germany *Judenrein*, or free of Jews, and in *Mein Kampf* he described how the Nazi state would breed a population of Aryans free of the sick, the weak, and, most important, the Jewish "contagion." As early as 1919, Hitler had written that "the final objective" of anti-Semitism must "unswervingly be the removal of the Jews altogether."[2]

After the seizure of power, Nazi policies had forced the vast majority of German Jews to emigrate, so that by 1939 few were left in the Reich. Once the war began, large-scale emigration became impossible, and Nazi officials evolved barbaric plans to deal with the millions of Jews in the conquered territories of Poland and eastern Europe. They first schemed to concentrate Europe's Jews in "reservations" in the Lublin district of Poland or on the island of Madagascar. As plans for the invasion of Russia progressed, the removal policy gave way to the Final Solution—the extermination of European Jewry.

Hitler gave SS leader Himmler orders for the Final Solution in the spring or early summer of 1941. As the German army pushed eastward, special SS units—*Einsatzgruppen* ("special-duty groups") commanded by police chief Reinhard Heydrich—herded Jews into ditches behind the front lines and shot them. Mobile gassing vans were also used. By fall the extermination process had been organized on a massive scale as Jews and other victims were transported by rail from all over the Continent to death camps in Poland.

The SS murdered millions in extermination camps such as Auschwitz, Treblinka, and Bergen-Belsen, where tens of thousands of men, women, and children were gassed to death each day. A precedent for the killing had been set earlier by the gassing of 70,000 mentally ill Germans. The bodies of the victims were stripped of clothing, hair, and gold teeth. Corpses were either processed for soap and fertilizer or burnt. Outside the camps, in Poland and

A group of Polish Jews are marched to the death camps flanked by German Gestapo agents. [UPI/Bettmann Newsphotos]

Russia, SS squads continued to slaughter many thousands more, shooting and burying their victims in mass graves.

The Nazis murdered a startling range of victims in their effort to purge Europe of "undesirable" elements, including gypsies, the infirm and mentally ill, Jehovah's Witnesses, and some 60,000 known German homosexuals. But their primary focus remained the Jews. Some estimates suggest that more than 6 million Jews perished in the Holocaust, more than three-fourths of Europe's Jewish population. Beyond the statistical enormity of the Holocaust lies the memory of the planned elimination of entire categories of human beings by a modern, technologically advanced society. Modern history has known no more heinous example of human barbarism.

🌸
ISABELLA KATZ
AND THE HOLOCAUST:
A LIVING TESTIMONY

No statistics can adequately render the enormity of the Holocaust, and its human meaning can perhaps only be understood through the experience of a single human being who was cast into the nightmare of the Final Solution. Isabella Katz was the eldest of six children—Isabella, brother Philip, and sisters Rachel, Chicha, Cipi, and baby Potyo—from a family of Hungarian Jews. She lived in the ghetto of Kisvarda, a provincial town of 20,000 people, where hers was a typical Jewish family of the region—middle-class, attached to Orthodox traditions, and imbued with a love of learning.

In 1938 and 1939 Hitler pressured Hungary's regent, Miklós Horthy, into adopting anti-Jewish laws. By 1941

Hungary had become a German ally, and deportations and massacres were added to the restrictions. Isabella's father left for the United States, where he hoped to obtain entry papers for his family, but after Pearl Harbor, Hungary was at war with America and the family was trapped. In the spring of 1944, when Hitler occupied Hungary, the horror of the Final Solution struck Isabella. On March 19 Adolf Eichmann, as SS officer in charge of deportation, ordered the roundup of Jews in Hungary, who numbered some 650,000. On May 28, Isabella's nineteenth birthday, the Jews in Kisvarda were told to prepare for transportation to Auschwitz on the following morning. Isabella recalled:

> And now an SS man is here, spick-and-span, with a dog, a silver pistol, and a whip. And he is all of sixteen years old. On his list appears the name of every Jew in the ghetto. . . . "Teresa Katz," he calls—my mother. She steps forward. . . . Now the SS man moves toward my mother. He raises his whip and, for no apparent reason at all, lashes out at her.

En route to Auschwitz, crammed into hot, airless boxcars, Isabella's mother told her children to "stay alive":

> Out there, when it's all over, a world's waiting for you to give it all I gave you. Despite what you see here . . . believe me, there is humanity out there, there is dignity. . . . And when this is all over, you must add to it, because sometimes it is a little short, a little skimpy.

Isabella and her family were among more than 437,000 Jews sent to Auschwitz from Hungary.

When they arrived at Auschwitz, the SS and camp guards divided the prisoners into groups, often separating family members. Amid the screams and confusion, Isabella remembered:

We had just spotted the back of my mother's head when Mengele, the notorious Dr. Josef Mengele, points to my sister and me and says, "Die Zwei" [those two]. This trim, very good-looking German, with a flick of his thumb and a whistle, is selecting who is to live and who is to die.

Isabella's mother and her baby sister perished within a few days.

The day we arrived in Auschwitz, there were so many people to be burned that the four crematoriums couldn't handle the task. So the Germans built big open fires to throw the children in. Alive? I do not know. I saw the flames. I heard the shrieks.

Isabella was to endure the hell of Auschwitz for nine months.

The inmates were stripped, the hair on their heads and bodies was shaved, and they were herded into crude, overcrowded barracks. As if starvation, forced labor, and disease were not enough, they were subjected to unspeakable torture, humiliation, and terror, a mass of living skeletons for whom the difference between life and death could be measured only in an occasional flicker of spirit that determined to resist against impossible odds. Isabella put it this way:

Have you ever weighed 120 pounds and gone down to 40? Something like that—not quite alive, yet not quite dead. Can anyone, can even I, picture it? . . . Our eyes sank deeper. Our skin rotted. Our bones screamed out of our bodies. Indeed, there was barely a body to house the mind, yet the mind was still working, sending out the messages "Live! Live!"

In November, just as Isabella and her family were lined up outside a crematorium, they were suddenly moved to Birnbäumel, in eastern Germany—the Russians were getting nearer and the Nazis were closing down their death camps and moving the human evidence of their barbarism out of reach of the enemy. In January, as the Russians and the frigid weather closed in, the prisoners were forced to march through the snows deeper into Germany, heading toward the camp at Bergen-Belsen. Those who could not endure the trial fell by the side, shot or frozen to death. On January 23, while stumbling through a blizzard with the sound of Russian guns in the distance, Isabella, Rachel, and Chicha made a successful dash from the death march and hid in an abandoned house. Two days later Russian soldiers found them. Philip had been sent to a labor camp, and Cipi made it to Bergen-Belsen, where she died.

Isabella later married and had two children of her own, making a new life in America. Yet the images of the Holocaust remain forever in her memory. "Now I am older," she says, "and I don't remember all the pain. . . . That is not happiness, only relief, and relief is blessed. . . . And children someday will plant flowers in Auschwitz, where

the sun couldn't crack through the smoke of burning flesh."[3]

The Grand Alliance: Victory in Europe

By 1942 the Grand Alliance of Russia, Britain, and the United States had been formed against Hitler's New Order. From the first the Allies were plagued by mutual distrust: Churchill feared Soviet territorial designs in Europe and what he believed was America's ignorance of European affairs; Roosevelt suspected Churchill's imperialist ambitions in the Mediterranean and Stalin's political motives; and Stalin suspected both Western statesmen, who hated communism, of wanting to deny the Soviet Union the fruits of victory. Nevertheless, they agreed to make military objectives—defeating first Germany and Italy, then Japan—their immediate goal, postponing political issues until the war was won. In January 1942 the three powers joined with 23 other nations in a United Nations declaration that reaffirmed these goals as well as the principles of the Atlantic Charter.

The tide of battle began to turn in favor of the Allies in 1942. In May and June, American forces stopped the Japanese advance in the Pacific in crucial battles in the Coral Sea and at Midway Island. In November the United States and Britain launched Operation Torch, the invasion of North Africa.

Under the pressure of the gigantic battles that were consuming Russian manpower on the eastern front, Stalin had repeatedly insisted on the opening of a major second front in the west. No nation sustained a greater burden of physical destruction and death than the Soviet Union, which lost some 20 million men, and no nation contributed more to the defeat of Germany. Since the winter of 1941 the German armies had continued to batter the Russians along an 1,800-mile front, but in August 1942 the German war machine was flung at the southern zone in a protracted battle for Stalingrad. The situation appeared hopeless when the Germans stormed the city in September. But Stalin's armies, circling around from the south and north, caught Hitler's forces in a gigantic pincer movement. Although winter fast approached, Hitler refused to withdraw his soldiers. On February 2, 1943, the last of the 500,000-man Sixth German Army surrendered. That July, German and Russian forces fought bitterly along the Kursk salient, southwest of Moscow, in the biggest tank battle of the war. A clear victory for the Russians, the engagement cost another half million German casualties and spelled ultimate defeat for Hitler.

Churchill and Roosevelt had met in January 1943 in Casablanca, where they made plans for opening the second front. To forestall the Soviets in central Europe, they chose Italy as the target, and in July, Allied troops landed in Sicily from their base in North Africa. The Sicilian in-

The female labor force in the United States more than doubled during World War II. Here women riveters work on an airplane. [UPI/Bettmann Newsphotos]

vasion precipitated a coup d'état against Mussolini by dissident Fascists and involved King Victor Emmanuel III and Marshal Pietro Badoglio. The king arrested Mussolini and appointed Badoglio prime minister, but Hitler quickly moved German troops into northern Italy and rescued the Duce. By early September, when the Italians signed an armistice and joined the Allies as a cobelligerent against Germany, the Allies had crossed to the mainland. In the north Mussolini established a puppet regime, the Italian Social Republic, under German auspices. Thereafter, for 18 months Italy became the scene of bitter fighting, not only between Allies and the Axis but also between Fascist loyalists and a massive partisan resistance movement.

In October, Allied foreign ministers meeting in Moscow reiterated their demand for unconditional surrender. They also agreed to the joint occupation of Germany, the purge of Nazism, and the creation of a United Nations organization. A month later Churchill and Roosevelt met with Stalin in Teheran for their first face-to-face conference. The talks focused on plans for the final attack against Hitler's "Fortress Europe." The three agreed to an invasion of western Europe in the spring of 1944.

Operation Overlord began on June 6, 1944—"D day." Under the supreme command of General Dwight D. Ei-

senhower (1890–1969), the Allies carried out the greatest amphibious landing in history on the coast of Normandy. More than 2 million men and millions of tons of equipment poured into northwestern France over the next few months. By the end of August, Allied armies had driven the *Wehrmacht* to the frontiers of Germany, but the drive stalled. In a desperate effort to stave off defeat, Hitler launched a counteroffensive in December, driving deep into the Allied sector in Belgium and Luxembourg, but the bloody Battle of the Bulge proved to be Germany's last major effort. From the east, Soviet armies poured into Germany in January, coming within 100 miles of Berlin, while British and American troops pushed toward Germany from the west, crossing the Rhine in March.

While the Allies were closing the ring around Germany, Churchill, Roosevelt, and Stalin met in February 1945 at Yalta, on the Black Sea. The Yalta conference revealed the growing tensions that would divide the Allies after the war. Roosevelt, eager to secure Soviet entry into the war against Japan, conceded some of Stalin's demands regarding the future governments of Europe. Soviet armies were already in Poland, Germany, eastern Europe, and the Balkans. Churchill, who had made a secret arrangement with Stalin regarding Soviet and British influence in the Balkans, joined Roosevelt in agreeing to a larger Russian role in eastern Asia and the transfer of Poland's eastern territory to Russia while compensating the Poles with German land. In return, Stalin promised to permit democratic elements in the postwar governments of Poland, Yugoslavia, and eastern Europe.

Three days after American and Russian soldiers met on the Elbe River on April 25, Mussolini was executed by Italian partisans. On April 30 Hitler committed suicide in a secret bunker beneath the ruined streets of Berlin. Ger-

man representatives signed the surrender in Eisenhower's headquarters on May 7, 1945.

The Atomic Bomb and the Defeat of Japan

With the European conflict at an end, American strategists turned their attention to the Pacific theater, where Japanese defeat was imminent. The naval battle of Midway in

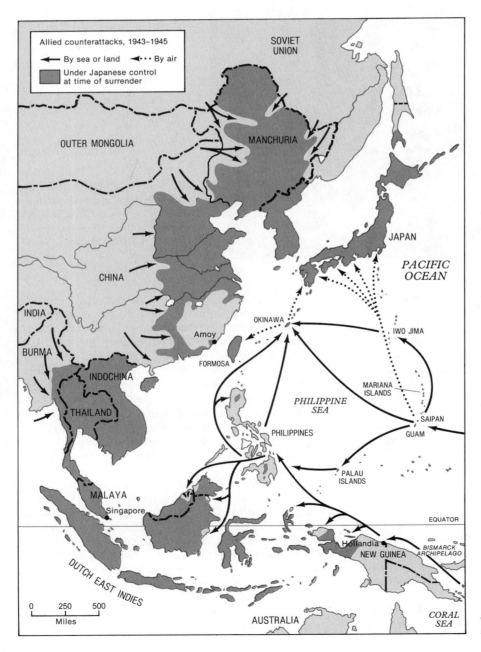

37.4 World War II in Eastern Asia

June 1942 had been won mainly by American aircraft carriers, which had been on patrol when Pearl Harbor was bombed, and by use of British-developed radar. A long island-hopping campaign began in which American and Australian troops retook the fiercely defended islands of the western Pacific one by one. Bloody battles in the jungles of New Guinea, the Solomon Islands, and the Bismarck Archipelago were followed by a slow northward advance, with hand-to-hand fighting and heavy losses on both sides. The Allies captured Saipan, within bombing range of Japan's big cities, in June 1944, and in October the Japanese suffered a major defeat in the Philippine Sea. By early 1945 the Philippines themselves were retaken, and in June the Allies seized Okinawa, part of Japan's home territory. Fanatical Japanese defenders often fought to the last soldier. Japanese pilots began to make suicidal *kamikaze* ("divine wind") attacks in planes loaded with bombs that purposely crashed into enemy ships. American losses, though serious, were soon replaced. Japan's fleet was by now almost entirely sunk, and American submarines had destroyed the majority of its supply and merchant ships. Meanwhile, American and Chinese forces had joined British and Indian troops in the liberation of Burma, while Allied naval dominance had cut the Dutch East Indies off from Japanese supply lines.

Japan was ready to surrender by the spring of 1945 and had begun peace feelers through the still neutral Russians. American bombers had destroyed nearly all of Japan's cities, using incendiary bombs to start giant firestorms. In one horrible night in Tokyo, fire bombing killed an estimated 100,000 people, the same number slain throughout the war in air raids over Britain. Many of the survivors in the gutted cities starved.

Events in the United States cut short plans for the final assault against the Japanese mainland. Working in secret laboratories on the so-called Manhattan Project, American, British, and European refugee scientists developed a primitive atomic bomb. The weapon was successfully tested on July 16 at Alamogordo in the isolated desert of New Mexico. Harry S Truman (1884–1972), who became president in April on Roosevelt's death, decided to use the awesome new weapon against Japan, a decision that subsequently aroused great controversy. On the one hand, some strategists argued that an invasion of Japan would cost heavy American casualties, although Eisenhower did not believe that the atomic bomb was needed to force Japan's surrender. On the other hand, at Yalta, Stalin had agreed to attack Japan within three months after the defeat of Germany, and Truman, with a decisive weapon at hand, may have been anxious to forestall the Russians. On August 6 an American plane dropped an atomic bomb on the medium-sized town and army base of Hiroshima, obliterating the city and killing over 78,000 civilians. Radiation fallout and other injuries eventually claimed thousands of additional victims. Truman called it "the greatest thing in history." Russia declared war on August 8 and swept into Japanese-occupied Manchuria. The next day the Americans leveled the city of Nagasaki with a second atomic device, with another large loss of life. On August 15 Emperor Hirohito announced the Japanese surrender.

The war had cost the lives of 2.5 million Japanese soldiers and sailors, and an additional million civilians had died in air raids. The country was in ruins. But the Japanese defeat of colonial regimes in the early years of the war had destroyed the myth of Western invincibility, and Japanese brutality had further stimulated Asian nationalism. Despite

◉ The End of Emperor Worship ◉

On August 15, 1945, after the atomic bombing of Japan by American planes, Emperor Hirohito spoke to his people for the first time over the radio and declared the war lost. Here is how one listener, 10 years old at the time, recalled the impact of the news.

The adults sat around their radios and cried. The children gathered outside in the dusty road and whispered their bewilderment. We were most confused and disappointed by the fact that the Emperor had spoken in a *human* voice, no different from any adult's. None of us understood what he was saying, but we had all heard his voice. One of my friends could even imitate it cleverly. Laughing, we surrounded him—a twelve year old in grimy shorts who spoke with the Emperor's voice. A minute later we felt afraid. We looked at one another; no one spoke. How could we believe that an august presence of such awful power had become an ordinary human voice on a designated summer day?

Source: O. Kenzaburo, *A Personal Matter*, trans. J. Nathan (New York: Grove Press, 1968), pp. vii–viii.

the Western victory in Asia, the old Western empires were irretrievably gone.

The United Nations

Allied plans for establishing a secure peace were based on the conviction that the fascist regimes had been responsible for the war and should be destroyed. The Allies imposed democratic and educational reforms on Germany, Italy, and Japan and removed compromised officials from positions of influence. They also supervised the drafting of new constitutions establishing parliamentary governments and civil liberties. Furthermore, the discovery of the Nazi death camps led to the establishment of the Nuremberg military tribunal to punish prominent Nazis for "crimes against humanity." Similar trials, on different grounds and sometimes under local jurisdiction, were held in Japan and Italy.

As in 1919, the victors in World War II placed great significance on the creation of an international organization to maintain the peace. Roosevelt, a Wilsonian idealist, was an ardent advocate of a new world body empowered to prevent aggression. The Allies dissolved the League of Nations and in its place created the United Nations, with headquarters in New York City. The formal charter, drafted at a meeting in San Francisco in April, was signed by 50 nations in June 1945.

The UN charter gave one vote to each member state in a General Assembly, which has since grown to more than triple its original size. But real power lay in the Security Council, whose permanent members were the United States, the Soviet Union, Britain, France, and China. Because each could veto Council decisions, the organization was mired in controversy from the start. Subsidiary agencies, such as the World Health Organization and the Food and Agricultural Organization, have, however, made important contributions in noncontroversial areas such as combating disease and starvation.

As the world began to recover from the ashes of destroyed cities and the loss of some 50 million lives, it could look back on a generation of economic depression, brutal dictatorship, ideological strife, and the bloodiest war in history. But even as the postwar recovery got under way, signs of further strife appeared. The peace settlements and the structure of the United Nations reflected the growing tensions that had already begun to divide the former Allies. Nations such as Britain, France, and Germany would never return to the positions of power they once commanded. Instead, two superpowers—the United States and the Soviet Union— would predominate in the postwar world. Moreover, the birth

of the atomic age, mirrored in the ruins of Hiroshima and Nagasaki, suggested the possibility that humans could one day destroy civilization.

Yet people everywhere could celebrate the triumph over European fascism and Japanese militarism. At the time, opportunity for rebuilding presented the world with a more immediate challenge. Moreover, out of the tragic and sobering legacy of the war, only the prospect of an end to the vast colonial empires that had once held in their grip the peoples of Asia, Africa, and Latin America, augured well for the future.

Notes

1. A. Hitler, *Mein Kampf*, trans. R. Manheim (Boston: Houghton Mifflin, 1962), p. 414.
2. L. S. Dawidowicz, *The War Against the Jews, 1933–1945* (New York: Holt, Rinehart and Winston, 1975), p. 153.
3. I. K. Leitner and I. A. Leitner, *Fragments of Isabella* (New York: Dell, 1988), pp. 18–19, 28, 31–32, 46–47, 102–103.

Suggestions for Further Reading

Boyle, J. H. *China and Japan at War, 1937–1945*. Stanford, Calif.: Stanford University Press, 1972.

Bracher, K. D. *The German Dictatorship*. New York: Praeger, 1970.

Butow, R. *Japan's Decision to Surrender*. Stanford, Calif.: Stanford University Press, 1954.

Calvocoressi, P., and Wint, G. *Total War*. London: Penguin Books, 1972.

Campbell-Johnson, A. *Mission with Mountbatten*. New York: Dutton, 1953.

Deutscher, I. *Stalin: A Political Biography*, 2d ed. New York: Oxford University Press, 1967.

Divine, R. A. *The Reluctant Belligerent: American Entry into World War II*. New York: Wiley, 1979.

Eubank, K. *The Origins of World War II*. New York: Crowell, 1969.

Friedrich, C. J., and Brzezinski, Z. *Totalitarian Dictatorship and Autocracy*. New York: Praeger, 1956.

Gilbert, M., and Gott, R. *The Appeasers*. Boston: Houghton Mifflin, 1963.

Havens, T. *The Valley of Darkness*. New York: Norton, 1978.

Hildebrand, K. *The Foreign Policy of the Third Reich*. Berkeley: University of California Press, 1973.

Hinz, B. *Art in the Third Reich*. New York: Pantheon Books, 1979.

Hsi-sheng Chi. *Nationalist China at War*. Ann Arbor: University of Michigan Press, 1982.

Ienaga, S. *The Pacific War*. New York: Pantheon Books, 1978.

Langer, W. L., and Gleason, S. E. *The Undeclared War, 1940–41.* New York: Harper & Row, 1953.

Lebra, J., ed. *Japan's Greater East Asia Co-prosperity Sphere in World War II.* Kuala Lumpur, Malaysia: Oxford University Press, 1975.

Myers, R. H., and Peattie, M. R., eds. *The Japanese Colonial Empire, 1895–1945.* Princeton, N.J.: Princeton University Press, 1984.

Robertson, E. M. *Mussolini as Empire Builder.* London: Macmillan, 1977.

Schoenbaum, D. *Hitler's Social Revolution: Class and Status in Nazi Germany.* New York: Anchor Books, 1967.

Tannenbaum, E. R. *The Fascist Experience: Italian Society and Culture, 1922–1945.* New York: Basic Books, 1972.

Taylor, A. J. P. *The Origins of the Second World War.* New York: Wiley, 1972.

Thomas, H. *The Spanish Civil War*, rev. ed. New York: Harper & Row, 1977.

Ulam, A. *Stalin: The Man and His Era.* New York: Viking, 1973.

White, T., and Jacoby, A. *Thunder Out of China.* New York: William Sloane Associates, 1946.

Wright, G. *The Ordeal of Total War, 1939–1945.* New York: Harper & Row, 1968.

C H A P T E R · 3 8

Revival and Revolution in East Asia

Much of Asia was devastated by World War II, and no part of it was unaffected. There were more war casualties in Asia than in all of the rest of the world. The heavy human and economic losses were, however, accompanied by the end of colonial rule and Western dominance in Asia. The Japanese conquest of Southeast Asia destroyed the image of Western superiority, while the war in Europe weakened both the power and the desire of the European powers to resume their former positions in Asia. The Japanese economy was destroyed by the war, and almost all of its cities were bombed to rubble. Japan lived under American military occupation from 1945 to 1952, but by 1950 the damage to the economy had been largely repaired and rapid new growth that would continue for decades had begun. By 1965 Japan had become the world's third industrial power, after the United States and the Soviet

The Cultural Revolution: Mao Tse-tung at a Peking University rally in 1966 where frenzied students wave their "Little Red Books." [East-foto/Sovfoto]

936

Union, and in the 1970s and 1980s it won a commanding position in world markets for its manufactured exports.

In China long-pent-up pressures for change resulted in civil war, from which the Communists emerged victorious over the Kuomintang (Guomindang) government in 1949. The new revolutionary government quickly repaired war damages, but in 1957 Mao Tse-tung, the Communist leader, launched the Great Leap Forward, a radical economic program that ended by plunging the country into mass starvation. It was followed in 1966 by the Cultural Revolution, a destructive effort to revive flagging revolutionary ardor, which ended only with Mao's death in 1976. China began to reopen its contacts with the West in the 1970s and to rejuvenate its economy. Korea was split by the Cold War into rival states; Vietnam, similarly divided, was unified by a successful war against the United States; and in Southeast Asia a number of new nations emerged, each following a different path.

The Recovery of Japan

Japan had been more completely destroyed by the war than any of the other belligerents. In addition to Hiroshima and Nagasaki, which had been leveled by the first atomic bombs, virtually all of Japan's cities, especially Tokyo and Yokohama, had been flattened and burned by massive conventional and incendiary bombing. A notable exception was Kyoto, the old imperial capital, which had been preserved by the intervention of American art historians. The government and what remained of the army in the home islands were still, however, in good order, and there was a smooth transfer of power to the American military government of occupation under General Douglas MacArthur. Japan had surrendered to the Allied forces, including Britain, China, Australia, Canada, New Zealand, and the Soviet Union, although the Soviets had intervened only in the last week of the war. But MacArthur permitted only token representation from each of the other allies in his SCAP (Supreme Commander Allied Powers) regime of occupation, over which he presided like a virtual emperor.

With very few exceptions, the Japanese people, including officials, officers, and troops as well as other civilians, accepted Emperor Hirohito's pronouncement of surrender and his call to "endure the unendurable." Most felt relief that the disastrous war was over. They soon found that the occupying Americans were not the devils some had feared and vented their bitterness on the now discredited military leaders who had so nearly destroyed the nation they were sworn to serve. In general, the occupation, which lasted from late August 1945 to late April 1952, was a period of peaceful reconstruction, with the Japanese doing most of the work of government under American supervision, except at the highest level.

38.1 *Modern Japan*

The American Occupation

Relief on finding the occupying forces bent on reconstruction rather than revenge was soon joined by gratitude for American aid. Most Japanese had lived at best on an austerity diet during the last years of the war, and many were half starved, living in makeshift shelters in the bombed-out cities. The winter of 1945–1946 would have been far harder if the Americans had not flown in emergency supplies of food and got the main rail lines working again to transport fuel and essential building supplies. Having expected far worse from their new rulers, the Japanese were pleasantly surprised. Many were even enthusiastic about the institutional changes that SCAP began to decree to root out the remnants of militarism and implant American-style democracy.

The big prewar industrial combines were broken up, although they subsequently re-formed. Thousands of political prisoners who had been accused of "dangerous thoughts" and jailed by the military-controlled government

The Japanese emperor Hirohito photographed with General MacArthur at the U.S. Embassy in 1945. [Bettmann Archive]

of the 1930s and 1940s were released. Other Japanese who were identified—sometimes wrongly—as having been too closely associated with Japanese fascism or militant imperialism were removed from their posts, including a number of senior officials. Several hundred Japanese were identified as suspected war criminals, and most were tried by a special tribunal in Tokyo that included Allied representatives. Seven were executed, including the wartime prime minister, Tojo, and 18 others were sentenced to prison terms. Nearly 1,000 minor war criminals in Japan and Southeast Asia, largely military men, were executed for gross cruelty to prisoners or to the inhabitants of conquered countries. This contrasted with the far more lenient treatment and in some cases even protection of all but the most major Nazi leaders by the United States and its allies in Europe.

A victor's justice in the aftermath of a bitter war is easily criticized, especially when racially tinged, but most Japanese accepted the tribunal's verdict as inevitable and perhaps even appropriate punishment. Most blamed their failed leaders rather than their new masters. The flexibility and adaptability of the Japanese in turn impressed the Americans, who had expected a sullen and resentful populace and found instead that they were to a surprising degree both liked and admired. Having fought ruthlessly and with immense dedication, the Japanese proved quite ready to accommodate to a relatively benign new order. Americans were admired because they had won and also because not only their relief and reconstruction program but also their efforts to democratize Japan were generally popular. The Japanese, after all, had suffered terribly under a militaristic police state and were ready to follow new paths. American ways were imitated uncritically by many, but the basic political reforms of the occupation sent down firm roots.

Most of the changes were reaffirmed after the occupation or, perhaps more accurately, were grafted onto earlier Japanese efforts to adopt Western institutions prior to the years of military government (1931–1945). In addition to a revitalization of electoral and party democracy, government was decentralized by giving more power to local organs. Public education, formerly supervised closely by the central government, was also decentralized and freed as much as possible from bureaucratic control. One of the most successful and permanent changes was the program of land reform, which compensated the large owners whose property was expropriated and sold the land to former tenants, thus ending the last surviving traces of the Tokugawa order. Japanese society began to evolve rapidly toward its present social system, in which status results from achievement rather than birth.

The new constitution drafted by SCAP officials retained the emperor as a figurehead but vested all real power in a legislature and prime minister elected by universal suffrage. There was a detailed bill of rights for the protection of individuals against arbitrary state power. Article 9 of the constitution forbade Japan to have any armed forces except for police and denied it the right to go to war. To most Japanese this was not only reasonable but welcome, given the ruin that arms had brought them and the aftermath of atomic warfare, of which they were the living witnesses. Japan, many felt, should set an example of the folly of war for the rest of the world. What disillusioned the Japanese about the occupation was the shift in American policy beginning in 1948 toward rebuilding Japan's military capacity and using it as a base of American strategic operation.

The goal of making Japan a Cold War ally of the United States soon took precedence over reform and reconstruction. The Berlin blockade, the final Communist victory in China in 1949, and the Korean War all further hardened the American line. Although President Harry Truman fired MacArthur in 1951 for his irresponsible management of the Korean War, Cold War considerations continued to dominate American policy. When the occupation ended in 1952, Japan was bound to the United States by a security

◉ MacArthur: An Assessment ◉

*Most observers described General Douglas MacArthur as a vain man,
ever conscious of his public image. Here is a leading Western historian's assessment of MacArthur in his role as the head of SCAP from
1945 to 1951.*

A tendency toward complacent self-dramatization was encouraged by the adulation of a
devoted wartime staff that he took with him to Japan. . . . They took almost ludicrous care
that only the rosiest reports of the occupation should reach the outside world. In their
debased opinion the slightest criticism of S.C.A.P. amounted to something approaching
sacrilege. MacArthur took up residence in the United States Embassy in Tokyo. Each day
at the same hour he was driven to his office in a large building facing the palace moat; at
the same hour each day he was driven home again. . . . He never toured Japan to see
things for himself. . . . The irreverent were heard to say that if a man rose early in the
morning he might catch a glimpse of the Supreme Commander walking on the waters of
the palace moat. There is no doubt that this aloofness impressed Japanese of the conservative type. . . . But it may well be doubted whether this kind of awed respect was
compatible with the healthy growth of democratic sentiment. . . . The Japanese perhaps
learned more about democracy from MacArthur's dismissal than from anything he himself
ever did or said.

Source: R. Storry, *A History of Modern Japan,* rev. ed. (New York: Penguin Books, 1982), pp. 240–241.

treaty that permitted the buildup of a Japanese "self-
defense force," the stationing of American troops, and
American use of several major bases in Japan. U.S. pressures for Japanese rearmament have continued, and the
bases remain, but Article 9 of the constitution still has the
support of most Japanese.

Economic and
Social Development

Whatever the political shifts as the occupation wore on,
economic reconstruction was almost miraculously rapid.
By 1950 the shattered cities, factories, and rail lines had
been largely rebuilt, and by the end of 1951 industrial production was about equal to what it had been in 1931, now
from new and more efficient plants. The Korean War provided an additional economic boost as Japan became the
chief base and supplier for American forces in Korea. By
1953, with reconstruction complete, personal incomes had
recovered to their prewar levels, and Japan was entering
a new period of rapid development. Some credit is due to
American aid in the hard years immediately after the war,
but the "Japanese miracle" was overwhelmingly the result
of the nation's own hard work, organization, and the pursuit of economic success through group effort. The growth

of production and income in Japan from 1950 to 1975 was
faster than has been measured in any country at any time;
in those 25 years, output and incomes roughly tripled. Yet
the Japanese continued to maintain a very high rate of
personal savings.

At the same time, production quality also rose impres-
sively, and in many respects Japanese goods, notably automobiles, cameras, sound reproduction equipment, optics, and many electronic items, became the best in the
world market. This was a tribute to advanced Japanese
technology and design, as well as to the efficiency of an
industrial plant rebuilt with the latest design and equipment. Similar factors were active in the postwar recovery
of Germany, while the victorious Allies, including the
United States, were saddled with their older and less efficient plants. After 1953 Japan dominated world shipbuilding, although it gave ground increasingly to South Korea
in the 1980s. By 1964 Japan had become the world's third
largest producer of steel, and by 1980 it had overtaken
both the USSR and the United States in steel output while
also becoming a major producer and exporter of automo-
tive vehicles. Japan also invaded European and American
markets on a large scale with its "high-tech" and industrial
goods.

Japanese democracy has retained healthy growth, although politics continue to be dominated by a conservative
coalition with no effective rival parties. High school edu-

cation is virtually universal, and literacy among the Japanese is the highest in the world. The press is of high quality and is avidly supported by a public that also buys and reads more books than in any other country. Over half of young Japanese continue with postsecondary education in a great variety of colleges, universities, and other institutions. Overall, the Japanese are now probably the best-educated population in the world.

Education was a major reason for Japan's spectacular economic success. Economic growth largely eliminated the nation's poverty and unemployment. With the postwar disappearance of aristocratic values, Japan became largely a nation of prosperous middle-class people in an orderly society. Despite crowded conditions—population density in its central urban corridor is the highest in the world—there are few slums, little violent crime, and few signs of social malaise. By 1980 Japan achieved the world's highest life expectancy and its lowest murder rate, less than one two-hundredth that of the United States.

Japanese disarmament, a condition at first imposed by the American occupation but now for many an ingrained social value, has also paid handsome dividends. Japan has thus been largely free of the crushing economic burden of maintaining the huge military establishment undertaken by most other large countries in the postwar world. Money was invested instead in economic growth, new technology, full employment, education, and a wide range of social services. Japan is virtually alone in the world in having escaped from most of the cankerous problems that breed in poverty, such as violence, hopelessness, and drugs. The national ethic of work, achievement, and high standards, now in the service of personal and group goals of economic advancement rather than imperial ambition, has produced a new and more constructive society.

Nevertheless, Japanese society has significant problems. The drive for achievement exacts a toll on schoolchildren as well as on adults. Pressures begin for admission to the "right" kindergarten and continue through elementary school, middle (high) school, and college or university. Each stage of schooling is accompanied by fiercely competitive examinations. Childhood, after the age of 5, is a stressful time for most Japanese. Extreme urban crowding and cramped living space add further burdens. Commuting time for people who work in downtown Tokyo *averages* nearly two hours each way and is only slightly less in other big Japanese cities. Parks and recreation facilities are extremely limited. Housing is fearfully expensive, and most urban Japanese, who constitute over 80 percent of the population, live in tiny apartments with minimal amenities. Yet as one of the best-informed and widely traveled people in the world, most Japanese know they are generally very well off despite their cramped quarters.

Notwithstanding the newer values of social equality and status based on achievement, traditional patterns remain,

Tradition meets modernity: woman at a bus stop dressed in the traditional kimono. [Ira Kuschenbaum/Stock, Boston]

especially the subordinate status of women. Deference to superiors or elders, and of all women to men, is still expected by older Japanese. New generations may well reshape their society on somewhat freer lines, but most would agree that it will be a long time before women achieve anything close to equality. In the workplace women are in subordinate or service roles, with very few exceptions. At the same time, women are often the real powers within the family and household. They usually have control of the family finances and have the preponderant role in the upbringing of children; most fathers work long hours, and their long commute usually gets them home only after the children are in bed. Nevertheless, about half of adult Japanese women work outside the house, close to the current American figure, often managing a small family business or neighborhood store. Equality in the professions remains a distant goal.

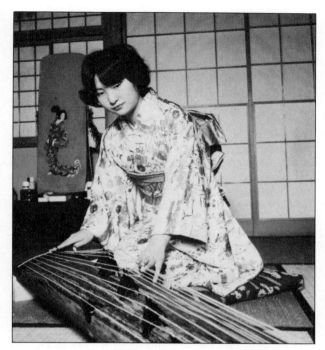

Modern Japanese women still learn traditional arts, and playing the *koto* is one. Koto
players, including learners, must wear the
traditional kimono, and usually practice in a
thoroughly traditional setting such as that
shown here, kneeling on a tatami (grass and
bamboo mat) in a traditional-style room.
[Shashinka Photo, Inc.]

Japan's International Role

Despite their global economic stature, the Japanese have
been reluctant to assume the role of a world power in
political terms, a role that has brought them tragedy in
the past. They have often been uncomfortably aware of
this disparity between their economic power and their
more hesitant political stance abroad. On a number of occasions they have felt their interests ignored in the ma-
neuverings of Cold War diplomacy. As an American client
and a bulwark against neighboring communist states, Japan
was dumbfounded when in 1971 Washington, reversing a
22-year policy, suddenly renewed contact with China without informing Tokyo in advance. The Japanese still refer
to this event as the "Nixon shock," and on many other
occasions as well, U.S. actions have caused the Japanese
to feel slighted or ignored.

It seems likely that in time Japan will come to play an
international diplomatic role more in keeping with its economic power, but most Japanese continue to hope that

this can be done without adding new military power. Some
Japanese have openly favored rearmament to compete in
a world dominated by nations with the greatest military
power, a policy that deeply concerns Japan's neighbors and
former victims of its imperialism. Although the Americans
have pressed for it, a rearmed Japan would no longer be
their client, which is indeed why some Japanese support
rearmament. More positively, by 1988 Japan had become
the world's largest donor nation of foreign aid.

Modern Japan has been a leader in other nonmilitary
directions, notably in the control of industrial pollution.
Japan is small, and most of its population, cities, and industry are crowded into a narrow coastal corridor only
about 400 miles long. Industrial concentration is higher
there than anywhere in the world, and hence Japan was
the first to notice the lethal effects of air and water pollution as one consequence of its postwar industrial growth.
Many deaths and many more health casualties derived
from heavy metal toxins and air pollution, traced to specific
plants and their poisonous discharges into the water or the
atmosphere. Once this became clear and public opinion
had been mobilized, national and municipal governments
quickly passed stringent legislation, beginning in 1969 with
the city of Tokyo, to limit emissions and effluents from
industry and vehicles. As industrial growth continues, concentration and crowding will go on generating the same
problems, and pollution levels are building up again, while
controls have remained incomplete. But Japanese organization, efficiency, and technology have demonstrated that
the problems can be managed, given the willingness to
confront them. The technology needed to control or even
eliminate pollution was developed quickly, and the added
expense was extremely modest, estimated at between 1
and 2 percent of total production costs.

Japan has also led the way in reducing energy use
through more efficient plants and better engine design.
Nearly all Japanese trains are electrified, including the
heavily used high-speed line that connects Tokyo with the
major cities to the south and southwest and Hokkaido to
the north. Trains leave Tokyo every 15 minutes for
Osaka, making the 310-mile trip in three hours, including
stops at Nagoya and Kyoto, running at speeds up to 140
miles per hour.

Urbanization is higher in Japan than anywhere else in
the world, and the coastal area from Tokyo to Osaka and
on to northern Kyushu is rapidly becoming a single vast
urban-industrial zone. Although the rural Japanese landscape, especially the mountains that cover much of the
country, is very beautiful, a good deal of the remaining
countryside is increasingly empty as people have flocked
to the cities in search of wider economic and cultural opportunity. On weekends and holidays urbanites rush to
natural beauty spots, temples or shrines, and resorts,
which are often excessively crowded. Crammed onto
overloaded trains or buses, most passengers must stand

Schoolchildren in front of the Heian Shrine in Kyoto. Japanese students wear uniforms, the boys' dating from Meiji times. [Steve Elmore]

for hours, while many others are locked into gigantic traffic jams on the highways. Much of traditional Japanese culture has been lost or discarded in this avalanche of change. Although many Japanese regret the price they have paid for development, their sense of national identity has remained strong, bound together with many symbolic survivals of traditional culture: customary food and rituals, aesthetic sensitivity, and the commitment to order, self-discipline, and group effort in the pursuit of excellence.

❀ TOKYO AND THE MODERN WORLD

By about 1965 Tokyo had become the world's largest city and a symbol of Japan's new economic leadership. The urban area had grown outward to merge with that of previously separate cities in the same lowland basin, including Kawasaki and Yokohama. By the 1980s this vast, unbroken conglomeration of dense settlement, commerce, industry, and government measured 50 miles across and included over 30 million people linked by the world's largest and most efficient subway system. Almost nothing is left of the Edo described in Chapter 28, most of which had been in any case periodically destroyed by fires. Modern Tokyo was also largely ruined by a catastrophic earthquake in 1923 and then again by American bombs and firestorms in 1944 and 1945.

The only part of the city that has survived all of these cataclysms unscathed is Tokugawa Ieyasu's massive sho-gunal castle, surrounded by its moats and stone walls, originally built in the early seventeenth century and since 1869 used as the imperial palace. In the middle of a huge and strikingly modern city of glass, steel, skyscrapers, and expressways, with traffic flowing around it, the palace still stands as a symbol of Japan's traditional past, both as a Tokugawa monument and as the home of a still enthroned emperor whose lineage goes back to before the dawn of Japanese history. Among Japan's many big cities, Tokyo still plays the role of the brash modernist, the focus of change, the center of everything new; but even in Tokyo the Japanese do not forget their past. The palace, though an anachronism, is nevertheless an appropriate focal point for the capital of Japan. For all its apparent emphasis on the streamlined or frantic present and future, Tokyo is also a city of the Japanese tradition.

That aspect of the city's character becomes clear beyond the immediate downtown and government areas. Except for the industrial clusters around the fringes of each originally separate municipality, Tokyo is primarily a vast collection of neighborhoods. Many are grouped around a surviving or rebuilt temple, shrine, former daimyo estate, or parklike garden. Wandering through the back streets and alleys of these neighborhoods, it is easy to imagine oneself in Tokugawa Edo. Clouds of steam escape from public bathhouses, enveloping the patrons, who include many dressed in traditional kimonos and walking in wooden clogs, especially in the evening after work. Inside countless tiny restaurants and teahouses with their tatami (bamboo mats), low tables, and wall scrolls, little seems to have changed since Ieyasu's time, including much of the food. Many inhabitants of the tiny houses or apartments maintain miniature Japanese-style gardens the size of a small tabletop or lovingly tend potted plants set out by the doorway or on small balconies to catch the sun. Street vendors, singing traditional chants, peddle roasted sweet potatoes, chestnuts, or *yakitori* (Japanese shish kebab).

Crowds of kimono-clad worshipers, or people simply on an outing, throng the courtyards of rebuilt temples and shrines, especially on festival days. Similar crowds fill the narrow streets and patronize street vendors or shops selling traditional as well as modern goods: fans both manual and electric, silks and nylons, horoscope fortunes and stock market guides, tea and beer, lacquer and plastic, scrolls and comic books. Like Japan itself, Tokyo is both very modern and very traditional, very Japanese and very Western.

China in Revolution

The cataclysmic changes that transformed twentieth-century China constitute the largest revolution in human history, measured by the numbers of people involved and the radicalness and speed of the changes. Although the events of 1911 leading to the overthrow of the Manchu dynasty are called a revolution, the pace of change was slow for many years, and the dominant political party, the Kuomintang, became in time largely a supporter of the status quo rather than a force for radical reform. The Chinese Communist party barely survived Kuomintang efforts to eliminate it, but during the anti-Japanese war from 1937 to 1945 it rapidly gained strength and support in the course of its guerrilla resistance to the invaders. The final contest between the two parties ended in Communist victory in 1949, and fundamental revolution began under a radically new set of ideals.

Postwar China and the Communist Triumph

The Japanese invasion and occupation of China from 1931 to 1945 fatally eroded the power and legitimacy of the Kuomintang government of Chiang Kai-shek. Buttressed by massive American military and economic support, it clung to a nominal authority while American representatives under General George C. Marshall tried to arrange a coalition with the Communists. When this effort predictably failed in 1947, China was torn by full-scale civil war. The Communist forces, meanwhile, had perfected a guerrilla strategy in their long struggle against the Japanese and had attracted millions of Chinese by their defense of the nation and their program of peasant-oriented reform.

Their leader, Mao Tse-tung (Mao Zedong, 1893–1976), offered a return to the simple virtues of hard work and self-sacrifice in order to build a new China, free from foreign influence and humiliation and free also from the now discredited and reactionary elitism of Confucianism and the old order it represented. The Confucian society had deteriorated sadly as China had sunk deeper into poverty, demoralization, and unwillingness to face drastically changed circumstances. People necessarily concentrated on ensuring their own survival rather than on responsibility for others or on group welfare. In their remote frontier base at Yenan (Yanan) in the northwest, where they were centered from 1934 to 1947, the Communists under Mao's direction had worked out a number of ideas for China's regeneration, while at the same time appealing broadly to the masses.

Mao himself, like several other Communist leaders, came from peasant stock, and their program emphasized peasant welfare and peasant values, as the Kuomintang had not. Landlordism and oppression of the peasantry were popular issues in the face of widespread rural poverty and mass suffering. Chinese who collaborated with foreign businessmen in the treaty ports prospered in league with a government that was prone to favor foreign influences. The cities, nearly all of which were foreign-dominated treaty ports as well as centers of Kuomintang

strength and the home of "running dogs" (collaborators with the foreigners), were obvious targets for a peasant-oriented revolutionary movement.

Success depended, however, on building a mass support base in the countryside, where most Chinese lived. The Communists initiated land reform programs in the areas they controlled—most of the north—as well as campaigns to politicize and organize the peasants. Intellectuals were also involved in an effort to create a new ideology that could appeal to peasants. Mao himself, though the son of a rich peasant turned grain merchant, was primarily an intellectual as well as a gifted poet in the tradition of the Confucian scholars and emperors. His prescriptions for art and literature that would "serve politics" and "serve the masses" attracted growing numbers of fellow intellectuals disillusioned with the corruption and spiritual bankruptcy of the Kuomintang. As an intellectual organizing peasant rebellion, Mao consciously followed an old Chinese tradition.

The civil war that broke out in 1947 soon became a rout, despite heavy American support for the Kuomintang. The Communists had few weapons except what they could capture from their opponents or make themselves, but their strength quickly multiplied as growing numbers of Kuomintang troops and officers surrendered to them, often voluntarily, with all their equipment. The close American connection, with its connotation of foreign dominance, probably weakened rather than strengthened the Kuomintang in its fight against the Communists and left a legacy of anti-American bitterness when the civil war ended. On October 1, 1949, Mao announced the inauguration of the People's Republic of China from a rostrum in front of the Forbidden City in Peking (Beijing), conscious, as always, of the tradition of China's imperial greatness, to which he was now the heir. "China has stood up," he said, and the great majority of Chinese responded with enthusiasm.

The revolution was the culmination of a long process that began with the overthrow of the old Ch'ing (Qing) dynasty in 1916. After the failure of Sun Yat-sen and the corruption of the Kuomintang, the Communists, originally appealing largely to intellectuals, had finally succeeded in creating a mass political base, with a peasant army forged in the fires of the Japanese war. They called their program "the mass line," claiming to represent the more than 80 percent of the Chinese people who lived in the countryside.

Reconstruction and Consolidation

Chiang Kai-shek and the remnants of the Kuomintang government and army fled to the offshore island of Taiwan (Formosa), where American aid helped them in time to build a prosperous economy and gain firm control of the island's population. From this tiny base, sheltered only by

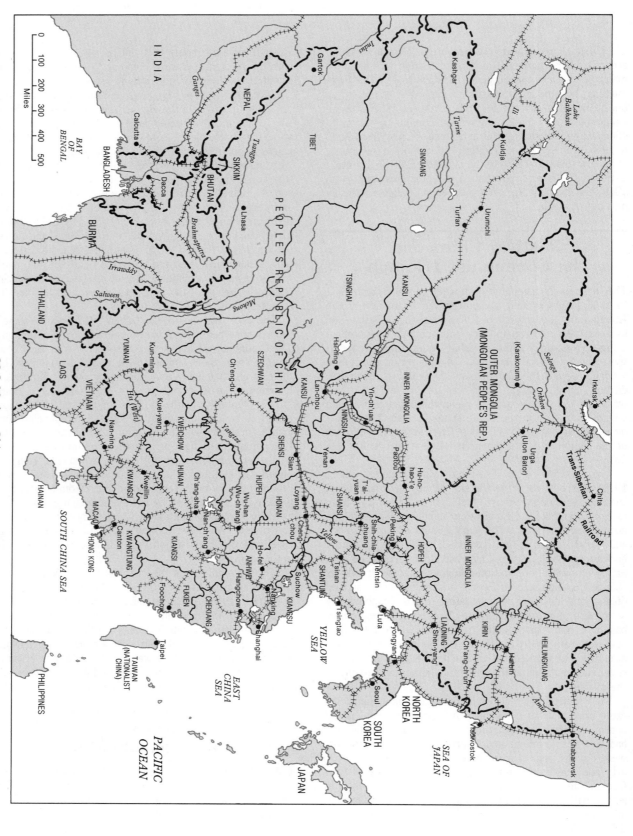

38.2 Modern China

American power, Chiang continued to claim sole legitimate authority over China. The United States supported the Kuomintang until the desire to exploit the split between the Chinese Communists and their erstwhile Soviet allies led belatedly to official American recognition of the government in Peking in 1979. Unofficial ties with Taipei (the Taiwan capital) remained, however. On the mainland the new government moved quickly to repair the physical damage of the long years of war and to extend its land reform and political education programs into the newly conquered south and southwest. All over the country what was still called land reform became more violent as party organizers, in an effort to create "class consciousness," encouraged peasants to "speak bitterness" and to identify their landlord-oppressors. Many thousands of the latter were killed by angry mobs, and their land was distributed among the poorer peasants.

Firm central government control was reestablished in all of the former empire, including Manchuria (now called simply "the northeast"), southern or "Inner" Mongolia, Sinkiang (Xinjiang), and Tibet, and a major program of industrialization was begun. War with the United States in Korea from late 1950 to mid-1953 and an American-sponsored embargo on trade with China slowed these efforts but also helped to radicalize the country and to strengthen dedication to the goals of self-reliance and reconstruction. By 1957 Mao judged that support for the new government was wide and deep enough to invite criticism. In a famous speech, he declared: "Let a hundred flowers bloom; let a hundred schools of thought contend." Many intellectuals and others, including many of China's ethnic minorities such as Tibetans and Muslims, responded with a torrent of criticism aimed at rigid party or government controls. Most of it was pronounced counterrevolutionary, and many of the critics were punished, jailed, or even executed.

The Great Leap Forward

Despite the evidence of dissent, Mao still felt secure enough in the support of the majority of his people that he moved swiftly to collectivize the land. By 1958 he moved beyond the Soviet model of collectivization as China's farms and fields were organized into new communes; private ownership was abolished, and all enterprises were managed collectively. The communes varied widely in area and population but averaged about 25,000 people, frequently incorporating large numbers of previously separate villages. Several villages made up a "production team," several teams a "production brigade," and several brigades a commune. Communes were supposed to include manufacturing enterprises as well, to bring industrialization to the rural areas. Communes were also set up in the cities but added little to existing factories, departments, or offices, and the experiment was short-lived.

Mao announced that 1958 would be the year of the "Great Leap Forward" in which China would overtake Britain in industrial output by united efforts within the commune structure. Communal dining halls were set up so that families need not lose work time by preparing meals. Backyard steel furnaces sprang up all over the rural landscape, using local iron ore and coal or other fuel. Communes were given quotas for production of specific agricultural and industrial goods, but too little attention was paid to the nature of local resources or to rational organization more generally.

The Great Leap was a dismal failure, and the country collapsed into economic chaos in 1959. Peasants had been driven to exhaustion in pursuit of unrealistic goals and by inefficient combinations of tasks and resources. Nearly all of the iron and steel from the backyard furnaces was of unusable quality, and the same was true of much of the other commune industrial output. Crops failed as labor was shifted arbitrarily between different tasks, and for at least three years food was scarce and famine widespread. Probably about 30 million people died of starvation or malnutrition in one of the worst famines in world history. Mao's radical policies had brought disaster, and for several years more moderate leaders such as Chou En-lai (Zhou Enlai, 1898–1976) and Liu Hsiao-chi (Liu Xiaoqi, 1894–1971) eclipsed him, although he remained the party chairman.

The Sino-Soviet Split

The Russians were alarmed by what they saw as the radical excesses of the Great Leap and its departure from the Soviet pattern. They were annoyed also by Mao's assertion that his version of socialism was superior to theirs, his continued support of Stalinist policies after they had been discredited in the USSR, and his accusations that Russia had now become ideologically impure, or "revisionist." The Russians saw Mao's bellicose stand on the reconquest of Taiwan, for which he requested Soviet nuclear aid, as a threat to world peace, and inevitable tensions arose out of the large-scale Soviet aid program and Soviet advisers in China. In 1959 the Russians withdrew their aid and advisers and moved toward a more antagonistic relationship with China. The next 15 years saw revived territorial disputes and armed border clashes between the two former allies on the long frontier between them, especially in the Amur region of northern Manchuria and along the northern border of Sinkiang.

Each claimed to be the true heir of Marx and Lenin and hence of the correct path to socialism, and in this ideological context long-standing historical conflicts between them surfaced. These dated back to the period of early tsarist expansion into Northeast Asia and to Russia's exploitation of Manchuria and its role as one of the Western imperialist powers during China's years of political weakness. On the other side, China's billion people, bordering thinly settled

◉ Attack on the "Revisionists" ◉ and "Imperialists"

At the Tenth Party Congress in 1973, Vice-Chairman Chou En-lai gave a long address in which he castigated the Russian "revisionists" and lumped them together with the American "imperialists."

There were many instances in the past where one tendency covered another and when a tide came, the majority went along with it, while only a few withstood it. . . . We must not fear isolation and must dare to go against the tide and brave it through. Chairman Mao states: "Going against the tide is a Marxist-Leninist principle. . . . The West always wants to urge the Soviet revisionists eastward to divert the peril toward China, and it would be fine so long as all is quiet in the West. China is an attractive piece of meat coveted by all. But this piece of meat is very tough, and for years no one has been able to bite into it. . . . The U.S.-Soviet contention for hegemony is the cause of world intranquillity. . . . They want to devour China but find it too tough even to bite. . . . U.S. imperialism started to go downhill after its defeat in the war of aggression against Korea. . . . [Khrushchev and Brezhnev in Russia] made a socialist country degenerate into a social imperialist country. Internally it has restored capitalism, enforced a fascist dictatorship and . . . exposed its ugly features as the new tsar and its reactionary nature, namely 'socialism in words, imperialism in deeds.' . . ."

If you are so anxious to relax world tension, why don't you show your good faith by doing a thing or two—for instance, withdraw your armed forces from Czechoslovakia or the People's Republic of Mongolia and return the four northern islands [the Kurile archipelago north of Hokkaido] to Japan? China has not occupied any foreign countries' territory. Must China give away all the territory north of the Great Wall to the Soviet revisionists in order to show that we favor relaxation of world tensions? . . . The Sino-Soviet boundary question should be settled peacefully through negotiations free from any threat. We will not attack unless we are attacked; if we are attacked, we will certainly counterattack.

Source: I. Hsu, *The Rise of Modern China* (New York: Oxford University Press, 1975), pp. 878–879.

Siberia and Russia's maritime provinces, were seen as an alarming threat to Soviet Asia. The rhetoric of accusation mounted on both sides; troops were stationed along the frontiers, and small clashes occurred. But China could not stand alone against the entire world, and its leaders began indirect overtures to the United States. More than a decade later, with the end of their misadventure in Vietnam in sight, the Americans finally responded. A cautious restoration of contact began when President Richard Nixon visited Peking late in 1971. This led to the establishment of diplomatic relations, with full U.S. recognition and an exchange of ambassadors with the People's Republic in 1979.

The Cultural Revolution

During the decade from 1966 to 1976, however, China passed through an unprecedented social cataclysm, the so-called Cultural Revolution, in which hundreds of millions of people suffered. The failure of the Great Leap Forward had necessitated more moderate policies and a period of recovery from economic disaster. By 1966 Mao judged the recovery to be complete, and he launched a new campaign designed to renew a revolution that he saw as having slipped into bureaucratic complacency and opportunism.

Mao remarked that he felt like "an ancestor at his own funeral and at the burial of his hopes." His cure was a purge, though his message was the old one of "serve the people," with its clear echoes of Confucian responsibility. The chief targets of his purge were the members of the elite: party managers and officials, teachers, writers, and intellectuals, as well as others who were allegedly tainted by foreign influence or bourgeois lifestyles or whose class origins were not appropriately peasant or proletarian.

The results were devastating. Millions were hounded out of their jobs. Artists and musicians who showed any interest in Western styles were attacked. Many intellectuals and other "counterrevolutionaries" were beaten or killed, and others were jailed, sent to corrective labor camps, or assigned to the lowest menial tasks as a means of "reeducation." Opera stars, writers, and concert violinists were set to cleaning latrines. All foreign music, art, and literature and the expression of all ideas not approved by the state were banned. Most books disappeared or were burned, to be replaced by the ever-present works of Mao himself and the *Little Red Book* of his sayings. Chinese who had studied abroad were particular targets. People were encouraged to inform on friends, colleagues, and even family members, causing deep trauma and division in a society based on traditional family ties. The accused were often jailed or condemned to corrective labor without evidence. Few people had the courage to try to help them, for fear that they too would meet the same

fate. The ensuing turmoil affected the lives of hundreds of millions of people and paralyzed the country. Nor were the rural communes exempt, for there, too, many were obliged to confess ideological sins and subjected to punishment and corrective labor.

During the height of the Cultural Revolution all universities and colleges were closed, as breeding grounds for a new elite. When they slowly began to reopen, it was only to the children of peasants, workers, and party loyalists still in power. The new curriculum concentrated on "political study." Most high school graduates in the decade after 1966, particularly those in the cities, were assigned to productive labor in the countryside, where, Mao felt, they would learn the value of simple toil and peasant virtues. This was partly a leveling alternative to the universities, partly a means to ease unemployment and housing shortages in the cities, and partly a way to reeducate

◉ Mao: The Revolutionary Vision ◉

The Communist revolution in China was in large part a peasant-based movement against the vested power of the cities. Mao Tse-tung put it dramatically.

Since China's key cities have long been occupied by the powerful imperialists and their reactionary Chinese allies, it is imperative for the revolutionary ranks to turn the backward villages into advanced consolidated base areas, . . . bastions of the revolution from which to fight their vicious enemies.

This equally famous statement of Mao's was published in the periodical Red Flag.

China's 600 million people have two remarkable peculiarities; they are first of all poor, and secondly blank. That may seem like a bad thing, but it is really a good thing. Poor people want change, want to do things, want revolution. A clean sheet of paper has no blotches, and so the newest and most beautiful words can be written on it, the newest and most beautiful pictures painted on it.

Still driven by his revolutionary vision, Mao the poet wrote in 1963, in traditional classic verse:

So many deeds cry out to be done,
And always urgently.
The world rolls on,
Time passes.
Ten thousand years are too long;
Seize the day, seize the hour,
Our force is irresistible.

Sources: Mao Tse-tung, *The Chinese Revolution and the Chinese Communist Party* (Peking: Foreign Language Press, 1954), p. 17 (written in 1939); *Red Flag,* June 1, 1958, pp. 3–4; "Reply to Kuo Mo-jo" (dated February 5, 1963), in *China Reconstructs* 16 (March 1967): 2.

Chinese too young to have shared the early years of hardship and sacrifice.

Some 17 million young people were sent down in this program by the time it was discontinued in the late 1970s. Most of them saw it as ruinous to their own ambitions and career plans, for which their urban origins and education had prepared them. Nor were most of them very helpful in agricultural or other development work. Their training had not in most cases been relevant, and indeed it had tended, as in China's past, to make them think of themselves as an educated elite who looked down on peasants and manual labor. The program was understandably unpopular with peasants too, since they had to feed and house disgruntled city youth who, with their higher level of education, were unprepared for farmwork. All white-collar workers were required to spend at least two months each year doing manual labor, mainly in the countryside, which not surprisingly met with resistance from professionals and others.

Mao called on teenagers and students to serve as shock troops for the Cultural Revolution. Like young people everywhere, they had little stake in the status quo, were filled with idealism, and were easily diverted from their studies. They welcomed their exciting new role and the opportunity to exercise authority over their elders. Mao called them "Red Guards" and permitted them to roam the country freely, ferreting out "rightists" and harassing everyone in responsible positions. Millions rode free or commandeered trains and buses to the cities, including Peking, where Mao addressed cheering crowds of Red Guards at mass rallies. Mao and his supporters promoted a personality cult; huge pictures and statues of the "Great Helmsman" and copies of his *Little Red Book* appeared everywhere. Rival factions quickly emerged among the Red Guards, each claiming to be followers of the true line. Many welcomed the opportunity to pay off old grudges and to denounce others, often anonymously. Uncontrolled violence broke out in many cities.

To halt the mounting chaos, Chou En-lai prevailed on Mao to call in the army in 1968. The Red Guards were suppressed, thus creating yet another embittered and dislocated group; the Guards felt they had been betrayed, a "lost generation." But the nightmare went on even after the Red Guards had been sent to the countryside. Even politicians at the top, except for Mao himself, were attacked for alleged deviations from the party line, which changed unpredictably. Liu Hsiao-chi (Liu Xiaoqi), a revolutionary comrade Mao had originally picked as his successor, was purged and accused of "rightist revisionism" because of his efforts to rebuild the economy after the disaster of the Great Leap Forward. He died under arrest after public humiliation and beatings. Other high officials suffered similar fates. Professionals in all fields were scrutinized for their political views and activism. Absence from the endless daily political meetings or silence during them was evidence of "counterrevolutionary tendencies." One

of the many slogans of the Cultural Revolution was "Better Red than Expert." No one at any level felt safe.

The Chinese Revolution remained primarily a peasant movement, a Chinese rather than a foreign-style answer to China's problems. This was appealing also on nationalist grounds, especially since nearly all the cities had been tainted by semicolonial foreign dominance. There was thus both a pronounced antiurban bias to the revolution and a determination to exalt the countryside, to put the peasants in charge, and to concentrate efforts at development in the rural areas, the supposed source of all revolutionary values.

This was the theme of both the Great Leap Forward and the Cultural Revolution. All movement of people was controlled, especially to the cities, where housing and ration books for food and household supplies were allocated only to those with assigned employment. Individuals could not chose jobs; they worked wherever the state sent them. In the 1970s a growing number of illegal migrants to the cities lived underground or on forged papers. Most of them are still there, their numbers apparently greatly increased; urban unemployment has become a major problem. Despite the official denigration of cities, they remained the places where most people wanted to be.

In the countryside each commune was designed to be self-sufficient as far as possible. The Cultural Revolution promoted a particularly extensive growth of small-scale rural industry, especially in what were labeled the "five smalls": iron and steel, cement, fertilizer, agricultural goods (including tools, machinery, and irrigation equipment), and electric power. There was also considerable production of light consumer goods for local use. Local manufacture did reduce the load on an already overburdened road and rail system and saved transport costs while providing employment and experience to the masses of rural people. But in most cases such production was considerably more expensive than that in larger-scale and better-equipped urban-based plants and of much lower quality. Decentralized industry has been considered as an alternative to the crowding, pollution, and dehumanization of industrial cities since the eighteenth century, but it has seldom proved economically practical. Mao's utopian vision of rural development was appealing as an attempt to alleviate the real poverty of the countryside, but it was pursued at dreadful cost. China, meanwhile, lagged farther and farther behind the rest of the world, technologically and educationally.

Mao had said that the major goals of the revolution should be the elimination of the distinctions between city and countryside, between intellectuals and manual workers, and between elites and common people. In pursuit of these aims, workers or janitors became plant managers and university officials; peasants were elevated to power in the communes' "revolutionary committees"; professors, technicians, and skilled managers were humiliated or reduced to the most menial jobs. Even "rich peasants"

◉ Revolution, Chinese Style ◉

From the beginning of their revolutionary victory, the Chinese asserted that their principles and experience should be the guide for the rest of the world, not the Russian way. Here is Liu Shao-ch'i in 1949.

The road taken by the Chinese people in defeating imperialism and in founding the Chinese People's Republic is the road that should be taken by the peoples of many colonial and semi-colonial countries in their fight for national independence and people's democracy. . . . This is the road of Mao Tse-tung. . . . This is the inevitable road of many colonial and semi-colonial peoples in the struggle for their independence and liberation.

Lu Ting-i, director of propaganda of the Central Committee, added in July 1951:

Mao Tse-tung's theory of the Chinese revolution is a new development of Marxism-Leninism in the revolutions of the colonial and semi-colonial countries. . . . It is of universal significance for the world Communist movement. . . . The classic type of revolution in colonial and semi-colonial countries is the Chinese revolution.

The Russians replied, in the words of Y. Kovalev, a leading propagandist:

The decisive prerequisites for the victory of the Chinese revolution were the October Socialist Revolution and the victory of socialism in the U.S.S.R., and the defeat of Japanese and German imperialism by the Soviet Union in World War II. . . . Stalin's analysis of the peculiarities of China as a semi-colonial country was taken as the basis for the working out of the strategy and tactics of the struggle for an independent and democratic China by the Chinese Communist Party.

Stalin's successor, Nikita Khrushchev, lectured Mao in 1958, after Mao suggested that the combined numbers of China and Russia could overcome the capitalist West.

Comrade Mao Tse-tung, nowadays that sort of thinking is out of date. You can no longer calculate the alignment of forces on the basis of who has the most men. Back in the days when a dispute was settled with fists and bayonets it made a difference who had the most men. . . . Now with the atomic bomb, the number of troops on each side makes practically no difference.

But the Chinese stuck to their insistence that theirs was the only true way. This editorial, in characteristic Cultural Revolution style, appeared in Liberation Army Daily *in May 1966.*

The thought of Mao Tse-tung is the sun in our heart, the root of our life, and the source of all our strength. Through it one becomes unselfish, daring, intelligent, and able to do anything; no difficulty can conquer him, while he can conquer any enemy. The thought of Mao Tse-tung transforms man's ideology, transforms the fatherland. . . . Through it the oppressed people of the world will rise.

Source: I. Hsu, *The Rise of Modern China* (New York: Oxford University Press, 1975), pp. 810–813, 859.

The leaders of Communist China in 1965: from left to right, Chou En-lai, Chu-Teh, Mao Tse-tung, and Liu Hsiao-chi. [Eastfoto/Sovfoto]

became targets. All those with any claim to expertise were suspect and were often hounded out of their positions in angry "struggle meetings"; those who refused to join in the denunciations risked being denounced themselves. The moral virtue and practical wisdom of the peasants and the countryside were extolled.

Mao drew heavily on traditional ideas in emphasizing the duty of those in positions of power and responsibility to serve the masses, and he, like the Confucians, used moral examples and slogans to inspire and mold group behavior. He also relied on the new technique of mass campaigns to galvanize people into action. Some were constructive, like the campaigns to eliminate flies or to build new dams and irrigation canals. But most were politically inspired and were aimed at "rightists" and "counterrevolutionaries." The Chinese revolution's radical phase lasted longer and went to greater extremes than similar phases of earlier revolutions, but in time it too faded, if only because the Chinese people were exhausted by constant political campaigns and by the terror itself. Mao's death removed the chief obstacle to a return to more normal conditions, and China turned with relief from its long ordeal.

China After Mao

As Mao lay dying in 1976, a few months after his old comrade-in-arms Chou En-lai had died of overwork and exhaustion while trying to hold the country together, a radical faction led by Mao's widow, Chiang Ch'ing (Jiang Qing), tried to continue his extreme policies. But in 1978

a more moderate leadership emerged under Hua Kuo-feng (Hua Guofeng), whom Mao had designated as his successor. Chiang Ch'ing and three of her associates, the so-called "Gang of Four," were tried and convicted of "crimes against the people" and sentenced to jail. China began to emerge from its nightmare and to resume cautious interchange with the rest of the world after 30 years of isolation. The universities and their curricula were slowly restored, and students now had to pass entrance examinations rather than merely to demonstrate proper "class origins." Efforts were made to provide somewhat greater freedom for intellectuals, writers, teachers, and managers.

Hua Kuo-feng was peacefully replaced by an old party pragmatist, Teng Hsiao-p'ing (Deng Xiaoping, born 1904), who returned to power in 1981 as the real head of state and chief policymaker. Most of Mao's policies were progressively dismantled. The new government acknowledged that China was still poor and technically backward, that it needed foreign technology and investment, and that to encourage production its people needed material incentives rather than political harangues and "rectification campaigns."

The communes were quietly dissolved in all but name. Agriculture, still by far the largest sector of the economy, was largely organized into a "responsibility system" whereby individual families grew the crops that they judged most profitable in an economy that was now market-oriented. The commune still nominally owned the land and the state still appropriated a share of farm output, but peasants were free to sell the rest in a free market. Those who did well under this system, and urban entrepreneurs who prospered in the small private businesses now permitted, felt free once again to display their new wealth. Expensive houses with television aerials sprouted here and there in the countryside, and in the cities motor scooters, tape recorders, and refrigerators became more common. The new rich and even party officials began to indulge personal tastes in clothing, including Western-style and fashionable outfits, which replaced the drab uniforms decreed in earlier years.

Rural industry remained where it had proved practical, but renewed emphasis was placed on large-scale and urban-based industrial production and on catching up with world advances in technology to make up for the lost years. Many factory and office managers and workers were now rewarded on the basis of their productivity. Technological, managerial, and educational elites also reappeared, and with them the bourgeois lifestyles denounced by Mao as the antithesis of revolutionary socialism. The new pragmatism was illustrated by Teng Hsiao-p'ing's pithy remark: "I don't care if a cat is red [socialist] or white [capitalist] as long as it catches mice." At the same time, he affirmed that China was still a socialist country under a Communist government that planned and managed the economy and aimed to provide social justice.

The decade after Mao's death saw a reappraisal of his legacy. The new leadership permitted controlled public criticism of the excesses of the Cultural Revolution and acknowledged the failures of Mao's economic policy. But much had also been accomplished. China remained poor,

but there was some growth in agriculture (except for the period 1958–1964), thanks in part to irrigation, better seeds, and fertilization. Industry grew rapidly, if unevenly, from what had been a very small and limited base. In 1964 China tested a nuclear bomb and thereby joined the ranks of the major powers. Thousands of miles of new railways and roads were built. China became a major industrial power. One of China's greatest successes was in delivering basic health care to most of its people, including for several years the system of "barefoot doctors" who traveled even to remote villages to provide basic care and the clinics established in every commune.

As in India, this greatly reduced the death rate, while the birthrate remained high. The result was a rapid growth in population, which nearly doubled between 1949 and 1982, when the first real census was taken. This growth placed great pressure on agriculture, where gains in production barely exceeded population·increase. As long as such growth continued, China could expect little progress in terms of the per capita welfare, by which real economic growth must be measured. In the 1970s the government began an attempt to control population growth. Beginning in 1983 families were penalized for having more than a single child, a policy seen as necessary for perhaps a generation if China was to escape from poverty.

Chinese socialism has also reduced gross inequities in wealth. Poverty at the bottom has not yet been eliminated, but increased production, better distribution, and the collective welfare system of communes and factories have benefited nearly everyone; recent inflation, however, has hurt many. Health levels, thanks in part to better nutrition as well as improved medical care, are in general high. Literacy has more than doubled since the revolution, and about half the population now gets as far as the early high school grades, although there are places for only about 3 percent in the universities.

Despite Mao's efforts, living standards in the cities have risen far more rapidly and substantially than in most rural areas. The growing division between urban and rural lifestyles and levels of affluence is a particular problem for the heirs of a peasant revolution, although it is shared by the rest of the developing world. China's cities are not yet disfigured by masses of visibly homeless and unemployed persons, as are many elsewhere in the developing and even the industrial world, but only because rigid controls on all movement and employment still prevent most rural people from migrating to the cities. Progress in other respects too has been won at the cost of state and collective social controls and the suppression of personal choice. This is not as disturbing to most Chinese as it might be to many Westerners, since the subordination of individualism to group effort and welfare has long been central to Chinese tradition.

China's past achievements and its revolutionary progress were due in large part to the primacy of responsibility and the pursuit of common goals over privilege and

Building an earthen dam for flood control on the Veniu River not far from Peking, 1971. Note the hand labor and absence of heavy machinery. [Sovfoto]

self-interest. Nevertheless, there have been protests and even student demonstrations against the continuing controls on free expression and choice of employment. As China opened its doors to more normal interchange with the rest of the world, more Chinese have come to see their political system as repressive. The political grievances resulting from this, along with the effects of Western cultural influence, led to remarkable demonstrations in Peking, Shanghai, and other major cities in the spring of 1989 that shook the party hierarchy. Most would argue that the system has other important virtues and that some controls remain necessary. Nearly all Chinese share a pride in their modern accomplishments as a nation. China has indeed stood up. Now it must make up for the years of isolation and move ahead with what it calls "modernization," recognizing that this must include a large infusion of foreign technology and perhaps also a greater scope for individual initiative and creativity.

Taiwan and Hong Kong

Taiwan had been taken over by the Japanese in 1895 as part of their colonial empire, but with Japan's defeat in 1945 the island was returned to Chinese sovereignty. In 1949 it became the sole remaining base for the defeated Kuomintang. Some 2 million mainland Chinese, including units of the Kuomintang army and government, fled to Taiwan, where they largely excluded the Taiwanese from political power.

The island had originally been settled by Chinese from Fukien (Fujian) province, just across the narrow strait that separates it from the mainland, beginning on a significant scale in the seventeenth century. They had retained their Chinese culture while developing some regional feeling, especially when the island was under Japanese control. They welcomed the mainlanders in 1945, but after repressive actions in 1947, and especially after the mass influx of 1949, they tended to regard them as oppressors.

Nevertheless, Taiwan in the 1950s began a period of rapid economic growth, at first with heavy American aid and then, by the early 1960s, on its own. A land reform program gave farmers new incentives as well as increased supplies of fertilizer, new crop strains, and new irrigation. Growing rural prosperity was matched and, by the 1970s, exceeded by industrial growth as Taiwan experienced a small-scale version of the Japanese "economic miracle." Taiwanese developments followed much the same path in technological achievements and both light and heavy manufacturing. Taiwan's trade with the rest of the world quickly exceeded that of mainland China. Taipei, the capital, became a large city and was joined by other rapidly growing industrial centers and ports.

Prosperity, wider relations with the rest of the world, and an unspoken acceptance of political realities in China and East Asia began by the 1980s to soften the harsher aspects of Kuomintang control. Taiwan remained a police state, but more representation and positions were offered to the Taiwanese along with a little more freedom of expression.

The tiny and rocky island of Hong Kong, just off the mouth of the West River, which leads to Canton, had been ceded to Britain by the Treaty of Nanking, which ended the Opium War in 1842. Additional territory was later leased on the adjacent mainland peninsula to supply Hong Kong with food and water as well as to provide room for expansion. Hong Kong grew rapidly in the nineteenth and twentieth centuries. Although under British control as a crown colony, it remained an overwhelmingly Chinese city, peopled by immigrants from overcrowded southern China who brought with them their interest and skill in commerce and their capacity for hard work. With the Communist victory in China, Hong Kong was isolated from its major market, for which it had served as a leading port for foreign trade. At the same time, it was flooded by waves of refugees from the mainland. The city and its resourceful people survived the crisis by developing a highly successful array of light industries, including textiles and electronics. Although dependent on imported raw materials, they were made profitable by inexpensive labor and efficient factories.

Hong Kong became even more prosperous than it had been before World War II. As China began to resume some trade outside the Communist bloc, Hong Kong regained its former role as a major distribution, commercial, and financial center, a function it also came to perform for much of Southeast Asia. By the 1980s the city and its adjacent territories had a population of nearly 6 million. But the Chinese government announced that when the lease on those territories expired in 1997, they and all of Hong Kong would be reclaimed. To this the British agreed. It remains to be seen how this citadel of capitalism will be integrated with the socialist system of the People's Republic.

Divided Korea

Korea had suffered perhaps more than any colonial country in the world under the exceptionally harsh Japanese rule that lasted from 1910 to 1945. Living standards fell sharply during this period as Japan milked Korea of much of its raw materials and food (see Chapter 33). Virtually all non-menial jobs were filled by Japanese. All efforts at political expression were ruthlessly suppressed, and activists were jailed, killed, or exiled. When the Pacific war ended in

1945, almost no Koreans had the educational or administrative experience to form a viable government.

In the confused weeks after the Japanese surrender, an ad hoc arrangement left Russian troops to occupy the northern half of the country above the 38th parallel while American troops occupied the southern half. The Cold War resulted in both a hardening of this division into a political boundary and the emergence of rival political regimes. A Russian-dominated government emerged in the north with its capital at Pyongyang, and an American client-state was formed in the south, headquartered at Seoul. The conservative, American-educated politician Syngman Rhee (1875–1965) became the first president of the Republic of South Korea, while the Communist leader Kim Il Sung (born 1912) headed the Democratic People's Republic of North Korea. When American and Russian troops withdrew from their respective areas, they left a United Nations commission to keep the peace but also left their two client regimes heavily armed with modern weapons.

On June 25, 1950, the North Koreans launched an invasion across the 38th parallel, although the South was clearly preparing its own strike. Because the Russians were then boycotting the United Nations Security Council, the United States was able to push through a motion condemning North Korea, which the government of the North ignored. A special United Nations emergency force was raised to combat North Korea, but the United States had already committed its soldiers to action, and the United Nations force was almost entirely American. By September the North Korean forces had overrun the entire peninsula except for a small section in the southeast. General Douglas MacArthur counterattacked behind enemy lines at Inchon. Ignoring his instructions from Washington, he pushed deeply into North Korea, bombed the bridges linking it with China, and massed troops near its frontier. The Chinese entered the war almost immediately, driving back MacArthur's forces and retaking much of the peninsula. At this critical point, MacArthur openly advocated attacking military bases in Manchuria and using atomic weapons against the Chinese. Enraged by this insubordination, President Harry Truman relieved him of duty, touching off a bitter domestic debate. Dwight Eisenhower, Truman's successor, ended the hostilities. Campaigning for the presidency in 1952 on a pledge that he would bring peace, he approved an armistice signed at Panmunjom in July 1953.

Most of Korea was devastated by the fighting, as the armies of both sides surged back and forth over the country. A million Koreans and a million Chinese (as compared with 150,000 Americans) died, and 3 million Koreans were made refugees from their shattered homes and villages. Coming on top of the ruthless exploitation of Japanese rule after 1910, the war further reduced Korea to poverty. Korea suffered as a pawn in the Cold War rivalries between the superpowers. Korea was left divided, its econ-

38.3 Modern Korea

omy further disrupted by the separation of its two halves, which were interdependent. The superpowers continued to supply the police-state regimes in both North and South with arms and economic aid, as their puppets, and the risk of another war between them remains, despite the fervent desire of most Koreans to see their country reunited.

American intervention in 1950 under its United Nations cloak was thus responsible for a fundamental worsening of the welfare of all Koreans. The alternative would have been a takeover of the entire country by the Communist government of the North, which, of course, is what prompted the American action. But the United States has belatedly come to accept a Communist government of China, among others, and it is not easy to argue that a Communist but unified Korea would be substantially worse, especially for Koreans, than the present situation, including its built-in tensions. American intervention in Korea formed the background for a similar policy in Vietnam, now generally acknowledged as a tragic mistake.

Although the war devastated both halves of the country, Korean culture, language, and national consciousness nevertheless remained one. Both states continued to pour scarce resources into their military establishments. This was a greater sacrifice in the less developed North than in the South, which included most of the best agricultural land and much of the industry, which the North had earlier supplied with most of its raw materials. By the 1960s South Korea had begun to recover from the war and by the 1970s to leap ahead economically, following the same path of rapid industrial development earlier pursued by Japan.

Syngman Rhee was forced to resign as president in 1960 after his dictatorial style had alienated many of his rivals, to be succeeded by a military junta and from 1963 by equally dictatorial rulers. President Chung Hee Park took office in 1963 but was assassinated in 1979 by his own Korean Central Intelligence Agency. His policies continued under Chun Doo Hwan, while the North remained under the tight control of Kim Il Sung. Both halves of Korea were police states in which free expression was savagely repressed. In 1987 a wave of student protests erupted in Seoul, and the government of Chun Doo Hwan was obliged to make a few concessions, among them the direct election of the president and somewhat more scope for political parties, including those in opposition. In the first direct presidential election in 16 years, the government's handpicked candidate, Roh Tae-woo, was chosen president in December 1987 amid charges of massive voting fraud, although he benefited from a split opposition.

Meanwhile Korean economic growth continued to produce growing prosperity for most people in the South. Rising incomes were spread widely among the population, and the gap between rich and poor was smaller than in most societies. South Korea began to invade world markets in a number of advanced manufacturing sectors, including automobiles. North Korea was largely closed to non-Communist outsiders, but economic development there was substantial, including industrial growth, although less impressive than in the South. As long as Korea remains divided between two implacably hostile governments supported by the United States and the Soviet Union, respectively, the peace of this chronically troubled part of the world will continue at risk, and the welfare of its people will suffer.

Southeast Asia Since World War II

China's revolutionary resurgence sent shock waves through Southeast Asia, where some 15 million Chinese resided. The Japanese had helped to destroy European colonialism in Asia before World War II, but the Chinese revolution now offered a new set of ideas. In neighboring Vietnam the Chinese government aided the Communist party under Ho Chi Minh (1890–1969) in its struggle first against French colonialism and then against an American invasion in support of a puppet government in the South (see Chapter 41). In the Philippines the Chinese example helped to inspire a peasant Communist uprising, the Hukbalahaps, whose successors still challenge the American-backed regime. In Indonesia reports of an alleged coup by Indonesian Communists and Chinese led to an American-supported counterstrike in 1965. Mass killings of innocent Chinese and suspected Communists resulted, and the toll of victims was probably over half a million. Malaya faced an insurrection between 1943 and 1957 by a small group of native Chinese guerrillas, but most Malayan Chinese refused to join it. The rebellion was suppressed by the outgoing British colonial administration when help from China did not materialize.

Neighboring Thailand was wary, but Thai Chinese, who had been assimilated into Thai society much more completely than in any other Southeast Asian country, remained peaceful. In Burma chronic tension existed between the majority Burmans and the numerous minority groups in the mountains around the Irrawaddy plain, and the small Chinese minority in Rangoon was expelled. The military government, which came to power in 1962 under General Ne Win (born 1911), however, modeled its policy in part on the Chinese example by cutting nearly all of Burma's ties with the rest of the world and attempting to promote domestic development through state-directed socialism.

The Philippines and Indonesia

The major event of the years after 1945 in Southeast Asia was the coming of independence to former colonial states. The Philippines in 1946 were the first to achieve it, as the Americans handed over the reins of government, although their continued presence was such that the country remained a virtual protectorate. The first two decades saw some token efforts at land reform. But in 1965 Ferdinand Marcos (1917–1989) became president and soon assumed dictatorial powers, which he used to favor the rich and to suppress free expression. For some 20 years his rule was firmly supported by successive American administrations. He was finally voted out of office in 1986, and a reformist government under Corazon Aquino began to attempt to repair the damage he had done.

Neighboring Indonesia won its armed struggle for freedom against the Dutch in 1949, who left the country unprepared for independence. Like the Koreans, few Indonesians had any administrative or technical experience, and the new government was unable to control inflation and corruption or to spur economic development. The outlying islands resented the dominance of Java, which contained the capital at Djakarta, and regional rebellion became chronic. President Achmed Sukarno (1901–1970), the leader of the independence movement, suspended the ineffective parliamentary government in 1956 and gradually took personal control, together with the army, in the name of what he called "guided democracy." This too failed to deal with Indonesia's mounting problems, and in 1966 General T. N. J. Suharto (born 1921), fresh from his CIA-supported purge of suspected Communists and Chinese, took over, confirming his rule by stage-managed elections in 1973 and 1978. The Suharto regime has made slow progress toward more orderly development despite its repressive nature, but this vast island country of some 175 million people stretched over a 3,000-mile-long archipelago has yet to evolve into full nationhood or to emerge from widespread poverty.

Indochina and the Vietnam War

When Japan surrendered in 1945, Ho Chi Minh, the head of Vietnam's Communist party, declared the independence of all Indochina. From the northern city of Hanoi, he began a war of liberation against French occupation. Under the leadership of General Vo Nguyen Giap, the Communists perfected guerrilla fighting techniques and conducted a war of attrition. Although the French retook southern Vietnam, Ho's forces controlled much of the north. In 1954, after the French-occupied fortress of Dien Bien Phu fell to Giap's forces, a hastily arranged summit conference in

Geneva brought together French, Vietnamese, British, American, Soviet, and Chinese representatives. They agreed to break up Indochina temporarily into separate states and to hold national elections to reunify Vietnam within a year. The government under Ho Chi Minh in the north of Vietnam was balanced by an American-backed dictatorship set up in the south under Ngo Dinh Diem based in Saigon, the old French colonial capital. Laos and Cambodia became independent nations.

Diem and the Americans, fearing a Communist victory, refused to permit the national elections agreed to at Geneva. Guerrilla warfare broke out in South Vietnam in 1957, but President Eisenhower limited American involvement to matériel and military advisers. The Kennedy administration escalated the local civil struggle into a major international conflict on the basis of the "domino theory" that a Communist victory in Vietnam would threaten all governments in Southeast Asia. Some 17,000 American military personnel were assigned to Vietnam, but the Communist-led National Liberation Front (NLF) succeeded in capturing most of the countryside. In 1963 Vietnamese generals abetted by the United States killed Diem and ushered in a succession of military regimes.

Under President Lyndon Johnson the conflict became a full-scale war. He ordered air strikes against the Communist North and in August 1964, following a staged naval incident in the Gulf of Tongking (Tonkin), secured passage of a resolution from Congress that gave the president carte blanche to enlarge America's role in the war. By the spring of 1965 the United States was carrying out massive bombardment of North Vietnam and had committed its soldiers to offensive operations. The number of American troops grew steadily, from 184,000 in 1965 to more than 500,000 by the end of 1968.

Indonesian rice fields, Sumatra. Rice remains the major crop of lowland Southeast Asia, and much of Java and Bali resemble this scene, as do the lowland rice-growing areas of Burma, Thailand, Vietnam, Malaysia, and the Philippines. [Henri Cartier-Bresson/Magnum]

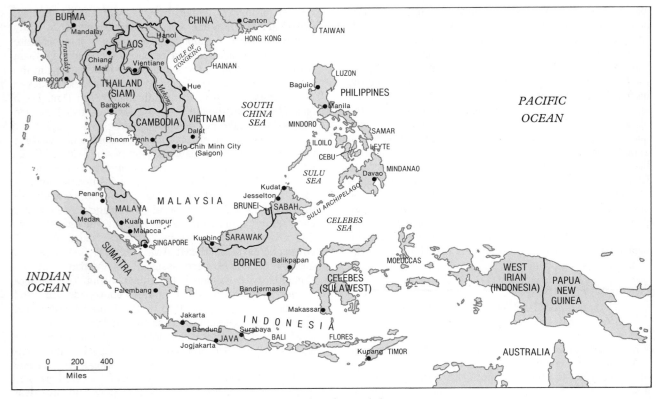

38.4 Southeast Asia

Despite this buildup, victory eluded the United States and its allies. The attempt to secure territory in the South by so-called search-and-destroy operations against the enemy proved futile, and the administration, fearing Chinese intervention as in Korea, declined to invade the North. Unable to gain victory on the ground, the United States dropped more explosives on Vietnam than the Allies had dropped on all fronts during World War II, and American troops killed thousands of civilians in fruitless efforts to prevent villagers from hiding Communist guerrillas.

The turning point in the war came in February 1968, when the NLF launched a wave of attacks against towns and cities in South Vietnam, the Tet Offensive. In April peace talks between the United States and North Vietnam opened in Paris, and in November, American voters elected the Republican Richard M. Nixon (born 1913) to the presidency. Nixon began the secret bombing of Communist supply routes in Cambodia and Laos in early 1969, concealing the operation through false reports. When Congress learned of the Cambodian bombings, it repealed the Tongking Gulf Resolution. In 1971 the publication of classified war documents heightened antiwar sentiments by revealing earlier deceptions by both Johnson and Nixon. Protests mounted as the 1972 presidential elections ap-

proached, but Nixon neutralized them by removing the last American ground troops. The Paris Accords, signed in January 1973, officially ended American involvement in the war. In April 1975 the North Vietnamese captured Saigon, ousted the government of President Nguyen Van Thieu, and unified the country.

The Americans claimed that the struggle was an example of "Communist aggression." Most Vietnamese saw it as a patriotic "war of national liberation" against French colonialism and U.S. imperialism. Peasants came to fear and hate the repressive policies of the puppet government of the South and of their American supporters, as they and most Vietnamese intellectuals had hated French oppression. There were some Vietnamese anti-Communists, including Catholic converts who fled the North, and some who supported the United States–backed government, but they were mainly relatively well-to-do elites and others who benefited from the widespread corruption of the Saigon government or who profited in various ways from the American presence. The war's outcome was ultimately decided by the support of most Vietnamese, including the peasants in this predominantly rural country, for the forces of the National Liberation Front, which they saw as a national rather than as a partisan effort.

In many ways the Vietnam war was a repeat of the long

struggle of the Chinese Communists against the Kuomintang. In Vietnam, too, the Communist party under Ho had captured the leadership of Vietnamese nationalism by the end of the Second World War. Like the Chinese, Vietnamese nationalists strove to free their country from foreign domination, and like them, they drew support against a corrupt and repressive regime domestically, which was further weakened politically by its subservience to foreign interests. Between 1.5 and 2 million Vietnamese gave their lives in the struggle; perhaps as many as 4 million were wounded, and over a million were refugees. The Americans suffered 57,000 dead and some 300,000 wounded.

As in Korea but to a far greater extent, American intervention produced in the end nothing but destruction and death. Official policy was based on almost total ignorance of Vietnam, its history of repeated success in repelling vastly superior Chinese armies, and the strength of Vietnamese nationalism. The small nation's guerrilla fighters humbled the military might of the world's greatest superpower, as the Chinese Communists had earlier defeated another United States client, the Kuomintang. But Vietnam suffered terribly. Its people and its economy have not recovered from what has been called the "endless war" from 1945 to 1975, although for many Vietnamese the struggle against the French had begun in the second half of the nineteenth century. The United States merely prolonged that struggle and, far from preventing a Communist

victory, had the effect of hardening the determination and the political rigidity of the government of the North. Since 1975 Vietnam has continued to suffer not only from the effects of unprecedented devastation but also from ideological tension and repression augmented by the long ordeal of conflict. If Ho had been allowed to prevail against the French in 1945 or 1946, as he clearly would have done without massive United States support for the French, most of these tragic problems would have been avoided.

Recovery from the war damage to the economy was slow. As after any civil war, bitterness remained between the Communist victors and those in the south who had opposed them. Many Vietnamese fled the country, including a large group who emigrated to the United States. But continued political and ideological tensions further slowed the recovery of Vietnam, which lagged behind much of the rest of Southeast Asia.

Vietnam's war of independence spilled over into neighboring Laos and Cambodia, with appalling human consequences. The overthrow of the neutralist ruler of Cambodia (now Kampuchea), Prince Norodom Sihanouk (born 1919), led to a civil war and subsequently to the genocidal Communist regime of Pol Pot, who was responsible for the deaths of perhaps a third of the country's people from 1976 to 1979 by forced labor, execution, or starvation. Vietnamese military intervention helped a more moderate rival government to win control of most of the country in 1979, but Pol Pot's Khmer Rouge forces remain active in

South Vietnam, 1967: a squad of American soldiers stops to watch as a target in a village burns. [Philip Jones-Griffiths/ Magnum]

their northern bases, supplied by China and the United States. Vietnam was still seen as the enemy of America and now again of China, and its move to eliminate Pol Pot was therefore resisted by both countries for political reasons. Those reasons included Russian support for Vietnam, which helped to sustain it in its war with the United States and which the Chinese also saw as a threat to themselves. Continuing Cold War rivalries in Indochina have thus prolonged its agony.

Malaysia, Singapore, and Thailand

Malaya's independence was delayed by the Communist insurgency, but once order was restored, the British quickly handed over power to the new state in 1957. Its major problem has been the diversity of its people. The Malays constituted a bare majority in their own homeland, thanks to massive Chinese immigration since the late nineteenth century. Most Malays were not interested in wage labor, and the booming growth of tin mining and rubber plantations brought in a wave of Chinese workers and entrepreneurs from overcrowded southern China. Many of them went on to become the dominant figures in the commercial life of Malaya and were joined by wives and families from China, as well as by immigrant laborers and merchants from India. By the time of independence Malays were only about half of the population.

This problem was eased in 1965 by the separation of the island of Singapore, overwhelmingly Chinese, as an independent city-state, and by the addition of former British colonies in northern Borneo, where Chinese were a minority. Since then the state has been called Malaysia, but there have been chronic conflicts between Malays and Chinese. The Chinese are effectively without a political voice, but Malays resent their economic power. A generally stable parliamentary system on the British model was marred in the 1980s by tendencies, like those in Singapore, toward authoritarianism and repression. The economy has remained relatively vigorous and has expanded from its colonial foundations in tin and rubber to include important palm oil production and a rapidly growing light industrial sector.

Independent Singapore continues as a high-income and high-growth center of trade for much of Southeast Asia and has become the world's fourth largest port in volume of traffic.

Thailand, just north of Malaya, was the only nation of Southeast Asia to retain independence throughout the colonial period. Since 1945 it has also enjoyed precarious political stability under democratic forms and has shared in the prosperous commercial growth of Malaya and Singapore through its port and capital of Bangkok, now a rapidly growing Western-style city.

Burma

Burma won its freedom from Britain in 1948 in the wake of India's independence, but it has been troubled by violence between the dominant Burmans and the diverse minorities who occupy the mountain fringes of the country. Chronic guerrilla-style civil war existed between government forces and rebel groups. General Ne Win's military government was not able to resolve this problem fully, and his policy of isolation from the rest of the world had the effect of further slowing Burma's already sluggish economic growth. Burma has begun to move cautiously toward resuming some external contacts and trade. A new and more responsive government may be able to build a more equitable and consensual national partnership among Burmans and non-Burmans, but the country still has far to go to attain viable nationhood.

For Southeast Asia as a whole, the transition from colonialism has been a hard one. Only Singapore and Thailand can be called fully successful states, and both may be regarded as special cases: Thailand never underwent colonial occupation and contains few non-Thai minorities. Singapore is in essence a creation of Western colonialism and capitalism. In the 1980s government policies in Singapore were often repressively applied and free expression curtailed or silenced. The countries of Southeast Asia are too scattered and too different from each other to work together as a unit, even for common economic purposes. It is a major sector of the world, but its diversity and the legacy of its colonial domination continue to retard its development.

Women Leaders in Modern East Asia

Several women have been prominent in positions of power in East Asia since 1945. Most traditional Asian societies were noted for the low status accorded to women, although Southeast Asia was a relative exception. In the modern period, however, some women have risen to great prominence, becoming heads of state in India, Sri Lanka, and the Philippines and political powers in Pakistan and China. Japan has produced notable women writers.

Chiang Ch'ing (Jiang Qing, born 1914), Mao Tse-tung's third wife, had been a minor movie star before she married him in Yenan in 1939. She assumed a prominent role in shaping party cultural policy, and with the Cultural Revolution in 1966 she emerged publicly as a member of the party's Central Committee in charge of cultural affairs. She was personally responsible for the persecution of writers and artists and for decreeing what was acceptable in music, art, literature, and drama. She reportedly used her power to pay off old scores against professional rivals and increasingly ignored or countermanded her husband's advice. She was often vituperative and spiteful in her personal style and ruthless in carrying out the policies she favored. Both traditional and foreign works were banned in favor of a rigid "socialist realism" whose overtly political message was designed to appeal to the masses of peasants and workers.

During Mao's last years, when ill health and advancing senility obliged him to withdraw from the day-to-day management of affairs, Chiang Ch'ing and her radical colleagues appear to have greatly enhanced their power, and they were probably the chief architects of the Cultural Revolution as a whole after 1968. They made a bid for full power after the death of Prime Minister Chou En-lai in January 1976 and while Mao was in his final illness. After Mao's death in September, Chiang and her colleagues were arrested and denounced. At her trial she insisted that she alone had been faithful to Mao's vision, but most Chinese had come to fear and hate her, and she is still seen as the archvillain of China's dark years.

Imelda Marcos (born 1930) acquired great political power as the wife of President Ferdinand Marcos of the Philippines. She became notorious for her ludicrously extensive wardrobe, including, reputedly, the world's largest personal collection of shoes and a huge hoard of jewelry. Far more important, however, was the worldwide real estate and investment empire she and her husband built for themselves with the help of Filipino tax money, American aid, and open corruption.

Mrs. Marcos played a prominent public role, opening public housing projects that proved to be shams, raising money to build a hospital in Manila that only the very rich could afford to enter, and speaking on behalf of her husband at rallies and functions. Ferdinand Marcos suffered periodic bouts of illness with advancing years, and it was rumored that his wife intended to succeed him.

But the Marcoses lost the elections of 1986, and a quite different woman, Corazon Aquino (born 1933), became president. Her husband, Benigno Aquino, had been the principal opposition leader until his murder in 1983 by guards assigned to him by Marcos on his return from exile. Assuming the leadership of his party, Mrs. Aquino ran a vigorous election campaign against Marcos and was elected and installed in office with belated American support.

As president she began the long task of rebuilding responsible government and countering the appeal of entrenched Communist rebels. This required a reduction in the great power of the rich landed and business families; but Mrs. Aquino, herself a member of this elite, needed their support. Continuing Communist insurgency, defections from her coalition by ambitious rivals, and plots by former Marcos loyalists have made her task difficult, although she has remained personally popular with most Filipinos. Her political power base remains precarious, like her tenuous control over the army.

Chiang Ch'ing and Imelda Marcos did not advance the cause of women's liberation in Asia, but many other women did, and the movement gathered new strength in all of Asia after 1945. Mao Tse-tung said that "women hold up half the sky," and although China has not yet approached gender equality, great strides have been made there, and even in Korea and Japan, away from traditional female subservience and toward greater recognition of women's rights and their coequal role in society.

Women in East Asian Society

The position of women in contemporary East Asia varies widely. In China life for women remained essentially unchanged from the time of Confucius to the beginning of the twentieth century. The Chinese woman was considered a temporary member of her parents' household, to be transferred to her husband's control at marriage. She adopted her husband's surname, only then followed by her own. Upon her death, only her husband's family surname was recorded in her husband's genealogy, so that her personal identity was permanently effaced. Despite the achievement of some women of rank in scholarship and the arts, the average woman was, at least until she bore a son, near the bottom of the status hierarchy.

The impact of Western imperialism in the late nineteenth century brought the first challenge to the traditional system. Mission schools and colleges began to educate women and added support to the movements against footbinding, chaste widowhood, and the general subjugation of women. After the revolution of 1911, the first women's magazines began to appear, and the demand of the younger generation for greater freedom from parental control opened up new secondary and university education to girls. Pioneer feminists became doctors, lawyers, teachers, and active revolutionaries; there were even banks staffed entirely by women and serving a female clientele. Missionary boarding schools provided an important avenue of mobility for aspiring village girls, while in the cities they offered daughters of the merchant class a Western-oriented education and social contact with foreigners. World War II, with its increased demand for labor power and its dislocation of families, also increased social and economic opportunities for women.

After the revolution of 1949, women in the People's Republic were given basic legal rights for the first time. The Marriage Law of 1950 not only gave women the right freely to choose their husbands and equal responsibility for the raising of children but also established the right of women to own property and to choose an occupation. The effect of this legislation was galvanic. A newspaper estimated in 1953 that 2 million persons had been affected by divorce in Shanghai, Peking, Tientsin, and Wuhan alone.

In the same year the Ministry of Justice reported that 70,000 to 80,000 women were being murdered or forced into suicide each year as a result of family conflict or oppression. This backlash presaged a long struggle for genuine equality. By 1958 women comprised 50 percent of the agricultural labor force but were far from equally compensated with men; nor had they advanced far in penetrating the manufacturing sector, where they were still largely confined to the textile and tobacco industries. The commune movement of the late 1950s also had the effect of regimenting women. The top political and professional echelons were still almost entirely reserved for men. Twenty years after the revolution, only 10 percent of the members of the Communist party itself were women.

Official policy toward women in the early decades of the revolution reflected the drive to mobilize labor in general. The traditional extended family was drastically affected by land reform, forced resettlement, and the commune system. Not until 1974, as part of a campaign against the Confucian ethos, was the position of women systematically addressed, particularly the residual dominance of the patrilocal family. Even then, however, the primary impetus was economic rationalization and increased productivity.

The other major prong of social policy affecting women has been the campaign for birth control. Since the late 1970s women have been under extreme pressure to reduce the birthrate, in many cases through late-term abortions. At the same time, the economic and social importance of male offspring remains very high, since daughters still join their husbands' families and family welfare depends critically on the number of working members, with males almost always better paid. The result has been a revival of female infanticide, which, though condemned by the government, is nonetheless a direct result of the combination of its demographic policies with a still largely unreformed social system.

The status of women in the newly industrialized nations of Taiwan and Korea, the city-state of Singapore, and the British colony of Hong Kong displays the tension between traditional Chinese or Chinese-influenced family culture and the needs of market capitalism, which tends to treat workers in isolation from the family or other social unit. On the one hand, wage remuneration has given women in these labor-intensive, export-oriented societies some potential economic independence; on the other, they are still expected to remain firmly under family control.

In Southeast Asia, where women have long had independent property rights and have been as active as men in the economy, the primary change in the past several decades has been the increasing differentiation between town and country life. The postwar constitutions of Burma, Thailand, and Indonesia gave legal equality to women, and in South Vietnam the Family Law Bill of 1958 spelled out such equality in detail. In the Islamic states of Malaysia and Indonesia, the special problem of women, apart from the general Islamic subordination of them, is

the persistence of polygamy and the ease of divorce, which has mounted in some areas as high as 60 percent.

The situation of Japan is unique in that it is the only East Asian nation in the front rank of the world's industrial powers. Before the twentieth century, women had been subservient to men, as in Confucian China, and unable to inherit property even when male descendants were lacking. As elsewhere in East Asia, a feminist movement had arisen early in the century, led particularly by Hiratsuka Raicho (1886–1971), who founded the first Japanese women's magazine, *Blue Stockings*, in 1911, and Ichikawa Fusae (1893–1981), who was later to serve in the House of Councillors almost continuously from 1953 until her death. A feminist organization, the New Women's Association, was founded after World War I, although it was not until the American occupation that women were able to win formal legal equality and the right to vote. Traditional patterns of deference continued to prevail, however. In 1980 fully 75 percent of the eligible women voted in the nationwide elections, as opposed to 53 percent of the male electorate; yet only 3 percent of the members returned to the Japanese Diet were women.

Social and economic inequality between the sexes continues to characterize Japan. The introduction of coeducation in 1950 led to a doubling of girls in secondary schools during the next decade and more than tripled the number of female university students. Yet university women are still regarded as exceptional in Japan. Women now comprise 35 percent of the work force but still lag far behind their male counterparts in earnings and benefits. They are exploited in every sector, including agriculture, where they constitute the majority of the labor force but are almost entirely unpaid workers on family farms. Most working women leave their employment upon marriage, only to reenter 10 to 15 years later at the bottom of the pay scale. Laws have recently been passed, however, providing child care and other benefits for working women. Japanese feminists are particularly active in such causes as consumer and environmental protection, peace and nuclear disarmament movements, and the fight against job discrimination.

Rewards and Problems of Modernization

East Asia as a whole had the highest economic growth rate of any part of the world in the decades following World War II, a pattern that still continues. Hong Kong, Taiwan, and South Korea rapidly developed in the wake of Japanese economic success after the mid-1950s. Much of this development was on the Japanese model, beginning in light industry and consumer goods and continuing into heavy manufacturing and precision goods. Singapore's growth paralleled that of Hong Kong; both were tiny Chinese city-states that had originally prospered as trade centers and then moved into "high-tech" industrialization and processing. In China, despite the drag exerted by antiurbanism and revolutionary ideology, industrial growth was impressive, and after 1980 overall economic development was rapid. In Southeast Asia several of the major cities besides Singapore, notably Bangkok in Thailand and Manila, the Philippine capital, grew enormously as booming commercial and light industrial centers.

Much of this growth rested on the East Asian tradition of disciplined hard work and organized group effort, but it was striking enough to attract world attention and speculation about its causes. East Asia does share, to varying degrees, an originally Chinese culture, which has for centuries stressed education, hard work, and group effort, perhaps enough to override other differences in the pursuit of advancement.

But modernization has brought new problems. These include the rapid erosion of traditional cultures (to the distress of many East Asians), the rise of huge cities inadequately supplied with basic services or housing, and fearsome pollution of urban and rural environments. Japan was only the first to suffer dramatically from industrial pollution as a result of the unprecedented concentration of cities and manufacturing in its lowlands. As a high-income and technologically developed society, Japan was also the first to deal successfully with at least some of those problems.

For the rest of East Asia, as in the developing world as a whole, largely unchecked pollution is still increasing, with deeply worrisome long-term consequences for human welfare. Other East Asian countries have passed environmental legislation too, but in most cases it is not effectively enforced. Chinese, Korean, Taiwanese, and Southeast Asian cities are dangerously polluted, their air heavy with soot and fumes, and their water supplies, often inadequate to supply their mushrooming populations and factories, are loaded with poisonous industrial residues. In rural areas heavy applications of chemical fertilizers, the use of largely unregulated chemical pesticides, and the development of factories cause additional environmental damage. Massive cutting of trees to feed the demand for new construction has exposed slopes to erosion, and silt chokes rivers and irrigation systems. In large parts of Southeast Asia the tropical rain forest that covers much of the area is rapidly being depleted to provide lumber for both domestic and world markets, with potentially serious effects on local and world climate.

Most of these countries are bent on rapid industrial and economic growth; they are reluctant to slow that growth or add to its costs, even by limiting the worst of the environmental damage. Such controls, many of them argue, are for rich countries. It may take more human disasters such as Japan experienced to persuade them that their own welfare is at stake. Japan, lacking most industrial raw materials and having to import nearly all of its oil, has invested proportionately more heavily in nuclear power than any country in the world, ignoring its location in one of the world's major earthquake zones. China has huge domestic supplies of coal, most of it with a high sulfur content, which supplies about three-quarters of the nation's energy. These problems may become future disasters as East Asia continues to modernize.

Urban growth in East Asia has taken place very rapidly and with minimal planning, especially outside China. Even in China industrial and residential areas have not been adequately separated; housing, water supply, and other urban services lag seriously behind demand; Peking has grown uncontrollably. These problems are equally pronounced in urban centers such as Seoul, Taipei, Bangkok, Manila, and Djakarta, where unchecked migration from rural areas has swollen city populations without a substantial increase in basic services.

While the problems of modernization seem especially serious in the cities, it is there also that the chief forces for economic growth are centered. The cities are the major industrial bases, educational centers, commercial and financial hubs, and centers of intellectual and cultural ferment, as they were in the history of the West. So far Asia has tended to repeat the Western experience of economic and industrial development, which in its early and middle stages was unpleasant and unhealthy for most people. As the process has gathered momentum in Asia after the Second World War, one may hope that the rest of the Western experience will be repeated too, as the cities become, like those in Japan, centers of improved welfare. Their advances can then spread more widely over each country.

꼬ᄀ   꼬ᄀ   꼬ᄀ

The years after 1945 were momentous for East Asia. New nations were born out of the former colonial regimes in Southeast Asia. Korea regained its independence, only to be torn by war and split by superpower tensions. China underwent the largest revolution in history, measured by the numbers of people involved, the scope of its change, and the length of both its gestation and its active course, including the convulsive struggles of the Cultural Revolution. A shattered Japan rebuilt its economy and rose to world industrial leadership. But although each of these major areas had its own internal problems, the dominant trend in all of them was economic growth and industrialization. East Asia as a whole, led by Japan, became the world's largest and most rapidly expanding commercial and industrial network, as it had long been its most populous geographic region. It remains to be seen whether the area's new economic power will be reflected proportionately in new political power on the world scene.

Suggestions for Further Reading

Japan

Dore, R. *City Life in Japan: A Study of a Tokyo Ward*. Berkeley: University of California Press, 1967.

Hane, M. *Modern Japan: A Historical Survey*. Boulder, Colo.: Westview Press, 1986.

Immamura, H. E. *Urban Japanese Housewives*. Honolulu: University Press of Hawaii, 1986.

Kawai, K. *Japan's American Interlude*. Chicago: University of Chicago Press, 1960.

Lebra, T. S. *Japanese Women: Constraint and Fulfillment*. Honolulu: University Press of Hawaii, 1984.

Minear, R. *Victor's Justice*. Princeton, N.J.: Princeton University Press, 1971.

New, C. *The Troubled Encounter: The United States and Japan*. New York: Wiley, 1975.

Reischauer, E. O. *The Japanese*. Cambridge, Mass.: Harvard University Press, 1980.

Stockwin, J. A. *Japan: Divided Politics in a Growth Economy*. London: Weidenfeld & Nicolson, 1975.

Storry, R. *A History of Modern Japan*, rev. ed. New York: Penguin Books, 1982.

Vogel, E. *Japan as Number One: Lessons for America*. Cambridge, Mass.: Harvard University Press, 1979.

China

Bonavia, D. *The Chinese*. New York: Harper & Row, 1984.

Ch'en, J. *Mao and the Chinese Revolution*. Oxford: Oxford University Press, 1967.

Dietrich, C. *People's China: A Brief History*. New York: Oxford University Press, 1986.

Fairbank, J. K. *The Great Chinese Revolution*. Cambridge, Mass.: Harvard University Press, 1986.

Johnson, K. A. *Women, the Family, and Peasant Revolution in China*. Chicago: University of Chicago Press, 1983.

Lee, H. Y. *The Politics of the Chinese Cultural Revolution*. Berkeley: University of California Press, 1978.

Leeming, F. *Rural China Today*. London: Longman, 1985.

Liang, H., and Shapiro, J. *Son of the Revolution*. New York: Knopf, 1984.

Murphey, R. *The Fading of the Maoist Vision*. New York: Methuen, 1980.

Nathan, A. *Chinese Democracy*. Berkeley: University of California Press, 1986.

Riskin, C. *China's Political Economy: The Quest for Development Since 1949*. New York: Oxford University Press, 1987.

Schram, S. *Mao Tse-tung: A Preliminary Reassessment*. New York: Simon & Schuster, 1984.

Selden, M. *The Yenan Way in Revolutionary China*. Cambridge, Mass.: Harvard University Press, 1971.

Terrill, R., ed. *The China Difference*. New York: Harper & Row, 1983.

White, M. K., and Parrish, W. *Urban Life in Contemporary China*. Stanford, Calif.: Stanford University Press, 1985.

———. *Village and Family in Contemporary China*. Chicago: University of Chicago Press, 1978.

Woronoff, J. *Asia's "Miracle" Economies*. New York: Sharpe, 1986.

Korea

Clough, R. N. *Embattled Korea*. Boulder, Colo.: Westview Press, 1987.

Lee, K. B. *A New History of Korea*, trans. E. W. Wagner. Cambridge, Mass.: Harvard University Press, 1985.

Southeast Asia

Greene, G. *The Quiet American*. New York: Viking, 1957. (A novel about the Vietnam War.)

Martin, L. K., ed. *The Asian Success Story*. Honolulu: University Press of Hawaii, 1987.

Steinberg, D., ed. *In Search of Southeast Asia: A Modern History*, rev. ed. Honolulu: University Press of Hawaii, 1987.

Nationalism and Revolution: India, Pakistan, Iran, and the Middle East

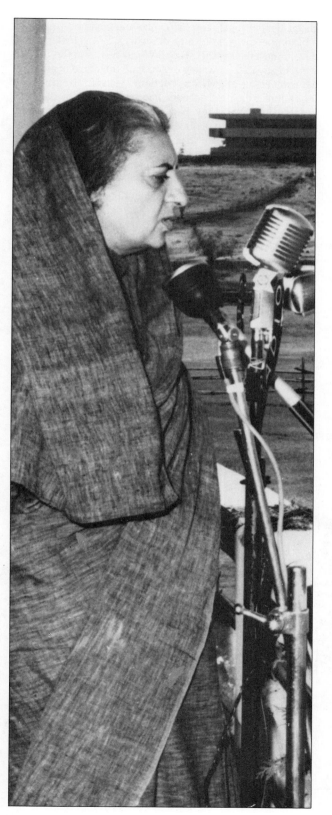

The postwar period was a time of rapid and radical change throughout the Middle East and central Asia. Britain and France withdrew or were forced from their colonial dominions, and a host of new nations emerged, some with ancient roots in the area, others the product of modern nationalism. Among the former, India and Egypt regained their old independence, one as a constitutional democracy, the other as a revolutionary socialist state. Among the latter, Pakistan, the world's third largest Islamic state (after Indonesia and India), emerged from the Muslim-majority regions of pre-1949 India. Some states, such as Jordan, were created primarily as buffer zones or as acts of political compromise, while in other cases nationalist movements, such as those of the Palestinians and the Kurds, remained frustrated. The most controversial new nation to emerge in the region was the state of Israel, where a powerful modern nationalism sought to revive the heritage of a kingdom that had flourished nearly 3,000 years before. Throughout the postwar decades, however,

Indira Gandhi in 1972, addressing a crowd at Kolhapur, India. [UPI/Bettmann Newsphotos]

the region as a whole has been characterized by turmoil and instability, culminating in the 1980s in a war between Iran and Iraq that now ranks as the fourth bloodiest conflict of the twentieth century.

South Asia: Independence and Political Division

The Indian subcontinent, known since 1947 as South Asia, is composed of the separate states of Pakistan, India, Bangladesh, Nepal, and Sri Lanka and contains well over a billion people, one-fifth of the world. British colonialism died in the ashes of the Second World War, and the British were in any case unwilling to continue their rule of an India determined to regain its freedom. Gandhi, Nehru, and other Indian political leaders had spent most of the war years in jail after they had refused to support the war without a promise of independence. Their example inspired many new followers, and by 1945 the independence movement was clearly too strong to be denied by a Britain now both weakened and weary of colonialism. The conservative wartime leader Winston Churchill was voted out of office. Churchill had been rigidly opposed to Indian independence. During the war he had declared, "I was not

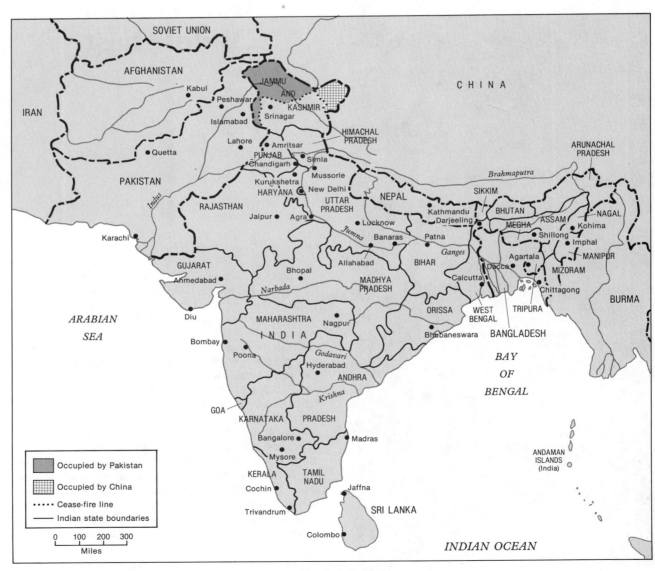

39.1 South Asia Today

made His Majesty's first minister in order to preside over the liquidation of the British Empire," and he was contemptuous of Gandhi. Lord Wavell, military commander in India and the first postwar viceroy, wrote in his diary: "Churchill hates India and everything to do with it. He knows as much of the Indian problem as George III did of the American colonies. . . . He sent me a peevish telegram to ask why Gandhi hadn't died yet."

The new Labour government under Clement Attlee moved quickly toward giving India its freedom. Elections were held in India early in 1946, but by then it had become clear that support for a separate state for Muslims had gained strength. The Muslim League, the chief vehicle for this movement, had been founded as early as 1906, but until 1945 it was supported by only a few Muslims, most of whom remained willing to work with the Congress party as the main agent of politically conscious Indians. The Muslim League's president, Mohammed Ali Jinnah (1876–1948), had earlier been a member of the Congress party and was even for a time its president. He and a few other Muslim leaders became dissatisfied with the Congress party's plans for a secular independent state that deemphasized religious identity and with the party's leaders' unwillingness to reserve what Jinnah regarded as adequate positions and representation for Muslims. Hindus and Muslims had lived together peacefully for most of nine centuries, even at the village level. Persian Muslim culture had blended in with indigenous elements to form modern Indian civilization. Both groups were long-standing

Mohammed Ali Jinnah in 1946. Note his totally Western dress. [India Office Library of the British Library.]

parts of the Indian fabric. It was hard to see them as irreconcilable.

Jinnah, like Nehru, was British educated. In his earlier career as a British-trained lawyer, he had paid little attention to Islam, and he knew no Urdu, the language of Islam

◉ Muslim Solidarity: Jinnah's Call ◉

Jinnah made a number of speeches during the Second World War in his effort to promote Muslim solidarity and political action. Here are excerpts from a 1943 speech.

The progress that Muslims, as a nation, have made during these [past] three years is a remarkable fact. . . . Never before has a nation, miscalled a minority, asserted itself so quickly and so effectively. . . . We have created a solidarity of opinion, a union of mind and thought. . . . Let us cooperate with and give all help to our leaders to work for our collective good. Let us make our organization stronger. . . . We, the Muslims, must rely mainly upon our own inherent qualities, our own natural potentialities, our own internal solidarity, and our own united will to face the future. . . . Train yourselves, equip yourselves for the task that lies before us. The final victory depends upon you and is within our grasp. You have performed wonders in the past. You are still capable of repeating history. You are not lacking in the great qualities and virtues in comparison with other nations. Only you have to be fully conscious of that fact and act with courage, faith, and unity.

Source: W. T. de Bary, ed., *Sources of Indian Tradition,* vol. 2 (New York: Columbia University Press, 1964), pp. 286–287.

in India. But as he saw his political ambitions threatened by the success of Gandhi and Nehru, he shifted his allegiance to the Muslim League and began to use it to persuade Muslims that a Hindu-dominated India would never, as he put it, give them "justice." He found support among some of the communal-minded (those who put separate group loyalty above national feeling) and also from Muslim businessmen, especially in the port city of Karachi, who saw a possible way of ridding themselves of Hindu competition. Nehru and others insisted that communalism had nothing to do with religion and that the exploitation of religious differences by a few politicians for their own ends fueled communal tensions. Hindus were often more active and more successful in business than Muslims, they were generally more educated, and as the great majority in India they also dominated politics and the professions. But they did not generally discriminate against Muslim intellectuals or professionals. Some other Muslim political figures, like Jinnah, saw greater opportunity for themselves if they could have their own state and supported the League in its campaign to convince Muslims that "Islam was in danger." When such relatively peaceful tactics did not produce enough result, Jinnah and the League began to promote terror and violence, urging Muslims to demonstrate and to attack Hindus in order to call attention to their cause.

The Congress party was slow to respond or to offer Muslims or the League a larger share in an Indian future. Gandhi and Nehru in particular were reluctant even to consider partitioning India just as it was about to win freedom. This tended to increase the League's fear of a Hindu threat to Muslims and its resort to tactics of violence. In the later stages of the long negotiations during 1946 and 1947 Jinnah offered to give up the demand for Pakistan (as the separate Muslim state was to be called) if he could be guaranteed the position of first prime minister of independent India. That demand was rejected, and Jinnah remained adamant in insisting on a separate state, of which he could be the head. Successive British representatives tried to work out a solution in sessions with the Congress party and the League, ending with the special mission in 1947 of Lord Louis Mountbatten (1900–1979), the wartime supreme commander in Southeast Asia. Mountbatten was appointed viceroy of India, with the sole charge of working out the terms for independence as quickly as this could be done.

If independence had been granted at any time before 1939, as most Indians and most British had wanted, the issue of partition would not have arisen. Jinnah was able to use the war years, while the Congress party leaders were in jail, to build his political base and then to spread the fear of cultural engulfment and oppression among his followers. Muslim-Hindu violence, once stirred up by the Muslim League, acquired its own dreadful momentum on both sides, especially in regions that were nearly evenly divided between the two religious communities, such as Punjab and East Bengal. Mob riots and mass killing spread widely. Although Mountbatten, like Nehru and Gandhi, hoped to avoid handing over power to a divided India, by July he as well as the party leaders recognized that partition and the creation of Pakistan were inevitable. Nehru

Nehru and Mountbatten in New Delhi, 1947. The two men developed an immediate liking for each other, which greatly eased the transition to independence. [UPI/Bettmann Newsphotos]

remarked bitterly that "by cutting off the head we will get rid of the headache," while Gandhi continued to regard partition as "vivisection."

Lines were drawn to mark off the predominantly Muslim northwest and western Punjab and the eastern half of Bengal as the two unequal halves of Pakistan, separated from each other by nearly 1,000 miles. At midnight on August 14, 1947, the Republic of India and the Islamic state of Pakistan officially won their independence. Gandhi boycotted the independence day celebrations in New Delhi, going instead to Calcutta to try to quell fresh outbreaks of mass violence there as refugees streamed in from eastern Bengal.

The first months of independence were tragically overshadowed by perhaps the greatest mass refugee movement in history as over 10 million people fled from both sides in 1947 alone, about a million of whom were victims of mob massacre along the route. When it was all over,

50 million Muslims continued to live in India much as before, and India still has more Muslims than Pakistan. For those who chose to migrate to Pakistan, including further millions after 1947, life in the new state (with an initial population of 70 million), was hard in the first chaotic years as Pakistan struggled to cope with the flood of refugees. Hindus remaining in Pakistan soon found that they had little place in an Islamic state that explicitly discriminated against all non-Muslims, and within a few years most of them had migrated to India, depriving Pakistan of many of its more highly educated and experienced people. For the educated elite of both countries, including the army officers who soon faced each other across the new boundaries, partition divided former classmates, friends, and professional colleagues who had shared a common experience, training, and values.

The partition lines also split the previously integrated cultural and economic regions of densely populated Punjab

◉ India and the Sense of History ◉

On the eve of independence, Nehru addressed the Constituent Assembly in 1946 with his characteristic eloquence, stressing the sense of history that many Indians share.

As I stand here, . . . I feel the weight of all manner of things crowding upon me. We are at the end of an era and possibly very soon we shall embark upon a new age. My mind goes back to the great past of India, to the 5000 years of India's history, from the very dawn of that history which might be considered almost the dawn of human history, until today. All that past crowds upon me and exhilarates me, and at the same time somewhat oppresses me. Am I worthy of that past? When I think also of the future, the greater future I hope, standing on this sword's edge of the present between the mighty past and the mightier future, I tremble a little and feel overwhelmed by this mighty task. We have come here at a strange moment in India's history. I do not know, but I do feel, that there is some magic in this moment of transition from the old to the new, something of that magic which one sees when the night turns into day and even though the day may be a cloudy one, it is day after all, for when the clouds move away, we can see the sun again. Because of all this I find a little difficulty in addressing this House and putting all my ideas before it, and I feel also that in this long succession of thousands of years, I see the mighty figures that have come and gone and I see also the long succession of our comrades who have labored for the freedom of India. And we stand now on the verge of this passing age, trying, laboring, to usher in the new. . . .

I think also of the various constituent assemblies that have gone before and of what took place at the making of the great American nation when the fathers of that nation met and fashioned a constitution which has stood the test for so many years. . . . [He then mentions the French and Russian revolutions also.] We seek to learn from their success and to avoid their failures. Perhaps we may not be able to avoid failures, because some measure of failure is inherent in human effort. Nevertheless we shall advance, I am certain . . . and realize the dream that we have dreamed so long.

Source: W. T. de Bary, ed., *Sources of Indian Tradition,* 4th ed., vol. 1 (New York: Columbia University Press, 1964), pp. 350–352.

and Bengal and caused immense disruption. Since the division was by agreement based solely on religion, nothing was considered except to separate areas with a Muslim majority, often by a thin margin. Many districts, villages, and towns were nearly evenly balanced between the two religions, which were deeply intertwined over many centuries of coexistence. The partition cut through major road and rail links, divided rural areas from their urban centers, and bisected otherwise uniform regions of culture and language.

The Kashmir Conflict

The still nominally independent native states, under their own Indian rulers, were technically given the choice to join India or Pakistan, but there was really no choice for the few Muslim-ruled states or smaller Muslim-majority areas surrounded by Indian territory, which were absorbed or taken over, including the large state of Hyderabad in the Deccan, Muslim-ruled but with a Hindu majority.

Kashmir, which lay geographically between the two rivals, had a Muslim majority but a Hindu ruler and its own hopes for independence. The ruler, Hari Singh, delayed his decision until his state was invaded by "volunteer" forces from Pakistan, and he agreed to join India in return for military help. Indian paratroops arrived just in time to hold Srinagar, the capital, and the central valley, the only economically important and densely settled part of the state. The cease-fire line, which still stands, gave roughly the western quarter of Kashmir to Pakistan, but the larger issue of which state Kashmir should belong to has never been resolved.

The Kashmir dispute has continued to poison relations between the two states and has sparked three inconclusive wars. Thus to the tragedy of partition and the violence following it has been added chronic Indo-Pakistani tension instead of the cooperation that would be more appropriate between two developing nations born out of the same context and sharing a common cultural tradition. Mahatma Gandhi, who had prayed and labored so hard to stop Hindu-Muslim violence, ironically became one of its victims when he was murdered on January 30, 1948, by a Hindu extremist who considered him too tolerant of Muslims. Nehru saw his death as "the loss of India's soul" and commented, "The light has gone out of our lives and there is darkness everywhere."

India After Independence

In the Republic of India, parliamentary democracy and British-style law have survived repeated tests and remain vigorous. Jawaharlal Nehru, who became prime minister at independence and served until his death in 1964, was a strong and revered leader who effectively dominated the new nation. He presided over the creation of 16 new language-based states within a federal structure. Federalism was necessary in any case given India's size and diversity, and language was the single most obvious basis of regional differences. Although Nehru and others were reluctant to acknowledge the importance of language-based regionalism, it became clear after several years of debate and negotiation that such a concession would have to be made. The states created by 1956 were the size of France, Germany, or Italy in population, and each coincided approximately with the distribution of what were officially declared to be "major" languages out of the many hundreds spoken. Each of these major languages had its own proud history and literary tradition, older, more extensive, and with more speakers than most European languages.

Hindi, the language of the Delhi area and the upper Ganges valley, was declared the official national language, to be used in national government and taught to all Indians in every region, while leaving each state its own regional language in its schools and legislatures. English, familiar to educated people in all the states, was retained as an "associate language" at the national level and continued to be taught in nearly all schools. Indian English has more speakers than American English, and it too has diverged from its British origins. Hindi is the mother tongue of only about 30 percent of the population, and even so consists of several mutually unintelligible dialects. No other native Indian language comes close. Hindi was therefore the obvious choice for a nationwide language, but for most Indians it remains a foreign tongue. It is resented especially by Dravidian-speaking southerners as yet another example of "northern domination" and the "oppression of Delhi."

India Under Nehru

Nehru saw India well launched on the path of economic development, both agricultural and industrial, but he acknowledged the Gandhian legacy by providing special government support for handicraft production and for small-scale rural industries, especially the hand weaving of cotton cloth. As in China, these were often not economically practical, but symbolically they were important because of their long association with the nationalist movement, and they also offered employment in rural areas, where most Indians still lived. Traditional village councils were revitalized and used as channels for new rural development in agriculture as well as other village enterprises.

But the most rapid growth was in the expanding cities, where industry and new economic opportunity were concentrated for the fortunate and which attracted streams of rural immigrants. Housing and other basic human services

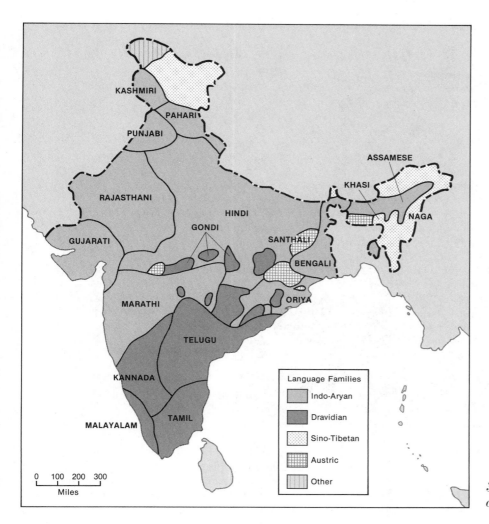

39.2 *Major Languages of India*

such as water, sewers, power, education, health care, and urban transport could not keep up with a mushrooming population, including many still unemployed, a familiar problem throughout the developing world. New immigrants took time to make a place for themselves and lived, or squatted, in slums or in the open air, but the wider opportunity that the cities potentially offered continued to draw them despite the squalor and hardships with which most of them had to contend. Calcutta, Bombay, and Delhi–New Delhi, the three largest cities, are among the largest in the world, but like most, including big American cities, combine luxurious lifestyles for a few and ragged poverty for many.

Despite government efforts to slow it down, India's population continued to grow, owing primarily to improved nutrition from agricultural gains and advances in public health that largely eliminated epidemic disease; life expectancy rose and death rates fell. But rising production, including new industrial output, more than kept pace, and

per capita incomes began a slow and steady rise, which still continues. A third or more of the population, however, remained in severe poverty as the top third won new wealth.

The Nehru years were marred by a border dispute with China, in the remote Himalayas, which erupted in brief hostilities in 1962. Fresh from their armed reoccupation of Tibet, the Chinese won a quick victory. The Chinese retained control of the small border area they had claimed, which they needed for access into western Tibet, where they were concerned to put down rebellion against their rule. India had refused to discuss the Chinese claim and foolishly tried to eject the Chinese troops, an effort for which the Indian army was poorly prepared. Nehru had attempted, with much success until then, to build pan-Asian friendship and cooperation in partnership with China as the other major Asian power and to promote India as the leader of the nonaligned nations. His death was hastened by the failure of relations with China, which he took

---

◉ India's World Role ◉

Nehru saw India as an emerging power in the modern world and as a major Asian leader. He wrote about this and about East-West relations.

One of the major questions of the day is the readjustment of the relations between Asia and Europe. . . . India, not because of any ambition but because of geography and history . . . inevitably has to play a very important part in Asia . . . [and is] a meeting ground between the East and the West. . . . The Middle East and Southeast Asia both are connected with India. . . . You cannot consider any question concerning the Far East without India. . . . In the past the West ignored Asia, or did not give her the weight that was due her. Asia was really given a back seat . . . and even the statesmen did not recognize the changes that were taking place. There is considerable recognition of these changes now, but it is not enough. . . . I do not mean to say that we in Asia are in any way superior, ethically or morally, to the people of Europe. In some ways, I imagine that we are worse. There is however a legacy of conflict in Europe. . . . We might note that the world progressively tends to become one. . . . [We should] direct [our] policy towards avoiding conflict. . . . The emergence of India in world affairs is something of major consequence in world history. We who happen to be in the government of India . . . are men of relatively small stature. But it has been given to us to work at a time when India is growing into a great giant again.

Source: W. T. de Bary, ed., *Sources of Indian Tradition,* 4th ed., vol. 1 (New York: Columbia University Press, 1964), pp. 352–353.

---

as a personal failure, calling it "a Himalayan blunder" (*Himalayan* is understandably used in India to mean "enormous").

With his passing, India felt it had been left leaderless and was fearful about finding an adequate successor. Nehru had been the symbol and architect of the new India and its dominant political figure for more than a generation. But the gap was filled through normal democratic processes by the old Congress party moderate Lal Bahadur Shastri as prime minister. His promising start, including an agreement with Pakistan to reduce tensions, was cut short by his death after only a year and a half. The party then chose Nehru's daughter, Indira Gandhi (no relation to the Mahatma), who quickly established her firm leadership and vowed to continue Nehru's and Shastri's policies.

India had maintained its political stability and democratic system through successive crises, despite a still largely illiterate electorate and the multiple problems of new nationhood, wars, internal and external tensions, and poverty, a record matched by few other new nations. Illiterate voters demonstrated a surprising grasp of political issues, and a far higher proportion of those over 18 voted than in the United States. The Indian press remained freely critical of government shortcomings and offered an open forum for all opinions. India's faithfulness to the system it inherited and has continued to cultivate stands in contrast to the failure of parliamentary democracy and the rise of totalitarianism, dictatorship, censorship, and the police state in so much of the rest of Asia and the world. American policy toward India has been slow to recognize the importance of this major democratic state, second only to China in total numbers.

☙ INDIRA GANDHI

Like her famous father, Indira Gandhi (1917–1984) was British-educated and widely traveled and came to office with long experience as her father's confidant after her mother's death in 1943, acting as hostess to streams of Indian and foreign visitors who sought Nehru's counsel or favors. Mrs. Gandhi had separated from her husband, Firoze, a journalist, a few years after their marriage, and she reared her two sons in her father's house. She impressed all who knew her with her razor-sharp mental powers and her keen grasp of political affairs, but during her father's lifetime she modestly eschewed any public role. After his death in 1964, she accepted the cabinet post of minister for information in Shastri's government, but only as one of many able women who had already held cabinet rank and who had been prominent earlier in the long struggle for independence.

The Ministry of Information gave her new public visibility, and when Shastri suddenly died, she entered the contest for Congress party leadership, which ended in her overwhelming victory and subsequent endorsement by the national electorate. She was a consummate politician within the Congress party, and many accused her of becoming merely a power broker, but without her father's charisma or deft diplomacy. Indira Gandhi shared her father's commitment to Western values but drew her political strength mainly from left of center. During her years as prime minister, from 1966 to 1977 and from 1980 to her death in 1984, she was a commanding figure.

Drought in 1965 and 1966, which caused much suffering but relatively few deaths, led India to become one of the first countries to launch a major campaign in the so-called green revolution, an agricultural policy that achieved higher yields with improved seeds and expanded irrigation and fertilizer production. By the end of the 1960s there had been a real breakthrough in production, and by 1975 India was again self-sufficient in grains and had a surplus for export, a situation it has since maintained. Industrial growth also continued, but the gap between rich and poor widened. The green revolution benefited farmers with enough land and capital to use and pay for the new seeds, irrigation, and fertilizers. Small farmers and people in non-agricultural areas sank further into relative poverty, and tenancy and landlessness rose. Upwardly mobile urban workers, managers, professionals, and technicians were more than matched by rising numbers of urban and rural poor. These growing pains were typical of economic development everywhere, including the nineteenth-century West.

In part to quash charges of corruption and to weaken her political opposition, Mrs. Gandhi in June 1975 proclaimed a state of national emergency in the name of "unity" and "reform." Civil rights were suspended, the press was controlled, opposition leaders and "trouble-makers" were jailed, the constitution was amended to keep the courts from challenging the government, and a series of measures was announced to control inflation, inefficiency, hoarding, and tax evasion. It seemed the end of India as the world's largest parliamentary democracy, but Mrs. Gandhi miscalculated her people's judgment. When she finally permitted a national election in January 1977, she and her party were defeated. The Indian democratic system and its tradition of free expression were soundly vindicated, but the coalition government of non-Congress parties that emerged under the aged Morarji Desai floundered and finally dissolved into bickering, paving the way for Mrs. Gandhi's return to power in the elections of January 1980.

Although she made no effort to reestablish the "emergency," Mrs. Gandhi's response to tensions and protests by disaffected regions and groups became increasingly rigid and authoritarian. Meanwhile, economic growth continued in agriculture and industry. By 1983 over a third of India's exports were manufactured goods, many of them from high-tech industries that competed successfully on the world market. India had become a major industrial power, and its pool of trained scientists and technicians, products of the British-inherited education system, was exceeded only by those of the United States and the Soviet Union. In 1974 its own scientists completed the first Indian nuclear test, though the government continued to insist it would not make nuclear weapons but would instead concentrate on the production of nuclear energy for peaceful purposes. Indian satellites joined American and Russian

Grain being fed into a storage silo in New Delhi: one of the fruits of the green revolution. [UPI/Bettmann Newsphotos]

ones in space, and Indian-made microchips began to revolutionize industry. At the same time, many rural sectors remained in the bullock cart age, and the urban poor slept under bridges near the new luxury apartments of those who had done well in the rapidly growing economy.

The Sikhs

Of the many groups that felt disadvantaged, the most continuously and effectively organized were the Sikhs of Punjab. Ironically, Punjab had led the nation in agricultural progress under the green revolution, and although not all Sikhs were well off, as a group they had prospered more than most others. Part of their discontent was no doubt related to the rising expectations common to periods of development. Having put the green revolution to work with their traditional entrepreneurial talents and hard work, the Sikhs grew increasingly angry at government controls on agricultural prices imposed by Mrs. Gandhi's fight against inflation, which severely restricted farmers' profits. A religious community founded in the fifteenth century as a reformist offshoot from Hinduism, the Sikhs also wanted greater recognition, increased political status, more control of Punjab state (where they were in fact a minority), and greater provincial autonomy.

Sikhs comprised only about 2 percent of India's population, and Mrs. Gandhi was reluctant to favor them or to make concessions on provincial autonomy when she had to confront so many similar demands from other discontented groups and protest movements. But her stance on the Sikhs was rigid to a fault; she met violence with more violence, capped by the storming of the Golden Temple in Amritsar, sacred to Sikhism, which a group of extremists had fortified. Four months later, in October 1984, she was gunned down by two of her Sikh guards in the name of Indian freedom. Many others had come to see her as corrupted by power.

India After Indira Gandhi

The Congress party chose Gandhi's son Rajiv (born 1944) to succeed her, and in January 1985 this choice was overwhelmingly confirmed in a nationwide election. Rajiv Gandhi offered peace to the Sikhs, granted many of their more reasonable demands (including new borders for Punjab that created a state with a Sikh majority), and in other ways as well showed himself to be a sensitive and responsible leader. As the grandson of Jawaharlal Nehru, Rajiv Gandhi had many of the same qualities of personal charm, ability, and diplomacy. He had never sought power and was accordingly trusted, but the reservoir of popular support for him began to decline as critics claimed that the Congress party under his leadership remained more interested in power-brokering than in serving all the needs of the people. India, in fact, has been a largely one-party

democracy since independence, although the Congress party was defeated in 1977 and after Nehru's death became increasingly split into rival factions. Many Indian voters have felt that they were not offered adequate alternatives and that government was often insensitive to their needs.

Three basic problems still resisted solution: miserable poverty for the bottom third or more of India's people, a population still growing too rapidly (one root of poverty), and continued outbreaks of violence among many of the groups in its highly diverse population. Caste continued to weaken slowly, especially in the cities, but most Indians remained in traditional village worlds, where caste connections still served an important function. Higher or "dominant" castes, as they were often called, resented and tried to suppress the rise of Untouchables. Hindus and Muslims fought one another in some areas. Sikh terrorism and Hindu reprisals threatened to plunge Punjab and Delhi into civil war.

Nationalism grew among Indian intellectuals late in the nineteenth century, but it did not stimulate a mass movement until the 1920s. Even Gandhi did not reach all Indians, and the country since independence in 1947 has been moving toward creating a single overriding sense of Indian identity that can take precedence over regional, religious, caste, and other group loyalties. India well illustrates the dictum of the British historian Lord Acton (1834–1902): "The nation is not the cause but the result of the state. It is the state which creates the nation, not the nation the state." To many—perhaps most—Indians it remains more important that they are Bengalis or Marathas or Tamils, Hindus, Sikhs, or Muslims, Brahmins or Untouchables, than that they are fellow Indians. It will take more time before such group loyalties can be merged into common "Indianness" through common experience in a single national state. This problem is shared with most new nations, many of which have difficulties comparable to India's. The difference is partly the scale of India's problem—some 800 million people with a diversity greater than all of Europe—and partly in the recency of its modern experience as a nation-state after 5,000 years of regional and group separatism. Since 1949 the traditional world of the village and its ties has expanded to include considerable integration with the modern world of the cities and with the larger world of regional states sharing a common language and culture.

Within India's federal political structure, central economic planning and an expanding national civil service also help to join people in mutual self-interest. Regular bus services on all-weather roads link every village with these wider worlds and with a national network. The sense of nationhood needs time to grow, but while it cannot come about in a single generation, that is clearly the hope of India's future.

The war against poverty, as the government called it, is of course related to communal and intercaste tensions

Women botany students at Ludhiana Agricultural University in Punjab. [© Marc and Evelyne Bernheim, 1981/Woodfin Camp]

and is the greatest challenge of all developing countries. India has done better economically than most of the so-called Third World, perhaps overall better than China, whose record has been praised by many economists in the West. But India's new wealth has not been well distributed. The hope is that as development proceeds and as efforts to limit population growth succeed, the fight against poverty may make significant headway. This is the same path followed by the West a century earlier as the fruits of the Industrial Revolution eventually raised the economic level of most people. Life expectancy rates and living conditions for most inhabitants are in fact better for modern Calcutta and Bombay than for nineteenth-century Manchester and New York. In India, as in most of Asia, the economic trends are strongly positive, and literacy is growing fast as universal free education spreads. This oldest of world civilizations still keeps much of its ancient tradition alive and draws strength from it as it also pursues the path of modernization.

Bangladesh and Pakistan

East Bengal, which became East Pakistan in 1947, was one of the subcontinent's poorest areas and had virtually no industry of any kind. It had been heavily dependent on Calcutta as its educational, cultural, commercial, industrial, and shipping center, through which its exports and imports moved and where nearly all transport lines were focused. East Bengal contained over half of Pakistan's population and produced three-quarters of its exports, mainly jute, but much of the profit went to Karachi. Moreover,

East Bengal was strikingly underrepresented in and underfunded by the national government. Even its language, Bengali, was not officially recognized.

Pakistan continued to be run by and for the small clique of Karachi and Punjabi businessmen and politicians who had pushed for its creation, although the faltering effort at parliamentary government was swept aside by a military dictatorship in 1958. When elections, finally held in late 1970, produced a victory for the East Pakistan party on a platform of greater autonomy, the military government in West Pakistan responded by arresting the party's leader, Sheikh Mujibur Rahman, and then turning its army and tanks against demonstrators in East Pakistan in a mass slaughter. About 10 million refugees poured across the nearby Indian border by the end of 1971, mainly to already overcrowded Calcutta. Guerrilla actions by Bengalis against the terrorism of the West Pakistani forces finally brought in the Indian army, which in ten days ended the slaughter.

With the Pakistani army defeated, East Pakistan became the new People's Republic of Bangladesh in December 1971. Sheikh Mujib, as he was called, became prime minister and the refugees returned home, but Bangladesh proved unable to achieve political stability or even effective government. Mujib was murdered by his own army in 1974, following charges of corruption. His military successor was assassinated in 1981, and no clear or successful political order has since emerged. Bangladesh remains one of the world's poorest nations, despite the agricultural productivity of its rice lands, burdened by a still too rapidly growing population and hampered by the lack of forceful planning and leadership. Periodic flooding caused in part by deforestation has compounded Bangladesh's problems.

What remained of Pakistan, in the west, continued to be governed by a military dictatorship, although there was some respectable economic growth in both agriculture and manufacturing. Jinnah died within a year of independence, and in 1958, after a series of corrupt and ineffective prime ministers, the country came under martial law, as it has been much of the time since. The army commander in chief, General Zia-ul-Huq, seized power in a 1977 coup d'état, dissolved the politically corrupt parliamentary system, and in 1979 executed the American-educated former prime minister, Zulfkar Ali Bhutto, after he was found guilty of conspiring in the murder of a political opponent. In an effort to break the connection with the "Karachi clique," the capital had been moved in stages between 1961 and 1965 to a new planned site called Islamabad ("City of Islam"), about 10 miles from the city of Rawalpindi in the northwest; the two cities operate as an urban unit, linked by commuting workers and civil servants, and now rival Karachi in size. Lahore, an older and larger city and the chief center of Muslim culture, was more central, but it was thought to be too close to the border with India to be safe. Pakistan lacks most industrial resources, except for some recently discovered oil, and it began in 1947 well below the all-Indian average economic level. Nevertheless, it has avoided major famine, greatly increased irrigation in Punjab and the Indus valley, and built a basic industrial structure. As in India and China, however, economic gains continue to be retarded in per capita terms by a growing population. As an Islamic state, Pakistan has been reluctant to promote family planning or to limit the growth of its population. Islamic fundamentalism similar to that in Iran has also won some support in Pakistan.

More recently the government became deeply involved in aiding and providing refuge for the Afghan guerrilla resistance to the Soviet-supported government in Kabul, the Afghan capital, only about 100 miles from the Pakistani frontier. Such activity further strengthened Pakistan's role as a Cold War client of the United States and produced a new flow of American military supplies. But such aid had little relevance to Pakistan's domestic problems and again prompted Indian complaints that the arms were being stockpiled for use against India. The two states have fought two small wars, in 1965 and 1971, in both of which Pakistan's military power came virtually exclusively from U.S. equipment. Pakistan has seemed useful to the United States as a regional anticommunist bulwark against the Soviet Union and as a friend and intermediary with China, particularly during America's resumption of relations with the People's Republic in the early 1970s.

When China became a Soviet rival instead of an ally and soon thereafter came into conflict with India over a border dispute, Pakistan took the Chinese side. American surveillance flights over the Soviet Union took off from bases in northwestern Pakistan, and in 1971 Washington used the Pakistan-China connection to respond to Chinese overtures, leading to President Richard Nixon's visit to Peking. But these international power ploys had little or nothing to do with Pakistan's people or their needs. Indeed, they put the Pakistanis at serious risk both by exposing them to the threat of war, the suffering resulting from further conflict with India, and the massive diversion of resources from urgently needed development into military expenditures. India and Pakistan, with so much history and so many problems in common, have more recently begun to move cautiously toward a less antagonistic relationship, but only after 40 years of tragic tension and conflict. This process has been helped by Soviet withdrawal from Afghanistan and by the death of General Zia in a plane crash in 1988. Bhutto's daughter, Benazir, was elected prime minister as Zia's successor in an open contest, thus becoming the first woman to govern an Islamic state, and Pakistan returned to a more democratic path.

Pakistan is a diverse state, resembling India on a smaller scale. It includes a majority whose mother tongue is not the official national language, Urdu, and many groups who feel unrepresented, neglected, or oppressed by the government. Outside the Indus valley and western Punjab, where most of the population is concentrated, Pakistan encompasses arid mountains along its western and northern borders, inhabited by people like the Baluchis and Pathans whose cultures and histories have little in common with those of the lowlands. A truly national state that can include them as partners has not yet emerged. The partition of India has become a permanent fact of life, but Pakistan has still to develop into a nation.

Sri Lanka

The island nation of Ceylon (which changed its name officially to Sri Lanka, an old precolonial name for the country, in 1975) lies across the Palk Strait from India. It made a relatively easy transition to independence in 1948, primarily as a consequence of Indian independence rather than of any strong nationalist movement on the island itself.

Sri Lanka had been under Western domination since the first Portuguese bases there early in the sixteenth century, and its small size and population were easily overwhelmed by foreign influences. Many of the elite were more British than Sinhalese (the majority inhabitants) in language and culture, and many regretted the end of their membership in the British Empire. But in the mid-1950s Ceylon was swept by what has been called "second-wave nationalism," a belated but emotional determination to rediscover and assert its own identity. In the elections of 1956 self-serving politicians stirred up communal feelings among the dominant Sinhalese against the minority Tamils, originally immigrants from nearby South India, who form about a fifth of the population. Approximately half of them had lived there, at the northern tip of the island, for over

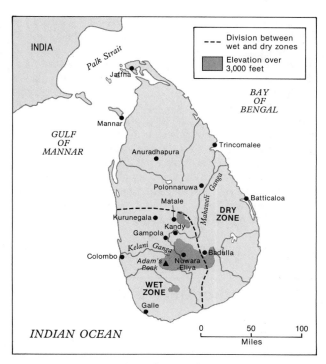

39.3 Sri Lanka

The Sri Lankan economy was disrupted by chronic fighting, which retarded its generally healthy growth after 1948. Nevertheless, Sri Lanka became self-sufficient in rice by the late 1970s, thanks to major investments in new irrigation and agricultural technology, and at the same time maintained the profitable plantation sector in tea, rubber, and coconuts, which continued to dominate its exports. Education, literacy, and public health were improved still further from the relatively high levels established under British colonial control, and per capita incomes remained somewhat higher than in any of the other South Asian states, thanks in part to the government's success in limiting population growth. But violence and terrorism on both sides, in an atmosphere close to civil war, eroded the British-inherited system of parliamentary government and the rule of law. In 1987, with Indian mediation and commitment to prevent clandestine support from South India to Tamil terrorists in Sri Lanka, an agreement was reached that gave some local autonomy to areas in which the Tamils were a majority and which aimed to end the fighting. But much bitterness and tension remained.

Sirimavo Bandaranaike is an example of the improving status of women in South Asia. Like China and Japan, South Asia traditionally accorded women a relatively low status, especially during the centuries of Muslim dominance in the north. There were exceptions, including even women military figures and heads of state among the Marathas and other groups and dominant figures at court such as Nur Jahan (see Chapter 19). The Westernization that accompanied British control led to increasing education for women; many educated women were prominent in the independence movement, and in government and the professions after 1947. In general this was a relatively small group, an intellectual and Westernized elite, while most South Asian women, especially in the villages, remained uneducated and subservient to their husbands to a degree that seemed extreme to Westerners. There were exceptions, particularly in South India and in the southern state of Kerala, where ancient matriarchal and matrilocal* social forms persisted to some degree. Husbands in this region commonly walk behind wives and defer to them, while property and family names often descend through the female line. Elsewhere in South Asia, women such as Sirimavo Bandaranaike and Indira Gandhi have achieved great prominence on the national scene since independence.

1,000 years, but the other half were more recently arrived laborers recruited to work the tea plantations in the central highlands. The Tamils are Hindu and speak primarily their own language, which has heightened their distinction from the Buddhist (or for the elite, nominally Buddhist) Sinhalese. They became a convenient scapegoat to stimulate the sense of Sinhalese nationalism, like the Chinese in many Southeast Asian countries.

The tragic pattern of communal violence between Sinhalese and Tamils began with the 1956 election of S. W. R. D. Bandaranaike, on a platform of Sinhalese-only nationalism. Like Jinnah, he had been educated in Britain and was thoroughly Westernized; his personal ambition and his keen mind turned to communalism, until then of little interest to him, as a means of creating a new political base for himself. Once called into existence by his campaign of discrimination, it could not be laid to rest, and he was assassinated in 1959 by a Sinhalese Buddhist who felt he had not gone far enough.

His place was taken by his widow, Sirimavo Bandaranaike (born 1916), the world's first woman prime minister. She continued most of his policies and ruled with a firm hand for two terms, 1960–1965 and 1970–1977. Like her husband, she was British-educated, sophisticated, and extremely able, showing a talent for both international and domestic diplomacy. Her authoritative rule restored order and relative stability at a time of domestic crisis. Tamils felt more and more excluded and oppressed and took to terrorism as a weapon, finally demanding a separate state.

The Turbulent Middle East

When World War II ended, Britain was still the paramount power in the Middle East, directly controlling Egypt, Pal-

---

*In a matrilocal society, a husband joins the wife's family.

estine, Transjordan, Iraq, southern Arabia, and the Persian Gulf. In the next decade, however, it withdrew almost completely from the region, leaving a vacuum of power that was filled by Arab nationalism, superpower rivalry, and the emergence of the state of Israel.

The Establishment of Israel

Britain's first withdrawal was from Palestine, where the conflict between Palestinian Arabs and Jewish settlers, compounded by an influx of refugees and Holocaust survivors, had reached a flashpoint. That conflict, in turn, represented a clash between the traditions of two great religions and the aspirations of two nascent nationalisms.

A small number of Jews had always lived in Palestine, to which the faithful believed their people would someday return to reestablish the ancient nation of Israel and await the coming of the messiah. In the mid-seventeenth century a messianic pretender, Sabbatai Zevi, had led an ill-fated expedition of thousands of Jews to Palestine. The serious immigration to the region that commenced two centuries later was spurred, however, not by millennial fervor but by a secular nationalist movement, Zionism.

The Zionist Movement

Zionism was a historic response to Jewish circumstances in nineteenth-century Europe. Emancipation had eliminated most of the civil restrictions that had confined Jews to the ghetto for centuries past without offering them a clear role or place in European society. Many Jews simply attempted to assimilate themselves into the larger nationalities among whom they lived, preserving their religious and cultural traditions while identifying themselves as Frenchmen, Germans, or Russians. To Zionist writers, however, as for other nineteenth-century nationalists, political identity as a nation was the final and necessary goal of every people's development. The Zionist position was supported negatively by anti-Semitic writers such as Count Gobineau (1816–1882), who argued that the Jews were an alien, unassimilable element that threatened the racial and cultural integrity of any nation that harbored them. The increasing tempo of anti-Semitic incidents in the late nineteenth century, culminating in the pogroms of Russia and, in the West, in the long, drawn-out agony of the Dreyfus affair (see Chapter 32), suggested to many that assimilation was a mirage. The result was a mass exodus of European Jews, particularly from Russia, from which 3 million emigrated between 1882 and 1914.

The great majority of Jewish emigrants went to the United States, Canada, South America, and Australia; scarcely 1 percent joined the trickle of earlier settlers in Palestine. The real impetus for creating a Jewish state in the Holy Land came from Theodor Herzl, the founder of modern Zionism. Herzl realized that the large-scale settlement necessary to provide a critical mass of population in Palestine would require both organization and capital. His solution was the Jewish National Fund, which undertook the purchase of all land to be occupied by the settlers. He envisioned a society whose growth would be rationally planned rather than subject to the vagaries of speculators and profiteers. New towns would be erected, carefully spaced and separated by belts of collective farmland and linked by express trains and superhighways. In short, the Zionist state was to be a utopian society in which mutualistic socialism was combined with technological progress and centralized planning.

Conflict over Palestine

Herzl's vision and Hitler's persecution combined to increase the Jewish population of Palestine tenfold between the end of World War I and the end of World War II. From less than a tenth of the total population of the territory in 1917, it had increased to a third by 1947. The Arab majority greeted the Jewish influx first with suspicion and then alarm. The entry of Western powers into the formerly Ottoman-controlled lands of the Middle East after World War I stimulated Arab nationalists. For such nationalists, the Jews were a spearhead unit of Western colonization. Their fears were underscored by the report of an American commission Woodrow Wilson sent to the area, which concluded that the Jewish National Fund intended the eventual purchase of the entire territory of Palestine, thereby dispossessing its Arab population. From an Arab perspective, Jewish socialism was simply the handmaiden of British imperialism.

Confronted by bitter and sometimes violent Arab resistance, the British government decided in 1939 to cap Jewish population in Palestine at one-third of the whole and to limit future land purchases severely. These new controls had broader implications, as Britain, the United States, and other powers sought to restrict Jewish emigration from Nazi-held Europe in general. When the dimensions of the Holocaust were discovered at the end of World War II, there was general humanitarian pressure to establish Palestine as a refuge for the remnants of European Jewry. The British Labour party, soon to be in power, endorsed Zionist demands for the immediate creation of a Jewish commonwealth and in December 1944 called for the transfer of Palestinian Arabs to neighboring countries. Nothing came of these or more moderate postwar proposals for a federated Jewish-Arab state, which were rejected by both sides. The British, unwilling to maintain their trusteeship in the face of mounting Jewish terrorist attacks and unable to contain the flood of illegal immigrants who ran their blockade, laid the problem before the United Nations in April 1947. After months of lobbying and debate, the General Assembly adopted in November a proposal to divide Palestine into three Jewish and three Arab sectors forming a Jewish and an Arab state, with Jerusalem as an international zone. All seven areas were to be linked in an economic union.

The General Assembly resolution was greeted with rejoicing by the Jews but unanimous rejection throughout the Arab world. The British refused to implement it on the grounds that it had not been accepted by both sides and withdrew their troops without making provision to transfer authority to either one. When the last units departed on May 14, 1948, the Jewish communal government proclaimed the state of Israel. A general struggle immediately

ensued for control of Palestine. Armies from Egypt, Syria, Lebanon, Jordan, and Iraq poured across the frontiers to assist the Palestinian Arabs, but the better-organized Jewish forces more than held their own. When a United Nations armistice halted the fighting in 1949, Israel controlled a third more territory than had been granted the Jews under the partition plan, while nearly 750,000 Palestinian Arabs had taken refuge in Lebanon, Syria, Jordan, and the Egyptian-occupied Gaza strip in southern Palestine.

While still fighting, Israel held its first elections in January. The fiery socialist David Ben-Gurion (1886–1973), founder of the first Jewish agricultural cooperative, or *kibbutz*, became Israel's first prime minister and its dominant political figure until his retirement in 1966, and the veteran Zionist leader Chaim Weizmann (1874–1952) was installed in the ceremonial office of president.

◉ Israel or Palestine? ◉

Two rival nationalisms with ancient roots in the same land put forward their claims to modern sovereignty over it.

The land of Israel was the birthplace of the Jewish people. Here their spiritual, religious, and political identity was shaped. Here they first attained statehood, created cultural values of national and universal significance, and gave to the world the eternal Book of Books. . . .

On the 29th November, 1947, the United Nations General Assembly passed a resolution calling for the establishment of a Jewish state in the land of Israel; the General Assembly required the inhabitants of the land of Israel to take such steps as were necessary on their part for the implementation of that resolution. This recognition by the United Nations of the right of the Jewish people to establish their state is irrevocable. This right is the natural right of the Jewish people to be masters of their own fate, like all other nations, in their own sovereign state.

THE PALESTINIAN NATIONAL CHARTER

Article 1: Palestine is the homeland of the Arab Palestinian people; it is an indivisible part of the Arab homeland, and the Palestinian people are an integral part of the Arab nation.

Article 2: Palestine, with the boundaries it had during the British mandate, is an indivisible territorial unit.

Article 3: The Palestinian Arab people possess the legal right to their homeland and have the right to determine their destiny after achieving the liberation of their country in accordance with their wishes and entirely of their own accord and will.

Article 4: The Palestinian identity is a genuine, essential, and inherent characteristic; it is transmitted from parents to children. The Zionist occupation and the dispersal of the Palestinian Arab people . . . do not make them lose their Palestinian identity and their membership of the Palestine community, nor do they negate them.

Sources: Declaration of the Establishment of the State of Israel, May 14, 1948; Decisions of the National Congress of the Palestine Liberation Organization, July 1–17, 1968.

❦
DAVID BEN-GURION, ISRAEL'S FOUNDER

The single most important figure in the establishment of modern Israel was David Ben-Gurion. Born David Gruen in Plonsk, Poland (then a part of the Russian empire), he was the son of a local Zionist leader. At 17 he startled the local Jewish community by calling for armed resistance against the state-backed pogroms. Three years later, in 1906, he emigrated to Palestine, where he worked as a farmer in Jewish settlements and adopted the Hebrew name Ben-Gurion ("son of the lion"). Expelled by the Ottoman Turks for his political activity at the outbreak of World War I, he eventually reached New York, where he met and married Pauline Munweis, his wife until her death in 1968.

Ben-Gurion responded to the Balfour Declaration by joining the British-sponsored Jewish Legion. Returning to Palestine after its capture from the Turks, he threw himself ardently into political organization and over the next two decades forged the institutions that were to become the nucleus of the Jewish state. In 1920 he founded the Histadrut labor confederation and ten years later its political arm, the Mapai, or Israeli Workers party, which later merged into the Labour party. Besides leading both organizations, he was elected chairman of the Zionist Executive, the supreme directive body of the Zionist movement, and head of the Jewish Agency, its executive branch.

When Britain, responding to Arab pressure, abruptly pulled back on its commitment to a Jewish homeland in 1939, Ben-Gurion urged and later led armed resistance to it. In May 1942 he assembled an emergency meeting of Zionists in New York that decided on the establishment of a Jewish state as soon as the war in Europe was ended. With the proclamation of Israel six years later, Ben-Gurion became simultaneously its first prime minister and minister of defense, welding its disparate and often conflicting resistance forces into a national army.

With a single brief interval, Ben-Gurion remained Israel's prime minister from 1948 to 1963, firmly shaping Israel's identity as a modern industrial state and a bulwark of Western influence in the Middle East. To critics of his frank espousal of Western interests, including the acceptance of $800 million in reparations from West Germany for Nazi war crimes, he replied characteristically, "What matters is not what Gentiles will say but what the Jews will do." Never wavering in his belief that modern Israel was the direct and legitimate heir of the ancient Jewish state, he was determined at all costs to establish it and to give no quarter to anyone who opposed it. This led him into an assault against Egypt's President Nasser in 1956 that brought about the fall of the Eden government in

A 1955 photo of Israeli leaders. David Ben-Gurion is on the right; from the left, the others are General Moshe Dayan, Premier Moshe Sharett and President Itzhak Ben-Zvi. [UPI/Bettmann Newsphotos]

Britain and contributed to the demise of the Fourth Republic in France, but left Ben-Gurion himself stronger than ever at home. Yet in his last years in office he attempted, though unsuccessfully, to institute peace talks with Arab leaders.

Ben-Gurion resigned abruptly in June 1963, in part because of dissension within the Labour party. He founded a new opposition party as a vehicle for his views, but it won only ten seats in the Knesset (parliament). Spent as a political force, he nonetheless remained a charismatic and controversial elder statesman, and to a world public the short, rotund man with the familiar pugnacious features and the halo of white hair remained the image of Israel itself. In failing health, he retired from all political activity in 1970 to spend his last years at the kibbutz of Sde-Boker in the Negev, writing his memoirs. He lived just long enough to see the twenty-fifth anniversary of the founding of Israel in 1973 and to experience the Yom Kippur War, which revealed how vulnerable, and how far from peace, the new nation still was.

Israeli Society: Challenge and Conflict

The new state chose a system of proportional representation rather than electoral districting for the Knesset, so each member represented the nation as a whole. This meant full representation for minority views but entailed coalition government as well; no single party has won a majority to date. Nevertheless, the Labour bloc, strongly Zionist, social-democratic and secular in character, controlled the government until 1977.

Despite its unity in times of crisis, Israel has been beset by contradictions from the beginning. The ideologically active left wing of the Labour bloc remained attached to the early Zionist ideal of social regeneration through physical labor and communal living exemplified in the kibbutz. The new Jewish man and woman, purged of the effects of centuries of ghettoization and bonded to the soil, would constitute the basis of a genuinely egalitarian society. What emerged instead, however, was an urbanized, consumer-oriented society that bore considerable resemblance to the social-democratic regimes of the West. Class divisions within the Jewish population intensified, particularly between the well-to-do eastern European settlers who dominated the Labour bloc and the so-called oriental Jews who flocked to Israel from the Arab states and Iran in the first two decades of independence and now comprise 65 percent of its Jewish population. This poorer and less literate group, wooed by the conservative Likud coalition of Menachem Begin (born 1913), turned the Labour coalition out of office after nearly three decades.

The tension between old socialist ideals and the reality of a consumer society is paralleled by that between religious fundamentalists and secular liberals. The fundamentalists, a hard core constituting 15 percent of the Jewish population, retain Orthodox diet, dress, and observance and have successfully insisted on religious controls over marriage, divorce, inheritance, and other social arrangements. Often confrontational, their influence derives not merely from their unity as a single-issue pressure group but from the unresolved debate over the nature of a "Jewish" state.

From its inception, Israel has advertised itself as the homeland of Jews the world over, and under the Law of Return, any Jew emigrating to it is automatically entitled to citizenship. Nonetheless, there is no generally accepted criterion of what defines a Jew, and a prolonged debate in the Knesset in 1960 and 1961 failed to produce one. Originally Semitic, the Jews have become racially heterogeneous through the long centuries of the Diaspora, and fair-haired Scandinavians mix today on the streets of Tel Aviv and Jerusalem with brown-skinned Indians, black Ethiopians, and even Chinese. Still more problematic is the attempt to define them as a "people," since they share few common customs, and fewer than half the population speaks the official language, Hebrew, as a native tongue. Least of all can they be distinguished on the basis of a common faith, since many secularized Jews in Israel and elsewhere no longer keep up religious observances. The fundamentalists alone have developed a clear standard, excluding anyone whose mother was not Jewish or who had not undergone Orthodox conversion. In practice, however, the authorities have simply accepted as a Jew anyone professing to be one. Even Israelis converting to Christianity have continued to be accorded the rights of citizenship.

The unresolved question of what defines a Jew goes to the heart of the central contradiction of present-day Israeli society: the situation of its Arab minority. Although enjoying formal equality, including the right to vote and to sit in the Knesset, the Arabs are clearly second-class citizens in the Jewish state, and their movements and activities are subject to regular military scrutiny and interference. Moreover, while Israelis can justifiably point to levels of health, literacy, and material prosperity among Arabs within their borders considerably higher than those of neighboring countries, they remain far below the national norm as a whole. The problem was compounded by Israeli occupation of the West Bank of the Jordan River as a result of the 1967 war; this doubled the number of Arabs under Israeli jurisdiction. For 20 years the occupation was relatively benign, but since late 1987 popular rebellion has repeatedly erupted.

Whether or not the Arabs under Israeli rule would be prepared to accept integration into a multiethnic state remains part of the larger question of Palestinian self-determination and the future of Arab-Israeli relations in general. In either case, their presence poses a challenge to an Israel defined, by whatever standard, as a purely Jewish state.

The Arab-Israeli Wars

The more immediate questions in the Middle East involve the general nonrecognition of the Israeli state by the other powers in the region apart from Egypt and the insistence of Palestinian Arab nationalists that Palestine be restored to them. Four wars have been fought to date over this question. All have resulted in military victories by the Israelis, none in settlement. The Palestine War of 1948–1949 established Israel as an independent state while creating a major refugee problem. The Israelis refused to allow the 750,000 Palestinians who had fled their homes to return without guarantees of security from their neighbors, a point that became moot as their abandoned homes and lands were occupied by the almost equal number of Jewish immigrants, mostly from the other countries of the Middle East, who flocked to the new state in the first two years of its existence. In effect, the massive population transfer envisioned by Zionists had taken place. But neighboring Arab states were both unable and politically unwilling to accept the tide of Palestinian refugees who crowded at their borders. Instead, the refugees were interned in squalid camps along the narrow Gaza strip and on the West Bank of the Jordan River, previously part of Palestine but now annexed by Jordan. The Palestinian Arabs thus became a people without a country.

Arab nationalists regarded Israel not only as a usurper in the region but also as an agent of Western interests. These suspicions were dramatically confirmed in October 1956 when Israel joined an amphibious Franco-British force in an invasion of Egypt, whose new president, Gamal Abdel Nasser (1918–1970), had nationalized the French- and British-owned Suez Canal Company in response to a cutoff of Western aid. For the British in particular, Egypt's control of the canal threatened important interests in the Far East, while Israel, alarmed at an Egyptian arms buildup, felt that a preemptive strike was essential to its security. With British air support, the Israelis swept across the Sinai peninsula to join assault troops at Port Said. But the war ended in fiasco. The United States, furious at the independent action of its allies, joined the Soviet Union in calling for an immediate cease-fire and withdrawal. Faced with the threat of ruinous economic sanctions, the British and French capitulated. Israel too withdrew, the damaging identification with colonial interests only partly compensated by the opening of the Gulf of Aqaba to Israeli shipping.

The long-term effects of the episode were profound. Nasser emerged as a hero and became the recognized leader of the Arab world until his death. The government of Sir Anthony Eden was forced from office in Britain, and with the assassination of the Iraqi king, Faisal II, and his prime minister, Nuri-es Said, in 1958 the British were forced from their last bases in the Middle East. The United States entered the breach to forestall Soviet influence, and in 1958 its own forces invaded Lebanon in support of pro-Western leadership. With Nasser and other Arab radicals looking to the Soviet Union for aid and the crucial oil resources of the region at stake, the Middle East became an important new area of superpower rivalry.

In the meantime, a new war brewed between the Arabs and the Israelis. In 1964 Israel began to divert water from the Jordan River to irrigate its southern Negev desert. Jordan protested, and an Arab summit conference in Cairo set up a command force that would coordinate guerrilla activities against Israel and serve as a provisional government for the refugees, the Palestine Liberation Organization (PLO). Terrorist attacks and retaliatory raids increased, while Egypt, Syria, and Jordan announced plans to attack Israel. When Nasser ordered United Nations peacekeeping forces to leave the Sinai in May 1967 and closed the Gulf of Aqaba, the Israelis struck first. In a campaign lasting only six days, Israel swept again across the Sinai, seized the West Bank, including the contested city of Jerusalem, and drove Syria off the strategic Golan Heights on the borders of eastern Galilee. Israel had occupied some 28,000 square miles, three times the size of its own territory. It was one of the swiftest and most decisive military victories in history. In November the United Nations Security Council adopted a resolution demanding Israel's withdrawal from the areas it had conquered but also calling for a settlement that would recognize its right to exist.

Humiliated by the Six Day War, Egypt rearmed with Soviet assistance and planned a new attack with Syria. This time preparations were secret. Israel was caught napping by the Yom Kippur War of 1973, so called because it began with a surprise attack on the annual Jewish day of atonement. Initially repulsed, Israeli forces quickly recovered and with American tactical assistance had regained the offensive when fighting was halted after 18 days on October 24. But they had suffered heavy losses on the ground and in the air, and the conflict brought the superpowers closer to confrontation in the Middle East than ever before.

The Yom Kippur War underlined the dangers posed by continued instability in the Middle East. It brought in its wake a threatened cutoff of oil exports that struck at the very heart of the Western economy. Accordingly, the American secretary of state, Henry Kissinger, conducted arduous "shuttle diplomacy" between the major Arab capitals and Jerusalem in an attempt to find a basis of accommodation. These efforts bore fruit in the Camp David accords of September 1978 between Egypt and Israel. The two parties agreed to a phased withdrawal of Israeli troops from the Sinai and a vaguely defined autonomy for the West Bank and the Gaza strip. President Sadat had ended the humiliating occupation of Egyptian territory and gained a major American subsidy for his ailing economy. Prime Minister Begin had won diplomatic recognition for the first time from an Arab state, secured Israel's western frontier, and divided its two principal antagonists, Egypt and Syria. Both men shared a Nobel peace prize. But Sadat was denounced in the Arab world for having made a separate peace with Israel and for failing to secure Palestinian rights. Egypt lost the position of leadership it had enjoyed for the previous quarter century, and Sadat himself was assassinated by Muslim fundamentalists in October 1981.

<hr>

♛
JERUSALEM: A CITY DIVIDED

<hr>

The divisions of the contemporary Middle East are nowhere more vividly symbolized than in the historic city of Jerusalem. Today, with its population of around 300,000, it reflects both a rich past and a divided present. The New City, to the west, is a modern capital, with fashionable shops, a convention center, and a Kennedy memorial. It also houses the Knesset, Israel's parliament, and the Israel Museum. The Old City, once shared by Arabs and Jews, is in the Arab quarter, a labyrinth of bazaars, market alleys, and narrow, winding streets. Administratively, the New and Old City are now one; politically, they are as far apart as ever.

After a long history as a religious center first of Judaism and then of Christianity, Jerusalem was conquered by the Muslims in 629. Unlike previous conquerors, they treated the city with great respect. It was sacred to Islam because the Jewish temple was the place to which Muhammad had been carried in his famous vision prior to ascending the seven heavens into the presence of the Almighty. Accordingly, the caliph Omar built a wooden mosque in the temple compound, above which rises today the gold-domed, octagonal structure known as the Haram el-Sharif (Dome of the Rock), still much as it was when completed in 691. For several centuries Christian and Jewish worship was permitted side by side with Islamic. As unrest increased in the Arab world, however, particularly after the ninth century, access to the holy sites became hazardous.

Crusader Europe recaptured Jerusalem and established Christian control of the city again for most of a century (1099–1187) and briefly from 1229 to 1244, expelling Jews and Muslims. Thereafter for nearly 700 years the city again reverted to Islam, first under the Mameluke Turks (1250–1517) and then under their Ottoman successors (1517–1917). It reached a low point in the seventeenth and eighteenth centuries as Ottoman rule decayed, but European influence began to revive it in the nineteenth century, and with the advent of Zionism it became a focus of Jewish immigration.

The British capture of Jerusalem in 1917 inaugurated its modern period. Extensive rebuilding took place, and access to the holy places was given to the three faiths, although at Muslim insistence the ban on Jews entering the Dome of the Rock on the site of the temple mount was maintained. Communal violence between Arabs and Jews erupted as early as 1929, and when the British withdrew from Palestine in 1947, the city (whose population was by now more than 60 percent Jewish) was besieged by the Arab Legion. The armistice of 1949 divided it into an Israeli and an Arab (Jordanian) sector, separated by barbed wire, sandbags, and sniper fire. The Six Day War gave Israel full control of the city, which was itself a major battlefront.

Jerusalem continues to house its three faiths. Its Christian community is particularly variegated, with Protestant, Catholic, Greek Orthodox, Armenian, Abyssinian, and Coptic churches represented. The city's shrines are once again open to all, but its future remains clouded by the Arab-Israeli controversy. As in the days of the prophet Ezekiel, it can be said of the city: "This is Jerusalem; I have set her in the midst of nations."

Arab Nationalism

Until the late nineteenth century communal identity among the various Arab peoples of the Middle East had little to do with political self-determination or territorial units. Under the Ottoman system members of each religious faith—Muslim, Christian, and Jewish—lived in an independent community governed according to its own law by its clerical hierarchy. Communal consciousness was therefore awareness of religious values and customs rather than ethnic differentiation. Although religious rivalries often had a territorial dimension, not until the final breakup of the Ottoman Empire and the arrival of Western imperialism did such rivalries become identified with control of political entities with discrete boundaries. The idea of nationhood in its modern meaning was, as in so many other parts of the world, a Western import that cut across religious, cultural, and tribal affiliations.

Despite a major Arab cultural revival in the nineteenth century centered in Cairo, Beirut, and Damascus, there was no serious call for Arab separation from the Ottoman Empire until Neguib Azouri, a Palestinian Arab living in Paris, published *The Awakening of the Arab Nation* in 1905, in which he envisioned a united Arab state stretching from the Persian Gulf to the Suez Canal. The revival of Turkish nationalism after the Young Turk revolution of 1908 galvanized its Arab counterpart. Moderate Arabs who had been content with the idea of greater political autonomy within the Ottoman framework rather than independence now faced a regime in Istanbul bent on more rigorous controls. When Turkey allied itself with the Central Powers in World War I, Britain, already in quest of oil for its modernized navy in the region, promised support for a united Arab state to the sharif of Mecca, Hussein ibn-Ali, in return for military assistance.

This promise was not kept. In 1920 Britain and France

divided the Arab provinces of the former Ottoman Empire between them as mandates under the League of Nations, with Britain adding Palestine, Transjordan, and Mesopotamia (Iraq) to its former protectorate in Egypt, and France gaining Syria and Lebanon. Although ibn-Saud united the vast interior of the Arabian peninsula as Saudi Arabia in the 1920s and proclaimed a kingdom in 1932, Britain remained in firm control of most of its coastline. At the same time, American companies began a vigorous exploitation of oil resources in Saudi Arabia and Iraq. World War II saw the Middle East turned into a major theater of operations, with Germany's failure to gain access to the oil fields a crucial factor in its defeat.

The status of some of the Arab trust territories evolved during the interwar period. Iraq had achieved at least enough of the appearance of a state to be admitted to the League of Nations in 1932, although British influence remained strong. In Transjordan a strongman who ruled with British backing, the Amir Abdullah, was recognized as a king in 1946, but British control was still so transparent that not until 1955 was the renamed kingdom of Jordan, including the West Bank area seized in the Palestine War, admitted to the United Nations. The pace of change was even slower in Syria and Lebanon, where the French showed little inclination to prepare their territories for statehood. French control lapsed during the Nazi occupation, however, and in 1946 both became independent. Although far more advanced economically than Britain's mandates, both countries faced special challenges. Lebanon had no sectarian majority; a variety of Muslim and Christian groups vied for dominance. Syria, despite its proud heritage, was fragmented by religious and tribal divisions among both its majority Muslim and minority Christian populations. In Syria these tensions remain barely under control; in Lebanon they erupted in 1975 in a civil war that precipitated anarchy, invasion, and foreign occupation.

The end of World War II brought rapid changes. In 1945 the League of Arab States was formed under British auspices, consisting originally of Egypt, Syria, Lebanon, Iraq, Transjordan, Saudi Arabia, and Yemen. Although many of these states were as yet in no credible sense independent, they rapidly became so as British influence waned, and it was the league that coordinated the 1948 invasion of Palestine. Defeat at the hands of the tiny Jewish army provoked a military coup in Syria, an upsurge in anti-Western sentiment, and an agonizing reassessment of the wider problems of Arab development and unity.

Nasser and the Egyptian Revolution

The most significant result of this ferment came in Egypt, where in 1952 the military revolution led by Gamal Abdel Nasser drove out the corrupt, British-supported King

Farouk, spelling the end of Britain's role in the Middle East and hence of the last direct Western presence in the region.

Nasser was born in 1918, the son of a postal clerk in upper Egypt. Like many young Egyptians of modest origin, he joined the army as a means of gaining educational opportunities and career advancement. His fellow graduates in the 1938 class of the military academy were mostly of similar background, the sons of minor officials, petty merchants, commercial agents, and small landowners. They shared a common sense of frustration at Egypt's continued dominance by Britain and a sense of alienation from the older and wealthier officer corps. Under Nasser's leadership they began to meet on a regular basis to discuss the nation's problems and to plan for its future. By 1942 this group had evolved into a central committee with smaller cells throughout the army. Contacts were also established with religious organizations and foreign Arab leaders. The army's humiliation in the Palestine War strengthened the resolve of the young officers to reform the nation. Now banded together as the Free Officers' Society, they staged a virtually bloodless coup on July 23, 1952, that brought a revolutionary council to power. At first the council attempted to govern the country through its civilian institutions and bureaucracy. When the latter refused to implement the council's directives on land reform, a military dictatorship was proclaimed.

The council's nominal head was a senior general, Muhammad Naguib, but Nasser remained its true leader. It was he who decided on the policy of "guided democracy." Political parties and parliamentary institutions remained the goal of the regime, he declared, but until the masses had been prepared for active political life by reform and education, these could only serve the interests of the few. The press was brought under government regulation, and political activity was exercised through a single mass party, the Arab Socialist Union. In 1954 Nasser assumed direct control of the revolution as prime minister, and two years later he unveiled a constitution guaranteeing basic rights, including racial, religious, and sexual equality.

Nasser's revolution was as much social as political. While most of Egypt's 25 million people lived on an annual per capita income of $60, an elite of 12,000 owned 37 percent of its arable land. Nasser broke up the great estates and distributed them among the peasantry, with the smaller lots subsumed into cooperative farms. The Permanent Council for National Production was established in 1953 to draft first a five- and then a ten-year plan for integrated industrial and agricultural development. Crucial to the success of these plans was the Aswan Dam, which aimed to increase cultivated land by a third by harnessing the Nile River. When the United States, alarmed at Nasser's rising popularity in the Arab world and irked by his lack of enthusiasm for an American-sponsored regional alliance, the Baghdad Pact, announced that it would not help fund the dam, Nasser responded dramatically. He nationalized the Suez Canal, with the stated purpose of using its income to build the dam, which had now become symbolic not only of his revolution but of Third World hopes in general for independent development. Launched in 1959 with a $300 million loan from the Soviet Union, the dam was completed in 1974 at a cost of more than $2 billion. Although its projected goals for irrigation and hydroelectric power were not fully met and ecological problems such as silting and stagnation continue to plague it, the dam enabled Egypt nearly to double its agricultural output.

Equally significant strides were made in the industrial sector, although much of it remained in handicraft and small-scale production. Nasser's record of accomplishment in one of the world's poorest nations, though politically and economically blemished by the disaster of the Six Day War, was impressive. Nonetheless, these gains were all but negated by unchecked population growth, running at some 3 percent a year. By the late 1970s Anwar el-Sadat had accepted a new client relationship with the United States as the price of economic survival, a policy continued since 1981 by his successor, Hosni Mubarak. The heroic age of Nasser had ended.

The Middle East in the Postwar World

Nasser's revolution was a model for many emerging nations in the postwar period, but its influence was most direct on Egypt's North African neighbors. By 1956 the French protectorates of Morocco and Tunisia and the British-occupied Sudan had achieved full self-government, largely under the impetus of Egypt's example, and the former Italian colony of Libya was also granted independence under a feudal monarch, King Idris. However, the French refused to consider withdrawal from Algeria, where a strong settler interest prevailed. A war of national liberation ensued between 1954 and 1962, marked by savagery on both sides and resolved only when Charles de Gaulle, whom the war had brought back to power, arranged a plebiscite.

The rapid formation of new states in the immediate postwar period failed to give definitive shape or stability to Arab nationalism. Tribal groups dispersed over various borders, such as the Kurds of Turkey, Syria, Iran, and Iraq, demanded a homeland of their own. Radical nationalist parties, such as the Ba'ath movement in Syria and Iraq, remained dissatisfied with the conservative, pro-Western regimes left behind in the wake of the imperial powers. Pan-Arabic pressures for political unification between separate states also remained strong. In 1958 Syria and Egypt combined to form the United Arab Republic, with Nasser as president. Ardent Arab nationalists, particularly Syrian Ba'athists, saw this union as the precursor

of a grand Islamic federation but were soon disillusioned when the Egyptians moved to take complete control of Syria's government and economy. Following a Syrian army rebellion in September 1961, the union was dissolved by mutual consent. Similar experiments with other partners have proved equally short-lived, but the dream of a single, unitary state remains deeply embedded in Arab nationalism.

OPEC and the Politics of Oil

The history of the modern Middle East has been to a large extent determined by oil. Otherwise sparing in its gifts, nature has endowed the region with 60 percent of the proven world oil reserves. Britain was already dependent on Iranian oil to power its fleet by the first decade of the twentieth century, and as the West converted rapidly from coal to oil-based energy, the strategic importance of the Middle East grew apace. The discovery of vast new reserves in the desert wastes of Arabia in the 1930s was immediately exploited by the California Arabian Standard Oil Company (later called Aramco) on concessions granted by King ibn-Saud. Almost overnight Saudi Arabia was transformed from a poverty-ridden principality of nomadic tribes to a nation with one of the highest per capita incomes in the world.

In 1960 the Saudis took the initiative in forming the Organization of Petroleum Exporting Countries (OPEC). Originally composed of Saudi Arabia, Iran, Iraq, the tiny and newly independent emirate of Kuwait, and Venezuela, it subsequently expanded to include Algeria, Ecuador, Gabon, Indonesia, Libya, Nigeria, Qatar, and the confederation of small Persian Gulf sheikhdoms known as the United Arab Emirates. At first OPEC confined its activities chiefly to gaining a larger share of the revenues produced by Western oil companies and greater control over levels of production. The persistence of the Arab-Israeli conflict, however, turned it from a simple cartel into a formidable political force. After the Six Day War the Arab members of OPEC formed a separate, overlapping group (OAPEC) for the purpose of concerting policy and exerting pressure on the West over Israel. Egypt and Syria, negligible oil producers but populous and militarily powerful, joined the latter group to underline its intentions.

The Yom Kippur War of 1973 galvanized Arab opinion. Furious at the emergency resupply effort that had enabled Israel to withstand the Egyptian and Syrian assault, the Arabs imposed an oil embargo against the United States, western Europe, and Japan. This was followed by a more than fourfold price increase in the price of oil, causing sudden inflation and economic recession in the noncommunist industrial world and even greater hardship among the underdeveloped nations. At the same time, the Saudis acquired operating control of Aramco, fully nationalizing it in 1980. As other OPEC nations followed suit, the cartel's

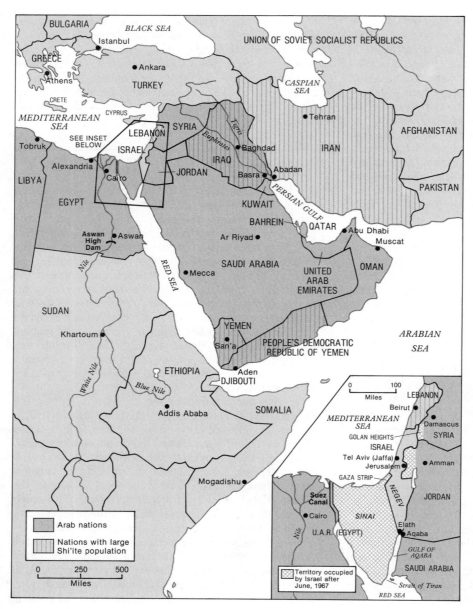

39.4 *The Modern Middle East*

income soared. Saudi Arabia, awash in profits, undertook a series of five-year development plans, of which the most ambitious, begun in 1980, called for the expenditure of $250 billion. Other cartel members also undertook major economic programs. For the first time, Third World nations whose resources and labor had long been exploited by the industrial giants had acquired control of a vital commodity, reversing the flow of capital. Some of this income was dispensed in the form of aid to other underdeveloped nations whose economies had been caught between higher prices for oil and the lower prices for their own commodities and raw materials caused by shrinking Western demand. Much of it, however, was reinvested in the West or absorbed in massive arms purchases that exacerbated political tensions, particularly in the Middle East. When reduced demand and overproduction produced a glut on the world market in the mid-1980s, oil prices plummeted and the cartel lost its unity. Producers such as Mexico, Nigeria, and Venezuela, whose economies had expanded recklessly, were plunged into near-bankruptcy, and even Saudi Arabia felt the pinch. The enormous reserves and relative underpopulation of the leading Middle East producers guaranteed the region its continuing strategic importance, but the politics of oil had proved dangerous for all concerned.

Modernization and Revolution in Iran

Iran, though ethnologically and linguistically distinct from its Arab neighbors in the Middle East, has shared its geographic destiny. As elsewhere in the region, social and political controls on the local level were traditionally exercised by the clergy on behalf of tribal landowning elites, with civil law and custom derived directly from religious precepts, although the merchant class of the larger towns had some independent influence. Patriarchal and hierarchical in structure, Iranian society was based on the absolute control of fathers over their families, khans or leaders over their tribes, and the shah as ruler over all, subject only to the ultimate authority of Shi'ite religious principles.

Iran's modernization began with its penetration by two conflicting imperial powers, Russia and Great Britain. In the 1860s and 1870s the first telegraph lines were set up with British assistance, thus ending the country's virtual isolation from the world. Concessions were given to build railroads and develop the country's resources. By 1907 the Russians and the British had formally divided Iran into spheres of influence, but a nationalist uprising in 1921 led by Reza Shah Pahlavi produced a modernizing dictatorship that, like Kemal Atatürk's in Turkey, attempted to introduce Western cultural and industrial models and to reduce the power of the clergy by stressing the nation's pre-Islamic past. New schools and industries were begun, and a conscript army was raised. A trans-Iranian railroad from the Caspian Sea to the Persian Gulf was built from the profits of state monopolies. Wide new avenues were cut through the major towns and named for national folk heroes. Sumptuary laws mandated the wearing of Western dress, and the traditional women's veil, the *chadar,* was made obsolete. In 1935 Reza Shah Pahlavi changed the country's Hellenistic name of Persia to Iran, meaning "land of the Aryans."

This last change was meant to reflect Iran's Indo-European roots but had contemporary significance as well. Reza Shah Pahlavi, dictatorial and often terroristic in his methods, was an ardent admirer of Hitler, and when an Allied force occupied Iran in August 1941, he was forced to abdicate in favor of his son, Muhammad Reza Pahlavi. For the next decade the country was once again a battleground of foreign interests, with the United States replacing Britain soon after World War II and the Soviet Union trying to regain its traditional foothold in the north. A new nationalist insurrection brought Muhammad Mossadegh, a prewar opponent of Reza Shah Pahlavi, to power as prime minister in 1951. Mossadegh nationalized the British-owned Anglo-Iranian Oil Company, thereby reasserting the country's independence. The West retaliated with a boycott of Iranian oil, and a CIA-led army coup deposed him in August 1953.

The shah, who had been briefly forced to flee the country by pro-Mossadegh crowds, returned with American blessing and remained a Western client thereafter. Like his father, however, he harbored grandiose ambitions. A "white revolution" was launched in the early 1960s to complete the process of modernization begun under Reza Shah Pahlavi, although the traditional landed elite remained firmly in control of the countryside. Using the massive oil profits of the 1970s, the shah attempted to turn Iran into the major military power of the Middle East, purchasing $15 billion worth of American arms between 1972 and 1978. But by the latter part of the decade his regime was under general assault. The land hunger of the peasantry remained unsatisfied despite promised reform, while the middle classes cultivated by the shah were frustrated by their exclusion from real power. Showy industrial projects and exotic weapons could not be operated without foreign advisers and technicians, reinforcing a painful sense of dependence on the West. Even the aristocracy, which had never accepted the Pahlavi dynasty, offered little support.

The Ayatollah Khomeini in 1979, addressing an adoring crowd from his home. [Alain Dejlan/Sygma]

The shah's most serious opposition, however, came from the Shi'ite clergy, which bitterly opposed what it took to be his promotion of corrupt Western values and mores. By raising a culturally sensitive issue that cut across class lines and evoked powerful religious and nationalist sentiment, the clergy brought to focus a general sense of grievance. Their exiled leader, the Ayatollah Ruhollah Khomeini (1900–1989), became the symbol of popular resistance.

The shah responded at first with repression and then, when crippling strikes brought the economy to the verge of bankruptcy, by desperate concessions. In January 1979 he fled into exile, and on February 1 Khomeini returned to Teheran as head of a revolutionary council, which proclaimed an Islamic republic. Real authority, however, emanated from Khomeini himself, who eliminated all political competitors and, armed with nearly absolute powers, embarked on a program of fundamentalist religious reform.

Khomeini's appeal reached far beyond the Shi'ites of Iran. His call to all Muslims to overthrow corrupt and tyrannical rulers and to return to the purity of Islamic law and ritual was particularly attractive to the migrant workers who maintained the economies of Saudi Arabia, Kuwait, and Bahrain. His order to seize 52 American em-

◉ Militant Islam ◉

The view of Islam as historically beleaguered by alien and hostile forces from the West is put forward by the Ayatollah Khomeini in his book, Islamic Government.

At its inception, the Islamic movement was afflicted by the Jews, who initiated a counter-activity by distorting the reputation of Islam, by assaulting it, and by slandering it. This has continued to our present day. Then came the role of groups which can be considered more evil than the devil and his troops. This role emerged in the colonialist activity which dates back more than three centuries ago. The colonialists found in the Muslim world their long-sought object. To achieve their colonialist ambitions, the colonists sought to create the right conditions leading to the annihilation of Islam. They did not seek to turn the Muslims into Christians after driving them away from Islam, because they do not believe in either. They wanted control and domination because during the Crusades they were constantly aware that the greatest obstacle preventing them from attaining their goals . . . was Islam with its laws and beliefs and with the influence it exerted on people through their faith. . . . Islam is the religion of the warriors who fight for right and justice, the religion of those seeking for freedom and independence, and those who do not want to allow the infidels to oppress the believers.

The role of women under revolutionary Islam is stated in the constitution adopted by the Islamic Republic of Iran on December 3, 1979.

In creating Islamic social foundations, all the human forces that had up to now been in the service of foreign exploitation will be accorded their basic identity and human rights. And in this regard it is natural that women, due to the greater oppression that they have borne under the idolatrous order, will enjoy more rights.

The family unit is the foundation of society and the main institution for the growth and advancement of mankind. . . . It is the principal duty of the Islamic government to regard women as the unifying factor of the family unit and its position. They are a factor in bringing the family out of the service of propagating consumerism and exploitation and renewing the vital and valuable duty of motherhood in raising educated human beings. . . . As a result motherhood is accepted as a most profound responsibility in the Muslim viewpoint and will, therefore, be accorded the highest value and generosity.

Source: T. Y. Ismael, *Iraq and Iran: Roots of Conflict* (Syracuse, N.Y.: Syracuse University Press, 1982), pp. 101, 147.

bassy officials and workers in November 1979 was the most dramatically popular act in the Middle East since the nationalization of the Suez Canal. Depicting the United States as a "great Satan" (while at the same time firmly repressing Iran's Communist party and doing pragmatic business with Israel, America's principal surrogate in the area), Khomeini skillfully combined Islamic revivalism with appeals to regional nationalism. In September 1980 Iraq's Saddam Hussein launched an ill-judged invasion of Iran that bitterly divided the Arab world, with Syria, Libya, and South Yemen backing Khomeini and Saudi Arabia and Jordan supporting Iraq. The war enabled Khomeini to keep revolutionary fervor high in Iran while consolidating a theocratic regime that may well outlast him and to burnish his image as the leader of Islam's *jihad,* or holy war, against the corrupting influence of the West. It was militarily inconclusive, however, and hostilities were halted by a truce in the summer of 1988.

Women and the Islamic Revolution

The resurgence of Islam has not been confined to Iran. From the Atlantic coast of North Africa to the islands of the Indonesian archipelago, across the great east-west belt where most of the world's 1 billion Muslims live, a major reawakening of Islamic culture has occurred since 1945. In part this has been associated with the emergence of new nation-states along this belt and the consequent testing of one of the world's most important religious traditions with the essentially secular ideology of modern nationalism. In part as well it reflects a struggle for identity

in a region whose people are skeptical of both Western materialism and Soviet atheism and are reluctant to align themselves with either of the superpower blocs. But it also has great significance for the social position of one-fifth of the world's women.

Koranic law continues to assign women a subordinate position in society. In the more conservative Middle Eastern states the law has continued to deny them equality in the public sphere and even access to it; in Saudi Arabia women were still not permitted to drive automobiles as late as 1980. In contrast, women had made significant strides in the postwar period in countries either heavily subject to Western influence or unified by socialist revolution. Tunisia, under the presidency of the strongly pro-Western Habib Bourguiba (born 1903), became in 1956 the first Islamic nation to replace the Koranic law on marriage, divorce, and childbearing by a civil code and the first Arab state to ban polygamy. Egypt under Nasser promulgated a constitution giving women full civil equality for the first time, and the socialist governments of Algeria and Yemen have included women's groups within their ruling party organizations. Such developments, however, have tended to affect only the urban middle class, with rural, tribal, and nomadic life continuing along traditional lines. The Iranian revolution of 1979 had a dramatic effect on women; Western attire vanished almost immediately, replaced by the traditional black or gray veil and a shapeless garment covering the entire body. Elsewhere too in the Middle East the *chadar* has again become the norm, sometimes as a symbol of resistance to Western mores, but often a matter of compulsion. Thus while Arab radicalism in the 1950s was at least rhetorically receptive to women's liberation, the fundamentalist revival of the 1980s has

Iranian demonstrators burn the American flag. [Jean Gaumy/ Magnum]

tended to consign women to their former roles, encouraging domesticity, public anonymity, and male dominance.

The Middle East Today

The hope of Camp David, that the Israeli-Egyptian accord would pave the way to a general settlement in the Middle East, has not been realized. No other Arab nation has moved toward recognition of Israel, while the Palestinian issue remains unresolved. During the 1970s the PLO was recognized as the legitimate government of the Palestinian people by many Arab, Soviet bloc, and Third World nations, and its leader, Yasir Arafat (born 1929), addressed the United Nations as a head of state. His influence declined precipitously in the early 1980s as the PLO's more militant factions fell under Syrian influence. In 1987, however, a popular uprising, the *intifada,* broke out on the West Bank against the Israeli occupation. Seizing this opportunity to reassert his leadership, Arafat began an intensive diplomatic campaign that climaxed in an address before the United Nations in 1988 and the initiation of direct bilateral talks with the United States.

The tragic clash between the Israelis and the Palestinians has become, for much of the international public, emblematic of the continuing appeal of nationalism in a globally interconnected world. The Palestinian poet Mahmoud Darwish spoke perhaps best for the common feeling on both sides of the conflict when he wrote:

> *Where shall we go, after the last frontier?*
> *Where will birds be flying, after the last*
> *   sky? . . .*
> *We will cut off the hand of song, so that our*
> *   flesh can complete the song.*
> *Here we will die. Here in the last narrow*
> *   passage. Or here our blood will plant—its*
> *   olive trees.*[1]

Legacy of Violence: The Lebanese Civil War

A tragic by-product of the Arab-Israeli conflict has been the civil war in Lebanon. On the surface, Lebanon had been one of the most successful of the states to win independence following World War II. Its thriving commercial economy had given it one of the Middle East's highest standards of living, and the political coexistence of a varied community of Christian, Jewish, and Muslim groups had made it a model of religious pluralism. Lebanon's equilib-

rium was, however, precarious. Urban prosperity masked rural poverty in the central valleys, a rising Muslim birthrate threatened the traditional Christian hegemony, and the country's semiofficial neutrality in the Arab-Israeli conflict brought it under increasing pressure from Arab nationalists. The sudden influx of some 300,000 Palestinian refugees after the Six Day War, followed by others expelled from Jordan in 1971, greatly exacerbated these tensions. The PLO made Lebanon its main base of operations, drawing retaliatory fire from Israel. The Lebanese divided sharply over the Palestinian presence, with Christian groups tending to regard them as unwelcome intruders and Muslims seeing them not only as victims seeking to regain their homeland but as patriots fighting in the common Arab cause against Israel. By 1975 the country had slid into full-scale civil war. When Syrian troops finally enforced a cease-fire 19 months later, 60,000 lives had been lost and nearly a third of the population displaced.

Syria's presence diminished the bloodshed but did nothing to restore stability. The PLO intensified its raids and attacks against Israel, while the Israelis sought to cultivate Christian allies in Lebanon. By 1980 there were approximately 40 separate armed groups in the country. Two years later the Israelis invaded Lebanon, driving the PLO from Beirut and occupying the southern third of the country. This defeat marked the temporary eclipse of Arafat, but the Israelis, now a target for all forces, soon withdrew after heavy losses. An American intervention in 1983 ended even more disastrously, with the death of 241 marines in a commando attack. By the late 1980s Lebanon had vanished as a nation in all but name, the epitome of sectarian anarchy and of the collapse of multiethnic community in the Middle East.

The increasing polarization of the Middle East was reflected in the prominence of revolutionary Iran; Syria, a state widely linked to support of terrorism; and Libya, whose ruler since 1969, Muammar al-Qaddafi (born 1942), has pursued a policy of military adventurism in North Africa while proclaiming the virtues of Arab unity. At the same time, the influence of militant Shi'ism has grown apace, particularly in countries with large Shi'ite populations, including (besides Iran) Iraq, Yemen, Bahrain, and Lebanon. In addition, economic pressures have intensified on many Middle Eastern countries that overextended themselves financially during the boom years of the 1970s and now face serious problems of unemployment and social unrest. The Iran-Iraq war demonstrated the fratricidal tendencies within Islam. Above all, the Arab-Israeli conflict continues to jeopardize hopes for the peaceful development of the region and, on a wider scale, international stability as well.

The forces of religion and nationalism created powerful tides in the postwar period along the great arc stretching from the Middle East to south-central Asia. The new states of India and Pakistan were born in an agony of civil war between their Hindu and Muslim populations, while the state of Israel was created in an equally bitter confrontation between Arab and Jew. Within Islam itself, divisions between Sunni and Shi'ite Muslims produced bloody conflict as well, most visibly in the Iran-Iraq war. At the same time, the unfulfilled national aspirations of the Palestinians and of the Kurds, the vulnerable oil economy, the problems of poverty and rapid social change, and the continuing unrest in Afghanistan and elsewhere all combine to make this region perhaps the most volatile in the world.

Notes

1.   M. Darwish, "Earth Scrapes Us," in *Modern Arabic Poetry: An Anthology,* ed. S. K. Jayyusi (New York: Columbia University Press, 1987), p. 208.

Suggestions for Further Reading

India, Pakistan, and Sri Lanka

Azad, M. *India Wins Freedom*. London: Longman, 1961.

Brown, J. *Modern India: The Origins of an Asian Democracy*. New York: Oxford University Press, 1985.

De Silva, K. M. *A History of Sri Lanka*. Berkeley: University of California Press, 1981.

Franda, M. *India's Rural Development*. Bloomington: Indiana University Press, 1980.

Gold, G. *Gandhi: A Pictorial Biography*. New York: Harper & Row, 1986.

Joshi, R., and Rindle, J. *Daughters of Independence: Gender, Caste, and Class in India*. London: Zed Books, 1986.

Kohli, A. *The State and Poverty in India*. Cambridge: Cambridge University Press, 1987.

Lamb, B. P. *India: A World in Transition*, 4th ed. New York: Praeger, 1975.

Mellor, J. *The New Economics of Growth: A Strategy for India and the Developing World*. Ithaca, N.Y.: Cornell University Press, 1976.

Moon, P. *Divide and Quit*. Berkeley: University of California Press, 1962.

Rosen, G. *Democracy and Economic Change in India*. Berkeley: University of California Press, 1966.

Swamy, S. *Economic Growth in China and India, 1952–1970*. Chicago: University of Chicago Press, 1974.

Tirtha, R. *Society and Development in Contemporary India*. Detroit: Harlo Press, 1980.

Wolpert, S. *Jinnah of Pakistan*. New York: Oxford University Press, 1984.

Ziegler, P. *Mountbatten*. London: Collins, 1985.

The Middle East

Abdulghani, J. *Iran and Iraq*. London: Croom Helm, 1984.

Ajami, F. *The Arab Predicament: Arab Political Thought and Practice Since 1967*. Cambridge: Cambridge University Press, 1981.

Anderson, J. N. D. *Islamic Law in the Modern World*. Westport, Conn.: Greenwood Press, 1975.

Avineri, S. *The Making of Modern Zionism: Intellectual Origins of the Jewish State*. New York: Basic Books, 1981.

Bakhash, S. *The Reign of the Ayatollahs*. New York: Basic Books, 1984.

Devlin, J. *Syria: Modern State in an Ancient Land*. Boulder, Colo.: Westview Press, 1983.

al-Fassi, A. *The Independence Movements in Arab North Africa*, trans. H. Z. Nuseibeh. New York: Octagon, 1970.

Kurzman, D. *Ben-Gurion: Prophet of Fire*. New York: Simon & Schuster, 1983.

Lacouture, J. *Nasser: A Biography*. New York: Knopf, 1973.

Mortimer, E. *Faith and Power: The Politics of Islam*. New York: Faber & Faber, 1982.

Rabinovitch, I. *The War for Lebanon, 1970–1983*. Ithaca, N.Y.: Cornell University Press, 1984.

Reich, B. *Israel: Land of Tradition and Conflict*. Boulder, Colo.: Westview Press, 1985.

Said, E. W. *The Question of Palestine*. New York: Times Books, 1979.

Salibi, K. *A History of Arabia*. Delmar, N.Y.: Caravan Books, 1980.

Sampson, A. *The Seven Sisters*. New York: Bantam Books, 1979.

Taryam, A. O. *The Establishment of the United Arab Emirates, 1950–85*. London: Croom Helm, 1987.

Waterbury, J. *The Egypt of Nasser and Sadat*. Princeton, N.J.: Princeton University Press, 1983.

Decolonization and Development: Africa and Latin America

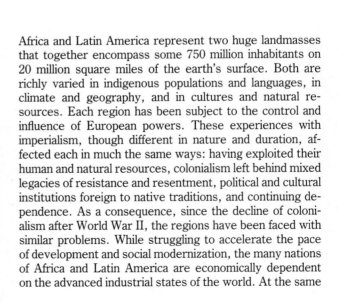

Africa and Latin America represent two huge landmasses that together encompass some 750 million inhabitants on 20 million square miles of the earth's surface. Both are richly varied in indigenous populations and languages, in climate and geography, and in cultures and natural resources. Each region has been subject to the control and influence of European powers. These experiences with imperialism, though different in nature and duration, affected each in much the same ways: having exploited their human and natural resources, colonialism left behind mixed legacies of resistance and resentment, political and cultural institutions foreign to native traditions, and continuing dependence. As a consequence, since the decline of colonialism after World War II, the regions have been faced with similar problems. While struggling to accelerate the pace of development and social modernization, the many nations of Africa and Latin America are economically dependent on the advanced industrial states of the world. At the same

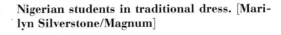

Nigerian students in traditional dress. [Marilyn Silverstone/Magnum]

time, the political record has been marked in many cases by instability and a pattern of repeated military-authoritarian governments. Most daunting of all remain the stark conditions of poverty and social inequality in which the vast majority of Africans and Latin Americans continue to live.

Europeans maintained control over their African territories in the decades before World War II. Few Africans held positions of influence or responsibility in their own lands. The Italian conquest of Ethiopia in 1935 and 1936 seemed yet again to demonstrate the Africans' helplessness in the face of Western power politics. Yet the colonial system in Africa disintegrated rapidly after 1945.

Conditions in Central and South America were different. Although unaffected directly by the fighting of the two world wars, Latin American economic strength was seriously undermined by the interruption of world trade. Equally serious were the effects of the Great Depression in the United States, which reduced the prices of Latin American exports. Thus whereas in Africa the years following World War II saw the Africans asserting a newfound strength over their exhausted European rulers, the same period in Latin America was marked by a precipitous economic decline. Outside influences grew, moreover, as the United States, fresh from victory in World War II, came increasingly to oversee developments throughout the Western Hemisphere.

Africa: The Seeds of Revolt

A prime factor in the early stages of the African independence movements was, paradoxically, the firmness with which European rule was enforced. Further, it was increasingly clear to the Africans that the colonial powers were not prepared to stimulate the economies of the countries they ruled. Railway networks, for example, had been constructed earlier in the colonial period, in the late nineteenth and early twentieth centuries; those of German East and Southwest Africa were built in the years before 1914 and that of the Gold Coast had been completed by 1903. By the 1920s, however, work and investment had virtually ceased. With the slump in works projects came a rapid decline in European emigration to Africa; most unskilled European workers preferred to seek a new life in North America.

Thus Africans found themselves increasingly responsible for performing work for governments over which they had no control and which were seemingly unconcerned for the present and future welfare of their subjects. The consequence was the formation throughout Africa of nationalist movements that sought complete independence and self-government. One of the first examples of this phenomenon occurred in North Africa, where Habib Bourguiba helped to found a Tunisian liberation party in 1934.

Four years later the party was banned and Bourguiba was thrown into jail, but the foundations of an autonomous Tunisian government had been laid.

The first political protest movements south of the Sahara developed in West Africa, where European rule had produced a class of Africans who were Western-educated but shut out from any control over their own destiny. In the British colonies African political associations such as the West African National Congress, formed in 1918, began to push for the conversion of legislative councils, which were generally made up of colonial officials and a few token Africans, into true African parliaments.

In the French territories, whose rule remained firmly based in Paris, would-be nationalist leaders found it necessary to spend time in France. Léopold Senghor (born 1906), the nationalist leader of Senegal, first established himself as one of the leading French poets of the period; J. B. Danquah, the founder of the movement to free the Gold Coast, published works on anthropology and religion. Inspiration came from similar movements in the United States and the West Indies, where figures such as W. E. B. Du Bois (1868–1963) and Marcus Garvey (1887–1940) were leading movements of black consciousness. These Europeanized African intellectuals tried to establish the concept of an African personality and to assert the intrinsic aesthetic beauty of African culture, which drew its strength from tribal roots. With this intellectual and moral foundation, they hoped to construct a new political status for people dominated by Europeans.

The main exception to this gradual stirring of independence was South Africa, although even there an organized opposition to white domination had been formed among the black labor force by 1912. The discovery of diamonds and gold there in the 1870s and 1880s led to the establishment of mining operations on a massive scale. Townships grew up around the mining camps, populated by unskilled African laborers who were recruited by the white-owned mining companies. Although in comparison with their skilled and unionized white coworkers black laborers were underpaid, their incomes were significantly higher than those elsewhere in black Africa. This had two consequences: black labor began to collect in shantytowns around the large South African cities, and the whites began to produce goods that could be sold to this new class of African consumers. The South African industrial revolution thus led to the appearance of a black proletariat rigidly governed by white masters. The profound racial tensions that followed have marked the history of South Africa to this day.

World War II hastened the process of resistance to colonial rule that had already begun. The bitter divisions of the European powers were plain for all to see. Indeed, some of the fiercest fighting of the British, French, and American forces against the Italians and Germans occurred on North African soil. In sub-Saharan Africa the colony of French Equatorial Africa, under the leadership of Félix Éboué, sent soldiers to fight against the Germans, even though the Vichy-dominated French West African administration supported Germany.

With the end of hostilities and the resumption of international trade, outside investment in Africa, both public and private, began to increase. In part this was due to the innate value of many of the continent's raw materials, including oil, copper, and cocoa. At the same time, the scale of foreign development projects reflected an increasing concern among the governing powers for the moral welfare of their subjects. Britain and France initiated colonial development schemes that involved the investment of large sums of public capital.

The independence movements that emerged after World War II were conditioned in large measure by the differences that had marked colonial rule among the great powers. The British supported Western-style education for Africans and involved them in the processes of colonial administration; after 1945 at least, most British politicians saw independence as the ultimate goal, for which they should prepare the people of their colonies. The French were less inclined to surrender control, preferring to assimilate their colonial populations with that of the motherland by offering access to French culture, including education in France itself.

Even by these standards, however, Portuguese and Belgian colonial policies were unenlightened and repressive. The Portuguese administrators did almost nothing to encourage, let alone finance, local economic or social development plans and concentrated instead on trade, and the standard of living of their subjects remained probably the most depressed in Africa. The Belgians ruthlessly exploited the Congo and provided almost no higher education or managerial experience for Africans.

It is not surprising, therefore, that the most successful of the new African states are mainly former British colonies, such as Kenya and Tanzania, even though not one has avoided disruptive problems and conflicts. Among the most strife-torn and chaotic have been Zaïre (the former Belgian Congo) and Angola (formerly Portuguese); Niger, Chad, and the Central African Republic, all former French colonies, have remained economically and militarily dependent on France.

In addition to economic improvements, the colonial powers began, partly in response to pressures from liberation movements, to improve living conditions in their African territories. In fields such as health and housing, sanitation and water supply, new developments were aimed at social as well as economic improvement. These were accompanied by an expansion in education. Beginning in 1943 Britain had formulated a scheme to set up universities in the colonies. Other colonial powers were less enlightened; in the Belgian Congo money was invested only in primary and vocational schooling, since the Belgians feared that it would be dangerous to allow their subjects to advance too quickly.

Postwar colonial Africa, then, was marked by a sense of transition. The stagnation of the previous decades gave way to an improvement in communications produced by road and air travel and a new social mobility. Many Africans benefited from the work of the teachers, welfare officers, surveyors, and other skilled professionals who came from Europe, but these outsiders reaped the major rewards of African economic progress. The imported planners, advisers, and researchers often earned large salaries; the Africans for whom they planned did not.

Black Africa: The Challenges of Nationhood

In the process of decolonization that marked the period from 1957 to 1975, the holdings of the four colonial powers that survived World War II—Britain, France, Belgium, and Portugal—acquired independence. Each of the colonial empires had combined a great variety of areas and peoples. By 1975 they had become 51 separate countries, very few of them with an understanding of nationhood and most of them uniting a variety of peoples, cultures, languages, and traditions. The first decades of independence were accordingly fraught with problems for most of them, some of which are still unresolved. The new states were relatively poor, although some had major natural resources awaiting fuller development. The progress of public health and medical care produced a rapid increase in population and a decline in infant mortality. Population in Africa is still growing faster than in most of the rest of the world, while economic development is only beginning.

In most African states today, tribal groups are still the most meaningful cultural and political units. Although most African nations were originally based on Western models, the majority of their citizens think of themselves as Kikuyu, Ibo, or Masai rather than as Kenyans, Nigerians, or Congolese. Even the relatively small state of Ghana in West Africa, about the size of Oregon, harbors ethnic groups speaking more than 35 languages, each with origins in long-standing tribal communities. The population of Nigeria, at nearly 100 million the largest in Africa, is split into some 200 similarly tribal-based language and cultural groups. Many of the new African communities, struggling with problems of poverty and internal diversity, have seen formal parliamentary democracy replaced by military or dictatorial regimes.

Most African nations began their independence under the leadership of charismatic figures such as Kwame Nkrumah (1909–1972) in Ghana, Patrice Lumumba (1925–1961) in the Congo (now Zaïre), Jomo Kenyatta (1891–1978) in Kenya, and Julius Nyerere (born 1922) in Tan-

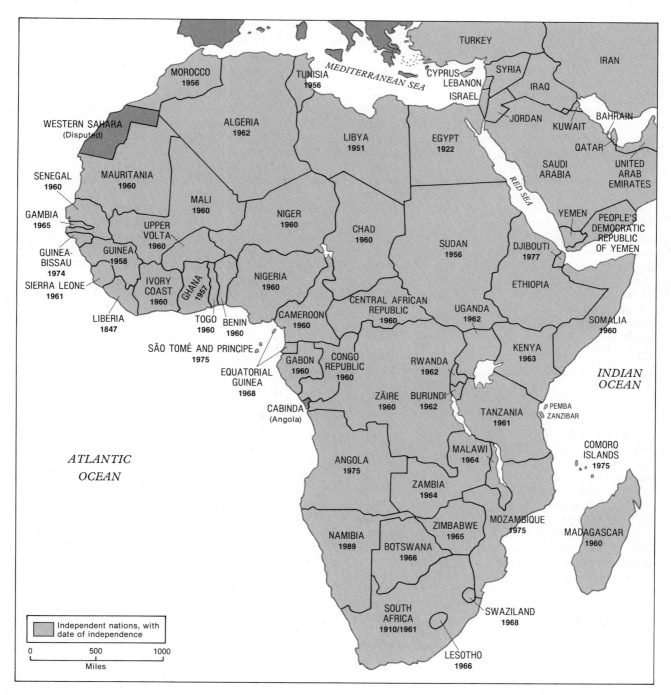

40.1 Africa Today

zania. Others relapsed after independence into one-man rule; the cruelest and most gruesome example is probably Idi Amin's dictatorship in Uganda from 1971 to 1979, when political opponents were brutally tortured and murdered.

Traditional tribal government, however, has its own democratic forms based on consensus, a process apparent even in many of the one-party states of contemporary Africa. Indeed, some of the new states, notably Kenya,

Tanzania, Senegal, and Zambia, have achieved considerable domestic stability based on well-established negotiating techniques between various interest groups. The success of this return to African tradition demonstrates that Western forms of government may not be the most appropriate vehicles of political stability.

The sheer number and diversity of the African states precludes all but the broadest generalizations about them. Throughout its history, Africa's physical geography has played a large part in establishing and reinforcing cultural patterns, and this remains true today, in spite of improvements in communications and transport. The Sahara remains a formidable barrier between northern and central Africa, although the new states of Mauritania, Mali, Niger, Chad, and Sudan straddle its southern limits. North and south of the Sahara are different worlds. To the north lies the Arab-dominated Mediterranean coastal plain known as the Mahgreb. South of the Sahara stretches a succession of semiarid savannah, rain forest, and mountain country. As we have seen, Islam crossed the great desert and spread into parts of black Africa, but the central rain forest area—the "big bush," as Africans still call it—repelled nearly all outside contacts until the imperialist rush of the late nineteenth century.

The Achievement of Independence

Ghana was the first African colony to win independence in 1957. It had been the British colony of Gold Coast, so named for the early coastal trade in gold. Its American-educated leader, Kwame Nkrumah, began to win a reputation as an oppressive dictator and in 1966 was overthrown. The effects of his mismanagement and his squandering of Ghana's resources outlasted his disappearance. The parliamentary democracy that was established in 1969, to the initial satisfaction of both the armed forces and the people, had little chance to show whether it could improve on the record of Nkrumah's one-party state, since it inherited the debts and empty treasury of its predecessors. In 1972 the army took control, and in succeeding years Ghana has yet to achieve effective cohesion or sustained economic growth.

Like Ghana, Nigeria was plagued by conflicts among its many tribal and cultural groups after achieving independence in 1960. Northern Nigeria extends into the savannah borders of the Sahara, while the southern and coastal areas are in the rain forest. Different cultures had evolved in each, breaking down in turn into distinct local or regional districts. The major rival groups were the Hausa of the north, who had been converted to Islam by the Mali traders of the fourteenth century, and the southern and coastal Ibo. These latter had benefited from the fact that Nigeria's colonial capital was at Lagos, on the coast. The effects of British administration were more pronounced in the

coastal region than in the interior, and the Ibo were thus in general better educated and more involved in the contemporary world.

When an Ibo army officer murdered the Hausa prime minister and seized power in 1966, Hausa tribesmen massacred Ibo living in northern Nigeria. In response, in 1967 the Ibo east of the Niger River seceded as the Republic of Biafra. The central government fought a long campaign against them, which dragged on with great suffering and bloodshed until the rebels surrendered in 1970 and were reincorporated into the Nigerian state. New discoveries of large coastal and offshore oil reserves brought a welcome infusion of revenues and general prosperity, helping to heal the internal divisions; in 1979 civil government was restored. Nigeria's economy has become one of the fastest-growing in Africa, although the fluctuating international price of oil has introduced elements of instability; it remains to be seen whether domestic differences can be managed in the long run.

In contrast to the more laissez-faire style of the British, the French attempted to mold the future destinies of their colonies by controlling the terms of their independence. The de Gaulle government offered to all French black African territories the choice of independence or autonomy as separate self-governing states within a French "community." This federation, presided over by France, would deal with matters of common interest such as foreign policy and defense. In the referendum that followed, France's technique for protecting its own self-interest seemed to have worked, since every territory except Guinea voted for autonomy within the community. By the end of 1960, however, virtually all of France's African possessions had followed Guinea's example and negotiated their independence.

Perhaps the most stable state to emerge from the French colonial empire has been Senegal, whose country's first leader, Léopold Senghor, retained power into the mid-1970s. Its stabilization was made easier by its relatively small size and by the fact that its capital, Dakar, the former capital of French Africa, was a modern center whose port provides access to international markets.

In 1960 Belgium abruptly pulled out of the Congo. Regional rivalries erupted into civil war, and the copper-rich southern province of Katanga seceded under its own leader, Moise Tshombe. After United Nations troops had helped to restore order, and following the CIA-sponsored assassination of Patrice Lumumba, the military regime of General Joseph Mobutu established firmer control and changed the country's name to Zaïre. Its subsequent history has been troubled by the conflicts of rival groups. Economic development has lagged, although Zaïre temporarily benefited from a rise in copper prices in the 1970s.

Trouble in the Congo spilled into neighboring Angola, where prolonged guerrilla warfare finally forced the Portuguese to withdraw in 1975 without establishing a fully effective government. The consequence was a civil war in which three separate liberation movements fought for control of the country. At first the right-wing Union for the Total Independence of Angola (UNITA), whose forces were reinforced by South African troops, seemed victorious, but the South African contingent provoked further intervention. The rival People's Movement for the Liberation of Angola (MPLA) received support from Communist countries, especially Cuba. With this help, the MPLA extended its control over the greater part of Angola, defeating both the forces of UNITA and of a third group, the National Liberation Front (FNL), whose main support came from across the border in Zaïre. The MPLA is generally recognized as the successor of the Portuguese governing authority, and a settlement of the fighting has been negotiated.

In East Africa, Tanganyika won independence in 1961 and in 1964 merged with the nearby island of Zanzibar to form the state of Tanzania. Its gifted leader, Julius Nyerere, attracted Chinese aid in railway building while adhering to the same neutralist course followed by many non-Western countries. Following Chinese and Indian models, he promoted cooperative schemes on a village basis to stimulate agricultural growth. Lacking Kenya's resources, Tanzania was further plagued by drought and poor soil. Nyerere retired from national politics in 1986; it remains to be seen if his country can survive its natural weaknesses and maintain a stable government.

Nyerere's generally high reputation was due in part to his style of rule. Unlike many of his fellow African leaders, he and his party maintained broad contact with Tanzanian society, avoiding the ostentatious paraphernalia of presidential palaces and limousines seen elsewhere. The moral authority gained from his concern with popular welfare buttressed Nyerere's main external concern: opposition to white oppression in southern Africa and help to black resistance there.

In Kenya the last years of British rule were rent by bitter conflict with the Mau Mau, a secret terrorist society among the dominant Kikuyu tribe sworn to kill or drive out all white settlers. By 1960 the movement was suppressed, and Jomo Kenyatta, the first president of independent Kenya, emerged from 11 years of prison and detention imposed for his involvement in the Mau Mau society. In power, Kenyatta proved moderate and led one of the most stable of African governments. By retaining the presence and support of at least some of the Europeans and Asians who had controlled Kenya's businesses during the colonial period, he avoided serious economic breakdown. By the time of his death in 1978, the country was sufficiently secure to allow for a peaceful transfer of power to his successor, Daniel arap Moi.

❧
JOMO KENYATTA: KENYA'S FOUNDING FATHER

The grandson of a Kikuyu medicine man, Kenyatta, who was himself uncertain as to the day and year of his birth,

---

◉ Black Power ◉

The aspirations of African blacks to direct their own destiny was eloquently stated in 1960 by Rashidi Mfaume Kawawa, who would later succeed Julius Nyerere as prime minister of Tanganyika.

The demand for Africanization is made by the black people and means a replacement by them of those of different origin. Despite the wider meaning that the term African has acquired today, the blacks are still at the bottom of every ladder and identify themselves completely and practically with the struggle for change. To ask the indigenous Africans to forget the agony of their past is to ask them to ignore the lesson that their experience has taught them. Asians and Europeans are crying in Tanganyika today for non-racial parties, but just how practical is this? Those non-racial political parties which have been formed in Tanganyika have never succeeded, for they never aimed at emancipating the African, but only at deluding him into satisfaction with the lowest rung. It is the experience of the present that will constitute African reaction in the future; and the place that the Asian and the European will build for themselves in Africa will be governed by the degree of sacrifice they are prepared to make in the cause of a life in joint advancement and dedication with and amongst the Africans.

Source: R. Segal, *African Profiles* (Baltimore: Penguin Books, 1962), pp. 113–114.

was probably born in 1891. The name by which he is known is a nickname: *Kenyatta* refers to the beaded belt, or *kinyata,* that he always wore, and *Jomo* means "burning spear" in the Kikuyu dialect.

Much of Kenyatta's youth was spent traveling in Europe. When he returned to Nairobi in the 1920s, he joined the Kikuyu Central Association and began to involve himself in his country's future. In 1929 and again in 1931 he went to London to argue his tribe's rights to the land on which it had settled. The British government refused to grant his request but allowed the Kikuyu to establish their own schools. Over the following years Kenyatta spent much of his time in Britain, studying at the London School of Economics and writing anthropological studies of his people, as well as an autobiography, *Facing Mount Kenya* (1938), that became a bible of the independence movement.

In October 1945 Kenyatta was one of the organizers of a pan-African congress in Manchester. The theme of the congress was "Africa for the Africans," and among the participants was Kwame Nkrumah, the future leader of Ghana. The congress emphasized the common goals of the independence movement for all Africans. When Kenyatta returned to Kenya, he was elected president of the Kenya African Union, a political party that sought to combine and unify Kenya's tribes. While urging his people to act with discipline and integrity, he fought for African voting rights, the elimination of discrimination based on race, and the return of land to its original owners.

In the face of British resistance to these demands, the Mau Mau movement developed. Kenyatta tried to dissociate himself and his party from the terrorists, but in 1952 he was accused of masterminding the Mau Mau and was put on trial. Despite questionable evidence, Kenyatta was convicted and sent to jail. Although much of his political base was drawn from Mau Mau support, he himself always professed his innocence.

By the late 1950s it became clear that Kenya would follow the example of Ghana and obtain independence. The principal political party, by now known as the Kenya African Nationalist Union, refused to make any moves to form a government as long as Kenyatta was imprisoned, and in 1961 he was finally freed from detention. Returning in triumph to his home territory, he became the first president of the new Republic of Kenya in 1964.

Avoiding recriminations or resentment against white Kenyans, Kenyatta aimed at forging a broad consensus of support among blacks and whites alike. He firmly rejected Communist efforts to gain a base in Kenya, declaring that his country would not "exchange one master for a new master." Although his government made every effort to involve native Kenyans in the economic and administrative organization of his country, it also encouraged European and Asian settlers to remain, as long as they accepted African leadership. For the first decade or so of Kenya's independence, Europeans continued to occupy key government posts. In neighboring Uganda, by contrast, non-Africans were expelled and their land was confiscated.

Kenyatta was married four times. A man of enormous vitality, he came to represent the new Africa on the international stage. Never losing his contact with his origins—while president he lived on a farm outside Nairobi, the capital, and regularly worked on the land—he was a familiar figure at international conferences and world assemblies such as the United Nations. Wearing alternately the finest of tailored suits and resplendent tribal robes, he represented not only his country but also the ideal of an African unity that combined modernity and tradition. A British administrator who worked with him described him as a man with "a sense of destiny but also a sense of humility." He died, still in office, in 1978.

Jomo Kenyatta, first president of independent Kenya. [© Jason Laure 1977/Woodfin Camp]

South Africa

The tormented history of South Africa is bedeviled not only by conflict between black and white but by division among the white ruling class as well. The British and the Dutch-descended Boers were the primary European settlers in the region, although the discovery of gold in the

1880s drew an influx of immigrants from eastern Europe, many of them Jews who founded important communities in and around Johannesburg. By the 1920s subsequent waves of immigration had swelled the Jewish population of South Africa to 100,000.

At the beginning of the twentieth century "race relations" referred to dealings between the British and the Boers. By the time the four British colonies that formed the Union of South Africa came together in 1910, the only nonwhite Africans permitted to vote were those of the former territory of the Cape of Good Hope, a right that was subsequently abolished. The division between the Afrikaners, as the Boers came to be called, and the English settlers effectively blocked any chance of the nonwhite population's obtaining political rights. Furthermore, although the Afrikaners led the opposition to nonwhite participation in government and in the country's social and economic management—all of South Africa's prime ministers from 1910 to the present have been Afrikaners—the British community did little to promote nonwhite interests. The United party, the main political opposition movement to the white Nationalists, advised moderation while never contesting the guiding principle of Nationalist policy, segregation.

By the end of World War II white South Africans made up less than a fifth of the country's population. Nonwhites included over a million Indians who had settled there since the nineteenth century and the descendants of mixed European and African parentage, officially called "Coloureds." The largest black groups were of the Bantu and Hottentot tribes. South African policy centered on *apartheid* ("separateness"), which segregated whites and nonwhites in separate living areas and denied nonwhites access to any but the most menial jobs. Black Africans were

assigned to drought-ridden and sparsely populated areas, first called "reserves" and then in the 1960s and 1970s nominally independent states, or "homelands," such as Bophuthatswana, Venda, and the Transkei.

The Afrikaners, who still speak a version of Dutch called Afrikaans, have retained their Calvinist religious beliefs, coupled with the conviction that the superiority of whites over blacks is God-ordained. African efforts at political expression are suppressed, the press is heavily censored, and "emergency laws," renewed at frequent intervals, have created broad police powers and subverted the constitutional system of justice. The largest black African resistance organization, the African National Congress (ANC), founded as early as 1912, helped to organize strikes, boycotts, and mass demonstrations. In 1959 a more radical alternative appeared in the Pan-African Congress, but antigovernment demonstrations led to reprisals by the whites, symbolized for many by the massacre of black demonstrators by white forces in 1960 at Sharpeville. The active black struggle for independence may be dated from that event. The violent suppression of political demonstrations, including a bloody police action in the black township of Soweto in 1976, has characterized the official South African response to the black demand for freedom.

The South African regime has persistently refused to accept the authority of the ANC to represent black interests. In 1983 nonwhites of Indian descent and Coloureds were admitted to a limited form of franchise with the formation of a "lower house of parliament," but black South Africans remain unrepresented and generally excluded from South Africa's economic prosperity. The ANC's leading spokesman, Nelson Mandela (born 1918), has been in jail for almost two decades; his wife, Winnie, kept his

Casualties of South Africa's brutal attempts to maintain apartheid: Sharpeville, 1960. [UPI/Bettmann Newsphotos]

⊛ Apartheid and the Oppression of Women ⊛

The brutality of apartheid is particularly apparent in its effects on black family life.

Widowhood—a life of void and loneliness; a period of tension, unbalance, and strenuous adjustment. And what can it be to those thousands of African women—those adolescent girls married before they reach womanhood, thrown into a life of responsibility before they have completely passed from childhood to adulthood; those young women in the prime of early womanhood left to face life alone, burdened with the task of building a home and rearing a family; those young women doomed to nurse alone their sick babies, weep alone over their dead babies, dress and bury alone their corpses? What can it mean to those young brides whose purpose has been snatched away, overnight, leaving them bewildered and lost, leaving them with a thirst and hunger that cannot be stilled?

And yet this is the daily lot of tens of thousands of African women whose husbands are torn away from them to go and work in the cities, mines, and farms—husbands who because of the migratory labor system cannot take their wives with them and, because of the starvation wages they receive, are forced to remain in the work centers for long periods—strangers in a strange land—but equally strangers at home to their wives and children.

These women remain alone in the Reserves to build the homes, till the land, rear the stock, bring up the children. They watch alone the ravages of drought, when the scraggy cows cease to provide the milk, when the few stock drop one by one because there is no grass on the veld, and all the streams have been lapped dry by the scorching sun. They watch alone the crops in the fields wither in the scorching sun, their labor of months blighted in a few days. They witness alone the hailstorm sweep clean their mealie lands, alone they witness the wind lift bodily their huts as if they were pieces of paper, rendering them and their children homeless. Alone they bury their babies one by one and lastly their unknown lovers—their husbands, whose corpses alone are sent back to the Reserves. For the world of grinding machines has no use for men whose lungs are riddled with . . . miner's phthisis [tuberculosis of the lungs].

Source: P. Ntantala, in *The Africa Reader: Independent Africa*, ed. W. Cartey and M. Kilson (New York: Vintage Books, 1970), pp. 306–307.

name—and his views—alive by her frequent public statements and appearances until the violence associated with her followers removed her from the scene. The main white opponent of apartheid throughout the 1960s and 1970s was also a woman, Helen Suzman. In the 1980s a new leader of moderate black African resistance appeared in the person of the Reverend Desmond Tutu, who was awarded the Nobel peace prize in 1984 for his efforts in the struggle against apartheid.

If there is any immediate sign of hope in the face of the regime's intransigence, it can perhaps be found in the informal dialogue between the ANC and some of the most prominent of South Africa's business leaders. The talks, begun in 1986, have continued sporadically. By far the richest and most industrially developed country in Africa, as well as the world's principal supplier of gold and dia-

monds, South Africa remains the last white-ruled state in sub-Saharan Africa.

North Africa

The world of North Africa was vastly different from that of the rest of the continent. Because it had been a center of Arabic culture for centuries, many of the newly emerging states either returned to earlier forms of government or at least had a single predominant cultural group formed by the native Arab population.

The independent nations of North Africa have been plagued by many of the same problems. Despite the predominance of Islam, tribal and religious divisions have ob-

Helen Suzman, a member of the South African Parliament, has been an outspoken opponent of apartheid. [William Campbell/Sygma]

structed the effectiveness of national governments. Most are dependent on the fluctuations of international commodity prices. Although population growth is unchecked, chronic food shortages and disease have caused widespread poverty and suffering. In addition, many nominally independent states continue to be dominated and manipulated by their former colonizers. The phenomenon of neocolonialism is particularly obvious in the case of France's former possessions.

The former French North African colonies have witnessed the triumphant revival of Islam. In Morocco and Tunisia the process of decolonization was relatively peaceful. Tunisia was allowed local autonomy in 1954 and became a republic in 1957, with Bourguiba as its president. The Islamic monarchy of Morocco was restored to its full powers in 1956. In Algeria, by contrast, the independence struggle was among the bitterest in Africa. Its liberation movement, the FLN, was openly aided by Egypt, Tunisia, and Morocco. Against the background of violent public

division at home, the French army in Algeria revolted, and in 1958 France's wartime hero, General de Gaulle, was placed at the head of the French state.

De Gaulle confounded the expectations of his military supporters by negotiating Algeria's independence. In 1962 the country became an independent Muslim republic, threatened in its first years by the attempts of the former Algerian colonists to undermine its existence as well as by divisions within the FLN. The combined wars of the French against the Algerian nationalists and the subsequent struggles of both French and Algerians to repress the colonists' resistance have left inevitable scars. In the late 1960s the Algerians retreated into a period of isolation from international affairs from which they emerged as an active neutralist state.

The French withdrawal from North Africa, together with the creation of the state of Israel and the resulting hostility of the Arab world, led to the disappearance of the Jewish communities that had flourished there under colonial protection since the nineteenth century. A large number of the Jews of Tunis and almost the entire Jewish population of Algeria migrated to France and Israel. The Jewish settlement in Morocco, which at 250,000 had been the largest in Africa, was reduced to a fifth of its former size.

The most extreme appearance of fundamentalist Islam in North Africa has been in Libya, a former Italian colony, which was administered by Britain from 1942 to 1951. With its independence it became a conservative Muslim kingdom, whose ruler was the spiritual leader of the Sanussi, a Muslim sect whose opposition to Mussolini's rule had resulted in brutal Fascist repression in the 1920s. In 1969, however, the monarchy was overthrown in a coup led by Colonel Muammar al-Qaddafi.

Qaddafi's histrionic ability to command world attention has depended on three factors: the vast revenues accumulated by Libya from its oil supplies, Soviet attempts to gain control in the region by providing Libya with military and financial aid, and Qaddafi's underwriting of terrorist groups operating in many parts of the world. The results have won Libya the hostility of much of the Western world, together with uncomfortable acceptance by many Arab neighbors. Since 1980 the Libyans have been embroiled in a civil war in neighboring Chad, a former French colony, that has brought them into open conflict with French forces. Skirmishes in 1985 and 1986 resulted in both sides retreating and the informal negotiation of an uncertain peace.

Libya's most dramatic, or at least most publicized, international activity has been the encouragement of terrorism on a worldwide scale. Much of this may well have been vocal rather than practical, principally intended to make headlines. In 1986, however, American planes bombed Libya in reprisal for alleged Libyan involvement in terrorist incidents and narrowly missed killing Qaddafi himself. The subsequent retaliation threatened by Libya did not materialize, and Qaddafi's own position may well have been shaken by the American attack, although the long-term consequences are impossible to foresee.

In Ethiopia, with the expulsion of the Italians in 1941, Haile Selassie returned to power. Unlike its neighbors, Ethiopia was Christian by tradition, although many of its customs, including slavery, had been adopted from Muslim practice. Ethiopia's geographic position at a key location on the Red Sea gave it an increasing importance following World War II, but imperial rule did little to modernize the country. After a period of growing chaos, characterized by student demonstrations, army mutinies, and reports of corruption in high circles, a serious famine brought the regime to crisis. In 1974 the emperor was deposed and replaced by a group of army officers; united only in their opposition to Haile Selassie, they ranged from moderates to extreme radicals.

Within a short time the radicals had gained control, and since then they have dismantled Ethiopia's traditional feudal system and replaced it with a repressive one-party state. The resulting disruption in food production has been only partly offset by Soviet aid after 1978. Soviet weapons and Cuban troops have been used against two of Ethiopia's long-standing enemies, Somalia and insurgents in the Ethiopian province of Eritrea. The latter staged a rebellion in the mid-1970s with the help of Arab states; by 1980 the revolt was firmly suppressed. The Somalis, meanwhile, have been forced to abandon their attempts to "liberate" the Ethiopian province of Ogaden, whose principal inhabitants are Somali nomads.

Throughout the Sahel region, which includes much of Ethiopia and Somalia, an already difficult situation was made even worse by a widespread famine that took a large toll of life in the mid-1980s. Western attempts to provide aid were in large measure frustrated by local bureaucratic inefficiency and corruption.

From the time it attained political independence in 1956, the Sudan was divided between its Muslim north and Christian south. The threat of an Egyptian attack, coupled with the increasing ineffectiveness of party government, provoked a military coup in 1958. Subsequent years have seen an alteration of democratic and military rule and the short-lived secession in 1974 of the southern part of the country. The deposition of the Sudan's military head, Colonel Gaafar Nimeiri, in 1985 has yet to lead to the secure return of democracy in a country devastated by famines in the mid-1980s.

In the decades following the end of World War II every part of the continent except for South Africa underwent significant political and social change. Despite modernization, however, women remain largely confined to traditional roles. Poverty and illiteracy continue to afflict the women of sub-Saharan Africa, who are also still subject to clan-arranged marriages and, in many places, polygamy. Drought, starvation, forced migration, civil war, and the AIDS epidemic have compounded these problems in re-

cent years, as has the urbanization that has broken up old communal relationships in which men and women worked side by side. In sub-Saharan countries a large proportion of women are involved in subsistence farming. In the cities female underemployment is particularly acute and paid jobs are the exception. Legal equality has gradually emerged, as elsewhere, and Ghana in 1960 took the unprecedented step of reserving ten seats in the national assembly for women. Women have long been active in handicraft production and trading, and when organized they have been formidable: thousands of Ibo women staged a tax rebellion in eastern Nigeria in 1923 that left 50 people dead.

Economic growth and political stability have proved hard to achieve and harder still to maintain, and the future of many African countries remains uncertain at best. If one cause unites so diverse a range of nations, it is opposition to continued white domination in South Africa. The Organization of African Unity, first formed in 1963, has articulated this common African concern while serving a broader, less tangible ideal, African "community," which inspired many of the leaders who guided their nations to independence.

South America: Reform and Revolution

Throughout most of Latin America the mood at the beginning of the twentieth century was one of confidence and optimism. But as the century nears its end, the economic and political progress of the early decades of independence after 1821 has been checked and, in some places, even reversed. Few Latin American governments, democratic or not, have found lasting solutions to the basic social and economic problems that beset the region.

Poverty and overpopulation remain endemic. Wealth and land continue to be concentrated in the hands of a privileged elite that sometimes represents as little as 2 percent of the population and has often protected its own landed and commerical interests by supporting undemocratic regimes. The deep-rooted social ills that afflict Latin American society are revealed in huge cities such as Buenos Aires and Mexico City, where millions live in overcrowded squalor. The Catholic church has maintained its influence throughout the region. Although at a local level pastoral workers have sought to improve living conditions for the poor, the official image of the church has been compromised in places by its lack of public opposition to repressive regimes.

The main force behind the maintenance of political repression has been the military. Since the mid-nineteenth century Latin American political life has been dominated by an endless series of crises and coups provoked by the

40.2 *Modern South America*

intervention of the army in civil affairs. Once in power, military leaders have retained control by co-opting the support of the landed and business classes. With the notable exception of Perón in Argentina, these so-called *caudillo* figures have lacked both charisma and broad-based popular support.

In economic terms, most Latin American countries are dependent on the export of raw materials and therefore at the mercy of world prices and demand. Continuing political instability has impeded the consistent development of natural resources and industrial production for the benefit of the population at large. The problems of financial

instability have been further compounded by the inability of countries such as Mexico and Brazil to repay the vast loans made to them by international organizations and foreign banks.

Each nation in Latin America faces its own special problems, in some cases created by its history and in others by its natural environment. Yet for the most part political life has been determined by a single basic principle: revolution, or sudden changes of authority, that merely redistribute power within the old elite. Only in a few instances has the new leadership produced significant change. In Chile a military coup overthrew a left-wing gov-

THE GROWTH OF LATIN AMERICAN CITIES

	Population (in thousands)					
	1940	1950	1960	1970	1980	Mid-1980s
Buenos Aires (Argentina)	2,410	5,213	7,000	9,400	9,927	10,728
Mexico City (Mexico)	1,560	2,872	4,910	8,567	12,000+	17,000
Rio de Janeiro (Brazil)	1,159	3,025	4,692	5,155	5,542	5,615
Lima-Callao (Peru)	—	947	1,519	2,500	4,601	6,000
Santiago (Chile)	952	1,275	1,907	2,600	4,309	4,750
Havana (Cuba)	936	1,081	1,549	1,700	1,935	1,970
Guayaquil (Ecuador)	—	259	450	800	1,279	1,387
Guatemala City (Guatemala)	186	294	474	770	754	1,800
La Paz (Bolivia)	—	300	400	500	635	950
San Salvador (El Salvador)	103	162	239	375	400	—[a]
Tegucigalpa (Honduras)	86	72	159	281	485	550
Managua (Nicaragua)	63	109	197	350	608	730

[a]*No accurate figures available after 1980.*

ernment in 1973 and installed a repressive right-wing dictatorship. In Bolivia the 192 changes of government that had taken place by 1985 only worsened its problems.

Since the days of the Monroe Doctrine, the United States has assumed an important and often decisive role in Latin American affairs. In its quest for territorial expansion in the 1840s, the United States seized huge tracts of Mexican territory that later became Texas and California, and in the 1890s it stripped Cuba and Puerto Rico from Spain. Thereafter, a combination of economic and security interests led Washington not only to limit the influence of European powers in Latin America but also to intervene unilaterally in the region. Yet the role played by the United States has varied greatly from one country to another. American involvement in Central American politics increased in the 1980s, and in more repressive regimes such as Chile, the United States has sometimes encouraged their leaders to mitigate the harsher effects of military rule. Direct U.S. intervention established and supported dictatorial regimes in Nicaragua, Haiti, Guatemala, and the Dominican Republic. Successive American administrations have never accepted a left-of-center regime except in Mexico or done more than tolerate centrist governments. When Argentina became embroiled with Britain in 1982 over the Falkland Islands (Islas Malvinas), Washington secretly supported its European ally while professing neutrality. In all cases, American authorities carefully monitor, influence, and often determine events throughout Latin America.

Brazil: The Unstable Giant

Brazil, which occupies almost half of the South American continent—some 3 million square miles—and has a population of more than 140 million, is a far more varied nation than its neighbors. Whereas the other countries in Central and South America speak the Spanish of their conquerors,

Brazil's cultural inheritance is mixed. The official language and culture derive chiefly from Brazil's Catholic Portuguese colonizers. That heritage is supplemented by the cultures of the indigenous Indian population and the Africans whose ancestors were imported as slaves in the seventeenth and eighteenth centuries.

The waves of European immigrants who came to Brazil in the nineteenth century included a sizable number of Jews. Continuing Jewish immigration was brought to a halt in 1930 by restrictive legislation, and in 1937 a secret order was circulated to all Brazilian consulates to reject visa applications submitted by Jews. In spite of official discrimination, however, small numbers of skilled workers and professionals escaped to Brazil from Nazi Germany. After World War II the Jewish population rose gradually to about 150,000, concentrating in the larger cities.

In Brazil during the 1930s and 1940s the rule of Getúlio Vargas introduced a period of relative economic and political stability. When Vargas died in 1954, the alliance between nationalism and capitalism that he had forged and maintained for a quarter of a century collapsed. The same forces that produced conflict elsewhere in South America now pitted themselves against each other in Brazil: the working class and the peasants on the one hand, and the landowning elite and the military on the other. This conflict unfolded against uncontrolled economic expansion based on foreign loans, used mostly for grandiose public works projects that resulted in profiteering and disastrous inflation.

Expensive public projects took an enormous toll in foreign exchange and political stability. The consequence was growing inflation and an increase in social tension. In 1964 a military government seized power, holding it for a generation. Successive military governments held occasional elections but refused to relinquish control. Although the country has made progress toward economic stability, the gap between the prosperous business class and the poor continues to widen. Uncontrolled development and specu-

The *favelas* of Rio de Janeiro: slums where a quarter of the city's people live in squalid shanties without water or sewers. [Bruno Barbey/Magnum]

lation have led to the spoliation of much of Brazil's land, especially in the Amazon basin. Political repression produced the familiar pattern of rigid censorship, police brutality, and human rights abuse.

By 1975 serious strains had developed in relations between Brazil and the United States. In addition to concern over Brazil's public image as a police state, Washington was alarmed at its growing involvement with nuclear technology. When the Carter administration reduced military aid, the Brazilians retaliated by canceling their military pact with the United States.

From 1979 to 1985 Brazil's military rulers slowly moved toward the reestablishment of civilian government. After parliamentary elections in 1982, a coalition of opposition groups, the Democratic Alliance, chose as its candidate for the presidency Tancredo Neves, a trusted and popular figure. His successor, José Sarney, lacked the ability to command a consensus, and the rest of 1985 was marked by a series of paralyzing strikes. Coming on top of a disastrous drought that devastated Brazil's coffee crop, a major source of exchange, the industrial unrest forced Sarney's government into action. Prices and wages were frozen, and negotiations with the International Monetary Fund and private banks rescheduled Brazil's debts.

Economically, Brazil's future seems unclear. A major steel industry has emerged; exports of goods such as chemicals, shoes, and automobiles are increasing; and minerals such as iron and bauxite are bringing in foreign currency. Nonetheless, the repayment of its foreign debts—the largest in the world—reached the breaking point in 1987, when Brazil suspended payments as inflation reached 365 percent per annum. The democratic govern-

ment has yet to deal with the country's social inequities and has failed to implement land reform. Yet the spirit of optimism that led to the creation of Brasilia is characteristic of Brazilian popular culture and may help the country weather its current crisis.

BRASILIA: THE PLANNED CITY

While Brazil faced financial collapse in the 1950s, its president, Juscelino Kubitschek, inaugurated the country's most ambitious public undertaking, a new capital city, Brasilia. The scheme, commissioned in 1957, was designed to give visible form to the government's faith in Brazil's future. The new capital was situated in the plains of the state of Goias, 600 miles inland. Within three years the master plan of Lucio Costa and the buildings of the architect Oscar Niemeyer had taken sufficient shape for the government to move there. As in Chandigarh, the Indian planned city designed by Le Corbusier, a major city was laid out from the beginning with an eye to its total physical and architecture design, as well as a concern for the day-to-day needs of its inhabitants.

The central part of the city, set on two main axes, north-south and east-west, is surrounded by an artificial lake that divides it from the suburbs. Most of the public buildings are set on the east-west—or "monumental"—axis. At its east end, in the Square of Three Powers, are the legislative, judicial, and executive buildings of government. Given the region's relative inaccessibility, it was necessary to construct a new highway system to connect

Brasilia with Rio de Janeiro, the former capital and Brazil's largest city. Brasilia boasts huge water and waste disposal systems and is entirely electrified.

Additional building projects were undertaken in the following decades. The University of Brazil is the center of the city's cultural life, with its auditorium and public library. Public services such as hospitals and clinics and fire and police departments are extensive and modern. By the late 1980s the population had reached about 1.4 million. Many of the original inhabitants came from economically depressed areas of the country to work on the construction of the city, but they have now been supplemented by those employed in local industries, which include printing, furniture, and services.

Brasilia has proved both daring and controversial. The notion of moving Brazil's capital to the interior goes back to the days of Portuguese rule and had been discussed again in the 1820s. Rio de Janeiro certainly exercised a cultural and social monopoly that many Brazilians found stifling. Moreover, the new city is a prosperous one. However, the architectural plans have been criticized as an example of utopian controlled design derived from a Bauhaus aesthetic with totalitarian overtones.

The artificial nature of the project has produced a city that is an exception to most great urban centers throughout the world, which have been almost always the result of a long period of human habitation, the products of accumulated human experience. Diplomats "exiled" to Brasilia complain of its arid climate and the shantytowns that have sprung up around it. Other countries that have followed Brazil's example, such as Nigeria with the construction of a new capital at Abuja, have met with mixed success. Yet the daring speed with which the scheme has been executed, together with the breadth of the concept, compels admiration. Certainly the creation of Brasilia has marked a commitment to urban living as the future basis of a nation that is still predominantly agrarian.

Argentina: Dictatorship and Democracy

Ever since Argentina's first struggles to win freedom from Spain in the early nineteenth century, political stability has proved elusive. The second largest country in Latin America, after Brazil, Argentina covers an area of just over 1 million square miles and is home to 30 million inhabitants.

Unlike Ecuador, which has a large Indian population, or Colombia and Paraguay, which have mestizo (mixed Spanish and Indian) majorities, Argentinians are overwhelmingly of European origin. The waves of immigrants, mainly Spanish and Italian, who flocked to Argentina in the nineteenth century produced conflicting interest groups that have proved difficult to reconcile. The industrialists of the capital city of Buenos Aires, the ranchers who control the great coastal estates, the farmers of the interior, and radical populists all vie for political recognition and power.

Among the European immigrants were large numbers of Jews attracted to Argentina by its relatively early industrialization. The Jewish community there, almost half a million in number, remains the largest in Latin America. The country's once liberal immigration policies changed, however, in the 1930s, when Argentina became a center of anti-Semitism. This trend continued after World War II as Argentina became a haven for escaped Nazi war criminals.

From the time of its rebellion against Spain in 1810, Argentina's history has been dominated by a series of caudillo rulers, most of whom were wealthy landowners or generals devoted to power and money. Only in 1916 were democratic radicals able to defeat the landowners and industrialists in Argentina's first open election and govern the country until 1930. But the Great Depression wrought havoc with the economy and induced the army to replace the government with a conservative coalition of bankers, landowners, and generals. This combination of interests has constituted the single most powerful force in Argentine politics ever since.

By the end of World War II the charismatic Colonel Juan Domingo Perón (1895–1974) had come to dominate the ruling clique. The archetypal caudillo, Perón's ability to mesmerize his fellow citizens owed much to the charm and brilliance of his wife Eva (1919–1952), once a popular radio announcer. By the time of her death, "Evita," who sponsored much of the regime's social reform programs despite her own opulent lifestyle, had become a popular folk heroine to her people. Her memory still remains a powerful force in Argentine politics.

With Eva's encouragement, Perón realized that his personal rule could not continue without the backing of the middle classes and the poor. Gaining control of the trade unions, he was elected president in 1946 with a large majority. Through skillful propaganda and careful attention to interest groups such as the church and the army, the Peróns retained the reluctant support of the right. At the same time, they introduced health and welfare benefits for the poor and stimulated jobs for the unemployed. These measures resulted in increased taxation, which brought a drop in agricultural production and export revenues. Financial chaos and corruption, together with the death of Eva, undermined support for Perón, who was deposed by the army in 1955.

A series of military regimes followed, alternating with brief periods of civilian rule. By 1973 Perón decided to end his exile in Spain and run for the presidency again. When the army refused to allow his candidacy, he put forward Hector Campora, a Peronist party worker, as his representative. Although Campora won, the Peronist victory led to a bloody civil struggle. In less than two months Campora was compelled to resign, Perón's opponents were forced into retirement, and new elections were

◉ Eva Perón on Peronism ◉

Juan Perón's dictatorship combined populism and nationalism into a political regime that in many ways resembled European fascism. Here Eva Perón, his wife and adviser and herself an important political figure, extolls Peronism with the kind of rhetoric that made the phenomenon so popular among Argentinians.

This is why we, the *peronistas*, may never forget the people; our heart must always be with the humble, the comrades, the poor, the dispossessed, for this is how to carry out best the doctrine of General Perón; and so that the poor, the humble, the working forces, and we ourselves, do not forget, we have pledged to be missionaries of Perón; to do this is to expand his doctrine, not only within our own country, but to offer it to the world as well, as a hope of the rewards always wished for by the working classes. . . .

General Perón has defeated internal capitalism, through social economy, putting capital at the service of the economy, and not vice versa, which only gave the workers the right to die of hunger: the law of the funnel, as it is called, the wide part for the capitalists and the narrow part for the people.

Perón has suppressed imperialist action. Now we have economic independence. He knows well all the insults he will receive for committing the "crime" of defending the country. Some Argentines allied themselves with foreigners in order to slander him, because General Perón was the first to make foreign powers respect Argentina, and treat it as an equal.

Source: E. Perón, *Historia del Peronismo* (Buenos Aires: Presidencia de la Nacion, 1951), trans. in R. Cameron, *Civilization Since Waterloo* (Itasca, Ill.: Peacock, 1971), pp. 529–531.

called. With his new wife, Isabel, as his running mate, Perón won by a large majority.

Perón's solutions to Argentina's massive problems were contradictory and self-defeating. While courting Communist countries such as Russia and Cuba, he instituted a repressive domestic policy. Liberal government officials and teachers were dismissed, and the left-wing opposition was crushed. Perón's failures may have been the result of ill health, which prevented him from controlling the conflicting forces within his coalition.

Isabel attempted to take her husband's place after his death in 1974, but the task proved impossible. Many Argentinians resented her efforts to portray herself as Evita's successor. Occupying the highest position ever held by a woman in the Western Hemisphere, the reclusive Isabel found herself unable to control her conspiring ministers. In the 21 months that she held office, she reorganized the cabinet ten times. Nor was she able to rectify Argentina's trade deficit or maintain a policy of economic

Juan and Eva Perón, who established a political system in Argentina that combined dictatorship with populist rhetoric and wide appeal. [Bettmann Archive]

austerity. Finally, the social life of the country was paralyzed by a rash of kidnappings and assassinations carried out by terrorists of both the left and the right. In 1976 yet another military coup—the sixth in 21 years—installed an army junta.

The army restored some order to the economy, increasing agricultural and industrial production and reducing inflation. The junta raised taxes and froze wages. In the face of mounting foreign debt, however, the value of the peso, the Argentine currency, fell, and the government devalued it by 70 percent. Thousands of political opponents were rounded up, tortured, and murdered. In protest, the United States suspended military aid to Argentina.

By 1982, with inflation and unemployment again increasing rapidly, the trade unions began a series of strikes, and the banned political parties called for a return to constitutional government. The regime, led by General Leopoldo Galtieri, sought to generate nationalist sentiment by challenging Britain for control of the Falkland Islands, a British Crown Colony. The Malvinas, as they are called in Latin America, are a group of barren, windswept islands off the southeast tip of Argentina inhabited mainly by sheepherders. In April 1982 Galtieri became an instant national hero when he ordered an invasion of the islands, but the government of British prime minister Margaret Thatcher, assisted by the United States, defeated Argentina.

The military government's popularity plummeted in the wake of its military defeat. The 1983 presidential campaign was won by a political moderate, Raúl Alfonsín. Despite his efforts to prosecute Galtieri and his associates for human rights violations, pressure from the army frustrated the process. Nevertheless, Alfonsín's election helped to restore international confidence in his country, and in 1986 he succeeded in negotiating loans from private banks in the United States and from the International Monetary fund. But lasting democratic solutions to the problems facing Argentina still remain an unrealized goal.

Chile and Peru: Socialism and the Military

Peru and Chile comprise most of South America's west coast. Both contain wide variations in climate and geography and have a population that is overwhelmingly mestizo. In Peru a left-wing military regime has given way to an unstable democracy, while in Chile a democratically elected socialist leader was replaced by a right-wing military dictatorship.

Throughout the nineteenth and early twentieth centuries Chilean politics were marked by continual struggles between the Liberal party, which first came to power in 1861, and the Conservatives, who represented the army and wealthy landowners. In 1920 the middle classes joined with the workers to bring the populist Arturo Alessandri Palma to power. While his government was ousted and reestablished, left-wing political parties continued to develop. In the 1930s the Radical party replaced the Liberals, while the Socialists and Communists grew in importance. Indeed, by the end of World War II the Communists were the focus of parliamentary opposition.

From 1946 to 1964, as coalitions formed by smaller parties replaced one another, public support for the left increased as a result of a well-organized labor movement. In 1970 Salvador Allende (1908–1973), a Marxist, came to power with a left-wing coalition government. Continuing support for Allende was demonstrated by large victories for his supporters in local elections the next year.

In his three years of power, Allende sought to redress many of Chile's social and economic inequities. Farms were distributed to peasants, who were provided with a wide range of social benefits. But Allende lacked the resources to pay for his programs, and deficit spending finally produced uncontrolled inflation.

Allende's government was isolated from abroad. His nationalization of American copper mines, together with other industries, led to the suspension of U.S. aid and trade. The United States even refused to sell food to Chile. The Soviets and the Chinese provided some help but not enough to offset a general boycott by non-Communist countries. Finally the army, with assistance from the American CIA, seized control in September 1973 and has remained in power ever since. Allende was slain during the coup.

Since the overthrow of Allende, Chile, one of South America's pioneers in democracy, has been governed by a repressive military dictatorship. Its leader, General Augusto Pinochet, proclaimed himself president. His well-documented policies of arbitrary arrests, torture, and executions led to a temporary suspension of American aid in 1979, although President Reagan restored it in 1981. Pinochet's constitution provided for his continued rule until 1997. Demonstrations of public opposition that marked 1985 and 1986 provoked brutal reprisals. Pinochet's presidential rule was repudiated in the elections of 1988, but he remains head of the armed forces and the effective head of the country. It is difficult to imagine a country more different from the revolutionary republic envisioned by its founders.

Like Chile, Peru was the scene of an experimental socialism, but under the unlikely direction of the army. A liberal reformist movement developed among the Peruvian educated classes in the early twentieth century. In 1924 this progressive coalition crystallized in the creation of the American Popular Revolutionary Alliance (APRA). Although anti-Communist, the APRA borrowed socialist ideas from Russia and western Europe and became the focus of an Indian rights movement. Most of Peru's history from the appearance of the APRA to 1968 consisted of periods of liberal government interrupted by army coups and military regimes.

The 1968 coup was unusual. The military leaders proclaimed a policy of "social democracy," intending to follow a middle way between capitalism and communism on the basis of a mixed economy. Banks, mines—some of them U.S.-owned—and other key industries were nationalized, and many large estates were distributed to peasants. Educational programs were expanded and social benefits introduced. The regime suppressed political opposition movements and censored the press.

The international effects of these policies were predictable. Russia sent money, weapons, and advisers, while in 1974 the Peruvian government expelled U.S. officials on charges of spying for the CIA. Peru became one of the leading advocates of Third World causes and an outspoken critic of American policies. As a result, foreign investment declined and Peru's economy began to collapse. Some industries were returned to their owners after 1975, but the damage had been done. By 1978 the regime returned the country to civilian rule.

Both of Peru's subsequently elected presidents have been drawn from the APRA. Their problems—a declining economy, massive debt, drug trafficking, and industrial unrest—have been compounded since 1983 by bands of guerrilla fighters in the countryside of southern Peru. Calling themselves *Sendero Luminoso* ("shining path," a quotation from Lenin), they are a splinter group of the Peruvian Communist party. In 1984 they were joined by another revolutionary movement, the *Tupac Amaru*, named after an eighteenth-century Indian who revolted against the Spaniards. The former group is active in rural areas; the latter operates primarily in the cities, including Lima, the capital. Together with the terrorist activites of cocaine traders, the guerrilla groups present serious problems. In 1987 President Alan García survived mutinies and public outrage against police and army brutality, but the future of his country remains troubled.

Bolivia: Land of Revolutions

Although the history of Bolivia, with its succession of military coups, superficially resembles that of Argentina, fundamental social differences prevail. The overwhelming majority of Bolivia's population is either of pure Indian or of mixed European and Indian descent. In the early days of independence after 1825 no educated middle class existed to run the state bureaucracy. Wealthy landowners were interested only in protecting their own interests. The military filled the vacuum with 50 years of misrule.

By the end of the nineteenth century political parties led by Bolivia's landed aristocracy had developed. The Liberal party exploited Bolivia's major resource, tin, and con-

structed road and rail networks throughout the country. The proceeds from these modernization programs further enriched the wealthy, who became known as the "tin barons," instead of improving living conditions for the poor.

By the 1930s most of Bolivia's mineral wealth had been sold to American investors, and the Great Depression devastated the economy. In 1932 conflict broke out between Bolivia and its southern neighbor, Paraguay, complicating an already difficult situation. The so-called Gran Chaco War ended in 1935 with Bolivia losing a sizable chunk of its territory.

Military governments continued into the postwar period. A brief attempt was made between 1937 and 1939 to introduce social reform for the workers, but its sponsor was murdered, and protests were brutally suppressed. Nevertheless, with great difficulty, Victor Paz Estenssoro managed to unify various urban protest groups into the National Revolutionary Movement (MNR) in 1941. A decade later the MNR won the national elections, but the army refused to allow Estenssoro to take power. Their action finally prompted a revolution that put Estenssoro in office as president.

In 1952 the new government took over the tin mines and raised workers' wages and benefits. Unfortunately, these moves coincided with a fall in tin prices on the world market, pointing up the danger of dependence on a single export. Not until 1966 did the mines return to their former profitability. Estenssoro also tried to redress the grievances of the Indians, most of whom lived in a condition of servitude that had changed little since the sixteenth century. The urban rebellion of the MNR had been accompanied by widespread uprisings and Indian land seizures in the countryside. The government recognized the claims of the Indians in 1953 and distributed land to the farmers.

The democratic government brought genuine social and economic improvement to Bolivia, but it failed to reduce the domination of the military, which seized power once more in 1964. Estenssoro returned to office in 1985 after 20 years marked by a succession of military coups. Most of the regimes were repressive and reactionary, although the pattern was briefly broken by General Juan José Torres, who seized power in 1970. Known for his left-wing sentiments, Torres relied on peasant, worker, and student support and convened a "people's parliament" to represent their views.

In 1972 he was deposed by Colonel Hugo Banzer, who remained in office for six years, a record in Bolivia's political history. Banzer attempted to introduce a coherent economic policy but also sold off the country's natural resources, including oil and natural gas, to foreign business interests. Although these measures stimulated economic growth, the rich gained most of the benefits. Another bewildering succession of coups marked the post-Banzer period. As unfavorable international reaction to drug trafficking and human rights violations grew, the United States broke diplomatic relations with Bolivia, forcing elections in 1982.

The new moderate government of Hernan Siles Zuazo appealed to foreign banks and the International Monetary Fund for help. The aid did little, however, to reduce inflation or satisfy worker demands. In the ensuing chaos, Estenssoro emerged once again, at the age of 77, as president. He promised economic and social reform, but lacking coherent political forces, or even a single charismatic figure such as Perón, Bolivia's history, already witness to 192 changes of government, persistently fulfills gloomy expectations.

Central America and the Caribbean

Private American businesses, especially the United Fruit Company and sugar, coffee, and tobacco firms, had entered Central America and the Caribbean in the late nineteenth century. The United States has maintained a more direct presence in the region since the Spanish-American War. In the wake of its victory over Spain in 1898, the United States declared a protectorate over Cuba and an-

nexed Puerto Rico. Five years later, when Panamanian rebels revolted against Colombia, which claimed the territory of Panama, Washington supported the rebels and quickly imposed its control over the newly formed republic. Americans then built the Panama Canal on land leased from its new dependency. The strategic importance of the canal for the United States, together with extensive economic interests, have maintained the U.S. presence in the area ever since.

The Cuban Revolution

Cuba has been one of the most prominent nations in Latin America since 1959, when the country experienced a dramatic political upheaval that has challenged America's sway over the Central American region.

Fidel Castro (born 1927), a charismatic leader and brilliant propagandist, united forces opposed to the corrupt dictator Fulgencio Batista, who had ruled the island since 1936. Yet when Castro's guerrilla campaign overthrew Batista in 1959, his goals were unclear. Although he had plans to hold elections, he quickly suspended them. By 1961 he had begun introducing state economic and social controls and declared himself a Marxist-Leninist.

Castro's revolution aimed at a radical transformation of Cuba's social and economic structure. His socialist pro-

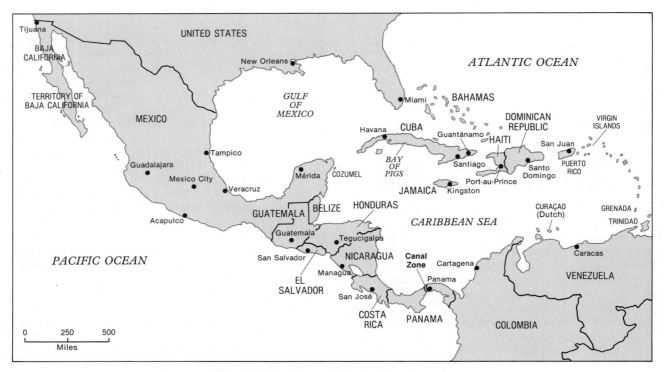

40.3 Mexico and Central America

grams drove much of the middle class—some 750,000 people—from the island, and many opponents who stayed were silenced by means of firing squads or imprisonment. Collective farms replaced the estates once owned by large landowners, and the government nationalized the sugar and tobacco industries. Moreover, significant social and educational reforms have improved the lives of Cuba's citizens, and today Cuba's infant mortality and illiteracy rates are the lowest in Latin America. Castro's reforms also gave women equality before the law and open access to education and the professions.

In many ways Cuba's history embodies the dilemma created by America's dealings with its southern neighbors. Batista's rule collapsed only after the withdrawal of informal American support in 1958. Yet Castro anticipated that his radical economic and social policies might bring American intervention. He therefore turned to the Soviet Union, which he hoped would serve as a counterweight to the United States. The Soviets proved powerful and willing patrons in return for a base of operations only 90 miles from the coast of Florida.

In April 1961 the United States sponsored a badly organized invasion by Cuban exiles at the Bay of Pigs on the southern coast of Cuba. The United States, reluctant to engage Cuban forces directly, refused air cover at the last moment, and the invaders were routed. The fiasco confirmed Castro's belief that American imperialism was poised to undermine him and encouraged the Russians to exploit their foothold in Cuba. Weapons, including intercontinental missiles, were deployed on the island, only to be withdrawn in 1962 when an alarmed American government confronted the Soviet Union.

In the 1960s Castro's Cuba served as a center for revolutionary aspirations throughout Latin America. Castro's chief aide in seizing power and organizing the new state had been Ernesto ("Che") Guevara (1928–1967). Guevara now became the principal theorist of guerrilla insurgency as a technique for bringing revolution to the rest of the Americas, personally encouraging rebel forces there and elsewhere. He was killed in Bolivia in October 1967 by U.S.-trained counterinsurgency forces, setting back Castro's policy of exporting revolution.

Despite this retrenchment, the Cuban regime has continued to defy American trade boycotts and the loss of the lucrative U.S. market. The stability of the Cuban economy is maintained largely by Soviet aid. In the 1980s Cuba began to involve itself in revolutions beyond Latin America, including those in Angola and Ethiopia. An apparent easing in relations with the United States in 1984 was reversed the following year, when a private American-based radio station, Radio Martí, began to transmit anti-Castro propaganda to Cuba. Castro himself has been elected president three times, and in 1986 he proclaimed a new emphasis on women, blacks, and young people and

Ernesto "Che" Guevara and Fidel Castro greet Soviet leader Anastas Mikoyan in 1961. [Sovfoto]

◉ Che Guevara on Guerrilla Warfare ◉

*In the course of the revolution against the Batista dictatorship in
Cuba, Che Guevara found it necessary to transform Marxist doctrine
and Leninist strategy to meet the conditions prevailing in the agrarian
societies of Latin America. Here he explains the fundamental principles
of guerrilla warfare.*

The armed victory of the Cuban people over the Batista dictatorship . . . forced a change
in the old dogmas concerning the conduct of the popular masses of Latin America. . . .

We consider that the Cuban Revolution contributed three fundamental lessons to the
conduct of revolutionary movements in America. They are:

(1) Popular forces can win a war against the army.

(2) It is not necessary to wait until all conditions for making revolution exist; the insurrection can create them.

(3) In underdeveloped America the countryside is the basic area for armed fighting.

Of these three propositions the first two contradict the defeatist attitude of revolutionaries or pseudorevolutionaries who remain inactive and take refuge in the pretext that
against a professional army nothing can be done. . . .

Naturally, it is not to be thought that all conditions for revolution are going to be
created through the impulse given to them by guerrilla activity. . . . People must see
clearly the futility of maintaining the fight for social goals within the framework of civil
debate. . . .

The third proposition is a fundamental of strategy. It ought to be noted by those who
maintain dogmatically that the struggle of the masses is centered in city movements, entirely forgetting the immense participation of the country people in the life of all the
underdeveloped parts of America.

Source: C. Guevara, *Guerrilla Warfare*, trans. J. P. Moray (Lincoln: University of Nebraska Press, 1985),
pp. 47–48.

appointed his sister-in-law as the first female member of
the party council.

Patterns of Violence

Military dictatorships have dominated Central American
politics since the turn of the century. In the 1970s elections in Guatemala, El Salvador, and Nicaragua were subverted by military intervention. In Guatemala, where half
the arable land is owned by 2 percent of the population,
each military regime tried to outdo its predecessor in violently repressing popular discontent. The result was some
of the bitterest guerrilla warfare in Latin America.

Haiti, which achieved independence from France in

1804 following a slave revolt, has been racked by violence
ever since. In 1957 François Duvalier established a police
state, which his family maintained for two generations by
a combination of brutality and superstition. After Jean-
Claude Duvalier succeeded his father, his wife exhausted
the country's treasury with extravagant shopping trips to
Paris while the people suffered the worst social conditions
in the Caribbean. When rioting broke out in 1986, the
Duvaliers fled the country, taking millions of dollars with
them. Family rule proved equally unstable in the Dominican Republic, where with American support General Ra-
fael Trujillo maintained a harsh but efficient dictatorship
from 1930 until his assassination in 1961. His son failed to
retain power and, together with his family, fled the island.
United States troops occupied the country between April

1965 and September 1966, thwarting the reformist candidacy of Juan Bosch and installing a rightist regime.

El Salvador, a coffee-producing country in which a tiny oligarchy controls three-fifths of the land, remains torn by a civil war that has claimed thousands of civilian casualties. In 1984 a moderate president was elected and negotiations were opened between the regime and the guerrillas, but no satisfactory end to the strife appears in sight. As in Guatemala, American aid, rationalized by a fear of communism, helps to finance the government's battle against the guerrillas.

The Nicaraguan Revolution

If fear of Castro's Cuba had earlier dominated American policy in Central America, the Nicaraguan revolution of 1979 set the tone for the 1980s. Like prerevolutionary Cuba, Nicaragua was harshly ruled for more than 30 years by a corrupt and stubborn dictator under American protection. When Anastasio Somoza García was finally ousted, the new revolutionary government and the United States confronted each other with mutual suspicion. Little has happened to dispel that mistrust.

The new ruling party, the *Sandinistas* (named for César Augusto Sandino, a guerrilla leader of the late 1920s and early 1930s), created a "national reconstruction government" under the presidency of Daniel Ortega. It has vastly improved public health, education, and food production through land reform. Sandinista economic policy contains a mix of capitalist and socialist elements. Nevertheless, much government spending has been devoted to fighting the U.S.-sponsored *contra* rebels in a war that has claimed over 30,000 lives to date. Much to the displeasure of Washington, the Ortega regime has not implemented Western-style democracy or guaranteed a free press. Whereas America has provided aid to the *contras*, Nicaragua has accepted Cuban, Soviet, and Swedish assistance. Nicaragua has undoubtedly aligned itself with Third World and Communist countries. Fears of intervention in the region were heightened by the American invasion of the Caribbean island of Grenada in 1983 and the installation of a pro-American government there.

At the beginning of that year, four Latin American

◉ A Sandinista Woman ◉

The revolutionary movement that toppled the repressive government in Nicaragua in 1979 drew dedicated militants from all walks of life, men and women who worked in the underground against difficult odds for years. Here a Sandinista woman leader, Dora Maria, explains the nature of her revolutionary commitment.

Sometimes I wonder, I ask myself why, given the brutal repression in 1973, when the people didn't yet support us, when they informed on comrades who carried out various actions, when they pointed them out on the streets, when the repression shattered us, when thousands of people fell—why did we keep on believing? And why in 1960, in 1961, in 1963, and in 1967 did the militants keep believing that one day the people would rise up?

What makes a man believe in his own potential as a man? What makes a woman believe that she is capable of anything? No one taught us. That is one of the great mysteries about the Revolution. They don't teach it to you at school. You don't learn to believe in humanity on the streets. Religion doesn't teach it. It teaches us to believe in God, not in men and women. So it's difficult to awaken that belief in yourself and in others. But in spite of all that, many women and men did develop that commitment.

It becomes an obsession—the people must rise up, they must. It begins with a vision, an imaginary idea. . . . We had to understand that people are historically capable of making revolutions. . . . But I never understood it as historical law. I think many people didn't. . . . All we knew was that we were going to make the Revolution, however long it took.

Source: M. Randall, *Sandino's Daughters: Testimonies of Nicaraguan Women in Struggle* (Vancouver, Canada: New Star Books, 1983), pp. 53–54.

A literacy campaign in Nicaragua. [Owen Franken/Stock, Boston]

countries—Venezuela, Colombia, Panama, and Mexico—met on the island of Contadora off the coast of Panama to develop a peace plan for Central America. The revelation late in 1986 that arms sales to Iran had secretly been used to fund *contra* forces caused a major scandal in the Reagan administration and undermined America's credibility as an opponent of international terrorism. Unlike Castro's Cuba, where the revolution developed in relative peace after 1962, Nicaragua's new regime has not had the opportunity to establish its domestic programs on a peaceful footing.

Mexico in the Twentieth Century

Although 300 years of Spanish control over Mexico ended in 1821, the modern republic was not inaugurated until 1920. The intervening century saw continuous conflicts between Mexico and the United States, culminating in the American annexation of Texas following the Mexican-American War. Attempts by Benito Juárez (1806–1872) to better the conditions of the Indian poor by a program of land reform from 1855 to 1876 were briefly interrupted by the intervention of the French emperor Napoleon III, who installed his relative Maximilian as emperor of Mex-

ico. After the death of Juárez, Porfirio Díaz (1830–1915) ruled despotically for nearly 35 years. By 1910 popular discontent had united peasants, workers, and intellectuals. The opposition was led by Francisco Madero (1873–1913), supported by bandit revolutionaries such as Pancho Villa and Emiliano Zapata. When Díaz fled in 1911, Madero assumed the presidency but was murdered in a military uprising openly encouraged by the United States ambassador to Mexico. The subsequent revolution led to the establishment of a republic.

Although since 1920 Mexico has had a parliamentary government, in practice the chief political force, the Institutional Revolutionary Party (PRI), has dominated the country, winning every election since 1929 and providing all of Mexico's presidents. Virtually every aspect of Mexican life is under PRI control, including political patronage, education, the economy, and cultural activities. Lázaro Cárdenas, who served as president from 1934 to 1940, introduced ambitious plans for the redistribution of land, causing confrontation with the Catholic church, and expropriated foreign-owned oil properties in 1938.

Mexico's population, currently more than 75 million, has doubled since 1960. Initial attempts to improve the lives of its vast and underprivileged peasant population gave way after World War II to a drive to industrialize. The result was the creation of large modern cities and an incipient middle class. Yet there has been little change in the lot of the urban or rural poor, whose numbers continue to swell. By the late 1960s the postwar economic boom had begun to decline, and in 1975 inflation had reached 40 percent. Following the killing of some 300 university students during a demonstration in 1968, unrest beset the country. In the 1970s the political leadership did little to arrest the erosion of public confidence, borrowing heavily from foreign investors attracted to Mexico's huge oil reserves, the fourth largest in the world.

With the fall of oil prices in 1981, Mexico's economy collapsed. The currency was drastically devalued, and the prices of electricity and gasoline increased. In the 1982 elections—which featured the candidacy of Rosaria Ibarra de Piedra, the first woman to run for president in the nation's history—the PRI presidential candidate, Miguel de la Madrid, won 74 percent of the votes, a small victory by Mexican standards. The challenge to PRI control was confirmed by a bitterly contested election in 1988.

Mexican society is beset by a wide range of natural and human problems. In 1985 a massive earthquake rocked the capital, Mexico City, leaving thousands dead or homeless. Even with international aid, the damage left irreparable wounds in a city already on the verge of collapse. The plight of Mexico City was, in fact, already one of the country's most serious problems. With more than 17 million people, many living in hovels, and plagued by pollution, it embodies the worst aspects of urbanization, with day-to-day difficulties in energy and public services. Like other Third World urban centers such as Calcutta, Mexico City symbolizes the crisis of city life in the late twentieth century.

Mexico's relations with the United States, always strained, deteriorated in the 1970s. Illegal immigration into America, formerly tolerated by both nations, was more tightly checked. Mexican drug trafficking, a national industry in which even the PRI was implicated, added to these tensions along with a rash of kidnappings and murders of Americans by Mexican bandits posing as policemen.

Mexico's immediate hope must be that oil prices will rise again. The elimination of the harsher inequities that pervade Mexican society represents the major challenge Mexico faces as one of Latin America's most populous countries.

Society and Culture in Latin America

It is difficult to generalize about so vast and varied a region as Latin America, but certain broad principles have applied during the twentieth century. The first is that democratic participation in the political process has been the exception rather than the rule. Paradoxically, because most citizens have been excluded from an active role in government, they have turned to direct political action far more than Americans or Europeans. The abuses of the secret police in Chile or Guatemala and the massive protests of the "mothers of the disappeared" (missing political prisoners) in Argentina have demonstrated how political realities affect the daily lives of Latin Americans in a direct and often violent manner.

The Catholic church has played an important, if inconsistent, role in Latin American society. Catholicism is deeply rooted in virtually every country of the region, although its external manifestations are often affected by indigenous Indian traditions and its influence varies from country to country. Hence whereas the church occupies an important position as a force for national unity in Argentina, Bolivian Catholicism represents only a thin veneer of European culture on an Indian civilization that goes back to pre-Columbian times. In Mexico the church has almost no influence in public affairs. In the 1970s Latin America saw the growth of so-called liberation theology, a philosophy of social activism that condones the use of violence to promote change in extreme circumstances. Generally developed by worker-priests closely involved in social reform in local communities, this philosophy met with a mixed reception from Catholic religious leaders, both in Latin America and in the church hierarchy. It was condemned by Pope John Paul II, most notably in his 1987 visit to Chile and Argentina.

The reactions of individual national clergy have been determined in part by local conditions. Whereas the archbishop of El Salvador played an important part in negotiations there before his assassination in 1979, the confiscation of church property by Nicaragua's Sandinista regime generated official Catholic protests. Yet even though Catholic influence varies throughout Latin America, the phenomenon of secularization that has swept Europe and North America has yet to make serious inroads there.

A third characteristic common to many Latin American countries has been the vitality and persistence of their popular cultures. With the possible exception of Mexico, more directly influenced by its powerful northern neighbor, Latin America shows less cultural conformity than Europe, where American influence has produced a degree of uniformity in popular music, television entertainment, and fast food. The folk songs and dances of Brazil's Carnival, the "reggae" music of Jamaica, the traditional pottery and weaving of Peru, all are manifestations of living and thriving cultural traditions.

Latin American achievements in the arts have also maintained a sense of national character. The Argentinian novelist Jorge Luis Borges (1899–1986) captured the blend of Spanish and Indian mysticism that pervades the life of his country while constructing parables of universal significance. Pablo Neruda (1904–1973), the Chilean writer and diplomat, is probably Latin America's best-known poet and one of four of the region's writers to win the Nobel prize for literature—the others being his compatriot Gabriela Mistral, the Guatemalan novelist Miguel Angel Asturias, and the Colombian novelist Gabriel Garcia Marquez (born 1928). If there is a feature common to the work of these writers, it is the use of fantasy and magic that provides an escape from reality: Marquez' novel *One Hundred Years of Solitude* describes life in an imaginary town in a remote region of Colombia, where extraordinary events are the order of the day.

Mexico has produced a number of major painters, including Diego Rivera (1886–1957), whose Communist sympathies influenced much of his work. Rivera's murals in Rockefeller Center, New York City, were removed after fierce controversy. Among his associates was José Clemente Orozco (1883–1949), famous for the bold realism of his frescoes. By contrast, Rufino Tamayo (born 1899) created a more cosmopolitan style that invokes a magical world comparable in painting to that of Borges' and Marquez' novels. On the whole, realistic depictions of the lives of workers and peasants have dominated Latin American painting, as in the moving frescoes of Rivera and the Brazilian Cândido Portinari (1903–1962), whose work can be seen at the United Nations building in New York.

Latin American composers have frequently been inspired by the folk music of their homelands. The Brazilian musician Heitor Villa-Lobos (1887–1959) wrote a series of works titled *Bachianas Brasileiras*, in which he treated

Brazilian folk motifs in a style reminiscent of Johann Sebastian Bach. Among the works of the Mexican Carlos Chávez (1899–1978), who founded the Mexican Symphony Orchestra, is the *Sinfonia India*, which uses folk motifs to evoke the country's Indian past. The generally underdeveloped state of musical conservatories in Latin America has forced most performing artists, including the famous Chilean pianist Claudio Arrau (born 1904), to study abroad. Yet many capital cities in the region have a thriving operatic tradition that goes back to the nineteenth century. The most famous and beautiful opera house in South America is the Teatro Colón in Buenos Aires, where performances meet international standards.

The best film production unit in Latin America is the Cuban Film Institute, where young directors and performers are encouraged to develop their skills at government expense. Elsewhere, filmmakers have used their works to document their country's history. The Argentinian film *The Official Story*, which describes events in Argentina after the fall of the military dictatorship in 1983, won an Academy Award as the best foreign film of 1985.

The thriving arts and popular culture of Latin America represent both a reminder of and an escape from the grim realities of everyday life. Unlike much of the rest of the world, the twentieth century has seen little change in age-old social patterns in the region anywhere but in Cuba and Nicaragua. Apart from Mexico, and to a lesser extent Argentina and Brazil, the population remains split into the wealthy few and the many poor, with little sign of a developing middle class. For example, in Brazil, Colombia, and Peru half or more of the households live in absolute poverty, defined as the ability to purchase the barest necessities for subsistence. Yet Latin America has the fastest-growing population in the world, increasing about 3 percent each year. In these same countries approximately one out of five adults is illiterate, and infant mortality remains high. Despite huge potential resources, most of the region is still predominantly agricultural. Industrial production is unequally distributed: as late as 1970 three nations—Argentina, Brazil, and Mexico—accounted for 80 percent of all industrial production in Latin America, and a third of that was confined to the cities of Buenos Aires, São Paulo, and Mexico City.

Women and the Culture of *Machismo*

Women in Central and South American society have only recently begun to regain the position they held in most communities before the Spanish conquest. Among the Aztecs, for example, women came close to legal equality with men. They could possess property, enter into contracts, testify before tribunals, seek divorce, and remarry freely. At the age of 50 they were accorded full equality and enjoyed equal status with men as elders.

Under the colonial regime, women lost most of their rights. The law presumed them to be mentally inferior, and the style of male bravado and presumption known as *machismo* that produced such laws became deeply ingrained in the culture. Yet in colonial times women were allowed to own property and to sign for mortgages in their own names. Independence brought little but lip service to the idea of greater equality for Latin American women. Not until the Mexican revolution in the early twentieth century was legal equality recognized. Argentina, Uruguay, and Chile followed suit in the 1920s and 1930s. Yet women in Argentina did not get the vote until 1947 and in Mexico only in 1953; with the passage of a female suffrage law in Paraguay in 1961, all women in the Americas had won the right to vote.

Despite progress, the goal of full equality remains elusive. Men are still recognized as head of the household in many Spanish-American countries, with the legal right to choose the place of domicile, direct the education of children, administer their property, and retain custody in case of divorce. *Machismo* enforces a double standard of sexual morality, with men permitted and even encouraged to form extramarital liaisons as proof of their virility. The result is a very high incidence of rape and illegitimacy, particularly marked in Brazil.

As elsewhere, the position of women is greatly affected by the variables of class, status, and income, by residence in town or country, and by skin color. The women of the elite are in many respects indistinguishable from their counterparts in the industrial West; for those trapped in rural poverty or urban squalor, the still-halting steps toward equality have had little effect. Eva and Isabel Perón notwithstanding, until recent years few women have played a visible part in public life. Beginning in the 1970s, however, more and more women have held appointed or elected positions in government. In Venezuela and Mexico women have served in presidential cabinets, and one woman became governor of the Mexican state of Colima.

Differences in education and training have generally relegated women to lower-paying jobs in the work force, and men usually displace women as a result of technological and unemployment cycles. Thus although women have been part of agricultural labor in Latin America for centuries, mechanization has made it difficult for them to obtain work in that sector. Similarly, ever larger numbers of Latin American women have moved into factory work, but they are generally paid less than men and hold less skilled jobs. Nevertheless, some exceptions hold out the promise of future change. In Brazil, for example, where the proportion of economically active women is lower than that of men, more women actually hold professional positions. Moreover, the number of working women doubled in the decade after 1970.

Experience has shown that when organized, women can exert a powerful force for change, as in the case of the Argentinian mothers of the disappeared. More revealing still, it has been estimated that women comprised as much as a third of the Sandinista People's Army in Nicaragua, where women now hold important government positions. In Cuba legislation passed in 1976 actually provided a legal basis for the sharing of housework and child care. Despite such transformation, however, the pattern of custom and prejudice dies slowly, and *machismo* continues to exert a powerful influence on male attitudes toward women.

The myriad of problems facing the global community as the second half of the twentieth century draws to a close can be seen as two broad challenges: the avoidance of a nuclear war that could destroy human society—an issue that will be examined in Chapter 41; and the securing of economic, social, and political well-being for the bulk of the world's inhabitants—an issue symbolized by the status of Africa and Latin America.

Both regions have undergone significant political change since the end of World War II as their peoples struggled against colonialism and continue to work to free themselves from dependency on the more advanced industrialized states. Yet the political systems under which many African and Latin American nations operate have been fraught with instability and a marked tendency toward authoritarianism. In part this political experience has been the result of the massive problems of development that each faces. The economic potential of the regions is vast, but immediate financial resources are limited. In most cases the small, privileged elites that control much of the wealth of these countries have neither directed resources toward the people nor been willing to extend democracy to them. In many areas racial and ethnic tensions contribute to political and social instability. Inefficiency, corruption, and the lack of appropriate technological capacity have combined to retard development, and despite productive agricultural soils, many states cannot feed their rapidly growing populations. Africa and Latin America are burdened with the fastest-growing populations in the world, high illiteracy, daunting health problems, and widespread poverty. Only far-reaching changes in the social and political structures of these regions can, in the long run, resolve such dilemmas.

Though these and other challenges appear at times insurmountable, the future holds substantial promise. Africa and Latin America possess not only extensive natural resources and rich cultural heritages but also populations that have repeatedly proved their creativity and resilience.

Suggestions for Further Reading

Africa

Bairoch, P. *The Economic Development of the Third World Since 1900*. London: Methuen, 1975.

Breese, G., ed. *The City in Newly Developing Countries*. Englewood Cliffs, N.J.: Prentice-Hall, 1972.

Elliott, C. *Patterns of Poverty in the Third World*. New York: Praeger, 1975.

Emerson, R. *From Empire to Nation: The Rise of Self-assertion of Asian and African Peoples*. Cambridge: Cambridge University Press, 1960.

Giliomee, H., and Elphick, R., eds. *The Shaping of South African Society*. Capetown: Longman, 1979.

Goode, W. J. *World Revolution and Family Patterns*. New York: Free Press, 1970.

Legum, C. *The West's Crisis in Southern Africa*. New York: Africana, 1978.

———, et al. *Africa in the 1980s: A Continent in Crisis*. New York: McGraw-Hill, 1979.

Lloyd, P. C. *Africa in Social Change*, rev. ed. Harmondsworth, England: Penguin Books, 1972.

Mazrui, A. A. *Protest and Power in Black Africa*. London: Oxford University Press, 1972.

Suckling, J., et al. *The Economic Factor of External Investment in South Africa*. London: Africa Publications Trust, 1975.

Wallerstein, I. *Africa: The Politics of Independence*. New York: Random House, 1963.

Latin America

Blasier, C. *The Hovering Giant: U.S. Responses to Revolutionary Change in Latin America*. Pittsburgh: University of Pittsburgh Press, 1985.

Booth, J. A. *The End of the Beginning: The Nicaraguan Revolution*, 2d ed. Boulder, Colo.: Westview Press, 1985.

Burns, E. B. *A History of Brazil*. New York: Columbia University Press, 1971.

———. *Latin America: A Concise Interpretive History*, 4th ed. Englewood Cliffs, N.J.: Prentice-Hall, 1986.

Keen, B., and Wasserman, M. *A Short History of Latin America*, 2d ed. Boston: Houghton Mifflin, 1984.

Meyer, M. C., and Sherman, W. L. *The Course of Mexican History*. New York: Oxford University Press, 1979.

Randall, M. *Sandino's Daughters: Testimonies of Nicaraguan Women in Struggle*. Vancouver, Canada: New Star Books, 1981.

Stepan, A., ed. *Authoritarian Brazil: Origins, Politics, and Future*. New Haven, Conn.: Yale University Press, 1976.

Thomas, H. *The Cuban Revolution*. New York: Harper & Row, 1977.

Maps and Their Makers (II)

The attempt to map the environment began with the earliest human societies. By the middle of the first millennium B.C., the first world map had been produced in Babylonia. Maps of considerable sophistication were drawn in the ancient West and China, but not until the discovery of the Americas and of the Pacific by Columbus and his successors in the late fifteenth and sixteenth centuries were the true dimensions of the earth known with any accuracy.

The discovery of the New World coincided with the development of movable type in the West. Printed maps circulated rapidly, facilitating trade and exploration. In 1570 Abraham Ortelius, a Flemish contemporary of Gerardus Mercator, published his *Theater of the World*, a collection of 70 maps covering the entire globe and incorporating the latest discoveries. It became a traveler's bible, going through 40 editions; a French reader enthused that it was the greatest work in the world after the Holy Scriptures.

Globes came into fashion too, and as Aristophanes had unfolded a map of the world on the ancient Greek stage, so William Shakespeare referred to the first English globe in *The Comedy of Errors*. Shakespeare remarked that "all the world's a stage," and it was no accident that the most important theater of his time

was called the Globe. The European imagination of the late sixteenth century was as fascinated with the idea of a knowable world as it was soon to be with its conquest.

The discovery of a new earth stimulated speculation about a new heaven as well. In 1595 the great Mercator's final work was published, called *Atlas*—the first collection of maps to bear this title—and subtitled *Cosmographical Meditations upon the Creation of the Universe, and the Universe as Created*. As this subtitle made clear, Mercator envisioned the mapping of the earth as only a first step toward a new understanding of the cosmos. Fourteen years later, in 1609, Galileo Galilei trained his telescope on the heavens and saw the four largest moons of Jupiter, the first new objects, apart from comets, to be observed in the heavens in thousands of years.

The discovery of these new celestial objects had a very different import from Columbus' discovery of the New World. Although pre-Columbian maps, based on Ptolemy, had underestimated the size of the globe, it was known and accepted that there were places on it where no humans lived and perhaps none had ever gone. The Ptolemaic heavens, however, for all their greater size, were believed to be fully mapped; nor

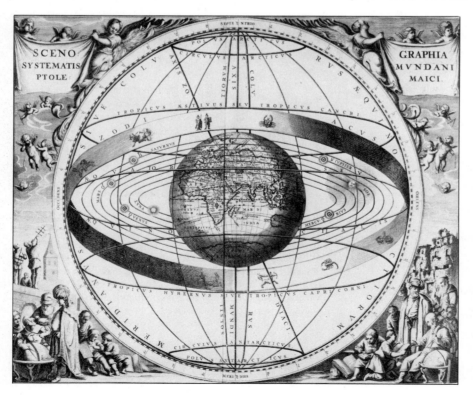

This elegant illustration of the Ptolemaic theory by Pieter Schenk and Gerard Valk dates from 1706, indicating that Ptolemy's model still had advocates into the eighteenth century. The earth is at the center, surrounded by a fiery atmosphere, while the sun, the moon, the five planets then known, and the heavens are represented by mythological figures and cherubs riding on a bed of clouds. At the edge of the system are the divisions of the Zodiac. [American Philosophical Society]

had the Copernican system, in transposing the earth and the sun, enlarged them. Galileo's four moons changed all that. The cosmos had begun to be explored; as much might be hidden as was known.

If the real exploration of the heavens had to await the development of radio astronomy in the twentieth century, the telescopes of the seventeenth were able to bring at least one celestial body within reach of the cartographers: the moon. Although only one side of it was visible from earth, some 48 craters had been located and named (mostly after ancient philosophers and modern scientists), as well as eight so-called seas. Celestial globes, depicting the sun, the earth, the planets, and the stars, became almost as popular as terrestrial ones. Such representations suggested an attempt to domesticate the cosmos. Europeans began to speculate whether beings like themselves might not inhabit other celestial bodies, and in 1639 the Italian friar Thomas Campanella published one of the earliest works of science fiction, *The City of the Sun*. With the publication of Sir Isaac Newton's *Mathematical Principles of Natural Philosophy* in 1687 (see Chapter 23), the distinction between celestial and terrestrial mechanics that had been maintained since the time of Aristotle collapsed, and it was soon generally accepted that the same physical laws governed both the earth and the heavens.

At the same time, cartography became a weapon in the struggle for commercial advantage and empire. As the imperial initiative passed in the seventeenth and eighteenth centuries from Iberia to England and France, both nations realized the crucial importance of reliable maps. Under Louis XIV mapmaking became a state enterprise. Astronomers were sent to Egypt, South America, and the West Indies to make the celestial observations essential for accurate mapping. The explorer La Salle was commissioned to survey the newly established colony of New France in North America, and a team under Jean-Dominique Cassini, director of the Royal Observatory, set out to produce a true map of France itself. Using the moons of Jupiter as a point of reference for sighting latitude, they discovered that previous maps had placed the port of Brest too far west, in what was actually open sea, and Marseilles too far south. When Louis XIV was shown these results, he exclaimed, "Your work has cost me a good part of my state!"

What France itself lost, however, its colonies regained in Guillaume Delisle's maps of Canada (1703) and Louisiana (1718), which extended French claims in the New World at the expense of England's. The British were not slow to respond, and a veritable war of maps ensued in fixing the boundaries of Nova Scotia, ceded by the French at the end of the War of the Austrian Succession (1748), with Britain ironically citing French maps to substantiate its claims to more

of the coastline with its rich fisheries and the French citing British maps to limit them.

Despite these conflicts, however, the two nations were able to cooperate occasionally in a common scientific interest. In the 1730s French expeditions to Lapland and Peru confirmed Newton's hypothesis that the earth was not a perfect sphere but, because of its variable motion, a prolate one, bulging at the equator and flattened at the poles. This was important to navigation, because it meant that degrees of latitude and longitude were not uniform but lengthened as they approached the equator and shortened as they receded. Fifty years later a joint team of British and French geographers measured the precise distance between Greenwich, England, and Paris, using French techniques of triangulation and a new British instrument, the theodolite, a 200-pound device consisting of telescopes, reflectors, and angle registers. One hundred years later, in 1884, an international conference established Greenwich as the prime meridian, that is, the point of 0 degrees of longitude from which all divisions of east and west would thenceforth be measured. Among other things, this made it possible to divide the earth into its present 24 time zones, each 15 degrees of longitude apart. Greenwich thus became, as Babylon, Jerusalem, and Ch'ang An had once been, the center of the earth.

Magellan had crossed the Pacific, but for the next 250 years little was reliably known about its western expanses. It found its geographer at last, however, in James Cook (1728–1779), the son of a Yorkshire laborer who worked himself up to a naval commission, driven by a passion for discovery that, as he confessed, "leads me not only farther than any man has been before me, but as far as I think it possible for man to go." Cook's three voyages set out in search of those will-o'-the-wisps of cartographers, a navigable shortcut to Asia through the Americas called the Northwest Passage and a great southern continent called Terra Australis, hypothesized by the ancient Greeks, popularized by Marco Polo, and still a standard feature of eighteenth-century maps. Cook found neither, but he did map thousands of miles of northwestern American coastline and virtually every island in the Pacific, and he did go farther than any man had been, sailing to within a few hundred miles of both the north and south poles.

Cook's voyages put a third of the world on the map, although it remained for others to complete his work. The Norwegian Roald Amundsen (1872–1928) finally traversed the chain of bays, straits, and sounds across northern Canada to the Beaufort Sea in 1903–1906. Antarctica, the true southern continent, was first sighted in 1820; the name Australia was given to the great landmass that the British explorer Matthew Flinders was the first to realize in 1801 was not an archipelago but a continent in its own right. Cook himself was tragically murdered in Hawaii, another of his discoveries, while preparing to make a fourth voyage.

The efforts of Cook, Flinders, and two other Englishmen, George Vancouver and Francis Beaufort, had given a tolerably good idea of the coastal contours of the six habitable continents by the mid-nineteenth century. It remained to map the equally challenging interiors of the Americas, Africa, and central Asia.

One of the first native surveyors of North America was George Washington, who as a young man charted the region between the Potomac River and Lake Erie, and, failing to persuade Congress of the urgency of a full geographic survey of the young American republic, left his countrymen at his death a full set of surveying instruments, including parallel rules, compasses, and a theodolite. The acquisition of the Louisiana Territory from France in 1803, however, provided the needed incentive. No one knew exactly what the country had bought. Some people speculated that the Missouri and Columbia rivers might provide a passage to the Pacific. Others imagined the West, as the Greeks had once imagined Terra Australis, as a land of milk and honey. The actual barrier of the Rocky Mountains was barely guessed at.

In 1804 the government dispatched a party of 45 men under Meriwether Lewis and William Clark that two years later, guided by Indian maps, reached the Pacific, laying claim to the western territories beyond Louisiana. They were followed by settlers, adventurers, and, after 1838, by the systematic surveys of the Army Corps of Topographical Engineers. In the 1870s John Wesley Powell rafted down the Colorado River, mapping much of the plateau and desert West, and in 1879 the United States Geological Survey was instituted. Its work continues today.

The British mapped India rapidly after its final conquest in 1818, proceeding northward to the Himalayas, where a Bengali clerk surmised that the mountain known as Peak XV, and called in Tibetan Chomolungma, or "Goddess Mother of the World," was the tallest in the world. It was named, however, after an Englishman, George Everest. Similarly, the mapping of Africa awaited its intensive colonization after 1870. In contrast, the Jesuits who reached China and Japan in the sixteenth century found an ancient and sophisticated cartographic tradition in both countries. When Matteo Ricci presented a world map to the Chinese emperor in 1602, he tactfully placed China in the center. The Italian Jesuit Martino Martini published the first European atlas of China in 1655, based on Chinese sources. But the Chinese, with their proud isolation, were slow to adopt Western mapping techniques or to accept the results of Western discoveries. The consequence was to place them at a considerable disadvantage in dealing with European imperialism in the nineteenth century.

While the true dimensions and contours of the earth were slowly yielding to exploration and measurement, a similar process was taking place with regard to the heavens. One of the stumbling blocks to the acceptance of the Copernican theory in the seventeenth century was that it suggested a far greater distance to the fixed stars than that of Ptolemy. By the latter part of the century, however, Copernicus had won the day, and French astronomers had calculated the distance between the earth and the sun with better than 90 percent accuracy.

A better appreciation of the scale of the cosmos, however, awaited one of the most important conceptual breakthroughs in history: the realization that the sun itself was a star. Only by means of this could even a rudimentary notion of the immensity of interstellar space be achieved. If any single individual may be credited with it, it was perhaps the martyred Giordano Bruno, who had argued—at the cost of his life—for the idea of an infinity of worlds and hence of an infinite space. A century later the great Dutch astronomer and mathematician Christiaan Huygens (1629–1695), hypothesizing that the star Sirius was a body as bright as the sun, calculated its distance as 27,664 times that of the earth from the sun. Sirius was in reality nearly 20 times farther away, but Huygens' estimate was at least a beginning. William Herschel (1738–1822) took a quantum leap by suggesting that the universe was a sea composed of great galactic islands, of which the sun's island, the Milky Way, was but one. Since Herschel had calculated the equatorial plane of the Milky Way at 7,000 light-years, and since the distance between galaxies must necessarily be far larger than their internal dimensions, he was faced with a universe that was, if not infinite, then perhaps ultimately incalculable.

Herschel was the first to realize that the light from the stars he gazed at had traveled so far—millions of years, he thought—that the bodies that had emitted them might no longer exist. At the same time, his slightly older contemporary James Hutton (c. 1726–1797) was suggesting, on the basis of his observation of geologic strata, that the earth itself was not (as had been thought only a century before) only a few thousand years old but many millions. The universe was receding in time as it was expanding in space.

These twin conceptions may have led to a fresh attempt to humanize space by populating it with intelligent life. In 1877 the Italian astronomer Giovanni Schiaparelli observed a network of fine symmetrical lines on the surface of Mars. An American, Percival Lowell, argued that these were elaborate canals built by a race of technologically advanced beings. This theory had wide credence in scientific circles and en-

A sketch of Herschel's 20-inch telescope. Later Herschel built a giant reflecting telescope with funds provided by Britain's King George III. [Yerkes Observatory]

tered popular culture as well; in 1938 millions of Americans were panicked by a radio hoax that announced that Martians had landed in New Jersey. Not until the Mariner 9 orbiting of Mars in 1971 and the unmanned Viking landing of 1976 were these fantasies laid to rest.

If the period from Columbus' discoveries and Copernican astronomy to Newtonian physics had seen an enormous advance in human knowledge of the earth and the heavens, and that from Newtonian to Einsteinian physics a similar one, the twentieth century marked the beginning of an era of unprecedented exploration and discovery. In 1909 Robert Peary reached the North Pole, and in 1911 Roald Amundsen reached the South Pole. Aerial photography of the Antarctic began in 1928, but not until the postwar period, particularly the International Geophysical Year of 1957–1958 and the U.S. Geologic Survey of 1961–1962, did the continent's true outlines begin to emerge.

At the same time, the oceans and their depths were at last surveyed. Magellan, having probed the depth of the Pacific to about 2,300 feet in 1521, pronounced it immeasurable, and many sailors indeed believed the seas to be bottomless. Not until 1856 was the Pacific's depth roughly ascertained (using tidal wave measurements), and only in the 1950s was the first map of the ocean floors produced. It revealed a planet beneath the planet, with mountain ranges greater than the Himalayas, chasms deeper than the Grand Canyon, and plains broader than the Russian steppe.

The discovery of the ocean's great topographic diversity, particularly of the earth's largest single feature, the Midocean Ridge in the Atlantic, led to the realization that the earth was dynamic and the continents themselves in motion. A theory of "continental drift" had been proposed 50 years earlier, to wide ridicule, by the German meteorologist Alfred Wegener. As the discovery of deep space had opened up the geographic dimension of time—as Herschel and his successors had realized that the image of the heavens was a record of past events—so the present generation of cartographers has begun to work backward to reconfigure the continents of past geologic ages. As Wegener had hypothesized, there may have been a single landmass or supercontinent, Pangaea, from which the present seven continents have emerged over the past 200 million years. Such projections may ultimately read forward too, enabling us literally to ascertain the shape of things to come.

At the beginning of the twentieth century the size of the universe was still estimated at no more than 10,000 light-years, and the existence of other galaxies was still an unproven hypothesis. The picture was rapidly transformed by the development of powerful new telescopes, the analysis of light spectra, and the discovery of stars whose variable luminosity enabled astronomers to use them as cosmic yardsticks, like beacons at sea. By 1930 Edwin Hubble (1889–1953) had demonstrated not only that other galaxies existed but also that they were receding at a velocity proportional

Kingdoms of space: the great spiral galaxy Andromeda, known as M 31, is roughly similar to our own Milky Way in shape although rather larger in size, with a diameter of about 180,000 light years. About 4 billion galaxies, each consisting of billions of stars, lie within reach of modern telescopes. [Observatories of the Carnegie Institution of Washington]

to their distance from our own. Hubble's law, as this discovery was called, suggested both that cosmic magnitudes were far greater than had been hitherto supposed and that those magnitudes were indefinitely expanding. Estimates of the present size of the universe have been extended continuously since then. Hubble calculated the edge of the universe as 500 million light-years away, but by midcentury that estimate had

doubled, and with the introduction of radio telescopes after World War II and the consequent discovery of quasars (quasi-stellar discrete radio sources), it was soon revised tenfold upward again. In the farthest reaches of space, stars may be beaming their light toward us while simultaneously receding from us at a speed nearly equal to that of light itself, and it appears certain that light has reached the earth that was propagated before our planet existed.

It has only been some thousands of years since humans first attempted to mark the distance between here and there on stone, skin, and sand, but our maps have now led us billions of years back in time and billions of light-years outward in space. As astronomers and geologists pursue their visions, the variety, utility, complexity, and sophistication of the mapmakers' art continues to increase. Maps are now indispensable for such diverse projects as weather prediction, flood control, agricultural and urban planning, mining, and—a sad commentary on the human adventure—arms control. At the same time, satellite photography, electronic data processing, and computer simulation have greatly increased the range and precision of mapping. The hand-drawn map, in use for scientific purposes until only a few years ago, may soon go the way of the hand-lettered book. Yet the caution of a nineteenth-century British surveyor remains valid: "All observations are liable to error; no telescope is perfect; no leveling instrument is entirely trustworthy; no instrumental gradations are exact; no observer is infallible."

Suggestions for Further Reading

Bagrow, L. *A History of Cartography*. London: Watts, 1964.

Bricker, C., and Tooley, R. V. *A History of Cartography: 2500 Years of Maps and Mapmakers*. London: Thames & Hudson, 1969.

Brown, L. A. *The Story of Maps*. Boston: Little, Brown, 1980.

Harley, J. B., and Woodward, D., eds. *The History of Cartography*. Chicago: University of Chicago Press, 1987–.

Kopal, Z. *Widening Horizons: Man's Quest to Understand the Structure of the Universe*. New York: Taplinger, 1970.

Schlee, S. *The Edge of an Unfamiliar World: A History of Oceanography*. New York: Dutton, 1973.

Sullivan, W. *Continents in Motion*. New York: McGraw-Hill, 1974.

Thrower, N. J. W. *Maps and Man*. Englewood Cliffs, N.J.: Prentice-Hall, 1972.

Wilford, J. N. *The Mapmakers*. New York: Knopf, 1981.

The Age of the Superpowers

The meeting of Soviet and American troops on the Elbe River in April 1945, amid the rubble of a continent, symbolized the eclipse of Europe as the dominant force in international politics. Germany had been decisively defeated and occupied. An exhausted Britain found itself the world's greatest debtor nation. France, overrun and occupied by Hitler's armies, had only de Gaulle's Free French and the internal resistance of the Maquis to remember with any pride. Few could deny that the Soviet Union and the United States had been the principal architects of victory or that their military strength would determine the future of the globe. The hegemony once exercised by western Europe was now to be shared by the two superpowers.

The Second World War transformed both nations, and each saw its role in a different light. Stalin, though a brutal dictator, represented the views of most Soviet peoples when he adopted a defensive posture toward postwar geopolitics. Since coming to power in 1924, his foremost concern in foreign affairs had been Soviet national interests. From that viewpoint, he saw the spread of communism primarily as an extension of Soviet influence and only secondarily as the success of an ideology. Three times in as

Leading Polish workers in a union movement of great political importance, Lech Walesa speaks to a crowd of strikers outside the Lenin shipyard in Gdansk in 1988. [Reuters/UPI Bettmann Newsphotos]

many decades Western powers had invaded his country, and the savage war fought on Soviet soil against the Nazis had taken an enormous toll on the Soviet Union's people and resources. Now he was determined to strengthen the USSR against a rearmed Germany and a hostile United States.

The American people emerged from World War II with a vastly different outlook. Attacked directly only at Pearl Harbor, the United States had lost some 390,000 soldiers in the war as compared to 20 million Soviet deaths. Wartime spending had brought full employment after more than a decade of economic depression. In 1945 a wealthy America towered above its devastated allies. In the face of shattered European economies, the United States could look eagerly toward the opening of vast new markets for the products of its businesses and farms. Secure behind the world's only nuclear capability, most Americans wanted rapid demobilization, lower taxes, more consumer goods, and an end to foreign political commitments. Only the Soviet Union threatened the global aspirations of American policymakers.

The Cold War

The conflict between Soviet and American national interests came to be known as the Cold War. As it grew in intensity after 1945, the Cold War assumed the public guise of a clash of ideologies. Many Americans saw themselves as defending capitalist democracy against communist totalitarianism, while the Soviets portrayed themselves as opponents of Western imperialism. In both

instances the rhetoric obscured the reality of the Cold War as a struggle for dominance between the world's strongest nations.

Potsdam and the Origins of the Cold War

Historians disagree as to when the Cold War began and who was responsible for breaking Soviet-American wartime collaboration. Some scholars place the beginnings as early as 1918, when American troops invaded northern Russia at Archangel to try to topple the Bolshevik regime. Others argue that the growing antagonism between the United States and the Soviet Union, already revealed in wartime discussions among the Allies, did not become irreversible until 1947 or 1948, when anticommunism became the guidepost of American policy. The consensus, however, is that the Cold War emerged out of the conflict between Stalin and Truman over the future of eastern Europe during the Potsdam Conference in the summer of 1945.

Stalin had made it clear at Yalta that he wanted a readjustment of borders and an extension of the Soviet frontier into Polish territory. In return, he promised to allow free elections in eastern Europe after the war. Between February and July, however, the situation had changed drastically, for the Red Army had overrun Poland, Romania, Hungary, Bulgaria, and most of Czechoslovakia and Yugoslavia, and pro-Soviet governments dominated by the Communists were installed. At Potsdam, with Truman now representing the United States and Clement Attlee, Churchill's successor, Great Britain, the issue resurfaced.

The Big Three at Potsdam, 1945: Churchill, Truman, and Stalin confer on post–World War II settlements. [Imperial War Museum, London]

Truman took an aggressive stance, charging that Stalin had betrayed the Yalta agreement. Stalin's goal was to establish a line of buffer states between Germany and the Soviet Union. With eastern Europe under Red Army occupation, the Soviet leader remained adamant in the face of what some historians believe was Truman's attempt to use America's atomic monopoly to blackmail the Russians into making concessions.

In any case, the division of Europe into Western and Soviet blocs was an accomplished fact when, in March 1946, former prime minister Winston Churchill set the tone for Cold War rhetoric by declaring that the Soviets had lowered "an iron curtain" across the continent, a term quickly adopted by Western cold warriors as a symbol of the division between East and West in Europe.

The Soviet-American clash soon took on a more global character. The United States blocked Soviet efforts to secure a foothold in Iran, and in August, when Stalin demanded a voice in controlling the Dardenelles straits, Truman sent an aircraft carrier to the eastern Mediterranean. The future promised a pattern of repeated and dangerous confrontations.

From the Truman Doctrine to the Berlin Blockade

While relying increasingly on the nuclear deterrent to safeguard American security, Truman insisted that the United States had to counter a growing communist challenge throughout the world, especially in Greece, China, and Indonesia, where communist movements were attempting to overthrow local governments. The Greek situation provided the president with an opportunity to arouse American public opinion. Since the liberation of Greece from the Axis in 1944, Britain had stationed troops there in support of a corrupt monarch in order to keep Soviet influence out of the Mediterranean. A civil war, led by procommunist wartime resistance fighters, now threatened the political stability of the country. Although Stalin abided by his wartime agreement to recognize Greece as an Anglo-American sphere of influence, the communist government of Yugoslavia was aiding the rebels, and the British could no longer sustain their effort on behalf of the rightist regime.

◎ The Iron Curtain ◎

As Cold War tensions with the Soviet Union grew, Western leaders adopted the powerful image of the "iron curtain" to describe the Soviet-controlled areas of Europe. The phrase originated in a speech given by British prime minister Winston Churchill while on a visit to the United States in 1946.

From Stettin in the Baltic to Trieste in the Adriatic, an iron curtain has descended across the continent. Behind that line lie all the capitals of the ancient states of Central and Eastern Europe. Warsaw, Berlin, Prague, Vienna, Budapest, Belgrade, Bucharest, and Sophia, all these famous cities and the populations around them lie in the Soviet sphere, and all are subject, in one form or another, not only to Soviet influence but to a very high and, in many cases, increasing measure of control from Moscow. . . .

The Communist parties, which were very small in all these Eastern states of Europe, have been raised to preeminence and power far beyond their numbers and are seeking everywhere to obtain totalitarian control. Police governments are prevailing in nearly every case, and so far, except in Czechoslovakia, there is no true democracy. . . .

Whatever conclusions may be drawn from these facts—and facts they are—this is certainly not the Liberated Europe we fought to build up. Nor is it one which contains the essentials of permanent peace. . . .

Last time I saw it all coming, and cried aloud to my fellow countrymen and to the world, but no one paid any attention. . . .

We surely must not let that happen again.

Source: R. R. James, ed., *Winston S. Churchill: His Complete Speeches, 1897–1963*, vol. 7 (New York and London: Chelsea House, in association with R. R. Bowker), pp. 7290–7293.

On March 12, 1947, Truman announced that America must assist nations that were "resisting attempted subjugation by armed minorities or by outside pressures. . . . The free peoples of the world look to us for support in maintaining their freedoms."[1] Urging Congress to appropriate $400 million in military aid to bolster the Greek and Turkish governments, the president inaugurated the Truman Doctrine, the cornerstone of American foreign policy for the next two decades. Soon the word *containment* was being used to describe the basic principle of the Truman Doctrine, according to which the United States should restrict communism to areas already under Soviet control. That July, Congress also passed a measure establishing the National Security Council, which was to coordinate military and diplomatic policy for the president with the assistance of the newly formed Central Intelligence Agency (CIA). Truman was especially concerned about Third World areas, where professed Marxists often led national anticolonial movements. Soviet propagandists answered the Truman Doctrine by accusing the United States of seeking to preserve colonialism and asserting that the Soviet Union spoke for national liberation.

Containment had its economic as well as its military side. The United States attempted to draw all European states into the American orbit through a massive program of economic development. In June 1947 Secretary of State George C. Marshall offered economic assistance to any European nation that promised to consult with the American government to determine its needs. Although Czechoslovakia, Poland, and Hungary were interested, the Soviet Union vetoed their participation in the Marshall Plan, fearing that Western economic penetration would weaken its hold on the eastern European states. In western Europe, however, the United States pumped $13 billion into Britain, France, Italy, Germany, and other countries. The Marshall Plan proved a huge success, inaugurating a sustained era of European prosperity that helped combat the growth of socialist and communist parties.

In response, the Soviet Union strengthened its hold on eastern Europe. In 1946 Stalin already controlled Poland, Romania, Bulgaria, and Albania, and over the next two years he consolidated Russian influence over Hungary and Czechoslovakia. The Soviet counterpart to the Marshall Plan was COMECON, an economic organization that claimed to integrate the economies of the eastern European states and the Soviet Union. Under the program, some nations, such as Czechoslovakia, were assigned industrial goals, while others, such as Bulgaria, were given agricultural quotas. In place of the old Communist International (Comintern), abolished during the war in the name of Allied cooperation, Stalin created the Communist Information Bureau (Cominform), designed to reassert Moscow's control over the world communist movement.

As the United States and the Soviet Union consolidated their respective positions in Europe, Germany assumed major importance. The future of Germany had been debated since Potsdam, when Stalin had insisted on moving Russia's borders westward at the expense of Poland, which in turn would receive portions of East Prussia as well as the city of Danzig, renamed Gdansk. Germany's eastern border was set at the Oder and Neisse rivers, and the country was broken into four occupation zones to be governed separately by Britain, France, the United States, and the Soviet Union. Berlin, inside the Russian zone, was similarly divided among the four powers. Yet no formal peace treaty or final resolution of Germany's status ever came, for disputes between Russia and the West left Germany broken into two separate states. The Soviet Union, which had suffered such massive casualties and destruction at the hands of Germany, preferred to see it permanently divided.

After 1946 the Western powers agreed to combine the three Western occupation zones into a single economic unit as a prelude to political sovereignty for a "West German" government. In 1948 self-government was instituted on a local level, and the Germans were permitted to write a new constitution. No postwar American action antagonized the Soviet Union as much as these efforts to reestablish a German nation, for Stalin feared both the industrial revival and the remilitarization of a new German state. That June, Stalin restricted access to West Berlin. The Americans promptly closed their sector to Soviet traffic. When Stalin blockaded all road, rail, and water access to Berlin, Britain and the United States followed suit with a counterblockade against goods moving from East to West Germany. Amid fear of war, the United States began to supply West Berlin by air, moving huge quantities of food, fuel, medicines, and other vital goods to the beleaguered city for almost a year until Stalin conceded defeat.

The Berlin blockade hastened the creation of a separate West German government, formally proclaimed on May 21, 1949, as the Federal Republic of Germany, with its capital at Bonn. Parliamentary elections brought to power as chancellor the Christian Democrat Konrad Adenauer (1876–1967), a former mayor of Cologne who had been imprisoned by Hitler. In contrast to Kurt Schumacher, the Social Democratic candidate who advocated nationalization of industry and banks, Adenauer represented America's Cold War position: cooperation with the West, rapprochement with France, and vigorous anticommunism. Five months after the creation of the Bonn government, the Soviet Union formed a Communist regime in the eastern sector, known as the German Democratic Republic, with its capital in East Berlin.

As the decade drew to a close, Cold War tensions heightened. In April 1949 the United States sponsored the North Atlantic Treaty Organization (NATO), a mutual-defense pact in which most Western nations, including Greece and Turkey, pledged to treat an armed attack against one nation as an assault against all. Although Soviet ground strength at the time outnumbered Western troops by about ten to one, in 1955 the Soviet Union established a similar defense system, dubbed the Warsaw Pact.

The relationship between the superpowers changed dramatically in September 1949 with news that the Soviet Union had detonated an atomic bomb. Several months later Communist forces under Mao Tse-tung (Mao Ze-dong) defeated the Nationalist armies of Chiang Kai-shek and seized power in China (see Chapter 38). The end of nuclear monopoly and the Communist takeover in China replaced confidence with uncertainty in American foreign policy.

The Cold War and American Politics

For Americans, the Cold War had powerful repercussions at home. In February 1950 Senator Joseph R. McCarthy (1908–1957) of Wisconsin claimed to have a list of Communists who held important positions in the State Department and accused Secretary of State Marshall of protecting them by inaction. McCarthy never produced the name of a single Communist and repeatedly changed the number of alleged "traitors" he had discovered in the government. But his message was clear: the Truman administration had bred and coddled the Communist enemy within the government.

That a senator could make such accusations against Truman appears incongruous in retrospect, for the president had shown himself to be an enthusiastic cold warrior,

had imposed a loyalty program on federal employees, and had jailed most leaders of the small and nearly impotent Communist party of the United States. Yet a wave of anti-Communist hysteria swept the country. It lasted for four years, and in some areas of American life, pools of suspicion lingered far longer.

McCarthy's "Red scare" campaign made him a national figure. Despite the election of a Republican president, Dwight D. Eisenhower (1953–1961), he continued to claim conspiracy in high places. The witch-hunt spread from Communists to other groups, including homosexuals. In televised hearings that ended in mid-1954, McCarthy finally overextended himself when he charged that the army itself was riddled with Communist spies. In December the Senate censured McCarthy, ending his influence. Yet imitators perpetuated his methods, especially in monitoring schoolteachers and blacklisting actors.

The Soviet Union and Eastern Europe

In the postwar period Stalin's immediate concerns were to establish a Soviet presence in eastern Europe and to undertake the domestic reconstruction of the Soviet Union. These goals were linked, for he regarded eastern Europe as a region whose economic resources could be used to rebuild Soviet strength.

The Cold War at home: Senator Joseph R. McCarthy of Wisconsin (seated) and his two chief aides, G. David Shine (left) and Roy Cohn (right). [Eve Arnold/Magnum]

Postwar Reconstruction in the Soviet Union

The Soviet Union faced an enormous task of reconstruction in the wake of a war that had destroyed much of its industry, many of its cities, and 30 percent of its national wealth. Not satisfied to restore conditions to the 1941 level, Stalin was determined to build an industrial base worthy of the USSR's new role as a world power. The Cold War increased the burden by adding massive expenditures for arms.

Stalin forced the USSR to return to the policies of the 1930s — extracting surplus capital for the development of heavy industry from the work of Soviet men and women. Although the exploitation of eastern Europe aided the work of reconstruction, most Soviets had to sacrifice their living standards again. Between 1946 and 1950 another five-year plan poured more resources into capital investment than had been spent during the 13 years after 1928, yet the economy produced only a minimum of consumer goods and began to stagnate by 1950. Housing remained so scarce that couples had to postpone marriage for years or live with in-laws in a single room.

Stalin's policies had a grimmer side. To meet the demand for workers, he deported huge numbers of people to labor camps, or *gulags*, across Siberia and central Asia, where thousands died from inadequate food, primitive conditions, and exhaustion. The inhuman conditions of life in the labor camps were brought to the attention of the Western world through the writings of Alexander Solzhenitsyn (born 1918), especially in his monumental work *Gulag Archipelago*. Harsh censorship policies and the repression of intellectuals remained a hallmark of Stalinist rule.

But Stalin's policies produced dramatic economic results. Tremendous increases were achieved in the production of iron, coal, steel, oil, chemicals, and electrical power, and science and technology moved ahead at an impressive rate. The USSR exploded an atomic bomb in 1949, tested a hydrogen bomb in 1953, and built high-quality fighter planes that proved themselves against American models during the Korean War (1950–1953). Most impressive, in 1957 the Soviet Union shocked the West by launching *Sputnik*, the world's first unmanned space satellite.

The war had relaxed social controls, but during Stalin's final years he reimposed ideological conformity. Secret police chief Lavrenti Beria began massive roundups of "enemies of the state" and transported them to the labor camps. There is also evidence that Stalin was planning another major purge, this time of Jews. He had already accused Soviet Jews of harboring pro-Western and anti-socialist views, and in January 1953 he ordered the arrest of nine Jewish physicians on charges that they had attempted to shorten the lives of Soviet officials. Before the alleged "doctors' plot" could unfold, however, a stroke took Stalin's life on March 5. His successors released the physicians and buried Stalin beside Lenin in the Kremlin's mausoleum.

From National Fronts to People's Democracies

The full extent of Stalin's plans for eastern Europe became apparent soon after the war. Unlike the Allies at the end of World War I, Stalin did not attempt to adjust frontiers along ethnic or national lines. Instead, he forcibly relocated entire populations to fit his notions of Soviet security. This entailed the removal of 13 million ethnic Germans, including families that had resided in the Czech Sudetenland, Silesia, and areas east of the Oder and Neisse rivers for centuries. He also moved about 4.5 million Poles westward, replacing them with Russians and Ukrainians, and about 600,000 Balts from their homelands in Estonia, Latvia, and Lithuania, sending half to East Germany and half deep into Russia.

Because most eastern European states had provided troops for Hitler's legions, Stalin forced those countries to pay reparations. The Soviet Union aligned the entire region with its economic system, chiefly as a source of raw materials that satellite states were compelled to sell to the USSR at low prices.

The Soviet Union constructed new governments in states occupied by the Red Army, setting up "national front" coalitions of Communist, Social Democratic, and peasant parties. Each coalition enjoyed a degree of autonomy that varied from country to country. Where Stalin feared a serious threat to Soviet security, as in Poland and Romania, the national fronts were a sham. Bulgaria fared better, since after the arrival of Russian troops in 1944, the Bulgarian army had joined in the war against Germany. Thus Stalin demanded no reparations from Bulgaria. However, when non-Communist members of the Bulgarian government sought assistance from the Western allies after the war, Stalin manipulated the regime to suit his aims. By contrast, between 1945 and 1947 the national front governments of Hungary and Czechoslovakia were true coalitions in which parties possessed a wide degree of freedom.

The national front regimes lasted less than three years, but they brought about fundamental changes. The Communists joined their coalition partners in breaking up the large, quasi-feudal estates that had characterized eastern European agriculture for centuries, distributing land to millions of peasant families. In addition, between 1945 and 1947 these governments nationalized the coal, steel, banking, and insurance industries.

In the late summer of 1947 Communist parties throughout the region began a concerted attack on their main rivals for popular support, the agrarian parties. Within six months all the national front regimes vanished. In their places appeared one-party Communist governments called "people's democracies." Two pressures probably led to the Soviet crackdown: the desire to use the area's wealth to support reconstruction at home and the decision to impose more direct control on the eastern European states in the face of the Marshall Plan.

The people's democracies geared their economic programs to meet Russia's needs. Governments forced the collectivization of small farms, thus releasing significant numbers of peasants for work in factories under a series of five-year plans. The Soviets intensified their policy of sending high-priced exports to the region while paying low prices for imports. In essence, eastern Europe, an area containing some 90 million people, became an adjunct to the Soviet system. This policy postponed eastern European recovery, leaving the region bleak for many years.

The Yugoslav Model

Direct Soviet hegemony stopped at Yugoslavia, which proved to be an important exception to Russian dominance in eastern Europe. Under the leadership of the Communist leader Marshal Tito (Josip Broz, 1892–1980), the Yugoslav resistance had liberated the country from the Nazis without significant aid from the Red Army. In the postwar period Tito rejected Stalin's claim to preeminence in the Communist world, engaging in a bitter confrontation with Stalin over national sovereignty and Communist strategy.

Tito had aided leftist rebels in Greece against Stalin's orders. When Tito urged Communist leaders in the region to follow his example and ignore Russia's strategic needs, Stalin vowed to discredit him and bring Yugoslavia into the Soviet orbit. In September 1947 Stalin located the headquarters of the newly created Cominform in Belgrade, the Yugoslav capital, hoping to use it to spy on Tito and undermine his support. When this tactic failed, Stalin responded in 1948 and 1949 by expelling Yugoslavia from the Cominform, placing an embargo on its economy, and isolating the country from its neighbors.

Within months the resourceful Tito applied for and received American economic assistance, simultaneously abandoning his support for world revolution while proclaiming the need for separate paths to socialism. In 1950 he initiated a policy of political decentralization by transferring authority from Belgrade to workers' councils and communes. These reforms gave workers a larger voice in the management of factories than anywhere else in the world. Tito had not only maneuvered Yugoslavia into a

position of nonalignment between the Soviet Union and the West but had also made his country the major world model of independent Marxism.

De-Stalinization and the Rise of Khrushchev

Stalin groomed no successor. In the power struggle that broke out after his death, his closest followers lost out. Beria, dismissed from his posts and expelled from the party, was executed. A collective leadership soon emerged that abolished the office of general secretary of the Communist party, Stalin's base of power for 30 years, and established party secretaries in its place. At the top of this group was Nikita Khrushchev (1894–1971), a miner's son who as party boss had governed the Ukraine from 1939 to 1950. By 1955 he was joined by Nikolai Bulganin and Vyacheslav Molotov, Stalin's longtime foreign minister, to form a three-man *troika*.

Khrushchev came to personify post-Stalinist Russia. Though he would never wield the arbitrary power that Stalin had, he stood out from his rivals. Illiterate until his twenties, his bald, rotund appearance and outgoing personality belied a keen intelligence. Khrushchev solidified his position in a speech before the Twentieth Congress of

Nikita Khrushchev, who emerged as the leader of the Soviet Union after Stalin's death, initiated a new stage in domestic development and confrontation with the West. [Sergio Larrain/Magnum]

the Communist party in 1956 that ranks among the most influential in Soviet history. This speech detailed Stalin's atrocities and attacked him for promoting a cult of personality. Later Khrushchev changed the name of Stalingrad to Volgograd and removed Stalin's body from the Red Square mausoleum. Official statues and portraits of Stalin also vanished.

As details of Khrushchev's speech became public, he began to take controversial action, dissolving the Cominform and meeting personally with Marshal Tito in a bid to improve relations with Yugoslavia. Stalinists on the Politburo attempted to depose Khrushchev, but the Red Army prevented the coup. In 1958 he assumed the office of premier, thus combining, as Stalin had done, the top party and state offices in his hands. The miner's son had become the leader of the Soviet Union.

Khrushchev introduced a wide range of reforms. Downplaying Stalin's emphasis on the development of heavy industry, he increased the supply of consumer goods and housing and stimulated agricultural production with modern technology. The new policies improved the Soviet standard of living, although shortages of appliances, clothing, and food continued. The judicial system replaced police terror for all but political crimes, and intellectuals had more freedom than ever before. The party bureaucracy, however, still represented a privileged elite.

Dissent and Diversity

Ten days after Khrushchev's meeting with Tito in June 1956, anti-Soviet riots broke out in Poznan, Poland. Stalinists were quick to blame them on the liberalized policy toward eastern Europe. Actually, the first serious disorders with the people's democracies had erupted in Czechoslovakia and East Berlin shortly after Stalin's death in 1953. Khrushchev's de-Stalinization program stimulated the discontent that already existed. His speech to the Twentieth Party Congress had undermined the legitimacy of the Stalinists in Poland by reporting that Russian agents had replaced Polish Communist leaders in 1948 with Soviet puppets. Thus in July 1956, when workers in Poznan began publicly demanding "bread and liberty," Polish police and military authorities refused to fire on them. Left with the option of calling in Russian troops or yielding to popular demands, the Polish government promised reforms. Wladyslaw Gomulka (1905–1982), a leader who had lost favor in 1947 for seeking a Polish way to socialism, convinced the Soviet Union to permit his return to power. Gomulka accepted spontaneously formed workers' councils in the factories and began making overtures to the peasants and to the Catholic church while remaining closely linked to Soviet foreign policy.

The October 1956 Hungarian revolution challenged the USSR more directly. When Hungarian police fired on protesters in Budapest, sparking anti-Soviet demonstra-

tions, the government called in Soviet soldiers. Throughout the country, workers' councils formed, demanding free elections, the end of the security police, and the withdrawal of Soviet troops. On October 28, when Imre Nagy (1896–1958) became premier and the Soviets began to withdraw, it appeared that the Hungarians had won. Nagy announced the reestablishment of a multiparty system and a return to the national front coalition of Communists, Social Democrats, and peasant leaders and proclaimed Hungarian neutrality between East and West. Convinced that a failure to respond would provoke further revolts throughout the Soviet bloc, Khrushchev ordered an invasion. Some 2,500 Russian tanks moved into Hungary, shelling Budapest and other cities. When the repression was over, thousands of Hungarians were dead and more than 200,000 refugees had fled. Though some Westerners had urged or expected American intervention, none came.

The new Soviet-installed Hungarian premier, János Kádár (1912–1989), cautiously led the nation to a more liberal form of communism over the next three decades. Imprisoned for nationalist activity earlier in his life, Kádár understood his country's desire for reform and independence. By the early 1960s he had removed Stalinists from the Hungarian Communist party and introduced programs that improved the standard of living. Although Kádár's role in the 1956 uprising undermined his leadership in the eyes of many, he remained in power until 1988.

By the early 1960s the countries of the eastern bloc had developed three different socialist systems: on the right stood the Yugoslavs, usually labeled "revisionists" because of their economic and political innovations; a number of "national Communists," such as Gomulka, straddled the middle ground, stressing solidarity with the Soviet Union in foreign policy but demanding domestic freedom to achieve communism; the "dogmatists," including the followers of Mao Tse-tung in China and the Albanian Stalinists, vehemently opposed revisionism and resisted liberalizing tendencies. Beyond Europe the most significant example of diversity has been the split between China and the Soviet Union (see Chapter 38). By the 1970s the Soviet Union remained the acknowledged leader of the Communist world, but its role was limited. The ideological unity of international communism was being eroded by diversity, internecine rivalry, and accommodation with the West.

Western Europe and North America

America's most immediate concern was Europe, to which it exported vast amounts of capital to stimulate economic reconstruction. The Marshall Plan also made possible an economic boom in the United States, for massive military outlays, together with the billions of dollars of aid sent abroad, stimulated the domestic economy. Although partly motivated by humanitarian concerns, that policy also reflected Cold War strategy: American policymakers believed that prosperity would diminish the appeal of communism and provide a basis for stable democratic governments.

The Political Revival of Europe

Much of western Europe's prewar leadership had been discredited by the policy of appeasement or collaboration with Hitler. In the former Axis countries the purges of fascist sympathizers opened bureaucratic positions to former resistance fighters. In Allied nations the disastrous economic conditions that followed the war forced some conservatives, even wartime leaders, out of office. No less a hero than Winston Churchill was defeated at the polls by the Labourite Clement Attlee (1883–1967) in the 1945 British elections because of his opposition to the extension of public assistance measures.

In France and Italy resistance leaders filled the power vacuum. General Charles de Gaulle, head of the exiled Free French movement, symbolized French efforts to erase the memory of Vichy collaboration with the Nazis,

President Charles de Gaulle of France and Chancellor Konrad Adenauer of West Germany symbolized the emergence of a western European community based on cooperation and autonomy. [Gamma-Liaison]

and in 1951 his followers emerged as the nation's largest political party. In Italy the liberal Ferruccio Parri (1890–1981) and the Christian Democrat Alcide De Gasperi (1881–1954), both former anti-Fascists, succeeded each other as prime minister. Because the Communists had been so prominent in the resistance movements, their support expanded enormously after the war. The Italian Communist party grew to some 2 million members by 1947, the largest in western Europe. In France the Communists were the strongest French party in 1945, and their vote rarely fell below the 25 percent level until 1958.

Despite the Marxist resurgence, western Europe did not face the prospect of social revolution, as it had in 1918 and 1919. The British Labourites and the West German Social Democrats were reformist rather than revolutionary parties. Probably at Stalin's orders, Communist resistance units stacked their arms and until 1947 participated in reformist governments. Moreover, American economic assistance encouraged the development of new center and moderate right parties, of which the progressive Catholic parties, most often called Christian Democrats, were the most significant.

Like the Communists, many of the new Christian Democratic leaders had been in the resistance, but they supported both democratic principles and capitalism. As parties based on Catholic religious loyalties rather than social class, the Christian Democrats appealed to a wide range of voters. The partition of Germany, which placed many Protestant areas under Soviet control, gave the Christian Democrats an unexpected advantage in West German elections, where Catholics predominated.

The potential for rebuilding lay in the destruction of the war, for it cleared away antiquated factories and outdated technologies. Moreover, refugees willingly offered inexpensive labor, and a rise in the birthrate provided larger internal markets. The Marshall Plan contributed significantly to the reconstruction. The major condition for participation in the program was a willingness to join the Organization for European Economic Cooperation, which encouraged planning and free trade. The Marshall Plan stimulated Europe's economy to such a degree that by the mid-1960s production was almost triple the prewar level, and some western European nations surpassed the United States in per capita standard of living.

Politically, the Marshall Plan weakened the extreme left and strengthened the Christian Democratic parties. When the USSR refused to allow eastern European participation in the plan, Communists in western Europe resigned from governing coalitions or were voted out of office. In the Federal Republic of Germany the Christian Democrats governed from 1949 to 1969, when the Social Democrats under Willy Brandt (born 1913) came to power in coalition with a minority party, the Free Democrats. The Social Democrats, who pumped considerable resources into social programs and education, ran the Bonn government until the early 1980s, when the Christian

Democrats under Helmut Kohl (born 1930) returned to office. In Italy, despite frequent changes of government, the Christian Democrats maintained de facto control from 1948 to 1982. The following year the Socialist Bettino Craxi (born 1934) became prime minister, but his policies proved little different from those of his predecessors. Similarly, centrist coalitions dominated France's Fourth Republic until its collapse in 1958 and de Gaulle's return to power. Thereafter, de Gaulle established a more centralized but equally anti-Communist Fifth Republic.

Between 1945 and 1951 Britain's Labourite prime minister Clement Attlee introduced the most far-reaching reforms of the period. Attlee nationalized utilities, railroads, airlines, coal mines, the Bank of England, and the iron and steel industries. His Social Welfare Acts covered public housing, free medical care, and national insurance benefits. The Conservatives came back into power in 1951 and

Margaret Thatcher, longtime Conservative prime minister of Great Britain, presided over the retrenchment of domestic welfare policies and a tough foreign policy. [Derek Hudson/ Sygma]

since then have alternated with the Labourites in heading the government. Although Conservative governments have not dismantled the British welfare state, since 1979 Margaret Thatcher (born 1925)—the United Kingdom's first woman prime minister—has favored private enterprise and imposed austere fiscal policies on the country. The result has been a reduction of inflation, but at the price of the highest unemployment since the Great Depression and the increasing polarization of society.

Women and Social Change in Western Europe and the Communist Bloc

While most western European governments avoided full-scale nationalization of industry, they did provide expanded welfare services. Low-cost medical care, family allowances, and unemployment compensation programs all became the rule.

Rapid modernization has marked European society since the end of World War II. Traditional class barriers relaxed, and a salaried managerial elite developed with the growth of public corporations and new technological industries. Social distinctions have also been blurred by a higher standard of living for many and the availability of mass-produced consumer goods. National television networks joined radio and film—which were already widely developed in the 1920s and 1930s—in reaching rural villages. Free higher education virtually eliminated illiteracy. The new prosperity, along with less expensive automobiles and highway construction, has made for a highly mobile society.

All European states except tiny Liechtenstein gave women the vote after the war, but in other ways the status of women varied greatly from one country to another. The Scandinavian and northern European nations generally adopted legal equality for women more readily than those in the south, but everywhere traditional values have given way to greater opportunity. In 1949 the prominent French intellectual Simone de Beauvoir (1908–1986) published her highly influential book *The Second Sex*, which demonstrated how women had been subordinated by tradition, social custom, and ideology. De Beauvoir's work provided an early theoretical basis for the women's liberation movements that developed in Britain, France, Germany, Italy, and Scandinavia in the 1960s. The revival of Socialist and Communist parties after the war gave practical reinforcement to the new feminist theory, for they combined a long tradition of female militancy with progressive social policies. Hence the representation of women is higher in Socialist and Communist parties than in bourgeois ones. Feminist coalitions and left-wing parties successfully fought for legalized abortion and more liberal divorce laws, even in some Catholic societies.

Women have made up a large percentage of the European work force since the Industrial Revolution. After 1945 they have had access to better jobs along with the growing availability of free higher education. About one out of every three wokers is now female, and women have also established a strong presence in labor unions. Nevertheless, most women are still excluded from high-level managerial positions and senior government posts and, like their American counterparts, continue to struggle for full equality.

In the Soviet Union, where women have made important gains since Stalin's death, more than half of the workers are female. Abortion was legalized, the divorce law was liberalized, and many more child-care centers were built. In the professions, women represented 67 percent of doctors, 35 percent of lawyers, and more than 58 percent of engineers by the 1980s. (In the United States, by contrast, women make up only 3.5 percent of all lawyers and 6.1 percent of all physicians.) Khrushchev appointed the first woman member of the Presidium of Ministers, but while some 29 percent of party members are women, they hold only 4 percent of the high party offices. In general, women's participation in Soviet and eastern European party politics is higher at local levels than in the central governments. For example, in East Germany about 25 percent of district committee members were women in 1981, whereas only 13 percent of the posts in the Central Committee were held by women. Differences in pay and political power between males and females, as well as social inequalities among Soviet women, continue to exist, but most Soviet women enjoy greater access to professions than women in the West.

Nevertheless, life is hard for most Soviet women, despite legal equality. They have few modern conveniences, and married women get almost no support from their husbands for the household duties they are expected to perform in addition to their paid jobs. Mikhail Gorbachev, the current Soviet leader, declared in 1987 that women have "inherent functions: those of mother, wife, the person who brings up children." Yet he has taken a greater interest in women's issues than any Soviet ruler since Lenin, supporting day-care expansion, flexibility in work schedules, and increases in the minimum wage for professions held mostly by women. Moreover, his campaign against alcoholism has received strong support from Soviet wives. Raisa Gorbachev, his wife, has proved to be a strong-willed and outspoken woman whose stylish life has become not a role model but a yardstick by which to measure the need for further improvements.

American Society in Transition

In the 1950s the United States entered an era of economic prosperity and apparent social tranquillity. President Ei-senhower attempted to moderate the trend that Roosevelt's New Deal had set in motion toward increasing government involvement in economic and social life. Yet as large numbers of Americans were driven to leave the farms and the cities for life in the suburbs, a federal highway program improved the country's transportation system and spurred the automobile industry. The Eisenhower government, which proved more sympathetic to business than any since 1932, reduced the federal role in the marketplace wherever possible.

Despite the withdrawal of government from social policy, the movement for racial equality made important strides in this period. In 1954 a landmark ruling by the U.S. Supreme Court (*Brown* v. *Board of Education*) found that segregated schools violated the constitution's Fourteenth Amendment, which guaranteed all citizens equal protection under the law. Correctly anticipating that the southern states would resist immediate integration, the Court ordered implementation of its ruling "with all deliberate speed." In 1957 Orville Faubus, the governor of Arkansas, summoned the National Guard to block entry of nine black children into Little Rock's Central High School. Eisenhower, who had not been enthusiastic about the *Brown* decision, nevertheless refused to allow such open flaunting of government authority. He ordered federal troops to Little Rock, forcing Faubus to back down.

❦
MARTIN LUTHER KING, JR., AND THE STRUGGLE FOR CIVIL RIGHTS

Black political activism, organized for the first time on a national level, was the driving force in the civil rights struggle. Dr. Martin Luther King, Jr. (1929–1968), a young black Baptist minister, led the first mass civil rights movement in America. Born in Atlanta, Georgia, King was the son of a Baptist preacher. While studying at Morehouse College, he gave up his interest in medicine and law to enter the ministry, eventually taking a Ph.D. in theology at Boston University.

King became active in civil rights in 1955, soon after becoming pastor of the Dexter Avenue Baptist Church in Montgomery, Alabama, when he was chosen to lead the fight against racial segregation on public buses. His eloquent rhetoric and inspiring personality introduced a dynamic new doctrine of civil struggle to the nation. A year later the blacks of Montgomery had achieved their goal.

To extend the successful Montgomery action throughout the nation, King organized the Southern Christian Leadership Conference (SCLC), which gave him a national platform. He was convinced that Mahatma Gandhi's tactic

Martin Luther King, Jr., who popularized the passive resistance strategy that led to victories in the civil rights movement, leads a march from Selma to Montgomery, Alabama in 1965. To his left is Coretta Scott King, his wife. [Bob Adelman/Magnum]

ject of covert FBI surveillance. In the spring of 1963 his efforts to end segregation in Birmingham, Alabama, resulted in national attention as police turned dogs and fire hoses on the demonstrators and arrested King along with hundreds of schoolchildren. From jail King wrote a letter of great eloquence explaining his nonviolent philosophy. In August 1963 King and other civil rights advocates marched on Washington. Before the Lincoln Memorial, his moral passion captivated some 200,000 peaceful demonstrators as he recounted his "dream" that one day blacks and whites would be brothers and sisters.

Kennedy's legislative proposal was blocked in Congress by a coalition of Republicans and southern Democrats and remained stalled in committee when he was assassinated in 1963. His more politically astute successor, Lyndon B. Johnson (1908–1973), obtained passage of the 1964 Civil Rights Act, which prohibited discrimination in public places and in the use of federal funds. For his contributions to civil rights, King was awarded the Nobel prize for peace.

In his final years King's leadership came under increasing pressure from more militant blacks, who faulted him for being too cautious. Riots in the Watts district of Los Angeles in 1965 brought attention to the enormous problems of blacks in northern and western cities, where his nonviolent tactics were questioned. King began to broaden his work to include housing discrimination in Chicago, and in 1967 he strongly opposed the war in Vietnam. In April 1968, while in Memphis, Tennessee, to support a strike of sanitation workers, he was gunned down by a white racist.

King's great contribution to civil rights had been his ability to turn regional protests into a national crusade. He had galvanized the black masses into action, and although complex racial problems continued to plague the nation, America would never quite be the same again.

The New Activism and American Women

The same year as the passage of the Civil Rights Act, Johnson ran for election on a platform calling for a "Great Society" made possible by a war on poverty. The voters returned him to office along with 40 additional Democratic members of Congress, giving the House of Representatives a progressive majority for the first time since 1938. The dramatic triumph of liberalism reflected a new social activism that had been stimulated by the struggle for racial equality.

Since the early 1960s university students in America had been in the forefront of social and political militancy, as they were in Europe. In June 1962 about 60 young people, members of a group known as Students for a Democratic Society (SDS), met at Port Huron, Michigan, to discuss civil rights, foreign policy, education, and welfare. The statement of principles they issued—the Port

of nonviolent disobedience was the answer to the civil rights struggle. In 1960 King became copastor with his father at the Ebenezer Baptist Church in Atlanta but devoted his energies to the SCLC and to a concerted drive against racial injustice. While protesting segregation at a lunch counter, he was arrested and sentenced to state prison on a pretext. The case aroused the interest of then–Democratic presidential candidate John Kennedy (1917–1963).

King's influence reached its peak in the years between 1960 and 1965. The nonviolent strategy of "sit-ins" and protest marches drew a huge following of blacks and whites and put pressure on President Kennedy, who proposed a comprehensive civil rights bill intended to end legal segregation. King's success also made him the sub-

◎ Letter from Birmingham Jail ◎

*After the arrest of Martin Luther King, Jr., in 1963, eight fellow clergy-
men published a statement calling his actions "unwise and untimely."
In April he wrote a lengthy response—scribbled in the margins of a
newspaper and on scraps of paper—explaining "why we can't wait."*

Perhaps it is easy for those who have never felt the stinging darts of segregation to say,
"Wait." But when you have seen vicious mobs lynch your mothers and fathers at will
and drown your sisters and brothers at whim; when you have seen hate-filled policemen
curse, kick, and even kill your black brothers and sisters; when you see the vast majority
of your twenty million Negro brothers smothering in an airtight cage of poverty in the
midst of an affluent society; when you suddenly find your tongue twisted and your
speech stammering as you seek to explain to your six-year-old daughter why she can't go
to the public amusement park . . . and see ominous clouds of inferiority beginning to
form in her little mental sky, and see her beginning to distort her personality by developing an unconscious bitterness toward white people; when you have to concoct an answer for a five-year-old son who is asking: "Daddy, why do white people treat colored
people so mean?" . . . when you are humiliated day in and day out by nagging signs
reading "white" and "colored"; when your first name becomes "nigger," your middle
name becomes "boy" (however old you are) and your last name becomes "John," and
your wife and mother are never given the respected title "Mrs."; when you are harried
by day and haunted by night by the fact that you are a Negro, living constantly at tiptoe
stance, never quite knowing what to expect next, and are plagued with inner fears and
outer resentments; when you are forever fighting a degenerating sense of "nobodiness"—
then you will understand why we find it difficult to wait. There comes a time when the
cup of endurance runs over, and men are no longer willing to be plunged into the abyss
of despair. I hope, sirs, you can understand our legitimate and unavoidable impatience.

Source: M. L. King, Jr., *Why We Can't Wait* (New York: Harper & Row, 1963), pp. 83–84.

Huron Statement—focused on the concept of "participa-
tory democracy," the notion that people should take part
in the decisions that affect their lives. SDS organized an
interracial movement of the poor in northern cities, took
part in sit-ins and demonstrations in the south, and became
increasingly militant over the Vietnam War. By the late
1960s SDS had begun to split apart, one faction forming
the Weathermen, an extremist group devoted to violent
action. Yet the Port Huron Statement left its mark on an
entire generation of Americans.

The civil rights movement and student activism transformed American society in other ways. The gay rights
movement, born in 1969 when a police raid in New York's
Greenwich Village sparked violent protests from men in
the Stonewall Bar, raised important issues about sexual
oppression and coincided with the emergence of a powerful new impetus toward women's liberation.

Many women who had left the home for the factory
during World War II sought job opportunities traditionally
closed to them. Feminists were encouraged by the controversial arguments of Betty Friedan (born 1921), whose
book *The Feminine Mystique* (1963) argued that women
should seek fulfillment beyond their ties to husbands and
children. After the war the number of women who worked
for pay outside the home rose dramatically, so that by
1960 twice as many women worked as in 1940. Equally
significant was the fact that whereas only 15 percent of all
wives worked in 1940, the figure exceeded 50 percent by
1980.

Two separate movements took up the challenge of feminism in the 1960s. The National Organization for Women
(NOW), representing older professionals, worked for
women's rights through the political and legal systems.
Friedan was elected president when it was formed in 1966.
The women's liberation movement, which attracted many
younger women who had been involved in antiwar and civil
rights efforts, was more confrontational. Beginning in 1968
it identified the patriarchial family and socially formed gen-

The new feminism began in the 1960s and has continued ever since. Here, at a 1970s fundraiser for the equal rights amendment, are Betty Ford, wife of former president Gerald Ford (speaking), with Bella Abzug on the far right and Betty Friedan on the left. [Alex Webb/Magnum]

der patterns as causes of oppression. Not only did feminists demand legal equality with men, but they also encouraged women to seek power through female solidarity and "gender consciousness."

Affirmative action regulations designed to enforce equal opportunity brought about improvement in employment patterns and wage scales for minorities and women. Yet in the 1970s a woman earned only 59 cents for every dollar earned by a man. In 1972 Congress passed the equal rights amendment to the constitution, but the measure failed when a number of state legislatures did not ratify it. Racial, ethnic, and sexual prejudice remains deeply entrenched in some segments of American society.

Canada: Economic Expansion and Social Change

Canada and the United States together make up most of the North American continent.* The two nations share a common 3,000-mile border that stretches from the Pacific to the Atlantic and along the eastern frontier of Alaska. Nevertheless, Canada possesses unique historical and cul-

---

*Mexico, though geographically part of North America, is usually grouped, for linguistic and historical reasons, with the other nations of Latin America.

tural traditions and, since World War II, has undergone its own social and economic transformation.

Despite an expanse of nearly 4 million square miles—making it, after the USSR, geographically the world's second largest nation—60 percent of Canada's 25 million people live in the Quebec-Windsor corridor, an industrialized region that hugs the U.S.-Canadian border from Detroit to the Atlantic. The remainder of the country represents a vast, sparsely populated territory of thick forests, productive agricultural prairies, and rich mineral deposits.

Canada's modern history has shown a gradual distancing from Great Britain, its traditional "mother country." The British North America Act of 1867 had defined its political and constitutional structure as a dominion within the empire. In 1931, however, the Statute of Westminster conceded full sovereignty to Canada, Australia, New Zealand, and the other dominions, which then became members of the voluntary Commonwealth of Nations. Today Elizabeth II serves as Canada's queen, but an elected prime minister and parliament actually govern. In 1947, after Canadian participation in World War II heightened national self-identity, parliament passed the Canadian Citizenship Act, which ended the granting of automatic citizenship to British subjects. Only in the mid-1980s did growing national sentiment result in the "patriation" of the constitution to Canada, that is, the replacement of the constitutional provisions of the British North America Act with a new constitution. The new Charter of Rights and Freedoms reinforced basic civil liberties. Throughout this century three major parties have dominated the political system. The Liberals, the largest party, have been in power for most of the modern period. The Progressive Conservatives, or "Tories," have a large following that is less inclined to support an extension of the welfare state. The left-of-center New Democratic party follows a social democratic program.

Persistent and at times violent tension has marked relations between Canada's chief linguistic groups, the English- and French-speaking populations. The abiding nationalism of Quebec province, where most French Canadians live, has grown into stiff political resistance against the nation's dominant English element. As a result of pressure from the Parti Québécois and other groups, in 1963 the Royal Commission on Bilingualism and Biculturalism was given a mandate to redress French grievances. The Official Language Act, passed in 1969, established both French and English as the official languages of the nation. Nonetheless, in 1970 the so-called October Crisis erupted in Quebec when a British trade commissioner was abducted and a provincial minister was murdered by the extremist Quebec Liberation Front. Martial law was imposed on the country, but French nationalism did not abate. Several years later the Parti Québécois won control of the provincial government on a separatist platform.

Despite such tensions, the Canadian economy expanded greatly. In the 1960s the diversified manufacturing sector spurred unparalleled prosperity, with the production growth rate reaching 7 percent in 1973 and the GNP jumping by 15 percent. Trade expanded, and agricultural exports soared with massive grain sales to China and the USSR. The discovery of large oil reserves in the western province of Alberta increased the nation's economic promise further. Real income rose as much as 6.5 percent a year. Indeed, Canada's growth was so rapid that it had negative consequences by the next decade. The problem, still to be resolved, centers on the fact that the greatly increased manufacturing sector is too large for the small size of the domestic market, which means that continuing prosperity relies too heavily on the vagaries of foreign exchange and economic conditions elsewhere.

Canada's growth in recent decades has been driven in large part by ever-increasing economic ties with the United States. American investments began pouring into Canada in the 1920s. Today about 70 percent of its manufacturing industries are owned and controlled by U.S. companies—the automobile industry, for example, is almost completely American-owned, and the oil and gas concerns are 80 percent foreign-owned. This pattern has meant that major decisions regarding Canadian subsidiaries, especially ones affecting labor and employment conditions, are made abroad. The integration of the two economies has recently been advanced by the signing and ratification of a free trade treaty that aims at creating a single market for the movement of goods across borders.

To the unequal economic relationship has been added the Americanization of the country's culture, increasingly resented by Canadian intellectuals, who are striving to create a unique cultural life of their own. From Canada's point of view, one of the most pressing issues of the future will be coming to grips with the pervasive feeling that the United States, with far greater wealth and population, is an overshadowing influence.

Canada's widening prosperity has had social consequences, especially in the growth of an affluent middle class, most of which lives in burgeoning urban centers. Toronto and Montreal, each with some 3 million people, symbolize the Canadian experience. While most of the nation's wealth is still controlled by the English population and centers on the modern financial network of Toronto, the French middle class has risen rapidly in recent years. Montreal, a sophisticated and cosmopolitan city, is the hub of a province, Quebec, that is now 70 percent urban and home to an ambitious entrepreneurial class. Although unemployment has been high in recent years, Canada's population has had since the 1960s one of the most advanced welfare states in the world, providing cradle-to-grave health care, social security insurance, and an array of other benefits. Canada's future, though faced with serious challenges, remains bright.

From Brinkmanship to Détente

By the early 1950s the superpowers were enmeshed in a struggle for hegemony. For 25 years the pattern of conflict set in 1947 remained fairly consistent: with American influence predominant in Latin America and western Europe and the Soviet Union supreme in eastern Europe, each power challenged the other in peripheral regions of the globe. The danger lay in the possibility that diplomatic confrontations would lead to local military conflict, which could in turn escalate into nuclear war. The Korean War (1950–1953) proved to be the first of several such situations (see Chapter 38).

Confrontation and Crisis

Eisenhower delegated exceptional authority to his secretary of state, John Foster Dulles (1888–1959). A man who combined a brilliant legal mind with righteous moralism, Dulles had been part of Wilson's delegation at the Paris peace conference in 1919. During his long tenure as secretary of state, he was one of the most strident voices of the Cold War, denouncing Truman's containment policy and advocating an offensive program to "liberate" areas under communist control. Dulles emphasized America's nuclear strength, basing foreign policy on repeated warnings that local communist aggression would lead to "massive retaliation" by the United States. The Dulles policy of rattling nuclear missiles whenever international crises erupted was dubbed "brinkmanship," but the eastern European revolts of the 1950s revealed the hollowness of these threats. America stood by in 1956 while anti-Soviet fighters in Hungary battled Soviet tanks with cobblestones and rifles.

The Eisenhower administration never abandoned containment. Using marines or covert operations directed by the CIA, the United States played a key role in overthrowing supposedly procommunist governments around the world, including those in Iran (1953), Guatemala (1954), and Chile (1973). The CIA also plotted the assassination of Congolese leader Patrice Lumumba in 1961 and, with the aid of American gansters, made several attempts against the Cuban leader Fidel Castro.

Under Kennedy, American Cold War strategy shifted again, but only in emphasis. Kennedy undertook a huge buildup of conventional and nuclear weapons. In his effort to close the "missile gap" with the Soviet Union, he accelerated the nuclear arms race, to which Russia responded in 1961 by detonating a hydrogen bomb in the atmosphere. Kennedy was fascinated with "counterinsurgency" operations, by which he meant the use of limited warfare against communist infiltration of Third World countries. One result of this was the Bay of Pigs fiasco in Cuba (see Chapter 40).

Encounters between Kennedy and Khrushchev brought the world to the edge of nuclear disaster. In the summer of 1961 Khrushchev tried to stem the flow of refugees from East Berlin to the West and threatened to sign a treaty with East Germany that would terminate Western rights in the city. Kennedy ordered reservists on military alert and urged Americans to build fallout shelters. This sharp response may have persuaded Khrushchev to back down, for on August 13 the East Germans sealed off their portion of the city by erecting a wall between the two sections of Berlin.

A year later Khrushchev intruded into the American sphere of influence in Latin America by constructing nuclear missile bases in Cuba. Khrushchev argued the need to prevent another American attempt to overthrow the Castro government, but Kennedy considered the action a direct military threat. In October 1962, when American air reconnaisance found Soviet missiles in Cuba, the president imposed a naval quarantine around the island and demanded the missiles' removal. For six tense days Soviet ships sailed toward Cuba and American forces went on war alert. Khrushchev finally drew back by sending Kennedy a letter deploring the horrors of nuclear war and offering a face-saving compromise. The Soviets agreed to withdraw their missiles in return for a public pledge from America not to invade Cuba; unofficially, the United States agreed to dismantle its own offensive missiles in Turkey.

Brezhnev and the Return to Repression

The turbulent Kennedy-Khrushchev era soon came to an end. Kennedy was assassinated in Dallas, Texas, on November 22, 1963. The following summer, while Khrushchev was vacationing in the Crimea, the Communist party's Central Committee stripped him of his power, charging him with a host of errors that included the Cuban crisis, the rift with China, and setbacks in Russia's agricultural and industrial growth. After a brief period of collective leadership, a veteran bureaucrat, Leonid Brezhnev (1906–1982), took Khrushchev's place. Brezhnev served as both Soviet president and Communist party secretary.

During the almost two decades that Brezhnev ruled, the Soviet Union underwent a return to government repression, although not to the extremes of the Stalin era. Party officials agreed on the need for stability and retrenchment after the changes wrought by Khrushchev. Restraints were reimposed on Russian intellectuals, symbolized by the expulsion of Alexander Solzhenitsyn in 1974. Despite Moscow's acceptance of the human rights provisions of the Helsinki Accords, criticism of government policy by prominent dissidents such as Andrei Sakharov, an internationally acclaimed physicist, brought persecution and long periods of Siberian exile. Recalling Russia's wartime sacrifices, Soviet leaders stressed nationalist traditions and the unity of the Soviet Union, crushing regionalism in the Ukraine and elsewhere.

The new wave of repression also affected the Soviet Union's 1.8 million Jews, who suffered from a long tradition of repression. In the Soviet system, state atheism discouraged Judaism along with all other religions, but the government also claimed that Jewish cultural identity and Zionism undermined the unity of the nation. Khrushchev's liberalization program had hardly affected the Soviet Union's Jews. In the 1960s they formed underground networks to keep Jewish tradition alive, circulating typewritten translations of books such as Leon Uris' novel *Exodus* (1958), which traced the emigration of the Jewish people to Palestine and the founding of the state of Israel. The Brezhnev regime, preoccupied with nationality problems within the Soviet Union and political dissidence, stepped up persecution of the Jews. Emigration to Israel, which had been virtually impossible before, was loosened as a result of international pressure in the 1970s. The exit rate reached a peak in 1979, when over 51,000 Jews left the Soviet Union, but declined steadily thereafter. Only in 1987, under Mikhail Gorbachev's more liberal policies, did the number begin to increase again. Western sources estimate that perhaps as many as 25 percent of Soviet Jews wish to emigrate.

◉ The Cuban Missile Crisis: Two Views ◉

The discovery by the United States in the fall of 1962 that the Soviet Union was installing missile bases in Cuba brought the world to the edge of nuclear war. The first of the following accounts of the crisis is by special White House assistant Arthur M. Schlesinger, Jr., who described President Kennedy's speech of October 19.

Then at seven o'clock the speech: his expression grave, his voice firm and calm, the evidence set forth without emotion, the conclusion unequivocal—"The purpose of these bases can be none other than to provide a nuclear strike capability against the Western Hemisphere." He recited the Soviet assurances, now revealed as "deliberate deception," and called the Soviet action "a deliberately provocative and unjustified change in the status quo which cannot be accepted by this country. . . ." He then laid out what he called with emphasis his *initial* steps: a quarantine on all offensive military equipment under shipment to Cuba; an intensified surveillance of Cuba itself; a declaration that any missile launched from Cuba would be regarded as an attack by the Soviet Union on the United States, requiring full retaliatory response upon the Soviet Union . . . and an appeal to Chairman Khrushchev "to abandon this course of world domination, and to join in a historic effort to end the perilous arms race and to transform the history of man."

Here is Soviet Premier Khrushchev's account.

I want to make one thing absolutely clear: when we put our ballistic missiles in Cuba, we had no desire to start a war. . . . In October, President Kennedy came out with a statement warning that the United States would take whatever measures were necessary to remove what he called the "threat" of Russian missiles in Cuba. . . . In our estimation the Americans were trying to frighten us, but they were no less scared than we were of atomic war. . . .

President Kennedy issued an ultimatum, demanding that we remove our missiles and bombers from Cuba. I remember those days vividly. I remember the exchange with President Kennedy especially well because I initiated it and was at the center of the action on our end of the correspondence. I take complete responsibility for the fact that the President and I entered into direct correspondence at the most crucial and dangerous stage of the crisis. . . .

The climax came after five or six days, when our ambassador to Washington, Anatoly Dobrynin, reported that the President's brother, Robert Kennedy, had come to see him on an unofficial visit. Dobrynin's report went something like this:

"Robert Kennedy looked exhausted. One could see from his eyes that he had not slept for days. He himself said that he had not been home for six days and nights. 'The President is in a grave situation,' Robert Kennedy said, 'and he does not know how to get out of it. We are under very severe stress. In fact we are under pressure from our military to use force against Cuba.' " . . .

We could see that we had to reorient our position swiftly. . . . We sent the Americans a note saying that we agreed to remove our missiles and bombers on the condition that the President give us his assurance that there would be no invasion of Cuba by the forces of the United States or anybody else. Finally Kennedy gave in and agreed to make a statement giving us such an assurance.

Sources: A. M. Schlesinger, Jr., *A Thousand Days: John F. Kennedy in the White House* (Boston: Houghton Mifflin, 1965), pp. 812–813; N. Khrushchev, *Khrushchev Remembers*, trans. S. Talbott (Boston: Little, Brown, 1970), pp. 496–498.

✿
MOSCOW: RUSSIAN CITY
AND SOVIET CAPITAL

One of the world's great cities, Moscow is not only the political capital of the Soviet Union but also the center of its industrial and cultural life. It embodies the sense of continuity that links the country's history from its early development to its status as superpower.

Moscow stands on the Moscow River, in the center of the vast plain of European Russia. Its origins stretch back to the twelfth century, when an early Russian prince built fortifications around an area known as the Kremlin ("Citadel"). The town gradually became a thriving trading site, and in 1326 the head of the Russian Orthodox church transferred his seat there. Moscow's rulers incorporated more of the surrounding countryside and provided defense against repeated Mongol invasions. By the fifteenth century it had become the undisputed core of a unified Russian state under Ivan the Great, who enlarged and strengthened the Kremlin with the crenelated red brick walls and towers that still give it its characteristic appearance.

The establishment of the Romanov dynasty in 1613 added employment in state administration to craft manufacturing. Commercial activity in Moscow centered in a large open market area called Red Square (in Russian, the word meaning "red" also means "beautiful"). In the second half of the eighteenth century Moscow University was founded, and architects from France and Italy were imported to design public buildings. Even after Peter the Great moved the capital to his new city of St. Petersburg, Moscow's industries continued to grow. By 1812, when Napoleon invaded Russia and occupied Moscow, its population had surpassed 275,000.

Following a disastrous fire during the occupation and Napoleon's withdrawal, a great program of rebuilding was undertaken that reconstructed the interior structures of the Kremlin and the Bolshoi Theater. The emancipation of the serfs in 1861 brought many of them to Moscow, whose population had increased to more than 600,000 by 1870. As new rail lines linked the city to the rest of the country during the 1890s, heavy engineering and metal industries developed. The number of inhabitants expanded rapidly, reaching almost 2 million before the outbreak of World War I.

The Soviets have given Moscow much of its modern appearance. Lenin moved the capital back to the city in 1918, and despite the ravages of the civil war its population had doubled by 1939 to more than 4 million, creating serious overcrowding and housing shortages. During World War II, Moscow withstood the onslaught of the German armies, which reached to within 25 miles of the city in late 1941. With Stalin remaining as a symbol of Russian resistance, the citizens of Moscow built antitank defenses, and the Red Army repulsed the *Wehrmacht*.

Recovery was rapid. In the late 1940s and early 1950s Stalin added ornate "wedding cake" skyscrapers to the Moscow skyline, and in the 1960s Khrushchev began the construction of extensive suburban apartment complexes to relieve the chronic housing shortage. Much of the country's modern industry is concentrated around the periphery.

The eclectic mix of Moscow's architecture reflects the richly diverse history of Russia. The Kremlin still dominates the city. Within its walls is one of the most striking and beautiful architectural ensembles in the world, over which rise the five golden onion-shaped domes of the fifteenth-century Cathedral of the Assumption and the white bell tower built by Ivan the Great. The nineteenth-century Kremlin Great Palace is now the seat of Soviet political power, while the Palace of Congresses, completed in 1961, is used for Communist party meetings. Along the east wall of the Kremlin lies Red Square, the ceremonial center of the capital. Today marchers in the annual May Day and the October Revolution parades pass by the squat bulk of the Lenin Mausoleum, as well as the domed sixteenth-century Cathedral of St. Basil the Blessed and GUM, the state department store. These sites symbolize the contradictions that mark Soviet life, while Moscow itself represents that peculiar combination of historical tradition and the legacy of revolution that is the Soviet Union.

Coexistence and Détente

In the 25 years following the clash over Cuba, American-Soviet disagreements remained sharp. Yet since the mid-1960s superpower relations have been partially clarified as both sides came to realize that nuclear confrontation would be a common disaster. Summit meetings and disarmament talks have formed the backdrop to a more fundamental trend toward the recognition of political realities that had been obscured by ideological rhetoric. If, in the 1960s, Cold War propaganda gave way to a public discussion of peaceful coexistence, so in the 1970s the United States and the Soviet Union began to define their relationship in terms of *détente,* literally a "relaxation of tensions."

American involvement in Vietnamese affairs (see Chapter 38) sparked a political and social crisis at home. The escalation of the war under President Johnson resulted in more than 500,000 American troops' being sent to Vietnam by the end of 1968. Unable to gain victory on the ground, the United States dropped more explosives on Vietnam than the Allies had used on all fronts during World War II, while American troops killed thousands of civilians in fruitless efforts to prevent villagers from hiding Communist guerrillas. By the mid-1960s a vigorous antiwar movement had begun to emerge in America. The protests started on college campuses, but outspoken opponents soon emerged in Congress and in the press. In 1967 demonstrations spread throughout the country, while thou-

South Vietnam's national police chief executes a Viet Cong officer on a Saigon street. Such scenes aroused opposition to the war in the United States and abroad. [Wide World Photos]

sands of young Americans declared themselves conscientious objectors or fled the United States to avoid the draft. Senator Eugene McCarthy (born 1916), campaigning on an antiwar platform, challenged President Johnson for the Democratic nomination. In March 1968, following McCarthy's strong showing in an early primary, the president announced that he would not seek another term.

After the Tet offensive in February 1968, peace talks with North Vietnam opened in Paris, and in November voters elected the Republican Richard M. Nixon (born 1913) to the presidency. Nixon began the secret bombing of Communist supply routes in Cambodia in early 1969, concealing the operation through false reports. In 1971 the publication of classified war documents heightened antiwar sentiments by revealing earlier deceptions by both Johnson and Nixon. Protests mounted as the 1972 presidential elections approached, but Nixon neutralized them by removing the last American ground troops. The Paris Accords, signed in January 1973, officially ended American involvement in the war.

The 1962 Cuban crisis and the Vietnam War provided the superpowers with an unstated but important lesson in international relations. In withdrawing Russian missiles from Cuba, Khrushchev had tacitly recognized America's predominance in Latin America. Vietnam had forced the United States to accept the limitations of its military strength. The leaders who followed Johnson and Khrushchev spoke increasingly of tempering Soviet-American relations with détente. Détente actually defined the process by which the superpowers agreed to formalize the dominance that the postwar settlements had given them.

This rapprochement was the work of an unlikely pair: Richard Nixon, a lifelong anticommunist, and Leonid Brezhnev, who had opposed Khrushchev's revisionist policies. Nixon repudiated the Dulles doctrine, which had de-

manded a rollback of Russian communism, while Brezhnev fell back on Lenin's notion that direct confrontation with the West was unnecessary in light of the inevitable decay of capitalism and the overthrow of colonialism by wars of national liberation.

The so-called Watergate crisis ended Nixon's presidency but not the era of détente. It was revealed that Nixon and his aides had illegally manipulated the campaign and had authorized surveillance and espionage against his political opponents. The crisis, which climaxed in 1974, exposed Nixon's efforts to cover up illegal White House operations. In August, faced with the possibility of impeachment, the president resigned in disgrace. Nixon's successor, Gerald R. Ford (born 1913), continued the policy of détente.

Détente contributed to the Helsinki Accords. In 1973 the United States and the Soviet Union joined Canada and almost all the European nations at the Conference on Security and Cooperation in Europe, held in Helsinki, Finland. In the final treaty, signed two years later, the Soviets endorsed political and human rights statements and agreed to encourage closer relations with the West. In return, the signatories guaranteed Europe's political boundaries, including the division of Germany into two states. Russia thus obtained formal recognition of the territorial adjustments in eastern Europe that had been arranged at Yalta and Potsdam. In effect, détente had served to achieve permanent agreement on the postwar settlements that had established the Russian—and, by implication, the American—sphere of influence in Europe.

American foreign policy remained basically unaltered under Ford's successor, Jimmy Carter (born 1924). Carter denounced repressive governments that violated basic human rights and decried the plight of political dissidents in the Soviet Union, but he continued to support dictatorships in Chile and Iran. He also cited the Soviet military buildup to justify an increase in American arms spending.

The Superpowers Challenged

In November 1979, after toppling Shah Muhammad Reza Pahlavi in Iran, Shi'ite Muslims under the leadership of the Ayatollah Ruhollah Khomeini seized the American embassy and captured 52 staff members. The unsuccessful American attempt to free the hostages was a major factor in determining the outcome of the 1980 American presidential elections, leading to the defeat of President Carter by Republican Ronald Reagan.

The hostage crisis demonstrated that the postwar world hegemony jointly exercised by the United States and the Soviet Union had not gone unchallenged. Smaller states have continually sought to mitigate superpower dominance and exert autonomy. In Europe and the non-Western world national leaders have employed a variety of techniques to maneuver between America and the Soviet Union. Within the Communist world ideological nonconformity has proved a powerful means of asserting independence, while in both western and eastern Europe nationalism has been used as a lever against Washington and Moscow.

Outside the immediate areas of superpower hegemony, states often exploited Cold War rivalries to extract economic and political concessions from each side. Neutralism and ideological nonalignment, especially among former colonies, have achieved the same results. The balance of nuclear terror actually enhances such possibilities, for to avoid mutual self-destruction over issues that do not threaten their vital interests, the superpowers are forced to act with restraint. Regional and economic organizations have exercised a moderating influence through the control of vital natural resources and markets. The revival of religious fundamentalism among Islamic states, so dramatically demonstrated in the United States–Iran crisis, suggests the availability of still other alternatives.

The Growth of European Autonomy

European efforts toward economic unity led to a subtle undermining of American influence. In 1950, against the background of the Marshall Plan, French foreign minister Robert Schuman (1886–1963) proposed a plan for cooperating in the production of steel and coal. Belgium, Luxembourg, and the Netherlands joined France, West Ger-

many, and Italy in forming the European Coal and Steel Community (ECSC), which quickly tripled iron and steel output and increased coal production almost 25 percent. By 1957 the ECSC concluded that further cooperation could strengthen Europe's economies and enable its members jointly to influence the superpowers. As a result, ECSC members created the European Economic Community, better known as the Common Market. Through the elimination of tariff barriers and the free exchange of labor and capital, the Common Market achieved remarkable success in economic integration. After years of French objection, Britain, Ireland, and Denmark became members in 1973. Although the United States still exercises a major influence in European economic life, Europe has escaped the direct dependency it once had on America. Indeed, while the Common Market brought an increase in American business in Europe, in the 1980s the flow of capital began to move in both directions as European products and investments entered the United States.

Charles de Gaulle, president of France from 1958 to 1969, led a more direct challenge to American hegemony. Proud and intensely nationalistic, he wanted to put France at the center of a Europe that would reassert its autonomy between the United States and the Soviet Union. For that reason, de Gaulle pulled French forces out of NATO, twice vetoed the entry of America's closest ally, Great Britain, into the European Common Market, and condemned America's escalating role in Vietnam. More grating still to Washington, the French leader tried to weaken the American economy by demanding gold for the large quantity of U.S. dollars held in Paris.

West Germany also demonstrated more autonomy. When the socialist Willy Brandt became federal chancellor in 1969, he embarked on a policy of reconciliation with the Communist bloc countries of eastern Europe. In exchange for guarantees of West Berlin's freedom and a mutual renunciation of force, Brandt concluded treaties with the Soviet Union, Czechoslovakia, and Poland that formally recognized existing frontiers. Of equal importance, he also began the normalization of relations with East Germany.

The success of the Common Market, together with the experience of de Gaulle and Brandt, led to Europe's increasing political independence from Washington. Although some Europeans have expressed anxiety at the prospect of an American missile withdrawal, since 1968 powerful grass-roots peace movements have challenged American nuclear policy. Moreover, most European states refused to follow the American lead in applying sanctions against the Soviet Union in 1979 after the Russian invasion of Afghanistan. A similar request was rejected in 1981 following the suppression of the Polish trade union movement, and in 1986 European states refused an American request for overflight permission during the bombing raid against Libya.

In eastern Europe the trend toward autonomy has been slower. Although the open revolts against Soviet authority in East Germany (1953) and Hungary (1956) were swiftly crushed, cautious ideological divergence from orthodox Communist policy drew many eastern European regimes away from Moscow. Combining Yugoslav nationalism with

doctrinal innovation, Marshal Tito steered his country into a quasi-neutral position even during the Stalinist period. Tito's example no doubt contributed to the harsh Soviet reaction against similar efforts in Czechoslovakia. In Jan-

41.1 *Europe Since World War II*

uary 1968 reformists within the Czech Communist party installed Alexander Dubček (born 1921) in office. Dubček lifted censorship and permitted local decision making in factories, unions, and the Communist party itself. The Czech example aroused demands for similar reforms elsewhere in eastern Europe. In August 500,000 Soviet and Warsaw Pact troops poured into Czechoslovkia and arrested Dubček and his reformist supporters. Brezhnev subsequently asserted the Soviet Union's right to intervene in the affairs of any socialist nation whenever necessary—the so-called Breshnev doctrine. By the 1970s a subtle shift in Soviet policy was introduced as Moscow sought to reduce the need for military intervention by stimulating economic integration with the eastern European region.

Efforts to achieve autonomy within the Communist world climaxed a decade later in Poland. In 1980 a rash of illegal strikes led to a massive work stoppage at the Gdansk shipyards and inspired the formation of the Solidarity movement, headed by Lech Walesa (born 1944), a tough but moderate organizer. With support from almost 10 million workers and the Catholic church, Solidarity won major concessions from the government before party leader General Wojciech Jaruzwelski (born 1923) imposed martial law and arrested union leaders. Walesa was eventually freed and Solidarity recognized. In the midst of a deepening economic crisis, partially free elections were held in 1989, leading to the formation of a coalition government headed by Tadeusz Mazowiecki of Solidarity.

The desire for ideological autonomy has also been linked to the growing identification of Communist parties with the idea of an independent Europe free from the influence of both superpowers. This trend gave rise to the phenomenon known as Eurocommunism, which found its first example in Italy, whose Communist party was inspired by the theoretical writings of Antonio Gramsci (1891–1937). Italian Communists have adopted considerable tactical flexibility based on Gramsci's notion that the history of a nation should guide the development of its Communist movement. Not unlike the European popular front policies of the 1930s, Italian Communist leaders have accepted both democratic principles and the possibility of sharing power in a coalition with bourgeois parties. The Communists of France, Spain, and most other Western countries have moved in the same direction, at times breaking with Moscow over international issues. In 1968 the Italian Communist party, together with its French counterpart, attacked the Soviet Union's invasion of Czechoslovakia.

The Nonaligned World

The colonial territories that gained nationhood after World War II found themselves economically dependent on the industrialized, wealthier Western states. Much-needed developmental resources came through assistance programs sponsored by the United States and the Soviet Union, which vied with each other to capture the political support of the newly independent countries. Yet, rather than becoming pawns in the East-West competition, underdeveloped states devised a strategy that turned the Cold War into what they called "creative confrontation"—playing off the superpowers to their own advantage while maintaining nonaligned status. India's Jawaharlal Nehru saw neutralism as a means of forging a "third force" among nonaligned nations, much as de Gaulle would attempt to do in Europe in the 1960s. The Egyptian leader Gamal Abdel Nasser maneuvered skillfully between the superpowers in pursuit of his goals.

In 1955 a large number of neutralist states convened the Afro-Asian Conference in Bandung, Indonesia, to discuss mutual interests and strategy. The United Nations soon became a focus of Third World nonalignment. The ranks of the General Assembly swelled rapidly as former colonies won independence, thus forming a substantial voting bloc with members from Latin America. Anticolonial sentiment, reinforced by the Soviets, often translated into anti-Western positions, but the primary agenda among nonaligned countries was to secure passage of social and economic assistance measures. Superpower refusal to fund such programs has often undermined the effectiveness of the neutralist coalition.

The Bandung conference symbolized continuing efforts to establish regional organizations designed to forge unity of policy and economic cooperation among Third World nations. The Organization of African Unity (OAU) was established because African leaders believed that disunity played into the hands of the superpowers. Founded in 1963, the OAU required a policy of nonalignment from each of its 30 member states and spawned a number of subregional economic groups similar in concept to the European Common Market. The OAU has also pursued a policy of political cooperation with other Third World regional coalitions, especially with Arab countries.

Much of the frustration expressed by nonaligned nations stemmed from the vastly unequal relationship separating rich and poor states. The resentment, strongest where key resources and local economies have been exploited by multinational Western corporations, has had a major impact on recent world events. The formation of the Organization of Petroleum Exporting Countries (OPEC) in 1960 reflects these concerns. OPEC devised the strategy of counterpenetration, whereby it hoped to make industrial economies that relied heavily on oil imports vulnerable to Third World pressures. Initially, the strategy had astounding success. Dwindling foreign aid from the United States and its allies, coupled with the West's pro-Israeli policy in the Middle East, angered the Arab nations in OPEC. In 1973 the group quadrupled the price of crude oil in one year. The sudden rise in fuel costs intensified inflation and recession in the West and underscored the interdependency of world societies. The next year the nonaligned bloc in the UN passed a resolution demanding the creation of a "new international economic order" in which resources, trade, and markets would be equally distributed.

Nonaligned states have forged still other forms of economic cooperation as leverage against the superpowers. OPEC, the OAU, and the Arab League have overlapping members, and in the 1970s the Arabs began extending huge financial assistance to African nations in an effort to reduce African economic dependency on the United States and the Soviet Union. At a 1977 Afro-Arab summit conference in Cairo, oil producers pledged $1.5 billion in aid to Africa. Recent divisions within OPEC have made concerted action more difficult. Nevertheless, the 1973 oil crisis provided dramatic evidence of the limitations of superpower hegemony.

The Nuclear Peril

Despite a history of ideological conflict and Cold War confrontations since the end of World War II, the United States and the Soviet Union have remained at peace with each other. Indeed, relations between the superpowers grew less tense in the 1980s, and efforts at political cooperation and disarmament held out the promise of a more peaceful world.

The Quest for Disarmament

Nuclear arms limitations talks have been a feature of diplomatic relations for more than 40 years. Some progress has been made; the superpowers have been forced to be sensitive to the demands of the international community, and their monopoly over nuclear arms has ended.

In 1946, when it still had the world's only atomic weapons, the United States suggested the creation of an international atomic development authority with the power to inspect all countries to prevent the manufacture of nuclear weapons. America proposed turning its research data and facilities over to the agency. The Soviet Union, in the midst of developing its own atomic capability, vetoed the proposal and in 1949 detonated an atomic weapon. Since then the United States and the Soviet Union have been engaged in a costly and dangerous nuclear arms race. Each now possesses enough nuclear weapons to exterminate most of the life on the planet.

During the height of the Cold War the superpowers developed their nuclear arsenals and delivery systems and conducted unrestrained testing of atomic weapons that threatened to destroy the environment. In 1952 the United States exploded a hydrogen bomb, an even more destructive weapon. The following year the Soviets announced their own hydrogen device, and in 1961 they tested a 50-megaton bomb, the equivalent of 50 million tons of TNT.

The first important step in nuclear disarmament came in 1963 with the signing of a test ban treaty that permitted only underground explosions. Although more than 100 nations signed the treaty, some states, hoping to achieve their own nuclear capability, refused. In 1968 the United States and the Soviet Union jointly sponsored a nonproliferation treaty that sought to restrict nuclear weapons to the five nations already in possession of them—the United States, the Soviet Union, Britain, France, and China. The pact called for international inspections to ensure that nuclear energy facilities would be used only for peaceful purposes. Eight countries (Argentina, Brazil, Egypt, India, Israel, Pakistan, Spain, and South Africa) did not sign the agreement. A similar pact in 1977 secured the agreement of 90 nations, but again, those approaching nuclear capacity refused. The limited success of the nonproliferation effort has not only made disarmament more difficult but also reflects the sobering failure of the superpowers to reach their own accord.

Little progress was made in American-Soviet disarmament until the 1972 SALT I treaty, which froze the number of offensive "strategic" intercontinental missile launchers for five years. The antiballistic missile (ABM) provisions of SALT I limited the number of ABM sites. In theory, ABMs could provide a nuclear defense by intercepting attacking missiles, although the cost would be prohibitive and decoys could make the system ineffective; in a nuclear exchange, even a small margin of error could result in tens of millions of fatalities. The ABM accord was based on the notion of deterrence, which argues that each side would not attack the other because it feared counterattack. By contrast, an unrestricted ABM race might tempt the nation that acquired an effective defense to consider a first strike against the other if nuclear war seemed "winnable."

The SALT I pact was imperfect. The United States possessed a manned nuclear bomber fleet that the Soviets could not match. Moreover, nothing prevented either side from equipping its missiles with multiple warheads (MIRVs), and no restrictions were placed on technical improvements in either missiles or warheads. The 1979 SALT II treaty limited each superpower to 2,400 nuclear launchers, of which only 1,320 could have MIRVs. But the U.S. Senate refused to ratify SALT II because of conservative opposition and the difficulty of maintaining true parity in the face of continued weapons research. The treaty was observed informally until President Reagan exceeded SALT II limits in 1986. Both the United States and the Soviet Union have continued to test nuclear weapons.

The Gorbachev Era

Recent changes in Soviet-American relations have further reduced superpower tensions. Brezhnev died in November 1982, only to be replaced in rapid succession by former secret police chief Yuri Andropov (1904–1984), the Politburo veteran Konstantin Chernenko (1912–1985), and, in March 1985, Mikhail Gorbachev (born 1931). Representing a younger generation, Gorbachev was reformist in outlook. He took symbolic steps to liberalize Soviet rule at home by permitting more open discussion—a policy known as *glasnost* ("openness")—releasing some prominent political dissidents, and establishing a commission to review censorship policies. In 1987 came news that *Dr. Zhivago*, Boris Pasternak's sweeping novel of love broken by the Russian Revolution, would be published, three decades after its appearance in the West.

The real focus of Gorbachev's domestic program concerned the Soviet economy. Administered through a central planning system that had originated with Stalin, economic policy was beset by a maze of bureaucratic processes that resulted in inefficiency, low-quality consumer goods, and outdated technology. Under Stalin the economy had grown rapidly until 1950 through an "extensive" method of expanding output by manipulating labor and capital. Growth slowed further in the 1970s, and the annual rate of the Soviet GNP dropped by half in the early 1980s. Gorbachev's reform program, which he has called *perestroika* ("restructuring"), called for an "intensive" growth fed by technological progress and efficiency and the cautious introduction of market incentives.

The climate for change stimulated by Gorbachev's reform program elicited a favorable response from the Soviet people. In the spring of 1989 elections were held for membership in the Supreme Soviet. For the first time in 70 years, citizens were free to vote for representatives from a long list of candidates, not all of whom had been nominated by the party or were party members. The results, dramatic in their implications, demonstrated popular discontent with party bureaucrats. Among those elected was Boris Yeltsin, a strong critic of the old party machine who had been ousted from his post as Moscow party boss because of his open criticism of bureaucratic vested interests. The elections, which strengthened Gorbachev's hand in his struggle with the older Communist party leadership, appear to have confirmed the impetus behind *perestroika*.

The early 1980s saw a steady buildup in the arms race. President Reagan increased military spending from one-fourth to one-third of the federal budget. The Soviets threatened to match the weapons escalation. The Reagan administration's arms policy aimed at achieving two goals: nuclear superiority over the Soviet Union and the development of the Strategic Defense Initiative (SDI). Dubbed "Star Wars" by the media, the SDI plan called for research and development of satellite-mounted lasers capable of destroying offensive enemy missiles in flight. SDI critics feared that the system might be intended to enable the

President Ronald Reagan and Soviet leader Mikhail Gorbachev meet in Moscow, May 1988. [Blanche/Gamma-Liaison]

United States to win a nuclear war, while advocates have argued that it would reduce the threat of war. Extensive research in space-based offensive weapons systems was simultaneously carried on under classified military budgeting.

Nevertheless, Gorbachev's reformist attitudes have had a positive impact on superpower relations. Beginning with a Geneva meeting in 1985, Gorbachev and Reagan held four summit meetings. At Reykjavik, Iceland, in 1986 the two leaders agreed in principle to a reduction of missile systems. Two years later, in Moscow, they signed documents that put into effect a treaty eliminating Soviet and American medium and shorter-range land-based missiles. Between 1985 and 1988 the two nations concluded more than 40 other treaties concerning a variety of issues from cultural exchanges to fishing rights. Still, they have made no headway on space-based defense systems, and the issue of long-range missiles remains unresolved.

Perestroika:
◉ Reform in Gorbachev's Russia ◉

In April 1985 Mikhail Gorbachev announced a policy of far-reaching reform that he called perestroika *("restructuring"). Gorbachev claimed that this policy of delegating more responsibility to the people, of encouraging initiative and openness, is the next natural stage in the development of the Soviet system. Here he describes his goals as a phase in the continuing revolution.*

We have come to the conclusion that unless we activate the human factor, that is, unless we take into consideration the diverse interests of people, work collectives, public bodies, and various social groups, unless we rely on them, and draw them into active, constructive endeavor, it will be impossible for us to accomplish any of the tasks set, or to change the situation in the country. . . .

It is wrong, and even harmful, to see socialist society as something rigid and unchangeable, to perceive its improvement as an effort to adapt complicated reality to concepts and formulas that have been established once and for all. The concepts of socialism keep on developing. . . .

Perestroika is a word with many meanings. But if we are to choose from its many possible synonyms the key one which expresses its essence most accurately, then we can say thus: perestroika is a revolution. A decisive acceleration of the socioeconomic and cultural development of Soviet society which involves radical changes on the way to a qualitatively new state is undoubtedly a revolutionary task. . . .

In accordance with our theory, revolution means construction, but it also always implies demolition. Revolution requires the demolition of all that is obsolete, stagnant and hinders fast progress. . . . Perestroika also means a resolute and radical elimination of obstacles hindering social and economic development, of outdated methods of managing the economy and of dogmatic stereotype mentality. . . .

And like a revolution, our day-to-day activities must be unparalleled, revolutionary. Perestroika requires Party leaders who are very close to Lenin's ideal of a revolutionary Bolshevik. Officialdom, red tape, patronizing attitudes, and careerism are incompatible with this ideal. On the other hand, courage, initiative, high ideological standards and moral purity, a constant urge to discuss things with people, and an ability to firmly uphold the humane values of socialism are greatly honored. . . . We still have a long way to go to achieve this ideal. Too many people are still "in the state of evolution," or, to put it plainly, have adopted a wait-and-see attitude.

Source: M. Gorbachev, *Perestroika: New Thinking for Our Country and the World* (New York: Harper & Row, 1987), pp. 29–55 passim.

Despite a record of slow and often interrupted disarmament negotiations, the superpowers have moved closer to the goal of reducing the nuclear peril. Indeed, the agreements reached in the 1970s and 1980s are far more hopeful than all pre- *vious disarmament efforts undertaken since the Great War. This advance must surely reflect the lessons derived from a century of war and strife and a realization that the world of tomorrow must rest on the basis of common purpose.*

Notes

1. F. Freidel, *America in the Twentieth Century* (New York: Knopf, 1960), pp. 475–476.

Suggestions for Further Reading

Brzezinski, Z. K. *The Soviet Bloc: Unity and Compromise.* Cambridge, Mass.: Harvard University Press, 1967.

Crankshaw, E. *Khrushchev.* New York: Viking Press, 1966.

Dawisha, K. *Eastern Europe, Gorbachev and Reform: The Great Challenge.* Cambridge: Cambridge University Press, 1988.

De Porte, A. W. *Europe Between the Superpowers.* New Haven, Conn.: Yale University Press, 1979.

Epstein, W. *The Last Chance: Nuclear Proliferation and Arms Control.* New York: Free Press, 1976.

Fejto, F. *A History of the People's Democracies: Eastern Europe Since Stalin.* New York: Praeger, 1971.

Freedman, L. *The Evolution of Nuclear Strategy.* New York: St. Martin's Press, 1982.

Gaddis, J. L. *The United States and the Origins of the Cold War, 1941–1947.* New York: Columbia University Press, 1972.

Herken, G. *The Winning Weapon: The Atomic Bomb in the Cold War, 1945–1950.* Princeton, N.J.: Princeton University Press, 1988.

Kolko, G. *The Politics of War.* New York: Random House, 1969.

Kriegel, A. *Eurocommunism.* Stanford, Calif.: Stanford University Press, 1978.

Laqueur, W. *Europe Since Hitler.* London: Weidenfeld & Nicolson, 1972.

Lovenduski, J. *Women and European Politics.* Amherst: University of Massachusetts Press, 1986.

Mastny, V. *Russia's Road to the Cold War.* New York: Columbia University Press, 1979.

Mazrui, A. A. *Africa's International Relations: The Diplomacy of Dependency and Change.* Boulder, Colo.: Westview Press, 1977.

Milward, A. S. *The Reconstruction of Western Europe, 1945–51.* Berkeley: University of California Press, 1984.

Pinkus, B. *The Jews of the Soviet Union: A History of a National Minority.* Cambridge: Cambridge University Press, 1988.

Ulam, A. *Expansion and Coexistence: The History of Soviet Foreign Policy, 1917–1967.* New York: Praeger, 1974.

Van der Wee, H. *Prosperity and Upheaval: The World Economy, 1945–1980.* Berkeley: University of California Press, 1988.

Von Laue, T. *The World Revolution of Westernization: The Twentieth Century in Global Perspective.* New York: Oxford University Press, 1987.

Civilization and the Dilemma of Progress

History, Time, and Progress

In the modern era, the prevailing view of historical process has been defined by the concept of progress, which sees history as a steady advance toward a better world. A century ago one proponent of progress, the American writer Edward Bellamy (1850–1898), wrote a popular novel that embodied this belief. In *Looking Backward,* Bellamy imagined a man who fell into a hypnotic sleep in 1887 and awoke in the year 2000. The man discovered a perfect world of universal peace and happiness in which all people shared equally in the wealth and benefits of a society freed from conflict, greed, and even the need for laws.

Repelled by the social evils of his own day, Bellamy believed that the future had to be better than the past and that it would inevitably lead to an ideal civilization. His

A powerful symbol of twentieth-century technology, the United States space shuttle *Discovery* roars off the launch pad in September of 1988. [UPI/Bettmann Newsphotos]

work belongs to a long utopian tradition that stretches back to Plato's fourth-century B.C. *The Republic*. Bellamy's optimism for the future stemmed from a prejudice against the past, for his vision of progress did not permit him to see the mixture of good and bad that is present in every period of history. Like many others then and now, he assumed that the passage of time automatically brought with it improvement over what had been before. Those who embrace this view generally assume that the closer in time to our own day, the better human life has been, that the present is superior to the past because it is now rather than then. Yet in his letter from Birmingham Jail, written in 1963, the American civil rights leader Martin Luther King, Jr., pointedly rejected the "strangely irrational notion that there is something in the very flow of time that will inevitably cure all ills."[1] The notion of progress has often obscured the fact that even at moments of relative peace and prosperity, certain groups without power or status—such as workers, racial minorities, and women—have not shared in the broad advances made by society at large.

Bellamy's understanding of progress reflects a relatively modern, peculiarly Western world view that broke with older Western and non-Western traditions alike. Earlier civilizations had viewed progress chiefly in spiritual or theological terms and tended to see history as cyclical rather than progressive. The ancient Greeks of the classical age believed that their ancestors of the archaic period had been more "heroic" and thus better. Confucius, whose ethical philosophy dominated Chinese thought, accepted the notion of social improvement through education and good example, but he also inculcated a respect for the knowledge and wisdom of the past and a measured view of the present and future. The Judeo-Christian and Islamic religions prophesied salvation and the attainment of a heavenly paradise through spiritual rectitude but had no place for a secular conception of progress. The Hindu and Buddhist concept of reincarnation, which stressed "progress" from lower to higher states of being, aspired to the ultimate spiritual state of Nirvana that would transcend the material world. Indian conceptions of history were decidedly cyclical; the period since about 900 B.C., in which we still live, the *Kali-yuga*, was conceived as one of decline and chaos.

Nineteenth-century Western thinkers were thus a minority in viewing progress in secular terms, based on belief in the material perfectibility of society. In this sense the human adventure is measured in terms of our ability to master the physical environment through scientific and technological advances and to improve the level of material well-being and comfort through the ever-increasing accumulation of wealth. Advocates of this conception of progress claimed that improvement would come through the application of knowledge to political, social, and economic problems. History, according to this view, would unfold as the natural laws that governed the universe were

discovered and manipulated in the interest of human improvement. The ethos of liberal capitalism sought to unfetter the laws of economics in order to achieve the greatest material good for the greatest number of people.

Even while this conception gained ascendancy in the West, a variety of reform-minded thinkers recoiled against the effects of industrialism by experimenting with socialist utopias in which private ownership of capital was replaced by communal property in rural egalitarian societies. Some utopian socialists even conceived of a technocratic society in which scientists and industrialists governed on behalf of the general populace. Then, in the mid-nineteenth century, "scientific" socialists explained history as the product of class conflict: categories of human beings—classes—competed for ascendancy by seeking control over the means of production and distribution. The Marxist utopia looked forward to the inevitable triumph of the working class over the capitalists and the ultimate creation of a classless society.

Bellamy's utopia was a combination of these visions. It imagined a highly organized industrial society in which a secular state exercised complete authority and evoked voluntary compliance from its citizens because it provided them with material comfort and well-being. Though repelled by the poverty and exploitation that characterized the expanding industrialization of his time, Bellamy remained a believer in the ability of technology to resolve the ills of modern society.

More than a century after the publication of *Looking Backward*, modern writers have become less sanguine about the benefits of a technological society. In 1932, in the midst of the Great Depression, the British author Aldous Huxley published *Brave New World*, a novel that depicted a totalitarian society in which people lacked no bodily comfort but were without freedom or creativity. In 1949, following World War II, George Orwell portrayed a dehumanized totalitarian society of the future in his book *1984*. The appalling nature of such totalitarian regimes as those of Hitler and Stalin and the specter of the atomic bomb provided the impetus for Orwell's novel and its bleak vision of the future. Orwell's message, in the words of the psychologist Erich Fromm, was intended to awaken us to the common "danger of a society of automatons who will have lost every trace of individuality, of love, of critical thought, and yet who will not be aware of it."[2]

Global Implications of Progress

The materialist theory of progress provided a powerful rationale for the imperialism that conquered much of the non-Western world in the late nineteenth century. Many

Europeans believed that they were bringing the benefits of their technologically superior civilization to unfortunate primitive peoples. Western science and industry, on which the theory of progress was based, in turn made possible imperialist domination over much of the rest of the world.

As we have seen, the reaction of the non-Western world to the Western intrusion has been mixed. The Chinese effort to keep all Western influences out of their country was by no means the norm, for the Japanese aggressively adopted Western-style industrialization and technology, both to resist Western domination and to extend their own hegemony over East Asia. Similarly, some southern African tribes conquered their neighbors with European firearms, and Arab traders used Western weapons to capture Africans for the slave market. In the early twentieth century Turkish and Iranian admirers of Western technology attempted to "modernize" their countries along the Western model, but more recently Islamic fundamentalists, particularly in Iran, have strenuously repudiated Western influences.

The Western idea of progress continues to influence both Western policies toward the nonindustrialized nations and Third World thinking about how to solve the immense social, economic, and cultural problems endemic to their own countries. Since World War II, industrialized nations have systematically exported their notion of progress to underdeveloped states as they emerged from colonial status to independence. In 1961 President John F. Kennedy announced a massive program of economic assistance for Latin America that he called the Alliance for Progress.

As Western developmental strategies for "modernization" replaced imperialism as the basis of the global dynamic, new forms of dependency have been substituted for older forms of subjugation. During the struggle for India's independence from the British, Mahatma Gandhi—who recognized the relationship between imperialism and the materialist notion of progress—rejected the Western model of development by urging his fellow Indians to adopt the traditional spinning wheel as the symbol of freedom and national regeneration.

Despite Gandhi's rejection of modern technology, his successors embraced Western-style industrialization, making India one of the first Third World countries to develop not only conventional electrical energy sources but a nuclear capability as well. Most other underdeveloped nations followed suit, generally adopting an enthusiastic attitude toward technology, with its capacity to enhance health as well as material comforts. Thus agricultural societies often seek to build huge dams, hydroelectric plants, and nuclear energy stations in order to electrify and industrialize their economies, but sometimes at the expense of destroying millions of acres of irreplaceable forests in the process of extracting raw materials and constructing factories. The problem is clearly one of balance; industrialization and conservation need not be mutually antagonistic.

Reliance on Western technology has at times been seriously disruptive to the Third World. The technology of advanced industrial nations and the accompanying infrastructures of such technology are not necessarily ideal or suited for developing countries. Historically, modern technology has been marked by its complex and large-scale character, and its success has depended on extensive national markets, skilled labor, and substantial investment capital. Because developing countries generally lack these resources, simple and inexpensive machinery that does not require extensive education and training may be more appropriate to agrarian societies. Moreover, since 1945 most technological development in the Third World has been undertaken with extensive loans borrowed from Western nations; the resultant economic dependency has crippled the debtor nations, most of which are unable to repay their huge obligations.

In recent years a rethinking of the Western notion of material progress has been unfolding. Not only has the idea of "appropriate technology" gained currency, but it is now increasingly recognized that Third World nations need not necessarily undergo the same stressful stages of development experienced by earlier industrial societies. It is probable, nonetheless, that the rapid transformation of the globe and of its human societies will continue, driven by technological change and its political ramifications.

Facing the Future: History as Freedom

As the twentieth century draws toward a close, civilization appears to be beset with a host of unparalleled problems. There is irony in the fact that science and technology have made the lives of many millions of people more comfortable, yet they have also been the source of unanticipated dilemmas. Advances in health care have resulted in a global population explosion that threatens to engulf the poorer societies of the Third World in a relentless cycle of poverty and social despair. Although new agricultural methods have increased food productivity, natural disasters and political upheavals periodically create crises of starvation and malnutrition for millions. The demands of industrialization have despoiled much of the earth's seas, rivers, forests, and air. Now that the depletion of finite energy resources looms as a distinct possibility, the harnessing of atomic power as an energy alternative is fraught with other dangers, as dramatized by the 1979 meltdown at the Three Mile Island nuclear power plant in Pennsylvania and the 1986 disaster at the Soviet plant in Chernobyl. And the entire human race faces the ultimate challenge of avoiding the folly of nuclear war.

Despite advances achieved in the struggle for human

rights by racial minorities, women, and other oppressed groups, vast inequities in economic justice and political freedom continue to exist—in Third World countries, in Communist-bloc nations, and in the Western world. These and other issues are compelling and dangerous, but the problems of our age are unique only in the particular forms they now assume. If nothing else, history provides us with perspective: war and conflict, disease and hunger, prejudice and exploitation, torture and state repression are some of the less pleasant features of history that our age has in common with all civilizations of the past. Over the course of 5,000 years, all societies have at times perceived the challenges facing them as insurmountable. Yet history also suggests that while the problems recur with relentless repetition, determined people have continued to seek durable solutions to them.

Change, often rapid and unpredictable, has been the hallmark of history. Even the most conservative of cultures, as in ancient Egypt or medieval China, underwent sudden and dramatic shifts in social and religious belief and political structure. Later generations do, of course, inherit traditions and values from the past, but they sometimes choose to discard them in the light of new circumstances. Those moments when men and women have successfully overcome adversity represent recurrent evidence of the open-endedness of history. Perhaps the only constraint under which our own age operates is the fact that as the world develops into a truly global community, we increasingly share the same human experience and thus equal responsibility for the world we make.

Notes

1.   M. L. King, Jr., *Why We Can't Wait* (New York: Harper & Row, 1963), p. 89.

2.   E. Fromm, "Afterword," in G. Orwell, *1984* (New York: New American Library, 1961), p. 267.

Aachen [*ah*-kun] (Aix-la-Chapelle), 265–266
Abbas, Shah, 471, 477–478
Abbasid [*ab*-uh-sid, uh-*bah*-sid] caliphate, 181–183, 265
Abdul Hamid II, 763, 882
Abdullah, Amir, 982
Abdullah al-Mansur, 181–182
Abelard [*ab*-uh-lahrd], Peter, 299–300
Abolitionist movement, 610–611, 782
Aborigines, 426
Abortion, 140, 512, 1030, 1031
Abraham, 26, 158, 179
Abstract Expressionism, 859
Abu Nuwas [ah-boo noo-*wahs*], 183, 187
Abyssinia. *See* Ethiopia
Academy (Florence), 349, 357
Acapulco, 571
Achaean [uh-*kee*-uhn] League, 109–110
Acre [*ah*-ker], 285
Act in Restraint of Appeals (1533), 389
Action française [ahk-syon frahn-sez], 836, 900
Actium [*ak*-tee-uhm], battle of, 131
Act of Supremacy (1534), 389
Adams, Abigail, 611–612
Adams, John, 586, 611–612
Addams, Jane, 782
Addaura Caves, 366
Adelard of Bath, 302
Adenauer [*ah*-d'n-ow-er], Konrad, 1024, 1029

Adler, Victor, 760
Adowa [*ah*-doh-wah], battle of, 803
Adrianople [ay-dree-uhn-*noh*-puhl], battle of, 144
Aegean [ee-*jee*-uhn] Sea, 76, 77, 80
Aegina [ee-*jye*-nah], 85
Aeneid [ih-*nee*-ihd] (Vergil), 133–134
Aeolian [ee-*oh*-lih-ahn] dialect, 80
Aequi [ee-kwye], 124
Aeschylus [*es*-kih-luhs], 101
Aetolian [ee-*tohl*-yuhn] League, 109–110
Afghanistan, 221, 466, 468, 472, 650, 663, 665, 813, 974, 1040
Africa: early history, 199–201; geography, 200; Sudan kingdoms, 201–207; Ghana, 202; Mali, 202–206; Songhay, 206–207; Swahili city-states, 207–208; southern Africa, 208–209, 803; Portuguese bases, 408–409; and New Imperialism, 802–807; seeds of independence, 991–992; granting of independence, 992–996; modern South Africa, 996–998; North Africa after World War II, 998–1000
African National Congress, 997–998
Afrikaners. *See* Boers
Afro-Asian Conference (1955), 1042
Agadir [ah-gah-*deer*] crisis, 839
Agesilaus [ah-jehs-ih-*lay*-uhs], 93
Agincourt [ah-zhan-*koor*], battle of, 324
Agra [*ah*-gra], 466, 470, 471, 475, 649, 650, 651, 657
Agricola, 139

Agricola, Rudolf, 351
Agriculture: Neolithic, 6–8, 12–13, 36, 77; origins in India, 36; in ancient China, 58–59, 62, 64; Hellenistic, 112; classical Roman, 132; Abbasid, 185; early African, 200–201, 205; Aztec, 215; Incan, 217; Chinese, 242, 488, 673, 674, 679; in medieval Europe, 269; in the Americas, 209, 572; in early modern Europe, 401–402, 408, 421; agricultural revolution in Europe, 697–699; in modern India, 809, 811; in modern Japan, 822
Agrippina [ag-rih-*pee*-nuh], 134
Ahimsa [ah-*hihm*-suh], 147, 878
Ahmedi, 465
Ahmet-elebi, Ahi, 465
Ahura-Mazda [ah-*hoo*-rah *mahz*-duh], 156, 157
Ainu [*eye*-noo], 258
Airplane, invention of, 717
Aix-la-Chapelle [*eks*-lah-shah-*pell*], Treaty of, 582, 655
Akbar [*ak*-bahr], 466, 467–470, 473
Akhenaton [ah-kuhn-*ah*-tahn], 23–25, 28
Akkadians [uh-*kay*-dee-uhnz], 16–17, 193
Alalia, battle of, 122
Alamogordo, nuclear testing at, 933
Alaric [*al*-uh-rik], 144, 173
al-Ashani, 186
Alaska, 586
al-Bakri [al-bah-*kree*], 202
Albania, 839, 906, 923, 1024, 1028; Italian invasion of, 923

Albert, Prince, 776, 777
Albertus Magnus [al-*bur*-tuhs *mag*-nuhs], 300, 301
Albigensian [al-bih-*jehn*-see-uhn] Crusade, 296
Albigensians, 296
Albizzi [ahl-*beet*-tsee] family, 338
Albuquerque, Affonso de [uh-*fahn*-zoh dih uhl-boo-*ker*-kuh], 411
Alcala [ahl-kah-*lah*], University of, 390
Alchemy [*al*-kuh-mee], 155, 185, 302
Alcibiades [al-sih-*bye*-uh-deez], 95
Alcuin [*al*-kwin], 266
Alemanni [*ahl*-eh-mahn-ee], 143
Alexander (Yugoslavia), 906
Alexander I (Russia), 636, 638, 721, 722, 723, 726, 727, 760–761, 764
Alexander II (Russia), 757, 761–762, 764, 788
Alexander III (Russia), 762
Alexander VI, Pope, 335, 337, 353, 375, 405
Alexander of Hales, 300
Alexander the Great, 24, 32, 33, 42–43, 47, 97, 107–110, 116, 179
Alexandra, 863
Alexandria, 47, 108, 109, 113–115, 130, 131, 133, 142, 159, 177, 181, 201, 321, 804
Alexius I Comnenus [uh-*lek*-see-uhs kuhm-*nee*-nuhs], 190, 264, 282, 283
Alfonsín, Raúl, 1006
Alfonso V, "the Magnanimous" (Aragon), 335
Alfonso VI (Castile), 286
Alfonso X, "the Wise" (Castile), 298, 310
Alfonso XII (Spain), 781
Alfred the Great (England), 306
Algeciras [ahl-jeh-*seer*-uhs] Conference, 838
Algeria, 803, 804, 983, 987, 999
al-Ghazzali [al-ga-*zah*-lee], Muhammad ibn, 187
Algiers, 762
Algoa [al-*goh*-uh] Bay, 408
Alhambra (palace), 287, 288
Ali [ah-*lee*], 184
Ali, Hussein [hoo-*sayn*] ibn-, 842, 981
Ali, Muhammad, 762
Ali, Sonni [*soh*-nee], 206
al-Khwarazmi [al-*khwah*-rahz-mee], Muhammad ibn-Musa, 185
Alkindi [al-*kihn*-dee], 186
Allende, Salvador [sahl-vah-*dohr* ah-*yane*-day], 1006
Alliance for Progress, 1049
All Quiet on the Western Front (Remarque), 848
Almagest (Ptolemy), 114, 428
Almohades [*al*-moh-haydz], 287
Almoravids [al-*moh*-rah-vyedz], 202, 204, 205, 286, 287
Alphabet, 81, 86, 121, 193, 195–196, 256, 257

Alsace [ahl-*zahs*], 334, 531, 759, 846
Alva, Duke of, 437
Amasis [a-*mah*-sis], 86
Amazon [*am*-uh-zahn] River, 209
Amboina [am-*boy*-nuh], 410
American Popular Revolutionary Alliance (APRA), 1006–1007
Americas, European conquest of, 414–419
Amerindians, 414–419, 584, 586, 709
Amherst, Lord, 678
Amiens [ah-*myahn*], 305
Amin, Idi [ee-dee ah-*meen*], 993
Amon-Re [*ah*-men-ray], 21
Amorites [*am*-uh-rites], 17
Amos, 159, 160
Amritsar [um-*riht*-ser], 473; massacre at, 814, 878
Amsterdam, 445–446, 530, 710
Amundsen, Roald, 1017, 1019
Amur [ah-*moor*] valley, 413, 675, 819
Anabaptists, 386–387
Anabasis [uh-*nahb*-uh-sis] (Xenophon), 104
Analects, 63–64
Anarchists, 788
Anastasius [an-ehs-*tay*-zhus], 173
Anatolia [an-uh-*toh*-lee-uh], 282
Anatomy, 142, 301, 552, 546, 687
Anaxagoras of Clazomenae [an-aks-*ag*-oh-rahs of klah-*zom*-eh-nee], 103
Anaximander, 427, 547
Ancestor worship, 59, 153, 213, 316
Andes [*an*-deez] Mountains, 209, 210, 217, 416
Andropov, Yuri [*yoo*-ree uhn-*droh*-poff], 1044
Angad, 473
Angelico, Fra [frah an-*jel*-ih-koh], 346
Anger, Jane, 612
Angevin [*an*-juh-vihn] Empire, 274
Angkor [*ahng* kohr], 234, 235–236
Angles, 265, 294
Anglo-Saxon Chronicle, 306
Angola, 408, 409, 803, 992, 994–995
Anguissola [ahn-*gwee*-soh-lah], Sofonisba, 361
Animals, domestication of, 7, 58
Anjou [*ahn*-zhoo], 274, 334
Ankara [*ang*-kuh-ruh], 883; battle of, 457
Annam [ah-*nam*], 236
Anne (England), 533, 543
Anne of Austria, 443
Anne of Bohemia, 327
Anne of Cleves, 397
Anschluss [*ahn*-schloos], 846, 919
Anselm [*an*-selm], 299
Antarctica, 1017
Anthony, 166
Anthony, Susan B., 613, 783
Anti-Comintern Pact, 918
Antigone [an-*tig*-uh-nee] (Sophocles), 102
Antigonus [an-*tig*-uh-nuhs], 109
Antioch [*an*-tee-ahk], 109, 112, 173, 284
Antiochus I [an-*tee*-oh-kuhs], 46, 109

Antiochus III, 112, 118, 127
Anti-Semitism: medieval, 308–309, 322; early modern, 394–395, 396, 609–610; modern, 764–765, 779, 831, 836, 893–894, 914–915, 928–930, 976, 1004
Antoninus (Caracalla) [an-toh-*nye*-nuhs], 135, 142
Antony, Mark, 130–131
Antwerp [*an*-twurp], 401, 422–423
Anuradhapura [ah-*noo*-rah-dah-*poo*-rah], 48, 49, 50, 231
Anyang [*ahn*-yahng], 58, 60, 74, 195
Apartheid [uh-*pahrt*-ayt], 997
Appeasement, policy of, 921–922
Aqaba [*ah*-kah-bah], Gulf of, 980
Aquinas [uh-*kwye*-nuhs], Thomas, 300, 301
Aquino [ah-*keen*-oh], Corazon, 954, 959
Aquitaine [*ak*-wih-tayn], 267, 274, 276, 324
Arabia, 177–178, 183–184
Arab-Israeli Wars: 1948–1949, 980; 1956, 978–979, 980; 1967 (Six-Day War), 980, 981, 988; 1973 (Yom Kippur War), 979, 980, 983
Arab League, 982, 1043
Arabs, 191, 202, 232; early history, 177–178; Mecca, 178; rise of Islam, 178–179; Umayyads, 180–181; Abbasids, 181–183; scripts of, 196–197; invasion of Europe, 267; in World War I, 842; between the world wars, 881–882; and nationalism, 981–982, 983; Egyptian revolution, 982–983
Arafat, Yasir, 988
Aragon [*air*-uh-gahn], 286, 287, 332–333, 433, 444
Arcadius [ahr-*kay*-dee-uhs], 173
Archaeology, 3, 5, 26, 27, 38, 41, 57–58, 78, 79, 123–124, 200, 202, 209, 211–212, 213, 229, 658
Archangel, 419, 535, 867
Archilochus [ahr-*kihl*-oh-kuhs], 83
Archimedes [ahr-kih-*mee*-deez] of Syracuse, 114–115, 551
Architecture: in Mesopotamia, 14, 18; in ancient Egypt, 19, 23–25; Persian, 33; in Ceylon, 49; in ancient China, 58–59, 60, 74; Greek, 98–100; classical Roman, 131, 135–136, 142; Islamic, 183; Mayan, 211; medieval Indian, 220, 229; Indonesian, 237; Romanesque, 302; Gothic, 304, 305; Italian Renaissance, 345, 361–362; in the Reformation, 396; baroque, 563; in Ch'ing China, 676; modern Western, 833–834, 852
Arezzo [ah-*rayt*-tsoh], 133
Argentina: colonial, 589, 717; modern, 1004–1006, 1013, 1014
Argos [*ahr*-gahs], 106
Arianism [*air*-ee-an-ism], 166, 201
Ariosto [ah-ree-*os*-toh], Ludovico, 560
Aristagoras, 427

Aristarchus [ar-ihs-*tahr*-kuhs] of Samos, 114, 428, 547
Aristodama [ar-ihs-toh-*dah*-mah] of Smyrna, 118
Aristophanes [ar-ihs-*toff*-uh-neez], 91, 427
Aristotle, 43, 91, 105–107, 116, 186, 190, 300, 301, 310, 547
Ark of the Covenant, 27
Arkwright, Richard, 700
Arles [ahrl], Council of, 166
Armenia [ahr-*mee*-nee-uh], 282
Armenians, 188, 667, 867
Arminians, 445, 447
Arms races: pre-1914, 838–839; post-1945, 1035–1036
Arno River, 344
Arrau, Claudio [*klow*-dyoh ahr-*rah*-oo], 1014
Arsinoe [ahr-*sihn*-oh-ee] II, 118
Arthashastra, 43, 44, 53
Arthurian legends, 307
Articles of Confederation, 586
Aryans [*ar*-yenz], 36, 147, 194; migrations of, 41; domination of India, 41–42; culture of, 42
Ashanti [ah-*shahn*-tee], 404
Ashikaga [ah-shee-*kah*-gah] Shogunate, 261–262, 682
Ashkenazim, 609
Ashoka [ah-*shoh*-kah], 46, 47, 53, 150, 194, 197
Ashurbanipal [ah-shoor-*bah*-nih-pahl], 18
Ashurnasirpal [ah-shoor-*nas*-ihr-pahl], 18
Asia Minor: ancient, 28–31, 32, 80, 81, 83, 86, 87, 108, 111; medieval, 178, 188, 193, 282–286 *passim*, 457
Assam, 812
Assembly of Notables, 617
Assyrians, 17–18, 24, 28, 31, 178
Astell, Mary, 450
Astrology, 185, 301
Astronomy: Hellenistic, 114, 547; in Ming China, 496; in the Scientific Revolution, 549–552, 554–555; modern, 730; and mapping, 1016–1020
Asturias [as-*tew*-rih-ahs], Miguel Angel, 1013
Aswan Dam, 982–983
Atahualpa [ah-tah-*wahl*-pah], 218, 416
Atatürk [ah-tah-*turk*]. *See* Mustapha Kemal
Athens, 79, 81, 131, 138, 173; development of democracy in, 86–87; during the Persian Wars, 87–88; in the Periclean Age, 88–92; role of women, 90–91; slaves and metics in, 91–92; criticism of, 92; visual arts in, 98–100; drama in, 100–103; philosophy in, 104–106, 119; rule of the Thirty Tyrants, 104; and Philip of Macedon, 106–107
Athletic festivals, 85–86
Atlantic Charter, 925, 929
Atomic theory, 54, 104, 119

Atomists, 104
Attalus III [*at*-uh-luhs], 128
Attila [uh-*till*-uh], 144, 173
Attlee, Clement, 965, 1022, 1029, 1030
Auclert, Hubertine, 783
Audiencias [ou-*thyen*-syahz], 416
Auerstadt [*ow*-er-shtaht], battle of, 636
Augsburg [*owks*-boork], 272, 279, 402; Diet of, 382; Peace of, 382, 441; League of, 531
August, Karl, 638, 729
Augustine [*ah*-guh-steen], 111, 166–167, 201, 383
Augustinians, 295
Augustus [ah-*guss*-tuhs], 131–134, 138, 198, 368. *See also* Octavius (Octavian)
Augustus the Strong (Saxony), 562
Aurangzeb [*ah*-rung-zehb], 472–475, 476, 477
Aurelian [ah-*ree*-lee-uhn], 143, 178
Auschwitz, 928, 929–930
Ausgleich [*ows*-glyek], 759
Austen, Jane, 733
Austerlitz [*os*-ter-lits], battle of, 636
Australia, 585, 588, 709, 824, 826, 842, 933
Australopithecus [ah-stray-loh-*pith*-ih-kuhs], 4
Austria, 341, 538, 605, 906, 1034. *See also* Holy Roman Empire: and the Napoleonic wars, 639; in the early nineteenth century, 721–727 *passim*; 1848 revolution, 740, 741–742; war with France (1859), 753; Austro-Prussian War, 757–758; Dual Monarchy, 759; in the Crimean War, 761; and the Congress of Berlin, 763; and the origins of World War I, 837–840; in World War I, 841–842; and the Peace of Paris (1919), 847; fascists in, 900; union with Germany, 919
Austrian Netherlands, 632
Austrian Succession, War of the, 582
Austro-Prussian War, 757–758
Autos-de-fé [ow-tohs duh *fay*], 434
Avars [*ah*-vahrs], 175, 177, 191, 265
Averroës [uh-*vehr*-oh-eez] (Ibn-Rushd), 186–187, 300
Avesta, 156–157
Avicenna. *See* Sina, Ibn
Avignon [ah-vee-*nyohn*], papacy at, 325–326
Ayuthia (Ayutia) [ah-*yoo*-tee-ah], 234, 235
Azerbaijan [*ah*-zer-bye-jahn], 867
Azores [uh-*zohrz*, *ay*-zohrz], 408, 416
Azouri, Neguib, 981
Azov [*ay*-zof], 535
Aztecs [*az*-teks], 198, 211, 214, 215, 414–415, 416, 417, 569, 1014

Ba'ath movement, 983
Babeuf, Gracchus [grah-*koos* bah-*burf*], 633
Babur [*bah*-ber], "the Tiger," 227, 466, 467

Babylon [*bab*-uh-lahn], 17, 18, 28, 29, 32
Babylonian Captivity (1309–1377), 325–326
Babylonians, 28, 427
Bacchae, The [*bak*-ee] (Euripides), 103
Bach, Carl Philipp Emanuel, 614
Bach, Johann Sebastian, 562, 614
Bacon, Sir Francis, 554, 556, 794
Bacon, Roger, 301
Bactria, 43, 111–112
Baden, 757
Badoglio, Pietro [*pye*-troh bah-*doh*-lyoh], 931
Bagehot [*bahj*-ot], Walter, 786
Baghdad [bagh-*dahd*, *bag*-dad], 180–188 *passim*, 458
Bahadur [bah-*hah*-dour], Teg, 473
Bahadur Shah, 665
Bahamas, 405
Bahrain [bah-*rayn*], 988
Baker, Josephine, 850–852
Baker, Sir Samuel White, 803
Bakewell, Robert, 698
Baki, Muhammad Abd ul-, 465
Bakunin, Mikhail [myih-kuh-*eel* buh-*koo*-nyin], 762, 788
Balabanoff, Angelica, 790, 868
Balboa, Vasco Núñez [*noh*-nyes] de, 406, 429
Baldwin, King of Jerusalem, 284
Baldwin, Stanley, 904
Balfour, Arthur, 766, 842
Balfour [*bal*-fur] Declaration, 842, 882, 978
Bali, 233, 816
Balkan League, 839
Balkans: early history, 173, 175, 188, 282; and the Ottomans, 457, 458, 762–763; and World War I, 837, 839–840, 841; in World War II, 931–932
Balkan Wars, 839–840
Ball, John, 322
Baltic Sea, 535
Baluchistan [bah-loo-chih-*stahn*], 6, 36
Balzac, Honoré de [oh-noh-*ray* duh bahl-*zak*], 704, 787
Bambuk [bahm-*book*], 202
Banaras [bah-*nah*-rahs], 46
Banda Bairagi, 474
Bandaranaike [buhn-druh-*nye*-uhk], Sirimavo, 975
Bandaranaike, S. W. R. D., 975
Bandung Conference. *See* Afro-Asian Conference
Bangkok, 235, 817, 958, 961
Bangladesh, 973
Banking: Muslim, 183; medieval European, 270, 308, 331; early modern European, 402, 403, 488, 571, 575–576, 580–581; modern Western, 696–697, 700, 714
Bank of Amsterdam, 543, 696–697
Bank of England, 543, 580–581, 697, 1030
Bank of France, 635

Bantu, 200, 208, 209, 316, 804, 997
Banzer, Hugo, 1007
Baptism, 158, 163, 165, 188
Baptists, 448, 450
Barbados, 574
Barbauld [*bahr*-bold], Anna, 612
Barcelona, 272, 324, 445, 833–834
Bar mitzvah, 162
Barnabites, 390
Baroque [buh-*roke*], 562–563, 645, 857
Basedow [*bah*-zee-doh], Johann, 607
Basel [*bah*-zuhl], 397; Council of, 383
Basil, 166
Basil II (Byzantium), 190, 282
Basque [bask] region, 781
Bastardy, 513, 1014
Bastille [bah-*steel*], 621, 622, 626
Batavia (Djakarta), 453, 816
Batista, Fulgencio [fool-*hahn*-see-oh bah-*tees*-tah], 1008–1009
Battisti, Cesare [*chay*-zah-ree baht-*tees*-tee], 889
Battle of Britain, 923
Battle of the Bulge, 931
Battle of the Nations, 639–640
Battle of the Saints, 585
Battuta, Ibn, 205–206, 208, 251
Batu [*bah*-too], 289
Baudelaire [bohd-ler], Charles, 833
Bauhaus [*bow*-hous] school, 853, 914
Bavaria, 265, 267, 395, 442, 582, 754, 757, 892
Bayezid I [bah-yeh-*zeed*], 457
Bayle [bel], Pierre, 559
Bay of Pigs invasion, 1009, 1036
Beard, Charles, 586
Beaufort [*bow*-fort], Francis, 1018
Beauharnais [bow-ahr-*neh*], Josephine de, 638
Beaumer [*boh*-mer], Madame de, 601
Beauvais [boh-*vay*], 304
Beauvoir [deh boh-*vwar*], Simone de, 1030
Bebel [*bay*-behl], August, 789, 791
Beccaria [bake-ah-*ree*-ah], Cesare [*chay*-zah-ray] Bonesana, Marquis de, 603
Bechuanaland, 805
Becket, Thomas à, 275, 276
Bede "the Venerable," 306
Beethoven [*bay*-toh-vehn], Ludwig van, 614–615, 638, 731, 732, 760, 796
Begin, Menachem [may-*nah*-kehm *bay*-ghin], 979, 980
Behn [bayn], Aphra, 356, 510, 612
Beirut [bay-*root*], 988
Belgian Congo, 803, 992, 994. *See also* Congo
Belgium, 735, 782, 900, 1040; in World War I, 840; in World War II, 922, 923, 931
Belgrade, 458, 609
Belisarius [bel-ih-*sar*-ee-uhs], 175, 176
Bell, Alexander Graham, 795
Bellamy, Edward, 1047–1048
Bellarmine, Robert, 548

Bellini, Gentile [jen-*tee*-lay bel-*lee*-nee], 458
Bellini, Giovanni, 346
Belsen, 928, 930
Benedictines, 293, 667
Benedict of Nursia [*ner*-shuh], 166, 293, 294
"Benefit of clergy," 275
Beneš [*beh*-nesh], Edvard, 907, 921
Bengal: medieval, 223–227 *passim*; early modern, 453, 468, 582, 649, 650; and the English, 652, 655, 656, 660
Bengal Renaissance, 658–660, 664
Ben-Gurion, David, 977–979
Benin, 409, 856
Bentham [*ben*-tham], Jeremy, 705, 707, 782
Bentinck, William, 662, 663
Beowulf [*bay*-oh-wulf], 305–306
Berbers, 201, 287
Berg, Alban, 760
Bergson, Henri [ahn-*ree* berg-*sohn*], 831
Beria, Lavrenti, 1026, 1027
Berkeley, George, 608
Berlin, 845, 894–897, 1024, 1028, 1036
Berlin, Congress of, 762, 763, 836
Berlin blockade, 1024
Berlin Conference (1885), 803
Berlin-to-Baghdad railroad, 838
Berlioz, Hector [*ek*-tor *ber*-lyohz], 731, 732
Bern, 383
Bernard of Clairvaux [klare-*voh*], 294, 303
Bernini [bur-*nee*-nee], Gianlorenzo, 562, 563, 645, 857
Bernstein, Éduard, 790–791
Besant, Annie, 774
Bessemer, Henry, 716, 769
Bethmann-Hollweg, Theobald von [*tay*-oh-bahlt fohn bate-mahn hole-vake], 839, 840
Bhagavad Gita [*bahg*-ah-*vahd gee*-tah], 147
Bhakti movement, 227, 228, 473, 642
Bhutto, Benazir, 974
Bhutto, Zulfkar Ali, 974
Biafra, 994
Bible, 375, 381, 384, 387, 392, 393, 559; New Testament, 162, 165, 376; Old Testament [Hebrew Scripture], 26–28, 114, 161, 165; English versions, 327, 389, 394; Geneva (1560), 394; King James (1611), 446
Biblical scholarship, 376, 379, 387
Bill of Rights (1689), 542
Bindusara, 46
Biology, 786
Birmingham, Alabama, 1032
Birth control, 709, 774
Bismarck, Otto von, 746, 751, 756–759, 763, 779–780, 795, 803, 837
Bismarck Archipelago, 933
Black Death. *See* Plague
Black Sea, 81, 603, 762

Blackshirts (Italy), 890–892
Blake, William, 608, 703
Blanc [blanh], Louis, 737, 738, 743
Blanqui [blanh-*kee*], Louis-Auguste, 737–738, 743
Blenheim [*blen*-im], battle of, 533
Blitzkrieg [*blits*-kreeg], 922–923
Blücher, Gebhard von [*gep*-hart fohn *blue*-ker], 640
Blue Rider movement (art), 834
Blue Shirts, 900
Blum, Léon [*lay*-on bloom], 905
Boccaccio, Giovanni [joh-*vah*-nee bohk-*kaht*-choh], 348, 356
Boccioni [boht-*choh*-nee], Umberto, 834, 835
Bodhisattvas [boh-dih-*saht*-vahz], 152
Bodin, Jean [zhan boh-*dahn*], 443
Boers [bohrz], 804–806
Boer War, 804–806
Bohemia, 270, 289, 327, 341, 441, 538, 605, 740, 759, 906
Böhme [*beh*-muh], Jacob, 607
Bohr [bohr], Niels, 852
Boleslav [*boh*-leh-slav] the Pious, 309
Boleyn [*buhl*-ihn, buh-*lin*], Anne, 388–389, 397
Bolívar [boh-*lee*-vahr], Simón, 589–590
Bolivia, 637, 1007–1008, 1013
Bologna [buh-*lun*-yah], University of, 297–298, 300, 301
Bolsheviks, 864–867, 869–871
Bombay, 652, 653, 657, 661, 811, 813
Bonaparte, Jerome, 637
Bonaparte, Joseph, 589, 637
Bonaparte, Louis-Napoleon, 746–747. *See also* Napoleon III
Bonaparte, Napoleon, 631–632, 634–640, 724, 731, 732
Bonaventure [boh-nah-vayn-*too*-rah], 300
Boniface VIII [*bahn*-ih-fuhs], Pope, 278, 281–282
Book of Changes, 60
Book of Common Prayer, 390, 394
Book of Lord Shang, 43
Book of Rituals, 60
Book of Songs, 60
Book of the Courtier, The (Castiglione), 349
Book of the Dead, 22, 314
Bora, Katherine von, 380
Bordeaux [bohr-*doh*], 272
Borges [bohr-hays], Jorge Luis, 1013
Borgia, Cesare [*chay*-zah-ray *bohr*-jah], 335, 337
Boris (Bulgaria), 906–907
Borneo, 816–817, 958
Borobodur [*boh*-roh-boo-*door*], 237
Borodin [buh-ruh-*deen*], Michael, 871
Borodino [buh-ruh-*dee*-noh], battle of, 639
Borromini, Francesco [frahn-*cheh*-skoh bohr-roh-*mee*-nee], 563, 564
Bosch, Hieronymus [hee-*rahn*-ih-muhs bahsh], 362

Bosch, Juan [hwahn bohsh], 1011
Bose, Subhas Chandra, 927
Bosnia, 762, 763, 836, 839
Bosporus, 175
Bossuet, Jacques [zhahk boh-*sway*], 528, 559
Boston, 585
Boswell, James, 614
Bosworth Field, battle of, 334
Bothwell, Earl of, 438
Botticelli, Sandro [*sahn*-droh baht-tih-*chel*-lee], 357, 857
Boucher, François [frahn-*swah* boo-*shay*], 613
Boulanger, Georges [zhorzh boo-lahn-*zhay*], 779
Boulton [*bohl*-ton], Matthew, 706
Bourbon [boor-*bohn*] dynasty, 442–444, 525–533, 617–618, 623–627 *passim*
Bourgeoisie, 695, 696; French, 617, 618–624, 626, 631, 633; Chinese, 680; Japanese, 686–687, 688; nineteenth-century European, 771–772, 774–775; after World War I, 849
Bourguiba, Habib [hah-*beeb* boor-*ghee*-bah], 987, 991, 999
Bouvines [boo-*veen*], battle of, 276, 282
Boxer Rebellion, 821
Boyars, 451–452
Boyle, Katherine, 510
Braddock, Edward, 582
Bradlaugh, Charles, 774
Brady, Mathew, 795
Brahe [brah], Tycho, 550, 555
Brahmins (Brahmans), 48, 149, 223, 235
Brahmi script, 194, 197
Brahms, Johannes, 760
Bramante [brah-*mahn*-tay], Donato, 361
Brancusi [brahng-koosh], Constantin, 859
Brandenburg, 441, 535, 539
Brandt, Willy [*vill*-ee brahnt], 1029, 1040
Braque, Georges [zhorzh brak], 834, 859
Brasilia, 1003–1004
Brave New World (Huxley), 1048
Brazil: discovery of, 405; colonial, 418, 419, 454, 572, 573, 574, 588, 590; modern, 900–902, 1002–1004, 1014; University of, 1004
Brecht, Bertolt [*ber*-tohlt brekht], 896–897
Brest-Litovsk [brest lih-tofsk], Treaty of, 844, 866
Brezhnev, Leonid [lay-*oh*-need *brehzh*-neff], 1036, 1039, 1042, 1044
Brezhnev Doctrine, 1042
Briand, Aristide [ah-ree-*steed* bree-*ahn*], 848
Bridge (art movement), 834
Bridget of Sweden, 325

"Brinkmanship," 1036
Brisbane, 824
Brissot, Jacques [zhahk bree-*soh*], 631
Bristol, 710, 737
Britain, 134, 139; age of Walpole, 579; triumph of the elite, 579–580; War of the Austrian Succession, 582; Seven Years' War, 582–583; and the American colonies, 584–585; and the Napoleonic wars, 636–640; in the First Industrial Revolution, 699–714; in the early nineteenth century, 721–724, 725–727, 736–737; in the Crimean War, 761; in the Second Industrial Revolution, 769–770; in the Victorian Age, 776–777; colonies in Africa, 803–806; colonial regimes in Southeast Asia, 814, 816–817; and Australasia, 824–825; and the origins of World War I, 836–840; in World War I, 840–844; and the Peace of Paris (1919), 846; fascists in, 900; and the Great Depression, 903, 904–905; in World War II, 922–925, 930–933; after World War II, 1029, 1030, 1040
British East Africa, 804
British North America Act (1867), 588, 1034
British Union of Fascists, 900
Brittany, 334
Brno [*ber*-noh], 366
Brontë [*bron*-tay], Charlotte, 734
Brontë, Emily, 645, 734
Bronze Age, 76–81, 99, 122, 123, 196
Bronzino [bron-*dzee*-noh], Alessandro, 857
Brown v. *Board of Education*, 1031
Broz [brawz], Josip. *See* Tito
Bruckner [*brook*-ner], Anton, 760
Brueghel [*bruh*-gehl], Pieter (the elder), 362, 363, 422
Bruges [broozh], 272, 422
Brunelleschi [broo-nel-*les*-kee], Filippo, 361
Bruni [*broo*-nee], Leonardo, 348
Bruno, Giordano, 393, 550, 1018
Brunswick, 324
Brussels, 625, 626
Bucer [*bew*-sur], Martin, 382, 384
Budapest, 609, 740, 1028
Buddha, Gautama, 53, 149–150, 152, 167, 368
Buddhism, 156, 166, 224, 315; in India, 46–47, 51–52; in Ceylon, 49; in Burma, 49; life of Buddha, 149–150; Four Noble Truths, 150; Hinayana and Mahayana schools, 150–152; role of women, 167, 168; in Southeast Asia, 231–237 *passim*; in China, 241, 242, 245, 246, 249; in Korea, 255, 256; in Japan, 259, 261, 642; Zen, 261; Tantric, 511
Budé, Guillaume [gee-*yohm* bew-*day*], 351
Buenos Aires [*bway*-nohs *ay*-rays], 1000, 1004, 1014

Bugenhagen [*boo*-gehn-hah-gehn], Johannes, 381
Bukharin [boo-*kah*-reen], Nicolai, 866, 871, 917
Bulavin, Kondraty, 535
Bulganin [bool-*gah*-nyin], Nikolai, 1027
Bulgaria, 763; in World War I, 837, 839, 842, 845, 847; between the wars, 871, 906–907; after World War II, 1022, 1024, 1026
Bulgars (Bulgarians), 188, 189, 190, 191, 267, 282
Bullinger [*bool*-ing-er], Heinrich, 383
Bundesrat, 758, 779
Buonarotti [bwo-nahr-*rot*-tee], Filippo, 737, 738
Burckhardt, Jacob [*yah*-kohp *boork*-hahrt], 363
Burgoyne [bur-*goin*], John, 585
Burgundians, 265, 324
Burgundy, 280, 334, 341, 432
Burial rites. *See also* Death: in ancient Egypt, 20–22, 314; in India, 53, 315, 643; in ancient China, 58–59, 316, 317; in ancient Greece, 77–78; in Greek art, 98–99, 315; Villanovan, 122; Hindu, 150, 315; Zoroastrian, 157; Early African 207; Neanderthal, 314; in Mesopotamia, 314; early Christian, 317; medieval Christian, 317–318; in Indonesia, 643; Huron practices, 644; in early modern Europe, 645; in the modern West, 645
Burke, Edmund, 585, 613, 625
Burma: ancient, 50; Buddhism in, 151; medieval, 232, 234–235, 253; attacked by China, 676; colonial rule, 814, 816; and World War II, 927, 928, 933; after World War II, 954, 958, 960; Bursa, 463, 465
Bush people, 201, 208, 209
Butler, Eleanor, 612
Butler, Joseph, 607
Byng, John, 582
Byron, Lord, 726, 731, 732
Byzantine Empire, 144–145, 188; early history, 173; society and government, 173–174; reign of Justinian, 174–175; Constantinople, 175–177; Islamic threat, 181, 188; and the Christian church, 188–190; Comnenian revival, 190–191; heritage, 191–192; relations with Franks, 266–267; and the Crusades, 282; after the Crusades, 286
Byzantium, 143. *See also* Constantinople

Cabalists, 310, 552
Cabot, John, 406, 419
Cabral, Pedro, 405
Cadiz, 724
Caesar [*see*-zuhr], Julia, 130
Caesar [*see*-zuhr], Julius, 121, 129–130, 139, 141
Caesarea [see-zah-*ree*-ah], 134

Caesaropapism, 294
Cagoulards [ka-goo-*lar*] (CSAR), 899
Cairo [*kye*-roh], 184, 188, 272, 321
Calais [kah-*lay*], 324
Calas, Jean [zhahn kah-*lah*], 598
Calcutta: in the eighteenth century, 650, 652–653, 655, 656, 657, 661; Black Hole of, 655; as a colonial capital, 660; modern, 811, 812, 927, 967, 973
Calderon de la Barca, Pedro, 561
Calendar, 121, 130, 213, 218, 538, 626
Calicut, 405, 409, 484
California, 419, 454, 586, 766, 1002
Caligula [kah-*lig*-you-lah] (Gaius), 134
Calixtus II, Pope, 279
Callicrates [kah-*lik*-rah-teez], 99
Calligraphy, 197, 516, 667
Calonne [ka-*lon*], Charles de, 617
Calvin, John, 167, 351, 376, 383–386, 395, 398
"Calvinist Fury," 437
Cambay, 232
Cambodia: Buddhism in, 151; early history, 232, 234, 235–236; colonial rule, 816; after World War II, 955, 956, 957, 1039
Cambrai [kahn-*bray*], 402; League of, 338
Cambridge, 272; University of, 298
Cambyses [kam-*bye*-seez], 32
Cameroons, 803
Campanella, Thomas, 1017
Campanus of Novara, 547
Camp David Accords, 980
Campo Formio, Treaty of, 632
Campora, Hector, 1004
Camus [ka-*moo*], Albert, 852
Canaanites, 26
Canada, 583, 644; dominion of, 587–588; westward expansion, 588; in the twentieth century, 1034–1035
Canadian Citizenship Act (1947), 1034
Canary Islands, 416
Candide (Voltaire), 598
Canisius, Peter, 395
Cannae [*kahn*-ee], battle of, 126
Canning, Lord Charles, 664
Canning, George, 736
Canon law, 301
Canossa, 279
Cánovas del Castillo [*kah*-noh-bahs del kahs-*tee*-lyoh], Antonio, 788
Canterbury Tales (Chaucer), 329, 348
Canticle of the Sun (Francis of Assisi), 296, 308
Canton, 409, 453, 493, 495, 675, 677, 681–682, 817
Canton (Guangzhou) delta, 64, 252
Cape Breton, 406
Cape Colony, 803, 804, 806
Cape Hatteras, 406
Capellanus, Andreas, 307
Cape of Good Hope, 405, 406, 409, 569, 724
Capet [*kay*-pit], Hugh, 276
Cape Verde Islands, 405, 408
Capital (Marx), 738

Capitalism, 270, 420–422, 695–697, 769–771, 800–801, 809, 902–903
Capone, Al, 904
Caporetto, battle of, 844
Capuchins [*kap*-yoo-chinz], 390
Capucines [kah-pyoo-*seen*], 390
Caracas, 589–590
Caraffa, Giampietro [jahm-*pyeh*-troh], 393
Caraka, 54
Caravaggio [kah-rah-*vahd*-joh], 562
Caravels, 403–404
Cárdenas [*kahr*-thay-nahs], Lázaro, 1012
Carlsbad Decrees, 727
Carlyle, Thomas, 706
Carmelites, 435
Carnegie, Andrew, 771
Carol (Romania), 906
Carolines, 826
Carolingian [kar-uh-*lihn*-jee-uhn] dynasty, 265–267
Carrà [kahr-*rah*], Carlo, 835
Carranza [kahr-*rahn*-sah], Bartolomé de, 434
Carter, James Earl ("Jimmy"), 1003, 1039–1040
Cartesianism, 554
Carthage [*kahr*-thij], 122, 126, 166, 201
Carthaginians, 122, 126–127
Carthusians, 294–295
Cartwright, Edmund, 699
Casablanca Conference, 929
Casimer-Perier [ka-zee-meer-pay-ryay], Jean-Paul, 734
Caspian Sea, 535, 985
Cassian, John, 293
Cassini [kah-*see*-nee], Jean-Dominique, 1017
Caste, 41, 147, 502–503, 972
Castellio [kas-*tell*-yoh], Sebastian, 387
Castiglione, Baldassare [bahl-dahs-*sah*-ray kah-steel-*yoh*-nay], 349–350
Castile [kah-*steel*], 286, 287, 332–333, 433, 444, 445
Castlereagh [kassl-*ray*], Viscount, 721, 723
Castro, Fidel, 1008–1010, 1036
Catalan rebellion, 445
Catalonia, 323, 445, 781
Cateau-Cambrésis [kah-*toh*-kahn-bray-*zee*], Treaty of, 432
Cathari [*kath*-uh-ree], 296
Catherine II, "the Great," 603, 605, 606
Catherine de Rambouillet [rahn-*boo*-yeh], 561
Catherine of Aragon, 334, 388–389
Catherine of Braganza, 652
Catherine of Siena, 325
Catholicism: struggle with Holy Roman Empire, 278–281; papal authority, 279, 281; Catholic Reformation, 390–394; and the *Kulturkampf*, 779–780; in Latin America, 1013

Catholic League (France), 439–440
Catholic League (German states), 441
Cato [*kay*-toh], 140, 141
Catullus [kuh-*tull*-us], 84, 141
Cavafy, Constantine, 114
Cavaignac [kah-veh-*nyak*], Louis-Eugène, 743, 746
Cavaliers, 448
Cave art, 5, 366
Cavell, Edith, 844
Cavour, Camillo [cah-*mee*-loh kah-*voor*], 746, 751–754, 780
Celebes [*sel*-eh-beez], 816
Cellini, Benvenuto [bayn-vay-*noo*-toh cheh-*lee*-nee], 357
Celsus, 115
Celts [selts, kelts], 124
Censorate, 69
Center party (Germany), 779, 780, 892
Centlivre [sent-*liv*-er], Susan, 612
Central African Republic, 992
Central Intelligence Agency (CIA), 1006, 1007, 1024, 1036
Cernavoda [*chehr*-nah-voh-dah], 367
Cervantes, Miguel de [mee-*gell* day suhr-*vahn*-tays], 435, 561
Cerveteri [cher-*veh*-tay-ree], 123
Ceuta [soo-tah], 404
Ceylon [see-*lahn*], 230, 724; early history, 48–50; Buddhism in, 150, 151; early modern, 409, 484, 651, 657–658; in World War II, 927
Cézanne [say-*zahn*], Paul, 833, 834, 859
Chabod, Federico, 364
Chad, 992, 994, 999
Chadar, 985, 987
Chaeronea [ker-oh-*nee*-ah], battle of, 107
Chakri [*chah*-kree] dynasty, 235
Chaldeans, 18
Chamberlain, Houston Stewart, 836
Chamberlain, Neville, 904, 921, 922
Chamber of Fasci and Corporations, 909
Chambord [shahn-*bawr*], 396
Champagne fairs, 298
Champollion, Jean [zhahn shahn-pawl-*yahn*], 24
Chancellor, Richard, 419
Chandigarh, 1003
Chandragupta Maurya [chun-druh-*goop*-tuh *mow*-ree-uh], 43–44, 46
Chang (Zhang) [chahng], 498
Ch'ang An (Qangan) [chahng-ahn], 44, 68, 73, 241, 244–245, 249, 272
Chang Chü-cheng (Zhang Juzheng), 496
Changsha [chahng-shah], 493
Chansons d'amour [shahn-*sohn* dah-*moor*], 306–307
Chansons de geste [shahn-*sohn* duh zhehst], 306, 307
Chardin [shar-*dan*], Pierre, 613

Charlemagne [*shahr*-leh-mayn], 189, 265–267
Charles I (England), 447–448, 594
Charles II (England), 449, 541, 652
Charles II (Spain), 445, 532–533
Charles III (Spain), 606, 724
Charles IV (Holy Roman Empire), 340
Charles V (Holy Roman Empire), 337, 340–341, 360, 379, 382, 388, 392, 394, 402–403, 408, 432
Charles VI (Holy Roman Empire), 539, 582
Charles VII (France), 324, 334
Charles VIII (France), 334, 337
Charles IX (France), 439
Charles X (France), 727, 734
Charles XII (Sweden), 535, 562
Charles Albert, elector of Bavaria, 582
Charles Albert (Piedmont), 740, 741, 751, 753
Charles Martel, 181, 265
Charles of Anjou, 286
Charles the Bold (Burgundy), 334
Charter Act (1833), 662
Chartist movement, 737, 740
Chartres [*shahr*-treh], 297, 304
Chateaubriand [sha-toh-bree-*ahn*], François-Auguste-René de, 732
Chaucer, Geoffrey [*jef*-ree *chahs*-uhr], 329, 348
Chávez, Carlos, 1014
Chavín [*chah*-vihn] culture, 210
Chemistry, 717
Chengdu, 493
Cheng Ho (Zhenghe), 484–486
Chernenko, Konstantin, 1044
Chernobyl Nuclear Plant, 1049
Chia Ch'ing (Ja Qing), 676
Chiang Ch'ing (Jiang Qing), 950, 958–959
Chiang Kai-shek [jee-*ahng* kye-*shek*], 871, 874, 876, 900, 925, 927, 943
Chiaroscuro [kyah-roh-*skoo*-roh], 356, 357
Ch'ien Lung (Qian Long), 673, 675–676, 678
Chile [*chil*-ee, *chee*-lay], 217, 590, 1006, 1013, 1014, 1036
Ch'in (Qin) [chihn, cheen] clan, 61
Ch'in (Qin) dynasty, 61–62, 64–66
China, ancient: geography of, 56; origins of, 57–58; Lung Shan culture, 57–58; Hsia dynasty, 57–58; Shang dynasty, 57–59; Chou (Zhou) dynasty, 59–61; age of warring states, 61–63; teachings of Confucius, 63–64; Ch'in (Quin) conquest, 64; Ch'in authoritarianism, 64–66; Han dynasty, 66–75; reign of Wu Ti, 66–69; early trading patterns, 69–70, 133; Han culture, 70–72; Han decline, 73–74; early cities, 57–58, 60, 74; Han legacy, 74–75; religion and philosophy in, 150, 152–156; writing in, 194–195, 197

China (sixth to fourteenth centuries): reunification, 241; T'ang dynasty, 241–247; Sung dynasty, 247–251; Southern Sung period, 251–252; Yuan dynasty, 252–253; culture, 254; influence on Japan, 258–259; missionaries in, 391
China, Ming: origins, 481–483; early European traders, 409, 495; missionaries in, 411–412, 413, 495; naval expeditions, 483–486; conservatism, 486–487; economy, 487–488; culture, 488–493; imperial Peking, 493–494; decline, 494–498; Manchu conquest, 498–499
China, modern: influence on eighteenth-century Europe, 614, 672–673; Manchu rule, 671–673; economic and demographic growth, 673–675; Kang Hsi and Ch'ien Lung, 675–677; Ch'ing decline, 677, 678–680; westerners in China, 677–678, 817–821; Opium wars, 680–682, 817, 818; Boxer rebellion, 821; in World War I, 842; 1911 Revolution, 872–873; May Fourth Movement, 873–874; Nanking decade, 874–876; Shanghai, 876–877; in World War II, 925–927, 933; postwar China, 943–945; Great Leap Forward, 945; Sino-Soviet split, 945–946; Cultural Revolution, 946–950, 958–959; China after Mao, 950–952, 961; women in modern China, 958–960
Chinese Revolution, 873–874, 942–943, 945
Ch'ing (Qing) dynasty, 499, 670–673, 675–678
Chinghis (Genghis) [*jehn*-gihs] Khan, 252, 256, 289
Chinoiserie [shin-*wahz*-uh-ree], 614
Chivalry, 307, 310, 328–329
Choiseul [shwah-*zul*], Duke of, 580
Chola, 47, 50, 229, 230–231, 237
Chopin, Frédéric [fray-day-*reek* shoh-*pan*], 733, 735
Chou (Zhou) [joh] dynasty, 59–61
Chou En-lai (Zhou Enlai) [joh en-lye], 945, 946, 948, 950, 959
Christian Brethren, 387
Christian Democratic party (Italy), 1029, 1030
Christian Democratic party (West Germany), 1029–1030
Christian Humanists, 376
Christianity: early history of, 155, 156, 158, 160–161, 178; in India, 47; in Roman Empire, 143–144, 165; life of Jesus, 162–163; Paul's contribution, 163–164; early growth, 164–165; early heresies, 165–166; monasticism, 166; role of Augustine, 166–167; women in the early church, 164, 167–168
Christianity, medieval: Byzantine, 188–190; Catholic-Orthodox split, 189; medieval church, 293, 375–376; monasteries, 293, 294–295;

medieval papacy, 293–294; mendicant orders, 295–296; heretics, 296–297
Christianity, early modern. *See also* Missionaries: humanist demands for reform, 376–378; Protestant Reformation, 378–390; Catholic Reformation, 390–394; eighteenth-century revival, 607–608
Chrysoloras [krih-suh-*lawr*-uhs], Manuel, 348
Chrysostom, John, 317
Ch'u (Qu) [choo], 61, 62
Chuang-tze (Zhuangzi) [jwahng-dzuh], 155
Chu Hsi (Zhuxi) [joo she], 153–154, 252
Chungking (Chongqing), 925, 926–927
Churchill, Winston: early career, 795, 842, 843, 880, 881; in World War II, 922, 923, 925, 930, 931–932; after World War II, 964–965, 1023, 1029
Church of England, 389–390
Chu Yüan-chang (Dzu Yüan-zhang), 481
Cicero [*sis*-uh-roh], Marcus Tullius, 141, 142
Ciompi [*chom*-pee] rebellion, 323–324, 338
Circumcision, 158, 164
Cistercians [sis-*tur*-shuhnz], 294, 311
Cities. *See also specific cities*: origins of, 14; Mycenaean, 79–80; early Greek, 81–83, 85–87; founded by Alexander, 108–109; Etruscan, 122–123; early Islamic, 184–185; medieval Indian, 229; in medieval Europe, 269–270, 272–273; Ottoman, 461–463; in modern Europe, 773–774; in modern Asia, 941–943, 951, 961, 968–969, 974
City of God, The (Augustine), 166
Civic Humanists, 348
Civil Constitution of the Clergy, 624
Civilization: definition of, 1; birth of, 8–9, 10–11, 12–17
Civil Rights Act (1964), 1032
Clarendon, Earl of, 541
Clare of Assisi, 292, 295–296
Clarke, Samuel, 607
Clarkson, Thomas, 610
Claudius, 134
Cleisthenes [*klice*-thee-neez], 87
Clemenceau, Georges [zhorzh klay-mahn-*soh*], 778, 779, 845, 846
Clement, 165
Clement V, Pope, 282, 325
Clement VII ("anti-pope"), 325
Clement VII, Pope, 341, 388
Cleomenes [klee-*ahm*-ee-neez], 87
Cleon [*klee*-ahn], 95
Cleopatra, 109, 112, 130
Clermont [klair-*mahn*], Council of, 282, 283
Cleves, 539
Climate, 4, 7–8, 11, 13, 30, 31, 36–37, 40, 48, 59, 217, 320
Clive, Robert, 655–656

Cloots [klohtz], Anarchasis, 625
Clovis [kloh-vihs], 265
Cluniac order, 294
Coal, 694, 700, 701, 714, 769–770, 823
Code Napoleon, 635, 637
Codreanu [koh-dray-ah-noo], Corneliu, 900
Coen [koon], Jan Pieterzoon, 453
Coffee, 651, 658
Cognac [kohn-yahk], League of, 341
Coinage, 31, 32, 85, 87, 110, 112, 126, 205, 207, 259, 270
Cokayne, Sir William, 420
Coke [cook], Sir Edward, 447
Colbert, Jean-Baptiste [zhahn kohl-bayr], 526–527, 555, 571, 701, 702
Cold War, 1022–1025, 1035–1036
Coleridge, Samuel Taylor, 731
Colet, John, 351, 378, 387
Coligny [ko-lee-nyee], Gaspard de, 439
College of Cardinals, 278
Cologne [koh-lohn], 270, 272
Colombia, 588, 590, 1004, 1008, 1012, 1013, 1014
Colombo, 50, 409, 410, 651, 657
Colonna, Egidio, 297
Colonna, Vittoria, 352
Colorado River, 1018
Colosseum (Rome), 136–137
Columbus, Christopher, 405, 406, 414, 416, 428–429
Combustion engine, 717
COMECON, 1024
Comintern (Third International), 871–872, 1024
Committee of Public Safety, 629, 630
Commodus, 142
Common Life, Brethren and Sisters of the, 329, 375, 376, 378
Common Market, 1040
Commonwealth of Nations, 1034
Communist Information Bureau (Cominform), 1024, 1027
Communist Manifesto, The (Marx and Engels), 739
Communist party (France), 1029, 1042
Communist party (Germany), 897–898
Communist party (Italy), 1029, 1042
Comnena [kohm-nee-nah], Anna, 190–191
Compostela, 302
Computers, 798
Comte [kohnt], Auguste, 734, 785–786
Concert of Europe, 722, 726, 759, 837
Conciliar Movement, 326
Concordat of 1801, 635–636
Condorcet [kon-dohr-say], Marquis de, 633
Condottiere [kohn-doht-tyay-ray], 335, 336
Confessions (Augustine), 166
Confucianism, 156, 166; Confucius and Mencius, 152–153; ideals, 153–154; role of women, 167, 168; revival in China, 246, 249, 250; in Korea, 255, 256; in Japan, 259; and Christianity, 412

Confucius [kohn-fyoo-shuhs], 63–64, 70, 152–153, 154, 168, 1048
Congo, 201, 803, 839, 1036. See also Belgian Congo
Congo River, 408, 569
Congregationalists, 448, 450
Congregation of the Holy Angels, 390
Congress of Vienna, 721–724
Congress party, 877, 878, 879, 880, 965, 966, 971, 972
Connecticut, 571
Conquistadores [kohng-kee-stah-doh-rays], 415–416
Conrad III (Holy Roman Empire), 284
Conscription, 66, 74, 128, 629
Conservative party (Britain), 777, 904, 1030
Consistory (Geneva), 385
Constance, 382; Council of, 326, 327, 378, 383; Peace of, 280
Constant, Benjamin, 732
Constantine, 140, 143, 160, 165, 166, 173
Constantine, Donation of, 350
Constantine V (Byzantium), 189
Constantinople: founding of, 143, 173; in the age of Justinian, 175–177; after Justinian, 181, 188, 189, 191; late medieval, 270, 285; fall of, 457, 461
Constitution of the Year I, 628
Constitutions of Clarendon, 275
Contarini, Cardinal, 352
Continental Congress, 585, 586
Continental System, 637, 638
Contraception, 140
Contra rebels, 1011, 1012
Conversos, 333, 434–435
Conway, Anne, Vicountess, 510
Cook, James, 426, 824, 1017–1018
Coolidge, Calvin, 904
Copernicus [koh-puhr-nih-kuhs], Nicolaus, 549–550
Coral Sea, battle of, 930
Corbusier, Le [leh kor-bu-zyay], 853
Córdoba [kohr-doh-vah], 186, 286, 287
Corinth, 82–83, 85, 93, 95, 106, 138; battle of, 128
Corneille, Pierre, 561
Cornelia, 139
Cornelisz [kor-nay-lihs], Cornelis, 697
Corporate system (Italy), 909
Corpus Juris Civilis, 174–175, 300
Corsica, 122, 634
Cort, Henry, 694
Cortes, 287, 333, 433, 445, 724, 725, 781
Cortés, Hernando [ayr-nahn-doh kohr-tehz], 215, 217, 415, 426, 569, 571
Cossacks [kahs-aks], 451, 452–453, 535
Costa, Lucio, 1003
Counter-Enlightenment, 607–609
Courbet [koor-bay], Gustave, 787
Courtier, The (Castiglione), 349–350

Courtly love tradition, 274, 307, 310, 311
Courtly romance, 307
Coverdale, Miles, 389, 423
Cracow, 395
Cranmer, Thomas, 374, 389, 390, 394
Crassus [kras-uhs], 129–130
Crates [kray-teez] of Thebes, 119
Craxi [krahx-ee], Bettino, 1030
Crecy [kray-see], battle of, 324
Credit-Mobilier [kray-dee-moh-bee-lee-yay], 747
Cremation, 317, 645
Creoles, 588, 589
Crete [kreet], 77, 78, 188, 458, 726
Crime, 519–522
Crimean [krye-mee-uhn] War, 749, 752, 761–762
Crispi, Francesco [frahn-cheh-skoh kris-pee], 781
Croatia [kroh-ay-shah], 538, 539
Croix de feu [krwah deh feh], 900
Cro-Magnon culture, 5
Cromwell, Oliver, 448–449, 454
Cromwell, Thomas, 389
Crossbow, 62
Croton, 81
Crusades, 190, 274, 282–286, 308
Crystal Palace (London), 716, 717
Cuba, 405, 416, 570, 588, 590; modern, 782, 1002, 1008–1010, 1036
Cuban missile crisis, 1036, 1037, 1039
Cubists, 834, 859
Cult of Death, 328
Cultural Revolution (China), 936, 946–950, 958–959
Cumae [kew-mee], battle of, 123, 125
Cumans [koo-mahnz], 289
Cuneiform [kyoo-nee-ih-form], 14, 15, 37, 58, 193, 196
Curie [kew-ree], Marie, 832
Curie, Pierre, 832
Custozza, battle of, 741
Cuzco [koos-koh], 217, 218, 416
Cyclades [sik-lah-deez], 77–78
Cylon, 86
Cynicism, 119–120
Cynics, 110
Cyprus, 435, 458
Cypselus [sihp-see-luhs], 82–83
Cyril [sihr-ihl], 190
Cyrus [sye-ruhs] the Great, 32, 87
Czechoslovakia, 846, 906, 907, 921; after World War II, 1022, 1024, 1026, 1028, 1041–1042

Dachau, 912
Dacians [day-shee-ahns], 139
Dadaists, 852–853, 896
Da Gama, Vasco [vash-koh dah gah-muh], 404, 405, 409, 411, 429
D'Ailly [da-yee], Pierre, 326
Daimyo [dye-myoh], 502, 682–683, 684, 688, 690
Dakar, 994
Daladier, Edouard [ay-dwahr dah-lah-dyay], 921
D'Albret [dal-breh], Jeanne, 386

Dalí [*dah*-lee], Salvador, 834, 853, 859
Dalmatia, 466, 724, 890
Damascus [duh-*mass*-kuhs], 27, 181, 184, 284
D'Amboise, Georges [zhorzh dahn-*bwaz*], 390
Danby, Earl of, 541
D'Annunzio [dahn-*noon*-tsyoh], Gabriele, 832, 890
Danquah, J. B., 991
Danse macabre [dahns ma-*kabr*], 328
Dante Alighieri [*dahn*-tay ah-lay-*gyeh*-ree], 329, 348
Danton, Georges [zhorzh dahn-*tohn*], 628, 630, 631
Danzig [*dahn*-tsig], 846
Darby, Abraham, 694, 699
Dardanelles [dahr-duh-*nelz*], 842, 1023
Darius I [duh-*ree*-uhs] (Persia), 32, 33, 88, 108
Darnley, Henry Lord, 438
Darwin, Charles, 768, 786
Darwish, Mahmoud, 988
Daumier, Honoré [oh-noh-*ray* doh-mee-*yay*], 719, 787
David, Jacques-Louis [zhahk dah-*veed*], 859
David (Israel), 27, 159–160
D day, 908, 931
Dead Sea Scrolls, 158
Death. *See also* Burial rites: in Mesopotamia, 314; in ancient Egypt, 314; in early Greece, 314–315; in ancient India, 315; in early China, 315–316; Hebrew view of, 316; in early Christianity, 316, 317; in Islam, 317, 642, 644; in medieval Christianity, 317–318; cult of, 328; in traditional Japan, 642; and the Protestant Reformation, 642, 645; African views, 642–643; in British India, 643; Sumbanese views, 643; Huron views, 644; suicide, 53, 643, 644; martyrdom, 644–645; Jewish views, 644–645; and the baroque, 645; and the Enlightenment, 645; in the modern West, 645–646
De Brazza, Pierre, 803, 804
Decadents, 832
Decameron (Boccaccio), 348, 393
Deccan, 47, 224, 225, 226, 229, 230, 231, 468, 473, 650
Decius [*dee*-shuhs], persecutions of, 165, 166
Declaration of Independence, 585
Declaration of the Rights of Man and the Citizen, 622–623, 624, 704
Declaratory Act (1719), 584
Decline of the West (Spengler), 852
Decretum [duh-*kree*-tum] (Gratian), 297, 301, 311
Deductive method, 106
Defender of the Peace (Marsiglio of Padua), 326
Defoe, Daniel, 543–544, 561, 612, 614, 701, 702

Degas [day-*gah*], Edgar, 786, 787
De Gasperi [day *gahs*-peh-ree], Alcide, 1029
De Gaulle [duh *gohl*], Charles, 923, 983, 994, 999, 1029, 1030, 1040
D'Eglantine [*deg*-lahn-tyne], Philippe Fabre, 626
Degrelle [deh-*grel*], Léon, 900
Deinocrates [dye-*nak*-rah-teez], 113
Deism, 595, 630
Dekker, Thomas, 561
De la Cosa, Juan, 429
Delacroix, Eugène [uh-*zhahn* duh-lah-*krwah*], 732, 734
Delagoa Bay, 408
De la Madrid, Miguel, 1012
De la Tour, George, 562
Delaware River, 454
Del Cano, Juan Sebastian, 406
Delhi: ancient, 46, 223, 224, 226; under the Mughals, 466, 475, 476, 649, 650; under the English, 656, 664
Delhi Sultans, 224–228, 231, 232
Delian [*dee*-lih-uhn] League, 93–94
Delisle, Guillaume [gee-*yohm* deh-*leel*], 1017
Delos [*dee*-lahs], 93, 116, 118
Delphi [*del*-fye], 85–86, 93, 100, 106, 110
Democritus, 104, 547
Demography: medieval, 269–270, 320, 321–322, 330; early modern, 401, 574, 673, 675, 677; modern, 693, 708–710, 740, 811, 1014
Demosthenes [dih-*mahs*-thuh-neez], 91, 106–107
Denmark, 441, 535, 607, 757, 782; Reformation in, 382; in World War II, 922; after World War II, 1040
Deraismes, Maria, 749
Derozio, H. L., 658–659
Dervishes, 458
Desai, Morarji, 971
Descartes, René [ruh-*nay* day-*kart*], 553–559 *passim*, 794
Desmoulins [day-moo-*lan*], Camille, 626, 630
D'Étaples, Lefevre [leh-*fevr day*-tapl], 351
Détente, 1038–1040
Devolution, War of, 530
Devotio moderna, 329
Devshirme [dev-*shir*-meh], 460, 461
De Witt, Jan [yahn deh *viht*], 530
Dharma [*dahr*-mah], 147, 149, 155
Dialectic method, 299
Dialogue Concerning the Two Chief World Systems (Galileo), 551
Dias, Bartholomeu [bahr-tuh-luh-*may*-uh *dee*-ush], 405, 409
Diaspora [dye-*ahs*-poh-rah], 114, 116, 159–160, 161
Díaz, Porfirio, 1012
Dickens, Charles, 713, 714, 787, 795
Dickenson, Emily, 734

Diderot, Denis [deh-*nee* dee-duh-*roh*], 597, 598, 601, 602, 614
Diem, Ngo Dinh [uhng-*oh* dihn zih-*em*], 955
Dien Bien Phu [dyen byen foo], battle of, 955
Diet, 254, 257, 269, 403, 419, 517, 773
Diet (Holy Roman Empire), 340
Dimini, 77
Dimitri [dee-*mee*-tree], Grand Prince, 332
Diocletian [dye-uh-*klee*-shuhn], 143, 165, 173
Diogenes [dye-*ahj*-eh-neez] of Sinope, 119
Directory, 631–632
Disease, 321–322, 417, 709, 712
Disraeli [diz-*ray*-lee], Benjamin, 704, 777, 804, 808, 814
Divan, 459
Divination, 59, 60
Divine Comedy, The (Dante), 329, 348
Divorce: in classical Athens, 91; in classical Rome, 140; view of Jesus, 162; in early modern Asia and Europe, 508; in modern Europe, 775, 1030, 1031; in modern Asia, 959, 960
Djakarta, 955, 961
Dodecanese Islands, 890
Dollfuss [*dole*-fuss], Engelbert, 900, 906, 919
Doll's House, A (Ibsen), 787
Dome of the Rock (Jerusalem), 181, 981
Domesday [*doomz*-day] Book, 274
Domestic (cottage) system, 421, 700–701
Dominic, 295
Dominican Republic, 1002, 1010–1011
Dominicans, 295, 300, 310, 311
"Domino theory," 955
Domitian [doh-*mish*-uhn], 134, 135, 136, 141
Domna, Julia, 142–143, 165
Donatarios, 418–419
Donatello [dahn-uh-*tell*-oh], 360, 857
Donation of Constantine, 350
Donatists, 166
Donne [dun], John, 552–553
Don Quixote [kee-*hoh*-tay] (Cervantes), 435, 561
Don River, 535
Dopolavoro, 910
Dorians, 80
D'Ors, Eugenio, 834
Dostoevsky [doss-tuh-*yev*-ski], Feodor, 727
Douglas, Alfred, 776
Dover, Treaty of, 541
Dow, Alexander, 659
Drake, Sir Francis, 419, 438, 447
Drama: Greek, 100–103; *Noh*, 261; early modern European, 561; *Kabuki*, 687; modern European, 896–897
Dreyfus Affair, 779

Drogheda [*draw*-uh-duh], Statutes of, 334

Drumont [droo-mon], Edouard, 764

Dual Alliance, 837

Dualism, 104, 155, 156–157, 296

Dualists, 104

Dual Monarchy, 759

Dubček [*doob*-chek], Alexander, 1042

Du Bois [doo *bois*], W. E. B., 991

Dulles, John Foster, 1035–1036

Duma, 536, 862, 863, 864

Dunkirk, evacuation from, 449

Dupleix [doo-*pleks*], Joseph, 655

Dürer, Albrecht [*ahl*-brehkt *dur*-uhr], 357, 397, 422

Durham Report, 588

Dutch East Indies (Indonesia), 453, 928, 933

Dutch War (1665–1667), 454

Dutch War (1672–1678), 530–531

Dutch West Indies Company, 454

Duvalier, François [frahn-*swah* doo-*vah*-yay], 1010

Duvalier, Jean-Claude, 1010

Eakins, Thomas, 786

Earth Mother, 8, 77–79, 116

East Bengal, 966, 967, 968, 973

East Germany, 1024, 1026, 1036, 1041

East India Companies: Dutch, 421, 445, 453, 569; English, 421, 453, 477, 569, 585, 648, 651–664 *passim*, 667, 680, 807, 816; French, 421, 655

Ebert, Friedrich [*free*-drik *ay*-bert], 892, 895

Eboué, Félix [fay-*leeks* eh-boo-*ay*], 992

Ecbatana, 32

Eck, Johann, 379

Eckhart, Meister, 329

Ecuador, 218, 590, 983, 1004

Eddas, 306

Eden, Sir Anthony, 978–979, 980

Edessa [ih-*dess*-uh], 284

Edict of Milan, 143, 165

Edinburgh, 272

Edirne [ee-*deer*-neh], 463, 465

Edison, Thomas Alva, 717

Edo [*ay*-doh], 414, 684, 688. *See also* Tokyo

Education: in ancient India, 54; in Confucianism, 64; in Legalism, 65; in China, 70, 493, 675, 677; in Sparta, 93; at Plato's Academy, 105; Carolingian, 266; in medieval Europe, 297–298, 311; humanist views, 349–350, 364–365; for Renaissance women, 351, 353; and Lutheranism, 380–381; in Calvin's Geneva, 386; and the Jesuits, 391; in early modern Asia, 513–514; in early modern Europe, 515–516, 530; in the Ottoman Empire, 516; in modern Europe, 775; missionaries in China, 820–821; in modern Japan, 939–940, 942

Edward I (England), 276, 309

Edward III (England), 324, 338, 344

Edward IV (England), 333, 334

Edward V (England), 333

Edward VI (England), 389–390

Edward VII (Britain), 828

Efendi, Mustafa Naima, 465

Egypt: birth of civilization in, 8–9, 18–19; Old Kingdom, 19–22; dynastic groupings in, 19; position of pharaoh in, 19–20, 22; society of ancient, 19–21, 25; religion of ancient, 19–23, 314; Middle Kingdom, 22; New Kingdom, 22–24; Alexander the Great's conquest of, 108; Hellenistic period, 81, 109; in the Roman period, 130, 131, 133; under the Byzantines, 173; early Muslim rule, 178, 181, 183, 184, 188, 193–194, 201, 267; writing in, 193–194; and the Crusades, 285; Ottoman rule, 458; and Napoleon I, 634, 637; modern, 762, 804, 882, 924, 977, 980, 982–983, 987, 999

Eichmann, Adolf, 929

Eiffel [*eye*-fel] Tower, 774

Eightfold path, 150

Einstein, Albert, 832

Eisenhower, Dwight D.: in World War II, 931, 932, 933; presidency of, 953, 955, 1025, 1031, 1035–1036

Eisenmenger, Johann Andreas, 609

Eisner [*eyes*-ner], Kurt, 892

Elbe [*ehl*-buh] River, 932

Eleanor of Aquitaine [*ak*-wih-tayn], 274–275, 307

Electricity, discovery of, 717

Elements, The (Euclid), 114, 301

Eleven Thousand Virgins, Brotherhood of the, 375

Elgin marbles, 726

Eliot, George (Mary Anne Evans), 734

Eliot, T. S., 852

Elizabeth I (England), 394, 419, 432, 438, 440, 441, 446, 447, 453, 454

Elizabeth II (Britain), 1034

Elizabeth of Austria-Hungary, 788

Elizabeth of Braunschweig [*broun*-shvyck], 380

Elizabeth of Valois [vahl-*wah*], 432

Elizabeth of York, 334

El Salvador, 1010, 1011, 1013

Emile [ay-*meel*] (Rousseau), 607

Empedocles, 103, 547

Ems Dispatch, 758, 795

Enclosure movement, 580, 698

Encomienda [ayn-koh-mee-*ayn*-dah], 570

Encyclopedia (Diderot), 597, 601, 602, 603, 612

Engels, Friedrich [*free*-drik *ehng*-uhls], 695, 739, 791

England, 265, 267, 270, 278. *See also* Britain: Norman Conquest, 274; Norman rule, 274–276; Edward I, 281; Wat Tyler rebellion, 322–323; Hundred Years' War, 324–325; Wars of the Roses, 333; Yorkists, 333–334; Henry VII's reign, 334; Renaissance in, 351, 361; humanists in, 378; Reformation in, 387–390;

Counter-Reformation in, 393–394; Anglo-Spanish War, 438–439; reign of Elizabeth I, 440–441; under the early Stuarts, 446–448; English Revolution, 448–450; early interests in Asia, 453; under the later Stuarts, 541–544; colonies of, 572, 574

English Revolution, 448–450

Enlightened despots: nature of, 601–603; Catherine the Great, 603; Frederick the Great, 604–605; Joseph II, 605–606

Enlightenment: roots of, 594–597; Deism, 594–595; idea of progress, 595–596; influence of Locke, 596–597; *philosophes*, 597–601; Voltaire, 597–598; Rousseau, 598–600; censorship, 601; *Encyclopedia*, 601, 602; and the Jews, 609–610; and abolitionism, 610–611; and women, 611–613; views on death, 645

Ennius [*en*-ee-uhs], 140

Enragés, 630

Entente Cordiale [ahn-*tahnt* kohr-*dyahl*], 838

Ephesus [*ehf*-uh-suhs], 100, 175

Epic of Gilgamesh [*gihl*-guh-mesh], 16, 314

Epictetus, 119

Epicureanism, 119

Epicurus [ehp-ih-*kyoor*-uhs], 104, 119, 141

Epirus [ee-*pye*-ruhs], Confederation of, 125

Equal rights amendment, 1034

Equestrians (Roman), 128, 129

Erasmus, Desiderius [des-ih-*deer*-ee-uhs ih-*rahz*-muhs], 330, 350, 351, 355, 376–378, 381, 387, 392, 396

Eratosthenes [er-uh-*toss*-thuh-neez], 114, 115, 427, 547

Erechtheum [ee-*rek*-thee-um], 99, 100

Eritrea, 803, 919, 1000

Ernst, Max, 834

Erzberger, Matthias, 893

Escorial [ays-*koh*-ree-ahl], 434

Eskimos, 426

Essex, 395

Estado Novo, 901–902

Estates General (Dutch), 445, 446

Estates General (France), 278, 282, 324, 334, 443, 526, 617, 618–620

Estenssoro, Victor Paz, 1007

Esterhazy [*ess*-ter-hah-zee] family, 614, 732

Estonia, 535, 866, 906, 922, 1026

Ethiopia, 200, 201, 803, 919, 1000

Etruscans [ih-*trus*-kenz], 85, 122–124, 135, 196

Euclid [*yoo*-klid], 114, 301

Eugene, Prince, 539

Eugénie, Empress, 748, 749

Eumenes [*yoo*-mee-neez] I, 111

Eumenes II, 111, 127–128

Euphrates [yoo-*fray*-teez] River, 9, 10, 13, 14
Euphrates Valley, 14
Euripides [yoo-*rip*-ih-deez], 101, 103, 117
Eurocommunism, 1042
European Coal and Steel Committee, 1040
Eusebius [you-*see*-bih-uhs], 144, 165
Evangelical Union, 441
Evans, Arthur, 78
Everest, George, 1018
"Ever-normal granary system," 67, 246, 519
Everyman, 308
Evolution, 786
Evolutionary Socialism (Bernstein), 790
Exchequer, 275
Excommunication, 293
Exekias, 86
Existentialism, 852
Experimental method, 301
Exploration, voyages of, 403–408, 483–486
Expressionism, 859
Eylau [*eye*-lou], battle of, 636

Fabian Society, 790
Fabliaux [fah-blee-*oh*], 308
Factories, 700–702
Factory Acts, 706, 707
Faerie Queene (Spenser), 441
Fa Hsien [fah-shyen], 50, 51
Faisal [*fye*-sahl], Prince (later Faisal I), 842, 881, 882
Faisal II (Iraq), 980
Falange [fay-lanj], 900, 921
Falkland Islands (Islas Malvinas), 1006
Family: in classical Rome, 133; and Confucianism, 152–153; in Islam, 184; in Asia, 505–506; in early modern Europe, 506–507; in Africa, 508; in the Industrial Revolution, 702–704
Famine, 320–321, 417, 443, 475, 498, 518, 532, 945
Fanti [*fahn*-tee], 404
Faraday, Michael, 717
Farel, Guillaume [gee-*yohm* fah-*rel*], 383
Farouk (Egypt), 982
Fascism: nature and origins, 887–888; in Italy, 888–892;, 909–912; in Germany, 892–899, 912–915; varieties of, 899–902
Fashoda incident, 804
Fatamid [*fat*-uh-mihd] family, 183
Fatehpur Sikri [*fut*-eh-poor *see*-kree], 470
Fathers and Sons (Turgenev), 787
Faubus, Orville, 1031
Faulkner, William, 852
Faust (Goethe), 730–731
Fauves [fohvz], 834
Fell, Margaret, 450

Feminist movement, 611–613, 748–749, 782–785
Ferdinand, Archduke Franz, 839, 840
Ferdinand I (Austria), 740, 742
Ferdinand I (Holy Roman Empire), 432
Ferdinand I (Naples), 725
Ferdinand II (Holy Roman Empire), 441
Ferdinand II (Naples), 740, 741
Ferdinand III (Holy Roman Empire), 538
Ferdinand VII (Spain), 405, 589, 724, 725
Ferdinand of Aragon, 332–333, 335, 338
Ferguson, Wallace, 364
Festivals, 299, 308, 471, 492, 511, 564
Feudal order, 310; parallels in ancient China, 60–61; parallels in south India, 229; Japanese, 260, 682–683, 684–685, 690; in Europe, 267–269; bastard feudalism, 333
Fichte [*fik*-teh], Johann, 625, 638, 720, 734
Ficino, Marsilio [mahr-*see*-lyoh fee-*chee*-noh], 349, 357
Fielding, Henry, 544, 614
Fiji [*fee*-jee], 824, 825
Filippo Maria (Milan), 336
Filmer, Robert, 443
Films, 1014
Finland, 866, 922; Reformation in, 382
Firdawsi (Firdausi) [fihr-*dow*-see], 187
First International, 788
Fischer, Fritz, 837
Fisher, John, 389
Fiume [*fyoo*-may], 890
Five-Year Plans (USSR), 915–917
Flagellants, 321, 644
Flanders, 270, 276, 324, 530, 531, 532, 533, 582, 583, 606
Flaubert [floh-*bair*], Gustave, 787
Flavians, 134–135
Fleury [flur-*ree*], Cardinal, 580
Flinders, Matthew, 1017
FLN (Algeria), 999
Florence, 270, 272, 323–324, 751; in the Renaissance, 338, 344–346, 348, 353–355
Florida, 391, 419, 454, 583, 585, 586
Fontenelle [fon-teh-*nel*], Bernard de, 595–596
Foochow (Fuzhou), 493
Food and Agricultural Organization (UN), 934
Forbidden City, 493, 494
Ford, Gerald R., 1039
Ford, Henry, 769
Forlì [fohr-*lee*], 337
Formosa, 453. *See also* Taiwan
Fort William. *See* Calcutta
Forty-two Articles, 390
Fourier [*foor*-yay], Charles, 715
Four Noble Truths, 150
Fourteen Points, 844–845
Fox, George, 450

Foxe, John, 394
Fragonard [fra-goh-*nar*], Jean-Honoré, 613
France, medieval, 267, 269, 270, 273, 274, 285; Capetian period, 276–278; reign of Philip IV, 281–282; Jacquerie, 322; Languedoc risings, 323; Hundred Years' War, 324–325; early Valois period, 334–335
France, early modern: Renaissance in, 351; civil war, 439–440; early Bourbons, 442–444; age of Louis XIV, 525–533, 580–581; colonies of, 572, 573, 574; in the War of the Austrian Succession, 582; in the Seven Years' War, 582–583; in the Revolutionary War, 585; Enlightenment in, 597–601; revolution of 1789, 616–626; the radical revolution (1792–1794), 626–631; the Thermidorian Reaction, 631–632; legacy of the revolution, 633–634, 720–721; the Napoleonic era, 634–640, 724, 727
France, modern: in the First Industrial Revolution, 714–715; in the early nineteenth century, 721–724, 725–727; revolution of 1830, 734–735; revolution of 1848, 719, 740, 742, 743; Second Republic, 743, 746–747; Second Empire, 747–749, 759; Franco-Prussian War, 758–759; Third Republic, 758, 777–779; in the Crimean War, 761; in the Second Industrial Revolution, 770; colonies in Africa, 804; colonial regimes in Southeast Asia, 816–817; and the origins of World War I, 837–840; in World War I, 837–840; after World War I, 840, 842–845; and the Peace of Paris (1919), 846; fascists in, 899–900; and the Great Depression, 904, 905; in World War II, 923, 931; after World War II, 1029, 1030, 1040
Franche Comté [frahnch kohn-*tay*], 334
Francis I (France), 328, 335, 341, 351, 396, 432
Francis II (France), 433
Franciscans, 296, 300, 311, 390
Francis of Assisi [ah-*see*-zee], 294, 295
Franck, Sebastian, 387
Franco, Francisco, 900, 921
Franco-Prussian War, 758–759
Frankfurt, 272, 625, 754
Frankfurt, Treaty of, 758–759
Frankfurt Assembly, 740–741, 742, 755
Franklin, Benjamin, 601, 717
Franks, 143, 181, 265–267
Franz Joseph I (Austria), 742, 753, 759, 760
Frederick, Elector of Saxony, 379
Frederick I, "Barbarossa" (Holy Roman Empire), 270, 280, 285, 297

Frederick II (Holy Roman Empire), 281, 285, 298, 310
Frederick II, "the Great" (Prussia), 540–541, 562, 581–582, 583, 598, 603, 604–605
Frederick III (Prussia), 540
Frederick V (Palatinate), 441, 447
Frederick William, "the Great Elector," 539–540
Frederick William I (Prussia), 540
Frederick William IV (Prussia), 625, 740, 742, 755–756
Free Corps, 892, 894
Free Democrats (West Germany), 1029
Free French, 923
Free Masons, 601, 727
French Academy of Sciences, 555
French Equatorial Africa, 804, 991–992
French Revolution (1789–1799): roots of the revolution, 617–619; the revolution of 1789, 619–623; the bourgeois order (1789–1791), 623–625; European reactions, 625; the fall of the monarchy, 625–626; the radical revolution (1792–1794), 626–631; the Thermidorian reaction, 631–632; the legacy, 633–634, 720–721
French Revolution (1830), 734–735
French Revolution (1848), 740
French Revolution (1870), 758, 777
Fresco, 356
Freud [froid], Sigmund, 760, 831–832
Friedan, Betty, 1033, 1034
Friedland [freet-lahnt], battle of, 636
Friedrich-Wilhelm University, 895
Fröbel [freh-behl], Friedrich, 607
Fronde [frohnd], 443–444
Frontinus, Sextus, 141
Fugger [foog-uhr], Jakob, 400, 402, 403
Fugger family, 402–403, 422–423
Fujiwara [foo-jee-wahr-uh] clan, 259–260
Fulton, Robert, 707
Funan, 235
Fur trade, 419, 571
Fusae, Ichikawa, 960
Futurists, 835–836
Fuzuli [foo-zoo-lih], Mehmet Suleiman, 465

Gabelle [gah-bell], 324, 526
Gabon, 983
Gainsborough, Thomas, 614
Galen [gay-luhn], 142, 185, 547
Galicia, 841
Galileo [gal-ih-lee-oh], 551
"Gallican Liberties," 333, 334
Gallipoli [gah-lip-oh-lee] campaign, 842
Galtieri [gahl-tyair-ee], Leopoldo, 1006
Gambia, 803
Gandhi [gahn-dee], Indira, 963, 970–972

Gandhi, Mohandas K., 147, 148, 814, 842, 877–880, 964–968, 1049
Gandhi, Rajiv, 972
Ganges [gan-jeez] Valley, 41, 42, 44, 46, 466, 650, 652, 657, 664, 665. See also Hindustan
"Gang of Four," 950, 959
Garcia, Alan, 1007
Gargantua (Rabelais), 351, 560
Garibaldi, Giuseppe, 753, 754
Garvey, Marcus, 991
Gascons, 324
Gascony, 276
Gaskell, Elizabeth, 713–714, 733, 734
Gaudí [gow-dee], Antonio, 833–834
Gaugamela [goh-ga-mee-lah], battle of, 108
Gauguin [goh-ganh], Paul, 833, 859
Gaul [gahl], 129, 130, 143, 181, 265
Gauls [gahlz], 109, 111, 124
Gay Rights movement, 1033
Gaza Strip, 980
Gdansk (formerly Danzig), 1042
Geisha [gay-shuh], 511, 687
General Association of German Women, 783
Generalife, 287–288
Geneva [juh-nee-vuh], 383, 385–386, 394; University of, 386
Genoa [jehn-oh-ah], 270, 272, 286, 338, 344
Gentile [jehn-tee-lay], Giovanni, 889
Gentry (English), 698
Geoffrey of Monmouth [jef-ree of mon-muth], 308
George I (Britain), 560, 579, 581
George II (Britain), 579, 582
George III (Britain), 584, 585, 678, 698
George IV (Britain), 726
Georgia, USSR, 867
Georgics (Vergil), 134
German East Africa, 803, 842
Germania (Tacitus), 141
Germanic tribes, 143, 144, 265
Germany, 267, 269, 270. See also Holy Roman Empire: prehistoric life in, 5; Renaissance in, 350–351; Reformation in, 378–382; Thirty Years' War, 441–442; victim of Louis XIV's aggression, 531–533; and Napoleon, 636, 638; in the First Industrial Revolution, 715; in the early nineteenth century, 723–724, 736; 1848 revolution, 740–741, 742; unification of, 750–751, 754–759; in the Second Industrial Revolution, 769–770, 771; Second Reich, 779–780; colonies in Africa, 803; and the origins of World War I, 837–840; in World War I, 840–845; and the Treaty of Versailles, 846–847; Nazism, 892–899, 912–915; in World War II, 922–925, 928–932; postwar division of, 1024
Gerson, Jean [zhahn zher-sohn], 326
Gestapo, 912

Ghana [gah-nah], 202, 203, 204, 409, 992, 994, 1000
Ghazis [gahw-zehs], 457
Ghent [gehnt], 272, 324
Ghibellines [gib-uh-leenz], 336
Ghiberti [gee-ber-tee], Lorenzo, 360
Giacometti [jah-koh-met-tee], Alberto, 834
Giap [jyopp], Vo Nguyen, 955
Gibbon, Edward, 2, 145
Gibraltar, 181, 533, 585, 724
Gilbert, William, 555
Gilbert Islands, 824
Gilchrist, Percy, 716
Gioberti, Vincenzo [veen-chayn-tsoh joh-bair-tee], 751
Giolitti [joh-leet-tee], Giovanni, 781, 891
Giotto [joht-toh], 356
Girondins [jih-rohnd-inz], 627–628, 631
Giudice [joo-dee-chay], Maria, 790
Gladstone, William, 776–777, 788
Glasnost, 1044
Gloire [glwahr], 526, 529, 530
Glorious Revolution (1688), 542–543
Gluck [glook], Christoph Willibald von, 614
Gnostics [nahs-tiks], 165
Goa [goh-uh], 408, 409, 411, 650, 651
Gobi [goh-bee] Desert, 321
Gobineau [goh-bee-noh], Arthur de, 836, 976
Go-Daigo, 261
Godfrey of Bouillon [boo-yohn], 283, 284
Godwin, William, 613
Goebbels [ger-buls], Joseph, 796, 894, 913
Goes [goos], Benedict de, 391
Goethe, Johann Wolfgang von [ger-tah], 187, 491, 638, 729–731
Gogol [goh-gol], Nikolai, 727
Gokhale [goh-kah-lay], G. K., 813
Golan Heights, 980
Gold Coast, 404, 991, 994
Golden Book, 338
Golden Bull, 340
Golden Horde, 289
Golden Lotus, The, 490
Gold rushes: California, 715; Australia, 715; South Africa, 716
Goldsmith, Oliver, 698
Gomulka, Wladyslaw [vlah-dihss-lahff guh-mool-kuh], 1028
Gonzalez, Julio, 834
Goodman, Christopher, 394
Gorbachev, Mikhail, 1031, 1036, 1044–1045
Gordon, Charles ("Chinese"), 804
Gordon riots, 705
Göring [gur-ing], Hermann, 894
GOSPLAN, 915
Gotha [goh-tah] Program, 789, 791
Gothic art, 304–305, 345
Göttingen, 380
Government of India Act, 808
Govind Singh, 473–474
Goya, Francisco, 637

Gracchus [*grak*-uhs], Gaius, 128–129, 137
Gracchus, Tiberius, 128–129
Gramsci [*grahm*-shee], Antonio, 1042
Granada, 186, 286, 287–288, 333
Gran Chaco [grahn *chah*-koh] War, 1007
Grand Alliance (World War II), 930–934
Grand National Consolidated Trades Union, 707–708
Granicus [gruh-*nee*-kuhs] River, battle of, 108
Granth Sahib, 473
Gratian [*gray*-shun], 297, 301, 311
Great Chain of Being, 594
Great Depression, 897, 901, 902–904, 1004, 1007
"Greater East Asia Co-prosperity Sphere," 928
Great Fear (France), 621
Great Interregnum, 281, 339
"Great Leap Forward," 945
Great Northern War, 535
Great Purges (USSR), 917–918
"Great Society," 1032
Great Trek (South Africa), 804
Great Wall, 64–65, 67, 241, 486, 494
Grebel, Conrad, 386
Greco, El [el *grek*-oh] (Domenico Theotokopoulos], 435, 857
Greece, ancient, 188, 282; Neolithic Age in, 76–78; Minoans 78–79; Mycenaeans, 79–80; Dark Age, 80–81; geography of, 81; age of expansion, 81–83; growth of the *polis*, 85–86; Athenian democracy, 86–87; Persian Wars, 87–88; Periclean Athens, 88–92; Spartan society, 92–93; Peloponnesian War, 93–95; the classical ideal, 97–99; classical art, 98–100; classical drama, 100–103; pre-Socratic science, 103–104; classical philosophy, 104–106; Macedonian conquest, 106–107; age of Alexander the Great, 107–109; Hellenistic Greeks, 109–114; Hellenistic science, 114–116; Hellenistic religion, 116; Hellenistic women, 117–118; later Greek philosophy, 119
Greece, modern, 458; in the early nineteenth century, 725–726; in the twentieth century, 836, 839, 906, 907, 922, 924, 1023
"Greek fire," 191
Greeks. *See also* Greece: in southern Italy, 122, 124–125; alphabet of, 196
Greenland, 267
Green revolution, 971, 972
Greenwich [*grehn*-ich] Mean Time, 1017
Gregory I, Pope, 294
Gregory VII, Pope, 279, 282
Gregory IX, Pope, 296, 298
Gregory XI, Pope, 325
Gregory XIII, Pope, 439, 440
Grenada, 1011

Grey, Lady Jane, 390
Grey, Lord, 736
Grey, Sir Edward, 840
Grimm, Jacob, 720
Grimm, Wilhelm, 720
Grocyn [*groh*-sin], William, 351
Groote [groht], Gerhard, 329
Gropius, Walter, 853
Grosseteste [*groh*-test], Robert, 301
Grosz [grohs], George, 896, 897
Grotius [groh-shih-uhs], Hugo, 445
Grumbach, Argula von, 380, 381
Grünewald [grew-neh-vahlt], Matthias, 397
Guadeloupe [gwah-thay-*loo*-pay], 573, 582, 583
Guam [gwom], 782, 826
Guarantees, Law of, 781
Guatemala [gwah-tuh-*mah*-luh], 211, 569, 1002, 1010, 1013, 1036
Gudea [goo-*day*-ah], 17
Guelfs [gwelfs], 336, 345
Guernica [gair-*nee*-kah], bombing of, 920, 921
Guernica (Picasso), 920
Guevara, Ernesto "Che" [air-*ness*-toh "chay" gay-*vah*-rah], 1009, 1010
Guiana, 454
Guicciardini, Francesco [frahn-*cheh*-skoh gweet-chahr-*dee*-nee], 355
Guilds: ancient, 124; medieval, 270, 272–273, 331, 344, 346, 510; Ottoman, 463; Chinese, 487, 674; early modern, 505, 510
Guillaume de Lorris [gee-*yohm* day lo-rees], 307
Guinea, 404, 994
Guise [gheez] family, 438, 439
Guizot, François [frahn-*swah* gee-zoh], 740
Gujarat [goo-jah-*raht*], 226, 232, 468, 651, 657, 811
Gulags, 1026
Gunpowder, 185, 207, 241, 242, 252, 577
Gupta dynasty, 197
Guptas, 50
Gurkhas, 678, 808
Gustavus Adolphus [guh-*stay*-vuhs uh-*doll*-fuhs], 441–442
Guston, Philip, 859–860
Gutenberg, Johann [*yoh*-hahn *goo*-tuhn-berkh], 355, 793
Guti [*goo*-tee], 17

Haarlem, 446
Habsburg [*habz*-burg] dynasty, 339–341
Habsburg-Valois Wars, 341
Haciendas, 416
Hadith [*heh*-deeth], 180
Hadrian [*hay*-dree-uhn], 135–136, 137, 138
Hafiz [hah-*feez*], Shams ud-din, 187, 188
Hagia Sophia [*hah*-juh soh-*fee*-uh], 173, 176–177, 462
Haiphong [hye-*fong*], 816

Haiti [*hay*-tee], 588, 1002, 1010
Hajj [hahj], 180
Halberstadt [*hahl*-ber-shtaht], 539
Halle [*hahl*-eh], University of, 515, 607
Hamburg, 267, 272, 297, 382
Hammurabi [hah-moo-*rah*-bee], code of, 12, 17
Hampton Court (palace), 396
Handel, George Friedrich, 614
Han [hahn] dynasty, 66–75
Han Fei [hahn fay], 67
Hangchow, 251, 252
Hankow (Hankou) [*hang*-kou], 493
Hannibal, 126–127
Hanoi, 236, 816, 955
Hanover, 380
Hanoverian succession, 543
Hanseatic [han-see-*at*-ik] League, 270, 331
Hanukkah, 116
Harappa [huh-*rahp*-uh], 36, 38, 39, 367, 658
Harappans, 148
Hardenburg, Prince, 638, 721
Harding, Warren G., 904
Hard Times (Dickens), 787
Hardy, Thomas, 706
Hargreaves, James, 699
Hari Singh, 968
Harold, 274
Harsha, 51, 52
Harun al-Rashid [hah-*roon* ahl-rah-*sheed*], 183, 187
Harvey, William, 552
Hasan, Abi bin, 207
Hasdai ibn-Shaprut, 310
Hasidim [hah-*see*-dim], 310, 610
Hasidism, 610
Haskalah movement, 610
Haskins, Charles Homer, 363–364
Hastings, battle of, 274
Hatshepsut [hat-*shep*-soot], 22–23
Hatt-i Humayun [hou-*mah*-yoon], 763
Hattusas [hat-too-shuhs], 28, 31
Hattusilis III, 29
Hausa [*hou*-sah], 994
Haussmann, Georges [zhorzh ohs-*mann*], 748, 749, 773
Havana, 583
Hawaii, 824, 825–826
Hawkins, John, 419, 438, 454
Hawkins, William, 651
Haydn [*hye*-d'n], Franz Joseph, 614, 732, 760
Haywood, Eliza, 612
Hébert, Jacques, 630
Hebrews. *See also* Jews: early history of, 26–28; ancient society of, 28; prophets, 29
Hebrew University of Jerusalem, 882
Hecataeus, 427
Hegel [*hay*-guhl], Georg Wilhelm Friedrich, 638, 720, 733
Heian [hay-ahn] Era, 259–260
Heidelberg, University of, 351
Heimwehr [*hyem*-vair], 900
Heine [*hye*-nee], Heinrich, 731

Heinsius [*hyen*-see-uhs], Antonius, 532, 533
Heisenberg [*hye*-zehn-berk], Werner, 852
Hejaz [hee-*jaz*], 881
Hejira [hih-*jye*-ruh], 179
Helena, mother of Constantine, 165
Hellenistic kingdoms, 108–112
Hellespont, 95, 175
Helsinki [hel-*sing*-kee] Accords (1973), 1036, 1039
Hemingway, Ernest, 904
Henlein [*hen*-line], Konrad, 921
Henrietta Maria, 447
Henry, Duke of Guise [gheez], 439
Henry I (England), 275
Henry I (Germany), 278
Henry II (England), 274, 275, 298
Henry II (France), 432
Henry III (France), 439–440
Henry IV (England), 333
Henry IV (France), 440, 442, 443, 594
Henry IV (Holy Roman Empire), 279
Henry V (Holy Roman Empire), 279
Henry VI (England), 333
Henry VI (Holy Roman Empire), 280–281
Henry VII (England), 334
Henry VIII (England), 328, 334, 361, 376, 378, 388–389, 396, 397
Henry of Navarre, 439, 440. *See also* Henry IV (France)
Henry the Navigator, Prince, 404, 429
Heraclitus [her-ah-*klye*-tuhs] of Ephesus, 104
Heraclius [heh-ruh-*klye*-uhs], 177
Herculaneum [her-kew-*lay*-nee-uhm], 138, 614
Herder, Johann Gottfried von, 614, 638, 720
Heresy, 165–166, 326–327, 385–386, 393, 394
Héricourt [ay-ree-*koor*], Jenny, 748
Herlihy, David, 364
Hermetic doctrine, 548–549
Herod, 160
Herodotus [hih-*rod*-uh-tuhs], 2, 18, 88, 95, 427
Herschel, William, 730, 1018, 1019
Hertz, Heinrich, 717
Herzegovina, 763, 837, 839
Herzen [*hair*-tsin], Alexander, 727, 762
Herzl [*herts*-l], Theodor, 764–766, 976
Hess, Rudolf, 894
Heydrich [*hye*-drich], Reinhard, 928
Hidalgo [ee-*dahl*-goh], Father, 590
Hidalgos [ee-*dahl*-gohs], 333
Hideyoshi [hee-deh-yoh-shee], Toyotomi, 257, 262, 683–684
Hieroglyphics [*hye*-ruh-*glif*-iks], 24, 79, 193–194, 197–198, 213
High Commission, Court of, 447, 448, 449
Himalayas, 969–970, 1018
Himmler, Heinrich, 894, 912
Hinayana (Theravada) Buddhism, 150–151

Hindenburg, Paul von, 841, 897, 898
Hinduism, 155, 156, 166; in India, 39, 41–42; in Ceylon, 49; writings, 147–148; belief in reincarnation, 148; evil and suffering, 148–149; diversity of, 149; role of women, 167, 168
Hindustan, 42, 43, 46, 51, 223, 226, 466. *See also* Ganges Valley
Hipparchus [hih-*pahr*-kuhs], 86, 114
Hippias [*hip*-ee-uhs], 86–87
Hippocrates [hih-*pahk*-ruh-teez], 54, 115
Hirohito [hee-roh-*hee*-toh], 933, 937, 938
Hiroshige [hee-roh-*shee*-geh], 687, 688
Hiroshima [hee-*rahsh*-mah], 933, 937
Hispaniola, 405, 416, 417, 569–570
History: nature of, 2–4, 733; sources for, 3, 60, 74–75, 141; fields of, 4
History of Rome (Livy), 134
History of the Peloponnesian War (Thucydides), 90, 94–95
History of the Persian Wars (Herodotus), 88
Hitler, Adolf, 760, 796, 886, 892, 893–899, 912–931 *passim*
Hitler Youth, 914
Hittites, 11, 13, 23, 41; early history, 28–29; society and religion, 29–31; trade of, 29–30; laws, 30; end of empire, 30–31
Hobbes, Thomas, 450, 557–558, 596–597, 599
Hobson, John A., 800, 801
Ho Chi Minh, 816, 871, 954, 955, 957
Hogarth, William, 505, 544, 614
Hohenlinden, battle of, 636
Hohenstaufen [*hoh*-uhn-*shtow*-fuhn] dynasty, 280–281
Hohenzollern [*hoh*-ehn-*tsol*-ern] dynasty, 539
Hokusai [hoh-koo-sye], 687, 688–689
Holbach, Baron d', 598
Holbein, Hans [hahns *hohl*-byne], 397–398
Hölderlin, Friedrich, 731
Holker, John, 714–715
Holocaust, 928–930
Holstein, 757, 758
Holy Alliance, 722, 724
Holy League (1494), 337; (1511–1513), 335, 338; (1571), 435–436
Holy Roman Empire, 276; early history, 278; struggle with Catholic church, 278–281; rise of the Habsburgs, 339–341; in the Thirty Years' War, 440–441; in the later seventeenth century, 450, 538–539; in the eighteenth century, 533, 539; in the War of the Austrian Succession, 582; in the Seven Years' War, 582–583; reign of Joseph II, 605–606; and the Napoleonic wars, 636, 638
Homer, 79, 80–81, 83, 103, 134, 196
Hominids, 4, 5
Homo erectus [*hoh*-moh ih-*rek*-tuhs], 4

Homo neanderthalis, 5. *See also* Neanderthal culture
Homo sapiens [*hoh*-moh *say*-pee-uhnz], 4
Homosexuals, 396, 513, 849, 929, 1033
Honduras, 590
Hong Kong, 817, 952, 960
Honshu, 684
Hoover, Herbert, 904
Hoplites, 83
Horace, 84, 134
Hortensia, 139
Hortensian Law, 124
Horthy [*hor*-tee], Miklós, 907, 929
Ho-shen (he-shen), 676–677
Hospitals, 301, 390, 465, 512; in India, 51; Byzantine, 176; Muslim, 186, 287; in Geneva, 386
Hottentot, 997
Hsia [shyah] dynasty, 57–58
Hsiung-nu (Xiung-nu) [shung-noo], 67–69, 71, 73
Hsuan Tsang [shwahn-dzahng], 52
Hsuan-tsung (Xuan Zong) [schwahn dzung], 246
Hsun-tzu (Xunzi) [shuhn-tsoo], 63
Hua Kuo-feng (Hua Guofeng), 950
Huáscar [*wahs*-kahr], 218
Hubble, Edwin, 1019–1020
Hudson Bay, 419
Hudson River, 454
Hudson Strait, 419
Hue [hway], 236
Hugo, Victor, 787
Huguenots [*hyoo*-guh-nots], 439–440, 443, 531, 533
Human figure, representations of, 5, 366–371, 855–860
Humanists, Renaissance, 346–352, 376
Human origins, 4–9
Human sacrifices, 214, 216–217
Humayun [hou-*mah*-yoon], 467
Hume, David, 608
Hundred Years' War, 324–325
Hungarians, 283
Hungary: medieval, 267, 284, 289, 341; early modern, 458, 466, 538, 539, 606; 1848 revolution, 740, 741–742; Dual Monarchy, 759; modern, 847, 871, 906, 929, 1022, 1024, 1026, 1028, 1041
Hung Hsiu-Ch'uan (Hong Xiuquan), 819
Hung-wu, 481–483
Huns, 31, 71, 144, 173, 191. *See also* Hsiung-nu
Hunter-gatherers, 5, 200
Hunyadi [*hoo*-nyo-dee], János, 341
Huron Indians, 644
Hus [huhs], John, 327, 375, 379
Husein [hoo-*sayn*], 184, 644
Hussein, Sadam, 987
Hutchinson, Anne, 612
Hutten, Ulrich von, 376
Hutton, James, 1018
Huxley, Aldous, 1048
Huygens [*hye*-genz], Christiaan, 1018
Huysmans [*hois*-mahns], J. K., 833

Hwan, Chun Doo, 954
Hyderabad, 650, 655, 657, 968
Hyksos [*hik*-sahs], 22, 25–27, 41, 79

Ibarra de Piedra, Rosaria, 1012
Iberian peninsula, 265, 286–288
Ibo, 994, 1000
Ibrahim [ib-rah-*heem*], 226–227
Ibsen, Henrik, 782, 787
Iceland, 267
Iconoclastic controversy, 189–190
Ictinos [ik-*tye*-nahs], 98, 99
Idealism, 608
Idris [ih-*drees*] (Libya), 983
Ikki, Kita, 900
Île de France [*eel* duh *frahns*], 276
Iliad, 80–81
Illuminated manuscripts, 303
Illyria, 126
Illyrian [ih-*lihr*-ee-ahn] War, 127
Imarets, 462, 463
Imhotep, 19
Imitation of Christ, The, 330
Impressionism, 787, 833
Incas, 217–218, 414, 416, 417, 508,
    519, 569
Index of Prohibited Books, 393, 601
India, ancient: geography of, 35–36;
    origins of civilization in, 36; Indus
    civilization, 36–41; Aryan invasion,
    41–42; Mauryan period, 42–47;
    Kushan and Greek invasions, 47;
    ancient Southern India, 47–48;
    Gupta period, 50–52; women in
    ancient India, 52–53; heritage of
    ancient India, 53–54; diversity of,
    53–54; invasion by Alexander the
    Great, 108; religions of, 147–152;
    Christianity in, 163; writing in,
    194, 197
India, medieval: spread of Islam,
    221–224; Delhi sultans, 224–228;
    southern India, 229–231
India, Mughal: origins, 466; age of
    Akbar, 467–470; Jahangir and Shah
    Jahan, 470–472; age of Aurangzeb,
    472–475; society and culture, 475;
    decline, 476–477
India, early modern: Mughal collapse,
    648–650; early westerners, 409,
    650–654; Anglo-French rivalry,
    655–656; early British rule,
    656–658; Orientalists and the
    Bengal renaissance, 658–660;
    subjugation of India, 660–664; 1857
    mutiny, 664–665, 807–808
India, modern: British rule, 807–808,
    811–812; growth, 808–811; New
    Delhi, 812–813; rise of nationalism,
    813–814; in World War I, 842;
    between the world wars, 877–881;
    in World War II, 927; independence
    and political division, 964–968;
    after independence, 968–973
India Act, 656
Indian Ocean, 409, 651, 724
Indochina, 925, 928, 955–958
Indo-European languages, 41
Indo-Europeans, 28, 31

Indonesia: early history, 232, 233,
    237, 410; colonial rule, 651, 814,
    816–817; in the twentieth century,
    928, 954–955, 960, 983
Inductive method, 106
Indulgences, 283, 327, 376, 379–380,
    383, 392
Indus civilization: origins of, 36–37;
    relations with Sumer, 37–39; cities,
    39–40; decline and fall, 40–41
Indus River, 10, 36, 38, 47
Industrial Revolution, First:
    demographic and technological
    roots, 693–695; capitalist society,
    695–697; agricultural developments,
    697–699; machine technology and
    the state, 699–700; the factory
    system, 700–702; impact on the
    family, 702–704; industrial workers,
    704–706; Robert Owen, 706–708;
    demographic growth, 708–710;
    Manchester, 711–714; the spread of
    industrialization, 714–716; applied
    science and engineering, 716–717
Industrial Revolution, Second,
    769–771
Industry, medieval European,
    330–331
Indus Valley, 35, 40, 42, 193, 657, 663
Infanticide, 140, 512, 709, 960
Ingria [*ing*-grih-ah], 535
Inheritance laws, 312
Innocent III, Pope, 275–276, 280, 281,
    285, 296
Innocent IV, Pope, 296, 298
Innocent XI, Pope, 539
Inquisition, 296–297, 333, 393,
    434–435
Institutes of the Christian Religion
    (Calvin), 383, 384, 385
Institutional Revolutionary Party
    (Mexico), 1012
Instrument of Government, 449
Integralists, 901
Intendants, 443, 526, 617
Interdict, 293
International Alliance of Women, 783
International Monetary Fund, 1003,
    1008
Intifada, 988
Investiture Controversy, 278–280, 301
Ionia [eye-*oh*-nee-uh], 87
Ionians, 80, 88
Iran [ih-*rahn*]: rise of the Safavids,
    477–478; in the eighteenth century,
    665–667; in the twentieth century,
    883, 884, 983, 985–988, 1036, 1040
Iranian Revolution, 985–988
Iraq [ih-*rak*]: origins of farming in, 6;
    in the twentieth century, 842, 882,
    977, 980, 982, 983, 987, 988
Ireland, 267, 334, 584, 740, 1040
Irene, 266
Irnerius, 300
Iron Age, 122, 201
Iron Curtain, 1023
Iron Guard, 900
Iroquois [*ir*-oh-kwoi] Confederation,
    586, 644

Irrawaddy Delta, 816, 954
Isabella (Castile), 332–333, 405, 433,
    440
Isabella II (Spain), 781
Isaiah [eye-*zay*-yuh], 28, 159, 162
Isaurians [eye-*sah*-ree-ehnz], 173
Isenheim altarpiece, 397
Isfahan, 477
Isherwood, Christopher, 895
Ishmael, 179
Isis [*eye*-sis], 116
Islam, 155, 156: Muhammad and the
    rise of, 178–179; teachings, 179–180,
    317, 642; spread of, 183–184;
    Sunni-Shi'ite split, 183–184; in
    Africa, 201, 202, 204–206, 208; in
    India, 221–228; in Southeast Asia,
    221, 231–233; and the Crusades,
    283–286
Islamabad, 974
Islamic civilization: early Islamic
    society and economy, 184–185;
    science and medicine, 185–186;
    philosophy, 186–187; literature,
    187–188
Ismail [ees-mah-*eel*] (Egypt), 804
Ismail (Iran), 477
Isocrates [eye-*sok*-rah-teez], 106
Isopolity, 110
Israel, 27, 28, 159, 976–981, 988
Issus [*ihs*-uhs], battle of, 108
Istanbul, 461–463
Istrian Peninsula, 890
Italian East Africa, 919
Italian League, 337
Italian Social Republic, 931
Italo-Turkish War, 839
Italy, 81, 85, 736; medieval, 175, 188,
    190, 265, 267, 270, 272, 278, 279,
    282, 334–339; Renaissance in,
    344–362 *passim*; and Napoleon,
    632, 636, 637–638; revolutions of
    1848, 740, 741; unification of,
    750–754, 759; in the
    Austro-Prussian War, 757–758; the
    Liberal state, 780–781; colonies in
    Africa, 803; and the origins of
    World War I, 837–839; in World
    War I, 842, 844; and the Peace of
    Paris (1919), 846; Fascism, 888–892,
    909–912; in World War II, 923–924,
    930–931, 932; after World War II,
    1029, 1030, 1040
Ito [*ee*-toh], Hirobumi, 823
Iturbide [ee-toor-*bee*-thay], Agustín,
    de, 590
Ivan III, "the Great" (Russia), 332,
    1038
Ivan IV, "the Terrible" (Russia), 451,
    452
Ivory Coast, 804

Jackson, Andrew, 766
Jacobins, 625–626, 627–628, 634
Jacquard [zha-kar], Joseph-Marie, 714
Jacquerie [zhahk-uh-*ree*], 322
Jahan [juh-*hahn*], Shah, 471–472, 473
Jahangir [jah-*hahn*-geer], 453,
    470–471, 651

Jahn [yahn], Friedrich Ludwig, 727
Jainism [jye-nizm], 149
Jamaica, 448, 574, 585, 588, 1013
James I (England), 446, 447, 453, 651
James II (England), 542
James IV (Scotland), 334
James VI (Scotland), 438, 446. See
    also James I (England)
Jameson Raid, 806
Jamestown, 454, 571
Jami [jah-mee], 187, 188
Janissaries [jan-ih-sar-eez], 460, 466
Jansen, Cornelius [kor-nay-lihs
    yahn-suhn], 559
Jansenists [jant-suh-nists], 515, 559,
    607–608
Japan, early: Buddhism in, 150, 152,
    155; Neo-Confucianism in, 154;
    Confucianism in, 155; Shinto in,
    155; geography, 257–258; early
    history, 258; Nara period, 258–259;
    Heian period, 259–260; Kamakura
    Shogunate, 260–261; Ashikaga
    Shogunate, 261–262, 682
Japan, early modern: early European
    traders, 409–411; reunification
    under the Tokugawa, 682–685;
    expulsion of foreigners, 685–686;
    culture, 686–688; foreign pressures,
    689–690
Japan, modern: modernization of,
    821–822; imperialism, 822–823; Ito
    Hirobumi, 823; in World War II,
    842; fascists in, 900; expansion in
    Asia, 918; in World War II,
    925–928, 930, 932–933; after World
    War II, 936–942, 961; women in
    modern Japan, 940, 960
Jarmo, 6
Jaruzwelski, Wojciech [voi-chek
    yah-roo-zehl-skee], 1042
Jati, 503
Jaurès, Jean [zhahn zhoh-res], 791
Java, 232, 233, 237, 238, 651, 816, 955
"Jazz Age," 849, 904
Jean de Meun [zhahn deh men], 307
Jebb, Ann, 612
Jebusites, 159
Jefferson, Thomas, 362, 585, 766
Jena [yay-nuh]: battle of, 636, 638;
    University of, 381
Jeremiah, 28, 159
Jericho [jehr-ih-koh], 6, 7, 367
Jerome of Prague, 327
Jerusalem: ancient, 27, 28, 128, 134,
    159–161, 175; and the Crusades,
    274, 284, 285; modern, 761, 981
Jesuits (Society of Jesus), 391,
    411–412, 413, 469, 495, 515, 562
    607, 667, 726
Jesus of Nazareth, 158, 160, 162–163,
    164, 167, 179
Jeunesses patriotes [zhe-nes
    pa-tree-ot], 899
Jews: in ancient Egypt, 22; in
    Alexandria, 114; Hellenistic, 116; in
    the Roman Empire, 134; medieval,
    272, 278, 283, 284, 285, 286, 287,

308–310, 339; in the Reformation,
    394–395, 396; in Brazil, 419; in
    Spain, 434, 435, 515; in the
    Netherlands, 446; in England, 449;
    in Poland, 451, 515; in the Ottoman
    Empire, 458; in the Holy Roman
    Empire, 538; in Rome, 564;
    emancipation of, 609–610; and
    death, 644–645; in Iran, 667; birth
    of Zionism, 764–766; migration to
    Palestine before World War II, 882;
    under Hitler, 914–915; and the
    Holocaust, 928–930; and the state
    of Israel, 976–981, 988; in North
    Africa, 999; in South America,
    1002, 1004; in the USSR, 1026,
    1036
Jihad [djih-hahd], 180
Jinnah [jihn-ah], Muhammed Ali,
    879–880, 965–966, 974
Joan of Arc, 324, 325
Johannesburg, 997
John II (Portugal), 405
John VI (Portugal), 725
John XII, Pope, 278
John (England), 274, 275–276, 277
John Albert (Poland), 341
John of Leiden, 387
John of Salisbury, 300, 301–302
John of the Cross, 435
John Paul II, Pope, 1013
Johnson, Lyndon B., 955, 956, 1032,
    1038–1039
Johnson, Samuel, 610, 614, 702, 733
John "the Baptist," 162
Joint-stock companies, 421–422
Joinville, Jean de [zhahn dur
    zhwahn-veel], 308
Jolson, Al, 796
Jones, Sir William, 658
Jonson, Ben, 561
Jordan, 977, 980, 982, 987, 988
Joseph, 22, 26
Joseph II (Austria), 605–606, 607, 609
Journal des dames, 601
Joyce, James, 852, 904
Juarez, Benito [bay-nee-toh
    hwah-rays], 1012
Judah [joo-dah], 27, 28
Judah ha-Levi, 310
Judaism, 155, 156, 165, 166;
    Covenant, 158; Torah, 158–159;
    Prophets, 159, 160, 162; role of
    Jerusalem, 159–161; Talmud,
    161–162; role of women, 167, 168;
    Haskalah movement, 610;
    Hasidism, 610; Reform movement,
    610; Reconstructionist movement,
    610; Conservative movement, 610;
    Orthodox tradition, 610
Judas Maccabaeus [mak-ah-bee-uhs],
    116
Judea [joo-dee-uh], 134
Jugurtha [joo-gur-thuh], 128
Julia Domna, 139
Juliana of Norwich, 561
Julian, "the Apostate," 144
Julio-Claudians, 134

Julius II, Pope, 335, 338–339, 346,
    359, 376, 378
Jumna River, 466
June Days (1848), 742
Jung [yoong], Carl, 832
Junkers [yoong-kers], 541, 756
Jurchen [joor-chehn], 251, 252
Justice and Liberty, 911–912
Justin, 174
Justinian, 173, 174–175, 176
Jutes [jootz], 265
Juvenal [joo-vuh-nuhl], 135

Kaaba [kah-buh], 178, 180
Kabir [kah-beer], 188, 642
Kabir of Banaras, 227, 228
Kabuki, 687
Kabul [kah-bool], 663, 974
Kádár, János [yah-nohsh kah-dahr],
    1028
Kaesong [kye-song], 256
Kafka, Franz, 852
Kaifeng [kye-fung], 244, 248, 251
Kalibangan, 36, 38
Kalidasa [kah-lee-dah-suh], 51, 514
Kalingas [kah-lihng-gahs], 46
Kalischer, Zevi-Hirsch, 764
Kamakura [kah-mah-koor-uh]
    shogunate, 260–261
Kamasutra, 511
Kamenev [kah-mihn-yif], Lev, 864,
    870, 871, 917
Kamikaze attacks, 933
Kampuchea. See Cambodia
Kandinsky, Wassily, 853, 859
Kandy [kan-dih], 50, 651
Kang Hsi (Kang Xi), 413, 670, 673,
    675
Kano, 201
Kansu (Gansu) [kan-soo], 247
Kant [kahnt], Immanuel, 597, 608,
    625, 732–733
Kappel [kahp-el], battle of, 383
Kapp Putsch, 892
Karacaoglan, 465
Karachi [kuh-rah-chee], 811, 966,
    974
Karanovo, 6
Karelia (Karelian Peninsula), 535
Karim Khan, 666–667
Karlowitz [kahr-loh-vitz], Treaty of,
    466, 539
Karma, 147, 148, 149, 150, 151
Karnak [kahr-nak], 23
Kashmir, 657, 663, 968
Kasim, Abul, 301
Kassites, 17, 41
Katanga, 994
Katip-elebi (Mustafa ibn Abdullah),
    465
Katz, Isabella, 929–930
Kaunitz [kow-nihts], Prince Wenzel
    von, 582
Kautilya [kow-tihl-yah], 43
Kawasaki, 942
Kay, John, 699
Keats, John, 731
Kellogg-Briand Pact, 848

Kemal Atatürk [keh-*mahl*
ah-tah-*turk*], Mustapha, 842,
882–883

Kempis, Thomas à, 330

Kennedy, John F., 955, 1032, 1036,
1049

Kenya [*ken*-yah, *keen*-yah], 200, 804,
842, 993, 995–996

Kenyatta [ken-*yah*-tuh], Jomo, 992,
995–996

Kepler, Johannes, 550–551, 552

Kerensky [kuh-*ren*-skee], Alexander,
864, 865

K'e t'ou (kowtow), 484, 678

Keynes [kaynz], John Maynard, 846

Khalji, Ala-ud-Din, 225–226

Kharijites, 184

Khartoum [kahr-*toom*], massacre at,
804

Khmelnitsky [hmil-*nyeet*-ski], Bogdan,
451

Khmer Rouge [kmehr rooj], 957–958

Khmers [kmehrz], 234, 235–236

Khoikhoi [koi-koi], 201, 209, 802

Khomeini [koh-*may*-nee], Ayatollah
Ruhollah, 985, 986–987, 1040

Khorsabad [*kohr*-sah-bahd], 18

Khrushchev, Nikita [niyh-*kee*-tuh
kroos-choff], 949, 1027–1028, 1031,
1036, 1037, 1039

Kibbutz, 882

Kiefer, Anselm, 860

Kiel [keel] mutiny, 845

Kierkegaard, Søren [*sur*-en
kyair-kuhgahr], 852

Kiev [*kee*-eff], 267, 288–289

Kikuyu [kee-*koo*-yoo], 511

Kilwa, 207–208

Kim il Sung, 953, 954

King, Martin Luther, Jr., 797,
1031–1032, 1033, 1048

King William's War, 532

Kipling, Rudyard, 660, 801

Kirov, Sergei [syir-*gay kee*-ruff], 917

Kissinger, Henry, 980

Kitchener, Horatio, 804

Klee [klay], Paul, 853

Kleist [klyest], Heinrich von, 731

Knesset, 979

Knights Hospitalers, 284

Knights of the Garter, 504

Knights Templars, 278, 284

Knossos [*nahs*-uhs], 77, 78, 79

Knox, John, 394, 438, 441

Koch, Robert, 709

Koguryo, 255

Kohl, Helmut, 1030

Kolikovo, battle of, 332

Kollontai [ko-lon-*tye*], Alexandra,
868–869, 917

Königgrätz [*ke*-nich-grets], battle of,
757

Königsberg [*ke*-nichs-berk], 539

Konoye [koh-*noh*-yee], Prince, 925

Koran, 179–180, 184, 198

Korea, 67, 241, 242, 247, 252, 253,
262, 497, 684, 821, 822, 823;
Buddhism in, 150, 152;

Neo-Confucianism in, 154; Paekche,
Silla, and Koguryo kingdoms,
255–256; Yi dynasty, 256–257;
influence on Japan, 258, 260–261;
after World War II, 952–954, 960

Korean War, 953–954

Kornilov, Lavr [*lah*-ver ker-*nyee*-luff],
864

Koryo, 256

Kossuth [koh-*sooth*], Louis, 740, 741

Kremlin, 332, 1038

Krishna, 147

Kristallnacht, 915

Kristeller, Paul, 364

Kronstadt [*krohn*-shtaht] mutiny, 869

Kropotkin [kroh-*pot*-kin], Peter, 788

Kruger [*kroo*-ger], Paul, 804, 805–806

Krupp, Alfred, 771

Krupskaya, Nadhezhda, 870

Kuan Yin, 167

Kubilai [*koo*-blye] Khan, 253, 260,
289

Kulaks, 870

Kulischiov, Anna, 868

Kulturkampf [kool-*toor*-kahmpf],
779–780

Kun [koon], Béla, 871, 906

Kuomintang [*kwoh*-min-tang]
(Guomindang), 871, 873, 874–876,
900, 925–927, 943, 945, 952

Kuprili [koo-pree-*lee*], Muhammad,
466

Kurds, 983

Kushans, 47

Kuwait, 983

Kweichou (Guizhou) [*kway*-chow;
gway-joh], 67, 673

Kyoto [*kyoh*-toh], 258, 259, 260, 682,
683, 684, 685, 937

Kyushu [*kyoo*-shoo], 684

Laborers, Statute of, 322

Labour party (Britain), 790, 904,
1029, 1030

Labour party (Israel), 978, 979

Labrador, 406

Laconia, 92

Lady Chatterley's Lover (Lawrence),
852

Lafayette [lah-fay-*et*], Marquis de,
619, 623, 735

Lafitte [la-*feet*], Jacques, 734, 735

Lagash [*lay*-gash], 14, 17

Lagos [*lah*-gohs], 994; battle of, 582

Lahore, 227, 650, 974

Lake Chad, 804

Lamarck, Jean-Baptiste, 786

Lamartine [lah-mar-*teen*], Alphonse
de, 746

Lamber, Juliette, 748

La Mettrie [la me-tree], Julian, 598

Lancashire, 711

Lancaster, house of, 333

Landtag (Prussia), 755–756

Land tenure (Europe), 401–402

Langland, William, 329

Langton, Stephen, 275

Languedoc [lahn-dok], risings in, 323

Laos [*lah*-ohs], 232, 236, 816;
Buddhism in, 151; after World War
II, 955, 956, 957–958

Lao-tze (Laozi) [laoh-dzuh], 154–155

Laplace [lah-*plahs*], Pierre Simon de,
565

La Rochelle [lah roh-*shell*], 443

La Salle, Sieur de [syur duh lah
sahl], 1017

Las Casas, Bartolomé de
[bahr-toh-loh-*may* day lahs
kah-sahs], 416

Las Navas de Tolosa [lahs *nah*-vahs
day toh-*loh*-sah], battle of, 286

Lassalle, Ferdinand, 789

Last Judgment: in Zoroastrianism,
157; in Islam, 179

Lateran Councils: Third, 309; Fourth,
296, 309; Fifth, 390

Lateran Pacts (1929), 909

Latifundia (estates)
[lad-uh-*fun*-dih-uh], 128, 129, 132

Latimer, Hugh, 394

Latin Kingdom of Constantinople,
285, 286

Latin language, 141

Latin League, 124

Latins, 122, 124

Latvia, 866, 906, 922, 1026

Laud [lawd], William, 447–448

La Venta, 209, 210

Law, John, 580–581, 702

Law: Roman, 121; in medieval
Europe, 300–301; Russian, 332, 534,
537; Ottoman, 459–460; and women
in early modern Europe, 511; Code
Napoleon, 635, 637; in British
India, 663–664

Lawrence, D. H., 852

Lawrence, T. E., 842, 881

League of Augsburg, 531

League of Nations, 845, 847–848, 918,
919, 982

League of the Three Emperors, 837

League of Venice, 334

Lebanon, 842, 881–882, 977, 980, 982;
civil war, 988

Lebensraum, 928

Le Bon, Gustav, 836

Le Chapelier [luh shah-peh-*lyay*] law,
626

Lechfeld [*lek*-felt], battle of, 278

Ledru-Rollin [le-*drew* roh-*lahn*],
Alexandre, 747

Legalism, 65–67

Lehar [*le*-hahr, *lay*-hahr], Franz, 760

Leibniz [*liep*-nitz], Gottfried Wilhelm
von, 555, 614, 672

Leignitz, battle of, 582

Leipzig, 639

Lend-Lease Program, 925

Lenin (Vladimir Ilyich Ulyanov), 801,
864–867, 869–870, 872

Leo I, Pope, 293

Leo III (Byzantium), 189

Leo III, Pope, 266

Leo IX, Pope, 278

Leo X, Pope, 354, 378, 379

Leo XIII, Pope, 780
Leon [lay-*ohn*], 287
Leonidas [lee-*on*-uh-duhs], 88
Leopold I (Holy Roman Empire), 531, 538, 539, 562
Leopold II (Austria), 625
Leopold II (Belgium), 303
Lepanto [lay-*pahn*-tok], battle of, 436, 458
Lermontov [*lyair*-mun-toff], Mikhail, 727
Lesbos, 84
Lesseps [luh-*seps*], Ferdinand de, 747
Lessing, Gotthold Ephraim, 609, 614, 731
Letters of Obscure Men (Hutten and Rubeanus), 376
Lettow-Vorbeck [*let*-oh *fohr*-bek], Paul von, 842
Leucippus [loo-*sip*-uhs], 547
Leuctra [*look*-trah], battle of, 106
Leuthen, battle of, 582
Levellers, 449
Leviathan [luh-*vye*-uh-thuhn] (Hobbes), 557, 558
Lewis, Wyndham, 836
Lewis and Clark expedition, 1018
Liberalism, 728, 776–782, 783
Liberal party (Britain), 777, 784
Liberal party (Canada), 1035
Liberation theology, 1013
Liberia, 803
Li Bing [lee bihng], 66
Libon of Elis, 98
Libya, 201, 839, 924, 983, 987, 988, 999–1000, 1040
Licinius [lih-*sihn*-ee-uhs], 165
Liebknecht [*leep*-k'nekt], Karl, 892, 895
Liebknecht, Wilhelm, 789
Liège [lee-*ayzh*], 272, 402, 694
Likud coalition, 979
Liliuokalani [lee-*lee*-oo-oh-kah-*lah*-nee] (Hawaii), 825
Lima [*lee*-mah], Peru, 416, 589
Linacre, Thomas, 351
Lincoln, Abraham, 766
Lindbergh, Anne Morrow, 900
Lindisfarne, 267
Linear A (script), 79
Linear B (script), 79
Linguet, Simon-Henri, 600
Li Po (Li Bo), 241, 244
Lippmann, Walter, 850
Lisbon, 286, 408
Li Ssu [lee *soo*], 43, 65, 66
List, Friedrich, 721
Lister, Joseph, 709
Liszt, Franz, 731
Literacy, 198; in Europe, 356, 365, 516, 601, 793–794; in Asia, 513–514, 793–794, 940, 951, 973, 975; in Latin America, 1012, 1014
Literature: early Greek, 80–81, 83–85; classical Roman, 133–134, 135, 140–141; Islamic, 187–188; Chinese, 241–242, 250–251, 488–492, 677;

Japanese, 259–260, 261, 262, 687; medieval European, 305–308; European Renaissance, 347–348, 351, 352; Ottoman, 465; early modern European, 435, 561; Romantic, 731–732; modern Western, 833, 834, 835–836, 852; South American, 1013
Lithuania, 290, 332, 341; in the twentieth century, 866, 906, 922, 1026
"Little Entente," 848
Little Ice Age, 217, 320
Little Red Book (Mao Tse-tung), 947, 948
Li Tzu-ch'eng (Li zi-cheng), 498, 499
Liubatovich, Olga, 868
Liu Hsiao-chi (Liu Xiaoqi), 945, 948, 949, 950
Liu Pang (Liu Bang) [lyoo bahng], 66, 70, 74
Liverpool, 575–577
Liverpool, Lord, 726
Livingstone, David, 803, 806
Livonia, 535
Livy, 127, 134
Lloyd George, David, 845, 846, 890
Locarno Treaties, 848, 919
Locke, Anne, 352
Locke, John, 542, 558–559, 595, 728
Lodis, 226–227, 466
Logical Empiricism, 852
Lollards, 327, 387
Lombard, Peter, 299, 312
Lombard League, 280
Lombards, 188, 265, 294
Lombardy, 280, 751, 753
Londinium (Roman London), 139
London, 272, 276, 277, 710, 772; late Stuart and Hanoverian, 543–544; Treaty of (1915), 890
London Workingmen's Association, 737
Long Depression, 773, 800
Long March, 874
Lope de Vega [*loh*-pay day *bay*-gah], 435, 561
Lord Shang, 65–66
Lord's Supper, 165
Lorrain [loh-*rehn*], Claude, 613
Lorraine [loh-*rehn*], 278, 334, 613, 759, 846
Lothal, 38, 40
Louis VII (France), 273, 274, 284
Louis IX (France), 277–278, 281, 298, 308, 309
Louis XI (France), 334, 335
Louis XII (France), 335, 338
Louis XIII (France), 443, 445
Louis XIV (France), 443, 525–533, 539, 562, 594, 1017
Louis XV (France), 580, 617, 699
Louis XVI (France), 617–618, 619, 623–627 *passim*
Louis XVIII (France), 640, 727
Louise of Savoy, 341
Louisiana, 580, 585
Louisiana Purchase, 586, 766, 1018

Louis-Philippe [loo-*ee* fee-*leep*] (France), 735, 737, 740
Lovett, William, 737
Lowell, Percival, 1018
Loyang [loh-yahng], 61, 71, 73, 74, 241, 252
Loyola, Ignatius of, 391–392, 434
Luanda, 409
Lübeck, 297, 324
Lublin, 395
Lucca, 338
Lucknow, 650, 664
Lucretius [loo-*kree*-shuhs], 141
Luddites, 705, 706
Ludendorff, Erich, 841, 845, 894
Luder, Peter, 351
Ludovico il Moro. *See* Sforza, Ludovico
Lüger, Karl, 764, 836, 893–894
Lu Hsun (Lu Xun), 874, 876
Lumumba, Patrice, 992, 1036
Lunéville [loo-nay-*veel*], Treaty of, 636
Lung Shan culture, 57–58, 74, 194
Lusitania, sinking of, 844
Luther, Martin, 167, 378–382, 384, 393, 395, 398, 704, 793
Lutheranism, 378–382, 387
Lützen [*lurt*-suhn], battle of, 442
Luxembourg, 531, 931, 1040
Luxemburg, Rosa, 789, 791, 892, 895
Lvov [lyuh-*voff*], Prince Georgi, 863, 864
Lycurgus [lye-*kur*-guhs], 93
Lydia, 32, 87, 116, 122
Lydians, 31
Lyell, Sir Charles, 786
Lyons [lee-*ohn*], 629
Lysippus [lye-*sihp*-uhs], 100

Macao [muh-*kow*], 410, 411
MacArthur, Douglas, 937, 938, 939, 953
Macartney, Viscount, 678, 679
Macaulay, Catherine, 612
Macaulay, Thomas Babington, 662, 663
Maccabees, revolt of, 128
McCarthy, Eugene, 1039
McCarthy, Joseph R., 1025
MacDonald, Ramsay, 904
Macedonia [mass-uh-*dohn*-yah] (Macedon), 127, 128; rule of Philip, 106–107; age of Alexander the Great, 107–109; Hellenistic period, 109–111
Machiavelli, Niccolò [nee-koh-*loh* mah-kyah-*vell*-ee], 2, 337, 352–355, 378
Machismo, 1014–1015
Machu Picchu [*ma*-choo *peek*-choo], 217, 416
McKinley, William, 788, 826
Madagascar, 804
Madeira [muh-*deer*-uh], 408
Maderna (Maderno), Carlo, 563
Madero, Francisco, 1012
Madison, James, 586
Madras [muh-*drahs*], 453, 582, 652, 653, 655, 657, 811

Madrid, 433–434
Madurai [*mahd*-oo-rye], 48, 229, 231
Magadha [*mahg*-uh-dah], kingdom of, 44
Magdeburg, 382, 539
Magellan [muh-*jel*-uhn], Ferdinand, 238, 406, 429
Magellan, Straits of, 406
Magic, 155, 322
Maginot [*mahzh*-ih-noh] Line, 923
Magna Carta, 276, 277
Magnetic compass, 185, 243, 251
Magritte [ma-*greet*], René, 834
Magyars [*mag*-yahrz], 191, 267, 278, 538, 539
Mahabharata [mah-*hah-bah*-rah-tah], 41, 42, 233
Maharashtra, 224, 657, 660, 811
Mahayana [mah-huh-*yah*-nuh] Buddhism, 150–152
Mahdali [mah-*dah*-lee] dynasty, 207–208
Mahgreb, 994
Mahler, Gustav, 760
Mahmud [mah-*mood*] of Ghazni [*gahz*-nee], 222, 224
Mahrathas [muh-*rah*-tehz], 224
Maimonides [mye-*mon*-ih-deez] (Moses ben Maimon), 300, 301, 310
Maine [mayn], France, 274, 334
Maine, New England, 454
Maintenon [man-teh-*nohn*], Madame de, 529–530
Mainz [myentz], 272
Maistre, Joseph de [zhoh-*zef* duh *mess*-truh], 601, 721
Majapahit [mah-jah-*pah*-heet], 237–238
Malabar coast, 409
Malacca [mah-*lak*-ah], 232, 237–238, 409, 411; Straits of, 409
Malaka, Tan, 871
Malatesta, Errico, 788
Malaya: early history, 230, 232, 233–234, 235, 237; colonial rule, 814, 816, 817; in World War II, 927–928; after World War II, 954, 958
Malaysia, 958, 960
Mali [*mah*-lee], 202–206, 409, 994
Mallarmé, Stéphane, 833
Malleus Maleficarum, 395, 396
Malpighi [mahl-*pee*-gee], Marcello, 552
Malplaquet [mahl-plah-*kay*], battle of, 533
Malta, 724
Malthus [*mahl*-thuhs], Thomas, 693, 709, 786
Mameluke [*mahm*-luk] dynasty, 184, 224
Manchester, 711–714
Manchu conquest, 498–499, 670–673, 675–678
Manchukuo [mahn-*choo*-kwoh], 918
Manchuria: early history, 67, 242, 247, 251, 254; and the Ming dynasty, 483; and early Manchu rule, 498, 671, 675; in the nineteenth and early twentieth centuries, 819, 821, 822, 823, 876; in World War II, 918, 925, 933; after World War II, 945
Manda, 207
"Mandate of Heaven," 60, 66, 69, 153, 481, 498, 677, 872
Mandates (League of Nations), 846, 847, 862, 881–882, 982
Mandela, Nelson, 997–998
Mandela, Winnie, 997–998
Mandeville [*man*-de-vihl], Bernard de, 600
Manegold of Lautenbach, 301
Manet [ma-*nay*], Edouard, 786
Manetho [*mahn*-e-thoh], 19
Manhattan Project, 933
"Manifest Destiny," 586
Manila [muh-*nihl*-uh], 408, 571, 583, 817, 961
Manila galleon, 408
Manley, Mary de la Riviere, 612
Mann [mahn], Thomas, 852
Mannerists, 857
Manors, 269
Mansa Musa [*moo*-sah], 206
Mantinea [man-tih-*nee*-uh], 111
Manucci, Niccolò [nee-koh-*loh* mah-*noo*-chee], 413, 479
Manutius, Aldus [*ahl*-duhs mah-*noo*-shee-uhs], 355
Manzikert [*man*-zih-kurt], battle of, 184, 190, 282
Maori [*mah*-oh-ree], 709, 824, 825
Mao Tse-tung [mou dzuh-*doong*] (Mao Zedong), 874, 936, 937, 943, 945–950, 959
Mapping, 404, 426–430, 1016–1020
Marat [mah-*rah*], Jean-Paul, 626, 628
Maratha Confederacy, 474, 649
Marathas, 473, 474–475, 649–650, 652, 657, 658
Marathon, battle of, 88
Marburg, 381, 442
Marchand [mar-*shahn*], Jean-Baptiste, 804
March on Rome (1922), 890, 891–892
Marcion [*mahr*-shuhn], 165
Marconi [mahr-*koh*-nee], Guglielmo, 717, 796
Marcos, Ferdinand, 954, 959
Marcos, Imelda, 959
Marcus Aurelius [*mahr*-kuhs ah-*ree*-lee-uhs], 119, 135
Marengo, battle of, 636
Margaret of Anjou, 333
Margaret of Austria, 341
Margaret of Parma, 436–437, 440
Marguerite d'Angoulême [dahn-goo-*lem*], 351
Marguerite of Navarre, 561
Marguerite of Valois [vahl-*wah*], 439
Marianas, 824, 825, 826
Marian exiles, 394
Maria Theresa (Austria), 581–582, 605–606, 609
Marie Antoinette, 627
Marie-Louise (Austria), 638
Marie of Champagne, 274, 307
Marie-Therese [ma-*ree*-tay-*rez*] (France), 530
Marinetti, Filippo T., 835
Marius [*mahr*-ee-uhs], 129
Marivaux [ma-ree-voh], Pierre de, 607
Marlborough, John Churchill, Duke of, 533
Marlowe, Christopher, 730
Marmora, Sea of, 175
Marne, battles of, 840, 845
Maronite Christians, 882
Marquez [*mahr*-kes], Gabriel Garcia, 1013
Marriage: in classical Athens, 91; in classical Rome, 133, 140; view of Apostle Paul, 164; Augustine's view, 167; in Islam, 180; Aztec, 216; in medieval Europe, 312; in Anabaptist Münster, 387; in early modern Europe, 506; in early modern Asia, 507–508; among the Incas, 508; in Africa, 508; Enlightenment views, 612; in modern Europe, 774, 775; in British India, 812
Marseilles [mahr-*say*], 270, 272
Marshall, George C., 943, 1024, 1025
Marshall Islands, 426, 826
Marshall Plan, 1024, 1026, 1028–1029
Marsiglio [mahr-*seel*-yoh] of Padua, 326
Martin V, Pope, 326, 335
Martineau [*mahr*-tih-noh], Harriet, 613, 708
Martines, Lauro, 364
Martini, Martino, 1018
Martinique [mahr-tih-*neek*], 573
Marx, Karl, 695, 705, 728, 738–739, 788
Mary, Virgin, 167, 311, 356, 369
Mary I (England), 390, 393–394, 432, 440
Mary II (England), 532, 542, 543
Maryland, 454
Mary of Burgundy, 340
Mary of Guise, 440
Mary of Hungary, 361
Mary Stuart, 438, 440
Masaccio [mah-*saht*-choh], 356–357
Masai [mah-*sye*], 511
Masaryk [*mah*-sah-rik], Tomáš, 907
Massachusetts, 454, 572, 585, 586
Massachusetts Bay Company, 422, 569
Masurian [mah-*zur*-ih-ahn] Lakes, battle of, 841
Materialists, 103
Mathematics, 54, 58; Pythagoras, 103–104; Hellenistic, 114–115; Islamic, 185; in the Scientific Revolution, 551
Mathiez, Albert, 633
Matisse, Henri, 834

Matteotti, Giacomo [*jaw*-ko-moh mah-tay-*oh*-tee], 891, 892
Matthias I Corvinus, 341
Mau Mau, 996
Maupeou [moh-*poo*], René Charles de, 580, 617
Maurice of Nassau, 445
Mauritania, 994
Mauritius [mo-*rish*-uhs], 724
Maurras [moh-ra], Charles, 836, 900
Maurya dynasty, 194
Mauryan [*mow*-ree-uhn] India, 42–47, 112
Maximian [mak-*sihm*-ee-uhn], 143
Maximilian [mak-sih-*mill*-yuhn], 334, 338, 376, 1012
Mayakovsky, Vladimir, 836
Mayans, 197–198, 210, 211–215
May Fourth Movement, 873–874
Mazarin [mah-zah-*ranh*], Giulio, Cardinal, 443–444, 526
Mazzini, Giuseppe [joo-*zep*-pay mah-*tsee*-nee], 735, 741, 751, 753, 767
Mecca, 178, 179, 180, 184, 185, 205
Medea (Euripides), 117
Medes [meedz], 18, 31, 32
Medici [*mehd*-ih-chee, *may*-dee-chee], Catherine de', 439, 440
Medici, Cosimo [*koh*-zee-moh] de', 338, 344, 349
Medici, Lorenzo [loh-*rehn*-tsoh] "the Magnificent," 338, 355
Medici, Marie de', 443
Medici, Piero de', 338, 353
Medici family, 338, 344, 354, 357, 402, 403
Medicine: in Mesopotamia, 17; in ancient India, 42, 54; Hellenistic, 115; Chinese, 155, 489; Islamic, 186; medieval European, 302; in the Scientific Revolution, 552; in the Industrial Revolution, 709
Medina [mih-*dee*-nah] (Yath'rib), 179
Medina Sidonia, duke of, 438
Meditations (Marcus Aurelius), 119
Mediterranean, 267
Medreses, 462, 465, 516
Megasthenes [mee-*gas*-thee-neez], 44, 45, 46, 112
Megiddo [me-*gihd*-oh], 28
Mehmet II, "the Conqueror," 457–458, 459, 461, 462, 465
Meiji [*may*-jee] Restoration, 690, 821–822
Mein Kampf (Hitler), 894, 895, 912, 928
Mekong [mee-kong] Delta, 236
Melanchthon [muh-*langk*-thuhn], Philip, 380
Melanesia, 824, 825–826
Melbourne, 824
Meleager [mel-ee-*ay*-jer], 84
Mencius [*men*-shuhs], 65, 152–153, 154
Mendelssohn, Moses, 610
Mendelssohn-Bartholdy, Felix, 731
Mendicant orders, 295

Menelik, 803
Mengele, Josef, 930
Mennonites, 387
Mensheviks, 864, 869
Mentuhotep, 22
Mercator, Gerardus (Gerhard), 429–430, 552, 1016
Merchant Capitalism, 420–422, 571–572, 573
Merchants (medieval European), 272
Merici [meh-*ree*-chee], Angela, 390
Meroë [*mehr*-oh-ee], 201
Merovingian [mehr-uh-*vin*-jee-uhn] dynasty, 265
Mersenne [mer-sen], Marin, 555
Mesoamerica: Olmecs, 209–210; Teotihuacán, 210–211; Mayans, 211–215; Aztecs, 215–217
Mesopotamia: birth of civilization in, 8–9; ancient civilization in, 12–18; religion of, 14–16, 314; Akkadian rule in, 16–17; writing in, 193
Messana, 126
Mesta [*may*-stah], 333
Mestizos, 418–419
Metals: discovery of, 8; copper, 11, 12, 28, 31, 58, 202, 402, 577; bronze, 11, 12, 28, 30, 57, 58, 60, 77, 201, 258; iron (in the ancient world), 11, 28, 29, 30, 31, 42, 60, 63, 81, 85; iron (in the Middle Ages), 122, 249, 258, 330; iron (in early Africa), 201, 208; iron (in the early modern era), 402, 577; iron (in modern industry), 694, 700, 716, 769, 770, 802, 823, 945; steel, 42, 249, 694, 716–717, 769–770, 811, 945; tin, 58, 816; lead, 58; zinc, 58; brass, 602; gold, 570–571, 715, 716; silver, 571, 674
Metalworking, 8, 12, 57, 77, 133, 201, 208, 218, 270
Metaphysics (Aristotle), 106
Metaxas [meh-tah-*ksahs*], John, 907
Methodists, 607
Methodius [mee-*thod*-ih-uhs], 190
Metics [*meh*-tiks], 92
Metternich [*meht*-ur-nik], Prince Klemens von, 639, 721–727 *passim*, 734, 740
Mexican-American War, 766
Mexico, 211, 415, 570, 571, 572, 589, 590. *See also* Mesoamerica: in the twentieth century, 984, 1012–1013, 1014; University of, 415
Mexico City, 415, 416, 1000, 1012, 1014
Michael II, 188
Michael VII, 282
Michelangelo [mee-kel-*ahn*-jeh-loh] Buonarroti, 352, 356, 359–360, 361, 857
Michelet [*meesh*-le], Jules, 633, 733, 749
Mickiewicz [meets-*kye*-veech], Adam, 721
Micronesia, 824, 825–826
Middleton, Thomas, 561

Midway Island, battle of, 930, 932–933
Mies Van der Rohe [*mee*-uhs vahn der *roh*-uh], Ludwig, 834
Mikveh Yisrael, 764
Milan [mih-*lahn*], 272, 334–346 *passim*, 402, 432, 740, 751
Miletus [mye-*lee*-tuhs], 83, 88
Mill, John Stuart, 782–783
Millets, 460
Miltiades [mihl-*tye*-ah-deez], 88
Milton, John, 561, 612
Milvian Bridge, battle of, 143
Minamoto clan, 260
Mindanao, 238
Ming dynasty, 480–498 *passim*
Mining, 330, 402, 416, 570–571, 705, 715
Minnesingers [*mihn*-ih-sing-uhrs], 307
Minoans [mih-*noh*-uhnz], 22, 79–80, 196
Minorca [mihn-*ohr*-kuh], 533, 582, 585
Minos [*mye*-nahs], 78
Mirabeau, Count Honoré [oh-no-*ray* mee-rah-*boh*], 626, 628
Miracle plays, 308
Miró, Joan [zhou-*ahn* mee-*roh*], 834
Miserables, Les [lay mee-zay-*rabl*] (Hugo), 787
Missionaries: medieval, 295; early modern, 391, 411–412, 413, 414, 419, 450; modern, 662, 686, 795, 801, 803, 807, 812, 818–819, 820–821, 824–825
Mississippi Bubble, 580
Mississippi River, 572
Mistral [mees-*trahl*], Gabriela, 1013
Mithraism, 157–158
Mixtecs, 198
Mnesicles [*nes*-ih-kleez], 100
Mobutu, Joseph, 994
Modena, University of, 393
Moderate Realists, 299–300
Mohács [mah-*hahch*], battle of, 341, 382
Mohenjo Daro [moh-*hen*-joh *dahr*-oh], 36, 38, 658
Moi, Daniel arap, 995
Moksha [*mok*-shuh], 148, 149, 315
Moldavia, 761, 762
Molière [moh-*lyair*] (Jean-Baptiste Poquelin), 561
Molotov, Vyacheslav [vyih-cheh-*slaff moh*-luh-toff], 1027
Moltke [*molt*-keh], Helmuth von, 758, 840
Moluccas, 408, 410, 816
Mombasa, 409
Monasteries, dissolution of, 380, 389
Monasticism, 151, 152, 166, 167, 188, 293, 294–295
Mondino de' Luzzi, 301
Mondrian [*mon*-dree-ahn], Piet, 853
Monet [moh-*nay*], Claude, 787, 833
Mongolia, 71, 241, 242, 247, 413, 483, 675, 945

Mongols, 68, 184, 225, 226, 234, 237, 256, 260–261, 486; conquest of China, 252–253; Yuan dynasty, 253; conquest of Russia, 288–290
Monotheism, 23, 25, 28, 116, 149, 159, 178, 179
Monroe Doctrine, 1002
Mons, 234
Montagnards, 628
Montagu, Mary Wortley, 612
Montaigne [mon-*tayn*], Michel de, 559
Monte Cassino [*mohn*-tay kahs-*see*-noh], 293
Montenegro [mon-te-*neh*-groh], 762–763, 837, 839
Montesquieu [mohn-tes-*kyoo*], Baron de, 600, 601, 609, 612
Monteverdi [mohn-tay-*vare*-day], Claudio, 562
Montezuma II [mahn-teh-*soo*-mah], 216, 217, 415
Montpellier [mon-peh-*lyay*], University of, 301
Montreal, 582, 1035
Moore, Henry, 859
Moors, 265, 286
Moravia [muh-*ray*-vee-uh], 289, 341, 538
Moravian Brethren, 607
More, Hannah, 612
More, Sir Thomas, 351, 376, 378, 389
Morelly, Abbé, 600
Morgan, John Pierpont, 771
Moriscos, 333, 435
Morocco, 202, 206, 762, 838, 839, 983, 999
Morse, Samuel F. B., 717, 795
Mosaics, 172, 175, 181, 191, 369
Moscow, 290, 331, 332, 639, 774, 1038; University of, 1038
Moses, 26, 27, 28, 158, 162, 179
Moshav, 882
Mosley, Sir Oswald, 900
Mossadegh [*moh*-sa-dek], Muhammad, 985
Mo-tzu (Mozi) [moh-*dzu*], 62
Mountbatten, Louis, 927, 966
Mozambique [moh-zuhm-*beek*], 409, 803
Mozarabs, 287
Mozart, Wolfgang Amadeus, 601, 614, 732, 760
Mozzoni [mots-*soh*-nee], Ann Maria, 783
Muawiya [moo-*ah*-wee-ah], 181, 184
Mubarak, Hosni, 983
Muftis, 460
Mughal (Mogul) [*moh*-guhl] dynasty: founding, 227, 466; from Akbar to Aurangzeb, 467–475; decline, 476–477, 649–653
Muhammad (Mohammed), 178–179, 180, 181, 184, 185
Muhammad Reza Pahlavi, 985–986, 1040
Muhammad Shah, 665
Mujib, Sheikh (Mujibur Rahman), 973
Mukden [*mook*-den], 498, 823

Mummification, 18
Munch [mungk], Edvard, 859
Munich [*myoo*-nik], 297, 845, 894
Munich Conference, 921
Munich *Putsch*, 894
Münster [*murn*-ster] (Germany), Kingdom of, 386–387
Müntzer [*meivn*-tser], Thomas, 387
Murasaki [moor-uh-*sah*-kee], Lady, 259–260, 514
Murat II, 465
Murmansk, 867
Muscovy, 331–332
Muscovy Company, 419
Music: in the Reformation, 398; baroque, 562, 614; Neoclassical, 614, 732; Romantic, 732; in Vienna, 760; Latin American, 1013–1014
Muslim League, 879, 880, 965–966
Mussolini [moos-soh-*lee*-nee], Benito, 888–892, 909–912, 918–919, 921–923, 931, 932
Mustafa, Kara, 531
Mycenae [mye-*see*-nee], 79–80
Mycenaeans, 41, 79–80, 196
Mysore, 649, 657
"Mystery cults," 116, 315
Mystery plays, 307–308
Mysticism, 147, 180, 225, 261, 310, 329–330, 349, 387, 435, 458, 503

Nabatea [nab-ah-*tee*-uh], 178
Nabateans, 196
Nadir Shah [*nah*-dur shah], 474, 650, 665–666
Nagasaki [nah-gah-*sah*-kee], 409, 414, 453, 686, 687, 933, 937
Naguib [*nah*-geeb], Muhammad, 982
Nagy, Imre [*im*-reh nazh], 1028
Nanak [*nah*-nuk], 473
Nan Chao [nahn chow], 253
Nanking (Nanjing), 241, 481, 483, 682, 819, 874–876, 925; Treaty of, 682, 817
Nantes [nahnt], Edict of, 440, 443, 531
Naples, 272, 334, 335–336, 341, 432, 445, 725, 754; University of, 298
Napoleon III, 747–749, 753, 757, 758, 788, 1012
Napoleonic wars, 636–640
Nara Period, 258–259
Naramsin [nah-rahm-*sin*], 17
Narva, battle of, 535
Naseby, battle of, 448
Nasrid dynasty, 287
Nasser, Gamal Abdel, 980, 981–982, 1042
Natal [nuh-*tahl*], 806
Nathan the Wise (Lessing), 609
National American Woman Suffrage Association, 783
National Assembly (France), 620–626 *passim*
National Convention (France), 626–628, 631
"National Fronts," 1026–1027

Nationalism: in the eighteenth century, 638, 687, 720–721, 751; in the nineteenth century, 724, 745–746, 767; in the twentieth century, 836, 906–907, 981–982
Nationalist party (Germany), 898
National Labor Front, 912
National Organization for Women, 1012
National Society for Women's Suffrage, 783
National Woman Suffrage Association, 783
NATO. *See* North Atlantic Treaty Organization
Naucratis [*nah*-krah-tihs], 85
Navarino [nah-vah-*ree*-noh], battle of, 726
Navarre [nuh-*vahr*], 286, 433
Navigation Acts (1651, 1660), 573, 700
Nazi party, 892–899 *passim*
Neander River, 5
Neanderthal culture, 5, 314
Nebuchadnezzar [neb-uk-uhd-*nez*-uhr], 18
Necker, Jacques, 617, 619, 620
Nefertiti [nef-uhr-*tee*-tee], 23–24
Negev Desert, 980
Nehru, Jawaharlal [jah-*wah*-har-lahl *nay*-roo], 877, 879–880, 964, 966–970, 1042
Nehru, Motilal, 813
Neisse [*nye*-suh] River, 1024, 1026
Nelson, Horatio, 636
Nemea [*nee*-mee-ah], 85
Neoclassicism, 732, 859
Neo-Confucianism, 154, 252, 300
Neo-Guelphs, 751
Neolithic Age, 6–9, 57–58, 76–78, 193, 195
Neoplatonism, 348–349, 352, 357, 359, 360
Nepal [nuh-*pol*], 224, 676, 678
Nerchinsk [*nyer*-chinsk], Treaty of, 413, 675
Nero, 134, 135, 141
Neruda [nay-*roo*-thah], Pablo, 1013
Nerva, 135
Netherlands: Renaissance in, 362; rebellion against Spain, 436–438; in the seventeenth century, 442, 445–446; early interests in Asia, 453; war with France (1672–1678), 530–531; Spanish, 533, 539; and Napoleon, 632, 636–637; capitalism in, 696–697; in the early nineteenth century, 723, 736; in the twentieth century, 782, 922, 1040; colonial regimes in Southeast Asia, 814, 816–817
Nevsky, Alexander, 289–290
New Amsterdam, 572
Newcastle, 694
Newcastle, Margaret Cavendish, Duchess of, 510
Newcomen, Thomas, 694, 699
New Deal, 905
New Delhi, 471, 812–813

New Democratic party (Canada), 1035
New Economic Policy (NEP), 870, 915
Newfoundland, 419, 533, 583, 584
New Granada, 569
New Guinea, 824, 826, 842, 933
New Harmony, Indiana, 707
New Heloise, The (Rousseau), 607
New Imperialism: historiographical
   debate, 800–801; in Africa, 802–807;
   in India, 807–814; in Southeast
   Asia, 814–817; in East Asia,
   817–823; in Australasia and the
   Pacific, 824–826
Ne Win, 954, 958
New Jersey, 454
New Lanark, 707
New Mexico, 586
New South Wales, 824
New Spain, 416–418, 569, 572, 590
Newspapers, 516, 538, 543, 626, 794,
   795, 796, 797
Newton, Sir Isaac, 554–555, 595, 1017
New York, 454, 572
New York City, 774, 903
New Zealand, 588, 709, 824–825, 826,
   842, 1034
Ngo Dihn Diem [noh-dihn-dyem],
   955
Nibelungenlied [nee-buh-lung-un-*leet*],
   306, 329
Nicaea [nye-*see*-uh], 288, 289; Council
   of, 166
Nicaragua, 590, 1002, 1010,
   1011–1012, 1013, 1015
Nice [nees], 632, 753
Nicholas I (Russia), 727, 735, 740,
   761, 762, 764
Nicholas II (Russia), 762, 776, 840,
   843, 862, 863
Nicholas V, Pope, 346, 350
Nicholas of Cusa [*kew*-suh], 548
Nicholas of Oresme [o-*rehm*], 548
Nicias [*nish*-uhs], 95
Nicopolis [nih-*kah*-puh-lis], battle of,
   457
Niemeyer [*nee*-mye-er], Oscar, 1003
Nietzsche [*nee*-chah], Friedrich, 831
Niger [*nye*-jer], 992
Nigeria, 201, 206, 510; modern, 983,
   984, 992, 994, 1000, 1004
Niger River, 204, 409, 803
"Night of the Long Knives," 912
Nijmegen [*nye*-may-guhn], Treaty of,
   531
Nikon, 537
Nile River, 9, 10, 11, 13, 18–19, 26,
   200, 803
Nimeiri, Gaafar [*gaf*-ahr nee-*mer*-ee],
   1000
Nimrud, 18
Ninety-five Theses (Luther), 379
Nineveh [*nihn*-uh-vuh], 18, 31
Nine Years' War, 532
Nirvana, 150, 315
Nixon, Richard, 946, 956, 974, 1039
Nkrumah, Kwame [*kwah*-may
   nkroo-mah], 992, 994, 996
NKVD (USSR), 917

Nobili [*noh*-bee-lee], Roberto de, 391
Nobility. *See also Daimyo*: ancient
   Egyptian, 20, 22–23; ancient
   Chinese, 59; ancient Athenian, 86;
   Roman, 124; Byzantine, 188;
   Mayan, 213; Aztec, 215; Incan, 218;
   Japanese, 260, 502; early modern
   European, 401–402, 503–504;
   Prussian, 540, 604–605; French,
   443, 617, 633; Russian, 451–452,
   536–537, 536; British, 579–580;
   nineteenth-century European, 771;
   after World War I, 848
Nobunaga, Oda, 261–262, 683
Noh [noh] drama, 261, 687
Nok culture, 201, 370
Nominalists, 299, 329
Nonaggression Pact (1939), 922, 923
Nonviolence, ideal of, 46, 147, 149,
   878, 1031–1032
Norman Conquest, 274
Normandy, 267, 274, 908, 931
Normandy invasion, 931
Normans, 190, 280, 282
Norsemen. *See* Vikings
North, Frederick Lord, 584
North Africa, 126, 175, 181, 188, 201,
   204, 265, 458, 930
North America, settlement of, 419,
   454, 572
North Atlantic Treaty Organization
   (NATO), 1024, 1040
Northern Wei [way] kingdom, 241
North German Confederation, 758
North Korea, 953–954
North Sea, 419
Northumberland, John Dudley, Duke
   of, 390
North Vietnam, 955–957
Northwest Ordinance, 586
Northwest Passage, 1017
Norway, 782; Reformation in, 382; in
   World War II, 922
Notables, Assembly of, 617
Nottingham, 710
Noucentisme, 834
Novalis [noh-*vah*-lis], Friedrich von,
   731
Novara, battle of, 741
Nova Scotia, 454, 533
Novels: Chinese, 73, 489–491, 677;
   Japanese, 259–260; picaresque, 520;
   English, 614; Romantic, 731–732,
   733–734; Realists, 787
Novgorod [*nov*-guh-rut], 290, 332
Novikov [*noh*-vee-kuf], Nikolai, 603
Nubia, 22, 23, 25
Nuclear weapons, 933, 951, 1025,
   1026, 1036, 1040, 1043–1045
Nuremberg, 382
Nuremberg Laws, 914–915
Nuremberg trials, 934
Nurhachi, 498
Nur Jahan [noor juh-*hahn*], 470, 471
Nurredin [noo-reh-*deen*], 284–285
Nyerere [nye-eh-*ray*-ray], Julius, 992,
   995
Nystad [*noo*-stahd], Treaty of, 535

Oceania, 824
Ochino [oh-*kee*-noh], Bernardino,
   352
Ockham, William of, 329
Octavia, 130–131
Octavius (Octavian), 130–131. *See also*
   Augustus
October Crisis (Canada), 1035
Odaenathus (Odenathus)
   [ahd-ee-*nay*-thuhs], 178
Oder [*oh*-der] River, 1024, 1026
Odyssey [*ahd*-ih-see], 80
Oedipus the King (Sophocles)
   [*ed*-ih-puhs], 102–103
Ogaden [oh-*gah*-dayn], 1000
O'Higgins, Bernardo, 590
Ohio Valley, 582
Okinawa, 933
Old Bolsheviks, 870, 917
Old Colonial System, 569–570
Oldenbarneveldt, Jan van [yahn vahn
   ol-den-*bahr*-nuh-velt], 445
Olivares [oh-lee-*vah*-rays], Count of,
   445
Oliver Twist (Dickens), 787
Olmecs [*ol*-meks], 209–210
Olympia, 85, 98, 99, 100
Omdurman [om-der-*man*], battle of,
   804
On Architecture (Vitruvius), 141
On Liberty (Mill), 782
Ontario, 588
On the Nature of Things (Lucretius),
   141
On the Origin of Species (Darwin),
   786
OPEC, 983–985, 1042–1043
Open Door policy, 689
Opera: Chinese, 492; European, 562,
   614
Operation Barbarossa, 924
Operation Overlord, 931
Operation Torch, 930
Opium Wars, 680–682
Oppenheimer, Samuel, 538, 609
Oprichnina, 451
Optics, 185, 302
Orange, house of, 445
Orange Free State, 804, 806
Oration on the Dignity of Man (Pico
   della Mirandola), 349
Oratory of Divine Love, 390
Oratory of Jesus, 515
Order of the Golden Fleece, 504
Oregon, 586
Oresteia [oh-rehs-*tee*-uh] (Aeschylus),
   101
Organization for European Economic
   Cooperation, 1029
Organization of African Unity, 1000,
   1042, 1043
Organon (Aristotle), 106
Orientalists (India), 658, 659, 663
Origen, 165
Orlando, Vittorio E., 845, 846, 890
Orléans [ahr-lay-*ahn*], 383; siege of,
   324
Orléans, Philip, Duke of, 580

Orozco [oh-*rohs*-koh], José Clemente, 1013

Ortega [or-*tay*-gah], Daniel, 1011

Ortega y Gasset [or-*tay*-gah ee gah-*set*], José, 848, 852

Ortelius [or-*tee*-lih-uhs], Abraham, 1011

Orwell, George, 1048

Osaka [oh-*sah*-kah], 262, 414, 683, 684, 685, 688

Oscans, 196

Osiris [oh-*sye*-ris], 21–22, 116, 314

Osman [*oz*-mun, os-*mahn*], 457

Osnabrück [*os*-nah-brook], 382

Ostrogoths, 144, 175, 265

Otto I, 267, 269, 278

Ottoman Empire, 725, 726; origins, 457; Mehmet the Conqueror, 457; Suleiman the Magnificent, 458; society, 459–461; urban life, 461–463; economy and culture, 463–466; war against the Holy League (1571), 435–436, 458; decline, 466, 665; education, 516; invasion of the Holy Roman Empire, 538–539; in the nineteenth century, 762–763; and the origins of World War I, 837, 843; in World War I, 842, 882

Otto of Brunswick, 281

Otto-Peters, Luise, 783

Oudenaarde [ou-duh-*nahr*-duh], battle of, 533

Oudh [oud], 650, 657, 664

OVRA, 909

Owen, Robert, 706–708, 738

Oxford, 298

Pacification of Ghent, 438

Pacific Ocean, 406, 429, 1019

Pacifism, 377, 386

Pact of Steel, 922

Padua [*pad*-yo-ah], University of, 298

Paekche [*payk*-cheh], 255

Paestum [*pes*-tuhm] (Poseidonia), 85

Pagan, Burma, 234

Pahlavi [*pah*-luh-vee] dynasty, 883, 985–986, 1040

Paine, Thomas, 610, 625, 631, 706, 794

Painting: in ancient Egypt, 24–25, 26–27; in ancient Ceylon, 49; Chinese, 72, 242, 244–245, 248–250, 480, 489, 497, 670, 855; Minoan, 78–79, 367; Greek, 83, 86, 99; Buddhist, 152; early medieval, 164; Byzantine, 190, 192, 264; early African, 200; Romanesque, 303–304; Italian Renaissance, 346, 356–360, 361, 856–857; Northern Renaissance, 362; Islamic, 369, 858; medieval Indian, 369; in the Reformation, 396–398, 435; baroque, 562, 571, 857; rococo, 613, 858; eighteenth-century English, 614; Goya, 637; early modern Indian, 468, 470, 648, 855, 858; Japanese, 684, 687, 688–689,

855–856, 858; Romantic, 730, 732, 734; Realists, 786–787; Impressionists, 787, 833; twentieth-century Western, 833, 834, 835–836, 852–853, 859–860, 896; Latin American, 1013

Pakistan, 881, 966, 968, 970, 973–974

Palatinate, 441, 531

Paleolithic Age, 4–5, 7, 58, 200

Palermo, 184–185

Palestine, 177, 188, 282, 284–285, 458, 760; origins of farming in, 6; Hebrew conquest of, 27; birth of Zionism, 764–766; modern, 842, 881, 882, 976–981, 982, 988

Palestine Liberation Organization (PLO), 980, 988

Palestinian National Charter, 977

Palestrina, Giovanni [joh-*vahn*-nee pah-lay-*stree*-nah], 398

Palk Strait, 409

Palladio, Andrea [ahn-*dray*-ah pah-*lah*-dee-oh], 361–362

Pallava, 47, 50, 229

Palma, Arturo Alessandri, 1006

Palmyra, 143, 178

Panama, Isthmus of, 406, 1012

Panama Canal, 1008

Pan Ch'ao (Ban Qao) [pahn chow], 71

Pandya, 47, 48, 50, 226, 229, 231

Pan-German League, 836

Panipat [*pah*-nih-put], battles of, 227, 466, 474

Pankhurst, Christabel, 784

Pankhurst, Emmeline, 783–785

Pankhurst, Sylvia, 784

Pan Ku (Bangu) [pahn goo], 75

Panmunjom Armistice, 953

Pan-Slav Movement, 836

Pantheon, 136, 142

Papacy, 279, 281, 293–294, 325–326, 781. *See also individual popes*

Papal bulls: *Clericis laicos* [*klehr*-ih-sis *lay*-ih-kos] (1296), 281; *Unam sanctam* (1302), 282; *Parens scientiarum* (1231), 298; *Exsurge domine* (1520), 379

Papal States, 335, 337, 338, 395, 725, 751, 753

Paper, 74, 185, 243, 255, 270, 330, 355, 547, 793

Paracelsus [par-uh-*sell*-suhs], 552

Paradise Lost (Milton), 561

Paraguay, 1004, 1007, 1014

Parakrama Bahu, 50

Pareto [pah-*ray*-toh], Vilfredo, 836

Paris: in the Middle Ages, 267, 272, 276, 297, 298–299, 324; University of, 297–298, 300, 326; early modern, 383; and the revolution of 1789–1799, 621, 623, 625–626, 634; modern, 710, 743, 748, 749, 774, 778

Paris, Peace of (1763), 583; (1856), 761, 762; (1919), 845–847

Paris, Treaty of (1783), 585; (1814), 640

Paris Accords (1973), 956, 1039

Paris Commune, 758, 778, 788

Park, Chung Hee, 954

Park, Mungo, 803

Parlement [pahr-luh-*mahn*], 277, 278, 443–444, 617, 618

Parliament (England): medieval, 276, 324; Reformation, 388–389; under Edward VI, 389–390; later Tudor, 394, 446, 447; early Stuart, 447; Short, 448; Long, 448; Rump, 448, 450, 454; Barebones, 448–449; Convention (1660), 541; Cavalier, 541; under William III and Anne, 542–543; age of Walpole, 579; Reform bills, 736–737; and the Chartists, 737

Parliament (France), 747, 778–779

Parliament (Germany). See *Bundesrat; Reichstag*

Parliament (Italy), 781, 890–892, 909

Parliament (Japan), 918, 960

Parma, Duke of, 438

Parmenides [pahr-*mehn*-ih-deez] of Elea, 104, 105

Parri [*pahr*-ree], Ferruccio, 1029

Parsees, 157

Parthenon, 98–100

Parthians, 67, 133

Parti populaire français [frahn-*say*], 899

Parti Québécois [kay-bay-*kwah*], 1035

Partnerships, 270

Pascal, Blaise [blays puhs-*kuhl*], 553, 559, 595

Passarowitz [pah-sah-*roh*-vitz], Treaty of, 466

Pasternak, Boris, 1044

Pasteur [pahs-ter], Louis, 709

Pataliputra [*pah*-tuh-lih-*poo*-truh], 43, 44–46, 47, 50

Patricians: Roman, 124, 128; early modern European, 504

Patronage, 346, 356, 360

Päts, Konstantin, 906

Paul the Apostle, 163–164, 167, 316, 383

Paul III, Pope, 391, 392

Paul IV, Pope, 395

Paul V, Pope, 563, 564

Paulette, 443

Pavia [pah-*vee*-ah], battle of, 341, 432

Pax Romana [paks roh-*mahn*-nuh]], 131, 134

Pays d'état [pay day-*tah*], 526, 527

Pearl Harbor, 925

Peary [*pir*-ee], Robert, 1019

Peasantry: in ancient Egypt, 20–21; in ancient China, 70–71; in ancient Athens, 86; Mayan, 213; Aztec, 215; in medieval Europe, 269; in early modern Europe, 401–402; French, 618, 619, 623, 633; in the agricultural revolution, 697–699; in nineteenth-century Europe, 772; after World War I, 848; in the USSR, 916

Peasants' Revolt (1524–1525), 382, 387, 397

Pechenegs [pech-uh-*negz*], 267, 282, 289
Pedro (Brazil), 590
Pegu [peh-*goh*], 234
P'ei Hsiu (Bei Xiu), 428
Peking (Beijing), 244, 253, 481, 485–486, 493–494, 498, 671, 818, 925, 952, 961
Pelagius [puh-*lay*-juhs], 166
Peloponnesian [pehl-uh-puh-*nee*-zhun] War, 93–95, 103
Peloponnesus [pehl-uh-puh-*nee*-suhs], 79, 95, 110
Penang [pee-*nang*], 816
Peninsular War, 637
Pennsylvania, 454, 572
Pentateuch [*pehn*-tah-tewk], 26
"People's Democracies," 1026–1027
Peoples of the Sea, 23, 31
Pepin [*pep*-ihn] the Short, 265
Perestroika, 1044, 1045
Pergamum, 111–112
Periander, 83
Pericles [*per*-ih-kleez], 88–90, 95
Peron [pay-*rohn*], Eva, 1004–1005
Peron, Isabel, 1005
Peron, Juan [hwahn] Domingo, 1004–1005
Perry, Matthew C., 689
Persepolis [per-*sep*-uh-lis], 33, 108
Persia, 133, 181, 183; rise of ancient, 31–32; imperial government of, 32; imperial capitals of, 32–33; wars with the Greeks, 87–88; renewed war with Greeks and Punic Wars, 126–127; Macedonians, 106–108; Pergamum 127–128; religions of, 156–158
Persian Gulf, 985
Persians, 18, 28, 31–33, 143, 178, 191. *See also* Persia
Persian Wars, 87–88
Perth, Australia, 824
Peru: Chavin culture, 210; Incas, 217–218; colonial rule, 416, 569, 570, 571, 572, 588, 590; in the twentieth century, 1006–1007, 1013, 1014
Pestalozzi, Johann Heinrich [*yoh*-hahn pest-ah-*lot*-see], 607, 704
Pétain, Henri [ahn-*ree* pay-*tenh*], 923
Peter I, "the Great" (Russia), 533–538, 562, 665
Peter III (Russia), 603
Peterloo Massacre, 712, 726
Peters, Karl, 803
Peter the Apostle, 163, 164
Peter the Hermit, 283
Petition of Right (1628), 447
Petrarch, Francesco [frahn-*cheh*-skoh *pee*-trahrk], 343, 347–348, 362
Petrograd (St. Petersburg), 863–865
Pfefferkorn, Johann, 376
Pharisees, 162
Pharsalus [fahr-*say*-luhs], battle of, 130
Phidias [*fid*-ee-uhs], 99

Philadelphia, 585
Philaret, 537
Philip, Arthur, 824
Philip II, "Augustus" (France) 276–277, 281, 285, 298, 309
Philip II (Macedon), 106–107
Philip II (Spain), 361, 394, 431–440 *passim*
Philip III (Spain), 444
Philip IV, "the Fair" (France) 278, 281–282, 309, 325
Philip IV (Spain), 444, 445
Philip V (Macedon), 127
Philip V (Spain), 533
Philip VI (France), 324
Philip of Hesse, 387
Philippi [fih-*lip*-eye], battle of, 130
Philippines: early history, 232–233, 238; colonial rule, 406, 408, 414, 416, 782, 816, 817, 826; in the twentieth century, 928, 954, 959
Philippine Sea, 933
Philip the Good (Burgundy), 334
Philistines, 27
Philosophes [feel-oh-*sohfs*], 597–598, 600–601, 603
Philosophy: in Vedic India, 42–43; in ancient China, 62–67; classical Greek, 104–106; Stoicism, 119; Epicureanism, 119; Cynicism, 119; Islamic, 186–187; Scholastic (Europe), 299–300, 329; Neoplatonic, 348–349; Descartes and Pascal, 553–554, 559; Hobbes, 557–558; Locke, 558–559; Skepticism, 559; Spinoza, 559–560; in the Enlightenment, 596–601; Idealism, 732–733; Nietzsche, 831; twentieth-century Western, 831, 852
Philostratus [fih-*los*-truh-tus], 142
Phnom Penh [peh-*nahm* pehn], 236
Phocas I [*foh*-kuhs], 188
Phoenicians [fih-*nee*-shuhnz], 26, 32, 196, 201
Phonograph, 796
"Phony War," 922
Photography, 795, 797
Phrygia [*frij*-ih-ah], 116
Phrygians, 31
Physics, modern, 832, 852
Physics (Aristotle), 106
Physiocrats, 699
Picabia [pee-*kah*-bya], Francis, 834
Picasso, Pablo, 834, 859, 920
Pico della Mirandola, Giovanni [joh-*vahn*-nee *pee*-koh day-lah mee-*rahn*-doh-lah], 349
Piedmont-Sardinia, Kingdom of, 751–753, 761, 780
Pietists, Pietism, 515, 607
Pilgrimages, 229–230, 327, 377, 380
"Pillars of faith," 179
Pillnitz, Declaration of, 625, 636
Pilsudski [peel-*soot*-skee], Józef, 906
Pinochet, Augusto [ow-*goos*-toh pee-noh-*chet*], 1006
Pinsker, Leo, 764

Pirandello [pee-rahn-*del*-loh], Luigi, 852
Pisa [*pee*-sah], 272, 345; Council of, 326
Pisan, Christine de [kree-*steen* duh pee-*zahn*], 351, 352, 353, 561
Pisistratus [pye-*sis*-truh-tuhs], 86, 87
Pissarro [pee-*sah*-roh], Camille, 787
Pitt, William, the Elder, 568, 582–583
Pitt, William, the Younger, 636
Pius II, Pope, 375
Pius V, Pope, 594
Pius VI, Pope, 624
Pius VII, Pope, 636
Pius IX, Pope, 740, 741, 751, 781
Pius XI, Pope, 909
Pizarro [pih-*zah*-roh], Francisco, 217, 218, 416, 569
Place, Francis, 706, 712, 737
Plague, 321–322, 345
Planck [plahngk], Max, 832
Plassey, battle of, 582, 655, 656
Plataea [plah-*tee*-ah], battle of, 88
Plato, 84, 104–106, 152, 186
Plautus [*plah*-tuhs], 140–141
Plebeians, Roman, 124, 128–129
Pliny [*plih*-nee], 67
Plombières [plon-byer], Treaty of, 751
Plows, 60
Plutarch, 91
Plymouth, Massachusetts, 454
Poem of My Cid, 306
Poetics (Aristotle), 106
Poetry: Tamil, 48; in India, 51; early Greek, 80–85; Hellenistic, 117–118; classical Roman, 141; Islamic, 181, 187–188; Chinese, 241–242, 250–251; Japanese, 262, 687; medieval European, 329, 330; Ottoman, 465; early modern European, 560, 561; Romantic, 731–732, 734; modern Western, 833, 836, 852; South American, 1013
Poggio Bracciolini [*pod*-joh braht-choh-*lee*-nee], 348
Pogroms, 609, 764
Poincaré [pwahn-kah-*ray*], Raymond, 904
Poitiers [pwah-*tyay*], 181, 274, 303, 307; battle of, 181
Poitou [pwah-*too*], 274
Poland. *See also* Grand Duchy of Warsaw: medieval, 289, 341; early modern, 395, 451, 535, 605; in the early nineteenth century, 722–723; 1830 revolution, 735; between the world wars, 846, 847, 848, 866, 867, 906; in World War II, 922, 923, 928, 931; after World War II, 1024, 1026, 1028, 1042
Pole, Reginald, 352
Policrates [poh-*lik*-rah-teez], 83
Polignac [poh-lee-*nyak*], Jules de, 734
Polis, 81–82, 85–87
Politburo, 870
Political theory: medieval European, 301–302; Machiavelli, 352–355; Hobbes and Locke, 596–597

Pollution, 941, 961, 1012
Polo, Marco, 223, 251, 253, 254, 403, 428
Polonnaruwa, 48, 50, 231
Pol Pot, 957–958
Poltava [pol-*tah*-vuh], battle of, 535
Polybius [poh-*lib*-ee-uhs], 2, 112–113
Polyclitus [pahl-ih-*klye*-tuhs] of Argos [*ahr*-gahs], 98, 134
Polynesia, 824, 825–826
Pomerania, 539
Pompadour [*pom*-pah-dohr], Madame de, 580
Pompeii [pahm-*pay*], 138–139, 614
Pompey [*pahm*-pee], 129–130
Pondicherry, 655
Ponet, John, 394
Ponsonby, Sarah, 612
Pontiac, 584, 586
Poona, 474
Poor Clares, 296
Poor Laws (England), 518, 703
Poor Relief: in Hellenistic period, 112; in Europe, 385, 386, 518; in Africa, 518–519; among the Incas, 519; in Asia, 519
Pop Art, 859
Pope, Alexander, 600, 612
Popular Front (France), 905
Popular Front (Spain), 919, 921
Porcelain: Asian, 74, 242, 255, 256, 403, 408, 409, 489, 688, 855, 856; European, 613, 614
Poros [*por*-uhs], 108
Port Huron Statement, 1032–1033
Portinari [por-tee-*nah*-ree], Cândido, 1013
Portolani, 404
Port Royal, Acadia, 454
Portugal, 286, 287, 607; voyages of exploration, 403–405; bases in Africa, 408–409; bases in Asia, 409–411; imperialism in Brazil, 418–419; annexed by Spain, 436; war of liberation, 445; colonies of, 572, 573; in the Napoleonic era, 637; in the early nineteenth century, 725, 736
Porus, 43
Poseidonius [pos-eye-*doh*-nih-uhs], 428
Positivism, 785–786
Postimpressionists, 833
Potosí [poh-toh-*see*], 416, 417, 570
Potsdam Conference, 1022–1023
Pottery, 36; prehistoric, 8, 12, 77; Chinese, 71, 245; Greek, 81, 83; Bronze Age, 123; classical Roman, 132–133; Olmec, 209; early Mexican, 211
Poverty, 54, 497, 512, 516–519, 544, 811, 814, 1003
Powell, John Wesley, 1018
Pragmatic Sanction (1713), 539, 582
Pragmatic Sanction of Bourges [*boorzh*], 334
Prague [*prahg*], 272, 441, 740, 742, 921
Prague, Treaty of, 758

Praise of Folly (Erasmus), 377
Praxiteles [prak-*siht*-el-eez], 91, 100, 117, 368
Predestination, 166–167, 383–384, 387
Presbyterians, 448
Pre-Socratics, 103–104
Prester (Elder) John, 404, 428, 429
Price, Richard, 612
Price Revolution (Europe), 419, 571
Priestley, Joseph, 730
Primo de Rivera, Jose Antonio, 900
Primo de Rivera, Miguel, 900
Primogeniture [*prye*-moh-*jen*-ih-chur], 64, 70, 312, 585
Prince, The (Machiavelli), 353–354, 355, 393
Printing: in Asia, 243, 250, 255, 256, 257, 488, 514; in Europe, 330, 355–356, 375, 381, 384, 423, 601, 793–794
Prints, Japanese, 688–689, 856
Procopius [proh-*koh*-pee-uhs], 174, 176
Progress, concept of, 2–3, 595–596, 729, 785–786, 1047–1049
Progressive Conservative party (Canada), 1035
Prohibition (United States), 904
Proletariat, 704–706, 772–773, 848–849
Prophets, Hebrew, 159, 160
Prostitution, 45, 48, 53, 54, 91; early modern, 216, 390, 511, 512–513
Proudhon [proo-*dohn*], Pierre-Joseph, 737, 738, 749
Proust [*proost*], Marcel, 852
Provence [pro-*vahns*], 334
Prussia, 779; rise of, 539–541; in the War of the Austrian Succession, 582; in the Seven Years' War, 582–583; Frederick the Great, 604–605; and the Napoleonic wars, 636, 638, 639; in the early nineteenth century, 721–724, 725–727; revolution of 1848, 740; and German unification, 754–759
Psychiatry, 831–832
Psychohistory, 3
Ptolemies [*tahl*-uh-meez], 109, 111, 112, 113–114, 160
Ptolemy [*tahl*-uh-mee], Claudius, 114, 185, 404, 428, 429, 547
Ptolemy I, 114, 116
Ptolemy IV, 112
Puduhepa, 29
Puerto Rico, 416, 570, 590, 782, 1002
Pufendorf [*poo*-fuhn-dorf], Samuel, 556
Pugachev, Emilian [yeh-myil-*yan* poo-gah-*choff*], 603; rebellion of, 603
Puhar, 50
Punic [*pyoo*-nik] Wars, 128
Punjab [*pun*-job]: ancient, 46; medieval, 223, 226, 227; early modern, 466, 473, 474, 649, 657, 663, 665; modern, 966, 967, 972, 974
Purdah, 233, 473–474
Purgatory, 378, 392

Puritans, 446, 447, 448
Pushkin [*poosh*-kyin], Alexander, 727
Putney Debates, 449
Pydna [*pihd*-nuh], battle of, 128
Pygmies, 802
Pylos [*pye*-lahs], 79, 80
Pyongyang [pyahng-yahng], 255, 953
Pyramids, 19, 25, 49, 211, 212, 213, 216
Pyrenees, Treaty of the, 442, 445
Pyrrhic [*pihr*-ik] Wars, 125–126
Pyrrhus [*pihr*-uhs], 125
Pythagoras [pih-*thag*-uh-ruhs] of Samos, 103, 427, 547, 551
Pythagoreanism, 103–104

Qaddafi, Muammar al- [moo-uh-*mar* el kah-*dah*-fee], 988, 999–1000
Qajar dynasty, 667
Qatar [*kah*-tur], 983
Quadrivium, 298
Quadruple Alliance, 722
Quakers (Society of Friends), 448, 450
Quebec [kwuh-*bek*], 454, 582, 588, 1035
Quebec Act, 585
Quesnay, François [frahn-*swah* keh-*nay*], 673, 699
Quiberon [keeb-*rohn*] Bay, battle of, 582
Quietism, 607

Rabelais, François [frahn-*swah* rah-*blay*], 351, 362, 560, 561
Racine, Jean Baptiste [zhahn bah-*teest* rah-*seen*], 561
Racism, 836
Radio, 796, 797, 798
Radischev, Alexander, 603
Raicho, Hiratsuka, 960
Railroads: in Asia, 663, 808–809, 816, 822, 941; in Europe, 695, 712, 715, 747, 766, 769; in Africa, 807, 991; in Australia, 824
Rajasthan [*rah*-juh-stahn], 223, 473, 657
Rajput Confederacy, 227
Rajputs [*raj*-pootz], 223, 226, 466, 468, 473, 650, 808
Rakoczi [*rah*-koh-tsee], Ferenc, 539
Raleigh, Sir Walter, 419, 454
Ramadan [rah-mah-*dahn*], 180, 233
Ramananda, 227
Ramayana, 41, 42, 233
Rambouillet, Catherine de, 561
Rameau [ra-*moh*], Jean-Philippe, 614
Ramillies [*ram*-ih-leez], battle of, 533
Ramses I [*ram*-seez], 23
Ramses II, 27, 29
Ramses III, 31
Ranade [*rah*-nah-day], Mahadeo Govind, 813
Randolph, Edmund, 586
Rangoon, 816, 954
Ranke [*rahng*-kuh], Leopold von, 733
Rapallo, Treaty of, 848
Raphael [*raf*-ay-uhl] Sanzio, 359, 361

Rasputin [rahs-*poo*-tyin, ras-*pew*-tin], Grigori, 863
Rastadt [*rah*-shtaht, *rahs*-taht], Treaty of, 539
Rathenau, Walther [*vahl*-ter *rah*-teh-now], 893
Rationalists, 387
Ravenna [rah-*vehn*-nah], 175, 188, 265
Ray, Man, 834
Raya, Krishna Deva, 231
Razin, Stenka, 452
Reagan, Ronald, 1006, 1012, 1040, 1044, 1045
Realist movement (art), 786–787
Realists (medieval), 299
Real Patronato, 333
Realpolitik, 756–757
Reconquista, 286–287
Red Fort, 650, 813
Red Guards (China), 948
Reflections on the Revolution in France (Burke), 625
Reform Acts: (1832), 736–737; (1867), 777, 782; (1884), 777
Reformation, Catholic (Counter): origins and characteristics, 390; Ursulines and Jesuits, 390–392; Council of Trent, 392–393; in England, 393–394
Reformation, impact of: on Jews, 394–395; witchcraft persecutions, 395–396; on art and music, 396–398
Reformation, Protestant: conditions in the late medieval church, 375–376; humanist demands for reform, 376–378; Lutheran movement, 378–382; Reformed tradition, 382–386; radical reformation, 386–387; English reformation, 387–390
Reformed Protestantism, 382–386
Reform movement (Judaism), 610
Regulated companies, 421
Reichstag [*ryechs*-tahk], 758, 779, 780, 897–898, 912
Reincarnation, 148, 149, 150, 315, 316
Reinhardt, Max, 897
Reinsurance Treaty, 837–838
Religion. *See also major religions by name*: origins of, 7–8; in Indus civilization, 39; Aryan, 42; in ancient China, 59, 74; Minoan, 79; Pythagoreanism, 103–104; Hellenistic, 116; functions of, 146–147; Asian attitudes, 155–156; Olmec, 209–210; Chavin, 210; early Mexican, 211; Mayan, 213–214; Aztec, 216–217; Incan, 218
Remarque [ruh-*mahrk*], Erich Maria, 848
Rembrandt van Rijn [reen], 562, 571
Remus, 124
Renaissance, European: urban context, 344–346; patronage, 346; humanists, 346–352; age of Petrarch, 347–348; civic humanists, 348; Neoplatonists, 348–349;

humanist education, 349–350; textual criticism, 350; northern humanists, 350–351; role of women, 351–352; Machiavelli, 352–355; printing revolution, 355–356; painting, 356–360, 362, 856–857; sculpture, 360–361, 857; women artists, 361; architecture, 361–362; historiography, 362–364
Renoir [ruh-*nwar*], Auguste, 787
Repartimiento, 570
Republic, The (Plato), 105
Republic of Virtue, 630
Return, Law of, 979
Reuchlin, Johann [*yoh*-hahn *roik*-luhn], 376
Revolutions of 1830, 734–736
Revolutions of 1848, 739–743
Rexist Movement, 900
Reynaud [ray-*noh*], Paul, 923
Reynolds, Joshua, 614
Reza Shah Pahlavi, 883
Rhee, Syngman [*sing*-muhn *ree*], 953, 954
Rheims [reemz], 297
Rhenish League, 270
Rhine, Confederation of the, 636
Rhineland, 395, 723, 846, 919
Rhode Island, 572
Rhodes, 458
Rhodes, Cecil, 804, 806
Rhodesia, 805
Rhone [rohn] Valley, 265
Riario, Girolamo, 337
Ribero, Diego, 429
Ricardo, David, 704, 705, 738
Ricci [*reet*-chee], Matteo, 391, 411–412, 495–496, 497, 1018
Richard I (England), 274–275
Richard II (England), 322, 323, 333
Richard III (England), 334
Richardson, Samuel, 607, 614
Richelieu [*ree*-sheh-lyuh], Cardinal, 443, 444
Riefenstahl, Leni, 913
Rigaud [ree-*goh*], Hyacinthe, 857
Rights of Man, The (Paine), 706
Rig Veda [rig *vay*-dah], 148
Rilke [*rihl*-kuh], Rainer Maria, 852
Rime of the Ancient Mariner (Coleridge), 731
Rio de Janeiro [*ree*-oh duh juh-*nayr*-oh], 419, 1003, 1004
Rio de la Plata, 406
Risorgimento [ree-sor-jee-*men*-toh], 751–754
Rivera [ree-*vay*-rah], Diego, 1013
Roads: in India, 45–46; in China, 64, 67, 241, 254, 671; Roman, 138; in Abbasid Caliphate, 182, 185; Incan, 218; in Iran, 477
Roanoke Island, 419, 454
Roaring Twenties, 904–905
Robespierre, Maximilien [max-see-mee-*lyenh* roh-bes-*pyair*], 601, 626, 628–630, 631
Robinson Crusoe (Defoe), 561, 614

Rockefeller, John D., 771
Rococo art, 613, 858
Rocque [rok], Colonel de la, 900
Rodin [roh-*danh*], Auguste, 367
Rodney, George, 585
Roe, Sir Thomas, 453, 651
Röhm [rurm], Ernst, 894, 912
Roland [ro-*lahn*], Madame, 630–631, 633–634
Romance of Reynard the Fox, 308
Romance of the Rose, 307
Romance of the Three Kingdoms, 73
Romanesque style, 303–304
Romania (Rumania), 762; and World War I, 837, 839, 848; between the world wars, 900, 906; in World War II, 922; after World War II, 1022, 1026
Romanov [ruh-*mah*-noff], Mikhail, 452
Romanov dynasty, 452, 760–762, 862–863
Romans, Classical: demand for Chinese silk, 67–68; contributions of, 121–122; origins of, 122, 123–124; rule of Etruscans, 122–123; origins of republic, 124; unification of Italy, 124–125; Punic Wars, 126–127; conquests in Greece and Asia, 127–128; decline of the republic, 128–131; age of Augustus, 131–134; literature, 133–134, 140–141; art and architecture, 134, 141–142; the empire (A.D. 14–138), 134–135; life in the city of Rome, 135–137; provincial life, 138–139; Roman women, 139–140; the empire (192–476), 142–145; adopt alphabet, 196; in North Africa, 201
Romanticism, 608, 645, 728–734
Rome, 265, 266, 272, 279, 344, 346, 401, 741, 753, 759. *See also* Romans, Classical: founding of, 122, 123–124; in the classical age, 135–137; early Christianity in, 164–166; University of, 298; Renaissance in, 359–360; in the age of the baroque, 562–564; under Mussolini, 911
Rome-Berlin Axis, 892, 919
Romulus [*rahm*-yoo-luhs], 124
Romulus Augustulus [ah-*gus*-tyoo-luhs], 144
Röntgen [*rent*-guhn], Wilhelm, 832
Roosevelt, Franklin D., 795, 796, 905, 925, 930–933, 934
Roosevelt, Theodore, 822–823
Roscellin [ro-seh-*lan*], 299
Rosenberg, Alfred, 894
Rosetta Stone, 24
Rossbach, battle of, 582
Rossi [*rohs*-see], Properzia, 361
Rouault, Georges, 834
Rouen [roo-*ahn*], 324
Roundheads, 448
Rousseau, Jean-Jacques [zhahn-zhahk roo-*soh*], 597, 598–600, 601, 603, 607, 609, 630, 704, 732, 794
Roux [roo], Jacques, 628